INTERNATIONAL BUSINESS

Pearson

INTERNATIONAL BUSINESS 7th Edition

Simon Collinson
University of Birmingham

Rajneesh Narula
Henley Business School, the University of Reading

Alan M. Rugman
Henley Business School, the University of Reading

 Pearson

Harlow, England • London • New York • Boston • San Francisco • Toronto • Sydney
Dubai • Singapore • Hong Kong • Tokyo • Seoul • Taipei • New Delhi
Cape Town • São Paulo • Mexico City • Madrid • Amsterdam • Munich • Paris • Milan

Pearson Education Limited
Edinburgh Gate
Harlow CM20 2JE
United Kingdom
Tel: +44 (0)1279 623623
Web: www.pearson.com/uk

First published by McGraw-Hill Inc. 1995
Sixth edition published by Pearson Education Limited 2012 (print and electronic)
Seventh edition 2017 (print and electronic)

ISBN: 978-1-292-06439-0 (print)
       978-1-292-06444-4 (PDF)
       978-1-292-17593-5 (ePub)

British Library Cataloguing-in-Publication Data
A catalogue record for the print edition is available from the British Library

Library of Congress Cataloging-in-Publication Data
A catalog record for the print edition is available from the Library of Congress

10 9 8 7 6 5 4 3 2 1
21 20 19 18 17

Cover: eternalcreative/Getty Images

Print edition typeset in 10/12.5 pt Times LT Pro by iEnergizer Aptara® Ltd
Printed in Slovakia by Neografia

CONTENTS IN BRIEF

CONTENTS IN DETAIL

Part One
THE WORLD OF INTERNATIONAL BUSINESS

Chapter 1
An Introduction to International Business   3

Chapter 2
General Frameworks in International Business   40

Chapter 3
Multinational Enterprises, Innovation, and Competitiveness   **90**

Part Two
THE ENVIRONMENT OF INTERNATIONAL BUSINESS

Chapter 4
International Politics   **123**

Chapter 5
International Culture   **152**

Chapter 6
International Trade 183

Chapter 7
International Financial Markets
and Institutions 218

Part Three

INTERNATIONAL BUSINESS STRATEGIES

Chapter 8
Multinational Strategy　255

Chapter 9
Organizing Strategy　290

Chapter 10
Corporate Strategy and National Competitiveness　318

Supporting resources

Visit **www.pearsoned.co.uk/rugman** to find valuable online resources

For instructors
■ Instructor's Manual
■ PowerPoints

For more information please contact your local Pearson Education sales representative or visit
www.pearsoned.co.uk/rugman

LIST OF FIGURES AND TABLES

Figures

Tables

PREFACE

Dedication

The seventh edition of *International Business* is dedicated to the memory of Alan Rugman, who began this textbook series over 30 years ago and invited me to join him as co-author for the fourth edition published in 2006. Our writing partnership began when I was a visiting professor at the Kelley School, University of Indiana in 2004 and I reflect on our collaboration in a volume dedicated to Alan, edited by Rob Van Tulder, Alain Verbeke and Rian Drogendijk (Collinson, 2015).[1] He was a great scholar and a much-missed mentor. For Alan this book series represented a lifelong project to continually improve the way we teach international business and engage people in a subject he was passionate about.

Alan would be extremely pleased to know that his colleague and friend, Rajneesh Narula has joined me to co-author this, the latest edition of his book. Alan's ideas and insights remain at the core of this book, but we have thoroughly revised and updated the text in step with the ever-changing world of international business. A brief biography of Alan can be found on page xxi.

Simon Collinson

The seventh edition of *International Business*

With a new co-author, Rajneesh Narula, we have three completely new chapters (Chapters 1–3) to open the book. As shown in these new chapters, we have significantly restructured the book to place a much greater emphasis on: (1) technology and innovation, as key drivers of international competitiveness; (2) institutions as mediators and moderators of MNE (multinational enterprise) activities; (3) small and medium-sized enterprises as important global players; and (4) how MNEs can be responsible businesses, taking a broader, more ethical stakeholder approach, rather than a narrowly profit-oriented shareholder approach.

The structure of the book has also changed, although we have kept the five main sections and made them more distinctive. A new introduction: "Frameworks for this Book: Our Approach to the Study of International Business" appears just before the start of Part One and the main chapters. It provides an overview of our approach and the structure of the book as well as the standard sections of each chapter. Figure 3 provides the new outline, linked to a description of how the book is organized.

The themes covered in the previous Chapter 11 have now been integrated into the new Chapter 3. Chapter 22 has been thoroughly revised and sits in Part Three, as the new Chapter 11. This leaves Part Five to focus on the five key countries and regions (Chapters 17–21).

Within the chapters the structure should be familiar to those who have used the book before. We have kept five case studies in each chapter (except Chapter 1, which introduces the field of international business). We have 100 case studies and almost one-quarter of these are entirely new. Most of the rest have been completely updated or rewritten. Every chapter has been thoroughly updated, with new data, trends, and references. A revised bibliography appears at the end of each chapter.

Acknowledgements

Our lead researcher on this project was Amir Qamar, a Ph.D. student at Birmingham Business School, the University of Birmingham, who deserves huge thanks for coordinating the revision process and updating large parts of the book. He also provided 12 of the new case studies and helped shaped the new emphasis described above. He was lead author on US manufacturing: from China to Mexico (Ch. 2); Worrying times for Singapore's SMEs (Ch. 2); R&D at Hewlett-Packard (Ch. 3); Greece: third (bailout) time lucky (Ch. 4); The

---

1 Collinson, Simon (2015). "Dedication: Yin and Yang: Integrating Disparate Perspectives for International Business Research and Teaching", in Rob Van Tulder, Alain Verbeke, and Rian Drogendijk (ed.) *The Future of Global Organizing* (Progress in International Business Research, Volume 10) Emerald Group Publishing Limited, pp. 27–35.

collective culture of the John Lewis Partnership (Ch. 5); China 2015: the start of the next global economic meltdown? (Ch. 7); End of an era: the Goodyear plant closure (Ch. 12); Adidas: promoting a global sports brand (Ch. 13); Primark: putting global stakeholders first (Ch. 14); Intel Effect (Ch. 15); Financial transparency at Siemens (Ch. 16); and VW scandal (Ch. 17). He is also the author for the Instructor's Manual.

Thanks also go to Dev K. (Roshan) Boojihawon, a Senior Lecturer in IB at the University of Birmingham, and another of our Ph.D. students, Emma C. Gardner, who also both provided excellent new case studies for

the book. Dev led on Floreal Knitwear (Ch. 10) and Mirum (Ch. 13). Emma was lead author for: Tesco at home and abroad (Ch. 2); The Big Four (Ch. 8); Glass ceiling (Ch.14); and Sony-diversifying into the automobile industry? (Ch. 18). Support for Rajneesh Narula was provided by Karim Kirollos, Teaching Fellow in International Business at Aston University, who helped edit and update the text and cases associated with Chapters 1–3. Further assistance was provided by Jong Min Lee and Maite Alvez Bezerra, doctoral researchers at Henley Business School, University of Reading.

ABOUT THE AUTHORS

Dr Simon Collinson is Dean of Birmingham Business School and Professor of International Business and Innovation at the University of Birmingham. He is also Chair of the Chartered Association of Business Schools (CABS), a member of the UK Economic and Social Research Council (ESRC) and the Council of the Greater Birmingham Chamber of Commerce, and a Fellow of the Royal Society (FRSA).

Previous roles include Professor of International Business at Henley Business School, University of Reading and Deputy Dean and Professor of International Business at Warwick Business School, University of Warwick (UK), where he was also Head of the Marketing and Strategic Management Group. He was an Academic Associate at the Centre for International Business and Management (CIBAM), Judge Business School, Cambridge, and a Research Associate at the Centre for Competitive Advantage in the Global Economy (CAGE) at Warwick University. During his time at Warwick he held the role of Lead Ghoshal Fellow (and then sat on the Board of Directors) in the Research Council UK- (RCUK-)funded Advanced Institute of Management (AIM) initiative. Prior to Warwick he was Lecturer and Senior Research Fellow at Edinburgh University Management School and the Assistant Director of the Japanese–European Technology Studies (JETS) Institute for seven years.

Simon has held visiting positions at Zhejiang University, the Australian Graduate School of Management (AGSM) in Sydney, the Kelley School of Business, Indiana University, Hitotsubashi University and the National Institute of Science and Technology Policy (NISTEP) in Tokyo, and the John Dunning Centre for International Business, Henley Business School, University of Reading. Following a Joint BA (Hons.) in Geography and Sociology at Leeds University and an MA in Human Geography at the University of Florida, Gainesville, Simon was awarded his D.Phil. from the Science Policy Research Unit (SPRU) at Sussex University in 1991.

His original research was on technology transfer and indigenous technological capabilities in Kenyan manufacturing firms. Since then projects and papers have focused on global innovation strategies, R&D, knowledge, and intellectual asset management in multinational firms; the competitiveness of international UK firms; national systems of innovation and emerging economies; high-technology entrepreneurship, small-firm networks, and regional development; Japan and China: local business practices and cross-cultural management, foreign direct investment, and economic change. Simon has received research funding awards from the UK ESRC and the Engineering and Physical Sciences Research Council (EPSRC), the UK government's Department of Trade and Industry, Japan's Science and Technology Agency, the British Royal Society, and European Commission Director General (/Directorate) XII (DGXII) of the European Union.

He has research, consulting, and executive teaching experience with a wide range of multinational firms. He has published a range of books and articles in refereed journals including *Journal of International Business Studies*, *Organization Studies*, *Business History*, *Research Policy*, *Multinational Business Review*, *International Journal of Technology Management*, *European Management Journal*, *R&D Management*, *Organization Dynamics*, and *Technology Analysis & Strategic Management*. His research has also featured in the *Independent*, *The Times*, *The Sunday Times*, BBC Radio 4, the *New Statesman* and the *U.S. News & World Report*.

While continuing to publish on China, innovation, and the evolving competitiveness of emerging economies, he has recently focused on two areas of research. First, the performance effects of organizational complexity. His most recent book, *From Complexity to Simplicity* was shortlisted for the Chartered Management Institute (CMI) business book of the year prize. Second, as joint-lead of City-REDI, the City-Region Economic Development Institute at Birmingham Business School, he has been working with regional policy-makers to accelerate local innovation and economic growth.

Dr Rajneesh Narula is the John H. Dunning Chair of International Business Regulation at the Henley Business School, University of Reading, UK. He has previously held positions at Copenhagen Business

School, the BI Norwegian Business School, the University of Oslo, and the University of Maastricht. He currently holds honorary appointments at UNU-MERIT, Norwegian Business School, and Oxford University.

His research and consulting have focused on the role of multinational firms in development, innovation and industrial policy, R&D alliances, and outsourcing. He has published over a hundred articles and chapters in books on these themes. He was Editor-in-Chief of *Multinational Business Review* from 2014 to 2016, and is currently Area Editor in development and international business for the *Journal of International Business Studies* (2016–20). He was Editor-in-Chief of *The European Journal of Development Research* from 2009 to 2013.

He regularly acts as a consultant and advisor to the European Commission, United Nations Industrial Development Organization (UNIDO), United Nations Conference on Trade and Development (UNCTAD), the Organization for Economic Co-operation and Development (OECD), and a variety of other international organizations. He has travelled widely, having undertaken research and consultancy projects or taught in Tanzania, Uganda, Thailand, China, Vietnam, Russia, India, Qatar, UAE, Colombia, Australia, Japan, Mauritius, Senegal, and Pakistan, in addition to almost all the countries of the EU.

He is listed as one of the top 20 most cited academic authors worldwide in the fields of international business, emerging markets, economics of innovation, and economic development. His publications with John Dunning and Sanjaya Lall on FDI-assisted development are especially well-cited contributions on the subject.

He is the author or editor of ten books, including *Globalization & Technology* (Polity Press, 2003), *Multinationals and Industrial Competitiveness* (with John Dunning, Edward Elgar, 2004), *Understanding FDI-assisted Economic Development* (with Sanjaya Lall, Routledge, 2004), and *Multinationals on the Periphery* (with Gabriel Benito, Palgrave, 2007). His publications have appeared in leading journals, including the *Journal of International Business Studies*, *Oxford Development Studies*, *Research Policy*, *Journal of Management Studies*, *Journal of World Business*, and *Management International Review*. His 2003 book *Globalization and Technology* has been translated and published in Chinese and Arabic.

He obtained his B.Eng. (Electrical Engineering, with Hons.) from Ahmadu Bello University, Zaria Nigeria, his MBA from Rutgers University and his Doctorate in International Business and Economics from Rutgers University, US. Before academia, Professor Narula worked as an Engineer in Nigeria, and later as a Planning Analyst at IBM Asia/Pacific Headquarters in Hong Kong.

Until his untimely death in July 2014, **Dr Alan M. Rugman** was Professor of International Business at the Henley Business School and Head of School, International Business and Strategy at the University of Reading, UK. Previously he was L. Leslie Waters Chair of International Business at the Kelley School of Business, Indiana University, from 2002 to 2009. He was Thames Water Fellow in Strategic Management at Templeton College, University of Oxford, from 1998 to 2001 and an Associate Fellow of Green Templeton College. Previously, he was Professor of International Business at the University of Toronto, Dalhousie University, and the University of Winnipeg. He was also a visiting professor at Columbia Business School, London Business School, Harvard University, UCLA, MIT, Warwick Business School, the University of Paris–La Sorbonne, University of Sydney, Saint Louis University, and the University of Lyon.

He earned his BA in economics from Leeds University in 1966, his M.Sc. in economic development from London University's School of Oriental and African Studies (SOAS) in 1967, and his Ph.D. in economics from Simon Fraser University in 1974. He was elected to an MA (Oxon) in 1998.

Dr Rugman published over 300 articles dealing with the economic, managerial, and strategic aspects of multinational enterprises and with trade and investment policy. These have appeared in such leading refereed journals as: *Journal of International Business Studies*, *Management International Review*, *The American Economic Review*, *Strategic Management Journal*, *Journal of Management Studies*, and *Journal of Business Ethics*. He is recognized as one of the ten most-cited scholars in the field of international business worldwide. (His Google Scholar Citations count is over 21,000 and his h-index 67.)

His books include: *Inside the Multinationals* (Columbia University Press, 1981 and Palgrave, 2006); *International Business* (McGraw-Hill, 1995); *Environmental Regulations and Corporate Strategy* (Oxford University Press, 1999); *Multinationals as Flagship Firms* (Oxford University Press, 2000); *The End of Globalization* (Random House, 2000); *The Oxford Handbook of International Business* (Oxford University Press, 2001, 2009); *The Regional Multinationals* (Cambridge University Press, 2005);

Regional Aspects of Multinationality and Performance (Elsevier, 2007); *Rugman Reviews International Business* (Palgrave Macmillan, 2009); and *Multinationals and Development* (Yale University Press, 2009).

As a leading authority in international business, Dr Rugman served as President of the Academy of International Business from 2004 to 2006, was elected a Fellow of the Academy in 1991, and served as Dean of the Fellows. He was also a Fellow of the Royal Society of Arts, elected 1998. He served on the Editorial Board of the *Journal of International Business Studies* and was the Editor-in-Chief of the *Multinational Business Review*.

In 2004 he received the Booz Allen Hamilton Award as Eminent Scholar in International Management, Academy of Management. He was also honored at a special plenary session of the European International Business Association annual meetings, Slovenia, December 2004 for the 25th Anniversary of his 1979 book, *International Diversification and the Multinational Enterprise*. In 2011, he received the Simon Fraser University Outstanding Alumni Award for Academic Achievement. His final plenary was at the Academy of International Business (AIB) conference in Vancouver, June 2014, fittingly an AIB Fellows Plenary with his peer group. A number of special issues of journals have been published in his honor, most recently a special section in *Journal of World Business*, edited by Rajneesh Narula and Alain Verbeke.[1] http://henley.ac.uk/news/news-item/in-memoriam-professor-alan-rugman/

---

1 Narula, R., and Verbeke, A. (2015). Making internalization theory good for practice: The essence of Alan Rugman's contributions to international business. *Journal of World Business*, 50(4), 612–22.

GUIDE TO THE CASE STUDIES

CHAPTER	TYPE OF CASE	ORGANIZATION/INDUSTRY	COUNTRY/ REGION	NEW/ REVISED	PAGE
Chapter 1 (n/a) An Introduction to International Business					
Chapter 2 General Frameworks in International Business	■ Active Learning Case	Starbucks: a global "coffee culture"	US	Revised	42
	■ International Business Strategy in Action	US manufacturing: from China to Mexico	US/Emerging Economies: China/Mexico	New	49
	■ International Business Strategy in Action	Worrying times for Singapore's SMEs	Singapore	New	71
	■ Real Case	Toys "Я" Us	US/EU/Japan	Revised	76
	■ Real Case	Tesco at home and abroad	US/Japan/UK	New	78
Chapter 3 Multinational Enterprises, Innovation, and Competitiveness	■ Active Learning Case	GE Healthcare in India: locally driven innovation	US/Asia		91
	■ International Business Strategy in Action	Spreadshirt: open innovation	EU	Revised	103
	■ International Business Strategy in Action	Innovation networks at IBM	US	Revised	112
	■ Real Case	Canon Group	Japan	Revised	115
	■ Real Case	R&D at Hewlett-Packard	US	New	117
Chapter 4 International Politics	■ Active Learning Case	How risky is foreign investment in Russia?	Emerging Economies	Revised	124
	■ International Business Strategy in Action	Greece: third (bailout) time lucky	Greece	New	129
	■ International Business Strategy in Action	Non-governmental organizations and political power	US/EU		136
	■ Real Case	How environmental regulations can be used as trade barriers	US/Emerging Economies		147
	■ Real Case	Embraer vs. Bombardier	Canada/ Emerging Economies: Brazil	Revised	148

CHAPTER	TYPE OF CASE	ORGANIZATION/INDUSTRY	COUNTRY/ REGION	NEW/ REVISED	PAGE
Chapter 5 International Culture	■ Active Learning Case	Cultures clash as big pharma gets bigger	EU: Sweden and Italy/US	Revised	153
	■ International Business Strategy in Action	McDonald's	US	Revised	158
	■ International Business Strategy in Action	The collective culture of the John Lewis Partnership	UK	New	173
	■ Real Case	Do not throw your *meishi*!	EU: UK/Japan		178
	■ Real Case	Sport can be local *and* global: Manchester United	EU/US/Asia	Revised	179
Chapter 6 International Trade	■ Active Learning Case	Trade of the triad and China	US/EU/Japan/ Emerging Economies: China	Revised	184
	■ International Business Strategy in Action	Microsoft shows the world is not flat	US/EU	Revised	192
	■ International Business Strategy in Action	Boeing versus Airbus	US/EU	Revised	197
	■ Real Case	Job losses and offshoring to China	US/Emerging Economies: China		207
	■ Real Case	Dumping on trade complaints	Canada/US		208
Chapter 7 International Financial Markets and Institutions	■ Active Learning Case	Barclays Bank international financial dealings	EU: UK	Revised	219
	■ International Business Strategy in Action	China 2015: the start of the next global economic meltdown?	China	New	231
	■ International Business Strategy in Action	AngloGold Ashanti	Emerging Economies: South Africa	Revised	241
	■ Real Case	HSBC	EU: UK	Revised	248
	■ Real Case	Rigging LIBOR	UK	New	249
Chapter 8 Multinational Strategy	■ Active Learning Case	Vodafone and the triad telecom market	EU	Revised	256
	■ International Business Strategy in Action	The Big Four	UK	New	261

CHAPTER	TYPE OF CASE	ORGANIZATION/INDUSTRY	COUNTRY/ REGION	NEW/ REVISED	PAGE
	■ International Business Strategy in Action	Fuji Xerox and Xerox	US/Japan	Revised	271
	■ Real Case	Mountain Equipment Co-op: a small business	Canada	Revised	278
	■ Real Case	Benetton	EU: Italy	Revised	279
Chapter 9 Organizing Strategy	■ Active Learning Case	Procter & Gamble	US	Revised	291
	■ International Business Strategy in Action	Sanofi-Aventis	EU: France/ Germany	Revised	295
	■ International Business Strategy in Action	Making the matrix work	EU/US/Japan		302
	■ Real Case	LVMH: organizing luxury products in the international arena	EU: France	Revised	312
	■ Real Case	Command Alkon: small but increasingly global	US		313
Chapter 10 Corporate Strategy and National Competitiveness	■ Active Learning Case	Worldwide operations and local strategies of ABB	EU	Revised	319
	■ International Business Strategy in Action	Nokia and Ericsson: moving beyond mobiles	EU	Revised	328
	■ International Business Strategy in Action	Renewed advantage through vertical integration at Floreal Knitwear	Asia	New	334
	■ Real Case	There is no global beer, only local	US/EU		342
	■ Real Case	IBM	US/EU	Revised	344
Chapter 11 Multinational Enterprises as Responsible Stakeholders	■ Active Learning Case	The environment, NGOs, and MNEs	EU/US	Revised	350
	■ International Business Strategy in Action	3M	US	Revised	354
	■ International Business Strategy in Action	Is The Body Shop an ethical business?	EU: UK	Revised	365
	■ Real Case	Dell: B2C	US/Emerging Economies: China		371
	■ Real Case	Maersk Group	EU: Denmark/ US/Asia		372

CHAPTER	TYPE OF CASE	ORGANIZATION/INDUSTRY	COUNTRY/ REGION	NEW/ REVISED	PAGE
Chapter 12 Production Strategy	■ Active Learning Case	GE production: from Six Sigma to the GE Store	US	Revised	382
	■ International Business Strategy in Action	Gap Inc.: a successful "hollow corporation"	EU/US	Revised	389
	■ International Business Strategy in Action	End of an era: the Goodyear plant closure	UK	New	391
	■ Real Case	Flextronics	Emerging Economies: Singapore	Revised	411
	■ Real Case	Nike	US	Revised	413
Chapter 13 Marketing Strategy	■ Active Learning Case	Adidas: promoting a global sports brand	UK/Brazil	New	417
	■ International Business Strategy in Action	Weeby buys Tappy	US/Emerging Economies: Vietnam	New	426
	■ International Business Strategy in Action	IKEA in international markets	EU: Sweden	Revised	428
	■ Real Case	Bang & Olufsen	EU: Denmark/ US	Revised	441
	■ Real Case	Mirum—never lose your sense of wonder!	US	New	443
Chapter 14 Human Resource Management Strategy	■ Active Learning Case	The Coca-Cola Company thinks local	US	Revised	448
	■ International Business Strategy in Action	The glass ceiling	UK	New	455
	■ International Business Strategy in Action	Primark: putting global stakeholders first	UK	New	463
	■ Real Case	Offshoring to India	US/Emerging Economies: India		472
	■ Real Case	Executive search firms	EU	Revised	473
Chapter 15 Political Risk and Negotiation Strategy	■ Active Learning Case	Nestlé in Nigeria	Emerging Economies: Nigeria	New	478

CHAPTER	TYPE OF CASE	ORGANIZATION/INDUSTRY	COUNTRY/ REGION	NEW/ REVISED	PAGE
	■ Real Case	Renault and Nissan: no pain, no gain	Japan/EU: France	Revised	610
	■ Real Case	Sony: diversifying into the automobile industry?	Japan	New	613
Chapter 19 North America	■ Active Learning Case	NAFTA	US/Emerging Economies: Mexico and Canada	Revised	620
	■ International Business Strategy in Action	Bombardier	Canada/ Emerging Economies: Brazil	Revised	625
	■ International Business Strategy in Action	Mexico and NAFTA	US/Emerging Economies: Mexico	Revised	637
	■ Real Case	Jumex of Mexico	Emerging Economies: Mexico	Revised	643
	■ Real Case	GlaxoSmithKline in the United States	UK/US	Revised	644
Chapter 20 Emerging Economies	■ Active Learning Case	Acer Taiwan goes international	Emerging Economies: Taiwan	Revised	649
	■ International Business Strategy in Action	From Oserian to Tesco: the Kenyan cut flower industry	Emerging Economies: Kenya	Revised	661
	■ International Business Strategy in Action	Korean *chaebols:* Hyundai and Samsung	Emerging Economies: S. Korea	Revised	669
	■ Real Case	The Indian IT, software, and services industry	Emerging Economies: India	Revised	673
	■ Real Case	Bumrungrad International in Thailand	Emerging Economies: Thailand	Revised	676

CHAPTER	TYPE OF CASE	ORGANIZATION/INDUSTRY	COUNTRY/ REGION	NEW/ REVISED	PAGE
Chapter 21 China	■ Active Learning Case	Oxford Instruments in China	EU: UK/ Emerging Economies: China	Revised	683
	■ International Business Strategy in Action	Airbus in China	EU/Emerging Economies: China		690
	■ International Business Strategy in Action	Haier goes global	Emerging Economies: China	Revised	701
	■ Real Case	Citigroup in China	US/Emerging Economies: China	Revised	705
	■ Real Case	Nanjing Auto makes the MG	EU: UK/ Emerging Economies: China	Revised	707

PUBLISHER'S ACKNOWLEDGMENTS

We are grateful to the following for permission to use copyright material:

Figures

Figure 2.10 adapted from The Handbook of Global Science, Technology, and Innovation (International R&D alliances by firms: Origins and development MERIT Working Papers 2014–058), Wiley-Blackwell (Narula, R., & Martinez-Noya A. (Editors: Daniele Archibugi and Andrea Filippetti) 2014) Wiley-Blackwell; Figure 2.11 from Decision-making and market orientation in the internationalization process of small and medium-sized enterprises, Management International Review, vol. 45, 4, pp. 413–426 (Collinson, S., & Houlden, J. 2005), Springer, With permission of Springer; Figure 2.12 adapted from Decision-making and market orientation in the internationalization process of small and medium-sized enterprises. Management International Review, vol. 45, 4 pp. 413–426 (Collinson, S., & Houlden, J. 2005), Springer, With permission of Springer; Figure 3.2 from IRI, R&D Magazine, International Monetory Fund, World Bank, CIA Factbook, OECDD, https://www.iriweb.org/sites/default/files/2016GlobalR%26DFundingForecast_2.pdf, Advantage Business Media; Figure 3.8 from The regional nature of Japanese multinational business, Journal of International Business Studies, vol. 39 (2) (Collinson S.C. and Rugman A.M. 2008), Palgrave Macmillan UK; Figure 3.10 adapted from Managing across Borders: The Transnational Solution, Harvard Business School Press (C. Bartlett and Ghoshal S. 2002) Harvard Business School Publishing; Figure 3.11 adapted from The Differentiated Network: Organizing MNCs for Value Creation, Jossey-Bass, San Francisco (Nohria N. and Ghoshal S. 1997) Wiley; Figure 5.2 from The cultural relativity of organizational practices and theories, Journal of International Business Studies, Fall ed., p. 92 (1982), G. Hofstede; Figure 6.1 from The Manager in the International Economy, 6 ed, Prentice Hall, NJ. (Vernon R. & Wells L.T., Jr 1991) p. 95, Pearson Education, Reprinted and electronically reproduced by permission of Pearson Education, Inc., New York, NY.; Figure 6.3 from The Manager in the International Economy, Prentice Hall (Vernon R. & Wells L.T., Jr. 1991) p. 85, Prentice Hall, Reprinted and electronically reproduced by permission of Pearson Education, Inc., New York, NY.; Figure 7.2 adapted from figure 1, St Louis Fed Review, March, p. 8 (Chrystal K.A. 1984), Federal Reserve Bank of St Louis; Figure 8.2 from Advanced Micro Deices: Poised for Chip Greatness. Unpublished student paper, Sloan School of Management, MIT (Scott Beardsley and Kinji Sakagami 1988) p. 46, Reported in Arnoldo C. Hax and Nicolas S. Majluf, The Strategy Concept and Process: A Pragmatic Approach (Englewood Cliffs, NJ: Prentice Hall, 1991); Figure 8.3 with the permission of The Free Press, a Division of Simon & Schuster, Inc., adapted from Creating and Sustaining Superior Performance by Porter M.E. Copyright © 1985 by Porter M.E. All rights reserved; Figure 8.4 with the permission of The Free Press, a Division of Simon & Schuster, Inc., adapted from Competitive Advantage by Porter M.E. Copyright © 1995, 1998 by Porter M.E. All rights reserved; Figure 9.11 adapted from Comparative and Multinational Management John Wiley & Sons, Inc. (Ronen S. 1986) John Wiley & Sons, Inc.; Figures 10.1, 10.2 with the permission of The Free Press, a Division of Simon & Schuster, Inc., adapted from Competitive Advantage of Nations by Porter M.E. Copyright © 1990 by Porter M.E. All rights reserved; Figure 10.3 from Fast Forward: Improving Canada's International Competitiveness, Diane Publishing Company (Rugman A. M. and D'Cruz H.R. 1991) p. 35, Diane Publishing Company; Figure 10.4 adapted from The 'Double Diamond' Model of International Competitiveness: the Canadian Experience, Management International Review, vol. 33 (Special Issue 2) (Rugman A.M. & D'Cruz J.R. 1993); Figure 10.7 adapted from Building and Managing the Transnational: the New Organizational Challenge in Competition in Global Industries,

Harvard Business School Publishing Corporation (Editor: Porter M.E. 1986) The Harvard Business School Publishing Corporation, all rights reserved; Figure 11.1 from Multinationals as Flagship Firms: Regional Business Networks, Oxford University Press Canada (Rugman A. and D'Cruz J.R. 2000) OUP Canada; Figure 11.2 from Multinationals as Flagship Firms: Regional Business Networks, Oxford University Press (Rugman A. and D'Cruz J.R. 2000) Oxford University Press Canada; Figure 12.4 adapted from United Nations Publication, http://unctad.org/en/Docs/wir2002_en.pdf, United Nations; Figure 14.1 from Who manages multinational enterprises?, Columbia Journal of World Business, Summer ed., p. 33 (Franco L.G. 1973), Elsevier Science Direct; Figure 14.4 from from page 2, Primark - engaging with stakeholders, http://business-cascstudies.co.uk/primark/engaging-with-stakeholders/what-is-a-stake-holder.html#axz4CIsRieom, Business Case Studies; Figure 18.1 from fig. 11.4, http://www.stat.go.jp/english/data/handbook/c0117.htm, © 1996 Statistics Bureau,Ministry of Internal Affairs and Communications; Figure 18.2 from figure 11.3, http://www.stat.go.jp/english/data/handbook/c0117.htm, © 1996 Statistics Bureau, Ministry of Internal Affairs and Communications; Figure 18.4 from Modern Japan: A Concise Survey, MacMillan (Cortazzi, Sir H. 1993) p. 132, MacMillan Publishers Ltd; Figure 18.6 from Groupe Renault Annual Report, 2014, https://group.renault.com/wp-content/uploads/2015/05/renault_ra_2014_en.pdf, Renault; Figure 18.7 from Groupe Renault 2014 Annual report, https://group.renault.com/wp-content/uploads/2015/05/renault_ra_2014_en.pdf, Renault; Figure 20.8 from http://www.ibef.org/industry/information-technology-india.aspx, Copyright © 2010-2016 India Brand Equity Foundation; Figure 20.9 from http://www.nasscom.in/it%E2%80%99s-growth-and-transformation-indian-itbpm-industry?fg=235321, Copyright © 2010-2014, NASSCOM.

Tables

Table 2.1 adapted from Location and collocation advantages in international innovation, Multinational Business Review, Vol. 20, no 1, pp. 6–25 (Narula, R. and Santangelo, G. D. 2012), Emerald Group Publishing ltd, Reprinted with permission from Emerald Group Publishing Limited; Table 2.4 adapted from 'A set of motives to unite them all ? Revisiting the principles and typology of internationalzation motives', Multinational Business Review, vol. 23 (1) (A. Cuerva-Cazurra and R. Narula 2015), Emerald Group Publishing Ltd, Reprinted with permission from Emerald Group Publishing Limited; Table 3.3 adapted from http://www.research.ibm.com/worldwide/index.shtml.; Tables 7.1 and 7.2 adapted from material sourced from Barclays Bank plc Annual Report; Table 8.1 adapted from Strategic planning for a global business, Columbia Journal of World Business, Summer vol. (Chakravarthy, B.S. and Perimutter, H.V. 1985), Elsevier Science and Technology Journals; Table 8.3 adapted from International Dimensions of Management, 2 ed., South-Western, a part of Cengage (Phatak A. 1989) South-Western Publishing; Table 12.1 from The New Competitors: They Think in Terms of 'Speed-to-Market, Academy of Management Perspectives, vol. 5 (no 2), pp. 23–33 (Vesey J.T.), The Academy of Management (NY); Table 13.1 from 'Measuring a promotional campaign' from "Planning Effective Marketing Strategies for a Target Audience", An Adidas Case Study, page 5, http://business-cascstudies.co.uk/adidas/planning-effective-marketing-strategies-for-a-target-audience/measuring-a-promotional-campaign.html#axzz4CIsRieom, Copyright © 1995-2016 Business Case Studies LLP; Table 15.4 from The influence of culture on the process of business negotiations: An exploratory study, Journal of International Business Studies, p. 88 (Graham J.L. 1985), Palgrave McMillan; Table 16.5 from Sovereign Wealth Fund Institute (updated November, 2015), http://www.swfinstitute.org/sovereign-wealth-fund-rankings/, Sovereign Wealth Fund Institute (SWFI).

Photographs
(Key: b – bottom; c – centre; l – left; r –-right; t – top)

Alamy Images: age fotostock 506, Agencja Fotograficzna Caro 625, ALANDAWSONPHOTOGRAPHY 429, Quentin Bargate 124, Joerg Boethling 242, Craig Joiner Photography 578, Yaacov Dagan 614, epa european pressphoto agency b.v. 670, 690, Russell Hart 179, Lou-Foto 701, David Lyons 708tl, Ingemar Magnusson 411, Iain Masterton 526, 583, Trevor Mogg 597, Patrick/SagaPhoto.com 313, Peter Probst 568, RosaIreneBetancourt 1 390, ScottyH 256, Helen Sessions 77, Trevor Smith 522, Peter Titmus 373, Kristoffer Tripplar 372; **Simon Collinson:** 683; **Fotolia.com:** WavebreakMediaMicro 42; **Getty Images:** Ulrich Baumgarten via Getty Images 550, Bettmann 620, Jean-Christophe Verhaegen/AFP 192, Francis Dean/Corbis via Getty Images 442, Matthew Lewis 708tr, Iain Masterton 344, Thomas Wirth/AFP 295; **Shutterstock. com:** Apples Eyes Studio 677, Roberto Caucino 278.

All other images © Pearson Education

FRAMEWORKS FOR THIS BOOK
Our Approach to the Study of International Business

Figure 1 sets the scene for this entire book. Our approach to understanding international business focuses on the interrelationships between the firm and its environment, at several connected levels. Multinational enterprises (MNEs) are firms (small and large) that have expanded to source inputs or sell outputs internationally. They are at the center of our framework.

Figure 1 The multiple, interacting levels and lenses of international business studies

International managers in MNEs make decisions based on their understanding of this environment and the (tangible and intangible) assets, resources, and capabilities they can coordinate internally to help their firms succeed. In this evolutionary sense, managers and their firms need to adapt in response to an ever-changing competitive environment in order to survive. There are opportunities to create alliances with partner firms, or benefit from new technologies, improve productivity, innovate, and develop new products and services to attract more customers. But there are also threats from competitors that can exploit these same opportunities faster or more effectively.

Overall then, we look at how well "firm-specific" assets (FSAs), resources, and capabilities are aligned with the host country environments (country-specific assets, or CSAs) in which MNEs operate. The "dynamic capability" of firms depends on the ability of decision-makers to maintain this alignment in a changing world, evolving FSAs to exploit external opportunities and cope with new threats. We make a distinction between the external industry environment and the external macro environment. The former is comprised of the specific threats and opportunities influencing the behavior of firms that collaborate or compete directly with each other in a particular industry sector (automotive manufacturing, insurance services, container shipping, etc.). The latter represents the broader, global context comprised of a complex range of different country markets, institutions, and cultures around the world. Country markets present opportunities (or "location advantages") such as access to inputs like lower-cost labor, cheaper resources, new technology or expertise, or access to new customers. But this access may be constrained by local competitors, institutions, and regulations or different ways of doing business. One core aim of international business studies is to better understand these differences and how MNE decision-makers can cope with them.

At the macro environment level it is important to understand how the interrelationships and interdependencies between countries are changing over time. The opening up of emerging markets, the growing dependence on China as a market and a source of manufacturing products, and the shifting nature of regional blocs (such as the EU) are the kinds of key changes that have implications for whole industries, each MNE, and individual decision-makers. Trade and FDI data help map these macro-level changes. As places (countries, regions, cities) compete to be net exporters and net recipients of inward investment, these empirical data show who are the winners and losers.

At the industry environment level, global value chains, buyer–supplier relationships, joint ventures, and alliances between co-dependent firms that specialize in different products and services all connect competing locations. MNEs derive competitive advantage by linking different places via these kinds of mechanisms. They leverage the benefits that come, for example, from buying or making products in one place (where cheap labor and other location advantages exist) and selling them in another, where disposable income and prices are high. They also benefit by integrating the knowledge and capabilities that exist in different locations to add value to products and services sold in other locations. All firms are brokers, but by definition MNEs are brokers that trade globally.

A full insight into the shifting complexities of international business requires a combination of theories, frameworks, concepts, tools, and examples from across the social sciences, including economics, political science, sociology, and human geography. Each of these disciplines explains a different set of factors operating at each of our levels of analysis, micro to macro. They also bring different "tool kits" to answer our questions. Put them together and we have more powerful and convincing explanations of how the world works. So our approach is multidisciplinary.

PRACTICAL THEORY

Kurt Lewin (one of the founders of social psychology) famously said, "There is nothing so practical as good theory." Good theory is useful as well as being evidence-based and broadly applicable to different contexts. Good theory, alongside key frameworks and concepts which simplify and explain the way the world works, can guide effective decision making by turning information into knowledge and knowledge into real-world wisdom.

This book takes a number of different perspectives to improve our understanding of international business. We take on the role of objective observers, compiling data and evidence to map trends and make predictions. Data on trade, foreign direct investment, global mergers and acquisitions (M&As), regulatory changes, the largest MNEs, and the fastest-growing SMEs (small and medium-sized enterprises) all help us understand what is going on in the world.

We also take on the role of decision-makers, putting ourselves in the shoes of government policy developers and (more often) practicing managers. A key question that runs through the book is: what are the main challenges facing an MNE manager, trying to enter new country markets and coping with very different country contexts?

Figure 2 outlines a series of decision stages for managers involved in the process of international expansion. The why, what, where, and hows (and really, how?) of internationalization are mapped on to some of the core concepts and frameworks featured in the book. Decision-makers have a wide range of strategic choices, which they make in the face of ever-changing opportunities and threats. The success of a firm, in fact its very survival, depends on its decision-makers making more right decisions than wrong ones. Firm sales revenues, profits, and other measures of performance allow us to judge whether the right decisions have been made, both over time (looking at data trends over the years) and relative to competitors (comparative benchmarking). The list in the right-hand column shows some of the main analytical concepts and frameworks we use to address the key questions for decision-makers that are guiding the international expansion of their firms.

One of the measures we use is the "Transnational Index" or TNI. This indicates how multinational a firm is by adding up three ratios: foreign sales as a percentage of total sales, foreign assets as a percentage of total assets, and foreign employment as a percentage of total employment. A low TNI (below 20 percent) shows that a firm is domestic market-oriented and not very multinational. Researchers have explored the relationship between multinationality and performance and found that there is no simple correlation. (See the top 100 MNEs listed by TNI in the appendix to Chapter 2.)

Both quantitative and qualitative approaches are necessary to get more complete explanations of the internationalization journey. Each of the chapters in our book (with the exception of Chapter 1) features five case studies of different kinds and these provide real-world stories about how specific firms (or, in some cases, industries or countries) have coped with particular international business challenges.

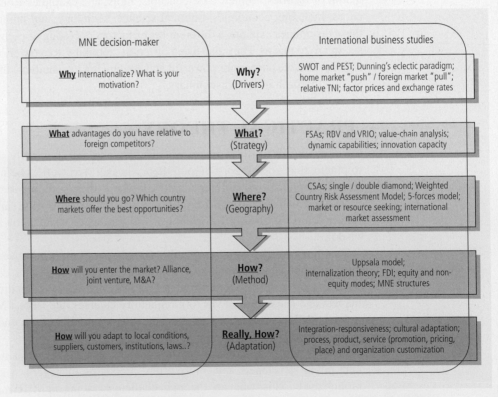

Figure 2 **The internationalization roadmap: decision stages for global expansion**

But our interest in this book goes beyond an understanding of what makes managers and firms successful—whether success is measured in profitability, providing employment, or just expanding in scale and becoming more powerful. We are interested in how MNEs and their activities affect the "rest of us". In responding to external change MNEs have a significant impact on our world. They provide most of our products and services and employ millions of people. *How* they do this and *where* they do this affects not just international trade and investment, but local communities, our shared environment, and most people's employment opportunities. One of our key aims is to help you, the reader, to *critically appraise* the effects of their actions. In what ways are they a positive or a negative force in our world? A substantial part of the book also discusses how government policies and the activities of non-government organizations (NGOs) influence the behavior of MNEs.

So our textbook uses multidisciplinary approaches, quantitative and qualitative methods, empirical data, and real-world case studies to examine and understand the motivations, actions, and effects of multinational firms, large and small, at multiple levels of analysis. In the final introductory section we provide an overview of how all of this material is structured through the book.

THE STRUCTURE OF THIS BOOK

Chapter 1 is slightly different in structure from the other 20 chapters in this book as it introduces the field of international business and contains no case studies. Each of the remaining chapters opens with a set of contents and key objectives and an "Active Learning Case", with learning checks throughout the chapter which ask (and answer) a series of questions relating the issues covered in the text to this opening case study. Two "International Business Strategy in Action" case studies and two "Real Cases" also feature, the latter coming at the end of each chapter. Key learning points and key terms as well as review and discussion questions also appear at the end of each chapter alongside a bibliography presenting references and further reading.

Figure 3 shows how the book is structured to cover the different aspects of international business across the levels of analysis outlined in Figure 1. There are five major parts. Part One contains the introduction and Chapters 2 and 3. We introduce some key frameworks and explore why and how firms become MNEs. Part Two covers the macro environment and discusses how political, cultural, and institutional contexts vary by region and require MNEs to adapt. Financial transactions and institutions and trade are given particular attention. This part looks at how places vary and how they interact, compete, and develop particular interdependencies.

Part Three shifts the emphasis toward the MNE and the decision-maker to examine how different international business strategies are appropriate in different global contexts. The interplay between strategy and structure (or "organizing strategy"; Chapter 9) is a central theme. As Alfred Chandler observed, these evolve in tandem. A firm's structure and organization enable some strategic options and limit or exclude others. So MNE structure shapes strategy. Strategic choices in turn require structural changes as the firm must reorganize its divisions, resources, and people to implement new initiatives, like entering a new overseas market. So strategy shapes structure. Chapter 10 focuses on the diamond models of advantage and the integration-responsiveness framework. Chapter 11 looks beyond performance and competitiveness to understand the wider obligations of MNEs to stakeholders, rather than just shareholders. We compare stakeholder approaches, in which ethics and corporate social responsibility are emphasized by "responsible businesses", with shareholder approaches where performance and profits dominate.

Part Four takes a more detailed look at some specific functions within MNEs: production, marketing, HRM (human resource management), and finance. These are specialist areas of business and management studies in their own right and we focus on the international dimensions of these functions and the ways in which they can facilitate effective international strategies. Chapter 15 presents the "Weighted Country Risk Assessment Model" as a framework for guiding the "where" and "how" decision steps outlined in Figure 2. It allows decision-makers to compare country markets and different modes of market entry as a precursor to investment.

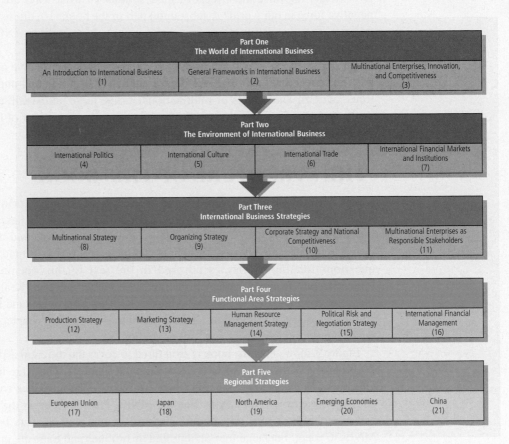

Figure 3 The structure of this book

Finally, Part Five presents five regional (macro) environments and discusses some specific international business strategies for "coping" with them. We provide an overview of the political, socio-cultural, economic and institutional characteristics of these key countries and regions, alongside case studies of both foreign MNEs and local firms. The former have successfully leveraged their FSAs to establish themselves in these markets, learning about the differences and adapting accordingly. The latter have evolved in these environments and reflect particular strengths, weaknesses, and characteristics that will underpin their ability (or inability) to expand internationally and become MNEs.

Part One

THE WORLD OF INTERNATIONAL BUSINESS

Chapter 1

AN INTRODUCTION TO INTERNATIONAL BUSINESS

Contents

Objectives of the chapter

In this chapter we are going to define the boundaries of the field of international business in an introductory overview of the main themes of this book. We will examine trends in international business, keeping in mind how globalization has evolved over the last century. We will examine some of the worldwide economic and political changes that are taking place and look at how globalization (and its constituent elements) is altering the way international business is conducted.

We will then focus on innovation and technology, and discuss how they lie at the core of greater interdependence, which is one of the defining features of globalization. After this, we look at social political developments and institutions, which effectively define how businesses conduct their operations. Understanding institutions, both formal and informal, is important for both firms and employees, so they can adjust their behaviors accordingly. We then discuss how supranational agreements try to harmonize some of these institutions, such as the World Trade Organization, which has led to the liberalizing of markets between member states and has been used to solve disputes. The next section looks at multinational enterprises (MNEs), which are at the core of spreading globalization, and we examine their controlling investments abroad, otherwise known as foreign direct investment, which will be a key feature throughout this book. We also trace the rise of MNEs to the present day. MNEs are not the only important actor in international business; so are small and medium-sized enterprises (SMEs), which will also be examined in this chapter. Finally, we discuss global value chains and networks, and show how products are assembled through firms that are based in several countries.

The specific objectives of this chapter are to:

1 *Define* the boundaries of the field of international business in an introductory overview of the main themes of this book.

2 *Examine* how worldwide economic and political changes have driven globalization and shape the way international business is conducted.

3 *Highlight* innovation and technology as major factors underlying global economic growth and greater interdependence between firms and countries.

4 *Introduce* some of the main actors that feature throughout this book: multinational enterprises and small and medium-sized enterprises, which are at the core of spreading globalization; value chains and networks, which connect firms globally; and institutions (national and global), which shape how these other actors evolve.

INTRODUCTION

Chapter 1 provides an introduction to the field of international business (IB). We begin by drawing the boundaries of the field of IB, its main definitions and concepts, and then introduce the main activities and stakeholders in IB and discuss their roles and inter-relations. We provide an overview of worldwide economic and political changes as a background to understanding the process of globalization and its main driver, the multinational enterprise. The section concludes with a discussion of new developments in international business. specifically, we discuss both the emergence of emerging economies and the growth of non-equity mechanisms, paying particular interest to the growth of global value chains.

WHAT IS INTERNATIONAL BUSINESS?

International business
The study of transactions taking place across national borders for the purpose of satisfying the needs of individuals and organizations

The world of **international business** is a wonderful and exciting field of study. The "international" in "international business" is superfluous because globalization has meant that all business is to some degree international. Today it is almost impossible to find a product or service that does not have an international aspect to its customer base, as well as at least one element of its supply chain. By supply chain, we refer to the chain inputs that come from other sources, including the raw materials, components, and equipment used to produce, store, and package the product or service. Therefore, in this book we approach IB as a study of business.

We define international business as the study of transactions taking place across national borders for the purpose of satisfying the needs of individuals and organizations. There are many forms of international business transactions. The "classical" view of international business has been international trade, in the form of **exporting** and **importing**. Trade is about transactions between actors that are physically located in different places. These actors may be in the same country, but located in different states or provinces, for instance. They may be in different countries, in which case the activity is known as **international trade**. International trade continues to grow, and remains core to the world economy. According to the United Nations Conference on Trade and Development (UNCTAD) the exports of goods and services in 2014 was worth US$23 trillion, an almost sixfold increase from US$4 trillion in 1990. (By definition, the total world exports will be equal to the total world imports, so it is axiomatic that imports have grown as fast as imports.) Trade is not new, as human beings have been engaged in bartering goods since the dawn of civilization. Indeed, as we shall discuss later, trade has been the driving force of economic growth and has been a driving force for globalization. The Appendix to this chapter lists the 25 largest exporters and importers.

Exports
Goods and services produced by a firm in one country and then sent to another country

Imports
Goods and services produced in one country and bought in by another country

International trade
The exchange of goods and services across international borders

Since the beginning of the twentieth century, the key change has been the growth of the international firm, with operations and activities that are directly controlled in overseas locations. Such operations are known as *affiliates* or *subsidiaries*. These international firms are known as **multinational enterprises (MNEs),** and although the casual observer may think of them as large behemoths like Google, Huawei, IBM, Iberia, Hon Hai, Reliance, etc., a majority of MNEs are small and medium-sized (e.g. Cobalt Light Systems, Acro Aircraft Seating, SafeGuard World International and Mind Gym).[1] For instance, firms with fewer than 200 employees accounted for 97.6 percent of all firms in Taiwan in 2013, and employed 78.3 percent of the workforce!

Multinational enterprise (MNE)
A multi-plant firm that controls and coordinates operations in at least two countries; or a firm that engages in value-added international business activities, that has affiliates in more than one country, and whose operations and activities in different locations are actively coordinated by one or more headquarters organizations

International firms are responsible for about one-third of global trade, much of which moves between affiliates: that is, these goods and services are being exchanged across borders but within the same MNE. Large MNEs—through various linkages—have considerable influence on other non-affiliated firms as well, because they depend upon a vast array of other firms to supply them with various inputs, intermediate goods, and supplies. Smaller firms are dependent upon a variety of larger MNEs as customers. Indeed, the total effect—which is hard to estimate accurately—is that possibly half of the global economic activity is in one way or another dependent upon international business and MNEs of all sizes.

The principles of trade are well known, having been a subject of study at least since the 1700s, and the principles and processes by which trade is undertaken are very unambiguous. Chapter 6 deals with international trade in considerable detail. Our interest in this opening chapter is to place the global economy and international business into context, and the novelty here is the role of the international firm, and how it undertakes international business.

The reader will have noted that we have not used the term "global firm," but instead we refer to "international firms" or "multinational enterprises." There are few firms that are truly global, and it is a common error to use the word "global" as a synonym for "international." This error lies in the failure to understand globalization, and therefore we begin this chapter by clearly defining globalization. We will then go on to explain how the MNE and international business have evolved, and how the intertwining of so many disparate factors has created the complex tapestry that is today's global economy.

GLOBALIZATION

There is little doubt that we live in a world defined by globalization. Globalization, however, remains a vague concept, used by different people in different ways. It is also a divisive subject because many of the social, political, and economic problems in the world today are attributed to the negative effects of globalization, while others regard it as a force for positive change. In this book we do not seek to take sides in the debate about the pros and cons of globalization, or to engage in a discussion of "making globalization good." It is simply a fact of the twenty-first century, and it is an ongoing *process*, rather than an *event*. In this book, we focus on **economic globalization**. We define economic globalization as *the growing interdependence of locations and economic actors across countries and regions.*[2]

Economic globalization
The growing interdependence of locations and economic actors across countries and regions

By referring to economic actors we are able to include very small actors (such as individual entrepreneurs), or very large ones (such as a nation-state, which itself consists of individuals), as well as firms of all sizes. We use the term "economic actor" deliberately to include not only MNEs, but all formally and systematically organized entities (such as non-governmental organizations, clubs, associations, charities, governmental organizations, state-owned firms, hospitals, research centers, and universities), each functioning (however imperfectly) as a clearly delineated single organization for the generation of a specific set of outcomes or goals defined by their stakeholders. These may be the generation of profits, the provision of jobs, reducing poverty, or some other goal, and they seek to act as a single cohesive unit toward the achievement of this goal. The logic of how each economic actor interacts internally follows similar principles, and they are seen by other actors as a cohesive single unit, regardless of the nature of its intended goal, or its size.

The outcomes of globalization

As summarized in Figure 1.1, globalization has manifested itself through certain very clear outcomes. Most obviously for the study of IB, there has been a greater interdependence of locations (whether countries, regions, or cities) and an interdependence of firms.

The *interdependence of locations* is an especially complex issue, and is associated with the growth of the international firm. At the most basic level, the growth of trade has reduced distances, and the concurrent growth of MNEs has accentuated this trend. The borders of countries (and cities and regions) have become increasingly blurred, because the economic actors located within that location also have operations in multiple other locations. At the country level, it affects the identity of the nation-state. On the one hand, countries remain sovereign and independent, while on the other hand, they are increasingly swayed by developments outside their borders. Currencies are floating, and their values are determined by

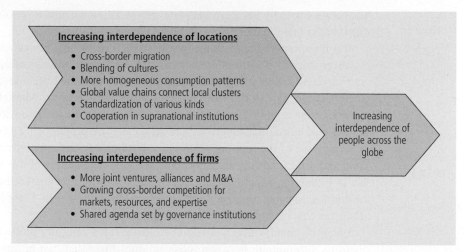

Figure 1.1 The consequences of globalization

the vagaries of currency traders the world over, and by political and economic developments not just in neighboring countries. Should a government decide to raise corporation taxes for companies located within its borders, this does not mean that there will be greater tax revenues. Higher tax rates in one country can motivate firms to relocate their operations to a lower-tax country. The declining sovereignty of countries reflects itself in the fact that home country governments can intervene directly to influence the investment decisions of their MNEs, and few countries can afford to make policy decisions without considering what other countries are doing. Government policies have to tread a thin line between responding to international developments and to domestic priorities. Countries in the EU cannot make laws that contravene EU laws; members of the World Trade Organization (WTO) must adhere to the rules of the WTO.

At the same time, this does not mean countries have no distinct identity: there are clearly defined characteristics and patterns that are history-dependent and idiosyncratic, such as areas of specialization, technological competences, structure of markets, consumption patterns, and culture. Although at a policy and international business level, countries have less independence, at a sociological, cultural, and political level they remain distinct. These differences continue to matter, and despite the rhetoric, there is little evidence that there is significant convergence at these levels.

The *interdependence of firms* has taken place through alliances, joint ventures, and outsourcing activities and is a distinctive feature of globalization. Collaboration by economic actors is happening in ever-greater numbers with every passing year. This is a phenomenon that has sparked the attention of managers, policy-makers, and academics alike. Some believe that this phenomenon is the death knell of the traditional firm, that firms will become increasingly "virtual," although we think this idea is somewhat exaggerated. Although collaborative activity is not a new practice, it is undeniable that there has clearly been a process of evolution whereby there is an increasing use of alliances explicitly for strategic purposes. Its novelty is not as an organizational form—economic units have collaborated for millennia. Intricate linkages between economic entities that create informal and formal networks to undertake value-added activity date back to before the seventeenth century. Rapid Japanese industrial growth over the last century has been partly attributed to the cooperation between interlinked firms with limited equity cross-holdings within industrial groups referred to in the post-World War II era as *keiretsu*. What is unique about today's cooperation between firms is its widespread use by firms of all sizes and nationalities, and its use in a growing variety of activities such as R&D. Furthermore, cooperative activity has a growing international element, and it is not just limited to related firms but is often undertaken with international competitors.

It is important to point out that just because it seems that globalization is leading toward a convergence of consumption patterns and the global presence of certain firms, products, and services, convergence does not imply uniformity. Just because consumer preferences have become similar, this does not mean they are the same. Markets are simultaneously local as well as global, and in some instances they may remain local. Coca-Cola is an example of a firm that advertises and sells the same product on a global basis. This seems to work most of the time for Coca-Cola, but homogeneity in consumption patterns in the food and drinks industry is rarely achieved. A good example of this is the soft drinks market in Indonesia, which, despite Coca-Cola's considerable marketing efforts, continues to be dominated by unsweetened and non-fizzy tea. A local firm, Sinar Sosro PT, continues to dominate this market, with a 58 percent share in 2014.

Large companies like Nestlé and Unilever have carefully plotted a course that allows them to differentiate between those product lines that can be marketed and produced regionally, locally, or globally (we will discuss the integration-responsiveness framework throughout this book, particularly in Chapters 8, 9, and 10). Other markets, such as banking services and mobile telephones, have shown considerable market convergence. Even in such sectors, there are limits to how far and how fast convergence has occurred. Despite HSBC's huge investment in announcing itself as a "global" bank operating under one brand since the 1990s, and with global technological platforms to allow seamless activity across borders, in 2015 HSBC announced its intention to disinvest from a number of key markets, and return to being a regional, Asia-based player.[3]

Understanding interdependence in globalization

Interdependence
Mutual reliance between groups of actors; individuals, firms, countries, or regions

There is a tendency to mistake internationalization for globalization, and the key to differentiating the two is the issue of **interdependence**. Interdependence is the essence of globalization, and as usual, it is a continuum, with firms, individuals and countries demonstrating different degrees of interdependence. Understanding globalization requires us to appreciate the increasing degree of interdependence between economic units, whether firms, individuals, or countries.

The term "interdependence" has a very specific meaning. It refers to a mutual reliance between groups of actors, and the degree of this mutual reliance can vary considerably. Members of a soccer team are typically deeply interconnected, with a high degree of interdependence. The sudden departure of a key player in a team can severely affect the efficiency of the team as a whole, and can endanger its very survival. The decision of the United Kingdom to withdraw from the European Union in June 2016 will prove to be very difficult to implement because both the EU and the UK are highly interdependent, and are bound very tightly together. The key issues are the degree of *centrality* and *reciprocity*. Reciprocity refers to the degree to which the reliance is two-way. Take the case of the USA and India. Their economies are obviously interdependent. However, the relationship is unequal. As an economic, political, and military superpower, the US has greater economic and political clout, and has greater influence in shaping the rules that define their interaction, while India remains peripheral in international affairs outside South Asia. Likewise, when it comes to economic activity, there is a strong imbalance. Over a third of India's exports go to the US, but for the US, India is only its thirteenth largest destination for exports, just after Taiwan, a country many times smaller. The United States enjoys a much more "central" status within the global economy, while India is less central and more toward the "periphery." On the other hand, India has a higher centrality than Vietnam or Kenya, given its larger economic size and its geopolitical position.

The last two decades have seen China, and some East Asian economies (such as Taiwan, Korea, Singapore, and Malaysia) become increasingly central compared with Laos, Vietnam, or Bangladesh. Much of Africa is firmly within the periphery. It is not only about physical size, or the lack of natural resources or markets. The Netherlands and Belgium are small in these terms, but have high centrality, whereas Norway, Finland, and New Zealand are on the periphery, but are less integrated into the world economy.

A more central economy is one which plays a significant role as either host or home to MNEs; engages in considerable trade in intermediate and manufactured goods; contributes greatly to innovation and scientific progress; is strongly linked or accessible physically to other central countries, through strong infrastructure, transport, and communication links; and plays a significant role in decision making within supranational organizations.[4]

It has become increasingly obvious that many more peripheral countries are unable to make and implement economic decisions unilaterally because in these economies MNEs from more central economies that are major players in international markets determine prices, and the central economies' banks determine lending, and therefore exchange rates, and the value and use of resources. Peripheral countries have to consider external and foreign conditions and actors in making economic decisions, and are thus more or less obliged to consider external (non-domestic) dimensions. They are *dependent* rather than interdependent on other more central countries, through supranational institutions as well as firms.

Interdependence is not just a country-level phenomenon. Economic actors come in all sizes. MNEs matter more than others because they are often large and powerful: the largest MNEs have revenues greater than the GDP of many countries. MNE-based industrial development policies are now commonplace among most countries.[5] There is also increased competition for MNE investment, particularly investments that provide opportunities for technology transfer, employment, and capital. Firms of all sizes are increasingly integrated with firms, customers, suppliers, governments, and organizations in other countries.

Regional integration

One of the most visible outcomes of globalization is economic integration, and this is happening naturally as a result of growing interdependence. However, at the same time as "natural" integration takes place because of growing MNE and trading activities, and the greater interdependence due to supranational organizations, common institutions, etc., there is also a process of *formal regional integration*. Most often, countries that are geographically proximate set up formal agreements to create "groups" that seek in large part to increase **foreign direct investment (FDI)** and trade within their region, consequent from increased opportunities to exploit economies of scale. Smaller and more peripheral countries also hope that it will increase their bargaining power with larger and powerful "central" economies. Interdependence caused by globalization is more a consequence of increased cross-border activity, while regional integration is intended to *cause* it.

There is no question that globalization has resulted in economic integration. This has led to a revival of previously unsuccessful or dormant schemes and the establishment of a number of new agreements. Although estimates vary, there are more than a hundred regional integration schemes in existence. Part of this enthusiasm has to do with the benefits that have accrued to members associated with the EU and NAFTA.

There are several similarities between globalization and regional integration. Both are processes and closely associated with cross-border economic activity, although globalization is more a consequence of increased cross-border activity, while regional integration is intended to cause it. Both globalization and regional integration are believed to provide opportunities for more rapid economic growth, associated in large part with increased FDI and trade that are consequent from increased opportunities to exploit economies of scale.

Foreign direct investment (FDI)
Equity funds invested in other nations. It is different from portfolio (financial) investment in that FDI is undertaken by MNEs which exercise control of their foreign affiliates

The single largest and most comprehensive regional integration scheme is the European Union. This group of nations, whose history and current developments will be discussed in Chapter 17, was formed by six countries in the late 1950s. Today there are 28 members of the EU.[6] This includes the EU15—Austria, Belgium, Denmark, Finland, Germany, Greece, France, Ireland, Italy, Luxembourg, the Netherlands, Portugal, Spain, Sweden, and the UK—an additional eight eastern European countries that joined on May 1, 2004—Czech Republic, Estonia, Latvia, Lithuania, Hungary, Poland, Slovenia, and Slovakia—as well as Cyprus and Malta. Bulgaria and Romania became members of the EU in 2007 and Croatia joined in 2013. The collective GDP of the EU is greater than that of the United States or Japan, and the economic data show how important the EU is in the international arena. For example, in terms of imports and exports, the EU accounts for 16 percent of world imports and exports.[7] A large portion of EU exports is in the form of intra-EU trade, which was 75 percent higher than EU exports leaving the EU (extra-EU trade) in 2014 (see Chapter 17).

Mapping globalization

It is not straightforward to map globalization: globalization has to do with the intertwining of a number of social, economic and political factors, and the problem is that it is all linked to human behavior and action. Understanding human behavior is unfortunately not a science but a *social science*. The beauty of science is in its clear-cut boundaries. An experiment in physics or biology can be repeated with exactly the same results, regardless of by whom or where or when. Furthermore, it is possible to exclude certain processes in the repetition, to create a "control," in order to clearly determine cause and effect. In the social sciences, we are obliged to throw in a *ceteris paribus* (Latin for "all else being equal") clause. In order to test arguments we sometimes introduce numerous restrictive and often implausible assumptions. Unfortunately all else rarely is equal. Thus with globalization we are only able to say that there are numerous factors that are interrelated, but we are unable to be certain about the causality or the relative importance of each factor.[8]

Figure 1.2 maps out the primary forces underlying globalization; the dynamic interactions and interdependencies that drive it forward. The main forces that shape globalization are:

■ Those associated with *socio-political developments*. Political decisions (or indecision) shape the success or failure of firms, and the competitiveness of countries. Liberalization and the preferred policy orientation of a country play a significant role in shaping economic policy.

■ Those associated with *technology* and *innovation*. The ability of firms to be successful depends ultimately on their ability to generate new ideas through innovation, and obviously firms shape the competitiveness of the location they are in. We discuss this in much greater detail in Chapters 3 and 10.

Upstream and downstream
Common terms in production process industries, such as oil and gas, metals, and biopharmaceuticals. They represent the beginning and end stages of the production process. Upstream production is the process of exploring and extracting raw materials, whereas the downstream stage involves processing the materials into a finished product and selling it

There are an assortment of "push" and "pull" factors as well, which affect the capacity of a firm to internationalize (Figure 1.2). At the **upstream** end of the firm's activities, it must balance push factors arising from rising prices of inputs that encourage it to go abroad to seek cheaper inputs. At the same time, these activities are "pulled" abroad because there are scale economies from relocating these activities in foreign locations.

Likewise, at the **downstream** end, closer to the final market and the customer, there are a variety of push and pull factors. The home market may be mature, and firms need to seek new opportunities for growth in new and faster-growing countries (push factor). On the other hand, there may be barriers to exports that encourage the firm to relocate production overseas, acting as a pull factor.

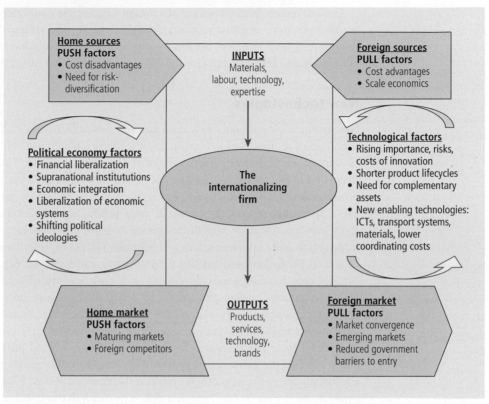

Figure 1.2 The dynamics of globalization

TECHNOLOGY AND INNOVATION

Technological change and innovation are acknowledged almost universally as determinants of globalization. Technology implies the application of scientific knowledge for practical aims. It involves applying scientific concepts that help us understand our environment, and allows us to convert this knowledge to develop and fabricate artifacts. Technology and science are *cumulative*, and build upon previous science and technology. The *practical* dividing line between science and technology is not always clear. Science and technology advance through *innovation*, which represents change in the stock of knowledge. Technology and science are subsets of knowledge.

Innovation means the introduction of *any* novelty, but there is an important distinction between "invention" and "innovation." An invention is an idea, sketch, or model of any new or improved device, product, process, or system. Innovations only occur when the new product, device, or process is involved in a commercial transaction. Multiple inventions may be involved in achieving an innovation. Technology represents the cumulative *stock* of these innovations. It therefore includes all activities that provide assets with which an economic actor can generate products or services. Science provides us with more generic knowledge, which may or may not generate products and services.

Innovation and technology lie at the core of the greater interdependence that we see as part of globalization. International business is tightly connected not only because it enables firms and countries to be interdependent (through communication technologies, transportation, logistics, etc.) but also because it is the source of economic growth and competitiveness (see Chapter 3).

Growth comes from the ability of a nation's industries to develop and sustain their competitive position, and this requires growth in the productivity of its capital and labor. Economic growth concerns not just the acquisition and development of knowledge through innovation and learning, but also the diffusion and efficient utilization of this knowledge.

New technologies

New technologies are only new until an even newer technology comes along. There have been numerous waves of new technologies, each of which has contributed to an industrial revolution, or, at the very least, to industrial *evolution*. The first industrial revolution was instigated in part by the development of centralized production units (the factory), the mass production of textiles, the use of waterpower, and access to cheap cotton (from the colonies). A century or so later, chemical mass production, the internal combustion engine, electricity, the telegraph, and the telephone brought about another. Some have argued that information and communications technologies (ICTs) represent a new "revolution." Each of the technologies credited has fundamentally affected the organization of economic activity, and has had knock-on effects on a wide variety of sectors. However, it is not always clear why certain technologies are regarded as more important than others. New technologies constitute a paradigm that shares the distinctive features of creating a technological *discontinuity*, and having significant cross-industry influences.

Each of these new technologies has, in its turn, promoted the increasing interdependence of economic units. Steam power made transportation much more reliable and rapid. Electricity and radio technologies improved communications. That the British managed to maintain an empire as far-flung as it did owes much to these technological changes: goods could be transported to and from colonies efficiently and cheaply; colonial administrators were able to keep in touch with London; civil unrest was curtailed by the use of machine guns. At the same time, these new technologies have allowed firms to coordinate and control (much more efficiently and reliably) their activities in different countries, and utilize differences in factor costs and inputs to better exploit comparative advantages and scale economies. The boundary-spanning MNE might never have come to exist in the absence of each of these "new" technologies.

Information and communications technologies are pervasive because they have affected numerous other industries. Biotechnology—another "new" technology—is highly dependent on advances in automation and data processing. In the absence of ICTs, mapping and cloning genes would be a tedious and slow process. Without these technologies, the human genome project might have taken several times as long. ICTs have affected other products where the importance of data processing and communications was hitherto marginal or negligible, such as the automobile, which was primarily a mechanical product. The average new automobile boasts several microprocessors controlling everything from the positioning of the seats and the anti-lock braking system, to electronic fuel injection and the ignition system. A whole gamut of new industries has evolved where ICTs are a core and central technology: internet service providers, e-bookshops, mobile telephony, and global positioning systems, to mention but a few.

ICTs are also a facilitating technology. Satellites, fixed-line networks, mobile networks, the internet, and networked computers have all acted to reduce costs of communications while improving reliability, efficiency and coverage. Distances have "shrunk."

ICTs also *facilitate* economic activity by disseminating information, collecting information, or reducing transaction, information, and communication costs. These developments have had a significant effect on the ability of the MNE to coordinate overseas activities (be they sales or manufacturing subsidiaries), as well as better undertake outsourcing and alliances.

The knowledge-intensive, multi-technology firm

It has long been the case that undertaking any form of economic activity has required access to a variety of skills and knowledge. There is an increasing need for non-traditional and non-intuitive skills. Many of the skills and much of the knowledge required in the workplace today require a certain level of education. "Basic skills" that one acquired through primary or secondary education are less relevant in today's workplace. Newer technologies have a greater non-intuitive aspect.

Two decades ago, subjects such as "principles of microprocessor design," "integrated circuit fabrication," or even "printed circuit board (PCB) design" were specialist topics in engineering departments, the subject of masters-level and doctoral theses. Today the first two of these are taught in advanced bachelor-level courses, and the last is such a general topic that amateur books teach one all there is to know. Technology matures over time: there is a proportional (but non-linear) decline in its uncertainty and a corresponding increase in its appropriability.

Products and production are increasingly multi-technology in nature. Seemingly independent technologies are required for products and processes, which have hitherto been seen as mono-technology products. This is not an entirely new phenomenon, but its intensity has increased. A car is no longer simply a mechanical engineering product, but requires technological competence in areas as diverse as ceramics, computing, communications, and plastics, among others. It is true that there are products and processes which are "simple" and will probably remain so. However, most firms need a larger base of knowledge. Multi-technology firms must maintain multiple competences, and maintain a minimum level of in-house expertise in several fields in order to monitor externally developed knowledge and integrate it with its other production inputs.

Even where products are mono-technology-based, the processes used to manufacture them often utilize several technologies. The increasing cross-fertilization of technologies across disciplines and resultant broader portfolio of competences has become fundamental to the competitiveness of technology-based firms. There has also, however, been a concurrent increase in competition, due to the liberalization of markets, and the reduction of transaction and transportation costs. This has led to a decline in profit margins due to increased cross-border competition. The increased costs of requiring more technology and knowledge across many sectors is not offset by greater profits. R&D in new technologies is increasingly expensive. Reducing costs (and maintaining profits) while maintaining the firm's technological assets has become an important managerial challenge.

SOCIO-POLITICAL DEVELOPMENTS

Economic interdependence is partly driven by political events, and most importantly by political stability. Stability of policies, and the creation and maintenance of the appropriate environment, plays a significant role in promoting the appropriate environment for firms to prosper. First, firms and entrepreneurs need to be able to claim and defend their property rights. Second, they need to be able to establish contracts that are legally enforceable, and to be able to do so at a reasonable cost and within a reasonable timeframe. The World Bank's Doing Business survey (Table 1.1) estimates the average time it takes to enforce a contract through the law courts, and it is easy to see the considerable differences between countries.

However, it is one thing to be able to enforce a contract within the same country; it is entirely more to enforce contracts across borders. Different legal systems means that a contract signed under one jurisdiction is invalid in another, and being able to enforce an

Table 1.1 Measures of institutions between countries

Country	Starting a business		Getting electricity		Dealing with construction permits		Enforcing contracts	
	Time	Cost	Time	Cost	Time	Cost	Time	Cost
US	4	1.4	60	0.3	89	14.6	370	22.9
Germany	14.5	8.8	28	1.1	96	94.4	394	14.4
UK	6	0.3	126	1.2	105	90.1	437	39.9
Japan	11	7.5	105	0.6	197	0	360	32.2
Poland	30	12.9	161	0.3	212	208	685	19.4
Russia	13	1.2	162	2	239	270	370	13.4
Turkey	6.5	16.4	70	433.3	169	3.5	420	24.9
Mexico	6	20	85	367.8	82	11.8	400	31
China	30	1	145	7.6	274	459.2	406	15.1
Egypt	8	9.2	54	1.9	179	304.6	1,010	26.2
South Africa	46	0.3	226	729.5	141	1.1	600	33.2
Nigeria	28	31.1	260	478	116	33.8	447	62
India	30	16.3	67	46.1	162	84	1,420	39.6
Peru	26	9.2	100	325.5	174	0.5	426	35.7
Kenya	30	42.7	158	1,020	125	9.3	465	47.2

Source: World Bank Doing Business survey (http://www.doingbusiness.org).

international contract requires nation-states to sign and enforce multilateral and bilateral agreements that allow this to happen. A Dutch firm undertaking a joint venture with a Brazilian company would typically sign three contracts: one under Dutch law, another under Brazilian law, and a third contract under US law, so that disputes could be managed by referring to the English text. This creates costs for both firms, since each needs to retain three legal teams in three different countries.

The ease with which goods and services move between countries can affect the competitiveness of firms that are engaged in international business. This has to do not only with the presence of roads, railways, and other transportation links, but also the *institutions* which we will discuss in the next section. A study by the Inter-American Development Bank found that the various problems in enforcing the regulatory and institutional frameworks between members of Mercosur, a free trade area in Latin America, suffered from a lack of enforcement. A truck carrying goods from Brazil to Chile required 200 hours for a 3,500 km journey, of which 50 percent is spent at the two border crossings. There is often a lack of common institutions, and a lack of political consensus in maintaining and properly enforcing these.

This leads us into the issue of institutions, a key concept in understanding business and strategy.

WHAT ARE INSTITUTIONS?

Institutions
The sets of common habits, routines, established practices, rules, or laws that regulate the interaction between individuals and groups

In the social sciences, **institutions** are not a synonym for "organizations." Institutions are the "sets of common habits, routines, established practices, rules, or laws that regulate the interaction between individuals and groups."[9] They are the "invisible glue" that holds all economic actors together. Several authors define institutions as being the "rules of the game," but this is an oversimplification. Institutions can be formal and informal.

Formal institutions
Rules that may be in the form of legal code, laws, and promulgations, government decrees that are legally laid out and codified

Informal institutions
Rules that are not always laid out in the form of written instruction, but come out of usage and tradition, and are often unwritten and tacit

Formal institutions are rules that may take the form of legal codes, laws, and promulgations, government decrees that are legally laid out and codified. Formal institutions can also exist in the form of rules within a firm. Responsibilities, job descriptions, codes of conduct, and accounting and financial regulations are all forms of formal institutions that are binding upon employees within a firm.

Informal institutions are—by definition—not always laid out in the form of written instruction, but come out of usage and tradition and are often unwritten and tacit. That is, people in that particular environment may "know" these rules, but to outsiders they are unknown, and are often transmitted simply by use. Countries have informal institutions, and some of these are often described as part of the national "culture." However, informal institutions are not entirely the same thing as culture. It is an unwritten rule (an informal institution) to shake hands with men, but not with women in South Asia. Firms also have informal institutions that are defined by interaction. IBM no longer formally requires male staff to dress in dark conservative suits, but should you wear the wrong outfit, you can be sure that someone will let you know that you have contravened an informal institution!

Institutions create the milieu within which economic activity is undertaken and establish the ground rules for interaction between the various actors; they represent a sort of "culture." Institutions will probably have taken years—if not decades—to create and sustain.

Formal institutions can be changed by senior management (the dress code in IBM used to be a formal institution) and by countries when new laws are passed by government, but this does not necessarily change the behavior of people. There may be a formal law that requires firms not to discriminate on the basis of age or gender, but this does not change the informal institution: there is still a glass ceiling for women in most companies. Habits and routines continue to prevail, often long after the formal institutions have changed. This is known as *institutional inertia*. In general, informal institutions are much harder to change than formal ones. Almost all European countries passed laws that forbade smoking in public spaces 20 years ago, but it took another 10 years before it became socially unacceptable to do so. The informal institutions were eventually modified to match the formal institutions, but it took a long time.

Introducing change in institutions is slow within countries, and within the same company; it is even more complex where the new institutions require synchronization between countries, or within an MNE that is located in several countries or regions.

Institutions and supranational agreements

Not all formal institutions are national or subnational. Globalization and the subsequent growth of international business have prompted the need to establish global and regional agreements to monitor and regulate economic activities.

World Trade Organization (WTO)
An international organization that deals with the rules of trade among member countries; one of its most important functions is to act as a dispute-settlement mechanism

General Agreement on Tariffs and Trade (GATT)
A major trade agreement that was established to negotiate trade concessions among member countries, and since superseded by the WTO agreements

The **World Trade Organization (WTO)** was established on January 1, 1995, and it is now the umbrella organization that governs the international trading system. It is the successor to the **General Agreement on Tariffs and Trade (GATT)**. The GATT was established in 1947 to liberalize trade and negotiate trade concessions among member countries. Although the early years saw a great deal of progress in reducing tariffs, by the 1980s there was a trend toward protectionism by many countries. At the GATT's eighth round of negotiations in 1986 (called the Uruguay Round because this is where the group met), negotiations dragged on for years before culminating in a number of agreements including reductions in industrial goods and agricultural subsidies, the increased protection of intellectual property rights under the Agreement on Trade-Related Aspects of Intellectual Property Rights (TRIPS), the creation of the General Agreement on Trade in Services (GATS), and the creation of the WTO to implement the GATT agreement. Today the WTO is enforcing these agreements. Presently, the Doha Round of the WTO has opened the door for further trade negotiations.

When member nations have a dispute, they can turn to the WTO to help resolve it. For example, the United States brought a case against the EU, charging it with a discriminatory banana import policy and the WTO ruled in its favor. In another case the United States requested that Japan be instructed to reorganize its commercial economy so that Kodak could better compete in that market against Fuji, its major rival, but the WTO rejected the claim and ruled in Japan's favor. In recent years many developing countries (in addition to the developed ones) have been using the WTO to help resolve trade disputes, and this bodes well for the future of the organization. The important thing to remember about the WTO is that it can enforce its decisions. Countries that refuse to comply can find themselves suffering severe consequences in the form of trade retaliation. Despite minor conflicts, international trade liberalization has arrived and this promises to help stimulate international business transactions.

In the financial services sector, there are a number of supranational agreements. It is worth highlighting developments connected with the Basel Accords. The Basel Accords refer to the banking supervision Accords—Basel I, Basel II, and Basel III—issued by the Basel Committee on Banking Supervision. They provide recommendations on banking regulations connected to capital risk, market risk, and operational risk. The purpose of the accords is to ensure that financial institutions have enough capital on account to meet obligations and absorb unexpected losses. From 1988 the Basel I framework was introduced initially in member countries: Belgium, Canada, France, Germany, Italy, Japan, Luxembourg, the Netherlands, Spain, Sweden, Switzerland, the UK, and the US. Over 100 other countries have also adopted the principles prescribed under Basel I. Basel II, first published in 2004, introduced risk weighting into the capital requirements for different activities. Basel III is still in its infancy stage, providing a framework on bank capital adequacy, stress testing, and market liquidity risk.

Globalization and liberalization

The liberalization of economic systems has been a decisive feature of the post-1945 "liberalization," and one of the underlying reasons behind the growth of international firms and international business, and the need for supranational organizations. Liberalization has come to have many meanings, and these include the liberalization of capital flows, the liberalization of trade regimes, and the liberalization of markets and economic systems. These are core to understanding globalization and the growth of interdependence.

International capital flows can be differentiated into several types:[10]

- foreign direct investment;
- international bank lending;
- international bonds and other credit instruments;
- portfolio investment, which implies ownership of shares or bonds of firms located overseas without the control associated with direct investment;
- international equities and other financial instruments (such as options and derivatives);
- development assistance and aid (both government-to-government aid, and NGO-controlled flows);
- monetary flows (through the sales and purchase of foreign currencies).

Liberalization has also occurred incrementally, but by far the most significant change goes back to the regulations (and organizations to monitor and enforce these regulations) established by the Bretton Woods agreement in 1944. It led to the growth of multinational banking, international money markets, derivatives trading, debt trading, and the cross-border listing and multiple listing of firms on several stock markets, to mention but a few developments. The growth of these new forms of investment has also caused new kinds of economic challenges, including the sub-prime mortgage crisis, and highlighted the need for greater cross-border regulation of MNEs that are able to take advantage of differences between national regulatory frameworks.

The liberalization of capital flows within the Bretton Woods agreement demonstrates its ideological origins, and reflects certain market capitalism-based value systems and institutions. A large number of countries liberalized capital flows in the mid-1980s, as a means to attract international investment. The increasing globalization of capital markets has led to considerable loss in economic autonomy of individual governments. The lack of control over domestic economic development has seen the need for governments to pursue policies designed to minimize disruptive financial flows, and this has pushed most to even greater levels of financial liberalization and greater engagement in IB.

Liberalization is an important force in economic globalization and promotes interdependence of economies. It is implicit within this view that FDI and MNE activity can be undertaken with much greater ease than previously, and the rest of this chapter looks into this in greater detail.

MULTINATIONAL ENTERPRISES

At the core of the twenty-first-century incarnation of globalization sits the multinational enterprise (MNE) or multinational corporation (MNC). There is good reason to take care in defining the MNE. Richard Caves defined the MNE as a multi-plant firm that controls and coordinates operations in at least two countries.[11] John Dunning focused on certain characteristics that distinguished MNEs from what we might call "firms with international activity," which is a definition still in popular use.[12] Essentially, this considers an MNE to be one which has substantial ongoing operations in foreign locations through FDI. Until the 1950s, many large MNEs were vertically integrated, which means that they engaged in almost all of the production from raw materials to finished goods within the same firm, and each country unit was largely self-contained. Ford owned rubber plantations in Brazil to manufacture its own tires in the early 1920s. It also invested in its own iron foundries, coal mines, glassworks, and railways. Most of these MNEs actively managed their foreign affiliates, and these affiliates were subsidiary to the parent firm, by which we mean they were highly dependent upon the parent firm for all major decisions. The foreign affiliate was actively managed by the parent, and in general, the affiliate did what it was told to do. Knowledge flowed primarily in one direction, from the parent to the subsidiaries.

Until the 1990s, FDI and MNE activity were considered synonymous because managing and coordinating a subsidiary across borders (in countries with different legal systems) and enforcing contracts across distances was considered difficult (and costly) to achieve. Thus ownership was considered to be the preferable option, rather than utilizing the market to transact with non-affiliated foreign actors. Most international and national agencies that maintain and collect data on MNE activity still generally define the MNE as a firm that *owns* and *controls* value-adding operations in more than one country.[13] However, globalization has played a significant role in changing the need to own assets in order to control them: as we shall discuss later in this chapter, and in Chapter 2, firms can engage in control with limited or no ownership.

Although FDI is one of the main modes by which MNEs engage in cross-border value-adding activities, today the MNE may also control and engage in value-adding activities through non-equity means, such as through strategic alliances, cooperative agreements, and outsourcing, sometimes without *legal* ownership of the various factories and plants, but *de facto* controlling the operations of the non-legally affiliated operation (see Chapter 2). Therefore, the use of the term "MNE" as a synonym for FDI is increasingly inaccurate.[14]

MNEs can and do organize activities through global production networks (GPNs) and global value chains (GVCs), and manage ongoing and systematic vertical transactions through multiple headquarters, which may or may not be associated with a singular "parent company."

The MNE has traditionally also been regarded as having a distinct "home country" where its headquarters are located, and which acts as the command center, providing primary strategic direction for its affiliates in various "host countries," as well as providing the primary or core assets on which the affiliates base their operations. Indeed, the home country establishment is referred to as the "parent firm," implying that the home country is at the top of a hierarchy of affiliates or subsidiaries. Furthermore, residents of the home country are assumed to own (and therefore control) the international operations of the MNE.

Although most MNEs are still organized along these lines, there are a growing number of firms where ownership and control are spread across several countries, as well as several cases where an MNE may locate its headquarters in a country other than its home country. Its stock may be traded on multiple stock exchanges in several countries. South African Breweries (SAB) is a South African-based MNE that is the historical "parent" of SABMiller, one of the world's largest brewers by volume, with more than 200 brands and brewing interests and distribution agreements in 75 countries across six continents. SABMiller has its primary listing on the London Stock Exchange, and for legal purposes it is a UK firm. However, its senior management, strategic decision making, and organizational culture remain very much South African.[15] SABMiller itself announced at the end of 2015[16] that it was to be acquired by its rival Anheuser-Busch InBev, which is also the result of a merger of Ambev, a Brazilian brewer, Interbrew, a Belgian-based firm, and Anheuser-Busch, a US brewer (and while Anheuser-Busch InBev is traded on the Brussels and the New York Stock Exchange, its management is dominated by its Brazilian partners, even though its corporate headquarters is in Belgium). The combined company would control 30 percent of the global market and have a 60 percent US market share. It is also an illustration of MNEs that have multiple headquarters located in different countries, with strategic control distributed along geographic, product, or functional lines.

The nature, structure, and organization of the MNE has changed quite considerably, and this change has been exacerbated by developments associated with the globalization of products, markets, and services, as well as political and economic developments associated with shifting political hegemonies and economic liberalization. Thus, a more accurate and current definition of an MNE is: *a firm that engages in value-added international business activities, that has affiliates in more than one country, and whose operations and activities in different locations are actively coordinated by one or more headquarters organizations.* Emphasis is placed on the presence of interdependencies between the various economic units in different locations, and their active coordination and control across borders, and not on the ownership structure.

Despite the importance given to MNEs, they do not account for a dominant or even a major share of the world's economic activity. In terms of employment, the world's largest MNEs employed 75 million *directly* in 2014, up from about 20 million in 2000. In terms of indirect effects—that is, people employed in firms that engage with MNEs, either as suppliers or through strategic alliances, or other partnerships—the figure is probably closer to 200 million. Put into context, with a world working population of about 3 billion, the direct number represented only 2.5 percent of total global employment, and the total number including direct and indirect employment is possibly no higher than 6 percent. Despite the relatively small role of MNEs on an aggregate level, however, the situation differs substantially across countries. MNEs account for less than 5 percent of the total employment in countries such as Japan and Indonesia, but this figure rises to well over 40 percent in countries such as Malaysia, Argentina, and Ireland. The significance of MNEs in terms of sales, value adding and ownership of assets is of similar magnitude.

However, two characteristics of the operations of MNEs stand out. First, larger MNEs have been found to be concentrated in the more "dynamic" sectors of the economy. Thus, even though they play a relatively small role in most economies in terms of the level of total employment, MNEs often play a disproportionately large role in two different types of industrial sectors. They tend to be most active in sectors typified by high growth rates, rapid innovation, and the use of new and emerging technologies (e.g., electronics, communication equipment, and industrial machinery), and also in mature sectors where economies of scale, branding, and advertising determine market share (e.g., petroleum products, chemicals, automobiles, food and beverages, and consumer goods). In mature sectors, while the technology underlying these industries may be diffused and codified, growing scale economies can result in a global oligopoly of a few MNEs maintaining a large share of the global market. A good example is the petroleum sector.

In general, a majority of MNEs come from developed-economy home countries. As we shall discuss later in this chapter, while the emerging economies are increasingly playing a greater role, it remains restricted to a handful of countries. These trends reflect the strong positive correlation between the level of economic development and the growth of firms from these economies that have the technological and organizational capabilities to compete globally with the more established MNEs in world markets.[17]

How do MNEs contribute to employment? The Economic Commission for Latin America and the Caribbean (ECLAC) suggests that it varies significantly by country and sector.[18] In the Caribbean, when investment targets the tourism sector, it estimated that each US$1 million of investment generated about six jobs, while the same investment in the financial sector, and mining and natural resource-intensive manufacturing, generated fewer than two jobs.[19] In Mexico and Central America, where the focus was on manufacturing, US$1 million generated four jobs on average. In South America, where investment tends to be linked to natural resources, the average number of jobs estimated to be created by $1 million was 2.5.

Proto-globalization and the MNE in historical context

Although the term "globalization" has recently been coined, the growing interdependence between countries and their firms is not new. All the constituent provinces of the Roman Empire shared a common set of laws and enforcement mechanisms. Tariff rates on trade were standardized, and they enjoyed the benefits of a common currency, a well-maintained transport infrastructure, and the financial and security apparatus to ensure safe conduct of these activities. Imports came from as far away as India and China to meet the demand for spices and silk,[20] while salt and leather came from West Africa. The Arabs and the Somalis were crucial in transporting these imports by sea and across the Sahara, while innumerable diplomatic treaties with neighboring states created the stability for these goods and services to be transported. Financial payment systems through moneylenders (who maintained an informal network with each other) allowed traders to travel without large amounts of gold and silver. These kinds of linkages and networks operated in a number of other large empires in the past two millennia, including the Parthians and the Ottoman, Malian, Austro-Hungarian, Spanish, and British empires.

Much of the IB activity was dominated by market transactions, with a flow of goods between locations in response to supply and demand. There was no systematic interaction between producers in country A and customers in country B. Such trading activities do not necessarily result in a high degree of interdependence. Raw materials were transported from one location to another, manufactured, and transported to other locations to be sold.

However, while there was significant movement of goods, and to some extent also of labor through immigration, most economic actors were immobile, and did not, as a rule, have operations in more than one location (until the last 100 years or so). That is, although financial capital was moved as individuals lent money to others in other locations, contracts were made between individuals in different locations; these were financial flows and flows of goods rather than a movement of physical assets or personnel. There was no significant integration of operations in different locations within the control and management of the same individuals. The idea of a "firm" as we understand it did not exist; rather these were most often entrepreneurs and family members, without an ongoing business enterprise that involved any sort of active coordination. These early "firms" were *international*, but not *multinational*. International business and economic activity was *extensive* in the sense that the value of goods and capital exchanged was considerable, and sometimes involved numerous countries and actors.[21] But it was not *intensive*, in that activities were largely not integrated across borders.

It was only later, somewhere in the late 1500s, that large trading companies and other state-sanctioned *de facto* monopolies such as the British or French East and West India companies came into being, and these were the first MNEs. Sea travel and international trade were hazardous and costly, and required considerable resources, and such ventures required widespread risk sharing. However, such firms were far and few between. Even as late as the 1780s, large firms were the exception rather than the rule in Europe and elsewhere—there were few firms with more than 30 employees.[22]

Although the economies of Asia during the 1700s accounted for 60 percent of the world's GDP, compared with about 25 percent for Europe,[23] the weakness of individual property rights and the feudal political structures[24] meant that most economic activity was similarly concentrated in the hands of the state or state-sanctioned actors, while much of private enterprise was small-scale, and international trade and cross-border flows of goods, services, and capital were small and sporadic.[25] Although data are scarce, there was considerably more trade between Europe and China and India than there was between China and India.

The industrial revolutions and the growth of private firms

The first industrial revolution (starting with the discovery of steam power, which in turn led to the growth of railways, steam-driven manufacturing, and powered ships), in conjunction with a number of important social and political developments, unleashed a period of rapid growth in Europe.[26] The economies of Europe expanded rapidly from the mid-1700s, leading to a consequent expansion and proliferation of firms in the modern sense—organizations with a recognizable structure, property rights, and ownership, engaged in ongoing, systematic, and regular economic transactions. This was also supported by the growth of stock markets, insurers, and banks that helped to reduce the risk to the individual entrepreneur. The legal and institutional setting also helped establish property rights and legal structures that permitted their growth. Two main consequences of this growth helped drive globalization further. First, there was a shortage of raw materials, and an international expansion to secure new supplies of inputs. Second, there was a shrinking of demand for "traditional" handmade products, which were more costly than factory-produced manufactures.

Parallel advances in transportation—especially shipping, and related fields such as map making, clocks, and astronomy—made transcontinental trade more reliable and subsequently cheaper. From the early 1800s, international trade grew by around 3.5 percent per annum for the rest of the century.[27] The British, Dutch, and French East India companies vied with each other to supply foreign markets with manufactured goods, as well as to acquire imports of raw materials.

The benefits of the new industrial technologies of steam power and automated mass manufacturing combined with declining transportation costs had the effect of displacing local manufacturing activities in Asia, South America, and Africa with imports from Europe. These new technologies also rapidly diffused to other countries, especially North America, which also sought overseas markets and cheaper raw materials, while raising tariffs on imported (European) goods. The adoption of the Gold Standard, which fixed the value of national currencies to the price of gold, reduced foreign exchange risks. A second industrial revolution helped cement the gains from the first industrial revolution, from the 1870s till the early 1900s. New important discoveries included telephony, telegraphy, electricity, a rapid expansion of railways, improved steel production, the internal combustion engine, and large-scale chemical production.

By 1913 most of the industrialized nations had become part of global capital markets. By the late 1800s the GDP of India and China had shrunk by about half of their pre-industrial revolution levels. Japan, on the other hand, had taken advantage of the new industries and by the early part of the twentieth century had become an industrialized nation (not, as many suppose, after World War II).

Assisted by the growing support infrastructure in finance, and the declining risks of investing abroad, private firms and entrepreneurs in the mid-1800s also began to make cross-border investments. European banking houses began opening up specialist facilities in the colonies to finance and support foreign investment.[28] For obvious reasons, opportunities were greatest in the new colonies and investors began to erect factories abroad. Many of these were what are known as "free-standing companies." Typically, they were legally incorporated in their home country. They usually specialized in a single commodity, product, or service, often in a single overseas country. As discussed earlier, one of the primary characteristics of the MNE is that control is exercised from head offices at "home." These were among the earliest private MNEs, although it is a matter of some debate to what degree these were established by residents of the "host" with a foreign passport and no apparent organizational link to a "parent" company at "home." During the 1800s a considerable amount of foreign investment in the European colonies abroad was carried out by free-standing companies.

Nevertheless, the first true multinational firms which were systematically coordinated and controlled by a parent firm in the home country came about around this time. Although this was initially an issue of natural resources, firms like Siemens and IG Farben from Germany, and Singer and Bell from the US, began expanding manufacturing activities abroad. By 1914, multinational manufacturing was also undertaken in a wide range of manufactured products, such as chemicals, pharmaceuticals, automobiles, and food products. These MNEs witnessed a continuous flow of knowledge and other resources across borders within the boundaries of firms.

FOREIGN DIRECT INVESTMENT

As discussed in the previous section, the first "modern" MNEs with coordinated activities that were controlled and systematically managed by parent firms began to emerge from about the late 1870s. By the 1900s, it became necessary to distinguish between foreign investment and foreign "direct" investment. The term "direct" is intended to indicate that this did not involve merely a movement of capital, as might be the case with "portfolio" investments in shares, stocks, and other financial instruments, which are sometimes referred to as "foreign portfolio investments." Foreign direct investment (FDI), in contrast, represented investments which provided the owners with not just ownership, but through that ownership, strategic and managerial control of an ongoing enterprise.

Measuring FDI and MNE activity

FDI has—since the 1950s—been the primary means by which governments, researchers, and supranational organizations have measured the level and intensity of MNE activity. This is because FDI is a measure that is readily available. All countries in the world are obliged to keep (and publish) records of long-term capital flows as a requirement by the International Monetary Fund and World Bank, and these are published as part of their balance of payments data. These data measure *flows* of FDI. Countries keep a record of monies that have been identified as being FDI, and this is recorded separately from portfolio capital transfers. *Inward FDI* flows to country A indicate money coming into country A during the reporting year, from foreign-owned MNEs to their subsidiaries in country A. In this case, country A is known as the *host country*. *Outward FDI* flows are monies going out, from firms that are registered in country A (known as the *home country*) to their subsidiaries in other countries.

Flows measure new money coming in or going out, and serve an important purpose for the IMF and central banks in working out the gross national product (GNP) and other statistical indicators of the amount of economic activity taking place in a country. It is also possible to estimate the growth of economic activity by MNEs (both outgoing and incoming). However, this does not tell us very much about *ongoing* economic activity. To take an example, suppose IBM built a large office in Tokyo in 1950, and this investment cost $50 million, which IBM transferred from the US to Japan in that year. As a result of this investment, it generated sales in Japan of $10 million a year, for the next 10 years. Let us suppose that IBM used the profits from these sales of $1 million a year to expand its operations by *reinvested earnings*. In other words, by 1960, the value of its investment was $60 million. If we relied on the flow data, we would only be able to see that IBM had FDI flows in 1950, and none thereafter, and we might wrongly conclude that there had been no increase in its activities in Japan or in its employment.

FDI stock data, on the other hand, are supposed to give us a more reliable estimate of the significance of MNE activity, and form a more reliable indicator of its contribution to the economy. MNEs might also build up their subsidiary by borrowing money locally. FDI stock allows us to estimate—more reliably—the sales and value-adding activity done by MNEs. However, FDI stock data are not completely reliable either, because they underestimate old investments. IBM's building in downtown Tokyo might be worth $1 billion by 2000, but you would not be able to estimate this from the flow data (assume there were no other inflows from IBM in the US to Japan) because the data from 1950 to 2000 would only record a zero for each year. The stock data would indicate $100 million (assuming an annual reinvested earning of $1 million). Reinvested earnings are not the only item missing: firms may raise capital locally from the sale of bonds, or from local loans. Nevertheless, FDI stock data (if properly and diligently calculated) give a more accurate idea of the contribution an MNE makes to the host economy, and have a monotonic relationship to its local value-adding activities. FDI stock also provides a better measure of how this significance changes over time, and by taking into account previous investments, it allows us to compare the relative importance of MNEs between countries.

Where FDI stocks are not available, international agencies such as UNCTAD estimate stocks by taking an accumulation of flows for a certain number of years as a rough proxy. Although such estimations are not always perfect, they still provide a better estimate of changing trends in the value of MNE activities than flow data.

Throughout this book we will try to refer to stock data wherever available, because they allow a fairer comparison between countries.

MNEs before World War II

Data from the early 1900s are hard to come by, but estimates suggest that about one-third of the US$40–50 billion in foreign investment in 1914 was FDI. As Figure 1.3 shows, the

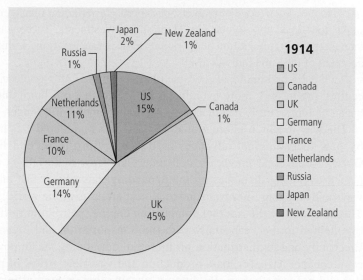

Figure 1.3 Estimated stock of outward FDI by country of origin, 1914

Source: Adapted from J. H. Dunning, *Multinational Enterprises and the Global Economy* (Wokingham: Addison Wesley, 1993).

major source of FDI stocks in 1914 was Britain, which accounted for 45 percent of the total, while western Europe as a region accounted for more than 80 percent of all FDI stock. Latin America and Asia were especially important as host economies, even though the largest individual host countries were the US and Canada.

Over 55 percent of the FDI in 1914 was directed to the primary sector, 20 percent to railroads, and only about 15 percent to manufacturing activities. Manufacturing investments were mainly concentrated in Europe, the US, and the UK colonies, but this was the era of large plantations (such as sugar, rubber, tea, coffee, cocoa, cotton, palm oil, and beef). These operations engaged in minimal local processing and were vertically integrated suppliers to parent firms that manufactured final products for consumers in the developed world. Vertical integration reduced the uncertainties of markets, while ensuring captive inputs. A number of major MNEs from that era are still major players in international business: firms like Shell, BP, Exxon, Unilever, Philips, Nestlé, Ford, Tata, Jardine Matheson, HSBC, BASF, and Agfa.

The rise of the modern MNE

In general, the early twentieth century showed the signs of a burgeoning economic interdependence between countries, and early cross-border interdependence between firms, both within countries, and between countries. Although international trade is not new, the beginning of the twentieth century saw an important change to international business with the growth of FDI and the multinational corporation.

Still further fundamental changes began to appear. The first firms began to *internationalize*— and by this we mean these "proto-MNEs" were interested in developing vertical linkages that led to a flow of goods through trade between locations, in response to varying elasticities of supply and demand. Later, this led to some degree of processing and coordination. Raw materials were transported from one location to another, manufactured, and transported to a third location for sale. These were the first *multinational enterprises* because they were not simply moving capital from one location to another to increase their returns. They were utilizing proprietary knowledge, knowledge capital embodied in physical assets or personnel, knowledge of markets, or expertise as efficient managers that allowed them to make significant and regular returns on their investments. There was also increasing (and later, significant) integration of operations in disparate locations within the control and management of the same individuals.

Such early multinationals became more and more commonplace, and, as the twentieth century progressed, more manufacturing MNEs that did more than just facilitate trade began to appear. Early manufacturing MNEs included Ford, Singer, and IG Farben.

The way in which international business was conducted was helped extraordinarily by new technological advances associated with the second industrial revolution. Goods—both final goods for consumers and raw materials—could be easily transported over long distances by the expanding network of fast and cost-effective railways and shipping lines from and to almost all parts of the world, and within countries. The invention of the internal combustion engine, petroleum refining and the automobile helped further, especially with the transportation and logistics within countries. Electricity and its distribution proliferated, outmoding steam power, but providing an even cheaper basis for mass production and vast new arrays of products and services that did not exist before. Production systems that created efficiencies for large-scale plants that allowed bulk chemicals to be synthesized cheaply led to growing vertically integrated operations and scale economies. Telegraph and telephones drastically improved the efficiency with which people could communicate across the world. This made possible mass production and mass marketing for the first time, allowing firms to take advantage of markets, while also increasing their need for raw materials from elsewhere.

Perhaps most importantly, the combination of a growing financial services industry and the availability of international sources of finance (manufacturing industries are by definition capital-intensive) and greater efficiencies of scale and efficiencies of scope led to the growth of large firms, and with it, the growth of professional management.[29] The era of the large firm naturally led to the era of the large MNE. One of the key developments was managerial—instead of owner-managers, the development of large corporations came out of the evolution of a new type of firm that was administered by a hierarchy of salaried professional managers.

The world economy became increasingly unstable from 1914. There was a severe recession in Europe soon after the end of World War I in 1918, and the US Great Depression in 1929 caused a worldwide economic shock. US GDP fell by almost a third between 1929 and 1933. Declining primary commodity prices caused sharp falls in real incomes for the producer countries in Latin America, Asia, Africa, and Australia. The Russian Revolution was followed by the sequestration of foreign-owned assets by the Soviet Union.

Political and economic nationalism was increasingly common in developing countries that were independent, such as in Latin America. They began to question foreign control and ownership over their natural resources and their dependence on imports for manufactured goods. Import substitution came to be seen as an important means to reduce their economic dependence on MNEs. A number of countries used tariffs, import quotas, and other trade barriers to help infant industries and foster their manufacturing sectors by import substitution. At the same time, dictatorships ruled Germany, Italy, and Japan, and foreign investments were either "pushed out," or were nationalized. Figure 1.4 gives data on FDI trends and patterns for 1938, and it is apparent that changes were marginal during this period: the dominance of Europe and particularly the UK as a source of FDI remained unchallenged, although the growth of US FDI and the decline in the importance of Germany as a source of FDI are also noticeable.

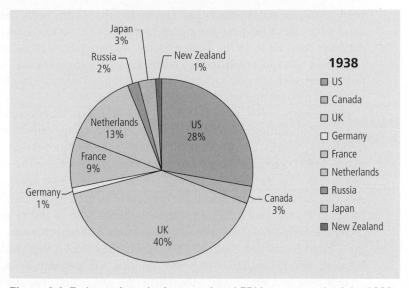

Figure 1.4 Estimated stock of accumulated FDI by country of origin, 1938

Source: Adapted from J. H. Dunning, *Multinational Enterprises and the Global Economy* (Wokingham: Addison Wesley, 1993).

INTERNATIONAL BUSINESS IN THE MODERN ERA

World War II (1939–45) represents a watershed in political, social, and economic terms, and can be taken to be a turning point in globalization. To be clear, it was not the physical and human losses as much as the outcomes from its aftermath that have shaped the world economy indelibly. On a political level, after 1945, the world economy was dominated by the US; the geopolitical stage was set through an East–West ideological divide between the two military superpowers, the United States and the USSR, and their spheres of influence. The reconstruction of Europe and Japan after the war was shaped by the US, and equally importantly, by the establishment of US-centric economic policies and economic systems that encouraged international trade and investment. The Bretton Woods agreement established a standardized economic system, payment systems, and regulatory mechanisms, along with organizations such as the World Bank and the International Monetary Fund. The first round of the General Agreement on Tariffs and Trade, signed by 23 countries, was a multilateral agreement that helped regulate international trade. In other words, many countries adopted similar formal institutions (at both a national and supranational level) that created a mechanism to engage in higher levels of trade (but not for FDI).

The various European colonial possessions in Asia, Africa, and Latin America became independent between 1945 and 1960, all seeking to become more economically prosperous, and to engage in the global economy to varying extents. China came out of its civil war by 1949 as a unified country, but chose to close its economy almost completely.

1950–90: the rise of the triad

During the 1950s, the world economy was dominated by the United States, which accounted for about 50 percent of the world's output and almost 80 percent of the FDI stock. The US dollar became the world's major reserve currency. US MNEs assumed leading positions in many industries. Much of the infrastructure of Europe and Japan had been destroyed, and the production facilities of these firms badly damaged, and they spent the first decade of the post-war era undergoing extensive reconstruction, heavily dependent on official aid from the United States. Many of the leading firms from Europe and Japan had either lost their foreign assets through war reparations, or sold them. Most of these countries had exchange controls which limited international capital movements and restricted their international expansion in any case.

By the early 1960s, there had been rapid growth in these economies, reflected in the growing competitiveness of their exports and increasing expansion of their MNEs. The developed countries accounted for 97 percent of the total global outward FDI stock in 1967, of which the US accounted for 57 per cent. The majority of inward FDI stocks—73%—were directed to other developed countries, while the largest host developing region was Latin America and the Caribbean with 18.5 percent. The most highly involved home countries of MNEs in Europe were Britain and the Netherlands, with 16 and 11 percent respectively.

By the early 1980s, the pace of globalization had further intensified. The influence of the United States had diminished somewhat, as wealth was more equally distributed between the triad countries of North America, Europe, and Japan, which accounted for around three-quarters of world manufacturing production. The domination of the triad is evident by the fact that even by 1990, the share of inward FDI to developed countries was 76.8 percent (Table 1.3).

In terms of host developing regions, the most important host regions were in Asia and Latin America. Even by 1990, China and India were largely unimportant as host countries, accounting for just 1 percent of the world total.

1990–2014: the rise of new players and forms of activity

During the 1990s, the pace of globalization intensified. National restrictions over cross-border capital flows were largely swept away as financial deregulation spread. The most striking changes were in emerging markets.

Some argue that China's move toward greater integration in the world economy was the beginning of this shift (officially, market-oriented policies were first introduced in 1979); others feel that the collapse of Communism in Russia and eastern Europe in the late-1980s was the turning point. Yet others point to Europe, where this was the beginning of important institutional changes, with the members of the European Economic Community (EEC) working hard toward the introduction of a Single European Market (SEM) in 1992. Negotiations for the North American Free Trade Agreement (NAFTA) were moving toward completion by 1994, but started much earlier. A number of other regional integration schemes also began around this time, including the Mercosur customs union inaugurated by Brazil, Paraguay, Uruguay, and Argentina in 1995. The Association of Southeast Asian Nations (ASEAN), which had started as largely a political effort to create cohesion in the region, set the basis for a degree of regional integration.

Not coincidentally, there was also a process of economic and financial liberalization in Africa, Asia, and Latin America, which led to widespread deregulation and privatization, and opened further opportunities. Negotiations for the Uruguay Round of GATT were also being undertaken concurrently, beginning in 1986 and completed in 1984. The Uruguay Round expanded GATT to include services, capital, intellectual property, and agriculture. It was the first set of multilateral trade negotiations in which developing countries played an active role.

With hindsight, it seems amazing that there were so many key socio-political and economic turning points across the world coming to a head at about the same time. It is difficult to be precise about causes and effects, but there is little doubt that these events were contemporaneous.

Table 1.2 FDI outward stock by countries (millions of US$), 1980–2014

Country	1980 Value	1980 % of total	1990 Value	1990 % of total	2000 Value	2000 % of total	2010 Value	2010 % of total	2014 Value	2014 % of total
World	548,198	100.0	2,253,944	100.0	7,298,188	100.0	20,414,081	100.0	25,874,757	100.0
Developed economies[a]	**477,203**	**87.0**	**2,114,508**	**93.8**	**6,535,722**	**89.6**	**16,978,445**	**83.2**	**20,554,819**	**79.4**
North America	239,158	43.6	816,569	36.2	2,931,653	40.2	5,446,299	26.7	7,033,195	27.2
United States	215,375	39.3	731,762	32.5	2,694,014	36.9	4,809,587	23.6	6,318,640	24.4
Canada	23,783	4.3	84,807	3.8	237,639	3.3	636,712	3.1	714,555	2.8
Germany	43,127	7.9	308,736	13.7	541,866	7.4	1,463,065	7.2	1,583,279	6.1
United Kingdom	80,434	14.7	229,307	10.2	923,367	12.7	1,635,791	8.0	1,584,147	6.1
Netherlands	41,867	7.6	109,870	4.9	305,461	4.2	1,004,454	4.9	985,256	3.8
Other developed economies[b]	*24,612*	*4.5*	*244,556*	*10.9*	*388,640*	*5.3*	*1,367,441*	*6.7*	*1,734,278*	*6.7*
Australia	4,983	0.9	37,505	1.7	92,508	1.3	449,740	2.2	443,519	1.7
Japan	19,612	3.6	201,441	8.9	278,442	3.8	831,076	4.1	1,193,137	4.6
Developing economies[a]	**70,995**	**13.0**	**139,436**	**6.2**	**762,065**	**10.4**	**3,400,014**	**16.7**	**5,264,911**	**20.3**
Asian NICs	*14,056*	*2.6*	*52,386*	*2.3*	*524,192*	*7.2*	*1,737,423*	*8.5*	*2,553,725*	*9.9*
Hong Kong	148	0.0	11,920	0.5	379,285	5.2	943,938	4.6	1,459,947	5.6
Singapore	772	0.1	7,808	0.3	56,755	0.8	458,650	2.2	576,396	2.2
Republic of Korea	127	0.0	2,301	0.1	21,497	0.3	144,032	0.7	258,553	1.0
Taiwan	13,009	2.4	30,356	1.3	66,655	0.9	190,803	0.9	258,829	1.0
Developing economies minus Asian NICs	*56,939*	*10.4*	*87,050*	*3.9*	*237,873*	*3.3*	*1,662,591*	*8.1*	*2,711,186*	*10.5*
BRICS	*44,164*	*8.1*	*60,633*	*2.7*	*128,917*	*1.8*	*1,055,010*	*5.2*	*1,741,303*	*6.7*
Brazil	38,545	7.0	41,044	1.8	51,946	0.7	191,349	0.9	316,339	1.2
China	0	0.0	4,455	0.2	27,768	0.4	317,211	1.6	729,585	2.8
India	78	0.0	124	0.0	1,733	0.0	96,901	0.5	129,578	0.5
Russia	n/a	–	n/a	–	20,141	0.3	366,301	1.8	431,865	1.7
South Africa	5,541	1.0	15,010	0.7	27,328	0.4	83,249	0.4	133,936	0.5
Developing economies minus *BRICS*	26,831	4.9	78,803	3.5	633,149	8.7	2,345,004	11.5	3,523,607	13.6
Developing economies minus *Asian NICs* and *BRICS*	12,775	2.3	26,417	1.2	108,956	1.5	607,581	3.0	969,882	3.7
Tax havens	**72**	**0.0**	**1,525**	**0.1**	**88,052**	**1.2**	**613,732**	**3.0**	**876,555**	**3.4**
British Virgin Islands	0	0.0	875	0.0	67,132	0.9	334,406	1.6	584,235	2.3
Mauritius	0	0.0	1	0.0	132	0.0	864	0.0	1,482	0.0
Cayman Islands	72	0.0	648	0.0	20,788	0.3	88,062	0.4	136,700	0.5
Panama	–	–	0	0.0	0	0.0	3,374	0.0	4,246	0.0
Luxembourg	0	0.0	0	0.0	0	0.0	187,027	0.9	149,892	0.6
Transition economies[c]	**0**	**0.0**	**0**	**0.0**	**400**	**0.0**	**35,623**	**0.2**	**55,027**	**0.2**

Notes:
[a] The value represents the sum of all countries included in the UNCTAD's classification; the countries listed are just a sample of the population.
[b] According to UNCTAD's classification, other developed economies include Australia, Bermuda Israel, Japan, and New Zealand.
[c] Although UNCTAD classifies Russia as a transition economy, we have included Russia's outward FDI stock at the developing economies' value. "FDI stocks are estimated by either cumulating FDI flows over a period of time or adding flows to an FDI stock that has been obtained for a particular year from national official sources or the IMF data series on assets and liabilities of direct investment" (UNCTAD, 2015).

Sources: Data for 1980: UNCTADSTAT (2015); data for 1990–2014: UNCTAD (2015).

Table 1.3 FDI inward stock by countries (millions of US$), 1980–2014

Country	1980 Value	1980 % of total	1990 Value	1990 % of total	2000 Value	2000 % of total	2010 Value	2010 % of total	2014 Value	2014 % of total
World	697,913	100.0	2,197,768	100.0	7,202,348	100.0	19,607,406	100.0	26,038,824	100.0
Developed economies[a]	**401,633**	**57.5**	**1,687,652**	**76.8**	**5,476,613**	**76.0**	**12,789,150**	**65.2**	**17,003,802**	**65.3**
North America	*137,209*	*19.7*	*652,444*	*29.7*	*2,995,951*	*41.6*	*4,014,166*	*20.5*	*6,041,200*	*23.2*
United States	83,046	11.9	539,601	24.6	2,783,235	38.6	3,422,293	17.5	5,409,884	20.8
Canada	54,163	7.8	112,843	5.1	212,716	3.0	591,873	3.0	631,316	2.4
Europe[a,b]	*230,849*	*33.1*	*932,579*	*42.4*	*2,263,007*	*31.4*	*7,910,159*	*40.3*	*10,049,259*	*38.6*
Germany	36,630	5.2	226,552	10.3	271,613	3.8	716,704	3.7	743,512	2.9
United Kingdom	63,014	9.0	203,905	9.3	463,134	6.4	1,094,833	5.6	1,562,858	6.4
Netherlands	19,168	2.7	71,828	3.3	243,733	3.4	647,723	3.3	564,442	2.6
Other developed economies[a,c]	*349,660*	*50.1*	*102,629*	*4.7*	*217,655*	*3.0*	*864,824*	*4.4*	*913,343*	*3.5*
Australia	24,776	3.6	80,364	3.7	121,686	1.7	527,064	2.7	564,608	2.2
Japan	3,270	0.5	9,850	0.4	50,322	0.7	214,880	1.1	170,615	0.7
Developing economies[a]	**296,280**	**42.5**	**510,107**	**23.2**	**1,702,016**	**23.6**	**6,579,217**	**33.6**	**8,688,598**	**33.4**
Asian NICs	*186,650*	*26.7*	*247,042*	*11.2*	*609,227*	*8.5*	*1,898,763*	*9.7*	*2,712,877*	*10.4*
Hong Kong	177,755	25.5	201,653	9.2	435,417	6.0	1,067,520	5.4	1,549,849	6.0
Singapore	5,351	0.8	30,468	1.4	110,570	1.5	632,766	3.2	912,355	3.5
Republic of Korea	1,139	0.2	5,186	0.2	43,738	0.6	135,500	0.7	182,037	0.7
Taiwan	2,405	0.3	9,735	0.4	19,502	0.3	62,977	0.3	68,636	0.3
Developing economies minus Asian NICs	109,630	15.7	263,066	12.0	1,092,788	15.2	4,680,454	23.9	5,975,721	22.9
BRICSs	*35,465*	*5.1*	*68,701*	*3.1*	*407,592*	*5.7*	*2,145,868*	*10.9*	*2,616,321*	*10.0*
Brazil	17,480	2.5	37,143	1.7	122,250	1.7	682,346	3.5	754,769	2.9
China	1,074	0.2	20,691	0.9	193,348	2.7	587,817	3.0	1,085,293	4.2
India	452	0.1	1,657	0.1	16,339	0.2	205,580	1.0	252,331	1.0
Russia	n/a	–	n/a	–	32,204	0.4	490,560	2.5	378,543	1.5
South Africa	16,459	2.4	9,210	0.4	43,451	0.6	179,565	0.9	145,384	0.6
Developing economies minus BRICSs	260,815	37.4	441,406	20.1	1,294,423	18.0	4,433,349	22.6	6,072,277	23.3
Developing economies minus Asian NICs and BRICSs	74,165	10.6	194,365	8.8	685,196	9.5	2,534,587	12.9	3,359,400	12.9
Tax havens	**249**	**0.0**	**4,318**	**0.2**	**65,136**	**0.9**	**567,937**	**2.9**	**900,275**	**3.5**
British Virgin Islands	1	0.0	126	0.0	32,093	0.4	236,858	1.2	511,367	2.0
Mauritius	26	0.0	168	0.0	683	0.0	4,658	0.0	4,586	0.0
Cayman Islands	222	0.0	1,749	0.1	25,585	0.4	133,421	0.7	187,094	0.7
Panama	–	–	2,275	0.1	6,775	0.1	20,742	0.1	35,917	0.1
Luxembourg	0	0.0	0	0.0	0	0.0	172,257	0.9	161,311	0.6
Transition economies[d]	**0**	**0.0**	**9**	**0.0**	**23,720**	**0.3**	**239,040**	**1.2**	**346,424**	**1.3**

Notes:

The value represents the sum of all countries included in the UNCTAD classification; the countries listed are just a sample of the population.

[a] According to UNCTAD's classification, Europe includes all countries from the European Union and also Gibraltar, Iceland, Norway, and Switzerland.

[b] According to UNCTAD's classification, other developed economies include Australia, Bermuda, Israel, Japan, and New Zealand.

[c] Although UNCTAD classifies Russia as a transition economy, we have included Russia's outward FDI stock at the developing economies' value. "FDI stocks are estimated by either cumulating FDI flows over a period of time or adding flows to an FDI stock that has been obtained for a particular year from national official sources or the IMF data series on assets and liabilities of direct investment" (UNCTAD, 2015).

[d]

Sources: Data for 1980: UNCTADSTAT (2015); data for 1990–2014: UNCTAD (2015).

The situation was almost certainly helped by new technological paradigms in transportation (the growth of containerization, improved air transport), and ICTs, which made it cheaper and faster to communicate across countries, and to conduct cross-border financial transactions. The advent of the internet played an important role in creating new markets, reduced coordination and search costs, and made it easier to enforce informal contracts.

New industries came about as a result of both these technologies and the new markets that opened up to international business. These include tourism, telecommunications, media services, software, banking, agriculture, utilities, and real estate. Many services sectors, which had long been closed to foreign investment and were often limited by law to domestic actors, grew rapidly: 63 percent of the total global inward FDI stock by 2012 was in the services sector, up from less than 10% in 1990. New technologies reduced the barriers to new, smaller firms entering these industries, which had in the past been restricted to a handful of large firms.

Modularization, outsourcing, and value chains

From the 1990s, there was also a relocation of labor-intensive industry functions from rich countries to lower-wage countries with skilled workforces. This followed a new tendency to "fine-slice" activities so that they could be modularized, thereby taking advantage of cheaper inputs wherever they might be. Back-office processing, call centers, accounting, and software maintenance and development all became growth industries for countries such as India, the Philippines, Egypt, Mauritius, Pakistan, South Africa, and others.

Modularizing products and services has led to a considerable geographic reorientation of the world economy. Outsourcing and the use of complex *global value chains* (GVCs) and *global production networks* (GPNs) has been especially important for the growth of international investment in the developing countries. In the case of manufacturing, the benefits of this expansion have been most keenly felt by the Asian economies, especially China, Korea, Taiwan, Malaysia, and Thailand.

Global value chains have played a large role in the expansion of retail and trading MNEs. Tesco, a British retail giant with operations in 12 countries, relies on complex webs of suppliers from around the world to ensure that it is able to sell its customers grapes sourced from India, tomatoes from Spain, and avocados from South Africa, all delivered at competitive prices and fresh, whether in the UK, Thailand, or Korea. Tesco is able to take advantage of its size by ordering in bulk and ensuring through the careful use of logistics and shipping that these perishable products are delivered fresh to its customers.

The continuing importance of the state-owned enterprise

The growth of commodities trade in developing countries (both agricultural and extractive) has been spurred by the privatization of state-owned enterprises (SOEs) in the countries that have liberalized their economies, and the rapid growth of the world economy from the mid-1990s to about 2013 has been fueled by high prices on traditional commodities, and subsequently the growth of MNEs in these areas.

While some countries privatized SOEs, they continued to flourish in other countries including China. Much of the growth in new MNEs from emerging markets reflects the growth of China. While the number of Chinese firms entering the Global Fortune 500 tripled between 2010 and 2014, the evidence suggests that few of them are truly internationalized. Indeed, the majority of the 73 large Chinese firms are SOEs and they have most of their total sales within China. They are still largely in the protected banking, insurance, natural resources, utilities, telecommunication, land and real estate and development, engineering and construction industries. Even where SOEs have been privatized, governments continue to exert considerable influence on their activities.

Many developing economies had nurtured SOEs and national champions as part of their economic and industrial policies since the 1950s, and these continue to be important—Brazil has Petrobras, Malaysia has PETRONAS, India has Indian Oil. They often also provided protection against competition, and subsidized their outward expansion. Although various agreements within the WTO (combined with economic liberalization) have led to the dissolution or at least weakening of such state support, this has provided them with the initial impetus to internationalize.

Emerging economy MNEs—significant but exaggerated

Although there is considerable hype about the growth of emerging country MNEs (EMNEs), the hard evidence is less impressive. Not all foreign investment is necessarily a foreign *direct* investment. Investments from developing countries may represent an institutional investment through a private equity firm, a sovereign wealth fund, or a portfolio investment. This is the case in many of the acquisitions by oil-exporting countries (including the Middle East countries, but also Russia) and China, where individuals or (state-owned or state-influenced) firms have access to capital, and acquire ownership in companies which gives them the *potential* to exert control, although in many cases they do not do so.

The acquisition of a dominant share in a foreign-based enterprise may be undertaken because it provides superior oversight and reduces the costs of shirking compared to non-equity modes of cooperation or a minority equity share. Thus firms may overvalue the benefits of having a dominant, majority or wholly-owned foreign affiliate, because the investor's home country does not provide it the experience of trusting other modes of entry share. Such investments are *de jure* FDI, but *de facto* portfolio investments.

Nonetheless, there is sufficient MNE activity from developing countries that is worthy of note. Although the growth of the Chinese economy over the last 25 years marks the single most important shift of economic power in the new global economy, the significance of the "four tigers," or Asian newly industrialized countries (NICs)—Hong Kong, Singapore, South Korea, and Taiwan—should not be underestimated. These four countries grew rapidly from the mid-1960s, and in terms of intensity of engagement with the world economy, and they are arguably more important in international business than China or India. Taiwan and Korea are deeply integrated in the global value chains of the electronics sector, while Singapore and Hong Kong are deeply linked within the transportation, finance, and logistics industries. Taiwan is the home country of Hon Hai/Foxconn, arguably the world's largest MNE with over a million employees. Indeed, in terms of income levels, all four countries are at a similar level of development to most of Europe and North America.

Table 1.2 gives the data of outward FDI stock for the NICs. They accounted for just 2.3 percent of the stock in 1990, but by 2014 this share had increased to 9.9 percent, significantly more than the BRICS, which consist of Brazil, Russia, India, China, and South Africa.

A number of studies point to the rapid growth of developing country FDI stocks. As a percentage of total outward stock this increased from 6.2 percent to 20.3 percent between 1990 and 2014. However, these data are misleading and do not indicate a broad phenomenon, but one that is limited to just a few countries. These data are summarized in Figure 1.5. Excluding the BRICS countries and the Asian NICs, we see only a slight increase in the outward FDI stock from developing countries as a share of total world FDI stock, from 1.2 percent to 3.7 percent over the period (which, given that these are nominal data, represents a real decrease). These data suggest that much of the growth in outward MNE activity from "developing countries" comes from a group of nine countries, some of which (the NICs) are to all intents and purposes developed countries, and have been so since the beginning of the new millennium. Indeed, the continued inclusion of the Asian NICs in the classification of developing countries seems somewhat strange and even problematic,

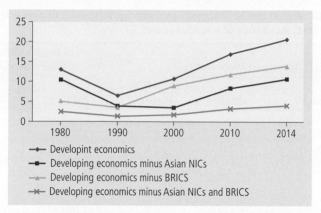

Figure 1.5 FDI outward stock from selected developing economies as a percentage of the world's FDI outward stock.

Source: Based on data taken from UNCTADSTAT

given that on a GDP per capita basis (whether real or nominal) they have clearly converged with the developed world.

Tables 1.2 and 1.3 also give data for offshore tax havens. In general, the use of these tax havens distorts the data. Some of these tax havens are ostensibly large outward investors, as well as large recipients of inward FDI. The British Virgin Islands inward FDI stock was $511 billion in 2014, higher than Russia or India, and close to that of Australia. Many of these funds move out equally fast — outflows from the British Virgin Islands were $54 billion and outward stock was $584 billion in 2014. Other tax havens include Mauritius, the Cayman Islands, Panama, and Luxembourg. Despite their heterogeneity, all these countries act as offshore investment hubs for MNEs. They tend to have low taxes and few legal requirements governing their activities. These operations are most often subsidiaries (and headquarters) "based" in these countries, which are "letterbox" companies with a legal address, but no local activities and little accountability. Such tax haven operations typically have FDI flows coming in, with the money subsequently leaving as outflows to third countries. Google achieved an effective tax rate of 2.4 percent on its non-United States profits in 2009 by routing profits to Bermuda. There is also round-trip investing, where FDI flows come in from a source country, and return to the same country. Information is understandably hard to obtain on these activities, but one of the largest inward investors to India is Mauritius, which is also a major destination for Indian outward FDI. This way, Indian firms move money abroad, and then take it back to India, where it is given tax and investment benefits normally reserved for foreign investors. In other words, significant investment in offshore financial centers means that outward FDI data may not accurately reflect reality.

Dominance of the triad continues

Table 1.4 gives us a sense of the significance and internationalization of the world's largest MNEs, and those coming from emerging markets. On average, these new MNEs have internationalized their sales and employment, but in terms of assets, they remain concentrated at home. Compared to the triad MNEs, however, they are on average much smaller, and considerably less internationalized.

The data for 2014 in Tables 1.2 and 1.3 are quite revealing. The triad countries still play a significant role in absolute terms, with the US alone accounting for 24.4 percent of all outward FDI stock, which is equivalent to the UK, France, Germany, and the Netherlands put together. Despite the rapid growth in flows from China, without including Hong Kong

Table 1.4 Internationalization statistics of the 100 largest non-financial MNEs worldwide and from developing and transition economies (billions of US$, thousands of employees and %)

	100 largest MNEs worldwide			100 largest MNEs from developing and transition economies		
	2013[a]	2014[b]	2013–14 % change	2012	2013	% change
Assets						
Foreign	8,249	8,266	0.2	1,506	1,632	8.4
Domestic	5,759	5,581	−3.1	4,025	4,403	9.4
Total	14,008	13,847	−1.1	5,531	6,034	9.1
Foreign as % of total	59	60	0.8	27	27	−0.2
Sales						
Foreign	6,053	6,132	1.3	1,690	1,806	6.8
Domestic	3,263	3,101	−5.0	2,172	2,415	11.1
Total	9,316	9,233	−0.9	3,863	4,221	9.3
Foreign as % of total	65	66	1.4	44	43	−1.0
Employment						
Foreign	9,562	9,599	0.4	4,103	4,226	3.0
Domestic	7,135	7,211	1.1	6,493	6,688	3.0
Total	16,697	16,810	0.7	10,596	10,914	3.0
Foreign as % of total	57	57	−0.2	39	39	0.0

Source: Adapted from UNCTAD, *World Investment Report,* 2015, table 1.6.

it has a stock value equal to Canada, and not much larger than Singapore. India and Malaysia show a similar level of outward FDI stock.

In terms of inward FDI, the story is similar. China's share of inward FDI stock has continued to rise, but is still about a quarter of that in the US, and only slightly more than Singapore.

Small and medium-sized enterprises

Whenever MNEs are discussed, it is common to hear about large firms. In fact, the best-known multinationals are companies that have become household words. Everyone knows of Honda, Unilever, Google, and Volkswagen. However, there are hundreds of thousands of **small and medium-sized enterprises (SMEs)**, many of which are suppliers to these MNEs.[30] Most of these companies have annual sales of less than $5 million, but they are able to compete effectively and perform functions that multinationals cannot do as efficiently. They are especially important in the global era because the improved enforceability of contracts and declining transaction and monitoring costs resulting from globalization have made it easier for SMEs to engage in international business.

Small and medium-sized enterprises (SMEs)
Defined by governments using different criteria for policy purposes. SMEs are firms with fewer than 250 employees in Europe, but fewer than 500 in the United States. Indian manufacturing firms qualify as SMEs if they invest less than US$2 million in plant and equipment

Since SMEs are small operations they are much more flexible in a variety of ways, and they are invaluable partners to larger firms because they can change direction, focus, and structure with relative ease. One of the major competitive advantages SMEs have over large firms is their flexibility. Larger firms wishing to outsource for various reasons tend to rely on SMEs because they are especially astute in utilizing external networks more efficiently.[31] SMEs overcome their biggest disadvantage—limited resources—by the skillful use of alliances.[32] SMEs also overcome their limited size and resources by being more innovative than larger firms in the same industry. SMEs have tended to have an innovation advantage in highly innovative industries where the use of skilled labor is relatively important.

Although SMEs have the advantages of being flexible and responding rapidly to change, there are also disadvantages due to their absolute size limitations. Nonetheless, SMEs are the backbone of many industries because of their efficiency and flexibility. In this book, we will be studying a large number of international business concepts that are used not just by large MNEs but also by smaller MNEs.

Part of the reason for the proliferation of smaller firms in developing countries is that inefficient regulations and poorly functioning institutions discourage entrepreneurs from entering the formal sector. The Indian manufacturing sector is dominated by micro-enterprises, of which the overwhelming majority are in the informal sector, and their productivity is half that of larger enterprises.[33] While small firms in India have achieved higher growth rates than larger firms in recent years, they also have a labor intensity that is almost four times higher than large enterprises.[34] The dominance of the informal sector is a result of India's labor legislation and pre-reform regulations that, on the one hand, provide special incentives to micro-enterprises by limiting the entry of larger firms in certain sectors, while on the other hand, limiting the ability of larger firms to lay off or replace workers, or declare bankruptcy. Firms, therefore, prefer to be capital-intensive rather than labor-intensive to avoid the complexities of becoming larger. Large firms also tend to fragment outsourced activities to a considerable number of small units (perhaps because the smaller firms predominate), creating further inefficiencies.

There is some evidence that SMEs are more innovative than their larger counterparts. According to the US Small Business Administration (US-SBA), firms of fewer than 500 employees in the United States represent 99.7 percent of all firms and employ just over half of all private sector employees.

Studying smaller international firms provides a useful contrast to large multinational firms. In particular, comparisons reveal the importance of scale and scope as sources of certain kinds of competitive advantages for internationalization, as outlined by Alfred Chandler.[35] Small firms have neither the manpower nor the financial resources to spread their options geographically or make many mistakes when they take their first steps into new markets. This means that they have to be particularly entrepreneurial, innovative, and adaptive when expanding abroad.[36]

The fragmented firm: global value chains and production networks

As we have discussed, control and coordination can be achieved through a minority ownership, and in some cases through non-equity means. Historically, FDI and MNE activities have been synonymous, partly a reflection of the way in which most international and national agencies maintain and collect data on MNE activity. Although FDI remains one of the main modes by which MNEs engage in cross-border value-adding activities, the MNE may also control and engage in value-adding activities through non-equity means, such as through cooperative agreements and outsourcing, sometimes without *de jure* ownership of the productive assets, but *de facto* controlling the operations of the non-affiliated operation. Therefore, the use of the term "MNE" as a synonym for FDI is increasingly inaccurate.[37] We emphasized in our definition of the MNE the interdependencies between the various operations in different locations, and their active coordination and control across borders, rather than the ownership structure. One of the powerful effects of globalization is that there is a shift away from traditional hierarchies toward a richer variety of organizational modes (see Chapter 2 for a discussion of entry modes). This has occurred along with a systematic shift in certain sectors and a variety of industries away from the vertically integrated firm. Globalization has made it easier for firms of all sizes to monitor, identify, and establish collaborative ventures than had previously been the case. In other words, hierarchical control and full internalization are no longer always a first-best option for MNEs.

Global value chains
Value chains are defined as the full range of activities bringing products or services from conception to production to consumption. Such chains that involve intra-firm or inter-firm economic activities beyond national borders are referred to as global value chains (GVCs).

Global production networks
Global production networks (GPNs) are organizational platforms where various actors from globally dispersed locations compete and cooperate for value creation, transformation and capture.

International production and trade are increasingly organized within **global value chains** (GVCs) or **global production networks** (GPNs) where the different stages of the production process are located across different countries. Globalization motivates companies to restructure their operations internationally through outsourcing and offshoring of activities. GVCs can be "producer-driven" or "buyer-driven" chains.[38] Producer-driven GVCs are more common in high-tech sectors such as pharmaceuticals. Lead or "flagship" firms are upstream and control the design of products, while the assembly is fragmented in different countries. In buyer-driven chains, retailers control the production taking place in other countries, but focus on marketing and sales. Such GVCs are common in the apparel and food and agriculture industries.

GVCs are typically coordinated by MNEs, with cross-border trade of inputs and outputs taking place within their networks of affiliates, contractual partners, and arm's-length suppliers. MNE-coordinated GVCs account for some 80 percent of global trade. MNEs coordinate GVCs through complex webs of supplier relationships and various governance modes, from direct ownership of foreign affiliates to contractual relationships (in non-equity modes of international production), to arm's-length dealings.[39]

The spread of GVCs is greater in industries where activities can be more easily separated and modularized, such as electronics, automotive, and garments, but GVCs increasingly involve activities across all sectors, including services. The majority of developing countries participate in GVCs. However, many poorer developing countries are still struggling to gain access to GVCs beyond natural resource exports.

Non-equity modes (NEMs) involve no FDI whatsoever (see Chapter 2 for a discussion on modes). The controlling MNE has no ownership stake, while maintaining a level of control over the operation by contractually specifying the way it is to be conducted. Outsourcing arrangements within a GVC most often require some degree of coordination by the MNE or lead firm of the outsourcing company. The defining features of NEMs—coordination and control of independent firms through contractual and non-contractual means, with a material impact on the conduct of their business—can blur the rigid distinction between FDI, NEMs, and trade.[40]

Nestlé has at least 600,000 contract farmers in over 80 developing economies as direct suppliers of various agricultural commodities. Table 1.5 gives some idea of the significance and size of NEM activity worldwide. In the electronics and automotive industries, contract manufacturing is very important, with firms typically outsourcing more than

Table 1.5 Key figures of cross-border non-equity mode activity, selected industries, 2010 (billions of US$ and millions of employees)

	Estimated NEM-related activity worldwide			
	Sales	Value added	Employment	Employment in developing economies
Contract manufacturing—selected technology/capital intensive industries				
Electronics	230–40	20–25	1.4–1.7	1.3–1.5
Automotive components	200–220	60–70	1.1–1.4	0.3–0.4
Pharmaceuticals	20–30	5–10	0.1–0.2	0.05–0.1
Contract manufacturing—selected labor-intensive industries				
Garments	200–5	40–45	6.5–7.0	6.0–6.5
Footwear	50–55	10–15	1.7–2.0	1.6–1.8
Toys	10–15	2–3	0.4–0.5	0.4–0.5
Services outsourcing				
IT services and business outsourcing	90–100	50–60	3.0–3.5	2.0–2.5
Franchising				
Retail, hotel, restaurant and catering, business, and other services	330–350	130–150	3.8–4.2	2.3–2.5
Management contracts—selected industry				
Hotels	15–20	5–10	0.3–0.4	0.1–0.15

Source: Adapted from UNCTAD, *World Investment Report,* 2011, table IV.4.

50 percent of production by cost of goods sold. In the electronics sector, a small number of contract manufacturers dominate the industry and produce for all major brands in the industry. By far the largest contract manufacturer is Taiwan's Hon Hai Precision Industry, which owns Foxconn. With an annual turnover of US$135 billion and a market capitalization of US$45 billion, it had net profits of US$4.2 billion in 2014.

The top developing country locations for outsourcing services (managed both by major developed country players and by local firms) are still in Asia. Three countries—India, the Philippines, and China—accounted for around 65 percent of global export revenues related to information technology/back-office processing services, partly because of locational advantages such as language and IT skills, the low cost of labor, and ICT infrastructure. However, the industry is expanding to countries such as Argentina, Brazil, Chile, the Czech Republic, Egypt, Morocco, and South Africa. UNCTAD estimates that worldwide, some 18 to 21 million workers are directly employed in firms operating under NEM partnership arrangements in selected industries and value chains.

This fragmentation of value chains has not happened in all industries and sectors, or even in all aspects of value added. For instance, the degree of outsourcing and NEM in R&D remains very low. In general, equity solutions such as FDI may provide the firm with greater control over foreign operations, reducing the risk of technology loss to suppliers and competitors, especially when the competitive advantage is based on easy-to-copy technology.[41] Some products and services are harder to modularize, and require large amounts of effort to reintegrate them. This may be because, in order to outsource, you need to invest heavily in codifying your knowledge, and this cost may also be prohibitive. Lastly, it is important that multiple alternative suppliers exist for what you want to outsource—where the firm becomes dependent upon one supplier, it can create a hostage situation.[42]

Indeed, because of all the challenges of outsourcing, firms often prefer to undertake *strategic alliances*.[43] We will discuss strategic alliances in some detail in the next chapter and in Chapter 8.

KEY POINTS

1 There is little doubt that we live in a world defined by globalization. Globalization, however, remains a vague concept, used by different people in different ways. This book defines economic globalization as the growing interdependence of locations and economic actors across countries and regions.

2 International business is the study of transactions taking place across national borders for the purpose of satisfying the needs of individuals and organizations. Two of the most common types of international business activity are export/import and foreign direct investment (FDI). In recent years both have been on the rise. Much of this is a result of large multinational enterprises (MNEs).

3 Small and medium-sized enterprises (SMEs) often function as the backbone of large MNEs, efficiently providing goods and services that are integrated into the latter's production process. SMEs also compete with MNEs in niche markets. SMEs are often more flexible then MNEs but struggle to match MNEs in terms of resources.

4 Institutions are defined as "sets of common habits, routines, established practices, rules, or laws that regulate the interaction between individuals and groups." Understanding institutions, both formal and informal, is important for both firms and employees, so they can adjust their behaviors accordingly.

5 Trade regulation has become an important issue in international business. Today, the World Trade Organization (WTO) is the major supranational body responsible for governing the international trading system.

6 There are two ways to measure FDI: FDI stock and FDI flow. Inward FDI flow is money coming into a country during the reporting year, from foreign-owned MNEs which have their subsidiaries in the recipient county. Outward FDI flows are monies going out from firms that are registered in the home country to another country through their subsidiaries abroad. FDI flow is different from FDI stock: the latter looks at the accumulation of FDI over time, whereas FDI flow only looks at FDI inflow or outflow in one reporting year. FDI stock is a more reliable indicator of FDI activity in countries.

7 International production and trade are increasingly organized within global value chains (GVCs) of global production networks (GPNs) where the different stages of the production process are located across different countries. Due to the globalized nature of some markets, it is advantageous for firms to develop products in different countries to benefit from home countries' location advantages.

Key terms

- international business
- exports
- imports
- international trade
- multinational enterprise (MNE)
- economic globalization
- interdependence

- foreign direct investment (FDI)
- upstream and downstream
- institutions
- formal institutions
- informal institutions

- World Trade Organization (WTO)
- General Agreement on Tariffs and Trade (GATT)
- small and medium-sized enterprises (SMEs)

NOTES

1 http://www.fasttrack.co.uk/fasttrack/leagues/ smeexport100leaguetable.asp?siteID=9&searchName=&yr= 2015&sort=num&area1=99

2 R. Narula, *Globalization and Technology: Interdependence, Innovation Systems and Industrial Policy* (Cambridge: Polity Press, 2003).

3 P. Jenkins and M. Arnold, "HSBC speeds up exit from emerging markets," *Financial Times* (2015). http://www.ft. com/cms/s/0/85642fcc-e50d-11e4-bb4b-00144feab7de.html

4 G. R. Benito and R. Narula, "States and firms on the periphery: the challenges of a globalising world." In G. R. Benito and R. Narula (eds.), *Multinationals on the Periphery* (Basingstoke: Palgrave Macmillan, 2007).

5 J. R. Markusen and A. J. Venables, "Foreign direct investment as a catalyst for industrial development," *European Economic Review*, vol. 43, no. 2 (1999), pp. 335–56; R. Narula and J. H. Dunning, "Multinational enterprises, development and globalization: some clarifications and a research agenda," *Oxford Development Studies*, vol. 38, no. 3 (2010), pp. 263–87.

6 Although, at the time of writing (June 2016), the UK had voted to leave the EU, this process is expected to be a complicated and time-consuming process, that is unlikely to be concluded by 2019. It is unclear what the new relationship between the EU and the UK will look like. As the UK will be a member of the EU until it concludes the exit negotiations, we continue to refer to the EU as having 28 members.

7 http://ec.europa.eu/trade/policy/eu-position-in-world-trade/; http://ec.europa.eu/eurostat/statistics-explained/index.php/ International_trade_in_goods

8 R. Narula, *Globalization and Technology: Interdependence, Innovation Systems and Industrial Policy* (New York: John Wiley & Sons, 2014).

9 B. Gregersen and B. Johnson, "Learning economies, innovation systems and European integration," *Regional Studies*, vol. 31, no. 5 (1997), pp. 479–90.

10 D. Held, *Global Transformations: Politics, Economics and Culture* (Stanford, CA: Stanford University Press, 2007).

11 R. E. Caves, *Multinational Enterprise and Economic Analysis* (Cambridge: Cambridge University Press, 1996).

12 J. H. Dunning, "The eclectic paradigm of international production: a restatement and some possible extensions," *Journal of International Business Studies* (1988), pp. 1–31.

13 J. H. Dunning, "Trade, location of economic activity and the multinational enterprise: a search for an eclectic approach." In P. J. Buckley and P. Ghauri (eds.), *The Internationalization of the Firm* (London: Thomson, 1999), pp. 61–79.

14 M. Wilkins, "The history of multinational enterprise." In A. Rugman and T. Brewer (eds.), *The Oxford Handbook of International Business* (Oxford: Oxford University Press, 2010), pp. 3–35.

15 H. Barnard, "Migrating multinationals and the theory of the multinational." In R. Ramamurti and A. Cuervo-Cazurra (eds.), *Understanding Multinationals from Emerging Markets* (Cambridge: Cambridge University Press, 2014), pp. 195–223.

16 A. Wexler, "SABMiller to keep South African listing, allays investors' fears," *Wall Street Journal*, 2015. Access: http:// www.wsj.com/articles/sabmillers-potential-sale-rattles-south-african-investors-1444214073

17 UNCTAD, *World Investment Report*, 2006.

18 Economic Commission for Latin America and the Caribbean, *Foreign Direct Investment in Latin America and the Caribbean, 2012* (Santiago, Chile: ECLAC, 2013).

19 Ibid.

20 E. H. Warmington, *The Commerce between the Roman Empire and India* (Cambridge: Cambridge University Press, 1974).

21 D. Held, *Global Transformations: Politics, Economics and Culture* (Stanford, CA: Stanford University Press, 1999).

22 F. Braudel, *The Perspective of the World: Civilization and Capitalism 15th–18th Century*, Vol. 3 (Berkeley, CA: University of California Press, 1992), p. 443.

23 A. Maddison, *The World Economy*, Vol. 1: *A Millennial Perspective*; Vol. 2: *Historical Statistics* (India: OECD, 2007).

24 F. Fukuyama, *The Origins of Political Order: From Prehuman Times to the French Revolution* (New York: Profile Books, 2011).

25 D. S. Landes, *The Wealth and Poverty of Nations: Why Some Are So Rich and Some So Poor* (New York and London: W. W. Norton & Co. 1999).

26 D. S. Landes, *The Unbound Prometheus: Technological Change and Industrial Development in Western Europe from 1750 to the Present* (Cambridge: Cambridge University Press, 2003).

27 G. Jones, *Multinationals and Global Capitalism* (Oxford: Oxford University Press, 2005).

28 Ibid.

29 J. H. Dunning, *Multinational Enterprises and the Global Economy* (Wokingham: Addison Wesley, 1993).

30 UNCTAD, *World Investment Report*, 2015, chapter 5.

31 Also see Paul Ellis and Anthony Pecotich, "Social factors influencing export initiation in small and medium-sized enterprises," *Journal of Marketing Research* (February 2001), pp. 119–30.

32 R. Rothwell and M. Dodgson, "Innovation and size of firm." In M. Dodgson and R. Rothwell (eds.), *The Handbook of Industrial Innovation* (Aldershot: Edward Elgar, 1994).

33 R. Narula, "R&D collaboration by SMEs: new opportunities and limitations in the face of globalisation," *Technovation*, vol. 24, no. 2 (2004), pp. 153–61.

34 S. M. Dougherty, R. Herd, and T. Chalaux, "What is holding back productivity growth in India? Recent micro evidence," *OECD Journal: Economic Studies*, vol. 1 (2009), pp. 1–22.

35 R. Narula, "The viability of sustained growth by India's MNEs: India's dual economy and constraints from location assets," *Management International Review*, 55 (2015), pp. 191–205.

36 G. A. Knight and D. Kim, "International business competence and the contemporary firm," *Journal of International Business Studies*, vol. 40, no. 2 (2009), pp. 255–73; G. A. Knight, "Entrepreneurship and strategy in the international SME," *Journal of International Management*, vol. 7 (2001), pp. 155–71; S. C. Collinson, *Small and Successful in Japan: A Study of 30 British Firms in the World's Most Competitive Market* (London: Avebury Press, 1996).

37 R. Narula and J. H. Dunning, "Multinational enterprises, development and globalization: some clarifications and a research agenda," *Oxford Development Studies*, vol. 38, no. 3 (2010), pp. 263–87.

38 K. De Backer and S. Miroudot, "Mapping global value chains," *OECD Trade Policy Papers*, no. 159 (Paris: OECD Publishing).

39 UNCTAD, *World Investment Report*, 2013.

40 UNCTAD, *World Investment Report*, 2011.

41 R. Narula and J. Hagedoorn, "Innovating through strategic alliances: moving towards international partnerships and contractual agreements," *Technovation*, vol. 19, no. 5 (1998), pp. 283–94.

42 R. Narula, "Choosing between internal and non-internal R&D activities: some technological and economic factors," *Technology Analysis and Strategic Management*, vol. 13, no. 3 (2001), pp. 365–87.

43 R. Narula and A. Martinez-Noya, "International R&D alliances by firms: origins and development." In Daniele Archibugi and Andrea Filippetti (eds.), *The Handbook of Global Science, Technology, and Innovation* (Hoboken, NJ: Wiley-Blackwell, 2015).

BIBLIOGRAPHY

Boddewyn, Jean J., Toyne, Brian, and Martinez, Zaida L. "The meanings of 'international management'," *Management International Review*, vol. 44, no. 2 (2004).

Cavusgil, S. Tamer, and Knight, Gary. "The born global firm: an entrepreneurial and capabilities perspective on early and rapid internationalization," *Journal of International Business Studies*, vol. 46, no. 1 (2015).

Collinson, Simon, and Rugman, Alan, M. "Case selection biases in management research: implications for international business studies," *European Journal of International Management*, vol. 4, no. 5 (2010).

Dicken, Peter. *Global Shift*, 6th ed. (London: Sage, 2011).

Driffield, Nigel, Jones, Chris, and Crotty, Jo. "International business research and risky investments, an analysis of FDI in conflict zones," *International Business Review*, vol. 22, no. 1 (2013).

Dunning, John H. "The study of international business: a plea for a more interdisciplinary approach," *Journal of International Business Studies*, vol. 20, no. 3 (fall 1989).

Forsgren, Mats, and Yamin, Mo. "A commentary on Adam Smith and international business," *Multinational Business Review*, vol. 18, no. 1 (2010).

Fruin, W. Mark. "Bringing the world (back) into international business," *Journal of International Business Studies*, vol. 38, no. 2 (March 2007).

Ghemawat, Pankaj. "Distance still matters: the hard reality of global expansion," *Harvard Business Review*, vol. 79, no. 8 (September 2001).

Ghemawat, Pankaj. *Redefining Global Strategy: Crossing Borders in a World Where Differences Still Matter* (Cambridge, MA: Harvard Business School Press, 2007).

Girod, Stéphane J. G., and Rugman, Alan M. "Regional business networks and the multinational retail sector," *Long Range Planning*, vol. 38, no. 4 (August 2005).

Jones, Geoffrey, and Khanna, Tarun. "Bringing history (back) into international business," *Journal of International Business Studies*, vol. 37, no. 4 (July 2006).

Lee, M., Yin, X., Lee, S., Weng, D. H., and Peng, M. "The impact of home country institutions on new venture export: examining new ventures in transition economies," *International Entrepreneurship and Management Journal*, vol. 11, no. 4 (2015), pp. 823–48.

Morck, Randall, and Yeung, Bernard. "History in perspective: comment on Jones and Khanna 'Bringing history (back) into international business'," *Journal of International Business Studies*, vol. 38, no. 2 (March 2007).

Porter, Michael E. *The Competitive Advantage of Nations* (New York: Free Press/Macmillan, 1990).

Rugman, Alan M. *Rugman Reviews International Business* (Basingstoke: Palgrave Macmillan, 2009).

Rugman, Alan M. "The international financial crisis and multinational enterprise strategy," *Transnational Corporation*, vol. 20, no. 1 (2011).

Rugman, Alan M., and Verbeke, Alain. "A new perspective on the regional and global strategies of multinational service firms," *Management International Review*, vol. 48, no. 4 (2008).

Rugman, Alan M., Verbeke, Alain, and Nguyen, Quyen T. K. "Fifty years of international business theory and beyond," *Management International Review*, vol. 51, no. 6 (November 2011).

van Hoorn, André, and Maseland, Robbert. "How institutions matter for international business: institutional distance effects vs. institutional profile effects," *Journal of International Business Studies* (2016).

Zott, Christoph, Amit, Raphael, and Massa, Lorenzo. "The business model: recent developments and future research," *Journal of Management*, vol. 37, no. 4 (2011).

APPENDIX: THE LARGEST IMPORTERS AND EXPORTERS

Table 1A Top 25 importers in the world, 2014 (billions of US$)

Rank	Country	Value	Share	% change
1	United States	2,413	12.6	4
2	China	1,959	10.3	0
3	Germany	1,216	6.4	2
4	Japan	822	4.3	(1)
5	United Kingdom	684	3.6	4
6	France	676	3.5	(1)
7	Hong Kong, China	601	3.1	(3)
8	Netherlands	151	3.1	0
9	Korea, Republic of	588	2.8	2
10	Canada	526	2.5	0
11	Italy	475	2.5	(2)
12	India	472	2.4	(1)
13	Belgium	463	2.4	0
14	Mexico	452	2.2	5
15	Singapore	366	1.9	(2)
16	Spain	358	1.9	5
17	Russian Federation	306	1.6	(10)
18	Switzerland	276	1.4	(14)
19	Chinese Taipei	274	1.4	2
20	United Arab Emirates	262	1.4	4
21	Turkey	242	1.3	(4)
22	Brazil	239	1.3	(5)
23	Australia	237	1.2	(2)
24	Thailand	228	1.2	(9)
25	Poland	220	1.2	6

Source: World Trade Organization, *International Trade Statistics*, 2015.

Table 1B Top 25 exporters in the world, 2014 (billions of US$)

Rank	Country	Value	Share	% change
1	China	2,342	12.3	6
2	United States	1,621	8.5	3
3	Germany	1,508	7.9	4
4	Japan	684	3.6	(4)
5	Netherlands	672	3.5	0
6	France	583	3.1	0
7	Korea, Republic of	573	2.8	2
8	Italy	529	2.8	2
9	Hong Kong, China	524	2.7	(2)
10	United Kingdom	506	2.7	(7)
11	Russian Federation	498	2.6	(5)
12	Canada	475	2.5	4
13	Belgium	471	2.5	1
14	Singapore	410	2.2	0
15	Mexico	398	2.1	5
16	United Arab Emirates	360	1.9	(5)
17	Saudi Arabia	354	1.9	(6)
18	Spain	325	1.7	2
19	India	322	1.7	2
20	Chinese Taipei	314	1.7	3
21	Switzerland	311	1.6	(13)
22	Australia	241	1.3	(5)
23	Malaysia	234	1.2	3
24	Thailand	228	1.2	0
25	Brazil	225	1.2	(7)

Source: World Trade Organization, *International Trade Statistics*, 2015.

Chapter 2

GENERAL FRAMEWORKS IN INTERNATIONAL BUSINESS

Contents

Objectives of the chapter

In this chapter, we introduce several important conceptual frameworks that provide the reader with a toolbox to understand international business. First we will introduce three important concepts: ownership advantages, location advantages, and internalization advantages, which are the pillars of two important frameworks, the eclectic paradigm and the FSA–CSA framework. The second part will introduce these two frameworks, which have many similarities and overlaps, and are both used frequently throughout this book. The FSA–CSA framework[1] is especially useful in understanding issues to do with strategy, while the eclectic paradigm helps to evaluate the broader aspects of international business. The eclectic paradigm, first developed by John Dunning, provides a consolidation of the literature on MNEs that draws on industrial organization theories, location theory, and market imperfections approaches. It is a basis for understanding almost all aspects of international business.[2] The two frameworks share two core concepts, which we will define first. Both approaches hold that firms with particular kinds of assets are able to make use of conditions and circumstances available in foreign locations to engage in value-adding activities in those locations. These assets are variously described as ownership-specific (O) advantages or firm-specific advantages (FSAs). Advantages that are not specific to a particular firm but are potentially available to all economic actors in a specific location (and are not mobile) are termed location-specific (L) advantages or country-specific advantages (CSAs). Each pair of terms is used interchangeably.[3]

The third part of this chapter will look at why firms become MNEs, more specifically at what are the motivations for them to go abroad. The fourth part will look at how firms engage in international activities and their internationalization process; this part introduces the Uppsala model and the concepts of liability of foreignness, psychic distance, and path dependence. The fifth part goes into detail of the entry modes that firms can opt for, such as greenfield, joint ventures, and mergers and acquisitions. The sixth part introduces the recent phenomenon of born global firms, which are firms that have had international activities from or near the start of their founding. The final part introduces the international activities of SMEs.

The specific objectives of this chapter are to:

1 *Introduce* some key conceptual frameworks from the international business "toolbox," including the eclectic paradigm and the CSA–FSA framework, which capture ownership advantages, location advantages, and internalization advantages.

2 *Explain* why firms become multinational enterprises (MNEs)—what motivates them to expand abroad.

3 *Understand* the internationalization process, the Uppsala model, and the concepts of liability of foreignness, psychic distance, and path dependence.

4 *Describe* the international activities of small and medium-sized enterprises (SMEs).

ACTIVE LEARNING CASE

Starbucks: a global "coffee culture"

From its first location in Seattle's Pike Place Market in 1971, Starbucks has grown into one of the largest coffee chains in the world. In 2014, Starbucks had 21,366 stores globally—an increase from the previous year, when it had 19,767. The company purchases and roasts high-quality coffee beans which are then brewed and retailed in trendy designer coffee shops that cater to a loyal following of young urban professionals, who appreciate the distinct taste of Starbucks' coffee. In 2014 its sales were US$16.45 billion.

The company's road to success began in 1985, when, after convincing the founders of Starbucks to test the coffee bar concept, the then director of retail operations, Howard Schultz, started his own coffee house to sell Starbucks coffee under the name Il Giornale. Within two years, Schultz purchased Starbucks and changed its company name to Starbucks Corporation. Since then, the company has expanded rapidly, opening stores in key markets and creating a "corporate coffee culture" in each of the urban areas in which it settled. Coffee bars are located in high-traffic areas and include large bookstores, suburban malls, universities, and high-traffic intra-urban communities.

Popularity has not come without a price for Starbucks. Coffee prices fell considerably in the late 1990s and led to the displacement of thousands of farmers. The main reason for a fall in the price of coffee was the oversupply that arose from improved production techniques and from a crop boom in the 1990s. Although Starbucks only purchases approximately 1 percent of the global supply of coffee, its high profile has made it a main target for protestors who accuse the coffee giant of not providing a fair price to coffee growers; despite Starbucks' policy of purchasing high-quality beans at premium market prices. To address the concerns of protestors, Starbucks introduced Fairtrade-endorsed coffee to its coffee houses. While the amount of Fairtrade coffee sold by the company is insignificant, at 1 percent of total sales, it is enough to portray the company as progressive and avert a consumer boycott.

The company directly operated 7,533 coffee houses in the United States in 2015. Unlike many coffee and fast-food chains, Starbucks does not franchise (license the right to operate one of its stores) to individuals in the United States. It does, however, negotiate licensing agreements with companies that have control over valuable retail space, such as an airport or hospital. In 2015, there were 4,962 Starbucks stores operating under licenses in the US.

With coffee houses in over 65 countries, today Starbucks has a global presence. In contrast to its domestic operations, the majority of Starbucks' international operations are through licenses. Indeed, of 9,404 international stores in 2014, 5,994 were licensed and in joint venture, while 3,410 were directly owned. Starbucks has also adopted different international strategies in different countries: for example, in 1998, when it expanded into the UK, it did so through an $83 million acquisition of Seattle Coffee Company which had 60 outlets. The outlets were then rebranded as Starbucks. After failing to make gains in 2007, Starbucks, in 2012 formed a 50:50 joint venture with Tata Global Beverages in India, called Tata Starbucks. The joint venture has so far been seen as a success—after opening its first outlet in October 2012, it opened its 75th outlet in April 2015, and now has a presence in seven cities.

While Starbucks has had many successes in its international ventures, it was not successful in expanding to Australia. Starbucks first entered in Australia in 2000 through a wholly owned subsidiary and opened several stores in quick succession. By 2008, however, it became apparent that Starbucks had troubles and, from both cultural and financial pressure, it closed 61 of its 85 outlets. While Starbucks adapted its product line in China to meet the different needs of their consumers, in Australia they failed to appreciate the differences between US and Australian preferences. Starbucks is branded as "affordable luxury," but as analysts point out, Starbucks' aggressive expansion meant its availability led it not to have a "luxury image" but to be a symbol of American consumerism. In fact, Australians prefer smaller boutique-style coffee cafés, with personal touch and stronger-tasting coffee than was on offer at Starbucks.

Sources: http://www.starbucks.in; http://www.statista.com/topics/1246/starbucks/; http://www.tataglobalbeverages.com/company/tgb-at-a-glance/about-us; "Starbucks in $83 million deal for British coffee chain," *New York Times*, April 30, 1998; P. Mercer, "Shunned Starbucks in Aussie exit," *BBC News*, August 4, 2008; A. Lutz, "Starbucks has failed in Australia," *Business Insider*, May 28, 2014.

1 What are Starbucks' firm-specific advantages?

2 Why is Starbucks focusing its international expansion on emerging countries, such as India?

3 Why did Starbucks fail in Australia?

4 What are the advantages of Starbucks using licensing and joint ventures when expanding abroad?

INTRODUCTION

Certain core concepts and frameworks are crucial to understanding international business activity and its relationship to strategy and innovation. These concepts are the focus of Chapter 2. There are two key frameworks that any student of international business needs to master: the eclectic paradigm and the FSA–CSA framework. The eclectic paradigm is a more general framework and is useful in understanding a variety of different issues. It is a toolbox in its own right, and helps us understand countries, modes of governance, and government policies, and it is used by policy-makers. It can be applied at a macro (country) level, as well as at an industry and firm level. The FSA–CSA framework finds its greatest application in understanding the strategy of firms. Both frameworks share two crucial aspects–ownership advantages/firm-specific assets, and location advantages/country-specific assets. The third "leg" of the eclectic paradigm is internalization advantages, which is a concept that is implicitly acknowledged by the FSA–CSA framework.

FIRM-SPECIFIC ASSETS/OWNERSHIP ADVANTAGES

Firms need to have assets that they are able to use in foreign locations to generate some kind of income. These assets are variously described as *ownership-specific (O) advantages* or *firm-specific assets (FSAs)*. The academic literature has tended to use these terms interchangeably.[4]

The understanding of ownership advantages in the international business field is based upon Hymer's (1976) monopolistic advantage theory. The theory was developed after neoclassical theories in economics failed to explain how foreign firms were able to compete against domestic firms. Hymer argued that MNEs hold "monopolistic advantages" (a term now replaced by "ownership advantages") to overcome the costs and disadvantaged position when they enter into a host country. These monopolistic advantages were either (a) not available to local firms or (b) superior to those of the local firms. Essentially, ownership advantages allow the business to overcome the barriers of entry into the host country. It is important to note that foreign firms are innately in a disadvantaged position in comparison to the home country's domestic companies when they enter the host country, considering they don't have networks, experience, or local knowledge, and therefore will need to offer something superior to compensate for this disadvantage.

A classification of O advantages

Ownership advantages are firm-specific in nature, and the competitiveness of firms is associated with the strength (or weakness) of their O advantages.[5] There are three types of O advantages (Figure 2.1).

Asset-type FSAs

This type of FSA involves the ownership of physical equipment, intellectual property, or privileged access to tangible and intangible resources (including knowledge possessed by employees). It is common to think of such FSAs as having to do with technology/engineering, such as new products, services and processes, machinery and equipment, and intellectual property. However, this type of FSA also includes privileged knowledge about where to find resources (i.e., in which particular locations), how to get privileged access to these resources, and at what price, relative to alternative locations. A firm may have the "know-who" which allows it to get a long-term lease to a copper mine in Zambia at a favorable price. Such knowledge is valuable to generating an income, even if it does not have technological assets, such as machinery or know-how. It can partner another firm that does have these assets, through either a non-equity partnership or an equity joint venture.

Transaction-type FSAs

These advantages are associated with conducting transactions efficiently. Firms can generate an income because they know how to organize themselves efficiently, both within countries and internationally. They are complementary to asset-type FSAs, and if a firm wants to be a successful MNE, it must know how to develop an organizational structure that allows it to benefit from the synergies of having operations in more than one country. This is known as *advantages of common governance*. If a firm has simply duplicated all its management and operations from its home country in the host country, it does not benefit from being an MNE. On the other hand, if it can establish a common human resource

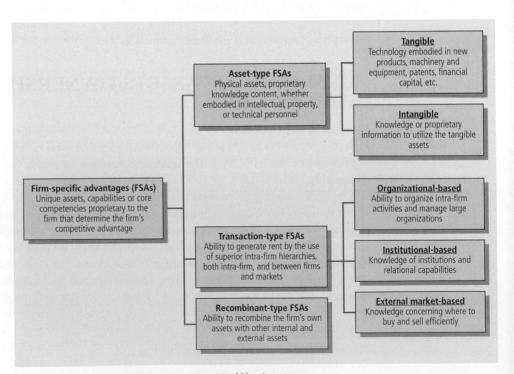

Figure 2.1 Classes of FSAs or ownership (O) advantages

management department, and common finance and accounting facilities, or is able to get loans more cheaply because it is borrowing for both operations at the same time, it is exploiting these economies of common governance. They are to do with managerial skills associated with efficiently running a complex organization, and encompass leadership, human resource capabilities, logistics, and creating and implementing organizational structures. They are about creating and maintaining routines within an MNE, and establishing efficient bureaucracies. In other words, the ownership of assets needs to be complemented by the ability to distribute these assets effectively to other constituent parts of the MNE so they can generate profits. However, simply having transaction-type FSAs without any asset-type FSAs rarely leads to rent generation.[6]

It is important to distinguish between the O advantages of the MNE at large, and those associated with individual establishments or subsidiaries (Rugman and Verbeke, 2001).[7] Much of the early literature on O advantages took a macro perspective, given the nature of the typical MNE and its centralized management structure. Such centralized MNEs had O advantages that were in principle available to all their subsidiaries. However, today this is not always so. The O advantages of the parent are not necessarily available to all its subsidiaries, and to each individual operating unit, and vice versa.

Transaction-type FSAs are about being able to conduct internal transactions efficiently, and the MNE should be able to conduct transactions more efficiently with external markets as well. An MNE must be a meta-integrator because it needs to do two things well. First, it must be able to move knowledge, goods, ideas, and people between its various establishments in different locations and countries to create this efficiency. Second, it must efficiently move goods, services, ideas, and people from and to unaffiliated firms outside the boundaries of its firm, especially where these are cheaper than those available internally. To do so requires knowledge of institutions. A familiarity with institutions plays an important part in reducing the coordination costs, the costs of opportunistic behavior, and other transaction costs.[8] Knowledge of institutions makes it cheaper to conduct transactions. Not least, a firm that is familiar with the major actors in its host economy and how to best approach them can be much more competitive than a firm that does not have good connections with state owned organizations, ministries, and policy-makers.

Recombinant FSAs

Recombinant advantages are an important set of FSAs, which represent capabilities for the recombining or "bundling" of complementary assets to improve their performance.[9] Firms require a certain threshold of assets—both transaction-type and asset-type FSAs—to successfully compete in any given country, and these different assets must be "bundled" together. Where a firm is deficient in one type of FSA, it can nonetheless continue to be competitive, overcoming this weakness by leveraging other assets outside its own boundaries. This is an expertise that is not easily acquired, or transmitted. Such expertise is a firm-specific asset in its own right.

Not all assets are equally mobile across borders. *Location-bound* O advantages allow the firm to generate profits, but only in a specific location. For instance, an MNE might have privileged access to natural resources, to capital, or specific infrastructure in its home country. It cannot use these FSAs in its host country, so they are considered to be location-bound.

MNEs can be part of large industrial group at home (sometimes with cross-holdings and common ownership) with interests in several industries. Appendix 2 lists the world's largest MNEs from a number of major home countries. Such linkages provide privileged access to intra-group transactions and intermediate goods within the same family of firms, but these advantages are not necessarily available when they move abroad. These may also derive from knowledge of institutions, by virtue of being an "insider." They may have close relationships with state-owned organizations, ministries, and policy-makers, and be able to influence domestic policy. They may be able to shape the technology and science infrastructure to their own needs, and in many cases, these will have evolved around and with their own domestic activities, often over a long period of time. Such linkages confer the basis to generate economic rent for incumbents, and are a cost to new entrants or those less entrenched in the domestic milieu. These advantages are not transferable to foreign markets, and establishing "membership" in business and innovation networks in new locations is not costless.[10]

✔ Active learning check

Review your answer to Active Learning Case question 1 and make any changes you like. Then compare your answer to the one below.

 What are Starbucks' firm-specific advantages?

The most obvious FSA of Starbucks is its brand. This is why it was so important for Starbucks to shift to fair trade, so it could keep up its image of luxury and maintain a good corporate social responsibility (CSR) image. Other FSAs include being able to identify prime and strategic locations, and benefit from economies of scale derived from its global distribution channels and bargaining power over suppliers.

LOCATION ADVANTAGES/COUNTRY-SPECIFIC ASSETS

Assets that are not specific to a particular firm but are potentially available to all actors in a specific location (and are not mobile) are termed *location-specific (L) advantages* or *country-specific assets (CSAs)*. L advantages are about the characteristics of specific locations, and are location-bound. Although it is increasingly popular to use country-specific assets as a synonym for L advantages, the term "L advantages" allows us to clearly distinguish between the various units of analysis, such as the country, national sub-regional, or supranational regions. Even within countries, sub-national regions have different types of assets. Supranational regions also exist—such as the European Union (EU)—which provide an additional layer of policies, regulations, and laws. An MNE may engage with all three levels of L advantage. For instance, consider an MNE with a production site in Maastricht, in the Netherlands. The MNE will need to consider the L advantages of the Netherlands at large, the Limburg province, as well as the EU.[11]

L advantages are in principle accessible and applicable to all firms equally that are physically or legally established in that location. We say "in principle" for three reasons. First, full information about L advantages associated with a specific location may not be readily available. Second, even where information is available, there may be costs associated with accessing this knowledge. This knowledge may be available to incumbents (whether domestic or foreign), and acquired through experience. Third, these L advantages may be made available (or denied) by the actions of governments that seek to encourage (or restrict) the activities of a particular group of actors by introducing barriers to their use of certain L advantages. This may be for commercial reasons (to favor a national firm over the MNE), or for strategic reasons such as national defense, or it may reflect the influence of interest groups that are able to influence government policy.

When location-bound assets are in the private domain (i.e., they are internalized by others), they are no longer L advantages but constitute O advantages, since they assist rent generation/market share retention by specific actors to the exclusion of other economic actors.

A classification of L advantages

It is important to understand that L advantages are about relevant complementary assets outside the boundaries of the MNE (or other firm actors) that are location-bound. Table 2.1 classifies L advantages into several broad categories. For each of these categories, we

Table 2.1 A classification of L advantages

Type of L advantages	Sources of L advantages	Example of L advantages
Exogenous L advantages	These derive from natural assets (independent of development stage)	• Sociological/anthropological • Culture, norms, religion, political stability • Land availability, rainfall, climate, extractive resources, basic population • Proximity and accessibility to other markets • Membership in a regional integration scheme
Fundamental L advantages	Basic infrastructure	• Primary schools • Health care • Transport (roads, railways) • Utilities (electricity, water) • Telecoms • Ports • Efficient bureaucracy • Public transport
	Legal infrastructure	• Legal system • Security and police • Tariff system • Property rights • Tax and excise
	Regulation and policy	• Incentives • Subsidies • Tax holidays • Regulatory agencies • Industrial policy • Competition policy • Capacity to enforce regulation
	Financial infrastructure	• Banking, insurance, stock exchange
Knowledge-related L-advantages	Knowledge infrastructure	• Tertiary education, universities • Public research institutes
Structural L advantages	Market and demand structure	• Income level and distribution • Size of potential market • Consumer sophistication • Wage rates • Skilled employee availability • Distribution channels • Competitors
Co-location L advantages	L advantages that derive from the presence of other actors in the same location	• Agglomeration economies • Networks of suppliers • Networks of customers • Presence of support industries
	Industrial policy	• Specific policies associated with given industry
	L advantages that derive from location-bound O advantages of other actors	• Presence of significant customer • Presence of significant supplier

Source: Adapted from R. Narula and G. D. Santangelo, "Location and collocation advantages in international innovation," *Multinational Business Review,* vol. 20, no. 1 (2012).

identify the specific type of L advantages and related sources and provide examples. As we discuss below, these categories have a certain degree of overlap.

Country-level L advantages

These are "contextual" in nature, because they provide the broad background of a location. They reflect the socio-economic and political environment. They remain macro and "generic" and are relevant to all firms, regardless of size, nationality, industry, or geographical unit of analysis. Some are exogenous, in the sense that they are independent of the economic stage of development, and are the natural assets of the location, such as population, climate, accessibility, etc. Others are generic because they "should" exist in all nation states, even though there are countries where they are not easily available—these include basic infrastructure, legal and financial infrastructure, and regulation and policy frameworks.

The last sub-category represents L advantages that are regarded as knowledge infrastructure. "Knowledge infrastructure" refers to public research institutes, universities, statistical organizations, national standards and testing laboratories, intellectual property protection, etc., that enable and promote science and technology development. For obvious reasons, this can also be categorized as an industry-level L advantage, since such assets may be specifically geared to a particular set of industries.

Industry-associated L advantages

In making an investment decision, MNEs seek specific, industry and market-related complementary assets. For instance, an IT firm will establish software design facilities where there is a large supply of IT graduates. Demand is also industry-specific. A luxury furniture firm will be interested in seeking out a market for other luxury goods, opportunities for distributing its goods through channels specific to luxury goods, and the competition within that specific sector. Industry policy is often industry-specific. A location which is home to a cluster of firms in a similar industry is likely to have access to a number of suppliers in support and related sectors. Governments may also provide specific incentives and policies to promote a specific sector, which may make a location more attractive for a specific industry, and not for others.

Informal institutions deserve special mention as an L advantage. Informal institutions shape the manner in which economic actors in a given location interact *in practice*. Such knowledge is also in principle available to all firms that seek to acquire it, but because informal institutions are largely tacit, physical proximity is crucial in its acquisition. In other words, it requires some degree of embeddedness to acquire. Embeddedness in a location provides membership to a "club" of complex relationships with suppliers, customers, and knowledge infrastructure through formal and informal institutions, and these institutions have taken years to evolve a stock of knowledge that is only available to members by virtue of their constant interaction.[12]

✔ Active learning check

Review your answer to Active Learning Case question 2 and make any changes you like. Then compare your answer to the one below.

 Why is Starbucks focusing its international expansion on emerging countries, such as India?

India has a fast-growing economy, with the second largest population in the world. With Starbucks targeting trendy 25- to 40-year-olds, the growing middle class and more Indians with disposable income, this is a good market opportunity. This is especially important for companies such as Starbucks where developed countries are increasingly seen as saturated markets.

INTERNATIONAL BUSINESS STRATEGY IN ACTION

US manufacturing: from China to Mexico

Offshoring has been reported as a declining trend for many nations and recently China has been under pressure concerning this strategy, as costs associated with wages, currency, fuel, and transportation are factors contributing to the decline of offshoring within China. Many firms are now appreciating the fact that offshoring in emerging countries, such as China, is costlier than initial predictions and are either moving production back home or finding alternative, cheaper locations, such as Mexico. Furthermore, analysts suggest that manufacturing in China is almost as expensive as manufacturing in the US.

With increasing costs in China, US manufacturing firms of all sizes are seeking to open plants in Mexico. Economists have reported that these US manufacturing firms are eager to expand operations in Mexico because, unlike China, it continues to hold relatively low labor costs. In addition, US firms opening plants in Mexico will have relatively low transportation costs with huge advantages in terms of ease when accessing the American market. Since 2010, the US's trade with Mexico has grown by approximately 30 percent, with annual figures of $507 billion. Furthermore, FDI figures from the US to Mexico reached $35 billion in 2013.

Figure 2.2 illustrates the comparative cost of shipping a 40 ft container to the US from China and Mexico. Due to the rise in oil prices, the cost of shipping from China to the US

increased from approximately $3,000 to $7,600 between 2000 and 2012. In contrast, the costs of shipping from Mexico to the US increased from approximately $1,900 to $2,800 within the same time period. Furthermore, factors such as distance and customs have resulted in the difference in time from Mexico to the US, and China to the US, reaching up to three weeks.

Evidently many US-based MNEs such as Caterpillar, Chrysler, Stanley Black & Decker, and Callaway Golf are moving or expanding into Mexico, which has helped Mexico secure billions of dollars of investment. Even though a growing number of firms producing high-technology products are reducing operations within China and moving to Mexico, it has been reported that firms producing low-technology products such as headsets (Plantronics), hula hoops (Hoopnotica), toilet brushes (Casabella), outdoor furniture (Meco Corporation), and industrial cabinets (Viasystems Group) have also reduced or closed operations in China and moved to Mexico.

The automotive industry has also been identified as an industry increasing operations in Mexico in comparison with China, following an increase of 16.8 percent in the average salary in the industry between 2009 and 2014. Observing Table 2.2, by 2013 Mexico had surpassed China in terms of global foreign direct investment in the automotive industry

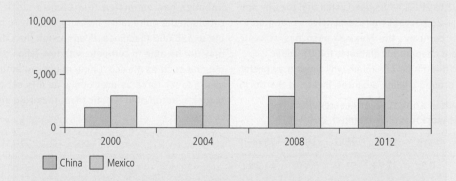

Figure 2.2 Cost of shipping a 40 ft container to the American East Coast (US$)

Source: CIBC.

Table 2.2 China's and Mexico's market share (%) in the global automotive industry, 2005–13

	2005	2006	2007	2008	2009	2010	2011	2012	2013
China	17.06	16.26	10.80	13.06	15.16	13.99	13.58	12.71	12.40
Mexico	1.93	4.28	3.85	4.35	5.75	4.53	5.05	9.05	12.56

Note: Based on number of greenfield FDI projects.

Source: fDi Markets.

as the number of greenfield FDI projects reached 12.56 percent. It is apparent that Mexico's market share in the global automotive industry has been increasing significantly, rising from 1.93 percent in 2005 to 12.56 percent by 2013. In contrast, China's market share in the global automotive industry decreased from 17.06 percent in 2005 to 12.4 percent in 2013. In 2015 Volkswagen announced that it would be investing US$1.5 billion in Mexico for the production of small SUVs. In addition, other automotive original equipment manufacturers (OEMs) such as Nissan Motors, General Motors, Ford Motors and Fiat Chrysler have also announced they will be increasing operations within Mexico.

Since 2009, wage rates have increased more dramatically in China than in Mexico. In absolute terms, wage rates in China are significantly higher than in Mexico for unskilled workers. For instance, in 2014, an average unskilled worker in an automotive plant located in Mexico could be expected to earn $3,645 annually, compared to $5,726 in China. However, wage rates remain lower in China for engineers and high-skilled workers. Table 2.3 illustrates the changes in annual salaries for the workforce in the automotive industry in China and Mexico. Even though the annual salary in the automotive industry increased by 16.71 percent in Mexico in 2014, the mean growth in salary for automotive workers between 2009 and 2014 was 4.9 percent in Mexico and 16.8 percent in China. It has been argued that Mexico's relatively predictable, steady wages offer firms a sense of certainty when forecasting manufacturing costs for the future.

Foreign exchange rates can also help to explain why firms may be favoring Mexico over China, as slight changes can have large effects on an organization seeking to expand operations. From 2003 to 2013, it has been noted that the Chinese yuan has become 26 percent more expensive in relation to the US dollar. In contrast, the Mexican peso has actually become 27 percent cheaper in relation to the US dollar.

Another factor that helps to explain why firms may prefer Mexico revolves around trading alliances. Including the North American Free Trade Agreement (NAFTA), Mexico currently has free trade agreements with 45 countries. Even though China aims to have 20 free trade agreements in place in the near future, as of 2015 they had only 12 agreements. Therefore, Chinese products are constantly hitting tariff barriers when entering crucial markets within North and South America.

Conclusion

Even though expanding operations in Mexico may result in job reductions in the USA, economists suggest that overall the American economy is likely to benefit more in the long run when firms decide to locate in Mexico rather than China. For instance, neighboring countries often share high levels of production levels. The National Bureau of Economic Research found that approximately 40 percent of the components identified in Mexican imports actually originated from the US itself, which is significantly higher than the 4 percent found in Chinese imports.

Multiple factors such as labor costs, currency trends, fuel costs, transportation, and trading alliances have inevitably led to many organizations favoring Mexico over China. However, this does not necessarily mean China's manufacturing industry will be diminished in the long run. Costs alone may not be sufficient for businesses to leave China, as the nation has been argued to contain some of the world's best supply chains of components and infrastructure. Furthermore, firms have already invested heavily in China. Having initially ventured there for low labor costs, they may not want to leave the country now, as the domestic market has itself become huge.

China displaced the US in 2010 as the largest manufacturing country in the world, and has invested heavily in automated manufacturing. The International Federation of Robotics has estimated that China's stock of operational robots in the automotive industry is likely to more than double to 428,000 machines. Even though the Chinese economy may not be able to compete with low labor costs from other nations such as Mexico, China might not actually require as vast a labor force as previously, as it is set to be the world leader in automated robotic manufacturing instead.

Table 2.3 Growth in annual salary costs within the automotive OEM workforce (% change), 2009–14

	2009	2010	2011	2012	2013	2014
China	14.4	8.92	32.93	22.31	11.07	11.25
Mexico	10.06	−8.93	6.12	−0.75	6.17	16.71

Source: fDi Benchmark.

Sources: http://tacna.net/mexico-vs-china/; Damien Cave, "As ties with China unravel, US companies head to Mexico," *New York Times*, May 31, 2014; James Kynge, "Mexico steals a march on China in car manufacturing," *Financial Times*, April 21, 2015; Reshoring Manufacturing, "Coming home," *The Economist*, January 19, 2013; Tia Nowack, "Manufacturers are leaving China, but where are they headed?," January 28, 2014, manufacturing.net; Schim Sau-wai, "Cheaper costs beckon manufacturers from China to Mexico," *South China Morning Post*, February 15, 2015.

Internalization advantages

The eclectic paradigm (see below) consists of three important building blocks, two of which are FSAs and L advantages. The third building block is the *internalization advantage*. This comes from internalization theory, pioneered by Peter Buckley and Mark Casson, and developed further by Alan Rugman, Jean-François Hennart, and Alain Verbeke, among others.[13] This is built on three premises. First, firms tend to maximize profits in the world of imperfect markets. Second, the existence of an imperfect market for intermediate goods provides firms with an incentive to create internal hierarchies to control such activities. Third, where imperfect markets exist, the internalization of markets creates MNEs because they are the most efficient way to facilitate and control the coordination of interdependent economic activities domestically or across geographies as compared to the coordination of such activities through the market. This is the internalization (I) advantage, and where there are advantages to the firm of internalizing such activities, it will do so. I advantages largely determine what entry mode (e.g., exporting, joint venture, or wholly owned subsidiary) the firm will adopt when it decides to operate in a foreign location. We discuss entry modes later in this chapter.

Internalization theory is linked closely with transaction cost theory (the cost associated with economic exchange). As there are costs with doing business in the market, a firm has to see whether keeping operations internally as opposed to leaving them to a third party would mitigate transaction costs. That is the main question internalization theory sheds light on. There are several reasons why a firm may want to keep its activities internal instead of leaving them to the market (e.g., outsourcing production). It could be that the firm's ownership advantage is in production and that outsourcing it to a third party could lead to some leakage to competitors. It could be that the firm is able to do it at a cheaper price internally or it could be that the company wants more control over quality.

THE ECLECTIC PARADIGM: PUTTING IT ALL TOGETHER

The eclectic paradigm[14] (sometimes known as OLI) connects the three building blocks together. It is easiest to think of the OLI framework as answering a set of three sequential questions (Figure 2.3):

1 Does the FSA of the firm provide it an advantage over other firms operating in the intended destination location? If the answer is "no," then the advantage is a domestic one, and the firm should not internationalize. Note that determining whether an FSA provides an advantage requires us to systematically analyze this, and this is best done

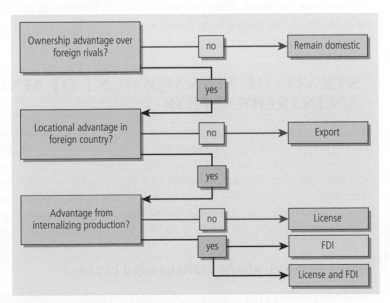

Figure 2.3 The OLI framework: a decision model

using the VRIO framework, which we introduce in Chapter 3. If the answer is "yes," the firm's FSAs provide it with an advantage over other firms in the foreign location, and we can move to the second question.

2   Can this FSA be used abroad, in conjunction with the location advantages of the host location? Are the location advantages of this location complementary to the FSAs of the firm? As we discussed earlier, not all FSAs are "stand-alone." They depend upon inputs that are location-bound. Let us suppose firm A (from Argentina) owns technology that provides it with an FSA (for instance, patented technology to produce rechargeable batteries), which it has hitherto been manufacturing in its home country. A key input for its manufacturing is specific raw materials, which the Argentinian government makes available at very low prices. This is a location advantage of its home country, and it is location-bound. If firm A wants to manufacture these batteries in Sri Lanka, the decision will depend upon whether these same raw materials can be acquired in Sri Lanka at a lower cost. It could also be that the raw material is not cheaper, but some other important input is low enough that it compensates for this, such as the cost of labor. If the answer is "yes," that is an overall advantage of producing in Sri Lanka rather than in Argentina (or another location) because of Sri Lanka's L assets, in which case we can move to the third question. If the answer is "no," then it needs to consider supplying the Sri Lankan market by exports, rather than FDI.

3   If there is a clear FSA, and there is a clear L advantage of the destination location, the next question the firm has to answer is: Are there any advantages for firm A from manufacturing in Sri Lanka itself, rather than allowing others to do so on its behalf? It may be that it does not have the prerequisite knowledge of the foreign market to be able to do this itself, or there may be barriers to entry of new foreign firms. If this is the case, it may prefer to license its technology to a local firm (or another firm already located there) rather than engaging in direct investment. In a service industry, the choice would be to franchise, rather than engage in FDI. The firm needs to conduct a cost–benefit analysis of the different entry modes to determine which would be economically most beneficial to it, and thereby to decide whether to internalize the foreign market or not, and if so, to what degree it wants to take on control and ownership of its foreign affiliate.

Of course, the issue of entry mode choice is a complex one, and firms can often undertake complex combinations—it may seek to license as well as make a joint venture, for instance. Furthermore, we know from Chapter 1 that it is possible to control a foreign operation without necessarily engaging in ownership. We will discuss this at some length later in the chapter.

STRATEGIC MANAGEMENT OF MNEs: AN INTRODUCTION

The strategic management process involves four major functions: strategy formulation, strategy implementation, evaluation, and the control of operations. These functions encompass a wide range of activities, beginning with an environmental analysis of external and internal conditions and an evaluation of organizational strengths and weaknesses. These activities serve as the basis for a well-formulated strategic plan, and by carefully implementing and controlling this plan, the MNE is able to compete effectively in the international arena.[15] Figure 2.4 illustrates the five specific steps in this overall process.

Steps in the strategic management process

Strategic planning typically begins with a review of the company's *basic mission*, which is determined by answering the questions: What is the firm's business? What is its reason for existence? By answering these questions, the company clearly determines the direction in

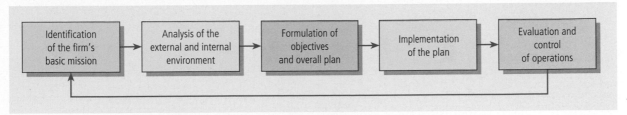

Figure 2.4 The strategic management process in action

which it wants to go. Shell Oil, BP, and Chevron, for example, see themselves as being in the energy business, not in the oil business, and this focus helps to direct their long-range thinking. AT&T and France Telecom view themselves as being in the communications business, not in the telephone business. Coca-Cola and PepsiCo see themselves in the food business, not in the soft drinks business.

A growing number of MNEs have revised their strategic plans because they realized that they had drifted too far away from their basic mission. Unilever, the giant Anglo-Dutch MNE, is a good example. After assessing its operations, the company concluded that it needed to adopt a "back to the core" strategy. As a result, it sold a wide range of peripheral operations, including transport, oil, milling, wallpaper, floor coverings, specialty chemicals, and turkey breeding. Today Unilever confines its business to consumer product goods: food, health and wellness products, personal care, and home care. The firm's strong research and development labs continue to develop new products in each of these areas, thus helping Unilever to remain competitive in worldwide markets.[16]

After determining its mission, an MNE will evaluate the external and internal environment. The goal of *external* environmental analysis is to identify opportunities and threats that will need to be addressed. The purpose of *internal* environmental analysis is to evaluate the company's financial and personnel strengths and weaknesses. Examining its financial picture will help the MNE decide what it can afford to do in terms of expansion and capital investment. Examining its financial picture will also help it to identify areas where cost cutting or divestment is in order. By making an evaluation of its personnel, an MNE will be able to determine how well its current workforce can meet the challenges of the future and what types of people will have to be hired or let go. In addition, the firm might like to include in its internal environmental analysis the reputation of its products, the structure of its organization, and its relationship with suppliers.

Internal and external analyses will also help the MNE to identify both long-range goals (typically two to five years) and short-range goals (less than two years). The plan is then broken down into major parts, and each affiliate and department is assigned goals and responsibilities. This begins the implementation process. Progress is then periodically evaluated and changes are made in the plan. For example, an MNE might realize that it must stop offering a particular good or service because the market is no longer profitable, or it might create a new product in order to take advantage of an emerging demand. Figure 2.4 describes the strategic management process. External and internal environmental assessments are discussed in more detail in Chapter 15.

A FRAMEWORK FOR GLOBAL STRATEGIES: THE FSA–CSA MATRIX

Although the eclectic paradigm and the FSA–CSA matrix serve similar purposes, the FSA–CSA matrix relies on only two blocks (absorbing the "I" aspect of the eclectic paradigm within these two). Thus, the two basic building blocks of the FSA–CSA framework are firm-specific advantages (FSAs) and country-specific advantages (CSAs) (see

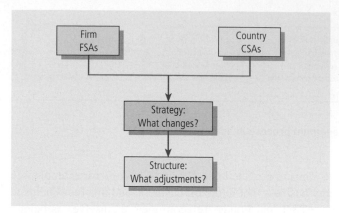

Figure 2.5 The basic components of international business

Figure 2.5). Managers of most MNEs use strategies that build on the interactions of CSAs and FSAs. They do this so that they can be positioned in a unique strategic space.

The CSAs represent the natural factor endowments of a nation; they are based on the key variables in its aggregate production function. For example, CSAs can consist of the quantity, quality, and cost of the major factor endowment, namely resources. Using Porter's terminology, the CSAs form the basis of the global platform from which the multinational firm derives a home-base "diamond" advantage in global competition.[17] Tariff and non-tariff barriers to trade and government regulation also influence CSAs. Building on these CSAs, the firm makes decisions about the efficient global configuration and coordination between segments of its value chain (operations, marketing, R&D, and logistics). The skill in making such decisions represents a strong, managerial FSA.

The FSAs possessed by a firm are based ultimately on its internalization of an asset, such as production knowledge, managerial or marketing capabilities, over which the firm has proprietary control. FSAs are thus related to the firm's ability to coordinate the use of its advantage in production, marketing, or the customization of services.

The FSA–CSA matrix

To help formulate the strategic options of the MNE, it is useful to identify the relative strengths and weaknesses of the CSAs and FSAs they possess. Figure 2.6, the FSA–CSA matrix, provides a useful framework for discussion of these issues. The "strength" or "weakness" of FSAs and CSAs is a relative notion, depending on the relevant market and the CSAs and FSAs of potential competitors. A strong FSA implies that, under identical CSAs, a firm has a potential competitive advantage over its rivals.

Quadrants (or cells) 1, 3, and 4 correspond broadly to three generic strategies: cost leadership, differentiation, and focus.[18] Quadrant 1 firms are generally resource-based and/or mature, globally oriented firms producing a commodity-type product. Given their late stage in the product life cycle, production FSAs flowing from the possession of intangible skills are less important than the CSAs of location and energy costs, which are the main sources of the firm's competitive advantage. Quadrant 2 firms represent inefficient, floundering firms with no consistent strategy, and no intrinsic CSAs or FSAs. These firms are preparing to exit or to restructure. Quadrant 2 can also represent domestically based small and medium-sized firms with little global exposure. Quadrant 3 firms can generally choose to follow any of the generic strategies listed above because of the strength of both their CSAs and FSAs.

The quadrants in Figure 2.6 imperfectly correspond to the three "generic strategies" utilized in the strategy literature: cost leadership, differentiation, and focus. These firms

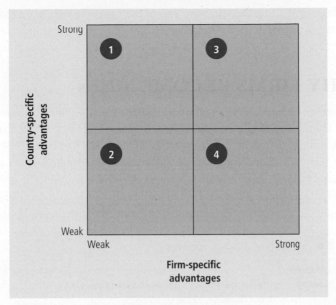

Figure 2.6 The FSA–CSA matrix

basically follow a differentiation strategy. In quadrant 4 the FSAs dominate, so in world markets the home-country CSAs are not essential in the long run. Thus these firms are following low-cost and price competition strategies.

In terms of business strategy, quadrants 3 and 2 are unambiguous in their implications. A quadrant 3 firm can benefit from strategies of both low cost and differentiation. Such a firm is constantly evaluating its production mix. As a product line matures and then declines, it eventually graduates to quadrant 2. However, by adopting new product lines, developing dynamic organizational capabilities, and maintaining an effective strategy, the firm can maintain its overall position in quadrant 3. In quadrant 2 there is no alternative but to restructure or to eventually leave the market.[19]

Quadrants 4 and 1 are credible positions for different types of firms. For instance, a quadrant 4 firm that has strong FSAs in marketing (customization) can operate globally without reliance on its home-market CSA, or the CSAs of the host nation. For such a firm, quadrant 4 does not signal a CSA weakness; the CSA is not relevant. In contrast, quadrant 1 has mature multinationals or product lines determined more by CSAs than by FSAs. By improving potential FSAs in marketing or product innovation and increasing value added through vertical integration, the quadrant 1 firm can move to quadrant 3, where its profitability should be enhanced.

Although quadrants 1, 3, and 4 represent appropriate strategic positioning for some firms, there exists an asymmetry between quadrants 4 and 1. A quadrant 4 strategic choice may be a stable one for some firms; however, quadrant 1 firms should be able to aim for quadrant 3. The reason for this asymmetry is rooted in the fact that CSAs are for the most part exogenous to the firm, whereas FSAs are not. Even to the extent that CSAs can be influenced by government protection, there is always increased uncertainty associated with such strategies. For the firm in quadrant 4 already following an efficiency-based strategy there is no incentive, or need, to move to quadrant 3.

It is useful to note the following two points. First, if the firm has a conglomerate structure, it would be more useful to situate each division or product line individually, recognizing that different units of the diversified firm would use different generic strategies. Second, changes in the trading environment—such as the EU 1992 single-market measures, or the EU 1999 single currency, or the United States–Canada Free Trade Agreement and

NAFTA—will affect the relative CSAs of the firms. To the extent that CSAs are improved, the firms will tend to move to quadrant 3, and, to the extent that the CSAs are hampered, the firm or some of its product lines may move to exit, as in quadrant 2.

WHY FIRMS BECOME MNEs

Companies become MNEs (internationalize) for a number of reasons. There have been many attempts to create classification schemes of internationalization motives. Of course, the most important motive that underlies all other motives is the profit motive. The purpose of the firm is first and foremost the generation of a greater return on its investment. The most complete set of motives was compiled by John Dunning in 1993, and these are listed in Table 2.4. Many of the firm's actions are driven by the need to sustain and utilize its FSAs. At the same time, internationalization is crucially driven by the need to engage with

Table 2.4 Internationalization motives

Types (adapted from Dunning, 1993)	Objectives/motives (inspired by and updated from Dunning, 1993)	The Cuervo-Cazurra et al. motives
Natural resource seeking	To acquire particular and specific resources of a higher quality at a lower real cost than could be obtained in their home country (e.g., physical resources, unskilled (or semi-skilled) labor, technological/managerial expertise, etc.)	"Buy better"
Market seeking	To supply goods or services to a particular country or region (from existing markets to new markets)	"Sell more"
Efficiency seeking	To rationalize the structure of established resource-based or market-seeking investment in such a way that the investing firm can gain from the common governance of geographically dispersed activities (e.g., economies of scale and scope)	"Buy better" and "Sell more"
Strategic asset seeking	To promote long-term strategic objectives—especially that of sustaining or advancing global competitiveness (e.g., augmentation of global portfolio of physical assets and human competences, which they perceive will either sustain or strengthen their ownership-specific advantages or weaken those of competitors)	"Upgrade"
Escape investment	To escape restrictive legislation, institutional voids, or macro-organizational policies by home governments (e.g., round-tripping investment, escaping from high levels of taxation or austere environmental regulation, etc.)	"Escape"
Trade-supportive investment	To promote and facilitate the exports and imports of goods and services from the investing (or other) firm	"Buy better" and "Sell more"
Finance-supportive investment	To support and assist in the purchasing of foreign-produced goods and services from the investing (or other) firm To establish domicile in a specific location for regulatory and tax reasons	"Buy better" and "Sell more"
Management-supportive investment	To support the control and coordination function on behalf of MNE headquarters (e.g., regional office, branch offices)	"Upgrade"
Passive investment	To arbitrage by buying and selling firms or assets with some involvement of direct managerial inputs (e.g., private equity capital firm, asset stripping, etc.)	"Buy better" and "Sell more"

Source: A. Cuervo-Cazurra and R. Narula, "A set of motives to unite them all? Revisiting the principles and typology of internationalization motives," *Multinational Business Review,* vol. 23, no. 1 (2015).

L advantages of a host country or location, or the FSAs of another firm located in the intended host location.

There is a crucial difference between the strategy of a firm, and its motivation to internationalize.[20] It may be a firm's strategy to do certain things, including internationalize, but to decide on a specific location requires the logic of location advantages to be included in the decision. The motivation to internationalize implies that the MNE seeks to utilize its FSAs in conjunction with location-specific assets.[21] Figure 2.7 summarises the options available.

The firm is intent on seeking to "squeeze" or exploit its existing FSAs as efficiently and as thoroughly as possible: in other words, to be *asset exploiting* in nature. However, as discussed in greater detail in Chapter 3, it is the very nature of FSAs that their value as a mechanism from which to derive income declines over time. That is, there are very few FSAs that are as valuable in ten years' time as they are today. This may be because other firms introduce products and services that compete directly, or create new products and services that supersede them. In other words, the FSA of a firm will become less valuable over time as a profit-generating mechanism, and the firm must seek to augment its existing assets, or develop and acquire new FSAs to supplement its older ones. Thus the second broad category of motives is associated with *asset augmentation* (Figure 2.6).

Under these two broad themes comes a variety of motivations (Figure 2.7). Firms may undertake *market-seeking internationalization* because they wish to "sell more." Firms may wish to capture economies of scale, thus expanding internationally. Many MNEs have targeted the United States because of its large population and high per capita income. Other firms sometimes need to diversify themselves in the face of the risks and uncertainties of the domestic business cycle. By setting up operations in another country, MNEs can often diminish the negative effects of economic swings in the home country. This has been widely done by Japanese MNEs, for example, which have found that, while their home economy has been in an economic slump since the 1990s, their US and European operations have done quite well.

Firms can internationalize to ensure access to important inputs to their activities by engaging in *resource-seeking investments*, creating "captive" input suppliers. This helps reduce the risk of opportunistic behavior by arm's-length suppliers, and the volatility of the market. In other words, they learn how to "buy better." These resources can include land, extractive mining assets, unskilled (or semi-skilled) labor, technological/managerial expertise, etc.

Firms can internationalize to be *efficiency seeking*. By setting up operations close to the foreign customer, these firms can eliminate transportation expenses, avoid the overhead associated with having intermediaries handle the product, respond more accurately and rapidly to customer needs, and take advantage of local resources. This process, known as internalization of control within the MNE, can help to reduce overall costs. Firms can rationalize the structure of established resource-based or market-seeking investment in such a way that the investing firm can gain from the common governance of geographically dispersed activities (e.g., economies of scale and scope).

Due to protective devices such as tariff and non-tariff barriers it may make sense to serve the market by FDI rather than through exports. The EU provides an excellent example. Firms outside the EU are subject to tariffs on goods exported to EU countries. Firms producing the goods within the EU, however, can transport them to any other country in the bloc without paying tariffs. This may be considered *trade-supportive* internationalization.

Firms may make *"escape investments"* because the home market is unstable, or increasingly risky because of political, social, or economic changes. A considerable number of emerging country MNEs seek to avoid institutional voids. That is, they seek to relocate their activities to places where the formal and informal institutions are more stable. HSBC began life as a Hong Kong-based bank, but due to the uncertainty of Hong Kong's status prior to the 1997 handover to China, it decided to move its headquarters and center of its operations to the UK.

It is important to distinguish escape investments from flight capital. *Flight capital* refers to investments whose primary purpose is to move financial resources out of a country that is considered risky, to another which is less risky. It is about financial movements of capital, and although these movements may be done through (and by) firms, the objective is similar to portfolio investments (discussed in Chapter 1).

Asset-augmenting internationalization is also referred to as *strategic asset-seeking* FDI in many academic texts. It describes an important reason for MNEs to internationalize, referring to investments by MNEs that are intended primarily to create learning opportunities that enhance their firm-specific assets. It involves the active augmentation of existing ownership advantages through R&D, or through the acquisition of FSAs as part of a cross-border M&A. However, it is not always the case that the acquiring firm has the capacity to internalize and efficiently utilize such knowledge. Asset augmentation is forward looking (and aspirational), and more than any other foreign activity of an MNE it depends upon the correct appraisal of the assets of other external actors. It is crucially dependent upon the existing FSAs of the MNE because the purpose is to "upgrade" these FSAs of the firm through internationalization.[22] Upgrading is not at all straightforward as we shall discuss in Chapter 3.

A single MNE may engage in multiple motivations in a given location. Motives, of course, are hard to determine accurately because firms are not willing to admit why they have engaged in a certain activity, since it will reveal their strategy to the public. Motives are always evolving, like strategies, because they are aspirational, and when they fail to produce the desired outcome, they require a revision in motivation, if not also in strategy. But crucially, they are also dependent upon actors outside the firm for their successful implementation. These actors are not passive, and also have their own motivations which are also evolving.[23] Relationships are rarely equal, and this can mean that firms with a weaker position (such as supplier firms to large MNEs) have their internationalization strategies dictated to them by their customers or, indeed, by their competitors (pro-active vs. reactive motives).[24]

Motives require information and the willingness of other actors to cooperate, which means that firms are constantly reconsidering their actions. HSBC may have withdrawn from being a Hong Kong (and Asia-centric) bank in the 1990s, but in 2015 it reconsidered this move, and discussed the possibility of returning to its pr-1997 roots as an Asian bank.

It is also worth remembering that MNEs do not always function as a single centrally managed firm in which all the parts are following the same strategy. The strategy of two

Figure 2.7 The motives of internationalization: a decision model

subsidiaries within the same MNE can differ, and the motives of the headquarters in under-taking certain actions may not be supported by the foreign subsidiary.[25] That is, there are differences in motives between units of the same MNE.

Over the last 30 years, MNEs have become increasingly sophisticated in managing and integrating activities across borders, and even relatively new and smaller MNEs are organized to maximize cross-border efficiencies and take advantage of the economies of common governance. Today, MNE operations increasingly tend to involve multiple motivations simultaneously.[26]

Firms also become MNEs in response to increased foreign competition and a desire to protect their home market share. Using a follow-the-competitor strategy, a growing number of MNEs now set up operations in the home countries of their major competitors. This approach serves a dual purpose: first, it takes away business from its competitors by offering customers other choices; and second, it lets competitors know that, if it attacks the MNE's home market, it will face a similar response. This strategy of staking out global market shares is particularly important when MNEs want to communicate the conditions under which they will retaliate.

How do firms engage in international activities?

Not all international business is done by MNEs. Indeed, setting up a wholly owned subsidiary is usually the last stage of doing business abroad. Why is it so? Why do firms wait to set up wholly owned subsidiaries and become MNEs?

Figure 2.8 outlines the typical process (or stages) by which a firm producing a standardized product will seek to develop its interdependencies with foreign markets. While this is apparently a generalization, as firms ultimately make decisions depending on their particular circumstances (i.e., industry, business model, etc.), this process is important because it is based on how the firm perceives risk and how it deals with it. In this process of internationalization, the firm *gradually* and *incrementally* develops its interdependencies with foreign markets because of the *liability of foreignness*—the inherent disadvantage that foreign firms experience in host countries due to their non-native status.[27]

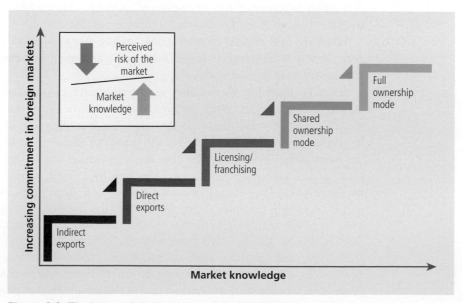

Figure 2.8 The internationalization process of the firm

The firm regards foreign markets as risky due to the fact that they involve a number of differences that are unknown or uncertain to the non-native firm. Foreign markets may have different *rules of the game* because they are governed by different formal and informal institutions. Thus, the (foreign) firm that is not well acquainted with the institutions in the host country is likely to face significant disadvantages (vis-à-vis a local firm) of doing business in host markets (i.e., higher transaction costs). To offset such disadvantages, the investing firm often has to deploy considerable resources and capabilities to engage in the foreign market. In general, firms are risk-averse. Therefore, firms often take an incremental approach to internationalization. This is known as the "Uppsala model"[28] because it was initially developed by scholars at Uppsala University in Sweden. This allows them to develop their knowledge of the host market at a gradual pace. The main argument of this model is that firms *incrementally* increase their commitment to foreign markets by gradually acquiring knowledge about foreign markets and operations through experience. Therefore, the Uppsala model shows that the firm's internationalization process is path dependent. *Path dependence* is the process where the accumulated knowledge from the firm's past international experience helps direct the firm's future trajectory.[29]

As shown in Figure 2.8, the gradually increasing approach to internationalization is shaped by the degree of *market commitment* the firm wishes to make, and the stock of *market knowledge* that the firm has of the host market. Market commitment is dependent upon the amount of resources devoted to enter the foreign market. By investing in a foreign market it is making a commitment, and the firm makes a deliberate choice in deciding its level of commitment.

Building up market knowledge is also a gradual process, shaped by experience, and what is generally known as *learning-by-doing*. Naturally, the commitment a firm makes to a foreign market is a function of its market knowledge. Initially firms usually perceive a high risk of making a commitment to foreign markets due to their lack of knowledge. Thus they typically start with low commitment to host markets, often using the services of specialists in local markets outside the firm. The accumulation of market knowledge will alleviate the perceived risk of the foreign market and gradually enable firms to make greater commitment to it (and develop deeper interdependencies with local actors). As illustrated in Figure 2.8, firms tend to increase their interdependencies with foreign markets in inverse proportion to *perceived risk* (blue-colored section), which gradually decreases over time with the increase of *market knowledge* (orange-colored section).

When the firm decides to enter a new market, it may want to avoid the risks of high commitment to unknown (foreign) markets by arranging non-equity-based agreements such as *licensing* or *franchising*.

Instead of licensing, the firm may see the potential for extra sales by exporting its products to foreign markets. When the firm has little knowledge of the foreign market, it may use a *local agent or distributor*. In this stage, the firm often uses exporting as a "vent" for its surplus production. Exporting has the benefit of requiring no long-run commitment to the international markets. As the firm acquires market knowledge it may set up its own local sales or marketing subsidiaries. This may be a *wholly-owned subsidiary*, controlled by the investing firm. It may be a *joint venture* with local firms, in which the firm has a partial ownership (and partial control). Both of these options are *equity modes of governance* (typically involving FDI) that involve relatively large commitments to the foreign market. This is distinguished from *non-equity modes of governance* such as *licensing*, *franchising*, and *exporting using agents*. Where exports become a significant part of the firm's sales, it will often set up a separate *export department* to manage foreign sales and production for such markets. Product design and the production process itself may also be modified to tailor products for export markets.

After the firm has become more familiar with the local market and accumulates more market knowledge, it may begin to locate higher value-adding activities such as production. This indicates a growing commitment to, and deeper interdependencies with, the foreign market. Even so, it is likely that such expansion will also be gradual. Initially, it may start with *local assembly and packaging* of its product lines, but later it may move toward deeper interdependencies by locating more strategic activities such as headquarter functions and R&D.

The Uppsala model is more complicated than it seems at first glance. Like all generalizations, it relies on simplifications. Not all firms necessarily follow the same sequence, or always begin the internationalization process with licensing or exporting. In reality, the process of internationalization and foreign entry is sufficiently complicated to depend on a careful weighting of many firm-specific and location-specific factors. The Uppsala model is not really about stages. It is built around the concept of learning and gradual evolution. Firms go from the familiar to the unfamiliar slowly and gradually, *if* they have a choice in the matter. Likewise, the Uppsala model also argues that (all else being equal) firms will decide where to go following a similar logic of incrementalism. The evidence indicates that, left to their own measures, firms conventionally prefer to engage with nearby countries first because these are likely to be similar to their home country— because they will have a smaller liability of foreignness in such locations. As they develop more confidence in internationalizing, they then further expand into more remote countries. Low-commitment entry modes, including joint ventures and alliances, rather than M&A or wholly owned greenfield investments, were seen as necessary stages in the learning process, to reduce risk and uncertainty.

"Neighboring" countries does not only mean neighboring in terms of geographical location, but also in terms of perceived similarities between the host and home country in a number of factors, including, religion, education, culture, language, industry development, and political systems. These factors make up the multidimensional concept of *psychic distance*, which is the perceived difference between two nations.[30] An example concerns the UK and the US. Although they are not neighboring countries, they share similar culture, language, business customs, and regulation. As a result, a UK firm will perceive it to be easier to do business in the US than in China, where there is a larger distance between the countries in terms of language, business customs, culture, and regulation. Therefore, according to the Uppsala model approach, the UK firm is likely to enter the US market before entering the Chinese market.

There are many caveats to such a general model, which people often take literally. There are industry-specific cases where low-commitment modes such as exporting are simply not an option. For instance, in the case of many service sector industries such as banking, finance, and insurance, foreign firms are required by host country regulators to establish a local presence as a condition for market access. In other instances, host country governments may impose punitive import duties and other tariff and non-tariff barriers to force firms to make a significant market commitment, and require that the foreign firm creates either a wholly owned subsidiary or a joint venture (for instance, in China).

That firms skip the exporting stage altogether and go immediately for FDI and a substantial local presence is not new. There are sectors where high transportation costs have always made exporting expensive (cement), while in others a local presence is necessary because of specific local consumption patterns and tastes, such as food products and beverages, because firms need to develop specific customized products for that market. In other cases, the firm may find that non-equity modes of governance do not sufficiently protect their FSAs from misuse by third parties. In such cases, firms choose to directly engage in full internalization by establishing a wholly owned subsidiary.

Psychic distance paradox

While, on the one hand, many researchers have found that firms find it easier to learn and have greater success when entering a foreign market where there are similarities between the two countries, on the other hand, research by O'Grady and Lane in 1996 showed the complete opposite. They concluded that "starting the internationalization process by entering a country psychically close to home may result in poor performance and, possibly, failure." The reason for this paradox is that the perceived familiarity led firms to underestimate the differences between the domestic market and the foreign market. Indeed, O'Grady and Lane (1996) showed that Canadian firms were performing poorly in the US market for that very reason.[31]

✔ Active learning check

Review your answer to Active Learning Case question 3 and make any changes you like. Then compare your answer to the one below.

❸ Why did Starbucks fail in Australia?

The main reason why Starbucks failed is because it underappreciated the differences between US consumers and Australasian consumers. Interestingly, Starbucks, in the past, has been more aware of the differences between its home market and the host country (such as when it expanded into China), and adapted its strategies and products accordingly. This is an example of a psychic distance paradox: with the US and Australia on the face of it having similar characteristics (e.g., language and culture), Starbucks underestimated the difference between the two countries and failed.

ENTRY MODES

When the firm decides to enter a new market, the first step is to decide whether it will opt for non-equity or equity entry modes. At the first stage, it may want to avoid the risks of high commitment to unknown (foreign) markets by arranging non-equity modes, such as exports and contractual agreements, and later move to equity modes (FDI), such as partial or full acquisition, which involve higher commitment to the foreign markets and often require higher knowledge or experience.

Non-equity entry modes

Exports are the most common or basic entry mode, often used by firms as a "vent" for their surplus production. Exporting is considered a potential source of extra sales, so in most cases the foreign markets are considered as an extension of the home country operations, providing economies of scale to firms that concentrate the production in the country of origin. Firms can opt for *direct* or *indirect exports*. In the latter case, firms may use a local agent or distributor to enter a particular market. By choosing this option, they do not need to be directly involved in the export process activities, such as shipping logistics or arranging appropriate distribution channels. However, two drawbacks may emerge. First, due to the minimal involvement in the process, firms will not learn from the experience of operating in foreign markets. Second, there is little or no control over products/services distribution.

Direct exports allow direct control of the distribution, branding, and pricing of products and services. Besides, it provides high involvement in the exporting process, allowing the understanding of consumers' needs and the identification of new opportunities. However, in comparison to indirect exports, this option has some drawbacks, such as higher costs, the need for a higher knowledge of foreign markets, and the liability of foreignness. Being a foreign company operating in the host country, the firm may face trade barriers from host country governments as well as difficulties in acceptance by host country customers.

Another non-equity mode of entry is via *licensing* or *franchising* agreements. Licensing is a contractual arrangement in which one firm (the licensor) provides access to some of its proprietary assets, such as patents, trademarks, or technology, to another firm (the licensee), in exchange for a fee or royalty. This fee often involves a fixed amount upon signing the contract and then an additive amount of 2–5 percent on sales generated by the agreement. A typical licensing contract will run for a fixed period of time (usually from five to seven years) and be renewable at the option of either or both parties. Franchising agreements are essentially similar to licensing agreements; however, they are typically used in the service industries.

The main benefit of non-equity agreements is that they require low initial investment and, therefore, risk only low financial losses if the foreign operations do not succeed. Moreover, the contracts may contain extremely detailed description of the licensee's or franchisee's obligations and conditions. Nonetheless, licensing and franchising agreements are more suitable for standardized products, services, or processes, where there is no risk of dissipation of the firm's technological or managerial advantages.[32] Indeed, one of the drawbacks is the high level of knowledge transfer, allowing not only the dissipation of the firm's FSAs, but also the development of competitors. The second drawback is low involvement in the daily licensee or franchisee operations, which may lead to limited control over marketing and production.

All the entry modes presented above are non-equity options. In most cases, non-equity entry modes involve less commitment to host countries, diminishing the uncertainty experienced when an enterprise is entering an unknown market. Indeed, when enterprises have low knowledge of the foreign market, non-equity entry modes are usually the less risky option. However, they can be considered an inefficient strategy when firms need to transfer intermediate goods across borders, because of market imperfections. Furthermore, they often involve less control of the firm's ownership, exposing the enterprise to the risk of creating competitors.

Equity entry modes

After the firm has become more familiar with the local market, some of the uncertainty associated with foreign involvement will have been overcome. The final stage of foreign involvement comes when the firm has generated sufficient knowledge of the host country to overcome its perception of risk. Because it is more familiar with the host country environment, it may now consider a foreign direct investment (FDI) activity. In this, it produces the entire product line in the host country.

The decision to invest in equity-based modes depends on several factors concerning the host and home country features. For instance, enterprises are more likely to invest in equity-based projects in host countries where governments offer policies that favor foreign direct investment. In a similar way, an equity mode is preferred when the host country's risk factors are perceived as low. FDI involves both contextual and transactional risks. Contextual risks are related to uncertainties about the foreign market environment, such as the instability of political systems, currency convertibility, price control, and the risk of intervention or expropriation. Transaction risks involve the risk of opportunistic behavior by local firms.[33] The perception of risks differs across firms from different countries, mainly because of cultural distance and managers' previous experience. However, the perception of risk tends to decrease when (foreign) market knowledge increases.

The equity modes can be classified into two types, shared ownership and full owner-ship. *Shared ownership* comprehends agreements between firms in which they have partial ownership, such as *international joint ventures*. An international joint venture is an agreement between two or more partners that involves setting up a new business entity overseas. It arises when two or more enterprises possess assets they want to combine, but assets both from the enterprise that is investing abroad and from the foreign enterprise are hard to sell or transact. For instance, when the efficient production of a product requires the combination of resources from enterprise X (local) and enterprise Y (foreign), but the transaction of the resources/knowledge is non-marketable due to market imperfections, such as high bargaining and information costs, the companies may engage in a joint venture. When the assets from only one company (in this case, enterprise X) are hard to sell, the best option is licensing (non-equity mode): that is, enterprise Y licenses enterprise X.[34] We explore strategic alliances and international joint ventures later in this chapter.

The benefits of this type of FDI are cooperation with partners that possess complementary resources and the sharing of risks and costs. Moreover, joint ventures are usually encouraged by governments. However, this type of agreement has a high rate of failure,[35] mainly due to conflicting goals, disputes about control, high instability, and poor decision making.

International joint ventures will be preferred to full acquisitions whenever firms want to combine resources, but the acquisition of the firm that possesses complementary resources (in this case, enterprise Y) is not possible due to legal barriers or market imperfections. They are also preferred when the complementary assets that enterprise X needs from enterprise Y are hard to separate from the assets that are not needed.

The last entry mode option is the *full ownership* of a subsidiary in a foreign country. Firms have the choice to set up subsidiaries through greenfield investment or acquisition. *Acquisition* will be the preferred choice whenever a firm wants to access assets that are embedded in another firm and the acquisition of the firm that possess the needed assets is legally possible, the market is efficient (i.e., the asset prices resemble their true value), and it does not involve high management costs.[36] The management costs depend on the compatibility between the resources of the acquirer and the acquired firms, as well as the earnings expectation after the payment of the acquisition costs. Acquisition is a faster way to enter foreign markets than greenfield investment, however it involves drawbacks. Acquisition is not always allowed, either by government barriers or by legal restrictions, and acquisitions may be considered to lead to ill will in some contexts. Moreover, the post-acquisition integration may be problematic.

A *greenfield* investment involves the establishment of a completely new business unit in a foreign market. This will be the preferred option whenever the integration of acquisitions is too costly and the assets needed can be accessed without the acquisition of an enterprise: for instance, when a company wants to access a skilled labor force available in a foreign country. The advantages of greenfield investment are that the enterprise has full control over the foreign operations and the firm's ownership, and the management of the unit is easier because it does not involve integration problems. The drawbacks are the high cost and the low speed involved in the establishment of new facilities from scratch. Furthermore, this type of investment usually requires high market knowledge and previous international experience. Figure 2.9 shows a summary of the advantages and disadvantages of each entry mode option.

On the flip-side, firms may choose *not* to proceed to higher degrees of foreign market commitment, and continue to service foreign markets by exporting, licensing, or franchising. This is especially so for SMEs, which may simply not have the resources to engage in FDI. For firms of all sizes, scale economies in production may already be achieved at home (or in another location). Take the automobile sector. Optimal economies of scale typically come from an annual capacity of over 150,000–200,000 units a year. Smaller markets may be better served by exports rather than investing in low-scale production.

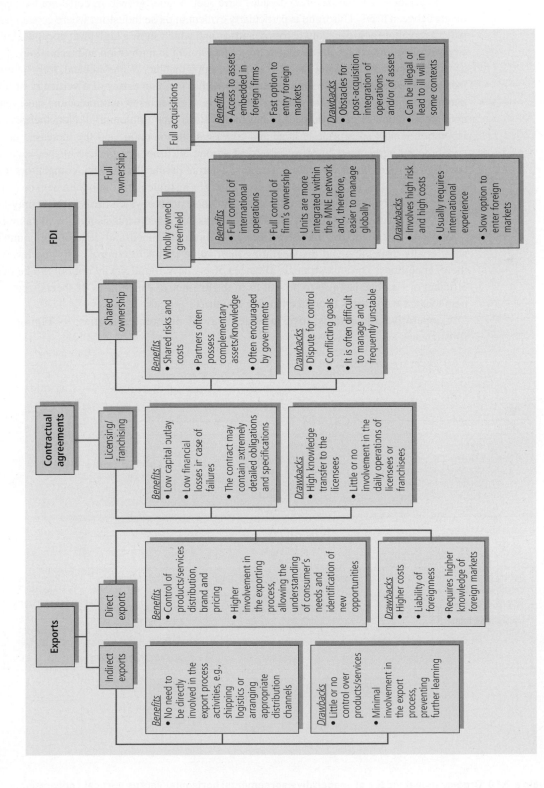

Figure 2.9 Entry modes: benefits and drawbacks

FDI

Full ownership

Full acquisitions

Benefits
- Access to assets embedded in foreign firms
- Fast option to entry foreign markets

Drawbacks
- Obstacles for post-acquisition integration of operations and/or of assets
- Can be illegal or lead to ill will in some contexts

Wholly owned greenfield

Benefits
- Full control of international operations
- Full control of firm's ownership
- Units are more integrated within the MNE network and, therefore, easier to manage globally

Drawbacks
- Involves high risk and high costs
- Usually requires international experience
- Slow option to enter foreign markets

Shared ownership

Benefits
- Shared risks and costs
- Partners often possess complementary assets/knowledge
- Often encouraged by governments

Drawbacks
- Dispute for control
- Conflicting goals
- It is often difficult to manage and frequently unstable

Contractual agreements

Licensing/ franchising

Benefits
- Low capital outlay
- Low financial losses ir case of failures
- The contract may contain extremely detailed obligations and specifications

Drawbacks
- High knowledge transfer to the licensees
- Little or no involvement in the daily operations of licensees or franchisees

Exports

Direct exports

Benefits
- Control of products/services distribution, brand and pricing
- Higher involvement in the exporting process, allowing the understanding of consumer's needs and identification of new opportunities

Drawbacks
- Higher costs
- Liability of foreignness
- Requires higher knowledge of foreign markets

Indirect exports

Benefits
- No need to be directly involved in the export process activities, e.g., shipping logistics or arranging appropriate distribution channels

Drawbacks
- Little or no control over products/services
- Minimal involvement in the export process, preventing further learning

Collaborative agreements/strategic alliances

It is no accident that the past few decades have seen a rapid growth in collaborative agreements between firms. This trend is particularly evident in those industries where consumption patterns are more homogeneous across countries, and which show a high level of capital intensity as well as knowledge intensity in terms of investment in innovation and technology.[37]

Cooperative arrangements have proven to be supplementary to hierarchical, fully internalized activities (such as those discussed above) within the boundaries of a vertically or horizontally integrated firm.[38] They are not entirely new either, as economic actors have relied upon cooperation to gain competitive advantage since time immemorial. Nonetheless, collaboration is now an especially large and pervasive phenomenon, and the increased use of collaborative agreements has been observed among all firms irrespective of their size and country of origin. Firms have always needed external partners (suppliers, competitors, customers, universities, technological research centers or institutes) to collaborate with on different, specific activities along their value chain, but the extent to which firms in the twenty-first century systematically exploit cooperative networks and agreements is quite breathtaking.

Nowadays, knowledge-intensive firms from both advanced and developing countries are globally dispersing and disintegrating their value chains to control costs and leverage their capabilities. Through strategic alliances, firms have found a way not only to be more efficient or flexible, but also to benefit from the distinctive capabilities of specialized partners located worldwide, even in emerging countries.

Cooperative agreements cover a wide array of different activities, as Figure 2.10 illustrates.

Figure 2.10 Organizational modes of cooperative agreements: horizontal versus vertical cooperation

Source: R. Narula and A. Martinez-Noya, "International R&D alliances by firms: origins and development." In Daniele Archibugi and Andrea Filippetti (eds.), *The Handbook of Global Science, Technology, and Innovation* (Hoboken, NJ: Wiley-Blackwell, 2015).

Horizontal versus vertical cooperation

It is important to distinguish between horizontal cooperation and vertical cooperation. Each has different primary motivations. *Horizontal cooperation* occurs among enterprises operating in the same industry, engaged in roughly the same kinds and types of value-adding activities. The opportunities for economies of scale and scope are here maximized, but there is also the possibility of conflict and leakage of intellectual property from one partner to the other. The cooperation between two biotechnology enterprises or between a human biotechnology enterprise and a pharmaceutical manufacturer would be considered a horizontal alliance. These are strategic in nature, and in general occur between large firms and organizations that are leaders in their field. They are commonly used to establish standards, and may often be seen by regulators as anticompetitive, as they involve some degree of collusion.

Vertical collaborations occur among enterprises operating in related industries along the same value chain, where one partner produces inputs for the other. The latter may be a larger enterprise assembling or sub-assembling products from parts and components acquired from different suppliers, including SMEs. It may also be a small systems integrator close to markets and obtaining equipment from larger suppliers. Vertical collaborations are less problematic, as the partners possess complementary but not competing capabilities and opportunities. Their primary (but not the only) motivation is toward reducing costs. Vertical alliances are especially important within global production networks and global value chains.

Defining strategic alliances

Strategic alliances are a particular subset of cooperative agreements, which have a significant *strategic* element to them. Strategic alliances are inter-firm cooperative agreements which are intended to affect the long-term product-market positioning of at least one partner.[39] In contrast to quasi-external, vertical solutions such as outsourcing and customer–supplier networks (which tend to involve lower levels of joint activity), strategic alliances are usually horizontal agreements (which tend to reflect a more complex strategic intent, and require closer collaboration).[40] The word "strategic" suggests that such agreements are aimed at the longer-term objective of enhancing the value of the firm's assets.

There are a variety of cooperative agreements that do not have a primary strategic intent, but are primarily cost-economizing: for instance, those associated with global value chains and production networks, where the primary objective is to reduce costs along a vertical chain. A strong strategic motive implies that the firm is often willing to forego (some degree of) cost savings in order to strengthen its portfolio of assets or its competitive position, or at least to defend its current position. Needless to say, most agreements have elements of both, but horizontal agreements tend to have a greater strategic aspect.

Alliances tend to create interdependence between the firms involved. The management interaction between the firms is coordinative and collaborative, and the collaboration is flexible and dynamic. The nature of the relationship may evolve through time; and the agreement may be terminated after achievement of the strategic goal. They tend to be objective (and short term) focused, although the same firms may engage in serial agreements. Strategic alliances are a compromise between short-term, pure market transactions (e.g., spot transactions) and long-term, pure organizational solutions.[41]

Cooperative agreements act as complements rather than as substitutes for traditional entry modes. This is because the excessive use of non-internal resources entails considerable risks and costs. As a general rule, firms find it costly and difficult to access competencies from other firms.

Alliances are notoriously costly in terms of resources, and suffer from a high failure rate. Common reasons for their failure include: unfulfilled expectations, lack of trust, asymmetry of learning, incompatibility of organizational cultures, unfair or unclear division of control and responsibilities, as well as certain government policies and regulations. Indeed, most alliances have a 70 percent failure rate, and even where successful, the majority of them last less than four years. A study[42] analyzing terminated research alliances in the biotech industry found that only 15 percent of the terminated alliances examined were successful, in the sense that they achieved their intended outcome (although an alliance may be a success from one partner's perspective and a failure from the other, because firms may learn asymmetrically). Given the strategic, uncertain and knowledge-based nature of the activities involved, these high rates of failure are not surprising.

Firms involved in alliances face a critical dilemma because they have to maintain the necessary knowledge exchange to achieve the alliance objectives, while at the same time avoiding the unintended leakage of valuable technology.[43] While this dilemma is common to most non-internalized modes of governance, it is more challenging in horizontal alliances. Although horizontal agreements provide opportunities for economies of scale and scope, there are also increased possibilities for the leakage of intellectual property from one partner to the other. Obviously, these managerial challenges become greater if the agreements are of an international nature. The higher the differences in their national and organizational cultures, language, or institutional environments, the higher the resources the partners need to invest in order to assure communication and control within the alliance. One of the main managerial challenges that firms face when doing alliances is associated with how to minimize the risk of opportunistic behavior by the partner. Managers have to be careful with how much they invest in the relationship because, although these relationship-specific investments may improve communication and coordination among partners, they may also be a platform for undesired technology transfers and asymmetric learning among partners.[44]

 Active learning check

Review your answer to Active Learning Case question 4 and make any changes you like. Then compare your answer to the one below.

4 **What are the advantages of Starbucks using licensing and joint ventures when expanding abroad?**

International joint ventures allow firms to combine resources, with Starbucks offering a globally recognizable brand, superior know-how in high-quality coffee, and economies of scale, but, as can be seen in 2007 when it failed to establish itself in India, joint ventures do have some weakness (e.g., lack of knowledge of the host country). In 2012, forming a joint venture with Tata Global Beverages allowed Starbucks to understand how to operate in the Indian market, while also leveraging off Tata well-known brand identity in the Indian market.

International new ventures and "born global" firms

An increasingly common term in the academic literature is the "born global" firm. Born global firms are also referred to as *international new ventures (INVs)* in the international entrepreneurship literature.[45] This is a term used to describe a firm that is immediately or very quickly reliant on a foreign presence to derive significant competitive advantage from the use of resources and the sale of outputs. Leveraging particular firm-specific advantages (FSAs), such as new technologies, unique products or services, or a valuable capability derived from one or more locations, such firms serve customers locally or globally. The very existence of born global firms can be due to their position as international entrepreneurial "brokers," exploiting commercial opportunities that arise from bridging resource inputs and market niches in different global locations.

International new ventures are subject to the multiple liabilities of smallness, newness, and foreignness. They tend to show a stronger home-region orientation than large-sized and already-established MNEs. Given their limited resources, small firms can be expected to reduce risk by selecting nearby countries in their home region as the final destination of their internationalization strategy from inception. As a result, international new ventures are likely to be born regionally, not globally, within their home region of the triad when going abroad into foreign markets.

The resource-based view (RBV) of firms proposes that, since international new ventures face a liability of foreignness by operating in unfamiliar and risky foreign markets, they should possess unique and distinctive resources and capabilities in order to overcome and counteract the liability effectively. The hard-to-replicate resources and capabilities internalized within firm boundaries are referred to as firm-specific advantages (FSAs), and they can be best exploited in similar institutional contexts within intra-regions than across inter-regions, because they are usually location-bound.

Transaction cost economics (TCE) also argues that international new ventures face a substantial level of transaction costs in both information search and monitoring processes when launching international operations across different foreign countries. We would normally expect transaction costs to be lower within the INV's home region of the triad due to spatial proximity, cultural and institutional similarities, psychical closeness, and, as a result, ease of transportation and communication. According to the organizational learning perspective, small and young ventures may be able to acquire hard-to-codify and tacit information about local customers' preferences and/or local business practices more easily within nearby countries in their home region than across different regions, because learning commonly takes place efficiently and effectively under culturally related and proximate external environments.

A number of commentators consider the growth of internet sales as an indication of the growing ease by which firms today can internationalize. While it is relatively costless to be able to sell goods and services by listing products on eBay, Alibaba, or Amazon, and become instantly international, such activities may distort the realities of their international business activities. A firm may be selling products or services abroad due to the marketing channel it is using (e.g. the internet); it does not mean it has operations abroad or that it tailors its marketing internationally.

THE INTERNATIONAL ACTIVITIES OF SMEs

How international are small firms? The data show that, in general, a relatively small number of SMEs sell products and services outside their domestic market, compared to the total number of active SMEs. When we consider another key measure of internationalization, foreign direct investment (FDI), again SMEs are less prominent than large multinational firms as sources of FDI. This makes sense when it is considered that the majority of small firms in most countries are likely to be family-owned shops or hairdressers, restaurants, and local tradesmen such as plumbers, painters, or carpenters.

In the European Union, just a quarter of all SMEs export or have exported at some point during the past three years. Moreover, their international activities are mostly geared toward other countries inside the internal European market and only about 13 percent of EU SMEs are active in markets outside the EU. However, SMEs are responsible for a larger proportion of total exports from some countries than we might expect.

Table 2.5 shows how international SMEs can be engaged in trade and/or FDI to access inputs or to sell outputs from abroad. If they stick to trading via imports (for inputs such as resources, materials, or expertise) and exports (for their outputs, i.e., products or services) then they are relying solely on international market transactions to underpin their relative

Table 2.5 Types of international SMEs by trade and FDI up and down the value chain

Different types of international SMEs	(1) International *inputs*: Foreign sourcing of materials or expertise ...		(2) International *outputs*: Foreign sales of products or services ...	
Internalization; foreign ownership?	(1a) Yes. Input-oriented FDI	(1b) No. Sourcing via markets	(2a) Yes. Output-oriented FDI	(2b) No. Selling via markets
For example?	Foreign greenfield production facilities, procurement offices, R&D JVs	*Imports* from foreign suppliers, outsourcing contractors or online service providers	Part or fully-owned foreign distribution, retail outlets, aftersales service providers	*Exports* direct to foreign customers or via distributors, or online service delivery
Company examples:				
Intamarque	None	None	None	Exports to wholesalers and retailers
SMS Electronics	None	Small volume of materials imports	None	Exports direct to manufacturers
Forward Internet Group	None	Offshore software developers	None	Online commissions from eBay and internet sales firms globally
Wilton Group	Limited input of expertise from Brazil-based offices	None	Sales and technical services offices in Brazil	Exports to clients
Ultimate Products	Offices in Belgium and Hong Kong for sourcing new products	Imports wide range of products for UK clients	Offices in Belgium and Hong Kong for selling products	Exports wide range of products for foreign clients

position in the industry value chain. As discussed earlier in this chapter, by engaging in FDI a firm "internalizes" a particular input or output activity based outside its home region. In this way it becomes a multinational firm.[46] So, for example, a small retailer might import products from abroad to sell locally, or export products to sell internationally. Only when this firm establishes its own shops abroad, to sell directly to customers, thereby internalizing the overseas sales function, do we refer to it as a multinational firm. Similarly, if it were to acquire a key supplier based abroad, thereby internalizing the overseas supply function (and engaging in vertical integration along the value chain), we would refer to it as a multinational firm.

The practical challenges for internationalizing SMEs

In Chapter 1, we discussed the competitive strengths of large multinational firms, some of which stem from what Alfred Chandler, an emeritus professor at Harvard Business School, described as scale and scope advantages. Scale provides financial power and various economies of scale across the functions of the firm. This is combined with scope, which refers to the breadth and diversity of assets and capabilities that provide large firms with a portfolio of geographic and innovation-related options, enhancing their ability to attain superior profits.[47]

SMEs face significant limitations compared to large firms, across both these dimensions, making internationalization strategies riskier. They do not have the financial muscle to "buy" their way into new markets, or spend on customizing products and brands for local customers. They also lack the range of specialists to draw on to shape and implement market-entry strategies, such as legal experts or managers with experience of local cultures. As described below, these limitations mean that small firms often need to be that much more entrepreneurial and innovative and/or take risky short-cuts, to expand across national borders. It also means that some elements of established theories of internationalization fail to adequately explain the patterns and processes of small firm internationalization.[48]

We already implied that the process of globalization has acted as an accelerator of the rapid expansion of SMEs into the international business arena. ICT advancements enabled smaller firms to reach customers and resources well beyond their domestic markets. Yet SMEs are still less likely to internationalize than large firms, mostly due to lack of sufficient knowledge and resources to overcome the liability of foreignness. However, we note large disparities between SMEs' international strategies across different national contexts.

In the deployment of resources to tap into the new opportunities, more successful SMEs pay close attention to the mode of entry. There are two main practices in which SMEs pursue internationalization: directly by entering foreign markets, or indirectly by staying in the domestic market. Each practice can be utilized via different entry modes as presented in Table 2.6 below.

SMEs are often assumed to opt for low equity and cooperative strategies because they have less access to financial assets or the level of human resources needed to support higher-commitment modes of entry. This also means that they have to quickly reach a level of profitability when they enter new markets because of their limited ability to raise investment capital. The specific challenges vary depending on the nature of the target country market and the individual firm. One in-depth study of British SMEs in Japan[49] confirmed the general conclusion above: SMEs tended to enter into joint ventures and collaborative alliances with Japanese enterprises in order to gain local knowledge and credibility with *keiretsu* networks and to share the investment risks. However, a study of the British exporters[50] shows that exporting SMEs are more geographically diversified than generally assumed, with a significant number engaged in export activities beyond the European region.

Table 2.6 SMEs' internationalization strategies

Direct entry modes to foreign markets	Indirect modes—staying in domestic markets
• Direct exports	• Indirect exports (via domestic intermediaries)
• Licensing/franchising	• Supplier to foreign firms
• Strategic alliances/partnerships	• Acquiring licenses/franchise from foreign firms
• FDI (greenfield wholly owned subsidiaries, M&As, joint ventures)	• Partners of foreign firms

INTERNATIONAL BUSINESS STRATEGY IN ACTION

Worrying times for Singapore's SMEs

Around 90 percent of corporations in Singapore are small and medium-sized enterprises (SMEs), so they play a significant role in the country's economy. Furthermore, Singaporean SMEs account for approximately 50 percent of the nation's GDP and 70 percent of all jobs in the domestic economy. In 2015, sentiment (business confidence) among Singapore's small firms fell to a three-year low. In particular, there were significant concerns about the expected decline of Singapore's economy, especially three major sectors: commerce and trading, construction, and the engineering and manufacturing sector.

This increasing lack of confidence in the economy was reflected in the SBF-DP SME Index, which fell to a three-year low: an average of 51.9. Since 2009, the Singapore Business Federation (SBF) has partnered with the DP info Group in order to provide an overall six-month outlook of the SME community as a whole, in relation to external conditions. The SBF-DP SME Index has played a crucial role in the SME community as an indicator of general business confidence and therefore the likelihood that SME investment will increase or decrease in future years.

Table 2.7 illustrates changes in SBF-DP indexes within each quarter of 2015. Even though all sectors portray a decreasing trend, the most worrying sectors seem to be commerce and trading, construction and engineering, and manufacturing, as between quarters 3 and 4 all three sectors illustrate a negative percentage growth by −2.6, −4.3, and −3.7 respectively. Furthermore, in between quarters 3 and 4, SME turnover expectations and profitability ▶

Table 2.7 Changes in SBF-DP SME Index in all four quarters of 2015

	1 1Q–2Q 2015	2 2Q–3Q 2015	3 3Q–4Q 2015	4 4Q15–1Q16	3–4 % change
Commerce and trading	54.0	53.9	53.0	51.6	−2.6
Construction and engineering	54.2	53.6	54.0	51.7	−4.3
Manufacturing	54.3	53.9	53.4	51.4	−3.7
Retail and food & beverage	54.7	51.5	51.0	51.2	0.4
Business services	54.9	54.4	54.4	54.8	0.7
Transport and storage	54.2	53.3	53.3	53.5	0.4
Total	54.4	54.0	53.5	51.9	−3.0

Source: SBF-DP SME Index St. Graphics.

expectations are shown as likely to drop from 5.55 to 5.38 and from 5.44 to 5.26 respectively.

To some degree the SBF-DP Index for this year reflected SME owner-managers' concerns about the global economic outlook and Singaporean exports with other parts of the world. Singapore's largest trading partners, China and Malaysia, were experiencing declining growth and challenging economic conditions. Economists suggested that lower turnover and profit expectations may lead firms to lay off staff, triggering an increase in unemployment across this small island economy. Ho Meng Kit, the CEO of the Singapore Business Federation (SBF), has stated that Singapore may be "hovering on the edge of recession."

A number of initiatives to help SMEs were launched in this period by the government and local banks. Singtel and DBS Bank, for example, launched the "99% SME Campaign" with the aim of providing free technological support and promotion for SMEs. At the policy level, Singapore and 11 other countries (the United States, Australia, Brunei, Canada, Chile, Japan, Malaysia, Mexico, New Zealand, Peru, and Vietnam) successfully negotiated a deal for the Trans-Pacific Partnership (TPP). The partnering countries account for approximately 40 percent of the global economy. The TPP aimed to change trading conditions by lowering tariff and non-tariff barriers (such as harmonizing regulations) to increase trade and investment across their borders. The Singaporean government joined the partnership partly to reduce dependence on China as a trading partner. Although the TPP negotiations took five years to finalize, the deal was struck at a point when the Chinese economy was starting to shows signs of weakness, increasing the significance of the partnership to Singaporean firms.

A select group of SMEs clearly were not feeling the effects of the local and international economic slowdown. The winners of the "Enterprise 50" (E50) competition, sponsored by OCBC Bank, were selected and ranked using both quantitative and qualitative criteria. The former included financial performance indicators such as operating profit before tax, turnover, and profit growth. The latter included management and marketing indicators, innovation, and export strategies. The top four firms show how diverse the SME sector is: Rotating Offshore Solutions Pte Ltd, Jumbo Seafood Pte Ltd, AllAlloy Pte Ltd, and Orange Valley Nursing Homes Pte Ltd. In contrast to the SBF-DP Index discussed above, 20 percent of the E50 firms were from the manufacturing sector. Other sectors represented were: real estate and construction (4 percent), wholesale trade and commission trade (2 percent), business services (6 percent), distribution (16 percent), engineering services (12 percent), hospitality and travel (2 percent), information technology (8 percent), logistics (4 percent), and other industries (26 percent).

Sources: Chloe Wang, "90% of SMEs in Singapore took steps to boost productivity: Survey," *Channel News Asia*, August 19, 2015; "SME's accounted for about half of Singapore's GDP in 2014: MTI," *Channel News Asia*, August 18, 2015; Mindy Tan, "Business sentiments of Singapore SMEs fall to three-year low," *Business Times*, September 10, 2015; Yasmine Yahya, "SME owners see tougher times ahead," *Straits Times*, September 10, 2015; Anne Williams, "Singapore companies, including SMEs, will benefit from TPP trade deal: Lim Hng Kiang," *Straits Times*, October 6, 2015; Annabeth Leow, "Push to support Singapore's SMEs," *Straits Times*, August 7, 2015; http://www.enterprise50.org/press_2015_nov.html

How do SME managers know which markets to enter?

Mathews and Zander[51] propose three milestones of international entrepreneurial processes: (1) the discovery of new opportunities; (2) the deployment of resources in the exploitation of these opportunities; and (3) engagement with competitors.[52]

The first major challenge for any firm looking to expand internationally is to decide which market location offers the best cost–benefit opportunity. Larger firms can invest in the due-diligence process underlying this decision. Managers can employ in-house resources and expertise and/or external specialists to help identify the most promising country markets in which to expand. As described in Chapter 15, this can entail a complex analysis comparing the relative risks and rewards of different country markets.

Decision-makers in both small and large firms also rely on their personal experience and existing international network relationships, both informal and formal, to assess the potential of different markets. This includes knowledge gained from existing buyers and suppliers and alliance partners, even when these are import and export contractors.[53] But there is evidence that these personal experiences and relationships are much more important to the decision-making process in small firms. Studies show how small firms, and particularly the smallest, owner-managed enterprises, tend to decide which markets to enter on the basis of fairly subjective evidence. This includes the views and opinions of personal contacts abroad and the experience and personal characteristics of small firm owners themselves.[54] A senior manager might spot a market opportunity during a family holiday abroad and this chance experience can be a strong influence on a small firm's market expansion strategy.

Mental maps
Cognitive representations of the nature and attributes of the spatial environment, showing how "psychic distance" operates in practice for SME managers

A study by Collinson and Houlden[55] used **mental maps** to capture the perceptions of decision-makers in a sample of British SMEs of the relative risks and rewards of foreign markets. Mental maps are defined as "cognitive representations of the nature and attributes of the spatial environment." They represent images of spatial environments developed by individuals based on their collated influences and experiences, and information available to them. Figure 2.11 shows the mental map for all of the firms in the study, with darker shading and higher numbers denoting more attractive foreign markets.

The map shows that mainland Europe and the United States represent the most attractive markets, given their size and familiarity to these British respondents. Much of Africa and parts of the Middle East, Southeast Asia and central Europe are either less well known or seen to be high-risk areas. Collinson and Houlden concluded that the mental maps of

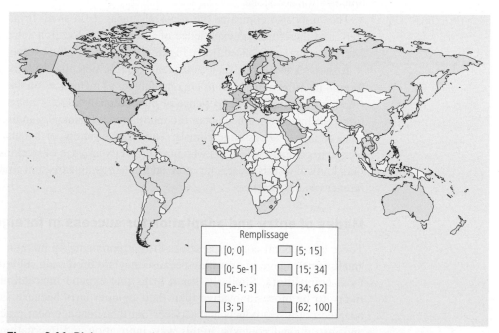

Figure 2.11 Risk vs. reward: country market attractiveness for SME managers

Source: S. Collinson and J. Houlden, "Decision-making and market orientation in the internationalization process of small and medium-sized enterprises," *Management International Review,* vol. 45, no. 4 (2005).

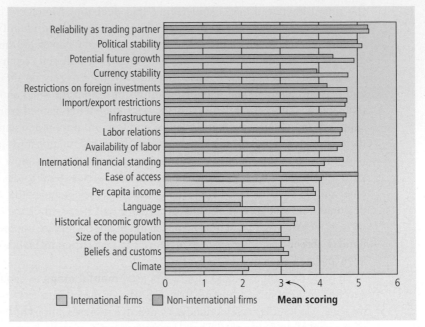

Figure 2.12 Foreign market selection criteria for international and non-international SMEs

Source: S. Collinson and J. Houlden, "Decision-making and market orientation in the internationalization process of small and medium-sized enterprises," *Management International Review*, vol. 45, no. 4 (2005).

decision-makers reflect their individual and group perceptions of opportunity and risk and subsequent geographical bias. They vividly illustrate how "psychic distance"—the perceived degree of cultural, social, and psychological differences between a home country and a foreign country—operates in practice. These perceptions form the basis of internationalization decisions.

The study also compared the views of managers in small firms that had internationalized, and therefore had experience of international location selection and market-entry, with non-internationalized firms. Figure 2.12 compares their responses.

It shows how factors such as language, future potential growth, currency stability, and foreign investment restrictions are rated higher as influences on the country selection decision for firms that have experience of internationalization. Managers in non-international firms are more concerned about the international financial standing of the target market, general ease of access, and climate. The relative ratings of language and climate show a complete contrast. Managers who have direct experience of working across language barriers know how this creates far more additional complexity, uncertainty, and risk than differences in the weather!

Modes of entry and adaptation for success in foreign markets

There is a general consensus across the entrepreneurship literature that more innovative small firms engage in exporting because they are producing superior products relative to local competitors. Similarly, small firms that expand internationally through FDI are likely to be more innovative than their counterparts because they have successfully adapted not just products and services but their management practices to other cultural and institutional contexts. In this way, innovation and internationalization are complementary activities.[56]

In terms of modes of market entry, studies suggest that firms tend to opt for higher-commitment and higher-risk entry modes (such as M&A or greenfield investments) with increasing firm size. SMEs are often assumed to opt for low equity and cooperative strategies because they have less access to financial assets or the level of human resources needed to support these higher-commitment modes of entry. This also means that they have to quickly reach a level of profitability when they enter new markets because of their limited ability to raise investment capital.[57]

Clearly the specific challenges vary depending on the nature of the target country market and the individual firm. One in-depth study of British SMEs in Japan confirmed the general conclusion above, showing that small firms tended to enter into joint ventures and collaborative alliances with Japanese enterprises in order to gain local knowledge and credibility with *keiretsu* networks and to share the investment risks. The study also showed how market barriers faced by all firms proved to be more challenging for small firms. These included:

- The high costs of start-up and operation, including costs of living and working in Japan, the high tax burden, and labor and property costs.

- Local recruitment difficulties, partly stemming from traditional lifetime employment and lack of status for the Japanese working in small foreign enterprises.

- Complex employment legislation and very different HRM practices, including the culturally embedded obligations of employers in Japan adding to the more generic barriers of language and culture.

- Market restrictions, including barriers associated with trading associations, "*dango*" and *keiretsu* structures, sometimes supported by government standards and trading legislation. The "tied" system of distribution in Japan, bound by strong face-to-face ties as well as cross-shareholding or financing arrangements between sellers and buyers at each level, proved to be a particular problem. These add to the costs and difficulties of getting products introduced into the market and distributed across different regional markets.

- Government-related complications such as local and national standards—accounting and taxation regulations are not "user-friendly" for non-Japanese and governance processes can be ambiguous.

- Demanding customers and intense rivalry, which have been the drivers of Japanese innovative capabilities in the past. These place huge pressures on foreign entrants to adapt marketing, product, and service quality and features, and after-sales support to meet the expectations of consumers and corporate customers.[58]

Small survivors are the SME success stories in large, complex markets like Japan. Their success is evidence of their dynamic capability to adapt and their ability to continually innovate. Lessons for other firms are relevant because these SMEs have proved their ability to adapt products and services as well as their own processes and management practices to the economic, institutional, and cultural contexts of foreign markets. Moreover, they have adapted not only to fit into these competitive environments but to succeed against local competitors. Their "fitness" is of a Darwinian kind.

KEY POINTS

1 For an MNE to be able to compete against domestic firms in the host county, they need ownership advantages or FSAs. There are three types of ownership advantages, asset-type FSAs, transaction-type FSAs and recombinant FSAs

2 Location advantages are an important determinant of where and how MNEs engage in international activities. There are a variety of motivations for, and modes of, internationalization, including market-seeking FDI, asset-augmentation and efficiency seeking FDI.

3 Modes of entry can be partially explained through internalization theory. These include non-equity modes (such as exports, licensing, and franchising) and equity modes (M&A, joint venture, and greenfield). An MNE has to decide whether to internalize its assets and engage in FDI.

4 The FSA–CSA matrix is a good tool to determine what strategies MNEs should adopt and helps explain how different firms operate in different markets. Some firms rely more on internalizing CSAs, for example, state owned oil companies, others are more reliant on the FSAs.

5 The accumulation of knowledge through some international activities, such as exports, may lead to a growing commitment to foreign markets (e.g. through FDI). This process is known as the Uppsala model. Firms are more likely to expand into countries which are psychically close to them, and once they acquire more experience in doing business abroad will expand to more psychically distant countries. "Born global" firms are different in that they internationalize near the beginning or at the point of their founding.

6 Because they lack resources and the scale and scope advantages of large MNEs, small and medium-sized enterprises (SMEs) that have managed to successfully internationalize often demonstrate some of the most effective dynamic and innovative capabilities.

Key term

● mental maps

REAL CASE

Toys "Я" Us

Toys "Я" Us opened its first international outlet in Canada in 1984 and then it expanded to parts of Europe, Hong Kong, and Singapore, where the company's "discount formula" was as popular as in the United States. The international business model applied to new markets was the same as that used by the company in the United States; identical stores with a self-service supermarket format that offered a great variety of toys sold at low prices. By 2015, Toys "Я" Us was present in 38 countries operating more than 755 international stores and over 250 licensed stores. These included 346 in Europe, 261 in Greater China and Southeast Asia, 83 in Canada, 59 in the Middle East, 34 in Australia, and 46 in Africa. Entering new markets, however, has not always been easy for the company. As this case shows, cultural and regulatory differences can make establishing a foreign business model very difficult.

Toys "Я" Us in Germany

Many foreign firms targeting the mainland European market start with the largest economy, Germany. It has a strong economy, a high per-capita GDP and a population with high levels of disposable income. It also greatly influences what happens in the rest of the EU. When Toys "Я" Us decided to enter the German market, it was greeted by a partial boycott and a public relations blitz that condemned the concept of a self-service toy supermarket as being alien and wrong. Even though the managing director of Toys "Я" Us was German, strong objections were directed against a US retailer wanting large-area sales space in Germany.

The company soon learned that legal and cultural barriers could be effectively used to block foreign competition. When Toys "Я" Us applied for a construction permit in Cologne, the city fathers asked the local chamber of

Source: Helen Sessions/ Alamy Stock Photo

commerce and retailers' association how they felt about the application. The latter replied that a toy store belongs in the center of the city, not on the edge of town. Yet this is exactly where Toys "Я" Us needed to be located so that it could build a sprawling store and a parking lot that was the size of a soccer field. In addition, the German Toy Manufacturers Association questioned why a toy store would sell so many non-toy items.

The managing director of Toys "Я" Us refused to allow these early setbacks to thwart his efforts. He continued making the rounds of trade shows, negotiating for store sites and presenting the company's plans to local officials; eventually he wore down the resistance. Even the competition began to realize that successful large toy stores could spark a boom in the toy market. Soon, competitors began copying some of the approaches used by Toys "Я" Us, such as piling shelves at the back of the store with baby food and diapers. Parents who came in to get diapers or baby food seldom leave without buying a toy for the child. The German experience taught the management that despite cultural, legal, and technical barriers, a foreign retailer can succeed in Europe if it is patient, maintains a strong consumer-oriented marketing focus, and is nationally responsive. By 2015 Toys "Я" Us had 66 stores in Germany and had expanded to establish 346 outlets across Europe, including 86 in the UK, 48 in France, and 50 in Spain.

Toys "Я" Us in Japan

The Japanese toy market is one of the largest, making it an attractive market for Toys "R" Us. But when the firm decided to enter this market in 1991, it had some major hurdles to overcome. Despite the rapid growth it had experienced, Japan's toy industry remained highly fragmented and locally focused. Japanese consumers appeared to prefer personal attention from the shop owner rather than low prices. In addition to customers' habits and personal loyalties, Japan's retail structure was also bolstered by a series of laws restricting the spread of larger retail stores. At the time, a typical Japanese toy store was less than 3,200 ft^2 (300 m^2) in area. Nearly all retail shops were domestically owned and bought their toys from local wholesalers, usually for 75–80 percent of the manufacturer's "suggested price." Retailers then sold the toys for the suggested price, deviating from it only rarely. Fragmented wholesalers served these shops. These wholesalers sold their products through a complex distribution system that typically involved between three and five layers of intermediaries.

The Toys "Я" Us business model clashed with traditional business structures. Its self-serve format put more attention on lower prices, minimizing personal attention to each customer, and cutting out intermediaries from the supply process. Japan not only presented great possibilities but also involved a high risk of failure, especially if the company didn't adapt its business model. To overcome the problems of Japanese culture and history being incompatible with the Toys "Я" Us business model, Den Fujita, who had successfully run McDonald's Japan, was enlisted as a local partner. At the time, he was the only Japanese business leader who had succeeded in bringing foreign non-luxury retail business into the restrictive Japanese market. His experience, political influence, vision, and unique understanding of both Japanese and US cultures enhanced the probability of success of Toys "Я" Us in Japan. With the help of Fujita, a powerful opinion leader who affected government policy making, and a younger generation that had started to realize that they were paying inflated prices for many consumer goods, many commercial restrictions were lifted. Toys "Я" Us was able to implement a business model that was closer to the one that underpinned its success in the United States. There are now more than 160 stores in Japan.

1 What are the firm-specific advantages of Toys "Я" Us?

2 What specific cultural and political barriers to entry does it face?

3 Why was Toys "Я" Us more successful in Japan than in Germany?

Tesco at home and abroad

The origins of Tesco can be traced back to when its founder, Jack "Slasher" Cohen, began selling food from a cart in Hackney in 1919, gaining his nickname from his "stack 'em high, sell 'em cheap" strategy. Since the opening of the first Tesco store in 1929, the company has flourished and it now operates in 12 countries across the globe, with 7,817 stores (including franchises) as of 2015. The UK is still the primary focus for the company, however, with over 310,000 of its 500,000+ employers working in Britain.

Over the decades the retailer has built up a dominant market share in its domestic market, peaking at over 30 percent in 2007 but slipping to 28 percent in 2016 as German newcomers Aldi and Lidl expanded across the UK. With the appointment of new CEO Phil Clarke in 2011 and a new cost-cutting initiative, the Big Price Drop, the retailer's prospects seemed very promising. In 2011/12 the future was still looking bright for the retail giant when it recorded profits of over US$5 billion; however the situation had sharply deteriorated by 2015, when the firm reported a US$9 billion loss. So what had gone wrong?

Tesco in the US

First, the US-based segment of the business, Fresh & Easy, which Tesco had established in 2007 under the leadership of Sir Terry Leahy, was failing to recoup the investment which the company had made. After six years in the market, the decision was made to withdraw from the US, leaving Tesco US$2.5 billion worse off. Observers pointed to a number of factors underlying its failure in the US market. One of the reasons was Tesco's focus on mid-sized shopping centers, whereas most American shoppers are used to larger-scale shopping centers. Tesco's self-checkout machines did not work well with American customers and the company's focus on its own-brand products meant there was not enough room to offer local shoppers their US favorites. Other details, like offering pre-packaged sandwiches instead of order in-store delis for shoppers to make custom-made sandwiches, which is norm in US supermarkets, contributed to this failure.

Retail analysts have also argued that despite Tesco conducting extensive research before entering the US market, the firm significantly underestimated the challenges. It failed to appreciate some key differences between the Americans and the British, just because they spoke the same language. The same observers note that this was not the case when Tesco entered new markets in Poland and China, where it appreciated the difference in shopping behaviors and adjusted its business model accordingly.

Tesco in Japan

Tesco's disappointing foray into the US market was not the first time it had called time on an international venture. Before this, in 2011, the firm announced that it was to exit the Japanese market and sell its stores to Aeon, a rival Japanese supermarket group. Having entered Japan in 2003 through the acquisition of C Two-Network convenience stores for about US$230 million, and despite having spent eight years trying to gain a foothold in the market, it had only managed to secure 1 percent market share. In line with Clarke's strategy of focusing solely on those regions where Tesco had the ability to become market leader, the company decided to exit Japan.

Tesco's lack of success in Japan was partly due to its inability to keep up with rapid changes in local customer tastes. The retailer did alter its business model to match the consumer behaviors in Japan, but not significantly enough. Costs are particularly high for stores in Japan. High rents coupled with a complex and expensive supply chain squeeze margins. The Japanese also have a strong preference for eating fresh foods that are locally sourced, making bulk buying difficult. The *Financial Times* once commented on this, observing in an article that there is a complete difference in the radishes eaten in Kyoto compared to those in Hokuriku. Finally, Tesco's small start with only 129 stores meant it failed to compete and develop brand awareness effectively when up against firms like Aeon, with 1,900 stores.

Tesco in Korea

In contrast to its performance in Japan, Tesco's Korean business, Homeplus, was going from strength to strength. Homeplus, a joint venture with Samsung, had almost 1,000 stores and was servicing around 6 million customers every week. Market analysts attributed this success to local chief executive Lee Seung-han of Samsung, who had managed to integrate Tesco into the Korean model and thus avoid the mistakes made by rivals Carrefour and Walmart. Korea was thriving, but all was not well on the home front.

Back in the UK

Back in the UK, the Big Price Drop had been coined the Big Price Flop by the media as rather than creating savings for the customer, prices on the shelves had actually increased. Tesco's large out of town supermarkets began to suffer as customer's habits changed, with people choosing to make smaller, more regular purchases at high street convenience stores. Meanwhile, discount retailers Aldi and Lidl were revolutionizing the supermarket industry and sparking a price war. The incumbents—Tesco, ASDA, Morrisons and Sainsbury's—were losing ground, demonstrated by Aldi's 15.4 percent increase in sales and Tesco's reduction in market share to 28 percent by 2015.

In particular, 2014 had been a challenging year for Tesco as pre-tax profits tumbled by 92 percent to only US$160 million, accounting irregularities were uncovered, and the firm's credit rating was dropped to Baa2 by Moody's. By January 2015, it had again been downgraded, this time to "junk" status. In the face of such strong competition from its German rivals, Tesco slashed its 90,000-product range by 30 percent in an attempt to follow the simpler model of its key competitors and cut costs, and announced the closure of 43 stores, but it seemed that nothing was going to rescue Tesco from this black hole.

With debts of over US$30 billion as of February 2015, Tesco was reviewing its portfolio in an attempt to see if it could strengthen its balance sheet, and in September it announced the sale of its Korean business, Homeplus, for US$6 billion. Although this by no means fixed the problem of Tesco's remaining debt, it opened up a number of options for restructuring and a new strategy.

Sources. Denise Winterman, "Tesco: How one supermarket came to dominate," *BBC News*, September 9, 2013; Kamal Ahmed, "Tesco posts record £6.4bn annual loss," *BBC News*, April 22, 2015; Kamal Ahmed, "Tesco sells South Korea stores for £4bn," *BBC News*, September 7, 2015; "Tesco timeline—the retail giant's rise and fall," *Guardian*, April 23, 2015; Nils Pratley, "Tesco's big price drop flop?," *Guardian*, December 8, 2011; Zoe Woods, "Tesco admits defeat and pulls out of Japan," *Guardian*, August 31, 2011; Simon Goodley, "Tesco names 43 stores to close in turnaround plan," *Guardian*, January 28, 2015; Andrea Felsted, "Philip Clarke failed to build on Leahy legacy at Tesco," *Financial Times*, July 21, 2014; Adam Jones, "Tesco announces retreat from Japan," *Financial Times*, August 31, 2011; Scott Campbell, "Tesco credit rating cut again by Moody's", *Telegraph*, June 16, 2014; Lianna Brinded, "Tesco, Sainsbury's, and Asda are being crushed by Aldi and Lidl," *Business Insider*, June 30, 2015.

1 What were the advantages of Tesco adopting a joint venture in Korea?

2 What are the advantages of Tesco using an M&A to enter into Japan?

3 What are the potential reasons why Tesco struggled to expand to the United States and Japan?

4 What are the FSAs of Aldi and Lidl to be able to compete successfully against Tesco in the UK?

NOTES

1 A. M. Rugman, *Inside the Multinationals: The Economics of Internal Markets* (New York: Columbia University Press, 1981); Alan M. Rugman (ed.), *International Business in Canada: Strategies for Management* (Toronto: Prentice Hall Canada, 1989), chapters 8, 13; Alan M. Rugman, *The Theory of Multinational Enterprises* (Cheltenham: Edward Elgar, 1996); S. C. Collinson and R. Narula, "Asset recombination in international partnerships as a source of improved innovation capabilities in China," *Multinational Business Review*, vol. 22, no. 4 (2014), pp. 394–417.

2 J. H. Dunning, "The eclectic (OLI) paradigm of international production: past, present and future," *International Journal of Economics and Business*, vol. 8, no. 2 (2001), pp. 173–90.

3 A. M. Rugman, "Reconciling internalization theory and the eclectic paradigm," *Multinational Business Review*, vol. 18, no. 2 (2010), pp. 1–12.

4 R. Narula and G. D. Santangelo, "Location and collocation advantages in international innovation," *Multinational Business Review*, vol. 20, no. 1 (2012), pp. 6–25.

5 R. Narula, "Keeping the eclectic paradigm simple", *Multinational Business Review*, vol. 18, no. 2 (2010), pp. 35–50.

6 J. Cantwell and R. Narula, "The eclectic paradigm in the global economy," *International Journal of Economics of Business*, vol. 8 (2001), pp. 155–72.

7 A. M. Rugman and A. Verbeke, "Subsidiary-specific advantages in multinational enterprises," *Strategic Management Journal*, vol. 22, no. 3 (2001), pp. 237–50.

8 G. D. Santangelo and K. E. Meyer, "Extending the internationalization process model: increases and decreases of MNE commitment in emerging economies," *Journal of International Business Studies*, vol. 42, no. 7 (2011), pp. 894–909.

9 A. Verbeke and N. S. Greidanus, "The end of the opportunism vs. trust debate: bounded reliability as a new envelope concept in research on MNE governance," *Journal of International Business Studies*, vol. 40 (2009), pp. 1471–95; J.-F. Hennart, "Emerging market multinationals and the theory of the multinational enterprise," *Global Strategy Journal*, vol. 2, no. 3 (2102), pp. 168–87.

10 R. Narula, *Multinational Investment and Economic Structure* (London and New York: Routledge, 1996); R. Narula, "Keeping the eclectic paradigm simple," *Multinational Business Review*, vol. 18, no.2 (2010), pp. 35–50.

11 R. Narula and G. D. Santangelo, "Location and collocation advantages in international innovation," *Multinational Business Review*, vol. 20, no.1 (2012), pp. 6–25.

12 U. Andersson, I. Bjorkman, and M. Forsgren, "Managing subsidiary knowledge creation: the effect of control mechanisms on subsidiary local embeddedness," *International Business Review*, vol. 522, no. 14 (2005), pp. 521–38.

13 P. J. Buckley and M. C. Casson, "The internalisation theory of the multinational enterprise: a review of the progress of a research agenda after 30 years," *Journal of International Business Studies*, vol. 40, no. 9 (2009), pp. 1563–80.

14 A. Rugman, A. Verbeke, and Q. T. K. Nguyen, "Fifty years of international business theory and beyond," *Management International Review*, vol. 51, no. 6 (2011), pp. 755–86.

15 J. Wolf and W. G. Egelhoff, "A reexamination and extension of international strategy–structure theory," *Strategic Management Journal*, 23 (2002), pp. 181–9.

16 Unilever, *Annual Report*, 2003.

17 See Michael E. Porter, *The Competitive Advantage of Nations* (New York: Free Press/Macmillan, 1990).

18 See Michael E. Porter, *Techniques for Analyzing Industries and Competitors* (New York and London: Free Press, 1980).

19 A. M. Rugman, C. Oh, and D. Lim, "The regional and global competitiveness of multinational firms," *Journal of the Academy of Marketing Science*, vol. 40, no. 2 (2012), pp. 218–35.

20 G. Benito, "Why and how motives (still) matter," *Multinational Business Review*, vol. 23, no. 1 (2015), pp. 15–24.

21 A. Cuervo-Cazurra and R. Narula, "A set of motives to unite them all? Revisiting the principles and typology of internationalization motives," *Multinational Business Review*, vol. 23, no. 1 (2015), pp. 2–14.

22 A. Cuervo-Cazurra, R. Narula, and C. A. Un, "Internationalization motives: sell more, buy better, upgrade and escape," *Multinational Business Review*, vol. 23, no. 1 (2015), pp. 25–35.

23 A. Cuervo-Cazurra and R. Narula, "A set of motives to unite them all? Revisiting the principles and typology of internationalization motives," *Multinational Business Review*, vol. 23, no. 1 (2015), pp. 2–14.

24 E. Beleska-Spasova, "The role of firm-specific advantages in UK export initiation," *Multinational Business Review*, vol. 19, no. 2 (2011), pp. 168–94.

25 S. Athreye, A. Tuncay-Celikel, and V. Ujjual, "Internationalisation of R&D into emerging markets: Fiat's R&D in Brazil, Turkey and India," *Long Range Plan*, vol. 47 (2014), pp. 100–14.

26 P. Criscuolo, R. Narula, and B. Verspagen, "Role of home and host country innovation systems in R&D internationalisation: a patent citation analysis," *Economics of Innovation and New Technology*, vol. 14 (2005), pp. 417–33.

27 S. Zaheer, "Overcoming the liability of foreignness," *Academy of Management Journal*, vol. 38 (1995), p. 341.

28 J. Johanson and J. E. Vahlne, "The internationalization process of the firm, a model of knowledge development and increasing foreign market commitment," *Journal of International Business Studies*, vol. 8, no. 1 (1997), pp. 22–32; J. Johanson and F. Wiedersheim-Paul, "The internationalization of the firm: four Swedish cases," *Journal of Management Studies*, vol. 12, no. 3 (1975), pp. 305–22.

29 K. Eriksson, A. Majkgard, and D. D. Sharma, "Path dependence and knowledge development in the internationalization process," *Management International Review*, vol. 40, no. 4 (2000), pp. 307–28.

30 P. Brewer, "Psychic distance and Australian export market selection," *Australian Journal of Management*, vol. 32, no. 1 (2007), pp. 73–92.

31 Shawna O'Grady and Henry W. Lane, "The psychic distance paradox," *Journal of International Business Studies*, vol. 27, no. 2 (1996), pp. 309–33.

32 J. H. Dunning and S. M. Lundan, *Multinational Enterprises and the Global Economy* (Cheltenham: Edward Elgar, 2008).

33 Y. Pan and D. Tse, "The hierarchical model of market entry modes," *Journal of International Business Studies*, vol. 31, no. 4 (2000), pp. 535–54.

34 J.-F. Hennart, "Down with MNE-centric theories! Market entry and expansion as the bundling of MNE and local assets," *Journal of International Business Studies*, 40 (2009), pp. 1432–52.

35 J.-F. Hennart, D. J. Kim, and M. Zeng, M., "The impact of joint venture status on the longevity of Japanese stakes in US manufacturing affiliates," *Organization Science*, vol. 9, no. 3 (1996), pp. 1–14.

36 P. Deng, "Why do Chinese firms tend to acquire strategic assets in international expansion?," *Journal of World Business*, vol. 44, no. 1 (2009), pp. 74–84.

37 R. Narula and G. Duysters, "Globalisation and trends in international R&D alliances," *Journal of International Management*, vol. 10, no. 2 (2004), pp. 199–218.

38 P. Dicken, *Global Shift: Mapping the Changing Contours of the World Economy*, 6th ed. (New York: Guilford Press, 2011).

39 J. Hagedoorn, "Understanding the rationale of strategic technology partnering: inter-organizational modes of cooperation and sectoral differences," *Strategic Management Journal*, vol. 14 (1993), pp. 371–85.

40 R. Narula and J. Hagedoorn, "Innovating through strategic alliances: moving towards international partnerships and contractual agreements," *Technovation*, vol. 19 (1999), pp. 283–94; R. Narula, "Strategic partnering by EU firms: a rejoinder," *Journal of Common Market Studies*, vol. 39 (2001), pp. 159–64.

41 R. Narula and A. Martinez-Noya, "International R&D alliances by firms: origins and development," in Daniele Archibugi and Andrea Filippetti (eds.), *The Handbook of Global Science, Technology, and Innovation* (Hoboken, NJ: Wiley-Blackwell, 2015), pp. 148–74.

42 J. Reuer and M. Zollo, "Termination outcomes of research alliances," *Research Policy*, vol. 34 (2005), pp. 101–15.

43 S. Mudambi and S. Tallman, "Make, buy or ally? Theoretical perspectives on knowledge process outsourcing through alliances," *Journal of Management Studies*, 47 (2010), pp. 1434–56.

44 A. Martinez-Noya, E. Garcia-Canal, and M. F. Guillen, "R&D outsourcing and the effectiveness of intangible relationship-specific investments: may proprietary knowledge be walking out the door?," *Journal of Management Studies*, vol. 50, no. 1 (2013), pp. 67–91.

45 B. M. Oviatt and P. P. McDougall, "Defining international entrepreneurship and modeling the speed of internationalization," *Entrepreneurship Theory and Practice*, vol. 29, no. 5 (2005), pp. 537–53.

46 This distinction lies at the heart of Oliver Williamson's "transaction cost economics" (TCE) between market and hierarchy. The latter refers to the situation where transactions are internalized within the firm ("hierarchy") because this incurs lower transactions costs compared to the market. In a similar vein, but with a different approach, in 1959 Edith Penrose asked "why do firms do what they do?" i.e. what determines the boundaries of the firm? She explored why firms left some business activities to the market and encompassed others internally. This is of central interest in international business theory, but only when the internalization involves incorporating overseas assets or business activities into the firm, rather than relying on (import–export) markets. By taking this step, firms become multinationals. E. Penrose, "Profit sharing between

producing countries and oil companies in the Middle East," *Economic Journal*, vol. 69, no. 274 (1959), pp. 238–54.

47 A. D. Chandler, *Strategy and Structure: Chapters in the History of the Industrial Enterprise* (Cambridge, MA: MIT Press, 1990).

48 For a summary, which particularly focuses on the reliance of small firms on intangible capabilities for successful internationalization, see G. A. Knight and D. Kim, "International business competence and the contemporary firm," *Journal of International Business Studies*, vol. 40, no. 2 (2009), pp. 255–73. Also: O. Burgel, G. Murray, A. Fier, and G. Licht, *The Rapid Internationalization of High Tech Young Firms in Germany and the United Kingdom: A Summary Report for the Anglo-German Foundation for the Study of the Industrial Society* (2000).

49 S. C. Collinson, *Small and Successful in Japan: A Study of 30 British Firms in the World's Most Competitive Market* (London: Avebury Press/Ashgate Publishing Group, 1996).

50 E. Beleska-Spasova and K. W. Glaister, "The geography of British exports: country-level versus firm-level evidence," *European Management Journal*, vol. 27, no. 5 (2009), pp. 295–304.

51 J. A. Mathews and I. Zander, "The international entrepreneurial dynamics of accelerated internationalization,"

Journal of International Business Studies, vol. 38, no. 3 (2007), pp. 387–403.

52 Ibid.

53 J. W. Liu and P. W. Beamish, "The internationalization and performance of SMEs," *Strategic Management Journal*, vol. 22 (2001), pp. 565–86.

54 S. McGaughey, D. Welch, and L. Welch, "Managerial influences and SME internationalization." In I. Bjorkman and M. Forsgren (eds.), *The Nature of the International Firm* (Copenhagen: Handelshojskolens Forlag, 1997), pp. 165–88.

55 S. Collinson and J. Houlden, "Decision-making and market orientation in the internationalization process of small and medium-sized enterprises," *Management International Review*, vol. 45, no. 4 (2005), pp. 413–26.

56 B. Cassiman and E. Golovko, "Innovation and internationalization through exports," *Journal of International Business Studies*, vol. 42, no. 1 (2011), pp. 56–75.

57 K. D. Brouthers and G. Nakos, "SME entry mode choice and performance: a transaction cost perspective," *Entrepreneurship Theory and Practice*, vol. 28, no. 3 (2004), pp. 229–47.

58 S. C. Collinson, *Small and Successful in Japan: A Study of 30 British Firms in the World's Most Competitive Market* (London: Avebury Press/Ashgate Publishing Group, 1996).

BIBLIOGRAPHY

Ambos, Björn, and Lars Håkanson. "The concept of distance in international management research," *Journal of International Management*, vol. 20, no. 1 (2014).

Buckley, Peter J., and Casson, Mark C. "The internalization theory of the multinational enterprise: a review of the progress of a research agenda after 30 years," *Journal of International Business Studies*, vol. 40 (2009).

Cavusgil, S. Tamer, and Knight, Gary. "The born global firm: an entrepreneurial and capabilities perspective on early and rapid internationalization," *Journal of International Business Studies*, vol. 46, no. 1 (2015).

Chandra, Yanto, Styles, Chris, and Wilkinson, Ian F. "An opportunity-based view of rapid internationalization," *Journal of International Marketing*, vol. 20, no. 1 (2012).

Chen, Shi-Fen S. "Extending internalization theory: a new perspective on international technology transfer and its generalization," *Journal of International Business Studies*, vol. 36, no. 2 (March 2005).

Ciravegna, Luciano, Lopez, Luis, and Kundu, Sumit. "Country of origin and network effects on internationalization: a comparative study of SMEs from an emerging and developed economy," *Journal of Business Research*, vol. 67, no. 5 (2014).

Collinson, Simon, and Morgan, Glenn. *The Multinational Firm (Images of Business Strategy)* (Chichester/Hoboken, NJ: Wiley, 2009).

Collinson, Simon, and Rugman, Alan M. "Relevance and rigour in international business teaching: using the CSA–FSA matrix," *Journal of Teaching in International Business*, vol. 22, no. 1 (2011).

Da Silva Lopes, Teresa. "The entrepreneur, ownership advantages, and the eclectic paradigm," *Multinational Business Review*, vol. 18, no. 2 (summer 2010).

Eden, Lorraine, and Li, Dai. "Rethinking the O in Dunning's OLI/eclectic paradigm," *Multinational Business Review*, vol. 18, no. 2 (summer 2010).

Hennart, Jean-François. "Down with MNE-centric theories! Market entry and expansion as the bundling of MNE and local assets," *Journal of International Business Studies*, vol. 40 (2009).

Johanson, Jan, and Vahlne, Jan-Erik. "The Uppsala internationalization process model revisited: from liability of foreignness to liability of outsidership," *Journal of International Business Studies*, vol. 40 (2009).

Lundan, Sarianna M. "What are ownership advantages?," *Multinational Business Review*, vol. 18, no. 2 (summer 2010).

Narula, Rajneesh. "Keeping the eclectic paradigm simple," *Multinational Business Review*, vol. 18, no. 2 (summer 2010).

Rugman, Alan M. "Reconciling internalization theory and the eclectic paradigm," *Multinational Business Review*, vol. 18, no. 2 (summer 2010).

Rugman, Alan M., and Oh, Chang Hoon. "Friedman's follies: insights on the globalization/ regionalization debate," *Business and Politics*, vol. 10, no. 2 (August 2008).

Rugman, Alan M., and Verbeke, Alain. "Liabilities of regional foreignness and the use of firm-level versus country-level data: a response to Dunning *et al.* (2007)," *Journal of International Business Studies*, vol. 38, no. 1 (January 2007).

Rugman, Alan M., and Verbeke, Alain. "Internalization theory and its impact on the field of international business." In Jean Boddewyn (ed.), *The Evolution of International Business Scholarship: AIB Fellows on the First 50 Years*, Research in Global Strategic Management, vol. 14 (Bingley: Emerald, 2008).

Rugman, Alan M., Verbeke, Alain, and Nguyen, Quyen T. K. "Fifty years of international business theory and beyond," *Management International Review*, vol. 51, no. 6 (2011).

Verbeke, Alain, and Yuan, Wenlong. "A strategic management analysis of ownership advantages in the eclectic paradigm," *Multinational Business Review*, vol. 18, no. 2 (summer 2010).

Zander, Ivo, McDougall-Covin, Patricia, and Rose, Elizabeth L. "Born globals and international business: evolution of a field of research," *Journal of International Business Studies*, vol. 46, no. 1 (2015).

APPENDIX: THE LARGEST GLOBAL MNEs

Table 2A The 25 largest global MNEs, 2015 ranking (billions of US$)

Rank	Company	Country	Revenue
1	Wal-Mart Stores	US	485.65
2	Sinopec	China	427.60
3	Royal Dutch Shell	Netherlands	420.40
4	Exxon Mobil	US	356.24
5	BP	UK	352.80
6	PetroChina	China	333.40
7	Volkswagen Group	Germany	268.50
8	Toyota Motor	Japan	252.20
9	Glencore International	Switzerland	220.90
10	Total	France	211.40
11	Apple	US	199.38
12	Samsung Electronics	South Korea	195.90
13	Berkshire Hathaway	US	194.70
14	Chevron	US	191.76
15	McKesson	US	174.00
16	Daimler	Germany	172.30
17	ICBC	China	166.80
18	EXOR	Italy	158.30
19	Gazprom	Russia	158.00
20	General Motors	US	155.93
21	AXA Group	France	153.80
22	Phillips 66	US	149.80
23	General Electric	US	148.45
24	E.ON	Germany	148.00
25	Eni	Italy	145.90
Total			5,842.11

Source: http://www.forbes.com/global2000/list/

Table 2B The 25 largest US MNEs, 2015 ranking (billions of US$)

Rank	Company	Revenue
1	Wal-Mart Stores	485.65
2	Exxon Mobil	356.24
3	Apple	199.38
4	Berkshire Hathaway	194.70
5	Chevron	191.76
6	McKesson	174.00
7	General Motors	155.93
8	Phillips 66	149.80
9	General Electric	148.45
10	Ford Motor	144.08
11	CVS Caremark	139.37
12	AT&T	132.54
13	Valero Energy	130.80
14	UnitedHealth Group	130.50
15	Verizon Communications	127.08
16	AmerisourceBergen	124.00
17	Fannie Mae	122.30
18	Costco Wholesale	115.60
19	Hewlett-Packard	109.76
20	Kroger	108.50
21	Express Scripts	100.90
22	JPMorgan Chase	97.80
23	Bank of America	97.00
24	CitiGroup	93.90
25	Cardinal Health	93.90
Total		3,923.94

Source: http://www.forbes.com/global2000/list/

Table 2C The 25 largest European MNEs, 2015 ranking (billions of US$)

Rank	Company	Country	Revenue
1	Royal Dutch Shell	Netherlands	420.4
2	BP	UK	352.8
3	Volkswagen Group	Germany	268.5
4	Glencore International	Switzerland	220.9
5	Total	France	211.4
6	Daimler	Germany	172.3
7	EXOR	Italy	158.3
8	AXA Group	France	153.8
9	E.ON	Germany	148.0
10	Eni	Italy	145.9
11	Allianz	Germany	128.4
12	Fiat Chrysler Automobiles	UK	127.5
13	BNP Paribas	France	124.5
14	Generali Group	Italy	111.7
15	BMW Group	Germany	106.6
16	Tesco	UK	102.6
17	Carrefour	France	101.2
18	Nestlé	Switzerland	100.1
19	GDF SUEZ	France	99.1
20	Prudential	UK	99.0
21	BASF	Germany	98.6
22	Siemens	Germany	97.4
23	Enel	Italy	97.3
24	EDF	France	96.7
25	Statoil	Norway	95.1
Total			3,838.1

Source: http://www.forbes.com/global2000/list/

Table 2D The 25 largest Japanese MNEs, 2015 ranking (billions of US$)

Rank	Company	Revenue
1	Toyota Motor	191.1
2	Honda Motor	117.1
3	IX Holdings	111
4	Nissan Motor	106.7
5	Nippon Telegraph & Tel	104.7
6	Hitachi	91.3
7	Toyota Tsusho	81.5
8	Softbank	80.6
9	Sony	76.9
10	Marubeni	74.1
11	Panasonic	73.5
12	Mitsubishi Corp	73.1
13	Tokyo Electric Power	63.9
14	Toshiba	63.2
15	Dai-ichi Life Insurance	60.9
16	Aeon	57.6
17	Seven & I Holdings	55.7
18	Nippon Steel & Sumitomo Metal	53.5
19	Itochu	53.1
20	Mitsui & Co	52.7
21	Mitsubishi UFJ Financial	49.2
22	Idemitsu	46.8
23	Fujitsu	45.1
24	MS&AD	44.3
25	KDDI	42.6
Total		1,870.2

Source: http://www.forbes.com/global2000/list/

Table 2E The 25 largest Chinese MNEs, 2015 ranking (billions of US$)

Rank	Company	Revenue
1	Sinopec	427.6
2	PetroChina	333.4
3	ICBC	166.8
4	China Construction Bank	130.5
5	Agricultural Bank of China	129.2
6	China State Construction Engineering	120.3
7	Bank of China	120.3
8	China Mobile	104.1
9	SAIC Motor	99.50
10	China Railway Group	96.80
11	China Railway Construction	94.10
12	Ping An Insurance Group	73.50
13	China Life Insurance	71.40
14	China Communications Construction	58.50
15	People's Insurance Company	55.70
16	Bank of Communications	53.60
17	China Telecom	52.70
18	China Unicorn	46.20
19	China Merchants Bank	45.50
20	CNOOC	44.60
21	Lenovo Group	44.30
22	China Minsheng Banking	40.00
23	China Shenua Energy	39.60
24	Industrial Bank China	39.40
25	China CITIC Bank	38.30
Total		2,525.9

Source: http://www.forbes.com/global2000/list/

Table 2F The 25 largest MNEs from emerging markets, 2015 ranking (billions of US$)

Rank	Company	Country	Revenue
1	Sinopec	China	427.6
2	PetroChina	China	333.4
3	Samsung Electronics	South Korea	195.9
4	ICBC	China	166.8
5	Gazprom	Russia	158.0
6	Petrobras	Brazil	143.7
7	Hon Hai Precision	Taiwan	139.0
8	China Construction Bank	China	130.5
9	Agricultural Bank of China	China	129.2
10	Rosneft	Russia	129.0
11	LukOil	Russia	121.4
12	China State Construction Engineering	China	120.3
13	Bank of China	China	120.3
14	SK Holdings	South Korea	105.3
15	China Mobile	China	104.1
16	SAIC Motor	China	99.5
17	China Railway Group	China	96.8
18	China Railway Construction	China	94.1
19	PTT PCL	Thailand	87.3
20	Itaú Unibanco Holdings	Brazil	76.6
21	Ping An Insurance Group	China	75.3
22	Indian Oil	India	74.3
23	Reliance Industries	India	71.7
24	China Life Insurance	India	71.4
25	Banco do Brasil	Brazil	68.8
Total			3,340.3

Source: http://www.forbes.com/global2000/list/

Table 2G The world's top 100 non-financial TNCs, ranked by foreign assets, 2013 (millions of US$ and number of employees)[a]

Ranking by: Foreign assets	TNI[b]	Corporation	Home economy	Industry[c]	Assets		Sales		Employment		TNI[b] (%)
					Foreign	Total	Foreign	Total	Foreign[d]	Total	
1	81	General Electric Co.	United States	Electrical and electronic equipment	331,160	656,560	74,382	142,937	135,000	307,000	48.8
2	34	Royal Dutch Shell plc	United Kingdom	Petroleum expl./ref./distr.	301,898	357,512	275,651	451,235	67,000	92,000	72.8
3	67	Toyota Motor Corporation	Japan	Motor vehicles	274,380	403,088	171,231	256,381	137,000	333,498[e]	58.6
4	56	Exxon Mobil Corporation	United States	Petroleum expl./ref./distr.	231,033	346,808	237,438	390,247	45,216	75,000	62.6
5	21	Total SA	France	Petroleum expl./ref./distr.	226,717	238,870	175,703	227,901	65,602	98,799	79.5
6	38	BP plc	United Kingdom	Petroleum expl./ref./distr.	202,899	305,690	250,372	379,136	64,300	83,900	69.7
7	9	Vodafone Group Plc	United Kingdom	Telecommunications	182,837	202,763	59,059	69,276	83,422	91,272[e]	88.9
8	68	Volkswagen Group	Germany	Motor vehicles	176,656	446,555	211,488	261,560	317,800	572,800	58.6
9	66	Chevron Corporation	United States	Petroleum expl./ref./distr.	175,736	253,753	122,982	211,664	32,600	64,600	59.3
10	36	Eni SpA	Italy	Petroleum expl./ref./distr.	141,021	190,125	109,886	152,313	56,509	83,887	71.2
11	73	Enel SpA	Italy	Electricity, gas and water	140,396	226,006	61,867	106,924	37,125	71,394	57.3
12	17	Glencore Xstrata PLC	Switzerland	Mining and quarrying	135,080	154,932	153,912	232,694	180,527	190,000	82.8
13	3	Anheuser-Busch InBev NV	Belgium	Food, beverages and tobacco	134,549	141,666	39,414	43,195	144,887	154,587	93.3
14	97	EDF SA	France	Utilities (electricity, gas and water)	130,161	353,574	46,978	100,364	28,975	158,467	34.0
15	1	Nestlé SA	Switzerland	Food, beverages and tobacco	124,730	129,969	98,034	99,669	322,996	333,000	97.1
16	33	E.ON AG	Germany	Utilities (electricity, gas and water)	124,429	179,988	115,072	162,573	49,809	62,239	73.3
17	75	GDF Suez	France	Utilities (electricity, gas and water)	121,402	219,759	72,133	118,561	73,000	147,199	55.2
18	59	Deutsche Telekom AG	Germany	Telecommunications	120,350	162,671	50,049	79,835	111,953	228,596	61.9
19	64	Apple Computer Inc.	United States	Electrical and electronic equipment	119,918	207,000	104,713	170,910	50,322	84,400	59.6
20	31	Honda Motor Co. Ltd	Japan	Motor vehicles	118,476	151,965	96,055	118,176	120,985	190,338[e]	74.3

(continues)

Table 2G (*Continued*)

Ranking by: Foreign assets	TNI[b]	Corporation	Home economy	Industry[c]	Assets Foreign	Assets Total	Sales Foreign	Sales Total	Employment Foreign[d]	Employment Total	TNI[b] (%)
21	88	Mitsubishi Corporation	Japan	Wholesale trade	112,762	148,752	17,645	75,734	19,790	65,975[e]	43.0
22	25	Siemens AG	Germany	Electrical and electronic equipment	110,462	137,863	85,441	99,543	244,000	362,000	77.8
23	8	ArcelorMittal	Luxembourg	Metal and metal products	109,602	112,308	74,369	79,440	175,565	232,000	89.0
24	46	Iberdrola SA	Spain	Utilities (electricity, gas and water)	108,679	127,235	23,534	44,106	18,702	30,680	66.6
25	58	Johnson & Johnson	United States	Pharmaceuticals	96,803	132,683	39,402	71,312	75,220	128,100	62.3
26	44	Nissan Motor Co. Ltd	Japan	Motor vehicles	95,228	143,029	81,172	104,606	93,240	160,530[e]	67.4
27	16	Hutchison Whampoa Limited	Hong Kong, China	Diversified	91,436	105,169	26,133	33,035	215,265	260,000	82.9
28	19	Fiat S.p.A.	Italy	Motor vehicles	90,985	119,474	106,053	115,263	163,082	225,587	80.2
29	69	Pfizer Inc.	United States	Pharmaceuticals	90,403	172,101	31,310	51,584	48,268	77,700	58.4
30	41	BMW AG	Germany	Motor vehicles	88,370	190,511	85,319	100,980	80,667	110,351	68.0
31	96	Wal-Mart Stores Inc.	United States	Retail and trade	88,206	204,751	137,613	476,294	800,000	200,000	36.1
32	78	Daimler AG	Germany	Motor vehicles	87,257	232,023	116,526	156,641	107,101	274,616	50.3
33	53	Telefonica SA	Spain	Telecommunications	87,156	163,654	58,237	75,758	76,969	126,730	63.6
34	48	Mitsui & Co Ltd	Japan	Wholesale trade	86,023	107,016	22,208	57,286	36,291	45,148[e]	66.5
35	87	Ford Motor Company	United States	Motor vehicles	79,092	203,752	61,458	146,917	97,000	181,000	44.7
36	100	CITIC Group	China	Diversified	78,602	565,884[f]	9,561	55,487	25,285	125,215	17.1
37	98	Statoil ASA	Norway	Petroleum expl./ref./distr.	78,185	144,741	23,953	105,446	3,077	23,413	30.0
38	35	Airbus Group NV	France	Aircraft	77,614	128,474	72,525	78,672	89,551	144,061	71.6
39	37	Novartis AG	Switzerland	Pharmaceuticals	71,941	126,254	57,185	57,920	73,081	135,696	69.9
40	60	Procter & Gamble Co.	United States	Diversified	70,981	139,263	51,342	84,167	88,751	121,000	61.8
41	13	Hon Hai Precision Industries	Taiwan Province of China	Electrical and electronic equipment	70,659	77,089	131,557	133,362	810,993	290,000	84.4
42	91	General Motors Co.	United States	Motor vehicles	70,074	166,344	56,900	155,427	104,000	219,000	42.1
43	2	Anglo American plc	United Kingdom	Mining and quarrying	68,955	71,165	27,266	29,342	95,900	98,000	95.9
44	50	BHP Billiton Group Ltd	Australia	Mining and quarrying	67,649	139,178	61,371	65,953	27,543	49,496	65.8
45	51	Repsol YPF SA	Spain	Petroleum expl./ref./distr.	66,011	89,613	35,019	74,012	21,510	30,296	64.0

46	62	International Business Machines Corporation	United States	Electrical and electronic equipment	60,841	126,223	64,942	99,751	306,758	431,212	61.5
47	49	BASF SE	Germany	Chemicals	58,323	88,644	79,032	98,212	59,683	112,206	66.5
48	45	Rio Tinto PLC	United Kingdom	Mining and quarrying	58,059	111,025	49,440	51,171	34,383	66,331	66.9
49	89	Microsoft Corporation	United States	Prepackaged software	57,087	142,431	36,505	77,849	41,000	99,000	42.8
50	18	Unilever PLC	United Kingdom	Diversified	55,769	62,664	48,182	66,114	140,000	174,000	80.8
51	20	BG Group plc	United Kingdom	Oil and gas field exploration	55,026	65,974	15,922	19,192	4,048	5,536	79.8
52	63	Hewlett-Packard Co.	United States	Electrical and electronic equipment	54,548	105,676	72,014	112,298	207,421	317,500	60.4
53	94	ConocoPhillips	United States	Petroleum expl./ref./distr.	54,430	118,057	26,459	54,413	5,266	18,400	41.1
54	26	Compagnie de Saint-Gobain SA	France	Non-metallic mineral products	53,704	62,957	40,204	55,795	140,794	187,726	77.5
55	7	SABMiller PLC	United Kingdom	Food, beverages and tobacco	53,332	53,751	18,492	22,311	59,997	70,486e	89.1
56	84	Orange	France	Telecommunications	52,362	118,178	23,238	54,409	85,472	165,488	46.2
57	85	RWE AG	Germany	Utilities (electricity, gas and water)	52,336	111,688	30,905	68,233	28,287	66,341	44.9
58	27	Roche Group	Switzerland	Pharmaceuticals	50,837	67,084	49,907	50,475	47,562	85,080	76.9
59	32	Mondelez International, Inc.	United States	Food, beverages and tobacco	50,834	72,557	28,308	35,299	76,428	107,000	73.9
60	55	Sumitomo Corporation	Japan	Wholesale trade	49,662	84,326	17,396	33,105	56,867	73,953e	62.8
61	30	GlaxoSmithKline PLC	United Kingdom	Pharmaceuticals	49,460	69,403	37,684	41,440	61,084	99,451	74.5
62	95	Petronas – Petroliam Nasional Bhd	Malaysia	Petroleum expl./ref./distr.	49,072	163,275f	71,939	94,543	5,244	46,145	39.2
63	52	AP Møller-Maersk A/S	Denmark	Transport and storage	48,730	74,451	43,931	47,397	29,701	88,909	63.8
64	65	Sanofi	France	Pharmaceuticals	48,403	132,266	40,199	43,748	55,786	112,128	59.4
65	42	Vattenfall AB	Sweden	Electricity, gas and water	47,667	75,105	18,491	26,363	22,301	31,819	67.9
66	83	Vale SA	Brazil	Mining and quarrying	47,247	124,289	38,734	47,130	15,894	83,286	46.4
67	70	Samsung Electronics Co., Ltd	Korea, Republic of	Electrical and electronic equipment	46,425	203,671	188,833	209,727	149,298	240,000	58.3
68	47	Schlumberger Ltd	United States	Other consumer services	45,507	67,100	31,369	45,266	76,857	123,000	66.5
69	24	Imperial Tobacco Group PLC	United Kingdom	Tobacco	45,444	45,872	36,301	44,115	19,200	35,300	78.6

(continues)

Table 2G *(Continued)*

Ranking by: Foreign assets	TNI[b]	Corporation	Home economy	Industry[c]	Assets Foreign	Assets Total	Sales Foreign	Sales Total	Employment Foreign[d]	Employment Total	TNI[b] (%)
70	90	United Technologies Corporation	United States	Aircraft	44,786	90,594	26,632	62,626	76,320	212,000	42.7
71	28	Christian Dior SA	France	Textiles	43,908	71,981	34,235	38,511	86,102	108,546	76.4
72	92	Tesco PLC	United Kingdom	Retail and trade	43,488	83,565	32,127	99,604	223,899	537,784[e]	42.0
73	80	China Ocean Shipping (Group) Company	China	Transport and storage	43,452	56,126[f]	19,139	29,101	4,400	130,000	48.9
74	5	Linde AG	Germany	Chemicals	43,048	45,090	20,357	22,112	54,218	63,487	91.0
75	76	Sony Corporation	Japan	Electrical and electronic equipment	42,239	149,161	55,565	77,510	94,071	146,300[e]	54.8
76	4	British American Tobacco PLC	United Kingdom	Food, beverages and tobacco	41,940	44,329	23,616	23,859	45,906	57,730	91.0
77	74	Caterpillar Inc.	United States	Construction	41,526	84,896	33,894	55,656	68,073	118,501	55.8
78	23	Lafarge SA	France	Non-metallic mineral products	41,484	51,046	15,787	20,178	49,256	63,687	78.9
79	15	Volvo AB	Sweden	Motor vehicles	41,185	53,242	40,477	41,862	72,945	95,533	83.5
80	93	Google Inc.	United States	Software	40,916	110,920	33,057	59,825	16,080	47,756	41.9
81	72	Renault SA	France	Motor vehicles	40,866	103,252	41,062	54,344	70,814	121,807	57.8
82	57	Marubeni Corporation	Japan	Wholesale trade	40,677	70,578	45,041	70,409	22,031	33,566[e]	62.4
83	40	ABB Ltd	Switzerland	Engineering services	39,893	48,064	27,463	41,848	82,700	147,700	68.2
84	14	AstraZeneca PLC	United Kingdom	Pharmaceuticals	39,700	55,899	23,892	25,711	44,892	51,600	83.6
85	39	Liberty Global plc	United Kingdom	Telecommunications	38,129	67,714	10,821	14,474	26,250	35,000	68.7
86	54	Carrefour SA	France	Retail and trade	37,913	59,981	51,594	98,644	267,590	364,795	63.0
87	29	OMV AG	Austria	Petroleum expl./ref./distr.	37,282	43,765	36,754	56,313	20,878	27,344	75.6
88	82	ITOCHU Corporation	Japan	Wholesale trade	37,075	76,347	17,502	55,193	47,269	77,513[e]	47.1
89	6	Barrick Gold Corporation	Canada	Gold mining	36,911	37,448	12,233	12,511	17,383	24,360	89.2
90	79	The Coca-Cola Company	United States	Food, beverages and tobacco	36,860	90,055	27,576	46,854	63,800	130,600	49.5
91	61	Cargill	United States	Food	35,928	59,880	86,092	136,654	87,000	140,000	61.7

		Corporation	Home economy	Industry[c]	Assets (Foreign)	Assets (Total)	Sales (Foreign)	Sales (Total)	Employment (Foreign)	Employment (Total)	TNI[b] (%)
92	86	PepsiCo Inc.	United States	Food, beverages and tobacco	35,863	77,478	32,789	66,415	106,000	274,000	44.8
93	10	WPP PLC	United Kingdom	Business services	35,649	41,236	15,018	17,229	105,190	117,115	87.8
94	43	Deutsche Post AG	Germany	Transport and storage	35,489	48,848	50,466	73,135	266,360	435,285	67.6
95	77	Merck & Co.	United States	Pharmaceuticals	34,552	105,645	25,787	44,033	46,900	76,000	51.0
96	11	Diageo PLC	United Kingdom	Food, beverages and tobacco	34,431	38,157	14,424	17,928	15,222	17,545	85.8
97	22	Teva Pharmaceutical Industries Limited	Israel	Pharmaceuticals	34,376	47,508	16,449	20,314	37,782	44,945	79.1
98	99	China National Offshore Oil Corp.	China	Petroleum expl./ref./distr.	34,276	129,834[f]	21,887	83,537	3,387	102,562	18.6
99	71	Japan Tobacco Inc.	Japan	Food, beverages and tobacco	34,054	44,858	11,640	23,948	24,397	49,507[e]	57.9
100	12	Koninklijke Philips Electronics NV	Netherlands	Electrical and electronic equipment	33,901	36,568	30,102	30,973	74,852	116,681	84.7

Notes:

[a] Preliminary results based on data from the companies' financial reporting; corresponds to the financial year from April 1, 2013, to March 31, 2014.

[b] TNI, the Transnationality Index, is calculated as the average of the following three ratios: foreign assets to total assets, foreign sales to total sales, and foreign employment to total employment.

[c] Industry classification for companies follows the United States Standard Industrial Classification as used by the United States Securities and Exchange Commission (SEC).

[d] In a number of cases, foreign employment data were calculated by applying the share of foreign employment in total employment of the previous year to total employment of 2013.

[e] Employment data refer to revised 2012 figures, as data were not yet available.

[f] Data refer to 2012.

Source: UNCTAD.

Chapter 3

MULTINATIONAL ENTERPRISES, INNOVATION, AND COMPETITIVENESS

Contents

Objectives of the chapter

Innovation is what enables firms to maintain their competitiveness, survive, and grow. It also goes hand-in-hand with internationalization. Firm-specific advantages (FSAs), such as technology, brands, or capabilities that can be used to compete effectively in other country markets, have to be adapted and developed to apply in different country contexts. Successful international expansion requires effective innovation.

The specific objectives of this chapter are to:

1 *Define* innovation and map out some innovation trends across firms and countries.

2 *Explain* how the resource-based view (RBV) and the VRIO framework connect innovation and competitive advantage.

3 *Understand* how dynamic capabilities underpin a capacity in firms to continuously innovate, alongside the R&D and technology development functions.

4 *Explore* different systems of innovation and the international dimensions of innovation.

5 *Examine* the MNE as a differentiated network, locating and linking different innovation activities in different locations.

ACTIVE LEARNING CASE

GE Healthcare in India: locally driven innovation

GE's Mac 400 is an ultra-portable electrocardiogram (ECG) which is made in India and has sold well locally, partly because it costs one-third of the price of an equivalent imported product. It is also light-weight, battery-operated, and easily serviced, making it ideal for India's rural areas where patients are far from specialist hospitals and power outages are common. The reason that the Mac 400 is so well suited to India is because it was conceptualized, designed, and sourced, as well as manufactured, in India, all following local customer requirements.

GE employs over 13,000 people in India and exports over $1 billion in products and services. One of its major business divisions, GE Healthcare, has invested in local joint ventures and manufacturing plants since the beginning of the 1990s, to reduce costs and increase local sales. But it is only much more recently that it has devolved some of the responsibility, capability, and resources to the local subsidiaries to pursue locally appropriate innovation.

The John F. Welch Technology Center (JFWTC) in Bangalore was established in 2000 and is GE's first and largest multi-disciplinary Research and Product Development Center outside of the United States. It collaborates with GE's four other R&D facilities that form the GE Global Research team (in New York, Munich, Shanghai, and Rio de Janeiro) to conduct R&D for all of GE's businesses worldwide. With over 4,000 employees and over 1,000 patents to its credit, it has hosted a range of technology development projects from train engines and aviation turbo fans to baby warmers in the healthcare field. These investments, together with the organizational and cultural changes underpinning the devolution of power and resources to the local management in India, are beginning to pay dividends. GE Healthcare's Global revenue is over US$18 billion, with the Indian subsidiary projected to reach over $1 billion in turnover in the coming years. The Indian subsidiary is increasingly seen to be an important part of GE

Healthcare as India's economic growth translates into increased buying power and better healthcare provision. At the same time, GE's India-based R&D efforts are creating products that are being sold globally. Of the first 7,500 Mac 400s that GE Healthcare had sold, about 2,000 had been bought by Indian customers; the rest had been bought by customers in other country markets.

The drivers that underpin the focus of healthcare product innovation in India, including accessibility, quality, and low cost, apply to other developing and emerging markets. So new products designed and developed in India are likely to sell well in these markets. This has been termed "low-cost" (or "frugal") innovation (Prabhu and Radjou, 2015) and "innovation for the bottom-of-the-pyramid" (Prahalad, 2006). By allowing local management to drive innovation, GE is able to target this rapidly growing market segment globally. Success in one market segment can, however, create challenges elsewhere. The fact is that products like the Mac 400 have the potential to significantly undercut more expensive (and profitable) products sold in more advanced markets like Europe and the United States. This leaves GE with a potential problem of its own making: new products from its emerging economy subsidiaries may increasingly "cannibalize" the firm's existing products in its more advanced markets.

Source: J. Prabhu and N. Radjou, *Frugal Innovation: How to Do More with Less* (London: Economist Books, 2015); V. Govindarajan, "On: innovation, strategy, global business: 10 tips for creating distinct-but-linked innovation groups," *Harvard Business Review* blogs (2010), at: http://blogs.hbr.org/govindarajan/2010/08/10-tipsfor-creating-distinct-.html; N. Mahajan-Bansal and M. Goyal, "Finger on the pulse, at last," *Forbes India*, at: http://www.forbes.com/2009/12/09/forbes-india-ge-healthcare-jeff-immelt-john-flannery.html; C. K. Prahalad, *The Fortune at the Bottom of the Pyramid: Eradicating Poverty through Profits* (Philadelphia, PA: Wharton School Publishing, 2006); "Reverse innovation: GE makes India a lab for global markets," May 20, 2010, in *India Knowledge@Wharton*, at: http://knowledge.wharton.upenn.edu/india/article.cfm?articleid=4476; http://www.ge.com/in/company/factsheet_in.html; GE Innovation timeline at: http://www.ge.com/innovation/timeline/index.html

1 Does GE have competitive advantages?

2 In what ways is GE's Mac 400 ECG the result of "local-for-local" innovation?

3 What indications are there that the Mac 400 ECG has become an example of "local-for-global" innovation?

INTRODUCTION

As we have discussed in Chapter 2, the key to a firm's competitiveness lies in its firm-specific assets (FSAs). FSAs come in many different forms, as Chapter 2 has also discussed. FSAs, however, need to be continuously upgraded, and this requires firms to be innovative. Innovation more broadly speaking can be thought of as "the successful exploitation or commercialization of new ideas." But an expanded and more useful definition is: "the renewal and enlargement of the range of products and services and the associated markets; the establishment of new methods of production, supply and distribution; the introduction of changes in management, work organization, and the working conditions and skills of the workforce."[1]

Chapter 1 made the point that innovation and technology are related. The stock of all innovations is regarded as being knowledge (of which technology is a subset). An asset that provides an advantage to company A today may not necessarily do so tomorrow, because its competitors may develop similar assets that compete with A's assets directly, or even make A's assets redundant. This does not have to be a radically new activity: if the competitor's product, process, or service can substitute for A's product, process, or service at a lower price, this may erode A's FSAs. Innovation and competitiveness are deeply inter-related, and in many instances the ability to innovate determines the competitiveness of both firms and countries.

Therefore, firms (whether uni-national or multinational, small or large) have to continuously seek ways of doing (at least) the same thing better for less money. FSAs do not have to be unique, but they do have to provide an *advantage* to the firm, relative to other firms.

Firms can also sell the same product or service at a higher price: but they do have to convince the customer that theirs is a better product or service, and this may be about learning how to better market their product. The ability to market a product successively is also a significant FSA. One of the reasons Apple is able to charge a premium for its products is the perception that its advertising and marketing have created of being a "cool," "must have" brand. Indeed, it is not uncommon for firms to have their marketing and R&D departments deeply intertwined.

Innovation
The renewal and enlargement of the range of products and services and the associated markets; the establishment of new methods of production, supply, and distribution; the introduction of changes in management, work organization, and the working conditions and skills of the workforce

Entrepreneurship and **innovation** also go hand-in-hand. Entrepreneurs, whether they are working in small or large firms, as owner-managers or employees, are distinctive because they have the capability and motivation to pursue innovative commercial opportunities that are riskier and more radical than normal. They identify such opportunities and assemble the resources and capabilities needed to create value.

The success of firms comes from continuously learning and innovating. All firms, regardless of their size, have to innovate to survive. However, firms do not innovate within a bubble. They are embedded in specific locations, and they have to interact with the environment into which they are embedded. The capacity to learn depends upon the location advantages/CSAs of their environment. The fundamental key to all creativity comes from the quality of people that the firm employs, and these are a function of the quality of the universities and the education policies of the government. It also depends upon the innovation policy chosen by the government, because countries (and regions within countries) give various incentives to attract and encourage firms to conduct R&D. As we shall discuss later in this chapter, the interaction of FSAs and CSAs underlies the competitiveness of firms, and because countries are sovereign, the policies of governments matter. MNEs are by definition located in many different locations, and this FSA–CSA interaction needs to be appreciated and understood in each location. One of the key advantages of being an MNE is the ability to take advantage of different opportunities within its portfolio of locations.

Politicians are interested in maintaining and upgrading their CSAs, and are increasingly interested in attracting the most innovative (and the most competitive) MNEs to choose their country and region. There is a *network effect* at work here: the more innovative firms there are in a specific location, the more attractive it is as a destination. Having high-quality knowledge infrastructure and human capital attracts more FDI. Countries monitor the quality of their CSAs continuously, and in this chapter we will take a look at one specific framework used to do so: the *systems of innovation* framework. This is not the only approach available; and Chapter 10 discusses CSAs and their relationship to competitiveness through other, complementary approaches.

Therefore, where firms locate innovation-related activities is of growing interest to managers, policy-makers, and international business researchers. Moreover, the ways in which multinational firms link and integrate inputs (specialist knowledge, capabilities, and ideas as well as assets and other resources) from various locations and connect these with market opportunities elsewhere is an increasingly important part of the "performance puzzle." The management of innovation and the location of innovation activities not only differentiate firms in terms of their performance, but have a significant impact on foreign direct investment flows and patterns of regional employment and development. In the first section of this chapter, we discuss and highlight the key trends in innovation at both the firm and country level. We then look at the resource-based view and introduce the VRIO framework, which is a useful tool to identify the FSAs that allow the firm to have a competitive advantage. Building upon the resource-based view of the firm, we introduce dynamic capabilities and look at how successful firms develop and maintain their competitive advantages in rapidly changing environments, driven by an increase in competition and technological advances. The next part of the chapter discusses the connection between FSAs and CSAs. The latter part of the chapter will introduce the work of Bartlett and Ghoshal (and their various co-authors) on the location of innovation activities and discuss how international innovation is about finding the right balance between integration and local responsiveness.

TRENDS IN INNOVATION AT THE FIRM AND COUNTRY LEVEL

The data on knowledge infrastructure and innovation at the country level mirror the evidence presented in Chapter 1. The developed countries still dominate the production of knowledge- and technology-intensive (KTI) industries (Figure 3.1). KTI industries accounted for 27 percent of world gross domestic product (GDP) in 2012.[2] They include high-technology manufacturing (such as aircraft and spacecraft; pharmaceuticals) and

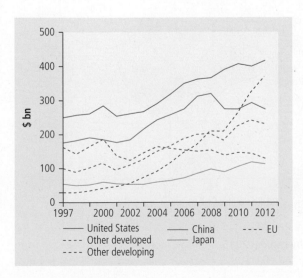

Figure 3.1 Output of high-tech manufacturing industries for selected economies, 1997–2012

Source: National Science Board, *Science and Engineering Indicators 2014 Digest*.
Notes: Output of high-technology (HT) manufacturing activities is on a value-added basis. Value added is the amount contributed by a country, firm, or other entity to the value of a good or service and excludes purchases of domestic and imported materials and inputs. HT manufacturing industries are classified by the Organisation for Economic Co-operation and Development and include aircraft and spacecraft, communications, computers, pharmaceuticals, semiconductors, and testing, measuring and control instruments. The EU excludes Cyprus, Estonia, Latvia, Lithuania, Luxembourg, Malta, and Slovenia. China includes Hong Kong. Developed countries classified as high-income countries by the World Bank. Developing countries classified as upper- and lower-middle-income countries and low-income countries by the World Bank.

knowledge-intensive services (such as commercial business, financial, and communication services).

The KTI share of the world's developed economies grew from 29 percent to 32 percent between 1997 and 2012.[3] This was due mostly to increases in commercial and public services, continuing a movement away from manufacturing and toward services. The growth of KTI activity in the developing world is most apparent in manufacturing and is largely due to China (Figure 3.1). Economic growth in other Asian locations has also contributed, growing in countries such as Brazil, Turkey, and South Africa. Between 2003 and 2012, China's HT manufacturing rose more than fivefold, resulting in its global share climbing from 8 percent to 24 percent in 2012. Despite this shift, the United States remained the largest global provider of HT manufacturing (27 percent of the global total).

In terms of R&D expenditures, the world's R&D expenditures are also dominated by the Triad (Figure 3.2). The top three R&D-performing countries accounted for over half of the estimated $1.44 trillion in global R&D in 2011 with the United States ($429 billion), China ($208 billion), and Japan ($147 billion) spending the most. The US share was 30 percent of the global total, compared with China (15 percent), Japan (10 percent), and the EU (22 percent).

Although absolute expenditures on R&D have been growing, the share of the developed countries declined in the last decade. Between 2001 and 2011, the US share declined from 37 percent to 30 percent of the global total, while the EU share dropped from 26 percent to 22 percent. During this period, China, India, Japan, Malaysia, Singapore, South Korea, and Taiwan all saw an increase in their combined share from 25 percent to 34 percent of the global total.

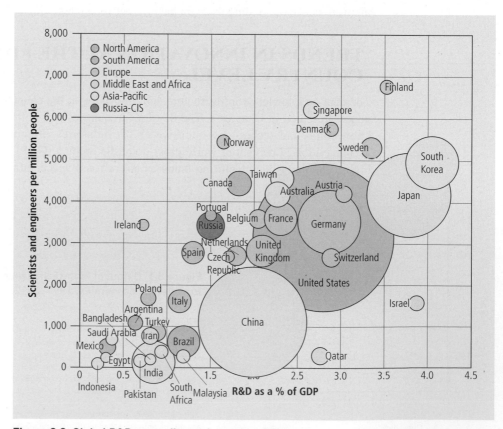

Figure 3.2 Global R&D expenditures by region, 2015

Source: Industrial Research Institute.

R&D expenditures are a measure of the *input* into innovation. Patents are an important measure of *output* of R&D. Not all patents become commercialized or lead to innovations, but they provide a good measure of the strength of the innovative capacity of firms. They are also indicative of innovation in knowledge and technology-intensive industries, and tend to exclude low-tech sectors where firms do not normally patent because the costs of filing a patent do not justify the effort. As Figure 3.3 shows, US patents granted tend to be dominated by the developed countries. The share of developing countries increased only marginally to 4 percent of the total in 2012. Figure 3.4 indicates the share of the largest emerging economies in US patenting.

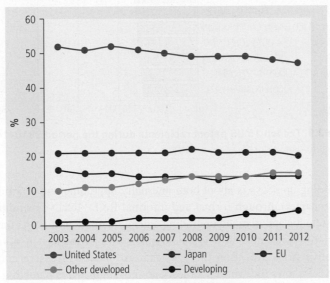

Figure 3.3 USPTO patents granted, by location of inventor, 2003–12

Source: USPTO, *Calendar Year Patent Statistics*, 2015.

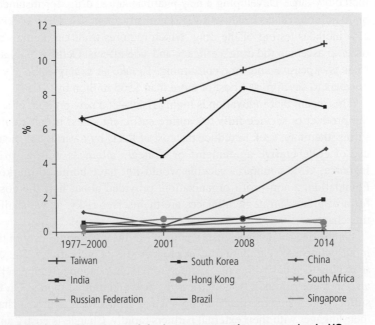

Figure 3.4 The share of the largest emerging economies in US patenting

Source: USPTO, *Calendar Year Patent Statistics*, 2015.

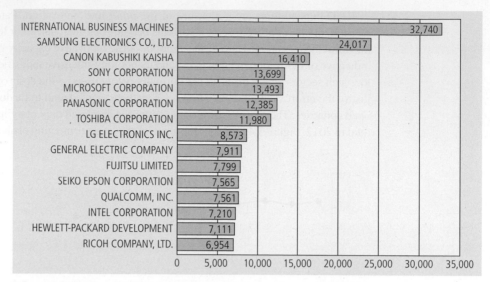

Figure 3.5 The top 15 US patent recipients during the period 2010–14

Source: USPTO, *Calendar Year Patent Statistics*, 2015.

Building up FSAs is about both internally upgrading and learning (as we shall discuss in this chapter) through formal and informal R&D. R&D expenditure by firms measures the systematic and planned upgrading and augmentation of FSAs through laboratory work, and in collaboration with external suppliers and partners. It is no accident that the most innovative firms are often the ones that are most aggressive about internationalizing. Figure 3.5 shows the world's largest and most aggressive patenting firms. Note that IBM, one of the most competitive MNEs in the world, registered more patents in a four-year period than most *countries* (for comparison, India-based firms were awarded fewer than 6,000 patents during the period). The amounts being spent on innovation by these firms is incredibly large. Developing a new pharmaceutical drug, for instance, can cost upward of $100 million. This is because R&D is not only about scientists working in a laboratory, but also includes testing of the drug, which requires trials on animals and human beings in order to ascertain the drug's efficacy and side-effects. Getting regulatory approval of these trials is expensive and time consuming. To take an example, GSK's malaria vaccine took 30 years to develop, at a cost of more than $565 million by 2015.[4]

This means that innovation is highly risky—if a new product or service is costly, and if the product or service fails to capture sufficient sales, it can easily bankrupt the firm. Firms, therefore, seek to reduce the cost of R&D by a variety of means, including greater use of collaborative agreements or strategic alliances with a variety of partners. For instance, GSK's malaria vaccine would not have come to market had not the Gates Foundation, a non-profit organization, provided about half the cost of the R&D in the form of grants. Strategic alliances are themselves risky, as we shall also later discuss in this chapter.

On the one hand, since costs are high, MNEs are continuously in the search for cheaper inputs while also searching for ways to increase their creativity. Therefore, they are always searching their environment (and therefore their location advantages) not only at home but also in their various host countries, for new and unique inputs. On the other hand, firms suffer from a deep inertia. They do not and cannot (and will not) change their location or their linkages with their external partners rapidly. Change is costly and, as we discussed in Chapter 1, institutions change only very slowly.

THE RESOURCE-BASED VIEW (RBV) AND THE VRIO FRAMEWORK

Resources and capabilities

Understanding that FSAs can provide a competitive advantage requires us to consider the resource-based view (RBV). RBV argues that the idiosyncratic, immobile strategic resources owned or controlled by a firm are its source of competitive advantage.[5] Each firm has a different mix of resources/competences and resource/competence gaps, and its strategic responses to these allow for the possibility of different paths to growth and internationalization,[6] and consequent heterogeneity in the international performance of the firm.[7]

One of the key strategic challenges in international business is the alignment of the firm-specific resources and capabilities (FSAs) with its host country environment (CSAs). To choose the best strategy, managers need to understand which resources in a firm create value and how they can sustain and develop that value creation. We will discuss this in greater detail later in the chapter.

First, we will explain the nature of resources and capabilities. "Resources" and "capabilities" are two different things (Table 3.1).[8] Resources are what a firm draws upon to create value, and valuable resources are embedded and difficult to trade in markets. Capabilities are the firm's ability to create, modify, reconfigure, and leverage resources. Essentially, it is the bundling of the resources that builds capabilities. Resources are not necessarily firm-specific, while capabilities are firm-specific and are the basis of FSAs.[9]

Table 3.1 Firm-specific resources and capabilities

Resources	
Tangible resources	• Financial assets: cash, stocks, loans • Physical assets: land, buildings, equipment, natural resources • Human capital: knowledge, skills, managerial know-how
Intangible resourcess	• Intellectual property: R&D knowledge, patents, copyrights, trademarks • Reputation: brand, corporate goodwill, formal and informal networks and relationships • Customer/supplier portfolio: exclusive contracts • Organizational culture: values, norms, tradition
Capabilities	
R&D and innovation capabilities	• R&D skills in new product and service development • Innovative organizational skills
Operational capabilities	• Process efficiency: Six Sigma, just in time, lean manufacturing
Marketing capabilities	• Market knowledge and responsiveness • Product development • Communication
Sales and distribution capabilities	• Sales skills and knowledge • Innovative sales channels • Efficient distribution model
Corporate management capabilities	• Strategy development and implementation structure • Leadership • Risk management
Dynamic capabilities	• Organizational ability to respond and adjust to internal and external shifts

Not all resources and capabilities have equal strategic importance or the potential to be a source of sustainable competitive advantage for a firm. The VRIO framework has been proven to provide a sound guidance in identifying the FSAs that can provide a competitive advantage.

The VRIO framework

Firms possess tangible and intangible assets, such as the firms' plant and equipment, training, experience, coordinating systems, and formal and informal planning. Nevertheless, not all attributes owned by firms will help them to develop value-creating strategies—in other words, only the ones that enable firms to increase or improve their efficiency and effectiveness are considered as strategically relevant resources. Therefore, *firm resources* can be any organizational process, capabilities, assets, or knowledge (strengths) owned by firms that allow them to generate and apply strategies in order to improve their efficiency and effectiveness.

Before exploring the VRIO framework, it is important to define the concepts of *competitive advantage* and *sustainable competitive advantage*. A firm has a competitive advantage when it applies a value-creating strategy not being utilized by existing or potential competitors. For this competitive advantage to be sustainable, competitors must not be able to replicate the strategy and the benefits originating from it.

In opposition to previous approaches used to understand the sources of sustainable competitive advantage for firms, such as SWOT analysis, this model is based on the assumption that firms have *tangible* and *intangible* resources that are not perfectly mobile and homogeneously distributed across competitors. In other words, firms' resources are *heterogeneous* and *immobile*.

The VRIO framework is a theoretical model based on the resource-based view (RBV) that helps to understand the sources of sustainable competitive advantages.[10] To hold the potential of sustainable competitive advantage, the firm's resources must fulfill four criteria: they must be valuable (V), rare (R), imperfectly imitable (I), and properly organized (O). The VRIO framework is summarized in Figure 3.6.

Valuable resources

Value can be determined by answering the question: *Do a firm's resources and capabilities add value by enabling it to exploit opportunities and/or neutralize threats?*[11] A resource can only be a source of sustainable competitive advantage when it adds value to the firm. A valuable resource helps the firm to exploit opportunities and nullify or overcome threats in the environment in which it operates. In other words, a valuable resource will allow firms to enhance their effectiveness and efficiency. Some examples of valuable resources are the organizational culture of 3M that prioritizes creativity, the Walt Disney brand name or Marks & Spencer's freehold ownership of the majority of its stores. In all those cases, the ownership of valuable resources allows the firms to operate more efficiently, more cheaply, or in a more effective way than its competitors.

It is worth noting that changes in the environment, such as changes in technology or customers' taste, may affect the value of resources over time. For instance, IBM's capabilities in mainframe computing became less valuable in the 1990s, with the spread of personal computers. IBM was fortunate that the internet era made mainframe machines valuable as they form the basis of internet servers. Therefore, managers should continuously verify whether the firm's resources continue to add value considering the environmental changes. The question of value combines both the external environment (opportunities and threats) and the firm's internal conditions (resources and capabilities).

Rare resources

Rarity can be addressed by answering the question: *How many competing firms already possess these valuable resources and capabilities?*[12] If several firms own a similar asset,

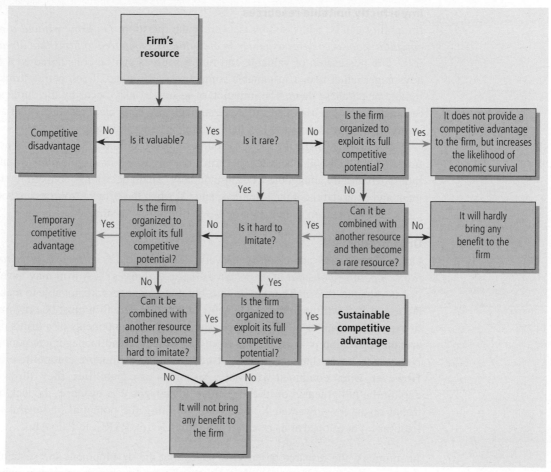

Figure 3.6 The VRIO framework: a decision-making process

Sources: Adapted from J. Barney, "Firm resources and sustained competitive advantage," *Journal of Management*, vol. 17 (1991); J. B. Barney, "Looking inside for competitive advantage," *Academy of Management Executive*, vol. 9, no. 4 (1995).

all of them will exploit this asset in a similar way. Therefore, it will cease to provide a sustainable competitive advantage for any of them. A sustainable competitive advantage requires the implementation of a value-creating strategy dissimilar to that of competitors. It implies that, to be a source of sustainable competitive advantages, a firm's resources must be rare among competing firms. An example was the Walmart's point-of-purchase inventory control system, which was no longer a source of sustainable competitive advantage once it had been imitated by Kmart.

In real life, it is very unlikely that a firm's resources can be considered unique, especially because it implies a comparison between all current and potential competitors' resources. Firms rarely have objective information about the tangible and intangible assets of their competitors, since such information is often uncodified, embedded in routines, equipment, and brands, embodied in individuals, and guarded jealously.[13] Indeed, the superiority of a technology or a specific knowledge asset over a rival's version is hard to judge, even after close examination. Besides, it is even difficult to value one's own assets—how much is a brand name really worth? Comparison is difficult even where knowledge is codified—for instance, in a patent. Thus the question that arises is: how rare must a valuable resource be in order to generate sustainable competitive advantage? Unfortunately, there is no straight answer to this question. In general, the firm's resources must be rare in comparison to its major competitors' resources.

Imperfectly imitable resources

Imitability can be addressed by answering the question: *Do firms without a resource or capability face a cost disadvantage in obtaining it, compared to firms that already possess it?*[14] The possession of valuable and rare resources can be considered as a first-mover advantage, rather than a sustainable competitive advantage, if competing firms can easily imitate or purchase them. The imitation of resources may occur by the duplication of the resource, or by the use of substitute or strategically equivalent resources that are no more costly than the resources used by the firm that is being imitated.

Three motives make the firm's resources hard to imitate: (1) unique historical conditions; (2) when the link between the firm's resources and its sustainable advantages is not intuitive (causally ambiguous), because of daily "small decisions" concerning the development and exploitation of the resources; and (3) when the firm's resources are socially complex, such as the firm's reputation or its relationship with suppliers.

Organization

Organization can be addressed by answering the question: *Is a firm organized to exploit the full competitive potential of its resources and capabilities?*[15] A firm may have a resource that is valuable, rare, and hard to imitate, but if the managers are not able to make appropriate use of it, it will not bring any benefits to the firm. The firm must be organized in order to exploit the benefits of its resources. The important components of a firm's organization are: compensation policies, formal reporting structure, and management control systems. None of those components can by itself generate sustainable competitive advantages. However, when combined with other resources or capabilities, they allow the firm to exploit the full potential of its competitive advantages. For instance, the lack of organizational resources prevented Xerox from exploiting the potential of several innovations (resources) developed at its research laboratory Xerox PARC, in Palo Alto.

In summary, the resource-based view states that the development and sustainability of a firm's competitive advantages rely on its tangible and intangible resources, which must be heterogeneous and immobile and present four attributes: value, rarity, imitability and organizational aspects. It is worth noting that, when a resource lacks one of the VRIO attributes, such as rarity, it may be combined with another resource that will add the missing quality, in this case rarity, to the old resource. The ability to combine resources is related to the concept of recombinant FSAs, explored in Chapter 2.

 Active learning check

Review your answer to Active Learning Case question 1 and make any changes you like. Then compare your answer to the one below.

1 Does GE have competitive advantages?

The best way to analyze this question is through the VRIO framework.

Value: *Do a firm's resources and capabilities add value by enabling it to exploit opportunities and/or neutralize threats?* YES

GE Global Research is well embedded in the firm.

Rarity of resources: *How many competing firms already possess these valuable resources and capabilities?* NOT MANY

As pointed out above, this is hard to assess, but very few organizations are of the same size, and have the same market experience and global presence as GE. Moreover, not many firms are able to invest as much in R&D as what GE does.

Imitability: *Do firms without a resource or capability face a cost disadvantage in obtaining it compared to firms that already possess it?* YES

With GE having over 1,000 patents, if they are utilized in their products, it means that their products are hard to imitate.

Organization: *Is a firm organized to exploit the full competitive potential of its resources and capabilities?* YES

GE has extensive experience of innovation and marketing products, and has a highly educated workforce (over 50 percent of its staff in the Indian R&D plant have either a Ph.D. or a master's degree).

DYNAMIC CAPABILITIES

Increasing competition and fast technology change in high-tech (KTI) industries has led scholars to explain how firms need to develop and maintain competitive advantages. Companies such as Philips and Texas Instruments have accumulated a large stock of valuable technological assets and proprietary knowledge following a "resource-based strategy." However, just the possession of valuable resources is not enough to explain the competitive advantages of these firms. Firms may have an extensive stock of valuable resources, but still have just a few effective capabilities. Even though Kodak owned a large portfolio of valuable patents, it was unable to continue to compete in the marketplace, filing for bankruptcy in 2012 and selling its patents for $525 million as part of its restructuring.[16]

Understanding how firms can sustain their competitive advantages at the same time they respond to environmental changes is a very ambitious goal, once it involves multiple levels of analysis, such as the external environment, the firm's routines and the managerial decision-process. Therefore, due to the complexity and broadness of topic, addressing this issue is one of the biggest challenges of the strategic management field.

To be successful in the global market, firms need to possess organizational capabilities to manage internal and external resources—that is, resources owned by the firm or external resources the firm can access and/or use—and to present quick and satisfactory reactions to environmental and technological changes. This is termed **dynamic capabilities**, where "dynamic" is associated with the unpredictability of the environment and "capabilities" refers to the ability of the firm to strategically manage internal and external resources and organizational skills in order to respond in a timely way to environmental changes.[17] Dynamic capabilities differ from other organizational capabilities because they are intentionally developed in order to modify or create a new resource base for the firm.[18]

Dynamic capability
The firm's ability to integrate, build, and reconfigure internal and external competences to address rapidly changing environments

In essence, firms need to be agile in order to respond in a timely fashion to environmental changes. They must be sensitive to existing and potential new opportunities and threats, act quickly after an opportunity is identified, and be able to efficiently manage their resources in order to maintain the firm's competitiveness. Firms need three main types of dynamic capabilities in order to respond to changes or new challenges: *quick learning*, the effective *integration of new assets/processes*, and the ability to *modify or transform existing assets/processes*.

Quick learning/incremental learning

Firms acquire knowledge by exploring in the vicinity of their existing knowledge assets, undertaking routines that lead to incremental innovations (*learning-by-doing*). Knowledge is acquired by the firm's interaction with its external environment. It may take place through interaction with customers, suppliers, competitors, or government agencies. In general, firms are averse to radical change, in that they are likely to "stay close" to patterns of behavior, learning, and interaction that have been successful in the past.

At a conceptual level, this is known as *incremental learning*. At a more operational level, it means that firms must also be quick to learn. Suppose a firm faces a new problem, for instance an unexpected error in the production process that stops the production line. The management teams may propose possible solutions. The proposed solutions may not work at first. However, after several tries the teams discover a particular solution that proves effective in restarting their production line. When a successful solution reaches this point of "maturity," it becomes the ideal approach to be used every time the same problem occurs. The continuous use of the same solution will then become an organizational routine. The action of proposing and testing new solutions for problems, and going through an extensive process of trials, is how firms learn in most circumstances, and is described as routinized or incremental learning. This is how the knowledge of a firm is translated into its organizational routines or processes. However, it is not only new internal problems that lead firms to "learn-by-doing". Firms may try new approaches when faced by environmental challenges, threats, technological changes, or new opportunities. This process of learning can be enhanced by the partnership with external actors, such as competitors or research centers, which can add different and complementary knowledge to the firm's existing resource base.

Integration of new assets/radical learning

The building of new assets is also fundamental to firms and it may occur by the combination of internal resources, the combination of internal resources with external resources, or even the combination of only external resources that the firm can assess and utilize. From an international business perspective, the internal resources include resources not only from headquarters, but also from subsidiaries located abroad. Likewise, the external resources include not only complementary home country specific assets, but also assets from the countries where subsidiaries are located (host countries). The combination may be between existing assets, between new assets, or between existing and new assets. This requires the firm to consider new and "radical" alternatives that are outside its existing paradigms.

Radical learning and applying new ideas requires a high degree of organizational efficiency from the firm, since it needs to be able to see the internal and external assets in a holistic fashion and, at the same time, recognize assets that, when combined, can be a source of competitive advantage. The efficient and effective integration and coordination of resources determines the firm's performance.

Modification and transformation of new assets

The success of firms relies not only on the development of new assets, but mainly on the enhancement or transformation of their existing asset base. The ability to identify dysfunctional routines is essential to firms' operation in high-velocity markets. Nevertheless, changing existing routines is neither easy nor costless. First, firms suffer from what is called organizational inertia. Organizations are constituted of individuals, who have a tendency to do things in the same way they have always been done, often resisting change. They also much prefer incremental change to radical change. Second, the improvement or transformation of resources is costly. Therefore, firms need to develop low-payoff changes as well as implementing strategies to ensure that the changes are effective.

Dynamic capabilities and small firms

The dynamic capabilities approach has also been seen as a useful conceptual and analytical framework for understanding small, adaptable firms. Because of their relative lack of financial and human resources and their often-cited need to respond quickly to temporary opportunities, such as new-technology waves or consumer fads, dynamic capabilities and organizational agility are seen to be more important to the survival and success of such firms.[19]

While it may not be particularly representative of small firms in general, the popular stereotype of a successful, fast-growing, high-tech start-up does seem to match what we might expect from a firm with the most dynamic of capabilities. They are the focus of attention partly because they are seen as the ideal-type of wealth-creating organization, but also because they are seen to hold lessons for other kinds of firms, large and small, looking to improve their responsiveness and innovativeness.

Research suggests that dynamic capabilities relate to the processes by which, and the success with which, small firms learn to grow and adapt to changing threats and opportunities in their surrounding competitive environment. This includes a heightened ability to sense external changes that present new threats or opportunities and the strategic and organizational flexibility to adapt to these. Dynamic capability theories refer to "search and selection" capabilities alongside "configuration and deployment" capabilities. Together these enable firms to orchestrate co-specialized assets, including outside knowledge and expertise, in a continuous way to maintain alignment with this changing environment. This way they are quicker at creating, extending, and modifying resources and assets to maintain competitive advantages, relative to firms with less dynamic capabilities.[20]

Studies of dynamic capabilities in firms of all sizes refer to the concept of capability life cycles. These depict how firms need to periodically renew their capabilities as they expand and evolve, either through internal upgrading and/or via acquisitions, joint ventures, and other kinds of external alliances. Failure to renew increases the dangers of other, newer, or faster firms developing capabilities that underpin superior competitive advantages.[21]

There are obvious parallels with Darwinian evolutionary theory and indeed dynamic capabilities approaches draw extensively from concepts such as "requisite variety," "selection and retention," and "evolutionary fitness," and from the work of evolutionary economists, such as Joseph Schumpeter. Schumpeter coined the term "creative destruction" to refer to the process by which superior new ways of doing things continually usurp old ways in an inevitable cycle of renewal. Schumpeter identified innovation as the critical dimension of economic change, contrary to the popular theories of the day, and placed the entrepreneur at the center of his view of economic systems.[22]

INTERNATIONAL BUSINESS STRATEGY IN ACTION

Spreadshirt: open innovation

In March 2001, a student in Leipzig (Germany) called Lukasz Gadowski developed an online company for designing and selling t-shirts. He was joined by Matthias Spiess, who financed the initial phase of the start-up, and by January 2002, 100 online affiliate ventures or "partner shops" had joined from around the world. Despite the enterprise being judged an "unrealistic business model" at the Cologne Business Plan Competition, 500,000 shops had joined by mid-2008 and the "Spreadshirt" company had made history. As of 2014, with over 3.4 million products sold, Spreadshirt has become a world leading e-commerce platform for consumers who demand custom printing of clothing and accessories.

The company's goal is to be "The creative apparel platform, inspiring people to create, buy or sell individualized fashion." It has an unusual business model, with customers playing the roles of buyers, sellers, and designers. They can buy customized t-shirts, hoodies, jackets, bags, or accessories directly from the online store. Whether they are individuals or corporate customers, they can also sell via the Spreadshirt online platform by setting up a shop. Firms like CNN, Holiday Inn, Nissan, and The Sun newspaper in the UK have done this to sell their own branded designs. But individual entrepreneurs anywhere in the world can also offer customized clothing through their own Spreadshirt shop website, while Spreadshirt takes care of inventory management, manufacturing, logistics, payments, and other aspects of customer service for their partner shops. This allows designers to sell their own designs without the investment

▶

required to establish their own full-service companies. Providing the capability for individuals to design one-off shirts without the need to set up a shop now makes up 40 percent of Spreadshirt's business.

Spreadshirt also runs "laFraise," Europe's largest t-shirt design competition, whereby each week designers from all over the world put forward their latest creations and the Spreadshirt community votes for the best. Winners get prizes as well as having their designs printed and sold globally. This is "crowd sourcing," effectively outsourcing the complex decision regarding which, out of hundreds of design options, a company should print and try to sell. By manufacturing a limited set of designs, a producer benefits from significant economies of scale and higher profits, but this requires a process for selecting the most popular designs. Rather than trying to assess this through market research, Spreadshirt and its "designer-seller-customers" use crowd sourcing.

Spreadshirt's primary activities take place via a range of online networks. It is both global and local in a way that firms with business models based on fixed assets can never be. As

partner shops join and leave, the firm's international portfolio of "resources" and its online profile in country markets change. But it does also have a physical presence of branch offices and customer service centers in France, Britain, the United States, Spain, Ireland, Italy, Poland, Brazil, the Czech Republic, Norway, Switzerland, Canada, Italy and the Netherlands, to support its head office in Germany.

Despite being the European market leader in its field, and being active in 19 different markets, as of 2015 Spreadshirt had a limited number of employees (450) and outsourced the "physical" aspects of its business on behalf of customers. Manufacturing, logistics, and supply chain management, and even elements of its marketing are done via contracts with other firms. The firm has half-a-million partner shops and millions of customers worldwide. Revenues grew from €12.2 million in 2006 to €15.3 million (125.7 percent) in 2007 and an estimated €70 million in 2014, although accurate figures are not available after 2007 (Krisch, 2009).

Source: http://eu.techcrunch.com/2010; http://www.spreadshirt.com; http://www.spreadshirt.co.uk; J. Krisch, "Spreadshirt swaps CFO; makes 21 million euro revenue," optaros.com blog (August 18, 2009).

CONNECTING FSAs TO CSAs

Developing new assets or improving existing ones requires the firm to find complementary assets that may be part of its location advantages. However, sometimes the assets in its immediate geographical vicinity are simply insufficient, and it needs access to location advantages elsewhere (see Chapter 2 for a discussion). At the same time, firms have finite resources. There are cognitive limits to what a firm can and cannot do, because it is constrained by its asset base or its potential to acquire assets. Moving abroad to do R&D is a daunting challenge. Small and medium-sized enterprises (SMEs), for instance, are limited by their size. A Kenyan IT firm with 100 employees may wish to establish R&D facilities in Silicon Valley, but there are limits to the size of any such affiliate. It might—with considerable additional capital—set up an R&D facility of 10, perhaps even 20 employees, but it is unlikely to be able to muster the resources to establish a facility with 500 employees. It is not only about having the money to internationalize. Resources also include managerial assets and other ownership advantages, and these are also finite. Although the resources available to mega-firms such as IBM, General Electric, and Sony are much larger, they too have their limits in terms of the breadth and depth of their firm-specific assets.[23] Firms in general are risk averse, and they are prone to minimizing the level of risk.

Firms ultimately depend upon CSAs for their resources. As discussed in Chapter 2, FSAs for most firms are location-bound to some extent. Knowledge is acquired by interaction with the external environment. It can take place through interaction with customers, suppliers, competitors, and government agencies. Firms are generally averse to radical change, in that they are likely to "stay close" to successful patterns of learning and interaction that have been successful in the past. This is referred to as routinized (or incremental) learning, which adds to the existing knowledge and competencies of a firm without fundamentally changing the nature of its activities. As we discussed in Chapter 2, MNEs proceed in roughly similar ways and steps to internationalize.

The location advantages of a country and the competitive advantages of its firms show a remarkable degree of interdependence. Firms of each country tend to embark on a path of knowledge accumulation that is shaped by its home country characteristics. Countries tend to sustain a distinct profile of national technological specialization.[24] The specialization of countries (and therefore their location advantages) changes very slowly, and the FSAs of firms closely overlap with the technological specialization of their home country.[25] As a literature inspired by Rugman and Verbeke[26] has shown, firms continue to show a strong bias toward home countries and regions, even where they have ostensibly become "global."

The *process* of interaction between O and L assets exists in every location. These processes are also broadly similar for all firms, regardless of nationality. The FSAs of firms in any given period tend to be a function of the home country's L assets. To understand the initial FSAs that a firm uses to internationalize, it is useful to understand the industrial and economic structure of its home country. To understand how its FSAs evolve when the MNE sets up an affiliate in another country, it is important to examine the location advantages of its home and its host location.

There are several frameworks to explain how FSAs and location advantages interact. Chapter 10 discusses some other frameworks, such as the diamond model and the double diamond model. In the next section we will discuss the systems of innovation model, which is directly linked to our specific interest in innovation and technology in this chapter.

SYSTEMS OF INNOVATION

Firms and their home country environment interact, and function as a "system." They are embedded through historical, social, and economic ties to other actors in the same location, and these constrain their actions. National contexts vary in terms of their economic, social, cultural, political, and institutional characteristics, and this variety underpins both of these kinds of innovation opportunity. These factors influence the kinds of resources and capabilities that are available in a particular location and the kinds of customers and markets that develop there. Studies also show how different forms of competitive advantage at the national, industry, and firm levels stem from the particular characteristics of the

Systems of innovation (SI) systems of innovation (SI).[27]

Systems of innovation (SI)
These stress the "importance of 'systemic' interactions between the various components of inventions, research, technical change, learning and innovation. The national systems of innovation (NSI) bring to the forefront the central role of the state as a coordinating agent" (Soete et al., *Systems of Innovation*, 2010)

The quality of local scientific, technological, design-related, and creative expertise, combined with institutional relationships between enterprises, universities, and government research organizations, underpins this competitiveness. These are one form of country-specific advantage (CSA) that supports the development of firm-specific advantages (FSAs). Firms that evolve in regions with high-quality capabilities and institutions benefit from this by gaining competitive advantages that help them expand internationally. These location endowments also make such locations attractive to other firms engaged in FDI.

Figure 3.7 gives a stylized version of a conventional innovation system. An SI approach essentially allows us to map the complex interactions between a firm and its environment. The environment consists, firstly, of interactions between firms—especially between a firm and its network of customers and suppliers. Secondly, the environment involves broader factors shaping the behavior of firms: the social, political, and cultural context; the institutional and organizational framework; infrastructures; the processes which create and distribute scientific knowledge, and so on. By economic actors we refer to two groups. The first group are firms—private and public—engaged in innovatory activity, and the second consists of non-firms that determine the knowledge infrastructure that supplements and supports firm-specific innovation. The knowledge infrastructure consists of public research institutes, universities, organizations for standards, intellectual

Figure 3.7 The conventional model of an innovation system

property protection, etc. that enable and promote science and technology development. For simplicity, we can broadly define the non-firm sector as consisting of: (1) a public R&D sector including various organizations conducting R&D activities; (2) an education sector consisting of universities, institutes, and other organizations providing training and education.

The interactions between the various actors within a system are governed by institutions, which we introduced in Chapter 1. Institutions are the "glue" that binds the various actors together, and determines the efficacy of their interaction (or lack thereof). Institutions are taken here to be of two types, informal and formal, and are generally assumed to be the "sets of common habits, routines, established practices, rules, or laws that regulate the interaction between individuals and groups."[28] Institutions create the milieu within which all economic activity is undertaken and establish the ground rules for interaction between the various actors. Formal institutions include the appropriate intellectual property rights regime, competition policy, the creation of technical standards, taxation, the establishment of incentives and subsidies for innovation, the funding of education, etc. They are codified and are administered by organizations that are often established by governments. Such organizations are designed to create and implement new and existing formal institutions. They are generally politically defined and provide legally binding rules, regulations, and institutions. Indeed, the political and economic spheres are rarely independent, and this is all the more so where a high degree of central planning was undertaken, whether in developing countries that implemented import substitution programs, or in the former centrally planned economies. In general, the policy environment in which economic actors function has a high degree of interdependency between the economic and political spheres.

Informal institutions are rarely codified. They are also necessary for creating and promoting links between the various actors, are closely tied to norms and values, and represent routines which are essential to the implementation of formal institutions. To modify and develop informal institutions is a complex and slow process, particularly since they cannot be created simply by government fiat. Perhaps the most important aspect of informal institutions is the "know-who."[29] For firms, these informal networks of government agencies, suppliers, politicians, researchers, and so on take considerable effort and often years—if not decades—to create, but once developed, they have a low marginal cost of maintenance.

INTERNATIONAL DIMENSIONS OF INNOVATION

A major defining feature of multinational enterprises (MNEs) is that they manage business operations across a range of country contexts, each of which represents a different set of opportunities for innovation, in two specific ways. First, country contexts provide a distinctive set of market opportunities, which offer the potential for an MNE to sell customized products and services to particular groups of customers across a variety of market locations. Second, they offer a unique set of resources or inputs into the innovation process, including scientific and technological assets and capabilities, and expertise and knowledge in R&D, engineering, or design, at a particular price. By continually linking innovation input opportunities and output opportunities, multinational enterprises, regardless of their size, are to a greater or lesser extent entrepreneurial.

Figure 3.8 outlines some of the main drivers for internationalization in relation to innovation in MNEs. The two main forms of internationalization, "asset exploiting" and "asset augmenting," were referred to in Chapter 2. Very often they go hand-in-hand because local specialists, whether engineers, plant managers, distribution specialists, or customer-relationship managers, are usually the best equipped to customize processes, products, and services to local conditions. Local assets and knowledge need to be leveraged to develop or adapt products and services for local customers.

Thus, in Figure 3.9, we show how an MNE with headquarters in one country is linked through its affiliates in other countries to the innovation systems of other countries. This may be because it is following its customers, and seeking to increase its market size. In this case, it will transfer knowledge from the parent to the affiliates through reverse and direct knowledge transfer (Figure 3.9).

As discussed in Chapter 2, MNEs can also internationalize as a way to upgrade through asset-augmenting activities. Thus they will engage in "reverse technology transfer," whereby MNEs undertake R&D abroad with the explicit intention of seeking and acquiring technological assets from the host country for use elsewhere in the MNE. Firms may

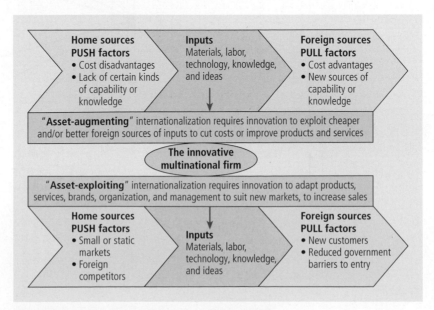

Figure 3.8 International dimensions of innovation

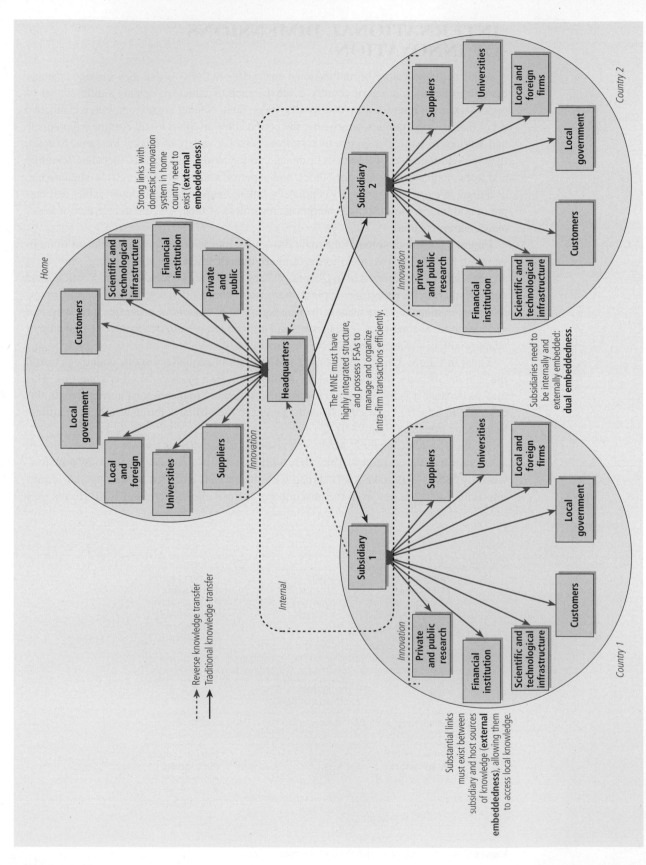

Figure 3.9 MNE headquarters linked through its affiliates in other countries to the innovation systems of other countries

Reverse knowledge transfer
Traditional knowledge transfer

Home

Scientific and technological infrastructure

Financial institution

Private and public

Customers

Local government

Local and foreign

Universities

Suppliers

Headquarters

Innovation

Strong links with domestic innovation system in home country need to exist (**external embeddedness**).

Internal

The MNE must have highly integrated structure, and possess FSAs to manage and organize intra-firm transactions efficiently.

Subsidiary 2

Country 2

Suppliers

Universities

Local and foreign firms

Local government

Customers

Scientific and technological infrastructure

Financial institution

private and public research

Innovation

Subsidiaries need to be internally and externally embedded: **dual embeddedness**.

Subsidiary 1

Country 1

Suppliers

Universities

Local and foreign firms

Local government

Customers

Scientific and technological infrastructure

Financial institution

Private and public research

Innovation

Substantial links must exist between subsidiary and host sources of knowledge (**external embeddedness**), allowing them to access local knowledge.

engage in R&D in a foreign location to gain access to complementary assets that are location specific. That is, foreign technological activities aim explicitly to benefit from the innovation system of the host location.

It is worth noting that not more than 30 years ago, countries had innovation systems that could be described as "closed." In the sense described in Chapter 1, they were poorly integrated into the global economy, and had few interdependencies with other actors in other countries. They engaged largely though trade, but experienced relatively little interdependence through FDI and intra-MNE flows. They were national systems of innovation because most linkages and interdependencies were based with the same country. Today few countries have closed systems. Of course, some innovation systems are more "national" than others, and the term is indicative rather than definitive.

The sources of knowledge available in today's typical "national" system are a complex blend of domestic and foreign ones. In some countries, it is increasingly difficult to separate foreign knowledge sources from domestic ones. MNE subsidiaries are sometimes so well embedded that they are regarded as part of the domestic environment. This reflects not just the length of time that these subsidiaries have been present (e.g., ABB in Norway), or the fact that the affiliate is jointly owned (e.g., Hindustan Unilever in India) or has been acquired (e.g., Nycomed Amersham, Reed Elsevier), but also the nature of the industry, and the growing trend toward consolidation in sectors with low growth and opportunities of global rationalization (e.g., metals, banking, automobiles). MNEs of any given nationality with subsidiaries in several countries may have links with several different universities in several different countries, and may receive research subsidies from several national funding agencies.

THE LOCATION OF INNOVATION ACTIVITIES IN THE MNE

As discussed elsewhere in this book, multinational enterprises have to cope with the competing pressures of integration and responsiveness: that is, to derive benefits such as economies of scale from the integration and standardization of their operations globally, while at the same time customizing and adapting in response to local customers and contexts.

As shown in Figure 3.10, adapted from the ground-breaking work of Christopher Bartlett and Sumantra Ghoshal, we can also feature innovation in this balancing act. In theory, some innovation activities should be centralized and/or standardized and some should be de-centralized and/or customized (or "localized"). We find this is also the case in practice, as described below.[30]

A second framework, developed by Nohria and Ghoshal, extends this logic by describing several archetypal MNE structures for managing different kinds of innovation.[31] Figure 3.11 shows this basic typology, differentiating between three generic forms of innovation activity: sensing, responding, and implementing. The framework shows how it may be appropriate either to separate or to combine these three activities, depending on industry conditions and the product or service in question.

In some industries, such as semiconductors, heavy engineering, and pharmaceuticals, innovation is predominantly technology-driven, rather than market-driven. This is normally because the needs of customers are clear-cut (faster processors, stronger bridges, or a cure for cancer) but difficult to achieve. Moreover, there are strong economies of scale in the centralization of R&D and innovation efforts to achieve scientific or technological breakthroughs ahead of competitors. Sensing opportunities for innovation, like new drug compounds to cure known diseases or faster semiconductor chip designs, and responding to these by allocating capital investment and putting together dedicated project teams, will tend to happen at one location. This specialist unit or "center of excellence" may also

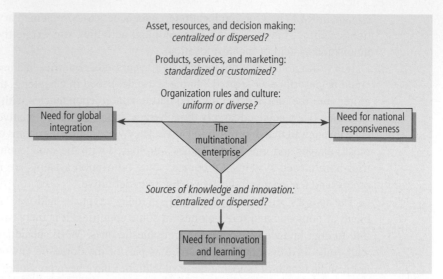

Figure 3.10 Structural, strategic, and organization dilemmas for the innovative multinational firm

Source: Adapted from C. Bartlett and S. Ghoshal, *Managing across Borders: The Transnational Solution* (Boston, MA: Harvard Business School Press, 2002).

Innovation processes	Location where different tasks are carried out		
	Sensing	Responding	Implementing
Center-for-global	At the center (possibly with input from a subsidiary)	Always at the center	In many units worldwide
Local-for-local	In a particular national unit	In the same national unit	In the same national unit
Local-for-global	In a particular national unit	In the same national unit, possibly with help from the center	In the national unit initially, then many units worldwide
Global-for-global	In many units, including the center, plus many subsidiaries	In many units, including the center, plus many subsidiaries	In many units worldwide

Figure 3.11 Global MNE structures for managing innovation

Source: N. Nohria and S. Ghoshal, *The Differentiated Network: Organizing MNCs for Value Creation* (San Francisco, CA: Jossey-Bass, 1997).

implement the innovation by developing and launching the product for sale around the world. This is referred to as **center-for-global** in the framework, in cases where the new technology or product is developed centrally but can be used at the local level. Nohria and Ghoshal use the example of telecoms switching systems, which have clear-cut technology development drivers and obvious economies of scale in R&D, making it appropriate for firms to focus resources and efforts in central R&D units. These create fairly standard components which can be used in telecoms networks around the world.

For market-seeking internationalization it may be appropriate for the local subsidiaries of a firm to sense the opportunity or need for product or service changes to suit local preferences.

Headquarters may then allocate to these subsidiaries the discretionary decision-making powers and the resources and capabilities to respond to these opportunities and implement changes to existing products or services, for the local market. These are labeled **local-for-local** innovations, where new or customized products and services are entirely developed by local subsidiaries because they suit the specific characteristics of the local market or country conditions.

✔ Active learning check

Review your answer to Active Learning Case question 2 and make any changes you like. Then compare your answer to the one below.

2 **In what ways is GE's Mac 400 ECG the result of "local-for-local" innovation?**

An R&D plant was set up to meet the demands of the local market. Medical products created through a process of "frugal innovation" were needed because Indian customers have low average levels of disposable income. This is different from GE Healthcare's other markets. Indian engineers have experience in frugal innovation and so were best placed to meet the needs of the market. Devolving the product development project to local management was therefore appropriate. GE leveraged its global differentiated network of assets and capabilities to innovate efficiently and effectively.

Center-for-global, local-for-local, local-for-global, and global-for-global
Structural archetypes for the location of three innovation-related activities: sensing, responding, and implementing. These result from the need for some innovation activities to be centralized and/or standardized and others to be de-centralized and/or customized (or "localized")

Local-for-global is where a locally developed product or service turns out to fit other markets beyond the location of the subsidiary responsible for creating it. Nohria and Ghoshal describe how Unilever gave its Indian subsidiary the remit for developing a new kind of clothes detergent to improve sales across the country. Because many people in India washed clothes by hand in rivers, a local team designed a soap bar with the same properties as soap powders (which had the inconvenient tendency to drift downstream and wash someone else's clothes!). This became a big-selling brand in India and then proved popular in developing countries in other parts of the world for the same reasons.

The fourth typology, **global-for-global**, is seen as the "ideal" organization structure for "transnational" corporations (as opposed to multinational corporations). Here firms pool inputs, including resources, knowledge, and capabilities, in response to changing technological and market opportunities globally. By effectively coordinating their many subsidiaries around the world, transnational companies can leverage the advantages of their size (scale advantages) and diversity (scope advantages), integrating specialist assets and expertise in response to their changing competitive environments. Nohria and Ghoshal also call this ideal organizational form the "differentiated network," building on previous studies of multinational networks.[32]

✔ Active learning check

Review your answer to Active Learning Case question 3 and make any changes you like. Then compare your answer to the one below.

3 **What indications are there that the Mac 400 ECG has become an example of "local-for-global" innovation?**

Innovation conducted at the local level, by the Indian R&D division, is already providing an input into designing and developing products to sell abroad. The Mac 400 ECG has had some success selling in countries outside India. Specifically, it provides a cheaper, simpler alternative for customers in low-income countries that are similar to India. So while the Indian R&D division was established to serve the Indian market, the locally appropriate, frugal innovation outputs it produces match the needs of other, similar markets.

Innovation networks at IBM

Between the summer of 2010 and early 2011, an IBM computer named "Watson" challenged and eventually beat other (human) contestants on the US game-show *Jeopardy!* It was seen to be a step-change in computing intelligence and a demonstration of the excellence of IBM's global R&D network. The computer, named after two of the firm's original founders, Thomas J. Watson Sr. and his son Thomas J. Watson Jr., can understand natural language and find answers to real questions across a wide range of subject areas. Built by linking 90 servers using IBM's "DeepQA architecture," it is the result of years of work by the company's leading researchers and is now being deployed as a support tool in healthcare, finance, and customer services.

IBM has long been a dominant global force in science and technology development. In 2014 the firm generated an average of over 20 patents per day, with a total figure greater than 7,000 US patents for the single year. IBM has continually positioned itself at the top of the patent list for 22 years and between 1993 and 2014 it received over 81,500 US patents (see Table 3.2). The firm invests over $6 billion in R&D annually, resulting in intellectual property (IP) income of about $1 billion each year as well as a stream of new technologies, products, and services. Ginni Rometty, IBM's chairman, president, and CEO stated that "IBM's continued investment in research and development is key to driving the transformation of our company, as we look to capture the emerging opportunities represented by cloud bug data analytics, security, social, and mobile."

In 2008 the incoming director of R&D at IBM, John Kelly, embarked on a restructuring program in response to both the development of new R&D competitors, such as Microsoft

and Google, and new opportunities in emerging economies. This took the lead from CEO Sam Palmisano, who had a clear view of what a "globally integrated enterprise" should look and act like: "a new kind of enterprise which is best understood as global rather than multinational." Kelly visited the eight IBM research labs around the world, including China, India, and Israel, to gain insights from the firm's global workforce of 3,200 researchers. On the basis of this, he decided to further internationalize the company's R&D structure and consolidate the fragmented allocation of resources into larger-scale, leading projects.

Both of these strategies have been seen by insiders as signaling a shift from the traditional US-based R&D centers to new initiatives in emerging economies. In 2010 the firm added R&D labs in Brazil and Ireland which looked into smarter natural resource management and innovations for societal and infrastructure transformations respectively. In 2011 IBM opened a R&D lab in Australia with a focus on smarter natural resource management related to resource discovery. In 2013 the company further expanded its worldwide portfolio of science and technology expertise by opening an R&D center in Nairobi, Kenya (see Table 3.3). A global network of 12 labs in six continents was established by 2016.

Global alliances and collaboration are also a central part of the strategy. Kelly uses the term *collaboratories* to denote "agile, in-market research" activities which connect with universities and science and technology institutes in different countries, rather than investing in large-scale, brick-and-mortar laboratories. Significantly, this also means conducting research closest to the problem. For example, instead of tackling transportation issues in the United States, where the infrastructure is in line with growth, he suggests that IBM will focus on a country, city, and area where road traffic is a primary problem, such as Mumbai.

IBM has developed a number of unique networking mechanisms for connecting researchers and employees for innovation. It holds a "smart camp" and uses Facebook to host discussions between its in-house researchers and other experts around the world. "Jams" or "jamming" are another unusual way the firm promotes technology-based creativity. These are online brainstorming sessions for huge numbers of people to share ideas and discuss key challenges which can be commercial or related to social or environmental issues. In 2006 the "Innovation Jam" connected over 150,000 people from 104 countries and 67 companies. Ten new IBM businesses were launched as a result, with seed investment totaling $100 million. An Innovation Jam in 2008 demonstrated

Table 3.2 Top ten patent recipients, 2014

Rank	Organization	No. of patents
1	IBM	7,534
2	Samsung	4,952
3	Canon	4,055
4	Sony	3,224
5	Microsoft	2,829
6	Toshiba	2,608
7	Qualcomm	2,590
8	Google	2,566
9	LG Electronics	2,122
10	Panasonic	2,095

Source: www.IBM.com

Table 3.3 IBM's research labs

Where?	Established when?	Doing what?
Almaden, San Jose, CA, USA	1955	Computer science, database, user interface, web software, storage systems software and technology, physical sciences, materials science, nanotechnology, life sciences, and services research
Zürich, Rüschlikon, Switzerland	1956	Nanoscience and technology, semiconductor technology, storage systems, advanced server technology, systems design, IT security and privacy, business optimization, mobile enablement, services research, and industry solutions lab
Watson, NY and MA, USA	1961	Computer science, database, data mining, business intelligence, user interface, storage systems software, materials science, nanotechnology, life sciences, services research, mathematics, and semiconductor technology
Haifa, Israel	1972	Storage and business continuity systems, verification technologies, multimedia, active management, information retrieval, programming environments, optimization technologies, and life sciences
Tokyo, Yamato, Japan	1982	Analytics and optimization, software engineering, middleware, system software, security and compliance, electronical and optical packaging technology, engineering and technology services, text mining and speech technology, and accessibility center
Beijing, China	1995	Business integration and transformation, information and knowledge management, future embedded systems and devices, resilient and pervasive infrastructure, and user interactions
Austin, TX, USA	1995	High-performance/low-power VLSI design and tools, system-level power analysis, and new system architectures
Delhi and Bangalore, India	1998	Speech technologies, pervasive computing, e-governance, information management, e-commerce, life sciences, distributed computing, and software engineering
São Paulo and Rio de Janeiro, Brazil	2010	Smarter natural resource management, smarter devices, smarter human systems, service systems and underlying technologies including analytics and optimization, distributed systems, mobile technologies, semiconductor packaging, and high-performance computing
Dublin, Ireland	2010	Innovations for societal and infrastructure transformations, with a focus on improving city operations and the well-being of citizens
Melbourne, Australia	2011	Smarter natural resource management related to resource discovery, production, supply chain and operations. Smarter natural disaster management including real-time event (stream) processing, weather modeling, traffic management, and mobility analytics
Nairobi, Kenya	2013	Developing commercially viable solutions to transform lives and spark new business opportunities in key areas such as water, agriculture, transportation, healthcare, financial inclusion, education, energy, security, and e-government

Source: adapted from http://www.research.ibm.com/worldwide/index.shtml.

how powerful "crowd sourcing" for new ideas could be. Since then IBM has coordinated online jams on governance, technology, and security. In 2011 the Prince of Wales in the UK kicked off "Start Jam," focusing on sustainable business practices.

Some of IBM's global networking efforts are clearly, at least in part, public relations exercises. But it has obviously developed a sophisticated range of networks and organization mechanisms to connect and leverage the huge range of in-house R&D expertise it has invested in and simultaneously tap into external sources of knowledge and capabilities for innovation. Doubling the number of patents within the last

five years leaves no doubt that IBM is a leader in R&D which covers a range of areas including cloud computing, analytics, mobile, social media, and security-related platforms.

Source: "Setting IBM's R&D Agenda," *Business Week*, April 2008; a video of John Kelly, Director of Research at IBM, is available at: http://www.businessweek.com/innovate/content/apr2008/id20080416_955900.htm; Samuel J. Palmisano, "The globally integrated enterprise," *Foreign Affairs*, May/June 2006; https://www.research.ibm.com/labs/; http://www.facebook.com/ibmwatson; http://www.ibm.com/developerworks/community; http://www.research.ibm.com/worldwide/index.shtml; http://www.youtube.com/watch?v=cU-AhmQ363I&feature=relmfu; http://www-03.ibm.com/press/us/en/pressrelease/32757.wss; https://www.collaborationjam.com; https://www-03.ibm.com/press/us/en/pressrelease/45793.wss

The innovative MNE as a differentiated network

MNEs, large and small, have to both adapt to local conditions and optimize their scale and scope advantages by standardizing products, services, brands, and organizational practices as much as possible. Hence, they face the dilemma of having to be both "global" and "local" at the same time. But one of the major natural competitive advantages of MNEs results from their ability to combine (and continually recombine) various inputs (particularly knowledge and expertise) into the innovation process, from different locations, to serve different customer needs across a variety of markets. Their ability to exploit this advantage depends to a significant degree on how they are structured to manage networks which connect these locations and incentivize specialists to connect across these networks to add value.[33]

Differentiated networks require strong integrative and dynamic capabilities to operate effectively. Not only must they integrate disparate resources and knowledge from the various parts of the firm, but they must also continually develop and recombine these assets in response to the complex and changing range of external innovation opportunities. In theory this is straightforward, but in practice there are many organizational barriers and constraints to resource and knowledge sharing. Moreover, which opportunities should be targeted and which areas of resource allocation or knowledge development should be prioritized is continually contested.

Firms that do develop more effective ways of integrating specialist knowledge for innovation tend to have a degree of "slack" in their configuration of assets, resources, and expertise. Clayton Christensen notes this in his analysis of how firms become locked into certain sets of markets, resources, and capabilities by focusing on cost cutting and efficiency. Over time they lose the flexibility to explore, experiment, and innovate their way on to a new "S-curve."[34] Firms that operate as dynamic networks also balance the division of decision-making responsibility for innovation between headquarters (the center) and subsidiaries (the periphery), and develop organizational mechanisms, such as project structures, incentives, communication channels, IT systems, roles, and responsibilities for connecting specialist sources of knowledge around the firm and leveraging these to serve clients and customers.

Research has shown how and why firms differ in their "integrative" innovation capabilities. Sony, for example, in comparison with counterparts like Panasonic (formerly known as Matsushita) and Philips, has a strong set of organization coordination mechanisms, communication practices, and employee incentives for connecting market opportunities with technological potential in its consumer electronics division.[35] This involves combining software and hardware specialists to create new functionalities in multimedia products and linking them effectively with consumers to develop some expertise in what drives patterns of adoption and use. Rather than relying on the marketing function to produce data and analysis on customers, Sony tends to encourage engineers and technologists to observe or work with customers directly to understand what kinds of innovation add value for them.

Ambidexterity
The ability of a firm to be aligned and efficient in its management of today's business demands while simultaneously being adaptive to changes in the environment

Compared to other Japanese firms, Sony is fairly unusual in its so-called **ambidexterity**: that is, its ability "to be aligned and efficient in its management of today's business demands while simultaneously being adaptive to changes in the environment."[36] Sony is continually coming up with new technology platforms (CDs, DVDs, minidisks, and so on) and new products based around these platforms. But it also invests in improving current product lines, with new models and new features, and it strives to make them cheaper through economies of scale and continuous improvement in manufacturing. Many Japanese firms are renowned for their incremental process and product innovation capabilities, but are weaker in terms of their radical or R&D-driven innovation. Moreover, they tend to be more locked into domestic market R&D and innovation networks, compared to counterparts from the United States or Europe.[37]

The original studies leading to the concept of the differentiated network focused predominantly on manufacturing firms, but as innovation in multinational networks has become more widely analyzed, knowledge-based services and other business sectors have also been examined.[38]

KEY POINTS

1 The VRIO framework, a theoretical model built upon RBV, helps us to assess and understand the FSAs that will lead to competitive advantages. For the firm to have competitive advantages, they must fulfill four criteria: the FSAs must be valuable (V), rare (R), imperfectly imitable (I), and properly organized (O).

2 Dynamic capability is the firm's ability to integrate, build, and reconfigure internal and external competences to address rapidly changing environments. The dynamic capabilities approach is useful to understand how successful firms are able to stay competitive in changing environments. If a firm fails to adapt to changing pressures and opportunities, or does not have the capabilities to do so, then it will lose it competitiveness and risk failing.

3 The quality of local scientific, technological, design-related, and creative expertise, combined with institutional relationships between enterprises, universities, and government research organizations, underpins the competitiveness of a region and is key in driving innovation. These are one form of country-specific advantage (CSA) that supports the development of firm-specific advantages (FSAs). Firms that evolve in regions with high-quality capabilities and institutions benefit from this by gaining competitive advantages that help them expand internationally. These location endowments also make such locations attractive to other firms engaged in FDI.

4 Firms centralize or de-centralize various innovation activities (sensing, responding to, and implementing) globally depending on the trade-offs between standardization and economies of scale and the need for national responsiveness. The center-for-global, local-for-local, local-for-global, and global-for-global typology and the concept of differentiated networks for innovation capture this key trade-off.

Key terms

- innovation
- dynamic capability
- systems of innovation (SI)
- center-for-global, local-for-local, local-for-global, and global-for-global
- ambidexterity

REAL CASE

Canon Group

Few companies can claim to be truly global multinationals, but with sales, revenues, production, and employees distributed across the world, the Canon Group of Japan comes as close as any to fitting that title. In 2010, Canon's sales grew 23 percent compared to the previous year, to a record high of US$42.225 billion. The company then seemed to struggle. By 2015 its revenues had dropped to US$31.54 billion, partly because of the declining popularity of cameras, as customers increasingly used their phones. But the firm's sales are spread evenly across the world's main markets, with over 80 percent of its products sold outside Japan. In 2015, 30 percent of its net sales were in the Americas, 28 percent in Europe, and 23 percent in Asia and Oceania.

Canon operates in three business segments. The Office segment provides office network, color network and personal multifunction devices, office, color and personal copy machines, laser printers, large-sized ink-jet printers and digital production printers, among others. The Consumer segment provides digital single-lens reflex cameras, compact digital cameras, interchangeable lens, digital video cameras, ink-jet multifunction devices, single-function ink-jet printers, image scanners, and television lenses for broadcasting use, among others. The Industrial Equipment and Others segment provides exposure equipment used in semiconductor and liquid crystal displays (LCDs), medical image-recording equipment, ophthalmic instruments, magnetic heads, micro motors, computers, handy terminals, document scanners, and calculators, among others. Canon is dual listed on the Tokyo Stock Exchange and New York Stock Exchange.

The company had its beginnings in 1933, when Precision Optical Instruments Laboratory was established to conduct research into cameras in Roppongi, Minato-ku, Tokyo. In 1947 the company changed its name to Canon Camera Co., and only in 1969 did the company take on the name Canon Inc.

Canon's international expansion started in 1955 with the opening of a New York branch. Initially, the company relied on sole distributors and established some in Europe and Latin America in the late 1950s and early 1960s. The sole distributor system was abolished in 1963 to make way for company-owned subsidiaries under the direct control of the Japanese headquarters.

International expansion goes beyond marketing to include production, research, and development. Taiwan became the site of Canon's first foreign production facility in 1970. Two years later the company opened a manufacturing plant in Germany. By 2001, the company had production facilities in all parts of the triad—Western Europe, the Asia–Pacific region, and North America. Nevertheless, the vast majority of Canon's production facilities remain in Asia, including Japan. So in contrast to the global distribution of its sales, 40 percent of its employees (almost 192,000 in 2015) were based in Japan and just 10 percent in Europe, 10 percent in North America, and 40 percent elsewhere, predominantly in Southeast Asian production centers.

From 1990 onwards, R&D centers were opened in the United States, Australia, France, Thailand, and the People's Republic of China. Each R&D facility specializes in a specific product line and is coordinated by a centralized R&D lab in Japan. Together with its R&D strategy, this has made Canon one of the best world innovators and the largest holder of patents after IBM and Samsung.

Canon is organized regionally. Canon USA oversees operations in the Americas. The subsidiary has its own marketing, R&D, and production facilities. Two companies oversee European operations. Together, they have two manufacturing plants in Germany and France, and R&D centers in the UK and France. Canon's operations in Asia and Oceania, excluding Japan, account for the largest number of employees in foreign countries. Region-wide activities for the Asian market are overseen by the Canon Asia Marketing Group, but marketing operations in this region are fragmented into sub-regional or national markets. The Southeast Asia region is the responsibility of Canon Singapore. Hong Kong has its own subsidiary that is also responsible for Taiwan and part of South Korea. The mainland Chinese market is the responsibility of Canon (China) Co. Japan's home market is still very important. Nearly half of Canon's employees are still working in Japan and company-wide R&D is still centralized there. Canon Australia is responsible for operations in the Oceania region.

The firm spends 8.3 percent of its revenue on R&D. Canon finds not only new technologies, but also new methods of manufacturing products. Canon has been reorganizing its production facilities to take advantage of its global scope, selecting suppliers and production facilities across the world to minimize costs and decrease production time. As a result, product design data can now be sent to plants around the world via computer. Information is translated through an automatic translation system allowing faster communication between subsidiaries. The firm is now using simulation technology to minimize the costly process of prototype production.

At a time when other Japanese and many other, large electronic companies are struggling to remain competitive, Canon's profits are soaring. The firm has been able to remain competitive by selecting those business lines in which it can be successful, given its strength in R&D and production technology. The firm abandoned the markets for personal computers, typewriters, and liquid crystal displays to concentrate on cameras, printers, and copiers.

Studies suggest that one of Canon's key competencies is its global system for new product development. In particular, it has evolved a number of organizational mechanisms for linking R&D and customer requirements globally. This is partly done through alliances and joint ventures in which Canon invests over the long term to derive the benefits of co-learning and joint resource development. Canon contributes its technological capabilities and supplier links, and local partners bring expertise relating to local customer preferences, distribution, and marketing.

On the plant floor, Canon's high productivity increases have been based on cell production technology. Here, a small number of workers have responsibility for the final assembly of the product. This type of production not only increases the amount of a product being produced per labor-hour, but also ensures quality as it is easier to backtrack the production process of a single product. It also saves floor space. Since 1998, Canon has decreased the length of its conveyor lines by 12 miles (19 km). However, the productivity increases of applying and perfecting cell technology to its operations are reaching a limit and now Canon is seeking ways of integrating automation technology into its production process.

In 2002, Canon made the unlikely decision to establish a facility in Oita, Kyushu, Japan, to produce digital cameras. CEO Fujio Mitarai's explanation is that "If we switch factories each time a place with lower labor costs is found, all investment in equipment is wasted. Instead, we should use our strengths in production, and manufacture products more cheaply than they could be manufactured in locations where the cost of labor is lower." Approximately 40 percent of Canon products are still manufactured in Japan. The company's long-term plan is to reach a balance between outsourcing and Japanese production. Mitarai's position is that anything for which labor costs are more than 5 percent of production costs can be outsourced to low labor-cost areas, such as China, and anything for

which labor costs are less than 5 percent of production—typically the more advanced technologically—can be produced domestically.

Website: www.canon.com.

Source: Canon, http://www.canon.com/ir/finance/highlight.html (accessed 2016); Canon, *Annual Report,* 2006–2014; "Can Canon keep printing money?," *Business Week,* September 5, 2005; "Hard to copy," *The Economist,* October 31, 2002; "(Still) made in Japan," *The Economist,* April 7, 2004; B. Bowonder and T. Miyake, "R&D and business strategy: analysis of practice at Canon," *International Journal of Technology Management,* vol. 13, nos. 7/8 (1997), pp. 833–53; H. Perks, "Exploring processes of resource exchange and co-creation in strategic partnering for new product development," *International Journal of Innovation Management,* vol. 8, no. 1 (2004), pp. 37–61; Thomson Reuters, *OneSource,* 2011.

1 Explain why, over the course of Canon's internationalization process, certain functions have been moved or expanded to certain global locations.

2 Why has it been important for Canon to internationalize its R&D activities?

3 Speculate as to why Canon is so unusual in its degree of independence from Japan's domestic market, compared to most other Japanese firms.

4 How is Canon still fairly dependent on Japan as a home base?

REAL CASE

R&D at Hewlett-Packard

Founded in a small garage by William Redington Hewlett and David Packard in 1939, The Hewlett-Packard Company (HP) is a multinational American organization that develops a range of computer hardware components. HP also provides software and IT-related services to SMEs and large organizations and is headquartered in Palo Alto, California, US. As of 2014, HP's net revenue was recorded as US$115.5 billion and its cash flow for operations was US$12.3 billion.

HP primarily has seven basic R&D centers: in Palo Alto, California; Cambridge, Massachusetts; Bristol, England; Galway, Ireland; Grenoble, France; Haifa, Israel; and Tokyo, Japan. These explore a wide range of technologies more or less linked to its product range. Its Advanced Studies Research Labs include a sub-group doing information theory research, linking the Mathematical Science Group based in Bristol with experts at the US universities at Stanford and Berkeley. Grenoble specializes in business PC design and development and Israel in image and document processing, among other areas.

These centers of research excellence are linked to HP's global product divisions, mainly headquartered in the United States, and its national subsidiaries around the world, which encompass most of its 85,500 employees.

The Palo Alto center pioneered HP's thermal ink-jet technology, for example. Its Consumer Products group, headquartered in San Diego, California, designed, developed, and led the manufacturing of a range of imaging products using this technology. The firm's subsidiary in Singapore customizes the design and produces thermal ink-jet printers for the Japanese and Asian markets.

The R&D structure of the firm evolved a step further when the Singaporean subsidiary took the lead from San Diego for the design, development, and manufacturing of a new range of portable ink-jet printers. It had built up a range of specialist capabilities, through learning from other parts of the internal network and through local Asian technical partnerships and subcontractors, which made it the best place to lead innovation efforts in this area for the firm as a whole. ▶

HP has developed a strong culture of creative innovation, going back to its roots as a garage-based start-up. In addition to the "formal" R&D function, with its global network of R&D centers, HP promotes innovation across all of its functions and employees. Continuous improvement of technologies, products, services, and solutions which exploit new technological trends and match these to the changing needs of customers is encouraged across the firm. HP focuses its efforts on areas where it believes it can make a unique contribution, which at times also include forming partnerships with other leading organizations.

In 2015 HP invested US$3.5 billion into R&D, up from US$3.45 billion in 2014 and US$3.14 billion in 2013. But the firm's R&D investment as a percentage of sales (a standard measure of R&D "intensity") declined from 3.9 percent in 2006 to less than 3 percent in 2015.

With the help of its R&D centers, HP has recently been able to develop new products and services around the cloud storage platform and related to "big data." In 2015, HP opened an 87,000 ft^2 Innovation Center in Ballybrit, Galway, Ireland, with a workforce of 700 engineers, consultants, and support team. With the opening of this new Innovation Center, HP is striving to become a leader in software R&D, cloud technology, and service innovation.

Conclusion

Even though HP's expenditure on R&D has been increasing, it is still relatively low compared to some of its competitors and particularly low as a percentage of sales. For example, Microsoft spends approximately 13 percent of its revenues on R&D, IBM 5–7 percent, and SAP 14 percent. However, in consecutive annual reports, HP states its intention to invest larger sums into R&D. The central belief of HP's founders, David Packard and William Hewlett, from the days of the garage in Palo Alto, that investing in R&D to drive continuous innovation is necessary for long-term competitive advantage, still runs strong.

Website: https://www.hpe.com/uk/en/home.html

Sources: HP, *Annual Report,* 2014; Cliff Saran, "HP CEO Meg Whitman pushes hardware R&D strategy," *Computer Weekly,* May 10, 2012; "HP opens new Innovation Facility in Galway", ARUP, May 13 2015, arup.com; "Invest in the West—MJ Conroy & HP Ballybrit," *Irish Building,* February 9, 2015.

1 Discuss if HP has competitive advantages and if there are examples of dynamic capabilities.

2 Discuss the interaction of CSAs and HP's FSAs in developing its competitive advantages.

3 Discuss whether the Singapore R&D subsidiary is: center-for-global, local-for-local, local-for-global or global-for-global.

NOTES

1 Although slightly dated, this definition is still one of the best. European Commission, "Green Paper on Innovation," *Bulletin of the European Union, Supplement 5/95* (Brussels: European Commission, 1995).

2 National Science Board, *Science and Engineering Indicators 2014* (Arlington, VA: National Science Foundation) (NSB 14-01).

3 Ibid.

4 http://www.theguardian.com/society/2015/jul/24/first-malaria-vaccine-given-green-light-by-european-regulators

5 E. T. Penrose, *The Theory of the Growth of the Firm* (New York: John Wiley, 1959); B. Wernerfelt, "A resource-based view of the firm," *Strategic Management Journal,* vol. 5, no. 2 (1984), pp. 171–80.

6 J. Bell, D. Crick, and S. Young, "A holistic perspective on small firm growth and internationalisation," Academy of International Business Conference, City University Business School, 1998.

7 E. Beleska-Spasova, K. W. Glaister, and C. Stride, "Resource determinants of strategy and performance: the case of British exporters," *Journal of World Business,* vol. 47, no. 4 (2012), pp. 635–47.

8 R. Amit and P. J. H. Schoemaker, "Strategic assets and organizational rent," *Strategic Management Journal,* vol. 14, no. 1 (1993), pp. 33–46; J. Barney, "Firm resources and sustained competitive advantage," *Journal of Management,* vol. 17 (1991), pp. 99–120.

9 R. Makadok, "Toward a synthesis of the resource-based view and dynamic-capability views of rent creation," *Strategic Management Journal,* vol. 22, no. 5 (2001), pp. 387–401.

10 J. Barney, "Firm resources and sustained competitive advantage," *Journal of Management,* vol. 17 (1991), pp. 99–120.

11 J. B. Barney, "Looking inside for competitive advantage," *Academy of Management Executive,* vol. 9, no. 4 (1995), pp. 49–61.

12 Ibid.

13 R. Narula, "Do we need different frameworks to explain infant MNEs from developing countries?," *Global Strategy Journal,* vol. 2, no. 1 (2012), pp. 41–7.

14 J. B. Barney, "Looking inside for competitive advantage," *Academy of Management Executive,* vol. 9, no. 4 (1995), pp. 49–61.

15 Ibid.

16 http://www.kodak.com/ek/US/en/Kodak_Announces_Sale_of_Patents.htm

17 D. Teece and G. Pisano, "The dynamic capabilities of firms: an introduction," *Industrial and Corporate Change,* vol. 3, no. 3 (1994), pp. 537–56.

18 C. Helfat, S. Finkelstein, W. Mitchell, M. Peteraf, H. Singh, D. Teece, and S. Winter, *Dynamic Capabilities: Understanding Strategic Change in Organizations* (Malden, MA: Blackwell, 2007).

19 See some of the original work on dynamic capabilities: D. Teece, G. Pisano, and A. Shuen, "Dynamic capabilities and

strategic management," *Strategic Management Journal*, vol. 18, no. 7 (1997), pp. 509–33; K. Eisenhardt and J. Martin, "Dynamic capabilities: what are they?," *Strategic Management Journal*, vol. 21 (2000), pp. 1105–22. Also see: S. A. Zahra, H. J. Sapienza, and P. Davidsson, "Entrepreneurship and dynamic capabilities: a review, model and research agenda," *Journal of Management Studies*, vol. 43, no. 4 (2006), pp. 917–55.

20 C. E. Helfat et al., *Dynamic Capabilities: Understanding Strategic Change in Organisations* (Malden, MA: Blackwell, 2007) is the best overview of the dynamic capabilities field, from a theory perspective. A good set of papers also appears in: M. Easterby-Smith, M. A. Lyles, and M. A. Peteraf, "Dynamic capabilities: current debates and future directions," *British Journal of Management*, vol. 20, no.1 (2009), pp. S1–S8. Some studies explicitly focus on dynamic capabilities in small firms, such as: E. Døving and P. Gooderham, "Dynamic capabilities as antecedents of the scope of related diversification: the case of small firm accountancy practices," *Strategic Management Journal*, vol. 29, no. 8 (2008), pp. 841–57.

21 Research on capability life cycles, such as: C. E. Helfat and M. A. Peteraf, "The dynamic resource-based view: capability lifecycles," *Strategic Management Journal*, vol. 24 (2003), pp. 997–1010, has obvious parallels with research on S-curves. S-curves show how firms can become over-dependent on and "locked" into an over-reliance on certain kinds of products, assets, and capabilities, such that when markets or technologies change they are unable to reinvent themselves and go into decline. See, amongst other work: C. Christensen, *The Innovator's Dilemma* (Boston, MA: Harvard Business School Press, 1997).

22 J. A. Schumpeter, *Capitalism, Socialism and Democracy* (New York: Harper, 1942).

23 R. Narula, *Multinational Investment and Economic Structure: Globalisation and Competitiveness* (London: Routledge, 2002).

24 J. Cantwell, *Technological Innovation and Multinational Corporations* (Oxford: Blackwell, 1989).

25 R. Narula, "Do we need different frameworks to explain infant MNEs from developing countries?," *Global Strategy Journal*, vol. 2, no. 1 (2012), pp. 41–7.

26 A. M. Rugman and A. Verbeke, "A perspective on regional and global strategies of multinational enterprises," *Journal of International Business Studies*, vol. 35 (2004), pp. 3–18.

27 C. Freeman, "The national system of innovation in historical perspective," *Cambridge Journal of Economics*, no. 19

(1995), pp. 5–24; B.-A. Lundvall, *National Systems of Innovation: Toward a Theory of Innovation and Interactive Learning* (London: Anthem Press, 2010); R. Nelson (ed.), *National Innovation Systems: A Comparative Analysis* (Oxford: Oxford University Press, 1993).

28 C. Edquist and B. Johnson, "Institutions and organizations in systems of innovation," in C. Edquist (ed.), *Systems of Innovation: Technologies, Institutions and Organizations* (London: Pinter Publishers/Cassel Academic, 1997).

29 R. Narula, *Gobalization and Technology* (London: Polity Press, 2003).

30 C. Bartlett and S. Ghoshal, *Managing across Borders: The Transnational Solution* (Boston, MA: Harvard Business School Press, 2002).

31 N. Nohria and S. Ghoshal, *The Differentiated Network: Organizing MNCs for Value Creation* (San Francisco, CA: Jossey-Bass, 1997).

32 In addition to Nohria and Ghoshal (1997, op. cit.), a range of related readings on this topic can be found in C. Bartlett, S. Ghoshal, and J. Birkinshaw, *Transnational Management: Text, Cases, and Readings in Cross-Border Management* (London: McGraw-Hill, 2004).

33 M. Adenfelt and K. Lagerström, "The development and sharing of knowledge by centres of excellence and transnational teams: a conceptual framework," *Management International Review*, vol. 48, no. 3 (2008), pp. 319–38.

34 C. M. Christensen, *The Innovator's Dilemma: When New Technologies Cause Great Firms to Fail* (Boston, MA: Harvard Business School Press, 1997).

35 S. C. Collinson, "Organising for multimedia product development: Sony and Philips compared," *Communications and Strategies*, vol. 19 (1995), pp. 47–77.

36 S. Raisch and J. M. Birkinshaw, "Organizational ambidexterity: antecedents, outcomes, and moderators," *Journal of Management*, vol. 34, no. 3 (2008), pp. 375–409.

37 S. C. Collinson and A. M. Rugman, "The regional nature of Japanese multinational business," *Journal of International Business Studies*, vol. 39, no. 2 (2008), pp. 215–30; S. C. Collinson and D. C. Wilson, "Inertia in Japanese organizations: knowledge management routines and failure to innovate," *Organization Studies*, vol. 27, no. 9 (2005), pp. 1359–87.

38 See, for example, M. L. Mors, "Innovation in a global consulting firm: when the problem is too much diversity," *Strategic Management Journal*, vol. 31, no. 8 (2010), pp. 841–87.

BIBLIOGRAPHY

Akhter, Syed H., and Beno, Colleen. "An empirical note on regionalization and globalization," *Multinational Business Review*, vol. 19, no. 1 (2011).

Bessant, John, and Tidd, Joe. *Innovation and Entrepreneurship* (London: John Wiley & Sons, 2nd ed., 2011).

Beugelsdijk, Sjoerd, Hennart, Jean-François, Slangen, Arjen, and Smeets, Roger. "Why and how FDI stocks are a biased measure of MNE affiliate activity," *Journal of International Business Studies*, vol. 41, no. 9 (2010).

Blundel, Richard, and Lockett, Nigel. *Exploring Entrepreneurship: Practices and Perspectives* (Oxford: Oxford University Press, 2011).

Brouthers, Keith D., and Dikova, Desislava. "Acquisitions and real options: the greenfield alternative," *Journal of Management Studies*, vol. 47, no. 6 (September 2010).

Buckley, Peter J., and Strange, Roger. "The governance of the multinational enterprise: insights from internalization theory," *Journal of Management Studies*, vol. 48, no. 2 (2011).

Chesbrough, Henry, Vanhaverbeke, Wim, and West, Joel. *Open Innovation: Researching a New Paradigm* (Oxford: Oxford University Press, 2008).

Collinson, Simon, and Rugman, Alan M. "The regional character of Asian multinational enterprise," *Asia Pacific Journal of Management*, vol. 24, no. 4 (2007).

Datta, Deepak K., Liang, Xin, and Musteen, Martina. "Strategic orientation and the choice of foreign market entry mode," *Management International Review*, vol. 49, no. 3 (2009).

Dhanaraj, Charles, and Parkhe, Arvind. "Orchestrating innovation networks," *Academy of Management Review*, vol. 31, no. 3 (July 2006).

Gronum, Sarel, Verreynne, Martie-Louise, and Kastelle, Tim. "The role of networks in small and medium-sized enterprise innovation and firm performance," *Journal of Small Business Management*, vol. 50, no. 2 (2012).

Helms, Marilyn M., and Nixon, Judy. "Exploring SWOT analysis—where are we now? A review of academic research from the last decade," *Journal of Strategy and Management*, vol. 3, no. 3 (2010).

Hennart, Jean-François (2009). "Down with MNE-centric theories! Market entry and expansion as the bundling of MNE and local assets," *Journal of International Business Studies*, vol. 40 (August 2009).

Hovhannisyan, Nune, and Keller, Wolfgang. "International business travel: an engine of innovation?," *Journal of Economic Growth*, vol. 20, no. 1 (2015), pp. 75–104.

Hutzschenreuter, Thomas, Voll, Johannes C., and Verbeke, Alain. "The impact of added cultural distance and cultural diversity on international expansion patterns: a Penrosean perspective," *Journal of Management Studies*, vol. 48, no. 2 (March 2011).

Javalgi, Rajshekhar (Raj) G., Deligonul, Seyda, Ghosh, Amit K., Lambert, Douglas M., and Cavusgil, S. Tamer. "Foreign market entry mode behavior as a gateway to further entries: the NAFTA experience," *International Business Review*, vol. 19, no. 3 (June 2010).

Kyläheiko, Kalevi, Jantunen, Ari, Puumalainen, Kaisu, Saarenketo, Sami, and Tuppura, Anni. "Innovation and internationalization as growth strategies: the role of technological capabilities and appropriability," *International Business Review*, vol. 20, no. 5 (2011).

Lambert, Susan C., and Davidson, Robyn A. "Applications of the business model in studies of enterprise success, innovation and classification: an analysis of empirical research from 1996 to 2010," *European Management Journal*, vol. 31, no. 6 (2013).

Makino, Shige, and Tsang, Eric W. K. "Historical ties and foreign direct investment," *Journal of International Business Studies*, vol. 42 (2010).

Mirus, Rolf, and Yeung, Bernard. "On the mode of international expansion: the role of agency costs," *Multinational Business Review*, vol. 18, no. 4 (2010).

Morschett, Dirk, Schramm-Klein, Hanna, and Swoboda, Bernhard. "Entry modes for manufacturers' international after-sales service: analysis of transaction-specific, firm-specific and country-specific determinants," *Management International Review*, vol. 48, no. 5 (2008).

Mudambi, Ram, and Swift, Tim. "Leveraging knowledge and competencies across space: the next frontier in international business," *Journal of International Management*, vol. 17, no. 3 (2011).

Nguyen, Quyen T. K. "The empirical literature on multinational enterprises, subsidiaries and performance," *Multinational Business Review*, vol. 19, no. 1 (2011).

Nieto, María Jesús, and Rodríguez, Alicia. "Offshoring of R&D: looking abroad to improve innovation performance," *Journal of International Business Studies*, vol. 42, no. 3 (2011).

Prabhu, J., and Radjou, N. *Frugal Innovation: How to Do More with Less* (London: Economist Books, 2015).

Prahalad, C. K., and Krishnan, M. S. *The New Age of Innovation: Driving Co-created Value through Global Networks* (New York: McGraw-Hill Professional, 2008).

Rugman, Alan M., and Verbeke, Alain. "Towards a theory of regional multinationals: a transaction cost economics approach," *Management International Review*, vol. 45, special issue 1 (2005).

Rugman, Alan M., Verbeke, Alain, and Nguyen, Quyen T. K. "Fifty years of international business theory and beyond," *Management International Review*, vol. 51, no. 6 (Nov. 2011).

Tidd, Joe, and Bessant, John. *Managing Innovation: Integrating Technological, Market and Organizational Change* (London: John Wiley & Sons, 2009).

Zott, Christoph, Amit, Raphael, and Massa, Lorenzo. "The business model: recent developments and future research," *Journal of Management*, vol. 37, no. 4 (2011).

Part Two

THE ENVIRONMENT OF INTERNATIONAL BUSINESS

Chapter 4

INTERNATIONAL POLITICS

Contents

Objectives of the chapter

Politics and economics are closely linked and often affect each other. A good example is the economic changes that are sweeping eastern Europe and Asia today. As these countries embrace open markets, their centrally planned economies are giving way to market-driven economies. However, this latter development would have been impossible had it not been preceded by the requisite political change as reflected by more democratic governments. The purposes of this chapter are to examine the linkage between political forces and economic change and then to review some of the major forms of economic integration that are being used to create regional trade areas and common markets. In future chapters these topics will be developed in more depth.

The specific objectives of this chapter are to:

1 *Compare and contrast* major political and economic systems and note the linkage among them.

2 *Examine* the primary reasons for the current privatization movement and the economic impact that this movement is having on selected countries.

3 *Describe* the five major levels of economic integration and how each works.

4 *Discuss* how MNEs are using strategic planning to benefit from current worldwide economic integration efforts.

5 *Discuss* the impact of non-governmental organizations (NGOs) on international business.

ACTIVE LEARNING CASE

How risky is foreign investment in Russia?

Making investments in any foreign country is a risky business. Each and every foreign country has a different set of legal, political, social, and economic institutions. Despite allegations that the world is flat, what we know is that there remains a large degree of variation in both country and regional institutional arrangements. So, no investor can afford to assume that doing business abroad is risk free. This logic applies to the current situation in Russia.

Source: Quentin Bargate/Alamy Stock Photo

A number of problems continue to plague Russia. Natural resources account for 80 percent of the country's exports, including oil and natural gas, making the economy susceptible to world price fluctuations. The banking system is weak and, after a series of crises dating back to 1998, generally distrusted. In 2004, for instance, smaller banks faced a liquidity crisis as depositors, afraid for their savings, withdrew large sums of money. In addition, widespread corruption and government interference in the judiciary process stymies both domestic and foreign investment. The country ranks as 136th out of 175 countries in Transparency International's "Corruption Perceptions Index" 2014 and among the worst in their "Bribe Payers Index."

A case in point is that of Yukos, one of Russia's largest oil companies, whose privatization was one of many corrupt undertakings in the transition to a market economy. The government sought to collect back taxes that are threatening to bankrupt the company. Yukos is charged with tax evasion, but critics claim the move was politically motivated and that the tools used to evade taxes were perfectly legal under Russian law when they were undertaken.

By 2010, the former Russian oil tycoon Mikhail Khodorkovsky of Yukos was already serving an eight-year jail term for fraud and tax evasion. In the verdict of the second trial on December 27, 2010, he and his business partner Platon Lebedev were found guilty of stealing billions of dollars from their own oil firm, Yukos, and laundering the proceeds between 1998 and 2003. They would have to stay in jail until 2017. Many critics believe the government wants the former tycoon kept behind bars for as long as possible because he challenged the president Vladimir Putin. As a result of this internal uncertainty, foreign investors continue to reassess their opportunities in Russia.

It is often argued that such political events in Russia make it far too dangerous a place to do business. This is not an accurate assessment of the political and economic situation in Russia. The nationalization of key resource-based companies and the perceived inappropriate treatment of some foreign investors undoubtedly reflect an increase in Russian economic nationalism. But it is an easier place to do business than many would suspect. It ranked 51st out of 189 countries in the World Bank "Ease of Doing Business" list in 2015 and 5th in the world in terms of "Enforcing Contracts," one of the key criteria (although this does fit the stereotype that many have of the country).

The reason that Russian authorities will not engage in massive nationalization of foreign assets is that the Russian economy remains dependent on foreign investment. Russia has large supplies of energy resources, but it needs to sell these to foreign consumers. Russia's resources will lose value if they are restricted to Russian consumers. There is as yet no economic evidence that Russia is seeking to be a self-contained, protected, and isolated economy. Instead, it relies upon trade and foreign investment. However, at a time of increased concern over energy security, Moscow has more than once reminded the rest of the world of the power it yields as a major energy supplier. In the past it cut gas to Ukraine after a row between the countries—a move that also affected the supply of gas to western Europe. This then led to armed conflict in the region.

Today Russia is one of the largest economies in the world. It is attracting large amounts of foreign direct investment from members of the European Union, especially Germany and the UK. But the Russian government is thought to have an "extensive shopping list of information" that it is trying to acquire through covert means—on the aerospace industry, defense, and information technology, as well as in politics and diplomacy, and significant cross-border political tensions continue. A long-running dispute that began with the apparent murder of Alexander Litvinenko in London in November 2006 led to diplomats being expelled from both countries. It continued over ten years and in January 2016 the findings of a public enquiry strongly suggested that President Vladimir Putin approved the murder.

Despite this reversion to Cold War diplomacy, it is not anticipated that British investment in Russia will decrease. Nor is it expected that London will stop being a second home for many wealthy Russian businessmen. In short, the British/Russian political difficulties appear to make less of an impact on the economic relationship between the two countries than one would expect.

In contrast to the British case, US political relations with Russia have been more benign. There have been a number of bilateral trade and investment agreements between the two countries. The United States also helped Russia with its application to join the World Trade Organization. In general, US officials encourage US investment in Russia, and also welcome Russian investment in the United States. It is unlikely that the US government will take any action to offset its ongoing concerns about human rights violations in Russia or an increase in Russian economic nationalism.

This long-run analysis of why Russia will remain an integral part of the world economic system does not mean that specific investment projects can escape risk. Russia is still at an early stage of economic development. It is not very long since the Berlin Wall crumbled and the former Soviet Union was opened to market forces. Russia has found it difficult to develop the appropriate market-based institutions to match its acceptance of worldwide capitalism.

Instead, Russia remains an autocratic regime, and foreign investors need to be careful in making commitments where the normal level and contractual arrangements available in the EU and North America do not yet fully exist. However, Russia is making progress in improving its institutional framework. Investors need to adopt a long-term view and should not be thrown off by short-term political developments in Russia. Foreign investors should seek to build lasting personal relationships with Russia's leaders in business and economics.

Websites: www.ford.com; www.imf.org; www.worldbank.org; www.tetrapak.de; www.pepsico.com; www.mcdonalds.com; www.yukos.com; www.telia.se; www.sonera.fi; www.telecominvest.com; http://www.transparency.org/cpi2014; http://www.doingbusiness.org/rankings

Source: Adapted from Alan Rugman, "Is it safe for Americans to invest in Russia?," Kansas City, *Sunday Star*, October 7, 2007; "Cinderella's witching hour," *The Economist*, July 8, 2004; "Court 'freezes' key Yukos assets," *BBC News*, April 19, 2005; Russia Country Profile, news.bbc.co.uk; "Prove my aid is Russian spy, says MP Mike Hancock," *BBC News*, December 5, 2010; "Russia postpones verdict on oil tycoon Khodorkovsky," *BBC News*, December 15, 2010; "Russian ex-tycoon Khodorkovsky appeals against jail term," *BBC News*, December 31, 2010; Transparency International, 2014 Corruption Perceptions Index, http://www.transparency.org/cpi2014; World Bank, Ease of Doing Business survey, 2015, http://www.doingbusiness.org/rankings

1 What type of economic system now exists in Russia: market-driven, centrally determined, or mixed?

2 Would Russia benefit by gaining admission to one of the major economic unions such as the EU? Why?

3 Is Russia a good potential investment for Western business? Explain.

INTRODUCTION

Over the past two decades, many countries have seen a dramatic change in their political systems. In general this has been characterized by a return to democracy for many developing and emerging economies and the development of more mature free market systems. Two significant examples are China and the Russian Federation. Each has a very different central government and governance system, but both have embraced free market economics and reforms are progressing across many fronts.

The movement toward market-driven economies of countries that were once controlled by the former Soviet Union is the result of historical political reforms. For example, Poland, Hungary, the Czech Republic, Latvia, Lithuania, and Estonia, to name but six, have all created market-driven economies. Years ago the former Soviet Union would not have permitted these satellite nations to abandon the command economy advocated by communist ideology and replace it with a free market system. Under Mikhail Gorbachev, however, the Soviet Union revised its political and economic thinking—and things have never been the same since. Although this has proved to be good news for the satellite countries, Russia, as seen in this chapter's Active Learning Case, remains a complex place to do business. Complexity and uncertainty create risk, which MNEs have to constantly monitor.

China has been much more open to FDI, but still walks a fine line between commitment to its political philosophy and the need to attract outside investments. At the turn of the century, former President Jiang Zemin noted that one of the country's primary economic objectives is to increase gross domestic product at an annual rate of 7 percent. During the interview, the president also said that capitalists should be welcomed into the Communist Party.[1] At the same time, China encouraged foreign capital investment in order to ensure that its economic engine continued to function efficiently—this implied a change in its political ideology. One development in this direction was a government announcement that the country could no longer ensure the survival of inefficient companies. Firms now have to be able to compete with MNEs or face the risk of going under. Workers, accustomed to job security, had to accept the fact that they could be laid off and be willing to be retrained in order to find employment in this new, competitive job market.[2] These reforms have come a long way. In 2005 the private economy accounted for nearly 40 percent of the gross product of Shanghai, China's largest urban center.[3] By 2015 it accounted for over 60 percent.

These governmental decrees certainly represent a big change in the way things have been done in China for the past 50 years. The same is true worldwide. International politics and economic integration are altering the way international business is being conducted, and those nations that cannot keep up with these developments are going to find themselves falling further and further behind. Free markets underpin the development of both small and large multinational firms. As political and economic changes take place everywhere, new opportunities open up for MNEs in some countries, just as other countries become more closed or risky because of military conflicts or changes in the political ideology which work against foreign investors. Chapter 15 provides further discussion of political risks and international business. In this chapter we will look at the major current economic and political systems and their impact on the world of international business. We will begin by examining political ideologies and economics.

POLITICAL IDEOLOGIES AND ECONOMICS

Ideology
A set of integrated beliefs, theories, and doctrines that helps to direct the actions of a society

An **ideology** is a set of integrated beliefs, theories, and doctrines that helps direct the actions of a society. Political ideology is almost always intertwined with economic philosophy. For example, the political ideology of the United States is grounded in the Constitution, which guarantees the rights of private property and the freedom of choice. This has helped lay the foundation for US capitalism. A change in this fundamental ideology would alter the economic environment of the United States. The same is true, for example, for China and the former Soviet Union republics. Simply put, the political and economic ideologies of nations help to explain their national economic policies.

Political systems

Democracy
A system of government in which the people, either directly or through their elected officials, decide what is to be done

In the extreme, there are two types of political systems: democracy and totalitarianism. **Democracy** is a system of government in which the people, either directly or through their elected officials, decide what is to be done. Good examples of democratic governments include the United States, Canada, the UK, and Australia. Common features of democratic governments include (1) the right to express opinions freely, (2) election of representatives for limited terms of office, (3) an independent court system that protects individual property and rights, and (4) a relatively non-political bureaucracy and defense infrastructure that ensure the continued operation of the system.

Totalitarianism is a system of government in which one individual or political party maintains complete control and either refuses to recognize other parties or suppresses them. A number of types of totalitarianism currently exist. **Communism** is an economic system in which the government owns all property and makes all decisions regarding the production and distribution of goods and services. To date, all attempts at national communism have led to totalitarianism. The best example of communism is Cuba. Another form of totalitarianism is **theocratic totalitarianism**, in which a religious group exercises total power and represses or persecutes non-orthodox factions. Iran and some of the sheikdoms of the Middle East are good examples. A third form is **secular totalitarianism**, in which the military controls the government and makes decisions that it deems to be in the best interests of the country. Examples of this are communist North Korea and Chile under Pinochet. Political systems typically create the infrastructure within which the economic system functions; in order to change the economic system, there often needs to be a change in the way the country is governed.

Economic systems

The three basic economic systems are capitalism, socialism, and mixed. However, for the purposes of our analysis it is more helpful to classify these systems in terms of resource allocation (market-driven versus centrally determined) and property ownership (private versus public). In a **market-driven economy**, goods and services are allocated on the basis of demand and supply. If consumers express a preference for cellular telephones, more of these products will be offered for sale. If consumers refuse to buy dot-matrix printers, these goods will cease to be offered. The US and EU nations have market-driven economies. In a **centrally determined economy**, goods and services are allocated based on a plan formulated by a committee that decides what is to be offered. In these economies people are able to purchase only what the government determines should be sold. Until recently, Cuba was the best example.

Market-driven economies are characterized by private ownership. Most of the assets of production are in the hands of privately owned companies that compete for market share by offering the best-quality goods and services at competitive prices. Centrally determined economies are characterized by public ownership. Most of the assets of production are in the hands of the state, and production quotas are set for each organization.

In examining economic systems, it is important to remember that, in a strict sense, most nations of the world have **mixed economies**, characterized by a combination of market-driven forces and centrally determined planning. Mixed economies include privately owned commercial entities as well as government-owned commercial entities. Governments in mixed economies typically own the utilities and infrastructural industries—railroads, airlines, shipping lines, and industries considered to be of economic and strategic importance—for instance, petroleum and copper. For example, the United States, a leading proponent of market-driven economic policies, provides healthcare and other social services to many of its citizens through government-regulated agencies, which gives it some aspects of central planning. Other democratic countries with mixed economies include the UK, Sweden, and Germany, all of which have even stronger social welfare systems than the United States.

Another role of government in the economy is that of promoting business and ensuring that local firms gain or maintain dominance in certain market areas. The US and EU governments continually pressure the Chinese to open their doors to foreign MNEs, and the Chinese government is very active in helping its local firms do business with the West.

Totalitarianism
A system of government in which one individual or party maintains complete control and either refuses to recognize other parties or suppresses them

Communism
A political system in which the government owns all property and makes all decisions regarding production and distribution of goods and services

Theocratic totalitarianism
A system of government in which a religious group exercises total power and represses or persecutes non-orthodox factions

Secular totalitarianism
A system of government in which the military controls everything and makes decisions that it deems to be in the best interests of the country

Market-driven economy
An economy in which goods and services are allocated on the basis of consumer demand

Centrally determined economy
An economy in which goods and services are allocated based on a plan formulated by a committee that decides what is to be offered

Mixed economies
Economic systems characterized by a combination of market- and centrally driven planning

As a result of such developments, there has been a blurring of the differences between market-driven and centrally determined economies. The biggest change has been the willingness of the latter to introduce free market concepts. Examples include Russia and other eastern European countries, which began introducing aspects of free enterprise such as allowing people to start their own businesses and to keep any profits that they make.[4] At the same time, however, many market-driven economies are increasingly adopting centrally determined ideas, such as using business–government cooperation to fend off external competitors, or political force to limit the ability of overseas firms to do business in their country. In the United States, for example, the government is frequently being urged to play a more active role in monitoring foreign business practices. On balance, however, we are now seeing a move from central planning to market-driven and mixed economies. The privatization movement that is taking place worldwide provides one prominent example.

GOVERNMENT CONTROL OF ASSETS

Privatization
The process of selling government assets to private buyers

Over the past decade or so, an increasing number of countries have begun moving toward **privatization**, the process of selling government assets to private buyers. To understand the reasons for, and the economic impact of, this process, it is helpful to examine both the potential benefits of government ownership and the advantages of moving to privatization.

Nationalization
A process by which the government takes control of business assets, sometimes with remuneration of the owners and other times without such remuneration

There are six common, and sometimes interdependent, reasons for countries to control business assets—a process known as **nationalization**. These comprise (1) promoting economic development, such as by coordinating the assets of many businesses into one overall master plan; (2) earning profits for the national treasury; (3) preventing companies from going bankrupt and closing their doors; (4) enhancing programs that are in the national interest; (5) increasing the political or economic control of those in power; and (6) ensuring goods and services to all citizens, regardless of their economic status.[5]

Divestiture
(also see *Privatization*)
A process by which a government or business sells assets

The opposite situation, privatization, can take two forms. The most common form is **divestiture**, in which the government sells its assets. The other is **contract management**, in which the government transfers operating responsibility of an industry without transferring the legal title and ownership. The major trend today is toward divestiture.

Contract management
A process by which an organization (such as the government) transfers operating responsibility of an industry without transferring the legal title and ownership

Some of the primary reasons for privatization are: (1) it is more efficient to have the goods and services provided by private business than by government-run companies; (2) a change in the political culture brings about a desire to sell these assets; (3) the company has been making money, and the government feels there is more to be gained by selling now than by holding on; (4) the purchase price can be used to reduce the national debt; (5) the company is losing money, and the government has to assume the losses out of the national treasury; (6) the company needs research and development funds in order to maintain a competitive stance and it is unwilling to make this investment; and (7) international funding agencies are making assistance to the country conditional on a reduction in the size of the government.[6]

Privatization in action

Many nations have privatization programs.[7] These include countries with moderate per capita gross domestic products, such as Argentina, Brazil, Chile, Mexico, and China, as well as economically advanced nations such as the United States, Japan, Germany, and the UK. All feel that their economies can be strengthened through privatization programs.

Greece: third (bailout) time lucky

Greece adopted the euro as its currency in 2001. This began a turbulent monetary relationship with the rest of Europe, leading to a near-exit from the EU in 2015. Even though Greece had been an EU member since 1981, its annual budget deficit was never low enough to satisfy the Eurozone's Maastricht Criteria. Initially, like neighboring Eurozone countries, Greece benefited with low interest rates and consistently received an inflow of investment capital and loans due to the financial power of the euro. However, in 2004, Greece announced that it had under-reported the level of its annual budget deficit in order to pass the Maastricht Criteria. Surprisingly, the EU did not permit any sanctions as other countries were also breaching regulations and it would not have been fair to sanction Greece without sanctioning the rest. Furthermore, the EU was uncertain of what sanctions to apply and overall did not want to weaken the power of the euro.

Despite these lessons Greece's debt continued to rise and in 2009 it became the epicenter of financial concerns in Europe as Greece again announced that it had been underestimating the scale of its budget deficit. The actual budget deficit was 12.9 percent of GDP, over four times the EU's 3 percent limit. Greece was forced to stop borrowing from financial markets and was heading toward bankruptcy. In 2010 it announced an austerity package designed to reassure the lending agencies that is was fiscally responsible and committed to lowering the deficit to just 3 percent of the GDP. Skeptical of this commitment the EU, the European Central Bank and the IMF decided to provide €240 billion as emergency funds in return for greater levels of austerity measures in Greece. This allowed Greece to keep up to date with interest payments on existing debts, while keeping its banks afloat. However, these measures proved to be ineffective in the face of a slowing economy, with tax revenues falling, reducing the government's ability to pay off the debt, and unemployment rising to 25 percent.

Following these events, the European Financial Stability Facility (EFSF) decided to provide Greece with an additional €190 billion to its original bailout in 2011. It was recorded that Greece's debt to GDP ratio had inclined to 175 percent, which was almost three times greater than the EU's limit of 60 percent. In turn, bondholders agreed to a financial haircut, exchanging €77 billion in bonds for debts which were actually worth 75 percent less.

With rioting in the streets, the tension between Greece and other European countries created an opportunity for the leftist Syriza party to win power. It rode a national wave of sentiment that blamed austerity measures forced on Greece by its creditors as the cause of the country's problems, rather than the solution. For a short while this seemed to blind the government and the nation to the harsh financial realities of indebtedness.

In 2015, Greece's debt to GDP ratio was projected to increase to almost 200 percent. In addition, the government missed two deadlines to pay almost €1.6 billion in debt interest on loans it had already received and it became the first Western economy to miss an IMF loan repayment. Greece's public debt was stated as highly unsustainable by the IMF. Furthermore, the IMF suggested this was down to deterioration in the domestic macroeconomic and financial environment due to the closure of the banking system. These poor economic factors resulted in a political debate determining whether Greece would remain in the EU. During mid-2015, with the help of the IMF, the European Stability Mechanism (ESM) decided to bail out Greece again, with a loan of €86 billion. Launched in 2012, the ESM is the Eurozone's only bailout fund, which is financed by all 19 member states and has Germany as its largest ESM contributor (€190 billion).

As the Greek situation has evolved it has proved to be the most important lesson so far on the risks of operating a single currency across independent economies with their own monetary policies and different levels of fiscal discipline.

Websites: www.bbc.co.uk, www.nytimes.com, www.economist.com

Source: Robert Peston, "Third time lucky for Greece?," *BBC Business News*, August 11, 2015; "Greece debt crisis: bailout deal at a glance," *BBC Business News*, July 13, 2015; "Greece debt crisis: IMF attacks EU over bailout terms," *BBC Business News*, July 15, 2015; "Greece's debt crisis explained", International Business, *New York Times*, November 9, 2015; "Greece and the euro: a third bailout gets the green light," *The Economist*, August 15, 2015.

In the case of Argentina, for example, the government has now ended the nation's phone monopoly and opened up the $10 billion market to outside investors. Previously the two telephone companies that monopolized all long-distance and local phone services had their territories firmly established, and neither could compete with the other. Now they can. Moreover, other telephone companies also have licenses to operate throughout the country. The Argentinean government believes that, as a result of privatization in this industry, competition will increase, phone rates will drop, and service will increase sharply.[8]

In the case of the UK, privatization and deregulation proved at one time to be a national boon, but also hugely contentious. Companies like British Telecommunications (now BT) and the Royal Mail significantly downsized their operations so as to increase their competitiveness and profitability. Critics said that privatization and deregulation were hurting the economy. Supporters pointed to the fact that many of the workers who were laid off began finding jobs with small and entrepreneurial telecoms and delivery firms that were springing up throughout the country. At the same time, there was an influx of large foreign competitors such as AT&T and AB L. M. Ericsson, in telecoms, which hired thousands of people. As a result, the number of jobs in the UK's telecoms industry increased, while prices decreased and service improved sharply.[9]

Another major group of nations turning to privatization is Russia and the eastern European countries. At the grassroots in Russia, a market economy has begun to evolve. Despite the lack of national or local laws to guide them, hundreds of small factories and service businesses are now privatizing themselves, and enterprises are pushing ahead with Russian-style versions of leveraged buyouts, employee stock ownership plans, and private spin-offs. Many are also taking their old, outmoded operations and modernizing them. A good example is the Vologda Textile Enterprise Company. By significantly reducing its workforce and rebuilding the looms, the firm has found that it can sell all of the textiles it produces to buyers in the EU.[10]

Privatization is not always a popular idea, and it is often part of election debates. Yet governments continue to assess the benefits of privatization against those of state ownership. Mexico and Japan provide two recent examples. In 2005 the Mexican government announced that it would privatize its two national airlines, Aeroméxico and Mexicana, in the hope that it could provide cheaper service and compete with low-cost services from the United States.[11] Despite opposition from civil servants and some political parties, Japan Post has been the focus of a slow privatization process for many years.[12]

GOVERNMENT–BUSINESS COOPERATION

The fact that governments are privatizing assets does not mean they are distancing themselves from business firms. Both Japan and the EU have seen a large amount of business–government cooperation that has been extremely beneficial to the business sector in these countries.

Japan and EU assistance

Ministry of Economy, Trade and Industry (METI)
A Japanese ministry charged with providing information about foreign markets and with encouraging investment in select industries and, in the process, helping to direct the economy. From the post-war period to 2001 it was known as the Ministry of International Trade and Industry (MITI)

After World War II, the Japanese government began formulating plans for regenerating its economy. In this vein, it gave responsibility for implementing the country's trade and industrial policy to the Ministry of International Trade and Industry (MITI). MITI ran Japanese industrial policy, funding research and directing investment. In 2001, its role was taken over by the newly created **Ministry of Economy, Trade and Industry (METI)**. The initial focus of the ministry was to provide protection to Japanese companies and to assist in marketing the products of four major industries: electric power, steel, shipbuilding, and fertilizers. Incentives were created to encourage investment in these industries and to help firms export their products. In recent years, METI's focus has been on targeting less energy-intensive industries for Japanese investment and growth. Prime examples include computers and chemicals, where it works cooperatively with Japanese businesses to help ensure success. METI's approach is less proactive ("command and control") and more cooperative.

Governments in the EU have also been very helpful in promoting businesses. One way has been to fund research consortia through research and development (R&D) support. One of the research programs that have been helped by EU governments is Research on Advanced Communications in Europe (RACE). Since the late 1980s, RACE has received billions of euros of government money to support its efforts in developing an integrated broadband telecommunications network. Another recipient of government largesse is the European Strategic Program for R&D in Information Technology (ESPRIT II). This consortium has engaged in hundreds of projects dealing with such high-tech areas as information technologies, microelectronics, and computer-integrated manufacturing. Perhaps the best-known R&D consortium is EUREKA, a pan-European group whose main objective is to create closer cooperation between private companies and research institutes in the field of advanced technologies for the purpose of exploiting commercial opportunities. The projects that are funded bring together companies throughout the EU and involve not only large firms but also small and medium-sized enterprises. Unlike many research consortia, however, EUREKA focuses on projects whose research is now ready to be applied.[13] (See the case **International Business Strategy in Action: Boeing versus Airbus** in Chapter 6 for a closer look at government-established consortia.)

US competitiveness

The results of such governmental efforts have not been lost on Washington, which has long recognized the value of an industrial policy that provides benefits similar to those offered by METI and EUREKA. As long ago as 1990, a special White House panel of experts from industry, academia, and the government released a list of 22 technologies that it deemed essential to US national defense and economic prosperity. Including composite materials, flexible computer-integrated manufacturing, and high-definition electronic displays, the list was intended to guide the Critical Technologies Institute, created by Congress in 1990 to conduct long-range strategic planning and to work closely with the private sector in developing important technologies.

Over the past two decades in particular, the US government has been active in supporting research consortia to help underwrite some of the costs associated with new technology development. A good example is Sematech, a consortium of 14 semiconductor manufacturing companies, which once received $100 million a year in subsidies from the US government to help shore up the chip-making equipment industry. By the mid-1990s these manufacturers were doing so well that Sematech's board voted to end federal funding, and the group is now funded entirely by private money.[14] Another consortium that has received government assistance is the National Center for Manufacturing Sciences, which has provided a host of important technology breakthroughs, including a method for hardening cutting tools by coating them with diamond film. A third has been the Microelectronics and Computer Technology Corporation, which has worked on advanced computing, software, and computer-aided design.

In the past, US administrations have supported research efforts that promoted industrial competitiveness and technological leadership. This often took one of two paths: (1) the funding of military research that could then be used to create commercially useful products; or (2) the direct funding of research efforts by US firms. The technology policy of the Obama administration has been to continue maintaining a strong focus on technology and progress has been made in the areas of: cybersecurity and internet policy; modernizing patent systems; transforming technology "from lab to market"; advanced manufacturing robotics; and open data initiatives.

Active learning check

1 **What type of economic system now exists in Russia: market-driven, centrally determined, or mixed?**

A mixed system currently exists. The country is moving away from a centrally determined economy, but there is a long way to go. As can be seen from the information in the case, the transition is causing a great deal of economic upheaval. This may even result in a regression toward some of the previously employed, centrally determined decision making. However, the country is not going to go back to the old way of doing things because it has too much committed to its current course of action. In particular, any further IMF loans or assistance from the United States, Japan, or the EU will depend on how well the country is holding the line and trying to make its market-driven economy work. So a mixed economic system will remain in place; in fact, this is really the only path the Russians can take in rescuing their economy.

ECONOMIC INTEGRATION

Economic integration
The establishment of transnational rules and regulations that enhance economic trade and cooperation among countries

Economic integration is the establishment of transnational rules and regulations that enhance economic trade and cooperation among countries. At one extreme, economic integration would result in one worldwide free trade market in which all nations had a common currency and could export anything they wanted to any other nation. At the other extreme would be a total lack of economic integration, in which nations were self-sufficient and did not trade with anyone. (The theory of these polar extremes will be discussed in Chapter 6.)

The concept of economic integration is attractive, but there are many implementation problems. In particular, it requires that the participants agree to surrender some of their national sovereignty, such as the authority to set tariffs and quotas. For example, if the United States and the EU agree to allow free trade of agricultural products, neither can restrict the other's right to export these commodities. So although free trade may lead to lower prices, those who are unwilling to give up the right to control goods being imported into their country may well be opposed to it.

A number of regional economic efforts have been undertaken over the past 30 years to promote varying degrees of economic integration. The most successful has been the EU, although less developed countries (LDCs) have also made integration efforts.

Trade creation and trade diversion

Before examining economic integration in more depth, it is important to realize that the agreement of countries to integrate their economies will bring about a shift in business activity. This shift can result in trade creation as well as trade diversion.

Trade creation
A process in which members of an economic integration group begin to focus their efforts on those goods and services for which they have a comparative advantage and start trading more extensively with each other

Trade creation occurs when members of an economic integration group begin focusing their efforts on those goods and services for which they have a comparative advantage and start trading more extensively with each other. For example, the United States and Mexico have an agreement that allows cars to be assembled in Mexico and shipped to the United States. As a result, Mexico, a low-cost producer, supplies a large number of vehicles sold in the United States, and both countries prosper as a result.

Trade creation results in efficient, low-cost producers in member countries gaining market share from high-cost member producers, as well as generating increased exports. In fact, a growing number of US companies have moved some of their operations to Mexico or hired Mexican firms to be their suppliers because this is a more efficient approach than making the goods in the United States. And when efficient regional producers are able to offer lower-price and higher-quality output than their competitors, trade creation results.

Trade diversion
Occurs when members of an economic integration group decrease their trade with non-member countries in favor of trade with each other

Trade diversion occurs when members of an economic integration group decrease their trade with non-member countries in favor of trade with each other. One common reason is that the removal of trade barriers among member countries makes it less expensive to buy from companies within the group, and the continuation of trade barriers with non-member countries makes it more difficult for the latter to compete. Thus, trade diversion can lead to the loss of production and exports from more efficient non-member countries to less efficient member countries that are being protected by tariffs or other barriers. Quite obviously, the creation of economic integration groups is beneficial only if trade creation exceeds trade diversion. Otherwise, the economic union impedes international trade.

Levels of economic integration

There are five levels of economic integration, which extend from simple economic trade arrangements to full political integration characterized by a single government. The following examines each of these levels, beginning with the simplest.

Free trade area

Free trade area
An economic integration arrangement in which barriers to trade (such as tariffs) among member countries are removed

A **free trade area** is an economic integration arrangement in which barriers to trade (such as tariffs) among member countries are removed. Under this arrangement, each participant will seek to gain by specializing in the production of those goods and services for which it has a comparative advantage and importing those goods and services for which it has a comparative disadvantage.

North American Free Trade Agreement (NAFTA)
A regional free trade agreement among Canada, the United States, and Mexico

One of the best-known free trade areas is the **North American Free Trade Agreement (NAFTA)**, which currently consists of Canada, the United States, and Mexico. NAFTA covers a North American economy with a combined output of US$17.0 trillion in 2014.[15] The United States and Canada created this free trade area with the US–Canadian Free Trade Agreement of 1989, and the arrangement has now been expanded to include Mexico.[16] While trade diversion can occur under free trade arrangements, NAFTA has led to a great amount of trade creation. In fact, trade among the three members of NAFTA is over $1 trillion annually![17]

Customs union

Customs union
A form of economic integration in which all tariffs between member countries are eliminated and a common trade policy toward non-member countries is established

A **customs union** is a form of economic integration in which all tariffs between member countries are eliminated and a common trade policy toward non-member countries is established. This policy often results in a uniform external tariff structure. Under this arrangement, a country outside the union will face the same tariff on exports to any member country receiving the goods.

Under a customs union, member countries cede some of the control of their economic policies to the group at large. None of the regional integration groups in existence today has been formed for the purpose of creating a customs union; instead, many of them have sought greater integration in the form of a common market or economic union. However, because of the difficulty of attaining this high degree of integration, some countries have effectively settled for a customs union. The Andean Community, which will be discussed shortly, is an example.

Common market

Common market
A form of economic integration characterized by the elimination of trade barriers among member nations, a common external trade policy, and mobility of factors of production among member countries

A **common market** is a form of economic integration characterized by (1) no barriers to trade among member nations, (2) a common external trade policy, and (3) mobility of factors of production among member countries. A common market allows reallocation of production resources, such as capital, labor, and technology, based on the theory of comparative advantage. Although this may be economically disadvantageous to industries or specific businesses in some member countries, in theory it should lead to the efficient delivery of goods and services to all member countries. The best example of a successful common market is the EU, although this group has now progressed beyond a common market and is now focusing on political and financial integration.

Economic union

Economic union
A form of economic integration characterized by free movement of goods, services, and factors of production among member countries and full integration of economic policies

An **economic union** is a deep form of economic integration and is characterized by free movement of goods, services, and factors of production among member countries and full integration of economic policies. An economic union (1) unifies monetary and fiscal policy among the member nations, including the same tax rates, and (2) has a common currency (or a permanently fixed exchange rate among currencies). Additionally, most of the national economic policies of the individual countries are ceded to the group at large. There are no true economic unions in the world, but the creation of a single currency, the euro, certainly moves the EU in this direction.

Political union

Political union
An economic union in which there is full economic integration, unification of economic policies, and a single government

A **political union** goes beyond full economic integration to encompass a single government. This occurs only when countries give up their individual national powers to be united and led by one government. One successful example is the United States, which combined independent states into a political union. The EU is now also on its way to becoming a political union. The European Parliament, for example, is directly elected by citizens of the EU countries, and its Council of Ministers, which is the decision-making body of the EU, is made up of government ministers from each EU country.

Economic integration: an overall perspective

Before concluding our discussion of levels of economic integration, four points merit consideration. First, a country does not need to pursue economic integration by starting with a free trade area and then working up to a common market or an economic union. For example, the UK was a member of a free trade area before deciding to leave and enter the EU. Many years later, in 2016 the country is considering whether to leave the EU. Simply stated, countries will choose the appropriate level of economic integration based on their political and economic needs.

Second, economic integration in the form of free trade typically results in a winning situation for all group members, since each member can specialize in those goods and services it makes most efficiently and rely on others in the group to provide the remainder. However, when a bloc of countries imposes a tariff on non-members, this often results in a win–lose situation. Those outside the bloc face tariffs, are thus less competitive with group member companies, and lose market share and revenue within the bloc. Among group members, however, increased competition often results in greater efficiency, lower prices, and increased exports to non-member markets.

Internal economies of scale
Efficiencies brought about by lower production costs and other savings within a firm

Third, and complementary to the above, bloc members often find that their businesses are able to achieve **internal economies of scale** brought about by lower production costs and other savings. So if a company in France was only moderately efficient when producing 1,000 units a week for the French market, it is now highly efficient producing 4,000 units a week for countries throughout the EU. The elimination of tariffs and trade barriers and the opening up of new geographic markets allow the company to increase production efficiency. In addition, since factors of production in a common market are allowed to flow

External economies of scale
Efficiencies brought about by access to cheaper capital, highly skilled labor, and superior technology

freely across borders, the firm may also achieve **external economies of scale** brought about by access to low-cost capital, more highly skilled labor, and superior technology. In short, in-group companies can draw on resources in member countries to help increase efficiency.

Finally, in the short run, some bloc countries may suffer because other member countries are able to achieve greater efficiency and thus dominate certain industries and markets in the bloc. The adjustment period may last as long as a decade as these less efficient countries scramble to improve their technologies, retrain their workforces, and redirect their economies to markets in the bloc where they can gain and sustain an advantage vis-à-vis other members. In the long run, however, economic integration results in all bloc countries becoming much more efficient and competitive.

Non-governmental organizations (NGOs)
Private sector groups that act to advance diverse social interests (see also *Civil society*)

Despite the logic of free trade and economic integration, many **non-governmental organizations (NGOs)** criticize MNEs and international institutions. We now discuss these issues. See also the case **International Business Strategy in Action: Non-governmental organizations and political power**.

Ethics, environment, MNEs, and the civil society

Many would argue that the real birth of modern-day civil society movements was in December 1999, when a coalition of NGOs and labor unions organized protests in Seattle that turned into riots, which hindered the launch of another round of the WTO. In July 2001, the violent riots in Genoa at the G7 Summit were another example of the work of some anti-globalization activists, mainly NGOs, attempting to prevent negotiations by world leaders.

Civil society
A group of individuals, organizations, and institutions that act outside the government and the market to advance a diverse set of interests

The **civil society** is a group of individuals, organizations, and institutions that act outside the government and the market to advance a diverse set of interests, including opposition to global business. Demonstrations against trade and investment agreements are mainly composed of environmentalists, anti-poverty campaigners, trade unionists, and anti-capitalists that are either part of an NGO or trade union, or simply individuals that share their views.[18] The lack of a common front across these organizations meant that, while some protestors are chanting and throwing roses, others are throwing rocks and charging at the police. The more extremist groups would like to see an end to multinationals and international trade. More moderate demonstrators would like a transformation in the rules of trade with less developed nations, debt forgiveness, and better labor and environmental standards.[19] Protestors also have different agendas. Trade unionists from developed countries are concerned about the alleged loss of jobs due to globalization, whereas human rights NGOs are much more concerned with the situation of workers in less industrialized nations.

The success of the NGOs in criticizing businesses, especially multinational enterprises (MNEs), builds on less spectacular but consistent progress in influencing the environmental agenda of international organizations. The first notable success of environmental NGOs occurred in NAFTA in 1993 when the Clinton administration inserted two side agreements on environment and labor after the first Bush administration had successfully negotiated NAFTA over the 1990–2 period.

The UNCED Rio Summit of 1992 reflected the agenda of environmental NGOs, leading to an agreement that sets commitments but which governments have been unable to deliver on. The Kyoto Summit in 1997 resulted in standards for reduction of greenhouse gas emissions; again, however, important economies—most notably the United States—would not meet them because of the economic and political costs of doing so.

Since then the activities of NGOs and civil society organizations (CSOs) more generally have grown and they have matured as institutions which government agencies and companies need to engage with. The 2015 United Nations Summit of NGOs saw a large number from a wide variety of thematic associations discussing their shared interests. Coalitions of NGOs have also evolved, like EURODAD.[20] EURODAD is the European Network on Debt and Development, a network of 54 NGOs from 17 European countries with a shared interest in debt, development finance, and poverty reduction. It has recently focused on "multilateral debt cancelation, debt sustainability, aid quality, conditionality and harmonization, and export credit debts."[21]

INTERNATIONAL BUSINESS STRATEGY IN ACTION

Non-governmental organizations and political power

When the topic of politics in the international business arena is discussed, one is likely to hear about such things as the impact of the government on international trade and the regulation of multinational enterprises (MNEs). In recent years another topic that has become more popular is the role of non-governmental organizations (NGOs) that have been gaining an increasing amount of political power.

An NGO is a non-profit organization run by volunteers with a specific mandate at a local, national, or international level. As such, NGOs take a number of different forms. Some are very large, such as the environmental group Greenpeace, the World Wildlife Fund (WWF), and Amnesty International, whereas others are smaller and less well known. NGOs' positions on international trade issues are as diverse as their mandates. For example, Oxfam, whose mandate is the long-term alleviation of poverty, suffering, and injustice, does not oppose trade itself. Indeed, it considers "fair trade" a means to achieve development in poorer countries and promotes other organizations that engage in this type of trade. The Institute for Leadership Development actively seeks to promote trade and the development of entrepreneurial skills in poorer countries. The US NGO Consumers for World Trade points out that protectionism is equivalent to a hidden tax and actively lobbies for free trade. Environmental and animal rights NGOs, on the other hand, lobby their governments and international bodies for trade rules that protect the natural environment. For example, in December 1997 at the Kyoto Summit, NGOs were instrumental in getting standards for the reduction of greenhouse gas emissions put into the agreement, even though the United States and other major economic powers refused to accept this standard because the technology was not available and the standard could not be met.

Protectionist or anti-trade NGOs often grab the headlines. For example, the American Farm Bureau seeks to improve the financial well-being and quality of life for farmers and ranchers in the United States and opposes government policies to liberalize agricultural trade by reducing subsidies to US farmers. Yet other NGOs are more generally opposed to

free trade and investment. In the 1997–8 period, for example, NGOs were extremely effective in defeating the Multilateral Agreement on Investment (MAI). The MAI was designed to make it illegal for signatory states to discriminate against foreign investors and to liberalize rules governing foreign domestic investment among the members of the Organization for Economic Cooperation and Development. NGOs contributed to riots in Seattle in December 1999 and violent clashes with the police in Genoa in July 2001. The NGOs influenced the Clinton administration to add two side agreements to NAFTA: setting up an environmental body in Montreal and a labor standard body in Dallas. In a nutshell, these NGOs managed to work outside the NAFTA agreement to get provisions incorporated into the overall contract. In the process, they showed that NGOs were becoming an important force in the international political arena.

Notwithstanding the variety of views emanating from NGOs, a select group is portraying MNEs as big, bad, and ugly. But is it an accurate portrayal? Starbucks, for instance, was heavily criticized for not selling Fairtrade coffee, yet it directly paid farmers a price higher than that received by farmers involved in fair trading. Being the best-known brand in North America was enough to make it the target of NGOs. In general, MNEs improve the well-being of workers across the world while manufacturing goods and providing services that improve the quality of life of consumers around the world. Given their rise in popularity over the last five years, NGOs are likely to be the focus of continuing interest among both international business analysts and local voters.

Websites: www.greenpeace.org; www.oxfam.org; www.fb.org; www.cwt.org; www.starbucks.com; www.oecd.org

Sources: James Harding, "Activists plan ocean-borne protests for WTO meeting," *Financial Times*, September 11, 2001, p. 1; Edward M. Graham, *Fighting the Wrong Enemy: Antiglobal Activists and Multinational Enterprises* (Washington, DC: Institute for International Economics, 2000); Alan M. Rugman, *The End of Globalization* (London: Random House, 2000); Sylvia Ostry, "The multilateral trading system," in Alan M. Rugman and Thomas Brewer (eds.), *The Oxford Handbook of International Business* (Oxford: Oxford University Press, 2000), pp. 232–58; Robert Weissman, "Why we protest," *Washington Post*, September 10, 2003.

These recent events show that the gulf between the agendas of NGOs and corporations as the economic drivers of global business is narrowing. There is no doubt that important conflicts of interest exist.[22] This is related to a traditional divide between the redistribution and equity concerns of NGOs and the economic and efficiency issues that drive business. Democratic governments in Western economies have incorporated these dual concerns in their political platforms, and, at least as part of a broader political package, voters have some say through the electoral process.

Complementary to the NGOs' perspective on international trade and investment is the intellectual failure of academic theory, in which the twin basic paradigms of economics and politics are found to develop explanations of today's global economy and the nature of foreign direct investment (FDI). In economics, the traditional efficiency-based neo-classical paradigm (with its associated theory of comparative advantages and the overall country gains from free trade) is unsuitable as an explanation of FDI. Despite the efforts by international business writers over the last 30 years to develop a modern theory of the MNE, most economists are unable to accept this explanation of the reasons for FDI. As a consequence, the GATT and WTO have developed institutional frameworks to deal with the "shallow" integration of tariff cuts, but have failed to deal with the "deep" integration of FDI.

Related to the out-of-date economics paradigm of free trade is the political science focus on the nation-state. Despite minor modifications to nation-state paradigms, such as to incorporate subnational units in decision making, there is a limited buy-in to the alternative international political economy (IPE) viewpoint. Indeed, there is another unfortunate parallel between economics and political science in that both sets of work on the role and power of the MNE have failed to change the out-of-date thinking of the majority of academics, despite the abundant evidence of the relevance of MNEs and the global economic and political systems of today. The NGOs have slipped into this vacuum with their view of MNEs as big, bad, and ugly. The NGO thinking is now more influential with governments in North America and Europe than is the work of serious academic scholars working on MNEs.[23]

The issue here is one of process. There is an "administrative heritage" of ideas. Today's media are poorly trained in economics, politics, and international business. Those few who have any training are usually victims of the out-of-date paradigms of traditional economics and political science, which cannot explain FDI and the MNEs. The MBAs of business schools, who are now exposed to the new thinking on MNEs, are in business rather than the media. The professional intermediaries, such as management consultants, focus on their business or government clients rather than the media, and their very skills of confidential advice and in-house retraining make them poor advocates compared to the NGOs. Finally, the civil service is basically useless in dealing publicly with anti-trade NGOs as bureaucrats attempt to support and influence ministers and other officials rather than entering into the public forum. This institutional failure of academics, consultants, and bureaucrats to prepare a credible case for initiatives such as the Multilateral Agreement on Investment (MAI) and be able to debate it publicly leaves the field open to NGOs.

During negotiations for the MAI, Canadian anti-globalization activists equated NAFTA's Chapter 11 provisions with investor protection mechanisms under MAI. Chapter 11 allows a company to sue national governments in trade matters that contravene NAFTA's principles. The provision had been used by Ethyl, a US company, to overturn a Canadian import ban on MMT, a gasoline additive that was deemed a health hazard. The Canadian Minister of the Environment could have averted litigation by banning the production of MMT as an environmental hazard, an internal matter subject to national law, but she ignored the advice of her bureaucrats and applied trade measures that came under the NAFTA. Several subsequent NAFTA Chapter 11 cases have been resolved on technical grounds with no loss of sovereignty to host nations in their environmental policies. The MAI had similar provisions to protect investors, which led to it being labeled a "NAFTA on steroids" by anti-globalization activists.

The late Edward Graham has exploded the myth that anti-global activists defeated the MAI.[24] Graham concludes that the draft MAI was a very weak document. In fact, the investment liberalization being negotiated in the MAI was so weak that the US business community had stopped supporting it long before anti-global activists started to protest against it in Paris. There was also a lack of leadership by the US government, tepid support in the EU, and eventually hostility to the MAI by the French government of Lionel Jospin, who was dependent on left-wing "green" support in his political coalition.

Perhaps what the MMT case really illustrates is the "dialog of the deaf" taking place between trade experts and activists. The latter used the MMT case in a general assault on the MAI and on subsequent international trade and investment liberalization initiatives at the WTO and G7 Summits. Graham argues that, as a consequence, the environmental NGOs missed the boat. He states that trade negotiators were open and willing to incorporate environmental concerns into the MAI but that violent opposition to it has now closed the window for cooperation between NGOs and governments.

Any more Seattles and Genoas, with the attendant violence, however, will probably alienate the general public from the anti-capitalist agenda of the more extreme anti-global activists. This small and over-publicized section of the NGO movement, with its apparent opposition to reforming global governance mechanisms, continues to protest violently against MNEs. Eventually, the most serious NGOs, such as WWF and Oxfam, must disassociate themselves from these violent activists in order to push forward a more sensible cooperative reformist agenda for civil society.

The European Union (EU)

After World War II, Europe needed to be rebuilt and economic cooperation among these countries was paramount. One of the earliest and most successful cooperative endeavors was the 1952 creation of the **European Coal and Steel Community (ECSC)** for the purpose of creating a common market that would revitalize the efficiency and competitiveness of these industries. Six countries (Belgium, France, Italy, Luxembourg, the Netherlands, and West Germany) created the ECSC, and its success set the stage for the creation of what would eventually become the European Union.

Formation

The foundation of the European Union was laid in 1957 by the Treaty of Rome. The six nations that created the ECSC were the original founders of what was initially called the European Economic Community (EEC) and later the European Community (EC). By 1991 six other nations had joined the EC (the UK, Denmark, Greece, Ireland, Portugal, and Spain)—and in 1995 with the admission of Austria, Finland, and Sweden, the EC was renamed the **European Union**. In 2004, ten new members joined the EU: Cyprus, the Czech Republic, Estonia, Hungary, Latvia, Lithuania, Malta, Poland, Slovakia, and Slovenia. In 2007 Bulgaria and Romania joined, followed much later by Croatia in 2013. Today the EU is a major economic group, and a growing number of countries have applied for admission. The main provisions of the founding treaty of 1957 were as follows:

1 Formation of a free trade area among the members would be brought about by the gradual elimination of tariffs, quotas, and other trade barriers.

2 Barriers to the movement of labor, capital, and business enterprises would eventually be removed.

European Coal and Steel Community (ECSC)

A community formed in 1952 by Belgium, France, Italy, Luxembourg, the Netherlands, and West Germany for the purpose of creating a common market that would revitalize the efficiency and competitiveness of the coal and steel industries in those countries

European Union (EU)

A treaty-based institutional framework that manages economic and political cooperation among its 28 member states: Austria, Belgium, Bulgaria, Croatia, Cyprus, the Czech Republic, Denmark, Estonia, France, Finland, Germany, Greece, Hungary, Ireland, Italy, Latvia, Lithuania, Luxembourg, Malta, the Netherlands, Poland, Portugal, Romania, Slovakia, Slovenia, Spain, Sweden, and the UK

3 Common agricultural policies would be adopted.

4 An investment fund to channel capital from the more advanced regions of the bloc to the less advanced regions would be created.

5 A customs union characterized by a uniform tariff schedule applicable to imports from the rest of the world would be created.

Some of the countries that were not members of the initial EEC felt that the objectives of this group went beyond what they were willing to do, but they did feel that a free trade agreement would be good for their own economies. As a result, these nations formed the **European Free Trade Association (EFTA)**, whose primary goal was to dismantle trade barriers among its members. Austria, Denmark, Norway, Portugal, Sweden, Switzerland, and the UK were the founding members. In time the distinctions between EFTA and the EC blurred, however, and some of the members (Austria, Denmark, Portugal, Sweden, and the UK) eventually joined the EC. Moreover, in 1992 EFTA signed a treaty that formally gives its members an economic association with the EU. Today EFTA members include Iceland, Liechtenstein, Norway, and Switzerland.

European Free Trade Association (EFTA)
A free trade area currently consisting of Iceland, Liechtenstein, Norway, and Switzerland; past members included the UK (before it joined the EU).

Growth and challenges

Over the years, the EU has made vigorous headways in pursuit of its objectives. For example, during the 1970s formal barriers to the free flow of labor and capital were gradually dismantled. The **Single European Act (SEA)**, which effectively prevents a country from vetoing any EU decision it deems to be in conflict with its vital interests, was enacted in the 1980s. In the past this veto power had often been used by EU members to protect their respective economic advantages, making it difficult for the group to make decisions.

Single European Act (SEA)
An Act passed by the EU that contains many measures to further integrate the member states, along economic and political dimensions, and that allows the Council of Ministers to pass most proposals by a majority vote, in contrast to the unanimous vote that was needed previously

Other major breakthroughs are occurring in the political and financial areas. With the EC 1992 measures, the EU transformed itself into a political, economic, and monetary superpower that can speak with one powerful voice about everything from interest rates to defense. By moving in this direction, the EU political leaders negotiated and implemented a method for ratifying two new treaties that would extend the community's powers from their present largely economic role to foreign and security policy and monetary affairs and, eventually, to defense.[25] The EU's integration includes consolidation of its financial and monetary system to facilitate the free flow of capital. The single European currency, the euro, was introduced to replace most national currencies. Closely linked to this was the establishment of a central European bank that regulates the money supply and is thus able to stabilize interest rates throughout the EU. The effect of these actions may well be the creation of a "United States of Europe."

However, the EU still faces a number of problems. One general disagreement among the members relates to the relationship that should exist between the community and the rest of the world. This has recently challenged the unity of EU members as they faced the difficult challenge of overwhelming volumes of inward migrants, in 2015. This influx was partly fueled by political upheavals in the Middle East and specifically Syria, creating unprecedented levels of refugees which EU member states had an ethical and humanitarian obligation to accept. These came alongside a growing flow of economic migrants, looking for better employment opportunities and to gain access to state-subsidized housing, health, and welfare benefits. Sharing the costs of dealing with migrants, across a set of countries with very different levels of resources for coping with the influx, tested the EU concord to its limits.

Another problem is the protection that countries give to their own industries, which is in direct contrast to the spirit of EU rules. A related area is the community's agriculture policies, which provide subsidies and rebates to farmers and have resulted in charges of unfair trade practices. There is also disagreement among the members regarding the amount of protection that poorer countries should be given before all trade barriers are dismantled. The Greek debt crisis in 2015 was related to this dilemma (see the case **International Business Strategy in Action: Greece**, above) and illustrates the major challenges of operating a monetary union with a single currency.

Even if all its goals have not been fully realized, the EU arguably remains the most powerful economic coalition in the international arena. Taken as a whole, it has 7 percent of the world's population, but is the largest economy and the largest participant in global trade, accounting for about 20 percent of global imports and exports. About two-thirds of EU countries' trade is with other EU member countries.

Organization

The major institutions managing the EU are: the European Council, the Council of the European Union, the European Commission, the European Parliament, the Court of Justice, and the Court of Auditors (see Figure 4.1). A brief description of each of these is set out below, but a full range of current facts and figures are at www.europa.eu

The **European Council** is composed of the heads of state of each EU member country as well as the president of the European Commission. The Council meets at least twice a year, and each head of state is typically accompanied to these meetings by a foreign minister. The purpose of the meetings is to resolve major policy issues and to set policy direction.

The **Council of the European Union** is the major policy decision-making body of the EU. Decisions are conducted by the relevant ministers from each country. If the environment is on the agenda, the 28 environment ministers from each EU country will compose the council. This body is responsible for all final EU decisions, except for the budget.

The **European Commission** currently has 28 members who are chosen by agreement of the member governments, each representing one country in the EU. The Commission, the executive branch of the EU, handles a great deal of the technical work associated with preparing decisions and regulations. The group is responsible for drafting legislation for proposal to the Council of the European Union, overseeing the implementation of EU policies, and carrying out studies on key policy issues.

The **European Parliament** currently has 751 members; 750 elected directly by the voters in each member country and one EU President. The Parliament serves as a watchdog on EU expenditures in addition to evaluating other decisions of the Council. More recently, the power of the Parliament has been expanded; it now has the right to vote on the appointment of commissioners as well as to veto matters related to the EU budget and single-market legislation.

European Council
Composed of the heads of state of each EU member country as well as the president of the European Commission. Meetings of the Council take place at least twice a year and their purpose is to resolve major policy issues and to set policy direction

Council of the European Union
The major policy decision-making body of the EU; it consists of one minister from each of the 28 member states and is one of four major institutions of the EU

European Commission
A 28-member group chosen by agreement of member governments of the EU; the Commission is the executive branch of the EU

European Parliament
A group of 750 representatives elected directly by voters in each member country of the EU plus the EU President; the Parliament serves as a watchdog on EU expenditures

Figure 4.1 The European Union's institutions

Court of Justice
A court that has one judge appointed from each EU member country; this court serves as the official interpreter of EU law

The **Court of Justice** has one judge appointed from each EU member country and serves as the official interpreter of EU law. In most cases this requires the judges to rule on the meaning or application of the Treaty of Rome, based on the actions of member countries, companies, and individuals. The Court of Justice has supremacy over national law, and as a result it is increasingly being used as a court of appeal over national decisions.

Court of Auditors
A court that has one judge appointed from each EU member country; this court monitors the financial aspects of the union

The **Court of Auditors** has one judge appointed from each EU member country and is responsible for ensuring that revenues and expenditures are implemented lawfully in accordance to the budget.

The future

The EU is a powerful economic union. Empirical studies show that the community has created much more trade than it has diverted from the rest of the world. Moreover, this market has a greater combined gross domestic product than either of the two other major triad markets: North America and industrialized Asia. At the same time it is likely that EU-generated projects will offer major competition to other worldwide industries. For example, Airbus, as will be seen in Chapter 6, is now a major force in the world aircraft manufacturing industry. Quite clearly, the EU promises tremendous economic gains for member countries.

Other examples of economic integration

While the EU is the most successful economic union, there are a host of others. The following briefly examines four of these.

Andean Community

Andean Community
An economic union consisting of Bolivia, Colombia, Ecuador, and Peru

The **Andean Community** is a customs union that was formed in 1969 with the signing of the Andean Pact by Bolivia, Chile, Colombia, Ecuador, and Peru. Venezuela was a member from 1973 to 2006, and Chile has withdrawn but remains an associate member country (www.comunidadandina.org). The union is also known as Comunidad Andina (CAN) or Andean Community (Ancom). The original objectives of the CAN countries were to integrate themselves economically, to reduce internal tariffs, to create a common external tariff, and to offer special concessions to the two smallest members, Bolivia and Ecuador. Initial restrictions that curtailed foreign investment led to Chile leaving the union. These restrictions have now been removed at the CAN level, but the legislation yields to individual national governments on the matter. Except for Peru, which is slowly removing its tariffs, the Andean Community is a customs union in which goods can travel free of duty among member states.

Mercosur

Mercosur is a free trade group that was formed by Argentina and Brazil in 1988 to promote economic cooperation. Today the group has been expanded to include Venezuela, Paraguay, and Uruguay, with Chile, Colombia, Ecuador, and Peru as associate members. In 2012 and 2015 Bolivia also signed the Accession Protocol and its membership status is "in accession process."

The members agreed to a five-year program under which they hoped to perfect their free trade area and move toward a full customs union. However, things have not worked out as planned with group members unable to agree on a common agenda. For example, Argentina imposed tariffs on Brazilian televisions, shoes, and other goods; Brazil does not recognize Argentina's food-quality standards; and external tariffs are often double charged.[26]

Mercosur and the Andean Community agreed in principle to work toward a "South American Community of Nations" that will encompass 360 million people and a GDP of $1 trillion. First, however, these countries must resolve their differences.[27]

Association of South-East Asian Nations (ASEAN)
An economic union founded in 1967 that includes Brunei Darussalam, Cambodia, Indonesia, Lao PDR, Malaysia, Myanmar, the Philippines, Singapore, Thailand, and Vietnam; this economic bloc focuses not on reducing trade barriers among members but, rather, on promoting exports to other nations

Asean

The **Association of South-East Asian Nations (ASEAN)** was founded in 1967 and now includes Brunei Darussalam, Cambodia, Indonesia, Lao PDR, Malaysia, Myanmar, the Philippines, Singapore, Thailand, and Vietnam. This economic bloc is different from most others in that the primary emphasis is not on reducing trade barriers among the members, although this has been done with the agreement on the ASEAN Free Trade Area (AFTA), but rather on promoting exports to other countries. Members have been particularly successful in promoting exports to the Japanese market and to the EU. Members of ASEAN have generally experienced rapid economic growth, thanks in no small part to the efficiency and productivity of their members as well as to their impressive marketing skills.

FTAA

The Free Trade Area of the Americas (FTAA) was relaunched in Quebec City in April 2001. All the economies of North, Central, and South America, along with all Caribbean economies (except for Cuba), agreed in principle to start the FTAA in 2005. While the US Congress approved the Central American Free Trade Agreement (CAFTA) in July 2005, the larger FTAA is in limbo. One main problem is that Latin American countries are wary of entering the agreement if it does not involve the elimination of US agricultural subsidies. The US objective for the FTAA is to build on the framework of NAFTA, discussed in Chapters 6 and 19 in detail. New attempts to revive the free trade agreement in 2008 and 2012 also failed.

 Active learning check

Review your answer to Active Learning Case question 2 and make any changes you like. Then compare your answer to the one below.

2 Would Russia benefit by gaining admission to one of the major economic unions such as the EU? Why?

Russia certainly would benefit by gaining admission to an economic union such as the EU. It could then take advantage of a wide variety of benefits, including free movement of goods and services across borders, trade creation, the possible development of internal economies brought about by the huge market that would then be available for Russian goods, and a strengthening of the nation's currency. Of course, admission to the EU or one of the other major economic unions is unlikely to occur, at least within the next few years, as the country is not stable. However, it would offer a very big boost to the nation's economy.

ECONOMIC INTEGRATION AND STRATEGIC MANAGEMENT

How can MNEs use strategic management planning to benefit from worldwide economic integration efforts? A number of steps are proving to be helpful, particularly the use of strategic alliances, acquisitions, and the localization of business operations.

Strategic alliances and acquisitions

One of the most common ways of benefiting from economic integration is by creating a strategic alliance, often in the form of a joint venture, with other firms that can provide important forms of assistance.

Strategic alliance
A business relationship in which two or more companies work together to achieve a collective advantage

A **strategic alliance** is a business relationship in which two or more companies work together to achieve a collective advantage. These alliances can take a number of forms. In some cases, companies jointly conduct research or combine their efforts to market a product. In other instances they license a firm to produce and sell a particular product in a specific market region. In the telecommunications industry, strategic alliances have been very important because of the high investment and the need to attain market penetration. An interesting example is the alliance between Apple and IBM launched in 2014. Given the long history of rivalry this could arguably only have happened as new CEO Tim Cook moved the company on from the legacy of Steve Jobs and looked to harness Apple's creativity and success with mobile "i-tech" with IBM's portfolio of software and services to corporations.

This is one, recent example of a long-term trend driven by the convergence of the three Cs—computers, communications, and consumer electronics. These industries have increasingly been developing joint products and services while expanding globally. The rapid rate of technological development and rising sophistication of consumers and their requirements has driven complexity and competition in the industry, leading to a growing range of strategic alliances. The alliance formed between Accenture and Huawei in 2014 to develop and market innovative solutions to address customer requirements in both the communications service providers (CSPs) and enterprise ICT markets illustrates these trends clearly.

There are examples from every industry sector showing how firms can gain a competitive advantage by combining assets, brands, technology, market positioning, finances, or capabilities. Volvo became the world's largest manufacturer of heavy-duty trucks through an alliance with the Dongfeng Motor Group, which involved joint investment in a new subsidiary. Abu Dhabi-based Etihad Airways invested in an alliance with India's Jet Airways to gain access to the rapidly growing Indian market. Jet Airways benefits from code sharing, which gives its customers access to international routes. This follows alliances between Etihad, airberlin, and Aer Lingus. The alliance between McDonald's, the leading global food service retailer, and Coca-Cola, the world's largest beverage company, has been running since 1955. Part of the success of both companies is due to the success of the other.

Localization of business operations

MNEs cannot conduct business overseas in the same way they do at home. They have to target their offerings carefully to the needs of the regional and local customers. These efforts result in the localization of business operations and typically focus on four areas: products, profits, production, and management.[28]

Localization of products
The localization of products requires the development, manufacturing, and marketing of goods best suited to the needs of the local customer and marketplace. This typically requires the modification of products that have sold well in other geographic regions. For example, in North America buyers use motorcycles primarily for leisure and sports, so they look for high horsepower output and speed. In contrast, Southeast Asians use motorcycles as a basic means of transportation, so they look for low cost and ease of maintenance; and in Australia, where shepherds use motorcycles to drive sheep, low-speed torque is more important than either high speed or ease of maintenance.[29]

MNEs commonly localize production by investing in research and development, so they can make the product that fits the specific needs of that market. This is sometimes more difficult than it appears, especially if the MNE has been successful with a product in the home market and is unwilling to change. A good example is provided by the Whirlpool Corporation, which dominated the US market before going to Europe in the late 1980s. Believing that the giant $20 billion European appliance market with its dozens of marginally profitable companies was on the verge of consolidation, Whirlpool wanted to be one of the major players. So it bought a majority stake in a struggling appliance operation belonging to NV Philips, the Dutch electronics giant, and acquired the rest of the operation two years later for $1.1 billion. Whirlpool believed that the European market was highly regionalized because there were so many diverse consumer preferences. For example, the Swedish liked galvanized washers that could withstand salty air; the British washed their clothes more often than many others, so they wanted quieter washing machines; and so on. Stoves provided even greater examples of product diversity. However, Whirlpool believed that the market was ready for product consolidation, and therefore lent its support to a "world washer," a single machine that could be sold anywhere on the Continent. As product diversity was reduced, Whirlpool believed, the marginal producers would be driven from the market and its own share would climb. What the company found was that the European market was a lot more competitive than it realized. Sweden's AB Electrolux and Germany's Bosch–Siemens Hausgeraete GmbH proved to be excellent competitors. In particular, they revamped their factories and drove costs down sharply. They also began introducing new products that kept customers coming back. By thus appealing to local tastes, Electrolux and Bosch–Siemens managed to keep Whirlpool's profits to a minimum, while preventing it from gaining market share.[30]

Localization of profits

Localization of profits
The reinvestment of earnings in the local market

Localization of profits is the reinvestment of earnings in the local market. MNEs do this by taking their earnings and using them to expand operations, set up new plants and offices, hire more local people, and make the investment more self-sufficient. In the United States, for example, Honda started out with an initial investment of $250,000 and has gradually reinvested its US profits. Today the company has almost $2 billion in its motorcycle, auto, and engine manufacturing plants in Ohio. At the same time it has reinvested almost $200 million in Honda Canada, a manufacturing plant making Honda Civics.

Localization of production

Localization of production
The manufacturing of goods in the host market

Localization of production involves the manufacture of goods in the host market.[31] Many MNEs, upon entering a foreign market, handle this function by exporting from the home country. For a successful relationship, however, this is often only a short-run strategy and is eventually replaced by a local manufacturing base.[32] One strategy for localizing production is to increase the amount of local content in the product by making more and more of the subunits in the host country. The ultimate step, of course, is to produce the entire product locally. Honda, for example, decided back in the late 1980s to turn its Ohio auto-manufacturing facility into a fully integrated, self-reliant entity. The plan involved a number of steps, including increasing the plant's production capacity so that it would be able to turn out 500,000 units annually and build them with at least 75 percent domestic content. In 2007 Honda started to build a parts plant in Greensburg, Indiana, employing workers within a one-hour drive of the plant. In the process, Honda localized its production.

The same is true for Toyota. The company increased the capacity of its Georgetown, Kentucky, and Princeton, Indiana, plants and its Ontario, Canada, facility. It also began production of its Lexus SUV in Canada. It increased the production capacity of its Burnaston, England, plant and increased auto production in its Thailand factory, while negotiating with the government to build an engine factory in Tianjin, China.[33]

Another way to localize production is to provide added value in operations by modifying the imported product and adapting it to local conditions and tastes. This approach is used when a product requires country-by-country (or regional) changes. Auto manufacturers, for example, take into account the terrain (unpaved roads require stronger underbody construction), the cost of gasoline (high costs often mean that the market wants smaller, more efficient cars), and which side of the road everyone drives on (right in the United States and Latin America; left in the UK and Asia).

The localization of production is often carried out in conjunction with a home-country partner which provides the plant and personnel, while the MNE is responsible for the initial product and the technology needed in assembling or modifying the goods. Sometimes, however, the MNE will own the entire operation and depend on local management to help run the organization.

Localization of management

There are a number of ways for MNEs to localize management. One is by encouraging home-office managers to learn the local culture and become part of the community. Research reveals that companies that staff their subsidiaries with older, mature senior managers from the home country who are fluent in the local language are often more highly productive than MNEs that staff operations with younger, less experienced managers.[34] A second way of localizing management is by delegating authority to host-country managers and developing and promoting these employees wherever possible. This strategy helps to create a bond between the host- and the home-country management. As one MNE spokesperson put it:

> we have become convinced that good communication between management and labor, as well as delegation of authority, elevate the employees' sense of participation in decision making. This, in turn, gives the employees a stronger sense of responsibility and motivation, which leads to improved productivity and maintenance of high-quality standards.[35]

✔ Active learning check

Review your answer to Active Learning Case question 3 and make any changes you like. Then compare your answer to the one below.

3 **Is Russia a good potential investment for Western business? Explain.**

Arguments can be made on each side. Untapped natural resources and potential consumer demand could provide billions of dollars of annual sales for investing companies. On the other hand, the economy is in terrible shape, and it is likely to take years before Russia begins to provide an acceptable return on investment for many current projects. One of the major reasons for getting in now, of course, is to try to gain a strong foothold in the market and effectively block future competition. If this should happen, those coming later would find slim pickings. However, this potential benefit is unlikely to attract many investors. Most are likely to conclude that the best strategy is to proceed with caution and wait for the current uncertainty and turmoil to settle.

KEY POINTS

1 Political ideologies and economic systems are interwoven. Democracies tend to have market-driven economies; totalitarian governments tend to have centrally determined economies. However, few nations fit totally into one of these two paradigms. Most use a mixed economic model such as that of the United States, which is mainly a market-driven economy with some central planning, or China, which still relies on central planning but is moving to allow some degree of free enterprise.

2 Another current economic development is the trend toward privatization. Many countries are selling their state-owned enterprises. A variety of reasons can be cited for these actions. In most cases these are economic in nature, including (a) increased efficiency, (b) reduction in government outlays, and (c) generation of funds for the national treasury.

3 Economic integration is the establishment of transnational rules and regulations that permit economic trade and cooperation among countries. Effective integration brings about trade creation, although in some cases these efforts result in trade diversion. There are five levels of regional economic trade integration: free trade areas, customs unions, common markets, economic unions, and political unions. The most successful examples have been the EU and the NAFTA. Some NGOs criticize such trade and investment agreements.

4 NGOs are an important new actor on the stage of international business, and MNEs need to take account of the civil society in their strategies.

5 MNEs use a variety of strategies to benefit from integration efforts. One is strategic alliances and acquisitions with which they are able to scale the economic wall and gain an inside position in the economic alliance or free trade area. Another is through the localization of operations by focusing on products, profits, production, and management. MNEs typically use both of these strategic approaches.

Key terms

- ideology
- democracy
- totalitarianism
- communism
- theocratic totalitarianism
- secular totalitarianism
- market-driven economy
- centrally determined economy
- mixed economies
- privatization
- nationalization
- divestiture
- contract management
- Ministry of Economy, Trade and Industry (METI)
- economic integration
- trade creation

- trade diversion
- free trade area
- North American Free Trade Agreement (NAFTA)
- customs union
- common market
- economic union
- political union
- internal economies of scale
- external economies of scale
- non-governmental organizations (NGOs)
- civil society
- European Coal and Steel Community (ECSC)
- European Union (EU)

- European Free Trade Association (EFTA)
- Single European Act (SEA)
- European Council
- Council of the European Union
- European Commission
- European Parliament
- Court of Justice
- Court of Auditors
- Andean Community
- Association of South-East Asian Nations (ASEAN)
- strategic alliance
- localization of profits
- localization of production

REVIEW AND DISCUSSION QUESTIONS

1 As political systems change, economic systems follow. What does this statement mean?

2 How does a centrally determined economy differ from a market-driven economy? Explain.

3 What are the benefits of privatization? Why will the trend toward privatization continue?

4 Why are government–business cooperative efforts beginning to increase? What benefits do they offer?

5 What is the purpose of research consortia? What is their future likely to be? Why?

6 How does trade creation differ from trade diversion? Compare and contrast the two.

7 There are five levels of economic integration. What is meant by this statement? Be complete in your answer.

8 How does the EU function? Identify and describe its organization and operation.

9 What is the purpose of the following economic alliances: the Andean Community, Mercosur, and ASEAN?

10 Some of the primary ways that MNEs use strategic planning to benefit from economic integration efforts is through strategic alliances and acquisitions. How do MNEs do this?

11 How do MNEs seek to localize their business operations? Describe three steps that they take.

REAL CASE

How environmental regulations can be used as trade barriers

With free trade areas evolving around the globe, many protected industries are now facing unwelcome competition. Free trade agreements generally include a principle of national treatment under which a country must treat all producers, domestic or foreign, equally. However, some seemingly neutral environmental regulations impose a greater burden on foreign producers than on their domestic competitors. Thus, they act as trade barriers under the disguise of environmental regulations.

For example, while environmental groups lobby for newsprint to contain a determined amount of recycled material and domestic producers of newsprint support the regulation, foreign newsprint companies, which have no recycling facilities in the host country, face a competitive disadvantage. This is what has been called a "Baptist–bootlegger" coalition. During the US prohibition era, Baptists were opposed to alcoholic consumption on moral grounds, while bootleggers actually benefited from prohibition by the sale of illegal alcoholic beverages. Today, environmental groups and domestic producers often form coalitions to promote their respective interests.

In the newsprint case, the foreign company would have two options if it were to continue to supply material from its home country. It could either open recycling plants in the host country and transport pulp from its own country to be processed there, so as to meet the environmental regulations, or take the recycling material to its home country to be processed. Both alternatives would pose significant transportation costs to the foreign producer.

A similar case is presented by the Ontario Beer Can Tax. In the early 1990s the province of Ontario levied a tax of $0.10 on each aluminum beer can. The province argued that these cans were not environmentally friendly and that the tax was designed to encourage the use of refillable glass bottles. US producers of beer and aluminum cans contended that this was a protectionist move and that the Ontario government was singling out the competition with its beer industry since it had no similar tax for soft drinks and juice cans. Moreover, research studies found that aluminum cans and glass bottles both have the same effect on the environment, and that 80 percent of all the cans were being recycled. They also found that the larger, heavier glass required more energy to transport than did the lighter aluminum cans. ▶

Source: Adapted from Alan M. Rugman, John Kirton, and Julie Soloway, *Environmental Regulations and Corporate Strategy: A NAFTA Perspective* (Oxford: Oxford University Press, 1999); M. Trebilcock and R. Howse, "Trade policy and domestic health and safety standards," in *The Regulation of International Trade*, 2nd ed. (London: Routledge, 1999); Julie Soloway, "Environmental trade barriers in NAFTA: the MMT fuel additives controversy," *Minnesota Journal of Global Trade*, vol. 8, no. 1 (1998); David Vogel and Alan M. Rugman, "Environmentally related trade disputes between the United States and Canada," *American Review of Canadian Studies* (summer 1997), pp. 271–92.

1 How can a health and safety regulation become a trade barrier? Provide examples.

2 How can different environmental circumstances make one country's regulations inefficient in another country?

3 What are some reasons why the government might not be willing to make allowances for different countries?

REAL CASE

Embraer versus Bombardier

Bombardier and Embraer compete in the mid-size aircraft market, the luxury jet market, and the military aircraft market. In 2004, both companies announced plans for bigger aircraft. In the United States, 61 percent of all flights take off with a higher number of passengers than either of their aircraft normally accommodated. Indeed, analysts believe that there has historically been a lack of flexibility from the two largest players, Boeing and Airbus, in supplying this category of aircraft.

In 1942 Joseph Armand Bombardier, a young Quebec mechanic turned industrialist, incorporated the world's first snowmobile manufacturer, L'Auto-Neige Bombardier. Although he had great plans for his innovative transportation inventions, he could never have foreseen the course his company would take in the next 50 years. For the year ended January 31, 2014, Bombardier was one of the world's top manufacturers of transportation products, including trains and aircraft, with yearly revenues of US$20.1 billion and over 74,000 employees of 95 nationalities speaking 20 languages in 60 countries (see Figure 4.2).

Bombardier's success is in no small part the responsibility of CEO Laurent Beaudoin, who over 30 years has followed a strategy of market entry and product improvement through acquisition, instead of relying strictly on R&D. This strategy has been exemplified by Bombardier's entry into the aerospace industry with the acquisition of Canadair in 1986.

In 1991, Bombardier took a risk on the undeveloped market of regional jets, which quickly paid off. Airlines could offer more short-haul flights at a more reasonable price at a time when airport hubs were overcrowded. Bombardier enjoyed a virtual monopoly on this airplane category until Embraer came along.

The beginnings of Embraer are very different. Founded in 1969 by a Brazilian military dictatorship, Embraer made its name building high-quality military and civilian aircraft. The airplanes were so expensive, however, that no one wanted to buy them, and for years the company lost millions in revenue. Then in 1994 it was privatized and given to Mauricio Botelho to turn around. He has. In 1995, the company launched a family of regional jets that were warmly received by US and European airlines. In 2009, Embraer had about half of the market; its sales reached $5.409 billion. Embracer's sales amounted to US$5.7 billion and it had acquired a workforce of approximately 19,000 people (see Figure 4.3).

Because direct subsidies by governments to domestic firms are illegal at the WTO, each company has attempted to obtain WTO approval on trade sanctions against its competitor in the late 1990s and early 2000s. Canada filed a complaint over Brazilian subsidies to Embraer. Brazil countered with its own complaint over Canadian subsidies to Bombardier. In total, there were four cases at the WTO:

1 WTO Dispute DS46: Brazil—Export Financing Program for Aircraft (Complainant: Canada), June 19, 1996.

2 WTO Dispute DS70: Canada—Measures Affecting the Export of Civilian Aircraft (Complainant: Brazil), March 10, 1997.

3 WTO Dispute DS71: Canada—Measures Affecting the Export of Civilian Aircraft (Complainant: Brazil), March 10, 1997.

4 WTO Dispute DS222: Canada—Export Credits and Loan Guarantees for Regional Aircraft (Complainant: Brazil), January 22, 2001.

Both countries were successful, and today they both have a green light to impose sanctions on each other. This is unlikely to happen, however, as it would strain bilateral relations between the two nations. Instead, both countries are seeking some form of a compromise.

Both companies argue that the other has an unfair advantage. Bombardier, argues Embraer, has access to top-of-the-line technology and low-interest loans from being located in an industrialized country. Embraer, argues Bombardier, has access to cheap labor and benefits from a weak currency. The initial WTO complaint was based on low-interest loans to Embraer customers by PROEX, a Brazilian agency set up to promote exports. In addition to the price of an Embraer airplane being lower by about $3 million, its customers could save even more by getting one of these loans. Brazil's complaint cited subsidies from the Canadian government to three small airlines as an incentive to purchase Bombardier airplanes.

Now that the WTO has ruled against both countries, instead of applying punitive tariffs, Brazil and Canada are seeking to negotiate an agreement. Both have amended their subsidies. In a market with increased competition for regional flights, a trade war must be averted. At stake are negotiations for the Free Trade Area of the Americas (FTAA). Indeed, the airplane dispute highlights the difficulties facing countries from the developed North and the developing South.

There are several reasons why a trade war should be avoided. The regional jet sector is facing increasing competitive pressure. Other companies are currently developing competitive products in the 40–100-seat category. These include the Commercial Aircraft Corporation of China Ltd. (COMAC), a state-owned company in which China Aviation Industry Corporation (formerly known as AVIC 1) holds an interest, Mitsubishi Heavy Industries Ltd. (MHI, Japan), and Sukhoi Company (JSC) (Sukhoi, Russia).

The financial crisis of 2008 continued to significantly affect the civil aerospace industry as a whole. Worsening economic conditions and restricted credit availability translate into a high level of order cancellations and deferrals of aircraft deliveries. This caused most of the original equipment manufacturers (OEMs) to reduce their production rates and has reduced their profitability. As a result, the world airlines' net loss was forecasted as being approximately $2.8 billion in 2010, compared to a net loss of $9.4 million in 2009. The limited availability of aircraft financing seen during 2009 also contributed to restraining airlines' ability to buy new aircraft in 2010. Given this climate and the planned production rate, Bombardier delivered approximately 20 percent fewer commercial aircraft in 2011 than in 2010. Bombardier's sales fell for the year ended in January 30, 2010 by 2 percent compared to those of 2009. Embraer also witnessed its sales decline by 25 percent in 2009 compared to the previous year's sales. Furthermore, as a result of the crisis Embraer also announced that it was reducing its operational workforce by 20 percent (4,000 jobs) from management and administrative positions in 2009.

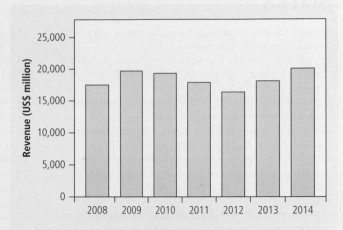

Figure 4.2 **Bombardier: revenue, 2008–14**

Source: Bombardier, *Annual Report*, 2008–14.

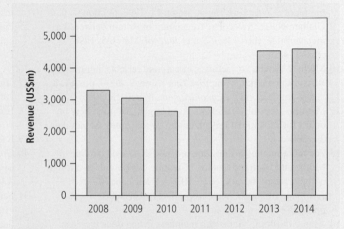

Figure 4.3 **Embraer: revenue, 2008–14**

Source: Embraer, *Annual Report*, 2008–14.

Websites: www.bombardier.com; www.embraer.com; www.boeing.com

Source: Rita Kolsélka, "Let's make a deal," *Forbes*, April 27, 1992, pp. 62–3; Clyde H. Farnsworth, "Bombardier snares DeHavilland," *New York Times*, January 26, 1992, p. 12; Jonathan Wheatly, "Embraer: the sky's the limit," *Business Week*, January 3, 2001; "Brazil's Embraer hits the stratosphere," *Business Week*, April 19, 2004; Bombardier, *Annual Report*, 2006–14; Embraer, *Annual Report*, 2006–14; "WTO rules against Canada over low interest loans for Bombardier deal," *CBC News*, October 19, 2001; "Embraer commercial aircraft deliveries drop 25% in 2009," *Air Transport Intelligence News*, www.flightglobal.com, January, 12, 2010; Andrew Downie, "Embraer: Brazilian group seeks military dividends," *Financial Times*, accessed from http://www.ft.com/cms/s/0/523a0782-cfe9-11de-a36d-00144feabdc0.html#axzz3wfUhmvzl

1 How do factor conditions differ for Embraer and Bombardier?

2 How does the dispute reflect the difficulties in drafting the FTAA?

3 Why are governments involved in this trade dispute?

4 Why are Canada and Brazil hesitant to apply the punitive tariffs they were awarded?

NOTES

1 Craig S. Smith, "Workers of the world, invest!" *New York Times*, August 19, 2001, section 3, p. 3.

2 For more on this, see Erik Eckholm, "Chinese president is optimistic about relations with the US," *New York Times*, August 10, 2001, pp. A1, A8.

3 "Private economy yields 40% of gross product in Shanghai," *People's Daily Online*, March 9, 2005.

4 Paul Starobin and Olga Kravchenko, "Russia's middle class," *Business Week*, October 16, 2000, pp. 78–84.

5 R. Molz, "Privatization of government enterprise: the challenge to management," *Management International Review*, vol. 29, no. 4 (1989), pp. 29–30.

6 Ibid., pp. 32–3.

7 For excellent coverage of privatization, see Dennis J. Gayle and Jonathan N. Goodrich (eds.), *Privatization and Deregulation in Global Perspective* (New York: Quorum Books, 1990).

8 Clifford Krauss, "Argentina to hasten end of phone monopoly," *New York Times*, March 11, 1998, Section C, p. 4.

9 Gautam Naik, "Telecom deregulation in Britain delivered a nice surprise: jobs," *Wall Street Journal*, March 5, 1998, pp. A1, A6.

10 Michael Wines, "A factory's turnaround reflects a glimmer in Russia's economy," *New York Times*, July 2, 2000, pp. A1, 8.

11 "Low-cost take off," *Economist.com*, March 23, 2005.

12 Mayumi Negishi, "Takenaka vows to get LDP members on board for Japan Post privatization," *Japan Times*, September 29, 2004.

13 For more on the current state of EUREKA, see Caroline Mothe and Bertrand Quelin, "Creating competencies through collaboration: the case of EUREKA R&D consortia," *European Management Journal*, December 2000, pp. 590–604.

14 Alan Goldstein, "Sematech members facing dues increase; 30% jump to make up for loss of federal funding," *Dallas Morning News*, July 27, 1996, p. 2F.

15 NAFTA fast facts (2015) http://www.naftanow.org/facts/default_en.asp

16 Larry Reibstein et al., "A Mexican miracle?" *Newsweek*, May 20, 1991, pp. 42–5; Paul Magnusson et al., "The Mexico pact: worth the price?" *Business Week*, May 27, 1991, pp. 32–5.

17 United States, BEA, *Survey of Current Business*, January and April 2005.

18 World Bank, "Defining the civil society", http://go.worldbank.org/4CE7W046K0 (2013); "Globalization, what on earth is it about?" BBC.co.uk, September 14, 2000.

19 "Who are the Prague protestors?" BBC.co.uk, September 26, 2000.

20 World Bank, "Civil society organizations," http://go.worldbank.org/KK5KGT24X0, September, 2015.

21 http://www.eurodad.org/

22 Alan M. Rugman, *The End of Globalization* (London: Random House, 2001).

23 Sylvia Ostry, "The multilateral trading system," in Alan M. Rugman and Thomas Brewer (eds.), *The Oxford Handbook of International Business* (Oxford: Oxford University Press, 2001), pp. 232–58.

24 Edward M. Graham, *Fighting the Wrong Enemy: Antiglobal Activists and Multinational Enterprises* (Washington, DC: Institute for International Economics, 2000).

25 Philip Revzin, "EC leaders adopt 2-year plan to forge political, monetary unity in Europe," *Wall Street Journal*, December 17, 1990, p. A6.

26 "A free-trade tug-of-war," Economist.com, December 9, 2004.

27 "Fraternity of 3,300 metres," Economist.com, December 9, 2004.

28 Hideo Sugiura, "How Honda localizes its global strategy," *Sloan Management Review* (fall 1990), pp. 77–82.

29 Ibid., p. 78.

30 Greg Steinmetz and Carl Quintanilla, "Whirlpool expected easy going in Europe, and it got a big shock," *Wall Street Journal*, April 10, 1998, pp. A1, A6.

31 Ferdinand Protzman, "Rewriting the contract for Germany's vaunted workers," *New York Times*, February 13, 1994, Section F, p. 5.

32 "Pepsi investing $350 million in China plants," *New York Times*, January 27, 1994, p. C3.

33 Brian Bremner et al., "Toyota's crusade," *Business Week*, April 7, 1997, pp. 104–14.

34 See Robert O. Metzger and Ari Ginsberg, "Lessons from Japanese global acquisitions," *Journal of Business Strategy* (May/June 1989), p. 35.

35 Ibid., p. 79.

BIBLIOGRAPHY

Czinkota, Michael R., Knight, Gary, Liesch, Peter W., and Steen, John. "Terrorism and international business: a research agenda," *Journal of International Business Studies*, vol. 41 (June/July 2010).

Dahan, Nicolas, Doh, Jonathan P., Oetzel, Jennifer, and Yaziji, Michael. "Corporate-NGO collaboration: creating new business models for developing markets," *Long Range Planning*, vol. 43, no. 2 (2010).

Dunning, John H. (ed.). *Governments, Globalization and International Business* (Oxford: Oxford University Press, 1997).

Eden, Lorraine. "The emerging North American investment regime," *Transnational Corporations*, vol. 5, no. 3 (December 1996).

Fratianni, Michele, and Oh, Chang H. "Expanding RTAs, trade flows, and the multinational enterprise," *Journal of International Business Studies*, vol. 40 (September 2009).

Gomes-Casseres, Benjamin. "Competitive advantage in alliance constellations," *Strategic Organization*, vol. 1, no. 3 (August 2003).

Graham, Edward M. *Fighting the Wrong Enemy: Antiglobal Activists and Multinational Enterprises* (Washington, DC: Institute for International Economics, September 2000).

Henisz, Witold, Mansfield, J., Edward, D., and Von Glinow, Mary Ann. "Conflict, security, and political risk: international business in challenging times," *Journal of International Business Studies*, vol. 41 (June/July 2010).

Hoffmann, Volker H., Trautmann, Thomas, and Hamprecht, Jens. "Regulatory uncertainty: a reason to postpone investments? Not necessarily," *Journal of Management Studies*, vol. 46, no. 7 (November 2009).

Jensen, Nathan M, Li, Quan, and Rahman, Aminur. "Understanding corruption and firm responses in cross-national firm-level surveys," *Journal of International Business Studies*, vol. 41 (2010).

Kobrin, Stephen J. "Sovereignty @ bay: globalization, multinational enterprises, and the international political system," in Alan M. Rugman (ed.), *The Oxford Handbook of International Business*, 2nd ed. (Oxford: Oxford University Press, 2009).

Kolk, Ans. "Social and sustainability dimensions of regionalization and (semi)globalization," *Multinational Business Review*, vol. 18, no. 1 (2010).

Lee, Seung-Hyun, Oh, Kyeungrae, and Eden, Lorraine. "Why do firms bribe?" *Management International Review*, vol. 50, no. 6 (December 1, 2010).

McCarthy, Daniel J., Puffer, Sheila M., and Shekshni, Stanislav Vladimirovich. *Corporate Governance in Russia* (Aldershot: Edward Elgar, 2004).

Muller, Alan, and Kolk, Ans. "Extrinsic and intrinsic drivers of corporate social performance: evidence from foreign and domestic firms in Mexico," *Journal of Management Studies*, vol. 47, no. 1 (2010).

Ostry, Sylvia. "The multilateral trading system," in Alan M. Rugman and Thomas Brewer (eds.), *The Oxford Handbook of International Business*, 1st ed. (Oxford: Oxford University Press, 2001).

Puffer, Sheila M., and McCarthy, Daniel J. "The emergence of corporate governance in Russia," *Journal of World Business*, vol. 38, no. 4 (November 2003).

Puffer, Sheila M., and McCarthy, Daniel J. "Can Russia's state-managed, network capitalism be competitive? Institutional

pull versus institutional push," *Journal of World Business*, vol. 42, no. 1 (March 2007).

Regnér, Patrick, and Edman, Jesper. "MNE institutional advantage: how subunits shape, transpose and evade host country institutions," *Journal of International Business Studies*, vol. 45, no. 3 (2013).

Rugman, Alan M. (ed.). *Foreign Investment and NAFTA* (Columbia, SC: University of South Carolina Press, 1994).

Rugman, Alan M. "Toward an Investment Agenda for APEC," *Transnational Corporations* (August 1997).

Rugman, Alan M. (ed.). *North American Economic and Financial Integration* (Oxford: Elsevier, 2004).

Rugman, Alan M., and Doh, Jonathan. *Multinationals and Development* (New Haven, CT: Yale University Press, 2008).

Rugman, Alan M., and Gestrin, Michael. "The strategic response of multinational enterprises to NAFTA," *Columbia Journal of World Business*, vol. 28, no. 4 (winter 1993).

Rugman, Alan M., and Verbeke, Alain. "Multinational enterprise and national economic policy," in Peter J. Buckley and Mark Casson (eds.), *Multinational Enterprises in the World Economy: Essays in Honor of John Dunning* (Aldershot: Edward Elgar, 1992).

Rugman, Alan M., and Verbeke, Alain. "Multinational enterprises and public policy," in Alan M. Rugman (ed.), *The Oxford Handbook of International Business*, 2nd ed. (Oxford: Oxford University Press, 2009).

Safarian, A. E. *Multinational Enterprise and Public Policy* (Cheltenham: Edward Elgar, 1993).

Sen, Amartya. *Development as Freedom* (Oxford: Oxford University Press, 1999).

Spar, Debora L. *Ruling the Waves: Cycles of Discovery, Chaos and Wealth* (New York: Harcourt, 2001).

Spar, Debora L. "National policies and domestic politics," in Alan M. Rugman (ed.), *The Oxford Handbook of International Business*, 2nd ed. (Oxford: Oxford University Press, 2009).

Trebilcock, Michael, and Howse, Robert. The *Regulation of International Trade*, 3rd ed. (London: Routledge, 2005).

Weintraub, Sidney, Rugman, Alan M., and Boyd, Gavin (eds.). *Free Trade in the Americas* (Cheltenham: Edward Elgar, 2004).

Chapter 5

INTERNATIONAL CULTURE

Contents

Objectives of the chapter

Places and people differ. The Japanese tend to be very polite, the Australians characteristically blunt. Red means "danger" or "stop" to the British, but in Turkey it signifies death and in China, good fortune. In France getting into a **grande école** tends to guarantee good job prospects whereas in Saudi Arabia the wealth and status of your family is far more important.

Patterns of global diversity and the implications of these differences have been studied from a range of perspectives, by sociologists, psychologists, anthropologists, and political scientists. Here we are concerned with how cultural diversity and related differences in the behavior, norms, and expectations of particular groups of employees, managers, colleagues, or customers affect management decision making and corporate organizations. After an introduction to the kinds of business contexts in which cultural differences matter, this chapter will describe some typologies of national cultural differences and discuss the implications of these for international managers.

The specific objectives of this chapter are to:

1 *Define* culture and explain the factors that underlie cultural differences.

2 *Show* where and why cultural differences matter to international managers.

3 *Explain* a number of frameworks that help identify important cultural differences.

4 *Examine* how firms can anticipate and cope with cultural differences.

ACTIVE LEARNING CASE

Cultures clash as big pharma gets bigger

A series of international mergers has made Pfizer one of the largest pharmaceutical firms in the world. In the process the firm has had to incorporate, integrate, and adapt to a wide range of different national cultures as it has absorbed new acquisitions into its expanding organization. We start the story with the merger of two firms, Pharmacia AB of Sweden (with operations in Italy) and Upjohn Company of the United States, which went through a steep cultural learning curve over 20 years ago, before being acquired in turn by Pfizer.

Senior managers leading the merger between Pharmacia and Upjohn only came to realize how significant the cultural differences were between Kalamazoo (Michigan, United States), Stockholm (Sweden), and Milan (Italy) after the merger took place in 1995. Everyday local preferences, beliefs and workplace practices underpin differences that can amount to major conflicts if they are not understood and incorporated into merged structures.

Swedes take off most of the month of July for their annual vacation; Italians take off most of August. Not knowing this, US executives scheduled meetings in the summer only to have to cancel many because their European counterparts were at the beach. As the more dominant US firm began to impose its way of doing things on the newly acquired European organizations, international relationships became increasingly strained.

Neither the Swedes nor the Italians were happy with impositions such as the drug and alcohol testing policy brought in by Upjohn, or the office smoking ban. These clashed with local ways of doing things and the more informal work environment that these cultures prefer. Although Upjohn later relaxed many of these work rules, allowing some local practices and preferences to prevail, ill-feeling and a degree of resistance had already developed among European colleagues.

The additional bureaucracy and the command-and-control style imposed by the Americans created more significant problems for the 34,000 employees and managers in Pharmacia and Upjohn Company. The Swedes were used to an open, team-based style of management where responsibilities are devolved; managers are trusted and not strictly monitored or closely managed. Swedish executives also tend to build up a consensus behind big decisions, "getting everyone in the same boat" (alla aer i baten) rather than handing orders down the hierarchy. As a traditional US multinational, however, Upjohn was more used to strong leadership and a centralized command-and-control structure. Its CEO, Dr. John Zabriskie, quickly created a strict reporting system, tight budget control, and frequent staffing updates, which clashed with the Swedish organization style. Swedish managers would leave meetings disgruntled, having been overruled by US executives keen to push their vision of the merged company.

The Swedes' own ways of doing things had already clashed with the Italian style of management, following the takeover of Farmitalia (part of Montedison) by Pharmacia in 1993. Italians are used to a distinctive division between workers (and their strong unions) and managers. Their steeper hierarchies contrast the more egalitarian Swedes. Italians also place a high value on families and will leave work to tend to sick relatives or help with childcare, which the Swedes frown upon. The addition of the Americans from Upjohn to this mix created further cultural confusion. Communication problems, beyond the obvious language differences, became a real barrier to honest dialog. "You go there thinking you're going to streamline the place," said American Mark H. Corrigan, Pharmacia and Upjohn Vice President for Clinical Development, "and you leave just having added five pounds from some wonderful meals."

These differences, many of them small but important at the local level, quickly began to have an impact on the overall performance of the merged company. In the months and years following the merger, unforeseen inefficiencies and added costs began to undermine the potential synergies of bringing together two such companies in the first place. At one level the problems amounted to things like canceled meetings, new organization demands (such as monthly report writing), and a general decline in staff morale. These and other changes added an estimated $200 million to the predicted costs of the restructuring, taking the total cost to $800 million. Even more seriously, for a pharmaceutical company heavily reliant on its new drugs pipeline to survive, delayed product launches and the loss of key staff (including the head of R&D at Pharmacia) had a longer-term impact. "There was probably an underappreciation . . . of these cultural differences," says Art Atkinson, former Vice President for Clinical Research and Development. Restructuring the firm's global R&D structure, with a new and neutral London-based center for the R&D function, did not help. This simply added a layer of management and a more complex matrix reporting structure, which further alienated key R&D personnel.

In 1997, after the stock price of the merged corporation had fallen significantly, CEO John Zabriskie resigned. Swede Jan Ekberg, the former head of Pharmacia, took over temporarily and began to rebuild aspects of the merged organization. ▶

After acquiring a major part of Monsanto in 2000, Pharmacia and Upjohn became Pharmacia, which was then itself acquired by the US giant Pfizer in April 2003 for $60 billion. The aim was to expand the portfolio of consumer health products, stronger oncology products and the Celebrex brand.

Pfizer then undertook a large-scale global restructuring and continued its pattern of acquisitions. In 2009 it bought Wyeth for $68 billion and tried to acquire AstraZeneca for over $100 billion in 2014, but this was blocked on the grounds that it would create a monopoly in certain pharmaceuticals product areas. Then in 2015 began a process of merging with Allergan (a £160 billion acquisition) to create the largest pharmaceuticals firm in the world with annual revenues of $64 billion. This created huge controversy because a major objective was to structure this with the smaller, Dublin-based Allergan buying Pfizer. This would both avoid competition policy restrictions and enable Pfizer to cut its tax bill by moving its registered HQ from the US to Ireland. This created a great deal of negative press for the firm, with the chair of a UK Parliamentary committee in 2015 calling it a "shark that needs feeding" because of its style of aggressive acquisitions.

Looking back, it is debatable as to whether the lessons of the earlier mergers and integrations were learned.

Cultural clashes still have a significant impact when firms try to integrate their organizations to create the kinds of strategic synergies that are clear on paper. There are strong signs, however, that Pfizer has focused in recent years on developing a strong corporate culture, partly to deal with this issue. HR training and internal communications under CEO Ian Read emphasize "ownership" and "straight talk" (http://pfizercareers.com/culture/own-it). Employees are known as "colleagues" and the firm has established a network of more than 100 "local, site-based Colleague Resource Groups (CRGs) affiliated with a variety of diverse communities." Depending on your perspective, this could mean their intention is to harmonize and integrate different national and corporate cultures as Pfizer progresses through each merger—or suppress differences and incorporate new cultures into its Anglo-American style of management.

Source: R. Frank and T. M. Burton, "Pharmacia & Upjohn faces culture clash: Europeans chafe under US rules," *Wall Street Journal*, February 4, 1997; R. J. Thomas, "Irreconcilable differences," *Accenture Outlook*, vol. 1 (2000); Pfizer, *Annual Report*, 2003; Ransdell Pierson and Bill Berkrot, "Pfizer to buy Allergan in $160 billion deal," *Reuters*, November 24, 2015; Steve Brozak, "No longer king of the north, Pfizer looks to recapture crown," *Forbes*, April 30, 2014; Sarah Gordon, "Honesty and quelling culture clash are vital for successful mergers," *Financial Times*, July 29, 2015. "MPs grill Pfizer and Vince Cable over AstraZeneca offer," *Telegraph*, May 12, 2014.

---

1 What kinds of cultural differences matter when organizations from different countries merge?

2 How well do the characteristics described in the case match the respective, stereotypical national cultures of these countries?

3 What could senior managers do before and after mergers to alleviate some of the problems that result from culture clash?

4 Explain why one organization might want to impose some of its ways of doing things on another, such as an acquired firm or subsidiary.

INTRODUCTION

Grande école
One of the "grand" or great schools considered to be the pinnacle of French higher education, highly selective and prestigious and the main source of the country's business and political leaders.

The number of workers employed by foreign-owned companies has grown significantly over the past 20 years as a result of the expanding activities of foreign affiliates of MNEs around the world. For many people, both employers and employees, this has brought home the realities of globalization. An estimated 75 million people globally now work for foreign companies, nearly three times the number in 1990. Companies such as Motorola, General Motors, British Petroleum, and General Electric are among the largest private sector employers in economies such as Malaysia and Singapore.[1]

This growing multicultural workforce, part of the increasingly global patterns of exchange and interaction discussed earlier in this book, makes it more and more important to understand how people's preferences, beliefs, and values differ. Understanding international cultural differences allows us to be aware of and adapt to the differences that matter for managers.

WHAT IS CULTURE?

Culture
The sum total of the beliefs, rules, techniques, institutions, and artifacts that characterize human populations or the collective programming of the mind

Socialization
The process of enculturation, or the adoption of the behavior patterns of the surrounding culture

Culture can be defined as "the sum total of the beliefs, rules, techniques, institutions, and artifacts that characterize human populations"[2] or "the collective programming of the mind."[3]

Sociologists generally talk about the **socialization** process, referring to the influence of parents, friends, education, and the interaction with other members of a particular society as the basis for one's culture. These influences result in learned patterns of behavior common to members of a given society.

As you can see, definitions of culture vary according to the focus of interest, the unit of analysis, and the disciplinary approach (psychology, anthropology, sociology, geography, etc.). This is significant in that studies of cultural differences adopt a specific definition and set of measurable criteria, which are always debatable. Research into culture and its impact in business and management studies is highly contentious and should not just be taken at face value, including the studies described below.

There is a strong consensus, however, that key elements of culture include language, religion, values, attitudes, customs, and norms of a group or society. Table 5.1 shows how the world's population is divided according to geography, language, and religion.

Language is perhaps the most important key to understanding culture in general and the specific values, beliefs, attitudes, and opinions of a particular individual or group. English is widely accepted as the language of business; many global institutions and companies have adopted English as their official language. For many firms, such as Toyota, NEC, Hitachi, and IBM Japan, English-speaking ability is a prerequisite for promotion.[4] However, any assumption that speaking the same language removes cultural differences is dangerous—it normally just hides them. Moreover, a reliance on English by British and American managers, and a lack of other language skills, can weaken their ability to empathize with and adapt to other cultures.

Religion, linked to both regional characteristics and language, also influences business culture through a set of shared core values. Protestants hold strong beliefs about the value of delayed gratification, saving, and investment. The sociologist Max Weber, writing in 1904, saw this Protestant work ethic as the "spirit of capitalism" during the Industrial Revolution.[5] Rather than spending, consuming, and enjoying life now, their religious beliefs prompted the Protestants to look to longer-term rewards (including those in the after-life). There are parallels with the Confucian and Shinto work ethics, which also view spiritual rewards as tied to hard work and commitment to the fruits of industry. Contrasting this, a more stoic attitude among some African populations partly

Table 5.1 World population percentages in terms of home region, language, and religion

Home region	%	Language	%	Religion	%
Asia	60	Mandarin	14.4	Christianity	33
Africa	15	Hindi	6.0	Islam	21
America & Caribbean	14	English	5.6	Hinduism	15
Europe	10	Spanish	5.6	Non-religious	16
Oceania	1	Bengali	3.4	Buddhism	6
		Russian	2.8	Chinese Traditional	6
		Portuguese	2.6	Prima-Indigenous	6
		Japanese	2.0	Other	1
		German	1.6		
		Korean	1.3		
		French	1.3		
		Other	54.4		

Source: www.nationsonline.org

explains their acceptance of the ways things are, because it is the "will of God" (*shauri ya Mungu*).

At the most general level, culture can refer simply to the lifestyle and behavior of a given group of people, so **corporate culture** is a term used to characterize how the managers and employees of particular companies tend to behave. But the term is also used by human resource managers and senior management in their attempts to proactively shape the kind of behavior (innovative, open, dynamic, etc.) they hope to nurture in their organizations. Promoting a distinctive corporate culture is also expected to enhance the sense of community and shared identity that underpins effective organizations.

Corporate culture
The shared values, traditions, customs, philosophy, and policies of a corporation; also, the professional atmosphere that grows from this and affects behavior and performance

THE IMPORTANCE OF CULTURE IN DIFFERENT BUSINESS CONTEXTS

Cross-cultural management issues arise in a range of business contexts. *Within* individual firms, for example, managers from a foreign parent company need to understand that local employees from the host country may require different organization structures and HRM procedures. In cross-border mergers and acquisitions (M&As), realizing the expected synergies very often depends on establishing structures and procedures that encompass both cultures in a balanced way. Cross-border joint ventures, alliances, or buyer–supplier relationships *between* two or more firms also require a cultural compromise. Finally, for firms to sell successfully to foreign customers requires culturally sensitive adaptations to products, services, marketing, and advertising.

Figure 5.1 outlines, at the most general level, links between business contexts and particular characteristics of individuals or groups that are influenced by social and cultural

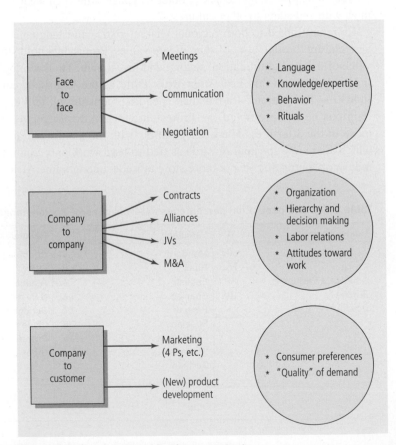

Figure 5.1 Cross-cultural business contexts

norms of a particular region. At the face-to-face level in meetings, the language and behavior of different peoples vary and their mutual understanding of each other's culture will influence the effectiveness and efficiency of communication between them. This influences how well multicultural workplaces operate at all levels, from strategy setting at the senior level to plant-floor operations.

Firms also tend to have different organizational and decision-making practices depending on where they have evolved and which cultures and subcultures they encompass. For firms to build successful alliances and partnerships, or for M&A activities to succeed at the company-to-company level, there needs to be an understanding of the organizational differences between them. This covers practically every element of corporate organizations from decision-making structures and systems and management–labor relationships to individual employees' attitudes toward their work and their employer.

Finally, culture influences the behavior and preferences of clients and customers. To sell successfully in a foreign market, a manager needs to adapt his or her product or service to meet the different needs of that particular group of customers. Any alteration in advertising, marketing, product or service features, after-sales support, technical back-up, documentation, etc., will be partly guided by cultural differences.

Failure to do this ends in the kinds of marketing mistakes and communication blunders that become marketing folklore. For example, Ford's low-cost truck was initially marketed as the Feira to Spanish-speaking people, but this means "ugly old woman" in Spanish. The Ford Comet, a high-end car, was sold as the Caliente in Mexico, which is local slang for "prostitute." Unsurprisingly, neither model did well in these markets. This reinforces the above point about the importance of language, but also demonstrates how some of the largest and most experienced companies do not appear to do the most basic cultural due diligence (their homework!) when launching products and services in foreign markets. Chapter 13 on marketing strategy examines these kinds of issues more closely.

Across all of the business contexts in Figure 5.1, ignorance of cultural differences represents a common stumbling block for international managers. **Ethnocentrism**, the belief that one's own way of doing things is superior to that of others, can also be a major barrier to good international management. The challenge lies in recognizing differences, combining the advantages that stem from different styles and approaches, adjusting and adapting to succeed with different people, in different partnerships, and in different markets.

Ethnocentrism
A belief in the superiority of one's own ethnic group; the dominance of the home-country culture in decision making, human resource management, and overall corporate culture in a multinational firm

---

 Active learning check

Review your answer to Active Learning Case question 1 and make any changes you like. Then compare your answer to the one below.

1 **What kinds of cultural differences matter when organizations from different countries merge?**

The definition of culture itself gives some indicators of the kinds of differences that matter. Organizations from different countries will have developed different beliefs, values, and patterns of behavior based on their underlying national culture. A wide range of differences could be important, including attitudes toward work and workplace practices, management–labor relations, the decision-making hierarchy, and division of responsibilities. Cross-border M&A often also requires changes to the marketing and branding of products and services as sales are expanded into new markets. Differences in the language, values, and preferences of customers in different countries also need to be taken into account.

Culture has always been important

Despite the various patterns and processes of globalization, cultural differences still remain important. Even with greater common access, via various media and the internet, to the same brands, rock icons, and sports stars, differences remain. Terms like **cultural convergence** or, simply, Americanization (the homogenization of global consumer preferences through the ubiquity of McDonald's, Coca-Cola, and Ford) overstate the similarities between groups of people around the world. (See the case **International Business Strategy in Action: McDonald's**.)

Cultural convergence
The growing similarity between national cultures, including the beliefs, values, aspirations, and the preferences of consumers, partly driven by global brands, media, and common global icons

---

INTERNATIONAL BUSINESS STRATEGY IN ACTION

McDonald's

When José Bové, a self-proclaimed leader of France's anti-globalization movement, was sentenced for vandalizing a McDonald's restaurant in 1999, he claimed to have the backing of the French people. That might have been an overstatement, but 40,000 French people were there to show their support. It was not only the French, however; in the 1990s McDonald's restaurants were vandalized in about 50 countries. At issue is the worldwide perception that McDonald's represents a particular friendly Ronald-McDonald type of US imperialism. Traditional lifestyles, critics say, are being eroded by McDonald's marketing practices, its value chain system, its fast-food concept, and the unhealthy food itself.

Yet, McDonald's bends over backward to blend into local cultures. The company advertises itself to its critics as a global company owned and run by local people. Indeed, the franchise system makes it so that McDonald's Japan is run by the Japanese and Israel's McDonald's restaurants are run by Israelis. Local business owners choose their menu's offerings to fit their culture, find alternative suppliers, and create suitable marketing for their culture. An American in Saudi Arabia might seat single men with families at a McDonald's opening, but a Saudi Arabian owner would know that this is unacceptable and the restaurant will be designed to accommodate the culture.

In the land of José Bové, Asterix, a French comic-strip character who stands for individuality and ironically symbolizes local resistance to imperial forces, replaced the goofy Ronald McDonald in the company's marketing in the early 2000s. In 1999, French McDonald's went the extra mile to prove how local it was by printing advertisements making fun of US eating habits. In one ad, a large American cowboy complains that McDonald's France does not import American beef to "guarantee maximum hygienic conditions." French restaurants are more fashionably and more comfortably designed than North American ones to create an environ-ment where customers may enjoy longer meals in accordance with French tradition. If they want, customers can order a beer from the menu.

In India, where local tastes are very different from those in the United States, the company crafted an entirely different menu that does not use beef or pork due to the mostly vegetarian population. The Indian Big Mac is made of lamb. In Israel, the locally owned McDonald's purchases over 80 percent of its ingredients from local producers, including 100 percent kosher hamburger meat, potatoes, lettuce, buns, and milkshake mix. There are no cheeseburgers in Israel's McDonald's because dairy products cannot be eaten together with meat.

On the other hand, McDonald's does bring its own culture to its foreign operations. In China, where children's birthdays are not traditionally celebrated, a successful McDonald's marketing strategy encouraged birthday parties at their establishments—not a bad deal for children, but still a cultural effect from a foreign multinational. More mundane things, such as combo meals, are popularized through McDonald's expansion. By promoting its carbonated beverages in India, the firm is unsettling the country's tea culture. The company's presence creates a cultural exchange, not a one-sided cultural takeover.

Beyond reactionary behavior against McDonald's cultural "impositions," McDonald's has had to suffer simply for being born in the United States. Just hours after the United States began bombing Afghanistan in 2001 McDonald's restaurants were vandalized in cities in Pakistan and Indonesia and Muslim clerics asked for the boycott of US products.

For activists and cultural protectors, the most frustrating thing is that their calls go unheeded. Owners of McDonald's franchises continuously remind customers that they too are locals, that their employees are locals, and that their suppliers are mainly local. In Brazil, some anti-war protestors on their way home will stop at a McDonald's for a bite to eat.

Some of McDonald's major troubles, however, are in its most established markets in the United States, Canada, and the UK. Russian and Chinese go-getters might think that a meal in McDonald's puts them in a class above, but in its two major markets of North America and Europe, where the firm derives over two-thirds of all revenue, the food is considered unhealthy. Indeed, both Canada and the UK considered imposing a tax on fatty foods on the grounds that it was damaging to people's health and it costs the healthcare system a substantial amount. The tax is unlikely to be imposed because of a strong backlash from poverty groups which argue that this tax would place an uneven burden on those who depend on cheap food for their everyday survival. In the United States, the firm is being sued over claims that it misled parents about the nutritional value of its products, leading their children to become obese and unhealthy. McDonald's in the UK reacted by eliminating supersized options from the menu. A set of healthier options has now been introduced in Europe and North America as the company fends off critics in some of its friendliest markets. The company has also embraced sustainability and extended its corporate social responsibility (CSR) activities and reporting in order to keep one step ahead of a wider set of critics. In 2011, McDonald's was among Fortune's top ten world's most admired companies and as of 2015 it remained among the top 50. Its recent decline in rating has been argued to be down to recent consumer criticism

concerning menu offerings in accordance with recent protests over minimum wages offered to workers.

What makes McDonald's such an admired, recognizable brand, even amid an enduring fast-food backlash? New items on the menu have helped: salads (with Newman's Own low-fat dressing), wraps, oatmeal, and apple dippers. In addition, the chain constantly adds to its dollar menu, catering to those who have felt the recession's crunch. McDonald's also operates a wide range of charity programs, including teacher awards and youth basketball games. And financially, the company has been reported to be doing fine. As of 2014, McDonald's operates in 120 countries with over 35,000 outlets which serve approximately 70 million customers on a daily basis. In addition, McDonald's has consecutively managed to acquire sales of approximately $27.5 billion in each of the last few years and as of 2014 it employed a global workforce of over 420,000 people.

Source: David Barboza, "When golden arches are too red, white and blue," *New York Times*, October 14, 2001; Tony Karon, "Adieu, Ronald McDonald," *Time*, January 24, 2002; Simon Romero, "War and abuse do little to harm US brands," *New York Times*, May 9, 2004; McDonald's corporate website: http://www.aboutmcdonalds.com/mcd/csr/report.html, downloaded June 2011; "The world's most admired companies", *Forbes*, 2011; http://money.cnn.com/magazines/fortune/mostadmired/2011/; http://fortune.com/worlds-most-admired-companies/mcdonalds-46/; McDonald's, *Annual Report*, 2014; Corilyn Shropshire, "McDonald's plunges on Fortune's list of most admired companies," *Chicago Tribune*, accessed from http://www.chicagotribune.com/business/ct-fortune-most-admired-0220-biz-2-20150219-story.html

Cultures vary and these variations lead to real and significant differences in the ways that companies operate and people work. Moreover, *because* of globalization more and more firms are coming head to head with the added complexity of doing business globally, which stems from the huge amount of variety in the world that still exists (and arguably will always exist).

Before moving on to examine some typologies of global cultures, here is a word of warning. Much of this section will describe how various kinds of individual and group behavior can be linked to specific cultural groups and associate these cultural dispositions with different business styles and company structures. Acting on the basis of cultural stereotypes is highly sensitive and can be problematic. For example, at the simplest level a banker may be able to prove empirically that Pakistanis are more successful than Jamaicans at starting and running small businesses around the world. Using this insight as the basis for discriminating against Jamaicans wanting bank loans for business start-ups is not only unethical, but in most countries falls foul of race discrimination laws.

NATIONAL STEREOTYPES AND KEY DIMENSIONS OF CULTURE

Culture at two levels

Psychic distance
A measure of the similarity or difference between two cultures; also commonly defined as the measurable distance between the home market and a foreign market resulting from the perception of cultural and business differences

There are traditionally two different approaches to looking at culture:

- The psychic or psychological level, which focuses on the internalized norms, attitudes, and behavior of individuals from a particular culture (**psychic distance** is a measure of differences between groups).

■ The institutional level, which looks at national (or group) culture *embodied* in institutions (government, education, and economic institutions as well as in business organizations).

In this chapter we will mainly discuss the first, culture as shared psychology, with a brief reference to national institutional differences at the end.

People who are born in, or grew up in, the same country tend to share similar cultural characteristics. Nordström and Vahlne examined a sample of Swedish firms to understand the effects of psychic distance on market-entry strategies and costs.[6] They ranked 20 particular countries according to a range of national characteristics that contribute to psychic distance and found, as you might expect, that Denmark is closest to Sweden (1/20), the UK comes in at 6/20, Portugal at 15/20, Japan 16/20, Brazil 17/20, and Australia 20/20.

Nationality and culture tend to coincide, although nations encompass a wide variety of institutions, religions, beliefs, and patterns of behavior, and distinctive subcultures can always be found within individual countries. The only way to make sense of this wide diversity is to characterize distinct cultural groups through simplified national stereotypes.

Many studies have attempted to create these stereotypes by mapping and comparing the shared characteristics of managers and employees in different countries.[7] Researchers then examine the effects of key differences on business behavior, organization, structure, and ultimately the performance of companies from different countries. The following describes the milestone studies of this kind in the management field.

Hofstede's four dimensions of culture

Geert Hofstede is a Dutch psychologist who conducted one of the earliest and best-known cultural studies in management, on IBM's operations in 70 countries around the world.[8] Getting answers to 32 statements from over 116,000 questionnaires, he mapped key cultural characteristics of these countries according to four value dimensions:

Power distance
A cultural dimension that measures the degree to which less powerful members of organizations and institutions accept the fact that power is not distributed equally

Uncertainty avoidance
The extent to which people feel threatened by ambiguous situations and have created institutions and beliefs for minimizing or avoiding those uncertainties

Individualism
The tendency of people to look after themselves and their immediate family only

Masculinity
The degree to which the dominant values of a society are success, money, and material things

1 **Power distance** is the extent to which a culture accepts that power in organizations is distributed unequally. High power distance equates with steep organizational hierarchies, with more autocratic leadership and less employee participation in decision making (see Figure 5.2 for examples).

2 **Uncertainty avoidance** is the degree to which members of a society feel uncomfortable with risk and uncertainty. High uncertainty avoidance (Japan, Argentina, France) will be reflected in the high priority placed on rituals, routines, and procedures in organizations and society in general. Countries with low uncertainty avoidance (Denmark, UK, India, US) tend to emphasize flexibility and informality rather than bureaucracy.

3 **Individualism** is the extent to which people are supposed to take care of themselves and be emotionally independent from others (see Figure 5.2 for examples).

4 **Masculinity** is the value attributed to achievement, assertiveness, and material success (Japan, Mexico, Germany, UK) as opposed to the stereotypical feminine values of relationships, modesty, caring, and the quality of life (Sweden, Netherlands, Denmark), according to Hofstede.

Figure 5.2 illustrates some of Hofstede's findings using two of the most useful dimensions, power distance against the degree of individualism/collectivism. It reflects some general stereotypes of the countries included, with clear grouping of Australia, the UK and the United States as highly individualistic and less hierarchical (small power distance)

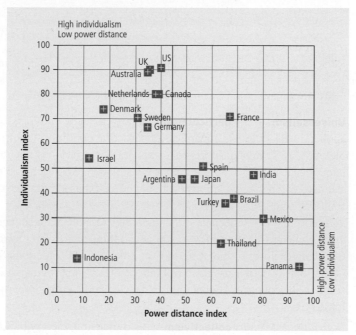

Figure 5.2 Hofstede's power distance against individualism for 20 countries

Source: G. Hofstede, "The cultural relativity of organizational practices and theories," *Journal of International Business Studies* (fall 1983), p. 92. Copyright © Geert Hofstede.

cultures against Mexico, Thailand, and Panama at the other extreme. We will elaborate on these definitions and their practical interpretation throughout this chapter.

Among his most important contributions, Hofstede provided strong evidence for the significance of national culture over professional role, gender, or race, as a determinant of variation in employees' attitudes, values, and behaviors, accounting for 50 percent of the differences his study observed. However, his studies have come in for significant criticism, despite widespread adoption of the four-dimensional framework. Three common criticisms are: (1) that the dimensions developed from data collected between 1968 and 1973 were relevant only for that particular period; (2) that corporate cultural and other influences from this one-organization study (of IBM) created significant bias; (3) that the sole use of attitude-survey questionnaires was not a valid basis for the resulting values and dimensions his study concluded with.[9]

Although Hofstede has continued to write on culture, organizations, and management,[10] it is useful to look more deeply into the work of another well-known Dutch culture guru.

Trompenaars' seven dimensions of culture

Fons Trompenaars built on Hofstede's work by expanding the framework for stereotyping and comparing different national cultures and by focusing more on the management implications of cultural differences. Using initial research involving 15,000 employees in 50 countries, Trompenaars explored the "cultural extremes and the incomprehension that can arise when doing business across cultures," even when people are working for the same company.[11]

Trompenaars arrived at seven distinctive dimensions of culture and used the questionnaire responses in his study to map a wide variety of countries along a continuum from one

Universalism
The uniform application of rules and procedures, regardless of situation, context, or individuals involved

Particularism
Judging a situation and adjusting rules and procedures according to the specific situation or individuals involved

Collectivism
The tendency of people to belong to groups who look after each other in exchange for loyalty

Neutral
A preference for unemotional, objective analysis of a situation or a decision and for limited displays of emotions and feelings in the workplace

Emotional
An acceptance of emotion and subjectivity as the bases for some decision making and a preference for explicit displays of emotions and feelings in the workplace

Specific
A tendency to limit workplace relationships and obligations, including relative status and hierarchical position, to the workplace

Diffuse
A tendency for workplace relationships and obligations, including relative status and hierarchical position, to extend into social situations and activities outside of work

Achievement oriented
Where status is earned rather than a right; recruitment and promotion opportunities tend to be more dependent on performance, as in a meritocracy

Ascription oriented
Where status is more of a right than earned; recruitment and promotion opportunities tend to be more dependent on seniority, ethnicity, gender, religion, or birth

extreme to the other within each dimension. The key to understanding this mapping approach is to identify where each country or culture is positioned *relative* to others on one or more of these dimensions.

Relative positioning gives insights into the kinds of conflicts, misunderstandings, and organizational and management problems that are likely to arise when individuals, groups, or firms from these countries interact in any of the ways described above.

1 **Universalism** *versus* **particularism**. In universalistic cultures, rules and regulations are applied in all situations, regardless of particular conditions or circumstances. The example used by Trompenaars refers to a salesman who does not fulfill his monthly sales quota because he was looking after his sick son. Should he be penalized according to standard company regulations or should he be excused because of the particular circumstances?

According to Trompenaars' findings, Switzerland, Canada, and the United States are among the most universalist. Australia and the UK are also toward this end of the scale. Germany is closer to the center, as is France, but the latter sits on the particularist side of the scale. Korea, Russia, and China are the most particularist of countries. (Note that some of the countries studied by Hofstede, like the strongly particularist Yugoslavia, no longer exist.)

2 *Individualism versus* **collectivism**. This dimension, clearly building on Hofstede, centers on whether individual rights and values are dominant or subordinate to those of the collective society.

The most individualist countries are Canada, the United States, Switzerland, and the UK. Among the most collectivist are Japan, Egypt, and India (and Nepal and Kuwait).

3 **Neutral** *versus* **emotional**. This reflects how much emotions are displayed in the workplace. More importantly, it indicates whether emotional or subjective (rather than objective) forms of assessment are thought to be the basis for good decision making in organizations. Some organizations emphasize reports, data, and analytical decision making by managers, whereas others feel that opinions, intuition, and gut feelings are credible or valid criteria. Predictably the most emotional countries include Italy and France and the least emotional groups (in the workplace at least) are the Japanese, Germans, Swiss, Chinese, and Indonesians.

4 **Specific** *versus* **diffuse**. Do work relationships (such as the hierarchical relationship between a senior manager and a subordinate) exist just in the workplace (are they specific), or do they extend into the social context outside the workplace (diffuse)? Here a telling example is whether an employee is willing to help paint a senior manager's house over a weekend. Clearly Australian bosses are likely to get a characteristically blunt answer to this request! China, Japan, India, and Singapore display highly diffuse relationships, Australia and the Netherlands the most specific.

5 **Achievement** *versus* **ascription**. This dimension refers to one's status within organizations, contrasting those cultures where status, credibility, authority, and ultimately power tend to be based on merit (achieved) against those where class, gender, education, or age tend to be the defining characteristics (status is ascribed).

Countries where status tends to be ascribed include Egypt, Turkey, and Argentina (and slightly less so, Russia, Japan, and France), and those where it is achieved include Norway, Sweden, and predictably the United States, Australia, Canada, and the UK.

Sequential
Cultures that view time in a sequential or linear fashion; order comes from separating activities and commitments

Synchronic
Cultures that view events in parallel over time; order comes from coordinating multiple activities and commitments

6 *Attitudes toward time.* **Sequential** (time as a sequence of events) versus **synchronic** (several events juggled at the same time) views of time tend to relate to punctuality for meetings and deadlines. Swedes and other northern European cultures tend to be punctual and plan according to specific timetables. Many southern European, Latin American, and Arabic cultures see punctuality and chronological precision as far less important. They also tend to naturally cope with a range of issues simultaneously, rather than one by one.

7 *Attitudes toward the environment.* This dimension reflects the emphasis a particular culture places on people's relationship with nature and the natural environment. On the one hand some cultures emphasize control and subjugation of environmental forces, whereas others emphasize the need to work with nature, in harmony with the environment. Clearly religious and philosophical differences around the world influence differences within this dimension.

Trompenaars' seven dimensions have been used in a variety of ways to gain insights into the kinds of problems that might arise in the contexts (face to face, company to company, and company to customer) outlined in Figure 5.1. In general they indicate the organizational characteristics we can expect from firms based in particular countries or dominated by certain nationalities. They are also used to measure changes in cultural values and behavior over time. Research shows that in both Japan and China, for example, achievement orientation is on the increase alongside some elements of individualism.[12]

The Japanese are moving away from a reliance on collectivism in the form of the state, large firms, and group associations, and placing more value on personal responsibility and individual performance. In China there is a shift in companies toward performance-related rewards and individual initiative, built on the changing views of the growing urban elite. But there are also wider concerns regarding the social costs as well as the benefits of self-interest.

The GLOBE project's nine dimensions of culture

More recent research has built on the Hofstede and Trompenaars research. The Global Leadership and Organizational Behavior Effectiveness (GLOBE) project began in 1992 and continues today. It has involved 150 researchers collecting data on cultural values and management and leadership attributes from 18,000 managers across 62 countries in the telecommunications, food, and banking industries.[13] In the same way as Hofstede and Trompenaars before them, the researchers place countries along a standard 1 to 7 scale. The GLOBE project, however, ends up with nine key cultural dimensions:

1 *Assertiveness.* The United States, Austria, Germany, and Greece are high; Sweden, Japan, and New Zealand are low.

2 *Future orientation.* A propensity for planning, investing, and delayed gratification: Singapore, Switzerland, and the Netherlands are high; Russia, Argentina, and Italy are low.

3 *Gender differentiation.* The degree to which gender role differences are maximized: South Korea, Egypt, India, and China are high; Hungary, Poland, and Denmark are low.

4 *Uncertainty avoidance.* A reliance on societal norms and procedures to improve predictability, and a preference for order, structure, and formality: Sweden, Switzerland, and Germany are high; Russia, Bolivia, and Greece are low.

5 *Power distance.* Russia, Thailand, and Spain are high; Denmark, the Netherlands, and Israel are low.

6 *Institutional collectivism (individualism vs. collectivism).* Promoting active participation in social institutions: Sweden, South Korea, and Japan are high; Greece, Argentina, and Italy are low.

7 *In-group/family collectivism.* A pride in small-group membership, family, close friends, etc.: Iran, India, and China are high; Denmark, Sweden, and New Zealand are low.

8 *Performance orientation* (much like achievement orientation). Singapore, Hong Kong, and the United States are high; Russia, Argentina, and Italy are low.

9 **Humane orientation**. An emphasis on fairness, altruism, and generosity: Ireland, Malaysia, and Egypt are high; Germany, Spain, France, Singapore, and Brazil are low.

Humane orientation
Cultures that emphasize helping others, charity, and people's wider social obligations

As you can see, many of these dimensions match those of Hofstede and Trompenaars, and the overall GLOBE framework is very much an extension of their approach.

The GLOBE researchers have examined the HRM implications of these cultural differences for practicing managers and looked at ways to avoid the pitfalls of ignorance and insensitivity.[14] A similar long-running study by the CRANET network has focused on European cultural differences and reports similar findings.[15]

As with the other cultural mapping studies by Hofstede and Trompenaars, GLOBE has faced some critical appraisal, which helps us understand the strengths and weaknesses of its concluding framework. A recent set of debates has usefully raised some methodological issues associated with these kinds of studies, and provides interesting points of contention we should be aware of, rather than blindly accepting the above kind of research.[16]

Applying the national culture frameworks

Different styles of communication and interaction result from the cultural differences listed above. These can lead to workplace misunderstandings, poor interpersonal and intergroup relationships, inefficiency, and higher costs. Three examples provide some insights into how we can apply the above typologies.

US managers, according to all of the above studies, are highly assertive and performance oriented relative to managers from other parts of the world (they come around the mid-point on all the other dimensions). Their interaction style is characteristically direct and explicit. They tend to use facts, figures, and logic to link specific steps to measurable outcomes, and this is the main focus of workplace interaction. Greeks and Russians are less individualistic, less performance oriented, and show lower levels of uncertainty avoidance (are less driven by procedures) than the Americans. When Russian and Greek managers, employees, customers, suppliers, or public sector officials interact with US counterparts, they may well find their approach too direct and results focused. For them communication is likely to be more about mutual learning and an exploration of relevant issues than an explicit agreement about specific expectations and end results. Similarly, the Swedes may find the US style too aggressive and unfriendly, working against the relationship-building process that for them is a major objective of workplace interaction.

The Koreans and Japanese have highly gender-differentiated societies with males tending to dominate decision making and leading most face-to-face communication. The agenda for discussion is likely set by males, and traditional language forms differ according to whether a man is addressing a woman or an older person talking to a younger person, and vice versa. Gender- (and age-) related roles, responsibilities, and behaviors are therefore deeply embedded in language and customs.[17] Poland and Denmark lie at the other end of the continuum on the gender-differentiation dimension. Perhaps even more than other Western managers, their lack of awareness of this cultural difference runs the risk of both embarrassing female employees and offending and alienating senior Japanese male managers. This kind of clash can make negotiations and interaction of all kinds between these groups that much more difficult.

Certain kinds of HRM techniques are inappropriate for organizations that show high power distance ratings. Companies and management consultancies in the UK, the United States, and northern European countries have developed fairly participative management systems to improve productivity, based on their characteristically low power distance and flat organizational hierarchies. Techniques such as 360-degree feedback systems for developing management–employee relationships are not likely to work, however, in Mexican, Panamanian, Thai, or Russian organizations, which have high power distance and steep hierarchies. Subordinates are uncomfortable being asked to evaluate senior managers, and managers would not see subordinates as qualified to comment on their performance. More than this, to employees in some countries this kind of consultation can give the impression that senior managers do not know what they are doing. The employees may lose faith in senior management's ability and leave!

None of the above examples means that international managers should (or ever could) entirely change their behavior to suit local values and practices. Like many of the challenges facing managers, cultural sensitivity and cross-cultural effectiveness come from striking a balance between one's own norms, values, and principles and those of the "foreigner." The lesson for multinational firms is that ethnocentric corporate cultures and completely standardized HR systems do not work. The key challenge is to adapt to get the best from local differences.

 Active learning check

Review your answer to Active Learning Case question 2 and make any changes you like. Then compare your answer to the one below.

2 **How well do the characteristics described in the case match the respective, stereotypical national cultures of these countries?**

According to the above frameworks they match reasonably well. The US culture is characterized as individualistic, achievement/performance oriented, and assertive. Most of these traits clash with the "feminine" (in Hofstede's characterization) values of relationships, modesty, caring, and the quality of life emphasized by the Swedes. Hofstede finds US managers less hierarchical than most cultures, which is not indicated in either Upjohn or Pfizer. However, as Figure 5.2 shows, both Sweden and the United States have a low power distance and high individualism rating, relative to other countries, but the latter has a slightly higher power distance (steeper management hierarchy) than the former. Sweden also has a relatively high uncertainty avoidance ranking, preferring order, structure, and formality, which does not stand out in the case study. Swedes are also high on institutional collectivism but low on family or small-group collectivism. The Italians are the opposite. Unlike the Americans, the Italians are not at all oriented toward achievement (Trompenaars) or performance (GLOBE). They are also more emotional than the Swedes and Americans according to Hofstede and have a relatively low future orientation (GLOBE).

"The way we do things here": the implications of cultural differences for organizations and managers

Mapping out a variety of national cultural typologies using the various dimensions of culture described above gives us some insights into the kinds of differences that exist among different groups of managers, employees, and organizations.

Two key questions about the role of the individual in a firm and the role of a firm in a society from Trompenaars' study give us a starting point to explore the management implications of cultural differences. The responses in Figure 5.3 reflect the degree of support for the particular proposition A or B for each of these questions.

Americans clearly display what has been termed (originally by the sociologist Max Weber) a mechanistic and functional view of the firm as an organization (A) and a shareholder-driven, profit-oriented view of this organization in society (although more than half the US vote in Figure 5.3 was for option B). The Japanese tend to have a more organic view of the firm, emphasizing the importance of social networks and the obligation of the firm to a wider constituency of stakeholders (although this is a characteristic of traditional Japan that has been strongly tested in the recent recessionary environment).

A wide range of factors within organizations are influenced directly or indirectly by the cultural predispositions of managers and employees. We know from the above studies and a wide range of other research that these factors include:

■ The general relationship between employees and the organization: their roles and responsibilities, obligations, and loyalties and the link these have with life outside the workplace.

■ Hierarchy, power and authority, and the accepted routes to attaining these, including factors that underpin status and credibility in different societies and organizations.

■ The role of formal rules and regulations versus the informal communication, personal networks, and hidden "rules of the game."

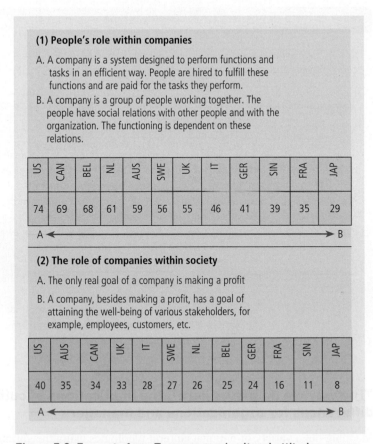

(1) People's role within companies

A. A company is a system designed to perform functions and tasks in an efficient way. People are hired to fulfill these functions and are paid for the tasks they perform.

B. A company is a group of people working together. The people have social relations with other people and with the organization. The functioning is dependent on these relations.

US	CAN	BEL	NL	AUS	SWE	UK	IT	GER	SIN	FRA	JAP
74	69	68	61	59	56	55	46	41	39	35	29

A ⟵——————————————————————⟶ B

(2) The role of companies within society

A. The only real goal of a company is making a profit

B. A company, besides making a profit, has a goal of attaining the well-being of various stakeholders, for example, employees, customers, etc.

US	AUS	CAN	UK	IT	SWE	NL	BEL	GER	FRA	SIN	JAP
40	35	34	33	28	27	26	25	24	16	11	8

A ⟵——————————————————————⟶ B

Figure 5.3 Excerpts from Trompenaars' cultural attitudes survey

Source: C. Hampden-Turner and F. Trompenaars, *The Seven Cultures of Capitalism: Value Systems for Creating Wealth in the United States, Britain, Japan, Germany, France, Sweden and the Netherlands* (New York: Doubleday, 1993).

- The accepted basis for decision making, including rationale, scientific, mechanistic, and objective versus subjective, tacit, rule of thumb, etc.
- The degree to which employees act and are treated as individuals or groups and the role of interpersonal relationships.
- Motivation and rewards systems.
- Interaction and communication mechanisms.

Work attitudes and the appropriate management of work attitudes have a significant influence on productivity and innovativeness in a company. Managers and employees who are motivated by their core social values to work hard and continually strive to improve their company's products and services and the processes by which they are produced are clearly a source of competitive advantage. It is interesting to note how social norms may drive a strong work ethic despite individual dissatisfaction with workload or job responsibilities. This has been shown in several companies between US and Japanese factory workers where the Japanese are found to be more loyal and aligned with company objectives but far less satisfied individually.[18]

Table 5.2 compares interview responses from sample workforces in seven countries. The resulting ranking of what it is that employees value most from their jobs shows that "interesting work" is what tends to engage most people, beyond everything else.

Table 5.2 Average and intra-country ranking of work goals: a seven-nation comparison

Work goals	Belgium	UK	Germany	Israel	Japan	Netherlands	United States
Opportunity to learn	5.8[a]	5.55	4.97	5.83	6.26	5.38	6.16
	7[b]	8	9	5	7	9	5
Interpersonal relations	6.34	6.33	6.43	6.67	6.39	7.19	6.08
	5	4	4	2	6	3	7
Opportunity for promotion	4.49	4.27	4.48	5.29	3.33	3.31	5.08
	10	11	10	8	11	11	10
Convenient work hours	4.71	6.11	5.71	5.53	5.46	5.59	5.25
	9	5	6	7	8	8	9
Variety	5.96	5.62	5.71	4.89	5.05	6.86	6.10
	6	7	6	11	9	4	6
Interesting work	8.25	8.02	7.26	6.75	6.38	7.59	7.41
	1	1	3	1	2	2	1
Job security	6.80	7.12	7.57	5.22	6.71	5.68	6.30
	3	3	2	10	4	7	3
Match between the people and the work	5.77	5.63	6.09	5.61	7.83	6.17	6.19
	8	6	5	6	1	6	4
Pay	7.13	7.80	7.73	6.60	6.56	5.27	6.82
	2	2	1	3	5	5	2
Working conditions	4.19	4.87	4.39	5.28	4.18	5.03	4.84
	11	9	11	9	10	10	11
Autonomy	6.56	4.69	5.66	6.00	6.89	7.61	5.79
	4	10	8	4	3	1	8

Notes:
[a] First row shows average rank on a scale of 1 to 10.
[b] Second row shows ranking of work goals within each country, with a rank of 1 being most important and 11 being least important.

Source: Adapted from Itzhak Harpaz, "The importance of work goals: an international perspective," *Journal of International Business Studies,* vol. 21, no. 1 (1990), p. 81.

CROSS-CULTURAL MANAGEMENT

Three key areas capture many of the factors covered by the above typologies and cultural stereotypes, where cultural differences can make a significant difference at the company-to-company and face-to-face levels. These are organization, leadership, and communication (see Figure 5.4).

Organization

Organization styles range from organic, informal, or people oriented to systematic or mechanistic, formal, or task oriented, in keeping with some common organizational dimensions described by sociologists throughout history (such as Max Weber and Emile Durkheim). Organizations that operate very much around personal relationships and social networks contrast those that are much more functional and logical. In fact different cultures and different firms display elements of both these characteristics, but the balance varies considerably and can create tensions when groups of people or firms from different ends of the spectrum interact or try to cooperate.

As an aid to predicting differences among individuals, groups, or firms, and understanding the significance of these variations, *relative* differences among countries, organizations, and groups of people are important, rather than any absolute scores. For example, family companies are characteristically directive, individual oriented but organic. Multinational firms are usually more autocratic and mechanistic. Consulting and professional services firms are often mechanistic and emphasize individual performance and rewards but may also be fairly team oriented. Entrepreneurial new ventures will usually be organic, unsystematic, and group oriented.

Leadership

Leadership styles range from individual oriented, directive, autocratic, top down, or authoritarian to group oriented, participative, democratic, bottom up, or egalitarian. Again, cultural groups and corporations often encompass both kinds of leadership but tend to reflect one dominant style.

Individual managers from cultures that score high on the power distance or assertiveness dimensions are likely to be viewed by those from other cultures as autocratic and directive, but will tend to view others as indecisive and too compromising. They will not want to spend too much time discussing issues to achieve a consensus. If they also reflect an organic or informal (low uncertainty avoidance) culture, this will result in an instinctive or unsystematic

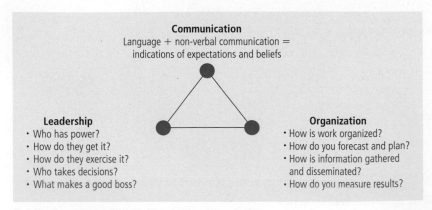

Figure 5.4 Management dimensions of culture

decision-making and implementation style, and they might be viewed as an unpredictable autocrat. This contrasts the combination of high power distance and high uncertainty avoidance, which results in a more directive and mechanistic style. Such leaders prefer established formal routines and a command-and-control bureaucracy, while other managers are likely to see this as over-regulated and inflexible. The Active Learning Case at the start of the chapter demonstrates a range of these styles and the problems that result from the imposition of a new style of organization and leadership within a corporate merger.

Communication

Clearly, at the face-to-face level language differences can be the most prominent barrier to communication and therefore to cooperation and coordination. English speakers tend to have an advantage in many situations since English has emerged as the main language of business globally. However, this has led to complacency among some indigenous English speakers, notably the British and the North Americans. First, less effort is often made to learn other languages and their associated cultures, which normally limits a manager's understanding of foreign colleagues, workers, or customers. Second, the assumption is often made that once the language barrier is broken cultural differences are also removed, whereas these may remain, causing miscommunication and misinterpretation. As for much of this chapter on culture, preparation and awareness are the best starting points for minimizing differences that can create problems.

It is through efficient communication that two parties steer toward an understanding—a mutually agreed basis for doing business. The signs and signals on this route to an understanding are strongly influenced by culture. Different groups have different ways of displaying approval or of showing frustration in negotiations and different ideas of what constitutes a final agreement. The Japanese do not really have an equivalent word for the English "no" and indicate disapproval in a range of non-verbal ways. The Japanese word *hai* does mean "yes" but it often means "yes, I understand what you are saying" not "yes, I agree with what you are saying." Germans place a lot of emphasis on written communications and documented evidence rather than verbal interaction, compared to the Spanish and Italians, to whom verbal interaction and agreement is recognized as binding in some contexts. The Americans prefer legal contracts and have armies of lawyers to make agreements highly specified. Other, more organic business cultures tend to work toward a relationship in which trust and understanding replace the need for legally binding contracts. Again, awareness through preparation and anticipation of differences is the best starting point for avoiding **culture clash**.

Culture clash
When two cultural groups (national or corporate) meet, interact, or work together and differences in their values, beliefs, rules of behavior, or styles of communication create misunderstandings, antagonism, or other problems

The corporate response

How have MNEs responded to the challenge of managing across cultural boundaries? What kinds of organization structures, HRM procedures, and corporate cultures have been developed to cope with the enormous differences among people and to unify this diversity toward a common purpose?

At a very general level, good transnational firms develop an *awareness* and appreciation of cultural differences among their managers and employees. They also take steps to encourage *adaptation* of personal behavior or organizational practices, or products and services, to suit the changing mix of cultures within the firm, in subsidiaries and in key markets. Training programs, including a range of activities at the induction stage, when new recruits join a firm or existing personnel take up a role in a new country, are a standard way for firms to do these things. Job rotation, with a focus on developing international managers with personal experience in a variety of different countries, is also practiced by a number of firms. It is normally very difficult to assess such practices using any form of cost–benefit analysis. The costs are usually easily identifiable, but the benefits are very often intangible. For many experienced international companies, such as Shell or Nestlé, a long-term commitment to (and investment in) cultural awareness is simply accepted as a necessary part of being global.

Beyond awareness and adaptation, the best firms aim to *leverage* the diversity of cultures within their organizations and combine the best aspects of different ways of doing things. Corporate culture, a shared identity spanning culturally diverse groups of employees, provides a way to do this. Companies can usefully invest in their own socialization mechanisms, such as social events alongside regular meetings and conferences. Company magazines, intranets, and even in-house television channels for corporate communications can all support this process. These may not only improve cross-cultural awareness, but also promote shared values, symbols, and even language to help bind employees together.[19]

Here is a list of other useful strategies for managing cultural diversity distilled from a number of research studies:[20]

1 Recognize diversity. Identify and map the various national cultures and ethnic groups within the firm and use this to understand which elements of consistency and standardization can or should be promoted.

2 Build diversity issues into recruitment, HRM planning, strategy, location decisions, alliances, and partnerships. This helps avoid clashes and inefficiency and supports cultural awareness.

3 Identify where and to what degree local divisions should be encouraged or empowered to take the lead in expressing and managing diversity. Some degree of devolution of responsibility away from the center of the firm allows local divisions to identify aspects of diversity that are most important to them and their operations.

4 Encourage cross-border discussion and interaction as well as focused training. Include specific kinds/combinations of international experience for fast-track managers.

5 Aim for a cultural balance in particular areas of strategic and tactical decision making (such as brand changes for foreign markets). Ensure a (numerically) balanced pool of managers or appropriately diverse inputs into decision making.

6 Lead from the top. Aim to match the geographic diversity of the firm's businesses with a culturally mixed senior management group and board of directors (as in the case of Sony and Unilever).

 Active learning check

Review your answer to Active Learning Case question 3 and make any changes you like. Then compare your answer to the one below.

3 **What could senior managers do before and after mergers to alleviate some of the problems that result from culture clash?**

A simple starting point would be to review the various frameworks (Hofstede, Trompenaars, and GLOBE, for example) to understand some generic differences between the national cultures involved in the merger and anticipate some of the likely problems. It would have also helped to examine the potential areas of organizational conflict with senior managers from each company and/or with managers with some experience of two or more of the countries and their ways of doing things. Some degree of cultural training or induction plus an investment in joint meetings and events to get to know each other could also have improved understanding and morale. However, the cost–benefit trade-off for these kinds of pre- and post-merger activity is difficult to precisely assess.

Multinational organization structures: imperialist or independent?

A key dilemma for international firms is the degree to which they promote or even impose a common, standardized corporate culture across the organization. Although this will create economies of scale and be more efficient in a number of respects, it will also stifle diversity and create clashes with local cultures and ways of doing things around the organization.

Firms respond to this dilemma in different ways, with different outcomes. At the simplest level we can map out a range of responses from what is termed *imperialist*, where a common culture is imposed wherever a company has a presence, to *federalist* or *independent* structures, where each national subsidiary bases its own culture on local norms and values. There are problems associated with either of these extremes and most firms try to steer a middle line, standardizing some elements across the whole organization to centralize and simplify some practices and unify employees, while allowing differentiation where necessary. This *transnational culture* allows for a compromise in work styles, values, and approaches, harnessing the strengths that lie in diversity.

Table 5.3 illustrates a range of organization types. In particular, it links elements of organization structure and design with cultural orientation, for example, in the relationship between headquarters and regional subsidiaries. It specifically extends the ethnocentric, **polycentric**, and **geocentric** typologies introduced by Perlmutter in the 1960s.[21]

Polycentrism
Each subsidiary, division, or function reflects the culture of its host country; local managers' cultural predispositions and decision making dominate over those of home-country managers in a multinational firm

Geocentrism
Neither home- nor host-country culture dominates decision making, human resource management, and overall corporate culture in a multinational firm

- *Ethnocentric* firms are where top management is dominated by home-country nationals, and procedures and management styles are transferred from the head office and imposed on regional subsidiaries in place of local ways of doing things.

- *Polycentric* firms tend to act like a federation of semi-autonomous organizations with financial controls or strict reporting structures holding them together. Subsidiaries are able to reflect the local cultural norms, and headquarters appreciates the need for different organization designs, procedural norms, rewards systems, etc., as long as profits flow to the center.

- *Geocentric* firms are seen as the ideal, collaborative, and meritocratic form of global organization. (Unilever is seen as an example based on the above statement.) They are characterized by: an equal sharing of power and responsibility between headquarters and subsidiary; senior management promoted according to ability rather than nationality; and subsidiaries that share worldwide objectives with managers focusing beyond national market interests.

In the geocentric organization the *benefits* of cultural diversity, such as knowledge of local customers and business practices, are harnessed for the good of the firm as a whole. The *costs* of diversity, such as language and communication problems, different values, and different attitudes toward work, are minimized. Firms moving toward this more balanced, geocentric approach have to recognize diversity and its effects and identify which elements of consistency in regulations and values should be promoted, where and when. Local divisions must identify aspects of diversity that are most important to them and their operations and take the lead in expressing and managing these differences. Discussion,

Table 5.3 Organization types reflecting cultural predispositions

	Imperialist	Interventionist	Interactive	Independent
Organization	Ethnocentric	Ethnocentric	Geocentric	Polycentric
Structure	Steep hierarchy	Flat hierarchy	Network	Federation
Strategy	Dictated	Centrally decided	Jointly specified	Locally specified
Decision making	Centralized	Distributed	Shared	Devolved

interaction, cross-divisional teamwork and job rotation, support, awareness, and understanding go alongside training programs, language courses, and cultural assimilation.

Unilever is an example of a firm that has closely examined the range of cultures it encompassed and made a deliberate attempt to use cultural differences as a strength rather than a weakness for fulfilling its strategic aims. As part of a high-profile internal campaign, the company described itself as a *multi-local multinational*, and this was used to explicitly inform employees of its cultural tolerance. According to a statement from a Unilever board chairman, one of the firm's objectives was to "Unileverize our Indians and Indianize our Unileverians."[22]

Culture clash in cross-border M&A and joint ventures

The range of organization styles in Table 5.3 also reflects the range of ways multinational firms approach the management of joint ventures or of firms acquired through merger and acquisition (M&A). They can either impose their own style of management on these organizations or allow them the independence to reflect their own cultural norms and existing corporate cultures.[23]

Cultural differences often prove to be a significant post-merger barrier for managers looking to realize the synergies and added value of pooling the resources and capabilities of two companies from different parts of the world. The Active Learning Case at the start of this chapter illustrates this clearly. Culture clash and its impact on the bottom line are often complex and difficult to predict. More often failure to anticipate culture clash results from the lack of awareness on the part of senior managers and deal-makers driving the M&A strategy. Financial analyses that focus on the due-diligence process of counting up assets and identifying cost-cutting benefits tend to miss any estimation of cultural and organizational synergy (or lack thereof). Anticipating such problems and preparing for the development of effective relationships between people from both sides of an M&A or an alliance is central to maximizing the rewards.

Daimler-Benz ran into these problems when it merged with Chrysler. A number of senior-level US managers either were asked to leave or left because they were unhappy about the style of management imposed by Daimler. Among these early leavers were members of the design team responsible for the PT Cruiser and other Chrysler successes of the late 1990s. Many went to arch-rival General Motors, which is not an unusual outcome. One study showed that on average 20 percent of a firm's top management will leave within one year of being acquired and 70 percent will go within five years.[24]

Cultural awareness and some degree of organizational adaptation can limit the number of key people who do leave following a cross-border M&A. Understanding how to predict and mitigate the negative effects of cultural differences should be on the agenda for all managers. Despite this, in some cases an ethnocentric, imperialist approach is precisely what is needed to drive a newly merged organization forward. When Carlos Ghosn led the partial takeover of Nissan by Renault, he imposed a very non-Japanese way of doing things on the firm. In terms of the firm within its broader economic and social context, breaking *keiretsu* ties and laying off employees were radical steps to take. Internally he instituted performance-related pay and promotion and cut through a range of traditional rituals around HRM, budget control, and decision making that were underpinned by the traditional Japanese culture of the company. These were the kinds of changes that needed to be made to reverse years of losses and indebtedness. It was also, arguably, impossible for the incumbent Japanese management to make such changes. (Chapter 18, on Japan, contains the full Nissan–Renault case.)

At the other end of the spectrum, reflecting again on Table 5.3, Tata Tea Limited, owner of 54 tea estates and the second-most popular tea brand in India, provides us with an example of a successful M&A which followed the "independent" approach vis-à-vis its newly acquired subsidiary. In March 2000 it bought one of the UK's top tea brands, Tetley Tea, some say on the basis of profits at Tata Consulting Services, the successful IT and software arm of the $9 billion Tata conglomerate. Coming more than 50 years after the end of 200 years of British colonial rule that had supported British ownership of tea estates in India, this shift of power is an appropriate symbol for the twenty-first century. But the takeover was barely noticed by the British public. In stark contrast to the imperialist approach of the British in India all those years ago, Tata took a hands-off approach, allowing the existing management, with its local knowledge and experience, to continue running Tetley. A federal structure with devolved decision making is supported by a polycentric organizational style.[25]

INTERNATIONAL BUSINESS STRATEGY IN ACTION

The collective culture of the John Lewis Partnership

Founded in 1864 in London, the John Lewis Partnership (JLP) is an employee-owned organization that primarily operates two businesses, John Lewis department stores and Waitrose supermarkets. This highly unusual ownership structure was established by John Spedan Lewis, the son of the founder, who signed away his ownership rights in 1929, paving the way for an "experiment in industrial democracy." At the heart of the company's constitution is the principle of establishing a "better form of business." Staff "happiness" and a democratic, inclusive culture, with management encouraging input and ideas from staff to help shape how the businesses are run, all continue to be central to the firm's ethos.

With a focus on delivering high-quality products and customer service, JLP has successfully grown to operate 340 Waitrose stores and 44 John Lewis retail stores with a workforce of over 90,000 employees. In 2014 JLP had revenues of £10.2 billion (£6.1 billion Waitrose and £4.1 billion John Lewis) and accumulated profits of £423.6 million (£310.1 million Waitrose and £226.1 million John Lewis). However, in 2015 JLP announced a large decrease in profits (26 percent down year-on-year) as a result of a number of market factors, including:

- supermarket price wars (as Lidl, Aldi and ASDA got into their stride on the UK high street), leading particularly to reductions in like-for-like sales with other supermarkets and a downward push on prices;

- a rise in pension costs, by £60 million, as the firm tackled its £1.2 billion pension deficit;

- redundancy payments offered to staff within three distribution centers set to close, affecting over 250 employees.

As an employee-owned organization, all staff within the JLP group receive a bonus based on their individual salary and the organization has been praised by various political factions in the UK as a model of caring capitalism. In 2014, all staff received a 15 percent pay out as a bonus, which was itself a reduction by 2 percent from the previous year. In 2015, following the above performance, the bonus payout was reduced to 11 percent.

The company's ownership model leads to a number of positive effects. First, the bonus structure means it is in the interests of all managers and staff to work hard, innovate, and continually improve because they personally benefit when the firm performs well. But equally important is the corporate culture that this structure promotes. It is a more egalitarian organization, with directors of the business paid substantially less than counterparts in rivals like Sainsbury's or Tesco and staff receiving perks including theater outings, access to holiday homes and various subsidized clubs. It is also one that is benchmarked because of the commitment, dedication, and friendliness of staff. Customers report excellent shop-floor service and this leads to more sales, but it also leads to greater employee satisfaction. Staff are rewarded and "empowered."

Finally, the "partnership spirit" at John Lewis benefits the wider communities in which the firm's offices and shops are located. The firm and its staff operate in the spirit of a social enterprise, working with local charities and volunteer groups. This is led from the top, by the Managing Director Andy Street, who is also Chairman of the Greater Birmingham and Solihull Local Enterprise Partnership (GBS-LEP). Andy Street has worked for many years with policy-makers and universities in the region to drive forward a renaissance in the Birmingham city region, where John Lewis built its flagship store in "Grand Central" Birmingham in 2015.

Source: JLP, *Annual Report*, 2014; Michael Pooler and Andrea Felsted, "Price war and pension costs hit John Lewis," *Financial Times*, September 10, 2015; Andrea Felsted, "John Lewis expected to cut staff bonuses," *Financial Times*, March 6, 2015; Graham Ruddick, "John Lewis profits fall as costs and competition increase," *Guardian*, September 10, 2015; "John Lewis says pensions to hit profits," *BBC News*, September 10, 2015; "John Lewis profits slide in 'difficult' market," *Sky News*, September 10, 2015; "Andy Street CBE delivers a compelling message for Birmingham," Birmingham Business School, University of Birmingham, December 8, 2015, birmingham.ac.uk.

Active learning check

Review your answer to Active Learning Case question 4 and make any changes you like. Then compare your answer to the one below.

4 **Explain why one organization might want to impose some of its ways of doing things on another, such as an acquired firm or subsidiary.**

Standardizing ways of doing things across the overall organization can be more efficient, to a certain extent. Differences can create difficulties in communication, teamwork, motivation, or coordination, and the impact on company performance can be significant. It is important to make the distinction between the values, beliefs, and norms, plus the associated work practices and management structures that stem from the dominant national culture (the imposition can then be described as ethnocentric) or from the corporate culture. In the latter case the firm will be aiming to derive the benefits of having a shared culture that bridges the national cultural differences across the overall organization.

Cultural differences between groups of people in the one firm, or between the employees of two firms engaged in a joint venture, are not necessarily a problem. However, when they do create difficulties in terms of communication, teamwork, motivation, or coordination, the impact on company performance can be significant, despite the fact that clear cause-and-effect relationships are often difficult to identify precisely. Rather than suggesting a single "best practice" for dealing with this, the examples above suggest that solutions are context specific.

CULTURE EMBODIED IN NATIONAL INSTITUTIONS

The second level at which we can analyze cultural differences and their effects is at the institutional level, where national cultural characteristics are *embodied* in institutions from government agencies and governance mechanisms to the education system, economic institutions, and business organizations.

Firms engaging in cross-border joint ventures or M&As need to take account of the national context in which the new partner or acquired firm is situated. Similarly, when marketing and selling products in a new national market, these broader differences matter. A country's distinctive political, legal, and institutional context partly reflects its dominant national culture. Education systems, labor laws, environmental regulations, capital markets, and the relationships between private sector businesses and public sector organizations will vary accordingly.[26]

Trompenaars uses his findings simply to divide various countries into subgroups reflecting shared characteristics stemming from common cultural influences (Figure 5.5).

■ *Western pluralism* emphasizes individual competitiveness, commonly represented by separate ventures competing in price-defined markets for success. Survival of the fittest is the catchphrase, and companies tend to be run as meritocracies.

■ *Command economies* are centrally planned hierarchies with less individualism and less individual incentive. Clearly, as global politics changes, countries are tending to move out of this category. For example, Poland is now an emerging capitalist country reflecting the characteristics of Western pluralism more than a command economy.

■ *Organic ordering* refers to the family-centered hierarchies of Asia, southern Europe, and Latin America. Inter- and intra-organization interaction is based around information sharing and collaborative competition.

Figure 5.5 Shared characteristics stemming from common cultural influences

Source: C. Hampden-Turner and F. Trompenaars, *The Seven Cultures of Capitalism: Value Systems for Creating Wealth in the United States, Britain, Japan, Germany, France, Sweden and the Netherlands* (New York: Doubleday, 1993).

■ *Structured networks* reflect the more equal, structured relationships between companies and with public sector organizations that exist in some countries.

France, with some comparisons with other Western economies and organizations, provides an example, giving a snapshot of some of the main characteristics that stem from the country's cultural distinctiveness.

France: cultural and social characteristics that create a national distinctiveness

National characteristics

■ Central planning, national protectionism for domestic industry, and strong government intervention in the market (compared to other European economies) lie at the heart of the French system. Civil servants are intellectual and respected as in Japan (but not the UK) and well paid (unlike in Japan).

■ Communication tends to be vertical (up–across–down). Bypassing official channels is not common: uncertainty reduction tends to predominate.

■ Hierarchy is important, bureaucracy respected. Clear hierarchy, divisionalization, and rules and regulations guide behavior. However, this exists alongside a respect for maverick gestures and individuals or groups that overcome the obstacles and beat the system.

■ Government-to-business links are formal and informal, with the elitist groups from the *grandes écoles* bridging public and private sectors at the senior level. Ascription dominates over achievement compared to the UK or the United States, again with parallels with Japan.

■ Competition occurs at school age when success determines assignment to a particular *cadre* or *echelon* inside and outside the workplace (depending on the school attended as much as individual performance).

■ France has a large number of family-owned and managed firms. It does not have the ***Mittelstand*** (small technical and engineering firms) that underpin the chemical and machine tool industries in Germany.

Mittelstand
About 3.4 million small and medium-sized firms defined as having less than €50 million turnover that make up the heart of the German economy

■ Capital markets are competitive but are not as "short-termist" as in the UK and the United States, with an overwhelming emphasis on share values and dividends. France does not have the strong interfirm networks that exist in Germany and Japan (*keiretsu*), which include links between financial institutions (banks, institutional shareholders) and the companies they fund.

French organizations

Esprit de corps
The spirit of a group that makes the members want the group to succeed

■ French companies also tend to be hierarchical, bureaucratic, and well structured, but there is a strong view of the company as a social entity (an **esprit de corps**) with an emphasis on obligation and loyalty rather than individual gain.

■ Despite moves toward a more equal relationship, French managers continue to have a supervisory role over workers. German and Japanese managers, by comparison, tend to be more collegiate and cooperative across levels of the hierarchy, including mentoring arrangements between senior and junior managers.

■ Hierarchical relationships are diffuse (in Trompenaars' terminology) rather than limited to the workplace (France ranks highest among European countries along this dimension). Companies have a responsibility toward the wider society, and managers, because of their professional status, have a role to play in society.

Gestion
The skill or practice of controlling, directing, or planning something, especially a commercial enterprise or activity

■ Scientific management techniques, termed **gestion**, dominate, which parallels German zeal for quantification and measurement to guide performance improvement.

■ There is a premium on technical and on-the-job training (similar to Germany and Japan). Marketing and accountancy skills are less valued than in the UK and the United States.

■ A surprise to many observers is that one-fifth of the labor force is unionized. French labor law (*Code du Travail*) is comprehensive and enforced. Companies are relatively loyal to their employees compared to British or US firms, but there is not the strong social contract that exists in Japan.

KEY POINTS

1 Culture can be defined as "the sum total of the beliefs, rules, techniques, institutions, and artifacts that characterize human populations."

2 Cultural differences can have an important effect at the face-to-face or company-to-company levels and need to be taken into account in dealing with different groups of customers around the world.

3 Culture can be analyzed at two levels: the psychic distance between groups of people, and the differences in culture embodied in national institutions and socio-economic systems.

4 Hofstede, Trompenaars, and the GLOBE researchers have constructed useful frameworks for understanding broad differences between national cultures which underpin differences in the design of organizations and the behavior of managers and employees.

5 Differences in organization, leadership, and communication can be used to measure differences in groups and individuals and help managers anticipate when and why cultures may clash.

6 Company responses to the challenges of managing diversity range from the imperialist to the independent approaches.

7 Ethnocentric firms impose a common culture on all subsidiaries, polycentric firms allow subsidiaries to reflect local ways of doing things, and geocentric firms maintain a balance between center and subsidiary.

8 When in Japan, do not throw your *meishi*!

Key terms

- *grande école*
- culture
- socialization
- corporate culture
- ethnocentrism
- cultural convergence
- psychic distance
- power distance
- uncertainty avoidance
- individualism

- masculinity
- universalism
- particularism
- collectivism
- neutral
- emotional
- specific
- diffuse
- achievement oriented
- ascription oriented

- sequential
- synchronic
- humane orientation
- culture clash
- polycentrism
- geocentrism
- *Mittelstand*
- esprit de corps
- gestion

REVIEW AND DISCUSSION QUESTIONS

1 In your own words, what is meant by the term *culture*?

2 In what way do ethnocentrism and misconceptions about other cultures inhibit those doing business internationally?

3 Why is language so critical in understanding international culture? How can this problem be dealt with effectively?

4 Why are cultural differences an important factor when adapting products for new overseas markets?

5 Use Trompenaars' seven dimensions of culture to compare and contrast your own national stereotype to another.

6 Why are work attitudes of importance to MNEs? Cite and describe two examples.

7 What kinds of reward systems are likely to be effective in more individualistic and achievement-oriented cultures like the United States?

8 Explain how the GLOBE project has extended the dimensions of national culture beyond the work of Hofstede and Trompenaars.

9 In the Pharmacia–Upjohn merger how did employment practices and workplace regulations differ among the Americans, the Swedes, and the Italians, and what impact did these differences have on the operational efficiency of the merged company?

10 Show with examples how managers in multinational firms could improve their employees' awareness of the important differences among cultures.

11 What are the benefits of and the problems for a polycentric MNE?

12 Why is an understanding of the institutional norms, regulations, and practices of other countries important for international firms? Give examples to illustrate your answer.

13 What does the French term *gestion* mean?

REAL CASE

Do not throw your *meishi*!

Some time ago the Competitiveness Division of the Department of Trade and Industry (DTI) in the British government commissioned research on British small and medium-sized enterprises (SMEs) that had managed to set up successful businesses in Japan, one of the toughest (though lucrative) global markets to break into for foreign firms (see Chapter 18). Numerous success stories from the study show how some firms managed to adapt to the differences in culture, society, and business practices that can act as barriers to foreign firms. But there are also numerous tales of the blunders that some managers made that undermined their efforts to establish themselves in Japan.

Meishi is Japanese for "business card," but has a deeper significance in Japan than elsewhere as a representation of the employee's allegiance to and respect for his or her company. The strong emphasis placed on loyalty and obligation between employees and their firms, lifetime employment based on a moral contract (rather than a price-based contract), and a manager's position as a member of a collective all have a strong influence on his (sometimes her) behavior when interacting with others. *Kaisha-in* literally means "company person," but it also denotes the individual as a representative of "our company" in the sense of a shared group consciousness. The company name comes first, before the individual's name on the *meishi* and when making introductions. The exchange of *meishi* also establishes relative rank within the strict corporate and social hierarchy, and therefore guides the correct behavior and even form of language used for interacting. Overall, for the Japanese exchanging *meishi* is an important symbolic ritual.

A senior technology manager from Scotland on his first assignment to Japan was attempting to establish a strategic alliance with a local firm as a starting point for marketing and selling his firm's products locally. In his first meeting he faced six senior executives from the Japanese firm, ranged across a boardroom table traditionally in order of seniority. Almost the first act of the Scottish manager was to *throw* his newly printed *meishi* across the table to each of the Japanese executives in turn!

There is no way of knowing how significant this single act was in undermining the firm's market entry in Japan. It failed in its attempt to forge an alliance with this particular Japanese firm and with others, eventually leading it to abandon its attempts. What we can say for certain is that a small amount of preparation by this manager to build even a basic understanding of business etiquette in Japan would have improved his company's chances of building a successful business in Japan.

The DTI study, including 30 detailed case studies of successful British firms in Japan, demonstrates very clearly that managers need to understand the cultural and social norms that underpin business practices in different countries if they are going to do business in those countries. The lesson applies to firms engaged in cross-border mergers and alliances, expanding into new markets through foreign direct investment activities, or even at the simple level, when hiring new recruits from overseas, outsourcing to foreign countries, or selling products and services abroad. Cultural awareness is critical to making business relationships work, at the face-to-face level or at the company-to-company level.

Source: S. Collinson, *Small and Successful in Japan: A Study of 30 British Firms in the World's Most Competitive Market* (London: Avebury Press/Ashgate Publishing Group, 1996); C. Nakane, *Japanese Society* (Tokyo: Charles E. Tuttle, 1973).

1 Explain what kinds of broad cultural differences we are likely to find between the Japanese and the British.

2 What impression do you think the Scottish engineer made on the Japanese executives?

3 What steps could the Scottish firm have taken to avoid this kind of mistake?

4 How easy is it to do a simple cost–benefit analysis on investments in improved cultural awareness among employees?

REAL CASE

Sport can be local *and* global: Manchester United

For most sports there appears to be a natural connection with the cultures and communities of particular locations and even individual venues. Often history plays a strong role, even when sports are played internationally. St. Andrews Links Course, Lord's Cricket Ground, and Wembley Stadium all have a particular symbolism to players and fans of golf, cricket, and soccer in and beyond the UK.

These contrast with more "placeless" global sporting events, particularly the Olympic Games, which involve most nations of the world. Rather than creating a sense of common identity, such events can reinforce national cultural identities through international competition.

Other sports remain local: Japanese sumo wrestling, Aussie rules football, and hurling in Ireland, for example, where the connection with national culture, community and history are strongest. American football is played in several countries but only seriously in the United States. It is not only a huge commercial enterprise but, like basketball and baseball, strongly embedded in local communities through schools and colleges, as an important symbol of US cultural identity.

Some sports could be defined as regional, such as baseball which is predominantly based in North America, but also popular in Japan and played little elsewhere. A few sports are marked on a global basis, although not all parts of the triad are fully involved. Golf, tennis, and soccer have global television audiences and advertising revenues. Among these, soccer is recognized as the biggest, played by an estimated 240 million people with 1.5 million teams and 300,000 clubs worldwide. Many countries, from Brazil to Cameroon, Italy to South Korea, would claim the game as an important part of their popular national culture. But soccer is not a major sport

in North America, where it ranks well behind American football, baseball, hockey, and car racing.

Europe hosts some of the major soccer club brands, with 52 leagues and a combined value over $20 billion. Within this the English Premiership is worth over $8 billion and as of 2015 it has been reported that eight of the top 20 most valuable teams are from this Premier League. It has been argued that the value of English soccer has been assisted by the rising value of the British pound in comparison with the US dollar and euro. One of the leading clubs in the Premiership is Manchester United—not your average soccer club, but certainly one of the best illustrations in the sporting world of the evolving mix between local cultural heritage and international business.

Born in 1878, Manchester United long epitomized the connection between the local team and the local community. Its fan base was dominated for over a hundred years by local people, with Trafford Park and the Manchester Ship Canal, one of the world's first industrial centers, at its heart. The grassroots, blue-collar, working-man's passion and fierce loyalty remain at the cultural heart of the club today. Rather than symbolizing English culture, it demonstrates the strength and persistence of the regional subculture of England's industrial northwest. This is reinforced by strong rivalry with other leading clubs such as Liverpool, Arsenal, and Chelsea. Now the brands of these teams are very multinational.

In the early 1990s, despite strong growth in international merchandising sales through Manchester United Merchandising, over 90 percent of revenues to the club still came from the domestic UK market. But a growing global fan club, the international spread of *Manchester United Magazine*, and the growing availability of televised games beyond the UK (particularly via Rupert Murdoch's global media networks) led to an export drive in the late 1990s and early 2000s. Countries with national teams but few big league teams, like Ireland, Scandinavia, and a range of Asian countries, where soccer is watched by millions on TV, became the club's best markets. By 2002 the global club membership had grown to 200 branches in 24 countries, and with profits of over $25 million on a turnover of over $100 million, it was considered the world's wealthiest club. MUTV, the club's own TV channel, and a large range of internet sites fueled interest in the team. By 2003 Manchester United had attracted an estimated global fan base of 53 million.

Major sponsorship deals with Nike and later Vodafone (at $15 million per year) boosted its finances and its global brand footprint. In 2014, Manchester United signed a new ten-year record-breaking sponsorship and licensing deal with Adidas, which guarantees the club an average income of £110 million per year. Furthermore, Manchester United signed a seven-year shirt deal with Chevrolet, which paid the club approximately $75 million during the 2014–15 season.

The cross-border takeover by the US-based Glazer family in 2005 made the club even more international by any definition. Boosted by wins in the Premiership, the FA Cup, and the European Champions League, the club's fan base had grown to an estimated 75 million worldwide. Significantly, 40 million of these were in Asia, compared to 23 million in Europe. Since then the actual number of global fans has been in dispute, ranging from "over 50 million" to "over 300 million."

In 2014 Manchester United generated revenues of $703 million, second only to Real Madrid's $746 million. As of 2015 Manchester United is worth $3.1 billion, and there are eight British clubs in the top 20 and five in the top 10, the others being Arsenal ($1.3 billion), Chelsea ($1.3 billion), Liverpool ($0.9 billion) and Manchester City ($1.4 billion).

By this time the club had a range of regional sponsors, with PepsiCo, Anheuser-Busch InBev, and Schick in North America, Ladbrokes in Europe, and Fuji Film and Air Asia in Asia. These were co-branding partners alongside global sponsors such as AIG, Vodafone, Nike, and Audi (and a few local partners like Dimension Data in South Africa). In some cases these have been the route to joint products and services, such as content services delivered by cell phone to Manchester United fans through Vodafone. Pre-

tax profits for the club are around $60 million and turnover, including merchandising and media partnerships, is over $250 million.

Despite the fact that, on average, over half the team comprises foreign players who play against the England national team in the World Cup, and despite the fact that the club's fan base is (in terms of pure numbers) more Asian than English, the passion for the club is still as strong as ever around Manchester. Global sports teams like Manchester United are embedded in local folklore, passionately discussed in bars and clubs around the world, part of the cultural identity of communities, but at the same time they are multinational businesses with global brands and international strategies.

Source: A. Rugman, *The End of Globalization* (London: Random, 2001); R. Bennet and J. Blythe, *International Marketing*, 3rd ed. (London: Kogan Page, 2002); W. Manzenreiter and J. Horne, *Football Goes East: Business, Culture and the People's Game in China, Japan and South Korea* (New York: Routledge, 2004); G. P. T. Finn and R. Giulianotti, *Football Culture* (New York: Routledge, 2000); "Neo-imperialism at the point of a boot," *The Economist*, March 11, 2007, p. 56; http://www.manutd.com; "Real top Man Utd in rich league," *BBC News*, February 14, 2008; "Manchester United can break £100m barrier for commercial turnover," *Guardian*, Friday, May 13, 2011; Mike Ozanian, "Real Madrid tops ranking of the world's most valuable teams," *Forbes*, accessed from http://www.forbes.com/sites/mikeozanian/2015/05/06/real-madrid-tops-ranking-of-the-worlds-most-valuable-soccer-teams/; https://www.soccerex.com/about; http://www.forbes.com/soccer-valuations/

1 What makes a sport local, regional, or global?

2 What major drivers are responsible for the internationalization of Manchester United?

3 How important are Manchester United's strong local roots to its international success?

NOTES

1 UNCTAD, *World Investment Report*, 2015, United Nations, Geneva; http://www.unctad.org

2 D. A. Ball and W. H. McCulloch, *International Business: The Challenge of Global Competition*, 7th ed. (Boston, MA: Irwin McGraw-Hill, 1999), p. 258.

3 G. Hofstede, *Culture's Consequences: International Differences in Work Related Values* (Beverly Hills, CA: Sage, 1980).

4 K. Voigt, "Japanese firms want English competency," *Wall Street Journal*, June 11, 2001, p. B7B.

5 M. Weber, *The Protestant Ethic and the Spirit of Capitalism*, 2nd Roxbury ed. (London: Roxbury, 1993).

6 K. A. Nordström and J.-E. Vahlne, "Is the globe shrinking? Psychic distance and the establishment of Swedish sales subsidiaries during the last 100 years," in M. Landeck (ed.), *International Trade: Regional and Global Issues* (Basingstoke: St. Martin's Press, 1994).

7 Many texts refer back to the work of Hall as one of the earliest authors in this field; E. T. Hall, "The silent language

of international business," *Harvard Business Review* (May–June 1960), pp. 87–96.

8 G. Hofstede, "The cultural relativity of organizational practices and theories," *Journal of International Business Studies* (fall 1983), p. 92; G. Hofstede, *Cultures and Organizations; Software of the Mind: Intercultural Cooperation and Its Importance for Survival* (London: Harper Collins, 1983).

9 B. McSweeny, "Hofstede's model of national cultural differences and their consequences: a triumph of faith—a failure of analysis," *Human Relations*, vol. 55, no. 1 (2002), pp. 89–118, cites additional problems in a stronger critique of Hofstede's approach. R. Jowell, "How comparative is comparative research?," *American Behavioral Scientist*, vol. 42, no. 2 (1998), pp. 168–78, meanwhile suggests that Hofstede and other analysts' cross-national data are too concerned with "league tables of distributions showing merely 'gee whiz' national differences" rather than offering explanations and interpretations.

10 G. Hofstede, *Culture's Consequences: Comparing Values, Behaviors, Institutions and Organizations across Nations*, 2nd ed. (Thousand Oaks, CA: Sage, 2001); G. Hofstede et al., "What goals do business leaders pursue? A study in fifteen countries," *Journal of International Business Studies*, vol. 33, no. 4, (2002), pp. 785–804.

11 F. Trompenaars, *Riding the Waves of Culture: Understanding Cultural Diversity of Business* (London: Nicholas Brealey, 1993); F. Trompenaars and C. Hampden-Turner, *Riding the Waves of Culture: Understanding Cultural Diversity in Global Business* (London: Nicholas Brealey, 1998); Fons Trompenaars and Charles Hampden-Turner also run a consultancy specializing in advice and training on cross-cultural issues. The website for the firm has some useful resources for further research: http://www.7d-culture.nl/. A similar site, with a range of tools and techniques for understanding and managing differences in European cultures, is: http://www.johnmole.com

12 C. C. Chen, "New trends in rewards allocation preferences: a Sino-US comparison," *Academy of Management Journal* (April 1995), p. 425; Y. Ono and B. Spindle, "Japan's long decline makes one thing rise: individualism," *Wall Street Journal*, December 29, 2000, pp. A1, 4.

13 M. Javidan and R. J. House, "Cultural acumen for the global manager: lessons from project GLOBE," *Organizational Dynamics*, vol. 29, no. 4 (2001), pp. 289–305.

14 D. A. Light, "Cross-cultural lessons in leadership", *MIT Sloan Management Review* (fall 2003), pp. 5–6.

15 This has involved 38 universities in annual surveys of around 7,000 organizations across Europe; C. J. Brewster and H. Harris (eds.), *International Human Resource Management: Contemporary Issues in Europe* (London: Routledge, 1999); C. Brewster, "HRM practices in multinational enterprises," in M. J. Gannon and K. Newman (eds.), *Handbook of Cross-cultural Management* (Oxford: Blackwell, 2001); J. Van Ommeren et al., "The Cranet Survey 1999," *UK Executive Report 1999*, Cranfield Network on European Human Resource Management, Cranfield, Bedford.

16 P. C. Earley, "Leading cultural research in the future: a matter of paradigms and taste," *Journal of International Business Studies*, vol. 37, no. 6 (2006), pp. 922–31; G. Hofstede, "What did GLOBE really measure? Researchers' minds versus respondents' minds," *Journal of International Business Studies*, vol. 37, no. 6 (2006), pp. 882–96; P. B.

Smith, "When elephants fight, the grass gets trampled: the GLOBE and Hofstede projects," *Journal of International Business Studies*, vol. 37, no. 6 (2006), pp. 915–21.

17 C. Nakane, *Japanese Society* (Tokyo: Charles E. Tuttle, 1973).

18 J. R. Lincoln, "Employee work attitudes and management practice in the United States and Japan: evidence from a large comparative survey," *California Management Review* (fall 1989), p. 91.

19 There are many firms that offer advice and training services to help companies improve their cultural awareness and the ability of employees to adapt to cultural diversity. A useful starting point, however, is G. Wederspahn, "Do your employees need intercultural services?" (2002), http://www.grovewell.com/pub-cultural-knowledge.html

20 Financial Times, *Managing Global Business, Mastering Management Series* (London: Pearson, 2000); M. C. Gentile, *Managerial Excellence through Diversity: Text and Cases* (Chicago, IL: Irwin, 1996); D. A. Thomas and R. J. Ely, "Making differences matter: a new paradigm for managing diversity," *Harvard Business Review* (September–October 1996), pp. 79–90.

21 H. V. Perlmutter, "The tortuous evolution of the multinational enterprise," *Columbia Journal of World Business*, vol. 4, no. 1 (1969), pp. 9–18.

22 Perlmutter in C. A. Bartlett and S. Ghoshal, *Text, Cases and Readings in Cross-Border Management*, 3rd ed. (Boston, MA: McGraw-Hill International Editions, 2000), p. 77.

23 S. C. Collinson, "M&A as imperialism?," in D. Angwin (ed.), *Images of M&A* (Oxford: Blackwell, 2006).

24 J. P. Walsh, "Top management turnover following mergers and acquisitions," *Strategic Management Journal*, vol. 9 (1988), pp. 173–83.

25 S. C. Collinson in D. Angwin, *Images of M&A* (Oxford: Blackwell, 2006).

26 R. P. Appelbaum, W. Felstiner, and V. Gessner (eds.), *Rules and Networks: The Legal Culture of Global Business Transactions* (Oxford: Hart Publishing, 2001); R. Whitley, *Competing Capitalisms: Institutions and Economies* (Cheltenham: Edward Elgar, 2002); R. Whitley, *The Multinational Firm: Organizing across Institutional and National Divides* (Oxford: Oxford University Press, 2001); R. Whitley, *Divergent Capitalisms: The Social Structuring and Change of Business Systems* (Oxford: Oxford University Press, 1999).

BIBLIOGRAPHY

Ashkanasy, Neil M., Trevor-Roberts, Edwin, and Earnshaw, Louise. "The Anglo cluster: legacy of the British empire," *Journal of World Business*, vol. 37, no. 1 (2002).

Barr, Pamela S., and Glynn, Mary-Ann. "Cultural variations in strategic issue interpretation: relating cultural uncertainty avoidance to controllability in discriminating threat and opportunity," *Strategic Management Journal*, vol. 25, no. 1 (2004).

Berry, Heather, Guillén, Mauro F., and Nan Zhou, "An institutional approach to cross-national distance," *Journal of International Business Studies*, vol. 41, no. 9 (2010).

Chevrier, Sylvie. "Cross-cultural management in multinational project groups," *Journal of World Business*, vol. 38, no. 2 (2003).

Collinson, Simon C., *Small and Successful in Japan: A Study of 30 British Firms in the World's Most Competitive Market* (London: Ashgate Press, 1996).

Collinson, Simon C., and Houlden, John. "Decision making and market orientation in the internationalization process of small and medium-sized enterprises," *Management International Review*, vol. 45, no. 4 (2005).

Collinson, Simon C., and Pettigrew, Andrew M., "Comparative international business research methods: pitfalls and practicalities." In A. Rugman (ed.), *The Oxford Handbook of International Business*, 2nd ed. (Oxford: Oxford University Press, 2009), Table 3.1 chapter 27.

Early, P. Christopher. "Leading cultural research in the future: a matter of paradigms and taste," *Journal of International Business Studies*, vol. 37, no. 6 (November 2006).

Fealy, Liz, and Kompare, Dave. "When worlds collide: culture clash," *Journal of Business Strategy*, vol. 24, no. 4 (2003).

Friday, Ernest, and Friday, Shawnta S. "Managing diversity using a strategic planned change approach," *Journal of Management Development*, vol. 22, no. 10 (2003).

Ghauri, Pervez. "Negotiating with the Chinese: a sociocultural analysis," *Journal of World Business*, vol. 36, no. 3 (fall 2001).

Hampden-Turner, Charles, and Trompenaars, Fons. *The Seven Cultures of Capitalism: Value Systems for Creating Wealth in the United States, Britain, Japan, Germany, France, Sweden and the Netherlands* (New York: Doubleday, 1993).

Han, Sam, Kang, Tony, Salter, Stephen, and Yoo, Yong Keun. "A cross-country study on the effects of national culture on earnings management," *Journal of International Business Studies*, vol. 41, no. 1 (2010).

Hofstede, Geert. "What did GLOBE really measure? Researchers' minds versus respondents' minds," *Journal of International Business Studies*, vol. 37, no. 6 (November 2006).

Holden, Nigel J. *Cross-Cultural Management: A Knowledge Management Perspective* (London: Prentice Hall, 2002).

Javidan, Mansour, House, Robert J., Dorfman, Peter J., Hanges, Paul J., and Sully de Luque, Mary. "Conceptualizing and measuring cultures and their consequences: a comparative review of GLOBE's and Hofstede's approaches," *Journal of International Business Studies*, vol. 37, no. 6 (November 2006).

Kostova, Tatiana, and Roth, Kendall. "Social capital in multinational corporations and a micro-macro model of its formation," *Academy of Management Review*, vol. 28, no. 2 (2003).

Leung, Kwok, Bhagat, Rabi, Buchan, Nancy R., Erez, Miriam, and Gibson, Cristina B. "Beyond national culture and culture-centricism: a reply to Gould and Grein (2009)," *Journal of International Business Studies*, vol. 42, no. 1 (2011).

McSweeny, Brendan. "Hofstede's model of national cultural differences and their consequences: a triumph of faith—a failure of analysis," *Human Relations*, vol. 55, no. 1 (2002).

Mead, Richard, and Andrews, Tim G. *International Management: Cross-cultural Dimensions*, 4th ed. (Oxford: Wiley-Blackwell, 2009).

Mole, John. *Mind Your Manners: Managing Business Cultures in Europe* (London: Nicholas Brealey, 1996).

Morgan, Glenn, Kristensen, Per Hull, and Whitley, Richard (eds.). *The Multinational Firm* (Oxford: Oxford University Press, 2001).

Muethel, Miriam, Hoegl, Martin, and Parboteeah, K. Praveen. "National business ideology and employees' prosocial values," *Journal of International Business Studies*, vol. 42, no. 2 (2011).

Ronen, S., and Shenkar, O. "Mapping world cultures: cluster formation, sources and implications," *Journal of International Business Studies*, vol. 44, no. 9 (2013).

Sarala, Riikka M., and Vaara, Eero. "Cultural differences, convergence, and crossvergence as explanations of knowledge transfer in international acquisitions," *Journal of International Business Studies*, vol. 41, no. 8 (2010).

Schneider, Susan C., and Barsoux, Jean-Louis. *Managing Across Cultures*, 2nd ed. (London: Prentice Hall, 2003).

Shao, Liang, Kwok, Chuck C. Y., and Zhang, Ran. "National culture and corporate investment," *Journal of International Business Studies*, vol. 44, no. 7 (2013).

Shenkar, O. "Cultural distance revisited: toward a more rigorous conceptualization and measurement of cultural differences," *Journal of International Business Studies*, vol. 43, no. 1 (2012).

Simon, David G., and Lane, Peter J. "A model of cultural differences and international alliance performance," *Journal of International Business Studies*, vol. 35, no. 4 (2004).

Sivakumar, K., and Nakata, Cheryl. "The stampede toward Hofstede's framework: avoiding the sample design pit in cross-cultural research," *Journal of International Business Studies*, vol. 32, no. 3 (fall 2001).

Smith, Peter B., Peterson, Mark F., and Thomas, David C. *The Handbook of Cross-Cultural Management Research* (Thousand Oaks, CA: Sage, 2008).

Triandis, Harry C. "The many dimensions of culture," *Academy of Management Executive*, vol. 18, no. 1 (2004).

Tung, Rosalie L., and Verbeke, Alain. "Beyond Hofstede and GLOBE: improving the quality of cross-cultural research," *Journal of International Business Studies*, vol. 41, no. 8 (2010).

Venaik, Sunil, and Brewer, Paul, "Avoiding uncertainty in Hofstede and GLOBE," *Journal of International Business Studies*, vol. 41, no. 8 (2010).

Von Glinow, Mary-Ann, Shapiro, Debra L., and Brett, Jeanne M. "Can we talk, and should we? Managing emotional conflict in multicultural teams," *Academy of Management Review*, vol. 29, no. 4 (2004).

West, Joel, and Graham, John L. "A linguistic-based measure of cultural distance and its relationship to managerial values," *Management International Review*, vol. 44, no. 3 (2004).

Zeng, Y., Shenkar, O., Lee, S. H., and Song, S., "Cultural differences, MNE learning abilities, and the effect of experience on subsidiary mortality in a dissimilar culture: evidence from Korean MNEs", *Journal of International Business Studies*, vol. 44, no. 1 (2013).

Chapter 6

INTERNATIONAL TRADE

Contents

Objectives of the chapter

An understanding of international trade is critical to the study of international business. The primary objective of this chapter is to examine key economic theories that help to explain why nations trade. In addition, the role and importance of a country's barriers to trade will be studied and discussion will focus on why most nations use trade barriers despite vigorous international efforts to eliminate them.

The specific objectives of this chapter are to:

1 *Define* the term *international trade* and discuss the role of mercantilism in modern international trade.

2 *Contrast* the theories of absolute advantage and comparative advantage.

3 *Relate* the importance of international product life cycle theory to the study of international economics.

4 *Explain* some of the most commonly used barriers to trade and other economic developments that affect international economics.

5 *Discuss* some of the reasons for the tensions between the theory of free trade and the widespread practice of national trade barriers.

Trade of the triad and China

Over the last three decades, new entrants into the world export market have transformed the economies of industrialized countries and the types of products they export. At the beginning of this time period, the Japanese were a growing force in the international arena. They dominated the 1980s and were able to make substantial gains at the expense of such dominant exporters as the UK and the United States. Indeed, between 1980 and 1990, both these countries lost worldwide market share to the Japanese in such industries as automotive products, office machines, telecom equipment, machinery and transport equipment, chemicals, and textiles.

In the late 1980s, however, the world economy began to see major changes. Asia, South Korea, Singapore, Taiwan, Thailand, and China were growing much more competitive on the world stage. South Korea, for example, started expanding its automotive industry, while China's market share of office and telecom equipment rose from between zero and about 1 percent of the market in 1990 to 4.5 percent by 2000; by 2009, it was 26 percent and by 2013 it had increased to 40 percent. Meanwhile, thanks to NAFTA—which decreased barriers to trade within North America—Mexico and Canada were increasing their market share of automotive products, machinery, and transport equipment. Such competition spurred the United States to radically restructure many of its industries; invest billions in new technology, plant, equipment, and information technology; and introduce improvement programs, such as Six Sigma, that allowed it to match the quality offerings of worldwide competitors. As a result, the US share of the world's export market in areas such as automotive products, machinery and transport equipment, chemicals, and textiles somewhat recovered. The big loser was Japan, which saw its export market share decline in most of these areas.

Today the biggest challenge to the export markets of industrialized countries is China. Between 2000 and 2013, China's share of the world's merchandise exports more than tripled—from 4.7 percent to 17.5 percent (see Table 6.1). This increase comes at the expense of exports by triad countries over the same period. By 2013, the core triad's share of world exports was 62.1 percent, with the EU accounting for approximately three-quarters of this (see Table 6.2). The United States and Japan were the hardest hit.

China's expansion is particularly evident in the clothing and textile markets. In 2013, the country held 38.6 percent and 34.8 percent of each market, respectively (Table 6.1). More impressive, however, were China's improvements in exports of office and telecom equipment and of machinery and transport equipment, both of which require significant technological know-how.

Table 6.1 China's share of the world's market for exports of manufactures, 2000–13

Industry	2000	2009	2013
All manufactures	4.7	9.9	17.5
Iron and steel	3.1	7.3	12.0
Chemicals	2.1	4.3	6.0
Machinery and transport equipment	3.1	n/a	n/a
Automotive products	0.3	n/a	1.9
Office and telecom equipment	4.5	26.2	33.9
Textiles	10.5	28.3	34.8
Clothing	18.3	34.0	38.6

Note: Manufactures are a subcategory within merchandise exports. These data include intra-regional EU exports.

Source: Authors' calculations based on data from World Trade Organization, *Statistics Database*, International Trade Statistics, 2014, tables 1.6, 2.36, 2.38, 2.40, 2.62, 2.67.

Table 6.2 The triad's share of world merchandise exports, 1993–2013 (%)

	1993	2003	2009	2013	1993–2013
US	12.6	9.8	8.7	9.8	−22
EU	45.4	45.9	41.2	45.9	1
Japan	9.9	6.4	4.8	6.4	−25
Triad	67.9	62.1	54.7	62.1	−9
Non-triad	32.1	37.9	45.3	37.9	18

Note: Data are calculated using world trade minus intra-regional EU trade.

Source: Authors' calculations based on data from World Trade Organization, *Statistics Database*, International Trade Statistics, 2014, table 1.5.

As can been seen in the tables, China's rise as a world exporter has decreased the share of the triad's share of world exports in manufactures. However, in terms of exports recent data show that the triad has been able to recapture some of the lost ground. In response to China's increased competitiveness, triad countries are trying to balance the need to integrate this new player into the international business arena with the negative short-term effects on their economies.

Japan's attitude toward China took a turn away from protectionism when it realized that this new trade partner could help it overcome some of the problems associated with its rigid economic system. Large amounts of inexpensive, low-skilled labor now allowed Japanese companies to outsource some of their manufacturing operations overseas, within its own region, while more skilled Japanese workers took care of the specialized areas of the production process. In addition, China eased Japan's long dependence on the US economy for its industrial and consumer products.

While US and EU companies have also moved operations to Japan, the governments are reacting more aggressively to pressure from special interest groups that see China as a threat to US businesses and jobs. The United States, which runs a large trade deficit with China, has argued that the yuan is undervalued, creating an unfair advantage for Chinese producers. The United States is threatening to impose tariffs on Chinese products. A bill is set to go before the Senate that would call for retaliatory trade sanctions against countries such as China that intervene to weaken their currencies in order to boost export at the expense of its trading partners. China relaxed the yuan's fixed exchange rate against the dollar in June 2010, but since then it has been allowed to appreciate by less than 3 percent. By November 2010, exports to the United States were up by 29.5 percent compared to a year earlier. China's exports increased amid inflation fears. China's November 2010 inflation figure was set to hit a new 28-month high of 5.1 percent versus October's inflation figure of 4.4 percent and above the official inflation target of 3 percent.

Japan has joined this wagon and is pressuring China to move to a more flexible exchange rate. Yet, critics argue that no one truly knows the market value of the yuan and that a fall in its price after deregulation could only worsen matters. For its part, the EU has reacted by asking China to curtail exports of textiles into the union after exports of clothing increased by 534 percent in less than six months in 2005. By November 2010, the overall figure was a 33 percent rise in exports to Europe.

An increase in exports by any nation does not necessarily mean that other countries are losing out. In terms of trade alone, any new entrant to the world exports market, other things being equal, will decrease the share of world exports of all other countries. This, however, does not mean that other countries are exporting less. They could be exporting, in value terms, a significantly higher amount because a new trade partner also means a new market to which they can export. More specifically, however, trade creates losers and winners. Triad economies are being forced to specialize. While those with most to lose pressure their governments to impose trade barriers, those with most to win—high-skilled industries—are expanding to serve the Chinese market. Further, customers' real incomes increase when they can purchase the same products at lower prices.

The data in this case help to reinforce an important principle of international trade: specialize in those products in which you can achieve an advantage. Over time, of course, competitors may erode this advantage by developing even better offerings for the export market. In this case, it is important either to counterattack by improving your own offering to win back this market share, or to find other markets where the country's skills and resources will allow it to compete effectively. In light of the emergence of more and more industrial countries in Asia, the growing competitiveness of Latin America, and the emerging industries of eastern Europe and the former Soviet Union, triad managers have their work cut out for them.

Sources: "Chinese urged to curb EU exports," *BBC News*, May 12, 2005; "China's yuan under fresh pressure," *BBC News*, May 6, 2005; "The halo effect," *The Economist*, September 30, 2004; "Chinese export jumps unexpectedly amid inflation fears," *BBC News*, December 10, 2010; "US ups China pressure on yuan," *BBC News*, October 9, 2010; "China stands firm over yuan move," *BBC News*, October 8, 2010; "Chinese exports and imports rise more than expected", *BBC News*, August 8, 2013; Kit Gillet, "China: despite US pressure, Beijing stands firm in currency spat," IPS News Agency, March 25, 2010, accessed from http://www.ipsnews.net/2010/03/china-despite-us-pressure-beijing-stands-firm-in-currency-spat/

1. How does the search for market niches by British firms help illustrate the theory of comparative advantage?

2. How does an EU manager's desire to buy domestic products illustrate the importance of consumer taste in international markets?

3. In what way could the EU use trade barriers to protect its markets from foreign competitors? Who can be affected by these trade barriers?

INTRODUCTION

International trade is the branch of economics concerned with the exchange of goods and services with foreign countries. Although this is a complex subject, we will focus on two particular areas: international trade theory and barriers to trade.

Some international economic problems cannot be solved in the short run. Consider the US balance of trade deficit. US trade with Japan and China heavily affects its overall imbalance. Moreover, this trade deficit will not be reduced by political measures alone; it will require long-run economic measures that reduce imports and increase exports. Other nations are also learning this lesson—and not just those that have negative balances. After all, most countries seem to want a continual favorable trade balance, although this is impossible, since a nation with a deficit must be matched by a nation with a surplus.[1]

International trade has become an even more important topic now that so many countries have begun to move from state-run to market-driven economies.[2] Inflation and, in many cases, unemployment are severe problems for these nations. Fortunately, enhanced international trade is one way to address a weak macro economy.[3] International commitment to a free market will bring prosperity to the world economic system. Since the time of Adam Smith in 1790, economists have shown that free trade is efficient and leads to maximum economic welfare. In this chapter we will discuss the economic rationale for free trade and the political impediments to it.

INTERNATIONAL TRADE THEORY

To understand the topic of international trade, we must be able to answer the question: why do nations trade? One of the earliest and simplest answers to this question was provided by **mercantilism**, a theory that was quite popular in the eighteenth century, when gold was the only world currency. Mercantilism holds that a government can improve the economic well-being of the country by encouraging exports and stifling imports. The result is a positive balance of trade that leads to wealth (gold) flowing into the country.

Neo-mercantilism, like mercantilism, seeks to produce a positive balance of trade but without the reliance on precious metals. Most international trade experts believe that mercantilism is a simplistic and erroneous theory, although it has had followers. For example, under President Mitterrand in the late 1970s and early 1980s, France sought to revitalize its industrial base by nationalizing key industries and banks and subsidizing exports over imports. By the mid-1980s the French government realized that the strategy was not working and began denationalizing many of its holdings.[4] More recently, China has proven to be a strong adherent of mercantilism, as reflected by the fact that it tries to have a positive balance with all of its trading partners.

A more useful explanation of why nations trade is provided by trade theories that focus on specialization of effort. The theories of absolute and comparative advantage are good examples.

Theory of absolute advantage

The **theory of absolute advantage** holds that nations can increase their economic well-being by specializing in the production of goods they can produce more efficiently than anyone else. A simple example can illustrate this point. Assume that two nations, North and South, are both able to produce two goods, cloth and grain. Assume further that labor is the only scarce factor of production and thus the only cost.

Labor cost (hours) of production for 1 unit

	Cloth	Grain
North	10	20
South	20	10

Thus lower labor-hours per unit of production mean lower production costs and higher productivity per labor-hour. As seen by the data in the table, North has an absolute advantage in

---

Mercantilism

A trade theory which holds that a government can improve the economic well-being of the country by encouraging exports and stifling imports to accumulate wealth in the form of precious metals

Neo-mercantilism

A trade theory which holds that a government can improve the economic well-being of the country by encouraging exports and stifling imports

Theory of absolute advantage

A trade theory which holds that nations can increase their economic well-being by specializing in goods that they can produce more efficiently than anyone else the production of cloth since the cost requires only 10 labor-hours, compared to 20 labor-hours in South. Similarly, South has an absolute advantage in the production of grain, which it produces at a cost of 10 labor-hours, compared to 20 labor-hours in North.

Both countries gain by trade. If they specialize and exchange cloth for grain at a relative price of 1:1, each country can employ its resources to produce a greater amount of goods. North can import 1 unit of grain in exchange for 1 unit of cloth, thereby paying only 10 labor-hours for 1 unit of grain. If North had produced the grain itself, it would have used 20 labor-hours per unit, so North gains 10 labor-hours from the trade. In the same way, South gains from trade when it imports 1 unit of cloth in exchange for 1 unit of grain. The effective cost to South for 1 unit of cloth is only the 10 labor-hours required to make its 1 unit of grain.

The theory of absolute advantage, as originally formulated, does not predict the exchange ratio between cloth and grain once trade is opened, nor does it resolve the division of the gains from trade between the two countries. Our example assumed an international price ratio of 1:1, but this ratio (P_{cloth} to P_{grain}) could lie between 2:1 (the pre-trade price ratio in South) and 1:2 (the pre-trade price ratio in North). To determine the relative price ratio under trade, we would have to know the total resources of each country (total labor-hours available per year), and the demand of each for both cloth and grain. In this way we could determine the relative gains from trade for each country.

Even this simple model of absolute advantage has several important implications for international trade. First, if a country has an absolute advantage in producing a product, it has the potential to gain from trade. Second, the more a country is able to specialize in the good it produces most efficiently, the greater its potential gains in national well-being. Third, the competitive market does not evenly distribute the gains from trade *within* one country. This last implication is illustrated by the following example.

Prior to trade, the grain farmers in North work 20 hours to produce 1 unit of grain that could be exchanged for 2 units of cloth. After trade, those who remain can exchange 1 unit of grain for only 1 unit of cloth. Thus, the remaining grain producers are worse off under trade. Cloth producers in North, however, work 10 hours, produce 1 unit of cloth, and exchange it for 1 unit of grain, whereas previously they received only half a unit of grain. They are better off. If grain producers in North switch to cloth production, then 20 hours of labor results in the production of 2 units of cloth, which they can exchange for 2 units of grain. Thus, international trade helps them. As long as North does not specialize completely in cloth, there will be gainers (cloth producers and grain producers who switched to cloth) and losers (those who continue as grain producers).

Because the nation as a whole benefits from trade, the gainers can compensate the losers and there will still be a surplus to be distributed in some way. If such compensation does not take place, however, the losers (continuing grain producers) will have an incentive to try to prevent the country from opening itself up to trade. Historically, this problem has continued to fuel opposition to a free trade policy that reduces barriers to trade. A good example is Japanese farmers who stand to lose their livelihood if the government opens up Japan to lower-priced agricultural imports.

A more complicated picture of the determinants and effects of trade emerges when one of the trading partners has an absolute advantage in the production of both goods. However, trade under these conditions still brings gains, as David Ricardo first demonstrated in his theory of comparative advantage.

Theory of comparative advantage
A trade theory which holds that nations should produce those goods for which they have the greatest relative advantage

Theory of comparative advantage

The **theory of comparative advantage** holds that nations should produce those goods for which they have the greatest relative advantage. In terms of the previous example of two countries, North and South, and two commodities, cloth and grain, Ricardo's model can be illustrated as follows:

Labor cost (hours) of production for 1 unit

	Cloth	Grain
North	50	100
South	200	200

In this example North has an absolute advantage in the production of *both* cloth and grain, so it would appear at first sight that trade would be unprofitable, or at least that incentives for exchange no longer exist. Yet trade is still advantageous to both nations, provided their *relative* costs of production differ.

Before trade, 1 unit of cloth in North costs (50/100) hours of grain, so 1 unit of cloth can be exchanged for half a unit of grain. The price of cloth is half the price of grain. In South, 1 unit of cloth costs (200/200) hours of grain, or 1 grain unit. The price of cloth equals the price of grain. If North can import more than half a unit of grain for 1 unit of cloth, it will gain from trade. Similarly, if South can import 1 unit of cloth for less than 1 unit of grain, it will also gain from trade. These relative price ratios set the boundaries for trade. Trade is profitable between price ratios (price of cloth to price of grain) of 0.5 and 1. For example, at an international price ratio of two-thirds, North gains. It can import 1 unit of grain in return for exporting 1.5 units of cloth. Because it costs only 50 hours of labor to produce a unit of cloth, its effective cost under trade for 1 unit of imported grain is 75 labor-hours. Under pre-trade conditions it costs North 100 labor-hours to produce 1 unit of grain. Similarly, South gains from trade by importing 1 unit of cloth in exchange for two-thirds of a unit of grain. Prior to trade, South spent 200 labor-hours producing the 1 unit of cloth. Through trade, its effective cost for 1 unit of cloth is $\frac{2}{3} \times 200$, or 133 labor-hours—cheaper than the domestic production cost of 200 labor-hours. Assuming free trade between the two nations, North will tend to specialize in the production of cloth, and South will tend to specialize in the production of grain.

This example illustrates a general principle. There are gains from trade whenever the relative price ratios of two goods differ under international exchange from what they would be under conditions of no trade. Such domestic conditions are often referred to as *autarky*, which is a government policy of being totally self-sufficient. Research shows that free trade is superior to autarky. In particular, free trade provides greater economic output and consumption to the trade partners jointly than they can achieve by working alone. By specializing in the production of certain goods, exporting those products for which they have a comparative advantage, and importing those for which they have a comparative disadvantage, the countries end up being better off.

The general conclusions of the theory of comparative advantage are the same as those for the theory of absolute advantage. In addition, the theory of comparative advantage demonstrates that countries jointly benefit from free trade (under the assumptions of the model) even if one has an absolute advantage in the production of *both* goods. Total world efficiency and consumption increase.

As with the theory of absolute advantage discussed previously, Ricardo's theory of comparative advantage does not answer the question of the distribution of gains between the two countries, or the distribution of gains and losses between grain producers and cloth producers within each country. No country will lose under free trade, but in theory at least, all the gains could accrue to one country and to only one group within that country.

Active learning check

Review your answer to Active Learning Case question 1 and make any changes you like. Then compare your answer to the one below.

1 **How does the search for market niches by British firms help illustrate the theory of comparative advantage?**

The theory of comparative advantage holds that nations should produce those goods for which they have the greatest relative advantage. By finding specific market niches overseas, UK firms "reveal" their relative advantage over the local competition. Success in terms of growing sales and profitability demonstrate that such firms are exploiting the UK's strengths in those markets. Given the rise of competitiveness in all areas of worldwide exports, few nations have been able to maintain their market share for very long. So the UK will have to continue to use this approach in order to remain one of the world's major export nations.

Factor endowment theory

A trade theory which holds that nations will produce and export products that use large amounts of production factors that they have in abundance and will import products requiring a large amount of production factors that they lack

Heckscher–Ohlin theory

A trade theory that extends the concept of comparative advantage by bringing into consideration the endowment and cost of factors of production and helps to explain why nations with relatively large labor forces will concentrate on producing labor-intensive goods, whereas countries with relatively more capital than labor will specialize in capital-intensive goods

Leontief paradox

A finding by Wassily Leontief, a Nobel Prize-winning economist, which shows that the United States, surprisingly, exports relatively more labor-intensive goods and imports capital-intensive goods

International product life cycle (IPLC) theory

A theory of the stages of production of a product with new "know-how": it is first produced by the parent firm, then by its foreign subsidiaries, and finally anywhere in the world where costs are the lowest; it helps explain why a product that begins as a nation's export often ends up as an import

Factor endowment theory

In recent years, more sophisticated theories have emerged that help clarify and extend our knowledge of international trade. The **factor endowment theory** holds that countries will produce and export products that use large amounts of production factors that they have in abundance, and they will import products requiring large amounts of production factors that they lack. This theory is also known as the **Heckscher–Ohlin theory** (after the two economists who first developed it). The theory is useful in extending the concept of comparative advantage by bringing into consideration the endowment and cost of production factors. The theory also helps explain why nations with relatively large labor forces, such as China, will concentrate on producing labor-intensive goods, whereas countries like the Netherlands, which has relatively more capital than labor, will specialize in capital-intensive goods.

However, the factor endowment theory has some weaknesses. One weakness is that some countries have minimum wage laws that result in high prices for relatively abundant labor. As a result, they may find it less expensive to import certain goods than to produce them internally. Another weakness is that countries like the United States export relatively more labor-intensive goods and import capital-intensive goods—an outcome that appears surprising. This result, discovered by Wassily Leontief, a Nobel Prize-winning economist, is known as the **Leontief paradox** and has been explained in terms of the quality of labor input rather than just labor-hours of work. The United States produces and exports technology-intensive products that require highly educated labor. The Leontief paradox not only shows one of the problems with factor endowment theory, but also helps us understand why no single theory can explain the role of economic factors in trade theory. Simply put, the subject is too complex to be explained with just one or two theories.

International product life cycle theory

Another theory that provides insights into international theory is Vernon's **international product life cycle (IPLC) theory,** which addresses the various stages of a good's life cycle. In particular, the theory helps explain why a product that begins as a nation's export often ends up becoming an import. The theory also focuses on market expansion and technological innovation—concepts that are relatively de-emphasized in comparative advantage theory. IPLC theory has two important tenets: (1) technology is a critical factor in creating

Figure 6.1 The international product life cycle

Source: Raymond Vernon and Louis T. Wells, Jr., *The Manager in the International Economy* (Englewood Cliffs, NJ: Prentice Hall, 1991), p. 85.

and developing new products; and (2) market size and structure are important in determining trade patterns.

Product stages

The IPLC has three stages: new product, maturing product, and standardized product. A new product is one that is innovative or unique in some way (see Figure 6.1(a)). Initially, consumption is in the home country, price is inelastic, profits are high, and the company seeks to sell to those willing to pay a premium price. As production increases and outruns local consumption, exporting begins.

As the product enters the mature phase of its life cycle (see Figure 6.1(b)), an increasing percentage of sales is achieved through exporting. At the same time, competitors in other advanced countries will be working to develop substitute products so they can replace the initial good with one of their own. The introduction of these substitutes and the softening of demand for the original product will eventually result in the firm that developed the product now switching its strategy from production to market protection. Attention will also be focused on tapping markets in less developed countries.

As the product enters the standardized product stage (see Figure 6.1(c)), the technology becomes widely diffused and available. Production tends to shift to low-cost locations, including less developed countries and offshore locations. In many cases the product will end up being viewed as a generic, and price will be the sole determinant of demand.

Personal computers and the IPLC

In recent years a number of products have moved through the IPLC and are now in the standardized product stage. Personal computers (PCs) are a good example, despite their wide variety and the fact that some versions are in the new product and maturing product phases. For example, the early version of PCs that reached the market in the 1984 to 1991 period were in the standardized product stage by 1995 and sold primarily on the basis of price. Machines that entered the market in the 1996 to 1998 period were in the maturing stage by 1999. PCs with increased memory capability that were in the new product stage in 1999 quickly moved toward maturity, and by 2002 they were being replaced by even better machines with faster processors and more multimedia capabilities. Today, diskettes are standardized and rarely used, while standard components include CD writers, DVD ROMs, DSL and wireless internet connectors, USB ports, advanced graphics and sound, flat LCD monitors, digital photography capabilities, etc.

Desktop computers have been replaced by laptop models that are lighter, faster, more sophisticated, and less expensive than their predecessors. In turn, these machines are being replaced by notebooks with advanced Pentium chips, long-term battery capability, and storage capable of holding billions of bytes complete with wireless equipment and serving as a complete communications center from which the international executive can communicate anywhere in the world. These machines will first be manufactured locally and then in foreign markets. This is largely because IBM (the inventor of the PC) computers became a commodity, and IBM's PC division was sold to the Chinese firm Lenovo in 2005. Lenovo has the benefit of low labor costs and it is better able to manufacture the laptops of today. Thus, computers will continue to move through an IPLC.

The IPLC theory is useful in helping to explain how new technologically innovative products fit into the world trade picture. However, because new innovative products are sometimes rapidly improved, it is important to remember that one or two versions of them may be in the standardized product stage while other versions are in the maturing stage and still others are in the new product phase.

Other important considerations

Many factors beyond those we have considered greatly influence international trade theory.[5] One is government regulation. Countries often limit or restrict trade with other countries for political reasons. For example, despite the benefits of international trade, the EU does not always see eye to eye with the United States on regulatory matters. As a result there are different government regulations affecting business in Europe than in North America. For example, EU competition policy differs from US antitrust policy; see the case **International Business Strategy in Action: Microsoft shows the world is not flat**. Other important factors include monetary currency valuation and consumer tastes.

Monetary currency valuation

Monetary exchange rate
The price of one currency stated in terms of another currency

When examining why one country trades with another, we need to consider the **monetary exchange rate**, which is the price of one currency stated in terms of another currency. In 2015 China's central bank devalued the renminbi by 2 percent against the US dollar. This made Chinese exports marginally cheaper relative to competitors. A more significant example was the long-term decline of the value of the Japanese yen from 1995 to 1998, resulting in a boost for Japanese exports to the United States and Europe. Imported products and services are also relatively more expensive for consumers in countries which experience currency devaluation, driving them to buy locally produced substitutes.

Another reason why monetary currency valuation is important is because a foreign firm doing business will report its revenues and profits in home-country currency. So if a British firm sold $10 million of machinery in Canada and the value of the Canadian dollar declined against the British pound, the UK company would report less revenue (in terms of British pounds) than if the Canadian dollar had remained stable or, better yet, increased in value against the pound. In mid-2005, the euro became so strong compared to the dollar that Volkswagen reported a 63 percent decline in pre-tax profits.[6] In the next chapter, we will discuss exchange rates in more detail.

Consumer tastes

International trade is not based solely on price; some people will pay more for a product even though they can buy something similar for less money. This willingness to pay more may be based on prestige, perceived quality, or a host of other physical and psychological reasons. Personal tastes dictate consumer decisions.

INTERNATIONAL BUSINESS STRATEGY IN ACTION

Microsoft shows the world is not flat

The dispute between Microsoft and the European Commission demonstrates that the world is not flat. Microsoft is a company that has ridden the wave of worldwide internet access and software applications. Yet, it has run into a brick wall in Brussels. There the EU Directorate General for Competition and State Aid (DG Comp) has imposed large fines for breaking its competition rules.

In March 2004, the DG Comp ruled that Microsoft is abusing its dominant market position with its Windows operating system. Since then the DG Comp has been threatening to impose large daily fines because it says Microsoft is failing to comply with that ruling. On September 17, 2007, Microsoft lost an appeal to the European Court of First Instance ending a nine-year battle with the EU. It paid fines to the EU of $1.4 billion. In December 2007, the EU launched a new antitrust investigation against Microsoft after Norway's Opera complained about its web browser. In January 2009, the EU Commission accused Microsoft of illegally tying Internet Explorer to Windows. The Commission's concern was that the US computer giant may have broken competition rules by bundling its web browser with its dominant Windows operating system. Internet Explorer is used by more than half of global business users, with Mozilla's Firefox at about 32 percent and Norway's Opera at 2 percent. In July 2009, Microsoft reached an agreement with EU antitrust regulators to allow European users a choice of web browsers. The accord ended 10 years of dispute between the two sides. Over that time, the EU imposed fines totaling €1.68 billion (US$2.44 billion, £1.5 billion). The European Commission said Microsoft's legally binding agreement ended the dispute and averted a possible fine for the company.

This case illustrates that even the world's most successful internet-based software company does not have unrestricted global market access for its products. Instead, the world is divided into a "triad" with strong barriers to entry into the key regional markets of the EU, North America, and Asia–Pacific. Microsoft is simply the latest large MNE to misread the world marketplace. Today, business activity is organized mainly within each region of the triad, not globally. For US firms, the process of going to a foreign triad market in Europe and Asia is fraught with peril.

The world's 500 largest firms, on average, sell 72 percent of their goods and services in their home region. Very few firms are truly global, defined as selling a significant percentage of their products in each triad region. For example, the world's largest firm, Wal-Mart, has 94 percent of its sales

Source: JEAN-CHRISTOPHE VERHAEGEN/AFP/ Getty Images

in North America. Microsoft discloses the geographic dispersion of its sales by geographic segments: sales in the United States and sales outside the United States. Over five years' average (2006–10), Microsoft generates 60 percent of its sales in the United States alone. If sales in Canada and Mexico are added on top of US sales, it is clear that the majority of its sales are in North America (see Figure 6.2). Firms like Wal-Mart and Microsoft need to understand that a business model developed for North America will need to be adapted when going to Europe and Asia.

In the case of Microsoft the key difference is in the way that the EU regulatory system operates. In Europe competition policy can be used as a barrier to entry. EU antitrust regulations have traditionally proven stricter than American ones. An individual firm (in this case, Sun Microsystems and Opera) can signal an EU-wide investigation. In this process the deck is stacked against the foreign firm. In 2001 the US firm General Electric also made a similar mistake in its planned acquisition of Honeywell which was disallowed by the EU.

While the United States has somewhat similar antitrust provisions, the application of these is more business friendly than in Europe. US antitrust policy aims to help consumers, whereas EU law helps competitors. Microsoft was able to settle its antitrust case with the Bush administration, but it failed to do so with the EU. The regulatory climate in Europe is harsher than in North America. Multinational firms like Microsoft which assume free trade, worldwide market entry, and other aspects of flat earth thinking are learning expensive lessons. In addition to differences in regulatory standards across the triad, there are major cultural, social, and political differences that deny globalization.

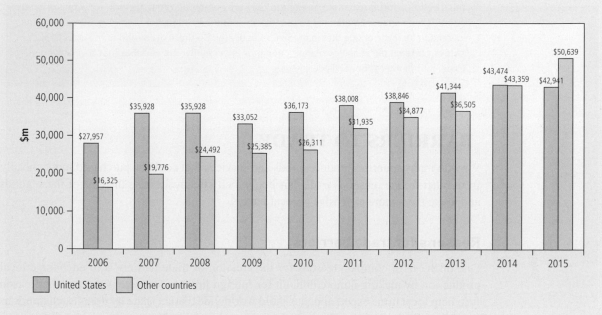

Figure 6.2 Microsoft: revenues by geographic segment (millions of US$, year ended June 30)

Source: Microsoft annual reports.

In terms of regulatory differences, antitrust is but one of an array of market-entry barriers. Even worse are anti-dumping and countervailing duty laws which are used to keep out foreign rivals. The United States itself administers its anti-dumping and countervailing duty laws in favor of the home team. In 2006, on security grounds, the US Congress overturned the executive branch decision to allow Dubai Ports International to acquire the US ports owned by P&O, a British firm. The Europeans perceive that the US commitment to free trade is weak; this is stiffening their spine with regard to Microsoft. The end result is typical triad-based economic warfare, where market entry is denied by the local bureaucrats and politicians.

While the US system is transparent, the EU investigation of unfair trade law cases, as well as antitrust, can be opaque and self-serving. The EU bureaucrats have continued the case against Microsoft even after Sun Microsystems and other business rivals in Europe, like Novell and RealNetworks, have settled their disputes. So now we can see the EU, as an institution, fighting a foreign multinational—not exactly a flat world.

The lessons of the Microsoft case are the following. First, globalization is a myth; instead world business is conducted mainly on an intra-regional basis within each part of the triad. Second, it is unlikely that the regulatory standards across the triad will be harmonized; thus, multinationals must be prepared to adapt their business models when they enter foreign regions of the triad. Third, even in high-tech areas such as software internet applications, the technology itself does not guarantee the flat promise of worldwide market access. The world is not flat; rather, there are very strong regional fault lines.

Sources: Indiana University CIBER Director's Message, May 1, 2006; *Financial Times*, September 18, 2007; *Wall Street Journal*, September 18, 2007; *Financial Times*, January 15, 2008; "EU fines Microsoft record 1.4 billion," *BBC News*, February 27, 2008; "Microsoft ends 10 year fight with Europe on browser," *BBC News*, December 16, 2009; "Microsoft in new EU browser offer," *BBC News*, July 2009; Microsoft, *Annual Reports*, 2006–15.

✔ Active learning check

Review your answer to Active Learning Case question 2 and make any changes you like. Then compare your answer to the one below.

2 How does an EU manager's desire to buy domestic products illustrate the importance of consumer taste in international markets?

This example shows that people often buy goods based on personal preference, rather than only on such characteristics as low price, high quality, or improved productivity. Of course,

►

this "Buy EU" focus will often come into play only when all other factors are approximately equal. The manager is unlikely to turn down a China-made product that is 30 percent less expensive in favor of one that is made domestically. So there are limits to the effects of consumer taste on purchase decisions, though it is certainly one variable that has proven very important in international trade.

BARRIERS TO TRADE

Why do many countries produce goods and services that could be purchased more cheaply from others? One reason is trade barriers, which effectively raise the cost of these goods and make them more expensive to local buyers.

Reasons for trade barriers

One of the most common reasons for the creation of trade barriers is to encourage local production by making it more difficult for foreign firms to compete there. Another reason is to help local firms export and thus build worldwide market share by doing such things as providing them with subsidies in the form of tax breaks and low-interest loans. Other common reasons include:

- to protect local jobs by shielding home-country business from foreign competition;
- to encourage local production to replace imports;
- to protect infant industries that are just getting started;
- to reduce reliance on foreign suppliers;
- to encourage local and foreign direct investment;
- to reduce balance of payments problems;
- to promote export activity;
- to prevent foreign firms from *dumping* (selling goods below cost in order to achieve market share);
- to promote political objectives such as refusing to trade with countries that practice apartheid or deny civil liberties to their citizens.

Commonly used barriers

A variety of trade barriers deter the free flow of international goods and services.[7] The following presents five of the most commonly used barriers.

Price-based barriers

Imported goods and services sometimes have a tariff added to their price. Quite often this is based on the value of the goods. For example, some tobacco products coming into the United States carry an ad valorem tariff (see below) of over 100 percent, thus more than doubling their cost to US consumers. Tariffs raise revenues for the government, discourage imports, and make local goods more attractive.

Quantity limits

Quota
A quantity limit on imported goods

Quantity limits, often known as **quotas**, restrict the number of units that can be imported or the market share that is permitted. If the quota is set at zero, as in the case of Cuban

Embargo
A quota set at zero, thus preventing the importation of those products that are involved

cigars from Havana to the United States, it is called an **embargo**. If the annual quota is set at 1 million units, no more than this number can be imported during one year; once it is reached, all additional imports are turned back. In some cases a quota is established in terms of market share. For example, Canada allows foreign banks to hold no more than 16 percent of Canadian bank deposits, and the EU limits Japanese auto imports to 10 percent of the total market.

International price fixing

Cartel
A group of firms that collectively agree to fix prices or quantities sold in an effort to control price

Sometimes a host of international firms will fix prices or quantities sold in an effort to control price. This is known as a **cartel**. A well-known example is the Organization of the Petroleum Exporting Countries (OPEC), which consists of Saudi Arabia, Kuwait, Iran, Iraq, and Venezuela, among others (see Table 6.3). By controlling the supply of oil it provides, OPEC seeks to control both price and profit. This practice is illegal in the United States and Europe,[8] but the basic idea of allowing competitors to cooperate for the purpose of meeting international competition is being endorsed more frequently in countries such as the United States.[9] For example, US computer firms have now created partnerships for joint research and development efforts.

Financial limits

Exchange controls
Controls that restrict the flow of currency

There are a number of different financial limits. One of the most common is **exchange controls**, which restrict the flow of currency. A common exchange control is to limit the currency that can be taken out of the country: for example, travelers may take up to only $3,000 per person out of the country. Another example is the use of fixed exchange rates that are quite favorable to the country. For example, dollars may be exchanged for local currency on a 1:1 basis; without exchange controls, the rate would be 1:4. These cases are particularly evident where a black market exists for foreign currency that offers an exchange rate much different from the fixed rate.

Foreign investment controls

Foreign investment controls
Limits on foreign direct investment or the transfer or remittance of funds

Foreign investment controls are limits on foreign direct investment or the transfer or remittance of funds. These controls can take a number of different forms, including (1) requiring foreign investors to take a minority ownership position (49 percent or less), (2) limiting profit remittance (such as to 15 percent of accumulated capital per year), and (3) prohibiting royalty payments to parent companies, thus stopping the latter from taking out capital.

Table 6.3 OPEC exports (000 barrels per day)

Algeria	1,206
Angola	1,639
Ecuador	430
Iran	1,579
Iraq	2,525
Kuwait	2,746
Libya	56
Nigeria	2,169
Qatar	1,117
Saudi Arabia	8,141
UAE	3,257
Venezuela	2,277
Total	27,142

Source: Adapted from www.opec.org.

Such barriers can greatly restrict international trade and investment. However, it must be realized that they are created for what governments believe are very important reasons. A close look at one of these, tariffs, helps to make this clearer.

Tariffs

Tariff
A tax on goods shipped internationally

Import tariff
A tax levied on goods shipped into a country

Export tariff
A tax levied on goods sent out of a country

Transit tariff
A tax levied on goods passing through a country

Specific duty
A tariff based on the number of items being shipped into a country

Ad valorem duty
A tax which is based on a percentage of the value of imported goods

Compound duty
A tariff consisting of both a specific and an ad valorem duty

Dumping
The selling of imported goods at a price below cost or below that in the home country

A **tariff** is a tax on goods that are shipped internationally. The most common is the **import tariff**, which is levied on goods shipped into a country.[10] Less common is the **export tariff** for goods sent out of the country, or a **transit tariff** for goods passing through the country. These taxes are levied on a number of bases. A **specific duty** is a tariff based on units, such as $1 for each item shipped into the country. So a manufacturer shipping in 1,000 pairs of shoes would pay a specific duty of $1,000. An **ad valorem duty** is a tariff based on a percentage of the value of the item, so a watch valued at $25 and carrying a 10 percent duty would have a tariff of $2.50. A **compound duty** is a tariff consisting of both a specific and an ad valorem duty, so a suit of clothes valued at $80 that carries a specific duty of $3 and an ad valorem duty of 5 percent would have a compound duty of $7.

Governments typically use tariffs to raise revenue and/or to protect local industry. At the same time, these taxes decrease demand for the respective product while raising the price to the buyer. This is illustrated in Figure 6.3, which shows how the quantity demanded declines from Q_1 to Q_2 when a tariff drives the price of a good from P_1 to P_2 (the world price plus the tariff). This price increase allows local producers to sell Q_3Q_2 and thus take market share away from foreign firms that were exporting Q_3Q_1 into the country. However, the figure shows this is done at the price of charging the consumer more money *and* reducing the number of buyers who purchase the product. At new price P_2, there are no longer any imports.

There are numerous reasons for using tariffs, such as to protect domestic industries or firms. The US government has used them to prevent foreign companies from selling goods at lower prices in the United States than back home. US auto makers have often accused their overseas rivals of using this tactic. In the case of Japanese car manufacturers, this was a particularly troublesome area when the value of the yen rose sharply in the early 1990s. As a result, argued the US car companies, imported parts and cars had to reflect the increased value of the yen or be subjected to tariffs.[11] Others have made similar arguments. Eastman Kodak, for example, asked the US Commerce Department to impose steep tariffs on the Fuji Photo Film Company. Kodak's argument was partially based on the rising yen. However, it also reflected a concern with **dumping**, which is the selling of imported goods at a price below cost or below that in the home country. In this case Kodak argued that Fuji sold color photographic paper for less than 20 cents per square foot in the United States, while charging almost 60 cents per square foot in Japan.[12]

Figure 6.3 Impacts of a tariff

Source: Raymond Vernon and Louis T. Wells, Jr., *The Manager in the International Economy* (Englewood Cliffs, NJ: Prentice Hall, 1991), p. 85.

Boeing versus Airbus

In 1970 a European consortium consisting of Germany, France, and the UK (Spain later became a member) created Airbus Industrie. The objective of the consortium was to build commercial aircraft, with Germany, the UK and Spain taking on the job of constructing the aircraft and France assuming responsibility for assembling it. The logic of the arrangement was fairly straightforward. Given the growth of international travel, there would be a continual need for new commercial aircraft, and Airbus wanted to be a major player in this industry.

Until this time, when major air carriers such as American Airlines, Japan Airlines, and Lufthansa needed to replace aging aircraft or increase the size of their fleet, they turned to Boeing or McDonnell Douglas, the two giant US aircraft manufacturers. Cargo carriers such as FedEx and DHL also bought aircraft from them, and, as international air shipments continued to grow rapidly, the annual demand proved to be a boon for Boeing and McDonnell.

The initial challenge for Airbus was to capture some market share and thus establish a toehold in the industry. This, fortunately, was not a problem. The consortium had divided up the responsibility for building the aircraft among its members. In this way, each country was guaranteed some of the work and, in turn, could count on its respective government to provide financial assistance and contracts. In particular, the consortium would have to spend large amounts of money for research and development in order to build competitive, state-of-the-art craft, but by getting support from their respective governments a great deal of the initial risk would be eliminated. This, by the way, was the same approach that had been used in the United States and helped account for much of Boeing's and McDonnell's success in building large aircraft. For example, much of the funding to build the giant C-5A cargo plane was provided by the US military. Then, by using this same technology, it was possible for Boeing to build its giant passenger aircraft.

Realizing that the consortium would eventually be able to build competitive commercial airplanes, Boeing and McDonnell lodged complaints with the US government claiming that Airbus was being subsidized by its governments, and Washington needed to take steps to protect the US commercial aircraft manufacturing industry. As the governments on both sides met to talk and discuss these issues, Airbus started building aircraft and by 1990 the consortium not only was becoming well established but had back orders for 1,100 aircraft; by 1997 this number had reached 2,300. In the process Airbus captured over 30 percent of the world market. One of the major reasons for its success was that it focused on building fuel-efficient craft at competitive prices. Its wide-body, medium-range models, the A300 and A310, for example, were very reliable and the orders started flowing in from a wide number of buyers including large US carriers such as American Airlines and Northwest Airlines. During the 1990s the battle in the aircraft market also saw Boeing and McDonnell Douglas merge their operations. McDonnell could not compete effectively in this new, highly competitive market, but when merged with Boeing it could provide the latter with a good chance to prevent Airbus from steamrolling the US aircraft manufacturing industry.

By 2001 Airbus was doing better than ever. Not only had it managed to catch up with Boeing and hold 50 percent of the overall market, but it was in the throes of making major decisions that could result in its becoming the dominant player in the industry. The company had decided to build a giant, double-decker superjumbo jet. Known as the A380, this aircraft is capable of carrying 555 passengers, and the first craft made its first commercial flight in 2007. A host of buyers signed firm orders with the company, including Qantas, which ordered 12 of the craft, Singapore Airlines, and Air France, which each placed orders for ten. In addition, Singapore Airlines took an option for 15 more. The Singapore deal alone was worth over $8 billion to Airbus, showing how lucrative the market for a superjumbo jet could be. By 2010, other A380 users are Lufthansa and Emirates. However, the engine explosion on one of Qantas' A380 on November 4, 2010 sparked a safety review, in what was considered to be the most serious safety incident yet for the superjumbo in its three years of operation. The plane experienced a mid-air explosion shortly after taking off, and the pilots of the flight made a successful emergency landing in Singapore. The aircraft underwent intensive work before they resumed flying three weeks later. The decision to restore A380 services followed an intensive Trent 900 engine inspection program carried out in close consultation with Rolls-Royce and Airbus. Modifications have been made to the Rolls-Royce engines used on 20 A380s by three airlines—Qantas, Lufthansa, and Singapore Airlines.

In response to Airbus's A380 aircraft, Boeing announced that it was going to build a smaller, faster, longer-range plane that would fly just below the speed of sound. Quite clearly the two competitors were moving in different directions.

Airbus was betting more than $12 billion that airlines will want a superjumbo jet that can carry a large number of passengers on long trips to a given region. Boeing was anticipating ▶

that there is a much larger demand for smaller, faster planes that can take people directly to their destination. In doing so, Boeing has ceded to Airbus a highly profitable jumbo market, wagering that the European group will not earn back its huge investment but rather end up stumbling badly. Boeing's decision to abandon the development of a larger plane (similar to what Airbus proposed) relied heavily on follow-on studies of the giant 747. The company's engineers concluded that, except in the case of a huge 800-passenger plane, a double-decker design had to be scaled back to a single decker to satisfy technical and safety standards. One reason, according to Boeing engineers, is because a double-decker arrangement is very inefficient. Another is that, in case of evacuation, a two-level aircraft can present major problems for those on board.

At this same time Airbus announced that its consortium arrangement was coming to an end and that the company would now be managed as a corporation. It could be said that this move effectively ended Airbus's life as an organization that operated in the world of business and politics and one in which each partner held a veto, politically motivated committees made many of the important decisions, and when things did not go well state funds could be counted on to prop up the consortium. Now, with all of that behind it, Airbus worked to streamline its operations and, according to the business partners, shave off about $400 million in annual expenses.

In 2015 Airbus broke even on the A380 project and in 2016 the company won a significant order from Iran, benefiting from radical changes in the geopolitics of the Middle East region. This included 12 A380s and over 100 other aircraft with an overall order value of $25 billion. Delivering on this required the approval of US export licenses as 10 percent of the components come from US suppliers.

Will Airbus continue to dominate the airways? Its initial challenge was to build the A380 superjumbo. If the demand for the huge craft does materialize, Boeing may find itself as a minor player in the industry. On the other hand, while in late 2001 Airbus recruited thousands of new workers to help with the project, it had trouble finding partners to help fund the venture. A number of European suppliers signed up but US and Japanese companies did not. For example, Airbus had offered Japanese manufacturers up to 8 percent of the work on the A380 in return for funding but had no takers. The company also wanted to get US firms to invest and thus defuse a potential political problem that could result in the US government making it difficult for Airbus to do business in the United States. When Airbus first got started, it relied

heavily on governmental support. Now that it was very successful, it no longer needed this type of help. However, the US government was unlikely to stand by and let this company dominate the industry while Boeing might be forced to take a back seat. In a way, the situation is similar to that in 1970 when Airbus first got started—the main difference is that the two companies now seem to be in opposite positions.

The United States and the EU have been involved in a long dispute on subsidies for Boeing and Airbus. In 2004, the United States lodged a complaint with the World Trade Organization (WTO). In 2010, the WTO ruled that the EU had paid illegal subsidies to Airbus. EU governments were found to have unfairly financed Airbus through risk-free loans, and research and infrastructure funding, although the WTO did not uphold all of the US complaints. However, the EU rejected the US claim that state support had materially impacted the sector and challenged the WTO ruling. The EU said that support for Airbus was not found to have affected jobs and profits in the US aircraft industry. And Airbus said that the support system itself—based on loans repaid as planes are sold—had not been faulted. Meanwhile, the EU has made a similar complaint over the US's alleged support of Boeing. However, the WTO's report into US government funding received by Boeing has been delayed.

Websites: www.boeing.com; www.airbus.com.

Sources: Adapted from Steven Greenhouse, "There's no stopping Europe's Airbus now," *New York Times*, June 23, 1991, section 3, pp. 1, 6; Stuart F. Brown, "How to build a really, really, really big plane," *Fortune*, March 5, 2001, p. 152; Anne Marie Squeo, "Boeing plans to build smaller, faster jet," *Wall Street Journal*, March 30, 2001, p. A3; Daniel Michaels, "Airbus signs up partners to help build jumbo jet," *Wall Street Journal*, June 21, 2001, p. A14; Mark Odell and Victor Mallet, "Airbus cuts back 2003 production targets," *Financial Times*, August 8, 2001, p. 15; Daniel Michaels, Zach Coleman, and Guy Chazan, "Airbus is in talks with Beijing on sale of jets," *Wall Street Journal*, August 21, 2001, p. A12; "Qantas resumes A380 flights after safety scare," *BBC News*, November 27, 2010; "EU Airbus subsidies illegal, says WTO," *BBC News*, June 30, 2010; "EU challenges WTO ruling on Airbus subsidies," *BBC News*, July 21, 2010; "Airbus signs $25bn deal to sell 118 planes to Iran," *BBC News*, January 28, 2016.

1   What are three reasons for the Europeans creating the Airbus consortium?

2   How will Airbus help the EU compete in the United States?

3   How will Airbus help the EU compete in Japan?

4   In what way did the Airbus consortium use a *keiretsu* approach to building the aircraft? Why do you think it opted for this approach?

Another reason for using tariffs is to raise government revenue. Import tariffs, for example, are a major source of revenue for less developed countries. A third reason is to reduce citizens' foreign expenditures in order to improve the country's balance of payments.

Tariffs continue to be one of the most commonly used barriers to trade, despite the fact that they often hurt low-income consumers and have a limited impact, if any, on upper-income purchasers. In recent years most industrialized countries have tried to reduce or eliminate the use of these trade barriers and to promote more free trade policies.[13] The United States is a good example. (The trade policies of the EU are discussed in Chapter 17 and those of Japan in Chapter 18.)

US trade policy

Despite being a highly protectionist nation in its early years, the United States has a policy today that generally strives to lower tariffs and trade barriers through the use of multilateral agreements. Since the protectionist disaster of the Depression years, the United States has sought to minimize the use of tariffs. It supported the General Agreement on Tariffs and Trade (GATT), and now it supports the 1994 World Trade Organization (WTO), which exists to liberalize trade and investment. Today US tariffs average only 2 to 3 percent advalorem to most countries of the world.[14]

The move away from tariffs does not mean US trade policy is completely open.[15] The US government employs a variety of approaches to promote or discourage international trade. For example, to encourage trade, there is the *North American Free Trade Agreement (NAFTA)*, which eliminates most trade restrictions (such as tariffs) among the United States, Canada, and Mexico and extends national treatment to foreign investment, and the **Caribbean Basin Initiative**, which eliminates tariffs on many imports from the Caribbean and Central American regions. Yet the *Trading-with-the-Enemy Act* disallows trade with countries judged to be enemies of the United States, including North Korea and Cuba. The US administration has the authority to prevent sales of goods to foreign governments when they are not deemed to be in the best interests of the United States. These goods can range from computers to chemicals to materials used for making nuclear weapons.[16]

The United States has also used negotiated agreements to limit the type or number of products entering the country. For example, a voluntary agreement with Japan restricts the number of cars imported to the United States. At the same time, exports are encouraged through legislation such as the **Foreign Sales Corporation Act**, which allows US exporters to establish overseas affiliates and not to pay taxes on the affiliates' income until the earnings are remitted to the parent company. The government also offers **trade adjustment assistance** to US businesses and individuals who are harmed by competition from imports. This aid takes such forms as loans for retooling and job counseling for those seeking alternative employment.

Caribbean Basin Initiative
A trade agreement that eliminates tariffs on many imports to the United States from the Caribbean and Central American regions

Foreign Sales Corporation Act
Legislation designed to allow US exporters to establish overseas affiliates and not pay taxes on the affiliates' income until the earnings are remitted to the parent company

Trade adjustment assistance
Assistance offered by the US government to US businesses and individuals harmed by competition from imports

---

 Active learning check

Review your answer to Active Learning Case question 3 and make any changes you like. Then compare your answer to the one below.

3 **In what way could the EU use trade barriers to protect its markets from foreign competitors? Who can be affected by these trade barriers?**

The EU could take a number of steps to protect its markets from foreign competitors. Examples include establishing or increasing ad valorem tariffs, placing quantity limits on various imports, and limiting foreign direct investment. Of course, other countries could retaliate and take similar action against EU-produced goods, so the use of these trade barriers must be selective and should not be undertaken unless efforts at negotiated agreements prove fruitless.

NON-TARIFF BARRIERS TO TRADE

Non-tariff barriers
Rules, regulations, and bureaucratic red tape that delay or preclude the purchase of foreign goods

Non-tariff barriers are rules, regulations, and bureaucratic red tape that delay or preclude the purchase of foreign goods. Examples include (1) slow processing of import permits, (2) the establishment of quality standards that exclude foreign producers, and (3) a "buy local" policy. These barriers limit imports and protect domestic sales.

The economic effects of non-tariff barriers (NTBs) on trade are roughly similar to those of tariffs. They are inefficient distortions that reduce potential gains from trade. Table 6.4 lists a wide range of NTBs.

NTBs have gained prominence and importance in recent years as nations have begun resorting to them more frequently for protection. Sometimes they are not imposed by countries to interfere deliberately with trade.[17] Rather, they arise out of domestic policy and economic management. Examples include tax breaks to reduce regional income disparities or regulations designed to increase local purchasing or employment. These, in turn, result in a type of indirect export subsidy. Other NTBs are more blatant devices that restrict imports or foster exports.

Quotas

The most important NTBs are quotas that restrict imports to a particular level.[18] When a quota is imposed, domestic production generally increases and prices rise. As a result, the government usually ends up losing tariff revenues.

Historically, the GATT and WTO have prohibited import quotas except on agricultural products, as emergency measures, or when a country has short-run balance of payments problems. Countries have circumvented this regulation most notably for textiles, footwear, and automobiles by negotiating voluntary export restraint agreements that are useful in preventing retaliatory action by the importing country. In general, business would rather be protected by quotas than by tariffs. Under quotas, if future domestic demand is known, companies can determine their future production levels. Under tariffs, domestic producers must estimate the elasticity of the demand curve for imported products and the future movements in world prices, which is a more difficult challenge.

Table 6.4 Common non-tariff barriers to trade

Specific limitation	Customs administrative rules	Government participation	Import charges
Quotas (including voluntary)	Valuation systems	Procurement policies	Import deposits
Import licenses	Anti-dumping rules	Export subsidies and incentives	Supplementary duties
Supplementary incentives	Tariff classifications	Countervailing duties	Import credits
Minimum import limits	Documentation needed	Domestic assistance programs	Variable levies
Embargoes	Fees	Trade diverting	Border levies
Sectoral bilateral agreements	Disparities in quality and testing standards		
Orderly marketing agreements	Packaging, labeling, and marketing standards		

"Buy national" restrictions

"Buy national" regulations require governments to give preference to domestic producers, sometimes to the complete exclusion of foreign firms. In Europe, for example, many of the telephone, telegraph, electric utility, airline, and railroad industries are government owned and buy from national firms only, thus closing a large market to exporters. On the other hand, countries like the United States have a similarly wide range of inefficient "Buy American" regulations at the national and state levels that discriminate against foreign suppliers. In 1976 the Tokyo Round of GATT discussions started a process that led to the Agreement on Government Procurement (GPA). In 2014 a total of 17 parties signed up to the revised version of the agreement, comprising 45 WTO members. The central aim of the GPA is to open up government procurement markets (worth an estimated US$1.7 trillion annually) to all members.[19]

Customs valuation

Considerable progress has been made in the area of customs valuation for the payment of duties. Value for duty is now generally based on the invoice cost, and the latitude of any country's customs office to reclassify products has been reduced.

Technical barriers

Product and process standards for health, welfare, safety, quality, size, and measurements can create trade barriers by excluding products that do not meet them. Testing and certification procedures, such as testing only in the importing country and conducting on-site plant inspections, are cumbersome, time consuming, and expensive. The costs must be borne by the exporter prior to the foreign sale. National governments have the right and duty to protect their citizens by setting standards to prevent the sale of hazardous products. But such standards can also be used to impede trade. For example, at one point Japan excluded US-made baseball bats from the market because they did not meet the country's standard. No product produced outside Japan (even products made by foreign subsidiaries of Japanese MNEs) could bear the certification stamp of the Japanese Industrial Standard (JIS) or the Japanese Agricultural Standard (JAS), and selling in Japan without the JIS or JAS logo was difficult. Similarly, at one time the regulations for automobile safety in the United States required that bumpers be above the height practical for imported subcompact cars, thus creating a technical barrier for these car manufacturers. Today the new code on technical barriers to trade requires consultation between trading partners before a standard that impedes trade is put in place. The code also requires that testing and certification procedures treat imports and domestic goods equally and that the importing country accepts certification testing conducted in the exporting country.

Anti-dumping legislation, subsidies, and countervailing duties

The GATT and WTO allow importing countries to protect their producers from unfair competition, such as "dumping" goods at extremely low prices in an effort to gain market share and to drive out local competition. Importing countries are allowed to impose additional duties on products that have received export subsidies or are "dumped." Before the duties are imposed, however, the country must show that its domestic industry has suffered "material" injury from dumped or subsidized imports. Although products at these artificially low prices provide consumers in the importing country with a "good buy," such competition is thought to be unfair to domestic producers, who object to dumping (and also to subsidized imports that can be offset by "countervailing" duties) if the domestic market of the exporting country is closed to them. A good example is the US auto industry, which claims that some Japanese cars are cheaper in the US market than at home, while Japan continues to impede exports of US cars into Japan.

The WTO has developed a code on countervailing duties and anti-dumping duties that now expedites the process of determining whether exports have been dumped or subsidized and whether the domestic industry has been injured. This subject is exceedingly complex. Here are some examples (and answers):

■ If the EU remits value-added taxes on exports by EU producers, is this a subsidy? (*No*)

■ If Canada subsidizes production in a specific sector in one of its depressed regions for domestic purposes, are the exports of a subsidized firm subject to countervailing action? (*Yes*)

■ If the British government subsidizes the British steel industry and its losses incurred by selling at home and abroad at prices below full cost, are its exports subject to anti-dumping or to countervailing duties? (*Maybe, sometimes*)

The problem is complex because of the difficulty in determining what material injury is and how it should be measured. This area is likely to be a point of contention for years to come.

Agricultural products

Trade in agricultural products is highly regulated by both quotas and fixed and variable tariffs. Domestic producers in most industrialized countries are often highly subsidized both directly and by artificially high domestic prices. Agricultural exports are often subsidized as well and, for example, the EU has strongly resisted changes to its Common Agricultural Policy (CAP) for some time. The CAP sets variable tariffs on imports to maintain high domestic prices by excluding or impeding imports. Major reforms in the CAP are now underway that will see continuing support for farmers but independently of production volumes. This is expected to improve the EU's negotiating position at the WTO. The United States is not without guilt in this area, however, since it also subsidizes the export of many agricultural products. The countries most affected by these subsidies are less developed countries with abundant and inexpensive labor and land, and thus a competitive advantage in agricultural products. Agricultural subsidies have often stalled trade talks as these countries refused to further liberalize while developed countries continued to subsidize agriculture.

Export restraints

Over the vigorous objections of countries exporting natural resources, the GATT (and WTO) rounds have moved to tighten the conditions under which exports can be restrained. In general, world tariffs increase with the level of processing: for example, import duties increase as copper is processed from concentrate to blister, to refined copper, to copper wire and bars, to copper pots and pans. This tariff structure makes upgrading of natural resources in the producing country difficult. Natural resource-producing countries have been largely unsuccessful in their attempts to harmonize tariffs on a sectoral basis in order to increase their ability to upgrade prior to export. However, they have argued successfully for their right to restrict exports to induce further domestic processing.

OTHER ECONOMIC DEVELOPMENTS

In addition to the above, other economic developments warrant consideration. These include countertrade, trade in services, and free trade zones.

Countertrade

Countertrade

Barter trade in which the exporting firm receives payment in products from the importing country

Countertrade is essentially barter trade in which the exporting firm receives payment in terms of products from the importing country. Countertrade is important to the airline industry (for example, the purchase of Boeing airplanes by British Airways if Boeing uses Rolls-Royce engines) and in defense (for example, the purchase of US jet fighters by Canada if some of the parts are locally sourced in Canada). Barter sometimes takes the form of a buyback in which the exporter agrees to take products that are locally produced.

Countertrade tends to decrease the efficiency of world trade because it substitutes barter for the exchange of goods by the price system. For example, a US exporter of machinery to Indonesia may have to take payment in an "equivalent value" of palm oil or rattan. The exporting firm will then have to either sell these products, in which it has no expertise, itself, or sell them through a broker or other firm. Some party to the trade—exporter, importer, or consumer—must bear these additional costs. Despite such obvious inefficiencies, countertrade appears likely to continue as an increasingly important factor in the international trade environment of the twenty-first century.

In one type of situation, however, countertrade may be beneficial. For example, if a US producer of textile machinery exports to China and agrees to take payment in the form of textile products, importers in the United States may perceive a lower risk of variability in product quality and delivery schedules (as a result of US technology and management), and the Chinese may perceive a lower risk of product failure in buying the machinery, since the selling firm will not be "paid" unless the machinery performs to specifications.

Trade in services

International trade in services has received relatively little attention from governments or trade economists during trade negotiations. Reliable statistics are seldom collected. However, as high-income countries move toward a service economy, trade in services has grown and become a significant component of the current accounts of many countries. In advanced countries like the US and the UK, for example, a long-running trade surplus in services (higher exports than imports) has provided a counterbalance to the trade deficit in goods (imports exceed exports). Figure 6.4 shows the main deficit and surplus components of the US current account balance. (The balance of payments account will be explained in the Appendix to this chapter.)

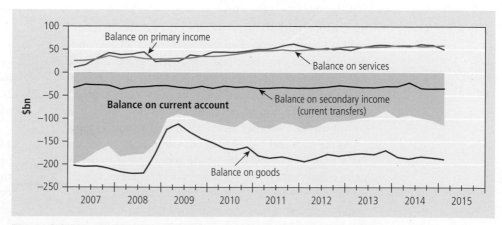

Figure 6.4 The US current account balance and its components, 2007–15

Source: http://blog.bea.gov/tag/current-account-deficit/

The flow of services across/among countries is highly regulated. Internationally traded services such as banking, investment income, insurance, media, transportation, advertising, accounting, travel, and technology licensing are subject to a host of national and international regulations for economic, social, cultural, and political reasons. In 1995, the General Agreement on Trade in Services (GATS) came into effect and now 140 WTO members are signatories. It covers all services except those provided by the government and those related to air traffic. Member countries are not forced to open all their service industries but can choose those areas for which they want to guarantee access to foreigners and, within a framework, how much access they want to provide. For example, a host nation might limit the scope of a foreign bank's operation through the use of licenses or by setting a maximum number of allowable branches.

Whatever forum is used, negotiating reductions in service trade barriers will be difficult, complex, and lengthy. The barriers are often difficult to list, much less quantify for purposes of negotiation. And the issues are often highly charged and not subject to rational analysis. For example, Canada imposes Canadian content requirements on television, radio, and print media to foster a "national cultural identity," to protect its cultural heritage, and to protect the domestic arts, theater, and movie industries. A government that reduced these trade barriers or even agreed to negotiate them would be in trouble with the (protected) Canadian media, as well as with the general public.

Free trade zones

Free trade zone
A designated area where importers can defer payment of customs duty while further processing of products takes place (same as a foreign trade zone)

A **free trade zone** is a designated area where importers can defer payment of customs duty while products are processed further (same as a foreign trade zone). Thus, the free trade zone serves as an "offshore assembly plant," employing local workers and using local financing for a tax-exempt commercial activity. The economic activity takes place in a restricted area, such as an industrial park, because the land is often being supplied at a subsidized rate by a local host government that is interested in the zone's potential employment benefits.

To be effective, free trade zones must be strategically located either at or near an international port, on major shipping routes, or with easy access to a major airport. Important factors in the location include the availability of utilities, banking and telecom services, and a commercial infrastructure.

More than 400 free trade zones exist in the world today, often encompassing entire cities, such as Hong Kong and Singapore. More than two-thirds are situated in developing countries, and most of their future growth is expected to occur there.

The advantages offered by free trade zones are numerous and mutually beneficial to all stakeholders. For private firms, the zones offer three major attractions. First, the firm pays the customs duty (tariff) only when the goods are ready to market. Second, manufacturing costs are lower because no taxes are levied. Third, while in the zone the manufacturer has the opportunity to repackage the goods, grade them, and check for spoilage. Secondary benefits to firms take the form of reduced insurance premiums (since these are based on duty-free values), reduced fines for improperly marked merchandise (since the good can be inspected in a zone prior to customers' scrutiny), and added protection against theft (resulting from security measures in the bonded warehouses).

At the state and local levels, advantages can be realized in terms of commercial services. On a more global level, free trade zones enable domestic importing companies to compete more readily with foreign producers or subsidiaries of MNEs, thereby increasing participation in world trade. Favorable effects are felt on the balance of payments because more economic activity occurs and net capital outflow is reduced. Finally, the business climate is improved due to reduced bureaucracy and resultant savings to business capital, currently inaccessible because of the delay in paying duties and tariffs. A free trade zone is a step toward free trade and can be an important signal by government to business that the economy is opening up. Opportunity replaces regulation, and growth of economic activity should result.

Before the establishment of more free trade zones becomes fully accepted and encouraged, governments must be convinced of their many economic benefits. Free trade zones are a vital necessity if nations are to remain competitive on an international scale. Not only will existing companies benefit from their use, but new industries will be attracted, keeping up the same benefits of world trade.

Maquiladora industry
Named after the practice of millers charging a _maquila, or_ "miller's portion," for processing other people's grain, this is a free trade zone that has sprung up along the US–Mexican border for the purpose of producing goods and then shipping them between the two countries

The **_maquiladora_ industry** along the US–Mexican border is an excellent example of a free trade zone. The low wage rate in Mexico and the NAFTA of 1994 make the _maquiladora_ region both accessible and important to labor-intensive firms in the United States and Canada. From only 12 _maquiladora_ plants in 1965, more than 570 now exist, providing over 100,000 jobs in Tijuana.

No Mexican taxes are paid on goods processed within the _maquiladoras_. Foreign companies doing such processing can benefit from lower wages and land costs than those in the United States as they increase the value added to their products. In return, Mexico attracts FDI into permanent plants, creates jobs, and collects taxes on any final products sold to the foreign firms, or within Mexico. Even though the United States has several hundred free trade zones of its own, many near seaports or airfields, these lack the low-wage workers of their Mexican counterparts.

Canada does not have free trade zones, but the federal government allows duty drawbacks, which arguably offer many of the same advantages. Unfortunately, these drawbacks, which are repayments of customs duties, apply retroactively and involve enough paperwork to discourage all but the largest or most dedicated organizations. As such, NAFTA and the lower-wage labor in Mexico have attracted Canadian firms producing labor-intensive products. Free trade zones exist in many other parts of the world than North America, and the advantages of these zones are enjoyed by businesses worldwide.[20]

KEY POINTS

1 International economics is the branch of economics concerned with the purchase and sale of foreign goods and services. This includes consideration of areas such as international trade, balance of payments, and barriers to trade.

2 A number of international trade theories help to explain why nations trade. These include the theory of absolute advantage, the theory of comparative advantage, the factor endowment theory, the Leontief paradox, and the international product life cycle theory. While no one theory offers a complete explanation of why nations trade, they collectively provide important insights. Other key considerations that offer explanations for why nations trade include monetary currency valuation and consumer tastes.

3 There are a number of barriers to trade. Some of the most common include price-based barriers, quantity limits, international price fixing, non-tariff barriers, financial limits, and foreign investment controls.

4 Although tariffs are often introduced to maintain local jobs and assist infant industries, they are inefficient. This economic inefficiency results in higher prices of imported goods for the consumers. The redistribution of resources from more efficient industry further adds to the cost of a tariff. Such costs do not occur under free trade.

5 Non-tariff barriers (NTBs) provide similar economic inefficiencies to tariffs. Unlike tariffs, however, NTBs are not imposed by nations to interfere deliberately with trade; they arise out of domestic policy. There are several types of NTBs, including quotas, "buy national" restrictions, technical barriers, and export restraints.

6 Countertrade is a form of barter trade in which the exporting firm receives payments in terms of products produced in the importing country. It is most pronounced in East–West trade, and although it may be beneficial to the trading partners, it increases the inefficiencies in the world trade system, which in turn raises costs and decreases trade volume.

7 Services are an important but somewhat misunderstood component of trade. Despite the trade of services in the billions of dollars among high-income countries, regulation has been less clear under GATT and the WTO.

8 A free trade zone is a designated area where importers can defer payment of customs duty while further processing of products takes place. In essence, it is an offshore assembly plant. The majority of these areas exist in developing countries and handle approximately 20 percent of worldwide trade. Free trade zones are advantageous to all because they provide benefits such as increased employment and lower business costs.

Key terms

- mercantilism
- neo-mercantilism
- theory of absolute advantage
- theory of comparative advantage
- factor endowment theory
- Heckscher–Ohlin theory
- Leontief paradox
- international product life cycle (IPLC) theory
- monetary exchange rate

- quota
- embargo
- cartel
- exchange controls
- foreign investment controls
- tariff
- import tariff
- export tariff
- transit tariff
- specific duty
- ad valorem duty
- compound duty

- dumping
- Caribbean Basin Initiative
- Foreign Sales Corporation Act
- trade adjustment assistance
- non-tariff barriers
- countertrade
- free trade zone
- *maquiladora* industry

REVIEW AND DISCUSSION QUESTIONS

1 Why is it difficult to solve international economic problems in the short run?

2 What is the supposed economic benefit of embracing mercantilism as an international trade theory? Are there many disadvantages to the use of this theory?

3 How is the theory of absolute advantage similar to that of comparative advantage? How is it different?

4 In what way does factor endowment theory help explain why nations trade? How does the Leontief paradox modify this theory?

5 If an innovating country develops a new technologically superior product, how long will it be before the country begins exporting the product? At what point will the country begin importing the product?

6 Of what value is the international product life cycle theory in helping to understand why nations trade?

7 How does each of the following trade barriers work: price-based barriers, quantity limits, international price fixing, non-tariff barriers, financial limits, and foreign investment controls?

8 What are some of the reasons for trade barriers? Identify and describe five.

9 How does the United States try to encourage exports? Identify and describe two ways.

10 Non-tariff barriers have become increasingly predominant in recent years. Describe a non-tariff barrier, and list four types, explaining how the United States does or could use such a device.

11 How does countertrade work? Is it an efficient economic concept?

12 What is a free trade zone? Is it an efficient economic concept?

13 What are two future problems and challenges that will have to be addressed by the international monetary system? Describe each.

14 What is meant by the term *balance of payments*?

15 What are the three major accounts in the balance of payments?

16 How would the following transactions be recorded in the IMF balance of payments?

a IBM in New York has sold an $8 million mainframe computer to an insurance company in Singapore and has been paid with a check drawn on a Singapore bank.

b A private investor in San Francisco has received dividends of $80,000 for stock she holds in a British firm.

c The US government has provided $60 million of food and medical supplies for Kurdish refugees in Turkey.

d The Walt Disney Company has invested $50 million in a theme park outside Paris, France.

REAL CASE

Job losses and offshoring to China

It was not a difficult choice to make. Over the last 10 years, US imports of manufactured goods from China shot up. Cheap labor—the cost of Chinese labor is six times lower than Mexican labor—accounts for this. Continuing manufacturing operations in the United States and remaining price competitive is simply not feasible. When jobs are outsourced across national borders—for example, from the United States to China—this is called offshoring.

Competition on quality, which can shelter domestic manufacturing from outsourcing to developing countries, was not an alternative because Chinese products for export are usually as good (although not in the case of toys, as Mattel found in 2007). When high labor intensity is tied to quality, the Chinese can outdo Western industrialized countries. Another factor is that the Chinese have a combination of highly skilled management and low-skilled labor, ensuring that production is efficient and that quality standards are met. This ability to produce high-quality goods is also what allows China to move from export manufacturing of Christmas decorations, toys, footwear, and clothing to household, consumer appliances, and, increasingly, the IT manufacturing sector.

National Presto, a US firm that makes high-quality pressure cookers and electric frying pans, had a difficult decision to make in the early 2000s. It could either offshore its production to China or see its market share continue to deteriorate. In 2002, the company closed plants in Mississippi and New Mexico, reducing its US workforce to less than half, and expanded its production in China. By 2003, all significant products marketed by the company were made in China.

Like many other US, European, and Japanese companies, National Presto uses an agent in Hong Kong to subcontract production to manufacturing plants in mainland China. Larger companies like Motorola, Philips, IBM, Toshiba, and GE have more control over their manufacturing plants in China. Kyocera of Japan, for example, invested $90 million in the early 2000s to construct a high-tech industrial park in Shilong Town of Dongguan City, Guangdong Province. Only 20 years ago Guangdong was dominated by paddy fields; today it is China's largest manufacturing cluster.

Proponents of free trade argue that political rhetoric against trade with China is meant to appease US fears of job losses. Yet, as seen in Table 6.5, 0.4 percent of all job losses ▶

Table 6.5 Outsourcing and job losses in the United States, third quarter of 2010

Reasons for job losses	Separations	% of total
With separations reported, of which:	3,074	1.64
Out of country relocation	737	0.40
Domestic relocation	2,337	1.26
Other	184,017	98.35
Total, private non-farm sector	187,091	100.0

Note: Data only cover layoffs in companies with at least 50 workers, who have filed for unemployment insurance for at least 50 workers, and where unemployment lasted more than 30 days.

Source: US Bureau of Labor Statistics, "Extended mass layoffs, third quarter 2010,'" November 12, 2010, tables A and 10.

in the United States in the third quarter of 2010 were the result of "out of country" relocation. While some argue that this percentage is undervalued because it does not take into consideration potential job gains that never materialized, others argue that, given economic conditions, there was no assurance that firms that created new jobs in China would have chosen to create these jobs in the United States if off-shoring to China had not been a possibility.

China has become the world's largest manufacturer, ahead of the United States, Japan, and Germany. It has out-paced Japan to become the country having the largest trade surplus with the United States. US politicians and lobby groups blame Chinese protectionist practices for the grow-ing trade deficit between the two nations, which in 2003 was estimated at $124 billion. In 2009, the deficit with China totaled $226.83 billion, still the largest imbalance with any nation, but down 15.4 percent from the all-time record of $268.04 billion set in 2008. The deficit with China was recorded as $273.04 billion in 2010 and it has continued to

rise as the US economy has recovered, reaching $367.17 bil-lion in 2015. Overall there has been a rise in orders for Chinese manufacturers of shoes, toys, and other low-cost items that are in high demand among American consumers.

Among the barriers that the United States claims prevent a free flow of its goods to China are import barriers, unclear legal provisions applied in a discriminatory manner against US imports, and an undervalued yuan. The last one has gen-erated the most controversy in the last few years. The Chinese yuan has been fixed at 8.28 to the dollar since 1994, a rate that critics argue to be up to 40 percent undervalued. China relaxed the yuan's fixed exchange rate against the dollar in June 2010, but since then it has been allowed to appreciate by less than 3%. Yet economists do not all agree that the yuan is undervalued. Some fear that a sharp deterioration would hurt not only the Chinese economy but also those trading partners that are most heavily dependent on Chinese imports.

Sources: "Chinese trade reform 'is failing'," *BBC News*, April 1, 2004; "China defiant on currency exchange," *BBC News*, September 2, 2003; Mary Hennock, "China: the world's factory floor," *BBC News*, November 11, 2002; www. worldbank.org; "Kyocera to build high-tech industrial park in Dongguan," *People's Daily*, September 13, 2000; "US trade deficit surges to $40.18 billion," *Associated Press*, www.msnbc.msn.com, October 2, 2010; Linda Levine, "Offshoring and job loss among US workers," Congressional Research Service, January 21 2011, accessed from http://forbes.house.gov/uploadedfiles/crs_-_offshoring_and_job_loss_among_u_s__workers.pdf

1 Does the theory of comparative advantage apply to China's trade with industrialized countries? How?

2 How does the factor endowment theory apply to China's trade with industrialized countries?

3 Are any of the countries mentioned operating in autarky?

4 How can distribution of gains from free trade cause much of the political debate regarding trade with China?

REAL CASE

Dumping on trade complaints

One of the biggest problems in international trade is the abil-ity of domestic producers to lobby their home governments to erect barriers to trade. In the past, the textile, apparel, and shoe industries were able to obtain protection from cheaper imports through tariffs, quotas, and special measures. Now multilateral trade agreements under the GATT and WTO (and also regional and bilateral agreements such as NAFTA and

the emerging Asian Pacific Economic Cooperation forum) outlaw such blatant instruments of protection. However, these agreements have been replaced by more subtle ones.

Prominent as a new type of protectionist device is the use of "unfair trade laws," especially anti-dumping (AD) and coun-tervailing duty (CVD) actions. The economic logic of AD and CVD makes some sense. It is unfair for a foreign producer to "dump" a product in your country below its price in the home country, or below the cost of producing it. Similarly, subsidized foreign products should be offset by a CVD of equivalent effect. The problem, however, lies with the administration of the trade laws, which is subject to political lobbying.

A variety of studies have found that the bureaucrats who administer AD and CVD laws are subject to capture by the home industries, which then use AD and CVD cases as harassment tools against often economically efficient foreign rival producers. For example, Rugman and Anderson (1987) found that the US administration of AD and CVD was used in a biased manner against Canadian producers, especially in resource-based industries such as softwood lumber, fishing, and agriculture. Thus, in the Canadian–US Free Trade Agreement of 1989, and again in NAFTA, five-person binational panels of trade law experts were set up to review the decision of the US (and Canadian) trade law agencies.

In a subsequent study, Rugman and Anderson (1997) found that these binational panels were able to remand back (i.e., successfully challenge) the decision of the US agencies twice as often in cases involving Canada as in AD and CVD cases involving the rest of the world. In related work researchers have found that the EU is just as bad as the United States when it comes to taking questionable AD

measures, especially against Asian countries. Indeed, one of the unresolved problems is how smaller countries can secure access to the protected markets of triad economies such as the United States and the EU. In Japan's case, there are similar arguments (including those from its triad rivals) that it has entry barriers in place preventing market access.

Website: www.wto.org.

Sources: Andrew D. M. Anderson, *Seeking Common Ground: Canada–US Trade Dispute Settlement Policies in the Nineties* (Boulder, CO: Westview Press, 1995); Alan M. Rugman, *Multinational Enterprises and Trade Policy* (Cheltenham: Edward Elgar, 1996); Alan M. Rugman and Andrew D. M. Anderson, *Administered Protection in America* (London and New York: Routledge, 1987); Alan M. Rugman and Andrew D. M. Anderson, "NAFTA and the dispute settlement mechanisms," *The World Economy*, December 1997, pp. 935–50; Alan M. Rugman and Michael Gestrin, "EC anti-dumping laws as a barrier to trade," *European Management Journal*, vol. 9, no. 4 (December 1991), pp. 475–82.

1 Why are AD and CVD measures brought and imposed?

2 What is the impact on a firm from a non-triad country if it faces an AD or CVD case in its major market?

3 What is the solution to the abusive use of AD and CVD measures by triad economies?

NOTES

1 Asra Q. Nomani and Douglas Lavin, "US and Japan nearing accord in trade dispute," *Wall Street Journal*, March 10, 1994, p. A3; and Richard McGregor, "Beans are on the Beijing menu as Bush prepares to talk trade," FT.com, February 21, 2002.
2 Douglas Harbrecht et al., "Tough talk," *Business Week*, February 20, 1994, pp. 26–8.
3 See, for example, Dana Weschler Linden, "Dreary days in the dismal science," *Forbes*, January 21, 1991, pp. 68–71.
4 Also see Steven Greenhouse, "French shift on state-owned sector," *New York Times*, April 8, 1991, p. C2.
5 For additional insights into trade theory, see Nicolas Schmitt, "New international trade theories and Europe 1991: some results relevant for EFTA countries," *Journal of Common Market Studies*, September 1990, pp. 53–74.
6 "Tested by the mighty euro," Economist.com, May 18, 2004.
7 See Richard W. Stevenson, "East Europe says barriers to trade hurt its economies," *New York Times*, January 25, 1993, pp. A1, C8.
8 Lucy Walker, "Sir Leon's cartel busters take to the road again," *The European*, April 12–14, 1991, p. 25.
9 Edmund Faltermayer, "Is 'Made in the USA' fading away?" *Fortune*, September 24, 1990, p. 73.
10 Edward Alden and Robert Shrimsley, "EU set to retaliate if US imposes steel tariffs," *Financial Times*, March 4, 2002.
11 See, for example, Doron P. Levin, "Honda to hold base price on Accord model," *New York Times*, September 2, 1993, p. C3.
12 Keith Bradsher, "Kodak is seeking big tariff on Fuji," *New York Times*, September 1, 1993, pp. A1, C2.
13 See, for example, Robert Cohen, "Grumbling over GATT," *New York Times*, July 3, 1993, p. 13.
14 Ed Gresser, "Tariffs biggest US tax on the poor," *Reuters*, September 10, 2002.
15 See, for example, Chris Adams, "Ailing steel industry launches a battle against imports," *Wall Street Journal*, October 1, 1998, p. B4; and "Steel vice," *Wall Street Journal*, October 1, 1998, p. A22.
16 As an example, see Clyde H. Farnsworth, "US slows computer for Brazil," *International Herald Tribune*, April 13–14, 1991, p. 5.
17 Claude Barfield, "Nerves of steel," *Financial Times*, March 1, 2002.
18 Sometimes these are voluntary quotas, as seen in Andrew Pollack, "Japan takes a pre-emptive step on auto exports," *New York Times*, January 9, 1993, pp. 17, 26.
19 WTO Agreement of Government Procurement, https://www.wto.org/english/tratop_e/gproc_e/gp_gpa_e.htm, accessed in September 2015.
20 Anthony DePalma, "Trade pact is spurring Mexican deals in the US," *New York Times*, March 17, 1994, pp. C1, 3.

BIBLIOGRAPHY

Anderson, Andrew D. M. *Seeking Common Ground: Canada–US Trade Disputes* (Boulder, CO: Westview Press, 1995).

Baggs, Jen, and Brander, James A. "Trade liberalization, profitability, and financial leverage," *Journal of International Business Studies*, vol. 37, no. 2 (March 2006).

Baldauf, Artur. "Examining determinants of export performance in small open economies," *Journal of World Business*, vol. 35, no. 1 (spring 2000).

Banalieva, Elitsa R., and Sarathy, Ravi. "The impact of regional trade agreements on the global orientation of emerging market multinationals," *Management International Review*, vol. 50, no. 6 (2010).

Barboza, Gustavo A., and Trejos, Sandra R. "Empirical evidence on trade reform, revealed trade openness, and output growth in Latin America: how far have we come?" *Multinational Business Review*, vol. 16, no. 4 (2008).

Beleska-Spasova, Elena, and Glaister, Keith W. "The geography of British exports: country-level versus firm-level evidence," *European Management Journal*, vol. 27 (2009).

Beleska-Spasova, Elena, and Glaister, Keith W. "Geographic orientation and performance evidence from British exporters," *Management International Review*, vol. 50, no. 5 (2010).

Beleska-Spasova, Elena, and Glaister, Keith W. "The role of firm-specific advantages in UK export initiation," *Multinational Business Review*, vol. 19, no. 2 (2011).

Bertrand, Olivier. "What goes around, comes around: effects of offshore outsourcing on the export performance of firms," *Journal of International Business Studies*, vol. 42 (2011).

Brewer, Thomas L., and Young, Stephen. "Multilateral institutions and policies: their implications for multinational business strategy," in Alan M. Rugman (ed.), *The Oxford Handbook of International Business*, 2nd ed. (Oxford: Oxford University Press, 2009).

Buckley, Peter J. "Government policy responses to strategic rent seeking transnational corporations," *Transnational Corporations*, vol. 5, no. 2 (August 1996).

Colantone, Italo, and Sleuwaegen, Leo. "International trade, exit and entry: a cross-country and industry analysis," *Journal of International Business Studies*, vol. 41, no. 7 (2010).

Collie, David R., and Le, Vo Phuong Mai. "Antidumping regulations: anti-competitive and anti-export," *Review of International Economics*, vol. 18, no. 5 (2010).

Curran, Louise, and Zignago, Soledad. "Intermediate products and the regionalization of trade," *Multinational Business Review*, vol. 19, no. 1 (2011).

Davis, Lucy. "Ten years of anti-dumping in the EU: economic and political targeting," *Global Trade and Customs Journal*, vol. 4, no. 7 (2009).

Deutsch, Klaus Gunter, and Speyer, Bernhard (eds.). *The World Trade Organization Millennium Round* (London: Routledge, 2001).

Dunning, John H., and Mucchielli, Jean-Louis (eds.). *Multinational Firms: The Global-Local Dilemma* (London: Routledge, 2002).

Fratianni, Michele U., Marchionne, Francesco, and Oh, Chang H. "A commentary on the gravity equation in international business research," *Multinational Business Review*, vol. 19, no. 1 (2011).

Fratianni, Michele U., and Oh, Chang H. "Expanding RTAs, trade flows, and the multinational enterprise," *Journal of International Business Studies*, vol. 40 (2009).

Fung, Hung-Gay, Yau, Jot, and Zhang, Gaiyan. "Reported trade figure discrepancy, regulatory arbitrage, and round-tripping: evidence from the China–Hong Kong trade data," *Journal of International Business Studies*, vol. 42 (2011).

Liu, Runjuan, Feils, Dorothee J., and Scholnick, Barry. "Why are different services outsourced to different countries?" *Journal of International Business Studies*, vol. 42 (May 2011).

Markusen, James R. "International trade theory and international business," in Alan M. Rugman and Thomas L. Brewer (eds.), *The Oxford Handbook of International Business* (Oxford: Oxford University Press, 2001).

Ostry, Sylvia. *The Post-Cold War Trading System* (Chicago, IL: University of Chicago Press, 1997).

Park, Soonchan. "The trade depressing and trade diversion effects of antidumping actions: the case of China," *China Economic Review*, vol. 20, no. 3 (2009).

Ramstetter, Eric D. "Export performance and foreign affiliate activity in Japan's large machinery firms," *Transnational Corporations*, vol. 6, no. 3 (December 1997).

Rugman, Alan M. *Multinational Enterprises and Trade Policy* (Cheltenham: Edward Elgar, 1996).

Rugman, Alan M., and Anderson, Andrew. *Administered Protection in America* (London: Croom Helm and New York: Methuen, 1987).

Rugman, Alan M., and Boyd, Gavin (eds.). *The World Trade Organization in the New Global Economy* (Cheltenham: Edward Elgar, 2001).

Rugman, Alan M., and Gestrin, Michael. "US trade laws as barriers to globalization," in Tamir Agmon and Richard Drobnick (eds.), *Small Firms in Global Competition* (New York: Oxford University Press, 1994).

Rugman, Alan M., and Verbeke, Alain. *Global Corporate Strategy and Trade Policy* (London and New York: Routledge, 1990).

Rugman, Alan M., and Verbeke, Alain. "Strategic trade policy is not good strategy," *Hitotsubashi Journal of Commerce and Management*, vol. 25, no. 1 (December 1990).

Rugman, Alan M., and Verbeke, Alain. "Location, competitiveness, and the multinational enterprise," in Alan M. Rugman (ed.), *The Oxford Handbook of International Business* (Oxford: Oxford University Press, 2009).

Vandenbussche, Hylke, and Zanardi, Maurizio. "The chilling trade effects of antidumping proliferation," *European Economic Review*, vol. 54, no. 6 (2010).

Zhang, Chun, Cavusgil, S. Tamer, and Roath, Anthony S. "Manufacturer governance of foreign distributor relationships: do relational norms enhance competitiveness in the export market?" *Journal of International Business Studies*, vol. 34, no. 6 (November 2003).

APPENDIX: BALANCE OF PAYMENTS

How well do we keep track of the millions of transactions that take place annually among exporters and importers, international banks, and multinational companies? The bankers who tabulate the foreign exchange dealings of their own banks are only a part of the picture. How well can we account for the part of direct investment that occurs through overseas borrowing, yet affects the home country's international economic position? Even more simply, how well can we measure "international" transactions that are simply transfers of funds from the account of an importer to the account of a foreign exporter in the same bank?

The realistic answer to these questions is: not very well. National governments create elaborate accounts for the transactions between their residents and foreign residents, but it is often very difficult to obtain full and accurate information. Putting that problem aside for the moment, let us consider the methods that governments use to record each country's international transactions.

Balance of payments (BOP)

The value of all transactions between a country's residents and the rest of the world; the three broad BOP categories are the current account, capital account, and official reserves

The most widely used measure of international economic transactions for any country is the **balance of payments (BOP)**. This record attempts to measure the full value of the transactions between residents of one country and residents of the rest of the world for some time period, typically one year. The balance of payments is a flow concept, in that it records flows of goods, services, and claims between countries over a period of time, rather than a stock of accumulated funds or products. It is a value concept, in that all the items recorded receive a monetary value, denominated in the given country's currency at the time of those transactions. *The balance of payments thus is a record of the value of all the economic transactions between residents of one country and residents of all other countries during a given time period.*

Why do we worry about measuring these transactions? We do so because if a country records a substantial imbalance between inflows and outflows of goods and services for an extended period of time, some means of financing or adjusting away the imbalance must be found. For example, if the Eurozone countries record a persistent trade deficit with China for several years, there will be pressure either to devalue the euro relative to the Chinese currency, the renminbi, or for Chinese investors to place large and continuing investments into euro-denominated securities. This pressure presents both a political outcome (pressure on the Chinese government to revalue the renminbi) and an economic outcome (pressure on the euro to devalue and on European producers to lower their costs, perhaps by producing in China).

So, the importance of the balance of payments is not only macroeconomic, in the domain of government accountants, but also managerial, since an imbalance provides guidance to managers about expected government policies as well as about opportunities to take advantage of currency opportunities. Since the relatively open foreign exchange markets of many countries today leave the exchange rate substantially to supply and demand, the balance of payments is an indicator of exactly that supply and demand for a country's currency that will lead to changes in the exchange rate.

The supply and demand for a currency come from both trade flows (exports and imports) and capital flows (investments and borrowing). So, the balance of payments implications for exchange rates must include both sides of the story, the "real" flows and the financial flows.

Balance of payments accounting

There is no such thing as the balance of payments, since the accounts are organized in a double-entry bookkeeping system, and for every debit entry there is a credit entry of equal value. There are half a dozen BOP measures, which group some international transactions together and leave others in a second, "everything else" category. In each case the intent is to place the fundamental economic causes of transactions in the first group and leave the payments for them in the second group. In the actual accounts, the former transactions are listed "above the line," and the payments are left "below the line."

Current account

Current account
A BOP category that consists of merchandise trade, services, and gifts (unilateral transfers)

The **current account** consists of merchandise trade, services, and unilateral transfers. (See Table 6A, parts A and B.)

Merchandise trade is typically the first part of the current account. It receives more attention than any of the other accounts because this is where the imports and exports of

Table 6A Balance of payments: IMF presentation

	Debits	Credits
I Current account		
A Goods, services, and income:		
1 Merchandise	Imports from foreign sources (acquisition of goods)	Exports to foreign destinations (provision of goods)
Trade balance		
2 Shipment and other transportation	Payments to foreigners for freight and insurance on international shipments; for ship repair, stores, and supplies; and international passenger fares	Receipts by residents from foreigners for services provided
3 Travel	Expenditures by residents (including internal transportation) when traveling in a foreign country	Receipts by residents for goods and services (including internal transportation) sold to foreign travelers in reporting country
4 Investment income	Profits of foreign direct investments in reporting country, including reinvested earnings; income paid to foreigners as interest, dividends, etc.	Profits of direct investments by residents in foreign countries, including reinvested earnings; income received by residents from abroad as interest, dividends, etc.
5 Other official	Foreign purchases by government not included elsewhere; personal expenditures of government civilian and military personnel stationed in foreign countries	Expenditures of foreign governments for goods and services, not included elsewhere; personal expenditures of foreign civilian and military personnel stationed in reporting country
6 Other private	Payments to foreigners for management fees, royalties, film rentals, construction, etc.	Receipts from foreigners for management fees, royalties, film rentals, construction, etc.
Goods, services, and income balance		
B Unilateral transfers:		
1 Private	Payments in cash and kind by residents to foreigners without a quid pro quo such as charitable gifts and gifts by migrants to their families	Receipts in cash and kind by residents from foreigners, individuals, or governments without a quid pro quo
2 Official	Transfers by government of reporting country for pensions, reparations, and grants for economic and military aid	Transfers received by government from foreigners in the form of goods, services, or cash as gifts or grants. Also tax receipts from non-residents
Current account balance		

Table 6A (*continued*)

	Debits	Credits
II Capital account		
C Capital, excluding reserves:		
1 Direct investment	(a) Increased investment in foreign enterprises controlled by residents, including reinvestment of earnings (b) Decreases in investment by residents in domestic enterprises controlled by foreigners	(a) Decreased investment in foreign enterprises controlled by residents (b) Increases in investment in domestic enterprises by foreigners
2 Portfolio investment	(a) Increases in investment by residents in foreign securities (b) Decreases in investment by foreigners in domestic securities such as bonds and corporate equities	(a) Decreases in investments by residents in foreign securities (b) Increases in investment by foreigners in domestic securities
3 Other long-term, official	(a) Loans to foreigners (b) Redemption or purchase from foreigners of government securities	(a) Foreign loan reductions (b) Sales to foreigners of government securities
4 Other long-term, private	(a) Long-term loans to foreigners by resident banks and private parties (b) Loan repayments by residents to foreign banks or private parties	(a) Long-term loans by foreigners to resident banks or private parties (b) Loan repayments by foreigners to residents
5 Other short-term, official	(a) Short-term loans to foreigners by central government (b) Purchase from foreigners of government securities, decrease in liabilities constituting reserves of foreign authorities	(a) Short-term loans to resident central government by foreigners (b) Foreign sales of short-term resident government securities, increases in liabilities constituting reserves of foreign authorities
6 Other short-term, private	(a) Increases in short-term foreign assets held by residents (b) Decreases in domestic assets held by foreigners, such as bank deposits, currencies, debts to banks, and commercial claims	(a) Decreases in short-term foreign assets held by residents. Increase in foreign liabilities of residents (b) Increase in domestic short-term assets held by foreigners or decrease in short-term domestic liabilities to foreigners
III Reserves		
D Reserves:		
1 Monetary gold 2 Special drawing rights (SDRs) 3 IMF reserve position 4 Foreign exchange assets	Increases in holdings of gold, SDRs, foreign convertible currencies by monetary authorities; decreases in liabilities to IMF or increase in IMF assets position	Decreases in holdings of gold, SDRs, foreign convertible currencies by monetary authorities; increases in liabilities to IMF or decrease in IMF assets position
E Net errors and omissions:	Net understatement of recorded debts or overstatement of recorded credits	Net understatement of recorded debts or overstatement of recorded credits
Balances:		
Balances on merchandise trade	A-1 credits minus A-1 debits	
Balance on goods, services, and income	A-1 through A-6 credits minus A-1 through A-6 debits	
Balance on current account	A and B credits minus A and B debits	

goods are reported, and these are often the largest single component of all international transactions. In this account, sales of goods to foreigners (exports) are reported as credits because they are a source of funds or a claim against the purchasing country. Conversely, purchases of goods from overseas (imports) are recorded as debits because they use funds. This payment can be made by either reducing current claims on foreigners or increasing foreign liabilities.

Merchandise trade transactions can affect a country's BOP in a number of ways. Assume that Nissan Motor of Japan has sold General Motors in the United States $600,000 worth of engines and these engines will be paid for from GM's account in a Detroit bank. In this case the imports are a debit to the current account (A-1) and a credit to the "other short-term, private" capital account (C-6b). Here is how the entry would be recorded:

		Debit	Credit
A-1	Merchandise imports	$600,000	
C-6b	Increase in domestic short-term assets held by foreigners		$600,000

The result of this purchase is that the United States has transferred currency to foreigners and thus reduced its ability to meet other claims.

Services

The services category includes many payments such as freight and insurance on international shipments (A-2); tourist travel (A-3); profits and income from overseas investment (A-4); personal expenditures by government, civilians, and military personnel overseas (A-5); and payments for management fees, royalties, film rental, and construction services (A-6). Purchases of these services are recorded as debits, while sales of these services are similar to exports and are recorded as credits. For example, extending the earlier example of Nissan and GM, assume that the US auto maker must pay $125,000 to Nissan to ship the engines to the United States. The transaction would be recorded this way:

		Debit	Credit
A-2	Shipment	$125,000	
C-6b	Other short-term private capital		$125,000

GM purchased a Japanese shipping service (a debit to the current account) and paid for this by increasing the domestic short-term assets held by foreigners (a credit to the capital account).

Unilateral transfers

Unilateral transfers are transactions that do not involve repayment or the performance of any service. Examples include the American Red Cross sending $10 million in food to refugees in Somalia; the United States paying military pensions to residents of the Philippines who served in the US Army during World War II; and British workers in Kuwait shipping money home to their families in London. Here is how the American Red Cross transaction would appear in the US BOP:

		Debit	Credit
B-1	Unilateral transfers, private	$10 million	
A-1	Merchandise exports		$10 million

Capital account

Capital account items are transactions that involve claims in ownership. Direct investment (C-1) involves managerial participation in a foreign enterprise along with some account that involves degree of control. The United States classifies direct investments as those investments that give the investor more than 10 percent ownership. Portfolio investment (C-2) is investment designed to obtain income or capital gains. For example, if Exxon shipped $20 million of equipment to an overseas subsidiary the entry would be:

		Debit	Credit
C-1	Direct investment	$20 million	
A-1	Exports		$20 million

"Other long-term" capital accounts are differentiated based on whether they are government (C-3) or private (C-4) transactions. These transactions have a maturity of over one year and involve either loans or securities. For example, Citibank may have loaned the government of Poland $50 million. "Other short-term" capital accounts are also differentiated based on whether they are governmental (C-5) or private (C-6). Typical short-term government transactions are short-term loans in the securities of other governments. Private transactions often include trade bill acceptances or other short-term claims arising from the financing of trade and movements of money by investors to take advantage of interest differentials among countries.

Official reserves

Official reserves are used for bringing BOP accounts into balance. There are four major types of reserves available to monetary authorities in meeting BOP deficits (D1 through D4 in Table 6A). These reserves are analogous to the cash or near-cash assets of a private firm. Given that billions of dollars in transactions are reported in BOP statements, it should come as no surprise that the amount of recorded debits is never equal to the amount of credits. This is why there is an entry in the reserve account for net errors and omissions. If a country's reporting system is weak or there are a large number of clandestine transactions, this discrepancy can be quite large.

US BOP

The official presentation of the US BOP is somewhat different from the IMF format presented in Table 6A. Because the United States plays such a dominant role in the world economy, it is important to examine the US system. Table 6B presents US international transactions for 2014.

A number of select entries in Table 6B help to highlight the US BOP. Lines 2 and 19 show that in 2014 exports of goods and services were $504.711 billion less than imports. The trade deficit has declined since 2008, when it was $695.936 billion, and 2006, when it stood at $763.267 billion. The United States continues to have trade deficit problems, but on a BOP basis this is improving.

To assess the trade situation accurately, however, we need to examine the data in more depth. This information is provided in Table 6C. The table shows that although US exports are strong in areas such as capital goods and industrial supplies and materials, the country also imports a large amount of these products. In addition, the United States is a net exporter of foods, feeds, and beverages, automotive vehicles and parts, consumer goods, and petroleum and products.

Table 6B US international transactions, 2014

Line	(Credits +; debits −)	2014 (in millions of US$)
	Current account	
1	Exports of goods and services and income receipts	3,291,353
2	Exports of goods and services	2,344,528
3	Goods, balance of payment basis	1,635,133
4	Services	709,395
12	Income receipts	819,705
14	Direct investment receipts	473,763
15	Portfolio investment income	307,627
16	Other investment income	31,135
17	Compensation of employees	6,878
18	Imports of goods and services and income payments	−3,701,981
19	Imports of goods and services	−2,849,239
20	Goods	−2,370,920
21	Services	−478,319
29	Income payments	601,801
31	Direct investment payments	178,181
32	Portfolio investment income	393,581
33	Other investment income	14,169
34	Compensation of employees	−15,871
71	Balance on goods (lines 3 and 20)	−735,787
72	Balance on services (lines 4 and 21)	231,076
74	Balance on primary income (lines 12 and 29)	217,904
75	Balance on secondary income	−123,821
76	Balance on current account (lines 1, 18, and 35 or lines 73, 74, and 75)	−410,628

Source: US International Transactions, 2014, table H.

Table 6C US merchandise trade, 2014

	2014 (millions of US$)
Exports	1,635,133
Foods, feeds, and beverages	144,176
Industrial supplies and materials	501,269
Capital goods, except automotive	457,655
Automotive vehicles, engines, and parts	159,453
Consumer goods, except automotive	198,452
Other	58,203
Imports	2,370,920
Foods, feeds, and beverages	126,644
Industrial supplies and materials	671,030
Capital goods, except automotive	453,743
Automotive vehicles, engines, and parts	328,493
Consumer goods, except automotive	559,309
Other	74,307
Balance on goods	−735,787

Source: US Bureau of Economic Analysis, *Survey of Current Business*, June 2015.

In the early 1980s US trade deficits were offset by large amounts of income generated by direct investments abroad. Later in the decade massive international borrowing offset these deficits. More recently the situation has improved somewhat, and dollar devaluation has helped to generate stronger demand for US exports, thus partially reducing the growth rate of its annual trade deficit. However, more concerted action will be needed if the United

States is to continue on this course. One way is to continue to increase US competitiveness in the international market. Another way is to get other countries to reduce their trade barriers and to make international markets more open.

When a country suffers a persistent balance of trade deficit, the nation will also suffer from a depreciating currency and will find it difficult to borrow in the international capital market. In this case there are only two choices available. One is to borrow from the IMF and be willing to accept the restrictions that the IMF puts on the country, which are designed to introduce austerity and force the country back on to the right economic track. The other approach is for the country to change its fiscal policy (tariffs and taxes), resort to exchange and trade controls, or devalue its currency. To prevent having to undertake austerity steps, the United States will have to continue working very hard to control its trade deficit.

Key terms

- balance of payments (BOP)
- current account
- capital account
- official reserves

Chapter 7

INTERNATIONAL FINANCIAL MARKETS AND INSTITUTIONS

Contents

Objectives of the chapter

This chapter considers financial markets that allow firms to find sources and uses of funds outside their home countries and to deal in currencies other than the domestic one. It also considers the risks involved in operating in these markets and the tools available to deal with those risks. The main risk has to do with dealing in foreign currencies, so **exchange risk** and the functioning of the **foreign exchange** market are key elements of the discussion. For example, when a German firm borrows from a bank in dollars, because of the low interest rate, the firm faces a problem of exchange risk. The firm has to decide what to do in case the dollar rises in value relative to the euro and makes loan repayment more expensive.

The specific objectives of this chapter are to:

1 *Review* the basic characteristics of all the financial markets that may be available to a firm in international business.

2 *Examine* the foreign exchange market, its operation, and the main participants.

3 *Explain* the fundamental economic factors that determine the exchange rates in the absence of government intervention in the foreign exchange markets.

4 *Show* how firms can operate successfully in more than one currency without facing unacceptable levels of exchange risk.

5 *Give insights* into domestic money and capital markets that exist around the world.

6 *Describe* the functioning of the euromarkets, both short term and long term.

7 *Explain* how the international monetary system functions and how it relates to both private sector firms and governments.

8 *Look at* a country's balance of payments and show what lessons can be drawn from it.

9 *Show* how firms can take advantage of the opportunities available in all of these markets.

ACTIVE LEARNING CASE

Barclays Bank international financial dealings

Barclays Bank is one of the largest banks in the world (around tenth when measured by capital assets according to Forbes, in 2015) and the second largest in the UK after HSBC. It has a worldwide spread of branches, representative offices, and other affiliates and is actively involved in businesses such as corporate finance for major firms around the world, retail banking in the UK and a few other countries in Europe, and in foreign exchange dealing in London, New York, Tokyo, and other financial capitals of the world. At the height of the financial crisis it avoided taking bailout funds from the UK government and survived 2008–09 better than most.

At the end of 2014 Barclays' business was divided among the currencies shown in Table 7.1. Growth in income and costs was constrained by foreign exchange translation movements. These are not necessarily major concerns for a multinational bank, since Barclays has lengthy experience in using these currencies, and the bank regularly deals with foreign exchange risk. Still, some banks had encountered huge crises due to foreign exchange losses. For example, National Australia Bank lost US$360 million in 2003/4 due to currency trading, and Allied Irish Banks lost more than US$770 million in 2002 from similar trading. Back in 1974 the entire world financial system was shaken by a pair of foreign exchange

losses that caused two banks to fail (Franklin National Bank in the United States and Bankhaus Herstatt in Germany) and the entire **eurocurrency** system to briefly come to a halt. (In 2008 the British government nationalized Northern Rock to prevent its failure, while banks in the United States also faced failure due to losses on the subprime mortgage market leading to the world financial crisis.)

Barclays is heavily involved in financial activities in more than 30 countries worldwide. However, at its heart Barclays is a home region bank, with 62 percent of its revenues in Europe (75 percent if we include off-balance sheet risks). A geographical analysis of revenues from external customers for continuing operations for the year ended December 31, 2014 (Table 7.1) shows that 38 percent of Barclays' revenues are in the UK, the bank's country of origin (47 percent if we include off-balance sheet numbers). Another 24 percent of the bank's business is in other European Union countries, about 29 percent in the United States and the remaining 10 percent in the remaining countries where it operates. With this exposure to risks in other countries, as Table 7.1 shows, Barclays has a large exposure in US dollars.

From another perspective, Barclays had an international financial exposure through its lending activities in various countries. Table 7.2 shows this distribution of activity.

Table 7.1 The Barclays Group's structural currency exposures as at December 31, 2014

Functional currency of operations	Foreign currency net investments £m	Borrowings which hedge the net investments £m	Derivatives which hedge the net investments £m	Structural currency exposures pre-economic hedges £m	Economic hedges £m	Remaining structural economic exposures £m
As at December 31, 2014						
US dollar	23,728	5,270	1,012	17,446	6,655	10,791
Euro	3,056	328	238	2,490	1,871	619
Rand	3,863	–	103	3,760	–	3,760
Japanese yen	364	164	208	(8)	–	(8)
Other	2,739	–	1,198	1,541	–	1,541
Total	33,750	5,762	2,759	25,229	8,526	16,703
As at December 31, 2013						
US dollar	34,220	5,555	12,558	16,107	5,812	10,295
Euro	9,336	538	5,570	3,228	2,833	395
Rand	3,835	–	114	3,721	–	3,721
Japanese yen	454	89	352	13	–	13
Other	2,850	–	1,101	1,749	–	1,749
Total	50,695	6,182	19,695	24,818	8,645	16,173

▶

Table 7.2 Analysis of loans and advances to customers as at December 31, 2014

Credit risk concentrations by geographical sector (£m)	United Kingdom £m	Europe £m	Americas £m	Africa and Middle East £m	Asia £m	Total £m
As at December 31, 2014						
The Group						
On-balance sheet:						
Cash and balances at central banks	13,770	12,224	9,365	2,161	2,175	39,695
Items in the course of collection from other banks	644	158	–	408	–	1,210
Trading portfolio assets	12,958	15,638	31,062	2,498	6,572	68,728
Financial assets designated at fair value	21,274	1,591	3,986	2,999	501	30,351
Derivative financial instruments	133,567	147,421	129,771	2,332	26,985	440,076
Loans and advances to banks	8,018	12,793	13,227	3,250	5,369	42,657
Loans and advances to customers	241,543	60,018	76,561	39,241	10,404	427,767
Reverse repurchase agreements and other similar secured lending	20,551	22,655	81,368	928	6,251	131,753
Available for sale debt securities	22,901	33,368	22,846	4,770	1,667	85,552
Other assets	837	–	232	483	128	1,680
Total on-balance sheet	476,063	305,866	368,418	59,070	60,052	1,269,469
Off-balance sheet:						
Contingent liabilities	10,222	2,542	5,517	2,757	225	21,263
Documentary credits and other short-term trade-related transactions	851	36	–	186	18	1,091
Forward starting reverse repurchase agreements	4,461	5,937	701	2	2,755	13,856
Standby facilities, credit lines, and other commitments	108,025	34,886	116,343	14,911	2,150	276,315
Total off-balance sheet	123,559	43,401	122,561	17,856	5,148	312,525
Total	599,622	349,267	490,979	76,926	65,200	1,581,994

A key concern of Barclays is how to manage these overseas and foreign currency activities, especially with respect to the risk of currency losses. As an international bank, Barclays wants to operate in major financial centers, but as a prudently managed firm, it doesn't want to take undue risk in foreign currencies or put significant amounts of assets in high-risk environments.

Website: www.barclays.com.

Source: Barclays, *Annual Report*, 2014.

1 What exchange risk does Barclays have as at December 31, 2014?

2 What should Barclays' expectation be about the value of the pound relative to the euro or the dollar?

3 How should Barclays deal with the risk involved in its foreign currency positions?

4 How can Barclays use the eurocurrency market in its international business, and will this help in dealing with the exchange rate problem?

INTRODUCTION

Exchange risk
The risk of financial loss or gain due to an unexpected change in a currency's value

International financial markets are relevant to companies, whether or not they become directly involved in international business through exports, direct investment, and the like. Purchases of imported products or services may require payment in foreign exchange, thus involving exchange risk. A company may choose to invest in a foreign business or security,

Foreign exchange
Foreign currency-denominated financial instruments, ranging from cash to bank deposits to other financial contracts payable or receivable in foreign currency

Eurocurrency
A bank deposit in any country that is denominated in a foreign currency. A yen-denominated bank deposit in Germany is a euro–yen deposit, a form of eurocurrency

and face both different interest rates and different risks from those at home. Often companies find that borrowing funds abroad is less expensive than borrowing domestically, in the United States or in any other home country. The relatively unrestricted "euromarkets" generally offer better terms to borrowers (*and* lenders) than do domestic financial markets in any country. Likewise, in today's global financial markets, investors are discovering more and more opportunities to diversify their portfolios into holdings of foreign securities. This chapter explores the various foreign and international financial markets, including the foreign exchange market, and examines ways to utilize them for domestic and international business.

FOREIGN EXCHANGE MARKETS

Currencies, like any other products, services, or claims, can be traded for one another. The foreign exchange market is simply a mechanism through which transactions can be made between one country's currency and another's. Or, more broadly, a foreign exchange market is a market for the exchange of financial instruments denominated in different currencies. The most common location for foreign exchange transactions is a commercial bank, which agrees to "make a market" for the purchase and sale of currencies other than the local one. In the United States, hundreds of banks offer foreign exchange markets in dozens of cities. However, over 40 percent of all foreign exchange business is done through the ten largest banks in New York.

Foreign exchange is not simply currency printed by a foreign country's central bank; rather, it includes such items as cash, checks (or drafts), wire transfers, telephone transfers, and even contracts to sell or buy currency in the future. Foreign exchange is really any financial instrument that carries out payment from one currency to another. The most common form of foreign exchange in transactions between companies is the draft (denominated in a foreign currency). The most common form of foreign exchange in transactions between banks is an online transfer, generally for transactions of $1 million or more. Far down the list of instruments, in terms of the value exchanged, is actual currency, which is often exchanged by tourists and other travelers.

Exchange rate
The value of one currency in terms of another; for example, US $1.2378/€1

Since no currency is necessarily fixed in value relative to others, there must be some means of determining an acceptable price, or **exchange rate**. How many British pounds (£) should one dollar buy? How many Brazilian reals should be paid to buy a dollar? Since 1973, most of the industrialized countries have allowed their currency values to fluctuate more or less freely (depending on the time and the country), so that the simple economics of supply and demand largely determines exchange rates. In graphic form, Figure 7.1 shows that the intersection of the supply curve and the demand curve for European euros (€) sets the price, or exchange rate, of euros in terms of dollars. Some of the participants in the foreign exchange market are listed below the graph; their specific activities are discussed in the following section.

The exchange rate of $1.2378 per euro is offered by one specific bank. This was the closing exchange rate quoted by Bankers Trust Company of New York for purchases of at least $1 million worth of euros on June 26, 2010. Another bank in New York may have quoted a slightly higher or slightly lower rate at the same time, and banks in San Francisco, London, or Tokyo probably quoted rates that differed even more. The rates quoted depend on each bank's interest in being involved in foreign exchange transactions and on the varying strategic positions and risks taken by the banks. Thus, the foreign exchange market among banks may be viewed as one large market or as many small markets with extensive (potential and actual) interrelations. Generally, the interbank market within any country is viewed as one market, and intercountry dealings are somewhat segmented by different rules and risks (though in the United States, the San Francisco market often

Figure 7.1 Foreign exchange market for euros in New York

offers quotations from various banks that differ noticeably from rate quotations in New York, due partly to the difference in time zones).

The differences in rate quotations may appear very small to an outsider. For example, euros may be quoted at $1.23236 at Citibank in New York and at $1.23386 at Bank of America in San Francisco. This difference seems small, but for every 1 million euros sold, the buyer of dollars in San Francisco receives an extra $1,500. Since the transactions are generally rapid, for values of $5 million to $10 million such differences may add up to a substantial gain (or cost) to the participant in the foreign exchange market.[1]

The various foreign exchange transactions just mentioned involve large commercial banks and large amounts of money. Most of the companies that do international business also utilize foreign exchange markets, but far less frequently than banks and for transactions that involve less money. Consequently, these companies' access to foreign currencies differs from that of the banks. (Specifically, banks make the market and companies pay for the use of this service.) The next section describes the various participants in the US foreign exchange market.

Foreign exchange markets in the United States

Figure 7.2 presents an overview of the foreign exchange markets operating today in the United States. This section discusses each of these markets in some detail.

The interbank market

Although the foreign exchange dealings of most managers involve a company buying from, or selling to, a bank, managers must understand the foreign exchange market among banks. This is because, as noted above, the vast majority of large-scale foreign exchange transactions are interbank, and these transactions tend to determine exchange rates, with which occasional market participants such as companies must deal.

Local and regional commercial banks may offer clients a foreign exchange service, which such banks provide on request by dealing through a larger bank, typically in a large city (such as New York, Los Angeles, or Chicago). If a local bank receives a request to buy Swiss francs (SF) for an importer in New Jersey, it will call its correspondent bank in

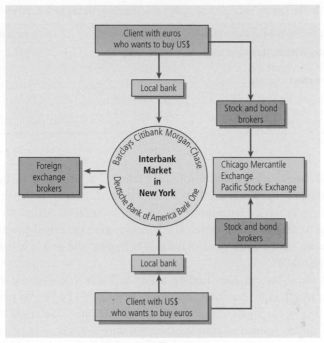

Figure 7.2 US Foreign exchange markets

Source: Adapted from K. Alec Chrystal, *St. Louis Fed Review* (March 1984), figure 1, p. 8.

New York (say, JP Morgan Chase Bank) and arrange to buy the SF for, say, $0.6753/SF. Then the local bank will add on its service charge so that the importer pays $0.6853/SF. Thus, the local bank earns $0.01 per SF, or about 1.5 percent on the transaction.

JP Morgan Chase Bank, in turn, will either take the requested Swiss francs from its own holdings of that currency or enter the interbank market to buy them. Assuming that Chase does *not* have the SF on hand, one of its **foreign exchange traders** will call several other major banks (or brokerage houses, which are discussed below) and contract to buy Swiss francs from the lowest bidder.

The interbank market generally operates with large transactions only of about $1 million to $10 million exchanged for the equivalent foreign currency. On a typical day in 2010, the more than 45 members of the main association of commercial banks in foreign exchange dealings (called the Clearing House Interbank Payments System, or CHIPS) transacted roughly $2 trillion in currency trades.[2] This had risen to over $5.2 trillion by 2015, well above the value of futures markets or stock market transactions.

The brokers' market

Another facet of large-scale foreign exchange dealing in the United States is the brokers' market. About six **foreign exchange brokers** make markets for foreign currencies in New York (as well as in London and elsewhere), creating trading in many currencies similar to that in the interbank market. In this case, the key differences are that the brokers seek to match buyers and sellers on any given transaction, without taking a position[3] themselves; they deal simultaneously with many banks (and other companies); and they offer both buy and sell positions to clients (where a bank may wish to operate on only one side of the market at any particular time). Also, the brokers deal "blind," offering rate quotations without naming the potential seller/buyer until a deal has been negotiated. Brokers play a large role in the total market, arranging about half of total interbank foreign exchange transactions.

Foreign exchange traders
Bankers who deal in foreign exchange, buying and selling foreign currencies on behalf of clients and/or for the bank itself; typically they deal in foreign currency-denominated bank deposits

Foreign exchange brokers
A company that provides specialized services to commercial banks in the interbank foreign exchange market, essentially functioning to unite interested buyers and sellers of foreign currency-denominated bank deposits; brokers intermediate about half of all wholesale foreign exchange transactions in New York and London

Table 7.3 Exchange rates in the interbank market, October 29, 2015

Foreign currency Exchange rates	UK sterling (£)	Europe euro (€)	Japan yen (¥)
Spot rate—closing (foreign currency units per US dollar)	1.5282	1.0958	0.00826
Forward rate—closing			
1 month outright	1.5150	1.0674	0.00816
3 months outright	1.4947	1.0950	0.00845
12 months outright	1.4518	0.9504	0.00742

Source: *Financial Times*, October 29, 2015.

Spot rate
The exchange rate offered on the same day as the request to buy or sell foreign currency; actual settlement (payment) may occur one or two days later

Forward rate
An exchange rate contracted today for some future date of actual currency exchange; banks offer forward rates to clients to buy or sell foreign currency in the future, guaranteeing the rate at the time of the agreement

Before moving on to other foreign exchange markets, let us consider an example in which the spot market is used by a tourist planning a trip to Japan. This person wants to visit Tokyo to see a friend during the Christmas vacation and to do some sightseeing. She is taking $1,000 with her and has already purchased the round-trip airline ticket. Since dollars cannot be used for most purchases in Japan, she needs to buy Japanese yen. How should she do it?

Looking at the currency trading listing in Table 7.3, she saw that Bankers Trust was offering to sell large quantities of yen at the rate of 120.98 yen per dollar. At the "retail" level—that is, for small transactions such as this one—she could expect to receive fewer yen per dollar. Instead of carrying the cash with her, she wanted to get traveler's checks. Upon calling the office of American Express in San Francisco, she found that yen-denominated traveler's checks are available but would cost her the exchange rate, plus a $5 service charge.

The tourist was willing to pay the extra cost to obtain the protection of traveler's checks, but one final problem arose. A friend who works in foreign exchange dealing at Wells Fargo Bank told her that the yen would probably decline in value relative to the dollar in the next few days. Since she would not leave for Tokyo for another week, she wondered whether it was worth waiting for the expected devaluation. The answer to this question is that no one knows! She could hope for a devaluation and delay purchase of the yen for a week, or ignore the potential gain or loss and buy the yen today. In such a short time period, it is probably better to ignore the few days' variability in the exchange rate—since it could be favorable or unfavorable—and just buy the yen at the most convenient time before departing for Tokyo. (One more point to confuse the matter: she could buy traveler's checks in US dollars and exchange them for yen in Japan when needed. Again, no one can be sure what the yen's value will be during her vacation time in Tokyo.)

Although this example does not offer a guaranteed way to make money from foreign exchange dealings, it does illustrate the kinds of problems that beset individuals and companies as they work with foreign currencies. Fortunately, there are some methods to help avoid the uncertainty involved in foreign exchange; they are discussed in the section below on "Protecting against exchange risk."

So far, our discussion has focused only on the *spot market*: that is, the market for immediate exchange of one currency for another. An additional, very large part of the US foreign exchange market is the set of instruments that allow contracting today for delivery of currency in the future. The main instruments of this type are forward contracts, foreign exchange futures contracts, and foreign currency options.

The forward foreign exchange market

The forward foreign exchange market at commercial banks in the United States offers banks, companies, and individuals the opportunity to contract *today* for a specific foreign exchange transaction in the *future*, at a fixed price (that is, exchange rate). Forward contracts are negotiated between the offering bank and the client as to size, maturity, and price. Referring to Table 7.3, we see that Bankers Trust was offering to sell British pounds for $1.4518/£ in 360 days on October 29, 2015 (for quantities of at least $1 million).

The rationale for forward contracts in currencies is analogous to that for futures contracts in commodities: the firm can lock in a price today to eliminate uncertainty about the value of a future receipt or a payment of foreign currency. A firm may undertake such a transaction because it has made a previous contract: for example, to pay €1 million to a supplier in three months for some needed inputs to its operations. If the firm wants to eliminate the risk that its payment in three months will change in dollar terms (that is, the €1 million may cost more dollars then), it can contract with a bank to buy €1 million three months forward, at a price established today. (From Table 7.3, we see that the price was $1.0958/€ for a contract with Bankers Trust on October 29, 2015.) Thus, firms can use forward contracts to eliminate the risk of variability in future dollar costs or revenues due to exchange rate changes. This concept, called *hedging*, and other motives for using the forward market are discussed later.

Notice that in the above example, the forward contract used for hedging is not the same thing as an insurance contract. The forward contract does fix a minimum "loss" for the firm by setting the guaranteed price of exchange in the future. Even if the dollar devalues to $0.95 per € in three months, the forward contract holder is still able to buy €1 million at a better rate than this to limit his/her losses. However, if the euro devalues over the next three months to, say, $1/€, the forward contract holder will have an opportunity cost of the difference between the forward rate and the (eventual) future spot rate. Thus, the forward contract insures against potential losses *and* against potential gains in foreign currency value.

Forward markets exist in any currencies and for any maturities that banks are willing to offer. Most of the forward contracts used in the United States involve exchanges of US dollars for euros, Japanese yen, British pounds, Swiss francs, and Canadian dollars. Maturities tend to be six months or less, though single-year and multiyear forward contracts are sometimes available.

The futures market in currencies

A very similar type of instrument is available on several securities exchanges in the United States and abroad. The foreign exchange futures contract is an agreement to buy or sell a fixed amount of foreign currency for delivery at a fixed future date at a fixed dollar price. The main difference between futures and forward contracts in the United States is that futures contracts have fixed sizes (about $50,000 to $100,000, depending on the currency) and pre-established maturity dates. (All are 3-, 6-, 9-, or 12-month contracts maturing on the third Wednesday of March, June, September, or December.) Also, futures contracts are available for only a few currencies (Canadian dollars, euros, Swiss francs, British pounds, Japanese yen, Mexican pesos, Australian dollars, and a few others), and only if a buyer and a seller can be found at the time.

The futures market at the Chicago Mercantile Exchange is currently very thin (that is, few contracts are traded) except for the three-month contracts denominated in Canadian dollars, euros, Swiss francs, British pounds, and Japanese yen.

Futures contracts are more widely accessible to firms and individuals than forward contracts because of their smaller value and the margin requirements that enable brokers to obtain collateral from market participants. (However, the currently thin nature of this market does not allow participants the wide range of currencies and maturities that are available for large-scale transactions in the forward market.) The standard contracts available at the Chicago Mercantile Exchange (CME) are described in Table 7.4. Trading hours have been extended via the GLOBEX system, which permits worldwide access to

Table 7.4 Currency futures contract specifications at the Chicago Mercantile Exchange

	British pound (£)	Eurozone euro (€)	Japanese yen (¥)
Trading unit	£62,500	€125,000	¥12,500,000
Quotations	US$ per £	US$ per €	US$ per ¥
Minimum price fluctuation	0.0001	0.0001	0.000001
Value of 1 point	$6.25	$12.50	$12.50
Months traded	Six months in the March quarterly cycle (Mar., June, Sep., Dec.) *GLOBEX (ETH): Sundays: 5:00 p.m.–4:00 p.m. Central Time (CT) next day*		
Trading hours	*Monday–Friday: 5:00 p.m.–4:00 p.m.* CT the next day, except on Friday—closes at 4:00 p.m. and reopens Sunday at 5:00 p.m. CT CME ClearPort: Sunday–Friday 6:00 p.m.–5:15 p.m. (5:00 p.m.–4:15 p.m. Chicago Time/CT) with a 45-minute break each day beginning at 5:15 p.m. (4:15 p.m. CT) *OPEN OUTCRY (RTH): 7:20 a.m.–2:00 p.m.*		
Last day hours	9:16 a.m. Central Time (CT) on the second business day immediately preceding the third Wednesday of the contract month (usually Monday)		

Source: Adapted from Chicago Mercantile Exchange, June 26, 2010.

E-resources: http://www.cmegroup.com/trading/fx/

CME contracts. In 2015, GLOBEX trading was available pretty much around the clock, around the world.

Foreign currency *options* are an additional instrument of the foreign exchange market in the United States; they offer participants the *right* to buy or sell foreign currency in the future rather than the obligation to do so. Foreign currency options are similar to foreign currency futures in the Unites States in that the contracts are for fixed quantities of currency to be exchanged at a fixed price in the future. The key difference is that the option may be *exercised*—that is, presented for currency exchange—at *any* time between its issuance and the maturity date, or not at all.[4]

Foreign exchange arbitrage involves simultaneous contracting in two or more foreign exchange markets to buy and sell foreign currency, profiting from exchange rate differences *without* incurring exchange rate risk. Foreign exchange arbitrage may be two-way, three-way, or intertemporal and is generally undertaken by large commercial banks that can exchange large quantities of money to exploit small rate differentials.

The simplest form of exchange arbitrage is two-way arbitrage, between any two currencies and between two places. Assume quotations for Swiss francs in the spot market on June 26, 2010, were:

At Bankers Trust in New York:	$0.91038/SF
At Bank of America in San Francisco:	$0.91158/SF
At Lloyds Bank in London:	$0.91398/SF

Arbitrageur
A person or firm that deals in foreign exchange, buying or selling foreign currency with simultaneous contracting to exchange back to the original currency; arbitrageurs thus do not undertake exchange risk

An **arbitrageur** can buy SF in New York and simultaneously sell them in London, making a profit of $0.0036/SF, or 0.37 percent per transaction. While the percentage gain is small, it translates to $3,600 for every SF1 million traded, and it involves no exchange risk. By repeatedly arbitraging this price (exchange rate) differential, the arbitrageur will make a profit until the exchange rate differential drops below the transactions cost (that is, the telephone bill, plus the arbitrageur's salary, plus other relevant costs).

The same two-way arbitrage may also occur in the forward market or between forward and futures markets. From the quotations here, we see that profitable arbitrage opportunities exist between the New York forward market and the Chicago futures market, as well as between the New York and San Francisco forward markets:

At Bankers Trust in New York: ¥109.00/$ for delivery in 90 days.

At Bank of America in San Francisco: ¥109.90/$ for delivery in 90 days.

At the Chicago Mercantile Exchange: ¥107.38/$ for delivery on June 26, 2010.

An arbitrageur can buy yen in New York and sell them in San Francisco, both for exchange in 90 days, and earn ¥0.9/$, or 0.77 percent per transaction. Similarly, an arbitrageur can buy yen in Chicago and sell them in San Francisco, to make ¥1.62/$, or 1.4 percent per transaction. The difficulties with the latter transaction are that contracts may not be available for the desired amount or maturity date and transaction costs are higher for the inter-market exchanges. Nonetheless, both transactions may be feasible and profitable, even after costs are considered.[5]

✔ Active learning check

Review your answer to Active Learning Case question 1 and make any changes you like. Then compare your answer to the one below.

1 What exchange risk does Barclays have as at December 31, 2014?

Barclays has exchange risk on the various assets and liabilities that were on its books at year-end 2014. These include exposures of £6,655 million in US dollars and £1,871 million in euros, among others. (It is interesting to note that in 2009, when we looked at this for the last edition of this textbook, these figures were £6,056 million in US dollars and £2,902 million in euros: i.e., not very different). From Tables 7.1 and 7.2, it appears that these exposures may be from lending to corporations in the European Union and the United States (though this is not certain, since some other activities are missing from the table). These are net asset exposures, or long positions, since Barclays will receive future cash flows in these currencies, and their values may change in terms of British pounds.

DETERMINATION OF THE EXCHANGE RATE

Exchange rates are determined by the activities of the various actors described earlier. If one could calculate the supply and demand curves for each exchange market participant and anticipate government constraints on the exchange market, exchange rate determination would be fairly simple. The composite supply and demand for foreign exchange would be as depicted in Figure 7.1.

Lacking this information, the analyst can still rely on two fundamental economic relationships that underlie exchange rate determination. Note that this section considers only economic factors; government restrictions on the exchange market are ignored.

The two fundamental economic relationships are **purchasing power parity** and the **international Fisher effect**. The former posits that shifts in exchange rates will occur to offset different rates of inflation in pairs of countries, and the latter proposes that exchange rates will shift to offset interest rate differentials between countries.

Purchasing power parity
The theory of exchange rate determination that states that differences in prices of the same goods between countries will be eliminated by exchange rate changes

International Fisher effect
The theory of exchange rate determination that states that differences in nominal interest rates on similar-risk deposits will be eliminated by exchange rate changes

Purchasing power parity

The purchasing power parity (PPP) theory[6] is based on the law of one price and explains the long-run exchange rates. If two countries produce an identical product and transportation costs are extremely low, the price of the product should be the same in two countries. Under the law of one price, the price of the product is the same not only in two countries but also around the world. If a standard ton of polyurethane plastic costs $200 in the United States and €190 in Germany, PPP requires an exchange rate of $1.05/€. The same reasoning could be used for all products whose production processes are equivalent in two countries and that are traded between these countries. The exchange rate that comes closest to simultaneously satisfying all of these equilibrium conditions is the PPP rate—a rate that equates the internal purchasing power of the two currencies in both countries.

Assuming we begin from that exchange rate, what will happen if Germany's inflation is 5 percent and the US inflation is 10 percent in the following year? PPP requires that the exchange rate adjust to eliminate this differential. Specifically, it requires that:

$$\frac{1 + \text{Infl}_{\text{US}}}{1 + \text{Infl}_{\text{Ger}}} = \frac{\text{XR}_{t+1}}{\text{XR}_t}$$

where:

Infl = inflation rate
t = time period

This means that inflation in the United States relative to inflation in Germany should be the same as the future exchange rate compared to the spot exchange rate. The relationship can also be written in a form similar to the interest parity equation by rearranging terms:

$$(1 + \text{Infl}_{\text{US}}) = (1 + \text{Infl}_{\text{Ger}}) \frac{\text{XR}_{t+1}}{\text{XR}_t}$$

Purchasing power in each currency will be retained if:

$$\text{XR}_{t+1} = \frac{1.10}{1.05} \ (\$1.05/€) = \$1.10/€, \text{ or } €0.909/\$$$

International Fisher effect

The international Fisher effect (IFE) translates Irving Fisher's reasoning about domestic interest rates to the transnational level. Fisher showed that inflation-adjusted (that is, "real") interest rates tend to stay the same over time; as inflation rises or falls, so do **nominal** (unadjusted) **interest rates**, such that **real interest rates** remain unchanged. At the transnational level, nominal national interest rates are expected to differ only by the expected change in the national currency's price (that is, the exchange rate). The international Fisher effect thus concludes that interest differentials between national markets will be eliminated by adjustments in the exchange rate. In terms similar to PPP, we see that:

Nominal interest rate
The actual rate of interest offered by a bank, typically given as an annual percentage rate

Real interest rate
The nominal interest rate adjusted for price changes. Domestically, this means adjusting for inflation; internationally, this means adjusting for exchange rate (currency price) changes

$$\frac{1 + i_{\text{US}}}{1 + i_{\text{foreign}}} = \frac{\text{XR}_{t+1}}{\text{XR}_t} , \text{ or } (1 + i_{\text{US}}) = (1 + i_{\text{foreign}}) \frac{\text{XR}_{t+1}}{\text{XR}_t}$$

where i = the interest rate, usually on a eurocurrency deposit denominated in the given country's currency.

If the eurodollar deposit rate is 3 percent/year and the euro–euro rate is 6 percent/year, the euro will be expected to devalue in the coming year by:

$$\frac{1.06}{1.03} = 1.029, \text{ or } 2.9 \text{ percent}$$

Notice that the international Fisher effect *will* operate in a free market, because investors will receive a higher return in euros otherwise. As more and more investors put their money in euros, the spot price of the euro will rise. Similarly, as US investors return their euro earnings to dollars at the end of the period (year), this increased demand for dollars will cause the euro to devalue (in the future). Thus, dollar and euro earnings will tend to be equalized.

Combined equilibrium relationships

The future exchange rate, XR_{t+1}, will be partially determined by both of the above factors (PPP and IFE), which can be viewed in a general equilibrium context as shown in Figure 7.3. This figure also demonstrates the interest parity relationship, which provides another link between current and future currency values. Remember that these relationships are *equilibrium* economic conditions, which hold only approximately since substantial uncertainty exists about future conditions. Also, if a government intervenes to prohibit the market from determining exchange rates, the relationships may diverge substantially from the equilibrium conditions. Figure 7.3 shows the main economic influences that, along with government policies and other factors, combine to determine exchange rates. Note that the expected exchange rate is in the top box, and the determinants of that rate (interest difference and inflation difference) are presented as fractions, so that they show the precise relationship between the spot exchange rate, XR_T, and the expected future rate, $E[XR_T]$.

A final caveat is in order. Despite the strong relationships among interest differentials, inflation differentials, and exchange rates, other important *economic* influences operate in international finance. Pure speculation can cause shifts in exchange rates, despite the fundamental economic conditions that have been described above. A country's balance of payments position may affect the exchange rate, even though that position also affects interest and inflation rates as well. Since the abandonment of the Bretton Woods system of

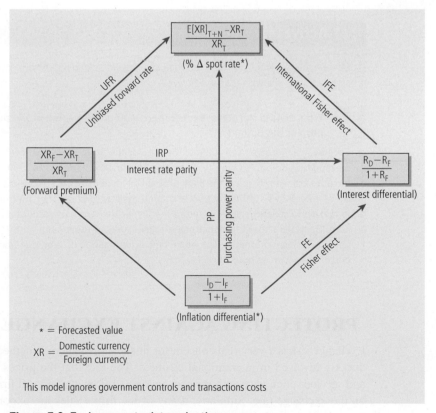

Figure 7.3 Exchange rate determination

fixed exchange rates, exchange rate determination has been extremely uncertain—perhaps similar to the determination of future values of stock exchange indexes.

Other factors determining exchange rates

PPP and IFEs explain overall exchange rate well, but other factors also determine exchange rates. In general, factors affecting the demand and supply of domestic products over foreign products determine exchange rates because these factors affect the demand and supply of local and foreign currencies in exchange rate markets. First, changes in demand affect the exchange rate. For example, the changes in trade barriers, such as tariffs and quotas, can affect the exchange rate. If the United States raises the tariff rates over Chinese products due to anti-dumping or countervailing regulation, the demand for domestic products increases over Chinese products and the US dollar tends to appreciate. Second, the changes in supply affect the exchange rate. For example, China becomes more productive than before. Chinese auto manufacturers recently developed their own models and produced them with great productivity, and the Chinese auto manufacturers can lower the price over foreign auto manufacturers. This affects the demand for Chinese automobiles, and the Chinese currency tends to appreciate. Third, national governments reserve foreign currencies and actively control foreign exchange rates to lower the price of exporting goods, to stabilize exchange rate volatility, and to protect the national economy from a currency crisis. According to the Central Intelligence Agency (CIA), China and Japan are the no. 1 and no. 2 countries in terms of reserves of foreign exchange and gold. China's combined value of reserves for foreign exchanges and gold amounts to $3.980 trillion (December 31, 2014 est.). Japan's combined value of reserves for foreign exchange and gold amount to $1.267 trillion (December 31, 2013 est.).

✔ Active learning check

Review your answer to Active Learning Case question 2 and make any changes you like. Then compare your answer to the one below.

2 What should Barclays' expectation be about the value of the pound relative to the euro or the dollar?

Barclays can forecast the value of the euro or the dollar based on PPP, the IFE, or a chartist method, in addition to simply using the forward exchange rate. Since Barclays' business includes currency trading, the bank probably should use one or more methods for the minute-by-minute activity in the foreign exchange market, and another method or methods for its longer-term concerns such as future maturities of loans and accounting reporting periods. In sum, Barclays should forecast using market-based tools such as IFE and PPP, as well as using additional methods such as technical forecasting or leading indicators for short periods of time such as hours or a few days.

PROTECTING AGAINST EXCHANGE RISK

Exchange risk is a very real concern for financial managers, whether or not their firms are directly involved in international business. The fact that the prices of imported products and services often vary with the exchange rate means that a local firm's costs may depend on the exchange rate. Similarly, if any of the firm's sales are exported, its earnings may vary as foreign sales change due to exchange rate changes. Even a purely domestic firm faces these problems, since suppliers and competitors that *are* doing international business will adjust to exchange rate changes, and this will affect the domestic firm.

From this perspective, exchange risk is *not* the risk that a local currency will decrease in value (devalue) relative to the home currency. *Exchange risk is the possibility that a firm will be unable to adjust its prices and costs to exactly offset exchange rate changes.* Thus, a US importer which faces 10 percent higher costs because of a dollar devaluation from €0.80/$ to €0.72/$ still has no exchange risk as long as the importer can raise its own prices by 10 percent without lowering total sales. (This result is the microeconomic version of PPP.) The problem may be viewed as one of "passing through" cost increases to the firm's customers via higher sales prices.

Similarly, the appropriate measure of exchange risk for financial instruments is the firm's possible loss or gain in purchasing power from exchange rate-adjusted interest rates. Investing in a US dollar account that pays 5 percent per year is better than investing in a Swiss franc account that pays 10 percent per year if, during the year, the franc devalues by 6 percent.

Alternatives to minimize exchange risk

Exchange risk exists whenever the firm's prices and costs cannot be exactly adjusted to offset changes in the exchange rate. Let us now consider a group of alternatives that will allow a firm to minimize (or at least reduce) its exchange risk. These alternatives fall into four categories:

1 Risk avoidance
2 Risk adaptation
3 Risk transfer
4 Diversification

INTERNATIONAL BUSINESS STRATEGY IN ACTION

China 2015: the start of the next global economic meltdown?

In 2015 much of the media attention was focused on Greece's financial meltdown. However, a crisis which may have global lasting impressions was actually occurring in China. Economists have consecutively reported the phenomena as "China's 1929", referring to the year of the largest stock market crash in history which resulted in the Great Depression era.

In late August 2015, the Chinese stock market witnessed a 30 percent decrease in value—a figure similar to the UK's entire economic output during 2014. This significant decrease had immediate consequences as it not only dragged down the Asian stock exchange but also the value of commodities too. Even though the Chinese government introduced a significant number of stimulus interventions, it

seemed as though investors were not willing to invest in Chinese stocks. Furthermore, over 940 organizations suspended trading on China's two main indices during this period. It has been reported that even China's media, who normally acclaim the Chinese economy, were labeling the day this occurred as "Black Monday."

Prior to the Chinese stock market crash in August 2015, observing Figures 7.4 and 7.5, we can see an inverse relationship between the Shanghai Composite Index and Japan's TOPIX Index. Before the events of China's "Black Monday," the Shanghai Composite Index had generally been decreasing and Japan's TOPIX Index had generally been increasing. However, during the stock market crash both indexes fell, as the Shanghai Stock Exchange decreased by 8.5 percent to a

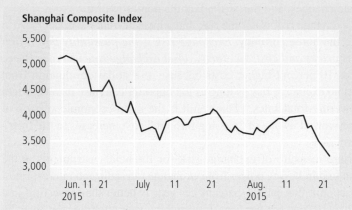

Figure 7.4 Change in the Shanghai Composite Index, June–August 2015

Source: Heather Timmons and Josh Horwitz, "Charts: this may be the start of the world's next financial crisis," *Quartz,* August 24, 2015.

Figure 7.5 Change in Japan's TOPIX Index, September 2014–July 2015

Source: Timmons and Horwitz.

Figure 7.6 Change in Hong Kong's Hang Seng Index, September 2014–July 2015

Source: Timmons and Horwitz.

value of 3,210 and Japan's TOPIX Index fell by 5.05 percent to a figure of 1,480. Furthermore, Figures 7.6 and 7.7 illustrate the change in Hong Kong's Hang Seng Index and Taiwan's TAIEX Index respectively. In accordance with China's stock market crash, Hong Kong's Hang Seng Index and Taiwan's TAIEX Index fell by 5.05 percent and 4.8 percent respectively. Furthermore, the Jakarta Stock Exchange Composite Index and Mumbai's Sensex Index also dropped by 4.04 percent and 4.55 percent respectively.

Even though Brent oil and copper prices were observed to have been generally declining in 2015, concerns regarding the future of China resulted in steeper falling demand for both commodities as the price of Brent oil fell to $45 and the average price of copper fell by 2 percent. It is important to note that after the crash the price of both commodities in 2015 were at a six-year low (Figures 7.8 and 7.9). The Chinese government pursued various strategies in an attempt to shore up the nation's $6 trillion stock market; however, declines in economic data clearly show these attempts as failing.

The future?

China is currently the world's second largest economy and any change there has the ability to significantly impact the global market. As a consequence of fears arising on the Chinese economy, it has been reported that London's FTSE 100 decreased by £70 billion in one day. The United States is particularly worried about the Chinese economy as over 30 percent of jobs which were created after the Great Recession era are export dependent. The total share of economic growth from emerging nations has significantly increased, from 20 percent of the global GDP during the 1990s to approximately 40 percent in 2015, and China alone has accounted for approximately a third of this global growth. With this in mind, there is no doubt that any fluctuations in China's economy will have global repercussions, but analysts have been debating if the significant deterioration within the Chinese economy will inevitably drag the US economy down too.

During the 1990s Asian financial crisis, many economists had predicted that there would be severe effects for the developed nations, particularly the United States. However, taking a glance at the US economy during the 1990s, it may be argued that these were some of the

Figure 7.7 Change in Taiwan's TAIEX Index, March–August 2015

Source: Timmons and Horwitz.

Figure 7.8 Change in the Brent oil price, August 2014–August 2015

Source: Timmons and Horwitz.

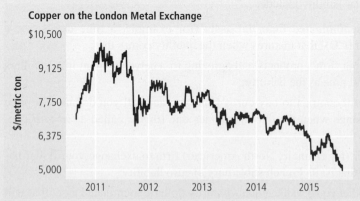

Figure 7.9 Change in the copper price, 2011–15

Source: Timmons and Horwitz.

best years the American economy has witnessed. There are multiple reasons why the Asian financial crisis did not spread among developing nations; however, a significant factor was the fact that the Asian financial crisis was significantly related to the flight of capital from emerging markets, as they had mismanaged their currencies. Developing nations experienced difficult times during the Great Recession which started in the United States. However, as developing economies relied heavily on exporting goods to developed nations, the Asian financial crisis ultimately resulted in the return of investment capital to developed nations, which in turn boosted stock markets, lowered interest rates, and caused growth to accelerate.

It is difficult to compare 1998 with the present, as Thailand and South Korea were clearly not such dominant forces in the global economy as China is now. Even though a deceleration in China's growth may have global repercussions, there are reasons to believe that this may not impact the United States seriously. For instance, exports only account for 15 percent of the nation's GDP and even if the United States were to experience a decline in trade by 10 percent, it has been reported that this would only reduce US growth by 0.2 percent.

The lessons?

It has been reported that the 2015 crash in China is similar to the US recession in 1929, as China today and the US in 1929 represent similar stages of economic development. For instance, the current rapid emigration of Chinese workers to industrial cities is similar to emigration trends of workers seeking jobs in steel and automotive manufacturing regions in the 1929 United States. With a world record growth in development, China has managed to position itself as a nation with vast economic power. Many lessons have been learned since 1929, such as that the "real" damage in a crash may not be the crash itself but the collapse of the banking sector. However, although stock markets may give advance warning of a credit crisis, many analysts are skeptical that China actually has a firm grasp on its banking sector. There ▶

is no doubt that a crash in the Chinese economy will have some global repercussions, but determining whether or not they will lead to a global economic meltdown depends on the response of China's policy-makers.

Sources: Jeremy Warner, "The real worrying financial crisis is happening in China not Greece," *Telegraph*, July 9, 2015; Julia Kollewe and Angela Monaghan, "Analysts fear China financial crisis as deflation looms," *Guardian*, January 9,

2015; Heather Timmons and Josh Horwitz, "Charts: this may be the start of the world's next financial crisis," *Quartz*, August 24, 2015; *Bloomberg News*, "Could China's yuan devaluation spark a new financial crisis?," August 23, 2015; Chris Matthews, "Will the crisis in China sink the US economy?," *Fortune*, September 2, 2015; Julia Kollewe and Angela Monaghan, "Analysts fear China financial crisis as deflation looms," *Guardian*, January 9, 2015; Lana Clements, "The five charts that show exactly why China's economic crisis is terrifying," *Express*, September 20, 2015; Lana Clements, "China crisis: Canada and Australia economies bitten by Beijing's financial meltdown," *Express*, September 2, 2015.

Risk avoidance

Exchange risk avoidance

An exchange risk management technique through which the firm tries to avoid operating in more than one currency

Exchange risk avoidance is the strategy of trying to avoid foreign currency transactions. A purely domestic firm can try to make all of its purchases from local suppliers of locally produced goods and make all of its sales to local buyers in competition only with other domestic firms. Obviously, this strategy is impractical, if only because all firms are affected by goods priced in foreign currency—automobiles, chemicals, steel, and so on. Also, there are very few industries that do not use imported materials, export some of their output, or compete with imported products.

Risk adaptation

Exchange risk adaptation

An exchange risk management technique through which a company adjusts its business activities to try to balance foreign currency assets and liabilities, and inflows and outflows

Exchange risk adaptation offers a more realistic alternative for protecting the firm against exchange risk. This strategy includes all methods of "hedging" against exchange rate changes. In the extreme, exchange risk calls for protecting all liabilities denominated in foreign currency with equal-value, equal-maturity assets denominated in that foreign currency. An illustration can best clarify this point.

Assume a French firm has contracted to buy $100,000 of machinery from a foreign supplier for use in its manufacturing operations. The purchase is payable in six months in US dollars. To eliminate foreign exchange risk completely, the firm may do two things. First, it may raise its own prices to customers once the six months pass to equate euro devaluation to price increase (note that this does *not* involve a foreign currency hedge). If this option is not available which is often the case, the firm may look to its other option: obtain some equal-value *dollar asset* maturing in 180 days. This may be as simple as depositing funds in a dollar-denominated bank account for six months or as arcane as arranging a swap of the dollar liability for some other firm's euro liability. Fairly standard methods of hedging an exposed dollar liability include:

- obtaining a dollar-denominated financial asset (for example, a time deposit or a Certificate of Deposit (CD)) that matures when the liability comes due;

- finding a buyer for your firm's products and agreeing to receive payment in US dollars for the same value and time as the liability;

- finding a bank that will contract to buy euros from you and sell you dollars at a price fixed today for exchange when the liability comes due (this is called a *forward contract*);

- agreeing with another (for example, North American) firm to exchange your dollar liability for that firm's (that is, its French subsidiary's) euro liability;

- contracting for any other equal-value, equal-maturity dollar-denominated asset that will offset the exposed liability.

The firm's goal in choosing among these methods is to minimize the cost of protection against exchange rate risk.

Risk transfer

Exchange risk transfer
An exchange risk management technique through which the firm contracts with a third party to pass exchange risk on to that party, via such instruments as forward contracts, futures, and options

The third strategy for reducing exchange risk is **exchange risk transfer**. This strategy involves the use of an insurance contract or guarantee that transfers the exchange risk to the insurer or guarantor. In many countries, the central bank offers exchange risk guarantees to importers and exporters of some products according to the bank's policies. Technically, though perhaps not realistically, any firm or government agency could issue a guarantee covering exchange rate changes to a local importer, at a price that would presumably reflect the risk.

Diversification

Currency diversification
An exchange risk management technique through which the firm places activities or assets and liabilities into multiple currencies, thus reducing the impact of exchange rate change for any one of them

The final strategy for reducing exchange risk is **currency diversification**. Here a firm can reduce the risk of unexpected local currency devaluations by spreading its assets and liabilities across several currencies (for example, euros, Swiss francs, and pounds in addition to US dollars). This strategy simply means, "Don't put all of your eggs in one basket." Domestically, a firm should deal with several suppliers and a variety of customers to reduce risk through diversification. Internationally, a firm should hold assets (and liabilities) in several currencies to reduce the impact of unexpected exchange rate changes.

The strategy that is probably most useful to the majority of firms is risk adaptation, or hedging. A key point of this section is to recognize that other alternatives may be used in many instances when hedging would be more expensive or otherwise less desirable. Nonetheless, the central problem in exchange risk management is hedging, and corporate treasurers should always be on the lookout for new instruments and techniques.

✔ Active learning check

Review your answer to Active Learning Case question 3 and make any changes you like. Then compare your answer to the one below.

③ How should Barclays deal with the risk involved in its foreign currency positions?

As an international bank, Barclays is constantly becoming involved in foreign exchange transactions. The bank needs to have a policy for its traders and its other bankers as to how much exchange risk the bank is willing to tolerate before looking for protection. The bank presumably knows more than most people about what to expect in the foreign exchange market, and it is very likely that Barclays will choose to run exchange risk without hedging because of this knowledge. Still, the bank must limit its exposure, and the usual hedging techniques for banks are forward contracts and matching loans with deposits in the same currency.

FOREIGN MONEY AND CAPITAL MARKETS

In each country an MNE enters, it will be able to obtain some degree of access to local financial markets. The MNE will generally utilize such markets to perform necessary local financial transactions and often to hedge its local asset exposure through local borrowing (or its local liability exposure through local deposits or investments). But the MNE can also utilize local financial markets to obtain additional funding (or place additional funds) for its non-local activities. A Mexican firm, for example, may choose to borrow funds through its Houston affiliate to finance its local needs in Texas *and* finance some of its needs in Mexico.

Usually national financial markets are not fully accessible to foreign firms; they are largely reserved for domestic borrowers and lenders. In these cases, use of local financial markets must be supplemented by use of the financial markets in the country of the parent company or elsewhere. Typically, such problems arise in countries that impose exchange controls, which limit the MNE's ability to put needed funds in the affiliate.

MNEs and national money markets

The advantages MNEs obtain from entering national money markets as *borrowers* of funds stem from the portfolio effect of holding liabilities in more than one (fluctuating) currency and from the local risk hedging that occurs as the MNE moves to balance local assets, such as plant and equipment, with local liabilities, such as local-currency borrowing. Additional benefits may occur if the local government subsidizes such loans through interest rate reduction, through tax breaks, or otherwise; a policy of this kind may be offered to attract the MNE's investment. This may lower the whole MNE's cost of capital if the subsidy does not disappear and if the interest rate remains below the comparable home-currency rate during the borrowing period.

The advantages MNEs obtain from entering national money markets as *lenders* of funds stem from the portfolio effect of holding financial instruments in more than one currency. There may also be a gain from balancing local-currency assets and liabilities if an excess of local liabilities was held previously. In addition, local financial investments may be a necessary strategy when exchange controls or profit remittance limits exist; such investments offer the firm an outlet for retained earnings that yield interest. Sometimes an exchange control policy may make the local-currency interest rates higher than those available in other currencies (after adjusting for expected exchange rate changes). In these cases, higher-than-normal profits can be earned by investing funds in local instruments, although exchange controls may limit conversion of the profits into the home-country currency, or a government-imposed exchange rate change may wipe out the advantage.

MNEs and national capital markets

The advantages MNEs obtain from entering national capital markets as *borrowers* are similar to those obtained from entering national money markets. However, the opportunities are generally much more limited. Very few countries have substantially developed stock markets, and those that do usually restrict the issuance of shares by foreigners. A few exceptions exist, such as the United States, the UK, Germany, and France, but even they serve only the largest and most creditworthy MNEs. National bond markets, when they exist, are also very restrictive. Thus far, virtually all of the **foreign bond** issues have taken place in New York (called "Yankee bonds"), London, Switzerland, Germany, and Japan (called "Samurai bonds").

Foreign bond
A bond issued by a foreign company in another country's financial market

Eurobond
A bond denominated in foreign currency issued in any country's financial market; most eurobonds are issued in London or in Luxembourg (for tax reasons)

The **eurobond** market, which functions mostly outside the United States, is dominated by dollar issues, which constitute about 40 percent of that total. In all, dollar-denominated issues account for about 36 percent of the two types of international bonds.

The advantages MNEs obtain from entering national capital markets as *lenders* come mainly from diversification and from higher returns that may be protected by exchange controls, just as in the short-term market. Since the national capital markets are generally small, opportunities to use them are quite limited for foreign as well as domestic investors. Of course, since the main currencies of interest to MNEs and other international investors *are* those of the few large industrial countries, opportunities in those national capital markets do exist.

REGIONAL MONEY AND CAPITAL MARKETS

Until recently, the scope of financial markets and instruments was predominantly domestic or fully international, but not regional. In the past two decades, however, the European Union has designed both a regional monetary system (the **European Monetary Union**, or EMU) and a regional currency unit (the euro) for intergovernmental financial transactions in the European Union.

European Monetary Union (EMU)
The agreement among, initially, 11 of the European Union countries to eliminate their currencies and create the euro; European Union countries do not necessarily have to join the EMU

Eurodollar
A dollar-denominated bank deposit outside the United States

The eurocurrency market

A **eurodollar** is a dollar-denominated bank deposit located outside the United States. This simple statement defines the basic instrument called the eurodollar. (Eurodollars are *not* dollars in the pockets of people who live in Europe! They are deposit liabilities of banks.) The widely discussed eurocurrency market is simply a set of bank deposits located outside the countries whose currencies are used in the deposits. Since over half of the deposits are denominated in US dollars, it is reasonably accurate to call this the eurodollar market. Notice that the eurodollar market is not limited to Europe; very large eurodollar markets exist in Tokyo, Hong Kong, Bahrain, Panama, and other cities throughout the world. For this reason, the eurodollar market is sometimes called the *international money market*.

What is the significance of the international money market? Since the eurocurrency market rivals domestic financial markets as a funding source for corporate borrowing, it plays a key role in the capital investment decisions of many firms. In addition, since this market also rivals domestic financial markets as a deposit alternative, it absorbs large amounts of savings from lenders (that is, depositors) in many countries. In fact, the eurocurrency market complements the domestic financial markets, giving greater access to borrowing and lending to financial market participants in each country where it is permitted to function. Overall, the eurocurrency market is now the world's single most important market for international financial intermediation.

This market is completely a creation of the regulatory structures placed by national governments on banking or, more precisely, on financial intermediation. If national governments allowed banks to function without reserve requirements, interest rate restrictions, capital controls, and taxes, the eurocurrency market would involve only the transnational deposits and loans made in each country's banking system. Instead, national governments heavily regulate national financial markets in efforts to achieve various monetary policy goals. Thus, the eurocurrency market provides a very important outlet for funds flows that circumvent many of the limitations placed on domestic financial markets. Many national governments have found the impact of the eurocurrency market on their firms and banks to be favorable, so they have allowed this market to operate.[7]

Since the eurocurrency market is a creation of the regulatory structure, it may be helpful to think about the key underpinnings of the system that allow eurodollars. Essentially three conditions must be met for a eurocurrency market to exist. First, some national government must allow foreign currency deposits to be made so that, for example, depositors in London can obtain dollar-denominated time deposits there. Second, the country whose currency is being used—in this example, the United States—must allow foreign entities to own and exchange deposits in that currency. Third, there must be some reason, such as low cost or ease of use, that prompts people to use this market rather than other financial markets, such as the domestic ones. The eurocurrency market has met these conditions for the past three decades, and its phenomenal growth testifies that the demand for such a market has been very large.

A wide range of countries allow foreign currency deposits to be held in their banking systems. Many of them impose restrictions (interest rate limits, capital controls, and so on) on these as well as on local-currency deposits, so that a free market does not exist. Other countries, including most of the developed countries and many of the newly industrializing countries, allow foreign currency deposits that are not subject to the regulations placed on domestic deposits. In such countries, participants find more favorable interest rates, greater availability of funds, and greater ease of moving funds internationally. These countries tend to be the euromarket centers.

Only a few currencies have become popular as eurocurrencies. Generally, these are the ones used widely in international trade—the US dollar, the euro, the British pound, and the Japanese yen. The governments of all the nations whose currencies are being used have consented (or, more accurately, have not objected) to allowing foreign banks, companies, and individuals to hold and use deposits denominated in those currencies. This may appear to be a trivial point, but any limitation on non-residents' use of dollar (or other eurocurrency) deposits would quickly eliminate that currency from the euromarket. The US government's temporary freeze on Iranian assets held in US banks in 1979 caused a tremendous crisis in the eurodollar market, because other participants saw the possibility of losing use of their eurodollars at the whim of the US government. The potential problem will continue to exist, but on the whole participants in the euromarket expect that full freedom to use the (dollar-denominated) deposits will continue indefinitely.

The third condition fundamental to the success of the euromarket is that it must possess advantages that will attract participants to the market. Those advantages include the ability to carry out dollar-denominated transactions outside the United States and the availability of favorable interest rates relative to rates in the domestic market. The first advantage clearly exists, because eurodollar account owners can sell their accounts to pay for other transactions, with no need to deal directly in the United States. The second advantage also exists, primarily because lack of regulation of the euromarket allows banks to reduce their costs and pass on the savings to clients in the form of lower loan rates and higher deposit rates. (The difference in lending rates to prime borrowers essentially disappeared during the 1980s.)

Eurocurrency interest rates

London interbank offered rate (LIBOR)
The interest rate on large-scale foreign currency-denominated deposits offered from one bank to another in London

The base interest rate paid on deposits among banks in the eurocurrency market is called **LIBOR**. (Outside London, which is the center of the entire euromarket, the base rate on deposits is generally slightly higher.) LIBOR is determined by the supply and demand for funds in the euromarket for each currency. Because participating banks could default (and, infrequently, do default) on their obligations, the rate paid for eurodollar deposits is always somewhat above the domestic Treasury bill rate. Also, because domestic banks must comply with Federal Reserve requirements, they offer slightly lower deposit rates than unregulated eurobanks. The history of the LIBOR rates is shown in Figure 7.10. The "Real Case" at the end of this chapter looks at how LIBOR was rigged in 2015.

The lending rate has no name comparable to the prime rate, but it is determined as LIBOR plus some margin, or spread, charged to the borrower. Banks generally do not require compensating balances or other implicit charges in addition to the spread over LIBOR in the euromarket. This also helps reduce the cost of using the euromarket for borrowers. The total cost of borrowing in the euromarket for a prime US corporation historically was marginally below the domestic US prime rate. Because of competition among lenders in both markets, prime borrowers have been able to obtain the same rate in both markets since the early 1980s.

Interest rates on other eurocurrencies generally follow the same pattern, though when capital controls exist in a particular country (say, France), borrowing rates may be higher in the euromarket (which is not restricted) than in the domestic market.

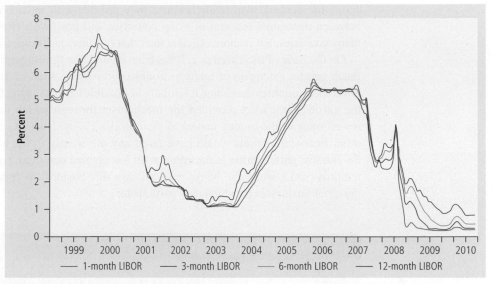

Figure 7.10 History of the LIBOR rates, January 1, 1999–December 31, 2010

Other market characteristics

Transactions in the eurodollar market generally involve $1 million or more, although in the past several years many deposits of $50,000 to $100,000 have been given at LIBOR, and loans of similar amounts have been offered at the analogous lending rates. The market is directly accessible to banks, which carry out about three-fourths of the total volume of transactions among themselves. Companies and individuals participate through their banks, generally at interest rates slightly less favorable than those offered among banks. (Investors may also participate in the euromarket indirectly by purchasing money market funds in the United States, when the funds themselves place large portions of their pooled investments in eurodollar accounts.)

Criticisms of the euromarkets

Over the years, the eurodollar market has been criticized as contributing to worldwide inflation and creating major new risks in the international banking system. While neither claim has been proved (or disproved) conclusively, each is worth considering here.

Because the eurodollar market adds to the worldwide volume of dollar-denominated assets, it has been accused of increasing the global money supply beyond the control of the US authorities. This may be true to some extent, but a number of factors mitigate the total impact of eurodollars. First, eurodollars exist only as time deposits and certificates of deposit, never as demand deposits or cash. Hence, in the narrow definition of money that includes only cash and demand deposits, eurodollars do not even appear at all. Second, as already noted, about three-fourths of all eurodollars are interbank deposits rather than new credit to companies or individuals that may use it for capital investment and thus economic growth. The interbank transfers (sometimes called *pyramiding*) do not create any new credit, however measured. Finally, the eurodollar deposits used by companies and individuals for investment and consumption probably replace other (for example, domestic) bank deposits that would have been used for the same purposes anyhow. That is, because the eurodollar deposits pay interest rates higher than domestic deposits, they often substitute for domestic deposits, and thus they are used for the same purposes that those deposits would have served. All in all, eurodollars probably add slightly to the total volume of economic activity worldwide because they provide a form of financial intermediation between depositors (savers) in many countries and borrowers (investors or spenders) in many countries that is more efficient than that of individual domestic financial markets.

On the issue of increased risk, it has been argued that the eurocurrency market has led to much greater extension of loans to troubled borrowers, such as the governments of less developed countries that found it virtually impossible to repay in the 1980s. Unquestionably, the eurodollar market provided the mechanism through which these governments borrowed most of the money loaned to them in the 1970s. It is not clear, however, that any other financial markets would have fared any differently in the absence of eurodollars. Essentially, participation in the euromarket has opened one more type of business to international banks, and these banks must manage this business as prudently as they manage the other businesses in which they participate.

 Active learning check

Review your answer to Active Learning Case question 4 and make any changes you like. Then compare your answer to the one below.

4 **How can Barclays use the eurocurrency market in its international business, and will this help in dealing with the exchange rate problem?**

Barclays can and does use the eurocurrency market for much of its international lending, since conditions in this market favor the large clients and banks with which Barclays deals extensively. Barclays can offer euro deposits for various maturities in various currencies to its clients, and the bank can use this market to find offsetting exposures such as loans or investments in those same currencies and maturities.

Eurobonds and euroequities

Eurobonds are the long-term analog of euro currencies. They are issued in countries of convenience and denominated in currencies other than the local one. With eurobonds, *taxation* of the interest income that investors receive is a key concern, so most of them are issued in tax jurisdictions that do not impose taxes on such interest payments (for example, Luxembourg). Eurobonds, like domestic US bonds, are issued by corporations and government agencies. They may be convertible into equity, and they may have fixed or floating interest rates.

Borrowers (namely, issuers of eurobonds) utilize this market for three main reasons. First, no regulatory agency establishes rules for disclosure by issuers, so substantial red tape is avoided; however, this generally limits participation to blue-chip corporations and governments. Second, the interest rates can be marginally lower than those on domestic issues, because investors can usually avoid taxes on their interest income. Third, the issuer gains access to potential investors in many countries simultaneously because the investment banks that place the issue offer it internationally. From time to time, eurobond issue is stimulated by additional reasons, such as domestic bond market restrictions that lead issuers to seek overseas funding. The United States, for example, established capital controls some time ago that made foreign bonds less attractive to US investors (the interest equalization tax was effectively a tax on interest received by US citizens from foreign bond investments) and limited lending by US parent companies to their foreign subsidiaries. As a result, both US and foreign issuers that were trying to place dollar-denominated bonds turned to the fledgling eurobond market for their funding.

For the investor, the eurobond market offers these advantages: (1) all issues are structured to allow exemption from interest withholding tax on the income earned; and (2) the terms of eurobond issues are more varied than those of domestic bond issues. For example, eurobonds usually have shorter maturities than domestic bonds (five to eight years) and often have floating-rate interest payments.

Euroequities

Euroequities have emerged in the past decade in the London Stock Exchange as another long-term euromarket, analogous to domestic stock markets. As the name implies, euroequities are shares of publicly traded stocks traded on an exchange outside the issuing firm's home country. They are bought and sold in shares denominated in the firm's home currency, so both company performance and exchange rate performance affect the returns on investments in euroequities.

In the United States, a market for such issues has operated for many years through an instrument called the American Depositary Receipt (ADR), which is essentially a claim on a share of stock in the foreign stock exchange intermediated by a securities broker who issues the ADR. Euroequities rival ADRs and offer the flexibility of being direct share issues by the non-local firms. The market exists primarily in London, and thus it encompasses non-British company shares. In fact, even the ADRs of British companies are now traded on the London Stock Exchange, so full global trading is possible through the exchange.

The London Stock Exchange euroequity market grew rapidly in the late 1980s. By 1989, 52 brokerage firms were making a market for euroequities issued by 707 firms. The monthly turnover during January 1989 was 278 million shares. The growing demand for these instruments (based on the firms available for investment and the tax-avoiding structure of the issues), as well as the growing supply (by firms that are blue chip and want to gain access to investors from many countries through the London Stock Exchange), make it likely that this market will increase in importance in global equities trading. By 2010, companies based in 22 different countries were listed in euroequity markets, with Japan and the United States followed by the United Kingdom (26), France (25), Canada (23), the Netherlands (19), Germany (15), and Sweden (13).

INTERNATIONAL BUSINESS STRATEGY IN ACTION

AngloGold Ashanti

When it comes to international finance, one of the primary concerns of MNEs is the ability to raise capital through new stock offerings and bank loans. For many years this was a major problem for the Anglo American Corporation of South Africa (AAC), which operated gold mines in that country. During South Africa's apartheid period, trade sanctions, controls on exchange currency, and protectionism all combined to isolate the AAC from outside financial markets. Unable to do business in the international arena, the AAC focused on expanding its domestic operations by acquiring holdings in a variety of industries including automobiles, newspapers, and vineyards.

As apartheid came to an end, however, there was a gradual liberalization of both trade and investment. And as its opportunity to move into the international arena began to increase, the firm put its gold mining activities into a new subsidiary, AngloGold, and began restructuring its operations. Non-core businesses were sold off and the company began focusing heavily on the development of its gold and uranium mines. However, its profitability and performance were handicapped by the small size of the South African economy and the fact that the Johannesburg stock market was not very influential in the worldwide financial markets. In addition, the local currency, the rand, was

▶

Source: Joerg Boethling/Alamy Stock Photo

the New York Stock Exchange, and today it is also listed on the Ghana and Australian Stock Exchanges. The firm now has access to equity capital in the EU and North America, as well as Australia. In 2003 AngloGold merged with Ashanti Goldfields. Further growth meant that by 2014 the organization encompassed 19 gold mine operations spread across nine different countries (Argentina, Australia, Brazil, DRC, Guinea, Ghana, Mali, South Africa, and Tanzania). In total, the firm produced 4.4 million ounces of gold, generating $5.2 billion in revenue, in 2014. This made it the third largest producer of gold, just behind Barrick Gold and Newmont Mining, with a workforce over 60,000 employees.

weak and the company needed to tie its operations to a stronger currency.

In response, AngloGold determined that it needed to link itself to the triad and expand its mining operations worldwide. As a result, in 1998 the company was listed on

While AngloGold Ashanti's main product is still gold, revenue is also derived from the sales of silver, uranium oxide and sulfuric acid, sold across a range of international markets.

Websites: www.anglogold.com; www.nyse.com

Sources: AngloGold, *Annual Report*, 2009 and 2014, and company web page.

Sometimes an MNE will lend money in the international money market. For example, if Bank of America finds that it can get a higher interest rate in Singapore than in the United States, it may deposit some money there. Similarly, if General Motors finds that there are limitations on the amount of profit that it can transfer out of a country, the company may invest in local financial instruments and thus gain interest on funds that would otherwise sit idle.

THE IMF SYSTEM

International monetary system
The arrangement between national governments/central banks that oversees the operation of official foreign exchange dealings between countries

International Monetary Fund (IMF)
The international organization founded at Bretton Woods, New Hampshire, in 1944 that includes most countries of the world and offers balance of payments support to countries in crisis along with financial advice to central banks

The last international financial market we will examine here may be viewed as either a very important framework for international financial dealings or a market that is generally irrelevant to private business managers. The **international monetary system** is a financial market in which only central banks and the **International Monetary Fund** (IMF, or "the Fund") operate, so private business plays no active role in it. On the other hand, rules for international financial dealings among countries are often set at the IMF, and substantial international loan decisions are made between governments and the IMF. Thus, the rules of the game in the other international financial markets are sometimes influenced by IMF activities.

The international monetary system oversees the exchange rate regime that prevails among the major developed countries, whose currencies are used for the vast majority of international payments. The IMF negotiates with governments of debtor nations (usually less developed countries) for loans directly from the Fund and for loan conditions that are used, subsequently, as a basis for lending by private banks to these same borrowers. In addition, the IMF serves as an intermediary for emergency loans between member governments to cope with the capital flow or exchange rate crises that occur from time to time due to speculation in foreign exchange markets or other causes. All in all, the international monetary system plays an important role in determining the rules of the game for private companies and banks in some spheres of international business, so managers need to understand its functioning.

The IMF was designed in 1944 at a conference of the Allied nations held at Bretton Woods, New Hampshire. Its general purpose was to provide a multilateral framework for avoiding international financial crises by establishing rules for national exchange rate policies and for adjustment to balance of payments disequilibria (discussed in the Appendix to Chapter 6). It was specifically intended to avoid the disastrous financial contraction that occurred during the 1930s. As originally negotiated, and as implemented in 1946 when the Articles of Agreement were signed by the initial 46 member countries, the IMF system required *fixed* exchange rates among member countries, with gold as the basis for currency valuation. The US dollar was initially fixed at a value of $35 per ounce of gold, and all other currencies were fixed at values expressed in both dollars and gold.

Fixed exchange rates were a fundamental base of the Bretton Woods system. Under the Articles of Agreement, each country was obligated to maintain its currency value at the initially set value (the "par" value), with a band of ±1 percent of flexibility around the par value. If a foreign central bank demanded to sell a country's currency back to the issuer, that country was required to pay the equivalent amount of gold, US dollars, or some other acceptable currency.

To join the IMF, a country was required to make a deposit of gold (25 percent), plus its own currency (75 percent), such that each member country's total deposit relative to the total of IMF deposits was roughly in proportion with its share of world trade. Then each member country received the right to borrow up to 200 percent of its initial deposit at the Fund, in any currency, to help pay for imbalances such as the one mentioned above. If a country borrowed more than its original deposit, the IMF would stipulate economic policies that the borrower had to follow to receive more financial support. (This imposition of policy demands by the IMF is called *conditionality*.)

While the IMF sought to provide assistance for nations facing balance of payments problems, its only resources were the contributions of its member countries: quotas based on each country's part in world trade, which initially constituted about $9 billion. This relatively small amount of liquidity was not sufficient to support the post-World War II economic recovery, or specifically the payments imbalances, of even the European countries.[8] Ultimately, the US Marshall Plan injected the needed funding into the international financial system, and specifically into Europe, during 1948–52.

In fact, the IMF provided very little funding to its member countries in its early years. During the Suez crisis in 1956, it loaned $1.7 billion to the UK, France, and India. Later, during speculative runs on the British pound (that is, periods when **speculators** sold large quantities of pounds for other currencies in expectation of a devaluation of the pound) in 1961 and 1964, it extended loans to the UK. By the end of the 1960s, the IMF was regularly providing credit to member countries, though still not at the levels that many analysts believed necessary to stabilize the system. (The alternative view is that the IMF should not provide credit to the member countries at all; rather, these countries should be forced to adjust their economies to escape balance of payments problems.)

At the end of the 1960s, the US dollar began to be the object of speculative pressure. The problem was severe, since the dollar constituted the base for the entire system of value (through its formal link to gold at $35 per ounce). The United States was unable to devalue to stop the speculation, and later it was unwilling to continue selling its gold holdings to foreign central banks that wanted to redeem their dollars. In August 1971, President Nixon announced that the United States would no longer sell gold to foreign central banks in exchange for dollars. In December 1971, he announced a devaluation of the dollar to $38 per ounce of gold; in February 1972 it was devalued to $42 per ounce, and later that year the United States declared that it would not support the dollar value at any price in gold.

Speculator
A person or firm that takes a position in foreign exchange with no hedging or protection mechanism to try to gain from expected exchange rate changes

These events essentially destroyed the Bretton Woods system of fixed exchange rates. Many initiatives to repair the system were presented during the following two years, but the United States would no longer accept the responsibility of providing the dollar as a fixed base for other currencies. In subsequent months, the IMF system was changed *de facto* to a floating exchange rate system that allowed each country to leave the value of its currency free to change with market forces or to fix that value to some other currency. Since that time, the United States has allowed the dollar to float in value relative to all other currencies, with occasional efforts by the Fed (the Federal Reserve System) to influence the dollar's relationship to particular currencies, such as the former German mark and the Japanese yen.

Under the current IMF system, no limitations are set on each member country's decision either to fix its currency value relative to some other currency or to allow it to fluctuate as supply and demand dictate. (Note that it is impossible for one country to keep its currency fixed relative to all others if the others are not fixed relative to one another.) In 1976, an accord called the Jamaica Agreement altered the IMF charter to formally allow for floating exchange rates. Today, the exchange rate regimes used by each nation are substantially unrestricted, and government strategies to influence exchange rates are altered as desired.[9]

> **Special drawing right (SDR)**
> The currency of the IMF; accounts at the IMF are denominated in SDRs, and the IMF has issued about $204 billion of SDRs as currency since its inception in 1969

At about the same time that the link between the dollar and gold was broken, the IMF's members agreed to create a new currency that the Fund would issue when authorized to do so by a vote of the members. This currency, called the **special drawing right (SDR)**, allows its holder to obtain (or draw) other currencies from the IMF (or from other members) when desired. SDRs have been created and issued on seven occasions to date. As of 2015, a total SDR of 204.1 billion existed. In each instance, the SDRs were allocated to Fund members according to their quotas. This new "international money" has served to support a number of countries that have encountered financial crises since 1971, allowing them to finance their imbalances, but it has not been a solution to imbalances in international financial flows. During the international debt crisis of the early 1980s, SDR use was wholly inadequate to deal with the more than $350 billion of debt owed by Latin American countries to foreign lenders. Total IMF resources include member country quotas, which totaled over $300 billion at the end of 2004. With a general SDR allocation that took effect on August 28 and a special allocation on September 9, 2009, the amount of SDRs increased from SDR21.4 billion to SDR204.1 billion (equivalent to about $280 billion, converted using the rate of September, 2015). So the Fund actually has quite substantial lending power today.

During the late twentieth century, SDRs became fairly widely used as a currency of denomination for private sector financial instruments such as bonds and long-term bank loans. Because the SDR has a value based on four currencies (see Figure 7.11), it is more stable as a borrowing or lending tool than any individual currency.

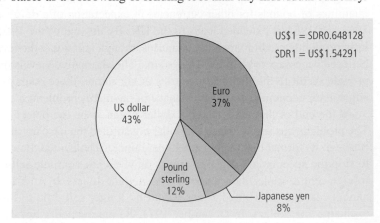

US$1 = SDR0.648128
SDR1 = US$1.54291

Euro 37%
US dollar 43%
Pound sterling 12%
Japanese yen 8%

Figure 7.11 **IMF special drawing rights (February 21, 2014)**

Source: Data from IMF.

When the dollar devalues relative to other widely traded currencies, so does the SDR—but only 43 percent of the SDR's value is affected negatively. The rest of the SDR's value is based on pounds, yen, and euros, and these currencies may rise or fall relative to the dollar in such a situation. Overall, the changes must net out over all currencies, and an instrument such as the SDR changes relatively little in value compared to any single currency. The SDR is really a "basket" of currencies whose value is generally more stable than that of any one of its components.

Just as the euro has gained wide acceptance as an instrument for denominating international financial transactions, so the SDR promises to maintain its acceptance as a risk-reducing instrument. (The SDR has the advantage of including the US dollar in the group of currencies that determine its value, whereas the euro is based only on European currencies.) At present, private sector investors and borrowers are using a much greater volume and value of euro-denominated instruments than SDR-denominated instruments.

Unresolved problems with the IMF system

The IMF system today differs dramatically from the model established at Bretton Woods in 1944. Flexible exchange rates have been substituted for fixed ones; gold has been greatly reduced as an international monetary asset,[10] and its link to the dollar has been severed; a new reserve currency, the SDR, has been created to increase world liquidity; and, perhaps most important, the US dollar is no longer the single base for the IMF system of value. These major changes have come in response to problems and crises that have occurred during the past 60 years—yet the IMF system itself survives. While few people would argue that the IMF has led directly to greater international financial stability over its history, at least the system has been flexible enough to accommodate the various crises that have threatened it.

Several problems that remain in the system deserve note. First, there has always been an uncomfortable tension between the countries that want to utilize the IMF simply as a bank for reducing the negative impacts of balance of payments difficulties and the countries that want to utilize it to subsidize economic development. The "link" between the IMF and development finance was originally delegated to the **World Bank** (the IMF's sister institution). Traditionally, the IMF has loaned funds only for short-term uses, sometimes extending to two or three years. Many borrowing countries, especially the less developed ones, have repeatedly called for greater use of IMF resources to finance development projects. While there are often no clear differences between financing payments imbalances and financing development projects that may later reduce those imbalances, the IMF has not substantially widened its scope. In the 1980s, under the cloud of multiple international loan renegotiations by Latin American countries, the Fund began to extend longer-term loans and to reconsider its strategy. The ultimate result of this crisis is that, in the early 2000s, the Fund retained its basic form, and the resources of the World Bank expanded to assist more heavily in economic development.

A second problem that continues to plague the Fund is the issue of exchange rate regimes. Even as the flexible rate system moves through its fourth decade, there are repeated calls for a return to fixed, or more tightly constrained, currency values. The great instability of international financial dealings during the period since the initial OPEC oil crisis of 1973–4 has led some analysts to argue for a return to fixed rates. The decision of most European Union countries to set up a single currency, the euro, has placed a regional fixed exchange rate regime alongside the floating rate system globally. The evidence of the entire twentieth century tends to suggest that no matter what exchange rate regime prevails, if international trade relations are unstable and payments imbalances are substantial, no exchange rate regime will be able to solve the problem. Thus, this problem most likely cannot be eliminated.

World Bank
The world's largest development bank, formed along with the IMF at Bretton Woods in 1944. Its original name was the International Bank for Reconstruction and Development (IBRD). The World Bank assists developing countries with loans and economic advising for economic development

On the whole, the international monetary system plays an important role in all international financial dealings by being the focal point for establishing rules on exchange rates, exchange controls, intergovernmental loans, and other official transactions. On a day-to-day basis, most international business people, especially in the triad countries, do not feel the international monetary system's impact.

MNEs AND INTERNATIONAL FINANCIAL MARKETS AND INSTITUTIONS

Whether or not a company or bank is involved in international trade, investment, or other international business, it is important that its managers understand some of the key aspects of international financial markets. The eurocurrency market may offer a low-cost borrowing opportunity, or the eurobond market may provide an outlet for selling new debt to a wider group of investors. The international monetary system establishes a framework within which governments set international financial policies that may affect many firms. The money and capital markets in foreign countries may offer opportunities to multinational firms that operate in those countries. The foreign exchange market determines the cost and availability of foreign currencies, used in business by many firms. Finally, all of these markets influence the functioning of the markets for real goods and services, the ultimate use for all financial claims.

KEY POINTS

1 Foreign exchange is any financial instrument that can be used to carry out payment from one currency to another. There are two major foreign exchange markets in the United States and the UK: interbank (including brokers) and futures/options (at stock and commodities exchanges). The most important participants in foreign exchange markets are banks—acting as traders, speculators, hedgers, and arbitrageurs. Exchange rates are determined by the activities of these four groups. The rates are also influenced by purchasing power parity, interest rates, and technical factors such as national economic statistics and seasonal demands.

2 There are a number of international finance strategies that can be of value to firms doing business overseas. Two of the most important are strategies for managing currency exchange rate risk and strategies for financing international operations.

3 The international monetary system is a market among central banks of the countries that belong to the International Monetary Fund (IMF). The IMF's objectives include the facilitation of balanced growth of international trade, the promotion of exchange stability, and the making of financial resources available to the members of the Fund. In recent years the fixed monetary system created by the IMF members in 1944 has been replaced by a managed float system. Currently the IMF faces a number of major problems, including helping Third World countries to deal with their international debt crises and increasing international liquidity.

Key terms

- exchange risk
- foreign exchange
- eurocurrency
- exchange rate
- foreign exchange traders
- foreign exchange brokers
- spot rate

- forward rate
- arbitrageur
- purchasing power parity
- international Fisher effect
- nominal interest rate
- real interest rate
- exchange risk avoidance

- exchange risk adaptation
- exchange risk transfer
- currency diversification
- foreign bond
- Eurobond
- European Monetary Union (EMU)
- eurodollar

- London interbank offered rate (LIBOR)
- international monetary system
- International Monetary Fund (IMF)
- speculator
- special drawing right (SDR)
- World Bank

REVIEW AND DISCUSSION QUESTIONS

1 If your firm had a subsidiary in Japan and about 100 million yen in exposed assets (that is, plant and equipment), how would you protect it against exchange risk?

2 If you managed the European operations of a large US-based MNE, in what market(s) would you seek long-term funding? Why?

3 If the euro area's inflation is about 3 percent per year and US inflation is about 2 percent per year, what would you expect to happen to the euro/dollar exchange rate in the next few months? Why?

4 What is the difference between a eurobond and a domestic bond in the United States? Which one would you prefer to issue as a company manager? Which one would you prefer to buy as an investor? Why?

5 How can a firm such as Ajax Steel in Peoria, Illinois, utilize the eurodollar market to minimize its financing costs? This firm is a medium-size manufacturer with no foreign sales.

6 Assume that the interest rate on 12-month US dollar deposits in London is currently 2.6875 percent per year and the rate on British pound deposits there is 4.1875 percent per year. The spot exchange rate is US $1.93/£. What do you expect the exchange rate to be in one year?

7 If you were offered the opportunity to establish a deposit in London-denominated euros, would you choose that rather than a deposit in British pounds or dollars? Why or why not?

8 What are the important differences between the Bretton Woods fixed exchange rate system and the current IMF system? How do these differences affect the MNE manager?

9 How may the International Monetary Fund affect companies' activities in international business?

10 How would you hedge the value of your export sale of €10 million of computers to a French customer? You will be paid in 180 days in euros. On what basis would you choose among hedging methods?

HSBC

Which bank is the world's largest? Prior to the merger of Citicorp and Travelers in 1998, it was the Hongkong and Shanghai Banking Corporation (HSBC). As of 2015, HSBC is the world's seventh largest banking and financial services group and the UK's no.1 largest banking group (Fortune Global 500, 2015 ranking). Formed in 1865 by a Scotsman in the then British colony of Hong Kong, HSBC grew to over approximately 6,100 bank offices in 73 countries with over 51 million customers by 2014. In the process it became the world's first truly global bank, offering a full range of financial services from retail to corporate banking to insurance and financial management. HSBC built this global business based on its strong Hong Kong base. The bank owns the Hongkong Bank and most of the Hang Seng Bank, giving it over 40 percent of the market in the Hong Kong Special Administrative Region of China that was created on July 1, 1997.

Perhaps less well known is that HSBC is also the owner of the former Midland Bank chain in the UK, the Marine Midland and Republic New York Banks and Household Finance in the United States, and the Hongkong Bank of Canada. It has also acquired large banks in Latin America, including Banco Bamerindus in Brazil and Bital in Mexico. In all these cases HSBC greatly improved the efficiency of the underperforming local banks through better systems and processes. For some time HSBC has operated a branding strategy under the HSBC title and logo, "the world's local bank". This captures one of the central dilemmas of global firms—to be both large and dominant, while being sympathetic to the needs of local customers. Branding, however, is only a start.

Today HSBC is well developed across the triad regions of Asia, Europe, and the Americas. It is a global bank in terms of assets, but not revenues. Its diversification strategy helped to insulate it from the Asian financial crisis of 1997–8.

There is an old saying that the best test of a business is how well it does in a downturn (because a "rising tide floats all boats," the strong and the weak). Again in the world financial crisis starting in 2007, HSBC looked pretty good. HSBC reported revenue of US$142.069 billion and profits after tax of US$5.728 billion for 2008. Although revenue was down 3 percent on a year earlier, that looked very healthy compared to sickly peers such as Citigroup, UBS, and Royal Bank of Scotland (RBS). RBS required a British government bailout.

HSBC was thriving because of its strong presence in emerging markets including India, China, the Middle East, and Brazil, cushioning it against the big losses it took in the US market due to the subprime mortgage crisis. Since 2007,

HSBC has expanded into Japan, Korea, Vietnam, and India by launching new branches and services, and by 2014 it had grown to employ 257,600 employees. Profits in some of HSBC's Middle East businesses, such as capital markets and private banking, were growing at a near 100 percent. HSBC reported revenue of US$61.248 billion and profits before taxation of U$18.7 billion for 2014.

Significant events in 2009 included its decision to sell landmark buildings in New York, London, and Paris to raise cash. HSBC agreed to sell its London base at Canary Wharf to the National Pension Service of Korea for $1.25 billion in cash and its New York headquarters to Israeli investment holding IDB Group for $330 million. HSBC sold its Paris building to private investors represented by French Properties Management for $573 million. HSBC would lease back these buildings. Importantly, HSBC announced in 2009 that it was relocating the principal office of the Group Chief Executive to Hong Kong. This underscores HSBC commitments to emerging markets' businesses and reflects the historic shifts now taking place in the world economy. HSBC's corporate headquarters remain in the UK where it continues to benefit from being at the heart of the world's financial centers.

Its first-mover advantage as a truly global bank may prove hard for its competitors to match. There is constant pressure in banking to reduce costs through greater scale economies and improved information technology. HSBC is well positioned to continue as an industry leader because of its successful strategy.

In retrospect, one of the world's largest banks came from one of the world's smallest economies. And it did this despite the regulatory barriers to entry for foreign-owned firms in Europe and North America. As a result HSBC is an example of a bank using modern management systems and market forces to win out over old-fashioned protectionism in a highly regulated worldwide industry.

Perhaps the biggest influence of HSBC and its new efficient banking methods has been on British banking. A further restructuring occurred in British banking in November 1999 when one of the country's four major banks (Lloyds, Barclays, NatWest, and HSBC) was taken over by a much smaller bank. NatWest was acquired by the Royal Bank of Scotland, only one-third the asset size of NatWest, in a drawn-out and controversial takeover. Another bank, the Bank of Scotland, first bid for NatWest and the takeover efforts of both the Royal Bank of Scotland and the Bank of Scotland were defended by NatWest Chairman, Sir David Rowland, who was also President of Templeton College, University of Oxford. The takeover was successful because investors were critical of NatWest's old-style management and were supportive of the cost-cutting and new information technology methods of the Royal Bank of Scotland. After the acquisition, many NatWest branches were closed; bank buildings were turned into coffee bars, restaurants, and hotels; and a leaner, more efficient bank emerged to reclaim its place in British retail banking.

The Bank of Scotland and Halifax, the largest mortgage lender in the country, finalized a merger in 2001. This fast-forwarded Halifax into mainstream banking and greatly increased the Bank of Scotland's scope of operations. Halifax then became a trading name of Bank of Scotland. The merger also allowed both banks to streamline their businesses and increase their market focus. These efforts toward restructuring operations and eliminating waste did not go unnoticed by rival banks. Barclays, for example, closed some of its branches in the early 2000s and introduced a wide array of tools and techniques designed to cut costs and increase operational efficiency. It realized that, to be a successful international operation, it needed not only to have wide geographic coverage but also to be able to offer efficient services. A takeover of Bank of Scotland by Lloyds TSB was approved by the Court of Session on January 12, 2009. On January 19, 2009, Bank of Scotland formally became part of Lloyds Banking Group.

In looking at these recent developments, it is clear that the steps taken by HSBC to modernize its own operations are proving to be a wake-up call for British banks as well. HSBC is also in the process of fundamentally changing its culture under the leadership of António Simões, the openly gay CEO of the bank. He has pushed for greater diversity and inclusivity in the workforce and is strongly supportive of a family-friendly approach to management. This is being reflected in the development of HSBC's UK head office, established in Birmingham in 2016, separate from the global group HQ in London.

Websites: www.hsbc.com; www.citigroup.com; www.bankofscotland.co.uk; www.royalbankscot.co.uk; www.natwest.co.uk; www.barclays.com.

Sources: "HSBC: world's strongest bank," *Bloomberg Business Week*, August 4, 2008; "HSBC to sell New York building for $330 million," *Bloomberg*, October 10, 2009; "HSBC sells Paris building for $573 million," *Reuters*, December 21, 2009; HSBC, *Annual Report*, 2008–14; Lloyds, *Annual Report*, 2009; "Fortune Global 500," *Fortune*, 2008, 2009, 2010, 2015 issues. "HSBC's António Simões says being gay was key to career success," *Guardian*, January 18, 2015.

1 Since HSBC does business with the People's Republic of China and has substantial holdings of Chinese yuan (renminbi) on hand, what risk does this pose for the bank?

2 How could HSBC manage its currency exchange rate risk?

3 As the British retail banks are merged to achieve cost savings and economies, does this increase or decrease the barriers to entry for foreign banks wishing to do business in the EU?

REAL CASE

Rigging LIBOR

In August 2015 a former bank trader, Tom Hayes, was found guilty of manipulating the LIBOR market and sentenced to 14 years in jail. His story illustrates how the complex interdependence of financial institutions across the world can be exploited for personal gain. It also highlights how individuals, firms, and institutions need to be held to account when this happens because the effects of their actions have widespread repercussions for the rest of us in terms of increasing the costs and risks of doing business.

The Intercontinental Exchange (ICE) London Interbank Offered Rate (LIBOR) is a benchmark rate used by many of the world's leading banks for setting the interest rate or charge for taking out short-term loans with each other. As it represents the average cost of borrowing for banks (calculated daily), it is also used to set interest rates for other loans, in different currencies and across different time periods. For example, the interest rates on a mortgage may be calculated by LIBOR + 3%, making the rate at which LIBOR is set significant for large numbers of private borrowers. Overall the value of more than US$350 trillion of loans and securities is set by the LIBOR and Tom Hayes was convicted on eight counts of conspiracy to rig it.

His involvement began in 2006 when he was working in Tokyo's financial district working for UBS Group AG. But the collapse of Lehman Brothers Holdings Inc. in September 2008 created the conditions for gaining control over the rate-setting network. In 2009, drawn by a US$3 million golden handshake, Hayes (given the nickname "Tommy Chocolate" because of his preference for hot chocolate over other drinks) took a job with Citigroup and it was there that senior management began an internal investigation of his activities. It took a further three years before he was arrested and charged after moving back to London.

The network of rate setters from 18 large banks were required to submit their internal rate to the British Bankers Association on a daily basis (it was called the BBA LIBOR then). The final rate was then set by taking an average of the submissions. They were reliant on a network of interdealer brokers to guide the rates they set. Tom Hayes managed to gain control over 25 traders and brokers across ten key firms, partly through bribery. Many of these have also stood trial and over 100 have been fired or suspended across the industry, with banks like Barclays, UBS and Deutsche Bank facing fines.

The LIBOR reflects the confidence banks have in each other's financial health and is also used as a measure of trust in the financial system. Because of this, monetary policy is also likely to have been influenced by the manipulation of the rate by a small network of self-interested bankers.

Bankers and banks might be forgiven if the rigging of the LIBOR rate stood as an isolated example of a corrupt, self-serving practice in the City. Unfortunately the sector and its highly paid employees have a history of illegal and unethical rogue trading, discriminatory practices, mis-selling of payment protection insurance, and insider trading.

Sources: Liam Vaughan and Gavin Finch, "Inside the LIBOR scandal: the story of how Tom Hayes manipulated the LIBOR market and ultimately lost," *Bloomberg News*, August 4, 2015; John Kiff, "What is LIBOR?," *Finance and Development*, December 2012, vol. 49, no. 4; Telegraph staff, "What is Libor and how is it manipulated?," *Daily Telegraph*, August 3, 2015; "The LIBOR scandal: the rotten heart of finance, a scandal over key interest rates is about to go global," *Economist*, July 7, 2012.

1 Explain, what is the London Inter-Bank Offered Rate (LIBOR)? And how is it determined?

2 How can LIBOR be manipulated?

3 Discuss the effects of the 2008 financial crisis in relation with LIBOR.

NOTES

1 Exchange rate quotations come as two-digit numbers, bid/asked, with the preceding numbers assumed. A British pound quote of 50/70 on October 14, 2004, meant an actual price of:

$1.7950 bid to buy one British pound.

£1.7970 asked for selling one British pound.

The bank is offering (bidding) to buy pounds for $1.795 per pound and also offering (asking) to sell pounds for $1.797 per pound. Of course, the actual transaction will involve $1 million or more, to be exchanged at those prices.

Rates are typically quoted on the *Continental basis*, as units of foreign exchange per dollar, everywhere. US banks have traditionally used the *American basis*, quoting US$ per unit of foreign exchange. Clearly, whether the quote is SF2.0/$ or $0.50/SF, the value is the same. The *Wall Street Journal* offers both types of quotations, as shown in Table 7.2.

Another means used to distinguish the two ways of presenting an exchange rate is to call a quotation of domestic currency/foreign exchange an *indirect quote*. Conversely, a quotation of units of foreign exchange/domestic currency is called a *direct quote*. This system has more general applicability to any pair of currencies, whereas the American/Continental system relates only to rates involving the US dollar.

2 See http://www.chips.org.

3 "Taking a position" means purchasing an asset (or a liability) denominated in a foreign currency without simultaneously matching it with a liability (asset) of the same value and maturity in the same currency. Realistically, if any one government disallows the euromarkets, they can still function almost as effectively in other countries and currencies. At present, the US government has the most important role, since about 80 percent of eurodeposits are denominated in US dollars. If a US bank buys Swiss francs, it takes a position in Swiss francs. When the bank sells those Swiss francs to a client, it eliminates the position.

4 A *foreign currency option* is a contract offering the holder the right to buy (namely, a *call option*) or sell (namely, a *put option*) a fixed amount of foreign currency for a fixed price during a fixed time period. The buyer of a call option on British pounds obtains the right to buy £31,500 at a fixed dollar price (that is, the *exercise price*) at any time during the (typically) three-month life of the option. The seller of the same option faces a *contingent liability* in that the seller will have to deliver the British pounds at any time if the buyer chooses to exercise the option.

The market value (that is, the price on "premium" that the buyer must pay to purchase the option) of an option depends on its exercise price, the remaining time to its expiration, the exchange rate in the spot market, and expectations about the future exchange rate. An option may sell for a price near zero, for thousands of dollars, or for anywhere in between. Notice that the buyer of a call option on British pounds may pay a small price to obtain the option but does *not* have to exercise the option if the actual exchange rate moves favorably. Thus, an option is superior to a forward contract having the same maturity and exercise price because it need *not* be used, and the cost is just its purchase price. However, the price of the option is generally higher than the expected cost of the forward contract, so the user of the option pays for the flexibility of the instrument.

5 Yet another kind of foreign exchange arbitrage involves comparing interest rates on similar investments between two currencies. Interest arbitrage is the choice of investing, say, $1 million in a eurodollar bank deposit, versus investing the same money in pounds, depositing in a europound deposit,

and contracting a forward contract to convert back to dollars. This comparison can be used for whatever currencies may be available, and the investor benefits from taking the highest return available, with the exchange rates guaranteed through forward contracts (that is, with no exchange risk).

6 This entire discussion refers to *relative* purchasing power parity (PPP). The stronger, absolute version refers to parity in the values of factor inputs used in the production of products whose prices reflect relative factor productivities. Relative PPP considers only *changes* in the relative price levels between countries, not the initial (absolute) levels.

7 Realistically, if any one government disallows the euromarkets, they can still function almost as effectively in other countries and currencies. At present, the US

government has the most important role, since about 80 percent of eurodeposits are denominated in US dollars.

8 See the Economic Cooperation Act of 1948 (Public Law 472, 80th Congress), US Code Congressional Service, 1948.

9 Exchange rate policies *are* constrained by the IMF if a country seeks to borrow more than its quota from the Fund. Also, a country does operate in violation of IMF rules if it imposes new exchange controls on current transactions without obtaining IMF approval; however, sanctions are seldom applied unless the country seeks to borrow as above.

10 Almost one-third of the world's monetary reserves were still being held in the form of gold at year-end 1991. See *IMF Survey*, November 8, 1993, p. 345.

BIBLIOGRAPHY

Agmon, Tamir. "Bringing financial economics into international business research: taking advantage of paradigm change," *Journal of International Business Studies*, vol. 37, no. 5 (September 2006).

Armstrong, Christopher S., et al. "Market reaction to the adoption of IFRS in Europe," *Accounting Review*, vol. 85, no. 1 (2010).

Banalieva, Elitsa R., and Robertson, Christopher J. "Performance, diversity, and multiplicity of foreign cross-listing portfolios," *International Business Review*, vol. 19, no. 6 (December 2010).

Bergh, Donald D., and Gibbons, Patrick. "The stock market reaction to the hiring of management consultants: a signalling theory approach," *Journal of Management Studies*, vol. 48, no. 3 (May 2011).

Blome, Constantin, and Schoenherr, Tobias. "Supply chain risk management in financial crises—a multiple case-study approach," *International Journal of Production Economics*, vol. 134, no. 1 (2011).

Boulton, Thomas J., Smart, Scott B., and Zutter, Chad J. "IPO underpricing and international corporate governance," *Journal of International Business Studies*, vol. 41 (2010).

Bowe, Michael. "International financial management and multinational enterprises." In Alan M. Rugman (ed.), *Oxford Handbook of International Business*, 2nd ed. (Oxford: Oxford University Press, 2009).

Bowe, Michael, Filatotchev, Igor, and Marshall, Andrew. "Integrating contemporary finance and international business research," *International Business Review*, vol. 19, no. 5 (October 2010).

Brown, Craig O., and Dinç, I. Serdar. "Too many to fail? Evidence of regulatory forbearance when the banking sector is weak," *Review of Financial Studies*, vol. 24, no. 4 (2011).

Campbell, John Y., Polk, Christopher, and Vuolteenaho, Tuomo. "Growth or glamour? Fundamentals and systematic risk in stock returns," *Review of Financial Studies*, vol. 23, no. 1 (2010).

Charupat, Narat, and Peter Miu. "The pricing and performance of leveraged exchange-traded funds," *Journal of Banking and Finance*, vol. 35, no. 4 (2011).

Chen, Huifa, Tang, Qingliang, Jiang, Yihong, and Lin, Zhijun. "The role of international financial reporting standards in accounting quality: evidence from the European Union," *Journal of International Financial Management and Accounting*, no. 21, no. 3 (2010).

Connelly, Brian L., Hoskisson, Robert E., Tihanyi, Laszlo, and Certo, S. Trevis. "Ownership as a form of corporate governance," *Journal of Management Studies*, vol. 47, no. 8 (December 2010).

Covrig, Vincentiu Lau, Sie, Ting, and Ng, Lilian. "Do domestic and foreign fund managers have similar preferences for stock characteristics? A cross -country analysis," *Journal of International Business Studies*, vol. 37, no. 3 (March 2007).

Cumming, Douglas, and Walz, Uwe. "Private equity returns and disclosure around the world," *Journal of International Business Studies*, vol. 41 (2010).

Doidge, Craig, Carolyi, Andrew, and Stulz, Rene M. "Why do foreign firms leave US equity market?," *Journal of Finance*, vol. 65, no. 4 (2010).

Eckert, Stefan, Dittfeld, Marcus, Muche, Thomas, and Rässler, Susanne. "Does multinationality lead to value enhancement? An empirical examination of publicly listed corporations from Germany," *International Business Review*, vol. 19, no. 6 (December 2010).

Eiteman, David K., Stonehill, Arthur I., and Moffett, Michael H. *Multinational Business Finance*, 12th ed. (Boston, MA: Pearson Addison Wesley, 2009).

Faccio, Mara. "Differences between politically connected and nonconnected firms: a cross-country analysis," *Financial Management*, vol. 39, no. 3 (2010).

Faff, Robert W., and Marshall, Andrew. "International evidence on the determinants of foreign exchange rate exposure of multinational corporations," *Journal of International Business Studies*, vol. 36, no. 5 (September 2005).

Forbes, Kristin J., and Warnock, Francis E. "Capital flow waves: surges, stops, flight, and retrenchment," *Journal of International Economics*, vol. 88, no. 2 (2012).

Giddy, Ian, and Dufey, Gunter. "Uses and abuses of currency options," *Bank of America Journal of Applied Corporate Finance*, vol. 8 (1995).

Grosse, Robert. *The Future of Global Financial Services* (Oxford: Blackwell, 2004).

Hearn, Bruce, Piesse, Jenifer, and Strange, Roger. "Market Liquidity and Stock Size Premia in Emerging Financial Markets: The Implications for Foreign Investment," *International Business Review*, vol. 19, no. 5 (October 2010).

Hejazi, Walid, and Pauly, Peter H. "Motivation for FDI and domestic capital formation," *Journal of International Business Studies*, vol. 34, no. 3 (May 2003).

Hejazi, Walid, and Santor, Eric. "Foreign asset risk exposure, DOI, and performance: an analysis of Canadian banks," *Journal of International Business Studies*, vol. 41 (2010).

Hutson, Elaine, and O'Driscoll, Anthony. "Firm-level exchange rate exposure in the Eurozone," *International Business Review*, vol. 19, no. 5 (October 2010).

Hutson, Elaine, and Stevenson, Simon. "Openness, hedging incentives and foreign exchange exposure: a firm-level multi-country study," *Journal of International Business Studies*, vol. 41 (2010).

Ito, Kiyohiko, and Rose, Elizabeth L. "The implicit return on domestic and international sales: an empirical analysis of US and Japanese firms," *Journal of International Business Studies*, vol. 41 (2010).

Johnson, Robert, and Soenen, Luc. "European economic integration and stock market co-movement with Germany," *Multinational Business Review*, vol. 17, no. 3 (2009).

Lessard, Donald R. "Finance and international business." In B. Toyne and D. Nigh (eds.), *International Business: An Emerging Vision* (Columbia, SC: University of South Carolina Press, 1997).

Leung, Kwok, Chahat, Rabi S., Buchan, Nancy R., Erez, Miriam, and Gibson, Cristina B. "Culture and international business: recent advances and their implications for future research," *Journal of International Business Studies*, vol. 36, no. 4 (July 2005).

Li, Siqi. "Does mandatory adoption of International Financial Reporting Standards in the European Union reduce the cost of equity capital?," *Accounting Review*, vol. 85, no. 2 (2010).

Lopez-Duerte, Cristina, and Garcia-Canal, Esteban. "Stock market reaction to foreign direct investments: interaction between entry mode and FDI attributes," *Management International Review*, vol. 47, no. 3 (2007).

Miller, Kent D., and Reuer, Jeffrey J. "Firm strategy and economic exposure to foreign exchange rate movements," *Journal of International Business Studies*, vol. 29, no. 3 (fall 1998).

Oxelheim, Lars, and Randøy, Trond. "The Anglo-American financial influence on CEO compensation in non-Anglo-American firms," *Journal of International Business Studies*, vol. 36, no. 4 (July 2005).

Pástor, L'uboš, and Veronesi, Pietro. "Political uncertainty and risk premia," *Journal of Financial Economics*, vol. 110, no. 3 (2013).

Purda, Lynnette D. "Risk perception and the financial system," *Journal of International Business Studies*, vol. 39 (2008).

Radebaugh, Lee H., Gray, Sidney J., and Black, Ervin L. *International Accounting and Multinational Enterprises*, 6th ed. (Hoboken, NJ: Wiley, 2006).

Remmers, Lee. "International financial management: 35 years later—what has changed?" *International Business Review*, vol. 13, no. 2 (April 2004).

Rugman, Alan M. *International Diversification and the Multinational Enterprise* (Lexington, MA: D. C. Heath, 1979).

Rugman, Alan M. "International diversification and multinational banking." In Sarkis J. Khoury and Alo Gosh (eds.), *Recent Developments in International Banking and Finance* (Lexington, MA: D. C. Heath, 1987).

Rugman, Alan M., and Li, Jing (eds.). *Real Options and International Investment* (Cheltenham: Edward Elgar, 2005).

Santos, Tano, and Veronesi, Pietro. "Habit formation, the cross section of stock returns and the cash-flow risk puzzle," *Journal of Financial Economics*, vol. 98, no. 2 (2010).

Shapiro, Alan C. *Multinational Financial Management*, 9th ed. (New York: Wiley, 2009).

Strange, Roger, Filatotchev, Igor, Buck, Trevor, and Wright, Mike. "Corporate governance and international business," *Management International Review*, vol. 49, no. 4 (2009).

Tong, Tony W., and Reuer, Jeffrey J. "Real options in multinational corporations: organizational challenges and risk implications," *Journal of International Business Studies*, vol. 38, no. 2 (March 2007).

Umutlu, Mehmet, Akdeniz, Levent, and Altay-Salih, Aslihan. "The degree of financial liberalization and aggregated stock-return volatility in emerging markets," *Journal of Banking and Finance*, vol. 34, no. 3 (2010).

Van Rooij, Maarten, Lusardi, Annamaria, and Alessie, Rob. "Financial literacy and stock market participation," *Journal of Financial Economics*, vol. 101, no. 2 (2011).

Yan, Shu. "Jump risk, stock returns, and slope of implied volatility smile," *Journal of Financial Economics*, vol. 99, no. 1 (2011).

Zhao, Hua. "Dynamic relationship between exchange rate and stock price: evidence from China," *Research in International Business and Finance*, vol. 24, no. 2 (2010).

Part Three

INTERNATIONAL BUSINESS STRATEGIES

Chapter 8

MULTINATIONAL STRATEGY

Contents

Objectives of the chapter

Multinational enterprises are businesses that are headquartered in one country but have operations in other countries. In such a complex environment, it is particularly important for these MNEs to have well-formulated strategic plans. Large MNEs do this by conducting a thorough analysis of their environments and often developing detailed, comprehensive plans for coordinating worldwide activities. These plans set forth objectives for all major divisions and units and provide for systematic follow-up and evaluation. Smaller MNEs may use less sophisticated plans. However, all multinationals that conduct strategic planning go through a three-step process: formulation, implementation, and control.

The specific objectives of this chapter are to:

1 *Define* the term *strategic planning* and discuss the strategic orientations that affect this planning process.

2 *Explain* how strategy is formulated, giving particular emphasis to external and internal environmental assessment.

3 *Describe* how strategy is implemented, with particular attention to location, ownership decisions, and functional area implementation.

4 *Discuss* the ways in which MNEs control and evaluate their strategies.

ACTIVE LEARNING CASE

Vodafone and the triad telecom market

Vodafone had its beginnings in 1982, when the Racal Electronics Group Board successfully bid for a private sector UK cellular license. The Racal Telecoms Division was established with 50 employees in the rural town of Newbury and launched the first cellular network on January 1, 1985. By the end of that year, Vodafone had 19,000 subscribers. For the year ended in March 30, 2013, London-based Vodafone was the world's second-largest cell phone company measured by revenue of £43.6 billion, of which 64 percent originated from Europe, and it had a workforce of approximately 100,000 employees. (China Mobile Communications with revenue of $107.529 billion and 800 million customers was the world's largest cell phone company according to Fortune Global 500, 2015 ranking.) As of 2014, it had approximately 434 million mobile customers around the world. It operates a network in over 27 countries and has a partner network in over 48 countries. Let's review its growth.

Vodafone expanded globally through a carefully crafted "triad" strategy. From 1991 to 1998 its focus was on Europe, where it developed one of the basic ideas that it continues to use in most cases—acquire companies in association with partners and pay for it with equity. This strategy has given Vodafone access to new markets while providing it with partners that help deal with local regulatory environment agencies and provide assistance in addressing local market needs. For example, in the case of Libertel of the Netherlands, Vodafone purchased 70 percent of the company while Dutch ING, the local partner, held the rest. The company had interests in companies across most European markets and over 50 percent of the shares in many of these companies. As of September 30, 2010, Vodafone had 124 million customers in Europe. In geographic terms, 37 percent of Vodafone's subscribers and 64 percent of its turnover were in western Europe.

To appease EU regulators during its acquisition spree in the 1990s, Vodafone had to divest itself of Orange, the UK's third largest wireless operator. European acquisitions could not, therefore, be the company's only growth strategy. Rather, the best strategy was to go international, gain market share in all major economies, then link together all these firms into a worldwide network. This is precisely what it did.

In June 1999, Vodafone took a major step in implementing its worldwide strategy when it overcame Bell Atlantic for AirTouch Communications, a California-based firm. Creating Vodafone AirTouch (VA) gave the overall company a market capitalization of $154 billion and a total of 35 million wire-

Source: ScottyH/Alamy Stock Photo

less customers worldwide. Soon after the acquisition, VA entered into an agreement with Bell Atlantic (which was soon to merge with GTE) that gave it a 45 percent stake in a venture called Verizon Wireless. This decision had proved to be a very good one; prior to the merger of Cingular and AT&T Wireless in 2004, Verizon was the largest US mobile telephone operator. Indeed, Cingular snatched AT&T Wireless from Vodafone, which was seeking to further cement its presence in the United States through a controlling interest in the company.

By 2001 the US market had relatively low penetration levels compared to Europe and Japan. Yet it has the highest potential for growth across industrialized countries. As of September 30, 2010, Vodafone's share in Verizon Mobile had 41.927 million subscribers compared to 38.9 million subscribers in 2001, a growth of 8 percent over ten years. In a major change to its strategy under CEO Vittorio Colao, Vodafone sold its shares in Verizon in 2014 for $130 billion, cutting its market value almost in half, to $100 billion. The core aim was to move away from all minority shareholdings and focus on investing in majority-owned acquisitions.

Vodafone cemented its position in Japan in late 2001 by increasing its share of Japan Telecom to 69.7 percent. That decision completed the firm's "triad" strategy. By 2001, Vodafone had 10.4 million subscribers in Japan—7.8 percent of the company's total subscribers. Yet on March 17, 2006, Vodafone announced an agreement to sell all its interest in Vodafone Japan to SoftBank for £8.9 billion, of which £6.8 billion was received in cash on closing of the deal. Vodafone Japan later changed its name to SoftBank Mobile. In November 2010, Vodafone sold its remaining minority interest in its

Japanese operations to current owner SoftBank for £3.1 billion and exited Japan, as part of its new strategy, "offloading non-core assets." Vodafone said it would focus on markets in Europe, India, and Africa.

To summarize, Vodafone was a major player in the EU with holdings in Omnitel, Mannesmann, and SFR. The company was a force in the US market through its minority holding in Verizon Wireless (until 2014). And in Asia, where the largest market for cell phones is in Japan, Vodafone held operating control of Japan Telecom and also owned J-Phone, a large cell phone operator. However, Vodafone eventually divested its investment in Japan.

By 2010, Vodafone had carefully ventured into other markets. In Australia and New Zealand, it had wholly owned subsidiaries and about 6.024 million subscribers. This represented 50 percent growth if compared to 4 million subscribers in 2001. In non-industrialized countries, where the risk is higher, it held minority interests in most of its operations. Only in Egypt did it have more than 50 percent ownership. In South Africa, Kenya, and Fiji, it held between 35 and 40 percent. In China, the market with the largest potential growth, it held a mere 3.2 percent ownership of the venture in 2000. In such a huge market, however, that accounted for nearly 5 million subscribers. In September 2010, Vodafone sold its stake in China's biggest operator, China Mobile, for $6.5 billion for cash, and achieved a near doubling of Vodafone's original investment. Vodafone continues to cooperate with China's leading telecommunication companies in areas such as roaming, network roadmap development, multinational customers, and green technology.

On February 11, 2007, the company agreed to acquire a controlling interest of 67 percent in Hutchison Essar Limited in India for US$11.1 billion. At the same time, it agreed to sell back 5.6 percent of its Airtel stake back to the Mittals. Vodafone would retain a 4.4 percent stake in Airtel. On September 21, 2007, Hutchison was rebranded as Vodafone in India. However, Vodafone has ongoing problems with the Indian tax authority, which claimed that Vodafone owed value added tax (VAT) on the purchase in 2007 of the Indian telephone assets of Hong Kong's Hutchison Whampoa. Vodafone decided not to set up provisions for this disputed £1.6 billion tax bill in India in its financial statements. As at September 30, 2010, Vodafone had 115.553 million mobile customers in India.

Vodafone's strategy is to maximize its footprint with a common technology and offer the largest possible "roaming" wireless capability, which lends itself to overall lower costs. Perhaps surprisingly, this roaming technology was more prevalent in Europe than in the United States, mostly due to EU-wide cooperation between governmental regulatory authorities regarding common platforms.

Vodafone is not only relying on geographic diversification of acquisitions. Technology plays a major role in this industry, and Vodafone, like its competitors, purchased licenses to operate 3G technology. When the industry overestimated the pace at which the technology was being developed, some providers stumbled badly, but this technology is now available in urban areas in Europe and Japan and is expanding quickly. Mobile telephones with video and picture technology are more established in the market, but it is data transfers that mobile service providers are counting on for increased profits. This new technology is expected to reduce overall costs and, competition permitting, might allow Vodafone to increase its revenue per subscriber.

The biggest challenge facing Vodafone will be that of coordinating all of its worldwide holdings so as to maximize shareholder value. In an effort to handle this problem, the company's head office has now abandoned the use of centralized control and opted for a decentralized type of operation. In the United States, for example, local partners and operating managers now make many of the major decisions regarding how to do business. The same is true in Europe. Vodafone is realizing that in order to manage all of these different units in worldwide markets where regulations and customer preferences are often quite different, the best approach is to create a strategic plan that recognizes and takes advantages of these differences.

Websites: www.vodafone.com; www.verizon.com; www.omnitelvodafone.it; www.mannesmann.de; www.nttdocomo.com; www.kddi.com

Sources: "Vodafone launches 3G in Europe," *BBC News*, May 4, 2004; Vodafone, *Annual Reports and Accounts*, 1999, 2000, 2004, 2009, 2010, 2014. News release, "Vodafone announces first half 2010/2011 results and strategy update," November 9, 2010. "Fortune Global 500," *Fortune*, July 26, 2010 issue, http://money.cnn.com/magazines/fortune/global500/2010; "Vodafone pockets $6.5bn in China mobile sales," *BBC News*, September 8, 2010; "Vodafone exits Japan and raises profit forecast," *BBC News*, November 9, 2010; "Fortune Global 500: China mobile communications," *Fortune*, 2015, http://fortune.com/global500/china-mobile-communications-55/; "Verizon sale cuts Vodafone value by half to $100 billion," *Bloomberg*, February 21, 2014.

1. Given the competitiveness of the environment, how much opportunity exists for Vodafone in the international cell phone market?

2. What type of generic strategy does Vodafone employ? Defend your answer.

3. What form of ownership arrangement is Vodafone using to gain world market share? Explain.

4. On what basis would a firm like Vodafone evaluate performance? Identify and describe two.

INTRODUCTION

In this chapter we provide an introduction to the key concepts of strategic management relevant to both MNEs and small and medium-size enterprises. We will review the rationale for strategic planning and the strategic orientation of firms (whether they are ethnocentric, polycentric, regiocentric, or geocentric). We will examine the process of strategy formulation and review the five forces of industry competitiveness. We then apply this thinking to analysis of a firm's value chain. We consider the basic generic strategies of firms. We apply these concepts to the implementation of strategy and discuss how this applies to different modes of entry, such as wholly owned subsidiaries, strategic alliances, and joint ventures. We will conclude with a section on the valuation of firm strategy and set the stage for discussion of relevant organization structures in Chapter 9.

Before becoming immersed in these details of strategic management, you should be aware of the linkages of strategy and structure to the previous work in this textbook discussing the theory of the MNE. In particular, the firm and country framework outlined in the opening chapters can be used to illustrate the special nature of strategic management as it applies to MNEs. In terms of the FSA and CSA matrix explained in Chapter 2, it is useful to review cells 1 and 4 at this juncture.

Cell 1 is a situation with low FSAs but strong CSAs. In terms of strategic management the firm will build competitive advantages due to its home-country CSAs. For example, firms from Canada will build CSAs based upon natural resources. They will exploit CSAs in the forest products sector, in minerals, and in cheap hydroelectric power. Firms from China will develop CSAs in manufacturing based upon cheap labor. Firms from India will develop CSAs in information technology based upon cheap skilled labor. Firms in the United States will develop economies of scale based upon the CSAs of its huge domestic market: such CSAs (in terms of scale economies) can then be exploited abroad. The challenge for MNEs is to combine the CSAs with strong FSAs, a situation in cell 3 of the FSA–CSA matrix. This chapter explores ways in which strategic management itself may be a type of FSA that can turn the CSAs of cell 1 into the combined country and firm advantages of cell 3.

In contrast, cell 4 of the FSA–CSA matrix is a situation of strong FSAs where these are independent of CSAs. This cell can best be described by the resource-based view (RBV) of strategy. The RBV is the basic theory of strategic management as explained in textbooks by Barney (2007), Grant (2008), Peng (2006), and Mintzberg et al. (1998). (These references are in the bibliography at the end of the chapter.) The core concept in the RBV is that a firm needs to develop a sustainable long-run competitive advantage, or capability. This is often called the core competence of the firm. In terms of international business, the core competence is identical to the concept of an FSA as discussed in earlier chapters. In other words, the RBV is simply a more detailed examination of the nature, extent, and strength of FSAs. The weakness of the pure RBV is that it is confined to cell 4 of the FSA–CSA matrix. In other words, it has no international component since CSAs are not relevant to a firm's success in cell 4.

Obviously, cell 3 of the FSA–CSA matrix is a most intriguing one. This is where country and firm effects are combined. Such complementary assets lie at the heart of the modern theory of the MNE in particular and international business in general. Cell 3 is a situation requiring the integration of firm and country advantages in a sustainable and long-run manner. In terms of the RBV, cell 3 is a situation requiring dynamic capabilities. In terms of mode of entry theory, it is a situation where network analysis can be applied to explain the generation of FSAs by subsidiaries within the network of the

MNE. Some cell 3 thinking can also be applied to analyze international joint ventures. But before proceeding to this depth of analysis, it is first necessary to review the basic issues of strategic management (in this chapter) and organization structure (in the following chapter). We will return to aspects of the RBV and the nature of location-bound or non-location-bound FSAs in Chapter 10 when we introduce the concept of national responsiveness.

Strategic planning
The process of evaluating the enterprise's environment and its internal strengths and then identifying long- and short-range activities

Strategic planning is the process of evaluating an enterprise's environment and internal strengths, identifying its basic mission and long- and short-range objectives, and implementing a plan of action for attaining these goals. MNEs rely heavily on this process because it provides them with both general direction and specific guidance in carrying out their activities. Without a strategic plan, these businesses would have great difficulty in planning, implementing, and evaluating operations. With strategic planning, however, research shows that many MNEs have been able to make adjustments in their approach to dealing with competitive situations and either redirect their efforts or exploit new areas of opportunity. For example, as a result of losing market share in Europe in recent years, General Motors cut its European capacity in an effort to stem further losses.[1] Meanwhile, Dell Computer expanded its international presence. In 2001 the company became the largest firm in the worldwide PC business, with a market share of 13 percent. On a different front, General Electric's strategy is to continue growing in spite of the European Commission's refusal to allow it to merge with Honeywell. GE Medical bought Data Critical, a maker of wireless and internet systems for communicating healthcare data; GE Industrial Systems acquired the Lentronics line of multiplexers from Nortel Networks; and GE Capital purchased Heller Financial, a company in the commercial financing, equipment leasing, and real estate finance business.[2] By carefully formulating their strategic plans, these MNEs are finding that they can better cope with the ever-changing challenge of worldwide competition.[3]

STRATEGIC ORIENTATIONS

Before examining the strategic planning process, we must realize that MNEs have strategic predispositions toward doing things in a particular way, which help determine the specific decisions the firm will implement. There are four such predispositions: ethnocentric, polycentric, regiocentric, and geocentric. Table 8.1 lists each predisposition and its characteristics.

Ethnocentric predisposition
The tendency of a manager or multinational company to rely on the values and interests of the parent company in formulating and implementing the strategic plan

An MNE with an **ethnocentric predisposition** will rely on the values and interests of the parent company in formulating and implementing the strategic plan. Primary emphasis will be given to profitability and the firm will try to run operations abroad the way they are run at home. Firms trying to sell the same product abroad that they sell at home use this predisposition most commonly.

Polycentric predisposition
The tendency of a multinational to tailor its strategic plan to meet the needs of the local culture

An MNE with a **polycentric predisposition** will tailor its strategic plan to meet the needs of the local culture. If the firm is doing business in more than one culture, the overall plan will be adapted to reflect these individual needs. The basic mission of a polycentric MNE is to be accepted by the local culture and to blend into the country. Each subsidiary will decide which objectives to pursue, based on local needs. Profits will be put back into the country in the form of expansion and growth.

Regiocentric predisposition
The tendency of a multinational to use a strategy that addresses both local and regional needs

An MNE with a **regiocentric predisposition** will be interested in obtaining both profit and public acceptance (a combination of the ethnocentric and polycentric approaches) and will use a strategy that allows it to address both local and regional needs. The company will be less focused on a particular country than on a geographic region. For example, an MNE doing business in the EU will be interested in all the member nations.

Table 8.1 Typical strategic orientations of MNEs

MNE orientation	Ethnocentric	Polycentric	Regiocentric	Geocentric
Company's basic mission	Profitability	Public acceptance (legitimacy)	Both profitability and public acceptance	Both profitability and public acceptance
Type of governance	Top down	Bottom up (each local unit sets objectives)	Mutually negotiated between the region and its subsidiaries	Mutually negotiated at all levels of the organization
Strategy	Global integration	National responsiveness	Regional integration and national responsiveness	Global integration and national responsiveness
Structure	Hierarchical product divisions	Hierarchical area divisions with autonomous national units	Product and regional organization tied together through a matrix structure	A network of organizations (in some cases this includes stockholders and competitors)
Culture	Host country	Home country	Regional	Global
Technology	Mass production	Batch production	Flexible manufacturing	Flexible manufacturing
Marketing strategy	Product development is determined primarily by the needs of the home-country customers	Local product development based on local needs	Standardized within the region, but not across regions	Global products with local variations
Profit strategy	Profits are brought back to the home country	Profits are kept in the host country	Profits are redistributed within the region	Redistribution is done on a global basis
Human resource management practices	Overseas operations are managed by people from the home country	Local nationals are used in key management positions	Regional people are developed for key managerial positions anywhere in the region	The best people anywhere in the world are developed for key positions everywhere in the world

Source: Adapted from "Strategic Planning for a Global Business," *Columbia Journal of World Business,* summer 1985. Copyright © Elsevier Science & Technology Journals. With permission from Elsevier Science.

Geocentric predisposition
The tendency of a multinational to construct its strategic plan with a global view of operations

An MNE with a **geocentric predisposition** will view operations on a global basis. The largest international corporations often use this approach. They produce global products with local variations and staff their offices with the best people they can find, regardless of country of origin. Multinationals, in the true meaning of the word, have a geocentric predisposition. However, it is possible for an MNE to have a polycentric or regiocentric predisposition if the company is moderately small or limits its operations to specific cultures or geographic regions.

The predisposition of an MNE will greatly influence its strategic planning process. For example, some MNEs are more interested in profit and/or growth than in developing a comprehensive corporate strategy that exploits their strengths.[4] Some are more interested in large-scale manufacturing that will allow them to compete on a price basis across the country or region, as opposed to developing a high degree of responsiveness to local demand and tailoring a product to these specific market niches.[5] Some prefer to sell in countries where the cultures are similar to their own so that the same basic marketing orientation can be used throughout the regions.[6] These orientations or predispositions greatly influence strategy.[7] For an example of strategic orientations, see the case **International Business Strategy in Action: The Big Four.**

INTERNATIONAL BUSINESS STRATEGY IN ACTION

The Big Four

The root of today's accountancy practices can be traced back to the Companies Act of 1900, a piece of legislation requiring all firms to undergo an annual audit, thus providing shareholders with a level of security that assertions about a company's financial performance were true and fair. Although accountancy was established as a profession by this time as a result of the growth of taxation since the turn of the nineteenth century, it was this legislation that really provided a level of consistency and allowed accountancy firms to flourish.

Unsurprisingly, the industry was quite fragmented, and despite many of the early firms hailing from Scotland, it wasn't long before London came to dominate. The 1920s and 1930s saw a series of mergers and acquisitions, and as there were fewer audits to be done, competition within the market increased, further polarizing the profession, which by this time was led by a handful of large firms. Since the 1960s further consolidation of the profession has resulted in the creation of the Big Four accountancy practices: PricewaterhouseCoopers, Deloitte, KPMG, and EY, which not only hold the top position in the UK market, but also have strong international networks enabling them to service clients across the globe. Table 8.2 illustrates the size of the Big Four in the UK versus globally in terms of revenue, highlighting the dominance of these firms at both a national and an international level.

Table 8.2 also shows a consistent pattern across all four in terms of the size of their UK operations relative to their global operations. All derive between 10 and 13 percent of global revenues from the UK market and employ between 6 and 9 percent of their overall employees in the UK. Although we could argue that PwC has a slightly larger dependency on the UK market, the difference is marginal.

Table 8.2 The Big Four

Firm	Global revenue (2014)	Worldwide staff	UK revenue (2014) (% of global)	UK staff (% of global)
Deloitte	$34.2bn	210,400	$3,914m (11%)	12,000 (6%)
EY	$27.4bn	188,292	$2,854m (10%)	12,000 (6%)
KPMG	$24.8bn	162,031	$2,876m (12%)	11,341 (7%)
PwC	$34.0bn	195,433	$4,319m (13%)	18,000 (9%)

Although by no means the only large accountancy practices, the Big Four are significantly larger than their peers with a combined UK fee income of over $13,650 million in 2015. The fee income of EY, the smallest of the group, came in at $2,790 million, in comparison to the Big Four's closest competitor, Grant Thornton, which raked in $772 million, and the Big Four firms typically have three times as many UK partners as their mid-tier counterparts. The contrast is evident, clearly distinguishing between the two levels of practices. Large accountancy practices, however, are fairly homogeneous in the services they provide to clients, and are typically comprised of Assurance (Audit), Taxation, and Advisory departments, although they also have more specialized sub-departments, such as Transaction Services and Insolvency.

In recent decades, the number of firms requiring an audit has undergone drastic change. In 1991, those with a turnover of less than £1 ($1.5) million were exempt, but this had leaped to over £5.5 ($8.3) million by 2004. The year 2009 saw the threshold raised to £6.5 ($9.75) million, before a dramatic increase in 2015 when the threshold reached £10.3 ($15.4) million. It is therefore no surprise that as fewer firms are required to undergo a statutory annual audit, the number of practices providing the service has decreased. In the half a decade to 2013, there was an 11.2 percent fall in the number of registered audit firms, and given that 98 percent of firms in the UK have a turnover of less than £10 ($15) million, the outlook for audit is rather bleak. Of those which are still in need of a statutory audit, many are of the size where only the Big Four firms have the scale and resources to carry it out.

With dwindling audit income, accountancy practices are looking to diversify their service offerings, and advisory work appears to offer the greatest opportunity for growth. Advisory work such as consultancy is typically more bespoke and is tailored to the individual client, and although overheads may increase as a result, this type of work is typically more profitable for the provider. It is therefore unsurprising that consulting services are expected to experience growth. The latest figures from Deloitte appear to confirm this, as the firm's UK practice saw consulting revenues increase by 10.5 percent on last year, in comparison to audit fees which rose by just 0.3 percent.

Not all consulting growth is organic, with over 150 mergers or acquisitions taking place in the first seven months of 2015, and in the past quarter of a decade the Big Four alone have been involved in 75 deals. Notably, PwC acquired Booz & Co. while Deloitte and EY have picked up firms such as

▶

MashUp and Silicon Roundabout respectively. KPMG has been particularly busy, accounting for 30 of these 75 deals, including its acquisitions of Boxwood and High-Point Rendel.

Many of these names, however, do not have a global reach, and although they add to the level of expertise of the Big Four, it remains to be seen to what extent they can help the Big Four to really dominate the global advisory and consulting sphere. With the Big Three, Bain & Co., Boston Consulting Group, and McKinsey & Co., dominating the management consulting industry, the Big Four currently appear to be very cautious in their deals, primarily opting for smaller, cutting-edge organizations specializing in innovative areas such as technology and analytics. With the economy picking up, the market seems to be big enough for everybody, and with the future for consulting looking bright, it will be very interesting to follow the progress of the Big Four. Whether or not they will one day rival the Big Three remains to be seen, but if recent M&A activity continues, and if the Big Four turn their attention to acquiring firms that will stretch their brand, it is certainly a possibility.

The Big Four have undoubtedly moved away from traditional accounting, and although they still provide standard services such as audit, they are constantly evolving and

developing new competencies; with fierce competition in the tier, innovation is obviously a differentiator for a firm. The development of consulting is not the only example of diversification, as recent years have also seen the development of legal services provisions enabled by the Legal Services Act of 2007, and firms are continually looking to expand their expertise and offerings. The Big Four are now undoubtedly multidisciplinary professional services firms, and they show no signs of stopping.

Sources: Liz Fisher, "Audit exemption threshold: what's the damage?," *ACCA*, November 25, 2015; Oliver Griffen, "Businesses want to raise audit threshold," *Economia*, April 30, 2015; Gavin Hinks, "Shrinking audit and KPMG SME offering means practice revolution," *Accountancy Age*, May 1, 2015; Richard Crump, "EY snaps up Silicon Roundabout firm in latest advisory push," *Accountancy Age*, August 18, 2015; Harriet Agnew, "Deloitte UK boosted by strong consulting growth," *Financial Times*, August 23, 2015; Margaret Cameron-Waller, "Opinion: consulting M&A deals among the Big Four could get big," *Accountancy Age*, July 20, 2015; "Attack of the bean-counters," *The Economist*, March 21, 2015; Statista, "Number of employees of the Big Four accounting/audit firms worldwide in 2015," 2015; PwC, *Annual Report*, 2014; PwC, *Facts and Figures*, 2015; PwC, *Global Annual Review*, 2015; Vincent Huck, "KPMG UK revenues up 5% but profits are down," *International Accounting Bulletin*, 18 December 2014; EY, "EY reports 2014 global revenues of US$27.4b," September 26, 2014, http://www.ey.com; Deloitte, "Deloitte announces record revenues of US$34.2 billion," 2015, http://www2.deloitte.com; "Top 50+50 Firms 2015", *Accountancy Age*, 2015; KPMG, *Annual Report*, 2014; "Business profile: Ernst & Young," *Telegraph*, May 19, 2014; Deloitte, "Deloitte UK," 2015, https://www.linkedin.com/company/deloitte-uk

STRATEGY FORMULATION

Strategy formulation
The process of evaluating the enterprise's environment and its internal strengths

Strategy formulation is the process of evaluating an enterprise's environment and internal strengths. This typically begins with consideration of the external arena, since the MNE will first be interested in opportunities that can be exploited. Attention is then directed to the internal environment and the resources the organization has available, or can develop, to take advantage of these opportunities.

External environmental assessment

The analysis of the external environment involves two activities: information gathering and information assessment. These steps help to answer two key questions: what is going on in the external environment; and how will these developments affect our company?[8]

Competitive intelligence
The gathering of external information on competitors and the competitive environment as part of the decision-making process

One of the most common ways to do this is through **competitive intelligence**, which is the use of systematic techniques for obtaining and analyzing public information about competitors. These data are particularly useful in keeping MNEs alert to likely moves by the competition.[9]

Information gathering

Information gathering is a critical phase of international strategic planning. Unfortunately, not all firms recognize this early enough. In the case of Harley-Davidson, the large US-based motorcycle manufacturer, it was not until the Japanese began dominating the motorcycle market that Harley realized its problem. A systematic analysis of the competition revealed that the major reason for Japanese success in the US market was the high quality of their products, a result of extremely efficient manufacturing techniques. Today, Harley is competitive again. It achieved renewed success because it rethought its basic business, reformulated company strategy, vastly improved product quality, and rededicated itself to its core business: heavyweight motorcycles.

There are a number of ways in which MNEs conduct an environmental scan and forecast the future. Four of the most common methods are: (1) asking industry experts to discuss industry trends and make projections about the future; (2) using historical industry trends to forecast future developments; (3) asking knowledgeable managers to write scenarios describing what they foresee for the industry over the next two to three years; and (4) using computers to simulate the industry environment and generate likely future developments. Of these, expert opinion is the most commonly used.[10] The Japanese and the South Koreans provide excellent examples. Mitsubishi has more than 700 employees in New York City, where its primary objective is to gather information on US competitors and markets. All large Japanese corporations operating in the United States employ similar strategies. The same is true for large South Korean trading firms, which require their branch managers to send back information on market developments. These data are then analyzed and used to help formulate future strategies for the firms.

Such information helps MNEs to identify competitor strengths and weaknesses and to target areas for attack. This approach is particularly important when a company is delivering a product or service for many market niches around the world that are too small to be individually profitable. In such situations the MNE has to identify a series of different niches and attempt to market successfully in each of these geographic areas.[11] The information is also critical to those firms that will be coming under attack.

Information assessment

Having gathered information on the competition and the industry, MNEs then evaluate the data. One of the most common approaches is to make an overall assessment based on the five forces that determine industry competitiveness: buyers, suppliers, potential new entrants to the industry, the availability of substitute goods and services, and rivalry among the competitors. Figure 8.1 shows the connections among these forces.[12]

Bargaining power of buyers

MNEs examine the power of their buyers in order to predict the likelihood of maintaining these customers. If the firm believes buyers may be moving their business to competitors,

Figure 8.1 The five forces of industry competitiveness

the MNE will want to formulate a strategy for countering this move. For example, the company may offer a lower price or increase the amount of service it provides.

Bargaining power of suppliers

An MNE looks at the power of the industry's suppliers to see if it can gain a competitive advantage here.[13] For example, if there are a number of suppliers in the industry, the MNE may attempt to play them off against one another in an effort to get a lower price. Or the company may move to eliminate any threat from the suppliers by acquiring one of them, thus guaranteeing itself a ready source of inputs.

New entrants

The company will examine the likelihood of new firms entering the industry and will try to determine the impact they might have on the MNE. Two typical ways that international MNEs attempt to reduce the threat of new entrants are by (1) keeping costs low and consumer loyalty high, and (2) encouraging the government to limit foreign business activity through regulation such as duties, tariffs, quotas, and other protective measures.

Threat of substitutes

The MNE looks at the availability of substitute goods and services, and tries to anticipate when such offerings will reach the market. There are a number of steps the company can take to offset this competitive force, including (1) lowering prices, (2) offering similar products, and (3) increasing services to the customer.

Rivalry

The MNE examines the rivalry that exists between itself and the competition and seeks to anticipate future changes in this arrangement. Common strategies for maintaining and/or increasing market strength include (1) offering new goods and services, (2) increasing productivity and thus reducing overall costs, (3) working to differentiate current goods and services from those of the competition, (4) increasing overall quality of goods and services, and (5) targeting specific niches with a well-designed market strategy.

As the MNE examines each of these five forces, it must decide the attractiveness and unattractiveness of each. This will help decide how and where to make strategic changes. Figure 8.2 shows the five-forces model applied to the semiconductor industry.

Notice in Figure 8.2 that at the time this analysis was conducted, the suppliers in the semiconductor industry were not very powerful, so they were an attractive force for the MNE. Buyers did not have many substitute products from which to choose (an attractive development), but there was some backward integration toward purchasing their own sources of supply (an unattractive development). Overall, the attractiveness of buyer power was regarded as inconclusive. The third force, entry barriers, was quite attractive because of the high costs of getting into the industry and the short product life cycles that existed there. It was very difficult for a company to enter this market. The fourth force, substitutes, was unattractive because new products were being developed continually and customer loyalty was somewhat low. The fifth and final force, industry rivalry, was also unattractive because of the high cost of doing business, the cyclical nature of sales, and the difficulty of differentiating one's products from those of the competition.

On an overall basis, however, the industry was classified as attractive. It also appeared that the industry would see consolidation of smaller firms into larger firms that would have greater resources to commit to research and development.

MNEs operating in the semiconductor industry would use this analysis to help them increase the attractiveness of those forces that currently are not highly attractive. For example, they could work to develop state-of-the-art semiconductors that might be substituted

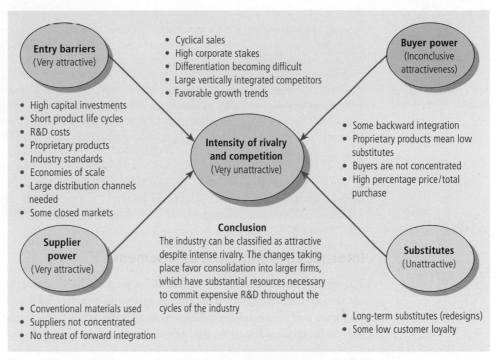

Figure 8.2 The five-forces model applied to the semiconductor industry

Source: Scott Beardsley and Kinji Sakagami, "Advanced micro devices: poised for chip greatness," unpublished student paper, Sloan School of Management, MIT, 1988. Reported in Arnoldo C. Hax and Nicolas S. Majluf, *The Strategy Concept and Process: A Pragmatic Approach* (Englewood Cliffs, NJ: Prentice Hall, 1991), p. 46.

for the competition's products, and they would attempt to maintain a technological advantage so that the substitute force would not become a problem for them. In the process, they would likely be better able to increase their power over the buyers since their products would be so high-tech that the customers could not do better by purchasing from a competitor. In summary, environmental assessment, such as that provided by an analysis of competitive forces, is used to determine MNE opportunities and threats, and to help identify strategies for improving market position and profitability.

 Active learning check

Review your answer to Active Learning Case question 1 and make any changes you like. Then compare your answer to the one below.

1 **Given the competitiveness of the environment, how much opportunity exists for Vodafone in the international cell phone market?**

As seen from the case data, the international opportunities in this industry are great. One reason is because the market is going to continue growing and updating itself with new technology that may allow Vodafone to increase its revenue per subscriber and carve itself a larger portion of the market. The number of cell phone users in the United States has increased sharply in the recent past, following the trajectory of Europe. New technology will allow for expansion in all three triad markets. The key to success in this industry is to have a presence in all major markets. China is an important market because of its large population and high average usage of mobile services, but the market is highly competitive and customers favor local mobile companies. In 2010, Vodafone sold its 3.2 percent stake of investment to the joint

▶

venture partner China Mobile. However, other emerging markets also represent opportunities for Vodafone. In 2003, Mobile signed a partner network with M1, one of the largest mobile companies in Singapore and a similar partner network agreement with Telekom Malaysia in 2006. In addition, Australia and New Zealand are important target markets. Finally, adoption in African counties is also growing rapidly, partly on the back of financial services such as M-Pesa. M-Pesa ("M" is for mobile, Pesa is Swahili for money) is Vodafone's mobile money transfer service which avoids the need for banks. It began in 2007 in Kenya and expanded across other parts of the continent (South Africa in 2010, Egypt in 2013) and beyond (India in 2013, Romania in 2014, and Albania in 2015). It points the way for Vodafone, not just in terms of future profitability, more of which will come from mobile services which add value to customers, but also in terms of the positive contribution the firm can make to supporting and enabling the poorest communities on the planet.

Internal environmental assessment

The internal environmental assessment helps pinpoint MNE strengths and weaknesses. There are two specific areas that a multinational should examine in this assessment: (1) physical resources and personnel competencies; and (2) the way in which value chain analysis can be used to bring these resources together in the most synergistic and profitable manner.

Physical resources and personnel competencies

The physical resources are the assets that the MNE will use to carry out its strategic plan. Many of these are reported on the balance sheet as reflected by cash, inventory, machinery, and equipment accounts. However, this does not tell the whole story. The location and disposition of these resources is also important. For example, an MNE with manufacturing plants on three continents may be in a much better position to compete worldwide than a competitor whose plants are all located in one geographic area. Location can also affect cost. In the 1980s it was possible for Japanese steelmakers to sell their products in the United States at lower prices than their US competitors. During the 1990s US firms improved their steel-producing technology and erected small mini-mills that were highly efficient, thus offsetting the location advantage of their foreign competitors. By 2000, European steelmakers, in particular, had sharply increased their efficiency and, along with Japanese firms, were able to compete in the US market.[14] Between 1997 and 2003, 41 US steel firms went bankrupt, which led the industry to lobby the US government for protection from imports. In 2002, tariffs of 8–30 percent were imposed on imports from most countries to help the US industry restructure.[15] These were removed in 2003, after complaints by other countries to the WTO. Facing increased competition from China and other Asian economies, in 2007 EU steel firms filed a complaint with the European Commission, seeking duties to be placed on goods imported from China, Taiwan, and South Korea. The European Confederation of Iron and Steel Industries (EUROFER) said the EU market had been "inundated" by imports. As a result EU prices had been undercut "by up to 25%" and threatened thousands of jobs. By 2014 China was by far the largest producer of crude steel (just under 50 percent of global production) and the biggest exporter.[16]

Another important consideration is the degree of integration that exists within the operating units of the MNE. Large companies, in particular, tend to be divided into **strategic business units (SBUs)**. These are operating units with their own strategic space that produce and sell goods and services to a market segment and have a well-defined set of competitors.[17] SBUs are sometimes referred to as "businesses within the business." Mitsubishi, the giant Japanese conglomerate, has a host of SBUs that constitute its corporate network, including steelmaking, auto production, electronics, and banking. So when a Mitsubishi

Strategic business units (SBUs)
Operating units with their own strategic space; they produce and sell goods and services to a market segment and have a well-defined set of competitors

SBU that manufactures and sells consumer goods is looking for help with financing, it can turn to the banking SBU. If the bank finds that a customer needs a firm to produce a particular electronics product, it can refer the buyer to the electronics SBU.

Vertical integration
The ownership of assets involved in producing a good or service and delivering it to the final customer

In fact, some large MNEs use **vertical integration**, which is the ownership of all assets needed to produce the goods and services delivered to the customer. Many large Japanese manufacturing firms, in particular, have moved toward vertical integration by purchasing controlling interests in their suppliers.[18] The objective is to obtain control over the supply and thus ensure that the materials or goods are delivered as needed. Many US and European firms have shied away from this strategy because "captured suppliers" are often less cost effective than independents. For example, a number of years ago *Time* magazine owned the forests for producing the paper it needed. However, the company eventually sold this resource because it found that the cost of making the paper was higher than that charged by large paper manufacturers that specialized in this product. So vertical integration may reduce costs in some instances, but it can be an ineffective strategy in others.[19] A particular problem with vertical integration is defending oneself from competitors which are less vertically integrated and are able to achieve cost efficiencies as a result. The latter rely heavily on outsourcers and employ **virtual integration**, which is the ownership of the core technologies and manufacturing capabilities needed to produce outputs coupled with dependence on outsourcers to provide all other needed inputs. Virtual integration allows an MNE to operate as if it were vertically integrated, but it does not require the company to own all the factors of production, as is the case with vertically integrated firms.

Virtual integration
A networking strategy based on cooperation within and across company boundaries

Personnel competencies are the abilities and talents of the people. An MNE should examine these because they reflect many of the company's strengths and weaknesses. For example, if an MNE has an outstanding R&D department, it may be able to develop high-quality, state-of-the-art products. However, if the company has no sales arm, it will sell the output to a firm that can handle the marketing and distribution. Conversely, if a company lacks a strong R&D department but has an international sales force, it may allow the competition to bring out new products and to rely on its own R&D people to reverse-engineer them—that is, to find out how they are built and develop technologies that can do the same thing—while relying on the sales force to build market share. This strategy has been used by many internationally based personal computer (PC) firms that have taken PC technology and used it to develop similar but far less expensive units that are now beginning to dominate the world market.

An understanding of what a company does well can help it decide whether the best strategy is to lead or to follow close behind and copy the leader. Not every MNE has the personnel competencies to be first in the field, and many are happy to follow because the investment risk is less and the opportunity for profit is often good.

Value chain analysis

Value chain
The way in which primary and support activities are combined in providing goods and services and increasing profit margins

A complementary approach to internal environment assessment is an examination of the firm's value chain.[20] A **value chain** is the way in which primary and support activities are combined to provide goods and services and increase profit margins. Figure 8.3 provides the general schema of a value chain. The primary activities in this chain include: (1) inbound logistics, such as receiving, storing, materials handling, and warehouse activities; (2) operations, in which inputs are put into final product form by performing activities such as machining, assembling, testing, and packaging; (3) outbound logistics, which involve distributing the finished product to the customer; (4) marketing and sales, which are used to encourage buyers to purchase the product; and (5) service for maintaining and enhancing the value of the product after the sale through activities such as repair, product adjustment, training, and parts supply. The support activities in the value chain consist of: (1) the firm's infrastructure, which is made up of the company's general management, planning, finance,

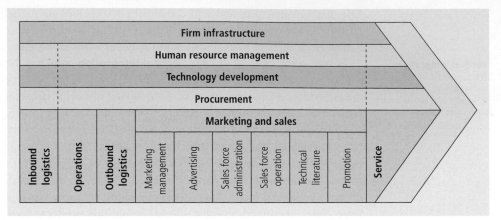

Figure 8.3 A basic value chain

Source: Adapted with the permission of The Free Press, an imprint of Simon & Schuster Adult Publishing Group, from *Competitive Advantage: Creating and Sustaining Superior Performance* by Michael E. Porter. Copyright © 1985, 1998 by Michael E. Porter. All rights reserved.

accounting, legal, government affairs, and quality management areas; (2) human resource management, which is made up of the selection, placement, appraisal, promotion, training, and development of the firm's personnel; (3) technology in the form of knowledge, research and development, and procedures that can result in improved goods and services; and (4) procurement, which involves the purchasing of raw materials, supplies, and similar goods.

MNEs can use these primary and support activities to increase the value of the goods and services they provide. As such, they form a value chain. Any firm can apply this idea of a value chain. For example, Makita of Japan has become a leading competitor in power tools for professional users worldwide because it was the first to use new, less expensive materials for making tool parts and to produce in standardized models. As of 2014, the company had 11 production bases, two located in each of Japan and China, and one each in the United States, Brazil, Canada, Mexico, the United Kingdom, Germany, and Romania. It then sold worldwide. During the fiscal year ended March 31, 2015, approximately 83.7 percent of Makita's sales were outside of Japan, most of them made to professional users worldwide, including those engaged in timber and metal processing, carpentry, forestry, and concrete and masonry works. During fiscal 2014 the organization acquired revenue of ¥414,718 million ($3.4 million), where Makita's primary products were power tools such as drills, rotary hammers, hammer drills, demolition hammers, grinders, and cordless impact drivers. Sales of these products accounted for more than 70 percent of Makita's total net sales.

Analysis of the value chain can also help a company determine the type of strategy that will be most effective. In all, there are three generic strategies: cost, differentiation, and focus.

Cost strategy
A strategy that relies on low price and is achieved through approaches such as vigorous pursuit of cost reductions and overhead control, avoidance of marginal customer accounts, and cost minimization in areas such as sales and advertising

1 **Cost strategy** relies on such approaches as aggressive construction of efficient facilities, vigorous pursuit of cost reductions and overhead control, avoidance of marginal customer accounts, and cost minimization in areas like R&D, service, sales, and advertising.

Differentiation strategy
A strategy directed toward creating something that is perceived as being unique

2 **Differentiation strategy** is directed toward creating something that is perceived as being unique. Approaches to differentiation can take many forms, including the creation of design or brand image, improved technology or features, and increased customer service or dealer networks.

Focus strategy
A strategy that concentrates on a particular buyer group and segments that niche based on product line or geographic market

3 **Focus strategy** involves concentrating on a particular buyer group and segmenting that niche based on product line or geographic market.

While low-cost and differentiation strategies are aimed at achieving objectives industrywide, a focus strategy is built around servicing a particular target market, and each functional policy is developed with this in mind.[21]

Figure 8.4 Generic strategies in worldwide shipbuilding

Competitive scope
The breadth of a firm's target market within an industry

In addition, the firm will determine its **competitive scope**, which is the breadth of its target market within the industry. Figure 8.4 provides an example of these generic strategies as applied to the worldwide shipbuilding industry.

The value chain can help an MNE create synergies within the organization's activities. For example, by combining the human resource talent of their sales people with the expertise of their design and styling personnel, firms like PSA Peugeot Citroën and Volkswagen have been able to increase their auto market share in western Europe in recent years.[22] In particular, Peugeot and VW have been able to cut costs and offer a wide range of new models. Their overall success is found in their ability to manage the flow of new products, so that the offerings remain reasonably fresh without spending money on excessive investment in updates or redesign. Firms that cannot get this aspect of the product cycle correct have been falling behind in the European market, as seen by Ford, General Motors, and, most significantly, Renault.[23] Simply put, by analyzing the ways of combining their primary and support activities, some automotive MNEs have been able to create a strategy that allows them to draw heavily on their strengths while minimizing their weaknesses.[24]

✔ Active learning check

Review your answer to Active Learning Case question 2 and make any changes you like. Then compare your answer to the one below.

2 **What type of generic strategy does Vodafone employ? Defend your answer.**

Vodafone uses a focus strategy that is geared toward identifying market niches and meeting the needs of the mobile customers in these target groups. Notice that in the earlier phase of growth it was comfortable with acquisitions which left it with a minority shareholding (a 35 percent stake in Verizon, for example). From 2014 onwards it wanted to be the major stakeholder, but also to have a partner which can help the company deal with the challenges in the local market. As the case notes, the company held over 50 percent of the shares in most of the European countries in which it operates and sold its minority stake in Verizon in the United States in 2014. Another generic strategy has been to pay for its acquisitions through equity, which saved it from the technology crash of the early 2000s and subsequent financial challenges. So the company targets selected markets in which there is little risk and provides innovative products at competitive prices in order to compete effectively.

Table 8.3 Typical goals of an MNE

Profitability	Marketing	Production	Finance	Human resource management
Level of products	Total sales volume	Ratio of foreign to domestic production share	Financing of foreign affiliates—retained earnings or local borrowing	Development of managers with global orientation
Return on assets, investment, equity, sales	Market share—worldwide, region, country	Economies of scale via international production integration	Taxation—minimizing the burden globally	Management development of host-country nationals
Annual profit growth	Growth in sales volume	Quality and cost control	Optimum capital structure	
Annual earnings per share growth	Integration of country markets for marketing efficiency and effectiveness	Introduction of cost-efficient production methods	Foreign exchange management—minimizing losses from foreign fluctuations	

Source: Adapted from *International Dimensions of Management*, 2nd ed., by A. Phatak © 1989 South-Western, a part of Cengage. Reprinted by permission www.cengage.com/permissions/

Goal setting

External and internal environmental analyses provide an MNE with the information needed for setting goals. Some of these goals will be determined during the external analysis, as the company identifies opportunities it wants to exploit. Others will be finalized after the value chain analysis is complete. In either event, one of the outcomes of strategy formulation will be the identification of goals.[25]

There are two basic ways of examining the goals or objectives of international business operations. One is to review them on the basis of operating performance or functional area. Table 8.3 provides an illustration. Some of the major goals are related to profitability, marketing, production, finance, and human resources. A second way is to examine these goals by geographic area, or on an SBU basis. For example, the European group may have a profitability goal of 16 percent, the North American group's profitability goal may be 17 percent, and the Pacific Rim group may aim for 18 percent. Then there are accompanying functional goals for marketing, production, and finance. If the MNE has SBUs, each SBU in these geographic locales will have its own list of goals.

This approach uses what is called a "cascading effect"—like a cascade of water rippling down the side of a hill, it reaches the bottom by moving from one level to the next. The MNE starts out by setting a profitability goal for the overall enterprise. Each geographic area or business unit is then assigned a profitability goal that, if attained, will result in the MNE reaching its overall desired profitability. The same approach is used in other key areas such as marketing, production, and finance. Within each unit, these objectives are further subdivided so that every part of the organization understands its objectives and everyone is working toward the same overall goals.

STRATEGY IMPLEMENTATION

Strategy implementation
The process of attaining goals by using the organizational structure to execute the formulated strategy properly

Strategy implementation is the process of attaining goals by using the organization structure to execute the formulated strategy properly. There are many areas of focus in this process. Three of the most important are location, ownership decisions, and functional area implementation. The case **International Business Strategy in Action: Fuji Xerox and Xerox** illustrates how these considerations can be used in gaining market entry.[26]

Location

MNEs have greatly expanded their international presence over the past decade. Some of the areas in which they have begun to set up operations include China, the former Soviet Union, and eastern Europe.

Location is important for a number of reasons. Local facilities often provide a cost advantage to the producer, particularly when the raw materials, parts, or labor needed to make the product can be inexpensively obtained close to the facility. Location is also important because residents may prefer locally produced goods. For example, many people in the United States like to "buy American." Some locations may also be attractive because the local government is encouraging investment through various means such as low tax rates, free land, subsidized energy and transportation rates, and low-interest loans while subjecting imported goods to tariffs, quotas, or other governmental restrictions, thereby making local manufacture more desirable. Finally, the MNE may already be doing so much business in a country that the local government will insist that it set up local operations and begin producing more of its goods there. This is a major reason why Japanese auto manufacturers began to establish operations in the United States.

INTERNATIONAL BUSINESS STRATEGY IN ACTION

Fuji Xerox and Xerox

Fuji Xerox was created in 1962 as a 50/50 joint venture between UK-based Rank Xerox and Fujifilm Holdings Corporation. It is regarded as the most successful partnership between US and Japanese firms. The arrangement developed from a sales operation for Xerox products in Japan into a fully integrated organization with its own R&D and manufacturing. By 1990, Fuji Xerox revenues were $4 billion and the company had a world product mandate to supply the entire Xerox Group with the low- to mid-range copiers that were the core of its business. Indeed, as Xerox's monopoly on large copiers began to dwindle in the 1970s, it was its Japanese partner, Fuji Xerox, that rode to the rescue with its new, high-quality smaller copiers.

In 1975, Xerox was forced by the US Federal Trade Commission to license its original core copier technology to rivals such as IBM, Kodak, Ricoh, and Canon. If it had not been for Fuji Xerox developing new copier technology, Xerox would have failed. The firm's early monopoly in the world copier business was eroded sharply by intense rivalry from Japanese competitors such as Canon and Ricoh as well as from Kodak and IBM. These rivals produced higher-quality, lower-priced, more technologically advanced, and more reliable copiers than Xerox.

When Fuji Xerox recognized the threat, its managers, acting autonomously, started R&D into new small copiers. The US head office was slow to take on board the technology and products of its Japanese partner. Loss of market share, however, especially to Canon, eventually led to ever-closer degrees of cooperation between Xerox and Fuji Xerox. In par-

ticular, the high quality standards of Fuji Xerox were spread throughout the Xerox Group, and its total quality management (TQM) techniques helped Xerox regain market. In this context, Xerox was helped by a partner that was the hotbed of TQM and copier innovation in the 1970s and 1980s.

One of the reasons for success in the collaboration between Xerox and Fuji Photo Films was that the latter acted as a silent partner in the 50/50 joint venture and allowed Fuji Xerox to develop its own management cadre, who became skilled in R&D and copier technology and in the manufacturing and marketing of small copiers. Fuji Xerox also transformed itself from a marketing subsidiary into a full-line business, thus ending up being more innovative and responsive to the market than Xerox itself.

In 2009, Fuji Xerox had revenues totaling US$11.080 billion with 40,646 employees. For its part, in 2014 Xerox's revenues totaled $19,540 million with over 100,000 employees. For the year ended March 31, 2014, Fujifilm Holdings Corporation reported revenue of US$20.23 billion (¥2,440.0 billion) and 78,595 employees. Fujifilm owned 75 percent of the company and Xerox owned the remaining 25 percent.

Websites: www.fujixerox.co.jp; www.xerox.com; www.fujifilm.com

Sources: Adapted from Benjamin Gomes-Casseres and Krista McQuade, *Xerox and Fuji Xerox*, Harvard Business School Case 9–391–156; David T. Kearns and David A. Nadler, *Prophets in the Dark: How Xerox Reinvented Itself and Beat Back the Japanese* (New York: Macmillan, 1992); Benjamin Gomes-Casseres, "Group Versus Group: How Alliance Networks Compete," *Harvard Business Review* (July/August 1994), pp. 62–74; www.hoovers.com; FujiFilm Holdings Corporation, *Annual Report*, 2010, 2014; Xerox, *Annual Report*, 2009, 2014.

Although the benefits can be great, a number of drawbacks are associated with locating operations overseas. One is an unstable political climate that can leave an MNE vulnerable to low profits and bureaucratic red tape. In Russia, for example, the government has encouraged joint ventures, but because of political and economic uncertainty many business people currently regard such investments as high-risk ventures. A second drawback is the possibility of revolution or armed conflict. MNEs with operations in Kuwait lost just about all of their investment in the Gulf War, and MNEs with locales in Saudi Arabia and other Middle East countries affected by the Gulf War also withstood losses in the region. Most recently, businesses in areas targeted by international terrorists have been making plans to reduce their risks. In some cases, firms are finding a way to "hedge their bets," as noted in the following example:

> Some . . . opt for locales where the cost of running a small enterprise is significantly lower than that of running a large one. In this way they spread their risk, setting up many small locations throughout the world rather than one or two large ones. Manufacturing firms are a good example. Some production firms feel that the economies of scale associated with a large-scale plant are more than offset by the potential problems that can result, should economic or political difficulties develop in the country. These firms' strategy is to spread the risk by opting for a series of small plants spread throughout a wide geographic region.[27]

Ownership

Ownership of international operations has become an important issue in recent years. Many Americans, for example, believe that the increase in foreign-owned businesses in the United States is weakening the economy. People in other countries have similar feelings about US businesses there. In truth, the real issue of ownership is whether or not the company is contributing to the overall economic good of the country where it is doing business. As one researcher noted, "because the US-owned corporation is coming to have no special relationship with Americans, it makes no sense for the United States to entrust its national competitiveness to it. The interests of American-owned corporations may or may not coincide with those of the American people."[28] Countries that want to remain economically strong must be able to attract international investors who will provide jobs that allow their workers to increase their skills and build products that are demanded on the world market. In accomplishing this objective, firms often engage in strategic alliances.

Strategic alliances

Sometimes companies prefer to invest in another country and maintain 100 percent ownership. This, however, is often very expensive and risky. Given that the MNE may not have much experience in that particular marketplace, local partners may be very helpful in dealing with all sorts of local barriers. As a result, it is becoming increasingly popular to find MNEs turning to the use of strategic partnerships. A strategic alliance or partnership is an agreement between two or more competitive MNEs for the purpose of cooperating in some manner in serving a global market.[29] The type of cooperation can be in marketing, research, or a more comprehensive manner. In recent years these partnerships have become increasingly popular,[30] although careful management of such agreements continues to be a critical area of concern.[31] An example of a strategic partnership is that of Matsushita Electric Industrial and Hitachi, Japan's two leading electronics manufacturers. These companies have jointly developed state-of-the-art technology in three areas: smart cards, home network systems, and recyclable and energy-efficient consumer electronics. In the past, both firms have developed their own products, but now they are turning to a strategic partnership to save money and shorten development time.[32] Another example of strategic partnerships is that between IBM and NTT. Under the terms of their agreement at the turn of the century, IBM provided outsourcing services to NTT, Japan's dominant telecommunications carrier. In turn, IBM was able to use NTT Comware staff in outsourcing and obtaining computer service contracts with other customers in Japan.[33]

International joint ventures

An **international joint venture (IJV)** is an agreement between two or more partners to own and control an overseas business.[34] This is a special type of a strategic alliance that involves setting up a new business entity, generally involving management separate from that of the partners' own management teams. IJVs take a number of different forms[35] and offer myriad opportunities.[36] One of these reasons is government encouragement and legislation designed to make it attractive for foreign investors to bring in local partners. A second reason is the growing need for partners which know the local economy, the culture, and the political system and which can cut through red tape in getting things done—something IJVs often do very well.[37] Indeed, IJVs are often the result of two or more companies identifying the potential for "synergies," wherein each partner brings to the venture what the other partner needs but is lacking in. For example, an MNE might provide a local partner with technology know-how and an infusion of capital that, in turn, will allow the local firm to expand operations, raise market share, and begin exporting. An example is Toyota and PSA Peugeot Citroën, which entered into an IJV to jointly develop and build a small, fuel-efficient car for the European market. The primary benefit for Toyota is the opportunity to expand its model line-up in Europe. The major advantage for Peugeot is that of gaining a new small car for its European product line while sharing the development costs with Toyota.[38]

Unfortunately, in many cases IJVs have not worked out well. Several studies found a failure rate of 30 percent for ventures in developed countries and 45–50 percent in less developed countries.[39] The major reason has been the desire by foreign MNEs to control local operation, which sometimes has resulted in poor decision making and/or conflicts with the local partners. In general, joint ventures are difficult to manage and are frequently unstable.[40] This issue of joint ventures and alliances is discussed further in Chapter 22 under the flagship firm analysis of business networks.

International joint venture (IJV)
An agreement between two or more partners to own and control an overseas business

 Active learning check

Review your answer to Active Learning Case question 3 and make any changes you like. Then compare your answer to the one below.

3 **What form of ownership arrangement is Vodafone using to gain world market share? Explain.**

Vodafone uses two basic approaches, but it is important to note that its strategy regarding ownership has changed a number of times during its growth. The most common approach is the international joint venture, which is seen by the company's decisions to acquire an ownership position in a local company but have a local partner hold the remainder of the ownership. Its minority stake in Verizon Wireless, which became the largest US mobile telephone operator in America, illustrates this. In some cases, however, Vodafone opts for total ownership and purchases the entire company, usually when it believes it does not need a local partner. An example is AirTouch Communications, where Vodafone acquired the entire firm. In both cases, of course, the ownership arrangement is designed to help Vodafone continue to increase its market share in that geographic region.

Functional strategies

Functional strategies are used to coordinate operations and ensure that the plan is carried out properly.[41] The specific functions that are key to the success of the MNE will vary, but they typically fall into six major areas: marketing, manufacturing, finance, procurement, technology, and human resources. For purposes of analysis, they can be examined in terms of three major considerations: marketing, manufacturing, and finance.

Marketing

The marketing strategy is designed to identify consumer needs and formulate a plan of action for selling the desired goods and services to these customers.[42] Most marketing strategies are built around what are commonly known as the "four Ps" of marketing: product, price, promotion, and place. The company identifies the products that are in demand in the market niches it is pursuing. It apprises the manufacturing department of any modifications required to meet local needs, and it determines the price at which the goods can be sold. Then the company devotes its attention to promoting the products and selling them in the local market.

Manufacturing

Designed to fit together with the marketing plan, the manufacturing strategy ensures that the right products are built and delivered in time for sale. Manufacturing also coordinates its strategy with the procurement and technology people to ensure that the desired materials are available and the products have the necessary state-of-the-art quality. If the MNE is producing goods in more than one country, it gives attention to coordinating activities where needed. For example, some firms manufacture goods in two or more countries, then assemble and sell them in other geographic regions. Japanese auto firms send car parts to the United States for assembly and then sell some of the assembled cars in Canada, Mexico, and South America. Whirlpool builds appliances worldwide with operations in Brazil, Canada, Mexico, the Netherlands, and seven other countries. Such production and assembly operations have to be coordinated carefully.[43]

Finance

Financial strategy often serves to both lead and lag the other functional strategies. In the lead position, finance limits the amounts of money that can be spent on marketing (new product development, advertising, promotion) and manufacturing (machinery, equipment, quality control) to ensure that the desired return on investment is achieved. In the lag position, the financial strategy is used to evaluate performance and provide insights into how future strategy should be changed.

Financial strategies used to be formulated and controlled out of the home office. In recent years, however, MNEs have learned that this approach can be cumbersome and, due to fluctuating currency prices, costly as well. Today's overseas units have more control over their finances than before, but they are guided by a carefully constructed budget that is in accord with the overall strategic plan. They are also held to account for financial performance in the form of return on investment, profit, capital budgeting, debt financing, and working capital management.

CONTROL AND EVALUATION

The strategy formulation and implementation processes are subject to control and evaluation. This process involves examining the MNE's performance to determine (1) how well the organization has done and (2) what actions should be taken in light of this performance. This process is tied directly to the overall strategy in that the objectives serve as the basis for comparison and evaluation.[44] Figure 8.5 illustrates how this process works.

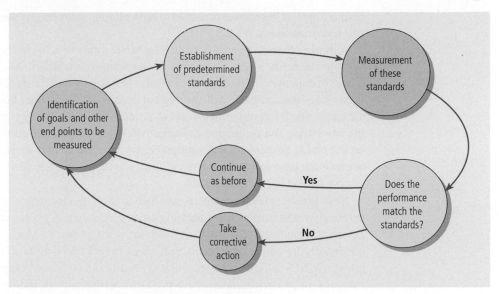

Figure 8.5 The control and evaluation process

If the comparison and evaluation show that the SBU or overseas operation is performing according to expectations, then things will continue as before. The objectives may be altered because of changes in the strategic plan, but otherwise nothing major is likely to be done. On the other hand, if there have been problems, the MNE will want to identify the causes and work to eliminate or minimize them.[45] Similarly, if the unit has performed extremely well and achieved more than forecasted, management may want to reset the objectives to a higher level because there is obviously greater market demand than was believed initially. In making these decisions, the company uses a variety of measures. Some are highly quantitative and depend on financial and productivity performance; others are more qualitative and judgmental in nature. The following discussion examines six of the most common methods of measurement used for control and evaluation purposes.

Common methods of measurement

Return on investment (ROI)
A percentage determined by dividing net income before taxes by total assets

Specific measures will vary depending on the nature of the MNE and the goals it has established. However, **return on investment (ROI)**, which is measured by dividing net income before taxes by the costs of investment, is a major consideration in most cases. There are a number of reasons why ROI is so popular as a control and evaluation measure: (1) it is a single comprehensive result that is influenced by everything that happens in the business; (2) it measures how well the managers in every part of the world are using the investments at their command; and (3) it allows a comparison of results among units in the same country as well as on an intercountry basis. Of course, there are shortcomings as well: (1) if one unit is selling goods to another unit, the ROI of the former is being artificially inflated; (2) the ROI in a growing market will be higher than that in markets that are just getting off the ground or are maturing, so that a comparison of the ROI performance between units can be misleading; and (3) the ROI is a short-term measure of performance that, if relied on too heavily, will not help managers develop the necessary long-term time horizons. Despite these shortcomings, however, ROI remains a major measure of performance.

Another measure is sales growth and/or market share. Units are given sales targets that usually require greater sales this year than last year. If the firm has made an estimate of the total demand, a market share figure accompanies the sales target for two reasons: (1) the MNE wants to increase its sales; and (2) the firm at least wants to maintain, if not increase, market share. If the market is judged to be declining, sales targets are lowered but the MNE still tries to maintain market share.

A third performance area is costs. The MNE wants to achieve increased sales and market share at as low a cost as possible. It also wants to maintain close control of production costs. So expenses are monitored carefully. This is particularly important in declining markets, where the company will want to cut costs as sales decline. For example, if an MNE estimates that it has only three years of product life in the market, it is likely that much of the advertising and promotion expenses will be dropped as the company focuses attention on supplying an ever-decreasing number of customers. This strategy is often successful because the remaining customers are highly loyal and do not need promotional efforts to convince them to buy the product.

New product development is another area of performance measure. This area is extremely important for firms that rely on new offerings. A good example is Nintendo, the Japanese manufacturer of such well-known video games as Mario Brothers, which must continually introduce new product offerings in order to maintain market share and sales growth. MNEs in high-tech areas such as electronic goods and computers also fall into this category. In an environment where product improvement or innovation is critical to success, new product development is a key area for control and evaluation.

MNE/host-country relations are another performance area that must be evaluated. Overseas units have to work within the cultural and legal framework of the host country. Many attempt to do this by blending into the community, hiring local managers and employees, adapting their product to the demands of that market, reinvesting part (if not all) of their profits back into the country, and working to improve the area's economic conditions. As a result, they get on well in the country and there are no problems with the government or other local groups. One thing MNEs know from long experience is that poor host-country relations can seriously endanger profits and even result in a loss of invested capital.

Finally, management performance must be considered. In rating this criterion, the MNE considers two types of measures: quantitative and qualitative. In the quantitative area, in addition to those discussed above, other common considerations include return on invested capital and cash flow. In the qualitative area, in addition to host-country relations, consideration is given to relations with the home office, the leadership qualities of the unit's managers, how well the unit is building a management team, and how well the managers of the unit have implemented the assigned strategy.

These methods of measurement are used in arriving at an overall assessment of the unit's performance. Based on the results, the MNE can then set new goals and the international strategic planning process begins anew.

Active learning check

Review your answer to Active Learning Case question 4 and make any changes you like. Then compare your answer to the one below.

4 On what basis would a firm like Vodafone evaluate performance? Identify and describe two.

Vodafone uses a number of bases on which to evaluate performance. One is market share. Note that the firm keeps track of how many subscribers it has by multiplying its ownership position in a venture by the venture's total subscription base. Another is overall worldwide market share. Finally, the firm evaluates its performance by its success in setting a footprint in all major markets.

KEY POINTS

1 Strategic planning is the process of determining an organization's basic mission and long-term objectives, then implementing a plan of action for attaining these goals. In carrying out their strategic plan, most MNEs tend toward one of four specific predispositions: ethnocentric, polycentric, regiocentric, and geocentric. Each was described in the chapter.

2 The international strategic planning process involves three major steps: strategy formulation, strategy implementation, and the control and evaluation of the process. Strategy formulation entails the evaluation of the enterprise's environment and the identification of long-range and short-range objectives. The analysis of the external environment typically involves information gathering and assessment, wherein consideration is given to the five forces that determine industry competitiveness: buyers; suppliers; new entrants to the industry; the availability of substitute goods and services; and rivalry among the competitors. The analysis of the internal environment involves consideration of the firm's physical resources and personnel competencies and the way in which a value chain analysis can be used to bring these resources together in the most synergistic and profitable manner.

3 Strategy implementation is the process of attaining predetermined goals by properly executing the formulated strategy. Three of the most important areas of consideration are location, ownership decisions, and functional area implementation.

4 The control and evaluation process involves an examination of the MNE's performance to determine how well it has done and to decide what action now needs to be taken. Some of the most common measures include return on investment, sales growth, market share, costs, new product development, host-country relations, and overall management performance.

Key terms

- strategic planning
- ethnocentric predisposition
- polycentric predisposition
- regiocentric predisposition
- geocentric predisposition

- strategy formulation
- competitive intelligence
- strategic business units (SBUs)
- vertical integration
- virtual integration
- value chain
- cost strategy
- differentiation strategy

- focus strategy
- competitive scope
- strategy implementation
- international joint venture (IJV)
- return on investment (ROI)

REVIEW AND DISCUSSION QUESTIONS

1 Define the term *strategic planning*.

2 In what way can the following basic predispositions affect an MNE's strategic planning: ethnocentric, polycentric, regiocentric, geocentric?

3 How will an MNE carry out an external environmental assessment? Identify and describe the two major steps involved in this process.

▶

4 Of what practical value is an understanding of the five-forces model presented in Figure 8.1. How would an MNE use this information in the strategic planning process?

5 In conducting an internal environmental assessment, why would an MNE want to identify its physical resources and personnel competencies?

6 What is a value chain? How can this chain be used in an internal environmental assessment?

7 What are the three generic strategies? When would an MNE use each? Support your answer with examples.

8 What are some typical MNE goals? Identify and briefly describe four major types.

9 One of the most important considerations when implementing a strategy is that of location. What does this statement mean?

10 When are MNEs likely to use an international joint venture? When would they opt for a strategic partnership? Defend your answer.

11 Functional strategies are used to coordinate operations and ensure that the plan is carried out properly. What are some of the most common types of functional strategies? Identify and describe three.

12 How do MNEs control and evaluate their operations? Describe the basic process. Then discuss some of the common methods of measurement.

REAL CASE

Mountain Equipment Co-op: a small business

Outside of Canada, few people have ever heard of the Mountain Equipment Co-op (MEC), but it is one of the most successful small businesses in the world. The company currently holds 65 percent of the Canadian market for outdoor equipment, far outdistancing all other competitive MNEs and retail brands in the country. In fact, MEC is so efficient that its products are priced lower than those of any North American competitor.

MEC was founded in 1969 when a group of six outdoor enthusiasts decided to get together and purchase expensive outdoor equipment. In August 1971 the organization was officially registered as a co-op and began operating under a member-elected board of directors that assumed responsibility for setting overall policy and overseeing management of all operations. As of December 2014, MEC had 4.3 million members, it operates stores in 18 cities across Canada, it has an international mail-order and online clientele, and a worldwide network of suppliers has helped it acquire revenues of CAD$336 million. For a one-time CAD$5 fee, members are able to enjoy a wide variety of benefits from an organization that focuses heavily on four primary objectives: keeping costs down, offering affordable goods, providing high-quality merchandise, and maintaining high ethical standards.

Source: Roberto Caucino/Shutterstock

Regarding the first of these, MEC takes a number of steps to control costs and offer affordable products. One is to use the clout of its large membership as a basis for extracting the best possible prices from suppliers, thus being able to offer low-cost products. Another is to keep the number of staff to a minimum. Two of the ways it does this are through the use of self-service in all stores and the promotion of its international mail-order business, which can be handled by a small number of personnel. In addition, the co-op minimizes overall marketing expenses by relying heavily on customer word-of-mouth and the mail-order network to help promote its products.

MEC also places a great deal of importance on the quality of goods. Its buyers and designers look not only for a low price from suppliers, but also for products that provide both functionality and durability. In addition, the co-op offers a lifetime guarantee on most of its products, regardless of whether it manufactured them, had them provided by an outsourcer, or purchased them from a large brand name company.

Co-op members are also assured that the company adheres to the highest ethical practices. MEC is an innovator in a number of areas, ranging from human rights to the environment. Its stores are designed with the utmost attention to the environment, using as much natural light as possible, high-efficiency HVAC (heating, ventilation, and air-conditioning), low-consumption water fixtures, and recyclable materials. As an example, its Ottawa store uses only half the energy of a conventional building. In addition, as a member of the organization "1% for the Planet," the co-op gives 1 percent of its gross sales each year to environmental and conservation groups. At the same time, its retail employees are among the best paid in the country and its buyers and inspectors are charged with ensuring that all factory workers in foreign countries receive a reasonable living wage and work under safe conditions.

MEC has undertaken many business initiatives to better serve its members, to secure long-term financial sustainability, and to promote its care of the environment. For example, in 1997, MEC introduced its popular and free of charge online gear swap where members can recycle used outdoor gear.

Some suppliers, such as Sierra Designs, Salomon, Arc'teryx, The North Face, and Patagonia, see MEC as a threat and have refused to sell to it. In many cases, however, this strategy has proven to be counterproductive, resulting in MEC designing and manufacturing these products and then successfully competing with the traditional brands that were unwilling to sell to it. In addition, the co-op's increased involvement in manufacturing has enabled it to monitor its suppliers' operations more closely.

Over the past couple of decades, MEC's strategy has been more emergent than calculated. Yet it has proven to be a successful business venture that has brought together a large group of dedicated environmentalists and other customers who need products for outdoor activities. In the process, the co-op has created a "style" and "brand" presence that appeals to outdoor enthusiasts. In fact, MEC's outdoor gear has become so popular that even urbanites, highly unlikely to go trekking or camping in the outdoors, are now becoming members. As a result, annual revenues are currently in the range of CAD$350 million and the company is continuing to expand operations across Canada.

MEC has been able to flourish as a result of the huge margins enjoyed by its competitors. This has allowed the co-op both to reduce prices and to maintain higher levels of environmental and labor practices than its competitors. Over the next few years, however, as competition grows and large outdoor retailers exert the same kind of pressure on suppliers that allowed it to sell at lower prices, MEC will have to switch its strategy to remain competitive. It has some advantages. For one, it has no shareholders and reinvests most of its surplus into the company. MEC still has to exploit to the fullest its community and environmental contributions. In the spirit of keeping advertising costs low, many members, not to mention potential members, have never heard of MEC's social policies or its charitable contributions.

Websites: www.mec.ca; www.sierra-designs.com; www.salomonsports.com; www.thenorthface.com; www.patagonia.com

Sources: www.mec.ca; "Mountain Equipment Co-op live with socially responsible retail," *PR Newswire*, May 22, 2001; "One of the greenest commercial buildings in the world," *Sustainable Sport Sourceline*, July 2000; "Mountain Equipment Co-op to stage outdoors skills challenge in celebration of its 2,000,000th member," *Canada NewsWire*, June 16, 2004; Martin Mittelstaedt, "Mountain Equipment pulls water bottles off shelves," *The Globe and Mail*, December 7, 2007; MEC, *Annual Report*, 2014.

1 How does the Mountain Equipment Co-op use value chain analysis to increase both its membership and its revenues?

2 What is the co-op's generic strategy? Describe it.

3 How does MEC measure its performance? What are two criteria it uses to evaluate how well it is doing?

REAL CASE

Benetton

Once famous for its shocking advertisements, Benetton was founded in 1955 by Luciano, Giuliana, Gilberto, and Carlo Benetton. Initially the family sold colored sweaters door-to-

door in Treviso, Italy. Over time, a regional network of family, friends, and agents set up a closely monitored set of distinctive retail outlets. Over a 15-year period, Benetton built up

300 affiliated but independently owned outlets in Italy and a factory with new methods to dye and condition wool. The company was not directly involved in the retail outlets, which received high-quality products at low costs. Part of the manufacturing savings was realized by outsourcing to neighboring subcontractors. For the year ended December 31, 2014, Benetton had total revenue of US$1.637 billion and a workforce of over 100,000 employees.

Benetton has kept its loose network of independent production subcontractors and distribution agents, but has now built up to a network of more than 5,000 retail stores in over 100 countries around the world. Only a small fraction of these are flagship stores owned by the group. The great majority of its retail stores are operated by independent entrepreneurs. About 90 percent of production still takes place in Europe, mainly in the northern Italian region around Treviso, and the group produces over 150 million garments every year. And the company is still 69.35 percent owned by the Benetton family. Yet the wool it uses to produce its clothing line is now imported from foreign countries. The parent company raises sheep on 900,000 hectares of land in Argentina.

Benetton is one of those companies that have succeeded partly because their production and design concept was built on a strong home base. It expanded the marketing end of its business through closely monitored (but not owned) independent stores, which were able to use the Benetton brand name and distinctive colors and were supported by clever international advertising.

Benetton does not advertise its clothes directly. Rather, its ads target a "lifestyle." The "United Colors of Benetton" ads were designed for a homogeneous global consumer interested in fast cars and a fast lifestyle. Benetton goes in for cutting-edge advertising that grabs public attention. This has created an image of new-age awareness, as the company's advertising ads have featured AIDS, capital punishment,

inter-racial relations, high art, and "attitude." The firm also sponsors a top Formula One team as well as teams in rugby, basketball, and volleyball, all of which contribute to the success of its brand name. Fabrica, Benetton's Communication Research Center just outside Treviso, is a mixture of philanthropy and advertising. The center sponsors 50 artists for a year, exhibits their work and publishes it in *Colors*, the company's art-focused magazine.

How well this plays out globally is uncertain. For example, Benetton had 700 retail stores in the United States in 1988, but only 150 by 1995. Is this because Benetton has too European an image to succeed in middle-America? How can an Italian family firm understand the American lifestyle from its European bases? Indeed, approximately 80 percent of its revenue was generated from its home region, Europe, of which roughly 45 percent was derived from Italy and 35 percent from the rest of Europe, 14 percent from Asia, only 3 percent from the Americas, and 1 percent from the rest of the world. The firm is now looking to expand into emerging markets where potential for growth among the growing middle class is greatest.

Website: http://www.benettongroup.com

Sources: Adapted from: *Benetton SpA: Industrial Fashion (A)*, Harvard Business School Case No. 9–685–614; *Benetton (B)*, Harvard Business School Case No. 9–685–020; INSEAD-CEDEP Case No. 01/97–4520, 1996; David Stillit, "Benetton: Italy's smart operator," *Corporate Finance*, June 1993; "Benetton's network," *Ivey Business Quarterly*, 1997; Benetton, *Annual Report*, 2009; Peter Crush, "CSR: diversity takes central stage," *PR Week*, April 18, 2005; "Benetton: IndíGenas Rechazan Oferta," bbc.co.uk, November 10, 2005; Edizone, *Annual Report*, 2014; www.benetton.com

1   Is Benetton a multinational enterprise?

2   What are the country-specific factors that have boosted Benetton's success?

3   What are Benetton's firm-specific advantages?

NOTES

1 Tim Burt, "GM outlines plans to cut European capacity," *Financial Times*, September 27, 2001, p. 19; Jorn Madslien, "General Motors gets ready to fix European subsidiaries," *BBC News*, March 3, 2011, http://www.bbc.co.uk/news/business-12625841

2 Matt Murray, "Merger machine: can GE keep growing through deals?" *Wall Street Journal*, July 31, 2000, pp. C1, 2; "General Electric debt rating cut," *BBC News*, March 12, 2009, http://news.bbc.co.uk/1/hi/business/7940191.stm

3 Also see Roland Calori, Leif Melin, Tugrul Atamer, and Peter Gustavsson, "Innovative international strategies," *Journal of World Business*, vol. 35, no. 4 (winter 2000), pp. 333–54; Kalevi Kyl-heiko, Ari Jantunen, Kaisu Puumalainen, Sami Saarenketo, and Anni Tuppura, "Innovation and

internationalization as growth strategies: the role of technological capabilities and appropriability," *International Business Review* (2010).

4 M. A. Hitt, "The meaning of organizational effectiveness: multiple domains and constituencies," *Management International Review*, vol. 28, no. 2 (1988), p. 28.

5 David Lei, John W. Slocum, Jr., and Robert W. Slater, "Global strategy and reward systems: the key roles of management development and corporate culture," *Organizational Dynamics* (August 1990), p. 29.

6 See David Norburn, Sue Birley, Mark Dunn, and Adrian Payne, "A four nation study of the relationship between marketing effectiveness, corporate culture, corporate values, and market orientation," *Journal of International Business Studies*, vol. 21, no. 3 (fall 1990), pp. 451–68.

7 For a good example, see Keith Bradsher, "Effective today, Chrysler and Daimler-Benz are one," *New York Times*, November 12, 1998, p. C 4; and Tim Burt, "Daimler chief to speak on strategy," ft.com, March 4, 2002.

8 For some specific applications of these ideas, see Michael M. Robert, "Managing your competitor's strategy," *Journal of Business Strategy* (March/April 1990), pp. 24–8.

9 Sometimes, of course, competitive intelligence degenerates into corporate spying, as seen in Andrew Edgecliffe-Johnson, "P&G admits spying on Unilever," *Financial Times*, August 31, 2001, p. 17; Rob Lemkin, "Dirty little secrets: corporate espionage," *BBC News*, 1 February 2008, http://news.bbc.co.uk/1/hi/business/7220063.stm; "US spy for China Noshir Gowadia jailed for 32 years," *BBC News*, January 25, 2011, http://www.bbc.co.uk/news/world-asia-pacific-12272941

10 J. E. Preble, P. A. Rau, and A. Reichel, "The environmental scanning practices of US multinationals in the late 1980s," *Management International Review*, vol. 28, no. 4 (1988), p. 10.

11 For more on this, see R. C. Hoffman, "The general management of foreign subsidiaries in the USA: an exploratory study," *Management International Review*, vol. 28, no. 2 (1988), pp. 41–55.

12 For more on this, see Michael Porter, *The Competitive Advantage of Nations* (New York: Free Press, 1990), chapter 2.

13 Andrew Pollack, "Nissan plans to buy more American parts," *New York Times*, March 26, 1994, pp. 17, 26; "Vauxhall boss warns over UK car making future," *BBC News*, April 24, 2011, http://www.bbc.co.uk/news/business-13179589

14 "A tricky business," *The Economist*, June 30, 2001, pp. 55–6.

15 "US steel tariffs," *Guardian*, November 11, 2003; "Steel firms oppose China imports," *BBC News*, October 29, 2007, http://news.bbc.co.uk/1/hi/business/7068142.stm

16 http://www.issb.co.uk/global.html. Accessed November 2015.

17 Arnoldo C. Hax and Nicolas S. Majluf, *The Strategy Concept and Process: A Pragmatic Approach* (Englewood Cliffs, NJ: Prentice Hall, 1991), p. 416.

18 Also see Julie Pitta, "Score one for vertical integration," *Forbes*, January 18, 1993, pp. 88–90.

19 For an excellent discussion of this topic, see Hax and Majluf, *The Strategy Concept and Process*, chapter 12.

20 C. K. Prahalad and Kenneth Lieberthal, "The end of corporate imperialism," *Harvard Business Review* (July/August 1998), pp. 69–79.

21 Hax and Majluf, *The Strategy Concept and Process*, p. 83.

22 Uta Harnischfeger, "Audi drives out VW's gloom," *FT.com*, March 1, 2002.

23 "The art of overtaking," *The Economist*, September 8, 2001, p. 68; "Car shares hit in latest market sell off," *BBC News*, 2 June 2011, http://www.bbc.co.uk/news/business-13627079

24 For another good example, see Seth Lubove, "Make a better mousetrap," *Forbes*, February 1, 1993, pp. 56–7.

25 Leslie Kaufman, "Avon's new face," *Newsweek*, November 16, 1998, pp. 59–60.

26 Also see W. Chan Kim and Peter Hwang, "Global strategy and multinationals' entry mode choice," *Journal of International Business Studies*, vol. 23, no. 1 (summer 1992), pp. 29–53.

27 Richard M. Hodgetts and Fred Luthans, *International Management*, 4th ed. (Burr Ridge, IL: McGraw/Irwin, 2000), p. 260.

28 Robert B. Reich, "Who is us?," *Harvard Business Review* (January/February 1990), p. 59.

29 Peter Lorange, Johan Roos, and Peggy Simcic Bronn, "Building successful strategic alliances," *Long Range Planning* (December 1992), pp. 10–17; Inkpen, Andrew C., "Strategic alliances," in Alan M. Rugman (ed.), *The Oxford Handbook of International Business*, 2nd ed. (Oxford: Oxford University Press, 2009).

30 See Masaaki Kotabe, Hildy Teegen, Preet S. Aulakh, Maria Cecilia Coutinho de Arruda, Roberto J. Santillan-Salgado, and Walter Greene, "Strategic alliances in emerging Latin America: a view from Brazilian, Chilean, and Mexican companies," *Journal of World Business*, vol. 35, no. 2 (summer 2000), pp. 114–32.

31 Mitchell Koza and Arie Lewin, "Managing partnerships and strategic alliances: raising the odds of success," *European Management Journal* (August 2000), pp. 146–51; Jorge Walter, Christoph Lechner, and Franz W. Kellermanns, "Disentangling alliance management processes: decision making, politicality, and alliance performance," *Journal of Management Studies*, vol. 45, no. 3 (May 2008), pp. 530–60.

32 Miki Tanikawa, "Electronics giants join forces in Japan," *Wall Street Journal*, May 24, 2001, p. W1.

33 Robert A. Guth, "IBM announces deal with Japan's NTT," *Wall Street Journal*, November 1, 2000, p. 23.

34 Audrey Choi, "BMW's chairman plans visit to Honda to discuss future of jointly held Rover," *Wall Street Journal*, February 18, 1994, p. A7.

35 Hemant Merchant, "Configurations of international joint ventures," *Management International Review*, vol. 40, no. 2 (2000), pp. 107–40.

36 Hong Liu and Kelvin Pak, "How important is marketing in China today to Sino-foreign joint ventures?" *European Management Journal* (October 1999), pp. 546–54.

37 Gautam Naik, "AT&T, BT form world-wide alliance," *Wall Street Journal*, July 27, 1998, p. A3.

38 John Tagliabue, "Toyota and Peugeot in pact to produce car for Europe," *New York Times*, June 30, 2001, p. B2.

39 Stefan H. Robock and Kenneth Simmonds, *International Business and Multinational Enterprises*, 4th ed. (Homewood, IL: Irwin, 1989), p. 216.

40 See Sing Keow Hoon-Halbauer, "Managing relationships within Sino-foreign joint ventures," *Journal of World Business*, vol. 34, no. 4 (winter 1999), pp. 344–70.

41 See, for example, Caron H. St. John, Scott T. Young, and Janis L. Miller, "Coordinating manufacturing and marketing in international firms," *Journal of World Business*, vol. 34, no. 2 (summer 1999), pp. 109–27.

42 Matt Marshall, "In Brazil, Coke sells foam as well as fizz," *Wall Street Journal*, July 28, 1997, p. A12.

43 Peter Marsh, "Pressing ahead with plastic," ft.com, March 4, 2002.

44 Jeffrey E. Garten, "Opening the doors for business in China," *Harvard Business Review* (May/June 1998), pp. 167–75.

45 Also see John Child and Yanni Yan, "Investment and control in international joint ventures: the case of China," *Journal of World Business*, vol. 34, no. 1 (spring 1999), pp. 3–15; John Child, "China and international business," in Alan M. Rugman (ed.), *The Oxford Handbook of International Business*, 2nd ed. (Oxford: Oxford University Press, 2009).

BIBLIOGRAPHY

Augier, Mie, and Teece, David J. "Dynamic capabilities and multinational enterprise: Penrosean insights and omissions," *Management International Review*, vol. 47, no. 2 (2007).

Asmussen, Christian G. "Local, regional, or global? Quantifying MNE geographic scope," *Journal of International Business Studies*, vol. 40 (September 2009). Banalieva, Elitsa R., and Athanassiou, Nicholas. "Regional and global alliance network structures of triad multinational enterprises," *Multinational Business Review*, vol. 18, no. 1 (2010).

Barkeman, Harry G., Shenkar, Oded, Vermeulen, Freek, and Bell, John H. J. "Working abroad, working with others: how firms learn to operate international joint ventures," *Academy of Management Journal*, vol. 40, no. 2 (April 1997).

Barney, Jay. *Gaining and Sustaining Competitive Advantage*, 3rd ed. (Upper Saddle River, NJ: Prentice Hall, 2007).

Buckley, Peter J., and Casson, Mark. "Edith Penrose's theory of the growth of the firms and the strategic management of the multinational enterprise," *Management International Review*, vol. 47, no. 2 (2007).

Dacin, M. Tina, Hitt, Michael A., and Levitas, Edward. "Selecting partners for successful international alliances: examination of US and Korean firms," *Journal of World Business*, vol. 32, no. 1 (spring 1997).

Davis, Peter S., Desai, Ashay B., and Francis, John D. "Mode of international entry: an isomorphism perspective," *Journal of International Business Studies*, vol. 31, no. 2 (summer 2000).

Demirbag, Mehmet, Tatoglu, Ekrem, and Glaister, Keith W. "Institutional and transaction cost influences on partnership structure of foreign affiliates," *Management International Review*, vol. 50, no. 6 (December 2010).

Egelhoff, William G. "Great strategy or great strategy implementation: two ways of competing in global markets," *Sloan Management Review*, vol. 34, no. 2 (winter 1993).

Ghemawat, Pankaj. *Redefining Global Strategy: Crossing Borders in a World Where Differences Still Matter* (Boston, MA: Harvard University Press, 2007).

Govindarajan, Vijay, and Gupta, Anil K. *The Quest for Global Dominance* (San Francisco, CA: Jossey-Bass/Wiley, 2001).

Grant, Robert M. *Contemporary Strategy Analysis* (Oxford: Wiley-Blackwell, 2008).

Hamel, Gary, and Prahalad, C. K. "Do you really have a global strategy?" *Harvard Business Review*, vol. 65, no. 4 (July/August 1985).

Hashai, Niron, Asmussen, Christian G., Benito, Gabriel R. G., and Petersen, Bent. "Technological knowledge intensity and entry mode diversity," *Management International Review*, vol. 50, no. 6 (December 2010).

Heracleous, L., and Collinson, Simon C. "HSBC's strategy and leadership." In K. Singh, N. Panagarkar, and L. Heracleous (eds.), *Business Strategy in Asia*, 3rd ed. (Singapore: Cengage, 2009).

Hitt, Michael A., Li, Dan, and Xu, Kai. "International strategy: from local to global and beyond." *Journal of World Business*, vol. 51, no. 1 (2016).

Hult, G., Tomas, M., Ketchen, David J., Griffith, David A., Chabowski, Brian R., Hamman, Mary K., Dykes, Bernadine

Johnson, Pollitte, Wesley A., and Cavusgil, S. Tamer. "An assessment of the measurement of performance in international business research," *Journal of International Business Studies*, vol. 39 (September 2008).

Jung, Jae C., Beamish, Paul W., and Goerzen, Anthony. "Dynamics of experience, environment and MNE ownership strategy," *Management International Review*, vol. 50, no. 3 (2010).

Kim, W. Chan, and Mauborgne, Renée A. "Making global strategies work," *Sloan Management Review*, vol. 34, no. 3 (spring 1993).

Kobrin, Stephen J. "Is a global nonmarket strategy possible? Economic integration in a multipolar world order." *Journal of World Business*, vol. 50, no. 2 (2015).

Koveshnikov, Alexei, et al. "A framework of successful organizational practices in Western multinational companies operating in Russia," *Journal of World Business*, vol. 47, no. 3 (2012).

Krishnan, Rekha, Martin, Xavier, and Noorderhaven, Niels G. "When does trust matter to alliance performance?," *Academy of Management Journal*, vol. 49, no. 5 (2006).

Merchant, Hemant. "Configurations of international joint ventures," *Management International Review*, vol. 40, no. 2 (2000).

Merchant, Hemant. "Cooperative strategy: economic, business, and organizational issues," *Academy of Management Review*, vol. 26, no. 2 (April 2001).

Meschi, Pierre-Xavier, and Riccio, Edson Luiz. "Country risk, national cultural differences between partners and survival of international joint ventures in Brazil," *International Business Review*, vol. 17, no. 3 (June 2008).

Mintzberg, Henry, Ahlstrand, Bruce, and Lampel, Joseph. *Strategy Safari* (New York: Free Press, 1998).

Mudambi, Susan M., and Tallman, Stephen. "Make, buy or ally? Theoretical perspectives on knowledge process outsourcing through alliances," *Journal of Management Studies*, vol. 47, no. 8 (December 2010).

Pak, Yong Suhk, Ra, Wonchan, and Lee, Jong Min. "An integrated multi-stage model of knowledge management in international joint ventures: identifying a trigger for knowledge exploration and knowledge harvest," *Journal of World Business*, vol. 50, no. 1 (2015).

Parkhe, Arvind. "Understanding trust in international alliances," *Journal of World Business*, vol. 33, no. 3 (fall 1998).

Piscitello, Lucia. "Multinationals and economic geography: location, technology and innovation," *Journal of International Business Studies*, vol. 44, no. 8 (2013).

Porter, Michael E. "The competitive advantage of nations," *Harvard Business Review*, vol. 68, no. 2 (March/April 1990).

Puck, Jonas F., Holtbrügge, Dirk, and Mohr, Alexander T. "Beyond entry mode choice: explaining the conversion of joint ventures into wholly owned subsidiaries in the People's Republic of China," *Journal of International Business Studies*, vol. 40 (April 2009).

Ricart, Joan Enric, Enright, Michael J., and Ghemawat, Pankaj. "New frontiers in international strategy," *Journal of International Business Strategy*, vol. 35, no. 3 (May 2004).

Roth, Kendall, Schweiger, David M., and Morrison, Allen J. "Global strategy implementation at the business unit level: operational capabilities and administrative mechanisms," *Journal of International Business Studies*, vol. 24, no. 2 (1993).

Rugman, Alan M. "Multinationals and global competitive strategy," *International Studies of Management and Organization*, vol. 15, no. 2 (summer 1985).

Rugman, Alan M., and Verbeke, Alain. *Analysis of Multinational Strategic Management: The Selected Scientific Papers of Alan M. Rugman and Alain Verbeke* (Cheltenham: Edward Elgar, 2005).

Rugman, Alan M., and Verbeke, Alain. "The theory and practice of regional strategy: a response to Osegowitsch and Sammartino," *Journal of International Business Studies*, vol. 39, no. 2 (2008).

Rugman, Alan M., and Verbeke, Alain. "A regional solution to the strategy and structure of multinationals," *European Management Journal*, vol. 26 (2008).

Tallman, Stephen B., and Yip, George S. "Strategy and the multinational enterprise." In Alan M. Rugman (ed.), *The Oxford Handbook of International Business*, 2nd ed. (Oxford: Oxford University Press, 2009).

Thakur, Manab, and Das, T. K. "Managing the growth–share matrix: a four-nation study in two industries," *Management International Review*, vol. 31, no. 2 (1991).

Tong, Tony W., and Reuer, Jeffrey J. "Competitive consequences of interfirm collaboration: how joint ventures shape industry profitability," *Journal of International Business Studies*, vol. 41, no. 6 (2010).

Vapola, Terhi Johanna, Paukku, Markus, and Gabrielsson, Mika. "Portfolio management of strategic alliances: an international business perspective," *International Business Review*, vol. 19, no. 3 (June 2010).

Verbeke, Alain. *International Business Strategy: Rethinking the Foundations of Global Corporate Success* (Cambridge: Cambridge University Press, 2009).

Verbeke, Alain, and Kano, Liena. "An internalization theory perspective on the global and regional strategies of multinational enterprises," *Journal of World Business*, vol. 51, no. 1 (2016).

Verbeke, Alain, and Yuan, Wenlong. "Entrepreneurship in multinational enterprises: a Penrosean perspective," *Management International Review*, vol. 47, no. 2 (2007).

APPENDIX: REGIONAL ASPECTS OF MULTINATIONALITY AND PERFORMANCE

The founder of this book series, Professor Alan Rugman, was a keen advocate of the need to robustly question established beliefs about the world and to look to the data and other empirical evidence to tell the real story. He focused on a number of key topics in international business studies and one of these was the relationship between multinationality and performance. This appendix, mainly written by him, outlines the main argument. More recent discussions have advanced his theories and one good summary appears in a special issue of *Journal of World Business* (vol. 50, no. 4, 2015), introduced by two of his co-authors, Chang Hoon Oh and Jing Li.

Introduction

A basic premise of international business is that foreign operations are profitable—otherwise, they would not take place! Thus it is hypothesized that the performance of the firm (usually an MNE) improves as its degree of foreign operations increases. Rugman (2005) has shown that the world's largest firms operate mainly on an intra-regional basis, in terms of both sales and assets. We relate traditional literature on multinationality and performance to the new metrics available, which includes new data on regional sales and on the return on foreign assets. Several papers examine regionalization and performance across industries, others over time and for various regions of the triad. This empirical work provides a very useful starting point in bringing the regional nature of MNEs into the literature on multinationality and performance.

In the field of international business one of the most basic issues is the relationship between multinationality and performance. Several hundred studies have examined the nature of this relationship, with somewhat inconclusive results. Here this literature is reviewed and extended and then related to the regional dimension of multinationality and performance. The regional aspects of multinational activity are explored in Rugman and Verbeke (2004) and Rugman (2005). The traditional empirical work on multinationality and performance can be extended by including this regional dimension.

Research on the *S* curve

Contractor (2007) presents a theoretical justification for the three-stage *S* curve (see Figure 8A). The horizontal axis represents the degree of multinationality, here proxied by the ratio of foreign (F) to total (T) sales, (F/T). The vertical axis represents a performance measure, here the return on total assets (ROTA). There is generally a positive relationship between these two variables. In an interesting twist, Contractor argues that the middle stage is consistent with the observations on the regional nature of multinational activity. He also suggests that the final stage, where performance suffers due to excessive multinationality, is typically populated by relatively few firms. This fall-off in performance beyond a certain threshold of multinationality may correspond to an attempt by some companies to reach a "global" stage. While these propositions remain to be tested, Contractor provides strong new insights into the possible relationship between the regional dimension of multinationality activity and the emerging literature on the *S* curve. He also reviews seven generic reasons why studies of multinationality and performance yield different results, and he provides an agenda for research to further test the viability of the three-stage *S* curve concept.

Regional versus total sales

Oh and Rugman (2007) provide new data examining the trends of regional sales between 2001 and 2005. They start with the 2001 benchmark year used in the pathbreaking paper by Rugman and Verbeke (2004) as further developed in the databank reported in the book by Rugman (2005). They find a remarkable degree of stability over time where the ratio of regional to total sales averages 75.7 percent. They also provide data for the first time on the regional nature of assets of the world's largest 500 firms. This averages 76.7 percent again with less than a 1 percent variation over the five-year period.

Osegowitsch and Sammartino (2007) conduct an analysis by taking the set of 380 firms reported in Rugman and Verbeke (2004) and going back to 1991 to find trends in regionalization over the period 1991–2001. One problem is that this yields a greatly reduced sample of 159 firms biased towards US firms. Indeed, most of their results exclude the Asian firms completely, and represent only 90 North American firms and 36 from Europe. Osegowitsch and Sammartino (2007) find that there is a reduction in intra-regional sales for this small set of US and European firms from 84 percent to 76 percent. Over this period they also find that some firms increase their sales outside their home region. They also find

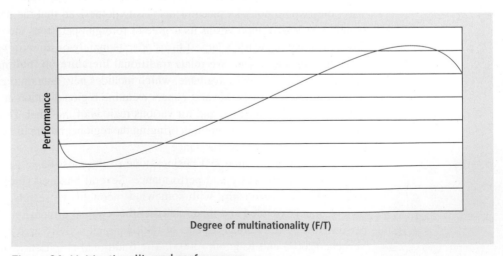

Figure 8A Multinationality and performance

that a somewhat larger percentage of firms can be classified as biregional in contrast to those found in the Rugman and Verbeke (2004) chapter. However, in contrast to their own conclusions their own data actually confirm the main two insights of Rugman and Verbeke (2004). First, the vast majority of firms remain home region oriented over the 1991–2001 period. Second, there are very few global firms. Their chapter is useful in provoking a debate about trends in regionalization and hopefully a more extensive dataset can be constructed to help reconcile their findings with those of Oh and Rugman (2007).

Goerzen and Asmussen (2007) use a set of Japanese MNEs to test the relationship between regional and global firms. They argue correctly that the performance of a firm is determined by its firm-specific advantages (FSAs). They show that regional firms build more upon location-bound FSAs, especially in the marketing area. In contrast, global firms have technological (R&D) FSAs, and these are presumed to be non-location bound. Goerzen and Asmussen find evidence that the FSAs of global firms are less location bound than the FSAs of regional firms. This work needs to be extended beyond the Japanese dataset in order to test the generalization of these findings. However, their theoretical logic is consistent with that of Rugman and Verbeke (2007), where it is argued that there is a liability of regional foreignness. In other words, the FSAs of MNEs are difficult to deploy and exploit outside the home region.

Gravity model

Hejazi (2007) introduces the logic of international economics and transaction costs to analyze the regional dimension of the activities of MNEs. He uses the well-known gravity model of international economics which has been used to analyze the importance of geography for the determination of international trade flows. He adapts the gravity model to measure foreign direct investment (FDI) instead of trade flows. The gravity model measures the country-level frictions affecting trade and can only be applied to FDI with some difficulty as FDI is partly a method to overcome such frictions. Thus the gravity model yields a new type of test of the activities of MNEs, although it is not a direct test of their strategies. Hejazi finds that there is a strong regional bias in the activities of MNEs from the EU, but he does not find this effect for North American MNEs, which is not surprising given the asymmetrical large size of the US market. (The size bias of the US market may also affect the results by Osegowitsch and Sammartino (2007).) While Hejazi does not test performance directly, his work offers new conceptual lenses on the nature of the regional dimension of multinationality. Such work using econometric techniques based on the gravity model needs to be taken up and related to the empirical literature on multinationality and performance.

Multinationality and performance

Bowen (2007) provides a theoretical critique of the extant empirical work in the multinationality and performance literature. He points out that basic statistical issues have not been resolved, including the issues of endogeneity and non-linearities in the tests. He argues that the multinationality and performance literature does not take into account the heterogeneous nature of firms, industries, or countries. Bowen argues further that the multinationality and performance literature needs to be much better integrated into basic international business theory and that the various "modes of multinationality" (exporting, FDI, outsourcing) can affect measurement. Such variations in types of multinationality are consistent with the observations of Rugman (2005) on the regional nature of multinational activity. A related criticism of the lack of theoretical underpinnings in the multinationality and performance literature has been advanced by Verbeke, Li, and Goerzen (2009). It is clear that much more effort needs to be put into the development of appropriate theoretical frameworks to model the observed empirical relationship between multinationality and performance.

Bausch et al. (2007) conduct a meta-analysis of a large set of previously published studies in the literature on multinationality and performance. They confirm a positive relationship between multinationality and performance. They have a broad definition of multinationality and include the traditional type of merger and acquisition (leading to wholly owned subsidiaries through the process of FDI) along with the non-traditional type of alliance formation. This leads them to invent yet another term for multinationality, namely international business combinations. It is unusual to include alliances in this type of work since it is difficult to assess the impact of alliances on firm performance in a direct manner, as can be done with the merger and acquisition mode of multinationality. Some challenging ideas are presented in this paper which attempts to extend the field of study by adding the alliance as an additional unit of analysis. It is particularly important to extend these tests to fully address the regional significance of different types of international business combinations.

Fortanier et al. (2007) offer a cautionary tale for researchers on multinationality and performance. They find that the empirical results testing this relationship are strongly affected by moderating variables. In particular the so-called "strategic fit" affects performance in a significant and positive manner. Strategic fit moderates the basic aspects of multinationality and performance including the shape, size, and direction of the relationship. Strategic fit is based upon the integration and national responsiveness framework, which is also used by Li and Li (2007). Fortanier and her coauthors (2007) collect archival data on the chain of ownership of multiple subsidiaries that allow them to conduct more robust econometric analysis on aspects of integration and responsiveness. They have data for 336 of the world's largest 500 firms for the year 2002. These variables enter as moderators when testing the basic relationship between multinationality and performance. The results indicate a significant positive relationship between multinationality and return on sales, but this relationship is not a stable one since the strategic fit varies by firm. In other words, firms with an integration strategy perform well internationally in industries which are integrated. In contrast, in multidomestic industries only firms with a national responsiveness strategy do well internationally, so industry effects matter, as also found by Li and Li (2007). While the paper is interesting because it attempts to introduce organizational structure and strategy issues more explicitly into the literature on multinationality and performance, the regional dimension is not explored.

Kumar and Gaur (2007) examine the relationship between multinationality and performance within the context of 240 of India's MNEs, many of which are smaller firms than the world's largest 500 for which the regional effect has been tested. They find strong evidence of a positive J-shaped exponentially increasing relationship between the internationalization of Indian firms and their performance. They also find that India's outward FDI differs between developing and developed economies and between manufacturing and service sectors. A key contribution is that their data include relatively small and medium-sized firms, not just the world's largest 500 firms. This helps us better understand the country context in studies of multinationality and performance, as India has many small multinational firms. Usually size of firms is a moderating or control variable, but Kumar and Gaur link it to a country factor for India.

Nachum and Wymbs (2007) offer an interesting contrast to the literature as their geographic unit of analysis is the city. This is a subnational unit of analysis, and it can be contrasted with the triad regions developed in Rugman (2005). A very good reason is given for choosing cities—namely, that the data tested relate to the financial and professional service industries. These are clustered in the world's major cities. The authors analyze 673 MNEs in these service sectors that entered New York and London through mergers and acquisitions. They find an interaction between geographic location and the FSAs of these MNEs. It is a useful idea to apply the location decision for an industry and firm at the appropriate geographic level. These findings can be usefully contrasted with other papers where regions cross national borders, rather than being subnational.

Regional aspects of multinationality and performance

Li and Li (2007) provide an innovative test of the regional aspects of multinationality and performance. The authors use the well-known integration and responsiveness matrix to distinguish between a "global" industry, which has a high degree of economic integration, and a "multidomestic" industry, which is nationally responsive. They choose the computer and office equipment industry as an example of a global industry, and the soap, cleanser, and toilet goods industry as an example of a multidomestic industry. They find significant differences between the two industries in terms of international strategies, which lead to confirmation of the regional dimension in multinational operations. Li and Li also test the impact of FSAs in the two industries in terms of both R&D and marketing intensity. Their results indicate that FSAs are largely non-location bound in the global industry, but much home-region bound in the multidomestic industry. In addition, they show that internationalization pace has a direct positive impact on firm performance in the global industry but not in the multidomestic industry.

Rugman et al. (2007) introduce a new dependent variable called return on foreign assets (ROFA). They contrast it with the traditional variable, return on total assets (ROTA). They also introduce a regional variable representing regional sales. Rugman and colleagues test the explanatory power of the regional sales variable with linear, quadratic, and cubic fits. They find that the regional variable explains ROTA in terms of the cubic fit, but not ROFA. These data are focused upon a set of 27 UK multinationals of which 8 are in manufacturing and 19 are in service sectors; the regional variable represents sales in the EU. The results indicate that the 27 large UK MNEs experience strong intra-regional sales and that the regional sales variable is a significant variable affecting firm performance in a positive but non-linear manner allowing for standard control variables.

In a related chapter Sukpanich (2007) also includes an independent variable representing intra-regional sales, this time across MNEs in the triad regions of North America and the EU. She has data on 91 firms of which 67 are from North America and 24 from Europe. Of the 91 firms, 66 are in manufacturing and 25 in services. Sukpanich uses the COMPUSTAT database to access data on the FSAs of MNEs. These FSAs include R&D and marketing variables. She finds a strong positive linear relationship between the measure of intra-regional sales and performance. Performance is higher for firms based in their home region. This result contrasts with that of Chen as discussed next.

Chen (2007) conducts a test of the multinationality and performance relationship across some service sector firms in an Asian context. He distinguishes between intra-regional sales and extra-regional sales for this set of service sector firms. He uses the same Osiris database as in Rugman et al. (2007). Chen does not find support for the hypothesis that intra-regional sales are a significant determinant of performance where performance is measured by return on total assets. Instead, he finds that extra-regional sales are significant, in contrast to Sukpanich (2007). To some extent this may support some findings by Osegowitsch and Sammartino (2007). Further research is required, but it is encouraging to see this focus on the Asian firms missing from Osegowitsch and Sammartino (2007).

Richter (2007) tests the importance of a regional sales variable across the UNCTAD set of the world's 100 largest firms as ranked by foreign assets. This is a somewhat unrepresentative sample as it consists of the world's most internationalized firms and is thus biased toward finding internationalization (and therefore regionalization). Richter uses the S curve and finds a significant cubic fit between performance and multinationality where the latter is measured by the UNCTAD transnationality index. When testing the foreign intra-regional sales variable, her results are ambiguous with either an *S* curve or inverted *U* curve being supported. However, as with other recent papers, Richter finds that this regional sales variable is a significant determinant of performance.

It would be useful to extend this type of research beyond the largest 100 firms (or the 500 largest in Rugman (2005)) to include many more MNEs that are small to medium sized. Indeed, it would be useful to test the regional dimension in the emerging literature on international entrepreneurship, some of which is focused upon the internationalization process of small and medium-sized firms. This will require some theoretical adjustments to the assumption that many of these firms are "born global." This literature seems to find relatively fast internationalization of small firms in the information technology and computer sector, but there has not been careful testing of the regional aspects of such internationalization, and other sectors need to be added. Furthermore, the normal metric used is a scope variable dealing with the opening of foreign subsidiaries, whereas a better metric is to use the ratio of foreign to total sales (in this case, regional to total sales).

While this work on international entrepreneurship remains to be undertaken, this recent empirical work provides a very useful starting point in bringing the regional nature of MNEs into the literature on multinationality and performance. There is uniformity in showing that the basic relationship between multinationality and performance is beset by issues of heterogeneity across countries, industries, and firms. Yet many of them also show that the regional nature of multinationality can be included in this work in a useful manner. Therefore, the regional dimension of strategy needs to be considered in future work analyzing the relationship between multinationality and performance.

References

Bausch, A., Fritz, T., and Bösecke, K. "Performance effects of internationalization strategies: a meta-analysis." In A. M. Rugman (ed.), *Regional Aspects of Multinationality and Performance* (Oxford: Elsevier, 2007).

Bowen, H. P. "The empirics of multinationality and performance." In A. M. Rugman (ed.), *Regional Aspects of Multinationality and Performance* (Oxford: Elsevier, 2007).

Carney, M., Gedajlovic, E. R., Heugens, P. P., Van Essen, M., and Van Oosterhout, J. H. "Business group affiliation, performance, context, and strategy: a meta-analysis," *Academy of Management Journal*, vol. 54, no. 3 (2011).

Chen, S. "Testing regional effects in the internationalization–performance relationship in Asia service firms." In A. M. Rugman (ed.), *Regional Aspects of Multinationality and Performance* (Oxford: Elsevier, 2007).

Contractor, F. J. "The evolutionary or multi-stage theory of internationalization and the regionalization of firms." In A. M. Rugman (ed.), *Regional Aspects of Multinationality and Performance* (Oxford: Elsevier, 2007).

Fortanier, F., Muller, A., and Tulder, R. van. "Internationalization and performance: the moderating role of strategic fit." In A. M. Rugman (ed.), *Regional Aspects of Multinationality and Performance* (Oxford: Elsevier, 2007).

Goerzen, A., and Asmussen, C. G. "The geographic orientation of multinational enterprises and its implications for performance." In A. M. Rugman (ed.), *Regional Aspects of Multinationality and Performance* (Oxford: Elsevier, 2007).

Hejazi, W. "The regional nature of MNE activities and the gravity model." In A. M. Rugman (ed.), *Regional Aspects of Multinationality and Performance* (Oxford: Elsevier, 2007).

Kirca, A. H., Hult, G. T. M., Roth, K., Cavusgil, S. T., Perryy, M. Z., Akdeniz, M. B., and Miller, J. C. "Firm-specific assets, multinationality, and financial performance: a meta-analytic review and theoretical integration," *Academy of Management Journal*, vol. 54, no. 1 (2011).

Kumar, V., and Gaur, A. S. "Internationalization and performance of Indian firms." In A. M. Rugman (ed.), *Regional Aspects of Multinationality and Performance* (Oxford: Elsevier, 2007).

Li, L., and Li, D. "Testing the global and regional strategies of multinational enterprises," in A. M. Rugman (ed.), *Regional Aspects of Multinationality and Performance* (Oxford: Elsevier, 2007).

Nachum, L., and Wymbs, C. "The location and performance of foreign affiliates in global cities," in A. M. Rugman (ed.), *Regional Aspects of Multinationality and Performance* (Oxford: Elsevier, 2007).

Oh, C.-H., and Rugman, A. M. "Multinationality and regional performance, 2001–2005." In A. M. Rugman (ed.), *Regional Aspects of Multinationality and Performance* (Oxford: Elsevier, 2007).

Osegowitsch, T., and Sammartino, A. "Exploring trends in regionalization," in A. M. Rugman (ed.), *Regional Aspects of Multinationality and Performance* (Oxford: Elsevier, 2007).

Richter, N. "Intra-regional sales and the internationalization and performance relationship." In A. M. Rugman (ed.), *Regional Aspects of Multinationality and Performance* (Oxford: Elsevier, 2007).

Rugman, A. M., Chang, H. O., and Dominic, S. K. L. "The regional and global competitiveness of multinational firms," *Journal of the Academy of Marketing Science*, vol. 40, no. 2 (2012).

Rugman, Alan M., and Verbeke, Alain. "A Perspective on Regional and Global Strategies of Multinational Enterprises," *Journal of International Business Studies*, vol. 35, no. 1 (January 2004), pp. 3–18.

Rugman, A. M., and Verbeke, Alain. "Liabilities of regional foreignness and the use of firm-level versus country-level data: a response to Dunning *et al.* (2007)," *Journal of International Business Studies*, vol. 38, no. 1 (January 2007).

Rugman, A. M., Yip, G. S., and Kudina, A. "The regional dimension of UK multinationals." In A. M. Rugman (ed.), *Regional Aspects of Multinationality and Performance* (Oxford: Elsevier, 2007).

Sukpanich, N. "Intra-regional sales and performance." In A. M. Rugman (ed.), *Regional Aspects of Multinationality and Performance* (Oxford: Elsevier, 2007).

Verbeke, A., Li, L., and Goerzen, A. "Toward more effective research on the multinationality–performance relationship," *Management International Review*, vol. 49, no. 2 (2009).

Additional bibliography

Banalieva, E., and Santoro, M. "Local, regional, or global? Geographic orientation and relative financial performance of emerging market multinational enterprises," *European Management Journal*, vol. 27, no. 5 (2009).

Beleska-Spasova, E., and Glaister, K. W. (2010). "Geographic orientation and performance," *Management International Review*, vol. 50, no. 5 (October 2010).

Chen, S., and Tan, H. "Region effects in the internationalization–performance relationship in Chinese firms," *Journal of World Business* (2010).

Oh, C. H. "The international scale and scope of European multinationals," *European Management Journal*, vol. 27, no. 5 (2009).

Oh, C. H. "Value creation and home region internationalization of US MNEs," *Multinational Business Review*, vol. 18, no. 4 (2010).

Oh, C. H., and Rugman, A. M. "Regional integration and the international strategies of large European firms," *International Business Review*, vol. 21, no. 3 (2012).

Qian, G., Khoury, T., Peng, M. W., and Qian, Z. "The performance implication of intra- and inter-regional geographic diversification," *Strategic Management Journal*, vol. 31 (2010).

Rugman, A. M., and Oh, C. H. "Does the regional nature of multinationals affect the multinationality and performance relationship?" *International Business Review*, vol. 19, no. 5 (2010).

Rugman, A. M., and Oh, C. H. "Methodological issues in the measurement of multinationality of US firms," *Multinational Business Review*, vol. 19, no. 3 (2011).

Rugman, A. M., and Oh, C. H. "Why the home region matters: location and regional multinationals," *British Journal of Management*, vol. 24, no. 4 (2013).

Rugman, A. M., and Verbeke, A. "Internalization theory and its impact on the field of international business." In J. J. Boddewyn (ed.), *International Business Scholarship: AIB Fellows on the First 50 Years and Beyond*, Research in Global Strategic Management, vol. 14 (Bradford: Emerald Group, 2008).

Rugman, A. M., Yip, G. S., and Kudina, A. "Testing the link between multinationality and the return on foreign assets," *Multinational Business Review*, vol. 17, no. 3 (2009).

Sullivan, Daniel. "Measuring the degree of internationalization of a firm," *Journal of International Business Studies*, vol. 25, no. 2 (1994).

Verbeke, A., and Brugman, P. "Triple-testing the quality of multinationality–performance research: an internalization theory perspective," *International Business Review*, vol. 18, no. 3 (June 2009).

Verbeke, A., Li, L., and Goerzen, A. "Toward more effective research on the multinationality–performance relationship," *Management International Review*, vol. 49, no. 5 (2009).

Wolf, J., Dunemann, T., and Egelhoff, W. G. "Why MNCs tend to concentrate their activities in their home region," *Multinational Business Review*, vol. 20, no. 1 (2012).

Yuan, L., and Pangarkar, N. "Performance implications of internationalization strategies for Chinese MNCs," *International Journal of Emerging Markets*, vol. 10, no. 2 (2015).

Chapter 9

ORGANIZING STRATEGY

Contents

Objectives of the chapter

The primary purpose of an organizing strategy is to help an enterprise implement its strategic plan. There are a number of basic organization structures from which to choose, although most MNEs tailor-make their design and sometimes use a combination of different structures. Another major area of organizing strategy is the organizational processes of decision making, communicating, and controlling. These processes are fundamental to the efficient operation of the structure, and management will need to decide how they should be carried out. This chapter examines the key elements of organizing strategy.

The specific objectives of this chapter are to:

1 *Examine* organization structures used by enterprises that are just beginning their international expansion.

2 *Describe* the international division and global structures that are used as firms increase their international presence.

3 *Analyze* the key structural variables that influence international organization designs.

4 *Review* the role of the organizational processes in ensuring that the structure is both effective and efficient.

Procter & Gamble

In 1837, William Procter, a candle maker, and his brother-in-law James Gamble, a soap maker, partnered to create a company that would manufacture and market soaps and candles from its base in Cincinnati, Ohio. When candles declined in popularity with the invention of the light bulb and production was eventually discontinued in the 1920s, soap became the basis from which the company built a successful product portfolio of cleaning products and eventually allowed Procter & Gamble to branch out into cosmetics, food, and pet products.

During P&G's first century, international expansion was an afterthought. In 1915, a Canadian plant was established, the first outside the United States. P&G's first overseas subsidiary was established with the purchase of Thomas Hedley & Sons Co., Ltd. in England in 1930. This coincided with the birth of P&G's brand management marketing system. Dedicated teams would work on marketing competing brands worldwide. In 1948, P&G established an overseas division to manage its growing international division, which at the time reached Asia, Europe, and Latin America. By 1963, as a result of European expansion, P&G established the European Technical Center in Belgium to serve common market subsidiaries. The Japanese market was entered in 1973 through the acquisition of the Nippon Sunhome Company, and in 1993 the Japan Headquarters and Technical Center opened in Rokkō Island in Kobe City.

By 1995, sales outside the United States had reached more than 50 percent of total sales, and a new top management team, headed by John E. Pepper, changed the organization structure of the firm from US and International to four regional sectors: North America; Latin America; Asia; and Europe, the Middle East, and Africa. All regional sectors reported to the chief operating officer.

By 2004, P&G had the workings of a global company in terms of its structure. Three interactive parts, whose subsidiaries are strategically placed around the world to best achieve cost-effectiveness, marketing and production, and design quality, were the basis of this structure. First, there were seven Market Development Organizations (MDOs) responsible for marketing products in the following regions: North America; ASEAN, India, Australia; China; North-East Asia; Central and Eastern Europe, the Middle East, and Africa; and Western Europe and Latin America. Second, these MDOs collaborated with any one of five product-based Global Business Units (GBUs) responsible for R&D, design, and the manufacturing processes. Third, there were Global Business Services (GBSs) located mainly in developing countries that provided accounting, human resource management, logistics, and system operations in a given region. Finally, a Corporate Functions (CF) segment oversaw operations but delegated decision making to each structural unit.

This basic structure has been sustained for over 10 years. In 2015 the GBUs had reduced to four: Baby, Feminine and Family Care; Beauty; Fabric and Home Care; and Health and Grooming. The MDOs were renamed "Selling and Market Operations" or SMOs, with dedicated retail customer and country-specific teams. There were six: Asia Pacific; Europe; Greater China; India and the Middle East and Africa (IMEA); Latin America; and North America. The GBS has also evolved and "provides technology, processes and standard data tools to enable the GBUs and the SMOs to better understand the business and better serve consumers and customers" (http://us.pg.com/who_we_are/structure_governance/corporate_structure).

In Figure 9.8 below, the SMOs are equivalent to marketing-based Area Profit Centers; the GBUs can be placed where the Business Profit Centers are. The GBSs, in turn, can take the place of Function Cost Centers. These three sectors interact with each other under the guidance of Corporate Functions.

This global three-axis matrix structure, however, has not resulted in an even distribution of sales across all three regions of the triad, or across P&G's seven-region segmentation. As of 2014, P&G had 118,000 employees and was ranked as the 100th largest company by sales ("Fortune Global 500," 2015) with total revenue of US$84.537 billion. A closer analysis indicates that revenues in North America were 39 percent, Western Europe 18 percent, Central and Eastern Europe 15 percent, Latin America 10 percent, and Asia 18 percent.

The firm's most important firm-specific advantage (FSA) is its ability to market products in multiple regions. It does this through product adaptation, marketing, and packaging to the needs of customers in diverse regions, and by creating successful brands. As of 2014 it has been reported that the top 70–80 brands are leaders within each respective industry and account for approximately 90 percent of P&G sales. Some of its most famous brands are Tide, Ariel, Pantene, and Crest.

P&G's strategy does not necessarily include developing global brands like Pringles, its most globally diversified brand. Instead, the firm might choose locally trusted brands to channel new products to multiple regions. Blendax, a European brand, is now the portal through which P&G markets Whitestrips, which are sold in North America under the

Crest brand. Many successful brands were carefully picked up through acquisitions and then revamped with new marketing. Between 1980 and 2000, P&G acquired CoverGirl, Noxzema, Clarion, Oil of Olay, Blendax, Old Spice, Max Factor, and Pantene, among others. In other words, the firm finds regional brands to develop regionally.

Another firm-specific advantage is that P&G's portfolio of products allows the diffusion of R&D to different product lines in all regions. For example, a fabric detergent discovery may create improved versions of Tide and Cheer in North America, Ariel in Latin America, and Bold in Japan. It might also spill over to non-fabric cleaners such as Salvo. This, and the GBUs' ability to coordinate production across the world, translate into scale economies that are difficult to rival in the industry.

P&G has gone further than most companies in creating a global structure that incorporates developing and emerging countries. For example, as far back as 2004, the GBS for the Americas was located in Costa Rica, while that in the Philippines provides services to the Asian region. Factories are located in Asia, eastern Europe, and Latin America as well as in more developed countries. R&D, usually reserved for developed nations, has also seen its way to developing countries like China.

Websites: www.pg.com; http://fortune.com/global500/procter-gamble-100/; http://us.pg.com/who_we_are/structure_governance/corporate_structure

Sources: Alan Rugman, *The Regional Multinationals* (Cambridge: Cambridge University Press, 2005); P&G, *Annual Report*, 2010, 2014; "Fortune Global 500," *Fortune*, July 26, 2010.

1 What type of organization structure does P&G have in place for its worldwide operations? Is this structure optimal?

2 Why was the international division replaced by the matrix structure?

3 Why does the company rely on decentralized decision making?

4 In controlling its operations, what are three areas that are paramount for the firm?

INTRODUCTION

This chapter on organization strategy is intimately related to the previous chapter on strategic management. Indeed, there is an unresolved debate about whether strategy follows structure or whether structure follows strategy. We do not need to resolve this debate, but simply to recognize the interconnections between strategy and structure. As shown in the introduction to the previous chapter, it is essential to link the issues of organization structure to the previous frameworks of international business. In particular, the FSA–CSA matrix of Chapter 2 is relevant.

In this chapter we will see that many firms operate in a centralized and hierarchical manner. These structures are suitable for firms pursuing strategies of economic integration, for example, where worldwide economies of scale are being obtained. As was shown in the previous chapter, a strategy of economic integration can occur in cell 1 of the FSA–CSA matrix. By the end of this chapter the student will realize that a centralized and hierarchical structure is usually followed by firms pursuing a cell 1 strategy of economic integration.

In contrast, firms which pursue marketing strategies and differentiate their products and or services by building strong brand names are best positioned in cell 4 of the FSA–CSA matrix. In cell 4, where FSAs are divorced from CSAs, the appropriate organization structure need not be one of hierarchy. A multinational firm may need to adapt its product or service to various foreign markets. This strategy of national responsiveness (discussed in Chapter 10) may require a decentralized organization structure, one where more autonomy is given to subsidiary managers.

Finally, in cell 3 of the FSA–CSA matrix it may be necessary to combine the advantages of both a centralized and decentralized organization structure. Somewhat paradoxically, this is often called a matrix structure. Such a matrix organization structure, where complementary assets need to be combined, is consistent with a strategy in cell 3 of the FSA–CSA matrix.

This chapter will now examine the various types of organization structures available to the senior management teams of multinational enterprises. We also examine how business networks can be managed. This thinking on strategy and structure is then applied in subsequent chapters to issues in production (Chapter 12); marketing (Chapter 13); human resource management (Chapter 14); political risk negotiations (Chapter 15); and international financial management (Chapter 16). This will then be applied as an example of regional strategy in the final set of chapters.

Organizations that have decided to expand internationally do so in a number of ways. Some simply ship their goods to a foreign market and have a third party handle sales activities. If a firm's international market is a large portion of its total operations, however, the enterprise may play a more active role in the distribution and sale of its products, and this requires a more complex organization structure. Often, firms start off as exporters and then, as their foreign sales grow, develop more intricate structures that can handle their foreign operations.[1]

Major MNEs such as IBM, General Motors,[2] Mercedes, and Mitsubishi have sophisticated global structures that form the basis of their organizing strategies. Sometimes these firms will also have subsidiaries or affiliates that are integrated into the overall structure. For example, Mitsubishi has 28 core groups that are bound together by cross-ownership and other financial ties, interlocking directorates, long-term business relationships, and social and historical ties. Among these are Mitsubishi Bank, Mitsubishi Heavy Industries, Asahi Glass, Tokyo Marine and Fire Insurance, Nikon Corporation, and Kirin Brewery.[3] The Mitsubishi Group obviously needs a carefully designed global structure that allows it to integrate and coordinate the activities of these many businesses. Sometimes this undertaking involves more time and effort than the formulation of the strategic plan.

ORGANIZATION STRUCTURES

Multinational enterprises cannot implement their strategies without an effective structure.[4] The strategy sets out the plan of action, but the structure is critical in ensuring that the desired goals are met efficiently. A number of choices are available to an MNE when deciding on an organizational arrangement, and a number of factors can influence this choice. For example, firms that are just getting into the international arena are likely to choose a structure that differs from that of firms with established overseas operations. Conversely, companies that use their structures as worldwide sales organizations will have a different arrangement from those that locally manufacture and sell goods in various international markets. International structures will change in compliance with the strategic plan, and a structure that is proving to be unwieldy or inefficient will be scrapped in favor of one that better meets the needs of the company.[5] The following discussion examines some of the most common organizational arrangements used by MNEs.

Early organization structures

When a company first begins international operations, such activities are typically extensions of domestic operations. The firm's primary focus continues to be the local market; international involvement is of secondary importance. International transactions are conducted on a case-by-case basis, and there is no attempt to consolidate these operations into a separate department. Under this arrangement, international sales are viewed as supplements to the income earned from home-country operations.

As international operations increase, however, the MNE will take steps to address this growth structurally. One way is by having the marketing department handle international

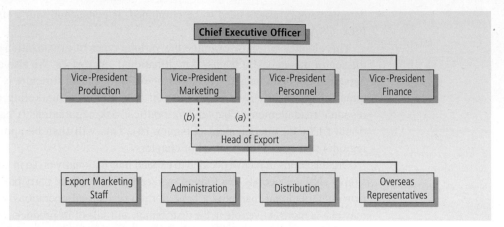

Figure 9.1 An export department structure

sales. All overseas operations are coordinated through this department; if sales warrant it, some of the salespeople will handle international transactions exclusively. In this way the company develops marketing specialists who learn the specific needs and marketing techniques to employ in overseas selling.

An alternative arrangement is to create an export department. This department may report directly to the chief executive officer (CEO) (Figure 9.1, line (*a*)) or be a sub-department within the marketing area (Figure 9.1, line (*b*)). If it operates independently of the marketing department (option (*a*)), it is either staffed by in-house marketing people whose primary focus is on the international market or operated by an outside export management company that is hired to provide the company with an international arm. Whichever approach is taken, MNEs planning to increase their international presence must ensure that the export department is a full-fledged marketing department and not just a sales organization.

Another possible arrangement is the use of overseas subsidiaries (see Figure 9.2). This is often a result of individual ventures in various geographic locales in which the head of the venture is given a great deal of autonomy and reports directly to the CEO. As long as the subsidiary shows sufficient profit, it is allowed to operate free from home-office interference.

As MNEs become more involved in foreign markets, the export department structure or subsidiary arrangement is generally discarded or supplemented because it cannot meet the organization's changing needs. As a result, the company will now look into joint ventures[6] and foreign direct investment, likely opting for an international division structure. To examine one company's international organization structure, see the case **International Business Strategy in Action: Sanofi-Aventis**.

Figure 9.2 Use of subsidiaries during the early stages of internationalization

INTERNATIONAL BUSINESS STRATEGY IN ACTION

Sanofi-Aventis

The French firm Sanofi-Synthelabo acquired Aventis, its most important and much larger French rival, in 2004, at the time creating the sixth largest pharmaceutical company in the world, Sanofi-Aventis. The new company is the result of a succession of approximately ten major mergers and acquisitions. Aventis itself was the product of a 1999 merger between French Rhône-Poulenc and Hoechst of Germany.

Sanofi-Aventis is a pharmaceutical group engaged in the research, development, manufacture, and marketing of healthcare products. Its business includes two main activities: pharmaceuticals and human vaccines through Sanofi Pasteur. It is also present in animal health products through Merial Limited (Merial). In its pharmaceutical activity, it specializes in six therapeutic areas: diabetes, oncology, thrombosis, cardiovascular, central nervous system (CNS), and internal medicine. The global portfolio of Sanofi-Aventis also consists of a range of other pharmaceutical products in Consumer Health Care (CHC) and other prescription drugs, including generics. It offers vaccines in five areas: pediatric combination vaccines, influenza vaccines, adult and adolescent booster vaccines, meningitis vaccines, and travel and endemic vaccines.

In 2014, Sanofi-Aventis had revenues totaling $36.340 billion, which made it the eighth largest pharmaceutical company in the world (see Table 9.1). The company continues to be based in France, but most of its sales are to foreign markets. Western Europe accounts for 23.3 percent of its sales, the United States for 32.6 percent, emerging markets for 33.6 percent, and the rest of the world for 9.5 percent.

Mergers in the pharmaceutical industry are the result of increasing pressures to consolidate in order to achieve

Source: THOMAS WIRTH/AFP/Getty Images

further economies of scale in R&D, marketing, and distribution. Aventis itself had managed to become one of the major competitors in its industry through mergers and acquisitions. Back in the mid-1980s Rhône-Poulenc was the 12th largest chemical firm in the world, with 80 percent of sales being generated in Europe. In this environment it competed with a large number of firms, including US-based giants DuPont and Dow Chemical, and leading European chemical companies such as Hoechst, BASF, Ciba-Geigy, and ICI.

During this period, the chemical industry was being increasingly structured on a "triad" basis. As a result, Rhône-Poulenc decided to consolidate its successful European base and move into the North American market. In the late 1980s the firm made 18 acquisitions in the United States, including Union Carbide Agrochemical Products and Stauffer Basic

Table 9.1 World's ten largest pharmaceutical companies, 2014 (based on revenue)

Rank	Company	Country of origin	Revenue (US$m)
1	Johnson & Johnson	United States	74,331
2	Novartis	Switzerland	57,997
3	Roche	Switzerland	49,860
4	Pfizer	United States	49,605
5	Sanofi	France	43,070
6	Merck	United States	42,237
7	GlaxoSmithKline	United Kingdom	37,960
8	AstraZeneca	Sweden	26,095
9	Bayer	Germany	25,470
10	Gilead Sciences	United Stated	24,474

Source: http://blog.proclinical.com.

▶

Chemicals. These acquisitions made the company the seventh largest chemical manufacturer in the world, generating over 20 percent of its total sales in the US market.

Managing its US operations was not easy. The takeover of Union Carbide worked pretty well because the latter's pesticide products were complementary to those of Rhône-Poulenc's herbicides and fungicides, and its corporate culture was similar. However, the Stauffer acquisition proved to be more difficult because there were overlapping product lines and the US managers at Stauffer had little international experience.

To improve the efficiency of its diverse US operations, Rhône-Poulenc adapted a highly decentralized organization structure, consolidating its US business operations into a US country group with headquarters at Princeton, New Jersey. The firm also established English as the official language of the company, even though its parent company was French.

And as an intermediate step on the path toward true globalization, the firm's US regional headquarters served to create a strong US presence in the face of vigorous competition from rivals with both efficient production and effective staffing. Rhône-Poulenc's plan for the future was to create a "transnational" structure.

The new Sanofi-Aventis can take advantage of the steps already taken by Aventis and its predecessor, Rhône-Poulenc, to maintain a strong presence in the US market.

Websites: http://en.sanofi-aventis.com; www.dupont.com; www.dow.com; www.hoechst.com; www.basf.com; www.ciba.com; www.novartis.com; www.ici.com

Sources: D. Hunter, "Reshaping Rhône-Poulenc," *Chemical Week*, vol. 156, no. 23 (1995), p. 30; Alan M. Rugman, *The Regional Multinationals: MNEs and "Global" Strategic Management* (Cambridge: Cambridge University Press, 2005); Matthew Herper, "Why Bristol and Sanofi shouldn't merge," *Forbes*, February 2, 2007; "Fortune Global 500," *Fortune*, 2010; Thomson Reuters, *OneSource*, 2011.

The international division

International division structure
An organizational arrangement in which all international operations are centralized in one division

The **international division structure** centralizes all international operations (see Figure 9.3), an arrangement that offers a number of advantages. First, it reduces the CEO's burden of direct operation of overseas subsidiaries and domestic operations.[7] Second, it creates a management team that prioritizes overseas operations. All information, authority, and decision making related to foreign efforts is channeled to this division, so there is one central clearing point for international activities. This structure also helps the MNE to develop a cadre of internationally experienced managers.

But the international division structure also has some significant drawbacks. One is that separating operations into two categories, domestic and international, can create rivalries between the two. Second, this arrangement puts pressure on the home office to think in global terms and to allocate resources on the basis of overall market opportunity. This can be extremely difficult for a management that has been domestically focused and makes the

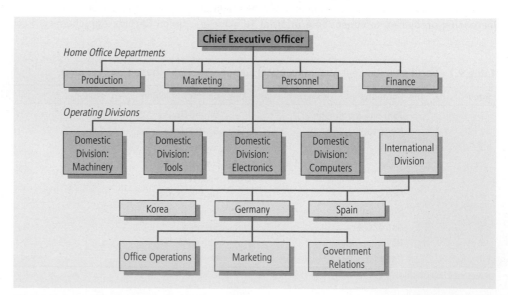

Figure 9.3 An international division structure

majority of its sales in the home market. Despite these drawbacks, the international division structure remains dominant among US MNEs.

Global organization structures

As MNEs generate more and more revenues from their overseas operations, their strategies become more global in focus and the structures used to implement them follow suit. European firms are a good example. Because their domestic markets are fairly small, these companies have traditionally had global structures. In all, there are six basic types: (1) global product, (2) global area, (3) global functional, (4) matrix, (5) mixed, and (6) transnational network.

Global product structure

Global product structure
An organizational arrangement in which domestic divisions are given worldwide responsibility for product groups

A **global product structure** is an arrangement in which domestic divisions are given worldwide responsibility for product groups. Figure 9.4 provides an example. In this arrangement, each product division sells its output throughout the world. As seen in the case of Product Division C, the European group operates in a host of countries. The same would be true for the other four geographic areas noted. In each case, the manager of the product division would have internal functional support for the entire product line. All production, marketing, personnel, and finance activities associated with Product C would be under the control of this individual. In recent years, Procter & Gamble has used this arrangement to market its wide assortment of products, from paper goods to beauty care, whereas Ford Motor Company has worked to establish a single automotive operation that relies on a global product structure.[8]

This arrangement employs a product division structure that relies on the "profit center" concept. Each product line is expected to generate a predetermined return on investment (ROI), and the performance of each line is measured on this profit basis. Each product line is also operated like an autonomous business, with the product division manager having a great deal of authority over how to run the operation. As long as the product line

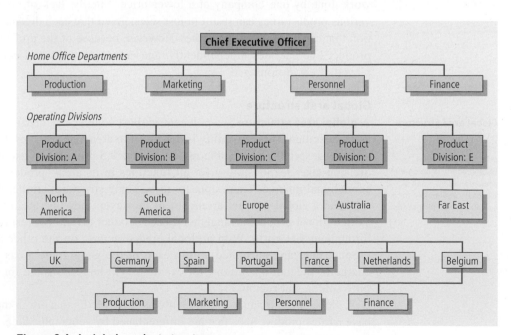

Figure 9.4 A global product structure

continues to generate the desired ROI, the division is usually allowed to operate unfettered by home-management controls. The only major exception is budgetary constraints that are imposed by central management.

A global product division structure has several benefits. If the firm produces a large number of diverse products, the structure allows each major product line to focus on the specific needs of its customers, which would be particularly difficult to achieve if the company were trying to sell all these products out of one centralized marketing department. The structure also helps develop a cadre of experienced, well-trained managers who understand a particular product line. And it helps the company match its marketing strategy to specific customer needs. For example, a product may be in the introduction stage in some areas of the world, and in the growth, maturity, or decline stage in others. These differing life cycles require close technological and marketing coordination between the home market and the foreign market, which can best be achieved by a product division approach. The product structure also helps the organization establish and maintain the necessary link between the product development people and the customer. By continually feeding back information from the field to the home office, product division personnel ensure that new product offerings meet consumer needs.

At the same time, there are drawbacks to the product division arrangement. One is the necessity of duplicating facilities and staff personnel within each division. A second is that products that sell well are often given primary attention, while those that need special handling or promotion are often sidetracked, even though this may result in the long-run loss of profit. A third is that an effective product division requires managers who are knowledgeable about the worldwide demand for their products. Most managers know the local market but do not know a lot about international markets. So it takes time to develop the necessary managerial staff to run this type of structure. A fourth shortcoming is the difficulty of coordinating the activities of different product divisions. For example, the electronics division may decide to subcontract components to a plant in Germany, while the computer division is subcontracting work to a firm in France. If the two divisions had coordinated their activities, it might have been possible to have all the work done by one company at a lower price. Finally, lack of cooperation among the various product lines can result in lost sales, given that each division may have information that can be of value to another. However, because of the profit center concept, each product line operates independently, and communication and cooperation are downplayed, if not discouraged.

Global area structure

Global area structure
An organizational arrangement in which primary operational responsibility is delegated to area managers, each of whom is responsible for a specific geographic region

A **global area structure** is a polycentric (host country-oriented) structure in which primary operational responsibility is delegated to area managers, each of whom is responsible for a specific geographic region. Figure 9.5 provides an example. Every regional division takes responsibility for all functions in its area—production, marketing, personnel, and finance. There appears to be some structural similarity between a global area and a global product arrangement; however, they operate in very different ways. With a global product arrangement, each product division is responsible for its output throughout the world. With a global area structure, on the other hand, the individual product lines are subsumed within each of the geographic areas. So the manager in charge of Belgian operations, for example, will be responsible for each of the product lines sold in that region.

A global area structure is commonly used by MNEs that are in mature businesses and have narrow product lines that are differentiated by geographic area. Food products are a good example.[9]

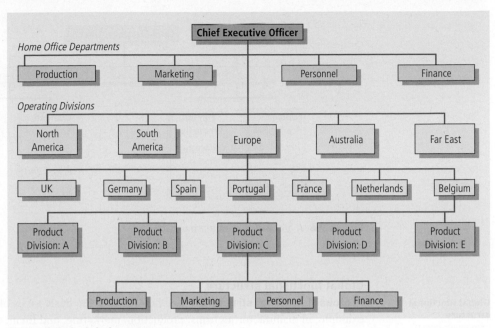

Figure 9.5 A global area structure

The global area structure provides division managers with the autonomy to make rapid decisions that depend on local tastes and regulations; because of this, the firm can become more "nationally responsive." Also, the company gains a wealth of experience in how to satisfy these local tastes, often building a strong competitive advantage in the process. The global area structure works well when economies of scale in production require a region-sized unit for basic production. For example, by setting up operations in the EU, a US company is able to achieve production cost advantages that would not otherwise be possible. Finally, the company can eliminate costly transportation associated with importing goods produced overseas.

If a product sells well in the United States, the company is likely to try to market it worldwide without making any modifications for local taste. Under the area structure, the opposite viewpoint holds: the product must be adapted to local tastes. But this means that the usual product emphasis in a company must be subsumed to the company's geographic orientation and the authority of the area managers. Another shortcoming with this organization structure is the expense associated with duplicating facilities. Each division has its own functional areas and is responsible for both production and marketing. Because production efficiency is often based on the amount of output, small plants are usually less efficient than large ones. Companies using a global area division structure also find it difficult to coordinate geographically dispersed divisions into the overall strategic plan. Quite often international cooperation and synergy among divisions end up being sacrificed. Finally, companies that rely heavily on R&D to develop new products often find that the global area divisions do not readily accept these offerings. This is because each group is trying to cater to the specific needs of its current market, and new products often require modification to meet those needs. Research shows that division managers prefer to sell products that have already been accepted by the market and are reluctant to take on new, untried products. Unfortunately, because most products have fairly short life cycles, this attitude is potentially dangerous to the long-term success of the MNE. The home office must continually fight such "anti-new product" drift.

Figure 9.6 A global functional structure

Global functional structure

Global functional structure
An organizational arrangement in which all areas of activity are built around the basic tasks of the enterprise

A **global functional structure** is one built around the basic tasks of the organization. For example, in manufacturing firms, production, marketing, and finance are the three primary functions that must be carried out for the enterprise to survive. Figure 9.6 shows such an arrangement. The head of the production department is responsible for all domestic and international manufacturing. Similarly, the head of marketing is responsible for the sales of all products here and abroad. This structure is most commonly used by MNEs with a narrow product line that has reached a stable plateau of global coverage and a level of demand that does not face major changes in a competitive attack.

The advantages of the global functional structure are allowing a small group of managers to maintain control over a wide-reaching organization, little duplication of facilities, and tight, centralized control. One disadvantage is difficulty in coordinating the production and marketing areas, since each operates independently of the other. This can be particularly troublesome if the MNE has multiple product lines. A second disadvantage is that responsibility for profits rests primarily with the CEO because there is little diffusion of operating authority far down the line.

Researchers have found that the global functional arrangement is most common among raw materials extractors with heavy capital investment. Energy firms also use it. However, this is not a structure that suits many other kinds of businesses.

Matrix structure

Matrix structure
An organizational arrangement that blends two organizational responsibilities such as functional and product structures or regional and product structures

Regional managers
In a geocentric matrix, managers charged with selling products in their geographic locale

Product managers
Managers responsible for coordinating the efforts of their people in such a way as to ensure the profitability of a particular business or product line

A **matrix structure** is an organizational arrangement that blends two organizational responsibilities, such as functional and product structures, or regional and product structures. The functional emphasis focuses on the activities to be performed, whereas the product emphasis focuses on the good that is being produced. This structure is characterized by a dual command system that emphasizes both inputs (functions) and outputs (products), thereby facilitating development of a globally oriented management attitude. Figure 9.7 illustrates a product–region matrix.

There are three types of managers in this geocentric matrix structure: regional managers, product managers, and matrix managers. **Regional managers** are charged with business in their markets. Their operation budgets include selling any of the products made by the MNE, subject to the decision of each regional manager. Their focus is polycentric. **Product managers** are responsible for coordinating the efforts of their people in such a way as to ensure the profitability of a particular business or product line. Their attitude is

Regions Products	Country A	Country B	Country C
Product 1			
Product 2			
Product 3			

Figure 9.7 A geographic matrix structure

ethnocentric. The matrix managers are responsible to *both* regional *and* product managers—they have two bosses.

With its three dimensions, the matrix design in Figure 9.8 is more complex than that in Figure 9.7. It illustrates how the matrix organizational arrangement can be used to coordinate and manage wide-reaching international operations. **Resource managers** are charged with providing the people for operations, whereas **business managers** are responsible for coordinating the efforts of these people to make profits for the product line. The resource managers are concerned with inputs, business managers with outputs. The bottom of Figure 9.8 shows functional specialists from such areas as marketing, manufacturing, and research. Individuals from each of these areas are assigned to each of the company's nine businesses. In turn, these nine profit centers operate in five different areas of the world, including the United States, Europe, and Asia. Each business is run by a business board (not shown in the figure) that reports to senior-level management.

Resource managers
In a matrix structure, managers charged with providing people for operations

Business managers
Managers responsible for coordinating the efforts of people in a corporate organization: for example, in a matrix structure

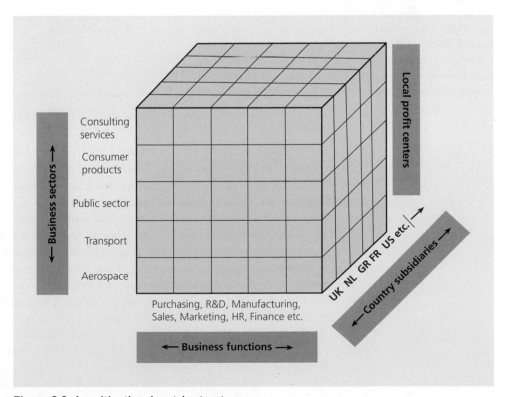

Figure 9.8 A multinational matrix structure

INTERNATIONAL BUSINESS STRATEGY IN ACTION

Making the matrix work

Many multinationals use matrix structures in their international operations. Some of these structures work out very well; some do not. Success can often be attributed to three important criteria: clarity, continuity, and consistency. If all three are achieved, the matrix tends to work well; if one or more are missing, the structural design is often ineffective.

Clarity refers to how well people understand what they are doing and why they are doing it. If the company's basic objectives are clear, if relationships in the structure are spelled out in direct, simple terms, and if the relevance of jobs is enunciated, there is a good chance that clarity will be achieved. A good example is NEC, the Japanese giant that decided to integrate computers and communication and to make this the focus of its business efforts. This message was clearly communicated to the personnel so that everyone in the organization understood what the company wanted to do. On the other hand, competitors like AT&T tried the same strategy but failed to clarify what they were doing. As a result, NEC has been more successful.

Continuity means that the company remains committed to the same core objectives and values. This provides a unifying theme and helps ensure that the personnel are committed. General Electric's Brazilian subsidiary is a good example of how a lack of continuity can hurt. In the 1960s the subsidiary built televisions. During the 1970s it was told to switch to large appliances. Then it was told to focus on housewares. By this time the company's dominant franchise in Brazil's electrical products market had all but dissipated. In contrast, Unilever set up operations in Brazil and, despite volatile changes in the economy, continued to focus its efforts on the electrical products market. By the 1990s Unilever had a thriving market in that country.

Consistency relates to how well all parts of the organization are moving in accord with each other. This is often a reflection of how well managers of the various operating divisions are pursuing the same objectives. For example, Philips NV launched an international strategy for its video cassette recording system, the V2000. However, its US subsidiary did not support these efforts because it felt that Matsushita's VHS format and Sony's Beta system were too well established. Because of this, Philips was unable to build the efficiency and credibility it needed to challenge the Japanese dominance of the VCR business.

Matrix structures can be complex organizational arrangements. However, if the MNE is able to achieve clarity, continuity, and consistency, the matrix approach can be very effective.

Websites: www.nec.com; www.att.com; www.ge.com; www.unilever.com; www.sony.com; www.philips.com

Sources: Christopher A. Bartlett and Sumantra Ghoshal, "Matrix management: not a structure, a frame of mind," *Harvard Business Review* (July/August 1990), pp. 138–45; Courtland L. Bovee et al., *Management* (New York: McGraw-Hill, 1993), pp. 321–3; Richard M. Hodgetts and Fred Luthans, *International Management*, 4th ed. (Burr Ridge, IL: Irwin/McGraw, 2000), chapter 7.

The matrix design in Figure 9.8 is sometimes referred to as a three-dimensional model because when it is drawn it has width, height, and depth. This multidimensional matrix addresses three major areas: function, product, and geography. So the structure is really a combination of some of the designs discussed earlier.

One of the major advantages of the multinational matrix is that it allows management to address more than one primary area of consideration. As Figure 9.8 shows, the company is able to focus on functional, product, and geographic considerations. MNEs that need to balance a product and a global location strategy can benefit from this type of structure.[10]

A drawback to the use of the matrix structure in international operations is the complexity of the design and the use of dual command, which can result in confusion about what everyone is responsible for doing and to whom one reports on various matters. A second drawback is the large number of meetings and discussions that often result from efforts to coordinate a variety of different groups, each with its own agenda. A third is that it often takes time for managers to learn to operate in a matrix structure, and if the enterprise has rapid turnover, there is always a significant portion of the personnel who do not fully understand how to function effectively in this environment. The case **International Business Strategy in Action: Making the matrix work** describes how some of these problems can be handled.

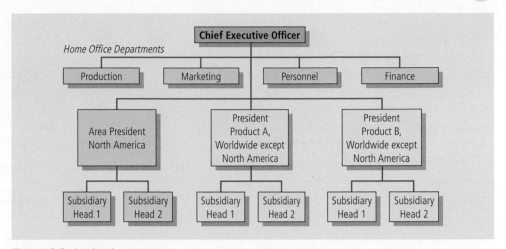

Figure 9.9 A mixed structure

Mixed structure

Mixed structure
A hybrid organization design that combines structural arrangements in a way that best meets the needs of the enterprise

A **mixed structure** is a hybrid organization design that combines structural arrangements in a way that best meets an enterprise's individual needs. Figure 9.9 provides an illustration. While pedagogically it is important to look at the models illustrated above, in practice a pure function, product, or area structure hardly ever exists. Most firms have some sort of mixed structure. Different businesses with different patterns of global demand, supply, and competition demand different management structures. Some structures might be very close to those mentioned above, but there is always some adaptation to be able to meet the needs of each specific enterprise.

Transnational network structure

Transnational network structure
An organization design that helps MNEs take advantage of global economies of scale while also being responsive to local customer demands

One of the newest forms of international organizational arrangements to emerge is the **transnational network structure**, which is designed to help MNEs take advantage of global economies of scale while also being responsive to local customer demands. This structural design combines elements of functional, product, and geographic designs, while relying on a network arrangement to link the various worldwide subsidiaries. At the center of the transnational network structure are nodes, which are units charged with coordinating product, functional, and geographic information. Different product group units and geographical area units have different structures depending on what is best for their particular operation. A good example of how the transnational network structure works is provided by Philips NV, which has operations in more than 60 countries and produces a diverse product line ranging from light bulbs to defense systems. In all, the company has six product divisions with a varying number of subsidiaries in each—and the focus of the latter varies considerably. Some specialize in manufacturing, others in sales; some are closely controlled by headquarters, others are highly autonomous.

The basic structural framework of the transnational network consists of three components: dispersed subunits, specialized operations, and interdependent relationships. *Dispersed subunits* are subsidiaries that are located anywhere in the world where they can benefit the organization. Some are designed to take advantage of low factor costs, whereas others are responsible for providing information on new technologies or consumer trends. *Specialized operations* are activities carried out by subunits that focus on particular product lines, research areas, and marketing areas, and are designed to tap specialized expertise or other resources in the company's worldwide subsidiaries. *Interdependent relationships* are used to share information and resources throughout the dispersed and specialized subunits.[11]

(a) **Global functional structure:** Decision making is centralized at headquarters.

(b) **Global area structure:** Decision making resides on each of the individual area regions.

(c) **Transnational network structure:** Individual units interact with each other and decision making is shared across the organization. Headquarters coordinates as another business unit and in cooperation with other units.

Figure 9.10 A transnational network structure

The transnational network structure is difficult to draw in the form of an organizational chart because it is complex and continually changing. Figure 9.10 gives a graphic scheme for the structure in comparison to the functional and area structures. The functional structure is one in which all decision making is made at headquarters, which coordinates all operations. The area, or geographic structure, is one in which each subunit acts independently from the others. That is, decision making is totally decentralized. The transnational network structure is a combination of both. Individual units interact with each other and decision making is shared across the organization. Headquarters is another business unit that coordinates the enterprise in coordination peripheral business units.

Let us now take a closer look at the transnational network structure. The peripheral circles represent the dispersed specialized subunits, each of which takes advantage of the different resources available in its environment to feed the organization. The connectors show the flows of components, know-how, labor, financial and marketing information, etc., among the different subunits. The central circle represents the headquarters, which helps to coordinate the interaction of the individual subunits using shared decision making.

✔ Active learning check

Review your answer to Active Learning Case question 1 and make any changes you like. Then compare your answer to the one below.

 What type of organization structure does P&G have in place for its worldwide operations? Is this structure optimal?

P&G follows a three-axis matrix structure in which the organizational responsibilities are divided among (a) regional marketing, (b) product-based R&D and manufacturing, and (c) regional logistics. These, in turn, are overseen by the Corporate Functions department. Because of the scale and international reach of its operations, a matrix structure allows high levels of national responsiveness in the marketing of P&G's branded products, economies of scale in R&D and production to be materialized through the Global Business Units, and economies of scale in logistics through the Global Business Services. Other types of organization structures would either constrain national responsiveness in marketing or undermine the company's capacity to achieve economies of scale at a regional level.

STRATEGIC MANAGEMENT AND ORGANIZING STRATEGY

Research has shown that effective organizations follow the adage "From strategy to structure."[12] They begin by formulating a strategy and only then design a structure that will efficiently implement this plan. In determining the best structure, three questions must be answered:

1 Can the company operate efficiently with domestic divisions or are international divisions also necessary?

2 On what basis should the organization be structured: product, area, function, mixed, or matrix?

3 How can the necessary coordination and cooperation be most effectively achieved?

These answers are usually determined through a careful analysis of five key variables.

Analysis of key structural variables

There are five key variables that MNEs examine in choosing from among alternative organization structures. In some cases one of these variables will outweigh the others, and the structure will be designed to accommodate this one. In most cases, however, there are three or four interacting variables that the structure must address.

First, the MNE will evaluate the relative importance of international operations at the time and project what the situation might be within three to five years. If the company is currently doing 5 percent of its business overseas and has an export department handling these sales, this organization structure may be adequate for now. However, if the MNE estimates that international sales will grow to 25 percent of total revenues in five years, the company will want to consider adopting an international division structure or one of the global arrangements. Unless the firm is prepared to make this transition, it may prove difficult to handle the anticipated rapid growth.

Second, the company will take into account its past history and experience in the international arena. If the firm has done very little business abroad, it is likely to choose a simple structure that is easy to understand and control. If the company has been doing business overseas for many years, it will probably have experienced managers who can work well in a more sophisticated structure, so it may choose a mixed design or a matrix.

A third area of consideration is the company's business and product strategy. If the company offers a small number of products and there is little need to adapt them to local tastes, a global functional structure may be the best choice. On the other hand, if the products must be tailored for local markets, a global product arrangement will usually be more effective. If the company is going to be doing business in a number of diverse geographic areas, a global area structure will typically be used. For example, to improve sales growth in Europe and Asia, Coca-Cola reinforced its global area organizational arrangement by putting new managers into positions overseeing operations in these regions.[13]

A fourth influencing variable is management's philosophy of operating. If the company wants to expand rapidly and is prepared to take risks, the firm will choose a structure that is quite different from that used by an MNE that wants to expand slowly and is conservative in its risk taking. Similarly, if the home office wants to keep a tight rein on operations, it will not use the same structure as a firm that gives local subsidiaries autonomy and encourages them to make decisions about how to keep the unit competitive at the local level. French and German subsidiaries, for example, tend to be more centralized than US units. There are also differences in the way operations are controlled. For example,

Japanese MNEs like to use face-to-face informal controls, whereas US multinationals prefer budgets, financial data, and other formalized tools.

A final key variable is the enterprise's ability to adjust to organizational changes. As MNE world sales increase, there are continual modifications in the structure. For example, when the company is small, the domestic divisions dominate. As the international side of operations grows, the managers of the domestic divisions have to cede some of their authority and influence. If they are unable or unwilling to do this, the structure is affected. Similarly, if international executives begin gaining greater authority and there is a need to revamp overseas operations, their willingness to adjust to organizational changes will affect the structure. In some cases MNEs have found that overseas managers, just like their domestic counterparts, build small empires and often are unwilling to give up this power.

The ultimate choice of organization structure rests with top management. However, this group seldom tries to force such a decision on those who will be directly affected. Instead, there is a give-and-take in which the needs of the enterprise and the personnel are considered.

In recent years the increase in mergers and acquisitions has had an important impact on MNE decision making. Deutsche Telekom's T-Mobile International provides a good example. As of 2014 the organization had 36,000 employees and had an ownership position in a large number of cell phone companies in a host of different countries (Austria, Croatia, Czech Republic, Albania, Germany, Hungary, Macedonia, Montenegro, the Netherlands, Poland, Romania Slovakia, the UK, the United States, and Puerto Rico), including VoiceStream (US), One2One (UK), Ben (Netherlands), max.mobil (Austria), and Radio Mobil (Czech Republic). In March 2011, Deutsche Telekom sold T-Mobile USA to rival AT&T for $39 billion, creating the largest US wireless network. The deal sent Deutsche Telekom shares surging. The deal still needs approval from regulators. Coordinating the operations of these holdings requires a carefully designed structure coupled with the appropriate amount of decentralized authority.[14] The result can be a structure that is both efficient and humanistic. In carrying this out, companies will address the organizational processes that take place within the structure.

✔ Active learning check

Review your answer to Active Learning Case question 2 and make any changes you like. Then compare your answer to the one below.

❷ Why was the international division replaced by the matrix structure?

The international division is a fairly primitive type of organization structure of an MNE. It is used at an early stage of international expansion (by P&G in the 1940s and 1950s). As P&G's sales in the international market increased beyond 20 percent or so, it turned to a more complex global organization structure, the three-axis global matrix, with which it could be nationally responsive and achieve economies of scale.

Coordination

The formal structure provides the skeletal framework within which the personnel operate. The structure is designed to answer the question: what is to be done? The organizational processes—decision making, communicating, and controlling—help make the structure work efficiently. These processes help answer the questions: who should do what, and how will they do it? These processes help put the organization structure into action.

Table 9.2 Factors that encourage centralization or decentralization of decision making in multinational operations

Encourage centralization of decision making	Encourage decentralization of decision making
Large enterprise	Small enterprise
Large capital investment	Small capital investment
Relative importance of the unit to the MNE	Relative unimportance of the unit to the MNE
Highly competitive environment	Stable environment
Strong volume-to-unit-cost relationship	Weak volume-to-unit-cost relationship
High degree of technology	Moderate to low degree of technology
Low level of product diversification	High level of product diversification
Homogeneous product lines	Heterogeneous product lines
High interdependence between the units	Low interdependence between the units
Few highly competent managers in the host country	Many highly competent managers in the host country
High experience in international business	Low experience in international business
Small geographic distance between home office and subsidiary	Large geographic distance between home office and subsidiary

Decision making

Decision making
The process of choosing
from among alternatives

Decision making is the process of choosing from among alternatives. In international operations one of the primary areas of consideration is where the ultimate decision-making authority will rest on important matters. If the home office holds this control, decision making is centralized; if the subsidiary can make many of these important decisions without having to consult the home office, decision making is decentralized. Table 9.2 provides some examples of factors that encourage both these types of decision making.[15]

Research shows that decision making in MNE subsidiaries tends to vary from country to country or culture to culture. For example, among British organizations there is a great deal of decentralized decision making. Many upper-level managers do not understand the technical nature of business operations, such as financial budgeting or cost control, so they delegate the authority for these matters to middle-level managers while they focus on strategic matters.

French and German subsidiaries tend to be fairly centralized in their decision making approaches. French senior executives like to maintain control of operations and tend to delegate less authority than do their British counterparts. German managers are hierarchical in their approach and most important decisions are made at the top.

In Scandinavian countries like Norway, Sweden, and Denmark, operations are highly decentralized both in Scandinavia-based firms and abroad. The Scandinavians place a great deal of emphasis on the quality of work life, and they are more interested in the well-being of the worker than in maximizing profit.

The Japanese use a combination of decentralization and centralization. They make heavy use of a decision-making process called *ringi*, or decision making by consensus.[16] At the same time, top management maintains a great deal of authority over what will be discussed at lower levels. Thus, senior-level management exercises both decentralization and centralization.

US MNEs, perhaps surprisingly, tend to use fairly centralized decision making in managing their overseas operations. This is particularly true in areas such as marketing policies, financial matters, and decisions on production capacity. Ford Motor, for example, in 2001 reduced the number of managers reporting to the CEO in order to better control operations.[17] On the other hand, Wal-Mart has been very successful in Canada by using a decentralized approach to accommodate the local market.[18] Moreover, this is the current trend worldwide as MNEs work to increase economies of scale and attain higher operational efficiency. One way in which many are doing this is through outsourcing, thus simplifying their structures and delegating the authority for some operations to their suppliers.[19]

> ✔ **Active learning check**
>
> *Review your answer to Active Learning Case question 3 and make any changes you like. Then compare your answer to the one below.*
>
> **③ Why does the company rely on decentralized decision making?**
>
> The primary reason why the firm relies so heavily on decentralized decision making is because the demands of the local areas are so great that it cannot make all important decisions from headquarters. This applies to the SMOs (previously MDOs), which must market to different cultures with different languages and business environments. But it also applies to the GBSs catering directly to a given region, which must function in the relevant languages and understand regionally specific logistics environments. Decision making is also delegated to the GBUs, which specialize to provide the most efficiency and innovation in each product category and to dissipate R&D knowledge across product families.

Communication

Communication
The process of transferring meanings from sender to receiver

Communication is the process of transferring meanings from sender to receiver. However, the way of doing this often varies from one MNE to another. For example, US MNEs use direct communications with their subsidiaries and overseas units.[20] Directives are spelled out clearly and precisely. Meanwhile, Japanese MNEs prefer more indirect communications in which things are implied and it is up to the listener to determine what to do. The direct approach works well for Americans, whose culture encourages openness and specific communications. The indirect approach works well for the Japanese, whose culture encourages indirect and implied communications.[21] Ouchi, after conducting a series of interviews with Americans working for a Japanese bank in the United States, found that this problem can be particularly disconcerting because each side is unable to understand the other's approach, as illustrated by the following:

American managers:
We have a non-stop running battle with the president. We simply cannot get him to specify a performance target for us. We have all the necessary reports and numbers, but we can't get specific targets from him. He won't tell us how large a dollar increase in loan volume or what percent decrease in operating costs he expects us to achieve over the next month, quarter, or even year. How can we know whether we're performing well without specific targets to shoot for?

Japanese bank president:
If only I could get these Americans to understand our philosophy of banking. To understand what the business means to us—how we feel we should deal with our customers and our employees. What our relationship should be to the local communities we serve. How we should deal with our competitors, and what our role should be in the world at large. If they could get that under their skin, then they could figure out for themselves what an appropriate objective would be for any situation, no matter how unusual or new, and I would never have to tell them, never have to give them a target.[22]

These types of culturally based differences can greatly affect an MNE's ability to get things done.

Kinesics
A form of non-verbal communication that deals with conveying information through the use of body movement and facial expression

Another communication-based problem is non-verbal messages. In international business these take two major forms: kinesics and proxemics. **Kinesics** deals with the conveying of information through the use of body movement and facial expression. For example, when verbally communicating with someone in the United States, it is good manners to look the other party in the eye. However, in many other cultures, such as the Arabic and Middle Eastern, this is not done, especially if one is talking to a member of the opposite sex. Such behavior would be considered rude and disrespectful.[23]

Proxemics
A form of non-verbal communication that deals with how people use physical space to convey messages

Proxemics deals with how people use physical space to convey messages. For example, in the United States, business people typically stand 2 to 3 feet (75 cm) away from those with whom they are communicating. However, in the Middle East and in many South American countries it is common to stand right next to the person. This often makes Americans feel very uncomfortable because this space is generally reserved only for family members and close friends. Business is not conducted at this distance. One group of authors summarized the problem this way:

> Americans often tend to be moving away in interpersonal communication with their Middle Eastern or Latin counterparts, while the latter are trying to physically close the gap. The American cannot understand why the other is standing so close; the latter cannot understand why the American is being so reserved and standing so far away; the result is a breakdown in communication.[24]

Another example of proxemics is office layout and protocol. In the United States, a large office connotes importance, as does a secretary who screens visitors and keeps away those whom the manager does not wish to see. In Japan, most managers do not have large offices; if they do, they spend little time in them since they are generally out talking to the employees and walking around the workplace. If the manager were to stay in the office all day, it would be viewed as a sign of distrust or anger at the work group. In Europe, many managers do not have walled-in offices. The bosses are out in the same large room as their people; there is no one to screen the brokers from the boss.

Every country has some unique communication patterns or behaviors.[25] These behaviors can be particularly troublesome to outsiders who are working locally and are unfamiliar with local approaches to communication. Figure 9.11 provides an interesting example in the form of epigrams that have been drawn from organization structures throughout the world.

United States	England	China	Norway
Americans believe that they all have a link to the top of the organization and, if need be, can drop by and talk to the president, regardless of their position in the hierarchy.	In England top managers and workers communicate among themselves, but there is no communication link between the two groups.	In China everyone is a small cog in a giant machine. As a result, there is a massive bureaucracy, with each person directly controlling a small number of subordinates.	In Norway the chain of command runs from the top to the middle management. Those at the bottom do not receive information from their boss; instead, they get it from the chief executive officer (CEO) who violates the chain of command and comes down the line. The person to whom the CEO passes this information then conveys it to all the other workers.

Figure 9.11 Organizational epigrams

Note: An epigram is a terse, witty statement. The organizational epigrams are designed to poke fun at the way communication flows in international organizations. Each was created by an individual with experience in the respective country. The explanation accompanying the respective epigram explains the logic behind the drawing. These epigrams illustrate that communication flows throughout the world are less efficient than the enterprise would like. They also illustrate that each country has its own unique approach to conveying information.

Source: Adapted from Simcha Ronen, *Comparative and Multinational Management.* Copyright © 1986 John Wiley & Sons, Inc. Reproduced with permission of John Wiley & Sons, Inc.

Controlling

Controlling
The process of determining that everything goes according to plan

Controlling is the process of determining that everything goes according to plan and that performance is rewarded. It consists of three steps: (1) establishing standards; (2) comparing performance against standards; and (3) correcting deviations. Controlling is closely linked to communication since it is virtually impossible to evaluate performance and make changes without communicating information. Many of the same organizational problems discussed above also apply here.

One of the major differences between US and Japanese firms is the use of explicit versus implicit control. A major difference between US and European firms is that US MNEs tend to rely more heavily on reports and other performance-related data, whereas Europeans make heavy use of behavioral control. US multinationals compare results of a foreign unit to those of other foreign units, as well as with domestic units, in evaluating performance. European MNEs tend to be more flexible and to judge performance on an individual basis rather than simply making a comparative judgment. Other differences include:

1 Control in US MNEs relies on precise planning and budgeting that is suitable for comparison purposes. Control in European MNEs takes into consideration a high level of company-wide understanding and agreement over what constitutes appropriate behavior and how such behavior supports the goals of the subsidiary and the parent company.

2 US multinationals do not encourage their managers to remain in overseas positions for a long period of time. As a result, they use large central staffs and centralized information gathering to carry out evaluations. European multinationals, on the other hand, encourage their managers to remain in overseas positions and rely heavily on these managers to provide input on how well the unit is doing.

3 Managers of US MNEs often report to a counterpart back in headquarters who, in turn, conveys information up the line. European multinationals have a more direct reporting channel so that the head of a foreign subsidiary reports to someone who is closer to the top of the structure.[26]

Another major difference is the way in which personnel are evaluated. In the United States and Europe, it is common to single out high performers and reward them. In Japan, however, credit is given to the entire group rather than just to one or two individuals. Singling people out for special attention is not regarded as complimentary. Rather, such attention would make individuals feel they were not regarded as team players, which would be insulting. Another important difference is the time period for personnel evaluations. Most US and European firms evaluate their people on an annual basis. However, in Japan the first major evaluation often does not occur until the employee has been with the firm for almost a decade.[27] These controlling differences greatly affect the way the structure is managed. As a result, running an overseas operation the same way as at home is often difficult.

 Active learning check

Review your answer to Active Learning Case question 4 and make any changes you like. Then compare your answer to the one below.

4 In controlling its operations, what are three areas that are paramount for the firm?

There are a number of areas P&G needs to control. One of these is profit. The company must ensure that its divisions are profitable in each market in which it operates. A second area is cost control. Presently, P&G's matrix structure is designed to be nationally responsive and decreases costs through economies of scale. A third area is innovation. One of the firm's principal competitive advantages is its ability to improve its brands against the competition; as a result, it must weigh its advances in R&D against that of the competition. A fourth area of control is the brand awareness of consumers for P&G's brands.

KEY POINTS

1 When a company first enters the international arena, it is common to find that these efforts are mere extensions of domestic operations. The MNE will typically handle foreign sales directly through its own marketing department, an export department, or an overseas subsidiary that is the result of a joint venture. As international operations become more important, however, the firm is likely to centralize these operations by adopting an international division structure. This organizational arrangement remains quite popular with many MNEs.

2 As multinationals generate increased revenues from their overseas operations, they are likely to adopt a global organization structure. There are six basic types: global product, global area, global functional, mixed, matrix, and transnational network. Each type has specific advantages and disadvantages.

3 There are five key variables that MNEs examine in choosing from among alternative organization structures: (a) the relative importance of international operations, (b) past history and experience in the international arena, (c) the company's business and product strategy, (d) management philosophy, and (e) the firm's ability to adjust to organizational changes.

4 The formal structure provides the skeletal framework within which the personnel operate. The organization processes of decision making, communicating, and controlling make the structure work efficiently. In the decision-making process, one of the key areas of consideration is the amount of centralization or decentralization that will be used by the home office. In communicating, culturally based differences will be of major importance, including non-verbal messages. In controlling, areas of concern include explicit and implicit control and the ways in which personnel will be evaluated.

Key terms

- international division structure
- global product structure
- global area structure
- global functional structure

- matrix structure
- regional managers
- product managers
- resource managers
- business managers
- mixed structure

- transnational network structure
- decision making
- communication
- kinesics
- proxemics
- controlling

REVIEW AND DISCUSSION QUESTIONS

1 How does an export department structure function? Who handles the overseas sales?

2 If a company's initial international expansion is conducted through the use of subsidiaries, how closely does it control these subsidiaries? Why?

▶

3 Why do MNEs use an international division structure? Are there any drawbacks to this organizational arrangement?

4 How does a global product structure work? Why would an MNE opt for this arrangement? What are two drawbacks to using this structure?

5 When would an MNE use a global area structure? When would the firm reject this structural arrangement in favor of a different structure?

6 How does a global functional structure work? When would it be a popular approach? When would it be of very little value in organizing international operations?

7 When would a company opt for a mixed structure? Why? Defend your answer.

8 How does a matrix structure work? When would an MNE opt for this organizational arrangement?

9 There are five key variables that MNEs examine in choosing from among alternative organization structures. What are these five? Identify and briefly describe each.

10 Why are some overseas operations highly decentralized while others are very centralized? What factors influence this arrangement?

11 Why are US international operations more centralized than those in Sweden? Why is the US model becoming more popular among MNEs?

12 In what way is implicit versus explicit communication important in understanding how home-office managements coordinate international activities?

13 What type of control techniques do US MNEs prefer? How does this preference differ from that of the Japanese? Compare and contrast the two.

REAL CASE

LVMH: organizing luxury products in the international arena

LVMH is the French-based, world-leading luxury goods group that was founded in 1987 with the merger of Louis Vuitton and Moët Hennessy. Christian Dior, Dom Pérignon, Givenchy, and Moët & Chandon are just a few of LVMH's world-famous luxury brand names. By 2014, revenues for the group totaled €30.638 billion, putting it among the top five marketers of luxury items (including wines). LVMH operates approximately 2,400 stores across the world and employs more than 80,000 people, where over 70 percent of employees work outside France. The company generates the bulk of its sales in foreign markets; only 10 percent of all revenues are earned in France. The United States is the company's single largest market, comprising 24 percent of revenues. It is important to note that although France earns a small fraction of LVMH's revenues, Europe as a whole (including France) accounts for 29 percent. Japan accounts for 7 percent, while Asia (excluding Japan) accounts for 29 percent. The remaining 9 percent is generated mainly in

the Pacific, Latin America, and Canada. With large shares of sales in each broad region of the triad, LVMH is a true global company.

LVMH's organizational arrangement is much more than that of a typical conglomerate. The whole organization focuses on shared costs and synergies, both backward and forward in its value chain. The five main lines of business are really strategic business units (SBUs) that are set up to market well-known, high-quality products while responding to local tastes and regulations. They are: (1) LVMH Fashion and Leather Goods; (2) Wines and Spirits; (3) Perfumes and Cosmetics; (4) Watches and Jewelry; and (5) Selective Retailing. By carefully overseeing major operations from the top while allowing the individual SBUs to make the decisions that directly affect their own local markets, LVMH employs a combination of "tight and loose" control to maximize its international presence. In the process, it has become the most global retail company.

Source: Patrick/SAGAPHOTO.COM/Alamy Stock Photo

high-quality luxury products. The company sources only in France, Italy, and Switzerland.

The vision of a totally integrated group was and continues to be an important part of the global strategy that has positioned LVMH as an industry leader. The company walks a fine line between the exclusivity required of luxury goods and the size and scope of its operations. It might operate around the world, but its products are not accessible to all.

Websites: www.lvmh.com; www.vuitton.com; www.moet.com; www.dior.com; www.givenchy.com

Sources: Adapted from www.lvmh.com; LVMH, *Annual Report*, 2010, 2014; Stéphane Girod and Alan M. Rugman, "Regional business networks and the multinational retail sector," *Long Range Planning*, vol. 38, no. 4 (2005), pp. 335–57.

The profit margin on luxury goods is very high, so control over production, distribution, and advertising is central to profitability. LVMH ensures that production standards in its manufacturing operations are the highest. It centralizes manufacturing by using a common laboratory for cosmetics research and integrates the operations for all the branch offices in each group to ensure maximum efficiency.

Marketing is a very important part of LVMH's strategy. The company spends 11 percent of all its revenues on worldwide advertising and purchases media products in bulk to receive the best value for its money. The "Made in France" label is stressed to appeal to its home country's reputation for

1 What type of organization structure does LVMH have?

2 What is the role of the SBUs in the organization structure of LVMH? What problems might arise if each SBU were run independently?

3 Compare the organization structure of LVMH to that of Procter & Gamble. Are there any similarities? How are these organizations different?

4 What are some of LVMH's FSAs that are listed in this case?

5 How would outsourcing to less developed countries affect LVMH?

REAL CASE

Command Alkon: small but increasingly global

Based in Birmingham, Alabama, in the United States, Command Alkon is the world leader in the design and supply of computer software for the construction business. With over $80 million in revenues, Command Alkon is a small to medium-sized MNE but it has tremendous capabilities in technology standardization and is number one in its niche software market segment in terms of market share, revenues, and distribution. Employing over 300 people, it has international offices in India, Colombia, France, the Netherlands, and the UK that market its products in each region through independent sales representatives. Roughly 20 percent of the company's business is now derived outside North America.

Command Alkon is the result of a merger in December 2000 of Command Data and Alkon, two construction material software and service firms. The merger was designed to

pool their R&D resources to compete more effectively in the fast-changing computer software business. Individual products were already compatible and the merger eliminated duplication of effort. The company specialized in the construction business, which was largely ignored by booming software firms, so it was able to become the largest player in a niche market. At present, it competes only with two smaller, local competitors and the systems developed in-house by customers.

It has internationalized with a number of small-scale mergers and acquisitions, including a French firm in 2008, a Dutch company in 2010, and a Brazilian firm in 2011. It focused on US-based takeovers through 2015 but also established offices in the UK, India, Malaysia, and Columbia.

Command Alkon has a largely ethnocentric strategy and organization structure. All decisions are centralized and ▶

hierarchical micromanagement is the name of the game. The dominant culture is that of the US home office. There is little customization, not much marketing, and investment in local offices is primarily to deliver the US products and services locally. It is not a "born global" firm; it is a US firm. Like most small businesses, Command Alkon is driven by its basic product or service, and it replicates its firm-specific advantage overseas.

One of the problems for small businesses is that the top management team is itself small. Often it comprises just the founder of the firm, his or her immediate family, and a few friends, so there is little managerial experience and a limited opportunity to develop international business skills, which leads to ethnocentric behavior. Indeed, most small business leaders do not have the internal resources to build an overseer business by foreign direct investment; instead, they are drawn to the export mode of foreign entry. Thus, they need an international division structure.

There are thousands of small and medium-sized enterprises (SMEs) like Command Alkon. Their business strategy is not as complicated as that of MNEs; usually SMEs are in only one line of business. The international experience of SMEs is usually through licensing and/or exporting. If they engage in foreign direct investment or develop global organization structure, it is usually to deliver a standard product globally, rather than to customize the product, service or organization to local markets.

Websites: www.commandalkon.com; www.systechsystems.com

Sources: www.commandalkon.com; Gilbert Nicholson, "Command Alkon found its niche and dug in," *Birmingham Business Journal*, November 2, 2001; Steven Lang, "The merits of specialization," *VARBusiness*, February 18, 2004; Thomson Reuters, *OneSource*, 2011.

---

1   Why does a small business like Command Alkon usually have little or no foreign direct investment? How does it go international?

2   What is the typical type of organization structure for a small business like Command Alkon?

3   Why are software businesses usually ethnocentric in their organization structure?

NOTES

1 See, for example, Yigang Pan and Xiaolian Li, "Joint venture formation of very large multinational firms," *Journal of International Business Studies*, vol. 32, no. 1 (2000), pp. 179–89; and Tim G. Andrews and Nartnalin Chompusri, "Lessons in 'cross-vergence': restructuring the Thai subsidiary corporation," *Journal of International Business Studies*, vol. 30, no. 3 (2000), pp. 77–93; and Namrata Malhotra and C. R. (Bob) Hinings, "An organizational model for understanding internationalization processes," *Journal of International Business Studies*, vol. 41 (2010), pp. 330–49; doi:10.1057/jibs.2009.75.

2 Brad Mitchener, "GM takes a gamble on eastern Europe," *Wall Street Journal*, June 23, 1997, p. A10.

3 William J. Holstein et al., "Mighty Mitsubishi is on the move," *Business Week*, September 24, 1990, p. 99; and Mure Dickie in Tokyo, "Japanese yards claim to have edge over rivals," *Financial Times Online*, February 7, 2011.

4 Robert L. Simison, "New data illustrate reshaping of auto parts business," *Wall Street Journal*, September 2, 1997, p. B4; and Lindsay Whipp in Tokyo, "Japan to invest in quake-struck auto-parts industry," *Financial Times Online*, May 29, 2011.

5 A good example is offered by Peter Siddall, Keith Willey, and Jorge Tavares, "Building a transnational organization for BP Oil," *Long Range Planning* (February 1992), pp. 37–45.

6 For some excellent examples, see Charles H. Ferguson, "Computers and the coming of the US keiretsu," *Harvard Business Review* (July/August 1990), pp. 55–70; and Benjamin Gomes-Casseres, "Joint ventures in the face of global competition," *Sloan Management Review*, vol. 30, no. 3 (spring 1989), pp. 17–26.

7 Richard M. Hodgetts and Fred Luthans, *International Management*, 4th ed. (Burr Ridge, IL: McGraw/Irwin, 2000), p. 303.

8 Joann S. Lublin, "Place vs. product: it's tough to choose a management model," *Wall Street Journal*, June 27, 2001, pp. A1, 4.

9 Hodgetts and Luthans, *International Management*, p. 306.

10 Yves L. Doz, Christopher A. Bartlett, and C. K. Prahalad, "Global competitive pressures and host country demands," *California Management Review* (spring 1981), p. 66.

11 See Sumantra Ghoshal and Christopher A. Bartlett, *Managing across Borders: The Transnational Solution* (London: Random House, 1998).

12 Alfred D. Chandler, Jr., *Strategy and Structure* (Garden City, NY: Anchor Books, Doubleday, 1966).

13 Betsy McKay, "Coke reorganization puts three as contenders for no. 2 position," *Wall Street Journal*, July 31, 2001, p. B2; and Louise Lucas in London, "Coca-Cola seeks cultural shift in Paris listing," *Financial Times Online*, May 23, 2011; and Jonathan Birchall in New York, "Coca-Cola sees broad global growth," *Financial Times Online*, February 9, 2011.

14 William Boston, "Can Telekom turn a David into a Goliath?" *Wall Street Journal*, June 1, 2001, pp. A11, 13; and Julia Caesar, "AT&T and T-Mobile create biggest US firm in $39bn deal," *BBC News Online*, March 21, 2011.

15 Also see Rebecca Blumenstein, "GM is building plants in developing nations to woo new markets," *Wall Street Journal*, August 4, 1997, pp. A1, 5; and Jorn Madslien, "Changed landscape for global carmakers," *BBC News Online*, May 10, 2011.

16 Raghu Nath, *Comparative Management: A Regional View* (Cambridge, MA: Ballinger, 1988), p. 125.

17 Tim Burt and Nikki Tait, "Ford refines chain of command in US," *Financial Times*, August 16, 2001, p. 13.

18 Bernard Simon, "Canada warms to Wal-Mart," *New York Times*, September 1, 2001, pp. B1, 3.

19 See, for example, "Japan Inc. on the Treadmill," *The Economist*, June 9, 2001, pp. 63–4; and Rakesh B. Sambharya and Kunal Banerji, "The effect of keiretsu affiliation and resource dependencies on supplier firm performance in the Japanese automobile industry," *Management International Review*, vol. 46, no. 1 (2006).

20 Bruce T. Lamont, V. Sambamurthy, Kimberly M. Ellis, and Paul G. Simmonds, "The influence of organizational structure on the information received by corporate strategists of multinational enterprises," *Management International Review*, vol. 40, no. 3 (2000), pp. 231–2.

21 For some excellent insights into how Japanese companies function, see Noboru Yoshimura and Philip Anderson, *Inside the Kaisha* (Boston, MA: Harvard Business School Press, 1997).

22 For an excellent contrast of American and Japanese communication problems, see William G. Ouchi, *Theory Z* (Reading, MA: Addison-Wesley, 1981), pp. 33–5.

23 Jane Whitney Gibson, Richard M. Hodgetts, and Charles W. Blackwell, "Cultural variations in nonverbal communication," in *Proceedings of the 55th Annual Convention of the Association for Business Communication*, 1990, p. 213.

24 Hodgetts and Luthans, *International Management*, p. 212.

25 David E. Sanger, "Tokyo's tips for New York," *New York Times Magazine*, February 6, 1994, pp. 28–9.

26 William G. Egelhoff, "Patterns of control in US, UK, and European multinational corporations," *Journal of International Business Studies*, vol. 15, no. 2 (fall 1984), pp. 81–2.

27 Ouchi, *Theory Z*, p. 22.

BIBLIOGRAPHY

Ambos, Björn, and Mahnke, Volker. "How do MNC headquarters add value?" *Management International Review*, vol. 50, no. 4 (August 2010).

Ambos, Björn, and Schlegelmilch, Bodo B. *The New Role of Regional Management* (Basingstoke: Palgrave Macmillan, 2010).

Ambos, Tina C., and Ambos, Björn. "Organizational capabilities and the effectiveness of knowledge flows within multinational corporations," *Journal of International Management*, vol. 15, no. 1 (2009).

Ambos, Tina C., and Birkinshaw, Julian. "Headquarters' attention and its effect on subsidiary performance," *Management International Review*, vol. 50, no. 4 (August 2010).

Andersson, Ulf, and Forsgren, Mats. "In search of center of excellence: network embeddedness and subsidiary roles in multinational corporations," *Management International Review*, vol. 40, no. 4 (2000).

Barkemeyer, Ralf, Preuss, Lutz, and Lee, Lindsay. "On the effectiveness of private transnational governance regimes— evaluating corporate sustainability reporting according to the Global Reporting Initiative." *Journal of World Business*, vol. 50, no. 2 (2015).

Barnard, Helena, and John Cantwell. "Knowledge in the theory of the firm and MNC: asset or action? A commentary on Foss N. 'Knowledge and organization in the theory of the MNC'." *Journal of Management and Governance*, vol.10, no. 1 (2006).

Bartlett, Christopher A., and Ghoshal, Sumantra. *Managing Across Borders: The Transnational Solution* (Boston, MA: Harvard Business School Press, 1989).

Bartlett, Christopher A., and Ghoshal, Sumantra. "Matrix management: not a structure, a frame of mind," *Harvard Business Review*, vol. 68, no. 4 (July/August 1990).

Beamish, Paul W., Karavis, Lambros, Goerzen, Anthony, and Lane, Christopher. "The relationship between organizational structure and export performance," *Management International Review*, vol. 39, no. 1 (1999).

Benito, Gabriel R. G., Grøgaard, Birgitte, and Narula, Rajneesh. "Environmental influences on MNE subsidiary roles: economic integration and the Nordic countries," *Journal of International Business Studies*, vol. 34, no. 5 (September 2003).

Bjorkman, Ingman, Barner-Rasmussen, Wilhelm, and Li, Li. "Managing knowledge transfer in MNCs: the impact of headquarters control mechanisms," *Journal of International Business Studies*, vol. 35, no. 5 (September 2004).

Bouquet, Cyril, Morrison, Allen J., and Birkinshaw, Julian M. "International attention and multinational enterprise performance," *Journal of International Business Studies*, vol. 40, no. 1 (2009).

Buckley, Peter J., and Carter, Martin J. "A formal analysis of knowledge combination in multinational enterprises," *Journal of International Business Studies*, vol. 35, no. 5 (September 2004).

Buckley, Peter J., and Strange, Roger. "The governance of the multinational enterprise: insights from internalization theory," *Journal of Management Studies*, vol. 48, no. 2 (March 2011).

Ciabuschi, Francesco, Dellestrand, Henrik, and Kappen, Philip. "Exploring the effects of vertical and lateral mechanisms in international knowledge transfer projects," *Management International Review*, vol. 51, no. 2 (April 2011).

Ciabuschi, Francesco, Martín, Oscar, and Ståhl, Benjamin. "Headquarters' influence on knowledge transfer performance," *Management International Review*, vol. 50, no. 4 (August 2010).

Collinson, Simon, and Morgan, Glenn. *Images of the Multinational Firm* (Oxford: Wiley-Blackwell, 2009).

De la Torre, José R., Esperança, José Paulo, and Martínez, Jon I. "Organizational responses to regional integration among MNEs in Latin America," *Management International Review*, vol. 51, no. 2 (April 2011).

Egelhoff, William G. "How the parent headquarters adds value to an MNC," *Management International Review*, vol. 50, no. 4 (August 2010).

Figueira-de-Lemos, Francisco, and Amjad Hadjikhani. "Internationalization processes in stable and unstable market conditions: toward a model of commitment decisions in dynamic environments," *Journal of World Business*, vol. 49, no. 3 (2014).

Foss, Nicolai J. "Knowledge and organization in the theory of the multinational corporation: some foundational issues," *Journal of Management and Governance*, vol. 10, no. 1 (2006).

Foss, Nicolai J., Husted, Kenneth, and Michailova, Snejina. "Governing knowledge sharing in organizations: levels of analysis, governance mechanisms, and research directions," *Journal of Management Studies*, vol. 47, no. 3 (May 2010).

Ghoshal, Sumantra, and Bartlett, Christopher A. "The multinational corporation as an interorganizational network," *Academy of Management Review*, vol. 15, no. 4 (October 1990).

Ghoshal, Sumantra, and Bartlett, Christopher A. *The Individualized Corporation: A Fundamentally New Approach to Management* (New York: HarperBusiness, 1997).

Heracleous, Loizos. *Strategy and Organization* (Cambridge: Cambridge University Press, 2003).

Inkpen, Aandrew C. "Knowledge transfer and international joint ventures: the case of NUMMI and General Motors," *Strategic Management Journal*, vol. 29 (2008).

Keupp, Marcus Matthias, Palmié, Maximilian, and Gassmann, Oliver. "Achieving subsidiary integration in international innovation by managerial 'tools,'" *Management International Review*, vol. 51, no. 2 (April 2011).

Kogut, Bruce, and Zander, Udo. "Knowledge of the firm and the evolutionary theory of the multinational corporation," *Journal of International Business Studies*, vol. 24, no. 4 (1993).

Lagerström, Katarina, and Andersson, Maria. "Creating and sharing knowledge within a transnational team—the development of a global business system," *Journal of World Business* vol. 38, no. 2 (2003).

Levy, Orly, Beechler, Schon, Taylor, Sully, and Boyacigiller, Nakiye A. "What we talk about when we talk about 'global mindset': managerial cognition in multinational corporations," *Journal of International Business Studies*, vol. 38, no. 2 (March 2007).

Li, Guey-Huey, Yu, Chwo-Ming, and Seetoo, Dah-Hsian. "Toward a theory of regional organization," *Management International Review*, vol. 50, no. 1 (February 2010).

Li, Jingxun, and Lee, Ruby P. "Can knowledge transfer within MNCs hurt subsidiary performance? The role of subsidiary entrepreneurial culture and capabilities." *Journal of World Business* (2014).

London, Ted, and Hart, Stuart L. "Reinventing strategies for emerging markets: beyond the transnational model," *Journal of International Business Studies*, vol. 35, no. 5 (September 2004).

Meyer, Klaus E. "Contextualizing organizational learning: Lyles and Salk in the context of their research," *Journal of International Business Studies*, vol. 38, no. 1 (January 2007).

Minbaeva, Dana, Pedersen, Torben, Björkman, Ingmar, Fey, Carl F., and Park, Hyeon J. "MNC knowledge transfer, subsidiary absorptive capacity, and HRM," *Journal of*

International Business Studies, vol. 34, no. 6 (November 2003).

Mudambi, Ram, and Navarra, Pietro. "Is knowledge power? Knowledge flows, subsidiary power and rent-seeking within MNCs," *Journal of International Business Studies*, vol. 35, no. 5 (September 2004).

Nachum, Lilach, "International business in a world of increasing returns," *Management International Review*, vol. 43, no. 3 (2003).

Oh, Chang Hoon, and Li, Jing. "Commentary: Alan Rugman and the theory of the regional multinationals." *Journal of World Business* vol. 50, no. 4 (2015).

Parkhe, Arvind. "Interfirm diversity, organizational learning, and longevity in global strategic alliances," *Journal of International Business Studies*, vol. 22, no. 4 (1991).

Piekkari, Rebecca, Nell, Phillip C., and Ghauri, Pervez N. "Regional management as a system," *Management International Review*, vol. 50, no. 4 (August 2010).

Rosenzweig, Philip M., and Singh, Jitendra V. "Organizational environments and the multinational enterprise," *Academy of Management Review*, vol. 16, no. 2 (April 1991).

Rugman, Alan M., and Verbeke, Alain. "A note on the transnational solution and the transaction cost theory of multinational strategic management," *Journal of International Business Studies*, vol. 23, no. 4 (fall 1992).

Rugman, Alan M., and Verbeke, Alain. "Extending the theory of the multinational enterprise: internalization and strategic management perspectives," *Journal of International Business Studies*, vol. 34, no. 2 (March 2003).

Rugman, Alan M., and Verbeke, Alain "A regional solution to the strategy and structure of multinationals," *European Management Journal*, vol. 26 (2008).

Sinkovics, Rudolf R., Roath, Anthony S., and Cavusgil, S. Tamer. "International integration and coordination in MNEs," *Management International Review*, vol. 51, no. 2 (April 2011).

Sullivan, Daniel. "Organization in American MNCs: the perspective of the European regional headquarters," *Management International Review*, vol. 32, no. 3 (1992).

Tallman, Stephen, and Chacar, Aya S. "Knowledge accumulation and dissemination in MNEs: a practice-based framework," *Journal of Management Studies*, vol. 48, no. 2 (March 2011).

Tran, Yen, Mahnke, Volker, and Ambos, Björn. "The effect of quantity, quality and timing of headquarters-initiated knowledge flows on subsidiary performance," *Management International Review*, vol. 50, no. 4 (August 2010).

Verbeke, Alain. "International acquisition success: social community and dominant logic dimensions," *Journal of International Business Studies*, vol. 41 (2010).

Verbeke, Alain, and Kenworthy, Thomas P. "Multidivisional versus metanational governance of the multinational enterprise," *Journal of International Business Studies*, vol. 39, no. 2 (2008).

Westney, Eleanor. "Challenging the transnational model," *Socio-Economic Review*, vol. 12 (2008).

Westney, Eleanor D., and Zaheer, Srilata. "The multinational enterprise as an organization." In Alan M. Rugman (ed.), *The Oxford Handbook of International Business*, 2nd ed. (Oxford: Oxford University Press, 2009).

Wolf, Joachim, and Egelhoff, William G. "Limitations of the network organization in MNCs," in J. Pla-Barber and J. Alegre (eds.), *Progress in International Business Research*, vol. 5 (Amsterdam: Emerald, 2010).

Wolf, Joachim, and Egelhoff, William G. "Network or matrix? How information-processing theory can help MNCs answer this question." In A. Bøllingtoft,

L. Donaldson, G. P. Huber, D. Døjbak Håkonsson, and C. C. Snow (eds.), *Collaborative Communities of Firms: Purpose, Process, and Design* (Springer Science, Business Media BV, 2011).

Zahra, Shaker A. "The dynamic firm: the role of technology, strategy, organization, and regions," *Academy of Management Review*, vol. 24, no. 4 (October 1999).

Chapter 10

CORPORATE STRATEGY AND NATIONAL COMPETITIVENESS

Contents

Objectives of the chapter

The primary objective of this chapter is to develop two frameworks for understanding how both nations and MNEs must fashion their strategies to achieve international competitiveness. In doing so, we give particular consideration to the regional economic integration of North America, although these frameworks are also relevant for other triad economies and also for emerging economy firms.

The specific objectives of this chapter are to:

1 *Examine* the determinants and external variables in Porter's "diamond" model of national competitiveness and critique and evaluate the model.

2 *Present* a "double-diamond" model that illustrates how firms in non-triad countries such as Canada are using their diamond to design corporate strategies for the North American market.

3 *Discuss* the benefits and effects of the North American Free Trade Agreement on both Mexico and Canada.

4 *Describe* how Mexico is using a double-diamond model to tap into the North American market.

5 *Define* the terms *economic integration* and *national responsiveness* and relate their importance to MNE strategies throughout the world.

Worldwide operations and local strategies of ABB

Headquartered in Zurich, Switzerland, Asea Brown Boveri (ABB) is one of Europe's major industrial firms. Since the merger in 1987 that created it, ABB has been acquiring or taking minority positions in a large number of companies throughout the world. In recent years it has purchased Westinghouse's transmission and distribution operations and Combustion Engineering, the manufacturer of power generation and process automation equipment.

ABB Ltd (ABB) provides power and automation technologies for its utility and industrial customers. It focuses on power transmission, distribution, and power-plant automation, and serves electric, gas, and water utilities, as well as industrial and commercial customers. ABB also delivers automation systems that measure, control, protect, and optimize plant applications across a range of industries. By 2014, the conglomerate, which employs approximately 150,000 people worldwide, had annual revenues of $39.83 billion; 34 percent of its revenues come from Europe, 29 percent from the Americas, and 27 percent from Asia. The remainder, 10 percent, comes from Africa and the Middle East.

ABB operates on both local and global terms. On the one hand it attempts to maintain deep local roots wherever it operates so that it can modify both products and operations for that market. For example, managers are trained to adapt to cultural differences and to learn how to communicate effectively with local customers. At the same time the company works to be global and to make products that can be sold anywhere in the world because its technology and quality give it a worldwide appeal.

ABB has five distinctive business divisions: discrete automation and motion accounted for 24 percent of total revenue in 2014, power products (also 24 percent), low voltage products (18 percent), process automation (18 percent), and power systems (16 percent).

This is possible for four reasons: (1) ABB's research and development makes it a leader in power and automation technology, enabling it to develop and build products and services throughout the world; (2) its operations are structured to take advantage of economies of scale and thus keep prices competitive; (3) it adapts to local environments and works closely with customers so that it is viewed as a national rather than a foreign company; and (4) it works

closely with companies in other countries that are favored by their own government but need assistance in financing and producing equipment for that market. As a result, ABB is able to capitalize on its technological and manufacturing expertise and develop competitive advantages in both triad and non-triad markets.

In some cases ABB has gone so far as to take an ownership position in companies located in emerging economic markets. For example, the firm purchased 76 percent of Zamech, Poland's leading manufacturer of steam turbines, transmission gears, marine equipment, and metal castings. And it has bought into two other Polish firms that make a wide range of generating equipment and electric drives. ABB reorganized these firms into profit centers, transferring its own expertise to local operations, and developing worldwide quality standards and controls for production. In Mexico, ABB acquired FIP SA in 2001, an oil and gas production equipment company. In October 2009, ABB Ltd. acquired Sinai Engineering Corporation to enhance its presence and capabilities in Western Canada. In January 2011, the company acquired Baldor Electric Company (the United States) at the value of $4.2 billion, including $1.1 billion of net debt.

More recently, in April 2015, the firm bought the small, Munich-based robotics firm, Gomtec GmbH. This makes sense when you know that ABB has installed more than 250,000 robots across the world. This merger and the large number of other acquisitions that have taken place throughout its history have to be fully incorporated into the ABB structure.

ABB works hard to be a "good citizen" of every country in which it operates, while also maintaining its supranational status. As a result, the company is proving that it is possible to have worldwide operations and local strategies that work harmoniously.

Website: www.abb.com

Sources: Adapted from William Taylor, "The logic of global business: an interview with ABB's Percy Barnevik," *Harvard Business Review* (March/April 1991), pp. 91–105; Carol Kennedy, "ABB: model merger for the new Europe," *Long Range Planning,* vol. 25, no. 5 (1992), pp. 10–17; Edward L. Andrews, "ABB will cut 10,000 jobs and switch focus to Asia," *New York Times,* October 22, 1997, p. C2; Alan M. Rugman, *The Regional Multinationals* (Cambridge: Cambridge University Press, 2005); ABB, *Annual Report,* 2009, 2014; Thomson Reuters, *OneSource,* 2011; "Fortune Global 500," *Fortune,* 2010. ABB website news, April 2015.

1 In what way does ABB's strategy incorporate Porter's four country-specific determinants and two external variables?

2 Why did ABB buy Gomtec GmbH? How can the company link this small firm into its global strategy and structure?

3 How does ABB address the issues of globalization and national responsiveness? In each case, cite an example.

INTRODUCTION

In this chapter, two frameworks are developed. Again it is useful to relate these to the basic firm and country model first outlined in the opening chapters of this textbook. In this chapter we will first review the single-diamond model of Michael Porter (1990). We will apply it to analyze the international competitiveness of large economies such as the United States, Japan, and Germany. We then introduce the double-diamond framework which is more suitable for somewhat smaller but open trading economies, such as Canada, New Zealand, Korea, Singapore, and, indeed, most countries in the world. Both the Porter single diamond and the double diamond deal with CSAs. There are rankings of countries based on the manner in which their CSAs are being utilized to improve their international competitiveness. Yet, in this work on international competitiveness, the manner in which CSAs are turned into FSAs is often not made explicit.

The second framework outlined in this chapter is the famous economic integration and national responsiveness matrix. The economic integration axis is largely explained by CSAs. The national responsiveness axis is a pure FSA. Indeed, only in international business can this type of FSA arise. The managers of a multinational enterprise (MNE) have a network of subsidiaries and national responsiveness is relevant when making decisions about the strategy and organizational structure of such firms. In contrast, purely domestic firms cannot experience FSAs in national responsiveness. Together, these two frameworks provide students with the basic insights necessary to analyze the complex nature of the strategy and structure of multinational enterprises and other firms involved in international business.

Some MNEs rely on their home market to generate the research, development, design, or manufacturing needed to sell their goods in international markets. More and more, however, they are finding that they must focus on the markets where they are doing business as well as on strategies for tapping the resources of those markets and gaining sales entry. In short, multinationals can no longer rely exclusively on the competitive advantage they hold at home to provide them with a sustainable advantage overseas.

In addition, many small countries realize they must rely on export strategies to ensure the growth of their economies. Those that have been most successful with this strategy have managed to tap into markets within triad countries. Good examples are Canada and Mexico, both of which have found the United States to be a lucrative market for exports and imports. As a result, many successful business firms in these two countries have integrated themselves into the US economy, while creating what some international economists call a North American market. In the future many more MNEs are going to be following this pattern of linking into the economies of triad members.

The basic strategy that these MNEs are following can be tied directly to the Porter model presented in earlier, although some significant modifications of this model are in order. We will first examine Porter's ideas in more detail and then show how these ideas are serving as the basis for developing corporate strategies and international competitiveness in Canada and Mexico.

THE SINGLE DIAMOND

At several points throughout this book we have referred to the four determinants of national competitive advantage, as set forth by Porter (see Figure 10.1). We noted that these factors can be critical in helping a country build and maintain competitive advantage. We now consider Porter's "diamond" framework in more depth, examining how his findings apply specifically to triad countries and determining how the ideas can be modified and applied to nations that are not triad members.

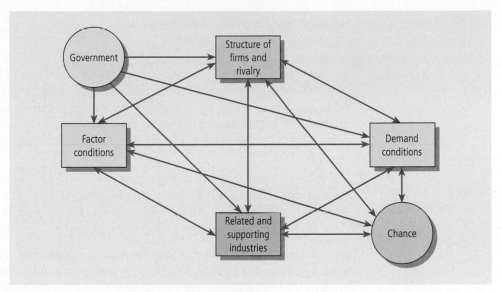

Figure 10.1 Porter's single-diamond framework

Determinants and external variables

Porter's "diamond" model is based on four country-specific determinants and two external variables. The determinants comprise:

1 *Factor conditions.* These include (a) the quantity, skills, and cost of the personnel; (b) the abundance, quality, accessibility, and cost of the nation's physical resources such as land, water, mineral deposits, timber, hydroelectric power sources, and fishing grounds; (c) the nation's stock of knowledge resources, including scientific, technical, and market knowledge that affect the quantity and quality of goods and services; (d) the amount and cost of capital resources that are available to finance industry; and (e) the type, quality, and user cost of the infrastructure, including the nation's transportation system, communications system, healthcare system, and other factors that directly affect the quality of life in the country.

2 *Demand conditions.* These include (a) the composition of demand in the home market as reflected by the various market niches that exist, buyer sophistication, and how well the needs of buyers in the home market precede those of buyers in other markets; (b) the size and growth rate of the home demand; and (c) the ways in which domestic demand is internationalized and pulls a nation's products and services abroad.

3 *Related and supporting industries.* These include (a) the presence of internationally competitive supplier industries that create advantages in downstream industries through efficient, early, or rapid access to cost-effective inputs; and (b) internationally competitive related industries that can coordinate and share activities in the value chain when competing or those that involve complementary products.

4 *Firm strategy, structure, and rivalry.* These include (a) the ways in which firms are managed and choose to compete; (b) the goals that companies seek to attain as well as the motivations of their employees and managers; and (c) the amount of domestic rivalry and the creation and persistence of competitive advantage in the respective industry.

The four determinants of national advantage shape the competitive environment of industries. However, two other variables, chance and government, also play important roles:

1 *The role of chance.* Chance events can nullify the advantages of some competitors and bring about a shift in overall competitive position because of developments such as (a) new inventions, (b) political decisions by foreign governments, (c) wars, (d) significant shifts in world financial markets or exchange rates, (e) discontinuities in input costs such as oil shocks, (f) surges in world or regional demand, and (g) major technological breakthroughs.

2 *The role of government.* Government can influence all four of the major determinants through such actions as (a) subsidies, (b) education policies, (c) the regulation or deregulation of capital markets, (d) the establishment of local product standards and regulations, (e) the purchase of goods and services, (f) tax laws, and (g) antitrust regulation.[1]

Figure 10.1 provides an illustration of the complete system of these determinants and external variables. Each of the four determinants affects the others, and all in turn are affected by the role of chance and government.

Critique and evaluation of the model

In applying this model to international business strategy, we must first critique and evaluate Porter's paradigm and supporting arguments. First, the Porter model was constructed based on statistical analysis of aggregate data on export shares for ten countries: Denmark, Italy, Japan, Singapore, South Korea, Sweden, Switzerland, the UK, the United States, and West Germany. In addition, historical case studies were provided for four industries: the German printing press industry, the US patient monitoring equipment industry, the Italian ceramic tile industry, and the Japanese robotics industry. In each case the country is either a member of the triad or an industrialized nation. Since most countries of the world do not have the same economic strength or affluence as those studied by Porter, it is highly unlikely that his model can be applied to them without modification.

Second, the government is of critical importance in influencing a home nation's competitive advantage. For example, it can use tariffs as a direct entry barrier to penalize foreign firms, and it can employ subsidies as an indirect vehicle for penalizing foreign-based firms. Government actions such as these, however well intentioned, can backfire and end up creating a "sheltered" domestic industry that is unable to compete in the worldwide market.[2]

Third, although chance is a critical influencing factor in international business strategy, it is extremely difficult to predict and guard against. In a similar vein, technological breakthroughs in computers and consumer electronics have resulted in rapid changes that, in many cases, were not predicted by market leaders.

Fourth, in the study of international business, the Porter model must be applied in terms of company-specific considerations and not in terms of national advantages. As Porter notes so well in his book, "Firms, not nations, compete in international markets."[3]

Fifth, in support of his model, Porter delineates four distinct stages of national competitive development: factor-driven, investment-driven, innovation-driven, and wealth-driven (see Figure 10.2). In the factor-driven stage, successful industries draw their advantage almost solely from the basic factors of production such as natural resources and the nation's large, inexpensive labor pool. Although successful internationally, the industries compete primarily on price. In the investment-driven stage, companies invest in modern, efficient facilities and technology, and work to improve these investments through modification and alteration. In the innovation-driven stage, firms work to create new technology and

Figure 10.2 The four stages of national development and the historical position of select nations

methods through internal innovation and with assistance from suppliers and firms in related industries. In the wealth-driven stage, firms begin to lose their competitive advantage, rivalry ebbs, and the motivation to invest declines. As seen in Figure 10.2, Porter believes that Singapore is in the factor-driven stage, Korea is investment driven, Japan is innovation driven, Germany and the United States are between the innovation and wealth-driven stages, and the UK is wealth driven. Because the stage of development greatly influences the country's competitive response, the placement of countries in Figure 10.2 is critical. So too is the logic that countries move from one stage to another, rather than spanning two or more stages, because there are likely to be industries or companies in all major economies that are operating at each stage.

Sixth, Porter contends that only outward FDI is valuable in creating competitive advantage, and inbound foreign investment is never the solution to a nation's competitive problems. Moreover, foreign subsidiaries are not recognized by Porter as sources of competitive advantage.[4] These statements are questionable and have already been rejected in this text. For example, scholars such as Safarian,[5] Rugman,[6] and Crookell[7] have all demonstrated that R&D undertaken by foreign-owned firms is not significantly different from that of Canadian-owned companies. Moreover, Rugman has found that the 20 largest US subsidiaries in Canada export virtually as much as they import (the rate of exports to sales is 25 percent, whereas that of imports to sales is 26 percent).[8]

Seventh, as seen in Figure 10.2, reliance on natural resources (the factor-driven stage) is viewed by Porter as insufficient to create worldwide competitive stature.[9] However, Canada, for one, has developed a number of successful megafirms that have turned the country's comparative advantage in natural resources into proprietary firm-specific advantages in resource processing and further refining-sources of sustainable advantage.[10] Moreover, case studies of the country's successful multinationals such as Alcan, Noranda, and NOVA help illustrate the methods by which value added has been introduced by the managers of these resource-based companies.[11]

Eighth, the Porter model does not adequately address the role of MNEs. Researchers such as Dunning[12] have suggested including multinational activity as a third outside variable (in addition to chance and government). Certainly there is good reason to question whether MNE activity is covered in the "firm strategy, structure, and rivalry" determinant, and some researchers have raised the question of how the same rivalry determinant can both include multinationality for global industries and yet exclude it for multidomestic industries. As Dunning notes, "There is ample evidence to suggest that MNEs are influenced in their competitiveness by the configuration of the diamond in other than their home countries, and that this in turn may impinge upon the competitiveness of home countries."[13] For example, in 2014, Nestlé earned over 98 percent of its sales outside Switzerland;[14] thus, the Swiss diamond of competitive advantage is less relevant than that of the countries in which Nestlé operates. This is true not only for MNEs in Switzerland but for 95 percent of the world's MNEs as well. For example, virtually all of Canada's large multinationals rely on sales in the United States and other triad markets. Indeed, it could be argued that the US diamond is more relevant for Canada's industrial multinationals than Canada's own diamond, since more than 70 percent of Canadian MNE sales take place in the United States. Other nations with MNEs based on small home diamonds include Australia, New Zealand, Finland, and most, if not all, Asian and Latin American countries as well as a large number of other small countries. Even small nations in the EU, such as Denmark, have been able to overcome the problem of a small domestic market by gaining access to one of the triad markets. So in applying Porter's framework to international business at large, one conclusion is irrefutable: *Different diamonds need to be constructed and analyzed for different countries.*

✔ Active learning check

Review your answer to Active Learning Case question 1 and make any changes you like. Then compare your answer to the one below.

❶ In what way does ABB's strategy incorporate Porter's four country-specific determinants and two external variables?

The strategy incorporates Porter's country-specific determinants as part of a well-formulated global strategy designed to tap the strengths of various markets. For example, the company draws on the factor conditions and demand conditions in Europe to support its power and automation business. It also draws on supporting industries to help sustain its worldwide competitive advantage in that industry. At the same time, the company's strategy, structure, and rivalry are designed to help it compete at the local level. The strategy incorporates the external variable of government by considering relations between countries as a lubricant for worldwide economic integration. It addresses the variable of chance by operating globally and thus reducing the likelihood that a war or a regional recession will have a major negative effect on operations. The firm's heavy focus on core technologies and R&D also helps minimize this chance variable.

THE DOUBLE DIAMOND

Researchers have recently begun using Porter's single diamond as a basis for analyzing the international competitiveness of smaller countries. This approach builds on Porter's theme of corporate strategy and process as a source of competitive advantage for a nation.

Canada and the double diamond

Figure 10.3 illustrates how Porter's single diamond would look if it were applied to Canada's case.[15]

Two themes have recurred consistently in Canadian industrial policy: export promotion for natural resource industries and import substitution in the domestic arena. The Canadian market has always been seen as too small to support the development of economies of scale required in modern industry. Hence it has been the practice in Canada to provide the

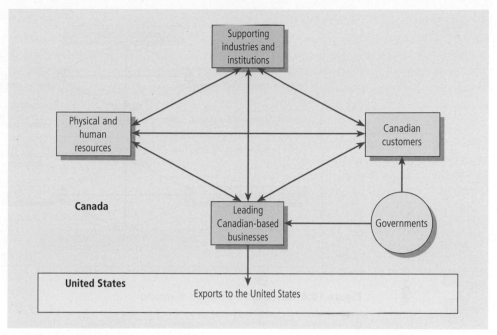

Figure 10.3 The single-diamond view

Source: Adapted from Alan M. Rugman and Joseph R. D'Cruz, *Fast Forward: Improving Canada's International Competitiveness* (Diane Publishing Co., 1991), p. 35.

base for developing large-scale resource businesses that are designed to exploit the natural resources found in the country. Export strategies have emphasized commodity products that have been developed in isolation from major customers. In the past these strategies had been encouraged by US government policies that removed or eliminated tariffs on imports of commodities that are not produced extensively in the United States. The Canadian government's role had been to help leading Canadian-based businesses by establishing relatively low taxes on resource extraction and by subsidizing the costs of capital through grants, low-interest loans, and loan guarantees.

With respect to import substitution, the Canadian goal had been to use tariff and non-tariff measures to provide a protected environment for developing secondary industry. Under this arrangement the country's approach to business was largely focused inwardly, relying solely on the extent and quality of natural resources as the basis for the creation of wealth.

By the mid-1960s, however, it had become clear that a more international focus was needed. The 1967 Canada–United States Auto Pact demonstrated that significant economic benefits would result from the elimination of tariffs on trade between the two countries in autos and parts. This agreement eventually became the model for the United States–Canada Free Trade Agreement.[16] In the process Canadian plants gained economies of scale by producing for the North American market as a whole rather than for the Canadian market alone. For corporate strategy, the result of North American economic integration has been the development of a Canadian–US "double diamond," which shows that the two countries are integrated for strategy purposes into a single market (see Figure 10.4).

Under this new arrangement, Canadian businesses are now in direct competition with firms operating in a diamond of their own in the United States.[17] To survive this rivalry with leading US firms, Canadian businesses have to develop competitive capabilities of a high order.[18] They can no longer rely on their country's home diamond and natural resource base. Innovation and cost competitiveness are equally important, and this

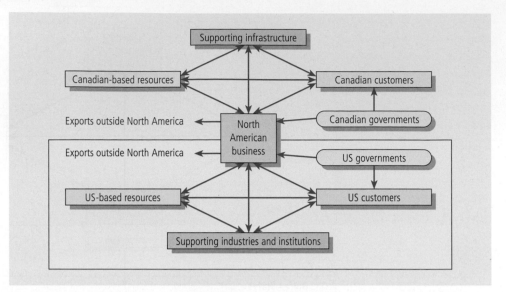

Figure 10.4 Canadian–US double diamond

Source: Adapted from Alan M. Rugman and Joseph R. D'Cruz, "The 'Double Diamond' Model of International Competitiveness: the Canadian Experience," *Management International Review*, vol. 33, Special Issue 2 (1993), p. 32.

requires strategies that are designed to access the US diamond. Now Canadian managers need a "double-diamond perspective" for their strategic decisions. The double diamond is, of course, relevant for other small, open economies such as Finland and Sweden. The case **International Business Strategy in Action: Nokia and Ericsson** provides an example.

The Free Trade Agreement has also created a series of unique pressures on the Canadian subsidiaries of US multinationals, many of which were created for the purpose of overcoming Canadian tariff barriers that were designed to encourage the development of local operations. These subsidiaries are now unnecessary, and many of them are currently in direct competition with their US-based parent. If they cannot compete successfully, future business will go south of the border.[19]

Meanwhile, major Canadian companies are working to develop competitive positions in the United States as well as worldwide.[20] A good example is Magna International, Canada's leading diversified automotive supplier headquartered in Aurora, Ontario, Canada. The company designs, develops and manufactures automotive systems, assemblies, modules and components, and engineers and assembles complete vehicles, primarily for sale to original equipment manufacturers (OEMs) of cars and light trucks in three geographic segments: North America, Europe, and rest of world (primarily Asia, and South America). It is Canada's largest automobile part manufacturer and also one of the world's 500 largest companies. The firm has now established a significant manufacturing and product development presence in the United States. As at September 2010, the company had 245 manufacturing divisions and 80 product development, engineering, and sales centers in 25 countries. In 2009, Magna derived 18.6 percent of its total revenues from Canada, 21.6 percent from the United States, 6.7 percent from Mexico (North America 46.9 percent), 38.6 percent from western Europe, 4.3 percent from the United Kingdom, 5.6 percent from other European countries (Europe 48.5 percent), and the remainder from rest of world.[21]

Bombardier Inc. provides another example. Beginning as a Canadian manufacturer of snow-going equipment, the company has now grown into a multinational firm with interests in aviation, transportation, and financial services. In the aviation/aerospace business, Bombardier has major operations in Canada and the United States, among other locations, and manufactures a line of business aircraft, commercial aircraft, including regional jets, turboprops, and single-aisle mainline jets, and amphibious aircraft. The company's transportation operations are located throughout North America and Europe and manufacture passenger trains, mass transit railcars, and engines. It also provides bogies, electric propulsion, control equipment and maintenance services, as well as complete rail transportation systems and rail control solutions.[22]

Other major Canadian firms are following suit, operating from a North American perspective in order to lay the groundwork for becoming globally competitive.[23] This involves viewing the United States and Canada as home-based markets and integrating the use of both "diamonds" for developing and implementing strategy. In particular, this requires:

- developing innovative new products and services that simultaneously meet the needs of the US and Canadian customer, recognizing that close relationships with demanding US customers should set the pace and style of product development;

- drawing on the support industries and infrastructure of both the US and Canadian diamonds, realizing that the US diamond is more likely to possess deeper and more efficient markets for such industries;

- making free and full use of the physical and human resources in both countries.[24]

Strategic clusters in the double diamond

The primary advantage of using the double diamond is that it forces business and government leaders to think about management strategy and public policy in a more productive way. Rather than viewing the domestic diamond as the unit of analysis, managers from smaller countries are encouraged to always be outward looking. Doing well in a double diamond is the first step toward global success.

Once a country has recognized the benefit of the double-diamond perspective, it should first identify successful and potentially viable clusters of industries within its borders and then examine their linkages and performances across the double diamond. A **strategic cluster** is a network of businesses and supporting activities located in a specific region, where the flagship firms compete globally and the supporting activities are home based, although some can be foreign owned. In addition, some of the critical business inputs and skills may come from outside the country, with their relevance and usefulness being determined by the membership of the strategic cluster. A successful strategic cluster will have one or more large MNEs at its center. Whether these are home or foreign owned is irrelevant so long as they are globally competitive. They are the flagship firms on which the strategic cluster depends. Ideally, they operate on a global basis and plan their competitive strategies within the framework of global competition. A vital component of the cluster is companies with related and supporting activities, including both private and public sector organizations. In addition, there are think tanks, research groups, and educational institutions. Some parts of this network can even be based outside the country, but the linkages across the border and the leadership role of the nation's flagships result in world-class competitive multinationals.[25]

Currently Canada has several strategic clusters. One is the auto assembly and auto parts industry in southwestern Ontario, led by the Big Three US auto multinationals with their related and affiliated suppliers and distributors. There are linkages to various high-tech firms and research groups that span the border, as does the auto assembly industry itself. Other strategic clusters are based in banking and financial services in Toronto, advanced manufacturing and telecommunications in Toronto, forest products in western and eastern Canada, energy in Alberta, and the fisheries in Atlantic Canada. Some are led by flagship Canadian-owned multinationals such as Bombardier, Magna International, and Research in Motion (RIM, best known as the developer of the BlackBerry smart phone); others are led by, or include, foreign-owned firms such as IBM Canada and DuPont Canada.[26]

Strategic cluster
A network of businesses and supporting activities located in a specific region, where flagship firms compete globally and supporting activities are home based

Nokia and Ericsson: moving beyond mobiles

Based in one of the world's smallest countries, Finland's Nokia was once the largest producer of cell phones. Founded in 1865, Nokia was a major manufacturer of paper products before it transformed itself into a high-tech producer of electronic products, especially cellular phones, starting in the 1970s. By 2014, based on turnover, Nokia was the second largest company in Finland with sales of €11.198 billion. It had production facilities spanning 13 countries and R&D in 13 locations worldwide. It generated sales in 140 countries and employed approximately 62,000 people. In 2014, Nokia derived €3,886 million of its total sales from Europe, €4,774 million from Asia–Pacific, including China, €1,100 million from the Middle East and Africa, €1,053 million from Latin America, and €1,919 million from North America.

At its height the firm was a pioneer in mobile telephones, riding the wave of first business users then regular consumers buying a series of Nokia's early models. Then in 2009 Nokia's sales dropped by 23 percent year-on-year and industry watchers commented that Nokia had been falling behind its competitors, particularly Apple, for some years. In February 2011, Nokia announced a strategic alliance whereby it planned to abandon its Symbian smartphone operating system in favor of Microsoft's Windows Phone 7, in order to challenge the growing popularity of phones powered by Google's Android operating software and the Apple iPhone. The Apple iPhone (driven by Apple's proprietary iOS) captured the top of the smartphone market, while devices powered by Android—free, open source software—were failing to fully challenge subsequent models of iPhones.

Between 2013 and early 2014 Nokia finally sold off its Devices and Services business to Microsoft, exiting the cell phone business. This left it with three major business divisions: Nokia Networks, its network infrastructure business; a location intelligence business (HERE); and Nokia Technologies, which includes intellectual property rights activities.

Finland has a population of approximately 5.5 million, so from the beginning Nokia has pursued foreign sales. Less than 1 percent of sales in 2014 were from its home country. Internationalization has always been essential for growth. The firm established itself initially as the cell phone leader in Scandinavia, despite competition from Ericsson of Sweden. From there it progressed to becoming the leader in the UK and then the rest of Europe, and formed strategic alliances with US distributors such as RadioShack and US telecom companies like AT&T. The firm also developed special phones for Chinese and Japanese users, spending a large percentage of sales on R&D, which allowed it to continuously introduce new handset models. For example, it pioneered the development of MP3 technology that allowed cell phones to evolve into portable music players.

Founded in 1876, L. M. Ericsson has grown to employ more than 115,000 people and had sales of US$26.67 billion in 2014, in the 180 countries in which it operated. Back in 1997, Ericsson was the world's largest producer of digital cell phones.

Unlike Nokia, which started as a paper and rubber producer, Ericsson has always been in telecommunications, beginning in 1876 as a telephone manufacturer. It has always been innovative, with one in four of its employees working in R&D. It has over 37,000 patents, giving it a strong portfolio of intellectual property rights. Many of these relate to telephone switches, helping it compete with firms such as Nokia Siemens Networks, France's Alcatel-Lucent, and Japan's NEC. Ericsson was well positioned to benefit from the telecom deregulation of the 1980s and 1990s. This created new demand, especially for new equipment like cell phones in areas with few local monopoly producers. By 2000 Ericsson was the world's leading supplier of 3G mobile systems.

Just like Nokia, Ericsson formed a range of alliances to access complementary technologies, including with Intel, Hewlett-Packard, and Texas Instruments. These firms acted as key suppliers of components and products that Ericsson used for voice and data transmission. An estimated 40 percent of global mobile traffic runs through Ericsson-developed networks, serving more than 1 billion subscribers around the world, every day. If it had a weakness, compared to Nokia and Motorola, this was perhaps its brand name and its direct consumer marketing capability. It has evolved as a strong B-to-B supplier, not as a B-to-C player.

Both Nokia from Finland and Ericsson from Sweden have successfully evolved from small domestic markets into global giants through technological innovation, complementary partnerships, and a constant focus on internationalization.

Websites: www.nokia.com; www.ericsson.com; www.motorola.com; www.nortelnetworks.com; www.alcatel.fr; www.att.com; www.compaq.com; www.hp.com; www.intel.com; www.ti.com

Sources: Richard Hylton, Nick Moore, and Roger Honor, "Making money in the tech market," *Fortune*, May 13, 1996; Erick Schonfeld, "Hold the phone: Motorola is going nowhere fast," *Fortune*, March 30, 1998; Caroline Daniel, "World's most respected companies," *Financial Times*, December 17, 2001; Nokia, *Annual Report*, 2009, 2014; Ericsson, *Annual Report*, 2009, 2014; Alan Cane, "Perspectives: longevity can be a tricky stunt to pull off," *Financial Times*, March 16, 2011, "HTC phone sales beat expectations," *BBC News*, July 6, 2010; "HTC profits double as smartphone demands grows," *BBC News*, June 6, 2011; S.C. Collinson and M. Jay, *From Complexity to Simplicity* (Basingstoke: Palgrave Macmillan, 2012).

Many Canadian clusters are resource based. The challenge for managers in these clusters is to continue to add value and eliminate the commodity nature of Canada's resource industries. One way to do this is to develop a global marketing strategy that builds on the Canadian–US double diamond instead of remaining as the extractor or harvester of resources. To implement such a global strategy requires a large investment in people who will bring strong marketing skills and develop a global intelligence network to identify the different tastes and preferences of customers. This network provides a role for smaller knowledge-intensive marketing research and consulting firms to participate in the resource-based cluster. There is also the potential for collaborative ventures.

The IMD World Competitiveness Scoreboard ranks Canada as one of the most competitive countries in the world. Yet, in contrast with the United States, Canada does not fare so well. According to the IMD, the United States is the world's most competitive nation.[27] A study of productivity (GDP per hours worked) by Statistics Canada shows Canada trailing the United States by about 6 percent. That is, for each hour of work, Canadians produce 94.2 percent, in dollar terms, of their US counterparts.[28]

Further research is required to investigate Canadian strategic clusters and their competitive advantages in comparison to rival clusters in North America and around the world. This will require two types of work. First, the intrafirm competition of clusters in North America needs new data that do not ignore the nature of foreign ownership and whether US and Canadian FDI by sector is inbound or outbound. Instead, direct investment in North America must be regarded as "domestic" and be contrasted with "external" direct investment from Japan[29] and the European Union.[30] Similarly, trade flows between Canada and the United States must be thought of as intrafirm when they occur between components of a cluster or even between and among clusters.

This approach is so radical that many existing concepts must be rethought. For example, the level and extent of subsidies available to clusters located in the United States (for example, in the Great Lakes region) must be related to those paid by provinces in Canada (such as Ontario). Yet there is little or no published work on state or provincial subsidies; even the work on federal subsidies in either country is extremely thin.

Finally, the real sources of Canadian competitive advantage are to be discovered not only by statistical analysis but also by interviews of managers and officials—that is, by fieldwork in the strategic clusters. Such "hands-on" research is exceptionally time consuming and expensive. However, to make the task feasible a number of important strategic clusters can be selected for analysis, self-audits can be made, conferences can be held, and so on. The future success of these efforts will depend heavily on leadership by Canadian business leaders and government officials.

Mexico and the double diamond

We can also adapt the Porter diamond model to analyze company strategies and international competitiveness in Mexico. The basic concepts in this framework are the same as those discussed in the Canadian diamond.

Linking to the US diamond

Mexico's linkage to the US diamond is somewhat different from Canada's. One reason is the fact that there are few home-based MNEs that have the capital to invest in the United States or Canada.[31] (Review Chapter 3 for information on how and why FDI is used by MNEs.) In fact, as seen in Table 10.1, during the period 2003–12 Mexico's FDI in the United States increased by $5,436 million and decreased by $31.6 million in Canada (2011). In contrast, by 2003 Canada had just $2,366.3 million invested in Mexico, whereas the United States had $56,851 million there. More important, by 2012 US FDI in Canada reached $351,460 million, and Canada's FDI

Table 10.1 FDI positions by Canada, the United States, and Mexico, 2003–14

Year	Canada's FDI in		US FDI in		Mexico's FDI in	
	US	Mexico	Canada	Mexico	US	Canada
2003	131,474.8	2,366.3	187,953.0	56,851.0	9,022	165.6
2004	163,083.5	2,143.5	214,931.0	63,384.0	7,592	238.5
2005	183,543.7	2,698.0	231,836.0	73,687.0	3,595	276.2
2006	192,231.6	4,425.2	205,134.0	82,965.0	5,310	199.1
2007	229,180.2	4,908.4	250,642.0	91,046.0	8,478	265.2
2008	243,111.6	3,491.0	246,483.0	87,443.0	8,420	268.2
2009	249,714.3	4,635.5	274,807.0	84,047.0	11,111	256.1
2010	251,342.0	4,902.0	295,206.0	85,751.0	10,970	191.0
2011	272,443.0	9,583.0	331,666.0	90,795.0	12,500	134.0
2012	275,598.0	10,109.0	351,460.0	101,030.0	13,618	n/a
2013	306,653.0	12,326.0	341,917.0	102,418.0	17,036	90.0
2014	349,965.0	13,046.0	361,372.0	107,825.0	17,710	884.0

Sources: http://www.international.gc.ca/economist-economiste/assets/pdfs/Data/investments-investissements/FDI_by_Country/CDIA_stocks_by_Country-ENG.pdf; http://stats.oecd.org; http://www.international.gc.ca/economist-economiste/statistics-statistiques/investments-investissements.aspx?lang=eng; http://www.bea.gov/international/di1fdibal.htm

in the United States was also similarly high at $275.598 million. Overall, over the ten years 2003–12, Canada's FDI in the United States more than doubled while the United States' FDI in Canada also went up by almost 1.9 times. Thus, Mexico's strategy with its North American neighbors relies more heavily on trade than on FDI for outward market access, while using inward FDI to help promote internal development.

As seen in Figure 10.5, in 2014 US exports to Mexico were $240.248 billion and its imports from Mexico were $294,074 billion, while Mexico's exports to the United States were $318.365 billion and its imports from the United States were $214.806 billion. Canada's exports to Mexico were $4.96 billion and its imports from Mexico were $28.6 billion, while Mexico's exports to Canada were $10.71 billion and its imports from Canada were $11.05 billion. Mexico is the United States' second largest trading partner, and although it has a negative trade balance with the world, it runs a positive balance with the United States. In fact, in recent years the latter has accounted for approximately 80 percent of Mexico's exports and approximately 50 percent of its imports. So Mexico is closely linked with the US economy, and its economic growth will depend heavily on participation in this North American market.[32]

Mexico is linking itself to the US diamond in a number of ways. One is by serving as a customer for outside goods. For example, Caterpillar supplies heavy equipment for road building in Mexico; Coca-Cola holds about half of the market for soft drinks in Mexico; and US soybeans dominate the Mexican oilseed market.[33]

At the same time, Mexican businesses and foreign subsidiaries based in Mexico are working to expand their links to the US market. Between 1993 and 2002, exports to the US market increased from $46 billion to almost $106 billion. Much of this output was in the form of manufactured goods, particularly automobiles. In fact, auto production in Mexico accounts for more than 450,000 workers and generates close to 1.5 million vehicles, most of which are targeted at the US market.[34] Ford, for example, is investing $1 billion in Hermosillo, Mexico, to develop a next generation of mid-sized vehicles.[35] At the same time, US firms are also investing in a wide array of non-automotive projects.[36] IBM, for example, now produces magnetic readers for computer hard-disk drives in Guadalajara and flies them to California on a daily basis. In the entertainment industry, Mexican productions have found an eager US audience with films like *Amores Perros* and *Y Tu Mamá También*.[37]

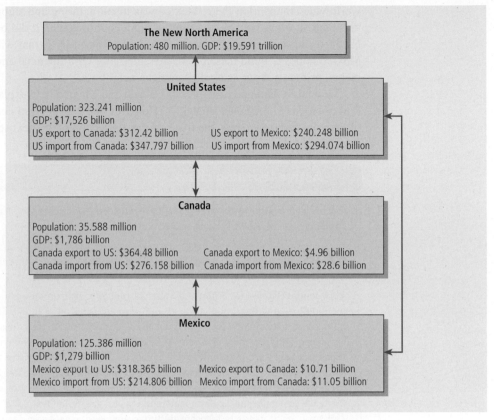

Figure 10.5 The shape of North America

Note: Population data, GDP and trade data are for 2008.

Sources: World Bank, 2010, 2014, http://data.worldbank.org/indicator; World Trade Organization, *International Trade Statistics*, 2009, 2014; http://www.wto.org/english/res_e/statis_e/statis_e.htm; IMF, *Direction of Trade Statistics Yearbook*, 2009, 2014.

Maquiladoras

In 1965 the Mexican government established the *maquiladora* industry to attract foreign manufacturing operations. Imported products for the *maquiladoras'* production are exempt from Mexican duties as long as they are used for exports. In recent years certain items not directly involved in production, such as transportation equipment and computers, have also been made exempt from duties. Moreover, *maquiladoras* are no longer restricted to the border zone, and some have been permitted to settle inland and sell finished products on the domestic market.

By the early 2000s the 12 original plants in 1965 had grown to 2,900.[38] Principally US owned, these businesses were widely considered to have established a basis for more intensified economic cooperation anticipated under an FTA.[39] Then competition from China and other emerging economies with cheap labor reduced the scale of the *maquiladora* industry.

Between 2009 and 2012, according to the *maquiladoras'* industry association, their exports and foreign investment each grew by more than 50 percent, to $196 billion and $7.4 billion respectively. Employment, having fallen sharply in the wake of the global financial crisis, rebounded by 25 percent to just over 2 million, slightly above the average for 2007–08. Carmakers, in particular, have been investing heavily in Mexico in response to a recovery in sales across the border in the United States.[40]

What will the future hold regarding Mexico and North America? The most likely developments will be continued investment by US and Canadian firms and the establishment of worldwide competition there. Mexico was manufacturing and shipping many more products back north as well as exporting to more countries than it did before NAFTA. Canada is still trying to create and nurture Canadian-owned MNEs that will compete worldwide. Mexico hopes to build these businesses internally with financial and technological investments, primarily from its North American neighbors.[41]

The double-diamond examples of Canada and Mexico help explain how MNEs can use Porter's ideas to formulate strategies. However, these firms also need to address the issue of national responsiveness, the focus of the discussion in the next section.

✔ Active learning check

Review your answer to Active Learning Case question 2 and make any changes you like. Then compare your answer to the one below.

 Why did ABB buy Gomtec GmbH? How can the company link this small firm into its global strategy and structure?

ABB bought Gomtec GmbH for a number of reasons. This small German firm provided new technologies and expertise in the area of human–robot interaction. The interface between humans and robots is a focal point for innovation and therefore competitive advantage in a number of ABB's product divisions. ABB has installed 250,000 robots in its own products and those of clients around the world. It therefore needs to keep ahead of the competition by developing or acquiring the leading technology and knowledge to improve both the robots and the interface between these and human controllers. Once a firm has selected a strategy, in this case to acquire particular assets and capabilities to innovate and add value to products and services, it needs to incorporate these acquired assets and capabilities into its global structure so it can leverage them effectively. So ABB needs to integrate this small firm, Gomtec GmbH based in Munich, within its global matrix structure, to ensure that it maximizes the added value obtained through the synergies it anticipated when it targeted this acquisition. In many cases, when giant multinationals buy SMEs, a key indicator of success is the retention of the key players in the small firm. If they leave, ABB will have lost the expertise that underpins the added value of the acquisition when combined with ABB's own people and assets.

INTEGRATION AND RESPONSIVENESS

Globalization
The production and distribution of products and services of a homogeneous type and quality on a worldwide basis

National responsiveness
The ability of MNEs to understand different consumer tastes in segmented regional markets and to respond to different national standards and regulations imposed by autonomous governments and agencies

A major trend that has affected the thinking of corporate MNE strategists over the last decade or so is that of balancing a concern for economic integration with national responsiveness. Somewhat unfortunately, economic integration has been known as "globalization" in the literature in this field. **Globalization** can be defined as the production and distribution of products and services of a homogeneous type and quality on a worldwide basis.[42] To a large extent, MNEs have homogenized tastes and helped to spread international consumerism. For example, throughout North America, the wealthier nations of Europe, and Japan there has been a growing acceptance of standardized consumer electronic goods, automobiles, computers, calculators, and similar products. However, the goal of efficient economic performance through a universal globalization strategy has left MNEs open to the charge that they are overlooking the need to address national concerns.

National responsiveness is the ability of MNEs to understand different consumer tastes in segmented regional markets and to respond to the different national standards and regulations imposed by autonomous governments and agencies. Throughout the coming years, multinationals will continually have to deal with the twin goals of economic integration and national responsiveness.[43] See the case **International Business Strategy in Action: Renewed advantage through vertical integration at Floreal Knitwear**.

Integration versus national responsiveness

To reconcile the twin issues of integration and national responsiveness, transnational MNEs can analyze them conceptually through the use of Figure 10.6, which has been adapted from Bartlett, and Bartlett and Ghoshal.[44] The vertical axis measures the need for globalization, frequently called "economic integration." Movement up the axis results in a greater degree of economic integration, which generates economies of scale as a firm moves into worldwide markets, selling a single product or service. These economies are captured as a result of centralizing specific activities in the value-added chain. They also occur by reaping the benefits of increased coordination and control of geographically dispersed activities.

The horizontal axis measures the need for corporations to be nationally responsive. Companies must address local tastes and government regulations, which may result in a geographic dispersion of activities or a decentralization of coordination and control for individual firms.

On the basis of the two axes in Figure 10.6, four situations can be distinguished. Quadrants 1 and 4 are the simplest cases. In quadrant 1, the need for integration is high and the need for awareness of sovereignty is low. This focus on economies of scale leads to competitive strategies that are based on price competition. In such an environment, mergers and acquisitions often occur.

The opposite situation is represented by quadrant 4, where the need for national responsiveness is high but the integration concern is low. In this case, companies adopt products

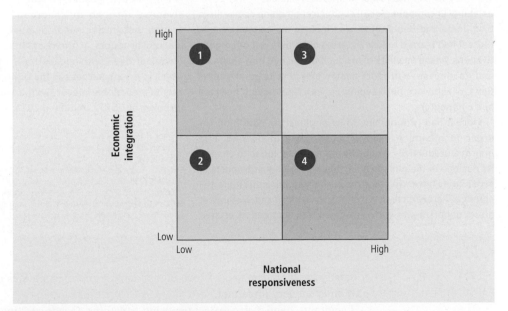

Figure 10.6 Integration and national responsiveness

Source: Reprinted by permission of Harvard Business School Press. Adapted from C. A. Bartlett, "Building and Managing the Transnational: the New Organizational Challenge," in *Competition in Global Industries*, edited by M. E. Porter, Boston, MA, 1986. Copyright © 1986 by the Harvard Business School Publishing Corporation; all rights reserved; and *Managing Across Borders: The Transnational Solution*, 2nd ed. by C. A. Bartlett and S. Ghoshal, Boston, MA, 1998. Copyright © 1998 by Harvard Business School Publishing Corporation; all rights reserved.

Renewed advantage through vertical integration at Floreal Knitwear

Based in Mauritius, Floreal Knitwear Ltd (Floreal) is the leading knitwear manufacturer in Sub-Saharan Africa and the second largest woolmark knitwear supplier in the world, after Benetton. Founded in 1971 by a group of Hong Kong investors, Floreal was the first African factory to produce sweaters of world-class quality. Its rapid success attracted attention and a larger textile conglomerate, named CIEL, acquired Floreal in 1973. The company enjoyed a period of steady growth and won several international awards and recognitions for its products up until the late 1990s.

The Asian crisis hit in 1997 and, up until 2000, several factors had culminated to have a significant impact on Floreal's operations. Among these were a fall in the price of sweaters in the United States and Europe (10 percent in three years); an appreciation of the Mauritian rupee against the euro by 20 percent in just a few months; a rise in labor costs by 27 percent in the garment sector; and an increase in production costs by 31 percent between June 1997 and April 2000. The cumulative effect of these factors was to drive down the profit of Floreal from Rs43 million ($US1.6 million) in June 1997 to a loss of Rs175 million ($US6.4 million) in July 2000. Its ability to compete globally with strengthening competition from India and Bangladesh was looking increasingly weak. Floreal had started to lose in terms of both its price competitiveness, based on costs of production that had now changed, and its innovative product design and development operations, which were not keeping up with fast-moving markets and competitors.

Floreal had rethink how to re-engineer its operations in order to minimize its overheads, keep innovating, and improve productivity as quickly as possible. It had to change its position in the global value chain for knitwear products in order to survive. So the firm embarked on a strategic re-engineering exercise in which the structures and systems of all its departments were reviewed and changed; it pruned

out all non-value-adding jobs, developed an outsourcing strategy, and established stronger performance control at all levels. The restructuring exercise reduced its workforce by 11 percent. Also, with further help from CIEL, it (vertically) integrated its R&D by establishing the Ferney Spinning Mills (a wool spinning factory with over 30 years of experience in high-quality wool and wool blend yarns), which now supplies 70 percent of its yarn needs and is its main source of innovation for its world-quality products. Floreal also invested in a world-class wet processing plant where it processed both cotton and wool garment dyeing. To counter the effects of rising labor costs, Floreal opened manufacturing operations in Madagascar and Bangladesh. Both locations have an abundance of cheap but highly talented labor, and they were also the prime sourcing destinations of its clients. Overnight, Floreal turned its head office in Mauritius into a knowledge-based hub for innovations, strategic thinking, and global marketing.

Vertical integration along the value chain continues to be a source of competitive advantage for Floreal today. It now has full control of the quality of the yarn fiber to the finished product. This, along with improved market responsiveness through quick product innovations, tailored around the specific needs of customers and markets. The leading products of the moment are its "vintage wool," "Tropical dye" (washed cotton), and "Total Easy Care," which is a huge success in the US market. Floreal is now an established global player, with a workforce of 5,500 and a turnover of US$77 million in 2014.

Sources: N. Rogovsky, P. Ozoux, D. Esser, T. Marpe, and A. Broughton, *Restructuring for Corporate Success: A Socially Sensitive Approach* (Geneva: International Labor Office, 2005); D. C. Wood, *Production, Consumption, Business and the Economy: Structural Ideals and Moral Realities* (Bingley: Emerald Group Publishing, 2014); "40 years of Floreal Knitwear: 'our strategy of diversification was good'," http://business.mega.mu, October 18, 2012; http://www.ide.go.jp/English/Data/Africa_file/Company/mauritius03.html; Michelle Russell, "Analysis: Mauritius apparel sector faces up to challenges," *Just Style*, May 22, 2014.

to satisfy the high demands of sovereignty and to ignore economies of scale because integration is not very important.

Quadrants 2 and 3 also reflect opposing situations. Quadrant 2 incorporates those cases where the need for both integration and national responsiveness is low. Both the potential to obtain economies of scale and the benefits of being sensitive to sovereignty are of little value. Typical strategies in quadrant 2 are characterized by increased international standardization of products and services. This can lead to lower needs for centralized quality control and centralized strategic decision making, while simultaneously eliminating requirements to adapt activities to individual countries.

In quadrant 3 the needs for integration and national responsiveness are both high. There is a strong need for integration in production, along with higher requirements for regional adaptations in marketing. Quadrant 3 is the most challenging and the one in which many successful "transnational" MNEs operate. Using this framework, we can analyze the impact of various exogenous policy shocks and trends on different industries, firms, banks, and other private sector institutions.

The Lexus and the Olive Tree

This economic integration and national responsiveness matrix can also be applied to analyze the influential book by Thomas Friedman, *The Lexus and the Olive Tree*.[45] Friedman uses the Lexus as a symbol of economic integration. In contrast, the Olive Tree is a symbol of the historical, political, religious, and social aspects which present obstacles to economic integration. Therefore, the logic of the Lexus view of globalization would fit on the vertical axis of Figure 10.6 whereas the Olive Tree would be assigned to the horizontal axis representing the need for national responsiveness. Friedman himself discusses the extreme cases of the Lexus in quadrant 1 and the Olive Tree in quadrant 4. However, based on our analysis of Figure 10.6 it is apparent that quadrant 3 represents another interesting case where both globalization and national responsiveness are equally important. The other point is that Figure 10.6 is a strategy diagram to be put into operation by managers of MNEs (or other firms). Therefore, it is the interpretation of the Lexus and the Olive Tree axes which is important for strategic management. A potential for strategy in quadrant 3 would require that an MNE is able to organize itself to cope with both axes.

In his later work Friedman argues that the Olive Tree is no longer relevant and that only globalization matters. In his book *The World is Flat*,[46] Friedman shows that there are three types of globalization, the latest version of which is driven by the internet and individual use of personal computers such that business can be done globally. Friedman calls this type of globalization 3.0. It has replaced globalization 2.0 which was led by MNEs and was organized at firm level rather than at individual level. In turn, this replaced globalization 1.0 which existed from 1492 to 1800, in which labor costs and natural resources were drivers of international trade and finance, and the world was organized at country level.

Balancing the trade-offs

MNEs in every industry apply the ideas in Figure 10.6, but they do so in a variety of ways. The following are select examples from three different industries: entertainment, personal computers, and automobiles.

Entertainment

One of the most successful entertainment firms in the world is the Walt Disney Company. Its Disneyland Paris operation in France is a good example of how integration and national responsiveness are balanced. The park offers many of the same features (integration) found in Disney's Orlando (Florida), Anaheim (California), and Tokyo operations, including amusement rides and cartoon characters such as Mickey Mouse, Goofy, and Donald Duck. The company has recently expanded its European facilities along the lines of its MGM studios near Orlando. Stressing uniformity among the geographically scattered parks, this integration focus is supplemented by national responsiveness that is designed to appeal to European visitors. English and French are the official languages of the park, and multilingual guides are conversant in Dutch, German, Spanish, and Italian. A second example of national responsiveness is found in the international emphasis the company has given its Disney characters: Pinocchio is Italian, Cinderella is French, Peter Pan is British. At its movie theater in the park, Disney shows a European history film offering (in the United States, the film is a travelog of America).

Another example of integration/national responsiveness is offered by Sega Enterprises, best known for its Sonic the Hedgehog video game character. Using computer simulation technology like that used to train airline pilots, Sega is developing small theme parks that will provide the same thrills as a roller coaster or a trip through space. By building a series of different amusement simulators, Sega intends to offer a wide array of "rides" without having to bear the expense of physically building the facilities. The idea is captured in the term *virtual reality*, which means that participants experience the effects of a situation without literally being there.[47] "Scramble Training," a Sega simulator that is part video and part movie, provides an example. This interactive game allows eight players to enter a small space capsule and take their position as pilot trainees. The captain appears on a screen in front of the simulator and gives orders to the players, who in turn launch the capsule and swerve through space, firing missiles and competing for points. When the captain is wounded, the controls are turned over to the player with the best score, who then steers the capsule in for a landing. Sega intends to develop a host of different interactive simulators that will allow it to compete with amusement parks such as Disney. (In fact, Sega's concept is often referred to as "Disney in a Box.") The simulators are uniform in design and construction, allowing the company to employ an integration emphasis. However, the types of games will vary from country to country (national responsiveness), depending on the entertainment interests of the local populace. For example, Sega has found that Americans are very sports oriented, so there is likely to be an opportunity for players to participate in a World Series baseball simulation. In Europe, this game would have little attraction, but many players there would like to participate in the World Cup soccer finals, so the company can modify its product characteristics to meet the needs of the customer.[48]

Personal computers

Most personal computer (PC) makers compete on the bases of technology and price. They offer state-of-the-art machines and try to hold down their costs by outsourcing components and improving assembly efficiency. This strategy is particularly important in markets such as Japan, where less than 25 percent of the population in the early 1990s owned PCs, and where local demands, such as the need to write in *kanji*, had discouraged foreign competition.

However, US firms have been making major headway in this market, thanks to their ability to exploit both integration and national responsiveness.[49] For example, Compaq and Dell have entered this market with low-priced units that were the same as those sold elsewhere (integration) but offered sharply lower prices (national responsiveness). As a result, both firms have been able to garner market share. IBM has employed a similar strategy in addition to addressing the desire of local customers to write in *kanji*. The company has now perfected a bilingual version of Microsoft's DOS, the standard operating system that controls approximately 80 percent of the world's PCs. This version allows these machines to prepare or search documents with Japanese characters, the Western alphabet, or both. Apple is also having very good success in Japan, thanks to its willingness to adapt to local needs. For example, the company has a Japanese management team that has helped to surmount local barriers to "buying foreign." It has also cultivated a strong network of dealers and worked to develop an image as an innovator, both of which are critical in the Japanese market. As a result of this careful balance of integration and national responsiveness, Apple and IBM alone accounted for almost 16 percent of the Japanese PC market in 2001 and approximately 15 percent in 2015. With the merger of HP and Compaq, and IBM divestment by selling its PC business to Lenovo (China) in 2004, HP and Dell are active in the Japanese PC market. According to Mintel Market Navigator, HP is the fourth largest laptop PC provider in Japan with a market share of 7.3 percent, whereas Dell had a modest market share of 2.7 percent by the middle of 2011.[50]

Other US firms are also using a carefully formulated integration/national responsiveness strategy to gain market share. Microsoft wrote a special version of Windows—one of the most popular PC software programs of all time—for the Japanese market. Until 1993, only 440,000 copies of the program had been sold, but when the company unveiled its newer version, more than 65,000 copies were snatched up in two days.[51]

Automobiles

Every car manufacturer uses economic integration by producing autos that can be made and marketed around the world. In a few cases, the Volkswagen Beetle being the best example, a car will not need to be modified for the local market.[52] Usually, however, an integration strategy is complemented by national responsiveness in the form of design, engineering, and manufacturing changes. Ford's Mondeo provides a good example. Developed for the world market, this car has uniform worldwide engineering standards with almost every specification expressed in the metric system. The company also has created uniform standards for raw materials, design, procurement, and manufacture of individual parts. Identical production tools are used at both European and US locations so that economies of scale can be maximized. At the same time, Ford has taken national responsiveness into consideration. European buyers prefer manual transmissions, whereas US buyers like automatic drive. Europeans demand cars that handle well, but this is not a priority issue with American customers. On the other hand, Americans want air-conditioned cars, and many Europeans do not. The overall cost of developing the Mondeo was $6 billion. However, initial sales in Europe were brisk and Ford believed it could maintain this momentum in the US market. It also believed it could create additional car models from the Mondeo program and thus develop a series of new offerings. If this is true, the integration and national responsiveness strategies used for the Mondeo will help smooth the way for future auto sales and help the company to recoup this enormous investment.[53]

Honda offers another example of integration and national responsiveness strategies. The firm now builds a variety of different car sizes from one production platform by bending and stretching the autos to fit the demands of the market. As a result, Honda is able to build cars in the United States that are longer and roomier, while offering smaller, more compact models of the same car in Japan. The company is now using this same approach to build sports utility vehicles for the world market.[54]

General Motors offers yet another example of integration and national responsiveness strategies. Like Ford, GM often develops cars for the European market, then introduces them into the United States. As a result, the cars are frequently identical in styling and design but have different features to accommodate local tastes. The Celta, a subcompact offering in Brazil, has fewer features and 50 percent fewer parts than competitive models. In collaboration with its suppliers, GM created a modular assembly plant with just-in-time supplier delivery. Efficiency costs of such an integration strategy allowed for an inexpensive subcompact for developing markets, where price and reliability are most important.[55] When the auto is made in another developing market, it will be possible to build and assemble each unit quickly because the process will have been perfected in Brazil. This integration focus is complemented by national responsiveness. In Brazil, marketing of the Celta stresses security locks and anti-theft devices, whereas in safer developing countries, the car's suspension system and handling on tough roads will receive more emphasis.

Competitiveness in the triad

From the viewpoint of MNEs, one of the most important business decisions concerns the trade-off between integration and national responsiveness. Successful MNEs know they can no longer afford to ignore the latter and concentrate solely on globalization through economic integration.

In the United States

The United States experiences considerable decentralization in economic decision making. It is a country in which subnational units continue to increase in importance. This issue should not be confused with pluralism. A variety of political opinions and parties is a strength of democracy. The problem arises when the institutional structure of the nation and its businesses cannot operate in an efficient manner, relative to global competitors.

The US Constitution was designed to allow Congress to be a broker for regional and special interests. On occasion, Congress works with the Executive branch to formulate and implement a coordinated economic policy and even a social policy. Examples of social reform and government economic activity in the Kennedy–Johnson years can be contrasted with a return to more market-based principles and a somewhat reduced role for government in the Reagan years.

However, in many areas affecting the private sector today, the overwhelming characteristic of doing business in the United States is the responsiveness of governments to special interest groups and lobbies. The more decentralized the level of government, the more responsive will be the regulatory activity to the lobbyist. On occasion businesses themselves can be lobbyists, but there are many other groups, such as environmentalists and social activists, who seem to be growing in power. Examples of conflicts in business lobbying occur in the areas of administration of US trade remedy laws and in the current US debate about the possible regulation of inward foreign direct investment (FDI).

Rugman and Anderson,[56] as well as others, have demonstrated that the current administration of US countervailing duty (CVD) and anti-dumping (AD) laws is highly responsive to domestic producer interests and biased against foreign firms. US corporations use CVD and AD as a competitive strategy to erect entry barriers against rival firms.[57] Between 1980 and 2003, US businesses filed 1,510 AD and CVD cases against foreign competitors with the US International Trade Commission; 37 percent of these cases, or 559, were found to be justified after the commission investigated the complaints. Table 10.2 lists a selection of products that were slapped with import tariffs in 2014.

Table 10.2 AD and CVD orders by product category, 2014

	No. of orders		
	AD	CVD	Total
Iron and steel products	121	31	152
Chemicals and pharmaceuticals	40	8	48
Miscellaneous manufactured products	45	12	57
Agricultural, forest, and processed food products	18	4	22
Minerals and metals	22	2	24
Plastic, rubber, stone, and glass products	9	2	11
Machinery and electronic/scientific equipment	2	1	3
Textiles and apparel	3	1	4

Source: http://www.usitc.gov/trade_remedy/731_ad_701_cvd/investigations/active/index.htm

Approximately 5 percent of all cases between 1980 and 2003 went against Canada.[58] Thus, even when the US government was pursuing negotiations for free trade with Canada, individual US corporations were still using the CVD and AD laws to help restrict Canadian imports. This is a clear example of US national interests being offset by selective producer interests. There were more than 22 CVD and AD cases against Canada in the 1990s.[59] More of the same is in store in the future, although Canadian concerns about the administration of CVD and AD laws have been somewhat answered by the establishment of binational panels under the terms of the FTA and then NAFTA.

Another area of concern is inward FDI, which some congressional leaders now wish to restrict, and some Americans seem concerned with the growing amount of Japanese FDI. Some members of Congress have urged more screening of such FDI, and there is a strong "Japan-bashing" stance in US trade policy. Yet at the same time, state officials have been actively seeking Japanese FDI because they want the jobs and the tax base that come with it. This potential clash between Washington "beltway" thinking (anti-Japanese) and state-level activity (pro-Japanese) parallels Canada's experience with the regulation of FDI.

The United States seems destined in the next ten years to repeat many of the mistakes made in Canada over the last 40 years. In 1974 the Trudeau government introduced the Foreign Investment Review Agency (FIRA), which was designed to screen FDI on economic criteria to assess whether there was a net benefit to Canada. Between 1974 and 1985, FIRA responded to Ottawa's political winds, at times rejecting as much as 30 percent of applications but at other times (especially from 1982 to 1985) approving virtually everything.[60] The administrators at FIRA and the responsible ministers made political decisions just as the US International Trade Commission and the US Commerce Department do today in US trade law cases.

In 1985, FIRA was abolished and a new agency, Investment Canada, was created with the mandate to attract FDI rather than scare it away.[61] This change in thinking about FDI came with a change in government, after the Progressive Conservatives were elected in 1984 with a mandate of job creation. Throughout the lifetime of FIRA, most provinces, especially those in Atlantic Canada, wanted FDI for jobs and taxes. The clash between the provinces that favored FDI and the central Canadian economic nationalists led to the federal government giving up many of its powers to regulate FDI by buying into the agenda of the provinces, especially their overwhelming priority for jobs. Perhaps this is some evidence of the triumph of decentralized economic power. But a paradox emerges. In Canada, the economic nationalists who have used central government power are in retreat, whereas it appears that in the United States economic nationalism is just beginning to take off. If Japan bashing continues, then the US proponents of restrictions on FDI will have the same unhappy experience with FIRA as did Canada. Private sector US corporate strategists will, therefore, need to respond to a large dose of economic nationalism and its associated protectionist inefficiencies.

In eastern Europe

Another example of the use of sovereignty and the destruction of centralized economic power and values was the 1989 revolution in central Europe and the collapse of the Soviet Union in 1991. The rejection of totalitarian communist regimes by the people of countries such as Romania, Belarus, and Russia has many implications for business. The key point is that these countries are very poor, with inefficient economic and financial systems. Their economic development will probably take place through FDI rather than through joint ventures. Popular wisdom to the contrary, joint ventures between poor nations and wealthy corporations rarely work. The preferable mode of international business is FDI because Western firms can then control their proprietary advantages and not risk dissipation through joint ventures.[62] Studies on joint ventures in developing countries have found a great deal of instability and failure.[63] Multinationals prefer FDI and countries such as India and Mexico, which once greatly restricted FDI, experienced inefficient economic development and eventually had to lift such regulations. This experience is relevant for eastern Europe.

Doing business in eastern Europe for the next 5–10 years will be dominated by the need for economic efficiency. The globalization concept will overwhelm concerns about adapting products for sovereignty. It is in the EU nations that national responsiveness will be important for corporations. In the wealthy triad powers, adapting to sovereignty matters; in the developing world and in eastern Europe, economic efficiency is what matters.

In Japan

A key explanation for the success of Japanese MNEs is that they benefit from a highly centralized home-market economy. This has permitted Japan to use levers of industrial and strategic trade policies that could not be implemented successfully in the other areas of the triad.

Centralized government policy is critical to implementing effective corporate strategy.[64] The Japanese cultural, religious, social, and political system is much more centralized in nature than other triad blocs, enabling the country's MNEs to follow globalization strategies. Thus, for example, after the two OPEC oil crises of the 1970s, Japanese industry was rapidly transformed out of shipbuilding, heavy engineering, and other energy-intensive manufacturing and into computer-based manufacturing, consumer electronics, and high value-added services, including banking and finance. The government and the MNEs worked together to implement a new industrial strategy in an effective and efficient manner.

Such radical restructuring through industrial policy is unlikely to work in North America and Europe because of the decentralized nature of economic power. Attempts by the United States or Canada to implement a new industrial policy are likely to fail. Whatever government incentives and subsidies are made available will be appropriated by industries seeking shelter from competitors in the triad. To erect entry barriers against foreign competitors, companies will use the decentralized nature of the economic system. This has already occurred in the United States, with companies seeking protection from competitors through the use of CVD and AD laws. US steel, forest products, fish, and semiconductor industries, among others, have been using short-term legal remedies instead of investing in the development of sustainable, proprietary, firm-specific advantages.

What are the implications for corporate strategy of these asymmetrical developments in the triad? Japanese MNEs will continue to pursue an integration/globalization strategy, but they may face difficulties when they need to operate in the decentralized environments of North America and Europe, since marketing-type skills will become more important than production skills. Over the last decade, MNEs from Europe and North America have often abused the nature of their home-country decentralized systems, and sovereignty has hindered efficient corporate development. However, MNEs from North America and Europe have a potential competitive advantage over Japanese MNEs if they can learn from their past mistakes. Awareness of sovereignty can make the former companies better equipped in the future to be more nationally responsive than their Japanese counterparts. Indeed, Japanese MNEs may become locked into a "globalization-only" strategy, just as the world begins to demand much more corporate responsiveness to sovereignty.

✔ Active learning check

Review your answer to Active Learning Case question 3 and make any changes you like. Then compare your answer to the one below.

3 **How does ABB address the issues of globalization and national responsiveness? In each case, cite an example.**

ABB addresses the issue of globalization by producing state-of-the-art products for worldwide markets. It may be necessary to make modifications to address local geographic and climatic conditions, of course, but the basic technology and manufacturing techniques are similar. At the same time, ABB addresses national responsiveness by trying to be a local firm that is interested in the needs of that market. As a result, the company balances globalization and sovereignty—a feat that most MNEs do not accomplish very well.

KEY POINTS

1 Porter's single-diamond model is based on four country-specific determinants and two external variables (chance and government). This model is extremely useful in examining strategies among triad and other economically developed countries. However, when applying the model to smaller, open, trading economies, a modification is in order.

2 Canada's economic success will depend on its ability to view itself as part of the North American market and to integrate itself into this overall market. This requires the use of a "double-diamond" model for corporate strategy, resulting in Canadian firms developing competitive capabilities that allow them to compete successfully with US firms in the United States. This is being done by (a) developing innovative products and services that simultaneously meet the needs of the US and Canadian customer, (b) drawing on the support industries and infrastructure of both the US and Canadian diamonds, and (c) making free and full use of the physical and human resources in both countries.

3 Mexico's economic success also depends on its ability to integrate itself into the North American market. However, this strategy is different from that of the Canadians because Mexico does not have the FDI to invest in the US market. Much of its linkage is a result of low labor costs that allow the country to produce inexpensive goods and export them into the United States. The North American Free Trade Agreement worked out with the United States and Canada in 1993 has continued to shape part of Mexico's on-going economic success.

4 A major trend that has affected the thinking of corporate MNE strategists over the past ten years is balancing a concern for economic integration and globalization with that of national responsiveness. Many MNEs have focused on integration without giving sufficient attention to the sovereignty issue. However, there will have to be a reversal of this trend and MNEs will have to become much more interested in national responsiveness if they hope to succeed in overseas markets.

Key terms

● strategic cluster   ● globalization   ● national responsiveness

REVIEW AND DISCUSSION QUESTIONS

1 Porter's diamond is based on four country-specific determinants and two external variables. What does this statement mean? Put it in your own words.

2 Porter notes, "Firms, not individual nations, compete in international markets." How does this statement help explain some of the major challenges facing MNEs?

3 Using Figure 10.2 as your point of reference, how does the current national development of the United States differ from that of Korea? How does the UK's differ from that of Singapore?

4 Why does Porter's diamond need to be modified in explaining the international competitiveness of countries such as Canada and Mexico?

5 How does the double diamond, as illustrated in Figure 10.4, help explain international competitiveness in Canada?

6 How can Canadian firms view the United States and Canada as home-based markets and integrate the use of both diamonds for developing and implementing strategy? Be complete in your answer.

7 Of what value are strategic clusters in the double diamond? Explain.

8 How does the double diamond in Figure 10.6 help explain Mexico's international business strategy?

9 How important are the *maquiladoras* to the growth of the Mexican economy? In what way do these businesses link Mexico with the Canadian–US double diamond?

10 In what way are economic integration/globalization and national responsiveness important to MNE strategies?

11 In the entertainment industry, which is more important, integration or national responsiveness?

12 Based on current developments in the PC market in Japan, which is more important for US MNEs, integration or national responsiveness? Why?

13 Which is more important for US auto makers doing business in Europe, integration or national responsiveness? Why?

REAL CASE

There is no global beer, only local

Beer is a good example of an industry that is local, not global. Indeed, beer is stubbornly local. Because beer is bulky and too expensive to export, it is brewed domestically; foreign producers will license their brand name products to local producers to gain a local market presence. In addition, imports of alcoholic beverages are traditionally heavily taxed. Rival domestic producers usually tie up local distribution channels. Governments also protect domestic breweries, such as in Germany, where the Reinheitsgebot

purity rules have protected indigenous beer for over 400 years.

In Canada, domestic brewers were exempted from the national treatment provision of the United States–Canada Free Trade Agreement of 1989 (and later from NAFTA in 1993). The reason is that, initially, each Canadian company needed to have a brewery in each province, resulting in rather small and inefficient breweries in the low-population Atlantic provinces. In light of such inefficiency and import protection, Labatt was taken over by the Belgian brewery, InBev, and Molson has merged with Coors.

The local, fragmented nature of the brewing industry can be offset by acquisitions. The half-dozen leading world brewers are constantly attempting to increase their market share in both developed and developing countries. Belgium's InBev has made huge gains in the world market, buying up such companies as Bass Brewers of the UK, Beck's of Germany, Labatt in Canada, Anheuser-Busch in the United States, and others. South African Breweries (SAB) merged with Miller. The new company, SABMiller, is now the world's second largest brewer.

There are a few premium "designer" beers (high-end beers that have been developed into global brands), but they are usually produced under license. This has led to cross-licensing and distribution arrangements as well as to mergers and acquisitions. Today there is some consolidation in this segment to a few large brewers such as Heineken and InBev. But the premium lager segment is a minority of the total world beer market, which still has mainly local beer.

Anheuser-Busch (in St. Louis, the United States) used to be the world's largest beer company and sold 90 percent of its Budweiser brand in the United States, a local beer. On July 13, 2008, Belgian brewing company InBev completed the acquisition of Anheuser-Busch for US$52 billion in equity, creating the world's largest beer company, Anheuser-Busch InBev. It has a portfolio of well over 200 beer brands. These include global flagship brands Budweiser, Stella Artois, and Beck's; multi-country brands, such as Leffe and Hoegaarden; and many local champions, such as Bud Light, Skol, Brahma, Quilmes, Michelob, Harbin, Sedrin, Klinskoye, Sibirskaya Korona, Chernigivske, and Jupiler. In 2009, its total sales were US$36.758 billion, of which 45.79 percent was generated in North America, 22.61 percent in Latin America–North, 5.61 percent in Latin America–South, 12.75 percent in Western Europe, 7.37 percent in Central and Eastern Europe, and 5.87 percent in Asia–Pacific. The Belgian brewery has aggressively gone the furthest in expanding from its EU base into North America since the 1990s. It purchased Canada's largest brewer, Labatt, in 1993. The company also produces and distributes soft drinks, particularly in Latin America.

In 2009, the Dutch brewery company Heineken generated a revenue of US$20.490 billion, of which 52.89 percent was within Western Europe, another 21.65 percent from Central and Eastern Europe, only 10.48 percent from the Americas,

Table 10.3 Largest worldwide brewers, 2009

Name	Country	Volume (million hectoliters)
Anheuser-Busch InBev	Belgium	350
SABMiller	UK	<250
Heineken	Netherlands	>200
Carlsberg	Denmark	125
Tsingtao	China	>50
Molson Coors	Canada/US	50
Modelo	Mexico	50
Yanjing	China	<50
Kirin	Japan	<50
Asahi	Japan	<50
Total (of above)		<50

Source: "Top four brewers make up half of the world beer market," *Reuters News*, February 8, 2010; "Top world brewer and brand sales – 2009," Plato Logic Limited, 2010.

12.29 percent from the Middle East and Africa, and the remainder, 2.69 percent, from Asia–Pacific.

According to the UK-based Plato Logic, in 2009 the world's four biggest brewers, Anheuser-Busch InBev, London-listed SABMiller, Heineken, and Denmark's Carlsberg accounted for over half of the world beer market. In fifth place was China's Tsingtao Brewery, in sixth place was the North America Molson Coors Brewing Co., while Mexico's Grupo Modelo, China's Beijing Yanjing Brewery Co. Ltd., and Japanese brewers Kirin Holdings Company Limited and Asahi Breweries Limited made up the rest of the top ten (see Table 10.3). These are "global" companies with local beer.

Websites: www.molsoncoors.com; www.heineken.com; www.ab-inbev.com; www.sabmiller.com; www.carlsberg.com; www.asahi.com; www.kirin.com

Sources: Reuters News, February 8, 2010; Anheuser-Busch InBev, *Annual Report*, 2008, 2009; Heineken, *Annual Report*, 2009; "Top world brewer and brand sales—2009," Plato Logic Limited, 2010; "Top four brewers make up half of the world beer market," *Reuters News*, February 8, 2010; Thomson Reuters, *OneSource*, 2011.

1 Is the production and distribution of beer nationally responsive?

2 If beer is mainly local, why are there mergers and acquisitions of beer companies?

3 In the integration/responsiveness matrix, where would you position the world's largest brand-name beer companies and why?

REAL CASE

IBM

In 1911, four recording and processing equipment manu-facturers in the United States merged to form the Computer-Tabulating-Recording Company (C-T-R). The new company merged its Canadian operations in 1917 under the name of International Business Machines Company. This name was adopted by all the company's operations in 1924; today, most people simply recognize it as IBM.

A pioneer of the personal computer (PC), IBM is also well known for leading the way to globalization. However, the computer industry is at a mature stage of manufacturing. Eventually in 2004, IBM got out of personal computers alto-gether, selling the business to China's Lenovo as PCs became commoditized.

In 2014, its operations spanned more than 200 coun-tries with over 400,000 employees worldwide and its research laboratories were located in 12 countries across the globe. According to "Fortune Global 500," IBM was ranked 82nd in terms of size and had revenues amount-ing to $92.8 billion in 2014. The organization derived 44.6 percent of all its revenue from the Americas, com-pared to 33.1 percent from Europe, the Middle East, and Africa, and 21.8 percent from Asia–Pacific. The remaining 0.5 percent of its revenue came from its uncategorized global operations.

Production is also spread around the world. Product lines are clustered in regions that offer plentiful labor or special-ized technology, depending on the nature of the product. ThinkPads used to be manufactured in Shenzhen, China; desktops in Guadalajara, Mexico. This reliance on develop-ing countries allows IBM to take advantage of low labor costs while placing the company inside some of the fastest-growing markets in the world.

IBM was an international company at its conception. C-T-R brought together the international operations of all its predecessors. In the decades following its establish-ment, the company aggressively pursued expansion across the world. In Latin America, an office opened in Brazil in 1917. Within the next 20 years, IBM secured con-tracts with governments and corporations in Argentina, Mexico, Ecuador, Chile, Cuba, Uruguay, and Peru. In Asia, the company opened its first office in Bombay, India, in 1920. The Philippine market was entered in 1925, fol-lowed the next year by the first IBM equipment being installed in Osaka, Japan, for the Nippon Mutual Life Insurance Company. In China, the first IBM machines

Source: Iain Masterton/Getty Images

were installed at the Peking Union Medical College in 1934.

IBM's entry into the European market started when a branch of the International Time Recording Company, an IBM forerunner, opened in France in 1914. It was only in 1919 that a consolidated IBM was introduced in Europe. In the 1920s and 1930s, IBM manufacturing facilities sprang up in Germany, France, England, and Italy.

Although IBM's organizational segments are product based, a company sales and distribution segment has a geo-graphic focus as well as a specialized and global industry focus. Small and medium business contracts are dealt with through a global sales and distribution segment. Its foreign subsidiaries share technology, logistics, business princi-ples, and a common source of manufacturing, but have the power to implement local strategies. In other words, they can choose their product lines and marketing strategy to respond to the needs of the local environment, including regulations, customer tastes, income levels, and the com-petitive environment.

In terms of production, IBM's highest commitment to glo-balizing production is its growing reliance on electronic manufacturing service providers. More than two-thirds of the company's Intel-based products are manufactured in worldwide factories by contract manufacturers, including Sanmina-SCI and Solectron. (See the **Real Case: Flextronics** in Chapter 12.)

IBM is one of only a few companies that have successfully penetrated foreign regional markets in terms of revenues and production. A main reason is that the computer, office, and electronics industry in which IBM operates is one of the most global, with average intra-regional sales of over 50 percent. Electronics are easy to transport and are standardized across all world regions. Seven of the nine largest global firms are from this industry. This extra-regionality is the result of standardized components that can be transported cheaply across the world, allowing for a global supply chain.

In terms of assets, however, IBM is highly intra-regional, as approximately 60 percent of its assets are in the United States. There are a number of reasons for this: (1) foreign production facilities are often owned by contract manufacturers; (2) the cost of land and equipment is higher in the United States than in many of the developing countries in which the company manufactures; and (3) the United States remains the most important market for IBM. Indeed, although IBM makes over 20 percent of its sales in each triad market, the

Americas continue to account for the largest portion. It is difficult to argue that this is merely the result of a home-region advantage. The United States is, after all, the largest triad economy and the largest market for technology products.

Sources: www.ibm.com; IBM, *Annual Report,* 2009, 2014; Alan M. Rugman, *The Regional Multinationals* (Cambridge: Cambridge University Press, 2005); "IBM outsourcing to Solectron, Sanmina-SCI," *Internet News,* January 7, 2003; "Fortune Global 500," *Fortune,* 2010, 2015.

1 Is IBM a multinational enterprise? Is it global?

2 How does contract manufacturing fit into IBM's strategy?

3 Using the integration and national responsiveness matrix, in what quadrant does IBM's strategy fall?

NOTES

1 For a detailed discussion of these variables and determinants, see Michael E. Porter, *The Competitive Advantage of Nations* (New York: Free Press, 1990), pp. 69–130.

2 Alan M. Rugman and Alain Verbeke, *Global Corporate Strategy and Trade Policy* (London and New York: Routledge, 1990).

3 Michael E. Porter, *The Competitive Advantage of Nations* (New York: Free Press, 1990), p. 33.

4 Ibid., p. 671.

5 A. E. Safarian, *Foreign Ownership of Canadian Industry* (Toronto: McGraw-Hill, 1968).

6 Alan M. Rugman, *Multinationals in Canada: Theory, Performance and Economic Impact* (Boston, MA: Martinus Nijhoff, 1980).

7 Harold Crookell, *Canadian–American Trade and Investment under the Free Trade Agreement* (Westport, CT: Quorum Books, 1990).

8 Alan M. Rugman, *Multinationals and Canada–United States Free Trade* (Columbia, SC: University of South Carolina Press, 1990).

9 See Alan M. Rugman, "Strategies for national competitiveness," *Long Range Planning,* vol. 20, no. 3 (1987), pp. 92–7.

10 Alan M. Rugman and John McIlveen, *Megafirms: Strategies for Canada's Multinationals* (Toronto: Methuen/Nelson, 1985).

11 Ibid.

12 John H. Dunning, "Dunning on Porter." Paper presented at the Annual Meeting of the Academy of International Business, Toronto, October 1990, and published in John H. Dunning, *The Globalization of Business* (London and New York: Routledge, 1993); and John H. Dunning, "Internationalizing Porter's diamond," *Management International Review,* vol. 33, special issue 2 (1993), pp. 7–16.

13 Ibid., 1990, p. 11.

14 United Nations, *World Investment Report* (New York: United Nations, 2000); and see also Nestlé, *Annual Reports,* 2006–14.

15 Alan M. Rugman and Joseph R. D'Cruz, *Fast Forward: Improving Canada's International Competitiveness* (Toronto: Kodak Canada, 1991); and Alan M. Rugman and Joseph R. D'Cruz, "The 'double diamond' model of international competitiveness: the Canadian experience," *Management International Review,* vol. 33, special issue 2 (1993), pp. 17–40.

16 For another view of the FTA, see John N. Turner, "There is more to trade than trade: an analysis of the US/Canada trade agreement 1988," *California Management Review* (winter 1991), pp. 109–19.

17 Alan M. Rugman, "The free trade agreement and the global economy," *Business Quarterly* (summer 1988), pp. 13–20.

18 Alan M. Rugman and Alain Verbeke, "Strategic responses to free trade," *Hitotsubashi Journal of Commerce and Management* (December 1988), pp. 69–79; and Alan M. Rugman and Alain Verbeke, "Foreign subsidiaries and multinational strategic management: an extension and correction of Porter's single diamond framework," *Management International Review,* vol. 33, special issue 2 (1993), pp. 71–84.

19 See, for example, Joseph R. D'Cruz and James Fleck, *Yankee Canadians in the Global Economy* (London, Ontario: National Centre for Management Research and Development, 1987); and Alan M. Rugman and Joseph D'Cruz, *New Visions for Canadian Business: Strategies for Competing in the Global Economy* (Toronto: Kodak Canada, 1990).

20 See Doug Struck, "Canada looks for spot in the big picture," *Washington Post,* December 29, 2004.

21 www.magna.com; Magna, *Annual Report,* 2009; "Global Fortune 500," *Forbes,* 2010.

22 www.bombardier.com; Bombardier, *Annual Report, 2010;* "Global Fortune 500," *Forbes,* 2010.

23 Doug Struck, "Canada looks for spot in the big picture," *Washington Post,* December 29, 2004.

24 Also, see Alan M. Rugman and Alain Verbeke, "Multinational corporate strategy and the Canada–US free trade agreement," *Management International Review*, vol. 30, no. 3 (1990), pp. 253–66; and Alan M. Rugman and Alain Verbeke, "How to operationalize Porter's diamond of international competitiveness," *International Executive*, vol. 35, no. 4 (July/August 1993), pp. 283–99.

25 For more details of this business network approach, see Joseph R. D'Cruz and Alan M. Rugman, *New Compacts of Canadian Competitiveness* (Toronto: Kodak Canada, 1992); Joseph R. D'Cruz and Alan M. Rugman, "Business networks for international competitiveness," *Business Quarterly*, vol. 56, no. 4 (spring 1992), pp. 101–7; and Joseph R. D'Cruz and Alan M. Rugman, "Developing international competitiveness: the five partners model," *Business Quarterly*, vol. 58, no. 2 (winter 1993), pp. 60–72.

26 D'Cruz and Rugman, *New Compacts of Canadian Competitiveness*, pp. 29–36; and see also "Global Fortune 500," *Forbes*, 2009–2011 issues, http://money.cnn.com/magazines/fortune/fortune500/.

27 IMD, *World Competitiveness Yearbook*, 2009.

28 John R. Baldwin, Jean-Pierre Maynard, and Fanny Wong, "The output gap between Canada and the United States: the role of productivity (1994–2002)," *Statistics Canada Analytical Papers*, January 2005.

29 Alan M. Rugman, *Japanese Direct Investment in Canada* (Ottawa: Canada–Japan Trade Council, 1990).

30 See Alan M. Rugman and F. Bill Mohri, "Trade and investment among Canada and the triad," Working paper, University of Toronto, July 1991; and Alan M. Rugman (ed.), *Foreign Investment and NAFTA* (Columbia, SC: University of South Carolina Press, 1994).

31 Alan M. Rugman and Alain Verbeke, "Foreign direct investment in North America: current patterns and future relationships in Canada, the United States, and Mexico," Ontario Centre for International Business, Research program working paper, no. 57, November 1991, p. 4, published in Khosrow Fatemi and Dominick Salvatore (cds.), *North American Free Trade Agreement* (London: Pergamon, 1994).

32 IMF, *Direction of Trade Statistics Yearbook*, 2000 and 2009.

33 Ben Juarez and Gabriel Hernandez, "Mexico's market a winning bet for US soybeans," *FAS Online*, December 2000.

34 "Why Mexico scares the UAW," *Business Week*, August 3, 1998, p. 37; and "US slowdown adds to Mexican auto industry's woes," Forbes.com, April 19, 2001 and www.amia.com.mx

35 Jamie Butters, "Mexico wins production of Ford Futura," *Detroit Free Press*, October 7, 2003.

36 Joel Millman, "High-tech jobs transfer to Mexico with surprising speed," *Wall Street Journal*, April 9, 1999, p. A18.

37 "The Mexicans are coming!" *The Economist*, October 3, 2002.

38 Rugman and Verbeke, "Foreign direct investment in North America," p. 12; and Geri Smith, "Made in the Maquilas again," *Business Week*, August 16, 2004.

39 United States International Trade Commission, *The Likely Impact on the United States of a Free Trade Agreement with Mexico*, USITC Publication 2353, February 1991, pp. 1–5.

40 "Mexico's maquiladoras: big maq attack," *The Economist*, October 26, 2013.

41 Also, see *Lloyd Economic Report* (Guadalajara, Mexico), March 1994.

42 For a discussion of various definitions of globalization, see chapter 1 of Alan M. Rugman, *The End of Globalization* (London: Random House, 2000 and New York: McGraw Hill/Amacom, 2001).

43 See Alan M. Rugman and Karl Moore, "How global is globalisation?" *FT Mastering Management Online*, November 2001.

44 Christopher A. Bartlett, "Building and managing the transnational: the new organizational challenge," in M. E. Porter (ed.), *Competition in Global Industries* (Boston, MA: Harvard Business School Press, 1986), pp. 367–401; and Christopher A. Bartlett and Sumantra Ghoshal, *Managing Across Borders: The Transnational Solution* (Boston, MA: Harvard Business School Press, 1989).

45 Thomas L. Friedman, *The Lexus and the Olive Tree* (London: HarperCollins, 2000).

46 Thomas L. Friedman, *The World Is Flat* (New York: Farrar, Straus and Giroux, 2005).

47 Andrew Pollack, "Sega takes aim at Disney's world," *New York Times*, section 3, July 4, 1993, pp. 1, 6.

48 For more on Sega, see Irene M. Kunii, "Sega: 'we're going to blow them out of the water'," *Business Week*, December 7, 1998, p. 108; and Dave Lee, "Twenty years of Sonic the Hedgehog," *BBC News Online*, June 23, 2011.

49 Brenton R. Schlender, "US PCs invade Japan," *Fortune*, July 12, 1993, pp. 68–73.

50 See also "PC market has ups and downs," *Asia Times*, December 5, 2001; Apple, *Guide to Japan for Macintosh Developers*, 2000 edition; and Mintel Global Navigator (Market research database), http://gmn.mintel.com/query/10056853/shares/single, 2011.

51 Schlender, "US PCs invade Japan," p. 73.

52 Gabriella Stern, "VW's US comeback rides on restyled Beetle," *Wall Street Journal*, May 6, 1997, pp. B1–2.

53 Alex Taylor III, "Ford's $6 billion baby," *Fortune*, June 28, 1993, pp. 76–81.

54 Keith Naughton et al., "Can Honda build a world car?" *Business Week*, September 8, 1997, pp. 100–8.

55 "GM do Brasil Launches the Chevrolet Celta," *Automotive Intelligence News*, September 5, 2000.

56 Alan M. Rugman and Andrew Anderson, *Administered Protection in America* (London and New York: Routledge, 1987).

57 Rugman and Verbeke, *Global Corporate Strategy and Trade Policy*.

58 United States International Trade Commission, "Import injury investigations statistics," November 2004.

59 International Trade Administration, *Antidumping and Countervailing Duty Cases Initiated Since January 01, 1980 Current Through January 01, 2000*, January 2000.

60 Rugman, *Multinationals in Canada*.

61 Alan M. Rugman and Leonard Waverman, "Foreign ownership and corporate strategy," in Leonard Waverman (ed.), *Corporate Globalization through Mergers and Acquisitions* (Calgary: University of Calgary Press, 1991), pp. 59–87.

62 Alan M. Rugman, *Inside the Multinationals: The Economics of Internal Markets* (London: Croom Helm and New York: Columbia University Press, 1981).

63 Paul W. Beamish, *Multinational Joint Ventures in Developing Countries* (London and New York: Routledge, 1989).

64 Rugman and Verbeke, *Global Corporate Strategy and Trade Policy*.

BIBLIOGRAPHY

Arregle, Jean-Luc., Beamish, Paul W., and Hébert, Louis. "The regional dimension of MNEs' foreign subsidiary localization," *Journal of International Business Studies*, vol. 40 (January 2009).

Asmussen, Christian Geisler, Pedersen, Torben, and Dhanaraj, Charles. "Host-country environment and subsidiary competence: extending the diamond network model," *Journal of International Business Studies*, vol. 40, no. 1 (2009).

Bartlett, Christopher, and Ghoshal, Sumantra. *Transnational Management* (Boston, MA: Irwin, 1992).

Bartlett, Christopher, and Ghoshal, Sumantra. *Managing Across Borders: The Transnational Solution*, 2nd ed. (Boston, MA: Harvard Business School Press, 1998).

Benito, Gabriel R. G., Lunnan, Randi, and Tomassen, Sverre. "Distant encounters of the third kind: multinational companies locating divisional headquarters abroad," *Journal of Management Studies*, vol. 48, no. 2 (March 2011).

Birkinshaw, Julian, and Pedersen, Torben. "Strategy and management in MNE subsidiaries." In Alan M. Rugman (ed.), *The Oxford Handbook of International Business* (Oxford: Oxford University Press, 2009).

Cho, Dong-Sung, and Moon, Hwy-Chang. *From Adam Smith to Michael Porter: Evolution of Competitiveness Theory* (Singapore and River's Edge, NJ: World Scientific, 2000).

Cho, Dong-Sung, Moon, Hwy-Chang Moon, and Kim, Min-Young, "Does one size fit all? A dual double diamond approach to country-specific advantages," *Asian Business and Management*, vol. 8, no. 1 (2009). ·

Collinson, Simon C., Sullivan-Taylor, Bridgette, and Wilson, David C. "Extending the integration–responsiveness framework: delivering a global service strategy at British Airways," *Strategic Innovators Journal*, vol. 3, no. 3 (2010).

Davies, Howard, and Ellis, Paul. "Porter's *Competitive Advantage of Nations*: time for the final judgement?," *Journal of Management Studies*, vol. 37, no. 8 (December 2000).

Dunning, John H. "Internationalizing Porter's diamond," *Management International Review*, vol. 33, no. 2 (1993).

Dunning, John H. "The geographical sources of competitiveness of firms: some results of a new survey," *Transnational Corporations*, vol. 5, no. 3 (December 1996).

Enright, Michael J. "The location of activities of manufacturing multinationals in the Asia-Pacific," *Journal of International Business Studies*, vol. 40 (June/July 2009).

Grant, Robert M. "Porter's 'Competitive advantage of nations': an assessment," *Strategic Management Journal*, vol. 12, no. 7 (October 1991).

Harzing, Anne-Wil. "An empirical analysis and extension of the Bartlett and Ghoshal typology of multinational companies," *Journal of International Business Studies*, vol. 31, no. 1 (2000).

Hutzschenreuter, Thomas, and Gröne, Florian. "Product and geographic scope changes of multinational enterprises in response to international competition," *Journal of International Business Studies*, vol. 40 (September 2009).

Kotler, Philip. *The Marketing of Nations* (New York: Free Press, 1997).

Mataloni, Raymond J. "The structure of location choice for new US manufacturing investments in Asia-Pacific." *Journal of World Business*, vol. 46, no. 2 (2011).

Meyer, Klaus E., Mudambi, Ram, and Narula, Rajneesh. "Multinational enterprises and local contexts: the opportunities and challenges of multiple embeddedness," *Journal of Management Studies*, vol. 48, no. 2 (March 2011).

Meyer, Klaus E., and Su, Yu-Shan. "Integration and responsiveness in subsidiaries in emerging economies," *Journal of World Business*, vol. 50, no. 1 (2015).

Moon, Hwy-Chang, Geddis, Lorna, and Jin Uk Kim. "A Fresh Look at an Old Debate on Globalization versus Localization,"*Journal of Organization and Management Development*, vol. 2, no. 1 (2009).

Moon, Hwy-Chang, Rugman, Alan M., and Verbeke, Alain, "A generalized double diamond approach to the global competitiveness of Korea and Singapore," *International Business Review*, vol. 7, no. 2 (April 1998).

Narula, Rajneesh. "Technology, international business and Porter's 'diamond': synthesizing a dynamic competitive development model," *Management International Review*, vol. 33, no. 2 (1993).

Peterson, Robert M., Dibrell, C. Clay, and Pett, Timothy L. "Long-vs. short-term performance perspectives of western European, Japanese, and US countries: where do they lie?," *Journal of World Business*, vol. 37, no. 4 (2003).

Piscitello, Lucia. "Multinationals and economic geography: location, technology and innovation," *Journal of International Business Studies*, vol. 44, no. 8 (2013).

Prahalad, C. K., and Doz, Yves L. *The Multinational Mission: Balancing Local Demands and Global Vision* (New York: Free Press, 1987).

Porter, Michael E. "The competitive advantage of nations," *Harvard Business Review*, vol. 68, no. 2 (March/April 1990).

Porter, Michael E. *On Competition*, updated and expanded ed. (Boston, MA: Harvard Business School Press, 2008).

Rizopoulos, Yorgos A., and Sergakis, Dimitrios E. "MNEs and policy networks: institutional embeddedness and strategic choice," *Journal of World Business*, vol. 45, no. 3 (2010).

Roth, Kendall. "International configuration and coordination archetypes for medium-sized firms in global industries," *Journal of International Business Studies*, vol. 23, no. 3 (1992).

Roth, Kendall, and Morrison, Allen J. "An empirical analysis of the integration–responsiveness framework in global industries," *Journal of International Business Studies*, vol. 21, no. 4 (1990).

Rugman, Alan M. "Diamond in the rough," *Business Quarterly*, vol. 55, no. 3 (winter 1991).

Rugman, Alan M. "Porter takes the wrong turn," *Business Quarterly*, vol. 56, no. 3 (winter 1992).

Rugman, Alan M., and D'Cruz, Joseph. "The double diamond model of international competitiveness: the Canadian experience," *Management International Review*, vol. 33, no. 2 (1993).

Rugman, Alan M., and D'Cruz, Joseph. *Multinationals as Flagship Firms: Regional Business Networks* (New York: Oxford University Press, 2000).

Rugman, Alan M., and Oh, Chang Hoon. "Multinationality and regional performance, 2000–2005." In Alan M. Rugman (ed.), *Regional Aspects of Multinationality and Performance* (Oxford: Elsevier, 2007).

Rugman, Alan M., and Oh, Chang Hoon. "The international competitiveness of Asian firms," *Journal of Strategy and Management*, vol. 1, no. 1 (2008).

Rugman, Alan M., Oh, Chang Hoon, and Lim, Dominic. "The regional and global competitiveness of multinational firms," *Journal of the Academy of Marketing Science*, doi 10.1007/s11747–011–0270–5 (2011).

Rugman, Alan M., and Verbeke, Alain. *Beyond the Three Generics*, Research in Global Strategic Management, vol. 4 (Greenwich, CT: JAI Press, 1993).

Rugman, Alan M., and Verbeke, Alain. "Foreign subsidiaries and multinational strategic management: an extension and correction of Porter's single diamond framework," *Management International Review*, vol. 33, no. 2 (1993).

Rugman, Alan M., and Verbeke, Alain. "How to operationalize Porter's diamond of competitive advantage," *International Executive*, vol. 35, no. 4 (July/August 1993).

Rugman, Alan M., and Verbeke, Alain. *Analysis of Multinational Strategic Management: The Selected Scientific Papers of Alan M. Rugman and Alain Verbeke* (Cheltenham: Edward Elgar, 2005).

Rugman, Alan M., and Verbeke, Alain. "A regional solution to the strategy and structure of multinationals," *European Management Journal*, vol. 26 (2008).

Rugman, Alan M., Verbeke, Alain, and Yuan, Wenlong. "Reconceptualizing Barlett and Ghoshall's classification of national subsidiary roles in the multinational enterprises," *Journal of Management Studies*, vol. 48, no. 2 (2011).

Rugman, Alan M., and Waverman, Leonard. "Foreign ownership and corporate strategy." In Leonard Waverman (ed.), *Corporate Globalization through Mergers and Acquisitions* (Calgary: University of Calgary Press, 1991).

Stone, Howard B. J., and Ranchhod, Ashok. "Competitive advantage of a nation in the global arena: a quantitative advancement to Porter's diamond applied to the UK, USA and BRIC nations," *Strategic Change*, vol. 15, no. 6 (2006).

Sun, Sunny Li, et al. "A comparative ownership advantage framework for cross-border M&As: the rise of Chinese and Indian MNEs," *Journal of World Business*, vol. 47, no. 1 (2012).

Vahlne, Jan-Erik, Ivarsson Inge, and Johanson, Jan. "The tortuous road to globalization for Volvo's heavy truck business: extending the scope of the Uppsala model," *International Business Review*, vol. 20, no. 1 (February 2011).

Venaik, Sunil, Midgley, David F., and Devinney, Timothy M. "A new perspective on the integration responsiveness pressures confronting multinational firms," *Management International Review*, vol. 44, special no. 1 (2004).

Yip, George S., Rugman, Alan M., and Kudina, Alina. "International success of British companies," *Long Range Planning*, vol. 39, no. 2 (June 2006).

Yu, Jisun, and Zaheer, Srilata. "Building a process model of local adaptation of practices: a study of six sigma implementation in Korean and US firms," *Journal of International Business Studies*, vol. 41 (April 2010).

Chapter 11

MULTINATIONAL ENTERPRISES AS RESPONSIBLE STAKEHOLDERS

Contents

Objectives of the chapter

"The only thing that is constant is change'. This is particularly the case
for the field of international business because it encompasses a wide
range of evolving factors at multiple levels: the manager, firm, industry
sector, country, and global. One of the most prominent changes is the
increased attention paid to corporate social responsibility and the
obligations of firms to wider stakeholders rather than just
shareholders. Business ethics and the ethical behavior of firms is a key
consideration for managers. In this chapter we explore two useful
frameworks to help analyze the future of international business. First,
we consider how multinational enterprises (MNEs) often serve as
"flagship" firms at the hubs of business networks. We relate this to
country-level (environmental) and firm-level strategies and future
trends. Second, we develop a framework to analyze the impact of civil
society on trade and investment agreements. This will incorporate a
discussion of corporate ethics and the role of non-governmental
organizations (NGOs) as they can affect such agreements.

The specific objectives of this chapter are to:

1 *Examine* how these changing developments will create both
   challenges and opportunities for MNEs over the next decade.

2 *Explain* why research will continue to be of critical importance to the
   field of international business.

3 *Examine* three frameworks in which MNEs can cope with their
   changing political and economic environments.

4 *Relate* the importance of the NGOs and ethical issues to the
   strategies of multinational enterprises.

ACTIVE LEARNING CASE

The environment, NGOs, and MNEs

What do Apple, Google, Berkshire Hathaway and Amazon.com have in common? In 2015, they were among the world's most admired companies in the *Fortune* annual ranking. The nine key attributes of reputation are innovation, people management, use of corporate assets, social responsibility, quality of management, financial soundness, long-term investment, quality of products and services, and global competitiveness. These rankings are calculated based on a survey of business people's perceptions. The top 20 firms according to business people are shown in Table 11.1.

Of course, non-governmental organizations (NGOs) may not like these companies and today, in a world of corporate social responsibility, the viewpoints of NGOs and other stakeholders are important. In particular, NGOs are often critical of the poor environmental performance of MNEs. Partly in response to this, the survey also highlights eight companies which are devising innovative ways to make their firms greener, including Coca-Cola, Southwest Airlines, Procter & Gamble, Google, Microsoft, FedEx, and Amazon.com.

Coca-Cola has developed technology to produce fully recyclable plastic bottles which are 30 percent composed of plastic made from sugar cane. This reduces the amount of petroleum by-products used to make the plastic. Coke wants to share the technology. The company has partnered with Heinz so the ketchup maker can use partially plant-based bottles for 120 million ketchup containers.

Southwest Airlines is one of the few airlines which wash the plane engines at night so that they burn fuel more efficiently during flights the next day. Southwest is also investing in the Federal Aviation Administration's updated navigation system, which helps planes fly the best routes and save excess fuel costs. The next initiative is to lighten the cabins of the planes. So, Southwest is adding lighter-weight carpeting, seat covers and life vests. The company is running its new cabin design by regulators and hopes to make an official announcement about it later this year. The end result will be even more fuel-efficient flights, which translate to an even greater profit margin for Southwest.

IT companies like Google and Microsoft are trying to focus on data center efficiency, which requires lots of power. Furthermore, Microsoft has formed partnerships with industry rivals to promote green technology. Along with AMD, Intel, Oracle, and other technology giants, Microsoft is on the board of a project called the Green Grid, which is designed to use IT to promote sustainability.

Table 11.1 The world's most admired companies, 2015

Rank 2011	Name	Country	Sector
1	Apple	United States	Computers
2	Google	United States	IT/search engine
3	Berkshire Hathaway	United States	Investment
4	Amazon.com	United States	Online retail
5	Starbucks	United States	Beverage
6	Walt Disney	United States	Media/leisure
7	SouthWest Airlines	United States	Airlines
8	American Express	United States	Credit card
9	General Electric	United States	Diversified
10	Coca-Cola	United States	FMCG
11	Johnson & Johnson	United States	Pharmaceuticals
12	FedEx	United States	Express courier
13	Nike	United States	Apparel
14	Nordstrom	United States	General merchandise
15	BMW	Germany	Automotive
16	Costco Wholesale	United States	Speciality retailers
17	Procter & Gamble	United States	Cosmetics
18	Whole Foods Market	United States	Food and drug stores
19	Singapore Airlines	Singapore	Airlines
20	Microsoft	United States	IT

Source: Adapted from "Survey of the world's most admired companies," *Fortune*, 2015 http://fortune.com/worlds-most-admired-companies/google-2/

Amazon.com doesn't make many tangible things, but it ships large quantities of books every day. And when the online store asked customers how it could improve the shopping experience, buyers said they wanted less packaging. Amazon has worked with suppliers such as Philips to cut out the clamshells and stick with boxes that are easy to open and made from recyclable materials. By cutting wasteful packaging, the company has also reduced its carbon footprint.

This was not enough for many of the firm's critics and in 2015, both to improve its reputation and to initiate some real changes to its strategy, Amazon appointed a "director of social responsibility". Christine Bader, a long-term advocate for large firms to be positive social and environmental forces in the world, took on the role. Her book, *The Evolution of a Corporate Idealist: When Girl Meets Oil* was a product of many years working at BP on social responsibility issues, although she left before the Deepwater Horizon oil spill when her expertise was needed most.

In general, the managers of both large MNEs and smaller firms are extremely aware of their wider social and ethical responsibilities. Most of these firms have developed explicit environmental programs and have appointed senior managers responsible for corporate social responsibility activities. Some firms have even hired former NGO activists and environmental politicians to help improve the firms' environmental policy and social programs. However, the success of these managerial initiatives remains open to question, as discussed in this chapter.

Websites: www.coca-cola.com, www.amazon.com, www.google.com, www.microsoft.com, www.fedex.com, www.pg.com, www.southwest.com

Source: "Survey of the world's most admired companies," *Fortune*, March, 2015 issue, http://money.cnn.com/magazines/fortune/mostadmired/2015/full_list/; "Eight green stars at most admired companies", *Fortune*, http://money.cnn.com/galleries/2011/fortune/1103/gallery.most_admired_green_leaders.fortune/7.html; Christine Bader, *The Evolution of a Corporate Idealist: When Girl Meets Oil* (Boston, MA: Bibliomotion, 2014).

① How have NGOs changed the external environment in which MNEs operate? Why is Apple the world's most admired firm among business people? Why is a firm like Google likely to be more admired by NGOs?

② As MNEs operate across the world and NGOs operate globally, why are there no "global" or "international" environmental agreements to set rules for sustainable development?

③ Where would a company like Coca-Cola, or others in Table 11.1, be positioned in Figure 11.7? Why?

INTRODUCTION

Many observers believe that paying attention to stakeholders, rather than just shareholders, is a relatively recent development for firms. Shareholders have an ownership interest. They make money if the firm makes money and this tends to drive firms to focus on performance and profits, sometimes regardless of other social or environmental considerations. Stakeholders represent a wider set of interests, including employees and customers, but also other interest groups that might be affected by (and/ or can affect) the behavior of firms. But while this shift toward the considerations of stakeholders is new for many Western MNEs, it is something that firms based in other countries have always practiced. Japanese firms have historically put employees above profits, and family businesses from other parts of Asia and the Middle East, for example, put the extended family group and the wider community ahead of other kinds of performance.

Those MNEs that have more recently started to pay attention to a wider set of interests, from environmental sustainability to employee welfare, have been motivated by two kinds of pressures. The first is external, from a wide range of increasingly well-informed, connected, and coordinated lobby groups. These include consumers (who want better, safer products and fairer pricing), suppliers (who want reasonable margins), employee groups (who want a fair wage and reasonable working conditions), and others who might be negatively affected by a firm's actions. The second driver for change comes from the firm's own leadership and management. "Enlightened" managers adopt a set of values or respect a code of ethics which influences their decisions and drives the firm to consider the wider interests of the communities affected by their actions. But there are also firms that adopt the appearance of being stakeholder oriented, by marketing themselves as caring and compassionate members of society, but really only when this attracts more customers and boosts profits. As increased attention is paid to corporate social responsibility, it is important to know how to differentiate firms that are genuinely focused on the needs of stakeholders and those that are only superficially concerned about non-shareholders.

Stakeholder theory argues that the purpose of a firm is to maximize value for stakeholders, rather than just shareholders. More broadly it represents a field of study which addresses how firms should, could, or do incorporate ethics and values in decision making.[1] We must not forget though that no firm can survive and therefore continue adding value for stakeholders and/or shareholders without sustaining some level of competitive advantage. If, by addressing the concerns of the wider society and "the planet," a firm ceases to be profitable, then it will cease to exist.

It is important to link the new frameworks developed here back to the familiar firm and country factors in the FSA–CSA matrix of Chapter 2. Essentially environmental regulations, and other societal pressures on the firm, can be regarded as CSAs. Whether they are positive or negative CSAs can be shown on the vertical axis of the FSA–CSA matrix. The novel thinking developed in this chapter is that the firm can evolve a sophisticated response to outside pressure groups and regulations which support stakeholders, such that it becomes an FSA. Of course, this FSA would be shown in quadrant or cell 3 of the FSA–CSA matrix. Thus this chapter is an extension of the thinking first developed in Chapter 2 and then related to strategic management (Chapter 8), organization structure (Chapter 9), and the integration/responsiveness framework (Chapter 10). Another way of looking at environmental regulations, or the activities of lobby groups, is as part of the home-country diamond (in Porter's single-diamond model). They can also be part of the host-country CSAs in terms of the double-diamond framework, as discussed in Chapter 10.

We will come back to corporate ethics and the challenges of "stakeholder capitalism" later in this chapter. First, we go back to some of the basics to understand how MNEs develop effective strategies more generally, in a changing environment. This involves introducing a number of useful frameworks, including the "five partners business network" framework and the idea of the "flagship firm," alongside the trade and investment framework.

DEVELOPING EFFECTIVE STRATEGIES

MNEs are supplementing or supplanting their old strategies in a number of ways in order to compete more effectively worldwide. Two of the most recent developments include going where the action is and developing new business networks with governments, suppliers, customers, and competitors.

Going where the action is

One strategy that is proving increasingly important is the need to go international in order to keep up with the competition. Successful multinationals have operations in the home countries of their major triad competitors. For example, IBM's strongest competitors are located in the United States, Europe, and Japan. In turn the company has facilities in all three places, to monitor the competition as well as to conduct research. Moreover, the communication network among the company's facilities allows each one to share information with the others and to provide assistance. This also helps the company to maintain a strong competitive posture.[2]

Another reason for locating near major competitors is that some markets develop faster than others and the experience and knowledge that is learned here can help in other markets.

For example, in the US market IBM is now trying to develop a strategy of providing the best service in the industry. In the past the company had often referred service problems to its dealers. However, now the firm is attempting to address these issues directly, ensuring a higher level of service and taking back customers who were lured away by smaller firms with better service, support, and prices. If this strategy works well, the company is likely to use it in other worldwide locations where small firms have been gaining market share. Today, IBM makes very sizable profits from software and services. Now IBM is customer-led, it is asked by its clients for what they want from IBM, and IBM is producing solutions rather than specific products to link together the complicated global infrastructure. IBM is also making a big push into cloud computing, developing software to move big corporate clients into the cloud and building vast data centers to host them. It is also looking at ways in which technology can make an impact in the healthcare sector, with sensors to monitor patients remotely. But these are competitive sectors where IBM may struggle to achieve the kind of market dominance it once achieved in mainframe computers.[3]

Another important aspect of a location-focused strategy is that MNEs often establish a home base for each major product line, and a multiproduct-line company will have "centers for excellence" all over the world. These centers are responsible for providing global leadership for their respective product lines. For example, Asea Brown Boveri, a Swiss firm, uses Sweden as the home base for transmission equipment. Research, development, and production are centralized in that country. Nestlé, the giant food company, has the world headquarters for its confectionery business in the UK because this home base is more dynamic in terms of the marketing environment and the high per capita consumption of confectionery products. At the same time Nestlé has made its Italian company, Buitoni, the world center for pasta operations. Meanwhile, Siemens has designated the United States as the world home base for medical electronics because this is where the market is most dynamic and will provide the company with the best chance of developing and maintaining state-of-the-art products.

It is also important to realize that the product line will dictate the degree of globalization. For example, food companies in Europe tend to be less international and more regional in focus. Local tastes vary widely and there are only modest gains to be achieved through large-scale operations, so European food companies tend to have an extensive local presence. The same is true for home appliances, which are often produced for regional markets. On the other hand, when European companies have become truly global, they have tended to focus on products that do not require high levels of integration on a worldwide basis.

So some companies have a need for global centers throughout the world, whereas others tend to stay in closer geographic proximity because of the nature of their product lines. Still others combine both of these approaches, as seen in the case **International Business Strategy in Action: 3M**.

✔ Active learning check

Review your answer to Active Learning Case question 1 and make any changes you like. Then compare your answer to the one below.

1 How have NGOs changed the external environment in which MNEs operate? Why is Apple the world's most admired firm among business people? Why is a firm like Google likely to be more admired by NGOs?

NGOs have captured public attention and won a lot of support in North America and western Europe for their "green" and anti-globalization agendas. MNEs cannot afford to ignore NGOs, especially US and EU MNEs whose home base "diamond" is threatened by NGOs which can influence government policy and regulation. Apple has gained recognition as the most successful MNE because it has an innovative approach to consumer electronics such as the iPhone and iPad, which are very successful with consumers around the world. In contrast, Google while still being consumer friendly has also developed an explicit environmental energy-saving strategy, making it more popular with green environmentalists.

INTERNATIONAL BUSINESS STRATEGY IN ACTION

3M

3M is a major MNE with over 55,000 products sold in 200 countries, comprising everything from office supplies to construction and building maintenance to chemicals. In 2015 it employed over 89,000 people and had operations in more than 70 countries. Taking this into account, one may question: how does the firm manage such a large international operation? One way is by matching its global strategies with the needs of the local market.

The company balances its global strategies and national responses on a region-by-region basis. For example, in Europe the company has set up a series of business centers to address local differences. The company also uses European management action teams (EMATs) to balance the needs of subsidiaries in responding to local expectations with the corporation's need for global direction. Today, 3M has 50 EMATs in Europe, each consisting of from 8 to 14 people, most of whom are marketing personnel. These groups are charged with bringing the firm's global plans to life by helping their execution at the local level. EMAT meetings, which usually occur quarterly, are designed to create action plans for the European subsidiaries. When the meetings are over, the members then return to their respective subsidiaries and begin executing the plans. In Asia the company uses a different approach, relying heavily on its Japanese operation to provide much of the needed direction to the subsidiaries. At the same time there are regional centers in Singapore and South Korea that help subsidiaries to address their local markets. In Latin America, meanwhile, 3M uses a macro approach, conducting business on a national rather than regional basis.

3M is seen by some as one of the first global manufacturing firms to integrate environmental sustainability into its global strategy, across all its operations, despite the obvious organizational complexity outlined above. It was among the first group of firms to be listed on the Dow Jones Sustainability Index when it started in 1999. In 2014 it won the US Environmental Protection Agency's (EPA) ENERGY STAR® award for the tenth year in a row for its worldwide energy-conservation efforts. These awards, alongside a range of indicators which the firm uses to measure its progress as a responsible company, suggest that it is genuinely concerned about its wider stakeholders. These examples come from its *Annual Sustainability Report* (2015):

■ 3M's Pollution Prevention Pays program has prevented nearly 2 million tons of air, water, and waste pollution, and the reduction of the company's global greenhouse gas emissions by 57 percent from 2002 to 2013 on an absolute basis (even as the company sales grew 30 percent over the same period of time).

■ Ongoing support to protect and restore vital ecosystems around the world. By working with partners such as The Nature Conservancy, the 3M Foundation has provided more than $21 million to preserve more than 1 million acres.

■ More than $61.6 million in global cash and in-kind product donations in 2013.

■ In 2014 3M joined the United Nations Global Compact, formalizing its commitment to the ten principles of the Compact in the areas of human rights, labor, the environment, and anti-corruption.

Some firms develop sophisticated vision and mission statements or advertising campaigns to promote their ethical or environmental credentials. It is always worth looking at the evidence and in 3M's case the rhetoric does seem to be matched by the numbers.

Website: www.3m.com

Sources: Adapted from Harry Mammerly, "Matching global strategies with national responses," *Journal of Business Strategy* (March/April 1992), pp. 8–13; www.3m.com; 3M, *Annual Report,* 2009–14; 3M *Sustainability Report* (2015) at: http://www.3m.com/3M/en_US/sustainability-us/

INTERNATIONAL BUSINESS RESEARCH FRAMEWORKS

No study of international business would be complete without paying attention to the role and importance of theoretical frameworks. In Chapter 2 we introduced the firm (FSA) and country (CSA) matrix, while in Chapter 10 we used the integration and national responsiveness matrix. Much of what has been discussed in this book is based on the research findings leading to such basic frameworks. In many cases the data were drawn from government statistics, company records, and business reports on recent developments and strategies. In other cases the information was garnered from formal studies that examined managerial behaviors among senior managers. Collectively, research provides important input for building international business theories and for formulating and implementing future strategies. As a result, it is useful to both academicians and practitioners.

Unfortunately, research findings can be confusing and contradictory. For example, many studies are extremely limited in focus and thus cannot be generalized to a universal setting. Similarly, when research is broadly based, it is likely that the findings cannot be generalized to specific situations. Porter's diamond, for example, helps to explain how triad nations develop competitive advantage. However, its value to non-triad nations, as explained in Chapter 10, is limited and the findings must be revised and modified in order to apply them. Despite such shortcomings, however, international business research will continue to be of critical importance to the field. Such research will allow us to test theories and to refine their practical applications.

Theories of international business

A great many theories have relevance to the study of international business. In some cases these are first constructed and then tested. A good example is Adam Smith's theory of labor specialization. Smith presented this concept over 200 years ago in his *Wealth of Nations*, and in recent years learning curve analysts have confirmed these findings. Of course, not all theories have had to wait centuries before being proven. However, this example does illustrate that international business research can be advanced through the formulation of useful theories.[4]

In other cases, theories are being tested for the purpose of reconfirming earlier findings. This is particularly important in learning how well a theory stands the test of time. A good example is the theory of lifetime employment in Japan. For many years, theorists have argued that lifetime employment creates a highly motivated workforce and Western organizations would be wise to copy this approach. More recent research, however, reveals that lifetime employment is less useful as a motivator than as a control tool for ensuring worker loyalty and performance. In return for guaranteed employment, workers stay with the firm for their entire career, work hard, and are compliant with management's wishes. Sometimes unions are employer dominated and then they serve more to maintain harmony within the employee ranks than to represent the workers.

Based on an analysis of empirical data collected on this topic, two researchers concluded: "lifetime employment is offered within a context of loyalty and benevolence based on cultural values. Its impact, however, is to increase the control of Japanese employees by managers."[5] Moreover, these researchers found that lifetime employment was not widely used by firms in tight labor markets because it was not possible to control the workers, who could easily find jobs with other companies and who derived little motivation from such guarantees.

This type of research is also important because it generates new hypotheses for testing. For example, as workers in large companies with guaranteed lifetime employment near retirement (55 to 60 years of age), will management replace them with younger people who are not given such guarantees? As the competitive environment increases, will companies stop offering these guarantees because they reduce the firms' flexibility in responding to changing conditions? Will young workers entering the Japanese workforce during this decade be motivated by such guarantees, or will they turn them down because they are unwilling to commit their career to one firm in return for job security? These types of questions will be focal points for future international business research efforts, since changing economic, cultural, and social environments are creating new conditions in which MNEs must compete. Research can help to shed light on the effect of these changes.

Practical applications of the theory

Research is also going to play an increasing role in helping to uncover how and why multinationals succeed. In particular, greater attention will be given to strategy research that is designed to explain why some firms do better than others and how these strategies are changing. For example, during the 1970s traditional international business strategy gave strong support to **strategic fit**, the notion that an organization must align its resources in such a way as to mesh with the environment. Auto firms had to design and build cars that were in demand, and this might mean a variety of models and accessories, depending on the number of markets being served. Similarly, electronics firms had to maintain state-of-the-art technology so as to meet consumer demand for new, high-quality, high-performance products. Today, however, successful multinationals realize that they must do much more than attempt to attain a strategic fit. The rapid pace of competitive change is requiring linkages between all segments of the business from manufacturing down to point-of-purchase selling, and in every phase of operation there must be attention to value-added concepts. So the basic strategic concepts of the past, once widely accepted, must be reconsidered and sometimes reformulated.

Other research areas likely to receive future attention will be cross-national collaborative research by individuals from two or more countries and joint efforts by international and non-international researchers. The world of international business is getting larger every day, and it is critical that research be designed not only to help explain what is happening and why it is occurring, but also to help predict future developments and thus better prepare students and practitioners for the international challenges of the twenty-first century.

Strategic fit
A strategic management concept which holds that an organization must align its resources in such a way as to mesh effectively with the environment

THE FIVE PARTNERS BUSINESS NETWORK FRAMEWORK

In the future governments will become more selective in their approach to industrial policy, aware that in the past billions of dollars have been wasted by bureaucratic efforts to streamline and refocus economic efforts. This recent trend is likely to result in more government–business efforts. However, the success of international business firms will depend more heavily on the companies themselves than on the government. Some of these developments will include the forging of new business networks for competitive advantage and the development of new relationships with non-business sector groups.[6]

Forging new business networks

Increasingly, the relationship of successful MNEs with their suppliers, customers, and competitors is changing. New strategies based on trust and reciprocal support are replacing the old business–client relationship in which companies sought to dictate the terms and conditions of sales and services.

In the case of suppliers, the current trend is toward reducing this number to a small group of reliable, efficient, and highly responsive firms. These suppliers are then brought into a close working relationship with the MNE so that both sides understand the other's strategy and plans can be formulated for minimizing working problems. The multinational will detail its needs and the supplier will draw up plans that ensure timely, accurate delivery. Another trend is the increase in the amount of responsibility being given to suppliers. Previously they were charged only with manufacturing, assembly, and delivery. Now many MNEs use their network partners to develop new materials and components, to perform industrial engineering functions, and to assume liability for warranties.

Flagship firms
Multinational firms characterized by global competitiveness and international benchmarks

In the case of customers, network linkages now involve changing the focus of the relationship from one in which sales representatives would work directly with MNE purchasing agents to one in which sellers interact more directly with their customers. D'Cruz and Rugman have explained this idea in the case of **flagship firms**, characterized by global competitiveness and international benchmarks.[7] In the conventional system the flagship firm and its customers maintain an arm's-length relationship. However, new relationships are now being forged in which there is a direct link between the flagship firm and its most important customers (see Figure 11.1, segments 1 and 2), whereas traditional relations are maintained with some distributors to serve the firm's less important customers. At the same time, network linkages are being developed with key distributors to serve other customers better (again see Figure 11.1, segments 3 and 4, etc.)

Network arrangements are also being created between international competitors in the form of joint ventures, technology transfers, and market-sharing agreements, such as a Japanese firm selling the product of a US firm in the Japanese market in return for a similar concession in the United States. Mazda and Ford Motor are excellent examples.

Figure 11.1 Network linkage and the changing shape of international distribution systems

Source: © Alan Rugman and Joseph R. D'Cruz, 2000. Reprinted from *Multinationals as Flagship Firms: Regional Business Networks* by Alan M. Rugman and Joseph R. D'Cruz (2000).

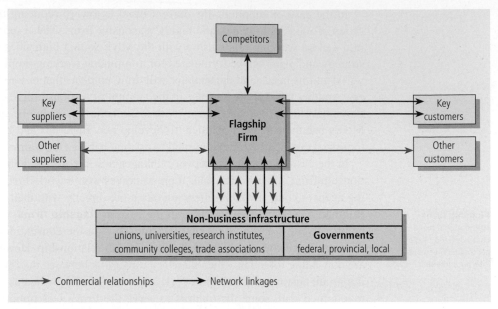

Figure 11.2 Network linkages for successful MNEs

Source: © Alan Rugman and Joseph R. D'Cruz, 2000. Reprinted from *Multinationals as Flagship Firms: Regional Business Networks* by Alan M. Rugman and Joseph R. D'Cruz (2000).

These strategic relationships among suppliers, customers, and competitors are becoming integral parts of MNE strategies, as are linkages to non-business organizations such as unions, with which multinationals are now sharing their strategies in the hope of creating a working relationship that will save jobs and ensure company profitability. Partnerships are also being fostered with universities that can help to educate and train human resources, and research institutions that can provide scientific knowledge that is useful for helping organizations to develop and maintain worldwide competitiveness. Another group that is getting increased attention is government, since this institution can be particularly helpful in supporting legislation that will encourage the upgrading of the workforce, development of state-of-the-art technology and products, exports, and the building of world-class competitors. Figure 11.2 provides an illustration of the basic structure of the **five partners** in an effective network. Notice how these relationships go beyond commercial transactions and involve network linkages to a wide variety of other groups. This is one of the waves of the future in international business.

Five partners
A business network consisting of five partner organizations: the flagship firm (a multinational enterprise), key suppliers, key customers, key competitors, and the non-business infrastructure

COPING WITH CHANGING ENVIRONMENTS

The international environment of the future will continue to be one of rapid change, and MNEs will have to stay abreast of a number of developments. The political and economic environments will present the greatest challenges.

Political environment

As already seen, the political environment affects MNE activities in many ways. For example, all major triad groups have trade barriers that are designed to limit the sale of foreign goods in their countries. This in turn typically results in trade negotiations that are designed to open up these markets and/or to reduce trade deficits. Protectionism trends are particularly treacherous because they are psychological as well as legislative. That is, even when trade barriers are lowered, there is a tendency for people to be protectionist and to "buy local."

Many managers say that they favor open markets, but, when questioned closely, they state strong support for protectionist strategies such as government assistance to domestic businesses and help for home-based firms that are seeking to go international.[8] In short, many business people speak out for free trade but advocate policies that put foreign firms at a distinct disadvantage. The Japanese are some of the strongest supporters of free trade. However, according to the US trade representative these opinions are not translated into action. For example, Japanese telecom fees make it difficult for foreign companies to compete effectively.

The ability of US firms to penetrate foreign markets will also be influenced by US government policies. US government trade policy toward Japan and Southeast Asia generally aims to open markets in the region. The objective was to increase the market share of US firms in this geographic triad region as well as to reduce the large trade deficit that the United States is running, most noticeably with China. The latter is likely to receive particular attention, given that in recent years China has sold far more to the United States than it has purchased from it.[9] The Bush administration reacted to the failure of the WTO Doha Round of multilateral trade negotiations by working out sets of bilateral free trade agreements, such as one with South Korea. In December 2010, both the United States and South Korea hailed their long-awaited free trade agreement as a "win–win" deal. President Barack Obama said the deal was "essential" in boosting US exports.

At the same time, overseas companies are lobbying their governments to negotiate greater access to the US market. For example, the governments of less industrialized countries are putting pressure on triad countries to liberalize agricultural trade. International institutions like the IMF, as well as non-governmental organizations (NGOs) like Oxfam, criticize the United States, the EU, and Japan, some of the more vocal supporters of free trade, for subsidizing their agricultural and manufacturing industries to the detriment of less developed countries.

A related issue is political risk. For example, in Latin America, Venezuela and Brazil have left-leaning populist governments. Venezuela is a large exporter of oil and Brazil is the manufacturing hub for Latin America, a host country for VW and Mercedes-Benz, among others.[10] The financial crisis in Argentina led to some factories being abandoned, followed by worker occupation of these factories. These workers started producing again and sought to be legitimized by the government as owners of the factory.[11]

Hong Kong, the former British colony, was returned to China in 1997. The Chinese government agreed to allow the region to maintain relative autonomy and to continue functioning under its own economic and political systems for 50 years after the takeover.[12] China is now heavily investing in Hong Kong and has more total direct investment there than in any other country. At the same time, two-thirds of foreign investment in China comes from Hong Kong Chinese. Many Hong Kong business people believe that relations with China have worked out for the betterment of both sides.

Another country where political risk is being re-evaluated is Vietnam.[13] Relations between the United States and Vietnam are now normalized, and the country has business ties with US multinationals that can provide assistance in helping to rebuild the economy. The IMF and the World Bank provided funds for critical highway and seaport projects. At the same time, Vietnam has been attracting billions of dollars in manufacturing investment from European and Asian companies. Now that the US trade embargo has ended, Vietnam has attracted US banks, aircraft, and power plant manufacturers to help in the rebuilding effort. One major reason that Vietnam is interested in rapprochement with the United States is that it sees it as a counterbalance to Japan and the growing military might of China. As relations between the two countries continue to thaw, political risk will decline and Vietnam will become an increasingly popular area for investment opportunities.

The continuing development of free trade agreements will also work to lessen political risk. For example, the North American Free Trade Agreement (NAFTA) binds Canada, the

United States, and Mexico together into an interdependent market in which each nation profits by working harmoniously with the others. The same is true for members of the EU as well as for other economic unions, from those being fostered in Latin America to those in Africa and the former Soviet Union. Firms doing business in these geographic areas will find that the greatest ongoing challenge is more likely to be economic than political. There will also be further consolidation of the world's trade agreements into a triad-based system (see Table 11.2).

Economic environment

The economic environment will be replete with opportunities for MNEs. US multinationals, for example, will continue to be a dominant force in the export market, as seen by the fact that the United States has consistently ranked as the world's largest exporter over the last decade. Meanwhile Asia–Pacific MNEs, except for those of Japan and Australia, will benefit from the comparatively lower cost of labor in their home countries.

New economic opportunities will also be provided by the rise of non-triad-based firms that become successful MNEs. In Mexico, for example, Anheuser-Busch, before being acquired by InBev, used to own approximately 50 percent of Grupo Modelo, maker of Corona and the country's largest brewer. In July 2008, Belgian brewing company InBev completed the acquisition of Anheuser-Busch for US$52 billion in equity, creating the world's largest beer company, Anheuser-Busch InBev. After years of unsuccessfully vying to be the market leader in Peru and losing to local Inca Kola, Coca-Cola's Peruvian bottling and distribution was transferred to its competitor. In turn, Inca Kola products are now sold in North America, mostly to immigrant South Americans, through the Coca-Cola Company. As non-triad countries develop, new opportunities for telecommunication and other infrastructure companies will materialize.

New goods and services will help to create new markets. An example is Apple's iPod, an MP3 player that can store a large quantity of music. Firms are competing to provide ever better MP3 players to gain a share of this growing market. New PC technology is also decreasing the weight of laptops while improving their processing speed, their graphics, and their multimedia capabilities. These products lend themselves to a globalization strategy since purchasers buy them based primarily on performance characteristics and not on cultural requirements. As a result, computer industry MNEs are likely to find this century offering both new opportunities and new challenges. The opportunities will come in the form of emerging markets, since sharp declines in PC prices tend to increase demand sharply. The major challenge will come in the form of increased competition, since PC technology tends to be easy to emulate, and so the barriers to entry for new firms are often quickly surmounted.

An accompanying development is the rise of the internet as a source of competition. Today a growing number of MNEs are becoming electronic companies, or e-corporations for short. The internet is driving down costs and helping companies reach thousands of new potential customers worldwide. As a result, MNEs are now throwing out their old business models and creating new ones that will help them do business electronically with customers who in the past were not accessible to them. One of the keys to this new development is the rapid rise of both businesses and households with internet access. By 2014 approximately 83 percent of the EU population and 77 percent of the US population had home access to the internet.[14] As a result, e-commerce is now accounting for a growing percentage of GDP in these economies.

Major MNEs that are finding themselves unable to compete in the ever-changing international arena are restructuring and realigning markets. Examples include (1) aircraft manufacturing, where Boeing is having to scurry to meet competition from Airbus and now the

Table 11.2 The world's major trade agreements

EU (15)	+EU (13)	EFTA (4)	NAFTA (3)	ASEAN (10)	Mercosur (4)	Andean Group (4)	OPEC (12)	Council of Arab Economic Unity (12)	CARICOM (15)	LAIA (12)	ECOWAS (15)	SADC (14)
Austria	Bulgaria	Iceland	Canada	Brunei Darussalam	Argentina	Bolivia	Algeria	Egypt	Antigua and Barbuda	Argentina	Benin	Angola
Belgium	Cyprus	Liechtenstein	Mexico	Cambodia	Brazil	Colombia	Angola	Iraq	Bahamas	Bolivia	Burkina Faso	Botswana
Denmark	Czech Rep.	Norway	United States	Indonesia	Paraguay	Ecuador	Indonesia	Jordan	Barbados	Brazil	Cape Verde	Dem. Rep. of Congo
Finland	Estonia	Switzerland		Laos	Uruguay	Peru	Iran	Libya	Belize	Chile	Côte d'Ivoire	Lesotho
France	Hungary			Malaysia			Iraq	Mauritania	Dominica	Colombia	Gambia	Madagascar
Germany	Latvia			Myanmar			Kuwait	Syria	Grenada	Cuba	Ghana	Malawi
Greece	Lithuania			Philippines			Libya	Yemen	Guyana	Ecuador	Guinea	Mauritius
Ireland	Malta			Singapore			Nigeria	United Arab Emirates	Haiti	Mexico	Guinea-Bissau	Mozambique
Italy	Poland			Thailand			Qatar	Kuwait	Jamaica	Paraguay	Liberia	Namibia
Luxembourg	Romania			Vietnam			Saudi Arabia	Palestine	Montserrat	Peru	Mali	South Africa
Netherlands	Slovakia						United Arab Emirates	Somalia	Saint Lucia	Uruguay	Niger	Swaziland
Portugal	Slovenia						Venezuela	Sudan	St. Kitts and Nevis	Venezuela	Nigeria	Tanzania
Spain	Croatia								St. Vincent and the Grenadines		Senegal	Zambia
Sweden									Suriname		Sierra Leone	Zimbabwe
UK									Trinidad and Tobago		Togo	

EU (28) spans EU (15) and +EU (13).

Key: EU—European Union; EFTA—European Free Trade Agreement; OPEC—Organization of Petroleum Exporting Countries; NAFTA—North American Free Trade Agreement; CARICOM—Caribbean Community and Common Market; ASEAN—Association of South-East Asian Nations; Mercosur—Mercado Comun del Sur; LAIA—Latin American Integration Association; ECOWAS—Economic Community of West African States; SADC—Southern African Development Community.

Sources: Adapted from http://europa.eu.int/abc-en.htm; www.opec.org; www.efta.int/abc-en.htm; www.caricom.org; http://wellsfargo.com/inatl/wrldalmn/intro/other/; www.sice.oas.org; and www.aladi.org

Chinese; (2) autos, where General Motors, Ford, VW, and Toyota are trying to stave off the onslaught of competition from China and the emerging markets in their home territories; and (3) household electronics, where such well-known manufacturers as Sony, Panasonic, and LG are finding that the acceleration of new product development cycles is allowing Chinese and other country firms to enter these markets.

New strategies, carefully crafted to the specific market, will offer increased opportunities for MNEs. In Japan, for example, the success of firms such as Toys "R" Us and Spiegel is a result of learning how to work within the system. Toys "R" Us set up its own retail stores by teaming up with the former director of McDonald's Japan for local knowledge and investment capital. It relentlessly pursued its objective of its discounted "category killer" toys despite vigorous opposition from small, local merchants who opposed letting Toys "R" Us into the Japanese market. Thanks to its dogged determination, the company was eventually given permission to open a large retail store and by 2009 it had 167 stores in Japan. Spiegel, famous for its mail-order business, formed a joint venture with Sumitomo Trading Company and introduced an upscale fashion catalog in Japan. The company directed its efforts at women from 20 to 40 years of age. Catalog selling proved successful and the firm inspired a range of copy-cat strategies among local Japanese companies. These efforts, which are characterized by strategies that are designed to circumvent problems in the distribution system rather than trying to meet them head on, are typical of those strategies that will be used in Japan and other foreign locations during the years ahead.

Business-to-business (B2B)

An example of an ethnocentric MNE is Air Liquide, the French manufacturer of industrial and medical gases. At its Paris headquarters, the vice presidents for each geographic region are all French. All regional managers in foreign offices are French and have previously worked in Paris. This allows Air Liquide to have a standardized, "global" strategy that treats the world as one integrated market. This works as the nature of the industry is B2B. The main customers of Air Liquide are other large industrial manufacturers in oil, iron and steel, and other types of chemicals. These companies depend on the gases supplied by Air Liquide. It has flagship relationships with many of those manufacturers.

The main competitors of Air Liquide are the UK-based BOC Group and Linde AG. While Air Liquide is more concentrated in the core gas business, its competitors are more diversified into the gases needed for consumers, transportation, etc.

In general, the largest number of B2B relationships would be between ethnocentric partners. Then there are clear rules of the game—both partners are in mature, standardized industries with easy-to-maintain, long-term relationships. So, B2B occurs in chemicals, autos and auto parts, oil, and other "commoditized" sectors.

THE TRADE AND INVESTMENT FRAMEWORK

The tendency toward international trade liberalization has been exemplified by two landmark historical developments, namely the North American Free Trade Agreement (NAFTA) of 1993 and the deeper integration of the European Union (EU). Both these regional triad agreements have developed from previous agreements. The principles of the 1989 United States–Canada Free Trade Agreement (FTA) are also the basis for NAFTA. Similarly, before 1995, the European Union was the European Community (EC). Albeit very different, in terms of goals and content, these two examples of trade and investment liberalization create a protected business environment for member countries, while in turn discriminating against third-country businesses.[15]

From the Canadian and Mexican perspective, the main rationale for negotiating the FTA, and subsequently NAFTA, was to secure access to the US market for both exports

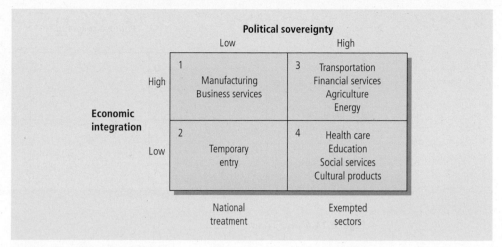

Figure 11.3 FDI and NAFTA

and FDI. Mexico also sought to create a secure economy for inward flows of FDI. In contrast, the EU's predecessor, the EC, was considered by many observers to create a "Fortress Europe" at the expense of third-country firms.[16]

Figure 11.3 classifies the different industries in the countries affected by trade liberalization in NAFTA. (It will also provide an initial framework for the EU.) The vertical axis denominates economic integration and the horizontal axis reflects the political sovereignty of nation-states. The left column therefore shows low political sovereignty in the form of national treatment. With national treatment, discrimination against foreign investors is not permitted; they are to be treated equally with domestic investors in the application of host-country laws and regulations.

Quadrant 1 refers to business sectors where there is high economic integration and low political sovereignty. But not all aspects of "free trade" agreements are here. Quadrant 2 refers to business sectors with low economic integration and low political sovereignty. These are sectors that tend to be naturally local, such as labor. Quadrant 3 refers to business sectors with combined high levels of economic integration and political sovereignty. While national treatment refers to the obligation of member states to treat all businesses from other member countries as if they were domestic businesses, this does not always apply; there are exempted sectors. Sectors in quadrant 3 are exempted from national treatment despite the efficiencies that would result from the application of national treatment. The last matrix section, quadrant 4, refers to sectors that are typically local and are exempted from national treatment.

According to the NAFTA document, national treatment in quadrant 1 applies to sectors such as manufacturing and business service. In quadrant 2 are the temporary entry permits for business service professionals (such as consultants and engineers). Exempted sectors are in quadrants 3 and 4. Those with a high level of economic integration in quadrant 3 include transportation, financial services, energy, and agriculture. Those with low levels of economic integration in quadrant 4 are health care, education, social services, and cultural products.

This framework was also a model for the Free Trade Area of the Americas (FTAA), agreed to at Quebec City in 2001. Unfortunately it was not implemented, due to opposition by Brazil. NAFTA was also the model for the Asia–Pacific Economic Cooperation (APEC), although this will not be fully effective until 2015 and 2020.

Figure 11.4 shows the more complex EU matrix. The two extra quadrants in the extreme left column capture the concept of an even lower level of political sovereignty, reciprocity.

	Political sovereignty		
	Reciprocity	National treatment	Exempted sector
Economic integration High	A	1	3
Low	B	2	4

Figure 11.4 NAFTA and the EU

The EU 1992 measures and subsequent "deepening" programs of political, social, and economic integration aim at quadrant A in everything but select sectors, such as culture. The manufacturing sector and business services are in quadrant A, which also includes banking and mutual funds, securities, insurance, transportation, broadcasting, tourism, and information services. In addition, there are harmonization laws regulating company behavior, including mergers and acquisitions, trademarks and copyrights, cross-border mergers, and accounting operations across borders. Another important objective of harmonization is the opening of public procurement. It is clear that such harmonization efforts place almost all economic sectors in quadrant A of Figure 11.4.[17] In conclusion, in contrast to NAFTA, the EU has a much deeper degree of economic, political, and social integration and a consequent loss of sovereignty for its member states.

Although both NAFTA and the EU can be analyzed in this way, many groups are opposed to such trade and investment liberalization. When they are opposed, they frequently cloak themselves in the guise of ethics, as we will see in the case **International Business Strategy in Action: Is The Body Shop an ethical business?**

 Active learning check

Review your answer to Active Learning Case question 2 and make any changes you like. Then compare your answer to the one below.

2 **As MNEs operate across the world and NGOs operate globally, why are there no "global" or "international" environmental agreements to set rules for sustainable development?**

The reason that there is no effective international environmental agreement is that there is no single international institution that can enforce one. The WTO deals with trade matters, not environmental issues. The United Nations deals with human rights in a political but not economic context. Further, the MNEs really do not operate globally, but are mainly "triad" based. And here, the US and EU triad blocs are often at odds on environmental, trade, and investment policies. Paradoxically, the NGOs are criticizing MNEs for something that they do not do: operate globally. The more responsible NGOs, which believe in sustainable development, should lobby the respective home-based triad authorities. This is where the power is—not with "global" governance. To ensure a safe environment, NGOs need to learn the realities of triad power.

ENVIRONMENT AND MNEs

The issue of globalization has opened up a gulf between representatives of civil society such as NGOs, on the one hand, and international business such as MNEs, on the other. Unfortunately these oppositions of opinion have become entrenched. In this section we will categorize perceptions regarding the role of international institutions and future alternatives for trade liberalization and indicate a range of more constructive responses for both MNEs and NGOs.

"Mobilizer" NGOs criticize the global trade and investment regime and believe that the major international institutions promoting free trade, such as the WTO, IMF, and World Bank, should be eliminated or fundamentally overhauled. "Technical" NGOs are relative insiders, willing to work with the mainstream international institutions in order to reduce perceived ineffectiveness or inequity in policy making. However, technical NGOs are now perceived by many national governments and business lobbies as having a common agenda with the mobilizers. This widespread perception has seriously affected the technical NGOs' capacity to achieve important objectives on their usually benevolent agendas.

In addition it is difficult to see how the WTO can address the multitude of goals prescribed by the anti-global mobilizers. The WTO is an understaffed bureaucracy with little political impact. The secretariat to the General Agreement on Tariffs and Trade (GATT) has successfully acted on behalf of national governments to cut tariffs, mainly on manufactured goods. Its value lies in the improved market access it opens to previously protected markets, thereby increasing overall economic efficiency; it functions by implementing rules of fairness agreed upon by sovereign states.

Unfortunately the WTO also embodies several asymmetric elements: on the one hand, it is consistently moving toward trade liberalization, but on the other, it is unable to eliminate the protectionist policies in some sectors put in place by many of its members.

Furthermore, a major structural change at the new WTO, as compared to GATT, is the increased use of trade law and litigation for dispute settlement. As the stream of disputes swells, the WTO is taking on a different shape. Instead of devoting most of its resources to promoting multinational trade liberalization and non-discrimination, the WTO is forced to focus much energy and expertise on resolving bilateral trade disputes. While the WTO has been successful for over 50 years in dealing with the technical tariff cuts, it is not very well equipped to deal with the new agenda of international trade and investment liberalization. Tariff cuts have allowed shallow integration across many manufacturing sectors. Today's agenda, with major implications for MNEs engaged in FDI, is one of deep integration.

INTERNATIONAL BUSINESS STRATEGY IN ACTION

Is The Body Shop an ethical business?

When it comes to the ethical company, The Body Shop is hailed as the prototype of the responsible firm. The company's website not only states the company's values but urges visitors to become active in the fight to end animal cruelty, to protect human rights, and to implement fair trade practices. Its founder, Anita Roddick, started the company in 1976 by open-ing a small store in Brighton, England, to support her family. In 1978, the opening of a small store in Brussels became its first overseas expansion. By the 1980s, the company was opening two stores per month. Today, The Body Shop provides a range consisting of over 1,200 products and has grown into an MNE with over 3,199 stores in over 60 countries around the world. ▶

The company has a lengthy résumé of its social achievements. In the animal rights arena, The Body Shop joined the campaign for a ban on animal testing for cosmetic products. This was a major factor in the 1998 decision of the UK government to ban animal testing in the industry. On the environmental front, the company has publicly joined NGO causes. For example, in the 1980s, the company sponsored Greenpeace posters, joined the "Save the Whales Campaign," and started a signature petition to ask the Brazilian government to halt the burning of the Amazon forest. The company also brought attention to Shell's involvement in Nigeria. Shell's operations were blamed for severe environmental deterioration, prosecution of protestors, and bribery of state officials. The Body Shop has converted many of its operations into Ecotricity, or energy from renewable resources, and helped create an academy of business with an ethical curriculum in the University of Bath.

The Body Shop's image is tied to that of its founder. Anita Roddick was an active participant on environmental rallies and fair trade missions, and in lobbying governments. She also defied the cosmetics industry's portrayal of women and urged women to accept cellulite and wrinkles as a natural part of their bodies. She stated publicly that cosmetics claiming to solve these problems do not really work—an assertion that has created a backlash from competitors. After the company went public in 1985, she often found herself at odds with shareholders. In fact, in 1998 shareholders pressured her to step down from the CEO chair in favor of Patrick Gournay, who oversaw a major restructuring that saw 300 job cuts, the company's withdrawal from manufacturing, and a management hiring spree to revitalize the company. In 2000, Roddick announced that she would slowly retire from managing The Body Shop to concentrate on her activism. She died in 2007. The Body Shop became part of the French company L'Oréal Group in 2006, but is run independently.

An important signature of The Body Shop is the "Trade not Aid" slogan. Under it, the company has sought to advance the plight of indigenous communities in Third World countries by promoting "Fair Trade." The goal is to support marginalized sectors of society to develop a livelihood within the context of sustainable development. Today, the company sources cocoa butter, babassu oil, and massagers, among other ingredients and products, from Community Trade suppliers in 26 countries, including India, Honduras, Nepal, and Mexico. In 2002/3, the company purchased £5 million in natural products through its Community Trade program.

In the 1990s, the company suffered a blow to its reputation when *Business Ethics* published an article by Jon Entine claiming that the company was the opposite of what it represented itself to be. Entine accused the company of selling drugstore quality products at a large premium by marketing cosmetics with petrochemical ingredients as natural products. In addition, the author claimed the company misrepresented the amount of its donations to charity, did not adhere to its own principles of "Fair Trade," and had itself committed unnecessary environmental damage. For instance, Entine mentions an incident in which The Body Shop went back on a contract to purchase large amounts of shea butter from suppliers in Ghana. This left the suppliers with a lot of stock that they could not sell anywhere else. There are also alleged incidents of the company forcing low margins on suppliers in Third World countries. And a franchisee in France claimed that The Body Shop dumped a load of plastic containers in a landfill site.

A number of consumer groups, NGOs, and internet websites have all jumped on the wagon. The website mcspotlight. com claims that The Body Shop sells products with ingredients that have been tested on animals, as long as the testing was not done for cosmetics, and that some of its products contain gelatin, an animal product. The same website claims that, in industrialized countries, The Body Shop pays its employees near minimum wages and is unwilling to recognize unions. The company is also accused of exaggerating the importance of its Community Trade program and of using the Kayapo Indians of Brazil for promotions without compensating them.

The Body Shop has denied most allegations and threatened a number of news media with legal action but has only taken action against a few, including Channel 4 in the UK. For the company, which was built on the confidence of the "conscious customer," the consequences of this bad publicity could be devastating. Premium prices are, after all, what customers are willing to pay for that extra social responsibility.

Whether the allegations are true or not, The Body Shop can still claim to be a pioneer of corporate responsibility because it brought the issues to the table. Many companies have emulated its principles, including Boots in the UK, which has developed its own brand of environmentally friendly cosmetics to compete with The Body Shop.

Websites: www.the-body-shop.com; www.greenpeace.org; http://www. loreal-finance.com/eng/brands/the-body-shop

Sources: Sharlene Buszka, "A case of greenwashing: The Body Shop," in *Proceedings of the Association of Management and the International Association of Management 15th Annual Conference, Organizational Management Division*, vol. 15, no. 1 (1997), pp. 199–294; www.mcspotlight.org; "Passion or profit," *Financial Times*, February 13, 2002; "Body Swap," *Financial Times*, February 13, 2002; Alison Smith, "US team hopeful of reviving flagging fortune," *Financial Times*, February 13, 2002, p. 20.

Figure 11.5 contrasts the various perceived roles and outcomes of the WTO. The institutional reality is largely that of quadrant 1, while the anti-global movement has been successful in creating an image of the WTO as in quadrant 4.

The technical NGOs' perspective is usually positioned in quadrant 2. Here, an assessment of the efficiency outcomes of improved market access is often combined with a belief in the power of the WTO to actually dictate fundamental national policy choices that could favor the redistribution of wealth. The dominant picture suggested by the stakeholders hurt by free trade and investment is positioned in quadrant 3. These stakeholders typically include labor, management, and owners of non-competitive firms in import-competing sectors, which lack exports or outward FDI. Their view is that the WTO may indeed be an implementation mechanism of sovereign governments' choices, but it results in increased inequality in the international distribution of economic power and wealth.

Two parameters critically determine the future options for further trade and investment liberalization: the choice between bilateral or regional and multilateral negotiations and between shallow or deeper integration. These choices are represented in Figure 11.6.

Quadrant 1 represents the old, highly successful GATT process of tariffs cuts and shallow integration. Quadrant 3 represents the new agenda of the WTO in terms of deep integration, including investment liberalization. Quadrant 2 represents the old regional trade agreements with tariff cuts (the Andean pact, the Caribbean initiative, ASEAN, etc.). Quadrant 4 represents the new type of regional trade agreements, such as NAFTA. These include national treatment for FDI and also enhanced market access for services and intellectual property. Quadrant 3, with deep multilateral integration, undoubtedly constitutes an optimal situation for all nations concerned in terms of long-term wealth creation, but at present it is not feasible because of constraints such as the structure of the WTO and US policy preferences. Quadrant 2 represents the worst-case scenario of shallow, regional integration.

This analysis demonstrates the perverse effects that mobilizers can have on trade and investment liberalization. Poor countries and groups always benefit more from multilateral

Figure 11.5 Different perceptions of the WTO

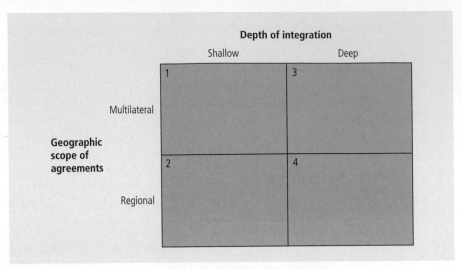

Figure 11.6 Institutional alternatives for trade and investment

than from regional agreements. They cannot be shut out from the former, and individual nations such as the United States always have less power in multilateral than in regional cases because of the number of countries involved. The strengthening, not the weakening, of mainstream global institutions such as the WTO—so despised by the mobilizers—may well represent the fastest route for poorer countries toward achieving fundamentally higher living standards for their population.

The pattern of MNE responses

Figure 11.7 categorizes MNE responses to civil society criticisms. The vertical axis distinguishes between a strategy that differentiates between stakeholders with whom a dialog is possible and those with whom it is not, and, on the bottom, a strategy of uniform response. The horizontal axis makes a distinction between a broad stakeholder perspective on the

Figure 11.7 MNE strategies and civil society

right, whereby goals other than shareholder wealth maximization are considered relevant, and, on the left, a narrower shareholder, profit-maximizing perspective.

Quadrant 2 reflects the outdated perspective on MNEs, paradoxically adopted by most mobilizers. They view MNEs as profit maximizers, which will systematically refuse a constructive dialog with any stakeholder representing civil society. Quadrant 1 represents an equally outdated response that is now being rejected by most large MNEs. Management has a shareholder perspective and its differential response is usually a PR exercise whereby an MNE provides lip service to the goals of friendly stakeholders but in fact is not serious about stakeholder management.

In fact, many MNEs are now positioned in quadrant 3. They pursue a stakeholder management model, perhaps driven by sustainable development environmental considerations. Here MNEs try to identify those salient stakeholders that can contribute to a win–win situation for the firm and society at large. These firms face the challenge of distinguishing between destructive mobilizers and benevolent, technical NGOs.

The main danger is for MNEs to fall in the quadrant 4 trap, whereby their stakeholder management approach can be abused by mobilizers, because the firm has not set up proper screening mechanisms to establish which stakeholder demands are legitimate and which are not. This problem is faced by many companies operating in both developing and advanced countries that are unfairly accused of unethical behavior (for example, Shell in the disposal of a North Sea oil rig, where Greenpeace misrepresented the position in order to win publicity).

A useful alliance could take place between MNEs with a quadrant 1 viewpoint in Figure 11.7 and the technical NGOs of quadrant 2. An example of this is the idea of sustainable development, whereby MNEs are the actors making new and environmentally sensitive investments. In contrast, alliances between the protected and inefficient firms in quadrant 3 and mobilizer NGOs in quadrant 4 are not useful. Yet this was exactly the type of coalition put together in Seattle in 1999 to disrupt the WTO meetings. There, labor, mobilizer NGOs, and even technical NGOs made common cause against business and governments.

Three suggestions are offered as to how MNEs should proceed:

1 The activities of external stakeholders should be discussed at the board and top management level, and an overall strategy should be developed to deal with them. It is important to make a distinction between technical NGOs and anti-global mobilizers. Initiatives should be developed to work with the former. Clear arguments should be developed to appropriately counter the discourse of the mobilizers, and this should be combined with an effective communication strategy to reach relevant audiences.

2 Sustainable development and ethical stakeholder perspectives should be embedded within the organization and its culture.

3 The firm should not engage in a debate with mobilizers (or even technical NGOs) through a small set of PR people; instead all senior managers should be trained to articulate the concept of stakeholder capitalism, rather than shareholder capitalism, and the contribution of the organization to the resulting wealth creation. In other words, all senior managers in the firm should engage with NGOs.

As a result of the above initiatives, firms should experience a dramatic improvement in both profile and performance. The firms that do best in future will be those that take leadership positions with respect to stakeholder management, capture the concept of values-driven rather than profit-driven capitalism, and respect their most important resource—namely, their employees. These policies will be the most effective tools at the microeconomic level against ideology-driven mobilizers.

For their part, NGOs, especially the technical ones, need to understand that anti-global rhetoric is leading to regional integration and bilateral agreements, as a politically more feasible—but ultimately less efficient—alternative to global integration. This does not benefit the objectives of civil society. Free trade and investment liberalization have not yet been achieved due to the vested interests and misperceptions of some components of civil society and affected stakeholders. We now need to recognize and correct these misperceptions as a precondition to achieving an overarching increase in world welfare and incomes.

✔ Active learning check

Review your answer to the Active Learning Case question 3 and make any changes you like. Then compare your answer to the one below.

3 **Where would a company like Coca-Cola, or others in Table 11.1, be positioned in Figure 11.7? Why?**

Coca Cola is probably positioned in quadrant 3 of Figure 11.7. In order to protect its worldwide brand, which has to be delivered locally through host-country partners and bottling subsidiaries, it is highly responsive to different stakeholder groups with whom it engages in a dialog to pursue a differential response. Such local responsiveness is particularly important to an MNE dealing with local host government regulations and NGOs. As a result, Coca-Cola is highly ranked as one of the more environmentally responsive and socially aware companies.

KEY POINTS

1 There will be an increase in the amount of international business research that is being conducted. This will come in the form of both theory testing and the practical application of information. Both academicians and practitioners will find this development helpful.

2 Multinationals, as flagship firms, are beginning to develop new business network relationships with suppliers, competitors, governments, unions, universities, and a host of other external groups. This networking relationship is proving particularly helpful in increasing productivity, profitability, and overall competitiveness.

3 The two environments that will present the greatest challenges for MNEs in the future are the political and the economic. The rising tide of protectionism will require that multinationals deal astutely with foreign governments. They will also have to weigh carefully the political risk associated with investing in countries that are now beginning to shed their central planning systems and to move toward free enterprise economies.

4 The principle of national treatment reduces political sovereignty, although some sectors are exempted in NAFTA, the FTAA, and APEC. In contrast, the EU has deep integration across political and social areas, as well as economic.

5 The interaction between MNEs and NGOs is complex but can be better understood by constructing an analytical framework.

Key terms

- strategic fit
- flagship firms
- five partners

REVIEW AND DISCUSSION QUESTIONS

1 Why is theory testing of value to the field of international business research? What can be learned from such information?

2 In addition to theory testing, how is international business research of value to both scholars and practitioners? In your answer, give an example of how each group can benefit from such research.

3 In what ways are MNEs developing new business networks? Give two examples and then explain why these developments are likely to help the companies maintain their competitive strengths.

4 How is the political environment likely to change during the future? Give one example and relate its significance for multinationals.

5 How is the economic environment likely to change in the future? Give one example and relate its significance for multinationals.

6 How does NAFTA differ from the EU?

7 Why are NGOs opposed to MNEs? What should MNEs do?

REAL CASE

Dell: B2C

Dell is a leader in personal computers. It competes with Toshiba, HP, Acer, Samsung, Sony, Lenovo, ASUSTeK, etc. Dell is based in Austin, Texas, and has production factories in Tennessee. It also produces in Ireland, Malaysia, Brazil, and China. Dell operates in four business segments: large enterprise, public, small and medium business, and consumer. It designs, develops, manufactures, markets, sells, and supports a range of products and services that can be customized to individual customer requirements. In February 2011, it acquired Compellent Technologies, Inc. During the fiscal year ended January 28, 2011, it completed five acquisitions: KACE Networks, Inc., Ocarina Networks Inc., Scalent Systems Inc., Boomi, Inc., and InSite One, Inc. For the fiscal year ended 28 January 2011, Dell's revenues increased 16 percent to $61.49 billion compared to the previous year. Net income increased 84 percent to $2.64 billion. Revenues reflect an increase in income from all four of its business segments. Dell generated 52 percent of its sales in the United States and 48 percent from foreign sales.

But its success lies in marketing directly to consumers rather than in any technological or cost advantages associated with production. Dell introduced the Dell Direct model, a business-to-consumer (B2C) concept, which has now been copied by major competitors. By eliminating retailers, Dell can deal directly with individual customers, offering detailed and richly configured systems. There is consumer customization, plus services and support. This method saves on inventory and introduces new technology quickly. Dell became a market leader with the first B2C direct business model.

The computer industry is at a mature stage of manufacturing. This means that there is pressure either to be extremely cost competitive or to develop value-added services that build on the computer itself. The five major computer manufacturers have responded to these market changes in different ways. IBM invented the personal computer and was perhaps the first to move strongly toward customer service. But eventually in 2004 it got out of personal computers altogether, selling the business to China's Lenovo as PCs became commoditized. In late 2002, Hewlett-Packard and Compaq merged to try to consolidate production but also to develop the service end. This left Apple and Dell as the firms driven by low cost and technology.

In China, Dell has developed an innovative B2C concept that is allowing it to quickly increase its market share. PC manufacturers have been flocking to China because of high expected growth. Dell entered the Chinese market in the 1990s, trailing behind IBM and Compaq. Soon Dell became the second largest foreign PC market player, after three local Chinese manufacturers. One way in which Dell was able to achieve this was by ▶

Source: Kristoffer Tripplar/Alamy Stock Photo

introducing the affordable Smart PC. Another has been to offer tailor-made PCs over the internet. A Chinese customer virtually builds his or her desired computer and then Dell assembles and delivers it. Implementing B2C retailing has not been easy because Chinese people are not used to credit cards. To overcome this obstacle, the company has made deals with major banks to allow customers to go to a branch and make a payment that is then reported to Dell. More recently, the largest Chinese computer manufacturers started to compete aggressively in the lower end of the market, forcing Dell to move upmarket where it expects to reap the benefits of a growing number of luxury-minded individuals. As of 2009, the top

five market leaders in China's laptop PC market, by volume and value, were as follows: Lenovo China Co., Ltd. 29.5 percent, HP Development Company 16.2 percent, ASUSTeK Computer Corporation 10.2 percent, Dell Group 9.2 percent, and Hasee Computer Co., Ltd. 6.5 percent.

Throughout the world, Dell has tried to add service value in its B2C process. It has 80 internet sites on which more than 65,000 institutional customers do business with Dell. Through www.dell.com customers can order, price, and configure products. Dell maintains after-sales service with customers. It also brings new technology quickly to the customer. In short, Dell's B2C system allows the MNE to engage in mass customization.

Websites: www.dell.com; www.dell.com.cn; www.hp.com; www.hp.com.cn; www.compaq.com; www.compaq.com.cn; www.ibm.com; www.ibm.com.cn; and www.acer.com

Sources: www.dell.com; Dell, *Annual Report*, 2009; Thomson Reuters, *OneSource*, 2011; "IBM at 100: from typewriters to the cloud," *BBC News*, June 14, 2011; Mintel Global Market Navigator database, China-Laptop PCs: company market share by volume and by value, 2009, http://gmn.mintel.com/query/10146777/shares/region; "Dell CTO Paul Prince: applications are the key," *BBC News*, January 20, 2011.

1 What is meant by B2C? How does Dell achieve B2C?

2 Why is Dell so successful in China?

3 Is B2C a viable strategy in the mature, competitive computer industry of today?

REAL CASE

Maersk Group

An example of the business-to-business (B2B) relational contracts found in the flagship model can be found in some of the operations of Maersk. This is the world's largest container-based shipping group. It has B2B relationships with companies that use its containers, with port authorities, and with supplies of its energy resources.

A.P. Møller-Maersk (APM) is a Denmark-based shipping group with sales of $56.1 billion and assets of $66.76 billion in 2010. The group owns and operates container carriers, bulk carriers, supply and specialty ships, and tankers. The group also provides various services in the areas of energy, shipping and offshore, and retail. The A.P. Møller-Maersk Group com-

prises approximately 1,100 companies. The group owns and operates more than 500 container vessels with a total capacity of around 3 million TEU (Twenty-foot Equivalent Units).

The main competitors to Maersk are shown in Table 11.3.

The Maersk Group divides its business into six segments: container shipping and related; tankers, offshore and related; terminals; oil and gas; retail and other; and technology. These are shown in Figure 11.8.

1 Container and related activities:
  ● Maersk Line
  ● Damco

- Maersk Container Industry
- Safmarine
- MCC Transport

2 Energy:

- Maersk Oil

3 Tankers and offshore-related activities:

- Maersk Tankers
- Maersk Drilling
- Maersk FPSOs
- Maersk Supply Services

4 Terminal activities:

- APM Terminals

5 Retail and related business (not discussed here):

- Dansk Supermarked
- Svitzer

6 Technology:

- Maersk Fluid Technology
- Maersk Maritime Technology

Source: Peter Titmus/Alamy Stock Photo

Maersk Line is one of the leading liner shipping companies in the world, serving customers all over the globe. The company also has nearly 3 million containers and operates across 130 countries. The Maersk Group provides similar container services across north/south trade lanes under the Safmarine name.

Maersk Logistics was combined with Damco in 2007 and no longer exists.

Damco offers services such as inland haulage, customs house brokerage, and refrigerated services. The company also offers customized and integrated solutions for operations such as supply-chain management; warehousing and distribution; and ocean freight. The company primarily provides its services to the retail, electronics, fast-moving consumer goods, and chemical industries.

APM Terminals is one of the world's largest operators of container terminals with over 50 container terminals spanning 34 countries and five continents. The company primarily engages in the development of port infrastructure necessary to meet the future demands of the global container trade. APM Terminals works closely with governments, country leaders, customers, truckers, and the entire shipping community to ensure supply-chain efficiency and world-class service.

Maersk Container Industry produces various types of reefer containers for the transportation of goods through ship, rail, or truck.

Maersk Oil operates the oil production of more than 700,000 barrels per day and more than 1,000 million cubic feet (28 million m^3) of gas production per day in the Danish and British parts of the North Sea, offshore Qatar, in Algeria, and in Kazakhstan. It conducts exploration activities in those areas as well as offshore Norway, the US Gulf of Mexico, Brazil, Angola, and Oman.

Table 11.3 Top six container shipping companies in order of TEU capacity, February 25, 2011

Company	TEU capacity*	Market share (%)	Number of ships
A.P. Møller-Maersk Group	2,176,416	14.6	586
Mediterranean Shipping Company SA	1,923,790	12.9	460
CMA CGM Group	1,231,245	8.2	399
Evergreen Marine Corporation	606,090	4.1	160
Hapag-Lloyd	593,798	4.0	132
CSAV Group	591,710	4.0	160

*TEU capacity and market-share figures from February 25, 2011, from *Alphaliner Report*, February 25, 2011, http://www.alphaliner.com/top100/index.php

Source: John Gapper, "Bye-bye, American shipping lines," *Financial Times*, February 23, 2011, http://www.ft.com

▶

Container shipping and related	Tankers, offshore and related	Terminal activities
Maersk Line	Maersk Tankers	APM Terminals

Container shipping and related
Maersk Line
Damco
Maersk Container
Industry
Safmarine
MCC Transport

Tankers, offshore and related
Maersk Tankers
Maersk Drilling
Maersk FPSOs
Maersk Supply Services
Maersk LNG

Terminal activities
APM Terminals

Oil and gas activities
Maersk Oil

Retail and other
Dansk Supermarked
Odense Steel Shipyard
Svitzer

Technology
Maersk Fluid Technology
Maersk Maritime Technology

Figure 11.8 Segmentation of the Maersk Group activities

Through Maersk Tankers, Maersk Contractors, and Maersk Supply Services the company offers solutions for the transport of crude oil, refined products, and gas; various supply vessel activities (including anchor handling, platform supply, and cable laying); drilling activities with mobile production units, and drilling rigs and ships, including advanced jack-up rigs, salvage and towage activities; and door-to-door transport and inter-European freight and passenger transport.

Maersk Tankers owns and operates one of the world's largest and most modern fleets of crude, product, and gas tankers. The fleet consists of more than 230 vessels.

Maersk Drilling (formerly known as Maersk Contractors) provides drilling and production services to oil companies. The company commands an extensive and technologically advanced fleet of some of the world's most advanced harsh environment jack-up rigs, 375 ft and 350 ft jack-up rigs, deepwater semi-submersibles, drilling barges, and workover barges.

Maersk Supply Services is primarily engaged in the field of tow-out and installation of large offshore installations, and other chartering services. The company maintains more than 50 offshore support vessels.

Examples of flagship partnerships

Maersk Line has flagship relationships. As explained above, it is one of the leading liner shipping companies. It operates over 580 container vessels and more than 3,000,000 containers. This amounts to 11,363.63 miles (18,288 km) of containers. Although the Maersk organization is extensively vertically integrated and produces vessels, containers, and oil through subsidiaries, Maersk Line is highly dependent on its business networks. Mr. Søren Skou, the Partner Chief Executive Officer of Maersk Line Business, recognizes the importance of partnerships, stating that "communication and partnerships are as important as the physical movement of goods."

Maersk Line maintains a strategically critical relationship with its competitors. In the midst of flattening sales, the beginning of 2008 saw agreements between the top three largest container ship lines of Maersk Line, Mediterranean Shipping Co., and CMA CGM sharing vessel space on the trans-Pacific trade. Government relations are also of high importance. In 2007, the Maersk Group spent $950,000 lobbying the federal government on issues such as port safety, railroad regulations, and ballast water legislation. The group is also a member of C–TPAT (Customs–Trade Partnership Against Terrorism), headed by the Department of Homeland Security. Maersk Line Limited, another Maersk Group subsidiary, transports more US government cargo related to military and humanitarian missions than any other company. In 2007, this amounted to 140,000 TEU of US military cargo alone. The Maersk organization also maintains ties with research and educational institutions. In Denmark, Maersk is engaged in a corporate partnership with the Copenhagen Business School designed to provide real-world business applications and attract talent. Additionally, Maersk Line is also engaged in development projects such as that of an energy-saving cooling system involving Wageningen University, sponsored by the Dutch government. Other flagship relationships include:

● **IBM:** In 2005, IBM and Maersk Logistics joined forces to bring real-time, enhanced visibility to global supply-chain operations by improving the quality of container tracking and enabling increased security of transported goods. The solution includes highly intelligent wireless tracking devices and an advanced technology network for use by manufacturers, retailers, logistics providers, carriers, and governments to share real-time cargo information.

● **NVOCCs:** As Non-Vessel Operating Common Carriers, larger freight forwarders compete directly with Maersk Logistics but also have attractive contracts with Maersk Line and Safmarine. In fact, it is possible that leading forwarders such as Kuehne & Nagel and ABX Logistics have more attractive contracts than Maersk Logistics.

1 Who are the major competitors of Maersk?

2 To what extent and to whom does Maersk act as a key supplier?

3 What is the key competitive advantage (firm-specific advantage) of Maersk?

Sources: www.maersk.com/en; Maersk, *Annual Report,* 2009; "Maersk spends $950,000 on lobbying," *Hellenic Shipping News,* 29 February 2008; analysis by authors of this book.

NOTES

1 Edward Freeman, *Strategic Management: A Stakeholder Approach* (Cambridge: Cambridge University Press, 2010).

2 Also see Howard Thomas, Timothy Pollock, and Philip Gorman, "Global strategic analyses: frameworks and approaches," *Academy of Management Executive* (February 1999), pp. 70–82; and Alan M. Rugman, *Regional Multinationals* (Cambridge: Cambridge University Press, 2005).

3 Also see David Kirkpatrick, "Why the internet is boosting IBM's mainframe sales," *Fortune,* January 11, 1999, pp. 148–9; and "IBM at 100: from typewriters to the cloud," *BBC News Online,* June 14, 2011, http://www.bbc.co.uk/news/business-13726776

4 Otto Andersen, "On the internationalization process of firms: a critical analysis," *Journal of International Business Studies,* vol. 24, no. 2 (1993), pp. 209–31; Sumantra Ghoshal and Nitin Nohria, "Horses for courses: organizational forms for multinational corporations," *Sloan Management Review* (winter 1993), pp. 23–35; see also John H. Dunning, "The key literature on international business activities: 1960–2006," in Alan M. Rugman (ed.), *The Oxford Handbook of International Business,* 2nd ed. (Oxford: Oxford University Press, 2009).

5 Jeremiah J. Sullivan and Richard B. Peterson, "A test of theories underlying the Japanese lifetime employment system," *Journal of International Business Studies,* vol. 22, no. 1 (1991), p. 79.

6 Alan M. Rugman and Joseph R. D'Cruz, *Multinationals as Flagship Firms: Regional Business Networks* (Oxford: Oxford University Press, 2000). This book is based on earlier work, such as: Alan M. Rugman and Joseph R. D'Cruz, *New Compacts for Canadian Competitiveness* (Toronto: Kodak Canada, 1992), p. 31; and Joseph R. D'Cruz and Alan M. Rugman, "Business networks for international competitiveness," *Business Quarterly,* vol. 56, no. 4 (spring 1992), pp. 101–7.

7 Rugman and D'Cruz, *Multinationals as Flagship Firms.*

8 For more on this, see Rosabeth Moss Kanter, "Transcending business boundaries: 12,000 world managers view change," *Harvard Business Review,* vol. 69, no. 3 (May/June 1991), pp. 151–64.

9 "China 'too slow' to open markets," *BBC News Online,* December 19, 2003; "US tells China to look to its own consumers," *BBC News Online,* May 9, 2011; and "US to meet China in Washington to tackle thorny issues," *BBC News Online,* May 8, 2011; "US China trade imbalance," *BBC News Online,* May 10, 2011.

10 Rob Hugh-Jones, "Analysis: Rice's Latin American tour," *BBC News Online,* April 20, 2005.

11 Alicia Jrapko, "Workers seize control of 150 plants," *Worker's World,* May 8, 2003.

12 "Country profiles: regions and territories: Hong Kong," *BBC News Online,* May 25, 2005.

13 Mark Landler, "Back to Vietnam, this time to build," *New York Times,* September 13, 1998, section 3, pp. 1, 11.

14 See www.internetworldstats.com; Eurostat, 2015, http://epp.eurostat.ec.europa.eu/portal/page/portal/statistics/search_database.

15 Alan M. Rugman and Alain Verbeke, "Corporate strategy after the free trade agreement and Europe 1992," in John Longair (ed.), *Proceedings: Regional Integration in the World Economy: Europe and North America* (Ottawa: Conference Board of Canada, March 1990).

16 See Gerard Curzon, "Ten reasons to fear Fortress Europe," Mimeo, Graduate Institute of International Studies, Geneva, 1989; and B. Burgenmeir and J. L. Mucchielli, *Multinational and Europe 1992* (London: Routledge, 1990) for an overview.

17 Rugman and Verbeke, "Corporate strategy."

BIBLIOGRAPHY

Bhagwati, Jagdish. *In Defense of Globalization* (Oxford: Oxford University Press, 2004).

Brewer, Thomas L., and Young, Stephen. *The Multilateral Investment System and Multinational Enterprise* (Oxford: Oxford University Press, 1998).

Clarkson, Max B. E. "A stakeholder framework for analyzing and evaluating corporate social performance," *Academy of Management Review,* vol. 20, no. 1 (January 1995).

Darnall, Nicole, Henriques, Irene, and Sadorsky, Perry. "Adopting proactive environmental strategy: the influence of stakeholders and firm size," *Journal of Management Studies*, vol. 47, no. 6 (September 2010).

D'Cruz, Joseph R., and Rugman, Alan M. "Developing international competitiveness: the five partners model," *Business Quarterly* (winter 1993).

D'Cruz, Joseph R., and Rugman, Alan M. "Business network theory and the Canadian telecommunications industry," *International Business Review*, vol. 3, no. 3 (1994).

Demirbag, Mehmet, et al. "Ethics and taxation: a cross-national comparison of UK and Turkish firms," *International Business Review*, vol. 22, no. 1 (2013).

Devinney, Timothy M. "Is the socially responsible corporation a myth? The good, bad and ugly of corporate social responsibility," *Academy of Management Perspectives*, vol. 23, no. 2 (2009).

Dunning, John H. *Multinational Enterprises and the Global Economy* (Reading, MA: Addison-Wesley, 1993).

Dunning, John H. *The Globalization of Business: The Challenge of the 1990s* (London and New York: Routledge, 1993).

Dyer, Jeff, and Chu, Wujin. "The determinants of trust in supplier–automaker relations in the US, Japan, and Korea: a retrospective," *Journal of International Business Studies*, vol. 42 (2011).

Fee, Anthony, and Gray, Sidney J. "Transformational learning experiences of international development volunteers in the Asia-Pacific: the case of a multinational NGO," *Journal of World Business*, vol. 48, no. 2 (2013).

Fortanier, F., Kolk, Ans, and Pinkse, Jonatan. "MNEs, global CSR standards and domestic institutions: harmonization and country-of-origin effects in CSR reporting," *Management International Review* (2011).

Giddens, Anthony. *Runaway World: How Globalization is Reshaping Our Lives* (London: Profile Books, 1998).

González-Rodríguez, M. Rosario, Díaz-Fernández, Carmen, and Simonetti, Biagio. "The social, economic and environmental dimensions of corporate social responsibility: the role played by consumers and potential entrepreneurs," *International Business Review* (2015).

Gray, John. *False Dawn: The Delusions of Global Capitalism* (London: Granta Books, 1998).

Guntz, Hugh P., and Jalland, R. Michael. "Managerial careers and business strategies," *Academy of Management Review*, vol. 21, no. 3 (July 1996).

Husted, Bryan W., and Allen, David B. "Corporate social responsibility in the multinational enterprise: strategic and institutional approaches," *Journal of International Business Studies*, vol. 37 (2006).

Husted, Bryan W., and Allen, David B. "Strategic corporate social responsibility and value creation," *Management International Review*, vol. 49, no. 6 (December 2009).

Jain, Subhash C., and Vachani, Sushil (eds.) *Multinational Corporations and Global Poverty Reduction* (Cheltenham: Edward Elgar, 2006).

Jean, Ruey-Jer (Bryan), Sinkovics, Rudolf R., and Cavusgil, S. Tamer. "Enhancing international customer–supplier relationships through it resources: a study of Taiwanese electronics suppliers," *Journal of International Business Studies*, vol. 41 (2010).

Kim, W. Chan, and Mauborgne, Renée A. "Effectively conceiving and executing multinationals' worldwide

strategies," *Journal of International Business Studies*, vol. 24, no. 3 (1993).

Kirton, John J., Daniels, Joseph P., and Freytag, Andreas (eds.). *Guiding Global Order: G8 Governance in the 21st Century* (Aldershot: Ashgate, 2001).

Kogut, Bruce. "Methodological contributions in international business research and the direction of academic research activity," in Alan M. Rugman and Thomas Brewer (eds.), *The Oxford Handbook of International Business* (Oxford: Oxford University Press, 2001).

Kolk, Ans. "Trends in sustainability reporting by the Fortune Global 500," *Business Strategy and the Environment*, vol. 12, no. 5 (September/October 2003).

Kolk, Ans. "Corporate social responsibility in the coffee sector: the dynamics of MNC responses and code development," *European Management Journal*, vol. 23, no. 2 (April 2005).

Kolk, Ans. "Environmental reporting by multinationals from the triad: convergence or divergence?" *Management International Review*, vol. 45, special issue 1 (2005).

Kolk, Ans. "Sustainability, accountability and corporate governance: exploring multinationals' reporting practices," *Business Strategy and the Environment*, vol. 17, no. 1 (January 2008).

Kolk, Ans. "Trajectories of sustainability reporting by MNCs," *Journal of World Business*, vol. 45, no. 4 (October 2010).

Kolk, Ans. "The social responsibility of international business: from ethics and the environment to CSR and sustainable development," *Journal of World Business*, vol. 51 (2016).

Kolk, Ans, and Pinkse, Jonatan. "Stakeholder mismanagement and corporate social responsibility crises," *European Management Journal*, vol. 24, no. 1 (February 2006).

Kolk, Ans, and van Tulder, Rob. "International business, corporate social responsibility and sustainable development," *International Business Review*, vol. 19, no. 2 (April 2010).

Li, Shaomin, Fetscherin, Marc, Alon, Ilan, Lattemann, Christoph, and Yeh, Kuang. "Corporate social responsibility in emerging markets," *Management International Review*, vol. 50, no. 5 (October 2010).

Marano, Valentina, and Pete Tashman. "MNE/NGO partnerships and the legitimacy of the firm," *International Business Review*, vol. 21, no. 6 (2012).

Martinez, Jon I., and Jarillo, J. Carlos. "Coordination demands of international strategies," *Journal of International Business Studies*, vol. 22, no. 3 (1991).

McDermott, Gerald A., and Corredoira, Rafael A. "Network composition, collaborative ties, and upgrading in emerging-market firms: lessons from the Argentine autoparts sector," *Journal of International Business Studies*, vol. 41, 308–29 (2010).

Narula, Rajneesh, and Alain Verbeke. "Making internalization theory good for practice: the essence of Alan Rugman's contributions to international business," *Journal of World Business*, vol. 50 (2015).

Nebus, James, and Rufin, Carlos. "Extending the bargaining power model: explaining bargaining outcomes among nations, MNEs, and NGOs," *Journal of International Business Studies*, vol. 41 (August 2010).

Nehrt, Chad. "Maintaining a first mover advantage when environmental regulations differ between countries," *Academy of Management Review*, vol. 23, no. 1 (January 1998).

Park, Byung Il, Chidlow, Agnieszka, and Choi, Jiyul. "Corporate social responsibility: stakeholders influence on MNEs' activities," *International Business Review,* vol. 23, no. 5 (2014).

Rugman, Alan M. "Multinationals and trade in services: a transaction cost approach," *Weltwirtschaftliches Archiv,* vol. 123, no. 4 (December 1987).

Rugman, Alan M. *The End of Globalization* (London: Random House, 2000). (Also published in 2001 by AMACOM/McGraw-Hill.)

Rugman, Alan M., and D'Cruz, Joseph R. "A theory of business networks." In Lorraine Eden (ed.), *Multinationals in North America* (Alberta: University of Calgary Press, 1993).

Rugman, Alan M., and D'Cruz, Joseph R. *Multinationals as Flagship Firms: Regional Business Networks* (Oxford: Oxford University Press, 2000, paperback, 2002).

Rugman, Alan M., and Doh, Jonathan. *Multinationals and Development* (New Haven, CT: Yale University Press, 2008).

Rugman, Alan M., Kirton, John, and Soloway, Julie. *Environmental Regulations and Corporate Strategy* (Oxford: Oxford University Press, 1999).

Rugman, Alan M., and Verbeke, Alain. *Corporate Response to Global Change*, vol. 3 of *Research in Global Strategic Management* (Greenwich, CT: JAI Press, 1992).

Rugman, Alan M., and Verbeke, Alain. *Beyond the Three Generics*, vol. 4 of *Research in Global Strategic Management* (Greenwich, CT: JAI Press, 1993).

Rugman, Alan M., and Verbeke, Alain. "Corporate strategies and environmental regulations: an organizing framework," *Strategic Management Journal*, vol. 19, special issue (April 1998).

Rugman, Alan M., and Verbeke, Alain. "Six cases of corporate strategic response to environmental regulations," *European Management Journal*, vol. 18, no. 4 (August 2000).

Rugman, Alan M., and Verbeke, Alain. "Toward a theory of multinational enterprises and the civil society," in A. Ghobadian et al. (eds.), *Strategy and Performance: Achieving Competitive Advantage in the Global Marketplace* (Basingstoke: Palgrave Macmillan, 2004).

Scherer, Andreas Georg, and Palazzo, Guido. "The new political role of business in a globalized world: a review of a new perspective on CSR and its implications for the firm, governance, and democracy," *Journal of Management Studies*, vol. 48, no. 4 (June 2011).

Stiglitz, Joseph E. *Globalization and its Discontents* (New York: Norton, 2002).

Tulder, Rob van, and Kolk, Ans. "Multinationality and corporate ethics: codes of conduct in the sporting goods industry," *Journal of International Business Studies*, vol. 32, no. 2 (June 2001).

Vachani, Sushil, Doh, Jonathan P., and Teegen, Hildy. "NGOs' influence on MNEs' social development strategies in varying institutional contexts: a transaction cost perspective," *International Business Review*, vol. 18, no. 5 (October 2009).

Wu, Jun, Li, Shaomin, and Samsell, Darryl. "Why some countries trade more, some trade less, some trade almost nothing: the effect of the governance environment on trade flows," *International Business Review*, vol. 21, no. 2 (2012).

Yaziji, Michael, and Doh, Jonathan. *NGOs and Corporations: Conflict and Collaboration* (Cambridge: Cambridge University Press, 2009).

Part Four

FUNCTIONAL AREA STRATEGIES

Chapter 12

PRODUCTION STRATEGY

Contents

Objectives of the chapter

Production strategy is critical to effective international operations. Most goods and services have very limited lives, so MNEs must continually provide new offerings, which can be accomplished only through a well-formulated production strategy. This chapter examines how MNEs carry out this process. In doing so, we will focus on the entire range of production strategies from research and development to manufacturing, shipment, and the final international destination. We will look at the most current approaches, including speed-to-market, concurrent engineering, and continuous cost reduction.

The specific objectives of this chapter are to:

1 *Understand* how firms organize their multinational production operations.

2 *Examine* the role of research, development, and innovation in production strategy.

3 *Relate* some of the most critical steps in generating goods and services, including global sourcing, costing techniques, quality maintenance, effective materials handling, inventory control, and the proper emphasis on service.

4 *Describe* the nature and importance of international logistics in production strategy.

5 *Review* some of the major production strategies being used by MNEs, including strategic alliances and acquisitions.

GE production: from Six Sigma to the GE Store

General Electric is a multibillion-dollar multinational corporation whose products range from 65 cent light bulbs to billion-dollar power plants. Based on revenues, assets, profits, and market value, the company was listed by *Fortune* magazine as number 8 in the world in 2015. One reason for GE's annual revenue of $148,321 million is its ability to manage a diverse multi product-line operation, handling such products as major appliances, lighting, medical diagnostic imaging equipment, motors, and commercial and military aircraft engines and engineering materials. GE also provides a range of services, including those related to electricity provision, media (GE owns NBC in the United States), and multimedia programming and distribution. Much of the company's success can be attributed to the production-related concepts it has employed over the last 20–30 years. During the 1980s, work-out, process mapping, and best practices were applied concepts at GE which spread to other large manufacturers.

Work-out is a training program designed to empower employees to implement their problem-solving ideas. A group of 40 to 100 people, picked by management from all ranks and functional areas, attend a three-day meeting. The first day consists of a manager leading the group in drafting an agenda addressing areas in which productivity can be increased. Then the manager leaves and for the next few days the group breaks into teams to tackle the agenda. On the last afternoon the manager returns and one by one the team members make their proposals for improved productivity. The manager can make only three responses: agree, disagree, or ask for more information; in the last case, an individual manager must empower a team to get the information by an agreed-upon date. These work-out sessions have proved extremely successful. In one case, a group of workers convinced management to allow their factory to bid against an outside vendor for the right to build new protective shields for grinding machines. As a result, the GE group completed the job for $16,000 versus $96,000 for the vendor.

The second method, *process mapping,* is to create a flow-chart that shows all the steps, no matter how small, involved in making or doing something. The map is analyzed for ways to eliminate steps and save time and money. One work group was able to reorganize production, cut manufacturing time in half, and reduce inventory by $4 million.

The third method, *best practices,* consists of finding companies that do things better than GE does and emulating them. GE personnel try to answer the question: what is the secret of this other company's success? Quite often the answer includes such things as getting products to market faster than anyone else, treating suppliers like partners, or having superior inventory management. As a result of best practices, GE is now keeping executives in their jobs for longer periods of time rather than rotating them quickly through new jobs; the best practices process revealed that frequent changes create problems in new product introductions. The company also learned how to use continuous improvement processes more effectively to bring a new product into the market ahead of the competition and then work on introducing new technologies. In the past, the firm would try to perfect all technologies first and then introduce the final product version.

In the 1990s, the dominant production concept was Six Sigma, a name that originates from a statistical method for deriving near-perfect quality, equal to 3.4 defects per million operations. The Six Sigma process allows GE to measure how many "defects" there are in a given process and then systematically work to eliminate them to approximate "zero defects." Six Sigma recognizes three elements: the customer, the process, and the employee. The customer is the key to defining quality. GE uses the term "Delighting Customers" to generate a mentality whereby customer expectations of performance, reliability, competitive price, on-time delivery, service, clear and correct transaction processing, and other customer needs become a key factor in all processes. The second element, the process, promotes "Outside-In Thinking Quality." GE must understand the transaction life cycle from the customer's point of view and identify significant value and improvement from that same perspective. Under the banner "Leadership Commitment People," the third element of Six Sigma, the employee, requires that all personnel use their talents and energies to satisfy customers. All employees are trained in Six Sigma, including statistical tools, strategy, and techniques of Six Sigma quality. At the core of the process is a workforce mentality on customer quality expectations, defect reduction, process capability, variation (the customer reacts to the variance rather than the average results), stability of operations, and designing processes to meet customer expectations.

GE's advantage over other production-oriented conglomerates is its ability to transfer knowledge over the whole company. This can be attributed to former CEO Jack Welch, who oversaw GE's transformation from a mainly manufacturing firm to a service-oriented, knowledge-based company. He defined GE's culture by creating a workforce that can identify opportunities and implement changes.

This approach continues to the present day. In 2016, under Jeff Immelt, GE announced it would move its global headquarters to Boston (MA) as part of a structural change to improve its innovative capabilities. It aspired to become the world's leading "digital industrial company" with the aim of "transforming industry with software-defined machines and solutions that are connected, responsive and predictive." GE Global Research became known as the "GE Store for Technology," a global network of nine technology centers hosting 3,600 scientists and engineers, working on advanced technologies across the company's industrial businesses. This was part of an on-going aim to structure the firm as an efficient "knowledge network," developing, integrating, and leveraging technological expertise across all parts of the firm to serve client needs.

Despite GE's firm-specific advantages (FSAs) in production, it has struggled to transfer aspects of its competitive edge equally to other parts of the world. While GE used to be a home-region company with the majority of its sales in the United States, now the company is slightly more diversified, but still regionally focused. It derives 48 percent of its revenues from the United States alone. Once its revenues from Canadian and Latin American operations are added on top of the US sales, the figure rises to nearly 57 percent. Europe, its largest foreign regional market, accounts for only 17 percent of revenues, closely followed by the Asian market which accounts for 16 percent of revenues. The remaining 10 percent are accounted for by other regions such as the Middle East and Africa.

Website: www.ge.com

Sources: "The world's super fifty," *Forbes*, July 27, 1998, p. 118; www.ge.com; General Electric, *10KSEC Filing*, 2002; "EU rejects latest GE offers," *BBC News*, June 29, 2001; "EU blocks GE/Honeywell deal," *BBC News*, July 3, 2001; "US Senators lash out at EU over GE deal," *BBC News*, June 15, 2001; "Fortune Global 500," *Fortune*, 2010, 2015, at http://money.cnn.com/magazines/fortune/global500/2010/; GE, *Annual Report*, 2009, 2014; GE, "The GE Store for Technology is open for business," 2016, http://www.geglobalresearch.com/impact/ge-store

1 How did GE use work-out to increase speed-to-market?

2 How has GE used Six Sigma to reduce cost and improve quality in consumer goods? In each case, give an example.

3 In what way could best practices help GE develop more effective international strategies? Explain.

INTRODUCTION

Production management has been responsible for many new goods and services. Examples are as varied as Palm's handhelds, Apple's iPad, Honda's hybrid cars, HP's digital cameras, eBay's internet auctions, and five-star hotel operations at the Ritz-Carlton. The nature of production management in the MNE is similar in many respects to that in domestic firms. Both are concerned with the efficient use of labor and capital. Both are also interested in investing in research and development (R&D) and in organizing operations to generate successful new product lines and increase production and service efficiency.

Like domestic firms, MNEs need to organize their production management so they can minimize operating costs through the use of logistics and inventory control. Canon, for example, relocates production to China only if labor accounts for over 5 percent of production costs.[1] Acer, the successful upstart from Taiwan, makes sure that computer parts with short product life cycles are shipped by air, and those with long product life cycles are shipped by sea (see the **Active Learning Case: Acer Taiwan goes international** in Chapter 20). However, pressures from host-country governments or special interest groups can affect a multinational's decision making in these areas. For example, host governments often criticize resource-based MNEs for their backward, forward, and horizontal integration. **Backward integration**, which is the ownership of equity assets used earlier in the production cycle (such as an auto firm acquiring a steel company), is criticized for doing little for employment or development in the host nation. **Forward integration**, which is the purchase of assets or facilities that move the company closer to the customer (such as a

Backward integration
The ownership of equity assets used earlier in the production cycle, such as an auto firm that acquires a steel company

Forward integration
The purchase of assets or facilities that move the company closer to the customer, such as a computer manufacturer that acquires a retail chain that specializes in computer products

computer manufacturer that acquires a retail chain that specializes in computer sales), is criticized on the basis that MNEs use the strategy to homogenize consumer tastes to the detriment of national identities. **Horizontal integration**, which is the acquisition of firms in the same line of business (such as a computer chip manufacturer that buys a competitor), is attacked for introducing similar product lines on a worldwide basis and undercutting the existence of local firms, most of which lack the economies of scale that can be achieved by MNEs.[2]

Horizontal integration
The purchase of firms in the same line of business, such as a computer chip firm that acquires a competitor

There are similar challenges in the industrial relations area, where MNEs must take into account different labor practices and wage rates. For example, multinationals are often under pressure from host governments to use local sourcing for their supplies, hire local workers, train home-country managers and supervisors, and help improve the production environment in the host nation. These decisions can sometimes result in higher production costs, although most international auto firms, for example, use local suppliers and workers to offset this problem.

The financing of operations is another production-related challenge. The choice between local and international borrowing and the use of internally generated funds to minimize the cost of capital is complicated by foreign exchange risk, international tax laws, and government controls on capital (see Chapter 16). Additionally, MNEs need to know where they are on their production cost curves in each country, as well as globally, so as to exploit any cost advantages with an appropriate organization structure. For example, as Toyota's worldwide market share began to stabilize, the firm found it needed to become increasingly more efficient.

The above examples illustrate some of the common production-related problems facing international firms. However, experienced MNEs have learned how to deal with these challenges. In doing so, they employ a wide gamut of production strategies that address research, development, innovation, global sourcing, costing techniques, and inventory control. The following sections examine each of these production strategies.

RESEARCH, DEVELOPMENT, AND INNOVATION

Production strategies do *not* begin with manufacturing. In the past many MNEs focused most heavily on this aspect of operations, failing to realize that an effective production strategy begins with new product development. We need to keep in mind that many of today's best-selling products and services had not been thought of a short while ago. Examples include laptops, tablets, cellular phones, satellite navigation devices, DVD and Blu-ray players, broadband DSL lines, and specialized discount stores that cater to selective product lines such as home-related goods or office supplies. Many other products and services have been greatly improved over the last decade or so. Examples include cell phones, antidepressant medication, automobiles, hazardous waste treatment services, home-delivery food services, online banking, medical diagnostic equipment, and televisions. MNEs have come to realize that if they are not developing new goods and services, they must be improving their current offerings. In either case the focus is on R&D and innovation.

Innovation can be broadly divided into product/service development and process development. The former refers to activities that support the creation of new products and services that customers want, or improvements to existing products/services that make more customers want them instead of those of rival firms. The latter refers to innovation activities that improve the way products/services are produced, making them quicker, cheaper, or better quality. Continuous innovation lies at the heart of sustained competitive advantage, and managing it effectively has a strong international business component.

Most large firms are involved in all of these activities. Sony, for example, is continually coming up with new technology platforms (CDs, DVDs, Blu-rays, 4K players) and new products based around these platforms. But it also invests in improving current product lines, with new models and new features, and it strives to make them cheaper through economies of scale and continuous improvement in manufacturing.

For us, concerned with the international strategy and organization of innovation and R&D, there are several key issues. The first is the question of how far products, services, and the processes that create them should be standardized across all locations, as opposed to customizing these to suit local markets. This lies at the heart of the "integration–responsiveness" theme that runs through this book. Despite the highly standardized nature of their products, even firms like McDonald's and Coca-Cola customize these for particular markets. Like all firms they have to manage a natural tension between country market managers who would like more customization to suit their local customer needs and head-office managers in the marketing, operations, human resource management, R&D, and strategy departments who would prefer to standardize across all markets.

A related issue is: where should firms locate different innovation-related activities? The answer to this depends on the industry and often the product or service in question. It is worth examining this by looking at the factors that influence the organization of R&D around the firm.

MNEs tend to operate several types of R&D networks, as shown on Figure 12.1. There is an innovation hierarchy from basic, long-term, or blue-sky R&D, which is often based around finding scientific breakthroughs, to applied, near-market, or demand-led innovation:

- Blue-sky or basic R&D centers are often linked to universities or government research institutes to tap into highly specialized expertise, wherever it is in the world.

- Technical design and development centers focus on more practical, near-market R&D and may be separate or co-located with regional headquarters or major business units.

- Applied technical development and customization departments, often situated within manufacturing centers, will focus on incremental improvements to production processes or minor adaptations to products to suit local markets.

Home country-based central R&D often sets the overall R&D strategy across a firm, but funding and other resources may partly come from country market managers who will

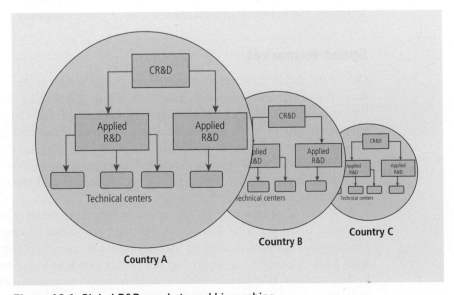

Figure 12.1 Global R&D: markets and hierarchies

push for more applied R&D activities to adapt products and services for their markets. For a large MNE, a few key locations may have R&D units, the firm's main markets may all have one or more applied R&D centers, and production locations will have technical centers. The complexity of managing strategy and implementation up and down the innovation hierarchy and across the different country locations should not be underestimated.

In terms of both product and process development, MNEs need to prioritize country locations according to both (1) local market requirements in terms of adaptation, design and development, and engineering support, and (2) local technological resources, expertise, contract companies, universities, and so on, often called the "national system of innovation."

The above organization structures are important because they affect how well firms leverage their R&D efforts for competitive advantage. The efficiency with which specialist knowledge inputs from experts around the firm are coordinated is paramount. For example, firms have to focus new product development (NPD) efforts at the point where technological opportunities meet market opportunities. Marketing departments and subsidiaries, distributors and retailers in country markets understand customer needs, whereas the central R&D department and technical design and development centers around the firm understand the potential of various technologies. These areas of specialist knowledge have to combine efficiently to direct NPD, and this is often done within cross-functional teams. NPD project teams are continually created and disbanded in manufacturing and service firms in response to the ever-changing technological and market opportunities they are faced with, and the strength of internal and external networks determines how well firms manage this process.[3]

Large MNEs that are good at managing knowledge networks are in a better position to leverage the scale and scope advantages that put them ahead of smaller or domestic market firms in terms of their innovativeness. They can afford large (scale) and specialist (scope) centers of excellence and can manage joint ventures with other big players to pool resources and spread the risk of R&D projects. They can then link these R&D centers to their markets around the world, prioritizing areas of development on which to focus their efforts to reap the most rewards in terms of sales of new and improved products.

Global innovation management and knowledge management are seen to be increasingly important to the long-run performance of all firms. Nohria and Ghoshal use the terms *distributed innovation* and *differentiated networks* to characterize how firms should learn globally and exploit this learning globally to improve production processes and products in all markets.[4] Other studies also emphasize the internal processes, within multinational structures, that constrain or facilitate this kind of global capability.[5]

Speed-to-market

One of the major manufacturing challenges facing MNEs is the speed with which they develop and get new products to market. In recent years, many firms have found that a "speed-to-market" strategy can be extremely profitable. Table 12.1 provides some data to support this statement. Notice that a company that enters the market one month ahead of the competition can increase annual gross profits by $150,000 on a product that generates $25 million and $600,000 on a product that generates $100 million. Simply put, by carefully designing the product and getting it out of the door fast, the company can dramatically increase profitability.

MNEs have taken a number of steps to ensure early delivery of their products. For example, Cisco Systems has outsourced the production of routers and switches to Flextronics, a contract electronics manufacturer. Flextronics receives an electronic order from Cisco, manufactures the product under the Cisco brand, and then delivers it directly to the customers. BMW has combined engineering, development, and production planning in bringing new cars to market in record time.[6]

Table 12.1 The cost of arriving late to market (and still being on budget)

If the company is late to market by:					
6 months	5 months	4 months	3 months	2 months	1 month
Gross potential profit is reduced by:					
233%	225%	218%	212%	27%	23%
If time-to-market is improved, profit will go up by:					
11.9%	9.3%	7.3%	5.7%	4.3%	3.1%
For revenues of $25 million, annual gross profit will increase by:					
$400,000	$350,000	$300,000	$250,000	$200,000	$150,000
For revenues of $100 million, annual gross profit will increase by:					
$1,600,000	$1,400,000	$1,200,000	$1,000,000	$800,000	$600,000

Source: Academy of Management Executive, "The New Competitors: They Think in Terms of 'Speed-to-Market'," by Joseph T. Vesey © 1991 The Academy of Management (NY).

Time-to-market accelerators
Factors that help reduce bottlenecks and errors and ensure product quality and performance

Modular integrated robotized system (MIRB)
A software-based production process that relies entirely on robots

Concurrent engineering
The process of having design, engineering, and manufacturing people working together to create a product, in contrast to working in a sequential manner

The strategic emphasis is on increasing speed by developing **time-to-market accelerators**, which are factors that help reduce bottlenecks and errors and ensure product quality and performance. These accelerators vary from firm to firm, but they all produce the same results. For example, in 2000, Pirelli, the Italian tire maker, unveiled its **modular integrated robotized system (MIRB)**, which enables the entire production system to be robotized. Small and flexible, MIRB allows smaller batches to be produced in different locations, potentially locating them next to Pirelli's industrial customers.[7]

In the past, many MNEs placed the bulk of their production attention on the manufacturing side of the operation. However, recent research shows that the best way to reduce defective products and speed delivery is by placing the greatest attention on product design and planning of operations. This is accomplished through what is known as **concurrent engineering**, which involves design, engineering, and manufacturing people working together to create and build the product. Concurrent engineering is useful for two reasons. First, if the product is carefully designed, fewer changes are needed later on and the good can be brought to market swiftly. Second, the costs associated with changes increase as the product gets closer to completion; that is, it is almost twice as expensive to correct a problem during production as during product design.

Once a product or service has been planned out, the MNE's attention turns to production. This strategy is focused very heavily on minimizing costs and increasing quality and productivity.

✔ Active learning check

Review your answer to Active Learning Case question 1 and make any changes you like. Then compare your answer to the one below.

1 How did GE use work-out to increase speed-to-market?

The primary way GE used work-out to increase speed-to-market was by looking for ways to eliminate production bottlenecks and streamline operations. The strategy of work-out asked the participants: how can we change the operation to get more done in less time? The workers who were familiar with the operations often had a wealth of information to share, and this was sometimes the first time anyone had asked them for their opinions. They were delighted to offer suggestions and recommendations. As a result, the company produced more products in less time than ever before.

GENERATION OF GOODS AND SERVICES

Most people think of the production process as one in which physical goods are produced. However, the process can also be used in generating services, and the two are quite often interlinked. For example, GM manufactures cars but also offers auto maintenance and repair services, whereas Boeing both builds and services aircraft. In other cases, services are primary, such as the Hilton Corporation offering hotel accommodations, Hertz and Avis leasing cars, and CNN providing international news coverage.

Sometimes goods and/or services are provided directly by the MNE; at other times the MNE has an arrangement with outside firms or suppliers (some of them being direct competitors) to assist in this process. For example, other firms make some of the HP printers, but HP has its name put on the units and assumes responsibility for marketing them. Service organizations follow a similar strategy. Some airlines purchase their in-flight food from companies like Marriott, and some rely on aircraft maintenance firms such as Ryder to service their craft. Many motels subcontract their food service to companies that specialize in this area, including fast-food franchisors such as McDonald's and Burger King. So there is often a mix of product/service strategies at work when generating goods and services. The following discussion examines some of the most important functions that are carried out in this process. The production of goods is emphasized most heavily because some of the areas under discussion do not lend themselves to services—although one that does is global sourcing, a primary area of consideration in production strategy.

Global sourcing

Global sourcing
The use of suppliers anywhere in the world, chosen on the basis of their efficiency

Sometimes MNEs produce all the goods and services they need. However, they often use **global sourcing** by calling upon those suppliers which can provide the needed output more efficiently regardless of where they are geographically located.

Global sourcing has become important for a number of reasons. The most obvious one is cost. If GM wants to be price competitive in the European Union, one strategy is to build and ship cars from Detroit to Europe at a price equal to, or less than, that charged by EU competitors. Because this is not possible, GM uses overseas suppliers and assembly plants to build much of what it sells in Europe. In deciding who will provide these parts and supplies, the company uses global sourcing, as do other MNEs.

Not all global sourcing is provided by outside suppliers. Some MNEs own their own source of supply or hold an equity position in a supplier. This relationship does not guarantee that the supplier will get the MNE's business on every bid. However, if the supplier is unable to match the cost or quality performance of competitive suppliers, the MNE will eventually terminate the relationship. So there is a great deal of pressure on the supplier to develop and maintain state-of-the-art production facilities. Additionally, because the supplier works closely with the MNE, the company knows how its multinational client likes things done and is able to operate smoothly with the MNE's design and production people.

In recent years, some giant MNEs have taken equity positions in a number of different suppliers. Japanese multinationals are an excellent example. These firms often have a network of parts suppliers, subcontractors, and capital equipment suppliers they can call on.

At the same time these suppliers often provide goods and services to other firms. This helps them to maintain their competitive edge by forcing them to innovate, adapt, and remain cost effective. If these suppliers are in similar or complementary industries, as in the case of NEC's suppliers, then technological innovations or revolutionary changes in manufacturing processes will be quickly accepted or copied by others. So the close proximity of the suppliers coupled with their business relationships helps to ensure that they attain and hold positions as world-class suppliers, and this advantage carries over to the customers, who gain both innovative ideas and high-quality, low-cost supplies.[8]

A good example is the leather footwear industry in Italy. Manufacturers regularly interact with leather suppliers, designers, and producers of other leather goods. As a result, the manufacturers are extremely knowledgeable about industry technology, production techniques, fashion trends, and supply sources.

These advantages also help explain why many US suppliers are going international. By setting up operations near world-class competitors, these suppliers find it easier to monitor developments, remain alert to changes in technology and production processes, and maintain state-of-the-art facilities. In fact, when manufacturers expand operations to another country, it is common to find their major suppliers setting up operations nearby in order to continue serving the manufacturers. The other reason is to prevent local competitors from capturing some of this business, which often happens when the supplier attempts to compete from the home country.

The global clothing industry provides a good example of these trends. The production of clothing sits within a broader value chain, which includes textiles and fibers for a range of both household and industrial goods. Upstream, the textile industry relies on access to sources of natural fibers, a "natural" factor endowment in Porter's diamond of advantage, compared to the "acquired" factor endowments associated with the chemicals industry for the production of artificial fibers. Clearly, each has favored different countries at different stages of the industry's development. Downstream, distribution and retailing and, in particular, branding and marketing have remained predominantly within the major markets of industrially advanced countries (and under their ownership). The case **International Business Strategy in Action: Gap Inc**. illustrates these patterns.

The clothing industry itself can be subdivided into three activities: design, preparation, and production. The last two have remained relatively labor intensive, which is why most preparation and production are done in cheap-labor locations. China's share of world exports in clothing grew from 4 percent in 1980 to over 20 percent in 2014, and it is now the world's dominant exporter.[9] Over 5 million Chinese are employed in the sector. By contrast, the United States has the biggest trade deficit in clothing ($94.3 billion in 2012).[10] Scotland and Italy, two dominant forces in textiles and clothing at one time, for example, have shifted upmarket to specialize in design and high-quality/fashion items. Employment has fallen drastically in these countries as a result and the patterns of trade have also reversed.

INTERNATIONAL BUSINESS STRATEGY IN ACTION

Gap Inc.: a successful "hollow corporation"

In 1999, after 28 years, founders Don and Doris Fisher still owned 24 percent of Gap Inc. and still played a leading role in managing the operations of this $2 billion clothing firm. By 2014 Gap had over 140,000 employees and its revenue had grown to $16,435 million, but the Fisher family was still very much involved with the shaping of the firm. As with other

▶

high-street clothing firms, its competitive advantage stemmed from linking cheap manufacturing in contract production facilities in around 45 countries, with design and fashion expertise and huge distribution and sales chains in the United States and Europe.

Just 1 percent of its own employees have any production-related role: 600 quality control employees in eight shipment processing facilities in North America, Europe, and Asia. Gap is essentially a distribution, retailing, sales, and, particularly, marketing firm—a specialty retailer operating 3,709 stores selling casual apparel, personal care products, and accessories. Its brands include Gap, GapKids, babyGap, Banana Republic, Old Navy, Althleta, and Piperlime. Gap measures its own success on its sales and its expansion rate, in terms of new stores, so in part it is also a real estate business. These provide an indication of its ongoing performance, its multinationality at any point in time, and its international expansion or retrenchment over time. In the late 1990s it was opening over 100 stores per year. More recently its overall growth and its international expansion have slowed (see Table 12.2). For example, due to losses, Forth & Towne brand stores were closed by the end of June 2007. From 2007 to 2010 the number of stores decreased from 3,167 to 3,095 (a decrease of 71 stores, or 2.3 percent). Despite Gap being a well-known brand in Europe, it is heavily reliant on its North American sales (87.8 percent), with only 10 percent of its stores situated in Europe and Asia, where it generates 12.2 percent of sales. Gap's product development offices are based in New York City, where product-managers, designers, and graphic artists monitor (and create) customer trends in its main consumer markets.

The Sourcing and Logistics Group, together with buying agents around the globe, draw up production schedules and place orders with the approved third-party clothes plants located around the world. Like other mid-range department stores, such as Neiman Marcus or Macy's in the United States, Marks & Spencer in the UK, and Karstadt in Germany, Gap's higher-quality, higher-priced garments are sourced from countries like South Korea, Taiwan, Hong Kong, Singapore, Turkey, Brazil, Mexico, and parts of India and China. In terms of the global clothing value chain, these garments sit "below" fashion designer clothing from Armani, Donna Karan, Hugo Boss, and Gucci, which is manufactured in small, high-quality batches in Italy and high-capability locations in Southeast Asia. But they sit "above" the discount chains like Wal-Mart and Kmart in the United States, ASDA and Matalan in the UK, and Carrefour in France, which source in bulk from lower-cost and lower-quality locations such as Malaysia, Indonesia, Vietnam, China, India, Mexico, Chile, Hungary, Kenya, and Pakistan. The value hierarchy in clothing is mirrored by a global hierarchy of locations, ordered by virtue of their cost base and local endowments that underpin quality, and speed of delivery, from related infrastructure to relevant expertise.

Each Gap brand has its own marketing team based in the San Francisco Bay area, which creates advertising posters, in-store design and graphics, and magazine and TV commercials. Distribution centers receive goods from overseas production plants, check the quality, sort the goods, and redistribute them to retail outlets in each of the country markets, the United States, Canada, Japan, the UK, and the Netherlands. The subcontracting arrangement with overseas manufacturers sometimes involves financial and technical support but mainly relies on imposing strict quality and cost limitations which independent suppliers must adhere to in order to maintain their contracts.

There are clear similarities in this strategy with Nike (see **Real Case: Nike**, below). Nike, however, has closer ties with its first-tier suppliers, often including some equity share, technology transfer, management, and design training.

Websites: http://www.gap.com; http://www.gapinc.com

Sources: P. Dicken, *Global Shift: Mapping the Changing Contours of the World Economoy*, 6th ed. (London: Sage, 2011); OECD, "A new world map in textiles and clothing: adjusting to change," Paris, at http://www.oecd.org; GAP, *Annual Report*, 2010, 2014.

When MNEs turn to global sourcing, there is typically a hierarchical order of consideration. The company gives first preference to internal sources, such as having subassemblies produced by the manufacturing department or the subsidiary that specializes in this work. However, if a review of outside sources reveals a sufficient cost/quality difference that would justify buying from an external supplier, this is what the company will do. In fact, sometimes an MNE will not attempt to make a particular part or product because it lacks the expertise to do so efficiently. The firm will simply solicit bids from outside suppliers and award the contract based on predetermined specifications (price, quality, delivery time, etc.). Over time the MNE will learn which suppliers are best at providing certain goods and services and will turn to them immediately.

When this process is completed, attention will then focus on the actual manufacture of the goods.

Recently, environmentalists have reviewed the global supply chains of MNEs. They argue that all suppliers to an MNE should follow environmentally sensitive policies—in other words, be "green."

Some firms face high risks due to dependence on global outsourcing. Outsourcing to suppliers may open up opportunities for competitors. Similarly, outsourcing production to different suppliers may prevent the development of new insights, innovations, and solutions which typically require cross-functional teamwork. Finally, outsourcing may risk key knowledge leakage.

Manufacturing of goods

MNEs face a variety of concerns in manufacturing goods and services. Primary among these are cost, quality, and efficient production systems.

Cost

Multinationals seek to control their costs by increasing the efficiency of their production processes. Often this means using new, improved technology such as state-of-the-art machinery and equipment. Although these purchases can be expensive, they may be the best way to raise productivity and lower costs, thus maintaining competitive advantage. A good example is provided by the automobile industry in Brazil, which is the heart of the South American automobile market. The country is host to 13 auto makers, including Daimler, Chrysler, Volkswagen, and Ford, which are investing over $20 billion to update Brazilian plants to modular manufacturing. **Modular manufacturing** allows suppliers of parts to take on some of the assembly. Dana Corporation, which has set up shop near a Chrysler factory in the city of Curitiba, is now responsible for the assembly of the Dakota's basic skeleton, which represents approximately 30 percent of the total cost of production. Once this skeleton reaches Chrysler, it is mounted with an engine and a body. Entire assembly lines had to be rebuilt to accommodate this process. Volkswagen, Ford, and General Motors are also developing similar assembly plants to test their efficiency for future implementation to their other factories.

Modular manufacturing
A manufacturing process that consists of modules that can be easily adapted to fit changing demand

A second approach is to faucet low-cost labor sources. A good example is the *maquiladora* industry (as discussed in Chapter 10) that has sprung up in Mexico just across the US border. Hundreds of US plants have been established in this area. Examples include

INTERNATIONAL BUSINESS STRATEGY IN ACTION

End of an era: the Goodyear plant closure

Founded by Frank Seilberling in 1898, Goodyear Tyre & Rubber Company is an MNE that manufactures tires for a range of vehicles including automobiles, trucks, airplanes, and farm equipment. With headquarters in Akron, Ohio, and a global workforce of approximately 75,000, in 2015 Goodyear announced its intention to close its plant in Wolverhampton (UK) by 2017, which would signal the end of a 90-year era and cause the loss of over 300 jobs. The closure brought much media attention and was labeled as controversial because since opening in 1927 the Wolverhampton plant had had a great deal of historical significance for the region. The plant was switched to war ▶

production in 1939 when employees worked consecutively for 20 days while just taking one day off. At its peak, the Wolverhampton plant had a workforce of approximately 7,000 employees.

Goodyear primarily manufactures tires, but the Wolverhampton plant had not been manufacturing tires for quite a few years. It had been involved in the production of rubber components for tire factories abroad, as well as other related products. Furthermore, all the raw materials required in the daily operations of compound mixing were imported and the final product was then exported to Goodyear plants abroad. This was no longer financially viable for Goodyear and it pledged to co-locate mixing processes and tire manufacturing plants globally to remove unnecessary transportation costs. At this stage, the Wolverhampton plant employed 330 workers in total, with 267 employees based in the mixing department, 53 in other tire-related goods divisions, and 10 in support roles at the factory.

Goodyear had been cutting operations in Europe as a whole and blamed these closures on factors such as currency trends, the state of the tire market in general, and China providing cheap tire alternatives. The Wolverhampton plant was based in the Midlands (UK), at the heart of Britain's automotive manufacturing sector, where closely located firms such as Jaguar Land Rover and Geely brought in over £1 billion of investment alone in 2015. Goodyear's closure in early 2015 brought negative media attention centered on the decline of manufacturing more generally within the region. Local MPs complained about the closure and unions urged the UK's Prime Minister, David Cameron, to seek greater protection for British workers. Erich Fric, the Managing Director of Goodyear Dunlop in the UK, stated that the closure was extremely saddening, but was required in order to strengthen Goodyear's competitive position, and he

reiterated that the company would honor its commitments to its workers.

Following the closure announcement, a report by industry experts Syntex was leaked to the media suggesting that Goodyear had not done enough to save the business. The report highlights three key findings regarding Goodyear's decisions:

- The company had failed to demonstrate that the Wolverhampton plant was loss making.
- It had taken "a passive approach" to seeking new buyers for the business.
- It had refused to provide statistical evidence backing up its claim that the plant was not competitive.

The company responded with several initiatives to support employees and their communities, working with unions and a taskforce group to finalize appropriate redundancy settlements. The taskforce provided support for the Wolverhampton employees through outplacements, careers guidance, interview skills training, and pension planning. Even though the Goodyear Wolverhampton plant closure was widely criticized by stakeholders as damaging to the employees and the region, the key question to ask is: did the firm have any real choice? MNEs can only act in the interests of their stakeholders if this does not ultimately harm their profitability to the degree that they go out of business entirely.

Sources: Andy Sharman, "Goodyear to close Midlands rubber operations," *Financial Times,* Business & Economy, June 25, 2015; "Goodyear will definitely shut Wolverhampton factory," *BBC News,* October 6, 2015; Tamlyn Jones, "Goodyear confirms Wolverhampton plant closure," *Birmingham Post,* October 7, 2015; Darren Campbell, "Union slams Goodyear over Wolverhampton plant closure," *Birmingham Mail,* October 7, 2015; "End of an era: Goodyear to close Wolverhampton factory," *Express & Star,* June 25, 2015; "Shock report on Wolverhampton's Goodyear plant raises questions over closure," *Express & Star,* October 12, 2015.

TRW Inc., which has a factory where workers assemble seat belts, and Mattel, which has a plant where workers turn out Barbie-doll houses and Disney teething rings. Labor costs in these facilities are less than 20 percent of those of similar workers in the United States. Also, because this is a free trade zone, US duties are levied on the imports only to the extent of the value added in Mexico, so low wage rates in Mexico help keep down the import duty.

A third approach is the development of new methods used to cut costs. For example, it is typical for a firm to calculate the selling price at an early stage in the new product development process. If the price is judged to be too high, the product is sent back to the drawing board to be reworked, or the company moves on to another project. Japanese firms pioneered the "parallel" new product development process now used by most firms. Rather than a sequential process whereby R&D handed over a product idea to manufacturing departments to make, project teams involving R&D, design, manufacturing, and marketing work together to build-in "manufacturability" and customer preferences throughout the development process. This saves unnecessary costs and shapes the product for specific markets as it evolves.

A fourth method that is gaining popularity with MNEs is that of costing products not on an individual basis but as part of a portfolio of related goods. Instead of evaluating the expenses of developing one new soft drink, for example, a company looks at the costs and revenues associated with the entire line of beverages. Coca-Cola of Japan provides an example. Every year it introduces more than 1,000 new soft drinks, fruit drinks, and cold coffees into the Japanese market. Ninety percent of them fail, but this does not stop Coca-Cola from introducing approximately one new product a month. From a cost accounting standpoint this is not a profitable strategy. However, as one Coca-Cola executive in Japan puts it, "We know that some of these products will survive only a month or two, but our competitors have them, so we have to have them." As a result, Japan is Coca-Cola's most profitable market and the company sells a variety of non-carbonated drinks to complement its main brand.

Quality

Quality has always been one of the major criteria for business success. As the president of an international consulting firm puts it, "Products are expected to be nearly perfect."[11] Nowhere is this more clearly reflected than in the auto industry, where the Japanese have garnered a large share of the international market by using what is called *kaizen*, or continuous improvement.[12] A good example is Toyota Motors, which has continually worked to reduce costs and improve quality. One way Toyota has achieved this goal is partly through large R&D expenditures. Another is through meticulous design, engineering, and production processes that ensure a proper fit of all parts and overall durability of the unit.[13] US and European auto manufacturers caught up with the Japanese some time ago, partly by imitating some of the above processes.

Other excellent examples of MNEs that have succeeded because of a strong focus on quality include such lesser-known firms as Stanley Works, the WD-40 Co., and A. T. Cross. Stanley Works manufactures tape measures in Asia then has the accuracy of samples checked by sophisticated laser computers back in New Britain, Connecticut, before selling them worldwide. Stanley has also developed a host of other high-quality products, from double-toothed saws that cut on both the upstroke and the down-stroke for the Asian market, to hammers without claws for carpenters in central Europe (who prefer to use pliers to pull out bent nails), to levels shaped like elongated trapezoids, which the French market prefers.

The WD-40 Co. of San Diego manufactures WD-40, a water-displacing lubricant that fights rust, cleans heel marks from linoleum and walls, and provides a variety of other services around the house. Car mechanics use it to loosen sticky valves and remove moisture from balky carburetors; odd jobbers apply it to frozen locks and screws. Today the blue-and-yellow spray can is found in stores throughout the world, where it enjoys fanatical customer loyalty. WD-40 is a best-seller in the UK and is rapidly gaining market share throughout Europe and Asia.

A. T. Cross of Providence, Rhode Island, has been manufacturing mechanical pens and pencils for almost 150 years. The units are assembled by hand and "every one of the company's hourly employees is a quality control expert who is responsible for checking the tolerances of the engraved grooves to within one ten-thousandth of an inch and for detecting nearly microscopic scratches or the slightest clotting of ink on a pen ball."[14] A. T. Cross's product quality is so high that, despite a lifetime guarantee, less than 2 percent of its products are ever returned for repair. Today these pens and pencils are one of the most popular US-made gifts in Japan.

Production systems

A **production system** is a group of related activities designed to create value. In the generation of goods and services this system includes location, layout, and material handling.

Location

Location is important because of its impact on production and distribution costs. Many MNEs have found that governments (national and local) are willing to provide tax breaks or other financial incentives to encourage them to set up operations. Accompanying considerations include the availability and cost of labor, raw materials, water, and energy as well as the development of the country's transportation and communication systems. As noted earlier, many suppliers set up operations near their major customers. So Ford has built up an integrated production network in western Europe. Ford suppliers are part of this production network so as to maintain their business relationship. Starbucks (see Figure 12.2) also acknowledges the importance of location and has primarily set up processing plants in close proximity to its coffee plantation sites. Location is also important to service enterprises because they usually require face-to-face contact with their customers. Hotels and airlines are typical examples. Personal service firms such as those of accountants, lawyers, and management consultants also fall into this category.

Layout

Plant layout is important because of its impact on efficiency. For example, most auto producers use an assembly line layout in which the workers remain at their station and, as the cars move past them, perform the necessary functions such as installing radios, air-conditioners, interior trim, and so on. In the case of Volvo, the employees work in small teams to build an entire car and the plant is laid out to accommodate this work flow. In other manufacturing settings, however, worldwide competitive firms tend to use U-shaped-cell flow lines, which are more efficient. Schonberger, an internationally known manufacturing expert, has noted that U-shaped production designs enable one person to tend several workstations and increase the speed at which materials can be delivered and defective parts can be reworked. Finally, Maytag has chosen to combine different layouts to cater to each production line in just one factory. A traditional long conveyer belt assembly line makes its standardized models. A second area makes more sophisticated models in smaller production cells instead of a long line. The third area makes the most sophisticated machines. In this setting, workers are craft workers putting together a substantial part of the machine.

Layout varies widely in service organizations, although it appears to be universal in use. Most hotels, regardless of the country, have the check-in and check-out areas in the same place as such support groups as the bellhops, concierge, and cashier. In fast-food units, the food preparation area is situated so that the personnel can quickly serve both in-unit and drive-through customers. In movie theaters, the concession area is located in the lobby and the projection room at the back of the theater.

Material handling

Material handling involves the careful planning of when, where, and how much inventory will be available to ensure maximum production efficiency. Part of this is resolved through careful inventory control processes. Part of it is handled when the production layout is determined. For example, General Electric uses **process mapping**, a flowchart that shows every small step in producing a product. As a result, the company is able to study every part of an operation and determine those that are redundant or that can be streamlined. Consequently, the company has been able to reduce work time on some jobs by as much as 50 percent.

Figure 12.2 Where Starbucks gets its coffee

Inventory control

Inventory control has received a great deal of attention in recent years because a well-designed inventory strategy can have dramatic effects on the bottom line.[15] One of the most popular concepts has been **just-in-time inventory (JIT)**, which is based on delivering parts and supplies just as they are needed. If this concept were carried to the extreme, it would mean that manufacturers would not need to store materials because suppliers would be delivering them just in time for shipment to the factory floor.

JIT is an important concept that has been adopted by MNEs throughout the world. However, the degree of use varies based on the product and the company's production strategy. In some companies it is used simply to keep inventory to a minimum. In more advanced firms, like one of the pioneers of the approach, Toyota, the concept is taken further and applied to link supply and demand in real time. Dealers order directly from the factory, which means that customers can get their built-to-order car in 7 to 10 days.

One of the major problems with JIT is that its success rests heavily on the quality and reliability of the suppliers. In Japan, where MNEs often have an equity position in these companies, suppliers will go out of their way to meet partners' demands. However, in the United States and Europe, most suppliers are independent businesses that work under a contract relationship, so the bonds are often not as strong between the two parties. A second problem with JIT is that, although it works well in managing delivery of parts to the assembly line, few firms have been able to apply the concept to the entire production process. Most firms still manufacture and ship their output to dealers to sell, in contrast to Toyota's approach of matching supply and demand before producing. One of the most important things to remember about JIT is that it needs strong support from the workers and the suppliers. Everyone must be operating in unison. If the workers are slow, there will be excess inventory on hand; if the supplier is late, the workers will be sitting by idly.

Demand-Flow™ Technology (DFT) is a production process that allows for flexible changes in the middle stages of production. Typically used to produce standardized assembly products, such as computers, DFT permits quick reactions to changes in demand and technology. A surge of demand for Intel i7 processors used within computers, for instance, would immediately shift inputs from other computers to be combined with i7 processor chips to respond to demand. This virtually eliminates inventories. Intermec, a company that makes bar code scanners, mobile computers, and related products, reduced inventory by 50 percent after implementing DFT. It was also able to consolidate five different printer lines into one flexible mixed-model line, decreasing the amount of required manufacturing floor space by 20 percent.

Developing a strong service orientation

As noted earlier, many products have a service element associated with them. Sometimes this element is more important than the product itself. For example, many people will not purchase a car or home appliance unless it can be serviced easily. Service is also important when choosing a bank, insurance agent, lawyer, or doctor. Many of the ideas we have discussed in this section, including sourcing, cost, and quality, are also key factors in shopping for services. In addressing this area, MNEs will do two things: (1) consider whether their strategy needs to be oriented toward a product, a service, or a combination of the two; and (2) determine the ideal degree of service to provide.

Determining the product/service balance

Some outputs lend themselves to a strong production orientation, whereas others require much more attention to service. Figure 12.3 offers an illustration. Designed more as a

---

Just-in-time inventory (JIT)
The delivery of parts and supplies just as they are needed

Demand-Flow™ Technology (DFT)
A production process that is flexible to demand changes

Product-dominated businesses	Equally balanced	Service-dominated businesses
Farm produce (corn, wheat, etc.)	Aircraft manufacturing	Advertising agency
Home construction	Fast-food unit	Theater production
Auto production	TV network	Teaching

Figure 12.3 Product- and service-dominated businesses

point of reference than as a factual source that addresses every firm in the respective industry, the figure nonetheless shows that some MNEs need to have a strong product-dominated focus whereas others benefit most from a service orientation. A good example is offered by aircraft manufacturers that must be concerned with both ends of the continuum. Olympus and Pentax, both manufacturers of flexible endoscopic equipment, provide another example. To develop their brand names in Latin America, these companies offer medical professionals the surgical training necessary to use their equipment. Because after-sales service is also an important consideration for prospective buyers, including hospitals, all major endoscope manufacturers have service stations in the region.

On the other hand, some manufactured products require far less service than they used to need. A good example is photocopiers. Manufacturers of these machines have improved product quality so substantially that many units are now sold on the basis of price. Service is no longer a major factor because everyone's product is of such high quality.

Knowing whether to sell on the basis of product or service (or a combination of the two) is critical to the success of many MNEs. A mistake at this point can result in emphasis on the wrong sales factors.

Providing the right amount of service

Once the MNE has determined the proper balance of product and service domination, it evaluates the specific type of service warranted. This is particularly important because many MNEs find that the strategy used in their own country does not work overseas. A good example is the Japanese approach to retail services. The amount of personal service provided in Japan would surprise many Westerners. For example, auto dealers typically provide pick-up and delivery for repair service customers and make new car sales calls to customers' homes. In department stores, it is common to find executives and sales clerks alike lined up to bow to the first customers in the store. Japanese banks often help their customers sell or buy homes, find distributors for merchandise, and provide them with tax advice.

Although these services help Japanese companies maintain customer satisfaction, research has found that they are of little value to doing business in other countries. For example, Japanese banks in the United States have discovered that US customers want only a limited amount of quality service; they prefer quantity and efficiency in the form of a variety of different services offered at low prices. As a result, Japanese banks here offer the same types of services as do other US banks. Would they be more successful if they changed this strategy and tried to emulate the approach used back home? Given the nature of the US market, they believe this would be a mistake. The lesson is clear: when competing in terms of service, one must match the competition but not exceed it unless the customer is willing to pay for this service. In the United States, the banking customer is not willing.

Review your answer to Active Learning Case question 2 and make any changes you like. Then compare your answer to the one below.

2 **How has GE used Six Sigma to reduce cost and improve quality in consumer goods? In each case, give an example.**

Six Sigma allows GE to use process mapping to reduce cost by identifying those activities that can be eliminated or combined in the production process. For example, can an individual who is performing one assembly-line task take on other tasks and thus reduce the number of people needed to produce the product? Can inventory be ordered and delivered in smaller amounts, thus making greater use of just-in-time? Consideration of these types of questions can help reduce cost. In improving product quality, the work group can examine how well all parts of the product fit together, examine the durability of the unit, and look for additional ways of testing the product to ensure that it measures up to quality standards.

INTERNATIONAL LOGISTICS

International logistics
The designing and managing of a system to control the flow of materials and products throughout the organization

International logistics is the designing and managing of a system to control the flow of materials and products throughout the firm. This includes the inflow of materials, movement through the production process, and outflow to the wholesale/retail firm or final consumer. International logistics is an important area of strategic consideration because these expenses can account for 10 percent of the total costs. The material management aspect of international logistics has already been addressed. The following discussion examines three other key topics: transportation, packaging, and storage.

Transportation

Container ships
Vessels used to carry standardized containers that can be simply loaded onto a carrier and then unloaded at their destination without any repackaging of the contents of the containers

In examining international logistics, we focus on the primary modes of transportation: ocean and air. The others—rail, pipeline, and motor carrier—are of importance in some regions (such as the European Union), but they are not as commonly used in moving goods from an MNE's plant to their final destination. Moreover, their use is highly dependent on the infrastructure of the country—that is, the extensiveness and quality of the nation's road system and rail network. In many non-triad countries the infrastructure is poor and the MNE's use of them is greatly limited.

Ocean shipping

Unconventional cargo vessels
Vessels used for shipping oversized and unusual cargoes

Roll-on-roll-off (RORO) vessels
Ocean-going ferries that can carry wheeled cargo such as automobiles, trailers, and trucks that drive onto built-in ramps and roll off at the point of debarkation

Lighter aboard ship (LASH) vessels
Barges stored on a ship and lowered at the point of destination

International firms can choose from a fairly wide variety of ocean carriers. The three most common carriers are conventional container ships, cargo vessels, and roll-on-roll-off (RORO) vessels. **Container ships** are used to carry standardized containers that can be simply loaded onto the carrier and then unloaded at their destination, without any repackaging of the contents of the containers. **Unconventional cargo vessels** are used for shipping oversized and unusual cargoes. **Roll-on-roll-off (RORO) vessels** are ocean-going ferries that can carry wheeled cargo such as automobiles, trucks, semi-trailer trucks, trailers, or railroad cars that drive onto built-in ramps and roll off at the point of debarkation. A carrier similar to the RORO is the **lighter aboard ship (LASH) vessel**, which consists of barges that are stored on the ship and lowered at the point of destination. These individual barges can then operate on inland waterways.

One of the major problems in planning an ocean shipping strategy is the limitations caused by the lack of ports and port services. In developing countries, for example, seaports sometimes lack the equipment necessary to load or unload container cargo, thus limiting the country's ability to export and import. In recent years a number of Third World countries have been working to improve their ports so they can become more active in the international trade arena.

Air shipping

Most countries have airports that can accommodate air freight. The problem with this mode of transportation is its high cost. Thus, although international air freight has grown dramatically over the last 30 years, it still accounts for less than 1 percent of the total volume of international shipments. It is used in trade more commonly among industrialized nations than any others, and it is usually restricted to high-value items that must reach their destination quickly.

Several developments have occurred over the past couple of decades that have helped increase the use of air shipments. These include more efficient ground facilities, larger aircraft, and better marketing of these services to shippers. In particular, the development by aircraft manufacturers of jumbo cargo jet planes and combination passenger and cargo aircraft has helped immensely.

Choice criteria

In deciding the best transportation mode to use, MNEs tend to focus on four important criteria: time, predictability, cost, and non-economic factors.

Time

The period between departure and arrival of a carrier can vary significantly between an ocean freighter and an aircraft. So one of the questions a firm must answer is: how quickly is delivery needed? A number of factors can influence the answer. One is the perishability of the product. Exotic flowers from South America are flown to the United States because they would not survive a sea voyage. A second factor is how soon the goods are needed to replenish current stocks. Autos from Japan are brought into the United States by ship because the length of the trip does not hurt the supply of cars on hand at local dealerships.

In businesses where speed is critical, companies are now coordinating their worldwide supply chains in order to reduce the amount of time needed to get the goods through the production cycle and to the customer. Victor Fung, Honorary Group Chairman (previously CEO) of Li & Fung, Hong Kong's largest export trading company and an innovator in the development of supply-chain management, has provided an example of how this is being done:

> Say we get an order from a European retailer to produce 10,000 garments. It's not a simple matter of our Korean office sourcing Korean products or our Indonesian office sourcing Indonesian products. For this customer we might decide to buy yarn from a Korean producer but have it woven and dyed in Taiwan. So we pick the yarn and ship it to Taiwan. The Japanese have the best zippers and buttons, but they manufacture them mostly in China. Okay, so we go to YKK, a big Japanese zipper manufacturer, and we order the right zippers from their Chinese plants. Then we determine that, because of quotas and labor conditions, the best place to make the garments is Thailand. So we ship everything there. And because the customer needs quick delivery, we may divide the order across five factories in Thailand. Effectively, we are customizing the value chain to best meet the customer's needs. Five weeks after we have received the order, 10,000 garments arrive on the shelves in Europe, all looking like they came from one factory, with colors, for example, perfectly matched.[16]

Predictability

Although both air and water transportation are basically reliable, they are subject to the vagaries of nature. Bad weather can close an airport; inadequate seaport facilities can slow the loading and unloading of cargo. Because of the great difference in delivery time between the two modes, the choice is often obvious. If a company needs to have a package delivered tomorrow, it will come by air; if the firm wants to clear merchandise out of the warehouse today but the international customer does not need it for 90 days, it will be sent by water. However, certain carriers are more reliable than others, and the MNE will use its experience in determining which companies to choose for delivery. Reliability is particularly important for air shipments, where a difference of one day could significantly influence the salability of the product.

Cost

The expense associated with shipping is a major consideration when choosing an international transportation mode. Because air freight is significantly more costly than shipment by water, the cost must be economically justifiable. Typically, an MNE will use air shipments only when time is critical and/or the product has high value. For example, if the company has purchased expensive watches in Zurich for its specialty outlets in New York and San Francisco, the watches will be flown to the retailers. Similarly, if a London-based MNE has bought a US-made supercomputer for the home office and wants it installed immediately, the unit will be flown over from the United States. On the other hand, if the merchandise is bulky or the cost of air freight is a significant portion of the value of the product, it will be sent by water. Autos are exported by ship, as are bulk commodities and resources such as oil and coal.

Non-economic factors

Sometimes non-economic factors influence the choice of transportation mode. For example, in the United States all government cargo must use national flag carriers when available, so there is seldom a question of how to send these goods. Similarly, other governments own or subsidize their carriers, and there is pressure on MNEs to use these transportation modes when doing business with those countries. Such political considerations must be taken into account when formulating the transportation strategy.

Packaging

Packaging is important in ensuring that a product is shipped in a safe container and arrives undamaged. When goods are transported a long distance or to areas with climates different from the one where they are manufactured, the container can prevent spoilage or leakage. Chemicals, for example, must be carefully sealed in containers that can withstand impact and will not crack open if tipped over or dropped. Machines, such as personal computers, must have interior packing that prevents damage during transit.

Packaging is also important because of its direct effect on cost. If units must be shipped in odd-shaped containers, fewer of them can be loaded into the hold of the transport than if they are shipped in square or rectangular containers and can be loaded atop and alongside each other. The weight of the packing material is also important, especially when goods are being shipped by air and costs are based on both distance and weight.

Intermodal containers
Large metal boxes that fit on trucks, railroad trains, and aircraft and help reduce handling costs and theft losses by placing the merchandise in a tightly sealed, easy-to-move unit

Packaging is also important in reducing loading and unloading costs and minimizing theft and pilferage. In recent years many shippers have begun using **intermodal containers**, which are large metal boxes that fit on trucks, railroad trains, and aircraft and help cut handling costs and theft losses by placing the merchandise in an easy-to-move unit that is tightly sealed.

As more goods are shipped internationally, packaging will continue to be a focal point of attention. Such considerations can help an MNE maximize shipping space and minimize transportation costs.

Storage

In some cases, goods that are shipped internationally have to be stored before being moved to their final destinations. In the United States, public storage is widely available. In other countries, including Japan, warehousing facilities are in short supply. Additionally, the configuration of many warehouses is different from that in the United States. Ceilings are often lower and there is little automation for handling such common chores as loading and unloading packages or stacking containers on top of each other. In such cases, the MNE must decide whether to invest in warehouse facilities or ship goods only when needed, thus eliminating the warehouse function.

Foreign trade zones
Areas where foreign goods may be held and processed and then re-exported without incurring customs duties (same as a free trade zone)

As discussed in Chapter 6, some countries have **foreign trade zones**, which are areas where foreign goods may be held and processed and then re-exported without incurring customs duties (same as a free trade zone). These zones are usually found at major ports of entry (including international air terminals). Their effective use can help an MNE: (1) temporarily store its goods while breaking a large shipment into smaller ones to be shipped to other locales; (2) combine small shipments into larger ones and then reship them; (3) process the goods and perform a host of value-added activities before repackaging them for the market; and (4) give those goods that will remain in the local market a "made in" status so that they can be sold as locally produced products.

An effective storage strategy can be particularly helpful in carrying out the final stages of an MNE's production plan. The strategy can also help minimize overall product cost, reduce delivery time, and increase customer satisfaction.

DIFFERENT KINDS OF GLOBAL PRODUCTION SYSTEMS

Location is a key factor in deciding the global structure of firms' production systems. But it needs to be considered alongside other factors which vary considerably by industry.

Companies tend to focus on the functions and innovation activities where they have the major advantage and often outsource activities, or parts of the value chain where they add less value. This determines the "boundaries" of the firm, what activities are internalized, and what are externalized or left to other firms to provide on a contract basis. Figure 12.4 shows a number of example industries and firms that have very different global production systems, determined by the functions and activities that add the most value.

Production system Where is the value added?	Internalized (within the firm's hierarchy)	Mixed	Externalized (to other firms in the market)
R&D/technology	Example: semiconductors (Intel)		Example: telecoms (Ericsson)
Manufacturing		Example: autos (Toyota)	
Marketing			Example: clothing (Gap)

Figure 12.4 Global production systems: where is the value added?
Source: Adapted from UNCTAD, *World Investment Report*, 2002.

Although Intel does a lot of marketing, its main competitive advantage lies in the continual development of new semiconductors, the heart of PCs and other IT and electronic devices. Product and process development are internalized and highly centralized because this suits the type of technology and product that the firm focuses on. At one point it accounted for around 25 percent of all R&D investment in the semiconductor industry. Much of its high-value manufacturing, particularly wafer production and fabrication, is done in the United States, where most of its manufacturing workforce is based. Other production sites are in Dalian (China), Israel, and Ireland. Much of its labor-intensive assembly and testing takes place in Malaysia, the Philippines, China, and Costa Rica, but is owned by Intel (internalized).

Ericsson also keeps much of its research, design, and development activities within the firm, but not so long ago it decided to let other firms make many of the components that make up its telecom systems. In 2001 Flextronics, a $14.5 billion Singaporean firm, took over much of Ericsson's manufacturing and supply-chain activities in Brazil, Malaysia, Sweden, and the UK. It externalized these activities because it decided they were not part of its core competencies, and it could safely contract other firms to supply these components. (See **Real Case: Flextronics** at the end of this chapter.)

Gap Inc. and other clothing firms have externalized the manufacturing function for many years now. Their focus is clothing design, marketing, branding, and real estate management. There are enough producers in cheap labor locations (such as China, which exports more garments than any other country by far) for Gap to use the market to contract out this activity to the cheapest and/or best. Intermediaries in this industry, like Flextronics in telecoms, include Mast Industries, which works with 400 factories in 37 countries, and Li & Fung, a $5 billion Hong Kong company that connects around 700 US and European brand owners with a network of 7,500 suppliers (1.5 million workers) around the world (of which 2,000 are active at any one time).

Toyota lies in the middle of these two extremes. Because manufacturing, and particularly maintaining continuous improvement in manufacturing, is so central to its competitive advantage, Toyota is partly vertically integrated down the supply chain. New product development (new car models and features) and process development (improving price and quality) are closely linked and involve good relationships with (and/or ownership of some) component suppliers. It cannot externalize car production because it is the source of many of its core competitive advantages.

Finally, for diversified or multiproduct firms, configuring the right kind of global production system can get complicated. Philips, for example, makes semiconductors, like Intel, but also has large consumer electronics and consumer products divisions. It has to manage both technology-driven and market-driven innovation and production activities.

STRATEGIC MANAGEMENT AND PRODUCTION STRATEGY

MNEs are currently focusing on a number of areas in improving their production strategies. Three that are getting particular attention are (1) technology and design, (2) continuous improvement of operations, and (3) the use of strategic alliances and acquisitions.

Technology and production design

MNEs are now spending more money on R&D than they have in the past. For example, Aventis, Eli Lilly, AstraZeneca, and Pfizer spend over 15 percent of their revenues on R&D, which provides the backroom for the introduction of new pharmaceutical products.[17] Yet, R&D is not only developing new products, but also helping firms find alternative parts as well as production techniques.

A second current trend is the use of concurrent engineering, which was discussed earlier in the chapter. Many MNEs are now realizing that a team approach to product development, which combines the talents of research, design, and manufacturing people as well as customers and clients, results in a more successful product. Ford Motors is an excellent example. Ford put together a group called Team Taurus to develop its Taurus and Sable automobile lines. Team members were drawn from designing, engineering, and production, and were brought together with customers. Collectively the group discussed how to build the new cars and replaced the sequential approach to manufacturing autos (first design the cars, then produce them, then market them) with a concurrent approach that involved addressing the design, production, and marketing issues all at the same time. The result of this strategy was a Taurus that captured a significant market niche and helped Ford close the gap between itself and the competition.

Coupled with these strategies are innovative human resource development programs that are designed around the concept of **empowerment**, which involves giving employees greater control over their work. This strategy is particularly effective because it creates a feeling of pride and ownership in the job and makes employees feel they are important assets. The use of empowerment is not limited to the research and design areas; it is important in all phases of production, beginning with product creation. Additionally, if things go smoothly at this early stage of the production cycle, there are likely to be fewer problems later on.

Empowerment
The process of giving employees increased control over their work

Continuous improvement

Due to the success of Japanese MNEs, *kaizen* (continuous improvement) has been emulated by MNEs worldwide. No matter what the good or service is, every day the company tries to do the job better. Some consultants have referred to this strategy as "rapid inch-up," which certainly captures the essence of the concept. US firms in particular have benefited from this idea. A good example can be found in the automotive industry. In the 1980s and 1990s, Toyota and Honda were able to offset the rising value of the yen with cost saving in their factories, thus allowing them to hold the price line on many of their new cars. These innovations were exported to US plants. By the early 2000s, however, US firms had successfully fought back by imitating and improving Japanese production techniques. By 2004, four of the five most efficient auto plants in the United States were owned by GM.[18] More recently auto plants around the world, including those based in emerging economies, compete for this accolade.

A large number of firms helped account for these results. One is Xerox, internationally known for its photocopiers. At the beginning of the 1980s the company was losing market share to overseas competitors. However, the firm then began implementing a production strategy for dramatically improving quality and reducing cost. Today Xerox is again a world leader in copiers. Another example is TPG, which services Ford's Toronto factory by arranging for 800 deliveries a day from 300 parts makers. The parts arrive at 12 different stages of production within 10 minutes of scheduled time to decrease the amount of parts inventory in the plant.

As discussed in an earlier section, JIT is a related concept that the MNEs are using to achieve continuous improvement. In the past JIT was used almost exclusively for managing inventory, but now the concept is being employed in other ways. For example, Toyota's use of JIT helps it assemble a car in 13 labor-hours, compared to 19 to 22 labor-hours for Honda, Nissan, and Ford.

Alliances and acquisitions

Alliances and acquisitions (M&As) continually change the global production map. Many MNEs cannot compete effectively without entering into joint ventures or other alliances with MNEs that can complement their production strategy. For example, Compaq is well known for its personal computers, but many of the components in these machines are purchased from outside suppliers or are developed by these firms under an alliance agreement. When Compaq needed a hard disk drive for its first laptops, it financed Conner Peripherals, a Silicon Valley start-up with a disk drive already underway, rather than develop the machine in-house. More recently, Compaq has ventured into the market for powerful desktop workstations used primarily by scientists and engineers. Instead of going head-to-head with market leaders such as Sun Microsystems and HP, the company assembled a dozen hardware and software firms, including these two computer giants, and put together an alliance aimed at defining a new technical standard for high-speed desktop computing. The objective of the alliance is to develop a standard that will suit any workstation, thus allowing customers the freedom to buy the latest, fastest machine without fear of being tied to any single manufacturer.

Compaq's approach is not unique; the Japanese *keiretsu* system has been using it for years (see Chapter 18). In fact, some researchers claim that industry alliances account for more of the success of Japanese firms than does JIT or any other manufacturing technique. Working in unison with each other, *keiretsu* companies have been able to wield a great deal of power. Many have monthly meetings in which they exchange information and ideas. Table 12.3 provides a brief overview of two of the country's major *keiretsu* members. Looking closely at the table, we see that it illustrates how valuable cooperation among the members can be. The idea has not been lost on US firms, among others, which are now beginning to put together their own "*mini-keiretsus.*" Eastman Kodak acquired a number of distributors in Japan and has taken small stakes in some 50 suppliers and customers, and IBM is investing venture capital in a host of small European computer-related firms. Motorola has not taken equity positions, but it uses a *keiretsu* approach by developing extremely close ties with suppliers.

Table 12.3 The Mitsubishi and Mitsui *keiretsu* in Japan

	Mitsubishi	Mitsui
Financial services and insurance	ACOM The Bank of Tokyo-Mitsubishi BOT Lease BOT Lease Defined Contribution Plan Consulting of Japan JACCS JALCARD Jibun Bank kabu.com Securities MDAM Asset Management Mitsubishi Auto Leasing Mitsubishi Corporation Capital Mitsubishi Corporation Futures Mitsubishi Electric Credit Mitsubishi UFJ Asset Management Mitsubishi UFJ Capital The Mitsubishi UFJ Factors Mitsubishi UFJ Financial Group Mitsubishi UFJ Lease & Finance Mitsubishi UFJ Merrill Lynch PB Securities Mitsubishi UFJ Morgan Stanley Securities Mitsubishi UFJ NICOS Mitsubishi UFJ Securities Holdings Mitsubishi UFJ Trust and Banking MMC Diamond Finance NBL Tokyo Credit Services Meiji Yasuda General Insurance Meiji Yasuda Life Insurance Mitsubishi Corporation Insurance Mitsubishi Estate Home MST Insurance Service Nippon Oil Trading Shunjusha Tokio Marine & Nichido Fire Insurance The Tokio Marine Life Insurance Union Bank of California NA	Japan Alternative Investment Co., Ltd. JA Mitsui Leasing, Ltd. Mitsui & Co. Energy Risk Mitsui & Co. Financial Services Ltd. Mitsui & Co. Financial Services (Asia) Ltd. Mitsui & Co. Financial Services (Europe) BV Mitsui & Co. Financial Services (USA) Inc. Mitsui & Co. Logistics Partners Ltd. Mitsui & Co. Precious Metals, Inc. Mitsui & Co. Principal Investments Ltd. Mitsui & Co. Realty Management Ltd. Mitsui & Co. Venture Partners, Inc. Mitsui Bussan Commodities Ltd. Mitsui Bussan Credit Consulting Co., Ltd. Mitsui Bussan Insurance Co., Ltd. Mitsui Bussan Precious Metals (Hong Kong) Limited Mitsui Bussan Trade Services Ltd. Mitsui Direct General Insurance Company, Limited MVC Corporation

Table 12.3 (*continued*)

	Mitsubishi	Mitsui
Computers, electronics, and electrical equipment	CHORYO CONTROL SYSTEM CHORYO DESIGNING DIA Instruments MC Medical Meiryo Technica Meldas System Engineering Mitsubishi Cable Industries Mitsubishi Electric Mitsubishi Electric Building Techno-Service Mitsubishi Electric Business Systems Mitsubishi Electric Consumer Products (Thailand) Mitsubishi Electric Engineering Mitsubishi Electric Home Appliance Mitsubishi Electric Lighting Mitsubishi Electric Micro-Computer Application Software Mitsubishi Electric OSRAM Mitsubishi Electric Plant Engineering Mitsubishi Electric System & Service Mitsubishi Precision Ryoden Kasei Ryoden Koki Engineering	
Information, communication, and IT	Bewith CHORYO DESIGNING Choryo Software Hiroshima Dia System Infosec Isuzu IT Frontier JAPAN SPACE IMAGING Material Business Support MCC Meldas System Engineering M.H.I. Digital System Mitsubishi C&C Research Association Mitsubishi Electric Control Software Mitsubishi Electric Information Network Mitsubishi Electric Information Systems Mitsubishi Electric Micro-Computer Application Software Mitsubishi Electric System & Service Mitsubishi Kagaku Media Mitsubishi Shoji & Sun MITSUBISHI SPACE SOFTWARE Mitsubishi UFJ Information Technology Mitsubishi UFJ Research and Consulting MTEC Nagoya Nikon Systems Ryoin Ryoka Systems Ryoyu Systems T-GAIA Tokio Marine & Nichido Systems	Grand Marche Co., Ltd. J-SCube Inc. Kids Station Inc. MITSUI & CO. VIXIA INC. Mitsui Bussan Secure Directions, Inc. Mitsui Electronics Inc. Mitsui Knowledge Industry Co., Ltd. Moshi Moshi Hotline, Inc. Nihon Unisys, Ltd. QVC JAPAN INC. ShopNet Co., Ltd. T-GAIA Corporation VIXIA INC. World Hi-Vision Channel, Inc.
Motor vehicles	Mitsubishi Automotive Engineering Mitsubishi Corporation Technos Mitsubishi Fuso Truck & Bus Mitsubishi Heavy Industries MITSUBISHI HEAVY INDUSTRIES TRANSPORTATION EQUIPMENT ENGINEERING & SERVICE Mitsubishi Motors Mitsubishi Nagasaki Machinery Mfg. RYOJYU COLDCHAIN	Car Sharing Japan Co., Ltd. Mitsui Automotriz SA Mitsiam Motors Co., Ltd. MITSUI BUSSAN AUTOMOTIVE INC. MITSUI BUSSAN MACHINE TEC Co., Ltd. Penske Automotive Group, Inc. PT Bussan Auto Finance PT Yamaha Indonesia Motor Manufacturing Toyota Canada Inc. Toyota Chile SA

Table 12.3 (*continued*)

	Mitsubishi	Mitsui
Food, beverages, feeds, and retail	ART COFFEE Coca-Cola Central Japan Dai-Nippon Meiji Sugar Kentucky Fried Chicken Japan Kirin Beverage Kirin Brewery Kirin Holdings KIRIN MC DANONE WATERS Koiwai Dairy Products KOIWAI FARM KOIWAI FARM PRODUCTS MARUICHI MC Beverage & Foods MC FOODS Mercian Mitsubishi-Kagaku Foods Mitsubishi Shoji Foodtech Nagano Tomato NITTO FUJI FLOUR MILLING Ryoshoku SAN-ESU SANYO FOODS TOSHO	Corner Stone Research & Development, Inc. Kadoya Sesame Mills Incorporated MCM Foods BV Mikuni Coca-Cola Bottling Co., Ltd. Mitsui Foods Co., Ltd. Mitsui Norin Co., Ltd. Mitsui Sugar Co., Ltd. Multigrain AG Novus International, Inc. PRI Foods Co., LTD. San-ei Sucrochemical Co., Ltd. Toho Bussan Kaisha, Ltd. United Grain Corp. Vendor Service Co., Ltd. Wilsey Foods, Inc.
Construction	Daiya Building Service DAIYA PR HIGASHI CHUGOKU RYOJU ESTATE Hiroshima Ryoju Kousan Kakoki Plant & Environment Engineering Kanmon Dock Service Kinki Ryoju Estate The Kodensha KOIWAI FARM Mitsubishi Cable Industries Mitsubishi Chemical Engineering Mitsubishi Chemical Functional Products Mitsubishi Electric Building Techno-Service Mitsubishi Estate Mitsubishi Estate Home MITSUBISHI HEAVY INDUSTRIES BRIDGE & STEEL STRUCTURES ENGINEERING Mitsubishi Jisho Sekkei Mitsubishi Materials Techno Mitsubishi Rayon Engineering Nagoya Ryoju Estate P.S. Mitsubishi Construction Ryoju Estate Ryoken Kiso Seibu Construction	Mitsui Bussan Construction Materials Co.
Metals, mining, and non-ferrous metal	Hosokura Metal Mining Isuzu Metal One Japan New Metals Kyushu Steel Center Metal One Corporation Metal One RYOWA Metal One Speciality Steel Metal One Steel Products Metal One Steel Service Mitsubishi Aluminum	Champions Pipe & Supply, Inc. Coil Center Co., Ltd. Coral Bay Nickel Corporation Inner Mongolia Erdos Electric Power & Metallurgical Co., Ltd. Japan Collahuasi Resources BV MBK Steel Products West Co., Ltd. Mitsui & Co. Steel Ltd. Mitsui Bussan Construction Materials Co., Ltd.

Table 12.3 (*continued*)

	Mitsubishi	Mitsui
	Mitsubishi Cable America	MITSUI BUSSAN KOZAI HANBAI CO., LTD.
	Mitsubishi Cable Industries	MITSUI BUSSAN METALS CO., LTD.
	Mitsubishi Corporation Exploration	MITSUI BUSSAN STEEL TRADE CO., LTD.
	Mitsubishi Corporation Unimetals	Mitsui Iron Ore Development Pty. Ltd.
	Mitsubishi Corporation Technos	Mitsui-Itochu Iron Pty. Ltd.
	Mitsubishi Materials	Mitsui Raw Materials Development Pty.
	Mitsubishi Materials Natural Resources Dev.	Limited
	Mitsubishi Nagasaki Machinery Mfg.	NIPPON AMAZON ALUMINIUM CO., LTD.
	Mitsubishi Nuclear Fuel	Nippon Steel Trading Co., Ltd.
	Mitsubishi Shindoh	Regency Steel Asia Pte Ltd.
	MOBY Suzuyasu	Shanghai Bao-Mit Steel Distribution Co., Ltd.
	Onahama Smelting and Refining Ryoko Lime Industry	Siam Yamato Steel Co., Ltd.
	Sus-Tech	Steel Technologies Inc.
		SUMIC Nickel Netherlands BV
		Valepar SA
Real estate	Chitose Kosan	Bussan Community Company
	HIGASHI CHUGOKU RYOJU ESTATE	Bussan Real Estate Co., Ltd.
	Hiroshima Ryoju Kousan	Mbk Real Estate Europe Limited
	IMS	Sumisho & Mitsuibussan Kenzai Co., Ltd.
	Izumi Parktown Service	
	Kinki Ryoju Estate	
	Marunouchi Yorozu	
	Mitsubishi Electric Life Service	
	Mitsubishi Estate	
	Mitsubishi Estate Building Management	
	Mitsubishi Estate Home	
	Mitsubishi Jisho Property Management	
	Mitsubishi Jisho Retail Property Mgmt.	
	Mitsubishi Jisho Towa Community	
	Mitsubishi Real Estate Services	
	Mitsubishi UFJ Real Estate Services	
	Nagoya Ryoju Estate	
	Ryoju Estate	
	Sotsu Corporation	
	Tamachi Building	
	Yokohama Sky Building	
Resources and energy	Astomos Energy Corporation	BHP Mitsui Coal Pty. Ltd.
	Marunouchi Heat Supply	Japan Australia LNG (MIMI) Pty. Ltd.
	MHI Nuclear Engineering	Kokusai Oil & Chemical Co., Ltd.
	Mitsubishi Chemical Functional Products	Kyokuto Petroleum Industries, Ltd.
	Mitsubishi Gas Chemical Company	Mit Energy Upstream LLC
	Mitsubishi Heavy Industries	Mitsui Coal Holdings Pty. Ltd.
	Mitsubishi Materials	Mitsui E&P Australia Pty Limited
	Mitsubishi Nuclear Fuel	Mitsui E&P Middle East BV
	Nippon Oil	Mitsui Gas Development Qatar BV
	Nippon Petroleum Refining	Mitsui LNG Nederland BV
	Nuclear Development	Mitsui Marubeni Liquefied Gas Co., Ltd.
		Mitsui Oil Co., Ltd.
		Mitsui Oil Exploration Co., Ltd.
		Mitsui Sakhalin Holdings BV
		Mittwell Energy Resources Pty., Ltd.
		Tensho Electric Industries Co., Ltd.
		United Petroleum Development Co., Ltd.
		Westport Petroleum, Inc.

Table 12.3 (*continued*)

	Mitsubishi	Mitsui
Chemicals	Asahi Glass Kibikasei Kyowa Hakko Kirin Mitsubishi Chemical Mitsubishi Chemical America Mitsubishi Chemical Analytech Mitsubishi Chemical Holdings Mitsubishi Chemical Medience Mitsubishi Engineering-Plastics Mitsubishi Gas Chemical Mitsubishi Gas Chemical Company Mitsubishi Kagaku Media Mitsubishi Pharma Mitsubishi Plastics Mitsubishi Rayon Mitsubishi Rayon America Mitsubishi Shoji Agri-Service Mitsubishi Shoji Chemical Mitsubishi Shoji Plastics Mitsubishi Tanabe Pharma MKV DREAM Nippon Polypenco RYOBI TECHNO Ryoden Kasei Ryouei Tokyo Shokai	Advanced Composites, Inc. DAIICHI TANKER CO., LTD. Daito Chemical Industries, Ltd. Japan-Arabia Methanol Company Ltd. Hi-Bis GmbH. Honshu Chemical Industry Co., Ltd. Mitsui AgriScience International SA/NV Mitsui Bussan Agro Business Co., Ltd. Mitsui Bussan Chemicals Co., Ltd. Mitsui Bussan Plastics Trade Co., Ltd. P.T. STANDARD TOYO POLYMER. P.T. Kaltim Pasifik Amoniak Sanko Gosei Ltd. Shark Bay Salt Pty Ltd. Soda Aromatic Co., Ltd. Tensho Electric Industries Co., Ltd.
Marine and aerospace		Mitsui Bussan Aerospace Co., Ltd. Orient Marine Co., Ltd.
Warehousing and transport	DAIYA LOGISTICS Isuzu Metal One SSS West Japan MHI AEROSPACE LOGITEM Mitsubishi Chemical Logistics Mitsubishi Corporation LT Mitsubishi Electric Logistics Mitsubishi Logistics Nippon Yusen Kabushiki Kaisha Ryowa Logitem	Intercontinental Terminals Company LLC TRI-NET (JAPAN) INC. TRI-NET LOGISTICS (ASIA) PTE LTD.
Pulp and paper	DIA HOZAI DIAMIC Mitsubishi Paper Mills Mitsubishi Paper Sales PICTORICO Tokyo Shokai	
Consumer service		AIM Services Co., Ltd. ALCANTARA SPA Burberry International KK BUSSAN REAL ESTATE CO., LTD. HANAE MORI Associates Co., Ltd. HOUSE DEPOT PARTNERS CO., LTD. Mitsui Bussan Inter-fashion Ltd. MITSUI BUSSAN PACKAGING CO., LTD. MITSUI BUSSAN TECHNO PRODUCTS CO., LTD. Mitsui Bussan Woodchip Oceania Pty. Ltd. SOGO MEDICAL CO., LTD. Storage Plus Corp. Sumisho & Mitsui Bussan Kenzai Co., Ltd.

Table 12.3 (*continued*)

Mitsubishi	Mitsui
Infrastructure project business unit	AES JORDAN HOLDCO, LTD.
	Atlatec Holdings, S.A. de C.V.
	Compañía de Generación Valladolid S. de R.L. de C.V.
	IPM Eagle LLP
	IPM (UK) Power Holdings Limited
	MBK Project Holdings Ltd.
	Mitsui & Co. Plant Systems, Ltd.
	Mitsui Power Ventures Limited
	MIT POWER CANADA LP INC.
	Mitsui Rail Capital Holdings, Inc.
	MRCE Group
	Mitsui Rail Capital Participações Ltda.
	MITSUI GAS E ENERGIA DO BRASIL LTDA.
	P.T. Paiton Energy
	Toyo Engineering Corporation

Sources: The individual websites of each business group (www.mitsubishi.com and www.mitsui.co.jp).

 Active learning check

Review your answer to Active Learning Case question 3 and make any changes you like. Then compare your answer to the one below.

3 **In what way could best practices help GE develop more effective international strategies? Explain.**

Best practices could help GE develop more effective international strategies by encouraging it to identify those MNEs that are most successful and then discover how they accomplish that feat. Do these firms manage to develop more new products than do their competitors? Or are they best at getting their new goods into the marketplace quickly? Do they produce the highest-quality goods? Or are they lowest-cost producers? What accounts for their ability to achieve such an excellent performance? By asking and answering these questions, GE can gain insights into how it needs to change its own production processes in order to emulate those MNEs successfully.

KEY POINTS

1 Many of today's goods and services will be replaced in the future with faster, more efficient, and cheaper substitutes. For this reason, MNEs need to continually research, develop, and bring new offerings to the marketplace. One way this is being done is through the use of time-to-market accelerators. A good example is concurrent engineering.

2 The generation of goods and services entails a number of specific functions. One is obtaining materials or supplies. Many MNEs have found that global sourcing is the best strategy because it helps keep down costs while providing a number of other benefits, including ensuring an ongoing source of supply and helping the company penetrate overseas markets.

3 In the production of goods and services, MNEs focus on a number of key factors, including cost, quality, and well-designed production systems. While these three factors are often interrelated, each merits specific attention. Multinationals have also developed very effective inventory control systems that help minimize carrying costs and increase productivity. Attention is also focused on gaining the proper balance between production and service domination.

4 International logistics is the designing and managing of a system to control the flow of materials and products throughout the firm. In addition to inventory control, this involves transportation, packaging, and storing.

5 MNEs are currently focusing on a number of areas in improving their production strategies. Three approaches that have been receiving particular attention are (a) technology and design, (b) continuous improvement of operations, and (c) the use of strategic alliances and acquisitions. These approaches are helping multinationals meet new product and service challenges while keeping costs down and quality up.

Key terms

- backward integration
- forward integration
- horizontal integration
- time-to-market accelerators
- modular integrated robotized system (MIRB)
- concurrent engineering
- global sourcing
- modular manufacturing
- production system
- material handling
- process mapping
- just-in-time inventory (JIT)
- Demand-Flow™ Technology (DFT)
- international logistics
- container ships
- unconventional cargo vessels
- roll-on-roll-off (RORO) vessels
- lighter aboard ship (LASH) vessels
- intermodal containers
- foreign trade zones
- empowerment

REVIEW AND DISCUSSION QUESTIONS

1 Why are MNEs so interested in new product development? Why do they not simply focus on improving their current offerings?

2 Why is speed-to-market such an important production strategy? Explain.

3 What are time-to-market accelerators? In what way is concurrent engineering one of these accelerators?

4 Why do many MNEs use global sourcing? Why do they not produce all the parts and materials in-house? Be complete in your answer.

5 Why are world-class suppliers often located next to world-class manufacturers? What forms of synergy often exist between the two groups?

6 How do MNEs try to cut production costs? Identify and describe three steps.

7 In what way is the continuous reduction cost method used by Japanese manufacturers different from the periodic cost reduction method employed by many US firms? Compare and contrast the two.

8 Some MNEs use a production strategy that involves costing a portfolio of related goods rather than just costing each individually. What is the logic behind this strategy?

9 How does *kaizen* help bring about increased quality? Is this approach limited to Japanese firms or are other MNEs using it as well?

10 What types of issues does an MNE confront when it seeks to improve its production system? Identify and describe three.

11 How does JIT help an MNE control its inventory? Give two examples.

12 How is employee training an important factor in implementing JIT and DFT production processes?

13 Why would an MNE want to determine the degree to which its primary business was product dominated and service dominated? Explain.

14 Why are MNEs concerned with international logistics? How does this help the companies increase their competitiveness?

15 In recent years MNEs have been focusing on a number of areas in improving their production strategies. What are two of these? Identify and describe each.

REAL CASE

Flextronics

You wouldn't think that company rivals such as Sony and Philips, or Ericsson, Alcatel, and Motorola, would choose to share the same factories to build competing products, but that is just what has been happening since the emergence of electronics manufacturing service providers (EMSPs). Contract manufacturing was a trend that changed the face of electronics manufacturing. Companies unknown to the public, such as Flextronics, Foxconn, Sanmina-SCI, Celestica, and Jabil, among others, now make such well-known products as IBM PCs, the Microsoft Xbox video console, Web TV set-top boxes for Philips and Sony, and portable phones for Ericsson, Alcatel, and Motorola. In 2006, EMSP industry revenues were estimated at over $200 billion and by 2013 they exceeded $1 trillion. In 2007 two of the largest EMSP companies, Flextronics and Solectron, combined when Flextronics, with revenues of $18.8 billion, acquired Solectron, with revenues of $10.6 billion. But this is a fast-moving industry sector and by 2015 Flextronics had slipped to fourth place in terms of revenues, behind the giant Hon Hai Precision industries, parent company to Foxconn and the main supplier to Apple, with revenues of almost $40 billion.

Flextronics remains one of the *Fortune* Global 500 companies, but most end-customers who use its products have never heard of it. Incorporated in Singapore in 1990, Flextronics is a provider of vertically integrated advanced design and electronics manufacturing services (EMS) to original equipment manufacturers (OEMs). It provides these

Source: Ingemar Magnusson/Alamy Stock Photo

services to various markets, which include infrastructure, mobile communication devices, computing, consumer digital devices, industrial, semiconductor capital equipment, clean technology, aerospace and defense, white goods, automotive and marine, and medical devices. As of 2015, Flextronics' total manufacturing capacity was approximately 27.2 million square feet. The company helps customers design, build, ship, and service electronics products through a network of over 100 facilities in 30 countries across four continents, and it has been recorded as employing approximately 200,000 employees. Though officially headquartered in Singapore, the company has strong ties to the US market and most of its customers are US companies. Flextronics is listed on ▶

NASDAQ (the United States) and the Frankfurt Stock Exchange (Germany).

Over the years Flextronics has expanded by purchasing smaller EMSP contractors and factories from its customers. In 2001, Flextronics purchased half of Xerox's office equipment-making operations for $220 million. The deal came with a five-year outsourcing contract for Flextronics to manufacture Xerox products. Currently its ten largest customers, including Sony-Ericsson, Motorola, and Hewlett-Packard, account for about 64 percent of net sales from continuing operations.

In 2014, Flextronics' total revenue was $26,108.6 million. It generated 53 percent of its sales from Asia, 31 percent from the Americas, and 16 percent from Europe. According to Rugman (2005), Flextronics is among nine "global" MNEs which derived 20 percent sales or more from each of the triad regions of North America, Europe and Asia.

Because of lower transportation costs as a percentage of total value, electronics can be transported by air, whereas cars are always transported by sea. This is one main reason why contract manufacturing has been so successful in the electronics industry, where parts might travel the world over before the product is finished.

Prior to the merger with Solectron, Flextronics had six industrial parks in low-cost regions near each large triad market. In Asia, two industrial parks in China, one in Malaysia, and one in India, and a network of regional manufacturing facilities, supply printers, cell phones, telephone switching boards, and PDAs, among other products. In the Americas, products from its two industrial parks (one in Mexico, one in Brazil) and its network of manufacturing facilities include automotive, telecommunications, networking equipment, and hardware products, among others. In eastern Europe, Poland and Hungary host two industrial parks and Ukraine one park, which are also supported by nearby manufacturing facilities and produce telecommunications infrastructure, electronics for automotives, printers, and disposable cameras, among other items.

The choice of location for production facilities is determined by the quality of the labor force, the cost of producing in the country, and the proximity to a triad market. Mexico, for example, is the low-cost region in the North American market. Brazil has the best industrial capabilities among countries in South America and strong ties to large international firms from Europe and North America. China has abundant labor, high expected economic growth, and proximity to the large Japanese market where international firms like Canon, NEC, and Sony are headquartered. Eastern Europe is the low-cost production area for western European markets. It is no surprise that the Flextronics industrial park in Poland is located near a university from which it can acquire skilled labor.

EMSPs do much more than provide cost-effective manufacturing. They help in the design of products to make them easier to manufacture; they also provide logistics services, such as material procurement, inventory management, vendor management, packaging and distribution, and automation of key components of the supply chain through advanced IT. In addition, they offer after-market services such as repair and warranty services.

Today's electronic manufacturers have come a long way from the cheap labor-based contractors that used to dominate the industry. Robotic automation is now a significant part of the production process and is handled mostly by specialists. It is their manufacturing expertise that makes for lower costs, but EMSPs provide many more advantages to OEMs. They decrease the risk of manufacturing because OEMs no longer need to make large investments in a new factory to create a new product that might or might not be successful. EMSPs can also purchase inputs at lower prices because they are making cell phones not only for Alcatel, but also for Motorola and Ericsson, increasing their purchasing power.

Contract manufacturing accounts for almost half of electronic manufacturing and this proportion has grown steadily since the early days of Flextronics. EMSP companies will increasingly dominate the industry in the future and this process will redefine the role of OEMs in the electronics industry as one of design and marketing.

Sources: Karyn McCormack, "Flextronics adds a key part," *Business Week*, June 4, 2007; "Let the bad times roll," *The Economist*, April 5, 2001; Jonathan Sprague, "Invasion of the factory snatchers," *Fortune*, August 15, 2002; Flextronics, *Annual Report*, 2010, 2014; Alan M. Rugman, *The Regional Multinationals* (Cambridge: Cambridge University Press, 2005).

1 Keeping in mind that Flextronics does not sell to end-customers, how does that change your interpretation of the regional sales data presented in this case?

2 What effect does the emergence of EMSPs have on new entrants into the electronics industry?

3 Why should OEMs be concerned about using EMSPs?

REAL CASE

Nike

One of the rules of international production strategy is: manufacture the highest-quality product and the world is likely to beat a path to your door. A number of firms help illustrate this rule. One is Nike, the sports shoe and clothing producer. Making a wide variety of high-quality shoes, Nike catalogs more than 800 models for use in approximately 25 sports. In 1999 it had 35 percent of the world's market for training shoes (and 45 percent in the United States) and these relative proportions have surprisingly not changed much. In 2014 its sales were $27,799 million. In an effort to keep ahead of the competition, Nike updates each shoe at least every six months. Most of these ideas are generated by Nike's R&D center in Beaverton, near Portland, Oregon, where physiologists and mechanical engineers study the stresses on an athlete's feet and collaborate with stylists on new shoe ideas.

The aim of the takeover of Umbro on March 3, 2008 was to extend these scale advantages. Although Nike sells its products in over 140 countries and produces in more than 33 countries, it is really a triad MNE. In 2014, approximately 80 percent of its sales were in the triad markets of the United States (44.2), Europe (22.9), and Asia (12.1), and 20 percent from emerging markets. Nike is still strong in its home market. In 2014, sales in the United States including US sales of other businesses accounted for approximately 44 percent of total revenues, which is remarkably consistent compared to 43 percent in 2008. It has maintained a steady share of the global market and has remained focused on its core home market.

Nike's high-quality production is matched by superb marketing skills. The world might be beating a path to Nike's door, but the company makes sure the world knows where it is. It has been reported that Nike spends 11 percent of its revenue on marketing, and its "swoosh" brand is recognized the world over. The company continues to use sports stars to endorse its products and is responsible for some of the biggest athlete endorsement deals of all time, including sponsorship of Michael Jordan and LeBron James. A deal for James in 2015 was worth an estimated $30 million, but brought in over $340 million for Nike through the launch of a line of branded sneakers. Besides American stars like Tiger Woods it has used European soccer players, such as Cristiano Ronaldo, and cricket players in India. The idea is: if you can make the "cool" guys wear your products, the rest will follow.

Perhaps the only thing Nike does not like to be remembered for is the bad publicity around its labor practices in Asia. Nike has outsourced all of its production to low-wage areas. By 2014, virtually all of Nike footwear was being produced by contract factories in Vietnam, China, Indonesia, Thailand, and India. Nike also had manufacturing agreements with independent factories in Argentina, Brazil, Mexico, and India to manufacture footwear for sales within those countries. In addition, all its apparel was produced in 33 host countries by independent contract manufacturers. Most of the apparel production occurred in China, Thailand, Indonesia, Malaysia, Vietnam, Sri Lanka, Turkey, Cambodia, El Salvador, Mexico, and Taiwan. And NGOs have criticized the poor working conditions in some of its Asian factories, from Pakistani children stitching Nike's soccer balls, to Vietnamese working in unsafe conditions. NGOs in the Western world started campaigns to boycott Nike, and demonstrators protested in front of Nike's stores. Allegations of long working hours, bad ventilation, and physical abuse of a mostly young female workforce have raised questions about Nike's reputation.

Nike's industry dominance was a main reason for its being severely targeted. Many of its competitors were found to have the same labor practices, but were not subjected to the same level of criticism. More recently Nike has acknowledged its corporate responsibility to improve working conditions in its own factories and help influence its suppliers.

Website: www.nike.com

Sources: Sydney H. Schanberg, "On the playgrounds of America, every kid's goal is to score: in Pakistan, where children stitch soccer balls for six cents an hour, the goal is to survive," *Life*, June 1996; Harry Dunphy, "Nike to improve conditions," *Associated Press*, May 12, 1998; Tom Braithwaite, "Nike moves closer to deal for Umbro," *Financial Times*, December 21, 2007; Nike, *Annual Report*, 2009, 2010, 2015; Total Sportek, "Biggest athlete endorsement deals in sports history," 2016, http://www.totalsportek.com

1   What is the key to Nike's production strategy? Explain.

2   What are the advantages of frequent design changes in Nike's sneakers?

3   Why was it important for Nike to clean up its labor practices in Asia? What more should the company do?

NOTES

1 "(Still) made in Japan," *The Economist*, April 7, 2004.

2 Also see Emily Thornton, "Mazda learns to like those intruders," *Business Week*, September 14, 1998, p. 172.

3 Simon C. Collinson, "Knowledge management capabilities in R&D: a UK–Japan company comparison," *R&D Management*, vol. 31, no. 3 (2001), pp. 335–47.

4 N. Nohria and S. Ghoshal, *The Differentiated Network: Organizing Multinational Corporations for Value Creation* (San Francisco, CA: Jossey-Bass, 1997).

5 T. W. Malnight, "Emerging structural patterns within multinational corporations: toward process-based structures," *Academy of Management Journal*, vol. 44, no. 6 (2001); and M. T. Hansen and B. Løvås, "How do multinational companies leverage technological competencies? Moving from single to interdependent explanations," *Strategic Management Journal*, vol. 25, no. 8/9 (2004).

6 Also see C. K. Prahalad and Kenneth Lieberthal, "The end of corporate imperialism," *Harvard Business Review* (July/August 1998), pp. 69–79.

7 Joseph T. Vesey, "The new competitors: they think in terms of 'speed- to-market'," *Academy of Management Executive* (May 1991), pp. 23–33; and "Re-inventing the wheel," *The Economist*, April 20, 2000.

8 Michael E. Porter, *The Competitive Advantage of Nations* (New York: Free Press, 1990), p. 103.

9 ILO, http://www.ilo.org/global/about-the-ilo/media-centre/press-releases/WCMS_008075/lang--en/index.htm

10 http://www.usitc.gov/research_and_analysis/tradeshifts/2012/textiles.htm

11 Erick Colonius, "Smart moves by quality champs," *Fortune* (spring/summer 1991), p. 24.

12 See, for example, Christopher Palmeri, "A process that never ends," *Forbes*, December 21, 1992, pp. 52–4.

13 "The car company in front," *Economist*, January 27, 2005.

14 Louis S. Richman, "What America makes best," *Fortune* (spring/summer 1991), p. 81.

15 Lucinda Harper, "Trucks keep inventories rolling past warehouses to production line," *Wall Street Journal*, February 7, 1994, p. B3.

16 http://www.lifung.com/leadership/victor-fung/ (2016); Joan Magretta, "Fast, global, and entrepreneurial: supply chain management, Hong Kong style: an interview with Victor Fung," *Harvard Business Review* (September/October 1998), pp. 105–6.

17 See Alan M. Rugman and Cecilia Brain, "Regional strategies of multinational pharmaceutical firms," *Management International Review*, vol. 44, no. 3 (2004), pp. 7–25.

18 "Fighting back," *The Economist*, September 2, 2004.

BIBLIOGRAPHY

Abdollahi, Mohammad, Arvan, Meysam, and Razmi, Jafar. "An integrated approach for supplier portfolio selection: lean or agile?," *Expert Systems with Applications*, vol. 42, no. 1 (2015).

Ambos, Björn, and Schlegelmilch, Bodo B. "The use of international R&D teams: an empirical investigation of selected contingency factors," *Journal of World Business*, vol. 39, no. 1 (February 2004).

Bellak, Christian, and Cantwell, John. "Revaluing the capital stock of international production," *International Business Review*, vol. 13, no. 1 (February 2004).

Bhuiyan, Nadia, and Baghel, Amit. "An overview of continuous improvement: from the past to the present," *Management Decision*, vol. 43, no. 5 (2005).

Brouthers, Lance Eliot, Werner, Steve, and Matulich, Erika. "The influence of triad nations' environments on price–quality product strategies and MNC performance," *Journal of International Business Studies*, vol. 31, no. 1 (spring 2000).

Cantwell, John. "Innovation and information technology in the MNE." In Alan M. Rugman and Thomas Brewer (eds.), *The Oxford Handbook of International Business* (Oxford: Oxford University Press, 2001).

Chan, Jenny, Pun, Ngai, and Selden, Mark. "The politics of global production: Apple, Foxconn and China's new working class." *New Technology, Work and Employment*, vol. 28, no. 2 (2013).

Chou, Yon-Chun, et al. "A framework of economic analysis for tapered technology-manufacturing alliances," *International Journal of Production Economics*, vol. 127, no. 2 (2010).

Collins, R., and Schmenner, R. "Taking manufacturing advantage of Europe's single market," *European Management Journal*, vol. 13, no. 3 (May/June 1995).

Collinson, Simon C. "Organizing knowledge to manage R&D: a UK–Japan company comparison," *R&D Management*, vol. 31, no. 3 (2001).

Contractor, Farok J., Kumar, Vikas, Kundu, Sumit, and Pedersen, Torben. *Global Outsourcing and Offshoring: An Integrated Approach to Theory and Corporate Strategy* (Cambridge: Cambridge University Press, November 2010).

Contractor, Farok J., Kumar, Vikas, Kundu, Sumit K., and Pedersen, Torben. "Reconceptualizing the firm in a world of outsourcing and offshoring: the organizational and geographical relocation of high-value company functions," *Journal of Management Studies*, vol. 47, no. 8 (December 2010).

Curran, Louise, and Zignago, Soledad. "How regional is the supply chain in the enlarged EU?," *Multinational Business Review*, vol. 18, no. 1 (2010).

Cusumano, Michael A. "Manufacturing innovation: lessons from the Japanese auto industry," *Sloan Management Review*, vol. 30, no. 1 (fall 1988).

Dyer, Jeffrey H., and Chu, Wujin. "The determinants of trust in supplier–automaker relationships in the US, Japan, and Korea," *Journal of International Business Studies*, vol. 42 (January 2011).

Flaherty, M. Therese. "Global sourcing strategy: R&D, manufacturing, and marketing interfaces," *Journal of International Business Studies*, vol. 24, no. 1 (1993).

Frost, Tony S., and Zhou, Changhui. "R&D co-practice and 'reverse': knowledge integration in multinational firms," *Journal of International Business Studies*, vol. 36, no. 6 (November 2005).

Griffith, David A., and Myers, Matthew B. "The performance implications of strategic fit of relational norm governance strategies in global supply chain relationships," *Journal of International Business Studies*, vol. 36, no. 3 (2005).

Hagedoorn, John, Cloodt, Danielle, and Kanenburg, Hans van. "Intellectual property rights and the governance of international R&D partnerships," *Journal of International Business Studies*, vol. 36, no. 2 (2005).

Hansen, Morten T., and Løvås, Bjorn. "How do multinational companies leverage technological competencies? Moving from single to interdependent explanations," *Strategic Management Journal*, vol. 25, nos. 8/9 (2004).

Hatani, Faith. "The logic of spillover interception: the impact of global supply chains in China," *Journal of World Business*, vol. 44, no. 2 (2009).

Helper, Susan, and Mari Sake. "Supplier relations in Japan and the United States: are they converging?," *Sloan Management Review* (2012).

Holweg, Matthias. "The genealogy of lean production," *Journal of Operations Management*, vol. 25, no. 2 (2007).

Kotabe, Masaaki, and Murray, Janet Y. "Linking product and process innovations and modes of international sourcing in global competition: a case of foreign multinational firms," *Journal of International Business Studies*, vol. 21, no. 3 (1990).

Kotabe, Masaaki, and Omura, Glenn S. "Sourcing strategies of European and Japanese multinationals: a comparison," *Journal of International Business Studies*, vol. 20, no. 1 (spring 1989).

Mehri, Darius. "The darker side of lean: an insider's perspective on the realities of the Toyota production system," *Academy of Management Perspectives*, vol. 20, no. 2 (2006).

Nieto, María, and Rodríguez, Jesús Alici. "Offshoring of R&D: looking abroad to improve innovation performance," *Journal of International Business Studies*, vol. 42 (April 2011).

Nohria, Nitin, and Ghoshal, Sumantra. *The Differentiated Network: Organizing Multinational Corporations for Value Creation* (San Francisco, CA: Jossey-Bass, 1997).

Ojah, Kalu, and Monplaisir, Leslie. "Investors' valuation of global product design and development," *Journal of International Business Studies*, vol. 34, no. 5 (September 2003).

Ørberg Jensen, Peter D., and Pedersen, Torben. "The economic geography of offshoring: the fit between activities and local context," *Journal of Management Studies*, vol. 48, no. 2 (March 2011).

Patel, Pari, and Pavitt, Keith. "Large firms in the production of the world's technology: an important case of 'non-globalization'," *Journal of International Business Studies*, vol. 22, no. 1 (1991).

Purvis, Laura, Gosling, Jonathan, and Naim, Mohamed M. "The development of a lean, agile and leagile supply network taxonomy based on differing types of flexibility," *International Journal of Production Economics*, vol. 151 (2014).

Quinn, James Brian, and Hilmer, Frederick G. "Strategic outsourcing," *Sloan Management Review*, vol. 35, no. 4 (summer 1994).

Reddy, Prasada. "New trends in globalization of corporate R&D and implications for innovation capability in host countries: a survey from India," *World Development*, vol. 25, no. 11 (November 1997).

Rondinelli, Dennis, and Berry, Michael, "Multimodal transportation, logistics, and the environment: managing interactions in a global economy," *European Management Journal*, vol. 18, no. 4 (August 2000).

Rugman, Alan M., and Bennett, Jocelyn. "Technology transfer and world product mandating," *Columbia Journal of World Business*, vol. 17, no. 4 (winter 1982).

Rugman, Alan M., and Brain, Cecilia. "Regional strategies of multinational pharmaceutical firms," *Management International Review*, vol. 44, special issue 3 (2004).

Rugman, Alan M., Jing, Li, and Oh, Chang Hoon. "Are supply chains global or regional?," *International Marketing Review*, vol. 26, no. 4/5 (2009).

Rugman, Alan M., and Verbeke, Alain. "Subsidiary-specific advantages in multinational enterprises," *Strategic Management Journal*, vol. 22, no. 3 (March 2001).

Serapio, Manuel G., Jr. "Macro-micro analyses of Japanese direct R&D investments in the US automotive and electronics industries," *Management International Review*, vol. 33, no. 3 (1993).

Shah, Rachna, and Ward, Peter T. "Lean manufacturing: context, practice bundles, and performance," *Journal of Operations Management*, vol. 21, no. 2 (2003).

Swamidass, Paul M., and Kotabe, Masaaki. "Component sourcing strategies of multinationals: an empirical study of European and Japanese multinationals," *Journal of International Business Studies*, vol. 24, no. 1 (1993).

Vandermerwe, Sandra. "Increasing returns: competing for customers in the global market," *Journal of World Business*, vol. 32, no. 4 (winter 1997).

Yip, George S. "Global strategy: in a world of nations?," *Sloan Management Review*, vol. 31, no. 1 (fall 1989).

Chapter 13

MARKETING STRATEGY

Contents

Objectives of the chapter

Every multinational has a marketing strategy designed to help identify opportunities and take advantage of them. This plan of action typically involves consideration of four primary areas: the product or service to be sold, the way in which the output will be promoted, the pricing of the good or service, and the distribution strategy to be used in getting the output to the customer. The primary purpose of this chapter is to examine the fundamentals of international marketing strategy. We will look at five major topics: market assessment, product strategy, promotion strategy, price strategy, and place strategy. We will consider such critical marketing areas as product screening, modification of goods and services in order to adapt to local needs, modified product life cycles, advertising, personal selling, and ways in which MNEs tailor-make their distribution systems.

The specific objectives of this chapter are to:

1 *Examine* the process used to conduct an international market assessment of goods and services.

2 *Study* the criteria that affect an MNE's decision to alter a good or service in order to adapt it to local market tastes.

3 *Describe* some of the ways in which MNEs use advertising and personal selling techniques to promote their products in worldwide markets.

4 *Review* some of the major factors that influence international pricing and distribution strategies.

ACTIVE LEARNING CASE

Adidas: promoting a global sports brand

Adidas was established in 1949 by Adolf Dassler and has become one of the largest brands in the sporting industry. The clever use of a three-stripe logo design has made the Adidas brand recognizable across the world. The Adidas Group consists of approximately 180 subsidiaries, which include Reebok, TaylorMade-Adidas Golf, Rockport, and CCM Hockey. The group's product portfolio is vast, ranging from footwear and clothing to accessories (bags, watches, eyewear, etc.). In 2014 Adidas employed 53,731 employees, 33 percent of whom were located in European emerging markets, 24 percent in North America, 21 percent in western Europe, 8 percent in China, and 8 percent in Latin America. The group's headquarters are located in Herzogenaurach, Germany and in 2014 the group's profit was recorded as $7.71 billion (€6.92 billion).

Global marketing strategy

Adidas's marketing beliefs revolve around the philosophy that consumers want choice; hence it incorporates the use of a multi-brand strategy which capitalizes on both a mass-market approach and a niche market or segmenting approach. The firm maintains a wide range of products but with a unifying brand, so managing and enhancing this brand is its main core competence. Recognizing the importance of effective international marketing, Adidas places the majority of its investments in the highest-potential markets. For instance, Adidas has been heavily investing in emerging markets, such as China and Russia, while simultaneously targeting underpenetrated markets such as the United States.

The ability to make slight modifications in the design of products has allowed Adidas to acquire a large catalog comprising a diverse range of sporting products ranging from mass to niche. Therefore, Adidas is able to take advantage of economies of scale and price its products accordingly in order to tap into nearly every country in the world, (ideally) overcoming any cultural differences. Furthermore, Adidas has established a series of promotional partnerships with an extensive range of sports associations, namely UEFA, FIFA, NBA, NFL, NHL, and the Olympic Games. In some cases, these partnerships date back to the earliest years of the firm. So, how has Adidas used these key sporting events to engage consumers across the world and promote its own brand identity? And how effective has this strategy been? We examine the firm's involvement with the 2012 Olympic Games and the 2014 FIFA World Cup to answer these questions.

2012 Olympic Games

With over 340 independent manufacturing partners spanning Asia, America, and Europe, Adidas continually develops innovative products which help athletes perform to their very best. Furthermore, Adidas has consistently built its marketing campaigns around various iconic athletes and sport personalities. Adidas's involvement with the Olympic Games can be traced back to the debut of Adidas's running shoes in Amsterdam (1928). In addition, multiple iconic achievements have involved athletes wearing Adidas's products in the Olympic Games such as:

- Jesse Owens, Berlin, 1936 (four gold medals);
- Muhammad Ali, Rome, 1960 (gold medal);
- Dick Fosbury, Mexico, 1968 (new back technique for high jump); and
- Nadia Comaneci, Montreal, 1976 (perfect 10).

Adidas anticipated that the London 2012 Olympic Games would be a key event at which it could promote its brand and expand its share of the performance sportswear and fashion sportswear market. The firm saw the UK as a style trendsetter in music and fashion for other parts of the world and this shaped the way it used the 2012 Olympic Games as a platform for targeting a more global audience. The sponsorship deal agreed by Adidas represented a new record as the broadest range of sportswear rights acquired in Olympic history. Adidas gained the right to be the "Official Sportswear Partner of the London 2012 Olympic Games" and positioned itself as the exclusive licensee of all branded London 2012 clothing items. To guide this investment Adidas set itself four marketing objectives:

- to ensure a clear association as Sportswear Partner of London 2012, Team GB, and Paralympics GB;
- to engage and excite the 14–19-year-old audience in order to drive brand preference in the UK;
- to deliver a licensed product return on investment (ROI) (branded and event branded licensee rights); and
- to become the most talked about sports brand in 2012.

One of the crucial factors for achieving its sponsorship goals was the company's direct involvement with the design and development of the athletes' kit. This provided a gateway for Adidas to connect with the target audience, while simultaneously developing new products to meet commercial sales targets. Adidas hired Stella McCartney (Paul's daughter) to

▶

create an innovative kit design and this led to the deconstructed union jack flag design.

Adidas involved the use of the likes of Jessica Ennis and Tom Daley when featuring TV adverts to increase support for Team GB. Furthermore, Adidas included TV adverts which highlighted the best UK talent across sport, including David Beckham, Wretch 32, and Derrick Rose. Adidas went on to exploit the use of social media when raising awareness of its campaign and #takethestage on Twitter became the prominent trend when supporting Team GB. In addition, Adidas used YouTube to increase awareness among customers—the reactions of individuals who were greeted with David Beckham's surprise appearance received over 3.2 million views. Adidas closely monitored every aspect of its promotional campaign, which enabled it to determine whether becoming the Official Sportswear Partner of the London Games and exclusive licensee of all branded products was financially effective. Table 13.1 illustrates how Adidas measured each of its marketing objectives. Observing this table, Adidas decided that its marketing campaign had paid off as each of its marketing objectives had been met in accordance with its measures.

2014 FIFA World Cup

Adidas not only targets the Olympic Games as an iconic event in order to promote its products, but regularly follows a similar social media strategy during prominent soccer tournaments. For the 2014 FIFA World Cup, Adidas was the official ball supplier and managed to drive up merchandise sales via the use of effective social media engagement. In order to engage with Brazilian fans prior to the 2014 World Cup, Adidas invited fans to cast votes regarding the official name of the match ball. After receiving over 1 million votes the ball was officially named as "Brazuca," which is an informal expression representing Brazilian Pride.

With a marketing slogan of "All In or Nothing," Adidas was directly competing against Nike's marketing campaign of "Risk Everything." Even though Nike had acquired Cristiano Ronaldo at $8.3 million as the second most expensive shoe endorser ever, Adidas's market research had identified that fans were interested more in receiving the latest information as quickly as possible rather than in the promotion of products. With this in mind, Adidas developed an innovative live hour-by-hour calendar which provided all the attention-grabbing information fans would need before a game even started. This required a heavy investment in marketing, but was deemed a success as Adidas's integrated marketing strategy generated millions of tweets while making it the most talked about brand during the 2014 World Cup. Furthermore, Adidas managed to gain the endorsement of two key players who reached the finals: Lionel Messi and Mesut Özil, who wore the Adidas Predator Instinct Battle Pack and F50 soccer boots respectively. Furthermore, capturing a global audience, Adidas has also partnered FIFA World Cup tournaments in order to reward players for outstanding achievements throughout the competition, such as the Adidas Golden Ball, the Adidas Golden Boot, and the Adidas Golden Glove.

Table 13.1 Adidas's marketing objectives and measurements

Marketing objective	Measurement
Ensure a clear association as Sportswear Partner of London 2012, Team GB, and Paralympics GB	• Adidas generated the highest number of articles among local sponsors (ranked third behind McDonald's and Coca-Cola). • 44 percent of 16–24-year-olds were aware of the sponsorship (Adidas's closest competitor achieved 16 percent).
Engage and excite the 14–19-year-old audience in order to drive brand preference in the UK	• YouGov (a measure of public opinion) score increased from 4.2 to 16.5 during the Games. • Adidas ranked no. 1 by London 2012 Nielsen audience tracking for categories "inspiring" and "empowering." • Adidas' "Don't stop me now" video was the most viewed video on www.bbc.co.uk during the Games. • 8 million views of #takethestage content on YouTube, including 2.5 million views from 14–24-year-olds.
Deliver a licensed product ROI (branded and event branded licensee rights)	• 2 percent market share growth. • 100 million total licensed product sales in 2012. • More sales at Adidas's Oxford Street store in London in one week than at any other Adidas store ever.
Become the most talked about sports brand in 2012	• Increased Twitter followers by 25 percent. • 32 percent share of sponsor traffic on Twitter. • 128 million Twitter impressions for #takethestage.

Source: Planning Effective Marketing Strategies for a Target Audience', an Adidas case study, businesscasestudies.co.uk.

As an MNE, Adidas's marketing mix is partly tailored for specific markets by identifying factors such as cultural and social differences. But it also benefits from the attractiveness and selling-power of global sporting superstars. Whatever their nationality or ethnicity, consumers from different nations and cultures all over the world venerate their prowess and see them as role models to emulate. The sports entertainment industry is also growing and Adidas has emphasized sports marketing within certain global regions, such as China, Russia, the UK, and the United States. Adidas aims to be a market-oriented organization which continually identifies and reviews consumer needs to guarantee that the products it releases meet customer requirements. Adidas aims not just to meet its customers' needs but to surpass their expectations by constantly adapting its products and acquiring key athletes and sporting personalities to showcase them. Even though gaining sponsorship deals with large sports events such as the

Olympic Games and FIFA World Cup is extremely expensive, via the use of well-organized marketing strategies and clear objectives, Adidas has identified a clear way of engaging deeply with consumers. It is important to note that Adidas was largely supportive of Team GB before, during, and after the Olympic Games, which helped it ensure the full support of the team's athletes. Effective marketing strategies, such as the London 2012 campaign and the "All In or Nothing" campaign during the 2014 World Cup, and the company's ability to deliver innovative products both underpin the continued success of Adidas.

Sources: Adidas, *Annual Report*, 2014; Leonid Bershidsky, "Why Adidas beat Nike at the World Cup," *Bloomberg View*, July 11 2014; *Times 100 Business Case Studies*, "Planning effective marketing strategies for a target audience: an Adidas case study," businesscasestudies.co.uk; http://www.dcmarketingpro.com/what-the-2014-world-cup-taught-us-about-effective-integrated-marketing; Chris Daniels, "Sponsors connect World Cup with US soccer growth," *PR Week*, December 20, 2013; Sebastian S. Vlasich, "Adidas—a global sports strategy", *Business Development Strategies*, January 1, 2012.

1 How could Adidas use international market assessment to maximize sales in different global markets?

2 Why does Adidas focus on promoting a single global brand and how do sports events help this strategy?

3 How would currency fluctuations affect Adidas's profit in the US market?

4 How does Adidas use online platforms and social media to promote its events, its sponsored athletes, and its products?

INTRODUCTION

International marketing
The process of identifying the goods and services that customers outside the home country want and then providing them at the right price and place

International marketing is the process of identifying the goods and services that customers outside the home country want and then providing them at the right price and location.[1] In the international marketplace, this process is similar to that carried out at home, but with some important modifications that can adapt marketing efforts to the needs of the specific country or geographic locale.[2] For example, some MNEs are able to use the same strategy abroad as they have at home. This is particularly true in promotions where messages can carry a universal theme (see the **Active Learning Case: Adidas**). Many fast-food franchises apply the same ideas because they have found that people everywhere have the same basic reasons for choosing their restaurants to eat in. In most cases, however, a company must tailor-make its strategy so that it appeals directly to the local customer.

In order to customize effectively, to enter a new market, MNEs must make a number of strategic decisions which fall into five broad areas: market assessment, product decisions, promotion strategies, pricing decisions, and place or distribution strategies. The latter four areas—product, promotion, price, and place—are often referred to as the four Ps of marketing,[3] and they constitute the heart of international marketing efforts.

INTERNATIONAL MARKET ASSESSMENT

International market assessment
An evaluation of the goods and services that the multinational can sell in the global marketplace

International marketing strategy starts with **international market assessment**, an evaluation of the goods and services that the MNE can sell in the global marketplace. This assessment typically involves a series of analyses aimed at pinpointing specific offerings and geographic targets. The first step is called the initial screening.

Initial screening: basic need and potential

Initial screening
The process of determining the basic need and potential of the multinational's goods and services in foreign markets

Initial screening is the process of determining the basic need and potential of the MNE's goods and services in foreign markets. This screening answers the question: who might be interested in buying our output? International auto manufacturers list the EU countries, North America, and Japan as potential buyers. Boeing targets the countries that will be rebuilding their air fleets in the next few decades. Kellogg's, General Mills, and Nestlé are interested in the United States and the European Union as well as any developing nations that offer potential new markets.

One way to carry out initial screening is by examining the current import policies of other countries and identifying the goods and services being purchased from abroad. A second way is by determining local production. A third is to examine the demographic changes taking place in the country that will create new, emerging markets. These cursory efforts help an MNE to target potential markets. Following the initial screening, the company begins to narrow its selection.

Second screening: financial and economic conditions

Secondary screening is used to reduce the list of market prospects by eliminating those that fail to meet financial and economic considerations. Financial considerations include inflation rates, interest rates, expected returns on investment, the buying habits of customers, and the availability of credit. These factors are important in determining whether markets that passed the initial, general screening are also financially feasible.

Market indicators
Indicators used for measuring the relative market strengths of various geographic areas

Market size
An economic screening consideration used in international marketing; it is the relative size of each market as a percentage of the total world market

Market intensity
The richness of a market or the degree of purchasing power in one country as compared to others

Market growth
The annual increase in sales in a particular market

Economic considerations relate to a variety of market demand influences, including market indicators. **Market indicators** are used for measuring the relative market strengths of various geographic areas, and focus on three important areas: market size, market intensity, and market growth. **Market size** is the relative size of each market as a percentage of the total world market. For example, industrialized countries account for a sizable part of the market for cellular telephones, and a few nations such as the United States and Japan account for the largest percentage of this total. Nevertheless, non-industrialized countries with large populations also have a significant market size. In fact, China, the world's largest country in terms of population, is also the world's largest cell phone market in terms of subscribers.[4] **Market intensity** is the "richness" of the market, or the degree of purchasing power in one country compared to others. For example, the United States and Canada are extremely rich markets for automobiles, telephones, and computers, so MNEs selling these products tend to highlight these two countries. **Market growth** is the annual increase in sales. For example, the market for cell phones and laptop computers in the United States will continue to grow in the years ahead, whereas the market for autos will grow much more slowly. However, given the large purchasing power in the US economy, MNEs selling these products will continue to target the United States. In recent years, other economies, such as South Korea, have become increasingly rich in terms of purchasing power, so they too are now target markets for high-tech products. Infrastructure and economic development can also influence market growth. For example, consumers in developing countries who have not yet been able to acquire a fixed line might choose instead to purchase a portable phone.

Trend analysis
The estimation of future demand by either extrapolating the growth over the last three to five years and assuming that this trend will continue or by using some form of average growth rate over the recent past

Estimation by analogy
A method of forecasting market demand or market growth based on information generated in other countries, such as determining the number of refrigerators sold in the United States as a percentage of new housing starts and using this statistic in planning for the manufacture of these products in other world markets

Regression analysis
A mathematical approach to forecasting that attempts to test the explanatory power of a set of independent variables

Cluster analysis
A marketing approach to forecasting customer demand that involves grouping data based on market area, customer, or similar variables

Quite often these data are analyzed through the use of quantitative techniques. Sometimes these approaches are fairly simple. **Trend analysis**, for example, is the estimation of future demand either by extrapolating the growth over the last three to five years and assuming that this trend will continue, or by using some form of average growth rate over the recent past. A similar approach is **estimation by analogy**, through which forecasters predict market demand or growth based on information generated in other countries. For example, if the number of refrigerators sold in the United States is 2.5 times the number of new housing starts, a US MNE that is planning to manufacture these products in the European Union will estimate demand based on the same formula. A more sophisticated approach is the use of **regression analysis**, a mathematical approach to forecasting that attempts to test the explanatory power of a set of independent variables. In the case of selling refrigerators in the European Union, for example, these variables would include economic growth, per capita income, and the number of births, in addition to other variables such as new housing starts. Another sophisticated approach is **cluster analysis**, a marketing approach that involves grouping data on the basis of market area, customer, and so on, based on similar variables, so that a marketing strategy can be formulated for each group. For example, US MNEs providing services in such areas as insurance, legal, financial, and management consulting know that their approaches must often vary from country to country.

Third screening: political and legal forces

The third level of screening involves taking a look at political and legal forces. A primary consideration is entry barriers in the form of import restrictions or limits on local ownership of business operations. Analysis of these barriers often results in identifying loopholes around the various restrictions or data that indicate barriers are far less extensive than initially believed. For example, some MNEs have been able to sidestep legal restrictions by forming joint ventures with local firms. Production restrictions or limitations on profit remittance that restrict operating flexibility must also be considered. Government stability is an important factor in starting a successful operation; however, it is often difficult to predict. Another consideration is the protection offered for patents, trademarks, and copyrights. In some countries, such as China and Taiwan, pirating has been fairly common, resulting in markets being flooded with counterfeit or look-alike products. (Country risk analysis is dealt with more extensively in Chapter 15.)

Fourth screening: socio-cultural forces

The fourth level of screening typically involves the consideration of socio-cultural forces such as language, work habits, customs, religion, and values. As noted earlier, culture greatly affects the way people live, and MNEs need to examine how well their operations will fit into each particular culture. For example, although Japanese auto manufacturers have set up assembly plants in the United States, those operations are not identical to the ones in Japan because of the work habits and customs of Americans. In the United States, the work pace is less frantic and most people are unwilling to work the typical 5½-day week which is so common in Japan. Moreover, US managers are accustomed to going home to their families after work, whereas Japanese managers often go out for dinner and drinks and discuss business until late in the evening. MNEs will examine these socio-cultural differences in determining where to locate operations.

Another study by an advertising firm shows that Muslims in the United States are among the richest and best educated of the US population. Their buying patterns are heavily influenced by Islamic law. The religious beliefs and cultural norms of this subgroup of the US population particularly influence their buyer preferences in the consumer markets of food, finance, and packaged goods.[5]

Fifth screening: competitive environment

The fifth level of screening is typically focused on competitive forces. If three or four locations are equally attractive, an MNE will often make a final choice based on the degree of competition that exists in each locale. In some cases, companies do not want to enter markets where there is strong competition. However, they will often decide to enter a competitive market because they believe the potential benefits far outweigh the drawbacks. By going head-to-head with the competition, the company can force itself to become more efficient and effective, and thus improve its own competitiveness. The MNE can take market share away from competitors and put them on the defensive, forcing them to commit more resources to defending the market under attack and thereby reducing their ability to retaliate effectively. Of course, these conditions do not always hold true, but they help illustrate why MNEs consider entering markets that are dominated by competitors.

Final selection

Before making a final selection, MNEs usually enhance their information by visiting the sites and talking to trade representatives or local officials. Such field trips are very common and can do a great deal to supplement currently available information. Sometimes these trips take the form of a trade mission: a visit sponsored by commercial officers in a country's local embassy and designed to bring together executives from MNEs that are interested in examining the benefits of doing business in the particular country.

Based on the outcome of the screenings and the supplemental data, the MNE chooses which goods and services to offer overseas. The marketing strategy employed in this process revolves around what are commonly called the four Ps of marketing: product, promotion, price, and place.

✔ Active learning check

Review your answer to Active Learning Case question 1 and make any changes you like. Then compare your answer to the one below.

 How could Adidas use international market assessment to maximize sales in different global markets?

Adidas could use a number of market assessment tools to help it target particular markets to enter and sell its products, or expand its current sales. Because it sells relatively high-end consumer goods, a screening of financial and economic conditions would provide data on disposable income, local consumer preferences, and trends in buying patterns to estimate current and future demand for its products. This should be done alongside analyses of social and cultural forces which will affect consumer preferences and the likely effectiveness of the firm's marketing strategy. Global sports celebrities are more attractive as fashion icons in some parts of world than others. Variations in religion, ethnicity, and cultural norms are important factors when planning a global marketing campaign. Political and legal factors are usually linked to the sociocultural context and will affect how easily the firm can enter the market and do business locally. These also influence the local media, which Adidas is heavily reliant on for its marketing approach. Finally, it should assess the degree to which competitor brands are targeting a particular country market. This may indicate that it is attractive and worth focusing on, but competition will add costs and put pressure on the firm to customize its product offering in a particular market.

PRODUCT STRATEGIES

Product strategies vary depending on the specifics of the product itself and the characteristics of the target market segment. Some products can be manufactured and sold successfully both in the home country and abroad by using the same strategies. Other products must be modified or adapted and sold according to a specially designed strategy. Figure 13.1 shows a range of possibilities. Products and services located on the left side of the continuum require little modification; those on the right must be modified to fit the market. To some degree this range of options parallels the more general international business manager's challenge to strike an appropriate balance between being "global or local," to standardize or customize, to integrate across all dimensions of the business or respond to local differences.

Little or no modification

Industrial goods and technical services are good examples of products that need little or no modification. A bulldozer, a laptop, and a photocopying machine serve the same purposes and are used the same way in the home country as they are abroad. Alterations would be minor and would include such things as adapting the machine to the appropriate electric voltage or changing the language used for its instructions and labels. The same is true for many types of services. For example, international engineering and construction firms find that their product strategies are similar worldwide. People interested in having a dam or power plant constructed use the same basic concepts and have similar needs throughout the world. In fact, experience is the greatest selling point in convincing clients to hire an MNE in engineering or construction. Foreign design and construction firms that proved themselves in the Burj Al Arab Hotel project in Dubai, for example, were invited to participate in the unprecedented Palm Jumeirah artificial island project.

Companies with a strong international brand image have also been able to succeed without a differentiation strategy. For example, the world-famous Scotch Chivas Regal is sold in many countries and is identical in each one. Schweppes (tonic water) and Perrier are internationally known and are also identical worldwide.

Moderate to high modification

A number of factors can compel an MNE to use moderate to high product modification. These include economics, culture, local laws, and product life cycle.

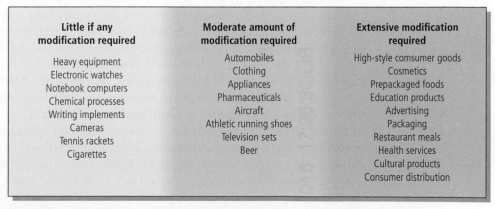

Little if any modification required	Moderate amount of modification required	Extensive modification required
Heavy equipment	Automobiles	High-style consumer goods
Electronic watches	Clothing	Cosmetics
Notebook computers	Appliances	Prepackaged foods
Chemical processes	Pharmaceuticals	Education products
Writing implements	Aircraft	Advertising
Cameras	Athletic running shoes	Packaging
Tennis rackets	Television sets	Restaurant meals
Cigarettes	Beer	Health services
		Cultural products
		Consumer distribution

Figure 13.1 Selected examples of product modification in the international arena

Economics

There are many examples of how economic considerations affect the decision to modify a product. For example, chewing gum packages often contain 10 to 20 sticks in the United States. But in many other countries, weak customer purchasing power necessitates packaging the gum with only five sticks. Countries vary in terms of the use of cars versus public transport and in terms of average house sizes (therefore storage space), so buying patterns also vary accordingly and firms must customize product size and packaging to suit local preferences.

Economics is also important when the cost of a product is either too high or too low to make it attractive in another country. For example, cash registers are electronic in economically advanced countries; virtually no one uses hand-cranked machines. However, in many other countries they are too expensive and sophisticated for most retail stores and small establishments, so MNEs like National Cash Roster continue to manufacture the hand-cranked versions. On the other hand, inexpensive calculators are widely used throughout the world, and many stores use handheld calculators to total customer purchases (although in some places calculations may be cross-checked for accuracy with an abacus).

Similarly, in economically advanced countries products are likely to have frills or extras, whereas only the basic model is offered in poorer countries. For example, bicycles in the United States are used for exercise and recreation and have a number of special features that make bicycle riding particularly enjoyable, whereas in many other countries they are a primary source of transportation. US bikes are built for comfort and ease of handling; elsewhere they are built for economy and ease of maintenance. As a result, manufacturers need to modify the product to fit customer needs.

Culture

A product must sometimes be adapted to different ways of doing things. Consider washing machines. The French prefer washers that load from the top, the British like front-loading units, the Germans prefer high-speed machines that take out most of the moisture in the spin-dry process, and the Italians like slower spin speeds because they prefer to hang-dry laundry in the sun. So manufacturers which sell washing machines in the European Union must produce a variety of different units.

Food is an item that often must be modified or sold differently. In fast-food franchises like McDonald's, portions of the menu are similar throughout the world while other items are designed to cater specifically to local tastes. Coffee in South American units tends to be a much stronger blend than that sold in North America. In certain parts of Europe and Asia, the food is more highly seasoned in keeping with local tastes. For products that are not modified, the marketing focus is different because of the way the item is used. Schweppes, for example, is typically served as a mixer in the United States and UK, where drinks like gin and tonic are popular. In France, however, it is drunk without alcohol. Clearly, marketing approaches differ in these two situations. The marketing message is also important when selling hard liquors. The products remain the same, but many places have social customs that frown on excessive consumption. In these cases, MNEs such as Seagram of Canada have tailored their advertising messages along the lines of moderate drinking and the use of mixers to reduce the alcoholic content per serving.

Culture also influences purchasing decisions on the basis of style or esthetics. Cosmetics and other beauty aids are good examples. Perfumes that sell well in Europe often have difficulty gaining market share in the United States because they do not appeal to American women. Similarly, many products that sell well in the United States, such as shampoos and deodorants, have limited market appeal elsewhere. People may not use these products, or they may find it hard to differentiate a product from local offerings. For example, Gillette has found it is difficult to develop a distinctive edge in selling toiletries because many people feel these products are all basically the same.

Convenience and comfort are other culturally driven factors that help explain the need for product modification. Early Japanese autos in the United States were designed to attack other foreign imports, specifically the VW Beetle. Researchers found that the two biggest complaints with the Beetle were the small amount of room in the back seat and the heater, which took too long to warm up the car. Aware that Americans wanted an economical car with these additional features, Japanese imports offered greater leg room for back seat passengers and a heater that was superior to the VW offering. Within a few years these imports had begun to erode VW's market share. Foreign manufacturers also identified a group that wanted several convenience and comfort features. The result has been the emergence of luxury Japanese and German cars that now compete extremely well with US models at the upper end of the market.

Other culturally based reasons for product modifications include color and language. In the United States, the color black is worn for mourning, whereas in other countries white is for mourning and thus is not used for consumer goods. Similarly, most American shampoos are light colored, whereas in some Oriental countries consumers prefer dark-colored shampoo. Language can be an important point of modification because a product may need to carry instructions about contents or use. In locations where two or more languages are spoken, such as Canada and Switzerland, this information is provided in all appropriate languages. Language is also important in conveying the right image for the product. Quite often it is difficult to replicate the message because the saying or slogan has no meaning in another language.

Local laws

Local laws can require product modification in order to meet environmental and safety requirements. For example, US emission-control laws have required Japanese and European car importers to make significant model changes before their autos can be sold in the United States. Food and pharmaceutical regulations require packaging and labeling that are often quite different from those in the home country. In Saudi Arabia, the label of any product containing animal fat or meat must clearly state the kind of animal used and the fact that no swine products are included. Brand name protection can also require product modification. Ford found that in Mexico it had to rename its Ford Falcon because this brand name was registered to another firm. The same thing happened to Ford in the case of the Mustang in Germany.

Product life cycle

Another reason for modifying a product is to cope with its limited product life cycle (PLC). Although Ford was extremely profitable in Europe during the 1980s, those earnings had disappeared by the early 1990s because Ford did not develop new, competitive products.[6] Contrast this to Coca-Cola of Japan, which introduces an average of one new soft drink per month and has the competition scurrying to keep up. Yet Kola Real has been particularly effective in offsetting the technology and marketing of Coca-Cola to bring its own products to market in Mexico.

One of the most effective strategies has been to shorten the PLC by offering new goods and services before the demand for the old ones has dropped significantly. Figure 13.2 provides a graphic illustration. Note that there are two types of PLCs: (1) the standard PLC, which covers an extended time continuum, often four to five years, and (2) a short life cycle that lasts a much shorter time. Many companies are discovering that by shortening the PLC and offering new product adaptations they are able to capture and retain a large market share. This is typically done by offering a new product, then modifying it, and

Weeby buys Tappy

The first Vietnamese technology company to be acquired by a Silicon Valley company was Tappy, bought by Weeby to gain access to the Asian mobile gaming market. Tappy was founded in January 2014 by Thuy Truong, a "serial entrepreneur" educated at the University of Southern California and now based in her native country, Vietnam, and Singapore. Her first start-up was "Parallel Frozen Yogurt," a frozen yogurt chain launched in 2008. She then co-founded GreenGar, in October 2010, which produced apps for iOS, Mac, and Android platforms. Among the popular of these was the "Whiteboard: Collaborative Drawing and Brain Tuner" app GreenGar, which achieved 13 million downloads in less than three years.

Tappy is a location-based social messaging application which enables people at a bar or an event to connect to each other. Weeby.co, based in Mountain View, California, is a cloud-based game-building platform which bought Tappy for an undisclosed seven-figure sum. Having raised $12 million in venture capital, Weeby.co has invested in messaging, gaming social networks, and game production, through its main product Weeby.co Producer. This allows anyone to create a game and launch it on Weeby.co's platform. Weeby.co's CEO, Michael Carter said:

> The team at Tappy are veteran operators in the Southeast Asia region. By acquiring Tappy and bringing on board the management team, we're jumping forward half a decade in business and strategic partnerships. The region is one of the fastest growing on the planet.

The investment is part of an upsurge in interest from foreign firms in the Vietnamese tech sector. First, it is a large and growing market, with an expanding middle class who tend to use their mobiles, rather than laptops or games consoles, to both play and communicate. It is also a potential entry point to other markets in Southeast Asia. Second, it is home to a rising number of high-tech start-ups in social media sector. Misfit Wearables, a small but very global high-tech firm based in San Francisco, Seoul, and Ho Chi Minh City, recently received a significant investment from Chinese smartphone manufacturer Xiaomi.

Foreign firms are entering into alliances or joint ventures with, or acquiring, local firms partly to tap into local skills and expertise to produce better products. They are following larger MNEs which have already invested in consumer electronics, computing, and communications sectors to take advantage of the country's cheap but well-educated labor force. Samsung is the largest foreign investor with almost $10 billion of FDI underpinning $20 billion in export turnover in 2013 (18 percent of Vietnam's total exports). But foreign firms are also using these "modes of entry" (alliance, joint venture or M&A) to access a growing market of young tech-savvy consumers who appear to be ahead of the curve in mob services. The Vietnamese are buying, adopting and co-developing online services in ways that are likely to be followed by Western consumers in the future.

The Vietnamese government is trying to make it easier for firms to set up in the country, partly by easing restrictions on foreign ownership. It is also investing in new business growth, with an emphasis on technology-based start-ups. Vietnam's Minister of Science and Technology, Nguyen Quan, said he believed start-ups should grow from universities or research institutes. "The country can now start with a start-up university, then a start-up city, to gradually become a start-up nation," he emphasized. Quan revealed the goal of having 5,000 tech companies by 2020.

If this is to happen, global entrepreneurs like Thuy Truong are an essential ingredient. They have the skills and the drive to build innovative new small firms. But they also bring an international network, from their personal experience living and working in different places, integrating skills and expertise (with different costs) from different locations to add value for consumers wherever they are located. Policy-makers like Nguyen Quan would do well to understand what attracts young entrepreneurs to return to their homeland. By developing the attractiveness of the home-country environment, Vietnam could encourage a growing number of entrepreneurs to invest their creative energies back in their home country.

Sources: Edward Barbour-Lacey, "Samsung increases investment into Vietnam's Saigon hi-tech park," *Vietnam Briefing*, October 8, 2014; Anh-Minh Do and Steven Millward, "Silicon Valley's Weeby.co leaps into Asia by acquiring Vietnam's Tappy," May 26, 2015; Duncan Riley, "Cloud games platform provider Weeby.co acquires Vietnamese social app Tappy," *Silicon Angle*, May 26, 2015; https://www.crunchbase.com; "Vietnam startup scene poised to takeoff as ecosystem comes together," *Deal Street Asia*, May 18, 2015; James Hookway, "Tech firms flock to Vietnam: global names accelerate one of the developing world's fastest transformations ever, *Wall Street Journal*, September 27, 2013.

bringing out a new version before the competition can effectively combat the first offering. For example, Intel first offered a Pentium processor. This was followed by the introduction of the Pentium II, Pentium III, and Pentium IV processor, each of which was faster than its predecessor. As processors get faster, they consume more energy and generate more heat, so for the meantime, until these issues are resolved, Intel cannot produce faster processors.

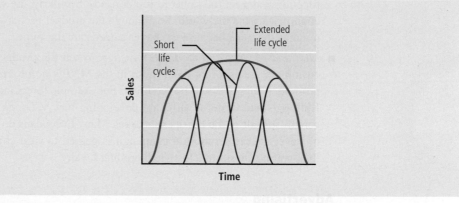

Figure 13.2 Product life cycles: two different approaches

As a result, more task-specific chips have been introduced.[7] The Centrino processor now caters to wireless users and the Desktrino caters to desktop users. The video game platform market provides another example of strategic continuous innovation. Nintendo and Sony constantly introduce new products and games to capture the market, always leaving the competition scurrying to keep up.[8] As long as a firm can continue such an adaptation strategy, it can outmode the old product (and those of competitors as well) and maintain market position. At some point the competition may gain the advantage by offering a product that revolutionizes the field, but as long as a product improvement strategy remains viable, the firm will continue to be the product leader. This strategy is being implemented by MNEs throughout the world.

PROMOTION

Promotion
The process of stimulating demand for a company's goods and services

Promotion is the process of stimulating demand for a company's goods and services.[9] MNEs promote their goods and services through advertising and personal selling. The specific approach used, however, will be determined by the nature of the product.

Nature of the product

In promoting a product, a company can use a variety of approaches. The choice is heavily influenced by whether the firm believes the same message can be used worldwide or needs to be adapted, and whether the product will remain the same or need to be modified. Here are four variations on this theme:

- *Identical product and identical message.* This approach is used when the MNE intends to sell the same product worldwide and believes that an identical promotional appeal can be used in all markets. A. T. Cross, for example, uses this strategy because writing instruments do not need to be adapted to local markets.

- *Identical product but different message.* This strategy is used when the product satisfies a different need in various markets. For example, in the United States many car companies tout the luxury and convenience of their products, whereas in other countries the same cars are promoted on the basis of their fuel efficiency or ability to meet basic transportation needs.

- *Modified product but same message.* This strategy is used when the market requires a different version of the product but the needs of the consumer are the same. For example, whether washing machines load from the top or the front, they provide the same function and meet the same customer needs. Similarly, the seasoning of foods differs in countries around the world. So although the product is changed, the promotion message remains the same because the buyer's needs are the same.

■ *Modified product and modified message.* When the product use and buying habits of customers are different from those in the MNE's home market, both the product and promotion message will be modified. For example, breakfast cereal companies such as Kellogg's and General Mills are developing new versions of their popular American cereals for sale in the European market. Many Europeans do not eat cereal for breakfast, however, so the promotion campaign is geared toward changing eating habits rather than getting consumers to switch product loyalty.

Advertising

Advertising
A non-personal form of promotion in which a firm attempts to persuade consumers to a particular point of view

Advertising is a non-personal form of promotion in which a firm attempts to persuade consumers to a particular point of view. In many cases MNEs use the same advertising message worldwide; again, because many products fulfill similar worldwide needs, a company can use a universal message and reduce advertising costs at the same time. However, there are times when the advertising must be adapted to the local market.[10] Two of the most common reasons are that (1) the way in which the product is used differs from that in the home country, and (2) the advertising message does not make sense if translated directly. An example of the latter is the Nike commercials that encourage the viewer to "Just do it," or Budweiser commercials that ask, "Why ask why?" These ads make sense to American viewers, but they are too culturally grounded to be used in many other countries, and would leave the viewer confused as to what the advertiser was saying. As a result, advertisers are very careful to tie their messages to buyer needs and wants. On the other hand, there are many advertisements that have been only moderately modified or carried in their entirety because they do make sense in other cultures. For example, Nike's ads featuring such internationally known sports stars as Tiger Woods and David Beckham transcend national boundaries, especially after the media exposure they have received. The case **International Business Strategy in Action: IKEA in international markets** provides some examples of how this is being done.

INTERNATIONAL BUSINESS STRATEGY IN ACTION

IKEA in international markets

From its founding as a small, private Swedish furniture retailer in 1943, IKEA has grown to become a multinational business with 147,000 employees and annual sales of €28.7 billion in 2014. As of 2014, the IKEA Group has operations in 42 countries, with 315 stores in 27 countries belonging to the IKEA Group. IKEA continues to grow with 716 million store visits and 1.5 billion visits to ikea.com in 2014, which represented increases of 4.7 percent and 15 percent respectively in comparison with 2013.

The parent company of the IKEA Group of companies INGKA Holding BV (the Netherlands) is owned by the Stichting INGKA Foundation in the Netherlands. The Foundation was founded in 1982 by the IKEA founder, Mr. Ingvar Kamprad, to create an ownership structure and an organization that stand for independence and taking a long-term approach. It has two purposes: to reinvest in the IKEA group and to fund charity through the Stichting Foundation. The company is headquartered in Delft, the Netherlands.

The 2014 annual report makes it clear that IKEA is a home-region-based multinational in terms of sales, purchases, and employees. For the year 2014, IKEA generated

69 percent of its total sales from Europe, 15 percent from North America, and 9 percent from Asia and Australia. In addition, IKEA purchases 59 percent of goods for sale from Europe, 35 percent from Asia, and 3 percent from North America. But this breakdown over-simplifies what IKEA does well. Muscovites and Londoners can buy towels produced in Turkey at any one of the retailer's warehouse stores. The firm has a standard product set worldwide, but benefits from huge economies of scale in sourcing (reducing cost) and creative product development (enhancing product attractiveness).

This internationalization process is all the more remarkable in that IKEA has remained true to the basic philosophy of its founder, Ingvar Kamprad, throughout its global expansion. Kamprad redesigned the furniture industry by introducing knock-down kits that customers could take away from the store and assemble themselves, enabling the company to stock larger quantities of furniture in its warehouses. Costs were lowered because these kits were easier to transport and took up less space in IKEA's large warehouse stores, and there was no need for assembly or delivery. In turn, customers could have their furniture immediately and could transport it in their own cars, saving on delivery costs. IKEA did a lot more than just provide convenient, easy-to-transport products, however. First, the products are carefully designed and more stylish than bargain do-it-yourself competitors. Second, IKEA changed furniture shopping from its traditional frosty "showroom" mentality to a more "fun" place with children's playpens, nurseries, and cafés in the stores. Indeed, a trip to an IKEA store is entertainment for the entire family. IKEA also built on the fast-growing informal suburban culture by providing abundant parking.

IKEA's relaxed, informal, yet efficient image was extended to Oslo and Denmark in the 1960s. It entered Switzerland in 1973, and Munich in 1974. By 1980, IKEA had opened an additional ten stores across Germany and followed this with an expansion through western Europe that culminated with its entry into the UK in 1987. In 1990, it entered the eastern European market with a store in Hungary; shortly after it entered Poland, the Czech Republic, and Slovakia. In 2000, it opened its first store in Moscow.

Expansion into other parts of the triad has been slower. In Asia and Oceania, IKEA opened its first store in Australia in 1975 and in Singapore in 1978. But its next expansion was in 1988, when it entered Hong Kong. Taiwan, Malaysia, and mainland China were added in the 1990s. In North America, IKEA opened a store in 1976 in Canada and used its Canadian operations to expand into the United States in 1985. The company also has operations in the Middle East.

Source: ALANDAWSONPHOTOGRAPHY/Alamy Stock Photo

IKEA also brought innovation to the logistics of furniture production by setting up groups of key suppliers to produce components at low cost. It has more than 1,000 suppliers in 51 countries around the world. These subcontractors, in turn, make money by getting large-volume orders for standardized components from IKEA.

The company also has kept tight control over product design and quality to maintain its brand name and the distinctive identity of its furniture. It was able to expand rapidly because it did not have to establish expensive manufacturing facilities around Europe, but rather retained centralized control over the subcontractors.

IKEA has recently been heavily investing in the sustainability of its operations as it currently owns 224 wind turbines and has installed over 700,00 solar panels on its buildings. In 2014 IKEA was recorded as producing 42 percent of the total energy consumption it requires from its own renewable sources. Furthermore, IKEA has predicted that by 2020 it will be energy independent as the energy produced from its renewable sources will exceed the total energy consumption it requires.

IKEA's marketing strategy has been to build on the Swedish home-base stereotype of clean and efficient service. All furniture is well designed, modern, functional, durable, of high quality, and price competitive. Its image and brand name are well established and have survived numerous imitators. As a result, IKEA has been able to move from its Scandinavian base to being a strong regional player in Europe, and is now competing successfully in the global arena. The firm increasingly relies on a web-based interface with customers, with different websites for different countries to reflect local tastes. As with many consumer products firms, this is evolving from being just a marketing and sales tool into a market-research tool. The 3D kitchen designer, for example, allows customers to design their own kitchens online using appliances and furniture from IKEA. IKEA can then use these designs to understand changing customer preferences.

▶

Overall, IKEA is a successful multinational business because it has introduced a highly differentiated product into a traditional industry and has built a globally recognized brand name for high-quality, inexpensive, and attractive furniture. It has also combined the generic strategies of differentiation, low cost, and niching, and has outsourced both production and delivery components of the value chain.

Website: www.ikea.com

Sources: IKEA, *Annual Report*, 2015; Christopher A. Bartlett and Ashish Nanda, "Ingvar Kamprad and IKEA," Harvard Business School Case No. 9–390–132; Joseph R. D'Cruz and Alan M. Rugman, "Developing international competitiveness: the five partners model," *Business Quarterly*, vol. 58, no. 2 (winter 1993), pp. 60–72; James Schofield, "IKEA wows the Russians," *BBC News*, February 22, 2002; Patrick Jackson, "IKEA's enormous niche market," *BBC News*, August 1, 2003; www.ikea.com; www.hoovers.com; Louise Armitstead, "Ikea reveals profits for first time to dispel 'secretive' image," *Telegraph*, October 1, 2010; IKEA, *Welcome Inside 2010 Update*, http://www.ikea.com/ms/en_GB/pdf/yearly_summary/Welcome_inside_2010_update.pdf

As in the United States, MNEs use several media to carry their advertising messages. The three most popular are television, radio, and newspapers. Some of the major differences between the approach used in the United States and that used in other countries include government regulation of media advertising and the fact that many stations do not carry advertising, although in recent years this has been changing. In particular, the use of television advertising has been increasing in Europe, whereas in other areas of the world, such as South America and the Middle East, newspapers remain the major medium for promotion efforts. However, there are restrictions on what can be presented. Examples include: (1) some countries prohibit **comparative advertising**, in which firms compare their products with those of the competition; (2) some countries do not allow certain products to be advertised because they want to discourage their use (such as alcoholic beverages and cigarettes) or because they want to protect national industries from MNE competition; and (3) some countries (such as Islamic nations) censor the use of any messages considered erotic.

Comparative advertising
The comparing of similar products for the purpose of persuading customers to buy a particular one

 Active learning check

Review your answer to Active Learning Case question 2 and make any changes you like. Then compare your answer to the one below.

2 **Why does Adidas focus on promoting a single global brand and how do sports events help this strategy?**

A simple answer to the first part of this question is: "because it can." Although it has a broad portfolio of products in terms of styles and types of sports equipment—particularly shoes—Adidas sells the kind of product that needs little or no modification or customization for local markets. Geographic segmentation is much less important than segmentation by income (luxury/premium to mass-market) and age group. Sports events help promote a standard brand because sport is a global phenomenon. There is arguably more of a shared interest in key sports (athletics, swimming, soccer, etc.) across different cultures than in music, art or cinema. This enables Adidas to reap huge economies of scale not just in manufacturing but more importantly in marketing and brand promotion.

Personal selling

Personal selling
A direct form of promotion used to persuade customers to a particular point of view

Personal selling is a direct form of promotion used to persuade customers to a particular point of view. Some goods, such as industrial products or those that require explanation or description, rely heavily on personal selling. Avon, the cosmetics company, has been very successful with this approach even in countries where people are unaccustomed to buying cosmetics from a door-to-door salesperson. In Mexico, for example, Avon managed to gain acceptance by first introducing the idea of personal selling through a massive advertising campaign, so that housewives became aware that the Avon salesperson was not a common door-to-door vendor but a professional trained to help clients look beautiful. Personal selling is also widely used in marketing products such as pharmaceuticals and sophisticated electronic equipment. For example, Pfizer and Upjohn use salespeople to call on doctors and other individuals who are in a position to recommend their products, and General Electric salespeople use the same approach in selling overseas that they use in the United States.

Because many international markets are so large, some MNEs have also turned to telemarketing. This approach has been very successful in the United States, and the overseas subsidiaries of such US firms as IBM and Ford have been using telemarketing to generate new sales. European firms such as Peugeot have been adopting this approach as well.

MNEs have also focused attention on recruiting salespeople on an international basis. In some countries this work is not highly regarded, so MNEs have given these people managerial titles that command importance, such as territory manager or zone manager. Recruiting local talent is extremely important because these people are often better able to sell to local customers. If the product requires special training to sell, MNEs often bring new salespeople to the home office for training, introduce them to those who are manufacturing the products, and create a feeling of teamwork among the field staff and personnel so that the salespeople are energized to go back into the field and sell.

PRICING

The pricing of goods and services in the international marketplace is often influenced by factors present in home-market pricing. These factors include government controls, market diversity, currency fluctuations, and price escalation forces.

Government controls

Every nation has government regulations that influence pricing practices. Some countries dictate minimum and maximum prices that can be charged to customers. Minimum prices can help protect local companies from more efficient international competitors because of a floor on price that can help ensure a profit for national firms. For example, if the minimum price for a particular type of personal computer is $1,000 and local companies can produce and sell the product for $700, they will make $300 a unit. Foreign competitors may be able to produce and sell the product for $500 and make a $500 profit per unit, but the minimum price laws prevent them from driving out local competition. Without this law, overseas competitors might price the unit at $600 and then raise the price dramatically after local competitors went out of business.

Governments also prohibit dumping, or the selling of imported goods at a price below cost or below the cost in the home country. The General Agreement on Tariffs and Trade (GATT) and WTO specifically prohibit this practice, which is designed to help MNEs drive out the local competition, establish a monopoly, and subsequently raise prices at will. A number of US firms have been influential in getting the US government to bring dumping charges against Japanese competitors.

Market diversity

Consumer tastes and demands vary widely in the international marketplace, resulting in MNEs having to price some of their products differently. For example, companies have found that they can charge more for goods sold overseas because of the demand. In the United States, there is a greater demand for light turkey meat than for dark turkey meat. The latter is typically sold at a lower price and is often purchased by animal food producers. However, the plump dark meat of turkey thighs has a strong market in Europe. As a result, firms like the Shenandoah Valley Poultry Company export thousands of metric tonnes of dark turkey meat to Europe each year.

A second factor influencing market diversity is the perceived quality of the product. For example, in the United States, German auto makers such as Mercedes found that some Americans were willing to pay a premium for German cars. In contrast, the Japanese are not willing to pay a premium for German autos, so Mercedes' pricing structure in Japan is different.

Another factor is the tax laws and attitudes about carrying debt. In the United States, some interest payments are tax deductible and most people have no aversion to assuming at least some debt. In many other countries, interest payments are not tax deductible and people are unaccustomed to carrying debt. In Japan, for example, little use is made of consumer credit. In pricing products, MNEs will adjust the local strategy to accommodate the impact of the tax laws and the consumer's willingness to assume debt.

Currency fluctuations

When selling products overseas, MNEs often end up assuming the risks associated with currency fluctuations (see Chapter 7). This risk is particularly important when the companies have a return on investment target because this objective can become unattainable if the local currency is devalued. For example, if it costs Mercedes $40,000 to manufacture and ship a particular model to the United States, and the company sells the car to its dealer for $50,000, Mercedes is making a 25 percent profit on the sale ($10,000/$40,000). However, if the dollar decreases in value by 10 percent against the euro, then the company's profit percentage will decline and the firm will have to choose between the following options: (1) increase the price of the car to the dealer to make up the loss of dollar value; (2) absorb the loss and leave the price the same; or (3) absorb part of the loss and raise the price to the dealer to make up the difference.

Price escalation forces

A problem similar to that discussed above is price escalation forces that drive up the cost of imported goods. In the case of Mercedes, for example, if the cost of the car rose from $30,000 to $33,000, the company would want to pass this along to the dealer. In the case of MNEs that sell through a marketing channel with a series of intermediaries, the effect of a price escalation can be even greater because everyone in the channel adds a percentage increase. For example, if an MNE exports and sells a consumer good for $10 to a large wholesaler and there are five additional intermediaries in the channel, each of whom marks up the good by 20 percent, as seen in Table 13.2, the final price to the consumer is $24.88. If the MNE's cost rises from $10 to $13, the final price to the consumer is now $32.35, a

Table 13.2 The effect of MNE pricing on final consumer costs

MNE price	Price charged by each intermediary				
	1	2	3	4	5
$10	$12.00	$14.40	$17.28	$20.74	$24.88
$13	$15.60	$18.72	$22.46	$26.96	$32.35

Ultimate effect of a $3 increase in MNE price: $32.35 − $24.88 = $7.47 or 30 percent.

30 percent increase. So price increases by the MNE can dramatically affect what the customer pays, and as long as the company continues to export rather than manufacture locally, price will be a key marketing consideration because of its effect on consumer demand. In this example it is likely that customer demand would drop substantially unless there were no effective substitutes for the product.

✔ Active learning check

Review your answer to Active Learning Case question 3 and make any changes you like. Then compare your answer to the one below.

③ How would currency fluctuations affect Adidas's profit in the US market?

To answer this question we need to understand where the firm's products are manufactured. According to its website (http://www.adidas-group.com/en/sustainability/supply-chain/supply-chain-structure/), 64 percent of its supply comes from Asian countries, including China, Vietnam, and Indonesia. We can then examine fluctuations in the US$ against a basket of these Asian currencies. So if the US$ fell in value by 10 percent against these other currencies, Adidas would earn 10 percent less from each sale *relative* to the costs of manufacture. Effectively its income in US$ is worth less in terms of the currencies which it uses to pay its suppliers. A more complex and real-world answer, however, would take into account other costs incurred by the firm. These include marketing, distribution, and sales in the United State (in US$) and across its European operations (in euros and possibly £s).

PLACE

The importance of international logistics was discussed in Chapter 12. The focus of attention here will be on the distribution differences among countries and conditions with which MNEs must be familiar. **Distribution** is the course that goods take between production and the final consumer. This course often differs on a country-by-country basis, and MNEs will spend a considerable amount of time in examining the different systems in place, the criteria to use in choosing distributors and channels, and how to employ distribution segmentation.[11]

Distribution
The course that goods take between production and the final consumer

Different distribution systems

It is often difficult to standardize a distribution system and use the same approach in every country because there are many individual differences to be considered. For example, countries such as Finland feature a predominance of general line retailers that carry a wide assortment of merchandise. In contrast, the wholesale and retail structure in Italy is characterized by a wide array of stores, many of which specialize or carry limited lines of merchandise. So in distributing goods in these two countries, MNEs need to employ different strategies.

Consumer spending habits can also negate attempts to standardize distribution. In the United States, many intermediaries are geared to handling credit sales, whereas in Japan most consumer purchases are on a cash basis. In both Germany and the United States, mail-order buying has increased dramatically in recent years, whereas in Portugal and Spain the market is quite small. So the route that the goods take to the consumer will vary.

The location where consumers are used to buying will also influence distribution. In economically developed countries where supermarkets have become commonplace, customers purchase a wide variety of food and other products under one roof. In most countries, however, purchases are made in smaller stores, and distribution requires the MNE or the local sales manager to deal with a large number of retailers, each of which is selling a small amount of merchandise. In recent years, some wholesalers and retailers have been expanding their operations to other countries. Wal-Mart, the giant US retailer, has expanded into Mexico and Europe; in 1999 it bought the British supermarket chain ASDA. However, most intermediaries operate exclusively within one country—another factor helping to explain why it is still difficult to standardize distribution on an international basis.

Choosing the best distribution system

MNEs use a number of criteria in creating the most efficient distribution system. One is to get the best possible distributors to carry their products. A key factor in evaluating potential distributors is the financial strength of the wholesaler or retailer, because the multinational wants to know that the distributor will be able to survive in the long run. MNEs that sell goods requiring periodic maintenance and servicing will be interested in businesses that can keep sufficient inventory on hand. This is particularly important when selling products such as autos, computers, and electronic equipment. A second factor is how well connected the distributor is in terms of knowing the right people and providing assistance in handling governmental red tape. This is a key consideration for Coca-Cola when choosing overseas distributors. A third factor is the number and types of product lines the distributor carries currently, so that the multinational can identify intermediaries that are most likely to give its goods a strong marketing push.

In many cases, distributors have competitive products or feel that they do not need to add any new product lines. If the multinational wants to tap into this distribution system, it will have to formulate an incentive program that is designed to convince the distributor to carry its products. Some of the ways in which this is done include (1) helping to pay for local promotion campaigns of the product, (2) providing generous sales incentives, (3) conducting marketing research to identify customer niches and sales forecasts to help the distributor decide how much inventory to carry,[12] and (4) ensuring that unsold or out-moded merchandise can be returned for a full refund.

Depending on the nature of the market and the competition, the multinational may give exclusive geographic distribution to one local seller or arrange to have a number of sellers jointly selling the product. For example, auto manufacturers often have more than one dealer in a major metropolis but are willing to give exclusive geographic distribution rights to dealers in rural areas. This is in contrast to food products that can be sold in a wide variety of outlets and for which exclusivity is unnecessary. In these cases the multinational will try to get a variety of distributors to carry the product.

STRATEGIC MANAGEMENT AND MARKETING STRATEGY

Marketing strategies play a key role in helping MNEs formulate an overall plan of action. Many approaches are directly related to the major areas that have been examined in this chapter, including ongoing market assessment, the use of effective pricing, internet marketing, and "open innovation." Table 13.3 illustrates the worldwide market penetration of several MNEs to be discussed in this section.

Ongoing market assessment

One of the major areas that MNEs are continuing to pay attention to is data collection and analysis for the purpose of developing and updating market assessments. In some cases

Table 13.3 International market penetration: location of subsidiaries, holdings, and joint ventures

General Motors (US)		Clarins (French)	Daewoo (Korean)	Mitsubishi Electric (Japanese)	Royal Dutch/Shell Group (Dutch/British)	
North America						
Canada		Canada	Canada	Canada	Canada	
Mexico		Mexico	Mexico	Mexico	Mexico	
US		US	US	US	US	
Western Europe						
Austria	Italy	Austria	France	Austria	Austria	Italy
Belgium	Luxembourg	Belgium	Germany	Belgium	Belgium	Luxembourg
Denmark	Netherlands	France	Greece	Denmark	Denmark	Netherlands
Finland	Norway	Germany	Ireland	Finland	Faroe Islands	Norway
France	Portugal	Italy	Italy	France	Finland	Portugal
Germany	Spain	Netherlands	Netherlands	Germany	France	Spain
Greece	Sweden	Portugal	Portugal	Greece	Germany	Sweden
Iceland	Switzerland	Spain	Spain	Iceland	Gibraltar	Switzerland
Ireland	Turkey	Switzerland	Sweden	Ireland	Greece	Turkey
	UK	UK	UK	Italy	Iceland	UK
				Luxembourg	Ireland	
				Netherlands		
				Norway		
				Portugal		
				Spain		
				Sweden		
				Switzerland		
				Turkey		
				UK		
Central and Eastern Europe						
Bulgaria	Malta	Russia	Croatia	Bulgaria	Bulgaria	Poland
Croatia	Montenegro		Czech Rep.	Croatia	Croatia	Romania
Cyprus	Poland		Hungary	Czech Rep.	Czech Rep.	Russia
Czech Rep.	Romania		Poland	Estonia	Estonia	Serbia
Estonia	Russian Fed.		Romania	Hungary	Hungary	Slovakia
Hungary	Serbia		Russia	Kazakhstan	Latvia	Slovenia
Latvia	Slovakia		Ukraine	Latvia	Lithuania	
Lithuania	Slovenia		Uzbekistan	Lithuania	Montenegro	
Macedonia				Montenegro		
				Poland		
				Romania		
				Russia		
				Serbia		
				Slovakia		
				Slovenia		
				Ukraine		
				Uzbekistan		
Asia and Oceania						
Australia		Hong Kong	Australia	Australia	Australia	Indonesia
China		Japan	Azerbaijan	Azerbaijan	Azerbaijan	Japan
Hong Kong		Malaysia	Bangladesh	China	Brunei	Kazakhstan
India		Singapore	China	Hong Kong	Cambodia	Malaysia
Indonesia		South Korea	Hong Kong	India	China	New Zealand
Japan		Taiwan	India	Indonesia	Fiji	Pakistan
Malaysia			Indonesia	Japan	Guam	Philippines
New Zealand			Japan	Malaysia	India	Singapore
Philippines			Malaysia	New Zealand		South Korea
Singapore			Myanmar	Pakistan		Sri Lanka

Table 13.3 (*continued*)

General Motors (US)	Clarins (French)	Daewoo (Korean)	Mitsubishi Electric (Japanese)	Royal Dutch/Shell Group (Dutch/British)	
Asia and Oceania					
South Korea		Philippines	Philippines		Taiwan
Taiwan		Singapore	Singapore		Thailand
Thailand		South Korea	South Korea		Vietnam
Vietnam		Taiwan	Taiwan		
		Thailand	Thailand		
		Vietnam	Vietnam		
South America, Central America, and the Caribbean					
Argentina		Argentina	Argentina	Argentina	Guatemala
Brazil		Brazil	Brazil	Barbados	Honduras
Chile		Chile	Chile	Bolivia	Nicaragua
Colombia		Colombia	Colombia	Brazil	Panama
Ecuador		Panama	Panama	Chile	Peru
Uruguay		Peru	Peru	Colombia	Puerto Rico
Venezuela		Venezuela	Venezuela	Costa Rica	Surinam
				Dominican Rep.	Trinidad &
				Ecuador	Tobago
				El Salvador	Venezuela
				French Antilles and Guiana	
Middle East					
Bahrain	Oman	UAE	Iran	Kuwait	Iran	Syria
Israel	Qatar		Iraq	Lebanon	Jordan	UAE
Jordan	Saudi Arabia		Israel	Saudi Arabia	Kuwait	Yemen
Kuwait	Syria		Jordan	UAE	Oman	
Lebanon	United Arab Emirates (UAE)		Libyan Arab Jamahiriya		Qatar	
			Saudi Arabia		Saudi Arabia	
			UAE			
Africa					
Egypt		Algeria	Egypt	Algeria	Libya
South Africa		Angola	South Africa	Angola	Madagascar
		Egypt		Benin	Mali
		Kenya		Botswana	Mauritius
		Morocco		Burkina Faso	Morocco
		Nigeria		Cameroon	Mozambique
		South Africa		Cape Verde	Namibia
		Tunisia		Congo	Nigeria
				Côte d'Ivoire	Senegal
				Djibouti	South Africa
				Egypt	Sudan
				Ethiopia	Swaziland
				Gabon	Tanzania
				Gambia	Togo
				Ghana	Tunisia
				Guinea	Uganda
				Kenya	Zimbabwe
				La Rion	
				Lesotho	

Sources: Adapted from www.gm.com; www.shell.com; www.mitsubishi.com; www.clarins-financials.com; www.daewoo.com. All data from websites were available as of June 2010.

this causes multinationals to change their market approach, whereas in other cases it supports maintaining a current strategy.

Clarins

The French cosmetics firm Clarins SA is a good example of a firm that is continuing to refine its market strategy based on market assessment data. For more than two decades the company has been gathering feedback from customers on what they like and do not like about the firm's cosmetics. From these surveys the company has learned that women want makeup that is long lasting, easy to choose, and easy to apply. This information has been invaluable in helping Clarins increase market share in an industry where competition is fierce. In fact, the company's growth rate in France has been more than twice the industry average, and Clarins is now achieving similar results in the US market. It is particularly interesting that this growth has been achieved despite the cost of Clarins' products. For example, one of its facial hydrating formulas sells for over $50. Aware of what up-scale customers are willing to buy, Clarins has been very successful in using market assessment information to develop and market high-quality skincare products. One marketing consultant has referred to Clarins as a "Body Shop for rich people;" certainly this target market has paid off well for the company.

Shell Oil

Shell Oil is an MNE whose market assessment has showed the importance of not making significant changes in product or delivery systems.[13] In recent years, Shell has limited its product diversification to tightly linked and synergistic energy and chemical businesses. The company has learned that it is most profitable when staying close to what it knows best. Today Shell works to balance its upstream (exploration and production), downstream (refining and marketing), and related chemical (industrial, agricultural, and petrochemical) businesses. It is also developing a strong network of service stations around the world and has learned that its ability to assess situations and react quickly is an important element in its marketing strategy.

Shell is also famous as both an active user and a developer of scenario planning.[14] These were historically used to examine energy futures, in terms of supply and demand, as well as exploration opportunities and relative risks. But they have expanded to encompass a range of socio-political, economic, and environmental trends and the likelihood and impact of specific disruptive events. Shell is now used by many firms as a benchmark firm for tools and practices to help "future-proof" strategies.

Effective pricing

Some MNEs use a high-price strategy and skim the cream off the top of the market. Others employ a low-price strategy designed to penetrate and capture a larger share of the middle and lower parts of the market. Depending on the nature of the market, both strategies can be successful.

Bang & Olufsen

Bang & Olufsen is a Danish electronics company that manufactures stereo components, televisions, and video equipment.[15] The firm targets the upper end of the market, selling to style-conscious consumers who are unlikely to flinch at paying $4,000 for an audio system, $7,100 for a wide-screen HDTV. One of the primary reasons customers buy from Bang & Olufsen is that the products are well engineered and designed. Televisions are sleek, thin, and modern looking; stereo consoles are trim, polished, and futuristic in design. But, rather than developing a stereotypical image as a provider of "boys' toys," the firm focuses heavily on women's design preferences as more than half of all buying decisions are made by women (and they exert a strong influence on the other half).[16] While many customers prefer to buy less stylish-looking products at one-third the price, Bang & Olufsen continues to have a steady stream of consumers who are willing to pay top dollar. Because of this, the company's worldwide sales in 2014 were approximately $350 million. See more about the company in **Real Case: Bang & Olufsen** below.

Internet marketing and "open innovation"

The internet is becoming a central tool, not just for marketing but for market research and innovation, for many multinational firms. Because consumers, and industry buyers, increasingly use the internet to assess the portfolio of products and services offered by a company, websites have become critically important for marketing purposes. They provide a window into the quality, credibility, achievements, and ethics of a firm, all of which underpin its corporate brand. Moreover, this now happens across a global platform that reaches more people in more countries than traditional marketing media such as radio or TV.[17]

Some large multinationals have been highly adaptive in keeping pace with the development of more sophisticated online platforms. Many have developed quite subtle positions in Facebook, for example, using these to promote specific products, but also convey a particular kind of image by interacting with young, early adopters on these kinds of user networks. This kind of online branding and marketing has evolved into a science of its own, partly because marketers have found online platforms play by different rules and often encourage a more liberal, unregulated environment than found in the "real" world. British advertisers, including Vodafone, Virgin Media, and insurance firm Prudential, withdrew adverts in the early days of Facebook when they found themselves next to the ultra right-wing British National Party (BNP), which was also promoting itself on the site.[18]

✔ Active learning check

Review your answer to Active Learning Case question 4 and make any changes you like. Then compare your answer to the one below.

** How does Adidas use online platforms and social media to promote its events, its sponsored athletes, and its products?**

Central to Adidas's marketing and promotion campaigns is the core principle that "being talked about" is the key to engaging customers and selling products. Innovative product designs and creative advertising is part of this, but the firm also needs to maximize its investment in iconic sports stars by showcasing them as fashion role models. Like all big global brands it is increasingly sophisticated in its use of online platforms and social media to achieve these aims. Online videos and YouTube campaigns engage audiences in the lives of sponsored superstars on and off the pitch. Team GB at the 2012 London Olympics was the focus of attention through the #takethestage twitter campaign. The firm also used the online voting competition to name the 2014 FIFA World Cup official match ball to engage the national passion of the Brazilian hosts. These methods attract attention to the brand generally and to specific product launches or promotions which are timed to align with big sporting events. The firm then uses social media to track, often in real time, the effectiveness and uptake of the marketing messages and the associated designs or products. It also attempts to measure the engagement levels of audiences with particular sponsored personalities in order to develop how and when they should be used for different promotion purposes.

As shown by the Adidas and IKEA case studies above, firms have moved beyond using websites as one-way channels to present information and images to customers; now they are interactive portals for developing a better understanding of, and relationship with, product and service "users." **Open innovation** is the term used to describe interactive, collaborative networks of product or service providers and customers. They allow users of products and services to help shape their development, and enable companies to design, develop, and distribute them more efficiently, by building in user preferences.[19] The internet has proved to be ideal for developing open innovation platforms.

Shell, above, provides a good example. It has established Shell "GameChanger"[20] as an online venturing network to gather radically new ideas for innovations in the "energy and mobility" industry. For the best ideas it can provide funds and contacts for would-be entrepreneurs and has a stage-gate process for assessing proof of concept into development. The firm is effectively using the internet to externalize part of its high-risk, blue-sky innovation activity.

Spreadshirt.com (www.spreadshirt.com) provides another good example. Rather than designing T-shirts and other clothing by second-guessing changing customer preferences, Spreadshirt invites customers to design their own online which can then be produced by the firm. This is similar to Dell's value-chain business model, whereby customers can piece together a preferred desktop PC before ordering it. Spreadshirt's production is outsourced abroad, so its main activity is to connect consumers with production processes. But, through the flow of design ideas coming from a global network of potential customers, it is able to: (1) achieve economies of scale by focusing on the standard clothing designs that attract the most customers; (2) assess changing customer markets, and changing market segments, as they evolve over time; and (3) innovate more efficiently by focusing resources on the best new product development opportunities.

It is important to understand the significance of these kinds of online activities as tools and techniques for helping solve some of the major dilemmas facing all multinational managers. Key questions faced by market analysts are: How much do we need to customize our products or services for particular market segments (geographic, demographic, cultural, etc.) to maximize market share and profitability? What kinds of product, service, design, marketing, and branding features can we standardize to optimize profitability? How are the preferences of different customer groups changing over time and where should we focus our innovation efforts? Open innovation and interactive internet networks, like the ones described above, can harness the direct input of (often unsuspecting) customers and users from all around the world to help solve these dilemmas.

Open innovation
Interactive, collaborative networks of product or service providers and customers or users which help firms innovate more efficiently

KEY POINTS

1 Marketing strategy begins with an international market assessment: the evaluation of the goods and services the MNE can sell in the global marketplace. There are a number of steps in this process, including an initial screening that is designed to determine the basic need potential of the company's goods and services, followed by additional screenings that culminate in a final selection of those outputs that the company will market internationally.

2 Product strategies will vary depending on the specific good and the customer. Some products need little or no modification, and others require extensive changes. Some of the factors that influence the amount of modification include economics, culture, local laws, and the product life cycle.

3 There are a number of ways in which MNEs promote their products, although the final decision is often influenced by the nature of the product. The two major approaches used in promotion are advertising and personal selling. Many multinationals try to use the same message worldwide because it is easier and more economical. However, this is not always possible because some messages either have no meaning in other languages or lack the impact of those in other markets. Similarly, while personal selling is used in some markets, in other markets the customer is unaccustomed to this promotion approach and non-personal approaches must be used, or the customer must be educated to accept this new form.

4 Pricing in international markets is influenced by a number of factors, including government controls, market diversity, currency fluctuations, and price escalation forces.

5 Place strategy involves consideration of distribution, or the course goods will take between production and final consumer. This course often differs on a country-by-country basis, and MNEs will spend a considerable amount of time in examining the different systems in place, the criteria to use in choosing distributors and channels, and how distribution segmentation can be accomplished.

6 MNEs are using a variety of marketing strategies when formulating their strategic plans. Three of the most important strategies are ongoing market assessment, effective pricing internet marketing, and "open innovation."

7 The internet has become an essential part of any firm's marketing and market analysis toolkit. It is also ideal for developing open innovation platforms to connect better with users and customers.

Key terms

- international marketing
- international market assessment
- initial screening
- market indicators
- market size
- market intensity

- market growth
- trend analysis
- estimation by analogy
- regression analysis
- cluster analysis
- promotion

- advertising
- comparative advertising
- personal selling
- distribution
- open innovation

REVIEW AND DISCUSSION QUESTIONS

1 How does initial screening help an MNE evaluate those goods and services that might be sold in the international market? What are some ways in which this screening is carried out?

2 After an MNE has completed an initial screening of its goods and services, what other steps can it take in further refining the choice of those products to sell internationally? Briefly describe the remainder of the process.

3 Why can some goods and services be sold internationally without having to undergo much, if any, modification? Explain.

4 What factors influence the need for moderate to high modification of goods and services that have sold well in the home country and will now be marketed overseas? Identify and describe three of the most influential factors.

5 When should an MNE use the same promotion strategy overseas that it uses at home? When should it modify the approach?

6 Many MNEs find that their advertising messages can be used in overseas markets without much, if any, modification. Why is this so?

7 Why do MNEs sometimes have to modify their personal selling strategies when marketing their goods in international markets?

8 What kinds of factors influence the pricing of goods and services in the international marketplace? Identify and describe three.

9 Why do many MNEs find that they cannot use the same distribution strategy overseas that they have used at home?

10 In choosing the best distribution system, what types of criteria do MNEs use? Identify and discuss three.

11 In what ways are multinationals using the following concepts to help them gain greater international market share: ongoing market assessment, effective pricing, internet marketing and "open innovation"? In each case, offer an example.

12 Explain how open innovation networks using the internet can help firms decide on whether to customize or standardize product features.

REAL CASE

Bang & Olufsen

Introduction

Headquartered in Denmark and dating back to 1925, Bang & Olufsen has evolved into the Rolls-Royce of the audio and visual industry. Producing luxury televisions, audio systems, loudspeakers, and telephones, B&O claims to be in the unique position of having no direct competitors. From a total of 1,400 stores in 60 countries, B&O sells select high-end, luxury niche products at high prices. The customer is typically male, over 35, and affluent, but B&O has also identified three other customer groups including the young and educated, the design fanatic, and the "gray gold" couples whose children have left the nest.

However, against the backdrop of economic downturn, the company experienced a sharp decline in sales and incurred significant losses. In fiscal year 2009/10, the result was (Danish Krone) DKK2,762 million in sales ($453 million) compared to DKK4,225 million sales in 2005/6, reflecting a sales decline of 34.62 percent. The company derived only 3.2 percent of its sales from foreign markets. Its revenue was 0.58 percent of Sony's 2009 revenue of $77,696 million. A restructuring plan included 300 layoffs in Denmark on October 21, 2008, and the abandonment of the development of new cell phones, MP3 players, and stand-alone systems like DVD2 and HDR2. The year 2009/10 also witnessed a decline in the company's B1 shops. At the end of May 2010, there were a total of 703 B1 shops across the world as against 758 shops at the end of the 2008/9 financial year. The company decided to focus on its traditional strengths: high-quality audio and video products as well as sound systems for the automotive industry.

The 4 Ps of B&O's marketing strategy are as follows.

Product strategies

B&O's approach to product development differs substantially from industry norms. Essentially, it is believed that consumers often are unaware of what they want. Instead, ideas are generated based on a deep understanding of how consumers live. Consumer research, corporate ethnographers, and creative teams are replaced with the visions of a handful of contract designers who enjoy unprecedented decision-making power. All of the designers can veto anything failing to meet their visionary standards and, in the past, product design clearly took precedence over engineering capability. The popular BeoSound 9000 CD player was conceived without consulting B&O engineers, who needed two years to produce the technology making the design possible. That particular piece was designed by David Lewis, knighted by the Queen of Denmark for his work, while three of his B&O products are ▶

featured in the Museum of Modern Art's permanent collection in New York. Unlike those produced by Sony and Samsung, new B&O products come few and far between; in fiscal year 2009/10, only seven new models were released. Instead products tend to follow differing life cycles. Many are kept on the market for up to a decade even without lowering prices. For example, the BeoLab 8000 speakers, first introduced in 1992 at a price of $3,000 a pair, are now selling well at $4,500. The BeoSound 9000, introduced in 1996, continues to demand a price of $4,750. Cutting-edge technology, coupled with legendary design, make this possible. In addition, each B&O product is part of an interconnected system, allowing B&O to offer living room solutions that are centrally controlled. Although it has proved successful in the past, relying on only a handful of designers can be a risky proposition. Key designers are growing older, and finding replacements can be troublesome.

Promotion

Demand for B&O products is stimulated in a variety of ways; however, the general message of pristine quality and design is central. With an estimated $50 million (£32 million) global media planning and buying account, B&O promotes through varying advertising vehicles and also engages in advertiser-funded programming. Consequently, B&O products have appeared in *The Apprentice* as well as films such as *Thunderbirds* and *Charlie's Angels*. Most of B&O's selling takes place in the retail stores located in major cities across the globe. Here, well-to-do customers can experience the powerful products first hand, frequently in private sessions catered to their needs. Lately B&O has engaged in symbiotic relationships with premium European car makers, supplying customized audio systems. The German car maker Audi was the first to offer the B&O sound system to its audience. The $6,155 option was expected to entice 100 Audi buyers in the first year. Instead, 15 percent of A8 Audi buyers opted for it, resulting in the system being installed in almost 4,000 cars. This success led to valuable promotional exposure and one additional agreement with British car maker Aston Martin. Although ten other European auto makers have expressed interest in cooperation, B&O chooses its partners carefully so as to protect the premium image. The agreement with Aston Martin was a result of the recognition of a similar culture and heritage rooted in passion, performance, design, and craftwork. B&O's other B2B offerings also provide substantial exposure, stimulating consumer demand. Later, in 2007, B&O secured an agreement with the luxury Grand Lisboa hotel located in Macau, China. At this hotel alone, an estimated 50,000 tourists annually will be exposed to B&O TV and speaker systems.

Source: Francis Dean/Corbis via Getty Images

Place

B&O products have been described as art in the living room. They need space and air to be fully appreciated, which means that they must be presented to the public quite differently from lower-priced alternatives. Worldwide, B&O relies primarily on company-owned stores and private retailers featuring premium products. In recent years, these locations have relied more heavily on customer databases to gain a better understanding of the individual customer. So far, B&O has resisted temptations of both the growing internet market and powerful big-box retailers, and instead continued to open company retail locations worldwide. Although selling premium solutions, B&O serves customers in both developed and developing economies worldwide. In fact, the two best-selling B&O retail locations are located in Moscow, where there exists a small set of extremely rich oligarchs. The emerging economies in Asia with otherwise low average incomes have also proven to be financially attractive due to the new millionaires and high-end luxury enterprises catering to world travelers. From the regional head office in Singapore, B&O is represented in ten countries in the Asia–Pacific region and its products are available from over 40 stores.

Price

Along with all other aspects of B&O communication with the public, selected retail prices match the general message of exclusivity. For example, retailing for $13,250, the 40-inch BeoVision 7 HDTV commands a premium price over other TV alternatives. The company targets a very limited segment (niche) of the world population, and can command these prices due to the documented premium quality and sustainability of its products. The substantial profit margin has the advantage of shielding the company against unfortunate economic conditions. In late 2007, the US dollar depreciated substantially against the world's premier currencies. If prices are left unchanged, this translates directly into lower profits for foreign companies operating in the United States and exchanging dollars into home currency. In the case of B&O, a substantial part of sourced components originated from the United States, which meant that production costs decreased accordingly.

Conclusion

In the coming years, B&O hopes to grow its market share by focusing on its niche. In doing so, the company must carefully consider what action to take and what message product, place, promotion, and price should send to make its goal a reality.

Websites: www.beoworld.org; www.bang-olufsen.com

Sources: "COO discusses Bang & Olufsen's opportunity to benefit from improving market conditions," twist.com, March 3, 2004; "Bang & Olufsen joins forces with Aston Martin for creative partnership," *Wireless News*, December 16, 2007; Tony Lewin, "Top marques turn to branded audio," *Automotive News Europe*, October 1, 2007; "Danish B&O eyes more automotive partnership deals in 2008," *Danish News Digest*, December 11, 2007; Gwendolyn Bounds, "A way to fight big rivals: play up style, service," *The Capital (Annapolis)*, April 1, 2007; Leo Jakobson, "Divine designs," *Incentive*, September 12, 2007; Christopher Lim, "Bang & Olufsen hot on customization," *Business Times Singapore*, September 22, 2007; "Denmark: B&O will double its size," *Esmerk Danish News*, September 26, 2007; Adeline Paul Raj, "Bang & Olufsen to jazz up image," *Business Times*, November 29, 2007; Ian Darby, "Bang & Olufsen reviews £50m global media," *Campaign*, April 14, 2006; Jay Greene, "Where designers rule," *Business Week*, November 5, 2007; Bang & Olufsen, *Annual Report*, 2009/10.

1 Why does Audi use B&O equipment in its high-end cars?

2 How does B&O combine actions on product, place, promotion, and price?

3 How can B&O double its market share by expanding on its successful niche in the future?

REAL CASE

Mirum—never lose your sense of wonder!

It is a complex time to be a big player in the global marketing communications ("marcomms") industry. The explosion of digital media means that every marketing idea is scrutinized by a variety of influencers with voracious demands for content, media outlets are merging overnight, and social media technologies are expanding rapidly. Multi-agency networks, like JWT, face the challenge of improving profitability through strategic integration.

Strategic integration, however, is hard to achieve. In principle, it entails exploiting the growth potential of the network by fully combining resources and competencies from business units or brands and directing those units toward new business opportunities that extend the existing corporate strategy of the network as a whole. In practice, how this is achieved is quite a delicate exercise in convergence, mainly because increased demands for transparency and authenticity mean that companies must speak with one voice to clients and markets. To stay ahead of the game in this industry, global marcomms networks have been converging rapidly as they continuously re-engineer to focus on the capabilities that would improve their speed, quality, efficiency, and responsiveness—and pruning business activities that no longer fit the value-creation logic of their corporate strategy.

In 2015, JWT made a similar attempt by creating a global multi-agency digital network called Mirum. Prior to Mirum, JWT had acquired a variety of digital agencies the world over.

Each of these agencies was a leader in its respective market, each hosting distinct talents and skills. JWT, however, struggled to bring them to work together—conflicting reporting lines, mixed digital fluency, and a complex digital landscape meant that it could not afford to deliver a siloed approach to communications. It had to find a single voice to bind them all, sharing common values, technological skills, and the ultimate desire to transform businesses through digital communications solutions.

Mirum was created to integrate JWT's digital expertise and promote greater agility and exchange between all agencies involved. Its website describes it as:

> a new agency created with a pioneering spirit, built by bringing together successful regional companies that have a deep understanding of local market needs. Our principles are rooted in innovation, design, data, marketing and technology to drive business transformation in a world of constantly evolving behaviors and expectations. Operating in 17 countries, with 40 offices and more than 2,200 professionals, Mirum is a global agency that is a part of the J. Walter Thompson Company and WPP family.

Mirum's capabilities are organized around "Strategy & Consulting" services, "Creative & Content," "User Experience & Platforms," "Analytics & Insight," and "Product Development & Mobile." Additionally, Mirum is able to provide deep vertical ▶

service offerings in Digital Retail, Behavioral Media, and Financial Services. Mirum allows JWT to provide more access to talent from around the globe, enabling the agency to tap into the expertise of different niches, while been able to deliver both the technology and innovative solutions that global brands demand.

Websites: http://strategyonline.ca/201501/30/twist-image-to-become-mirum/; http://www.wpp.com/wpp/press/2015/jan/29/introducing-mirum-a-modern-global-company/; https://www.jwt.com/en/mirum/; http://www.mirumagency.com/london

Source: R. A. Burgelman and Y. L. Doz, "The power of strategic integration," *MIT Sloan Management Review* (spring 2001); T. Zenger, "Trial and error is no way to make strategy," *Harvard Business Review*, vol. 19, no. 4 (April 2015).

1 Explain, what was JWT's rationale in the creation of Mirum?

2 How does JWT benefit from the creation of Mirum?

NOTES

1 See, for example, Graham Hooley, John Saunders, Nigel F. Piercy, and Brigitte Nicoulaud, *Marketing Strategy and Competitive Positioning*, 4th ed. (Harlow: Prentice Hall, 2008).

2 Nanda K. Viswanathan and Peter R. Dickson, "The fundamentals of standardizing global marketing strategy," *International Marketing Review*, vol. 24, no. 1 (2007), pp. 46–63.

3 Philip Kotler and Gary Armstrong, *Principles of Marketing,* 12th ed. (Harlow, Prentice Hall, 2007).

4 "China goes mobile crazy," *BBC News*, August 15, 2001.

5 "Food, fashion and faith," *The Economist*, August 4, 2007.

6 Richard A. Melcher and John Templeman, "Ford of Europe is going in for emergency repairs," *Business Week*, June 17, 1991, p. 48; and Daniel Howes, "Ford's blue oval takes on added luster in Europe with Thursfield," Detnews.com, December 4, 2001.

7 "Intel's right-hand turn," *The Economist*, May 12, 2005.

8 "Hand-to-hand combat," *The Economist*, December 16, 2004.

9 See Hooley et al., *Marketing Strategy and Competitive Positioning*.

10 In a *Wall Street Journal* interview Martin Sorrell, CEO of the advertising conglomerate WPP, argues that standardized advertising is practically impossible; Erin White and Jeffrey A. Trachtenberg, "One size doesn't fit All," *Wall Street Journal—Eastern Edition*, October 1, 2003, pp. B1–2.

11 Joan Magretta, "Fast, global, and entrepreneurial supply chain management, Hong Kong style," *Harvard Business Review* (September/October 1998), pp. 103–14.

12 See, for example, Robert T. Green and Ajay K. Kohli, "Export market identification: the role of economic size and socioeconomic development," *Management International Review*, vol. 31, no. 1 (1991), pp. 37–50.

13 Keetie E. Sluyterman, *Dutch Enterprise in the Twentieth Century* (London: Routledge, 2005).

14 For a wealth of resources, see www.shell.com/scenarios.

15 Andrew Tellijohn, "Bang & Olufsen will bring high-end audio to galleria," *Business Journal*, November 15, 2002.

16 Andrew Davidson, "Bang & Olufsen's Mr Cool," *Sunday Times*, January 6, 2008.

17 Richard Gay, Alan Charlesworth, and Rita Esen, *Online Marketing: A Customer-led Approach* (Oxford: Oxford University Press, 2007).

18 Carlos Grande, "Facebook loses more ads in BNP row," *Financial Times*, August 3, 2007.

19 Henry William Chesbrough, *Open Innovation: The New Imperative for Creating and Profiting from Technology* (Boston, MA: Harvard Business School Press, 2003).

20 See http://www.shell.com/home/content/gamechanger-en.

BIBLIOGRAPHY

Alexander, Nicholas, Rhodes, Mark, and Myers, Hayley. "International market selection: measuring actions instead of intentions," *Journal of Services Marketing*, vol. 21, no. 6 (2007).

Almodovar, Paloma, and Rugman, Alan M. "The regionalization and performance of standardizing versus customizing firms," Henley Business School, University of Reading, Dunning Center for International Business Discussion Paper Series, mimeo (2011).

Aspelund, Arild, Madsen, Tage Koed, and Moen, Øystein. "A review of the foundation, international marketing strategies, and performance of international new ventures," *European Journal of Marketing*, vol. 41, nos. 11/12 (2007).

Auger, Pat, Devinney, Timothy M., Louviere, Jordan J., and Burke, Paul F. "The importance of social product attributes in consumer purchasing decisions: a multi-country comparative study," *International Business Review*, vol. 19, no. 2 (April 2010).

Blois, Keith. *The Oxford Textbook of Marketing* (Oxford: Oxford University Press, 2000).

Boehe, Dirk M. "Captive offshoring of new product development in Brazil," *Management International Review*, vol. 50, no. 6 (2010).

Broderick, Amanda J., Greenley, Gordon E., and Mueller, Rene Dentiste. "The behavioral homogeneity evaluation framework: multi-level evaluations of consumer involvement in international segmentation," *Journal of International Business Studies*, vol. 38, no. 5 (September 2007).

Ching, Ha Lau, and Ellis, Paul. "Does relationship marketing exist in cyberspace?," *Management International Review*, vol. 46, no. 5 (2006).

Constantinides, Efthymios. "The marketing mix revisited: toward the 21st century marketing," *Journal of Marketing Management*, vol. 22, no. 3–4 (2006).

Czinkota, Michael R., and Ronkainen, Ilkka A. "A forecast of globalization, international business and trade: report from a Delphi study," *Journal of World Business*, vol. 40, no. 2 (May 2005).

Ellis, Paul D. "Is market orientation affected by the size and diversity of customer networks?," *Management International Review*, vol. 50, no. 3 (2010).

Eng, Teck-Yong, and Spickett-Jones, J. Graham. "An investigation of marketing capabilities and upgrading performance of manufacturers in mainland China and Hong Kong," *Journal of World Business*, vol. 44, no. 4 (2009).

Gabrielsson, P., and Gabrielsson, M. "Globalizing internationals: business portfolio and marketing strategies in the ICT field," *International Business Review*, vol. 13, no. 6 (December 2004).

Gabrielsson, Peter, Gabrielsson, Mika, and Gabrielsson, Hannele. "International advertising campaigns in fast-moving consumer goods companies originating from a SMOPEC country," *International Business Review*, vol. 17, no. 6 (December 2008).

Grewal, Dhruv, et al. "Evaluation of subsidiary marketing performance: combining process and outcome performance metrics," *Journal of the Academy of Marketing Science*, vol. 37, no. 2 (2009).

Griffith, David A., Yalcinkaya, Goksel, and Calantone, Roger J. "Do marketing capabilities consistently mediate effects of firm intangible capital on performance across institutional environments?," *Journal of World Business*, vol. 45, no. 3 (2010).

Hewett, Kelly, Roth, Martin S., and Roth, Kendall. "Conditions influencing headquarters and foreign subsidiary roles in marketing activities and their effects on performance," *Journal of International Business Studies*, vol. 34, no. 6 (November 2003).

Il Park, Byung, Whitelock, Jeryl, and Giroud, Axèle. "Acquisition of marketing knowledge in small and medium-sized IJVs: The role of compatibility between parents," *Management Decision*, vol. 47, no. 8 (2009).

Jain, Subhash C. *Handbook of Research in International Marketing* (Cheltenham: Edward Elgar, 2003).

Jiménez, Nadia Huitzilin, and San Martín, Sonia. "The role of country-of-origin, ethnocentrism and animosity in promoting consumer trust: the moderating role of familiarity," *International Business Review*, vol. 19, no. 1 (February 2010).

Kanso, Ali M., and Nelson, Richard Alan. "Multinational corporations and the challenge of global advertising," *International Marketing Review*, vol. 24, no. 5 (2007).

Kotabe, Masaaki, "Contemporary research trends in international marketing: the 1990s." In Alan M. Rugman and Thomas Brewer (eds.), *Oxford Handbook of International Business* (Oxford: Oxford University Press, 2001).

Lim, Lewis K. S., Acito, Frank, and Rusetski, Alexander. "Development of archetypes of international market strategy," *Journal of International Business Studies*, vol. 37, no. 4 (July 2006).

Manolopoulos, Dimitris, Papanastassiou, Marina, and Pearce, Robert. "Technology sourcing in multinational enterprises and the roles of subsidiaries: an empirical investigation," *International Business Review*, vol. 14, no. 3 (June 2005).

Michael, Steven C. "Determinants of the rate of franchising among nations," *Management International Review*, vol. 43, no. 3 (2003).

Ngo, Liem Viet, and O'Cass, Aron. "Performance implications of market orientation, marketing resources, and marketing capabilities," *Journal of Marketing Management*, vol. 28, no. 1–2 (2012).

Norburn, David, Birley, Sue, Dunn, Mark, and Payne, Adrian. "A four-nation study of the relationship between marketing effectiveness, corporate culture, corporate values, and market orientation," *Journal of International Business Studies*, vol. 21, no. 3 (1990).

Okazaki, Shintaro, and Taylor, Charles R. "Social media and international advertising: theoretical challenges and future directions," *International Marketing Review*, vol. 30, no. 1 (2013).

Papu, Ravi, Quester, Pascale G., and Cooksey, Ray W. "Country image and consumer-based brand equity: multi-level evaluations of consumer involvement in international segmentation," *Journal of International Business Studies*, vol. 38, no. 5 (September 2007).

Powers, Thomas L., and Loyka, Jeffrey J. "Market, industry, and company influences on global product standardization," *International Marketing Review*, vol. 24, no. 6 (2007).

Reynolds, Nina L., Simintiras, Antonis C., and Diamantopolous, Adamantios. "Theoretical justification of sampling choices in international marketing research: key issues and guidelines for researchers," *Journal of International Business Studies*, vol. 34, no. 1 (January 2003).

Ripollés, Maria, and Andreu Blesa. "International new ventures as 'small multinationals': the importance of marketing capabilities," *Journal of World Business*, vol. 47, no. 2 (2012).

Rubera, Gaia, Ordanini, Andrea, and Griffith, David A. "Incorporating cultural values for understanding the influence of perceived product creativity on intention to buy: an examination in Italy and the US," *Journal of International Business Studies*, vol. 42 (2011).

Rugman, Alan M. "The myth of global strategy," *International Marketing Review*, vol. 18, no. 6 (2001).

Rugman, Alan M. and Verbeke, Alain. "Trade policy and global corporate strategy," *Journal of Global Marketing*, vol. 2, no. 3 (spring 1989).

Rugman, Alan M., Oh, Chang H., and Lim, Dominic S. K. "The regional and global competitiveness of multinational firms," *Journal of the Academy of Marketing Science* (2011).

Samiee, Saeed. "Brand origin recognition accuracy: its antecedents and consumers' cognitive limitations," *Journal of International Business Studies*, vol. 36, no. 4 (July 2005).

Samiee, Saeed, and Walters, Peter G. P. "Relationship marketing in an international context: a literature review," *International Business Review*, vol. 12, no. 2 (April 2003).

Schlegelmilch, Bodo B., and Chini, Tina Claudia. "Knowledge transfer between marketing functions in multinational companies: a conceptual model," *International Business Review*, vol. 12, no. 2 (April 2003).

Schmid, Stefan, and Kotulla, Thomas. "50 years of research on international standardization and adaptation: from a systematic literature analysis to a theoretical framework," *International Business Review*, vol. 20, no. 5 (October 2011).

Sharma, Piyush. "Country of origin effects in developed and emerging markets: exploring the contrasting roles of materialism and value consciousness," *Journal of International Business Studies*, vol. 42, no. 2 (February/March 2011).

Singh, Jagdip, Lentz, Patrick, and Nijssen, Edwin J. "First- and second-order effects of consumers' institutional logics on firm consumer relationships: a cross market comparative analysis," *Journal of International Business Studies*, vol. 42, no. 2 (February/March 2011).

Solberg, Carl Arthur, and Durrieu, François. "Access to networks and commitment to internationalization as precursors to marketing strategies in international markets," *Management International Review*, vol. 46, no. 1 (2006).

Taylor, Charles R., and Okazaki, Shintaro. "Who standardizes advertising more frequently, and why do they do so? A comparison of U.S. and Japanese subsidiaries' advertising practices in the European Union," *Journal of International Marketing*, vol. 14, no. 1 (2006).

Theodosiou, Marios, and Leonidou, Leonidas. "Standardization versus adaptation of international marketing strategy: an integrative assessment of the empirical research," *International Business Review*, vol. 12, no. 2 (April 2003).

Townsend, Janell D., Yeniyurt, Sengun, Deligonul, Z. Seyda, and Cavusgil, S. Tamer. "Exploring the marketing program antecedents of performance in a global company," *Journal of International Marketing*, vol. 12, no. 4 (2004).

Veale, Roberta, and Quester, Pascale. "Do consumer expectations match experience? Predicting the influence of price and country of origin on perceptions of product quality," *International Business Review*, vol. 18, no. 2 (April 2009).

Vorhies, Douglas W., and Morgan, Neil A. "Benchmarking marketing capabilities for sustainable competitive advantage," *Journal of Marketing*, vol. 69, no. 1 (2005).

Walters, Peter G. P., and Zhu, Mingxia. "International marketing in Chinese enterprises: some evidence from the PRC," *Management International Review*, vol. 35, no. 3 (1995).

Wu, Jie. "Marketing capabilities, institutional development, and the performance of emerging market firms: a multinational study," *International Journal of Research in Marketing*, vol. 30, no. 1 (2013).

Yang, Deli, and Fryxell, Gerald E. "Brand positioning and anti-counterfeiting effectiveness," *Management International Review*, vol. 49, no. 6 (2009).

Zeugner Roth, Katharina Petra, Diamantopoulos, Adamantios, and Montesinos, M. Ángeles. "Home country image, country brand equity and consumers' product preferences: an empirical study," *Management International Review*, vol. 48, no. 5 (2008).

Chapter 14

HUMAN RESOURCE MANAGEMENT STRATEGY

Contents

Objectives of the chapter

Human resource management strategy provides an MNE with the opportunity to truly outdistance its competition. For example, if HP develops a laser printer that is smaller, lighter, and less expensive than competitive models, other firms in the industry will attempt to reverse-engineer this product to see how they can develop their own version. However, when a multinational has personnel who are carefully selected, well trained, and properly compensated, it has a pool of talent that the competition may be unable to beat. Products and brands may, to some extent, be imitable; knowledge and capabilities, and the processes that combine and leverage them for competitive advantage, tend not to be. For this reason, human resource management (HRM) is a critical element of international management strategy. This chapter considers the ways in which multinationals prepare their people to take on the challenges of international business. We focus specifically on such critical areas as selection, training, managerial development, compensation, and labor relations.

The specific objectives of this chapter are to:

1 *Define* the term *international human resource management* and discuss human resource strategies in overseas operations.
2 *Describe* the screening and selection criteria often used in choosing people for overseas assignments.
3 *Relate* some of the most common types of training and development that are offered to personnel who are going overseas.
4 *Discuss* the common elements of an international compensation package.
5 *Explain* some of the typical labor relations practices used in the international arena.
6 *Describe* some of the human resource management strategies that are currently receiving a great deal of attention from MNEs.

The Coca-Cola Company thinks local

The Coca-Cola Company has been operating internationally for most of its 130-year history, since it first started operations in Canada in 1906. With revenues amounting to $45,998 the company operates in 200 countries and employs 129,200 people. Its human resource management (HRM) strategy helps explain a great deal of its success. It now follows a strategy of "national responsiveness" by adapting to local market conditions. For example, it transferred more than 300 professional and managerial staff from one country to another under its leadership development program, and the number of international transferees is increasing annually. One senior-level HRM manager explained Coca-Cola's strategy by noting:

> We recently concluded that our talent base needs to be multilingual and multicultural … To use a sports analogy, you want to be sure that you have a lot of capable and competent bench strength, ready to assume broader responsibilities as they present themselves.

In preparing for the future, Coca-Cola includes a human resource recruitment forecast in its annual and long-term business strategies. It also has selection standards on which management can focus when recruiting and hiring. For example, the company likes applicants who are fluent in more than one language because they can be transferred to other geographic areas where their fluency will help them to be part of Coca-Cola's operation.

The firm also has a recruitment program that helps it identify candidates at the college level. Rather than just seeking students abroad, Coca-Cola looks for foreign students who are studying in the United States at domestic universities. The students are recruited in the United States and then provided with a year's training before they go back to their home country. Coca-Cola also has an internship program for foreign students who are interested in working for the company during school breaks, either in the United States or back home. These interns are put into groups and assigned a project that requires them to make a presentation to the operations personnel, including a discussion of what worked and what did not. The interns are then evaluated individually and management decides their future potential with the company.

Coca-Cola believes these approaches are extremely useful in helping to find talent on a global basis. Not only is the company able to develop internal sources, but its intern program provides a large number of additional individuals who would otherwise end up with other companies. Coca-Cola earns a greater portion of its income and profit overseas than it does in the United States. Its HRM strategy helps explain how, despite the success of its policies, Coca-Cola found itself facing a series of problems as it entered the millennium. During the 1980s the firm expanded its global reach and began to centralize control and encourage consolidation among all bottling partners. In the 1990s, however, the world began to change. Many national and local leaders began seeking sovereignty over their political, economic, and cultural futures. As a result, the very forces that were making the world more connected and homogeneous were also triggering a powerful desire for local autonomy and the preservation of unique cultural identity. Simply put, the world was demanding more nimbleness, responsiveness, and sensitivity from MNEs, while Coca-Cola was centralizing decision making, standardizing operating practices, and insulating itself from this changing environment. It was going global when it should have been going local.

Former CEO, Neville Isdell, helped Coca-Cola turn around during the late 2000s by focusing on marketing-led growth. In particular, he helped Coca-Cola implement three principles designed to make it more locally responsive. First, it is instituting a strategy of "Think local, act local" by putting more decision making in the hands of local managers. Second, it is focusing itself as a pure marketing company that pushes its brands on a regional and local basis. Third, it is working to become a model citizen by reaching out to the local communities and getting involved in civic and charitable activities. In the past, Coca-Cola succeeded because it understood and appealed to global commonalities; in the future it hopes to succeed by better understanding and appealing to local differences.

Websites: www.cocacola.com; www.cokecce.com

Sources: "The veteran," *The Economist*, June 2, 2007; Coca Cola, *Annual Report*, 2010, 2014; Thomson Reuters, *OneSource*, 2011.

1. Does the Coca-Cola Company have a local perspective regarding the role of human resource management?

2. On what basis does Coca-Cola choose people for international assignments? Identify and describe two.

3. What type of training does Coca-Cola provide to its interns? Of what value is this training?

4. How useful is it for Coca-Cola's managers to be fluent in more than one language? Why?

INTRODUCTION

International human resource management (IHRM)

The process of selecting, training, developing, and compensating personnel in overseas positions

Home-country nationals

Citizens of the country where the multinational resides

Expatriates

Individuals who reside abroad but are citizens of the multinational's parent country; they are citizens of the home, not the host, country

Host-country nationals

Local people hired by a multinational

Third-country nationals

Citizens of countries other than the one in which the multinational is headquartered or the one in which they are assigned to work by the multinational

International human resource management (IHRM) is the process of selecting, training, developing, and compensating personnel in overseas positions. This chapter will examine each of these activities. Before doing so, however, it is important to clarify the general nature of this overall process, which begins with selecting and hiring.

There are three basic sources of personnel talent that MNEs can tap for positions.[1] One is **home-country nationals**, who reside abroad but are citizens of the multinational's parent country. These individuals are typically called **expatriates**. An example is a US manager assigned to head an R&D department in Tokyo for IBM Japan. A second is **host-country nationals**, who are local people hired by the MNE. An example is a British manager working for Ford Motor Company in London. The last is **third-country nationals**, who are citizens of countries other than the one in which the MNE is headquartered or the one in which it has assigned them to work. An example is a French manager working for Sony in the United States.

Staffing patterns may vary depending on the length of time the MNE has been operating. Many MNEs will initially rely on home-country managers to staff their overseas units, gradually putting more host-country nationals into management positions as the firm gains experience. Another approach is to use home-country nationals in less developed countries and employ host-country nationals in more developed regions, a pattern that is fairly prevalent among US and European MNEs.[2] A third pattern is to put a new operation under the supervision of a home-country manager but turn it over to a host-country manager once it is up and running. Figure 14.1 provides an illustration of the types of managers, by nationality mix, required over the stages of internationalization. When an MNE is exporting into a foreign market, host-country nationals will handle everything. As the firm begins initial

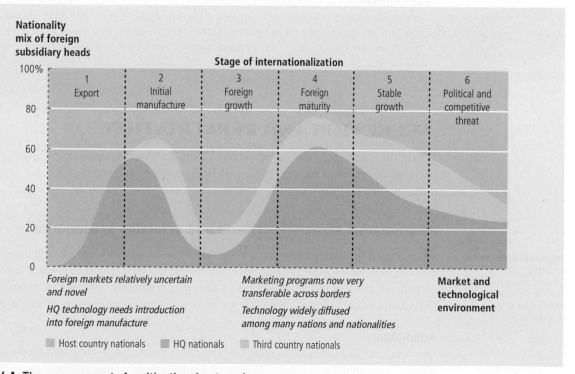

Figure 14.1 The management of multinational enterprises

Source: Reprinted from *Colombia Journal of World Business*, Summer 1973, Lawrence G. Franco, "Who manages multinational enterprises?" p. 33, Copyright 1973, with permission from Elsevier Science.

manufacture in that country, the use of expatriate managers and third-country nationals begins to increase. As the company moves through the ensuing stages of internationalization, the nationality mix of the managers in the overseas unit continues to change to meet the shifting demands of the environment.

In some cases, staffing decisions are handled uniformly. For example, most Japanese MNEs rely on home-country managers to staff senior-level positions. Similarly, some European MNEs assign home-country managers to overseas units for their entire careers. US MNEs typically view overseas assignments as temporary, so it is more common to find many of these expatriates working under the supervision of host-country managers.

The size of the compensation package also plays an important role in personnel selection and placement. As the cost of sending people overseas has increased, there has been a trend toward using host-country or third-country nationals who know the local language and customs. For example, many US multinationals hired English or Scottish managers for the top positions at subsidiaries in former British colonies such as Jamaica, India, the West Indies, and Kenya in the early days of their international expansion.[3]

The above factors influence IHRM strategies and help MNEs integrate an international perspective into their human resource policies and practices.[4]

 Active learning check

Review your answer to Active Learning Case question 1 and make any changes you like. Then compare your answer to the one below.

1 **Does the Coca-Cola Company have a local perspective regarding the role of human resource management?**

The company certainly does have a local perspective regarding the HRM role. Coca-Cola is interested in recruiting people from anywhere in the world, training and developing them, and sending them to assignments around the globe. It does not confine itself to recruiting, training, developing, or promoting people from any one particular region or country. Both Americans and non-Americans have equal opportunities in the company, further reinforcing this international perspective.

SELECTION AND REPATRIATION

Two of the major HRM challenges facing MNEs are those of selecting qualified people for overseas assignments and, in the case of home-country nationals, effectively repatriating them into the workforce upon their return. Each presents a significant challenge.

International screening criteria and selection procedures

International screening criteria
Factors used to identify individuals regarded as most suitable for overseas assignments

International screening criteria are those factors used to identify the individuals regarded as most suitable for overseas assignment. Some MNEs use an extensive list, whereas others rely on only a handful of factors. A number of screening criteria are commonly used in determining whom to send overseas. These criteria focus on both individual and family considerations.

Adaptability

One criterion is an individual's ability to adapt to cultural change. Research shows that many managers are initially pleased to learn they are being sent overseas. However, within a few months many of them begin to suffer from culture shock brought on by the large number of changes to which they are subjected. This often results in a decline in job satisfaction. However, as they continue their overseas assignment, satisfaction goes back up. Research by Torbiorn as long ago as 1982, for example, reported that by the end of the first year most managers are through the cultural change phase and are beginning to adjust to their new conditions. Among those who stay overseas for two or more years, Torbiorn found that satisfaction reaches new heights and continues rising.[5] This general pattern has not changed as much as we might think. Researchers have also found that men tend to adjust slightly faster than women, and that people over the age of 35 have somewhat higher levels of satisfaction after the first year.

In determining how well an individual will adapt to cultural change, MNEs examine a number of characteristics, including (1) work experiences with cultures other than one's own, (2) previous overseas travel, (3) knowledge of foreign languages (fluency is not generally necessary), (4) the ability to solve problems within different frameworks and from different perspectives, and (5) overall sensitivity to the environment.[6]

Self-reliance

Managers who are posted to overseas assignments must be self-reliant and independent because they often have to make on-the-spot decisions without consulting the home office. In determining self-reliance, MNEs evaluate the amount of field experience the individual has had, as well as experience in special projects and task forces—assignments that often require and nurture self-reliance. Consideration is also given to hobbies or avocations that require a high degree of personal independence.

Age, experience, and education

MNEs often find that young managers are eager for international assignments and want to learn more about other cultures. On the other hand, older managers have more experience and maturity to bring to the assignment. To balance the strengths of the two groups, many firms send both young and seasoned personnel to the same overseas post so that each can learn from the other.

Some MNEs believe that a college degree, preferably a graduate degree, is important for international managers. However, there is no universal agreement on this point. Multinationals who sell highly technical products tend to prefer people with science degrees. Others hold that a good education helps develop logical thinking, creative ideas, and a broad perspective of the world, so they prefer individuals with a liberal arts education.

Health and family status

Expatriates must have good physical and emotional health. Those with physical problems that will limit their activities are screened from consideration. So are those judged less likely to withstand culture shock.

Multinationals also take into account a person's family situation. An unhappy family life will hurt employee productivity. One survey of US multinationals found that the primary reason for expatriate failure was the inability of the manager's spouse to adjust to a different physical or cultural environment. For this reason, some firms interview both the spouse *and* the manager before deciding whether to approve the assignment.[7]

The increasing number of dual-career families in Western countries creates a further challenge for MNEs. Equally career-minded spouses might find their careers interrupted during their spouses' overseas assignments. In fact, a study of 332 repatriates and spouses found most dissatisfaction with MNEs resulted from lack of employment support for the trailing spouse.[8]

Motivation and leadership

Another selection criterion is the individual's desire to work abroad and potential commitment to the new job. Many people who are unhappy with their position at home will consider an overseas assignment, but this is not sufficient motivation. Motivational factors include a desire for adventure, a pioneering spirit, a desire to increase one's chances for promotion, and the opportunity to improve one's economic status.[9]

Additionally, one group of researchers recently examined the factors associated with employee willingness to work overseas and concluded the following:

- Unmarried employees are more willing than any other group to accept expat assignments.

- Married couples without children at home or those with non-teenage children are probably the most willing to move.

- Prior international experience seems associated with willingness to work as an expatriate.

- Individuals most committed to their professional careers and to their employing organizations are prone to be more willing to work as expatriates.

- Careers and attitudes of spouses will likely have a significant impact on employee willingness to move overseas.

Employee and spouse perceptions of organizational support for expats are also critical to employee willingness to work overseas.

Applicants are also evaluated on the basis of their leadership potential, since most expatriates end up supervising others. Although this is a difficult factor to assess, a number of characteristics are commonly sought when making this evaluation, including maturity, emotional stability, the ability to communicate well, independence, initiative, and creativity. These characteristics are good indications of leadership potential.

Selection procedures

The most common selection procedure is the interview. A general consensus is that extensive interviews of candidates and their spouses by senior executives still ultimately provide the best method of selection. For example, 52 percent of the US MNEs that Tung surveyed conducted interviews with both the manager and the spouse, whereas 47 percent conducted interviews with the candidate alone. In the case of technically oriented positions, these percentages were 40 and 59 percent. Other MNEs follow a similar pattern. Based on her research, Tung has concluded that multinationals are becoming increasingly cognizant of the importance of interviewing in effective performance abroad.[10]

Some companies also use tests to help in making the final choice of who will perform well in overseas assignments. However, this approach has not gained a great deal of support because it is expensive and many MNEs feel that tests do not improve the selection process. As a result, the candidate's domestic record and evaluations from superiors and peers, along with the interview, tend to be relied on most heavily.

Repatriation of expats

Repatriation
The process of returning home at the end of an overseas assignment

Repatriation is the process of returning home at the end of an overseas assignment. Managers are repatriated for a number of reasons. The most common one is that the predetermined time assignment is completed. For expatriates, an overseas assignment usually lasts two to three years, although some companies are now encouraging their people to consider making the international arena a lifetime career choice. Another reason is the desire to have their children educated in the home country. The expatriate may be unhappy overseas and the company may feel there is more to be gained by bringing the person back than in trying to persuade the individual to stay on. Finally, as in any position, if a manager has performed poorly, the MNE may decide to put someone else in the position.

Readjusting

Although many expatriates look forward to returning, some find it difficult to adjust. A number of reasons can be cited. One is that the home-office job lacks the high degree of authority and responsibility the expat had in the overseas job. Another is that the expat feels the company does not value international experience and the time spent overseas seems to have been wasted in terms of career progress.[11] A third reason is a change in the standard of living. While overseas, many expats have generous living allowances and benefits that they cannot match back home. An accompanying problem is the change in cultural lifestyle. For example, a person who is transferred from a cosmopolitan city such as Vienna to a small town in Middle America may find it necessary to make major adjustments, ranging from social activities to the pace of life in general. Additionally, it is common to find that those who sold their house before leaving and have been overseas from three to five years are stunned by the high price of a replacement home. Not only have they lost a great deal of equity by selling, but they must also come up with a substantial down payment and much larger monthly mortgage payments. Some companies do not have plans for handling returning managers. If these individuals are assigned jobs at random, they can find their career progress jeopardized.

Recent research shows that the longer people remain overseas, the more problems they are likely to have being reabsorbed into the operations back home. In addition to the factors considered above, several factors make repatriation of such people after longer periods difficult: (1) they may no longer be familiar to people at headquarters; (2) their old jobs may have been eliminated or drastically changed; or (3) technological advances at headquarters may have rendered their existing skills and knowledge obsolete. In many cases, it takes from 6 to 12 months before a returning manager is operating at full effectiveness.

Adjustment strategies

Transition strategies
Strategies designed to help smooth the move from foreign to domestic assignments

Repatriation agreement
An agreement that spells out how long a person will be posted overseas and sets forth the type of job that will be given to the person upon returning

In recent years, MNEs have begun to address adjustment problems faced by returning expatriates. Some have now developed **transition strategies** that are designed to help smooth the move from foreign to domestic assignments.

One of these strategies is the **repatriation agreement**, which spells out how long a person will be posted overseas and sets forth the type of job the person will be given upon returning. The agreement typically does not spell out a particular position or salary, but it does promise a job that is at least equal in authority and compensation to the one that the person held overseas. Such an agreement relieves a great deal of the anxiety expatriates encounter because it assures them that the MNE is not going to forget them while they are gone and that there will be a place for them when they return.

A second strategy is to rent or maintain the expatriate's home during the overseas tour. Both Union Carbide and the Aluminum Company of America have such arrangements. These plans help reduce the financial burden managers face when they go on a three-year or four-year tour.

A third strategy is to assign a senior executive as a sponsor for every manager posted abroad. This ensures that there is someone looking after each expatriate and ensuring that his or her performance, compensation, and career path are on track. When the expatriate is scheduled to return home, the sponsor begins working internally to ensure a suitable position. Companies such as IBM and Union Carbide use this form of the mentoring process, which is proving to be very effective.

A fourth strategy is to maintain ongoing communications with expatriate managers, ensuring that they are aware of what is happening in the home office. If they are scheduled to be home on leave for any extended period of time, the company works them into projects at headquarters. In this way they can maintain their visibility at headquarters and increase the likelihood that they are viewed as regular members of the management staff rather than as outsiders.

These strategies that help MNEs maintain a proactive approach in dealing with expatriate concern are becoming more widespread. The best-managed multinational firms tend to have (1) mentor programs consisting of one-on-one pairing of an expatriate with a member of the home-office senior management staff, (2) a separate organization unit with primary responsibility for the specific needs of expatriates, and/or (3) maintenance of constant contacts between the home office and the expatriate.[12]

✔ Active learning check

Review your answer to Active Learning Case question 2 and make any changes you like. Then compare your answer to the one below.

 On what basis does Coca-Cola choose people for international assignments? Identify and describe two.

One of the bases on which Coca-Cola chooses people is the ability to speak at least two languages fluently. A second is familiarity with at least two cultures. Both are viewed as critical for success in international assignments.

TRAINING AND DEVELOPMENT

Training
The process of altering employee behavior and attitudes in a way that increases the probability of goal attainment

Managerial development
The process by which managers obtain the necessary skills, experiences, and attitudes that they need to become or remain successful leaders

Training is the process of altering employee behaviors and attitudes in a way that increases the probability of goal attainment. **Managerial development** is the process by which managers obtain the necessary skills, experiences, and attitudes they need to become or remain successful leaders. Training programs are designed to provide those who are going overseas with information and experience related to local customs, cultures, and work habits, thus helping them interact and work more effectively with local employees. Development is typically used to help managers improve their leadership skills, stay up to date on the latest management developments, increase their overall effectiveness, and maintain high job satisfaction.[13]

Types of training

MNEs use several types of training and development programs.[14] These can be grouped into two general categories: standardized and tailor-made.

Standardized training programs
Generic programs that can be used with managers anywhere in the world

Standardized training programs are generic and can be used with managers anywhere in the world. Examples include programs for improving quantitative analysis or technical skills that can be used universally. Research reveals that many behaviorally oriented concepts can also be handled with a standardized program (although follow-up programs must be tailor-made to meet specific country needs). Examples include programs designed to acquaint participants with the fundamentals of communicating with, motivating, or leading people. Another form of standardized training presently offered by large MNEs addresses cultural differences on a global scale. For instance, with operations in 200 countries, managers of Colgate-Palmolive are often exposed to more than one foreign culture. To address this, the company has offered cultural diversity training to its managers.[15]

Tailor-made training programs
Programs designed to meet the specific needs of the participants, typically including a large amount of culturally based input

Tailor-made training programs are designed to meet the specific needs of participants and typically include a large amount of culturally based input. These programs are more commonly developed by large MNEs and by multinationals that need a working knowledge of the local country's beliefs, norms, attitudes, and work values. Quite often the input for the programs is provided by managers who are currently working in the country (or have recently worked there) and by local managers and personnel who are citizens of that country. In most cases this training is provided to expatriates before they leave for their assignment, but in some cases it is provided on site.

Research shows that the following six types of programs are most popular:

1 Environmental briefings used to provide information about such things as geography, climate, housing, and schools.

2 Cultural orientation designed to familiarize the participants with cultural institutions and value systems of the host country.

3 Cultural assimilators using programmed learning approaches designed to provide the participants with intercultural encounters.

4 Language training.

5 Sensitivity training designed to develop attitudinal flexibility.

6 Field experience, which sends the participant to the country of assignment to undergo some of the emotional stress of living and working with people from a different culture.[16]

Typically, MNEs use a combination of the above programs, tailoring the package to fit their specific needs. A good example is provided by Underwriters Laboratories Inc., which uses a two-day, in-house program to train those personnel who will be dealing extensively with Japanese clients in the United States. The program is designed around a series of mini-lectures that cover a wide range of topics, from how to handle introductions to the proper way of exchanging gifts. It employs a variety of training techniques, including lectures, case studies, role-playing, language practice, and a short test on cultural terminology. The two-day training wraps up with a 90-minute question-and-answer period during which participants are given the opportunity to gain additional insights into how to develop effective client relationships.

Some firms extend their training focus to include families. In addition to providing language training, firms such as General Electric Medical Systems (GEMS) Group, a Milwaukee-based firm with expatriates in France, Japan, and Singapore, match up the family that is going overseas with another family that has been assigned to this country or geographic region. The latter family will then share many of the problems it faced during the overseas assignment and relate some of the ways these situations were resolved. It is also common to find MNEs offering cultural training to all family members, not just to the manager. This helps create a support group that will work together to deal with problems that arise during the overseas assignment.

INTERNATIONAL BUSINESS STRATEGY IN ACTION

The glass ceiling

The glass ceiling has been a hot topic ever since the term was coined almost three decades ago and the sometimes controversial debate over its existence and possible solutions shows no signs of cooling down. The term, which was first seen in the *Wall Street Journal* in 1986, has come to collectively symbolize the range of barriers which may be faced by women attempting to make their way up the promotions ladder to higher management levels in the corporate world.

Despite the fact that women make up, for example, 50 percent of the UK's workforce, they only account for 32 percent of managers and 28 percent of senior executives. This begs the question: what is happening to result in men disproportionally advancing through the organizational ranks? Several factors appear to be at work.

Women are normally the principal caregivers for children or other dependents within the family unit and this can lead to a range of potential explanations. First, women appear to undertake a process of self-selection, whereby they actively opt out of particular types of roles, such as those which cannot be easily combined with family responsibilities. According to a study by the ILM, 66 percent of women cited predictable working hours as being important to them, and as a result, women may typically opt for part-time roles or those which may allow for breaks in employment, or choose to remain in a more junior role, thus accounting for the imbalance in gender at more senior levels.

For women who don't opt out, work–life balance challenges can prove to be quite an obstacle to progression. Working hours can be intense and erratic, particularly in professional service sectors like law, accountancy, and management consulting. Many top-level positions also require the individual to travel, and having a level of mobility and flexibility is a key to advancement in many firms.

In response to the problem of the glass ceiling and gender disparity, many firms have looked to develop their maternity leave arrangements and flexible working opportunities, and advances in technology now allow the option of working from home. Leading by example also plays a very important role, with 41 percent of women surveyed by the ILM citing the lack of female role models as a barrier to progression. Furthermore, it was highlighted that there was a lack of role models (and therefore a lack of individuals?) who manage to successfully combine a career and family life, rather than those who have made sacrifices in this area to reach their senior position.

Perhaps most important of all, however, is raising awareness of the glass ceiling in men. In the banking sector, for example, only one-fifth of men acknowledge its existence. This is a major barrier to progressing gender equality and arguably acts as a limitation on firm performance. According to a study by McKinsey & Company, those firms which have the greatest number of women on their senior teams reported increased operational results, growth in equity, and a rise in share price. Furthermore, based on nine different criteria for organizational excellence, those firms in which women account for a third of the senior team perform better than those with no women at senior level. Having more women in senior positions therefore undoubtedly has a positive impact on company performance.

According to the *Harvard Business Review*, research has also shown that, although women tend to receive mentoring, they rarely have a sponsor to help them progress. In fact, males are 46 percent more likely to have a sponsor and, in turn, receive clear support and advice. PricewaterhouseCoopers (PwC), the UK's largest professional service firm offering assurance, advisory, and tax services, has taken steps to change this. In order to aid some of the organization's most talented females in achieving their full potential, in 2010 PwC launched its Female Board Mentoring Sponsorship program involving 26 employees, with 7 more joining since then. They were matched with senior male executives who in turn introduced them to their networks and worked with them on high-profile projects. Impressively, 60 percent of the women were selected for leadership roles and 90 percent had been promoted in the first three years of the program. PwC was awarded the "Opportunity Now Advancing Women in the Workplace" award in 2013 in recognition of its efforts.

Sources: Elizabeth Antoniou, "Glass ceiling – thing of the past?," *Performance Psychology*, OPM Consulting; Claire Cohen, "Women can be CEOs and mothers. But Marissa Mayer's maternity leave is a bum idea," *Telegraph*, September 5, 2015; Institute of Leadership & Management, "Women in banking," accessed from https://www.i-l-m.com/~/media/ILM%20Website/Downloads/Insight/Reports_from_ILM_website/Research_womeninbanking_march12%20pdf.ashx; Helen Briggs, "ONS: mothers' average age hits 30," *BBC News*, July 16, 2014; Emma Jacobs, "Sponsors crack glass ceilings," *Financial Times*, July 8, 2013; Rachel Savage, "Female managers aren't 'working for free'—but they are missing out on promotions," *Management Today*, August 25, 2015; PwC, "PwC—champion of gender equality," accessed from http://workplace.bitc.org.uk/ChampionPwC; Emily Stewart, "The diamond ceiling: women CEOs aren't hauling in gaudy pay packages like male peers", *The Street*, August 27, 2015; Equality and Human Rights Commission, *Employment and Earnings in the Finance Sector: A Gender Analysis*, 2009; McKinsey & Co., *Women Matter: Gender Diversity, A Corporate Performance Driver*, 2007; Sylvia Ann Hewlett, with Kerrie Peraino, Laura Sherbin, and Karen Sumberg, *The Sponsor Effect: Breaking through the Last Glass Ceiling*, December 2010, accessed from http://30percentclub.org/wp-content/uploads/2014/08/The-Sponsor-Effect.pdf

 Active learning check

Review your answer to Active Learning Case question 3 and make any changes you like. Then compare your answer to the one below.

3 **What type of training does Coca-Cola provide to its interns? Of what value is this training?**

The company puts interns into groups and assigns projects that require them to investigate or study certain areas of operations. The interns are then evaluated on the outcome. This training is useful in helping the firm identify those individuals who offer the most promise for the company.

COMPENSATION

In recent years compensation has become a primary area of IHRM attention.[17] On the one hand, multinationals want to hire the most competent people. On the other hand, they want to control costs and increase profits. Sometimes these two objectives are not compatible; it can be expensive to relocate an executive overseas. A close look at the breakdown of international compensation packages helps to make this clear.

Common elements in an international compensation package

A typical international compensation package includes base salary, benefits, and allowances. In addition, most packages address the issue of tax protection and/or tax equalization. The following examines these four elements.

Base salary

Base salary is the amount of cash compensation an individual receives in the home country. This salary is typically the benchmark against which bonuses and benefits are calculated. Survey research reveals that the salaries of expatriates are tied to their home country, so a German manager working for a US MNE and assigned to Spain will have a base salary tied to the salary structure in Germany.[18] This salary is usually paid in the home currency, the local currency, or a combination of the two.

Salary has become an issue when foreign firms have merged or acquired companies in other countries where salaries are significantly higher. For example, when Chrysler and Daimler-Benz merged, the Chairman and CEO of Chrysler had a salary of $1.6 million, whereas his Daimler-Benz counterpart was earning $1.1 million.[19] Moreover, international differences in salaries also create difficulties, as discussed below.

Benefits

Benefits often make up a large portion of the compensation package. There are also a number of difficult issues that typically must be resolved, including how to handle medical coverage, what to do about social security, and how to handle the retirement package. Some of the specific issues that receive a great deal of attention are:

- whether or not to maintain expatriates in home-country programs, particularly if the company does not receive a tax deduction for it;
- whether companies have the option of enrolling expatriates in host-country benefit programs and/or making up any difference in coverage;
- whether host-country legislation on termination affects benefit entitlements;
- whether expatriates should receive home-country or host-country social security benefits; and
- whether benefits should be maintained on a home-country or host-country basis, who is responsible for the cost, whether other benefits should be used to offset any shortfall in coverage, and whether home-country benefit programs should be exported to local nationals in foreign countries.

Most US MNEs include their expatriate managers in the company's benefit program and the cost is no more than it would be back home. In cases in which a foreign government also requires contribution to a social security program, the company picks up this expense for the employee. Fortunately, in recent years a number of international agreements have been signed that eliminate requirements for dual coverage.

MNEs also provide vacations and special leave to expatriates. This often includes company-paid air fare back home for the manager and family on an annual basis, as well as emergency leave and expense payments in case of death or illness in the family.

Allowances

Cost-of-living allowance
A payment to compensate for differences in expenditures between the home country and the foreign location

Allowances are another major portion of some expatriate compensation packages. One of the most common is the **cost-of-living allowance**, which is a payment to compensate for differences in expenditures between the home country and the foreign location. Designed to provide employees with the same standard of living they enjoyed in the home country, this allowance can cover a wide variety of areas, including relocation, housing, education, and hardship.

Relocation expenses usually include moving, shipping, and storage charges associated with personal goods that the expatriate is taking overseas. Related expenses can include perquisites such as cars and club memberships, which are commonly provided to senior-level managers.

Housing allowances cover a wide gamut. Some firms provide managers with a residence while overseas and pay all expenses associated with running the house. Other firms provide a predetermined amount of money each month, and the managers can make the housing choice personally. Some MNEs also help individuals sell their houses back home or rent them until their return. The company usually pays expenses associated with these activities. Other MNEs such as General Motors encourage their people to retain ownership of their homes by paying all rental management fees and reimbursing the employees for up to six months' rent if the house remains unoccupied.

Education allowances for an expatriate's children are an integral part of most compensation packages. These expenses cover such things as tuition, enrollment fees, books, supplies, transportation, room, board, and school uniforms. In some cases attendance at post-secondary schools is also provided.

Hardship allowance
A special payment made to individuals posted to geographic areas regarded as less desirable

A **hardship allowance** is a special payment made to individuals who are posted to areas regarded as less desirable. For example, parts of Europe, China, and some Middle East countries typically receive a hardship premium as an inducement to accept the assignment. These payments can be in the form of a lump sum ($10,000 to $25,000) or a percentage (15 to 50 percent) of the individual's base compensation.

Taxation

MNEs provide tax protection and/or tax equalization for expatriates. For example, a US manager sent abroad can end up with two tax bills: one for income earned overseas and the other for US taxes on these monies. Section 911 of the US Internal Revenue System code permits a deduction of up to $70,000 on foreign-earned income. For some executives, however, some US taxes might still be due. In handling these situations, most MNEs have a tax equalization program under which they withhold an amount equal to the home-country tax obligation of the manager and then pay all taxes in the host country. With tax protection, the employee pays up to the amount of taxes equal to those he or she would pay based on compensation in the home country. In this case, the employee is entitled to any difference if total taxes are less in the foreign country than in the home country. Other MNE tax considerations involve state and local tax payments and tax return preparation.

The most common approach is for the MNE to determine the base salary and other extras (bonuses etc.) the manager would make while living in the home country. The taxes on this income are then computed and compared to the total due on the expatriate's income, and the multinational pays any taxes over and above the amount that would have been due in the home country.

Compensation trends and comparisons

In terms of compensation, the MNE's objective is to ensure that expatriates do not have to pay any additional expenses as a result of living abroad. Figure 14.2 illustrates this idea. The income taxes, housing, goods and services, and reserve from the home country are protected so that the individual's out-of-pocket expenses remain the same. As we see from the figure, the overall package can be substantial. This is why there is a trend toward not sending expatriates to overseas positions unless there is a need for their specific services. In fact, the costs have become so prohibitive that firms like Dow Jones & Company, owner of the *Wall Street Journal*, long ago radically revised its formula for paying allowances for housing, goods, and services.[20] In addition, MNEs are increasingly replacing permanent relocation and long-term assignments with as-needed short trips that typically last less than a year.[21]

Another trend is the creation of special incentive systems designed to keep expatriates motivated. In the process, a growing number of MNEs are now dropping bonuses or premiums for overseas assignments and replacing them with lump-sum premiums. This approach has a number of benefits. One is that expatriates realize they will be given this payment just once—when they move to the international locale. So the payment tends to retain its value as an incentive. A second is that the costs to the company are less because there is only one payment and no future financial commitment.

The specific incentive program used will vary. Researchers have found that some of the factors that influence the type and amount of incentive include whether the person is moving within or between continents and where the person is being stationed. Table 14.1 provides some of the latest survey information related to these incentive practices.

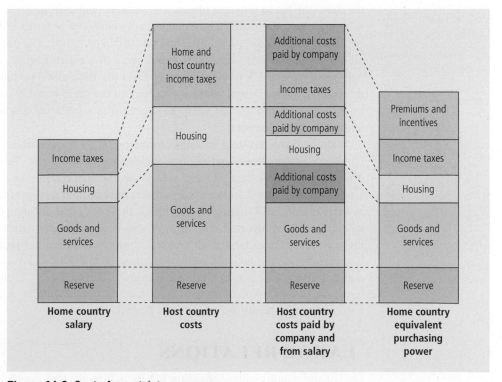

Figure 14.2 Cost of expatriate managers

Source: C. Reynolds, "Compensation of overseas personnel," in J. J. Famularo (ed.), *Handbook of Human Resource Administration,* 2nd ed. (New York: McGraw-Hill, 1986), p. 51.

Table 14.1 Employer incentive practices around the world

Type of premium	Asia (%)	Europe (%)	North America (%)	Total (%)
Respondents paying for moves within continent				
Ongoing	62	46	29	42
Lump sum	21	20	25	23
None	16	27	42	32
Respondents paying for moves between continents				
Ongoing	63	54	39	49
Lump sum	24	18	30	26
None	13	21	27	22

Source: Geoffrey W. Latta, "Expatriate incentives: beyond tradition," *HRfocus*, March 1998, p. S4. © *HRfocus*, March 1998. 212/244–0360. http://www.ioma.com

Finally, it is important to realize that many companies are beginning to phase out incentive premiums. Instead, they are focusing on creating a cadre of expats who are motivated by non-financial incentives.

More companies are starting to take an entirely different approach, paying *no* premiums to expatriates regardless of where they send them. According to this philosophy, an assignment itself is its own reward. It is an opportunity for an employee to achieve personal and career growth. In some organizations, succession planning for senior-level positions requires international experience. Others view expatriate assignments as a step toward achieving globalization. Companies that subscribe to the philosophy of paying no premiums only consider cost-of-living issues, not motivational rewards, when designing pay packages.

When we step back and compare salaries across countries, we get an insight into some of the difficulties maintaining parity or equality across groups of managers doing basically the same job but in different places. The starkest contrasts appear when we compare CEO salaries around the world. The United States stands out in terms of the average remuneration for CEOs compared to any other industrialized nation. For example, a group of non-US advanced countries (including Japan, most of western Europe, and Canada) averaged only 33 percent of US foreign CEO pay. Over the 1988–2003 period, US foreign CEO pay increased by 196 percent, whereas CEO pay in the set of non-US countries only increased by 129 percent.[22] This has been the source of a significant amount of criticism in the United States and beyond.[23]

What is also interesting in terms of international compensation comparisons is the gap between CEO pay levels and workers' salaries around the world. Table 14.2 shows the ratio difference between the CEO and average workers in a range of countries. CEOs in the United States are paid far more than in other nations, and earn over twice as much as CEOs in Switzerland and Germany. Even though there are clear differences between CEO wage rates, it has been reported that this may still be an underestimation of the gap in most of these countries because certain areas of compensation are not included in the figures.[24] The variation across national systems seems to be symbolic of broader socio-economic and cultural differences between these countries.[25] Differences in corporate governance systems, the role of financial incentives, and, more fundamentally, differences in the role of corporations in society are reflected in these data.

LABOR RELATIONS

One of the major challenges facing MNEs is that of orienting their strategy to meet the varying demands of organized labor around the world (see Figure 14.3). National differences in economic, political, and legal systems create a variety of labor relations systems,

Table 14.2 Ratio between CEO and average worker pay, 2014

Country	Ratio
US	354
Switzerland	148
Germany	147
Spain	127
Czech Republic	110
France	104
Australia	93
Sweden	89
UK	84
Israel	76
Japan	67
Norway	58
Portugal	53
Denmark	48
Austria	36
Poland	28

Source: Roberto A. Ferdman, "The pay gap between CEOs and workers is much worse than you realize," *Washington Post,* September 25, 2014.

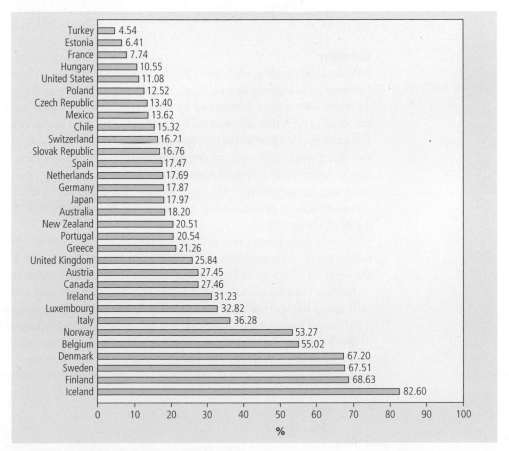

Figure 14.3 Trade union density, 2012

Note: Trade union density corresponds to the ratio of wage and salary earners that are trade union members, divided by the total number of wage and salary earners (OECD *Labour Force Statistics*). Density is calculated using survey data, wherever possible, and administrative data adjusted for non-active and self-employed members.
Source: OECD.Stat.

and the strategy that is effective in one country or region can be of little value in another country.

In managing labor relations, most MNEs use a combination of centralization and decentralization, with some decisions being made at headquarters and others being handled by managers on site.[26] Researchers have found that US MNEs tend to exercise more centralized control than European MNEs such as the British ones. A number of factors have been cited to explain this development: (1) US companies tend to rely heavily on formal management controls and a close reporting system is needed to support this process; (2) European companies tend to deal with labor unions at an industry level, whereas US MNEs deal at the company level; and (3) for many US firms the domestic market represents the bulk of their sales (a situation that is not true for many European MNEs) and the overseas market is managed as an extension of domestic operations.[27]

Labor relations practices

Labor relations practices vary widely. In some countries the economy is strong and unions are able to make major demands; in other countries the economy is weak and the unions' ability to bargain is diminished. Similarly, some countries have strong pro-management governments whereas others are heavily union oriented. A third factor is the willingness of unions to strike or walk out as opposed to continuing to talk with management in the hope of resolving differences. Germany and Japan provide some interesting contrasts.[28]

Germany

Labor unions traditionally have been strong in Germany. Although a minority of the labor force is organized, unions set the pay scale for about 90 percent of the country's workers, with wages determined by job classifications. Union membership is voluntary, but there is only one union in each major industry. This union negotiates a contract with the employers' federation for the industry, and the contract covers all major issues, including wages and terms of employment. If there is a disagreement over the interpretation or enforcement of the contract, the impasse is typically resolved between the company and the worker with the participation of a union representative or work council. If this procedure is unsuccessful, the matter can then be referred to a German labor court for final settlement.

Despite their power, unions have a much more cooperative relationship with management than do their counterparts in the United States. One reason is that workers serve on the board of directors and can ensure that the rank and file are treated fairly.

Strikes tend to occur after the contract has run out and a new one has yet to be ratified by the workers. As in the United States, several agreements may be in force in a particular company, and they do not have the same termination dates. So one group of workers may be striking or working without a contract while another is working under contract. On occasion, and in violation of the law, there may be strikes in the middle of a contract period, but this is rare and union and management typically have a good working relationship. However, whether this will continue in the future is difficult to say.

Japan

In Japan, union–management relationships are extremely cooperative. Social custom dictates non-confrontational behavior. So although labor agreements are often general and vague, disputes over interpretations tend to be settled amicably. Sometimes it is necessary to bring in third-party mediators or arbitrators, but there are no prolonged, acrimonious

Primark: putting global stakeholders first

Established in 1969, Primark is a subsidiary company of Associated British Foods (ABF) and is currently one of the largest clothing retailers in Europe. In 2014, Primark had 278 stores which employed 54,000 people in the UK, the Republic of Ireland, the Netherlands, Belgium, Austria, and France. Primark's competitive success is based on providing fashionable goods at the lowest possible price. With this unique strategic combination Primark has continually been able to increase its range, covering womenswear, menswear, children's wear, footwear, lingerie, accessories and homeware. In order to provide goods at the lowest possible price, Primark sources its goods from developing countries such as China, Bangladesh, India, and Vietnam. In 2014 Primark's total revenue was £4,950 million with a profit margin of 13.4 percent. As part of the ABF Group, Primark shares important ethical values in relation to its employees and wider stakeholders. These broadly include taking care of their people, being a good neighbor, respecting human rights, and engaging with stakeholder organizations. This case study looks at the different ways in which Primark engages with key external stakeholders. Figure 14.4 highlights a selected range of these stakeholder groups.

Primark incorporates a range of techniques in order to effectively engage with different stakeholder groups. For instance, when looking to engage with workers and communities within a given country, Primark uses the model of the community engagement program which it first used in India. However, one key lesson from Primark's experience in India was the importance of understanding the needs of specific groups of stakeholders in different countries and adapting its approach accordingly.

Trade unions and civil society groups

With the aim of protecting workers, Primark has been working closely with a range of global civil society groups and trade unions. The firm successfully engages with these groups by listening and learning about their concerns, often

Figure 14.4 Primark's key stakeholders
Source: Business Case Studies.

with the partnership of multiple stakeholders. They then jointly develop ways to overcome these issues. Two key organizations which assist Primark with this approach are the Ethical Trading Initiative (ETI) and the International Labor Organization's Better Work Program.

The ETI is an alliance of organizations, trade unions and other voluntary organizations that simultaneously work together in order to improve the lives of workers who produce their goods. Primark has been a member of the ETI since 2008 and was awarded "Leader" status by the ETI in 2011 and 2012. The "Leader" status is the highest possible status and demonstrates continuous and robust improvements in auditing and training programs and substantial engagement with external stakeholders.

In 2010, Primark became a member of the Better Work Program, which is a global partnership initiated by the UN's International Labor Organization to improve global labor practices. Being part of this program involves regular factory ▶

assessments, which seek to ensure adherence to international standards. Primark believes that collaboration with key external stakeholders helps generate innovation and sustainability in the global garment manufacturing industry as well as promoting fairness through improved wealth distribution.

Workers and communities

Primark primarily sources its products from garment world leaders such as China, Bangladesh, India, and Vietnam. As workers from these countries have often been recognized as being the most vulnerable within the supply chain, successful engagement within these communities is a critical component of Primark's ethical approach. Primark often works with local non-government organizations (NGOs), which have the local knowledge to support Primark's initiatives. A series of joint programs with NGOs demonstrates its commitment.

For instance, in Bangladesh, 16 factories which Primark continually buys from have been working closely with Nari Uddug Kendra (NUK), an NGO that focuses on women's rights. Working with NUK, Primark has introduced training schemes in factories with the aim of managing workers more fairly and educating them as to their rights. One report suggests that over 1,000 workers have been involved with this scheme. Since 2011, in Bangladesh, Primark has also introduced the HERproject, which has provided over 5,000 women workers with support in education, hygiene, sexual, and reproductive health issues. The HERproject has apparently led to an increase in the number of women now being able to access appropriate health clinics (by 89 percent) and contraception services (by 55 percent).

Furthermore, in China and Bangladesh, Primark has introduced projects with the aim of developing long-term improvements in labor standards and providing workers with living wages. In southern India, Primark has been working closely with another NGO to identify workers and families who may be at risk in regard to certain issues via the use of surveys, which guide initiation of education, hygiene, and gender projects in the region. Since 2011, Primark has also teamed up with Business for Social Responsibility (BSR), a corporate social responsibility organization with over 250 members, in order to identify labor migration trends within China.

Customers

Primark's competitive strength revolves around providing consumers with the latest fashionable goods at the lowest possible price. However, Primark does not have a significant advertising and marketing budget, as its strategy is to get consumers themselves to spread the word about its products. Even though Primark aims to provide consumers with products at the lowest possible price, it also actively seeks to ensure that it is complying with ethical guidelines. This is demonstrated on its ethical trading website, which provides Primark with a platform when communicating with its customers. Furthermore, Primark has been engaging with its customers via The School Project. The School Project aims to bring awareness among young people surrounding the topic of ethical trading.

Shareholders

As Primark's shareholders own the company, they ultimately have the power when making key decisions. For instance, shareholders are able to suggest and select individuals among the board members. Shareholders expect Primark to adopt ethical business practices among all its stakeholders. ABF issues a separate corporate social responsibility (CSR) report to its shareholders, which demonstrates the ways in which Primark has been acting upon its ethical and social responsibilities.

Conclusion

Primark is a successful clothing retailer in Europe which provides consumers with the latest fashionable goods at the lowest possible prices. Promising consumers low-priced products has often attracted negative media attention for the firm over the pay rates and conditions of its workers in developing-country factories. A closer look at the company's practices reveals that Primark acknowledges these concerns and is working closely with retailers, other brands, industry bodies, trade organizations, advocacy groups, NGOs, suppliers, workers, and communities to ensure their concerns are heard. Primark thoroughly believes that working together with stakeholders as a team can ensure all issues are appropriately raised and successfully addressed.

Sources: ABF, *Annual Report*, 2014; "Primark: engaging with stakeholders," *Business Case Studies*, accessed from http://businesscasestudies.co.uk/primark/engaging-with-stakeholders/introduction.html#axzz3l9A7QUpg; "Working with stakeholders", accessed from http://www.abf.co.uk/responsibility/our-actions/working_with_stakeholders_primark; Primark Ethical Trading, "Our work in Bangladesh," accessed from http://www.primark-bangladesh.com/our-work-in-bangladesh/; "Primark ethical trade team," accessed from http://www.abf.co.uk/responsibility/our-actions/primark_ethical_trade_team

---

disputes that end up in a plant being closed down because the two sides cannot work together. Typically, a strike is used merely to embarrass the management and seldom lasts longer than one week. Although it is possible to resort to legal action in resolving strikes, this is typically frowned upon by both labor and management, and both sides try to stay away from using this means of bringing about solutions to their problems.

Japanese unions are most active during the spring and at the end of the year, the two periods during which bonuses are negotiated. However, these activities do not usually end up in a union–management conflict. If there is a strike, it is more likely to be at a time when a Japanese union is negotiating with management during industry-wide negotiations. Even here, the objective is to show that the workers are supportive of the union and not to indicate a grievance or complaint with management. In overall terms, Japanese workers tend to subordinate their interests and identities to those of the group. This cultural value helps account for a great deal of the harmony that exists between labor and management.[29]

Industrial democracy

Industrial democracy
The legally mandated right of employees to participate in significant management decisions

Unlike the United States, many countries have **industrial democracy**, which is the legally mandated right of employees to participate in significant management decisions. This authority extends into areas such as wages, bonuses, profit sharing, work rules, dismissals, and plant expansions and closings. Industrial democracy can take a number of different forms.

Forms of industrial democracy

At present there are a number of forms of industrial democracy. In some countries one form may be more prevalent than others, and it is common to find some of these forms existing simultaneously. The following describes three of the most popular forms.

Codetermination

Codetermination
A legal system that requires workers and their managers to discuss major strategic decisions before companies implement the decisions

Codetermination is a legal system that requires workers and their managers to discuss major strategic decisions before companies implement them. It has brought about worker participation on boards of directors and is quite popular in Europe, where Austria, Denmark, the Netherlands, and Sweden have legally mandated codetermination. In many cases the workers hold one-third of the seats on the board, although it is 50 percent in private German companies with 2,000 or more employees. On the negative side, some researchers report that many workers are unimpressed with codetermination and feel that it does not provide sufficient worker input to major decisions.

Work councils

Work councils
Groups that consist of both worker and manager representatives and are charged with dealing with matters such as improving company performance, working conditions, and job security

Work councils are groups that consist of both worker and manager representatives and are charged with dealing with such matters as improving company performance, working conditions, and job security. In some firms these councils are worker or union run, whereas in others a management representative chairs the group. The councils are a result of either national legislation or collective bargaining at the company–union level, and they exist throughout Europe. However, their power varies. In Germany, the Netherlands, and Italy, work councils are more powerful than they are in the UK, France, and Scandinavia.

Shop floor participation

Shop floor participation takes many forms, including job enrichment programs, quality circles, and various other versions of participative management. These approaches give workers an opportunity to make their voices heard and play a role in identifying and resolving problems. Shop floor participation is widely used in Scandinavian countries and has spread to other European nations and the United States over the last two decades.

Industrial democracy in action

Industrial democracy can be found in different forms throughout the United States, Europe, and Asia. The following discussion examines three examples.

Germany

Industrial democracy and codetermination are both very strong in Germany, especially in the steel and auto industries. Private firms with 2,000 or more employees (in the steel industry it is 1,000 employees) must have supervisory boards (similar to a board of directors in the United States) composed of workers as well as managers. There must also be a management board responsible for daily operations to which company employees elect members.

Researchers have found that codetermination works well in Germany. Some critics have argued that too many people are involved in the decision-making process, which slows things down, resulting in inefficiencies. However, Scholl reports that a study he conducted of both managers and work councils found no such problems.[30]

Denmark

Industrial democracy in Denmark gives workers the right to participate in management on both a direct and an indirect basis. The direct form maintains that employees are members of semi-autonomous work groups that provide ideas on how to enhance productivity and quality, and how to schedule work. In the indirect form, shop stewards on the floor represent fellow workers on the board of directors, and on cooperation committees that consist of both management and worker representatives. Industrial democracy works exceptionally well in Denmark, where researchers have found that cooperation committees contribute substantially to openness, coordination of effort, and a feeling of importance on the part of workers.

Japan

Japan's use of industrial democracy concepts is not tied to political philosophy as in Europe; rather, it is oriented more to Japanese culture and the belief in group harmony. Moreover, Japanese industrial democracy is not as extensive as that in the West. Japanese workers are encouraged to identify and to solve job-related problems associated with quality and the flow of work. Management in turn is particularly receptive to worker ideas that will produce bottom-line results. This process is carried out in a paternalistic setting in which the company looks after the employees and the latter respond appropriately.

Unions play virtually no role in promoting industrial democracy or participative management because they are weak and, in many cases, only ceremonial. One group of researchers put it this way:

> In truth, most workers think of themselves as company employees who are simply associated with the union. Moreover, it is not uncommon to find a union strike in a company with two or three work shifts and no loss of work output. This is because, when the strikers are done picketing or marching, they then go to work and the group coming out of the factory takes up the strike activity. In a factory with three shifts, a line employee will work a full shift, picket for a while, go home to eat and sleep, and then return to the factory for her or his shift.[31]

As a result, Japanese MNEs face the greatest challenge from industrial democracy because they are least accustomed to using the idea.

STRATEGIC MANAGEMENT AND IHRM STRATEGIES

A number of HRM strategies are currently receiving attention from MNEs.[32] Four that do warrant consideration are language training, cultural adaptation, competitive compensation, and specially designed HRM programs.

Language training

English is the primary language of international business. However, training in the host-country language can be particularly useful because it allows managers to interact more effectively with their local colleagues and workers, and communicate more directly with suppliers and customers. Another advantage is that the training allows the manager to monitor the competition more effectively. For example, in recent years a growing number of US MNEs have set up operations in Japan, including DuPont, Eastman Kodak, Hewlett-Packard, IBM, Procter & Gamble, and Rockwell International. Many of these MNEs' expatriate managers and R&D personnel have been given language training, which has paid off handsomely. For example, when Rockwell International entered into negotiations with a Japanese firm over royalties on a patent it holds on advanced semiconductor processing technology, the Japanese company said it had no intention of using Rockwell's patent. However, the company negotiators were able to show the Japanese an article from a Japanese newspaper in which their company had boasted about using the new technology. As a result, Rockwell now receives royalties on the use of this technology by the Japanese company. In fact, thanks to language training, Rockwell was able to discover a host of patent infringements on the same technology by other Japanese firms.

Language training is useful in recruiting local talent and developing good relations with local organizations. IBM Japan, for example, hires 30 percent of its research scientists from Japanese universities or companies. Other US firms follow a similar pattern, offering large salaries ($150,000 and up) to attract senior Japanese scientists who can help create new high-tech products. Language training also comes in handy in developing and sustaining relationships with universities and government agencies. In fact, Dow Chemical has created a team for just this purpose.

Another benefit of language training is the ability to monitor competition. MNEs often locate near their major competitors because new developments by these firms are most likely to be reported in local newspapers and other sources. It is often possible to learn more about what a competitor is doing through local news media than one could ever find out from an investigation conducted by MNE headquarters. Many foreign MNEs have personnel who are fluent in English, peruse the *Wall Street Journal*, *New York Times*, and US industry publications on a daily basis, then compile a thick folder on the strategies of their US competitors.

Language training is also useful in helping to learn about a country's culture and to interact socially with the people. Research reports that most US expatriate managers give little importance to the value of a second language. In contrast, executives from South America, Europe, and Japan place a high priority on speaking more than one language. Fortunately, universities in the United States are now stepping in to help. For example, the Massachusetts Institute of Technology and other institutions of higher learning now offer courses in how to read technical Japanese and understand the Japanese research culture; this educational focus is likely to expand to other countries in the future. For the moment, however, language training continues to be a weak link in the development of an effective IHRM strategy for many MNEs.

 Active learning check

Review your answer to Active Learning Case question 4 and make any changes you like. Then compare your answer to the one below.

4 **How useful is it for Coca-Cola's managers to be fluent in more than one language? Why?**

Coca-Cola's managers must be fluent in other languages because the company believes this allows them to operate effectively in at least two different cultures. This permits the company to transfer managers from one geographic region to another and to know that the managers will be able to become acculturated within a minimum time period. Moreover, because there are common languages in many regions of the world, a manager who is fluent, say, in English and Spanish could be transferred to countries throughout North America, South America, Europe, Africa, and Australia. Thus, bilingualism provides the company with a cadre of managers who can literally span the globe.

Cultural adaptation

Closely tied to language training is the need for managers to understand the culture of the country to which they are assigned. The importance of culture was discussed in Chapter 5, where it was noted that major differences exist between cultural clusters. In preparing managers for overseas positions, MNEs are now using three basic approaches. The simplest and least expensive is to design a program that provides cultural orientation by familiarizing individuals with the country's cultural institutions and value systems. This is often done through a formal training program and/or meetings with company personnel who have just returned from a posting in that country. The second is to provide individuals with language training and, if time and money permit, allow them to visit the country. Some MNEs tie this approach to a manager's assignment by setting aside the first couple of weeks on site for orientation and acculturation. A third approach that is fairly expensive but has received high marks for its value is the use of cultural assimilators.

Cultural assimilators

Cultural assimilator
A programmed learning technique designed to expose members of one culture to some of the basic concepts, attitudes, role perceptions, customs, and values of another culture

A **cultural assimilator** is a programmed learning technique designed to expose members of one culture to some of the basic concepts, attitudes, role perceptions, customs, and values of another. Cultural assimilators are developed for pairs of cultures, such as familiarizing managers from the United States with the culture in Germany. Of course, an assimilator can be developed for expatriates who are assigned to any culture in the world, and the approach almost always takes the same format: the person being trained is asked to read a short episode of a cultural encounter and then choose an interpretation of what has happened and why. If the response is correct, the individual goes on to the next episode. If not, he or she is asked to reread the episode and then make another choice.

Cultural assimilators use critical incidents as the basis for training. These incidents are typically ones in which (1) the expatriate will be interacting with a host nation, (2) the situation may be misinterpreted or mishandled if the expatriate is not properly trained, and (3) the event is relevant to the expatriate's task or mission requirements. The incidents are provided by expatriates who have served in this particular country, as well as by members of the host nation. Once they are written, they are tested on people who have had experience in the country in order to ensure that the responses are realistic and that one choice is indeed preferable to the others. Typically, 150 to 200 incidents are developed and the list is pruned to 75 to 100 incidents, which are eventually included in the assimilator booklet.

Assimilators can be expensive to create. The typical cost for developing one is approximately $50,000. However, for MNEs that are continually sending people to a particular overseas location, the cost can be spread over many trainees and the assimilator can remain intact for a number of years. A $50,000 assimilator that is used with 500 people over a five-year period costs the company only $100 per person, and the cost of revising the program is often quite small, so over the long run the assimilators can be very cost effective.

Competitive compensation

MNEs are also beginning to evaluate more carefully the cost of sending people overseas as well as to review the expense of maintaining executive talent in the international arena. The first of these concerns focuses on all expatriates. The second addresses top-level managers only.

Compensation costs vary widely because goods and services in some countries are sharply higher (or lower) than in others. For example, food, clothes, and entertainment in the United States are fairly inexpensive compared to Japan, Hong Kong, Taiwan, or the UK (see Table 14.3). In particular, the cost-of-living allowance for managers in Europe and Japan adds significantly to the MNE's overhead. For this reason, major MNEs, from

Table 14.3 Cost of living in select cities (New York = 100), 2015

Location	Cost	Location	Cost
New York City	100.0	Montreal	58.9
Zurich	92.6	Brussels	57.3
Geneva	91.8	Rome	57.1
Oslo	79.9	Buenos Aires	56.1
London	79.5	Munich	56.1
Hong Kong	76.8	Amsterdam	55.5
Chicago	76.7	Manama	55.4
Copenhagen	74.3	Frankfurt	55.1
Sydney	72.5	Shanghai	54.3
Tokyo	70.6	Vienna	53.4
Miami	67.7	Beijing	53.2
Auckland	67.6	Istanbul	53.0
Los Angeles	67.4	Berlin	51.3
Luxembourg	66.1	Lyon	51.2
Dubai	66.1	Barcelona	50.5
Milan	64.5	Madrid	50.4
Seoul	64.2	São Paulo	49.5
Paris	63.8	Rio de Janeiro	49.2
Toronto	63.7	Nicosia	48.4
Helsinki	63.2	Athens	47.5
Dublin	63.1	Bangkok	46.4
Stockholm	62.8	Mexico City	46.2
Taipei	62.7	Lisbon	45.3
Tel Aviv	61.4	Moscow	45.2
Doha	61.4	Santiago de Chile	44.0

Source: https://www.ubs.com/microsites/prices-earnings/edition-2015.html

General Motors to IBM to TRW, are looking for ways to recruit and develop local talent to staff operations and thus reduce their reliance on expatriates.

The other major area of compensation that is receiving increased attention is hiring and retaining top management talent. Research shows that the cost of hiring senior-level managers is extremely high, and in most cases these individuals received a substantial salary raise when they moved into their new position. Moreover, as the demand for talented executives rises, the salaries of international managers will continue to rise. This is one reason why many MNEs are now hiring people for specific locations and leaving them in place for extended periods of time. This strategy is less costly than continually moving managers from one geographic location to another.

HRM strategy will become an increasingly important part of the overall MNE strategic plan. Rising compensation costs are one of the major reasons for this trend.

Specially designed HRM programs

Another emerging trend is specially designed HRM programs. In recent years a growing number of MNEs have begun to realize that HRM practices have to be tailor-made. This has been clearly illustrated by Sparrow and Budhwar, who compared data from 13 different countries on the basis of HRM factors. Five of these factors included the following:

1 Structural empowerment characterized by flat organization designs, wide spans of control, the use of flexible cross-functional teams, and the rewarding of individuals for productivity gains.

2 Accelerated resource development characterized by the early identification of high-potential employees, the establishment of both multiple and parallel career paths, the

rewarding of personnel for enhancing their skills and knowledge, and the offering of continuous training and development education.

3 Employee welfare emphasis characterized by firms offering personal family assistance, encouraging and regarding external volunteer activities, and promoting a culture that emphasizes equality in the workplace.

4 An efficiency emphasis in which employees are encouraged to monitor their own work and continually improve their performance.

5 An emphasis on long-term results such as innovation and creativity rather than just weekly and monthly short-term productivity.[33]

Research suggests that countries are unique in their approach to HRM. What works well in the United States may have limited value in France. This is even the case across Anglophone nations such as the United States, Canada, Australia, and the UK, where differences in employee welfare emphasis, accelerated resource development, long efficiency orientation, and long-term vision show different HRM profiles for each.

These findings point to the fact that MNEs in the future will have to focus increasingly on HRM programs designed to meet the needs of local personnel. A good example is provided in eastern Europe, where international managers are discovering that in order to effectively recruit college graduates their firms must provide training programs that give these new employees opportunities to work with a variety of tasks and help them specialize in their particular fields of interest. At the same time, the MNEs are discovering that these recruits are looking for companies that offer a good social working environment. A survey of more than 1,000 business and engineering students from Poland, the Czech Republic, and Hungary found that almost two-thirds of the respondents said they wanted their boss to be receptive to their ideas, 37 percent were looking for managers who had strong industry experience, and 34 percent wanted a boss who was a good rational decision-maker. These findings indicate that multinational HRM is now becoming much more of a two-way street: both employees and managers need to adjust continually to emerging demands.[34]

KEY POINTS

1 International human resource management (IHRM) is the process of selecting, training, developing, and compensating personnel in overseas positions. IHRM strategies involve consideration of staffing, selecting, training, compensating, and labor relations in the international environment.

2 A number of screening criteria are used in choosing people for international assignments. These include adaptability, self-reliance, age, experience, education, health, family status, motivation, and leadership. The most common selection procedure is the interview, although some firms also use testing. In recent years MNEs have also begun formulating repatriation strategies for integrating returning managers back into the workplace at home.

3 Training and development programs are another key part of IHRM strategies. There are a wide variety of these programs, ranging from environmental briefings to language training.

4 There are a number of common parts in a typical international compensation package, including base salary, benefits, allowances, and tax protection and/or equalization. In essence, the package's objective is to ensure that the expatriate does not have to pay any additional expenses as a result of living abroad.

5 Labor relations practices vary widely in the international arena. For example, union–management relations and industrial democracy approaches are different throughout Europe, and these differ dramatically from those in Japan.

6 A number of HRM strategies are currently receiving a great deal of attention from MNEs. Three of these are language training, cultural adaptation, and competitive compensation.

Key terms

- international human resource management (IHRM)
- home-country nationals
- expatriates
- host-country nationals
- third-country nationals
- international screening criteria

- repatriation
- transition strategies
- repatriation agreement
- training
- managerial development
- standardized training programs

- tailor-made training programs
- cost-of-living allowance
- hardship allowance
- industrial democracy
- codetermination
- work councils
- cultural assimilator

REVIEW AND DISCUSSION QUESTIONS

1 Many US MNEs are accused of not focusing their efforts sufficiently on internationalization. How can they develop an international perspective among their managers? Offer three suggestions.

2 What are some of the most common screening criteria for individuals being chosen for international assignments? Identify and discuss four of them.

3 Why do MNEs tend to prefer interviews to testing when selecting people for international assignments?

4 In what way is repatriation proving to be a major problem for MNEs? How can they deal with this issue? Offer two substantive recommendations.

5 What are some of the most common forms of training and development offered to people going international or already operating abroad? Identify and describe three of them.

6 What are the most important parts of an international compensation package? Identify and describe three of them.

7 Why do some compensation packages have a hardship allowance?

8 In terms of compensation, why do many MNEs prefer to use a local manager rather than bring in an expatriate?

9 What are some of the primary differences in labor relations practices between Germany and Japan? Identify and discuss two of them.

10 How does industrial democracy work? Compare and contrast its use in Denmark, Germany, and Japan.

11 How are MNEs attempting to improve the language training given to their personnel being posted overseas?

12 How would an MNE use a cultural assimilator to prepare people for overseas assignments?

13 What are some of the latest trends in competitive compensation in the international arena? Identify and describe two of them.

REAL CASE

Offshoring to India

When outsourcing crosses national borders it is called offshoring, but over the last few years, British trade unions and US politicians have been campaigning to stop offshoring—at a time when a growing number of firms, including Lloyds TSB, HSBC, Abbey, IBM, and JP Morgan, are using India's service professionals. In the mid-2000s, India's high-tech sector was growing at 30 percent per year and the volume of outsourcing contracts at 50 percent per year. IT sector exports were $12 billion in 2004 and rose to $32 billion by 2007 and again to $55 billion by 2014.

The growth of the Indian IT sector is surprising because it lacked the domestic factors typically associated with the development of a competitive industry. First, local demand for software was non-existent. Second, related and supporting industries such as telecoms or computing were highly underdeveloped. Third, the national communication infrastructure was among the worst in the world. Fourth, despite India's relatively higher level of education in relation to other countries, it was nowhere near the level of the triad countries. Finally, financial capital was in short supply.

Clearly, some general conditions help account for the time of the growth period, not least the global shortage of software programming skills relative to demand. The imbalance between supply and demand pushed up the price of software skills, globally increasing the cheap labor advantage held by Indian firms. This, coupled with strong English language skills, made Indian programmers good substitutes for more expensive Western programmers. Software engineers technically trained in the United States and Europe had developed customer links to the major customer firms (banks, telecoms, IT companies, and so on) in the West and then returned to India to establish their own ventures. New technologies enabled Indian firms to service the needs of overseas customers via satellite and the internet. Transportation costs are insignificant and the geographic time difference can be an asset, allowing Indian firms to work through the "Western night." Finally, the Indian government had identified software as an area of potential growth in the 1970s and supported it through the 1990s, when the industry began to explode. Another important factor has been the willingness of computer firms, such as Computer Associates, to invest in the Indian market.

In the United States, fears of job losses are forcing politicians to take a stand. A US government regulation now prohibits the offshoring of government services. This, however, has little effect on India's industry, which has traditionally relied on private contracts. Supporters of outsourcing argue that it is beneficial to customers who can now pay less for services and that the rise in wealth in India would increase bilateral trade, creating opportunities for US firms. Indeed, a recent study by McKinsey estimates that for every dollar of US outsourcing,

78 cents are value created in the United States and only 22 cents are retained by the foreign country. The British government is taking a different stand from the US government and is offshoring to India the IT systems for the National Health Service. It is no longer just IT jobs. Offshoring of accountant services, medical services, research, and data entry to India is also growing.

Offshoring does not always run smoothly. In the case of call centers, despite employee training in different English accents, customers have complained of problems communicating. In addition, the cultures might clash. On the other hand, many argue that Indian workers are more professional and better educated than their Western counterparts. The industry might be attracting a disproportionate number of bright minds in India because of the relatively higher standard of living enjoyed by those in the industry.

Today, Indian IT firms like Tata Consultancy Services, Infosys Technology, Wipro Technologies, and Satyam Computer Services are diversifying their portfolios and increasingly relying on e-commerce and other internet-related businesses to cushion themselves against changes in the outsourcing market. Four factors drive this diversification: political risk from protectionists, rising wages, the rising value of the rupee, and growing competition from other nations such as China and Russia.

Websites: www.ca.com; www.wipro.com; www.infosys.com; www.tata.com; www.satyam.com

Sources: http://www.nasscom.in/india-itbpm-exports, 2015; Zuhair Ahmed, "India dismisses outsourcing fears," BBC News, February 9, 2004; "US outsourcing is 'accelerating'," *BBC News*, June 17, 2004; Kaushik Basu, "Outsourcing: long-term gains for all," *BBC News*, March 29, 2004; NASSCOM–McKinsey, *Extending India's Leadership in the Global IT and BPO Industries*, New Delhi, 2005; http://www.nasscom.in/

1 Porter's well-known 1990 study on the competitive advantage of nations describes factors that have promoted high rates of innovation in certain industries in certain countries. These are summarized as the Porter diamond framework showing how factor conditions, related and supporting industries, demand conditions, and the strategy, structure, and rivalry of other local firms can force continual improvements in productivity and new product development. How does the development of Indian IT fit into this framework?

2 What are the threats and opportunities for Western software firms arising from this shift in the competitive landscape? How are they strategically responding to these?

3 What factors must a firm considering outsourcing take into account?

Executive search firms

Commonly known as headhunters, executive search firms (ESFs) are a specialized branch of management consulting that work directly with clients, usually MNEs, to identify, evaluate, and recruit senior executives. Most *Fortune* 1,000 companies use ESFs to fill positions ranging from entry level to CEO and board member. Worldwide ESFs are an $18 billion industry. Their fees are a percentage of the salary (including equity) that the chosen candidate will receive in the first year of employment, which creates the right incentives for bargaining for high salaries by their executives. The largest firms are shown in Table 14.4. These firms are highly competitive, particularly in North America and Europe. There are also many small local boutique firms, but these often work with the major international chains for MNE recruiting.

After several years of dot.com-driven prosperity, the slowdown of the world economy hit the ESFs hard. Between 1998 and 2000, the industry had enjoyed a boom with annual growth of over 20 percent. In the United States, growth was even higher at 31 percent in 2000. By the first few years of the new century, however, the crash of the IT industry and the US recession had reduced the number of executive spots and put a freeze on new hiring for many positions. Between 2000 and 2003, almost all ESFs were reporting losses and many headhunters were looking for work themselves. By 2004, things had started to turn around for ESFs, especially in financial services, real estate, security, and construction, which once again began to hire. Since then business has picked up once again: 2006 saw a 9 percent increase in searches and a 13 percent increase in revenues for ESFs.

To offset the strong dependence on the business cycle, ESFs are increasingly diversifying. Korn Ferry and Heidrick & Struggles now offer strategic management assessments and executive development services. A third of Egon Zehnder International's revenues come from non-search work. The

Table 14.4 Top executive search firms, 2014

Rank	Name	Number of offices	Corporate headquarters
1	Boyden	70	US
2	Korn Ferry	80	US
3	TRANSEARCH	55	France
4	Egon Zehnder	60	Switzerland
5	N2Growth	6	US
6	Heidrick & Struggles	75	US
7	Russell Reynolds	40	US
8	Spencer Stuart	50	Netherlands, Ireland, and US
9	Stanton Chase International	70	UK
10	Bo Le Associates	25	China
11	Signium	40	US
12	Slayton Search Partners	-	US
13	Witt/Kieffer	9	US
14	DHR International	50	US
15	CTPartners	24	US
16	Polachi	-	US
17	Ridgeway Partners	3	US
18	Wyatt Jaffe	-	US
19	John Peebles Associates	-	New Zealand
20	RSR Partners	5	US

Note: In order to qualify for the Top 20 Executive Search Firms list, organizations must be retained search firms, have multiple practice areas, have displayed recognized thought leadership, and have completed signature searches for global brands in multiple geographies. The ranking order for the Top 20 Executive Search Firms list is derived algorithmically based upon a proprietary weighting of the following criteria: annual revenue, number of placements, number of ancillary services or practice areas, level of searches handled by average salary, completion ratio, average time to complete, stick rate, client satisfaction (testimonials/votes), social media presence, and executive thought leadership. The algorithm also negatively weights adverse circumstances (e.g. candidate exited based upon discovery which the search firm should have filtered, client litigation, poaching, etc.).

Source: http://www.topexecutivesearchfirms.com/top-executive-search-firms/

▶

company has become a consultant for private investors who want to evaluate a firm's quality of management. Like its competitors, it has entered the human resource development business by providing mid-sized MNEs with an assessment team. It now has 283 consultants serving client needs from 58 offices worldwide. Diversification has allowed these companies to reduce reliance on executive searches as a line of business; branching into consulting, however, is unlikely to provide much respite for ESFs since consulting firms face similar challenges.

Alongside some degree of diversification, ESFs have significantly internationalized in recent years, following the relocation of clients and the growth of executive search services outside the triad regions.

Korn Ferry, for example, has 500 consultants in 80 offices in 39 countries and has expanded its presence in China and India considerably over the past few years. Research by Faulconbridge et al. has shown how the industry has evolved through several stages: organic growth after the 1960s, M&A from the late 1970s, and the development of a variety of alliance networks more recently. This expansion path has given rise to several distinctive organizational forms: the wholly owned multinational, such as Heidrick & Struggles International, Spencer Stuart, and Egon Zehnder International; the networked transnational, such as the Globe Search Group; and hybrid organizations, such as Korn Ferry, which adopt either structure, depending on the market context or client needs.

But analysis of the figures in *Executive Grapevine* in 2010, an annual report on headhunting, suggests that some parts of the industry face pressure from business networking websites such as LinkedIn, which completed a successful initial public offering in May 2011. More significant is the way that companies are using business networking websites to negotiate better rates for external searches. The report indicates that employers no longer need headhunters to put names on a shortlist. They need them to do the selling, to persuade people to move. At the top levels people are still not used to social networks. They tend to be older and once they step outside certain sectors, like technology, the social networks have not really had an impact. Headhunters themselves are divided over the impact of business networking websites. Some believe they can be useful in executive searches. Historically, it might have taken ten days or so to find a particular person who had disappeared off the radar. Now it takes you 20 seconds. Some do not believe it will replace executive search firms any time soon. Even so, some practitioners believe that the continued growth of networking websites may force headhunters out of the market at the lower end of their current business model, because they will make it hard for search firms to raise fee levels even when general market conditions improve. This would leave the headhunters even more heavily exposed to the fortunes of the high earners in the financial sector, for example in the UK, than they are already.

Websites: www.kornferry.com; www.heidrick.com; www.spencerstuart.com; www.russreyn.com; www.zehnder.com; www.hhgroup.com; www.rayberndtson.com; www.onrec.com/newsstories/; www.amrophever.com

Sources: James R. Faulconbridge, Sarah J. E. Hall, and Jonathan V. Beaverstock, "New insights into the internationalization of producer services: organizational strategies and spatial economies for global headhunting firms," *Environment and Planning A*, vol. 40, no. 1 (2008), pp. 210–34; www.kornferry.com; Kathy Showalter, "Headhunting firm benefits from stable relationships," *Columbus Business First*, September 19, 2003; Alison Smith and Gill Plimmer, "Headhunters track down fee increases," *Financial Times*, July 10, 2011.

1   When staffing the needs of the foreign subsidiary of a German company, what pool of candidates can the ESF choose from? Why would an international ESF be more capable of performing this task than the MNE's internal human resources department?

2   How would compensation negotiations differ for home-, host-, and third-country candidates?

3   What types of factors would the ESF use to identify a potential candidate for an overseas assignment?

NOTES

1   Chris Brewster and Wolfgang Mayrhofer, *Handbook of Research on Comparative Human Resource Management* (London: Edward Elgar, 2012).

2   Rosalie L. Tung, "Selection and training procedures of US, European, and Japanese multinationals," *California Management Review*, vol. 25, no. 1 (fall 1982), p. 59.

3   Richard M. Hodgetts and Fred Luthans, *International Management*, 4th ed. (Homewood, IL: Irwin/McGraw, 2000), p. 430.

4   Anne-Wil K. Harzing and Joris Van Ruysseveldt (eds.), *International Human Resource Management: Managing People Across Borders*, 2nd ed. (London: Sage, 2003).

5   Ingemar Torbiorn, *Living Abroad* (New York: Wiley, 1982), p. 98.

6   Hodgetts and Luthans, *International Management*, p. 434.

7   Bernd Kupka and Virginia Cathro, "Desperate housewives—social and professional isolation of German expatriated spouses," *International Journal of Human Resource Management*, vol. 18, no. 6 (2007), pp. 951–68.

8   Michael Harvey, "Dual career expatriates: expectations, adjustments and satisfaction with international relocation," *Journal of International Business Studies*, vol. 28, no. 3 (winter 1997). See also Hung-Wen Lee, "Factors that influence expatriate failure: an interview study," *International Journal of Management*, vol. 24, no. 3 (2007), pp. 403–13.

9 Torbiorn, *Living Abroad*, pp. 156–61.

10 Tung, "Selection and training procedures," p. 64.

11 Helene Mayerhofer, Linley C. Hartmann, and Anne Herbert, "Career management issues for flexpatriate international staff," *Thunderbird International Business Review*, vol. 46, no. 6 (2004), pp. 647–66.

12 Chris Brewster, Paul Sparrow, and Guy Vernon, *International Human Resource Management*, 2nd ed. (London: Chartered Institute of Personnel and Development, 2007).

13 Jie Shen, "International training and management development: theory and reality," *Journal of Management Development*, vol. 24, no. 7 (2005), pp. 656–66.

14 Paul R. Sparrow, "Globalization of HR at function level: four UK-based case studies of the international recruitment and selection process," *International Journal of Human Resource Management*, vol. 18, no. 5 (2007), pp. 845–67; Steven H. Rhinesmith, "An agenda for globalization," *Training and Development Journal*, February 1991, pp. 22–9.

15 "Company culture in the global village," *Philips' What's Up Archive*, July 12, 1999; see also Leandra Celaya and Jonathan S. Swift, "Pre-departure cultural training: US managers in Mexico," *Cross Cultural Management*, vol. 13, no. 3 (2006), pp. 230–43.

16 Tung, "Selection and training procedures," p. 65.

17 Brewster et al., *International Human Resource Management*.

18 Peter J. Dowling and Randall S. Schuler, *International Dimensions of Human Resource Management* (Boston, MA: PWS-Kent Publishing, 1990), p. 121. Also see Marion Festing, Judith Eidems, and Susanne Royer, "Strategic issues and local constraints in transnational compensation strategies: an analysis of cultural, institutional and political influences," *European Management Journal*, vol. 25, no. 2 (2007), pp. 118–31.

19 Greg Steinmetz and Gregory L. White, "Chrysler pay draws fire overseas," *Wall Street Journal*, May 26, 1998, p. B1.

20 Alex S. Jones, "Dow Jones plans to tighten foreign policy for workers," *New York Times*, September 9, 1991, p. C6.

21 "Nasty, brutish and short," *The Economist*, December 14, 2000.

22 John Alexander Burton and Christian E. Weller, "Supersize this: how CEO pay took off while America's middle class struggled" (Washington, DC: Center for American Progress, May 2005).

23 Eduardo Porter, "More than ever, it pays to be the top executive," *New York Times*, May 25, 2007.

24 Burton and Weller, "Supersize this."

25 Marion Festing, Judith Eidems, and Susanne Royer, "Strategic issues and local constraints in transnational compensation strategies: an analysis of cultural, institutional and political influences," *European Management Journal*, vol. 25, no. 2 (2007), pp. 118–31.

26 See, for example, Laurie Hays, "IBM's finance chief, ax in hand, scours empires for costs to cut," *Wall Street Journal*, January 26, 1994, pp. A1, A6.

27 C. K. Prahalad and Y. L. Doz, *The Multinational Mission: Balancing Logical Demands and Global Vision* (New York: Free Press, 1987).

28 Howard F. Gospel and Andrew Pendleton, *Corporate Governance and Labour Management* (Oxford: Oxford University Press, 2005).

29 Mari Sako, *Shifting Boundaries of the Firm: Japanese Company–Japanese Labour* (Oxford: Oxford University Press, 2006).

30 Wolfgang Scholl, "Codetermination and the ability of firms to act in the Federal Republic of Germany," *International Studies of Management & Organization* (summer 1987), pp. 27–37.

31 Hodgetts and Luthans, *International Management*, p. 504.

32 Günter K. Stahl and Ingmar Björkman, *Handbook of Research in International Human Resource Management* (Cheltenham: Edward Elgar, 2006).

33 Paul R. Sparrow and Pawan S. Budhwar, "Competition and change: mapping the Indian HRM recipe against world-wide patterns," *Journal of World Business*, vol. 32, no. 3 (fall 1997), p. 231.

34 Bodil Jones, "What future European recruits want," *Management Review* (January 1998), p. 6.

BIBLIOGRAPHY

Athanassiou, Nicholas A., and Roth, Kendall. "International experience heterogeneity effects on top management team advice networks: a hierarchical analysis," *Management International Review*, vol. 46, no. 6 (2006).

Bhanugopan, Ramudu, and Fish, Alan, "Replacing expatriates with local managers: an exploratory investigation into obstacles to localization in a developing country," *Human Resource Development International*, vol. 10, no. 4 (December 2007).

Bolino, Mark C. "Expatriate assignments and intra-organizational career success: implications for individuals and organizations," *Journal of International Business Studies*, vol. 38, no. 5 (September 2007).

Briscoe, Dennis R., and Schuller, Randall S. *International Human Resource Management* (London: Routledge, 2004).

Caprar, Dan V. "Foreign locals: a cautionary tale on the culture of MNC local employees," *Journal of International Business Studies*, vol. 42 (2011).

Carr, Stuart C., Inkson, Kerr, and Thorn, Kaye. "From global careers to talent flow: reinterpreting 'brain drain'," *Journal of World Business*, vol. 40, no. 4 (November 2005).

Chen, Stephen, Geluykens, Ronald, and Choi, Chong Ju. "The importance of language in global teams: a linguistic perspective," *Management International Review*, vol. 46, no. 6 (2006).

Chiang, Flora F. T., and Birtch, Thomas A. "Appraising performance across borders: an empirical examination of the purposes and practices of performance appraisal in a multi-country context," *Journal of Management Studies*, vol. 47, no. 7 (November 2010).

Collings, David G., Scullion, Hugh, and Morley, Michael J. "Changing patterns of global staffing in the multinational enterprise: challenges to the conventional expatriate assignment and emerging alternatives," *Journal of World Business*, vol. 42, no. 2 (June 2007).

Fang, Yulin, Jiang, Guo-Liang, Frank, Makino, Shige, and Beamish, Paul W. "Multinational firm knowledge, use of expatriates, and foreign subsidiary performance," *Journal of Management Studies*, vol. 47, no. 1 (January 2010).

Fey, Carl F, Morgulis-Yakushev, Sergey, Park, Hyeon Jeong, and Björkman, Ingmar. "Opening the black box of the relationship between HRM practices and firm performance: a comparison of MNE subsidiaries in the USA, Finland, and Russia," *Journal of International Business Studies*, vol. 40 (May 2009).

Gammelgaard, Jens, McDonald, Frank, Tüselmann, Heinz, Dörrenbächer, Christoph, and Stephan, Andreas. "Subsidiary role and skilled labor effects in small developed countries," *Management International Review*, vol. 49, no. 1 (2009).

Goerzen, Anthony, and Beamish, Paul W. "The Penrose effect: 'excess' expatriates in multinational enterprises," *Management International Review*, vol. 4, no. 2 (2007).

Gooderham, Paul N., et al. "National and firm-level drivers of the devolution of HRM decision making to line managers," *Journal of International Business Studies* (2015).

Holtbrügge, Dirk, and Mohr, Alex T. "Subsidiary interdependencies and international human resource management practices in German MNCs," *Management International Review*, vol. 51, no. 1 (2011).

Iles, Paul, Xin Chuai, and Preece, David. "Talent management and HRM in multinational companies in Beijing: definitions, differences and drivers," *Journal of World Business*, vol. 45, no. 2 (2010).

Jun, Sunkyu, Gentry, James W., and Hyun, Yong J. "Cultural adaptation of business expatriates in the host marketplace," *Journal of International Business Studies*, vol. 32, no. 2 (June 2001).

Kirkman, Bradley L., Lowe, Kevin B., and Gibson, Cristina B. "A quarter century of *Culture's Consequences*: a review of empirical research incorporating Hofstede's cultural values framework," *Journal of International Business Studies*, vol. 37, no. 3 (March 2006).

Kostova, Tatiana, Valentina Marano, and Stephen Tallman. "Headquarters–subsidiary relationships in MNCs: fifty years of evolving research," *Journal of World Business*, vol. 51, no. 1 (2016).

Lawler, John J., Chen, Shyh-jer, Wu, Pei-Chuan, Bae, Johngseok, and Bing Bai, Bing. "High-performance work systems in foreign subsidiaries of American multinationals: an institutional model," *Journal of International Business Studies*, vol. 42 (October 2010).

Loess, Kurt H., and Yavas, Ugur. "Human resource collaboration issues in international joint ventures: a study of US–Japanese auto supply IJVs," *Management International Review*, vol. 43, no. 3 (2003).

Mäkelä, Kristiina, et al. "Determinants of strategic HR capabilities in MNC subsidiaries," *Journal of Management Studies*, vol. 49, no. 8 (2012).

Maloney, Mary M., and Zellmer-Brun, Mary. "Building bridges, windows and cultures: mediating mechanisms between team heterogeneity and performance in global terms," *Management International Review*, vol. 46, no. 6 (2006).

Mezias, John M., and Scandura, Terri A. "A needs-driven approach to expatriate adjustment and career development: a multiple mentoring perspective," *Journal of International Business Studies*, vol. 36, no. 5 (September 2005).

Minbaeva, Dana, et al. "MNC knowledge transfer, subsidiary absorptive capacity and HRM," *Journal of International Business Studies*, vol. 45, no. 1 (2014).

Morris, Shad S., and Snell, Scott A. "Intellectual capital configurations and organizational capability: an empirical examination of human resource subunits in the multinational enterprise," *Journal of International Business Studies*, vol. 42 (August 2011).

Newenham-Kahindi, Aloysius. "Human resource strategies for managing back-office employees in subsidiary operations: the case of two investment multinational banks in Tanzania," *Journal of World Business*, vol. 46, no. 1 (2011).

Nielsen, Sabina. "Top management team internationalization and firm performance," *Management International Review*, vol. 50, no. 2 (2010).

Punnett, Betty Jane, Greenidge, Dion, and Ramsey, Jase. "Job attitudes and absenteeism: a study in the English speaking Caribbean," *Journal of World Business*, vol. 42, no. 2 (June 2007).

Reiche, B. Sebastian, Kraimer, Maria L., and Harzing, Anne-Wil. "Why do international assignees stay? An organizational embeddedness perspective," *Journal of International Business Studies* 42 (May 2011).

Robson, Matthew J., Paparoidamis, Nicholas, and Ginoglu, Dimitrios. "Top management staffing in international strategic alliances: a conceptual explanation of decision perspective and objective formation," *International Business Review*, vol. 12, no. 2 (April 2003).

Schuler, Randall S. *Managing Human Resources in Cross-Border Alliances* (London: Routledge, 2004).

Shaffer, Margaret A. "Dimensions, determinants, and differences in the expatriate adjustment process," *Journal of International Business Studies*, vol. 30, no. 3 (September 1999).

Shay, Jeffrey P., and Baack, Sally A. "Expatriate assignment, adjustment and effectiveness: an empirical examination of the big picture," *Journal of International Business Studies*, vol. 35, no. 3 (May 2004).

Smale, Adam, Björkman, Ingmar, and Sumelius, Jennie. "Examining the differential use of global integration mechanisms across HRM practices: evidence from China," *Journal of World Business*, vol. 48, no. 2 (2013).

Taylor, Sully. "Creating social capital in MNCs: the international human resource management challenge," *Human Resource Management Journal*, vol. 17, no. 4 (2007).

Taylor, Sully, Beechler, Schon, and Napier, Nancy. "Toward an integrative model of strategic international human resource management," *Academy of Management Review*, vol. 21, no. 4 (October 1996).

Thomas, David C., Lazarova, Mila B., and Inkson, Kerr. "Global careers: new phenomenon or new perspectives?" *Journal of World Business*, vol. 40, no. 4 (November 2005).

Welch, Denice E. "Globalization of staff movements: beyond cultural adjustment," *Management International Review*, vol. 43, no. 2 (2003).

Yamazaki, Yoshitaka. "Expatriate adaptation," *Management International Review*, vol. 50, no. 1 (2010).

Zellmer-Bruhn, Mary, and Gibson, Cristina. "Multinational organization context: implications for team learning and performance," *Academy of Management Journal*, vol. 49, no. 3 (June 2006).

Chapter 15

POLITICAL RISK AND NEGOTIATION STRATEGY

Contents

Objectives of the chapter

For international managers, different countries represent different business contexts with new sources of opportunity and risk. Political change, whether gradual or sudden, can be a source of both, and tends to be a particularly important factor in emerging and developing countries. Changes in institutions, governance systems, and business-related legislation are frequent in such countries and can radically change the local "rules of the game." An important management priority is to fully assess the risks as well as the potential rewards before and after investing in these kinds of new markets. Major political changes in China and India in the early 1990s, for example, opened up these economies for foreign investors. They had always been attractive markets, but were made accessible by government-led liberalization. However, the high level of control still held by these governments over their economies, combined with the continued uncertainty regarding political change, results in a high level of political risk for investors.

Beyond these major political shifts, smaller changes in any government's policies toward foreign investors—from taxes and tariffs to profit repatriation to local input content to employment legislation to corporate governance practices—can tilt the balance between profit and loss.

This chapter examines political risk in the context of overall country risk assessment. We look at how multinational enterprises (MNEs) try to forecast this risk, how they can understand governments' policy agendas, and how they can use negotiating tactics to minimize their political risk.

The specific objectives of this chapter are to:

1 *Examine* the nature of political risk.

2 *Understand* how to apply some of the tools and resources that companies can use to measure and forecast political risk.

3 *Discuss* some of the ways that firms manage risk.

4 *Review* typical strategies and tactics used in negotiating agreements.

Nestlé in Nigeria

Nestlé is one of the largest multinational firms in the world with operations in 197 countries, 442 factories in 86 countries, and almost 340,000 employees. It first entered the Nigerian market as a trading company in 1961 and has recently invested over $500 million to expand its operations. In 2014/15 it focused on a major project investing $28 million for bottled water production across a distributed set of plants near the main cities, under the "Nestlé Pure Life" brand. It has also expanded the Nestlé Flowergate Factory, a Maggi production facility near Sagamu in the Nigerian state of Ogun. This was opened in 2011 and employs over 4,000 people. The Maggi brand is part of Nestlé's food seasoning and culinary products division and is also very popular in India.

Nigeria is a country of contrasts. It has a GDP estimated at over $560 billion, making it the largest economy in Africa, substantially larger than South Africa. It has been listed among the "MINT" countries (Mexico, Indonesia, Nigeria, and Turkey), seen as the next group of large, fast-growing economies after the BRICs (Brazil, Russia, India, and China). It also boasts Africa's richest man, Aliko Dangote, whose $23 billion-plus industrial conglomerate produces cement, flour, and sugar, while 60 percent of his 175 million countrymen live in severe poverty. Literacy rates and mortality rates are very low, placing Nigeria firmly in the developing country category.

One of the earliest attractions for foreign firms investing in Nigeria was the local oil industry. It is the biggest oil exporter in Africa and has the largest natural gas reserves in the continent. This industry is currently suffering from the downturn in global prices, but theft and corruption have also undermined the development of the industry, forcing many foreign investors to close down operations. More recently, strong growth in cell phones (it has 70 percent mobile penetration), banking, and the "Nollywood" movie industry have attracted inward investment via joint ventures and alliances.

Local purchasing power is also growing. According to the African Development Bank (ADB), the Nigerian middle class consists of 23 percent of the population with average households having a monthly income ranging between $600 and $850. This buying power is a key attraction for Nestlé and a wide range of global consumer products companies. The food and beverages sectors, key to Nestlé, grew by 60 percent between 2007 and 2011.

But entering this market and operating a business in Nigeria carries significant risks for multinational firms, compared to other country markets. Underdeveloped infrastructure, weak institutions, and cultural and social tensions all add to the normal complexities of management. In the World Bank's "ease of doing business" rankings, it is listed at 170 out of 189.

The poor energy infrastructure (ranked 187 out of 189 countries for "getting electricity" in the above ranking) means that to avoid outages manufacturers have to establish a reliable alternative source of power. This can cost 25 percent of their overall start-up costs. The weak transport infrastructure adds to the costs of product distribution and has risen by 15 percent in the past two years. For Nestlé specifically, distribution and selling expenses have grown ahead of turnover at 11 percent over the past few years, as have the cost of sales, by 8.6 percent. Finally, like other firms it is dependent on imports. Inefficient transport facilities combined with corrupt officials create expensive delays. Goods that are not fast-tracked are said to take about 60 days at the port in Lagos. Predicting which costs will grow and how quickly is a key to estimating future profitability or economic viability for foreign investors.

Economic inefficiency, uncertainty, and instability in Nigeria are exacerbated by a range of political risks. Nigeria's 200 ethnic groups, 500 indigenous languages and complex regional politics underpin long-running tensions alongside the more recent impact of Islamist insurgents. Religious terrorist activity tended to affect the poorer northeast in the past, but has recently struck in the capital, Abuja. There have been over 4,000 deaths in the past four years and a large number of kidnappings, including the 200 schoolgirls taken by the infamous Boko Haram sect in 2014.

Corruption is also a major hurdle for all managers, foreign and local. Transparency International ranks Nigeria 136 out of 175 in its "Corruption Perception Index" and the "misuse of public power for private gain" affects business at the national and local levels. In a long-running scandal over oil revenues, the Central Bank governor, Lamido Sanusi, was suspended after exposing a multibillion-dollar hole in the oil accounts. Despite assurances President Goodluck Jonathan's administration was unable to answer whether $3 billion, $10 billion, or $20 billion was missing! In 2015 Goodluck's administration was replaced by one led by Muhammadu Buhari.

Nestlé is one among a group of mature multinationals in Nigeria, including Heineken, Cadbury's, and Unilever, and more recently General Electric, Procter & Gamble, and Nissan, that have learned to cope with such uncertainties.

They have the people, resources, and experience to mitigate the severest risks and adapt as Nigeria develops into a mature economy.

Sources: "Investing in Nigeria," *Financial Times*, May 5, 2014; Thando Matutu, "$28 million boost for Nestlé Nigeria," *CNBC Africa*, 12 February 2015; https://www. transparency.org; http://www.worldbank.org/en/country/nigeria; http://www. nestle.com/asset-library/documents/library/documents/about_us/quick-facts-2014-en.pdf; http://www.doingbusiness.org/reports/global-reports/~/media/GIAWB/Doing%20Business/Documents/Annual-Reports/English/DB15-Chapters/DB15-Country-Tables.pdf; http://www.doingbusiness.org/data/exploreeconomies/nigeria

1 Why has Nestlé increased its investments in Nigeria in recent years?

2 What kinds of country risks have Nestlé and other MNEs faced when doing business in Nigeria?

3 What are the pros and cons of MNE investment for Nigeria as a nation?

4 What are the lessons for other firms looking to invest in developing countries like Nigeria?

INTRODUCTION

A range of strategy frameworks in this book—such as the strategy matrix, Porter's value chain, competitor analysis, and Porter's five forces—help managers understand their competitive environment and identify their firm's unique competitive advantages. Country risk analysis can build on these approaches by providing insights into the country-level factors that will affect the leveraging of these advantages in a particular country, and help managers balance potential risks against rewards. **Country risk analysis** examines the chances of non-market events (political, social, and economic) causing financial, strategic, or personnel losses to a firm following FDI in a specific country market. Rather than looking at a market, industry, or group of competitors, country risk analysis tries to predict macroeconomic and political sources of change that might undermine a firm's position in a local market.[1] This kind of analysis is used to compare country markets before making investment decisions. Decision-makers supplement strategic information about market size, market growth, presence of local suppliers, support industries, and the strengths of local competitors with, for example, estimates of current and future socio-economic and political risks that are country specific. In this chapter we will particularly examine political risk, but first we will examine a well-known, general framework for analyzing and comparing country conditions: PEST analysis.

Country risk analysis
Examines the chances of non-market events (political, social, and economic) causing financial, strategic, or personnel losses to a firm following FDI in a specific country market

Generic PEST analysis

One of the simplest, most general, and multidisciplinary frameworks for understanding change at the broadest level is the **PEST framework** (Figure 15.1). This is used to map out particular competitive environments or investment *contexts* for firms at the regional or national level, compare country conditions, and build future scenarios to understand short-term and long-term threats and opportunities. Influential factors are divided into political, economic, social or socio-cultural, and technological (PEST), which in combination create particular opportunities and threats for firms. PEST can be extended to PESTLE by adding legal factors, reflecting national legislative institutions and policies, and environmental factors, including local policies on waste and pollution. It can be used specifically to assess new investment environments as an input into global expansion and market-entry strategies.

PEST framework
Examines the political, economic, socio-cultural, and technological conditions in particular country markets

Clearly, there are strong interactions between the categories of factors. Political developments have a strong influence over economic change, particularly in emerging markets

Figure 15.1 PEST framework for country analysis

like China. Similarly, economic, social, and technological factors are interdependent. However, the PEST breakdown makes the task of analyzing a complex range of influences more manageable.

On the face of it, this kind of framework may look too general and simple to guide management strategy. The general PEST overview shown above, however, is just a starting point to organize more focused analyzes. Rigor can be added and accuracy improved in two ways:

1 *Add depth.* To fully understand the nature of the changes taking place within each of the categories, further tools and techniques are needed:

   ■ Political scientists and analysts conduct formal risk assessments on political change within regions or countries. Formal rankings are published to guide investors along the same lines as insurance assessors (see related discussions later in this chapter). Such analyses also map out the key political constituencies, central and regional agencies, key ministers and bureaucrats, as well as changing forms of legislation in different countries as an input into MNE strategy and implementation (for example, aiding the development of personal contacts and networks in target countries).

   ■ Economic analyses cover everything from national-level to industry-sector or market-specific trends. Companies compiling return on investment (ROI) projections need to know something about productivity levels that can be expected in would-be plants, encompassing data on employees, technologies, support industries, local utilities, and so on. Any investment that relies on some element of local financing will need data on local interest rate trends, lending conditions, and the general stability of domestic capital markets, for example.

   ■ Social trends analyses are relevant for firms looking to market new products and services in new countries. Mapping patterns of disposable income, customer preferences, and regional differences in these requires a combination of quantitative and qualitative analyses. Statistical overviews covering demographics, buying patterns, and market research need to be complemented with insights into socio-cultural norms and changing patterns of expectations if advertising messages are to be pitched correctly.

2 *Add foresight.* Arguably the most difficult challenge facing any decision-maker is to predict the future. The complexity that results from the variety of factors that managers need to consider when making international business decisions adds immeasurably to this uncertainty. Accurate scenario building is central to the strategic planning and future success of any firm and can be done using the PEST framework as a starting point. Rather than creating grandiose visions of the future, managers need to extrapolate accurately and objectively from the past and current trends across all the PEST dimensions to map out the likelihood of different futures and the implications of these for particular global strategies.

✔ Active learning check

Review your answer to Active Learning Case question 1 and make any changes you like. Then compare your answer to the one below.

❶ Why has Nestlé increased its investments in Nigeria in recent years?

A PEST analysis would suggest that favorable economic and socio-cultural trends are most relevant to Nestlé's decision to increase investment in specific product lines. Higher levels of disposable income and a growing middle class are key attractions, alongside a 7 percent growth in GDP. We should note that the company also uses Nigeria as a base to export to other parts of Africa, where similar trends exist. Technological trends are less relevant, although better local support for customizing products in general and specifically for supporting the firm's investment in clean water production could be cited.

Political trends are probably unfavorable to further investment, given the failure of the government to deal decisively with terrorist groups at one level, or endemic corruption at another. However, Nigeria's position in the World Bank's "ease of doing business" rankings has improved from 175/189 in 2014 to 170 in 2015. Given that Nestlé is investing in the country, we can only assume its senior management feels that the positives outweigh the negatives.

POLITICAL RISK

Risk

Danger   +   Opportunity

This is the Chinese character for "risk." The first symbol is for "danger," the second symbol is for "opportunity." Risk is seen as danger and opportunity combined.

Political risk
The probability that political forces will negatively affect a multinational's profit or impede the attainment of other critical business objectives

Political risk is the probability that political forces will negatively affect a firm's profit or impede the attainment of other critical business objectives. The study of political risk addresses changes in the environment that are difficult to anticipate. Common examples include the election of a government that is committed to nationalization of major industries or one that insists on reducing foreign participation in business ventures.

Most people believe that political risk is confined to Third World countries or to those with unstable governments. However, the shifting policies of triad region governments illustrate that political risk is also an issue for firms doing business in highly industrialized nations. Governments routinely protect key industries for reasons of national security, self-sufficiency, or national culture. Examples include US restrictions on foreign investment in the banking, defense, and commercial airline industries; Japanese protection of its rice producers; and France's limitations on foreign involvement in its movie and media businesses. The EU and US governments have long supported their regional champions in the aerospace industry, partly for security reasons, partly to protect local firms. Airbus spent $11 billion on building the A380 double-decker jumbo jet, one-third of which came from European taxpayers. This exacerbated the trade battles in this industry, refereed by the WTO.[2]

Much of this political sparring is predictable. It is unanticipated change stemming from complexity and uncertainty that creates more dangerous kinds of risk. However, these examples indicate the pervasiveness of political risk. Given the large number of international markets in which MNEs operate, political risk is going to remain an area of concern. In dealing with this issue, effective negotiating can help to reduce and contain problem areas. This will be explained later in the chapter.

Deregulation and political risk

Overall there has been a general trend toward liberalization, deregulation, and the opening up of national borders over the past 15 to 20 years, and this has been a major driver of globalization. Table 15.1 shows the growing number of regulatory changes that have been favorable to FDI. In particular, the progressive liberalization of countries with large domestic markets and extensive privatization or denationalization programs underway, such as China, Brazil, and India, has significantly changed the global economy. Huge opportunities exist for MNEs in these countries, and they have responded by investing to establish themselves in these new markets.

FDI inflows into these countries, particularly China, have grown immensely. India recorded inflows of only $237 million in 1990, and these increased to $2,151 million in 1995. The inflows jumped to $6,598 million in 2000 following the politically led liberalization process. By 2008, FDI inflows into India had reached $41,554 million but they had declined to $28,153 by 2013. In 2008, FDI into developing countries rose to $620,733 million compared to $36,897 million in 1990, representing an increase of 1,682 times. Furthermore, as of 2013 FDI into developing countries had increased to $759 billion and accounted for an estimated 56 percent of global FDI inflows, compared to 18 percent in 2000.[3] China, in particular, has risen to be a leading recipient of FDI each year. In 2013, FDI inflows to China were $347,848 million (see Chapter 20, Emerging Economies).

For these giant emerging markets, major political shifts led to the start of the process of integrating with the global economy and the opening up of their borders to foreign investors. Continuous, small, but significant changes to their policies and legislation regarding FDI and the activities of MNEs mean that ongoing assessments of political risk in these countries are of paramount importance to investors. The governments of these countries, together with their massive, complex civil service bureaucracies, maintain a strong level of control over their economies, and the direction and pace of change remains unpredictable.

Table 15.1 Changes in national regulations on FDI, 2000–13

	2000	2001	2002	2003	2004	2005	2006	2007	2008	2009	2010	2011	2012	2013
Number of countries that introduced changes	46	52	44	60	80	78	71	50	41	47	55	49	54	59
Number of regulatory changes	81	97	94	125	164	144	126	79	68	88	121	80	86	87
Liberalization/promotion	75	85	79	113	142	118	104	58	51	61	80	59	61	61
Restriction/regulation	5	2	12	12	20	25	22	19	15	23	37	20	20	23
Neutral/indeterminate	1	10	3	n/a	2	1	n/a	2	2	4	4	1	5	3

Source: World Investment Report, 2013.

The nature of political risk

We can examine political risk at two different levels, as seen in Figure 15.2.[4] Legal/ governmental risks are potentially harmful to foreign businesses but are the product of, or permissible within, the existing political, economic, and legislative system. Non-legal or extra-governmental risks lie outside this system and are a violation of existing laws. Macro-level risks affect all foreign firms evenly, and micro-level risks harm individual or specific groups of firms.

Macro political risk

Macro political risk
A risk that affects all foreign enterprises in the same way

Expropriation
The governmental seizure of private businesses coupled with little, if any, compensation to their owners

Indigenization laws
Laws which require that nationals hold a majority interest in all enterprises

A **macro political risk** is one that affects all foreign enterprises in the same general way. **Expropriation**, the governmental seizure of private businesses coupled with little, if any, compensation to the owners, is an example of a macro political risk. Communist governments in eastern Europe and China expropriated private firms following World War II. Fidel Castro did the same in Cuba from 1958 to 1959. In more recent years, governments in Angola, Chile, Ethiopia, Peru, and Zimbabwe have expropriated private enterprises. In some cases this stems from **indigenization laws**, which require that nationals hold a majority interest in all enterprises. The privatization of a range of state-owned industries in Russia marked a turning point in that country's history. However, the corruption and racketeering that led to politically connected individuals building massive fortunes from, for example, the oil and aluminum industries may have triggered another turning point (see **Real Case: Yukos and the Russian oligarchs** in this chapter). The government has threatened to re-nationalize key industries.[5]

Macro political risk can also be the result of political boycotts. During the war in Iraq, following 9/11 in the United States, American consumers boycotted French imports and avoided holidaying in France because the French were unsupportive of the military invasion of Iraq.[6] In all these cases, both large and small businesses feel the impact of the political decision.

Micro political risk

Micro political risk
A risk that affects selected sectors of the economy or specific foreign businesses

A **micro political risk** is one that affects selected sectors of the economy or specific foreign businesses. These risks are typically a result of government action in the form of industry regulation, taxes on specific types of business activity, and local content laws.

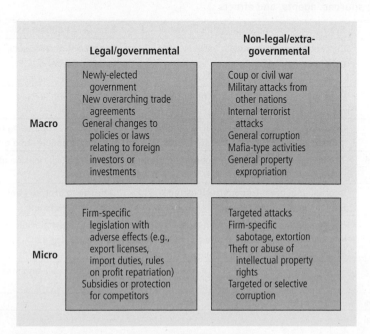

Figure 15.2 Types and levels of political risk

A number of factors help to determine the degree of micro political risk. One is the dominance of foreign firms or the growing competitiveness of their products in an industry. For example, small and medium-sized makers of precision tools for the electronics industry in the United States have joined forces to lobby for higher tariffs on imports that compete with their products, including those made by large US firms offshore. Prompted by the growing trade deficit and job losses in manufacturing, they have used the National Association of Manufacturers to push the government to defy WTO regulations and protect their particular businesses by increasing specific tariffs.[7]

The end of the global textile quota system in January 2005 drastically changed the competitive environment for countries like Kenya and Pakistan. Under this system the United States and the European Union restricted textile imports according to their country of origin. This had the effect of partly protecting these countries from direct competition with countries like India and China, because they had a guaranteed volume of exports to the big markets. Up to 60 percent of Pakistan's annual export income came from the textile sector, which employed more than half of the country's industrial workforce, so this change has had a significant impact on its economy.[8]

This last example shows that some political risks are predictable and can be partly planned for. Others are not and tend to have a more significant effect. The changing priorities of governments, often swayed by powerful interest groups, are an important source of this kind of risk. As discussed below, governments have specific economic, social, and often military agendas, and changes in these will result in adjustments to the various levers that control trade and the activities of foreign investors.

Sources of political risk

There are a number of sources of political risk. Table 15.2 presents some important sources and their effects.

So a variety of motivations help to explain political risk. The MNE's challenge is to identify these motivations and then to decide how to manage them.

Table 15.2 Political risk: sources, agents, and effects

Sources of political risk	Groups that can generate political risk	Effects of political risk
Political philosophies that are changing or are in competition with each other	Current government and its various departments and agencies	Expropriation of assets (with or without compensation)
Changing economic conditions	Opposition groups in the government that are not in power but have political clout	Indigenization laws
Social unrest	Organized interest groups such as teachers, students, workers, retired persons, etc.	Restriction of operating freedom concerning, e.g. hiring policies and product manufacturing
Armed conflict or terrorism	Terrorist or anarchist groups operating in the country	Cancelation or revision of contracts
Rising nationalism	International organizations such as the World Bank and the United Nations	Damage to property and/or personnel from terrorism, riots, etc.
Impending or recent political independence	Foreign governments that have entered into international alliances with the country or that are supporting opposition to the government	Loss of financial freedom such as the ability to repatriate profits
Vested interests of local business groups	—	Increased taxes and other financial penalties
Competing religious groups	—	—
Newly created international alliances	—	—

COUNTRY ANALYSIS AND POLITICAL RISK ASSESSMENT

As described above, the PEST framework provides a simple way of mapping the pros and cons of foreign investment opportunities in particular countries for MNEs. There are many other analytical tools and techniques to measure the cost–benefit or risk–reward ratio for a specific investment proposition. These range from scenario planning, Delphi exercises, and multivariate risk analyses to simple observation. The degree to which companies actually use these techniques before investing abroad varies a great deal.

Small firms, especially owner-managed firms, often move from simple exporting to engage in FDI on the basis of the owner, CEO, or senior manager seeing an opportunity when on holiday in a foreign country! Little or no rigorous risk analysis or comparison of opportunities between countries is conducted, partly because it takes time and is expensive, but often because managers are unaware of the need for analysis and/or ignorant of the tools, techniques, and information resources that can help them make these decisions.[9] Most firms, however, will conduct some level of analysis to capture the likely costs and benefits and probable risks relating to a particular overseas investment.

There are many sources of information on the PEST conditions in different country markets for use in comparative risk analysis. Country risk rating services are provided by a range of agencies that produce general reports and may conduct specific analyses on behalf of client companies. Such agencies include the Bank of America World Information Services, the Business Environment Risk Intelligence (BERI) SA, the Control Risks Information Services (CRIS), the Economist Intelligence Unit (EIU), Standard & Poor's Ratings Group, the Political Risk Services (ICRG), and Moody's Investor Services.

BERI political risk services, for example, began in 1966 using 15 variables, such as bureaucratic delays, monetary inflation, and political stability, to "isolate to the degree possible the political process affecting business." It contained a weighting to emphasize certain criteria (such as political stability) over others in terms of their significance and impact. The sum of the weights was 25 and each of the 15 factors was then scored at four times its weight, so the highest possible points and lowest risk was 100. A global panel of experts (although US-based experts dominated) then assessed the score for each variable in a Delphi-style validation to help rank 40 to 50 countries according to the resulting consensus. Scores between 70 and 56 were defined as moderate risk, denoting overall stability despite the varied risk of complications that might affect day-to-day operations for businesses. Any country with a rating under 56 was considered unstable.

The FORCE Country Reports from BERI also provide a qualitative analysis of sociopolitical, economic, and financial forecasts. They include scenario analyses and so-called political, operations, and remittance/repatriation risk indices and profit opportunity recommendations (POR). The BERI risk measurement components include several categories of information, such as political factionalization, linguistic/ethnic/religious tension, coercive measures to maintain the regime, prevalence of corruption, radical left strength, dependence on major external power, and so on.[10]

Online risk information resources

An increasing number of country rating and indexing schemes are available online. One of the best is the World Bank and IMF site (http://rru.worldbank.org/DoingBusiness/), which is a useful resource for off-the-shelf reports, such as *Doing Business* in country X this year. But it also allows users to create customized reports using an online database of indicators across 189 economies. This is linked to specialized topic areas covering practical guidelines for investing and managing in different countries, including Starting a Business,

Hiring and Firing Workers, Enforcing Contracts, Getting Credit, and Licensing and Inspections. The World Bank's Multilateral Investment Guarantee Agency (MIGA) is also a good source (http://miga.org).

One of the most widely used and well-respected sources of information is the Economist Intelligence Unit (EIU) (www.eiu.com). Alongside fairly general information it has a host of interactive services, most of which are for subscribers only. It also describes some of the indicators and the methodology underlying its Country Risk Service.

The Fraser Institute, with its very overt political view, compiles the Index of Economic Freedom (http://www.fraserinstitute.ca and http://www.freetheworld.com). This compares 23 components across seven areas (economic structures, monetary policy, etc.) to measure the degree to which host-country institutional arrangements and policies intervene in or influence the operation of the economy. It also attempts to assess how predictable these arrangements and policies are and therefore how important they are as a source of market uncertainty.

PricewaterhouseCoopers (PwC) compiles an opacity index, which is closer to the kinds of analyses that examine non-legal activities by governments that might influence or intervene in business. This measures the impact of business, economic, legal, and ethical opacity on the cost of capital around the world.

Finally, as an indication of the importance of these kinds of analyses, the World Economic Forum (WEF) has developed a Public Institutions Index as an input for its overall annual global competitiveness ranking (http://reports.weforum.org/global-competitiveness-report-2014–2015/methodology/). This index comprises a Contracts and Law sub-index (covering judicial independence, property rights, organized crime, favoritism in government decision making) and a Corruption sub-index (including irregular payments for imports and exports, tax collection, and public utilities).

Quantifying risk vulnerability

As shown by the above risk ratings services, all risk is relative. Measuring risk therefore involves comparing options, one investment proposition against another. This means combining investment appraisal and country appraisal techniques. There are factors that may be more important for one kind of investment than another—a production plant will have different requirements from a distribution or marketing operation, or an offshore IT service office, for example. Therefore different risk criteria are more or less relevant at the country level. Table 15.3 shows the **Weighted Country Risk Assessment Model** for combining both.

Weighted Country Risk Assessment Model
Combines an investment project appraisal with country risk analysis

Two different country cases (A and B) are compared using 30 different criteria; 15 are political in nature and 15 are economic, although many of the latter are also directly or indirectly influenced by the governments. The Risk column gives a rating (1 is low risk; 5 is high) comparing Country A and Country B on this criterion and can represent either a direct comparison (for example, high or low current disposable income levels) or a risk measure—the potential for change that would harm the investment proposed (for example, the likelihood that disposable income levels will fall significantly in the future). So, for example, Country A is rated as more politically stable than B and has a lower likelihood of internal conflicts, more predictable policies, a more stable tax and tariff regime, and fewer (less likelihood of) bureaucratic delays. Economically, the two countries are a little more similar, although Country A, for example, clearly rates higher in terms of upholding intellectual property rights, so there is less risk of breaches of copyright, patents, or brands. They have fairly similar domestic economic environments in terms of the listed criteria, with Country A having experienced better growth in the past five years, but expecting the same growth prospects as B for the next three years. This relative country rating across the three categories is summarized by the totals at the foot of the table: 67 for Country A and 101 for Country B.

Table 15.3 The Weighted Country Risk Assessment Model

		Selected criteria	Country A			Country B		
			Risk (5 = high)	Importance (5 = high)	Combined score (/25)	Risk (5 = high)	Importance (5 = high)	Combined score (/25)
Political environment	1	Stability of the local political system	2	4	8	4	4	16
	2	Likelihood of internal conflict	1	4	4	4	4	16
	3	External threats to stability	3	3	9	3	3	9
	4	Harmful government intervention in the economic system	1	4	4	4	4	16
	5	Reliability of the country as a trading partner	3	4	12	3	4	12
	6	Policy continuity/predictability	2	5	10	4	5	20
	7	Stability of tax and tariff regime	1	4	4	3	4	12
	8	Effectiveness of public administration	2	3	6	3	3	9
	9	Prevalence of corruption	1	3	3	5	3	15
	10	Bureacratic delays	1	4	4	5	4	20
	11	Enforceability of contracts	2	4	8	4	4	16
	12	Corporate governance and ethics legislation	3	2	6	4	2	8
	13	Labor unions and labor relations	3	5	15	3	5	15
	14	Linguistic/ethnic/religious tensions	2	1	2	3	1	3
	15	Social stability	2	2	4	3	2	6
International economic environment	16	Import restrictions	4	4	16	4	4	16
	17	Export restrictions	3	5	15	3	5	15
	18	Attitudes toward foreign investors	2	3	6	3	3	9
	19	Respect for intellectual property rights (patents, brands)	2	4	8	5	4	20
	20	Restrictions on monetary transfers	3	5	15	3	5	15
	21	Revaluation of the currency during the last 5 years	3	2	6	4	2	8
	22	Balance of payments situation	2	2	4	2	2	4
Domestic economic environment	23	Per capita income	3	1	3	3	1	3
	24	Economic growth over the last 5 years	2	1	2	4	1	4
	25	Potential growth over the next 3 years	2	1	2	2	1	2
	26	Inflation over the past 2 years	3	3	9	4	3	12
	27	Accessibility of domestic capital markets to outsiders	2	4	8	2	4	8
	28	Availability of high-quality local labor force	2	5	10	2	5	10
	29	Availability of energy resources	2	4	8	2	4	8
	30	Infrastructure; transportation and communication systems	3	4	12	3	4	12
		TOTALS	67	100	223	101	100	339

Sources: The approach and the items in the table were developed by Simon Collinson, drawing from prior risk assessment models and studies, including D. W. Conklin, "Analyzing and managing country risks," *Ivey Business Journal*, vol. 66, no. 3 (January/February 2002), pp. 36–42; S. T. Cavusgil, "Measuring the potential of emerging markets: an indexing approach," *Business Horizons*, vol. 40, no. 1 (1997); A. I. J. Dyck, *Country Analysis* (Boston, MA: Harvard Business School Press, 1997); and E. Dichtl and H. G. Köglmayr, "Country risk ratings," *Management International Review*, vol. 26, no. 4 (1986), pp. 4–12. This latest version of the framework benefited from the advice and feedback of Professor Derek Condon, Professor of International Business and Corporate Governance, Birmingham Business School.

The Importance column rates each of the same 30 criteria in terms of relevance to the kind of investment proposed. This example has been designed to reflect an overseas investment for a production facility, mainly for exports. Criteria such as export restrictions, the availability of high-quality labor, the stability of taxes and tariffs, policy continuity, bureaucratic delays, and enforceability of contracts, for example, are considered important (rating 5 or 4). Economic growth and per capita income, for example, are considered less important. These would be important if we were considering a sales and distribution operation for consumer products. As this illustration shows a country comparison, not a comparison of different types of investment, the Importance columns for Country A and Country B are identical. If we were to compare types of investment, we would change the ranking of the various criteria (between 1 and 5), but the total for this column would still need to add to 100, otherwise the weighting method would not work. In this case we would simply be changing the *relative* importance of different risk factors to suit a different type of invest-ment proposition.

The combined score weights each country criterion according to respective importance to the type of investment under consideration, and the combined totals provide an overall comparison of the two countries. The higher the final score, the riskier the combination of investment and location. Country A, with 223 out of a possible 500, appears to be a better option for this kind of investment than Country B with 339.

Table 15.3 presents a fairly basic example. The list of criteria can be changed and extended to far more than 30 and sub-criteria (for example, different kinds of bureaucratic delays under item 10) can be added. The balance among political, economic, social, tech-nological, and legal criteria can also be altered according to the investment proposition and/or the countries to be considered. We could also use a different Likert scale, such as from 1 to 10 rather than 1 to 5. The model can be extended to compare more than two country cases. For any extension of the model, it is important to remember that the ratings are *relative*. For example, the above-mentioned BERI political risk ratings show Zimbabwe as riskier than Peru. We might give the former 5 for some of the political criteria in the Risk column and the latter a comparative 2 or 3. If we were to add Sweden to the compari-son, the rating in the Risk column would need to reflect the change, perhaps by giving Zimbabwe and Peru 5 in some categories and Sweden 1. So the rating scores are not abso-lute. They depend on the country comparison being made.

Note that this model only provides a summary framework for estimating relative coun-try risk. In practice it will only reflect the intelligence that goes into the relative risk rat-ings. A thorough and rigorous analysis of all the factors that underlie even the limited number of 30 criteria in Table 15.3, in terms of both current and future investment condi-tions, is not easy. In some cases quantitative data are available, including from some of the agencies and sources listed above. For other criteria, such as political stability or the likely impact of corruption, there is no such thing as perfect information, and assumptions, esti-mates, and some subjective guesswork are always necessary. However, the better the expertise, information, and experience that can be leveraged to make such assessments, whether from inside or outside the firm, the more accurate the relative final scores are going to be.

What the model also helps decision-makers do is identify the kinds of risks they may be able to reduce, adapt to, prepare for, or guard against prior to or following an investment. Knowing which sources of risk you can influence, and which you cannot, puts you in a better position to manage a market-entry strategy. Negotiating with government agencies, customs officials, or local unions; establishing alliances with local recruitment agencies or banks; or generally developing networks of local contacts and advisors can all help moni-tor and alleviate some of these risks and are essential.

In practice, a common problem is for managers to fail to consider the full range of coun-try risks that might affect an investment or to make uninformed assumptions in their appraisal. A project team responsible for capital budgeting in an accounting or finance department of a firm may not know a great deal about different country conditions. Project investment models and financial scenarios may be transferred with a range of built-in assumptions that can hide additional costs or risks from the appraisal. For example, differ-ences in labor rates are a key driver for the movement of manufacturing plants and for offshoring. Many companies build in the reduced labor cost, which makes savings and resulting profits look impressive, but assume similar levels of productivity and transactions costs for the new overseas operation. The additional costs and risks may become more obvious over time, with experience, and profit can quickly turn to loss. This has happened to some of the large numbers of companies that have outsourced parts of their IT and back-office operations to India, for example.[11] So how can we build country risk analysis into our financial planning tools?

Accounting for country risk

International managers can incorporate elements of the above kinds of risk analysis into financial appraisal models when considering FDI. A five-year return on investment (ROI) or return on assets (ROA) model should take account of a range of risks as an input into financial estimates of costs and revenue. This enables a more realistic comparison between countries as locations for various kinds of investment. Although never perfect, because we have incomplete information about the past and present, and it is impossible to accurately forecast the future, this can still help decision-makers build better estimations. They can develop a better understanding about the likely impact of certain events or changes on specific investment propositions; they can compare investment propositions across different country contexts; and they can revise estimates for investment returns on the basis of this kind of analysis.

Companies that try to incorporate risk estimation in financial appraisals tend to build on standard financial models at the project level. The most common work on the basis of net present value (NPV), ROI, or internal rate of return (IRR) calculations, and these can incorporate country risks in a number of ways. A common approach is to increase the hurdle rate for ROI at the pre-project consideration stage, which will deselect the riskiest propositions. The hurdle rate is the set rate of financial return over a period of time that covers both project costs and the cost of the capital needed for the investment. Companies or business units will often have a set rate of return below which they will not invest. A simple rule of thumb would be to increase the rate of return in line with the additional risks associated with locating the investment in a particular country, compared to another.

Also common is to adjust the cash flows of the project to reflect the potential impact of a particular event on the value of the project. So, for example, if policy changes that will lead to an increase in tax rates, import duties, or labor costs are likely, this risk needs to be built into the long-run calculation of the break-even point of an investment. There is a probability that costs will rise and net revenues will decline, so this can be built into a five- or six-year forecast for an investment. The term **adjusted present value (APV)** is sometimes used to denote an NPV that takes into account the riskiness of the project's expected future cash flows.

Adjusted present value (APV)
An NPV that takes into account sources of country risk that might impact a project's expected future cash flows

More sophisticated techniques for accounting for country risk have been developed. Some firms attempt to place specific probabilities on certain events taking place and calculate the direct cost implications for the project. This approach works well as an extension of the above country risk assessment model, but again relies on accurate information and intelligence to derive realistic probabilities. If political analysts estimate that there is, say, a 20 percent chance that the government of a particular developing country will change in the next three years, resulting in a radical change in policies toward foreign investors, this risk can be reflected in a higher hurdle rate for the APV and an alternative location for the investment might look more promising. This kind of approach is often termed *sensitivity analysis* and can be combined with formal *scenario analyses*. More sophisticated real-options analyses might attempt to calculate relative costs and benefits of, for example, closing a facility, moving it to another country, scaling down operations, or continuing in the face of a significant economic or political shock.

Active learning check

Review your answer to Active Learning Case question 2 and make any changes you like. Then compare your answer to the one below.

2 **What kinds of country risks have Nestlé and other MNEs faced when doing business in Nigeria?**

Companies like Nestlé experience the full range of legal/governmental and non-legal/extra-governmental risks at the macro and micro levels in Nigeria. Policies and laws for foreign investors change regularly for reasons that are often politically motivated. This can create higher costs, which affect all firms, or other disadvantages, such as import tax duties or export licensing costs, which can have a greater impact on MNEs. The threat of terrorist attacks is ever-present as is the impact of corruption in its various forms.

These techniques not only alert managers to relative sources of risk when comparing investment propositions, but also can help develop strategies to reduce risk. In the case of the developing country where the change of political party is likely to adversely affect foreign investors, this may lead to political lobbying by foreign firms with investments at risk. It also leads, unfortunately, to MNEs actively intervening in unethical ways in the national politics of smaller nations to secure their interests.

NEGOTIATION STRATEGIES

There are two key steps in developing effective negotiating strategies. First, MNE managers need to evaluate their own position and that of the other group(s) in order to determine how the interests of both can fit together. Second, they need to understand the "modus operandi" of the other groups: who has the power to make what kinds of decisions and what negotiating style are they likely to adopt?

Earlier in this chapter we discussed how widespread deregulation and liberalization were opening up emerging markets, like China and India, to foreign investors. Central and regional government agencies still maintain a strong control over these economies and the rules of engagement for foreign investors, so it is imperative that MNE managers understand: (1) their political, economic, and social policy objectives; (2) their levers of power, the mechanisms by which they can influence the costs and benefits of doing business (taxes, tariffs, quotas, regulations on capital transfers, local input requirements, etc.); (3) the structures, networks, and institutional agencies through which they operate (who has the power to influence what?); and (4) their negotiation style and tactics. These represent the whys and hows of government intervention in market forces, and firms have to adapt to these to improve their chances of investment success.

Figure 15.3 depicts the interplay among: (1) the elements that attract multinational firms to a particular region, which have been discussed throughout this text (central column); (2) the strategic aims of MNEs; and (3) some general policy aims of governments. MNE objectives may or may not fit with government aims and this will affect the investment decision.

Taking this a step further, the most effective negotiation strategies are those that incorporate (1) the relevant risk criteria in Table 15.3 that can be influenced through negotiation, (2) the evolving government policy priorities, and (3) the appropriate government agencies, local organizations, and key individuals who should be approached. This helps reduce the risk or increase the potential rewards from cross-border investments. If energy

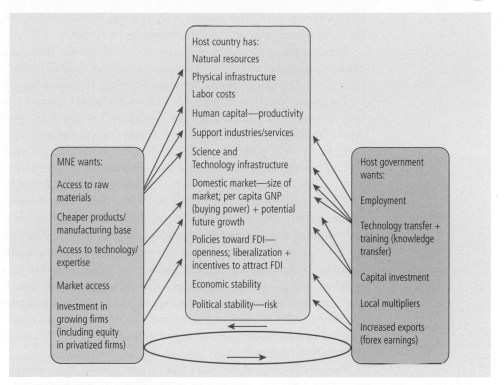

Figure 15.3 FDI drivers: the strategic objectives of MNEs, host-country attractiveness, and host-government requirements

resources are important for a large-scale manufacturing facility, can local authorities guarantee energy supplies at a particular cost over a particular period in return for the plant being located in their region? If labor costs are an important factor, can these be fixed for a period of time through negotiations with local trade unions?

Negotiations between MNEs and national governments or local organizations are a two-way bargaining process where each party has something the other wants. We can identify power resources or bargaining chips held by MNEs looking to invest globally on the one hand and by the governments of host countries on the other. Governments look for inflows of capital and technology, for large local employers, and for access, via MNEs, to overseas markets to boost exports and foreign exchange reserves. To get these they leverage their attractiveness, which may consist of large or growing domestic markets, natural resources, cheap or productive labor, and economic and political stability, to which they may add specific incentives, such as tax breaks or higher levels of foreign ownership or profit repatriation than normally allowed.

The bargaining strength of both firms and governments is limited by the degree of competition. If other MNEs offering similar levels of capital investment, employment, or technology exist, the negotiating position of one MNE is weakened. If other regions offer cheaper labor, more economic or political stability, or better incentives to foreign investors, the negotiating position of the government is weakened.

The bargaining strengths for an MNE may come from its technology, products, services, managerial expertise, and capital. For example, when General Motors sets up a new operation in Mexico, the company invests capital, uses modern technology to build the autos, and employs managerial expertise in getting the operation up and running. When the Hilton Corporation builds a new hotel in Germany, it invests capital, employs managerial expertise, and offers a variety of world-class hospitality services to the guests. MNEs also hire local personnel, stimulate the economy, and, in industries such as manufacturing, textiles, and mining, help to generate exports for the country.

The bargaining strengths of the country will include such factors as large consumer markets, economic and political stability, sources of capital, tax breaks, and an appropriate labor force. The United States, for example, offers all these strengths to MNEs. As a result, the bargaining position of foreign MNEs vis-à-vis the US government is diminished. This is in contrast to the situation faced by companies looking to set up operations in less developed countries, where the latter have a weak bargaining position because of their small consumer market, political instability, and/or relative financial weakness.

Other parties involved in a negotiation will also have specific strengths. For example, in many cases a local partner knows the market and has conducted business there for years. This makes the partner valuable to the MNE. Other contributions of local partners can include capital, a well-trained workforce, factories or retail outlets for moving the goods to the customer, and government contractors that can help to eliminate red tape.

Other parties to the transaction can include stockholders or other interest groups that monitor the company's operations. During the 1980s many MNEs stopped doing business in South Africa because of pressure from these investor groups. Companies involved in manufacturing war material, producing chemicals, and building nuclear energy plants have also come under investor and social pressure. MNEs may also encounter complaints from partners in other joint ventures who feel that this latest investment will negatively affect their current venture.[12]

The membership of the WTO and various trading blocs around the world, particularly the EU and NAFTA, directly affect the degree to which national governments *can* intervene in trade and FDI. Governments in emerging markets and developing countries have more direct influence over the running of the economy and the rules and regulations governing trade and investment. However, once they have joined the WTO their use of legislation governing foreign equity participation, profit repatriation, cross-border M&A, and local content rules, as well as tax and investment incentives, becomes more restricted. At this stage, though, and in the foreseeable future for such countries, a higher level of direct control over the economy and foreign relations represents a significant influence over the ever-changing opportunities and risks for investors.

Finally, individual politicians and civil servants in less developed countries are able to use their own influence more effectively to block or to facilitate a particular MNE investment. This is partly due to the higher level of government control over the economy and individual businesses, but also because of the relative lack of legal or institutional recourse to challenge government actions. Couple this with the fact that salaries for government officials and bureaucrats in poorer countries tend to be very low and you get an insight into why corruption is so much more prevalent in developing countries, as discussed in the following section.

Behavioral characteristics of the participants in negotiations

When it comes to the actual process of cross-border negotiations there is a range of cultural, behavioral, and tactical differences between groups that international managers need to understand if they are to negotiate effectively.

Cultural differences

Although the objective of the negotiation process may be universal (strike as good a deal as possible), the way in which the process is carried out will be greatly influenced by the cultural values and norms of the participants. Many of the following observations build on Chapter 5, which examines cultural differences between people from different countries around the world.

INTERNATIONAL BUSINESS STRATEGY IN ACTION

Political risk for De Beers

Established in 1888 in Johannesburg, South Africa, De Beers is the largest mining company in the world. The De Beers name is synonymous with diamonds and is a leading organization in terms of diamond exploration, mining and trading. As of 2014, the organization was operating in 28 countries and has been reported as selling 35 percent of global diamond production. De Beers has two shareholders, whereby 85 percent of the organization is owned by the mining company Anglo American, while the government in Botswana owns the remaining 15 percent. Furthermore, as of 2014 the organization employed approximately 20,000 employees and had a revenue of £7.1 billion.

But De Beers once controlled (not directly mined) about 80 percent of the world supply of rough stones. The De Beers Groups Diamond Trading Company (DTC), formerly the Central Selling Organization (CSO), maintained a cartel for limiting supply and driving up prices. Competitors have reduced this share by challenging its single-channel distribution system and by developing other sources of diamonds outside of its control. In Canada, Australia, and Russia, rival mining firms like BHP Billiton, Rio Tinto, and ALROSA have found huge deposits of lucrative stones and developed new technologies to mine them efficiently. As recently as 1998 De Beers' share was down to around 65 percent, and today production from its own mines gives it just a 45 percent share. Add to this its contract to sell Russian stones and its overall market share is around 55 percent, in a global market for rough diamonds worth about $8 billion.

De Beers faces a range of political risks. It is under threat from anti-globalization and ethical business groups for its involvement in civil wars in Sierra Leone, Angola, and Congo. It is also facing potentially damaging political and governance changes in South Africa, including calls to re-nationalize and/or place into "black hands" a range of natural resource-based industries including mineral mining. More worrying for the Oppenheimers is a legal campaign by activists who want reparations from firms that worked in apartheid South Africa. This is not currently being supported by South Africa's

government, but this may change. De Beers has some leverage since its operations have resulted in lucrative and stable tax revenues for the South African government, as well as for Botswana, Namibia, and Tanzania.

It has also built more stable relationships with some governments through joint ventures and cross-shareholdings. Debswana, for example, is jointly owned (50–50) by De Beers and the Botswana government. It supports local supplier development and training programs, as well as boosting the country's diamond exports (which account for four-fifths of total exports). The Botswana government currently owns 15 percent of De Beers.

The firm has been trying to cope for some time with other sources of political risk, hindering its expansion into the end-consumer markets of the triad. De Beers was banned from directly entering the US market because of an antitrust legal ruling that sees it as a monopoly. Under the CSO, the group's market dominance had allowed it to manipulate market prices by accumulating inventory. De Beers is allowed to operate in the EU, but has faced anti-competition action, particularly in relation to its Russian and eastern European operations. A major watershed occurred in 2004 as De Beers finally pleaded guilty to charges of price fixing of industrial diamonds in an Ohio court and agreed to pay a $10 million fine, thereby ending a 60-year-long lock-out of the US market. De Beers is now working directly in the largest diamond market, the United States. This might help it further leverage its recent partnership with luxury products firm LVMH to sell De Beers-brand diamonds.

Websites: www.billionaires.forbes.com/topic/Nicky_Oppenheimer; www.debeersgroup.com; www.lvmh.com; www.adiamondisforever.com

Sources: UNCTAD, *World Investment Report 2007: Transnational Corporations, the Extractive Industries and Development* (Geneva: UNCTAD, 2007), http://unctad.org; "The cartel isn't for ever," *The Economist*, July 17, 2004; T. Buck and N. Innocenti, "De Beers offer set to end EU probe," *Financial Times*, December 21, 2004; "South Africa's Cuban missile," *The Economist*, August 9, 2003; R. Smith, "Diamonds aren't forever," *BBC News*, July 26, 2001; "De Beer's worst friend," *The Economist*, August 20, 1998; "De Beers sells diamond mine for $210m," *BBC News*, January 21, 2011; "De Beers plans $1bn rights issue to cut debt," *BBC News*, December 1, 2009.

Commenting on the difference between Arab and US negotiators, one group of researchers noted:

> [Arabs] treat deadlines as only general guidelines for wrapping up negotiations. They tend to open negotiations with an extreme initial position. However, the Arabs believe strongly in making concessions, they do so throughout the bargaining process, and they almost always reciprocate an opponent's concessions. They also seek to build a long-term relationship with their bargaining partners. For these reasons, Americans typically find it easier to negotiate with Arabs than with representatives from many other regions of the world.

✔ Active learning check

Review your answer to Active Learning Case question 3 and make any changes you like. Then compare your answer to the one below.

❸ What are the pros and cons of MNE investment for Nigeria as a nation?

Nigeria benefits from FDI worth billions of US dollars each year. About half of it comes from Europe and much of it goes into the gas and oil sectors. These investments boost imports and exports and help the country develop its local industry. They also create employment and a so-called regional "multiplier effect" by stimulating growth in other businesses. These include suppliers and contractors that sell to foreign firms in the country, but there are also indirect effects on retailers, restaurants, cinemas, and other consumer services from the additional disposable income created by the growing numbers of employees. Technology transfer and training also takes place, enabling local firms to improve their production and innovation capabilities. Finally, Nestlé and other MNEs advertise the support they provide for local charities, education foundations and poverty-alleviation projects in the towns and villages where they manage their operations.

On the downside, open markets that encourage inward FDI can create "unfair" competition when large and powerful MNEs force smaller local firms out of the market. Some degree of protection for "infant industry" development is advocated by some policy-makers so long as it targets specific sectors for growth. More critical observers argue that the repatriated profits of MNEs represent a form of exploitation. Their view is that added value and wealth created from oil and other local natural resources should be reinvested in the domestic economy.

One of the major differences is the amount of authority that the negotiator has to approve an agreement. In some societies, such as the United States and UK, negotiators are given authority to make deals or at least to express agreement on the basic arrangement that is being negotiated. This approach works well when doing business with many Western firms, as well as with Chinese negotiators. However, it is often of limited value when dealing with people from other cultures. In fact, the other parties may not have the authority to give the go-ahead on anything. For example, Japanese and Russian negotiators are often lower-level personnel who are not authorized to approve agreements. This can be frustrating to Americans who feel that they are wasting their time. The lack of face-to-face interaction with those who will be making the final decision can be unsettling. On the other hand, many foreign negotiators use this ploy because they have learned that it often leads to greater concessions from US business people, who become anxious to sign a deal and thus are more flexible on terms.

INTERNATIONAL BUSINESS STRATEGY IN ACTION

Intel effect

Established in 1968, the Intel Corporation, also known as Intel, is an American multinational technology organization headquartered in Santa Clara, California. Currently, Intel holds global market dominance as a high-value semiconductor computer chip manufacturer.

In 1996 Intel announced that it would be opening a $300 million test plant in Costa Rica. Intel not only planned to open a single test plant, but wanted to open a campus that would accommodate four plants with the potential of employing 3,500 employees over time for a total investment of $500 million. Intel began to work in Costa Rica in 1997 with an assembly and test plant, and by 2013 it had expanded its activities to make it one of the largest R&D centers in the country. In 2013, Intel employed over 3,000 employees covering design, prototyping, testing, and validity of software solutions.

The presence of Intel in Costa Rica came with positive effects on the economy as it provided jobs and support for local industries. Furthermore, Intel was identified as a "catalyst" within Costa Rica when attracting FDI. In 2014 Intel was certified as "Essential Costa Rica," which was the nation's brand license. However, in the very same year, reacting to a very difficult competitive environment, Intel decided to close its microprocessor assembly plant in Costa Rica. This decision to leave Costa Rica was likely to be triggered more by its lack of success to compete successfully in the global market than by any particular problem with its local operations or the attractiveness of the country as a high-technology center. But it had significant effects on the local economy.

Intel had failed to capitalize on providing chipsets for the smartphone industry, where rivals such as Qualcomm, NVidia, and Texas Instruments dominated. The closure was inevitably felt across the economy, as Intel operations in Costa Rica alone were valued at approximately $2 billion per annum. Furthermore, Intel accounted for 20 percent of the country's exports, which was over twice the size of the nation's traditional exports of bananas and coffee. It has been reported that from 2000 to 2012 Intel accounted for 11 percent of net FDI. Even though Intel hired 200 employees in 2014 in its engineering and global services department in Costa Rica, this would clearly

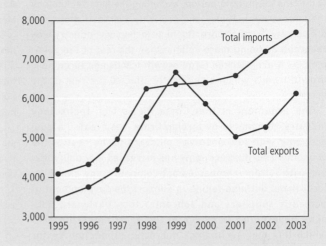

Figure 15.5 Costa Rica: imports and exports, 1995–2003

Source: Central Bank of Costa Rica, Customs, Export Promotion (PROCOMER).

not fully compensate for the closure of the assembly plant. Figures 15.4 and 15.5 highlight Costa Rica's boom in terms of FDI flows and exports and imports following Intel's arrival.

It is difficult to assess how Intel's exit affected Costa Rica's ability to attract inward investment. But the firm left over 1,500 employees who have acquired key skills as engineers or technicians, and they could be viewed as a prize asset for any organization seeking to expand its business to or within Costa Rica. In addition, it has often been ignored that the service industry also plays a crucial part in Costa Rica's exports. Even though tourism is the largest industry, IT services are the second largest, contributing $1.9 billion toward the economy. It is also important to acknowledge the large volume of profit outflows from foreign organizations in Costa Rica, which reached $800 million in 2013. With the dramatic downsizing and lower profits expected from Intel, Costa Rica may benefit from an improvement in income deficit levels.

Acknowledging the fact that Intel was a crucial source of GDP growth, it is still difficult to decide whether Costa Rica will face serious long-term difficulties. Costa Rica publishes a monthly economic activity index (IMAE), and during 1997–2004, including the high-technology sector, the economy grew by an average of 5 percent. In contrast,

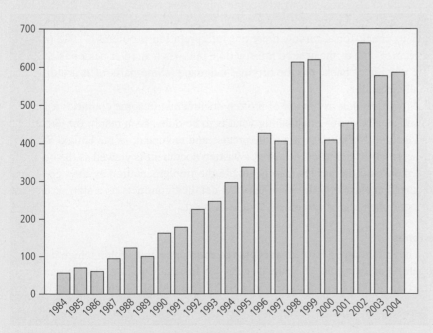

Figure 15.4 FDI flows in Costa Rica, 1984–2004

Source: Central Bank of Costa Rica, Customs, Export Promotion (PROCOMER).

within the same time period, excluding the high-technology manufacturing industry, the economy averaged growth of 4.2 percent. Furthermore, the high-technology industry was recorded as being more volatile than the rest of the economy, as it experienced large growth trends and large non-growth trends which significantly affected the rest of the economy.

One argument is that Costa Rica's high-technology industry, dominated by foreign firms, has created a dual economy with few positive spillovers to the rest of the economy. This dual economy has increased inequality levels, with foreign companies out-competing any emerging local firms but also failing to support the development of domestic suppliers and subcontractors. Backward linkages have failed to evolve in the short timescale over which this high-technology microchip production sector has developed.

A new hope

More recently there are signs of accelerated economic growth for Costa Rica, as the government spreads the net more widely to attract other foreign firms into the country. In 2015 President Luis Guillermo Solis ended a ten-day tour of four US cities with promises of investment from organizations such as Dole Food Co. and Bridgestone Corporation, to help reduce unemployment levels which had by then risen to 10.1 percent. After experiencing difficulties following the closure of Intel, it seems that Costa Rica is learning from its narrow focus on the high-technology sector and seeking to benefit from other kinds of inward investment.

Sources: www.intel.com; R. Aguilera, "Costa Rica: life after Intel," *The World Post*, July 1, 1014, accessed from http://www.huffingtonpost.com/rodrigo-aguilera/costa-rica-life-after-int_b_5246788.html; S. Jose, "Intel outside," *The Economist*, April 19, 2014; E. Martin and M. McDonald, "Costa Rica sees 'Intel effect' ending as GDP poised for pickup," *Bloomberg*, June 1, 2015; *The Impact of Intel in Costa Rica: Nine Years after the Decision to Invest*, World Bank Group, 2006.

Another cultural difference in negotiating style is the objective of the negotiators. As the typologies in Chapter 5 show, American, German, and British managers, for example, tend to be very practical and to focus on short-term results. Negotiators from the Far East tend to move more slowly, like to get to know the other party, and have a more long-run focus. Gift giving, social custom, and certain rituals can play an important part in negotiations and are part of the initial process of developing trust and mutual respect.[13]

Language is also a key factor. When negotiators do not speak the same language and must use interpreters, there are more chances for a misinterpretation or misunderstanding to occur. This problem also exists in written communications. Schermerhorn, for example, has found that, when documents are translated from one language to another and then translated back to check for accuracy, there are interpretation problems.[14] The original translation appears to convey the desired information, but, when another person is called in to translate the document back into the original language, some parts of it are different from that initially intended.

A related cultural problem is the use of written documents. In some countries a written document is used as a basis for establishing what is to be done. As a result, the document is detailed and factual. In Germany it will be precise and technical; in the United States it will be legalistic. In other countries, however, a written document is viewed as the basis for a general agreement and the parties then negotiate the implementation as they go along. Chinese and other Far East negotiators often view detailed contracts as a sign of distrust and believe a more open-ended agreement should be used.

Acceptance zones

Acceptance zone
An area within which a party is willing to negotiate

Each party to a negotiation will have an **acceptance zone** or an area within which it is willing to negotiate. For example, if Anheuser-Busch InBev, Belgium (InBev acquired Anheuser-Busch in 2008) wants to buy a brewery in Düsseldorf, Germany, the Belgium MNE will determine three prices: the highest price it is willing to pay, the price it would like to pay, and the offer at which it will begin the bargaining. For purposes of illustration, assume that Anheuser-Busch InBev, Belgium is willing to pay up to €25 million for the company but hopes to make the acquisition for €23 million and intends to start the negotiation at €20 million.

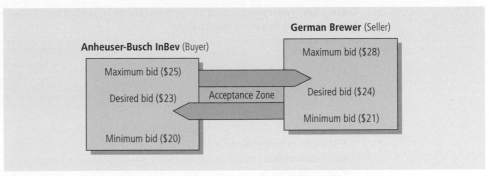

Figure 15.6 Zones of acceptance in the negotiating process (in millions of US$)

Will Anheuser-Busch InBev be successful? This depends on the acceptance zone of the Düsseldorf brewer. If the company will not sell for less than €27.5 million, there will be no deal because the buyer's maximum offer is less than the seller's minimum acceptance. However, assume that the German firm will not sell for less than €21 million, would like to get €24 million, and intends to start the negotiation at €28 million. In this case the two sides should be able to strike a deal, since they have overlapping zones of acceptance, as illustrated in Figure 15.6.

Notice from Figure 15.6 that, when the acceptance zones of the two parties overlap, there is common ground for negotiating. Additionally, keep in mind that, if the zones do not overlap, negotiations will not always end in a stalemate. After listening to each other, the parties may agree to change their respective bids and offers, adjust the acceptance zones, and end up with common negotiating ground.

In the case of Figure 15.6 the two parties would eventually negotiate within a range of $21 million (the least amount the seller will take) and $25 million (the most the buyer will pay). It is not possible to say what the final price will be because this will depend on how willing each side is to concede ground to the other. However, whatever the final price, the seller is going to get at least the desired minimum and the buyer will not pay more than the established maximum.

Bargaining tactics

Negotiators use a range of bargaining tactics, including promises, threats, rewards, commitments, and the use of self-disclosure, in their drive for a better deal. Some of these are also linked to different cultural characteristics, as shown in Table 15.4. Keeping silent is a standard Japanese practice when negotiating with each other as well as with foreigners. Table 15.4 shows that each group of Japanese, American, and Brazilian negotiators has a series of behaviors that make it different from the other two. For example, the Japanese like to make recommendations, the Americans make wide use of promises, and the Brazilians rely heavily on self-disclosure.[15]

These behaviors and tactics are often used in international negotiations. Effective negotiators learn how to use them and how to counteract their use by the opposition. Some examples are provided in the next section.

Transparency and corruption: politically sensitive political risk

One of the most difficult aspects of foreign business for international managers is how to cope with corruption. A very large number of firms engage in bribery of various kinds, but the ethical issues are not straightforward. In many cases they argue that to opt out would simply mean they lose out to less ethically minded competitors. In other cases it is

Table 15.4 Twelve examples of the differences in verbal behaviors among Japanese, American, and Brazilian negotiators

Behavior (description)	Number of times behavior was used in a 30-minute negotiating session by members of each group		
	Japanese	American	Brazilian
1 Making promises	7	8	3
2 Making threats	4	4	2
3 Making recommendations	7	4	5
4 Giving warnings	2	1	1
5 Offering rewards	1	2	2
6 Making commitments	15	13	8
7 Asking questions	20	20	22
8 Giving commands	8	6	14
9 Revealing personal information about oneself	34	36	39
10 Making a first offer	61.5	57.3	75.2
11 Granting initial concessions	6.5	7.1	9.4
12 Using the word "no"	5.7	9.0	83.4

Source: Adapted from John L. Graham, "The influence of culture on the process of business negotiations: an exploratory study," *Journal of International Business Studies* (spring 1985), p. 88, Palgrave Macmillan. Reproduced with permission of Palgrave Macmillan.

genuinely difficult to know whether such practices are simply the accepted local rules of the game. In the UK an extra payment to rail companies buys you a better seat on the train in a less crowded compartment. This is called "First Class." In India an extra payment may get you onto a train that is already overbooked (or that you are told is overbooked). The only difference is that the payment will go straight into the ticket collector's pocket, rather than the railroad company. However, in many places it is accepted that workers in national industries or officials in government agencies will top up their incomes by offering these kinds of "discretionary services."

There are very different levels of corruption, from the small scale to the very large scale. Our Indian ticket collector may make a few extra rupees each month from small-scale bribes. One estimate suggests that Mohamed Suharto, President of Indonesia from 1967 to 1998, built a personal fortune of between $15 billion and $35 billion through embezzlement, in a country with an average GDP per capita (an indication of average annual salaries) of $695.[16]

Governments, particularly those in previously centrally planned economies, are directly responsible for a large volume of purchasing. The volume of government expenditure on public procurement in China jumped from $0.4 billion in 1998 to $18.7 billion in 2003, as its economy and the need for large-scale infrastructure projects grew. By 2011 Chinese officials' overseas trips, the procurement and maintenance of government cars, and the fees for official receptions alone cost an estimated $132 billion a year. The country attracted a great deal of international attention for the 2008 Olympic Games in Beijing and Expo 2010 in Shanghai. Government-funded events such as these pushed the government to limit corrupt practices through policies such as the Public Procurement Act. But such activities are not confined to emerging and developing countries. Bid rigging is widespread in Japan, particularly in the construction industry. The 2003 Act on Elimination and Prevention of Involvement in Bid Rigging was an attempt by the Japanese government to curb such practices, which involve collusion among powerful *keiretsu*, industry bodies, and government agencies. The amount lost due to bribery in government procurement globally is thought to be at least $400 billion.

The Berlin-based organization Transparency International (TI) produces a number of reports each year, of which the best known is the Corruption Perceptions Index (CPI). The

Corruption
The misuse of public power for private benefit

CPI has promoted research into, and more open discussion of, the causes and consequences of corruption. **Corruption** is defined by TI as "the misuse of public power for private benefit," and each year TI has evolved the methodology to improve consensus and acceptance of the metrics that underlie the country rankings.

The extent of corruption is a measure of the *frequency* and *value* of corrupt payments and the resulting obstacle imposed on businesses. A composite index from different polls and surveys from independent institutions, including the World Economic Forum, the World Business Environment Survey of the World Bank, the Institute of Management Development (in Lausanne), PricewaterhouseCoopers, the Economist Intelligence Unit, and Gallup International on behalf of Transparency International, are used in the CPI. The 2014 survey shows Denmark, New Zealand, and Finland as the least corrupt economies, Germany 12th, the UK 14th, Japan 15th, the United States 17th, France 26th, Spain 37th, Italy 69th, Brazil 69th (joint), India 85th, China 100th, Russia 136th, and the most corrupt countries as Sudan 173rd, North Korea 174th, and Somalia 174th (joint).

Another report is the *Bribe Payers Index* (BPI), which measures the "propensity of companies from 30 leading exporting countries to bribe abroad." It is based on the responses of more than 11,000 business people across 125 countries, polled in the World Economic Forum's Executive Survey. Although multinational firms from advanced countries usually rank high in the index, they still regularly pay bribes. Companies from emerging economies, including the BRIC countries, tend to rank among the worst. Despite high-profile campaigns to reduce the amount of local corruption in these countries, their firms actively bribe when abroad.

Other reports by TI examine other elements of corruption, including the most prominent offenders in specific countries, usefully comparing, for example, the judiciary, customs, police, local administrators, registry and permit officials, tax officials, and traffic police in various countries. Case studies and intra- or inter-regional comparisons also make up much of TI's analysis.[17]

The global corruption report by TI shows a clear correlation between corruption and income. Poorer countries (like Bangladesh) tend to have the highest incidence of corruption. In low-income, developing, and emerging markets, transparency is also more of a problem. **Transparency** reflects the *clarity* and *consistency* of policies and legislation applied in the governance of businesses and is strongly associated with corruption. There is considerable debate about the relative levels of corruption and transparency prevalent in developing and advanced countries. The latter do tend to have more governance checks and balances, and arguably more freedom of the press and leeway for interest groups to reveal and oppose corrupt practices and transparency problems.

Transparency
The *clarity* and *consistency* of policies and legislation applied in the governance of businesses

There is, however, a socio-cultural dimension to such issues, and in some countries certain established, recognized, and accepted business practices are considered to be the "local rules of the game" that should simply be respected and adapted to, rather than criticized as non-Western. Again, China provides a useful illustration. One of the key obligations for China as it joins a growing range of international organizations (such as the WTO) and legal treaties is to improve its transparency. In the past, import duties have been found to vary between 10 and 20 percent for the same product because customs officers across the country do not have a standard definition or system for categorizing product types. This has not just led to MNE managers and local importers having to engage in extended discussions with local officials regarding product categorization, but significantly increased the incentive and opportunity for bribery.

Government clean-up campaigns in China have focused on the standardization of rules governing both domestic and foreign businesses. The licensing procedures for both have tended to be unregulated and very much at the discretion of local officials, who are said frequently to abuse the yearly check-up system (*Nianjin*) to earn additional fees before approving licenses. However, foreign firms without the necessary *guanxi* (informal, reciprocal obligation networks) connections are subject to these and other additional charges. The more bizarre include the "spiritual civilization fee" and a "wall-cleaning fee" that can run into thousands of US dollars.

STRATEGIC MANAGEMENT AND POLITICAL RISK

MNEs take many steps to ensure that their strategies do not go awry because of unexpected developments. One of the most beneficial steps is the use of integrative and protective/defensive techniques.

Use of integrative and protective/defensive techniques

Integrative techniques
Strategies designed to help a multinational become a part of the host country's infrastructure

There are a variety of stratagems that MNEs employ in reducing risk. Some are collectively known as **integrative techniques**, which are designed to help the MNE become a part of the host country's infrastructure.[18] The objective of an integrative technique is to help the company blend into the environment and to become less noticeable as a "foreign" firm. One of the simplest ways is to use a name that is not identified with an overseas company and, if an acquisition is made, keep the old name in place. For example, Bridgestone is a Japanese tire company, but no one would know this based on the name of the company. Additionally, Bridgestone owns Firestone Tire and Rubber, but few Americans are aware of this fact. Similarly, Hoechst of Germany owns the Celanese Company, and most people do not know this. Nor do many people realize that almost 25 percent of the banks in California are Japanese owned; their names provide no clues to their real owners. This tactic deflects public attention and concern that US assets are being swallowed up by overseas investors.

Another common integrative technique is to develop good relations with the host government and other political groups and to produce as much of the product as possible locally. In turn the MNE will hire and promote local personnel and use them to run a large portion of the operations. This strategy endears the company to the government and, if any action is taken against foreign firms, these firms are likely to be spared.

Protective and defensive techniques
Strategies designed to discourage a host country from interfering in multinational operations

Protective and defensive techniques are strategies that are designed to discourage a host country from interfering in multinational operations. In contrast to integrative techniques, protective and defensive measures are aimed at fostering *non-integration* of the MNE into the local environment. A good example is conducting research and development (R&D) at other geographic locales and importing this knowledge as needed. Should the government suddenly decide to seize the firm's facilities, the company's R&D base would not be threatened.

Another protective and defensive technique is to limit the role of the local personnel to those operations that are not vital to the running of the facility. So if the government decides to take over the operation, the host-country personnel will not be able to handle things efficiently. Those with the requisite knowledge and training are overseas personnel who are sent on site by the multinational.

A third technique is to raise as much capital as possible from the host country and local banks. When this happens, the government is reluctant to interfere in operations because this may threaten its own investment and that of the home-country banks. In a manner of speaking, this strategy co-opts the government and brings it onto the MNE's team. Any strike against the multinational is a blow against the host country.

A fourth technique is to diversify production among a number of countries. In this way, if the government seizes the MNE's facilities, only one area of production is disrupted. The company can then reallocate production and get back on stream in short order.

Combination strategies

MNEs often use a combination of integration and protective/defensive techniques to reduce and manage their political risk. Figure 15.7 provides an example of how companies can do this. In the case of the low-technology manufacturing firm (#1 in Figure 15.7), the only way to employ a protective/defensive strategy is to raise capital locally. As a result, this firm will work to integrate itself into the country and to act very much like a local firm.

An international air carrier (#2 in Figure 15.7) will use an integrative strategy by setting up local operations and by hiring people to staff the facilities, to maintain the aircraft, and to handle arrivals and departures. The airline will also help to generate money for the country by bringing in tourists and business people. At the same time, the company will seldom have more than a small percentage of its aircraft in this locale on any one day. Additionally, the pilots will often come from other countries and be highly skilled individuals, and the top management team will be operating out of headquarters in the home country. So while the air carrier will take some steps to accommodate the country, it will also be well positioned should the country decide to seize its aircraft or to increase taxes or airport fees. Moreover, aside from facilities at the airport, the company will usually have no other fixed assets except for the aircraft. Therefore any crackdown on the airline might result in retaliatory action by other airlines, which would refuse to fly into the country. Such action could seriously hamper the country's economic growth. Consequently, a strategy that provides for the intermediate use of both integrative and protective/defensive techniques often works extremely well.

A high-technology R&D firm (#3 in Figure 15.7) will not put much emphasis on integrative techniques because it does not want to become integrated into the local economy. The firm may be situated where it is because the company finds that it is easier to recruit top talent to live in that region. Or other competitors may be headquartered there, and the company finds that it is easier to keep tabs on these firms by situating nearby. So while the company may hire local people to staff basic operations, personnel from other countries who live locally will handle all the R&D and other sophisticated functions. If the firm should hire local people for some of these R&D positions, the company will work to keep them loyal to the firm and not to the country. Thus if there is an attempt to seize the firm's R&D facilities, the loss will be minimized.

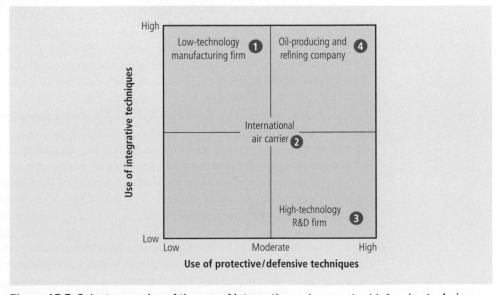

Figure 15.7 Select examples of the use of integrative and protective/defensive techniques

In the case of an oil-producing and refining company (#4 in Figure 15.7), the firm is likely to make strong use of both integrative and protective/defensive techniques. The company will need to get on well with the government, since it is tapping the country's natural resources. There is likely to be a great deal of hiring of local personnel for routine jobs. The firm will also work hard to generate as much revenue as possible, since the government is unlikely to interfere with the operations of a revenue-producing firm. At the same time, the MNE will maintain control of the more sophisticated jobs so that these cannot be carried out by anyone else. If the company were to be taken over, local workers would be unlikely to know how to operate the machinery and equipment efficiently.

✔ Active learning check

Review your answer to Active Learning Case question 4 and make any changes you like. Then compare your answer to the one below.

 What are the lessons for other firms looking to invest in developing countries like Nigeria?

One overriding lesson from Nestlé's experience in Nigeria is that understanding economic and political risks and their underlying sources can significantly increase your chances of making a successful investment in an uncertain emerging market. The company has taken the time and made the effort to understand what the risks are and reduced some of the potential impacts by adapting to the local business environment. It hires a large number of local nationals in senior management positions to guide the local subsidiaries, and provides training and education to build understanding in its local workforce.

A second lesson is not to make assumptions based on your understanding of operating in other economies. Any manager who fails to build in the additional costs that arise from poor energy infrastructures or transport systems, the length of time and expense of importing components, or the possible additional costs of thefts, will fail to invest wisely. Accurate estimates of the probable profit and loss scenarios of any investment project must be based on current costs and likely future conditions encompassing all of these risks and uncertainties.

Companies like Nestlé are also highly sensitive to local politics, investing in strong relationships with key agencies to monitor developments and be ready to respond to the threats and opportunities that stem from shifts in government policy.

We must remember that Nestlé is a very large MNE, with the global scale and the financial muscle to invest to fill gaps in local infrastructure, resist excessive demands from corrupt officials, and cope with the turbulence and uncertainties of country markets like Nigeria. Most international firms do not have this level of assets, resilience, or experience and this can make the task of successfully investing in somewhere like Nigeria even harder and far riskier.

Identifying sources of potential risk and assessing the possible impact on foreign investments of all kinds is difficult to do. Emerging and developing countries generally represent riskier markets, as well as potentially more rewarding markets for MNEs. Their rapid rate of growth, strongly interventionist policies, less mature government institutions, and evolving governance systems all create additional uncertainties for foreign investors. These add to the existing complexities of trying to cope with different economic, social, and cultural ways of doing things. International managers looking to invest in these countries need to develop an in-depth understanding of the ever-changing official, formal rules and regulations governing different kinds of investment. In addition to the country risk analysis techniques introduced here, there is no substitute for direct experience. Only by visiting and learning about the geographic, socio-cultural, economic, and political context in which business takes place can managers develop a qualitative, tacit understanding about the official, formal and the unofficial, informal local rules of the game.

KEY POINTS

1 Country risk analysis examines the chances of non-market events (political, social, and economic) causing financial, strategic, or personnel losses to a firm following FDI in a specific country market.

2 A PEST analysis provides a starting point for examining and comparing political, economic, socio-cultural, and technological conditions in countries that present investment opportunities. Add depth and foresight to make PEST a little more rigorous.

3 Political risk is the probability that political forces will negatively affect an MNE's profit or impede the attainment of other critical business objectives. This risk can be examined in terms of macro and micro factors. A macro political risk is one that affects foreign enterprises in the same general way. A micro political risk is one that affects selected sectors of the economy or specific foreign businesses.

4 General trends toward liberalization and deregulation have opened up a range of emerging markets to FDI, but governments maintain a strong level of control over the economy and the activities of foreign firms. Their ever-changing policies are a source of both new opportunities and risk.

5 There are a number of sources of political risk. Among others, these include the political philosophy of the government in power, changing economic conditions, rising nationalism, social unrest, terrorism, the vested interests of local business groups, and newly created international alliances.

6 There are numerous sources of information on political risk and global rankings of various kinds showing how countries compare. Online resources provide a quick and convenient way of starting a country risk analysis.

7 When assessing risk vulnerability at the project level, quantitative and qualitative information needs to be combined in an analysis of both the investment proposition and the country conditions. The Weighted Country Risk Assessment Model can provide a framework for this. Information gaps and uncertainty will always remain, but the process can improve FDI decision making.

8 Country risk analyses can be incorporated into financial forecasts to produce revised NPV, ROI, or IRR calculations. The adjusted present value (APV) takes into account country risk estimates.

9 Understanding the policy objectives, policy tools, institutional structures and networks, and negotiating tactics of government agencies will help foreign managers negotiate better local conditions for FDI.

10 Power resources are the bargaining chips used by companies and governments in investment negotiations.

11 Corruption is defined by Transparency International as "the misuse of public power for private benefit." It can be difficult to distinguish between corrupt practices and local rules of the game that stem from differences in local market structures and business cultures.

12 There are three key steps in developing effective negotiating strategies. First, the MNE evaluates its own position and that of the other parties to the negotiation. Second, the firm examines the behavioral characteristics of the other parties in order to better understand their style of negotiation. Third, the MNE uses this information to hammer out an agreement that is acceptable to both sides. Identifying the acceptance zone of the other party is an important step.

13 MNEs tend to use a combination of integrative and protective/defensive techniques in minimizing political risk.

Key terms

- country risk analysis
- PEST framework
- political risk
- macro political risk
- expropriation
- indigenization laws
- micro political risk
- Weighted Country Risk Assessment Model
- adjusted present value (APV)
- acceptance zone
- corruption
- transparency
- integrative techniques
- protective and defensive techniques

REVIEW AND DISCUSSION QUESTIONS

1 How can a country risk analysis help an international manager making decisions about which countries to invest in?

2 How can we make a simple PEST analysis more robust, accurate, and useful?

3 What is meant by the term *political risk*? Is there political risk in every country of the world? Explain.

4 Show, with an example, how the process of deregulation and liberalization is opening up opportunities for foreign investment in emerging markets.

5 How does macro political risk differ from micro political risk? Compare and contrast the two.

6 What are some factors that help to determine the degree of micro political risk? Identify and describe three of them.

7 What resources are available online for comparing political risk in two or more countries? Give two examples and say how their measures and rankings differ.

8 What difficulties would a manager face in compiling an accurate Weighted Risk Assessment Model for two emerging market countries?

9 What is an adjusted present value calculation? Give examples of the kinds of country risks that could be incorporated into an APV calculated for a manufacturing investment in a less developed country.

10 When predicting political risk, why will an MNE be interested in examining the economic development agenda and policies of the government?

11 Choose a well-known MNE and describe the kinds of power resources or bargaining chips it could use in FDI negotiations with a country government.

12 Why does corruption tend to be more prevalent in poorer countries?

13 Describe one method for comparing the levels of corruption to be expected in two different countries.

14 Why is improving transparency important for investors and for local populations in less developed countries?

15 Why will an MNE be interested in the behavioral characteristics of the participants in a negotiation? How can such information help to improve its negotiating position?

16 In a negotiation, why would an MNE be interested in the acceptance zone of the other party?

17 What are some bargaining tactics that are used in international negotiating? Identify and describe three of them.

18 How do MNEs use integrative techniques in order to reduce their political risk? Describe an example.

19 How do MNEs use protective/defensive techniques in order to reduce their political risk? Describe an example.

Yukos and the Russian oligarchs

Russia has been making overtures toward a free market economy for a considerable time. During the early 1990s investment from the West was seen as a way to improve the economy. However, significant changes needed to take place to reduce political risk in Russia. Initially, five steps were recommended by outside experts: (1) change the relationship between the national government and the republics in order to set up a federal political system in which central powers are limited; (2) eliminate or slash most state subsidies, including defense spending, and create a uniform sales tax and personal and corporate income tax system; (3) establish a commercial banking system, boost interest rates, and create an independent bank that will halt current inflationary practices; (4) break up state monopolies and industrial cartels; and (5) free the price of most goods immediately and gradually add to this list those changes that must be phased in more slowly: energy, public transportation, housing, and basic consumer goods such as milk, bread, and meat.

By 1997, the private sector accounted for more than half of Russia's output. Some 18,000 industrial firms had been privatized and over 1 million new businesses created. The old Russia, its ideology and institutions, appeared to have gone. Despite currency and interest rate problems in the late 1990s, by 2001, for the first time since the end of communism, Russia had a balanced budget, a trade surplus, reserves, and a growing economy. Inward foreign direct investment (FDI) also surged, growing tenfold between 2000 and 2009, with a peak of almost $80 billion in 2008. It jumped again in 2011, with high investments by firms like BP and PepsiCo.

But foreign investors in Russia have learned to be cautious. Government bureaucracy, endemic corruption and periodic interference in the economy by political leaders, including a habit of re-nationalizing assets in particular industries, have proved to be enduring characteristics of the country. The practice of giving preferential treatment to oligarchs, the powerful individuals who span the political and business worlds, also continues. This biased system, where the state uses an administrative mechanism, rather than a market one, to distribute assets, property, and commercial opportunities to powerful individuals in return for their political support, was favored by Yeltsin. President Vladimir Putin came to power promising to end it, but has a tendency to slide back into these old ways.

The turbulent history of Yukos, Russia's largest oil company, provides an interesting example. It was privatized in the 1990s along with a number of government-owned utilities and natural resource companies. These included Sibneft, the oil company in which the flamboyant Roman Abramovich had the major shareholding, and the source of the wealth with which he bought the English soccer club Chelsea. Other well-connected individuals made fortunes from the sell-offs, which were generally well below market prices. Some channeled surplus funds offshore, including the head of Yukos, Mikhail Khodorkovsky. A US investor, Kenneth Dart, who had unwisely bought stakes in Yukos's production subsidiaries, lost many millions of dollars as Mr. Khodorkovsky stripped their assets and siphoned money into offshore accounts.

Putin appeared to be trying both to stem the flows of capital from these previously state-owned enterprises and to transfer power to his own favored oligarchs. As Mr. Khodorkovsky's political ambitions grew, he was sent to jail on flimsy charges of tax evasion. The Russian state subsequently seized a large stake in Yukos, its Yuganskneftegaz subsidiary, which represented 60 percent of its oil production capacity, apparently to pay some of Yukos's unpaid taxes. It then sold this for $9.35 billion, well below market value, to the Baikal Finance Group in December 2004. It then emerged that Rosneft, a state-owned oil company headed by Igor Sechin, a close confidant of Mr. Putin, had bought Baikal for an undisclosed sum. So the state had taken back Khodorkovsky's prime asset by the back door. A close advisor to Putin, Andrey Illarionov, said at the time that this constituted "expropriation of private property" and should take the prize for the "swindle of the year." He has since lost his job.

Around this time Putin also directed the Russian government to limit foreign firms' involvement in a range of industries for "strategic" reasons. In early 2005 the Ministry of Natural Resources stated that foreign groups and Russian companies with more than 49 percent foreign ownership would be banned from participating in tenders to exploit oil and metal deposits. Officials argued, for example, that Siemens, the German industrial giant, should be barred from buying a stake in Power Machines Engineering Company, on national security grounds. It just so happens that a company controlled by one of Russia's most powerful and Putin-friendly oligarchs, Oleg Deripaska, expressed a strong interest at the same time.

Illarionov's verdict was that Russia had shifted, regrettably, to "an interventionist model of economic development, with extremely incompetent intervention in economic life by ▶

state officials." While the Kremlin still argues for entry into the World Trade Organization and Russia's integration into the global economy, in practice it has been raising barriers.

Sources: Alexey Kuznetsov, "Inward FDI in Russia and its policy context," Vale Columbia Center on Sustainable International Investment, 2010, http://www.vcc. columbia.edu/files/vale/documents/Profiles_Russia_IFDI_Final_ November_30_2010.pdf; "The outspoken silenced," *The Economist*, January 8, 2005; "Method and madness: Yukos, Putin and the oligarchs," *The Economist*, January 1, 2005; "And the owner is?" *The Economist*, November 8, 2003; R. Norton and K.-L. Hubert, "The good news about Russia," *Fortune*, April 14, 1997, p. 32; S. H. Hanke, "Is the rouble next?," *Forbes*, March 9, 1998, p. 64; D. Yergin and T. Gustafson, "Don't write off Russia—yet," *Fortune*, September 28, 1998, pp. 99–102; D. F. Cavallo, "The immensity of Russia's problems," *Forbes*, August 24, 1998, p. 263.

1 What political risks do MNEs face in Russia? Identify and describe three of them.

2 What strengths would a foreign oil or energy firm bring to the country? What Russian needs would it help to meet?

3 How could this firm employ integrative or protective/ defensive techniques in the country? Identify and describe one approach that could be used for each.

REAL CASE

Problems with ports

Ports are important. Despite the shift to services and intangibles, trade in physical goods has continued to grow significantly. Today, almost 10 billion tons of seaborne trade flows through the world's ports each year. But there is a great deal of variability in the costs of using different transport routes and shipping infrastructures. Shipping a container from a company in Sub-Saharan Africa costs almost twice as much as shipping it from India and it takes six times longer than shipping it from the USA. To address these problems, significant aid funding, particularly from the World Bank, has focused on reducing these trade costs and improving shipping infrastructure to support trade. In the process we have learned more about how various forms of corruption create some of these additional costs and inefficiencies in many ports around the world.

Here we focus primarily on ports in Sub-Saharan Africa, because the higher costs and risks associated with these undermine the growth of trade, FDI, and the development of local firms in countries that desperately need this development. However, a brief comparison with Japan also shows that different forms of political risk are prevalent in ports around the world.

Over 90 percent of African imports and exports go via the continent's 100-plus port facilities. These handle 6 percent of the world's shipping cargo traffic and an estimated 3 percent of the world's container traffic. Seven key ports manage the bulk of this traffic: Durban (South Africa), Mombasa (Kenya), Djibouti, Lagos (Nigeria), Abidjan (Ivory Coast), Suez Canal (Egypt), and Tangier (Morocco). Durban

Source: age fotostock/Alamy Stock Photo

alone handles over 4,500 vessels yearly and about 83,000 containers per month, and manages trade worth over $45 billion.

Some of the relatively higher costs of African ports are due to the lower economies of scale associated with their smaller size as well as poorer dockside infrastructure and facilities. It is also clear that corruption plays a major role in increasing costs, delays, and uncertainty. One study of firms' behavior in relation to corruption in ports, with evidence from Maputo (Mozambique) and Durban, found that public officials in charge of service delivery in ports can engage in "collusive corruption" and/or "coercive corruption," depending on the context. The first is when public officials and private sector managers collude to share the profits of illegal transactions; the second is when a public bureaucrat coerces a private sector manager into paying an additional fee to gain access to the service. The study concludes that "collusive corruption" is associated with higher usage of the corrupt port and "coercive corruption" is associated with reduced demand for port services (Sequeira and Djankov, 2014).

This study finds that "bribes are high, frequent and not equalized across ports." In Maputo there is a 53 percent probability that a bribe will need to be paid, compared to 36 percent in Durban. Moreover, the amount paid is three times as high in Maputo as in Durban. The average bribe paid in Maputo increases the total port costs for a 20-foot container by 129 percent (compared to 32 percent in Durban) and adds 14 percent (compared to 4 percent in Durban) to the total shipping costs on any route connecting southern Africa to the Far East. However, it is worth noting that some bribes are paid for avoiding tariff duties, so they can reduce the overall costs of trade to the private agent but reduce the amount of funds received by legitimate public sector organizations.

The incentives for bribery are clear, given that the average bribe in Maputo represents about a quarter of the monthly salary of a customs official (but just 4 percent in Durban), and taking bribes can increase annual salaries by 600 percent. But the beneficiaries vary across ports, depending on the context and conditions. The Sequeira and Djankov (2014) study found that the main recipients of bribe payments in Maputo are customs officials (80 percent) and the primary reason for payment is for tariff evasion (41 percent of the time). However, in Durban, clerks in the document department and security agents receive over 50 percent of all bribes. The latter are paid extra to watch over cargo on the docks and prevent it being stolen or removed while waiting for clearance (i.e., for doing their job).

Further up the east coast of Africa, Kenya's main port of Mombasa has also been studied to understand the cause of higher costs and delays for international shipping firms. According to one study, the key reasons are, in order of importance: security and theft; bureaucratic forwarding and clearing procedures (cost increases due to procedural delays); customs and excise harassment (leading to corruption, otherwise further delays); obsolete, poorly maintained port handling and lifting equipment (leading to further delays); high tariffs for poor service; and just plain corruption.

As with many other kinds of support infrastructure and service operations owned or regulated by government agencies in less developed countries, what they do, how they do it, and how much it costs vary a great deal depending on the institutional structures and values that dominate locally. In some parts of Africa, a generic "culture of corruption" stems from the short-term and self-serving perspective of individuals in positions of power. This may be because of the fragile nature of the political systems in which they operate. A change of government, or the replacement of one senior-level patron with another, triggered by tribal or other conflicts, can mean officials can lose their jobs and their means to an above-average existence.

Many forms of corruption exist in Kenya, including petty corruption (to obtain a small service or get it done faster), corruption by harassment (where the private sector is harassed into bribing), political corruption (soliciting bribes for favors), and grand-scale corruption (evading tax on a grand scale or fixing government tenders worth hundreds of millions of dollars). Political interference in Kenya's ports takes a number of forms. Particularly important are:

1 Political appointments to key management functions, resulting in unqualified and sometimes corrupt personnel in critical power positions.

2 Political undercurrents in labor recruitment; tribal affiliations and ruling political party affinity lead to biases in the recruitment of low-wage labor as well as more senior posts.

3 Regular interference in tender allocations; for government-related tenders, kickbacks (bribes) are necessary to win contracts.

4 Well-connected port users have an advantage and can queue-jump or get better services or security protection, creating frustration for other port users.

Beyond these kinds of problems, small-scale corruption is rife. Port users may need to bribe petty officials to release goods or pay security guards protection money to avoid theft (which they can often be responsible for). The uncertainty for foreign managers unfamiliar with these local rules of the game is increased by the constant change in key officials and their political affiliations. Moreover, bribing the wrong person not only is a waste of money, but also can create big problems for anyone caught "playing the game" during sporadic government crack-downs.

Finally, by way of contrast, it is worth noting that ports in other parts of the world are not immune from these problems. Japan's ports have long been slower and more expensive than most other ports in the Asia region. Part of the explanation lies in another form of corruption, a complex cartel which the Japanese government, with pressure from the USA, has finally started to tackle. At the end of the 1990s, when the problem was at its worst, it took three to four days to clear customs and immigration in a Japanese port and cost $36,000 to $40,000 to unload a vessel, compared to one day in most other ports and $11,000 in Singapore and $16,000 in the United States.

One major source of these additional costs was the near-monopoly power of the Japan Harbor Transportation Association (JHTA). At its height the JHTA was a cartel of 2,000 member organizations encompassing the waterfront services (stevedoring, cargo handling, and transfer ▶

documentation) across 130 ports in Japan. It was run by Chairman Takashima, the so-called king of the waterfront, eight vice chairmen and 85 directors from the various port companies. The JHTA was responsible for two kinds of anti-competitive practices. First, the system of prior consultations between shipping companies and the labor unions of cargo-handling companies took place via JHTA. Foreign firms could not select which firm handled their cargo on the basis of quality or cost; JHTA chose for them. It also controlled schedule changes, changes in berths and route calls, and centrally regulating and slowing down the entire process. There was no formal documentation, application, or appeals procedure; the system operated through informal lobbying. Second, licensing requirements for technical operators and stevedoring firms acted as barriers to foreign firms (and to non-cartel Japanese firms) entering the market. Foreign firms were not allowed to perform stevedoring or port services for themselves or appoint third parties without the consent of JHTA.

The JHTA connected both government departments and *yakuza* (mafia-like groups in Japan) in ways that non-Japanese cannot easily understand. A US Embassy study found that 110 ex-officials from the Ministry of Transport had moved to senior management positions in waterfront companies. This is *amakudari* (literally, "descent from heaven"), a system of secondment or "semi-retirement" for bureaucrats common in Japan. In 2005 the Japanese government

promised to take measures to reduce the cost of using its main ports by 30–40 percent to "arrest a dramatic drop in competitiveness" in relation to other Asian ports. However, the anti-competitive networks described above still persist as a symbol of the socio-political nature of this sector in Japan.

Sources: Sandra Sequeira and Simeon Djankov, "Corruption and firm behavior: evidence from African ports," London School of Economics and Political Science, 2014, http://www.nes.ru/dataupload/files/JIE_Corruption%20in%20Ports%20 2014.pdf; "Africa's biggest shipping ports," *BusinessTech*, March 8, 2015, http://businesstech.co.za/news/general/81995/africas-biggest-shipping-ports/; Mariko Sanchanta, "Japanese government to cut main port costs by up to 40%," *Financial Times*, January 7, 2005, p. 3; Michiyo Nakamoto, "Port city seeks to nurture new enterprises," *Financial Times*, April 27, 2004, p. 3; Parit Shah, "A strategy for the port of Mombasa," unpublished MBA dissertation, Warwick Business School, Coventry, 2004; US Embassy in Tokyo, *Third Report to the Leaders on the US–Japan Regulatory Reform and Competition Policy Initiative*, June 8, 2004, http://tokyo.usembassy.gov/e/p/tp-20040609–01.html; Lucy Kilalo, "10 charged with stealing at port," *The Daily Nation*, March 12, 2003; UNCTAD, *Review of Maritime Transport 2014*, http://unctad.org/en/PublicationsLibrary/rmt2014_en.pdf

1   What are the main differences in the barriers and risks faced by foreign firms across the different port systems referred to in the case?

2   Why is it difficult for foreign firms to challenge these unfair practices in either Africa or Japan?

3   How could a manager looking to use these ports minimize the risk and uncertainty created by local ways of doing things?

NOTES

1 Witold J. Henisz, Edward D. Mansfield, and Mary Ann Von Glinow, "Conflict, security, and political risk: international business in challenging times," *Journal of International Business Studies*, vol. 41, no. 5 (2010), pp. 759–64; S. Sakarya, M. Eckman, and K. H. Hyllegard, "Market selection for international expansion: assessing opportunities in emerging markets," *International Marketing Review*, vol. 24, no. 2 (2007), pp. 208–38; S. Bridgewater, "Assessing market attractiveness," in S. Bridgewater and C. E. Egan (eds.), *International Marketing Relationships* (Basingstoke: Palgrave, 2002); W. J. Henisz, *Politics and International Investment: Measuring Risk and Protecting Profits* (Cheltenham: Edward Elgar, 2002); K. D. Miller, "A framework for integrated risk management," *Journal of International Business* (summer 1992), pp. 311–31; D. Kern, "The evaluation of country risk and economic potential," *Long Range Planning*, vol. 18, no. 3 (1985), pp. 17–25; and M. Perlitz, "Country portfolio analysis—assessing country risk and opportunity," *Long Range Planning*, vol. 18, no. 4 (1985), pp. 11–26.

2 D. O'Connell, "Dogfight," *Sunday Times*, September 19, 2004.

3 Adapted from United Nations, *World Investment Report*, 2006 and 2009, key data downloads at http://www.unctad.org

(Geneva: United Nations Conference on Trade and Development).

4 This framework partly comes from C. R. Kennedy, Jr., *Managing the International Business Environment: Cases in Political and Country Risk* (Englewood Cliffs, NJ: Prentice Hall International, 1991).

5 A. Ostrovsky, "Economics minister hits at Putin policy," *Financial Times*, January 12, 2005.

6 D. Brewster and A. Hill, "US opts for homegrown products," *Financial Times*, April 1, 2003.

7 E. Alden, "Small manufacturers drive trade protectionism up the US agenda," *Financial Times*, February 1, 2005.

8 F. Bokhari, "Pakistan weaves into a new era," *Financial Times*, January 12, 2005; H. K. Nordas, "The global textile and clothing industry post the agreement on textiles and clothing," *World Trade Organization*, 2004, http://www.wto.org/english/res_e/booksp_e/discussion_papers5_e.pdf.

9 S. C. Collinson and J. Holden, "Decision-making and market orientation in the internationalization process of small and medium-sized enterprises," *Management International Review* (MIR), vol. 45 (2005), pp. 413–36.

10 The Business Environment Risk Information (BERI) model contains a variable that it calls "Mentality" in its formula for national risk assessment. The idea behind inclusion of this

concept is that there can be a national attitude, a mentality that would be resistant or corrosive to foreign investment and prevent efficient and productive investment and business operations. Details about the criteria and methodology used by BERI are available at http://www.beri.com.

11 Ilan Oshri, Julia Kotlarsky, and Leslie P. Willcocks (eds.), *The Handbook of Global Outsourcing and Offshoring* (Basingstoke: Palgrave, 2009).

12 The bargaining environment can be captured by the structure of a complex, interrelated network. The bargaining power of individual constituencies is related to their basis of power, network position, bargaining outcome preferences, and motivation to influence bargaining (James Nebus and Carlos Rufin, "Extending the bargaining power model: explaining bargaining outcomes among nations, MNEs, and NGOs," *Journal of International Business Studies*, vol. 41, no. 6 (2010), pp. 996–1015).

13 Nancy J. Adler, *International Dimensions of Organizational Behavior*, 2nd ed. (Boston, MA: PWS-Kent Publishing, 1991), p. 197; Fons Trompenaars and Charles HampdenTurner, *Managing People Across Cultures*, Culture for Business series (London: Capstone, 2004).

14 John R. Schermerhorn, Jr., "Language effects in cross-cultural management research: an empirical study and a word of caution," *National Academy of Management Proceedings*, 1987, pp. 102–5; S. C. Collinson and A. M. Pettigrew "Comparative international business research methods: pitfalls and practicalities," Chapter 27 in A. M. Rugman (ed.), *The Oxford Handbook of International Business,* 2nd ed. (Oxford: Oxford University Press, 2009).

15 For additional insights into negotiating, see Carl Rodrigues, *International Management: A Cultural Approach* (Thousand Oaks, CA: Sage, 2008).

16 Transparency International, *Global Corruption Report 2010*, http://www.globalcorruptionreport.org.

17 See http://www.globalcorruptionreport.org and http://www.transparency.org/index.html.

18 For a good example of how Japan does this, see Andrew Pollack, "Japan takes a pre-emptive step on auto exports," *New York Times*, January 9, 1993, pp. 17, 26; and Richard W. Stevenson, "Japanese cars get British accents," *New York Times*, February 25, 1992, pp. C1, C14.

BIBLIOGRAPHY

Alessandri, Todd M., Ford, David N., Lander, Diane M., Leggio, Karyl B., and Taylor, Marilyn. "Managing risk and uncertainty in complex capital projects," *Quarterly Review of Economics and Finance*, vol. 44, no. 5 (December 2004).

Aulakh, Preet S., and Mudambi, Ram. "Financial resource flow in multinational enterprises: the role of external capital markets," *Management International Review*, vol. 45, no. 3 (2005).

Chatterjee, Sayan, et al. "Integrating behavioral and economic concepts of risk into strategic management: the twain shall meet," *Long Range Planning*, vol. 36, no. 1 (2003).

Chen, Charles J. P., Yuan Ding, Kim, and Chansog, Francis. "High-level politically connected firms, corruption, and analyst forecast accuracy around the world," *Journal of International Business Studies*, vol. 41, no. 9 (December 2010).

Click, Reid W. "Financial and political risks in US direct foreign investment," *Journal of International Business Studies*, vol. 36, no. 5 (September 2005).

Coeurderoy, Régis, and Murray, Gordon. "Regulatory environments and the location decision: evidence from the early foreign market entries of new-technology-based firms," *Journal of International Business Studies*, vol. 39, no. 4 (June 2008).

Desbordes, Rodolphe. "The sensitivity of US multinational enterprises to political and macroeconomic uncertainty: a sectoral analysis," *International Business Review*, vol. 16, no. 6 (2007).

Di Gregorio, Dante. "Re-thinking country risk: insights from entrepreneurship theory," *International Business Review*, vol. 14, no. 2 (2005).

Figueira-de-Lemos, Francisco, Johanson, Jan, and Vahlne, Jan-Erik. "Risk management in the internationalization process of the firm: a note on the Uppsala model," *Journal of World Business*, vol. 46, no. 2 (2011).

Filatotchev, Igor, Strange, Roger, Piesse, Jenifer, and Yung-Chih Lien. "FDI by firms from newly industrialized economies in emerging markets: corporate governance, entry mode and location," *Journal of International Business Studies*, vol. 38, no. 4 (July 2007).

Gaba, Vibha, Pan, Yigang, and Ungson, Gerardo R. "Timing of entry in international market: an empirical study of US Fortune 500 firms in China," *Journal of International Business Studies*, vol. 33, no. 1 (2002).

Goerzen, Anthony, Sapp, Stephen, and Delios, Andrew. "Investor response to environmental risk in foreign direct investment," *Management International Review*, vol. 50, no. 6 (December 2010).

Heidenreich, Stefan, Mohr, Alexander, and Puck, Jonas. "Political strategies, entrepreneurial overconfidence and foreign direct investment in developing countries," *Journal of World Business*, vol. 50, no. 4 (2015).

Henisz, Witold, and Delios, Andrew. "Uncertainty, imitation and plant location: Japanese multinational corporations, 1990–1996," *Administrative Science Quarterly*, vol. 46, no. 3 (2001).

Henisz, Witold J., and Zelner, Bennet A. "Legitimacy, interest group pressures and change in emergent institutions: the case of foreign investors and host country governments," *Academy of Management Review*, vol. 30, no. 2 (2005).

Hillman, Amy, and Keim, Gerald. "International variation in the business–government interface: institutional and organizational considerations," *Academy of Management Review*, vol. 20, no. 1 (January 1995).

Hoti, Suhejla, and McAleer, Michael. "An empirical assessment of country risk ratings and associated models," *Journal of Economic Surveys*, vol. 18, no. 4 (2004).

Inkpen, Andrew C., and Beamish, Paul W. "Knowledge, bargaining power, and the instability of international joint ventures," *Academy of Management Review*, vol. 22, no. 1 (January 1997).

Jiménez, Alfredo, Luis-Rico, Isabel, and Benito-Osorio, Diana. "The influence of political risk on the scope of internationalization of regulated companies: insights from a Spanish sample," *Journal of World Business*, vol. 49, no. 3 (2014).

Keating, Robert J., and Abramson, Neil R. "A new framework in the quest for cultural understanding using Australia, Thailand and Japan as an example," *International Journal of Business Studies*, vol. 17, no. 1 (June 2009).

Keillor, Bruce D., and Hult, G. Tomas M. "Predictors of firm-level political behavior in the global business environment: an investigation of specific activities employed by US firms," *International Business Review*, vol. 13, no. 3 (June 2004).

Kobrin, Stephen. "When does political instability result in increased investment risk?" *Columbia Journal of World Business*, vol. 13, no. 3 (1978).

Kumar, Rajesh, Rangan, U. Srinivasa, and Rufin, Carlos. "Negotiating complexity and legitimacy in independent power project development," *Journal of World Business*, vol. 40, no. 3 (August 2005).

Mudambi, Ram, and Navarra, Pietro. "Political tradition, political risk and foreign direct investment in Italy," *Management International Review*, vol. 43, no. 3 (2003).

Peng, Mike W., Wang, Denis Y. L., and Jiang, Y. "An institution-based view of international business strategy: a focus on emerging economies," *Journal of International Business Studies*, vol. 39, no. 5 (July/August 2008).

Ramamurti, Ravi. "Reassessing risk in developing countries," *Long Range Planning*, vol. 36, no. 4 (August 2003).

Ramamurti, Ravi, and Hashai, Niron (eds.). *The Future of Foreign Direct Investment and the Multinational Enterprise: 15*, Research in Global Strategic Management series (Bingley: Emerald Group Publishing, 2011).

Reuer, Jeffrey J., Shenkar, Oded, and Ragozzino, Roberto. "Mitigating risk in international mergers and acquisitions: the role of contingent payouts," *Journal of International Business Studies*, vol. 35, no. 1 (2004).

Rothaermel, Frank T., Kotha, Suresh, and Steensman, H. Kevin. "International market entry by US internet firms: an empirical analysis of country risk, national culture, and market size," *Journal of Management*, vol. 32, no. 1 (2006).

Sauvant, Karl, *Yearbook on International Investment Law and Policy 2009–2010* (New York: Oxford University Press, 2010).

Scherer, Andreas Georg, and Palazzo, Guido. "The new political role of business in a globalized world: a review of a new perspective on CSR and its implications for the firm, governance, and democracy," *Journal of Management Studies*, vol. 48, no. 4 (2011).

Stasavage, D. "Private investment and political institutions," *Economics and Politics*, vol. 14, no. 1 (2002).

Strange, Roger, Filatotehev, Igor, Yung-chih, Lien, and Piesse, Jenifer. "Insider control and the FDI location decision," *Management International Review*, vol. 49, no. 4 (August 2009).

Tahir, Rizwan, and Larimo, Jorman. "Understanding the location strategies of the European firms in Asian countries," *Journal of American Academy of Business*, vol. 1, no. 2 (2004).

WWW RESOURCES

http://www.tdctrade.com
http://www.wto.org
http://www.worldbank.org/wbi/governance/govdata2001.htm
http://www.worldbank.org/data/countrydata/countrydata.html
http://rru.worldbank.org/DoingBusiness/
http://miga.org
http://www.countryrisk.com

http://www.economist.com/countries
http://www.eiu.com
http://transparency.org
http://www.globalcorruptionreport.org
http://www.opacity.index.com
http://www.fraserinstitute.ca
http://www.freetheworld.com

Chapter 16

INTERNATIONAL FINANCIAL MANAGEMENT

Contents

Objectives of the chapter

This chapter discusses the opportunities and problems that face multinational enterprises (MNEs) because they operate in a multicurrency, segmented-market world.

The specific objectives of this chapter are to:

1 *Compare* and *contrast* how polycentric, ethnocentric, and geocentric solutions are used in determining the financial planning and controlling authority that is given to subsidiaries.

2 *Study* some of the most common techniques that are used in managing global cash flows, including funds positioning and multilateral netting.

3 *Examine* foreign exchange risk strategies that are used to protect the multinational against transaction, translation, and economic exchange risks.

4 *Explain* how capital budgeting is carried out in a multinational firm.

5 *Describe* how international financing opportunities for an MNE differ from those available to a domestic firm.

6 *Provide* examples of international financial strategies currently being used by multinationals.

ACTIVE LEARNING CASE

Financial transparency at Siemens

Siemens was founded by Werner von Siemens and Johann Georg Halske in 1847, with the invention of the telegraph. Headquartered in Germany, Siemens has grown to become a global diversified technology company primarily specializing in energy, healthcare and infrastructure industries. In 2014 Siemens' revenue totaled €71.92 billion, 10 percent of which was profits. With a workforce of 357,000, located in nearly every country of the world, Siemens has truly become a global MNE.

In 2006 Siemens faced a major corruption scandal which spanned over 60 percent of total global operations, with fines amounting to €2.5 billion. Corrupt activities involved the securing of contracts to provide power generation equipment in Italy, telecommunications infrastructure in Nigeria, and national identity cards in Argentina via the use of bribes. The firm's corporate governance structures and culture came into question as its values and ethics appeared to be compromised by an aggressive growth strategy and a complicated, decentralized structure with little oversight from the main headquarters.

Most of the German investigation focused on a vast number of artificial consulting contracts and a tortuous system of accounts which helped the organization secure business from overseas. Ironically, the findings illustrated how a particular Saudi Arabian organization threatened to expose the bribes to the Securities and Exchange Commission (SEC), unless Siemens cooperated by supplying an additional $910 million in consulting fees. Siemens ended up paying an additional $50 million in order to settle this form of "blackmail," leading to observations that there really is "no honor among thieves." Organizations that frequently use "fly-by-night" consultants and "off the books" accounts have tended to signal to various authorities that they may be engaging in illegitimate practices.

Replacing Klaus Kleinfeld, Peter Löscher was appointed as the new CEO in 2007 and was primarily responsible for developing a culture of integrity among the Siemens workforce. This was a major challenge as many board members had resigned and several executives were facing legal prosecution. Following his appointment, Löscher drastically restructured the top three levels of management and approximately 65 percent of senior executives were replaced. Löscher was the first outsider appointed as CEO and he invested a significant amount of time overseeing the detailed operational activities of employees within the organization. He discovered a widespread sense of disappointment among workers, stemming from past leadership failures which had ultimately impacted workers' engagement and productivity levels.

Tackling corrupt practices head on, with the exclusion of directors Siemens offered their workforce an "amnesty." This meant that employees who came forward and admitted to being involved in bribery were guaranteed that they could keep their job. In contrast, employees who did not wish to share any information and who later were found to be involved in such matters were to be fired. It has been reported that approximately 130 staff members came forward.

Key changes were made involving the corporate governance and structure of the board. Previously, it had been operating on two tiers, where reports were issued to the executive board, which lacked an in-depth understanding of the business as a whole. In essence, Siemens was passing down preapproved decisions without evaluating them effectively. Löscher enforced the breakdown of the original two-level system into a single board which consisted of eight individuals who had acquired a deep understanding of each of the industries within Siemens. In addition, this board included two new positions overseeing supply chain management and sustainability, and legal counsel and compliance. Prior to 2007, operations across 190 different countries had been organized into 70 global clusters. This was reduced to a total of 20 clusters in order to reduce the complexity of operations and increase accountability and oversight. By 2012 the number of clusters was further reduced to 12, managed by a steering group who met every quarter.

One of the key changes to the board was the appointment of US lawyer Peter Solmssen, who was responsible for compliance within Siemens. The compliance team held positions in crucial functions within Siemens and expanded from 170 employees to approximately 600 employees in 2011. The Siemens Compliance Organization became independent from Siemens itself, reporting directly to Siemens' main board.

Solmssen highlighted the need for sustainability. However, unlike conventional visions of sustainability, where firms prioritize the reduction of emissions and improve efficiency levels, Solmssen believed sustainability should be viewed more broadly as underlying every aspect of a global business culture. Solmssen argued that anti-corruption practices could be established at little cost and with minimal disruption. John Garred, Siemens' UK Regional Officer, suggested that Siemens' anti-corruption policy was built on three fundamental principles: prevent, detect, and respond. In essence, this meant training the workforce regarding anti-corruption policies, monitoring whether these policies were indeed working, and responding robustly when violations were uncovered. Garred also identified the importance of management accountants as key compliance regulators.

Management accountants consistently conduct control checks on payments and can explore anomalies in the system to assess compliance; they are the "eyes and ears" of the compliance team. Furthermore, management accountants play a vital role in guiding the ethics of decision making in conjunction with the procedural and regulatory aspects of compliance. In essence, management accountants often go well beyond simply adding and subtracting, but can analyze and interpret information from a range of perspectives, adding significant value to an organization's strategic goals.

Following the corruption scandal, Siemens recognized that in order to rebuild trust both internally and externally, structural, procedural, and cultural interventions had to be implemented simultaneously. Siemens has consistently highlighted the need for open communication and transparency. The firm has introduced global programs which aim to bridge the gap between top management and lower-level employees via the use of middle management. For example, "integrity dialogs" are mentioned during sales meetings, to openly discuss any ethical issues and how these should be handled as part of the contracting process. In order to improve transparency, Siemens also externally reports compliance-related developments. The reporting of ethical information is seen as one important dimension of good corporate governance, as it allows both management and stakeholders to gain an insight into the impact of leadership activities within the firm.

Siemens Chief Financial Officer, Joe Kaeser, was appointed as the new CEO in 2013 and revised the company's long-term strategy. Kaeser once stated that "Compliance is not a program, but the foundation of sustainable business," and suggested that focusing on the long term, developing real and sustainable values, and considering stakeholders are principles which ensure good corporate governance.

Conclusion

Siemens experienced a difficult period during the corruption scandal, but via the use of effective corporate governance, financial reporting, and auditing practices, it has managed to get back on track. The firm needs to continually demonstrate that it has the appropriate monitoring and compliance processes in place, as its current and past activities are still under scrutiny. In 2015 an investigation found that corrupt practices within Siemens could be traced back to 1998 when €70 million in bribes were paid in order to secure the sale of equipment to Greece's dominant telecom operator, OTE.

So lessons remain to be learned. There are significant costs involved in compliance and firms also need to accept that they may lose contracts to less ethical companies. But there are also significant costs not only in legal expenses and fines, but also in terms of lost trust and reputation, when corrupt practices are uncovered.

Sources: Siemens, *Annual Report*, 2012, "Rethinking the value chain, ethical culture change at Siemens: a case study", *CGMA Briefing*, 2014; Graham Dietz and Nicole Gillespie, "Rebuilding trust: how Siemens atoned for its sins," *Guardian*, March 26, 2012; Bruce Watson, "Siemens and the battle against bribery and corruption," *Guardian*, September 18, 2013; Donna Boehme and Joe Murphy, "No place to hide: early lessons from the Siemens case," *ETHIKOS* (November/December 2007), accessed from http://compliancestrategists.com/csblog/wp-content/uploads/2014/01/NovemberDecember-2007-Ethikos-PDF-Download.pdf; Siri Schubert and T. Christian Miller, "At Siemens, bribery was just a line item," World Business, *New York Times*, December 20, 2008.

① How did Siemens restructure its parent–subsidiary relationships between 2007 and 2012 in terms of using a polycentric, ethnocentric, or geocentric solution?

② How is Siemens exposed to exchange rate risks and what kinds of hedging strategies could it employ to mitigate these risks?

③ If Siemens believes that the euro is going to appreciate in relation to the US dollar, how is it likely to deal with receivables and payables?

④ When Siemens is looking to invest in its foreign affiliates around the world, what are some of the important considerations in choosing among alternative financing sources?

INTRODUCTION

Any firm with affiliates in at least two countries (even with a simple sales office abroad) needs to deal with differences in the financial environments of those countries—differences in their tax systems, their currency systems, and numerous other areas. Can you imagine trying to keep the books of a company such as Johnson & Johnson, which is required to maintain financial records according to the different accounting standards in the dozens of countries where it operates, plus records for use in internal control? Beyond the chores of record keeping, the firm operating at this level obtains opportunities to transfer funds (and products) between countries, utilize financial markets in each country to serve its global needs, and diversify its risks internationally. Increasing numbers of MNEs, such as Ford and General Electric, are building internal financial institutions so that they can take advantage of these opportunities around the world. This chapter explores the opportunities and problems of firms in such an environment.

National financial markets and the euromarkets were discussed in Chapter 7; here the emphasis is on using these markets to optimize the financial position of the multinational firm. The issue of transaction exchange risk was treated in Chapter 7; this chapter considers such risk in the context of a firm that does repeated international business and maintains long-term assets abroad. Finally, we consider the full set of financial issues in a firm whose subsidiaries in different countries compete for use of the available financial resources. This chapter treats the topic of multinational financial management as a whole.

The chapter is structured to cover major issues in corporate finance as they apply to the international context. Basic financial management can be divided into two broad headings: (1) choice and management of *sources* of funds; and (2) choice and management of *uses* of funds. At the international level, exchange risk management must be added. Figure 16.1 depicts the topics that constitute the substance of the chapter. Overall financial management requires *control* over each type of decision depicted in the figure, especially since financial managers in each affiliate may make decisions that affect the total corporation's financial position.

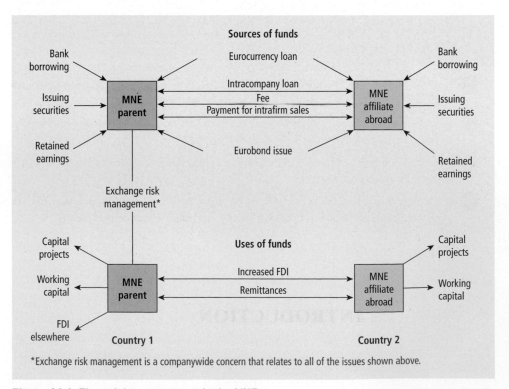

Figure 16.1 Financial management in the MNE

In the next section, we explore aspects of the parent–subsidiary financial relationship within the MNE. Then the discussion turns to the issue of managing cash flows in the MNE. Next, we consider a more comprehensive presentation of exchange risk management than that given in Chapter 7. After that, we look at the two sides of financial management in the context of the MNE: namely, use of available funds (particularly for capital budgeting) and financing for the firm's short- and long-term needs. A section on control of the financial activities in an MNE follows. And finally, some strategic considerations for the firm in international finance are presented.

DETERMINING PARENT–SUBSIDIARY RELATIONSHIPS

Because finance is such an important area of operations, it is critically important that parent companies firmly establish the relationships that will exist regarding financial planning and control authority. On the one hand, each branch or subsidiary should be responsible for its own planning and control system. On the other hand, there must be some central control in order to coordinate overall operations and to ensure both efficiency and profitability. In addressing this challenge, MNEs tend to opt for one of three managerial solutions: polycentric, ethnocentric, or geocentric, just as these choices are used in other strategic areas.

Polycentric solution

Polycentric solution
A decentralized decision-making framework in which financial decisions are largely allocated to foreign affiliates and financial evaluation of affiliates is done in comparison to other firms in that context

A **polycentric solution** is to treat the MNE as a holding company and to decentralize decision making to the subsidiary levels. In this arrangement, financial statements are prepared according to generally accepted accounting principles in both the overseas subsidiary's and the parent's home country, and the subsidiary's performance is evaluated against that of similar domestic and foreign concerns.

The advantages of the polycentric approach are those commonly obtained with decentralization. Decisions are made on the spot by those most informed about market conditions, and international subsidiaries tend to be more flexible, motivated, efficient, and competitive. On the other hand, this solution reduces the authority of the home office, and senior corporate management often dislikes this dilution of its authority. Additionally, an MNE may find that a polycentric approach results in competition between different international subsidiaries and lowers overall profits for the company.

Ethnocentric solution

Ethnocentric solution
A centralized decision-making framework in which financial decisions and control for foreign affiliates are largely integrated into home-office management

Working capital
Short-term financial instruments such as bank deposits and marketable securities that can be optimized by the MNE on a global basis

The **ethnocentric solution** is to treat all foreign operations as if they were extensions of domestic operations. In this case each unit is integrated into the planning and control system of the parent company.

The advantage of this system is that management is able to coordinate overall operations carefully. This usually results in centralization of the finance function so that cash not needed for day-to-day operations can be invested in marketable securities or transferred to other subsidiaries or branches that need **working capital**. The primary drawback of this solution is that it can cause problems for the individual subsidiary, which may feel that it needs more cash than is left on hand or that it is hindered in its efforts to expand because the parent company is siphoning off necessary resources.

Geocentric solution

Geocentric solution
A decision-making framework in which financial decisions and evaluation related to foreign affiliates are integrated for the firm on a global basis

The **geocentric solution** is to handle financial planning and controlling decisions on a global basis. These decisions are typically influenced by two factors. One is the nature and location of the subsidiary. For example, British investment in North America has predominantly been via holding companies, the polycentric approach, since the quality of local management largely rewards decentralization. Conversely, investment in developing countries has typically been more centralized, with the parent company maintaining close control of financial expenditures. The second influencing factor is the gains that can be achieved by coordinating all units in a carefully synchronized way. When an MNE's overseas units face a myriad of tax rates, financial systems, and competitive environments, it is often more efficient to centralize most of the financial control decisions because this is the best way to ensure that profit and efficiency are maximized. For example, if two subsidiaries are equally able to sell a particular product to a major customer, with centralized financial planning the parent company could ensure that the sale would be made by the unit located in the country with the lowest corporate income tax rate. Additional examples of the ways in which financial operations could be directed by using a geocentric solution are seen in the management of global cash flows.

✔ Active learning check

Review your answer to Active Learning Case question 1 and make any changes you like. Then compare your answer to the one below.

 How did Siemens restructure its parent–subsidiary relationships between 2007 and 2012 in terms of using a polycentric, ethnocentric, or geocentric solution?

Arguably Siemens moved from a polycentric structure toward a more ethnocentric structure, because of its concerns over corruption and compliance. More control and oversight was brought under the main board and decision-making power became more centralized.

MANAGING GLOBAL CASH FLOWS

One of the key areas of international financial management is the careful handling of global cash flows. There are a number of ways in which this is done. Three of the most important ones are the prudent use of internal funds flows, the use of funds positioning, and the use of **multilateral netting**. The following sections examine each of these three.

Multilateral netting
Payment of net amounts due only between affiliates of an MNE that have multiple transactions among the group, which can be partially netted out among them, so then only the net funds need to be transferred

Internal funds flows

When an MNE wants to expand operations or fund activities, one of the simplest ways of obtaining the needed monies is by getting them from internal sources such as working capital, which is the difference between current assets and current liabilities. For example, if General Electric's German subsidiary wants to hire more employees, it may be able to pay for this payroll increase out of the funds it generates from ongoing operations. Another way of raising money internally is by borrowing from a local bank or from the parent company. For example, an MNE's Chilean subsidiary will get a loan

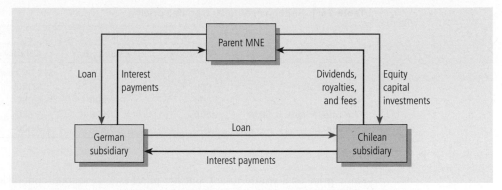

Figure 16.2 Common examples of internal sources and flows of funds

from the parent company or the German subsidiary and then repay the money with interest out of operations. A third way is by having the parent company increase its equity capital investment in the subsidiary. In turn the subsidiary could pay the parent dividends on the investment. These examples are illustrated in Figure 16.2 and help to show that there are many ways for multinational firms to generate internal cash for operations.

Which method is most likely to be used? The answer will depend on a number of factors, including government regulations regarding intercompany lending. For example, when tax rates are high for a profitable subsidiary, it is common to find those units willing to lend money at low rates of interest to other subsidiaries in the MNE that need funds to expand into growth markets. The logic behind this strategy is quite simple: the highly profitable unit does not need to charge a high interest rate because much of this interest earning will be lost to the high local taxes. Conversely, the subsidiary that is borrowing the money needs low interest rates so as to conserve its cash for expansion purposes. By shifting the money around in this fashion, the MNE is able to support expansion efforts, to minimize taxes, and to increase the sales potential of the subsidiaries. In an effort to prevent multinationals from taking advantage of such tax loopholes, in recent years some governments have changed their tax laws and established a minimum rate that can be charged on these intercompany loans.

Another area of concern is government limits on a parent company's ability to charge subsidiaries a licensing or royalty fee for the use of technology or to assess a management fee that covers the subsidiary's fair share of corporate overhead. When there are no government restrictions in these areas, the MNE has greater freedom in drawing funds from subsidiary operations, thus providing the parent with a pool of money that can be used for other worldwide operations. The ways in which this is done are commonly referred to as funds positioning techniques.

Funds positioning techniques

Funds positioning techniques are strategies that are used to move monies from one multinational operation to another. While there are a variety of approaches, three of the most common are transfer pricing, use of tax havens, and fronting loans.

Transfer pricing

A **transfer price** is an internal price that is set by a company in intrafirm trade, such as the price at which the Chilean subsidiary will purchase electric motors from the German subsidiary. An initial conclusion would be that the German firm will sell the motors at the

Funds positioning techniques
Mechanisms such as transfer pricing, intercompany loans, and timing of payments that are used to move funds from one affiliate to another in a multinational firm

Transfer price
The price used for an intracompany payment for shipment of products or services from one affiliate to another in an MNE; these prices can be used to reduce taxes, move funds to desired locations, and so on

Table 16.1 Shifting profits by transfer pricing

	Arm's-length price		Transfer price	
	Country A	Country B	Country A	Country B
Sales	$10,000 exports	$12,000	$12,000 exports	$12,000
Costs of sales	8,000	10,000	8,000	12,000
Profit	2,000	2,000	4,000	Nil
Tax rate (A: 40%, B: 50%)	800	1,000	1,600	Nil
Net profit	1,200	1,000	2,400	Nil

same price as it would to any outside purchaser. A second conclusion is that the Chilean subsidiary will receive a discount because it is an intrafirm transaction and the parent will not allow its subsidiaries to profit at the expense of each other. However, both of these conclusions are incorrect when a transfer pricing strategy is employed. The final price will be determined by local regulations and will be set at a level that allows the MNE to achieve certain desired goals, such as to increase profit, to reduce costs, and/or to move money among the subsidiaries.

A good example is provided by a multinational that has a subsidiary located in Country A, which has a low corporate income tax and is selling goods to a subsidiary located in Country B, which has a high corporate income tax. If the transfer price is set carefully, it is possible to reallocate taxable income away from the highly taxed subsidiary to the subsidiary with the low tax rate. Table 16.1 provides an example by contrasting arm's-length pricing with transfer pricing. An **arm's-length price** is the price a buyer will pay for merchandise in a market under conditions of perfect competition. As seen in the table, it cost the subsidiary in Country A $8,000 for the goods it is selling to the subsidiary in Country B. Under an arm's-length price the seller is adding $2,000 for profit and selling the goods for $10,000. In turn the second subsidiary is selling these goods for $12,000. Thus both subsidiaries are making a profit of $2,000. As also seen in the table, the tax rate in Country A is 40 percent, whereas in Country B it is 50 percent. So the first subsidiary will have a net profit of $1,200, whereas the second subsidiary will net $1,000.

Under a transfer price arrangement, however, the objective is to maximize profits in the low-tax-rate country and to minimize them in the high-tax-rate country. In this case, as seen in Table 16.1, the first subsidiary sells the goods for $12,000, and after paying 40 percent tax on the $4,000 profit, it ends up with a net profit of $2,400. The second subsidiary sells the goods for $12,000 and makes no profit. However, thanks to the transfer pricing strategy, the multinational's overall profit is greater than it was with arm's-length pricing ($2,400 versus $2,200).

Note that taxes are not the only considerations. Import tariffs also influence the decision to use transfer pricing. If the importing country has high tariffs, the firm needs to consider whether a high or low transfer price will maximize after-tax, after-tariff profits.

One of the obvious benefits of transfer pricing is that it allows the multinational to reduce taxes. A second benefit is that the strategy lets the firm concentrate cash in specific locales such as with the first subsidiary, or to move funds away from a country facing significant exchange rate risk, or to reduce payment of import tariffs. One of the problems with transfer pricing is that the financial statements do not accurately reflect subsidiary performance because the profit margins are manipulated. A second problem is that the strategy may not encourage efficient performance by the seller in a low-tax jurisdiction, whose primary objective is to unload merchandise on the other subsidiary at a profit as high as can be justified.

Arm's-length price
The price that exists or would exist on a sale of a given product or service between two unrelated companies—as contrasted with an intracompany transfer price

Table 16.2 Transfer pricing through tax havens

	Country A subsidiary	Country B subsidiary (tax haven)	Country C subsidiary
Sales	$8,000 exports	$12,000 exports	$12,000
Costs of sales	8,000	→8,000	→12,000
Profit	—	—	—
Tax rate (A: 40%, B: 0%, C: 50%)	—	—	—
Net profit	0	4,000	0

In recent years, countries have been rewriting their tax codes to prevent arbitrary transfer pricing. In the United States, for example, the Internal Revenue Service (IRS) now asks multinationals to apply for an advanced determination ruling before establishing a transfer pricing policy. After the firm submits the request, the IRS will determine whether or not the policy is appropriate. The objective of the tax agency is to ensure that MNEs charge their overseas subsidiaries the same price for components and products as they charge independent third parties, thus effectively eliminating price manipulation for tax purposes. Because a large part (about one-third) of international trade in the early twenty-first century is intrafirm, transfer prices are a necessary aspect of much of international business.

Use of tax havens

Tax havens
Jurisdictions that offer the MNE a lower tax rate (or no tax) than in other places, so that MNEs can locate some of their business activities there and thus reduce overall tax payments

A second funds positioning technique is the use of **tax havens**, which are low-tax countries that are hospitable to business (see Table 16.4). This strategy is typically used in conjunction with transfer pricing and involves a subsidiary selling its output at a very low cost to a subsidiary in a tax haven, which in turn sells the merchandise at a very high price to a third subsidiary.[1] Table 16.2 provides an example, which is similar to that in Table 16.1, except that the sales are now routed through a subsidiary located in a tax haven, Country B, where no tax is paid at all. The result of the example in the table is a net profit of $4,000. This is greater than that illustrated in Table 16.1, where a simple case of transfer pricing was employed. For more on the matter of tax havens, see the case **International Business Strategy in Action: Worldwide tax havens**.

Fronting loans

Fronting loan
A third-party loan in which an MNE home office deposits funds with a financial institution, which then lends to the MNE's affiliate in a country where the MNE faces political risk or currency transfer restrictions

A **fronting loan** is a funds positioning strategy that involves having a third party manage the loan. For example, if a US multinational decided to set up operations in China, the MNE might be concerned with the political risk that accompanies such a decision. Is it possible that the government might expropriate the subsidiary's assets, including all the cash on hand? In an effort to protect its investments, the parent company could deposit funds with a major international bank that has strong ties to China and is on good terms with the government. In turn the subsidiary would apply for a loan with this bank and the multinational company's deposit would be given to the subsidiary in the form of a loan. It is highly unlikely that the Chinese government would expropriate the subsidiary and endanger the loan or its relationship with the international bank. Thus the MNE has successfully positioned its funds.

Funds positioning strategies are important in moving money around a multinational, as well as in helping the MNE to cope with political and legal roadblocks that stand in the way of such action. However, an internally operated netting process that controls the flow of funds and ensures that bills are paid promptly always complements these strategies. This process is often collectively referred to as multilateral netting.

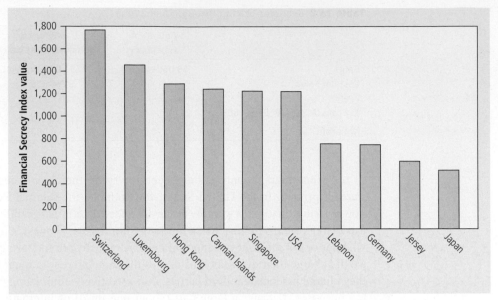

Figure 16.3 World's top tax havens based on Secrecy Index value, 2015

Source: City A.M., "Mapped: the world's biggest tax havens," February 12, 2015.

Multilateral netting

When subsidiaries do business with each other, each may owe money to the others and in turn be owed money by them. Figure 16.4 provides an example of four subsidiaries that have both amounts due and amounts payable from each of the others. Over time, of course, these obligations will be resolved by the individual subsidiaries. In an effort to make the process more efficient, however, many multinationals have now set up **clearing accounts** in a certain location and assigned the manager at this location the authority to make the transfers that are necessary to pay intracompany subsidiary obligations. This process of multilateral netting, which involves a determination of the net amount of money owed to subsidiaries through multilateral transactions, begins with a computation of the amounts owed to each. Table 16.3, which has been constructed based on the information in Figure 16.4, shows these net positions. Based on this information, those that owe money are required to transfer it to a centralized clearing account (see Figure 16.5), whereas those that are owed money are paid from this central account.

The clearing account manager is responsible for seeing that this process occurs quickly and correctly. Typically, this manager will receive monthly transaction information from all the subsidiaries and will use these data to determine the net position of each unit. The manager will then see that the necessary transfers are made. These transfers usually take place in the currency of the payer, so the German subsidiary will pay its obligation in

Clearing account
A centralized cash management bank account in which one MNE affiliate reviews payment needs among various MNE affiliates and arranges to make payments of net funds due from each affiliate to others through the clearing account

Table 16.3 Net cash positions of subsidiaries

Subsidiary	Total receivables	Total payables	Net positions
German	$300,000	$225,000	$75,000
Chilean	125,000	150,000	225,000
Japanese	200,000	275,000	275,000
Mexican	225,000	200,000	25,000

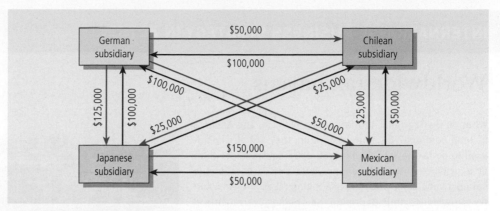

Figure 16.4 Multilateral dollar flows between subsidiaries

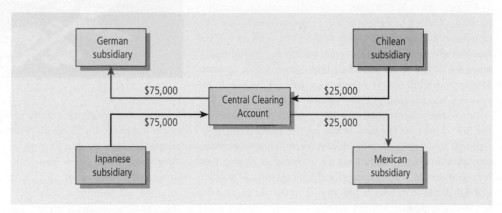

Figure 16.5 Centralized netting process in action

euros, whereas the Mexican subsidiary will pay in pesos. The clearing account manager's staff will handle the process.

There are a number of reasons that multilateral netting has become popular. One advantage is that it helps the parent company to ensure that financial interactions between the units are quickly brought to completion. If bills are allowed to be outstanding for months at a time, it can result in the other units not wanting to do business with slow-paying subsidiaries. Netting helps to reduce the likelihood of such problems. A second advantage is that those units that are owed money have faster access to their funds. A third advantage is that the parent company knows which subsidiaries are amassing large amounts of cash and can tap these sources if necessary to support activities in other locales. A fourth advantage is that the cost of converting foreign exchange is minimized because the central clearing account manager can convert large amounts at the same time.

There are also some problems associated with multilateral netting. One is that many governments place controls on these operations by allowing them only for trade transactions. So the MNE's ability to use netting for moving funds can be limited. A second problem is that in other cases governments have required that payment for imports be delayed until these goods clear customs, thus slowing down the netting process by as much as 60 to 90 days. A third is getting local subsidiary managers to cooperate and keep the central clearing account manager fully apprised of all transactions affecting this process. Sometimes there is a reluctance to cooperate on the part of those managers whose cash outflows are substantially larger than their inflows. Under a netting process they can no

INTERNATIONAL BUSINESS STRATEGY IN ACTION

Worldwide tax havens

What do Switzerland, the Bahamas, Monaco, and Andorra have in common? By some definition, they are all considered to be tax havens. In general, a tax haven is a country or a jurisdiction that allows individuals or corporations to set up a subsidiary and to avoid paying taxes in their country of residence, thus depriving their home governments of some tax revenues that are used to provide government services.

An estimated $25 trillion of private financial wealth is located, untaxed or lightly taxed, in tax havens or "secrecy jurisdictions" across the world. African countries as a group are thought to have lost over $1 trillion in "capital flight" since the 1970s. Given that their total external debt amounts to less than $200 billion, Africa is a major net creditor to the rest of world because of these practices.

Source: Trevor Smith/Alamy Stock Photo

One of the main reasons for the creation of tax havens in the first place was the lack of any single, overarching international tax standard. Individual governments have different tax policies, so MNEs have an incentive to deploy their financial assets across their worldwide network of subsidiaries in order to minimize taxation. It would not be possible for MNEs to do this if there were a common unitary world tax system. The MNEs are reacting to the lack of a global standard in government tax policy, yet governments then blame them for using legal tax havens to reduce overall taxes paid.

Each tax haven jurisdiction has its own sets of laws on taxation and levels of transparency. Tax havens are also sometimes accused by governments and NGOs such as Oxfam as being a means for money laundering and for hiding the proceeds of criminal activity, including political corruption, illicit arms dealing, and drug trafficking. Governments have come together more recently to reduce the potential for tax havens to be used for these purposes, but accurate data to map trends in the criminal exploitation of tax havens is not readily available. The United Nations has also actively been trying to curb the use of tax havens for money laundering.

The OECD lists a number of factors used to identify a tax haven. Among these, a tax haven is a country or jurisdiction that: (1) imposes no or nominal taxes and is used by foreigners to escape taxes in their own countries (this includes "ring-fencing" jurisdictions that reserve preferential

treatment to foreigners, thus shielding the country from tax avoidance by its own residents); (2) has laws or administrative practices that prevent the exchange of information with other governments on taxpayers benefiting from low taxation; (3) lacks transparency; and (4) does not require substantial productive operations in the country, suggesting policies geared to attracting income only on a preferential tax basis. Of all these factors, only the first one is necessary for the identification of a tax haven.

The Financial Secrecy Index (FSI) ranks countries according to the secrecy and the scale of their activities and claims to be a politically neutral ranking tool. Table 16.4 provides the latest ranking from 2015 data. The aim of the Tax Justice Network which developed the ranking is to improve our understanding of global financial secrecy, tax havens, and illicit financial flows.

In recent years, the OECD has been pressuring countries and jurisdictions to reverse what it calls harmful tax competition and lack of transparency. The EU has also challenged the use of unfair tax competition by US exporters in the World Trade Organization and won. Under US law, US exporters could set up a sales operation in an offshore tax haven and avoid paying taxes on the proceeds of this business. The British and French governments have also each targeted their own tax haven jurisdictions, the British challenging the Channel Islands and Isle of Man offshore tax havens.

Table 16.4 The world's top tax havens, 2015

Rank	Jurisdiction	FSI value	Secrecy score	Global scale weight*
1	Switzerland	1,466.1	73	5.625
2	Hong Kong	1,259.4	72	3.842
3	USA	1,254.8	60	19.603
4	Singapore	1,147.1	69	4.280
5	Cayman Islands	1,013.2	65	4.857
6	Luxembourg	817.0	55	11.630
7	Lebanon	760.2	79	0.377
8	Germany	701.9	56	6.026
9	Bahrain	471.4	74	0.164
10	United Arab Emirates (Dubai)	440.8	77	0.085
11	Macao	420.2	70	0.188
12	Japan	418.4	58	1.062
13	Panama	415.7	72	0.132
14	Marshall Islands	405.6	79	0.053
15	United Kingdom	380.2	41	17.394
16	Jersey	354.0	65	0.216
17	Guernsey	339.4	64	0.231
18	Malaysia (Labuan)	338.7	75	0.050
19	Turkey	320.9	64	0.182
20	China	312.2	54	0.743
21	British Virgin Islands	307.7	60	0.281
22	Barbados	298.3	78	0.024
23	Mauritius	297.0	72	0.049
24	Austria	295.3	54	0.692
25	Bahamas	273.1	79	0.017
26	Brazil	263.7	52	0.678
27	Malta	260.9	50	0.990
28	Uruguay	255.6	71	0.037
29	Canada	251.8	46	1.785
30	Russia	243.3	54	0.397
31	France	241.9	43	3.104
32	Isle of Man	228.6	64	0.068
33	Liberia	218.2	83	0.006
34	Bermuda	217.7	66	0.042
35	Cyprus	213.9	50	0.518
36	Liechtenstein	202.4	76	0.010
37	Ireland	187.4	40	2.313
38	Belgium	181.2	41	1.863
39	Guatemala	177.2	76	0.007
40	Israel	173.8	53	0.166
41	Netherlands	168.4	48	0.322
42	Chile	166.7	54	0.120
43	Saudi Arabia	163.9	61	0.037
44	Australia	148.1	43	0.586
45	India	148.0	39	1.487
46	Philippines	146.1	63	0.020
47	Vanuatu	142.8	87	0.001
48	Ghana	139.2	67	0.010
49	Korea	124.3	44	0.302
50	US Virgin Islands	118.2	69	0.004

* The global scale weight represents a jurisdiction's share in global financial services exports.

Source: http://www.financialsecrecyindex.com/introduction/fsi-2015-results

Reluctantly, many of these countries have responded to OECD pressures and reformed their policies. The Channel Islands and the Cayman Islands both have anti-money-laundering legislation. Under pressure from the French government, Monaco also signed an agreement to prevent money laundering, increase transparency, and remove some tax concessions.

Yet the total eradication of tax havens will not come without confrontation. For one, tax havens and their financial institutions depend heavily on these deposits. The Bahamas, which considers itself a major international financial hub, can foresee a tremendous loss of income, especially if other countries, including Switzerland and Luxembourg, are not ready to implement the same policies. The Bahamas has argued that the OECD is using a two-tier system, cooperatively designing legislation with its member countries and then imposing this regime on smaller, less developed, non-member countries.

Since the financial crash of 2008 efforts to improve transparency and regulate tax havens have gathered momentum. In 2015 a number of national governments launched investigations into the activities of HSBC's private bank in Switzerland, which was accused of helping clients evade tax payments through a range of illegal mechanisms. This gave added momentum to steps that the Swiss government was already making to change its status as the world's largest tax haven. Other tax havens including Singapore, Dubai and Monaco have been following suit and promised to open their financial records to scrutiny by tax authorities from around the world by 2017 or 2018.

Websites: www.oecd.org; www.oxfam.org; www.financialsecrecyindex.com

Sources: "A progress report on the jurisdictions surveyed by OECD Global Forum in implementing the internationally agreed tax standards, progress made as at January 4, 2011" (original progress report April 2, 2009), OECD, www.oecd.org; Vanessa Houlder, "The tax havens hidden in plain sight," *Financial Times,* February 13, 2015.

longer delay payments for three or four months while working to reverse the flow and to pay their bills out of current earnings.

Multilateral netting can help an MNE to ensure that intersubsidiary accounts are balanced, and the process is extremely useful in assisting the parent company in managing global cash flows. However, there is an inherent problem in this process that requires special attention and which netting cannot resolve: foreign exchange risk as typified by the fluctuating value of international currencies. This risk is particularly important when MNEs do business with buyers who are paying in weak currencies. In dealing with this dilemma, MNEs often formulate a foreign exchange risk management strategy.

Managing cash

Consider a multinational firm such as Nestlé (based in Switzerland) whose network of affiliates extends around the world. Each affiliate has its own customers and suppliers, as well as financial ties to the rest of the company. Viewing the company as a single unit for purposes of cash management can yield far better results than would be obtained if each affiliate managed its cash independently. For example, much less foreign exchange protection is generally needed if all of the affiliates are evaluated together than if each affiliate **hedges** its own position. The French subsidiary may have a large number of accounts payable in euros that can be hedged simply by consolidating the German affiliate's excess cash, which is also in euros. Similarly, the Canadian subsidiary may possess a large amount of Canadian dollar assets that can be hedged by having the US company contract some liabilities (for example, by purchasing equipment or taking out loans) denominated in Canadian dollars. The whole company may coordinate its borrowing efforts through the British subsidiary, which uses the London eurocurrency market.

Hedge
A strategy to protect the firm against risk, in this case against exchange rate risk

Centralized cash management offers five kinds of potential gains to the MNE:

1 By pooling the cash holdings of affiliates where possible, the MNE can hold a smaller total amount of cash, thus reducing its financing needs.

2 By centralizing cash management, it can have one group of people specialize in the performance of this task, thus achieving better decisions and economies of scale.

3 By reducing the amount of cash in any one affiliate, it can reduce country risks as well as financial costs.

4 As noted previously, it can net out intracompany accounts when there are multiple payables and receivables among affiliates, thus reducing the amount of money actually transferred among affiliates.

5 Its central cash management group can ensure that cash management decisions aim at corporate goals rather than the goals of individual affiliates when these might conflict.

The first kind of gain results simply from better use of the cash held by the firm. If each affiliate holds enough cash to meet its transactions needs, precautionary needs, and speculative needs (following the Keynesian categories of money demand), far more cash is likely to be held than is needed *company-wide*. A domestic company centralizes the cash management function at one location (usually the home office), and an MNE can do the same. The key difference between the two is that the MNE is often restricted in its ability to shift funds among affiliates internationally; thus, less centralization is possible at the MNE level. Any reduction in cash holdings, however, enables the firm to reduce its financing needs, thus lowering costs.

The second kind of gain relates to the development of management skills. By centralizing the cash management function, even if funds are left in the affiliates for the most part, the firm can utilize the skills of a specialized group of cash managers. Gains from this group's decision making should include economies of scale in borrowing, since the group can borrow to meet the entire company's needs and then distribute funds to affiliates as required. Also, the group should develop detailed knowledge of financial opportunities worldwide, thus enabling the firm to borrow at lower cost or lower risk than firms lacking such expertise.

If the MNE reduces its total assets through centralized cash management, it also reduces both its exchange risk and its country risk, in that fewer assets are at risk worldwide. The country risk does not change, but the exposure of the company to that risk decreases. Country risk may also be hedged or transferred by the decision-makers in the cash management group, who have greater access to protection tools than do managers in any one affiliate.

The fourth kind of benefit, from multilateral netting of accounts, is primarily cost savings from the reduced need to transfer funds between affiliates.

The fifth kind of gain from centralized cash management relates to business strategy. Placing the cash management function in one location, either at the home office or at a location closely monitored by the home office, makes better control possible. In this way, the firm can ensure that cash management decisions are made to meet global corporate needs rather than to improve an affiliate's position, possibly at the expense of the rest of the company. This is especially true with respect to hedging, which should be decided at the corporate level, since virtually every affiliate is likely to have assets or liabilities in another currency that are partially or totally hedged by balance sheet items of other subsidiaries.

While centralized cash management offers obvious and potentially very large benefits, it also presents some problems. Most importantly, if freedom to manage cash is taken away from the affiliate manager, some of the affiliate's ability to improve its performance is also removed. The evaluation of each affiliate must recognize this point. (This idea is discussed further in the section on controls.)

Another problem with internationally centralized cash management arises when national rules restrict financial transfers into or out of some countries. Virtually all less developed countries and many developed ones limit funds outflows through exchange controls or taxation. Some countries specifically disallow international netting of payments. Because of such restrictions, international cash management today requires a great deal of knowledge about national financial constraints and often requires a decentralized strategy of funds transfers due to these constraints.

The whole idea of international funds transfer and management is a major opportunity for firms that have operations in multiple countries. Not only can transfer pricing, multilateral netting, and so on be used to move funds as needed in the firm, but other policies such as dividend remittances, payment of royalties and fees, and intracompany loans are among the many alternatives that can be used to optimize the firm's overall financial situation.

INTERNATIONAL BUSINESS STRATEGY IN ACTION

Sovereign wealth funds

In terms of international financial management, a recent development illustrates the tensions between the workings of financial markets and the sovereignty of nations. Mainly due to its large and persistent balance of trade deficit, the United States has long been a destination for inward financial flows. Basically, the US trade deficit has to be balanced by a surplus on its capital (monetary) accounts. Another way of saying this is that, as Americans consume more in imports than they export, leading to a trade deficit, it is necessary to sell US financial assets to foreigners to balance the books. The end result of these financial capital inflows is that foreigners own more American assets.

►

For many years, foreigners bought US Treasury bonds and other financial assets. However, as the value of the US dollar decreased in 2007 and 2008, the yields on US financial investments also started to fall. Financial assets denominated in US dollars became less valuable compared to assets in other currencies such as the euro. Even the Canadian dollar was worth more than a US dollar in late 2007.

The result of the falling US dollar was that foreigners switched from financial investments into the US stock market. Equity ownership of US firms became a substitute for US bonds for foreigners. Many US firms welcomed such foreign investment, even as it diluted American ownership of their companies. For example, some US financial institutions, such as Citigroup, Merrill Lynch, and Morgan Stanley, were bailed out by foreign private equity funds in early 2008. However, this has raised issues of sovereignty as the richest private equity funds are owned by governments from the Middle East and China. They are called sovereign wealth funds.

For example, one of the world's richest sovereign wealth funds is owned by the government of Dubai. Some time ago the takeover of some US ports by Dubai Ports was criticized by Senator Hillary Clinton and many of her colleagues in the US Congress. President George W. Bush was forced to reopen the process by which Dubai Ports had been allowed to take over US ports. Senator Clinton argued that US ports should not be foreign owned, but seemed to have forgotten that the firm was already foreign owned, by a British company, P&O. What she and her congressional colleagues really objected to was that Dubai Ports was a Middle Eastern government-owned financial company, against which discriminatory measures should be used.

Ultimately the US government can discriminate against foreign investors on the grounds of national security. In the case of US ports there is some logic to such discrimination, especially in a post-9/11 world. However, it is difficult to apply this logic of national security to many of the protectionist arguments raised by labor groups and others opposed to foreign investment. The confusion arises because the large state-run private equity funds of the Middle East and China are seen as instruments of their governments. They are not seen as purely financial investment houses, although they operate in world financial markets in the same way as the banks and financial institutions of Western economies.

The control of strategic entities in the United States will continue to be controversial. The Dubai Ports case sparked discussion of whether any of the 360 US ports should be allowed to be operated by foreign entities. Three out of five terminals in New York and New Jersey, and 80 percent of the Port of Los Angeles, are now being operated by foreign firms. At the time of the controversy, only about 5 percent of the approximately 26,000 containers arriving daily at the US coasts were inspected by the US government, leaving the responsibility of screening the rest to companies that own and operate the ports. One of these companies is Denmark-based Maersk Group, vertically integrating into port management from its core business of vessel operation. In operating terminals in 12 different ports across the United States, the company plays a part in US national security efforts.

This issue is also relevant in Europe, where European firms such as Swiss bank UBS received funds from the Singapore Investment Corporation (GIC). The British bank Barclays also received investments from Temasek of Singapore.

The world's largest sovereign wealth funds are reported in Table 16.5. The largest sovereign wealth fund is Norway's Government Pension Fund—Global founded in 1990, while Singapore's Temasek was set up in 1974. The China Investment Corporation, a much newer fund, invested $3 billion in US buyout firm Blackstone.

It is not clear how the issue of sovereign equity funds will be resolved. At a macro-economic level it is necessary for world financial and trade imbalances to be reconciled. As long as the United States has a large trade deficit there will need to be inward flows of foreign investment. If a large proportion of these inward flows are from private equity funds, then there is little that the United States can do to avoid this.

Sources: Financial Times, January 24, 2008; Mimi Hall, Bill Nichols, and Sue Kirchhoff, "Security issues go beyond ports flap," USA Today, February 23, 2006; Jessica Holzer, "Dubai's Olive Branch," Forbes, October 3, 2006; David Shuster, "Who owns the United States ports?" MSNBC, February 22, 2006; www.maersk.com; Sovereign Wealth Fund Institute, http://www.swfinstitute.org/sovereign-wealth-fund-rankings/ (November 2015).

Source: Iain Masterton/Alamy Stock Photo

Table 16.5 Largest sovereign wealth funds by assets under management, 2015

Country	Fund name	Launch year	Billions of US$	Origin
Norway	Government Pension Fund – Global	1990	873	Oil
UAE—Abu Dhabi	Abu Dhabi Investment Authority (ADIA)	1976	773	Oil
China	China Investment Corporation	2007	746.7	Non commodity
Saudi Arabia	SAMA Foreign Holdings	n/a	671.8	Oil
Kuwait	Kuwait Investment Authority	1953	592	Non commodity
China	SAFE Investment Company	1997	547 (est.)	Non commodity
China—Hong Kong	Hong Kong Monetary Authority Investment Portfolio	1993	417.9	Non commodity
Singapore	Government of Singapore Investment Corporation (GIC)	1981	344	Non commodity
Qatar	Qatar Investment Authority	2005	256	Oil
China	China National Social Security Fund	2000	236	Non commodity
Singapore	Temasek Holdings	1974	193.6	Non commodity
UAE—Dubai	Investment Corporation of Dubai	2006	183	Non-commodity
UAE—Abu Dhabi	Abu Dhabi Investment Council	2007	110	Oil
Australia	Australian Future Fund	2004	95	Non commodity
South Korea	Korea Investment Corporation	2008	84.7	Non commodity

Source: Sovereign Wealth Fund Institute, http://www.swfinstitute.org/sovereign-wealth-fund-rankings/ (updated November 2015).

EXCHANGE RISK MANAGEMENT

We have discussed exchange risk primarily in relation to *transactions* denominated in foreign currency. In addition, exchange risk exists in the translation of financial statements and, in principle, for future, so-far unspecified activities of the firm. Three kinds of exchange risk should be differentiated: (1) transaction risk; (2) translation risk; and (3) economic risk. Each kind of risk is important to the MNE, and each leads to somewhat different conclusions for hedging strategies.

Transaction risk

Transaction risk
The risk of financial loss or gain to an MNE due to unanticipated exchange rate changes affecting future cash flows from transactions that are denominated in foreign exchange

When a specific contracted asset or liability is denominated in a foreign currency, it is subject to **transaction risk**, or the risk of an unexpected change in its home-currency value during the time to maturity. Accounts payable and receivable, loans, and bank deposits denominated in foreign currencies are examples of items that are subject to such exchange risk. Each foreign currency transaction can be hedged (or not) with some offsetting transaction in the same currency and with the same maturity. This topic was discussed in Chapter 7, and a new example is presented at the end of this section.

Translation risk

Translation risk
The risk of losses or gains on the MNE's balance sheet, due to unhedged exchange rate changes during an accounting period

Translation risk, or accounting risk, is the risk of value changes in foreign currency assets and liabilities on the balance sheet, whether or not the transactions occur during the accounting period. For example, the plant and equipment of foreign subsidiaries is subject to valuation change even if no purchase or sale of such items takes place during the accounting period. Because balance sheet information is reported in most countries to securities regulators and in published financial statements, valuation changes in the foreign operations of multinational firms become public knowledge. Loss in the value of foreign currency assets, regardless of its impact on company earnings, may negatively affect investors' perceptions of a firm. To avoid the appearance of weakness due to the devaluation of foreign assets, firms often try to hedge their balance sheets through financial contracts (such as forward contracts or money market hedges).

A good example of this exposure for a US MNE is when the currency of a local country weakens in relation to the dollar. For example, if the Chilean peso declined by 10 percent against the dollar, the value of the Chilean subsidiary's peso account at the local bank would also decline when translated into dollars in the **consolidation** process. If the company had the equivalent of $100,000 (US) on deposit, this account would now be worth $90,000 in translation and consolidation. Of course, this decline would not affect the number of pesos on deposit, and the local purchasing power of these pesos, at least in the short run, would remain the same. However, the decline would negatively affect the subsidiary's ability to purchase imports from countries with strong currencies since it would now take more pesos than before to buy these goods.

Conclusions as to the desirability of **balance sheet hedging** are ambiguous. On the one hand, since investor decisions may be based on valuation changes in foreign currency assets, the firm should hedge to avoid investor preoccupation with such changes. On the other hand, since the valuation of foreign currency assets may not affect the economic viability of the project, it would be a waste of effort for the firm to deal with such changes.

Economic risk

Economic risk is the risk of unexpected changes in future cash flows from foreign operations (and from activities denominated in foreign currencies, wherever they occur). Such risk is most important to the firm, since future cash flows are the basis for the firm's value. Unfortunately for the manager, it is not possible to know with certainty the full set of future cash flows that will occur. Thus, a hedging strategy cannot be perfectly matched with such cash flows. To deal with economic risk, the firm may choose to follow a generalized strategy of hedging transactions when they are contracted and trying to balance foreign currency assets and liabilities as they appear on the balance sheet. Or the firm may choose not to hedge at all, on the assumption that future currency fluctuation will be approximately offset by price changes in each country (that is, purchasing power parity will approximately hold). Despite the inherent difficulty of predicting future foreign exchange exposures, ultimately the firm should be concerned about economic (foreign exchange) risk as the key variable in exchange risk management.

Consider the economic risk involved with a subsidiary's assets. If the value of the local currency strengthens, the sale of inventory will generate larger dollar profits. However, would it be wiser to lower the price, to take less profit per item, but to generate more demand? Similarly, would it be wise now to sell fixed assets such as buildings or factories and then to lease them back from the purchaser? Some US firms in Tokyo found that by the early 1990s the land and buildings that they had bought years before were now worth hundreds of times their original purchase price. Believing that the local real estate market was as high as it was going to go and feeling that it would be more advisable to sell the properties and rent them back, these firms sold their office buildings and made tremendous profits. The ensuing decline of Tokyo real estate prices showed that these firms had made very wise (lucky) decisions.[2]

Another example of economic exposure is the risk that companies take when selling to a country with a weakening currency. In this case many MNEs have sought to increase their own production efficiency, lower their costs, and continue to generate acceptable profit. Firms such as Honda, Nissan, and BMW have complemented this strategy by setting up operations in the United States, their largest international market.[3] In the process, the firms have reduced their economic exposure.

In fact, all three kinds of foreign exchange risk play important parts in the management of an international firm. No single hedging strategy can cover them all, so the MNE

Consolidation
The translation of foreign affiliate accounts and addition to home-country accounts for the purpose of reporting the complete (global) condition of a company; consolidation of foreign affiliate accounts that are denominated in other currencies necessarily produces translation risk

Balance sheet hedging
The use of financial instruments denominated in foreign currency to eliminate exchange rate (translation) risk from the balance sheet of a company

Economic risk
The risk of financial loss or gain to an MNE due to the effects of unanticipated exchange rate changes on future cash flows that are denominated in foreign currencies

Table 16.6 Exchange risk hedging techniques*

To hedge an exposed liability	To hedge an exposed asset
Buy foreign exchange in the forward market	Sell foreign exchange in the forward market
Buy foreign exchange in the futures market	Sell foreign exchange in the futures market
Buy foreign exchange call options	Buy foreign exchange put options
Invest/deposit in a foreign exchange instrument	Borrow in a foreign exchange instrument
Incur accounts receivable in foreign exchange	Incur accounts payable in foreign exchange
Swap liabilities with another firm	Swap assets with another firm
Obtain any other foreign exchange asset	Obtain any other foreign exchange liability

* These techniques assume no expectation about the direction of exchange rate change. If devaluation is expected, then creation of a net liability position is attractive, and vice versa for expected revaluation. In each instance, the hedge must produce an equal-value asset (liability) in the same currency with equal maturity to offset the exposed liability (asset).

manager must devise plans for dealing with each. Fortunately, both transaction and economic risk deal with future cash flows; thus, the management of these two kinds of risk can be combined fairly readily. For example, the firm can hedge all occasional exports denominated in foreign currencies and seek local-currency financing for the entire production of its foreign affiliates. Then, if it does not employ balance sheet hedging (as suggested earlier), it can follow a consistent and simple hedging strategy. Judging from the immense volume of material dealing with corporate foreign exchange management strategies, it is safe to say that MNEs generally do *not* follow such simple strategies. Instead, they combine some hedging with some speculation in an effort to maximize their results from foreign exchange dealings. Table 16.6 lists a range of exchange risk hedging techniques that can be used to deal with one or more of these exchange risk categories.

 Active learning check

Review your answer to Active Learning Case question 2 and make any changes you like. Then compare your answer to the one below.

2 **How is Siemens exposed to exchange rate risks and what kinds of hedging strategies could it employ to mitigate these risks?**

As a major MNE, Siemens is exposed to all three of the main types of exchange rate risk, namely: transaction risk, translation risk, and economic risk. It is continually moving goods, services, and funds across borders, so any changes in the exchange rates between countries will have an effect on its finances. Given its main operating regions, the changing value of the euro against the US dollar and the Chinese renminbi are likely to be particularly important. Because it has manufacturing assets distributed around the world, it is subject to translation risk. This means that its balance sheet assets and liabilities (plant and equipment) change in value according to shifts in exchange rates, even if none of these are bought or sold in the accounting period. Siemens should, and probably does, employ most if not all of the hedging strategies listed in Table 16.6.

An example of exchange risk management

Consider the situation faced by a US-based firm such as American Express Company (Amex) when its subsidiary in the UK reports the purchase of £5 million of office equipment (mainly furniture and computer terminals) for the subsidiary's tourist service offices throughout that country. This equipment is to be paid for in 180 days in British pounds.

The strategies for dealing with exchange risk in this transaction depend on the whole firm's position in British pounds. The problem can be analyzed as follows.

First, if American Express already has an existing asset exposure in the UK due to its subsidiary's ongoing activities, that position may partially or wholly cover the new transaction. In other words, if American Express (UK) has a balance sheet that shows net sterling (pound) assets, typically because foreign subsidiaries have some dollar liabilities, the new account payable may partially offset that asset exposure.

Second, the same results may occur even if the British subsidiary has been operated to cover ongoing exchange risk in the UK. In the event that American Express has placed funds in euro–British pound deposits in one of its other subsidiaries (for example, in France or Germany), the new account payable may offset the existing exposure. *Note that the exposure is still not covered unless the maturity of the existing asset matches the six-month maturity of the new liability.*

Third, American Express can look for a financial hedging technique to avoid the exchange risk. For example, some new asset such as a bank deposit or short-term security could be purchased with a maturity of 180 days and a value of £5 million. Or a forward contract could be arranged with a bank to sell dollars and buy pounds in 180 days. Through the London International Financial Futures Exchange (LIFFE) or through one of the US futures exchanges, American Express could arrange a futures contract or **currency option** contract to hedge the account payable. The alternatives are numerous, but the basic goal is to find a British pound asset that matures in 180 days, worth £5 million, to hedge the new liability that calls for a cash outflow of £5 million in 180 days.

The following table lists relevant financial information if American Express were making this hedging decision on January 13, 2011:

Currency option

A derivative financial instrument where the owner has the right but not the obligation to exchange money denominated in one currency into another currency at a pre-agreed exchange rate on a specified date. The right to buy is the call option and the right to sell is the put option. It allows the company to take advantage of favorable movements in exchange rates. Options are the only form of hedging that does this

Spot exchange rate	US$1.57680/£1
180-day forward exchange rate	US$1.57350/£1
180-day LIBOR rate in pounds is 1.06375%	2.1275%/year
180-day LIBOR rate in dollars is 0.45681%	0.91362%/year
6-month sterling call option (to buy) strike price:	
The options cost US $875 per contract at the CME, with £31,250 per contract	US$1.5840/£1
For this option, the premium is US $0.0072/£	
6-month sterling futures contract rate:	
The futures contracts have £62,500 per contract	US$1.5800/£1
Ignore commissions and other transaction costs for these instruments	

Sources: Financial Times, http://markets.ft.com/markets/currencies.asp; *Wall Street Journal,* http://online.wsj.com/mdc/public/page/2_3020-moneyrate.html; http://www.global-rates.com/interest-rates/libor/libor.aspx

American Express can use this information to evaluate various financial hedges for the sterling account payable.

First, the firm can use a simple forward contract to hedge the exposure. A forward exchange contract to buy British pounds would cost about US$7.8675 million in six months, as follows:

$$£5,000,000 \times US\$1.57350/£ = US\$7,867,500$$

This forward exchange contract completely hedges the account payable, because it will result in receipt from the bank of £5 million in 180 days, which will be used to pay the supplier of office equipment.

A second alternative is called "money market hedging." The first step is to place funds now into a pound-denominated investment that matures in six months. The choice shown above is a eurosterling account that pays 2.1275 percent per year for the six-month period.

The dollar value of pounds for American Express to buy today can be calculated by discounting the future pounds that are needed to a present value of pounds that must be deposited today to achieve that sum in six months. The calculations are as follows:

$$£5,000,000/(1.043003) = £4,793,850.17$$

This first step shows that the interest earned in the eurosterling deposit for 180 days will be 1.06375 percent (that is, 2.1275%/2) and that £4,793,850.17 must be deposited today to reach the value needed to pay the account payable. Next, the dollars that must be used today to buy these pounds is:

$$£4,793,850.17 \times US\$1.57680/£1 = US\$7,558,942.95$$

The hedging cost is lower for this alternative, since the funds must be paid *now* rather than in 180 days. To compare the two choices, they must be placed in the same time period. This requires discounting the forward contract value using the relevant discount rate, which would be a deposit interest rate in dollars for the same time period:

$$US\$7,867,500/(1.018421) = US\$7,725,194.28$$

The discount amount (1.018421) is the implicit return to depositing funds in a eurodollar account (comparable to the europound deposit) for six months at 0.91362 percent per year. This results in a lower cost of hedging in the money market hedging (US\$166,251.79).

A third alternative is to use a futures contract hedge in the LIFFE or the Chicago Mercantile Exchange (CME). Using the CME's quotes, we see that American Express could buy future pounds for US\$1.5800 per pound in contracts worth £62,500 per contract. Multiple contracts could be bought, so that with 80 contracts the company could obtain the needed £5 million. However, since the exchange rate is worse than the forward rate (that is, it costs more dollars to buy the pounds), American Express will not consider a futures hedge.[4]

Each of these financial hedges can protect American Express against foreign exchange risk. The company will want to choose the least costly hedge in this case, namely the forward market hedge. In other situations, one or another of these three alternatives will be the most beneficial to the firm. Beyond these choices, American Express should consider the possibility of structuring its business such that it could use British pound assets (for example, accounts receivable, investments, etc.) to hedge liabilities such as this purchase of equipment.

Developing forecasting and reporting systems

The management of foreign exchange risk can be both complex and cumbersome. A multinational with 20 subsidiaries can present a formidable challenge to the parent company because so many foreign exchange risk decisions need to be made and monitored. However, there are a number of steps that MNEs typically take in creating the necessary system for managing these decisions. They may:

1 Decide the types and degrees of economic exposure that the company is willing to accept.

2 Develop the necessary expertise (in-house personnel and/or outside economists or consultants) for monitoring exchange rates and for forecasting those rates that are applicable to the identified exposures.

3 Construct a reporting system that allows the firm to identify exposed accounts, to measure this exposure, and to feed back information on what the firm is doing and the status of these decisions.

4 Include all MNE units in this reporting system so that each better understands the risks it is assuming and is aware of the actions that must be taken to deal with these risks.

5 Keep senior-level management fully apprised of what is going on in each area of responsibility so that every regional or divisional manager is able periodically to revise the exposure risk and to make those strategy changes that will help more effectively to manage the process.

As firms begin to implement these five steps, they are better able to deal with the management of foreign exchange risk.

✔ Active learning check

Review your answer to Active Learning Case question 3 and make any changes you like. Then compare your answer to the one below.

 If Siemens believes that the euro is going to appreciate in relation to the US dollar, how is it likely to deal with receivables and payables?

If Siemens believes that the euro is going to get stronger against the US dollar, and if it is owed US dollars, the firm will try to collect them immediately before their value declines. At the same time Siemens will delay payment of those obligations that are fixed in US dollars because it will get more US dollars per euro after the appreciation, thus making it easier to pay those bills. The firm will lead collections and lag payables.

CAPITAL BUDGETING IN THE MNE

Capital project evaluation follows many of the same principles in an international firm as in a domestic firm, though additional variables and risks must be considered. Specifically, foreign projects must be evaluated for exchange risk, country risk, different financing costs, and any problems associated with the transfer of products, services, or funds due to government controls in any of the relevant countries. To see how these factors appear in the analysis, consider the following example of a food processing plant to be constructed by a US-based company in Qamaria (a fictitious country).

The company has developed the following pro forma income statement for the proposed investment project:

Proposed Qamaria processing plant pro forma income statement, typical year (in local currency)

Sales	10,000,000
Cost of goods sold:	
Local materials	1,000,000
Imported materials	2,000,000
Labor	3,000,000
Overhead expenses	600,000
Interest on loan from parent firm	400,000
Net income before tax	3,000,000
Local tax: 50%	1,500,000
Net income after tax	1,500,000

Assuming the investment made by the parent firm is 4 million in local currency, the project appears to have a simple return on capital of about 38 percent per year

(1,500,000/4,000,000). As long as the firm's cost of capital is less than 38 percent, the project is worth undertaking.[5] The normal, domestic concerns apply to this project evaluation: that is, the estimate is only as good as the forecasts of costs and sales. In addition, this foreign project faces potentially important considerations such as exchange risk, currency inconvertibility and other country risks, and preferential local borrowing opportunities. Chapter 15 provides more detailed discussion of this problem of country risk evaluation and management.

Exchange risk will affect the US dollar value of the profits earned, potentially raising or lowering them substantially. For example, if the local-currency value rises by 10 percent in relation to the dollar, net income after tax will rise (in dollar terms) by 10 percent, other things equal. However, if imported materials come from the United States, that cost (in local currency) will fall. Similarly, if the loan is made in dollars, interest cost (in local-currency terms) will fall. Sales, if any are exported from Qamaria, may decrease due to the exchange rate change.[6] In sum, a rise in the value of the local currency relative to the US dollar will tend to cause an increase in dollar profits from the affiliate, and such profits will tend to fall if the local currency devalues relative to the dollar.

Country risk (defined in Chapter 15) is another concern in the attempt to evaluate this project properly. If the host government decides to restrict profit remittances, then, no matter how profitable the project, the MNE will not be able to utilize its earnings elsewhere in the firm or to distribute them to shareholders. This problem is known as **currency inconvertibility**, regardless of whether the cause is a political decision or simply an economic reality. If discontent with the Qamaria government leads to strikes or violent confrontation between the government and opposition groups, the plant may be damaged or its production curtailed. Not all country risk is negative; if the government chooses to reduce corporate taxes to stimulate greater investment, the project may generate greater profitability than that shown above. In sum, country risks need to be considered when the full set of the project's financial implications is being judged.

Borrowing costs may differ in Qamaria and the United States. Thus, if the firm uses its **weighted-average cost of capital** in capital budgeting decisions, this project should be adjusted to account for any locally subsidized borrowing opportunity that exists. Many countries (and states or provinces within countries) offer low-interest loans to corporate investors to attract production facilities and jobs. If this is true in Qamaria and if the firm chooses to borrow some funds locally, the subsidized capital cost should be reflected in the capital budget. The project as shown uses an intracompany loan whose interest may be charged at the parent's actual cost of funds or marked up (or down) to achieve greater (or lesser) transfer of funds to the parent.

Finally, recall that the capital budget measures the project's *incremental impact* on the whole firm. Thus, if there are export sales from the parent to this new affiliate, those new sales must be counted in the evaluation. If the project replaces sales that were formerly exported to Qamaria, those lost sales must be counted. Any other intracompany impacts should also be measured in the project evaluation. This means the project should be judged in comparison to other alternatives available to the firm serving the Qamaria market. If exports from the United States offer a greater incremental profitability than the proposed plant, exports should be chosen. In summary, the incremental gains to the firm from the proposed project should be compared to the potential gains from other international business alternatives that may be available.

In contrast to domestic projects, one additional key question must be answered: who should conduct the analysis, the parent or the foreign subsidiary? Typically, the initial analysis is done at the subsidiary or branch level and then passed up to the head office for modification and/or approval. For example, two subsidiaries may both want to build a new tire plant and sell to the same market. Without coordination, they would compete against

Currency inconvertibility
The inability of a firm to transfer profit from a subsidiary in a host country to other areas of the organization or to shareholders because of host-government restrictions on profit remittances

Weighted-average cost of capital (WACC)
The firm's cost of obtaining funds from the various sources available. Each source of funds is weighted (multiplied) by the percentage of total capital it provides. Thus, the WACC is W_1 (cost of using retained earnings) + W_2 (cost of bank borrowing) + W_3 (cost of other source of funds), where each cost is stated as an annual percentage rate and each W is the percentage of total capital from that source

each other and the expected profits would not materialize. So the parent corporation will make a decision that benefits the entire organization. In this latter role the parent may have to turn down a positive NPV project from one subsidiary in favor of a higher NPV project from another subsidiary. The same process applies in reverse to plant closures: the shutdown will be at the plant with the largest negative NPV. Similarly, factories or holdings that do not generate sufficient profit may be sold.

Use of NPV

The parent company will review expenditure proposals because it has the necessary overall information to make these decisions. Moreover, such expenditure decisions will often be different from those of the subsidiary because the latter may use faulty valuation techniques or fail to address adequately the impact of political risk. In explaining why these differences occur, we must first review the basic NPV criterion. This criterion separates the financing and operating parts of the problem by discounting operating cash flows by a weighted-average cost of capital that embodies the financing decision. The NPV equation is:

$$\text{NPV} = \sum_{t=0}^{T} \frac{I_t + C_t}{(1 + K_A)} \qquad (16.1)$$

where:

$$K_A = k_e \frac{S}{V} + k_d(1-t_x)\frac{D}{V} \qquad (16.2)$$

The definitions of the terms are:

I_t = investment cash outlays in year t

C_t = cash inflows in year t

T = terminal date or end of project

K_A = weighted-average cost of capital

k_e = cost of equity capital

k_d = cost of debt financing

t_x = tax rate

D/V, S/V = debt and equity ratios, respectively

NPV = incremental net present value for the project.

In examining what determines the NPV, we must realize that disagreement between parent and subsidiary can arise because of the discount rate K_A, investment cost, and annual cash flows. Political risk can also affect all values. For example, the risk of foreign currency controls can cause some of the future cash flows to be largely ignored by the parent. From the parent's perspective, if funds can no longer be remitted, their value is substantially reduced, since they are not available for dividend payments or for reinvestment elsewhere. Conversely, once foreign exchange controls are in place, the parent will often treat blocked funds as being less valuable. From the parent's perspective, the cost of future investments in the country, financed by these blocked funds, is reduced. In both cases the subsidiary is not directly concerned with the problem of foreign exchange controls, and it will discount all cash flows that are incremental from its own perspective.

Similarly, country risk may cause the parent to increase the discount rate or required return to reflect that risk. However, if the subsidiary does not agree with that perception, it will not increase the discount rate, so its calculation of the present value of the cash inflows and NPV will be higher. Moreover, if foreign exchange controls are enforced, the local capital markets can be isolated from the international capital market. From the subsidiary's perspective, the result may be lower local real interest rates, which make local investment opportunities seem attractive. However, the parent, looking at global opportunities, may decide that it will make more sense to draw capital out of the country for reinvestment elsewhere.

Another reason that parent and local NPVs may differ is faulty application of the NPV framework. The most common errors are in incorrectly choosing t_x and K_A. The tax rate t_x is relevant in two places: the incremental tax that results from the incremental profits and the incremental tax shield that results from debt financing. Here, the errors usually come from a failure to determine the incremental tax rate. From the subsidiary's perspective the tax rate is the extra tax that it pays locally. However, the parent must also consider any incremental tax that it will pay once dividends are remitted.

In determining the discount rate K_A, several problems emerge. First, it is common that discount rates differ by several percentage points. The reason is obvious: inflation differs across different countries, and thus the inflationary premium built into the discount rate will differ. What the firm can never do is to use a discount rate from one country to evaluate cash flows denominated in another currency. The correct procedure is to calculate the real discount rate and then to "gross it up" for the inflationary expectations of the relevant country.

Additionally, debt ratios differ across subsidiaries, and the weights in Equation 16.2 may alter the cost of capital. This will inevitably occur if the multinational maximizes the use of debt financing in a country with subsidized borrowing rates. However, the debt ratio of that country is then not appropriate for determining the cost of capital, since the excess debt can be carried only because that subsidiary is part of a multinational. Similarly, it is a mistake to use the local real cost of debt to determine the cost of capital. In both these examples, if the MNE uses local debt norms and local debt costs, it is negating the advantage of being a multinational. That advantage is the ability to raise debt internally where it is the cheapest. As a result, in a country with a high debt cost the firm may have very little debt, whereas in a country with subsidized interest costs it may have a large amount of debt. In both cases there is no effect on the overall cost of funds to the multinational. Hence local debt norms and interest costs will be ignored unless local regulations restrict the use of debt funds to projects within that country. In this instance, if the firm accepts a local project, it can also raise more subsidized foreign debt. If the money cannot be removed from the country by transfer pricing or whatever, then its cost is relevant in Equation 16.2.

Institutional features

Thus far the focus has been on the technical question of how to evaluate capital expenditures. However, a very important institutional factor that warrants attention is the impact of government policies such as subsidies and controls.

Government intervention can affect the profitability of a project or its financing. For example, in considering foreign investments, countries such as Australia and Canada have **foreign investment review agencies**, which review these investments to ensure that they benefit the local economy. As a result, foreign investment is often contingent on factors such as local employment quotas, local sourcing of components, the transfer of technology, and a degree of local ownership. This intervention can obviously complicate capital expenditure analysis. Frequently the result is to forecast specific, quantitative outcomes. For example, if technology is locally licensed, what is the possible impact of its being leaked to different countries? If the MNE has to train local middle management and to sell shares locally, how does this affect the probability of forcible divestiture at some future date? In many cases the result of local content regulations is to expropriate all the

Foreign investment review agency
A government agency that reviews applications for foreign direct investment projects and approves or disapproves the projects, according to standards established by the government

advantages possessed by the multinational. One of the particular problems here is local ownership requirements. The parent's viewpoint is dominant on the assumption that the objective of the firm is to maximize its market value, which is owned by shareholders in the home country. However, once joint ventures and significant minority shareholdings are traded locally, this solution breaks down. The problem now becomes whose market value should be maximized? The result is that while minority ownership reduces the political risk of expropriation, it restricts the multinational's freedom of action. It is, therefore, not surprising that, where political risk is lowered, minority shareholders get bought out.

However, government regulation is not all bad. Outside North America the interventionist approach of most governments creates unique opportunities for the MNE. For example, most countries provide concessionary financing that is contingent on the use of certain local resources. The British Export Credits Guarantee Department (ECGD) has some of the lowest-cost money for export financing as long as the borrower uses British equipment. By structuring an investment to use British equipment, a multinational might be able to borrow $10 million at 3 percent interest instead of at a market rate of, say, 9 percent. In effect, this subsidized loan represents a gift by the British taxpayers. This value has to be factored into the analysis. The inclusion of subsidies also occurs in domestic capital expenditure analysis, for example, with the proliferation of small-business financing programs. However, in an international project, rather than being unusual, it is rare not to determine the value or cost of a particular government program. Recently, government regulation of MNEs has been falling, leading to more cross-listings on the world stock exchange.

INTERNATIONAL FINANCING IN THE MNE

The home office of an MNE should have available to it funding from the domestic money and capital markets, as well as from international money and capital markets. The funding sources available to a *foreign affiliate* of an MNE include debt and equity from the parent and local financing in the host country. Table 16.7 presents a view of these sources that expands on the view presented in Figure 16.1 and on the discussion in Chapter 7. The sources of credit to the MNE are divided between short- and long-term loans and between direct and intermediated provision of funds through a bank or some other financial institution.

Table 16.7 International sources of credit (including markets and intrafirm transfers)

Borrowing	Domestic inside the firm	Domestic market	Foreign inside the firm	Foreign market	Euromarket
Direct, short term	Intrafirm loans, transfer pricing, royalties, fees, service charges	Commercial paper, other promissory notes, commercial credit	International intrafirm loans, international transfer pricing, dividends, royalties, fees	Commercial credit	Eurocommercial paper
Intermediated, short term	Short-term bank loans, discounted receivables	International back-to-back loans	Short-term bank loans, discounted receivables	Euro short-term loans	
Direct, long term	Intrafirm loans, investment in affiliates	Stock issue, bond issue	International intrafirm long-term loans, FDI	Stock issue, bond issue, ADR issue	Eurobonds, euroequity
Intermediated, long term		Long-term bank loans	International back-to-back loans	Long-term bank loans	Euro long-term loans

Note: Direct means borrowing from owners of wealth (e.g., investors); *intermediated* means borrowing from a financial intermediary (e.g., a bank). International back-to-back loan means a loan in which two companies in different countries borrow offsetting amounts from one another in each other's currency.

Notice that in addition to the funding that was discussed earlier in the intrafirm context, numerous sources of external funding are available to the MNE. These sources include funding from domestic money and capital markets in each country where the firm operates, as well as funding from the euromarkets in money centers such as London, New York, and Tokyo. A large firm from Norway, for example, could seek financing in the US market through international bank loans, through bond issue, or even through issuing stock shares or American Depositary Receipts.[7]

Financial structure

Debt–equity ratio
The value of a firm's total debt divided by the value of its total equity; a higher ratio implies greater leverage, and potentially greater risk

Financial structure in an MNE is complicated by the fact that the "normal" **debt–equity ratio** differs from industry to industry and from country to country. For example, the average debt–equity ratio in large Japanese companies is about 2.75 to 1. In the United States, this ratio is generally far less than 1, averaging about 0.6 for non-financial industries as a whole. As a rule, the total financial structure of an MNE follows the standards of the home-country financial market, since shares are usually traded there. On the other hand, a US company's affiliate in Japan may be able to operate successfully with far higher leverage than that of the parent, given local conditions in Japan. Thus, the financial structures of foreign affiliates may differ from that of the overall firm or that of the parent in particular. The only limitation is that the financial structure of the affiliate must not cause the financial structure of the entire firm to deviate from acceptable standards in the home country.

The entire MNE may choose to meet its external financing needs by borrowing through an affiliate in a low-interest country if such funding is available and if exchange rate protection still leaves financing costs lower than those in other currencies. As already noted, since the MNE is evaluated by investors in the home country, its overall debt–equity structure must satisfy the financial community in that country. However, if the firm sells shares of an affiliate in the host country's financial market, the debt–equity position of the affiliate is an important issue.

For a wholly owned foreign subsidiary that does not sell shares in the host country, the debt–equity ratio should be determined by overall corporate needs. If funding is available at low cost (adjusted for expected exchange rate changes), local borrowing is appropriate. If a substantial amount of assets is exposed locally, local borrowing provides a hedge to both exchange and country risks. If the local currency is expected to devalue substantially, then, even if local interest rates are high, it may make sense to borrow locally, assuming the expected post-devaluation interest costs would be lower than the home-country costs.

Local equity financing may be forced on the firm if the host government demands partial local ownership of foreign enterprises. This situation exists today in many less developed countries and in most of the formerly communist countries. In this case, the affiliate's debt–equity ratio may be skewed toward equity, especially if the parent seeks to avoid sending funds into that country. That is, financing for the affiliate would come from the local partner's equity investment plus retained earnings, and other funding would be sought only after these sources were used up.

In countries with restrictions on funds transfers, such as profit and royalty remittances, equity financing would again be sensible—using those funds that cannot be taken out of the country. That is, if funds are blocked from transfer abroad, the MNE must reinvest them locally; investing the funds in the existing operation (that is, profit reinvestment) may offer a greater benefit than placing them in local financial instruments such as bank deposits or government securities. This strategy is widely used by multinationals, though most would prefer the freedom to take their funds out of the host country.

Finally, notice that *if* the MNE is able to lower its total borrowing costs by utilizing foreign sources of funds, it has gained an advantage relative to domestic firms that limit themselves to domestic financial markets in any country. If the MNE has a lower weighted-average cost of capital for any given capital budget, it will undertake more projects than the purely domestic firm (or will be more profitable in the same projects).

✔ Active learning check

Review your answer to Active Learning Case question 4 and make any changes you like. Then compare your answer to the one below.

 When Siemens is looking to invest in its foreign affiliates around the world, what are some of the important considerations in choosing among alternative financing sources?

When Siemens is looking to invest in its foreign affiliates around the world, two important considerations are the size of the investment and the timescale involved. For large investments it will normally go to domestic or foreign funding markets for loans, rather than rely on internal financing mechanisms. As listed in Table 16.7 there are a variety of options. To reduce risk it can spread its borrowing across a portfolio of loans and institutions. By using eurocurrency markets in London or mainland Europe, it can minimize its short-term borrowing costs, and it can also issue commercial paper in New York or London to obtain working capital. For longer-term borrowing, Siemens could issue shares in the United States or in another money center such as Frankfurt or Tokyo, as well as issuing bonds in a low-tax jurisdiction such as Luxembourg. The choices depend on interest rates, exchange rates, and currencies in which Siemens will have cash flows in the future.

CONTROL: IDENTIFYING OBJECTIVES, EVALUATING AFFILIATE PERFORMANCE, AND MAKING PERFORMANCE CONSISTENT WITH GOALS

Control
The fundamental function of management that involves developing profit plans for the firm and its divisions and then deciding what to do when actual operating results differ from those planned

Control is the fundamental function of management that involves developing profit plans for the firm and its divisions and then deciding what to do when actual operating results differ from those planned. For a foreign investment project, the financial control process generally begins with putting together a set of pro forma financial statements (income statement, balance sheet, cash flow report). Then detailed budgets are developed for individual divisions, allocating the full capital budget to the specific purposes for which it will be used. During the time period after the creation of these plans, the firm's management observes the results and notes any deviations from the budget. Usually, of course, actual results differ from budgeted ones. Finally, the firm develops and implements a management plan for dealing with the deviations. The process is cyclical—as each planning period ends, another begins—and new budgets and managerial contingencies may be developed.

In the multinational firm, the potential for substantial home-office control over affiliates exists because major capital budgeting usually requires more resources than those available in an affiliate, and home-office assistance is needed to carry out capital projects. In addition, financial reporting to the parent company provides an informational basis for controls, which may or may not be exercised, depending on the extent of the firm's decentralization. Finally, because the people assigned to manage foreign affiliates are usually well known to the home-office managers, an informal, personal contact ties affiliates to the home office. All of this means that the home office has the potential to impose heavy controls on the activities of foreign affiliates.

The process described so far is substantially equivalent to the one used to evaluate and control domestic divisions in a firm. But foreign affiliates face a wide range of additional factors that may affect their performance, and these factors should be considered when setting the goals and judging the performance of affiliates. How should the managers of foreign affiliates be evaluated for their financial performance? If they are evaluated in local-currency terms, the home office must worry about hedging foreign currency exposures and about remitting or reinvesting profits. If they are evaluated in home-currency terms, affiliate managers must deal with exchange risk and remittance policy. If they are limited in their financial dealings due to centralized cash and foreign exchange management policies but are evaluated in home-currency terms, it must be recognized that their options are limited. On another issue, if transfer prices are set to move funds to the home office, foreign profitability will look lower than it would if these prices were set to keep more funds in the affiliates. Correct evaluation of the performance of affiliate managers must take into account the constraints imposed on the affiliates.

Most managers and outside analysts agree that foreign affiliates must be evaluated in home-currency terms, since home-currency investors judge the firm as a whole. Therefore, the firm must create an evaluation scheme that produces home-currency performance measures, adjusted to account for the limitations placed on the affiliate by the home office.

STRATEGIC INTERNATIONAL FINANCE

There are a number of ways in which MNEs apply the international financial concepts that have been discussed in this chapter. One way is by employing a geocentric approach that helps to coordinate subsidiary operations and ensures that there is a uniform, harmonious strategy. This approach is particularly evident in the way that some multinationals are now closing local operations in favor of overseas production and are using joint ventures and other partnership arrangements to reduce their financial risk.[8] Another approach is the manner in which financial management analysis is used in choosing sites for overseas operations. This is particularly true for foreign firms with strong currencies.

Establishing overseas operations

Because the United States is a major market for many international firms, foreign MNEs have been particularly concerned about the value of the US dollar. For example, when Ford Motor acquired Volvo's automotive business, the Swedish firm insisted on receiving the purchase price in krona. In 2009, when GM and Chrysler filed for bankruptcy and were bailed out by US taxpayers, Ford had to sell its luxury division, which included Jaguar, Land Rover, and Volvo cars.[9] This concern has also resulted in foreign firms setting up operations in the United States in order to offset the competitive impact associated with having a currency that is very strong vis-à-vis the US dollar. For example, BMW built an auto production facility in South Carolina because it found it was 20 percent less costly to produce cars in South Carolina than to bring them in from Germany.[10] Other companies have made acquisitions in the US market in order to protect their overall profitability. For example, BASF has acquired a Mobil plastic unit for $330 million; Benckiser purchased Coty, the fragrance maker, from Pfizer for $440 million; Siemens spent $1.2 billion to purchase ROLM, a manufacturer of telecommunications equipment, from IBM; and Daimler-Benz bought Chrysler for almost $40 billion. However, the buyout failed to produce the trans-Atlantic automotive powerhouse dealmakers had hoped for, and DaimlerChrysler announced on May 14, 2007 that it would sell Chrysler to Cerberus Capital Management of New York, a private equity firm that specializes in restructuring troubled companies. On October 4, 2007 a DaimlerChrysler extraordinary shareholders' meeting approved the renaming of the company. From October 5, 2007, the company has been titled Daimler AG. The US company adopted the name Chrysler LLC when the sale completed on August 3, 2007.[11]

At the same time, US firms are continuing to move abroad, especially since many Asian currencies are at a low ebb and purchase prices have fallen. General Motors, for example, is now producing light trucks in China, has 16 ventures there related to producing auto components, and has opened a Buick plant in Shanghai. Atlantic Richfield and Phillips China have invested in ventures for drilling for methane gas, IBM is expanding its investment there, Telluride International Energy is building a power plant, and Lucent Technologies has earmarked millions of dollars to expand its internet backbone in the country. All of these moves to overseas operations give the multinational firm a reduced currency risk by diversifying the company's cash flows into additional currencies.

European and US firms are not alone in their efforts to establish overseas operations. Pacific-based MNEs are also realizing the benefits of going local, and this group is not limited to auto makers. South Korean firms such as LG Group and Samsung are now using direct investment and joint ventures to help open markets in Europe and the United States. High labor costs, runaway interest rates, and low-cost competition are battering these firms at home, and local content laws have been holding down market acceptance abroad. In an effort to circumvent these problems, LG is using alliances to widen its market share, as seen by its collaboration with Gepi of Germany and Iberna of Italy to produce refrigerators for the European market. LG designs the units in its Ireland facility, Gepi supplies the components, and Iberna assembles the finished products. Samsung purchased Werk für Fernsehelektronik, a former East German picture tube maker, and spent $120 million to upgrade the plant to produce 1.2 million television sets annually. Again, the issue of concern here is that these firms are achieving a financial goal along with their strategic choices to go abroad; they are reducing exchange rate risk by diversifying their cash flows into different currencies.

Reducing financial risk

Although some of the above strategies are useful in reducing risk, there are other tactics that are also particularly useful, including mergers, acquisitions, joint ventures for new, high-risk projects, partnering with established MNEs in order to gain international market share, and cutting operating costs through new plant design.

KEY POINTS

1 International financial management encompasses a number of critical areas, including the management of global cash flows, foreign exchange risk management, capital expenditure analysis, and international financing. In carrying out these financial activities, MNEs can use three approaches or solutions: polycentric, ethnocentric, or geocentric.

2 There are three main areas of consideration in managing global cash flows. One is the movement of cash so that each subsidiary has the working capital needed to conduct operations. A second area is the use of funds positioning techniques that can help to reduce taxes and to deal with political and legal roadblocks that impede cash flows. A third is multilateral netting, which ensures that transactions between the subsidiaries are paid in a timely manner.

3 Foreign exchange risk management encompasses a variety of financial strategies that are designed to limit the multinational's exposure to exchange rate fluctuations. In particular, the MNE will want to reduce translation, transaction, and economic exposure. One of the most common ways of doing this is through hedging. Examples include the purchase of forward exchange contracts and the balancing of foreign currency assets with foreign currency liabilities.

4 A third major strategic financial issue is capital expenditure analysis. This entails computation and deliberation of such matters as the weighted cost of capital and the degree of political risk that is being assumed. Some of the methods of dealing with these issues were discussed, with attention given to the fact that the final decision on capital expenditures is often affected by subjective considerations as well as by objective evaluations.

5 At present MNEs are taking a number of important international financial steps. Some of the primary ones include designing global foreign exchange management programs, establishing international cash management centers, and creating coordinated international borrowing programs for affiliates.

Key terms

- polycentric solution
- ethnocentric solution
- working capital
- geocentric solution
- multilateral netting
- funds positioning techniques
- transfer price
- arm's-length price
- tax havens
- fronting loan
- clearing account
- hedge
- transaction risk
- translation risk
- consolidation
- balance sheet hedging
- economic risk
- currency option
- currency inconvertibility
- weighted-average cost of capital (WACC)
- foreign investment review agency
- debt–equity ratio
- control

REVIEW AND DISCUSSION QUESTIONS

1 In determining parent–subsidiary relationships, how does a polycentric solution differ from an ethnocentric or geocentric solution? Compare and contrast all three.

2 What is meant by the term *working capital*, and what are two of the most common ways in which parent companies can provide this capital to their subsidiaries? What are two ways in which the parent can obtain funds from the subsidiaries?

3 How can an MNE shift profits through the use of transfer pricing? Provide an example.

4 Of what value is multilateral netting in helping MNEs to manage cash flows? Give an example.

5 If a foreign country is facing high inflation, what are three financial strategies that the local multinational unit might employ? Identify and describe each.

6 Why are MNEs interested in translation and consolidation of financial statements? Of what practical value is this activity to the company?

7 Under what conditions will an MNE face translation exposure? What financial strategy might the organization use to minimize this exposure?

8 When might an MNE face transaction exposure? What is a financial strategy that the firm could use to minimize this risk?

9 What is meant by the term *economic exposure*? What is a financial strategy that an MNE could use to minimize this risk?

10 When would a multinational use a lead strategy to hedge a risk? When would a multinational use a lag strategy for this purpose? In each case, give an example. A lead strategy is a choice by an MNE to make intracompany payments (for example, from an affiliate to the home office) earlier than in an arm's-length situation, to move funds out of the country of the affiliate more rapidly. A lag strategy is a choice by an MNE to make intracompany payments (for example, from an affiliate to the home office) later than in an arm's-length situation, to hold funds longer in the affiliate country.

11 When might an MNE use a forward exchange contract (a contract with a bank to buy or sell foreign exchange at a future date, with the exchange rate and value fixed today)? When might the firm decide to forgo this strategy and leave a particular foreign currency transaction unhedged?

12 What role does net present value (NPV) play in the review of capital expenditure proposals? Give an example.

13 How can country risk affect the computation of NPV? Will the risk result in the MNE wanting a higher or a lower NPV? Explain.

14 Why do parent and local subsidiaries sometimes differ in their calculation of NPV for a particular project or expenditure? How can this difference be resolved?

15 What are some of the financing alternatives available to MNEs that are not available to domestic firms? Give an example.

REAL CASE

Skandia

Information technology has transformed the financial services and insurance business into a universal product. Instead of large numbers of white-collar clerical workers toiling in large local banking and insurance halls (like Bob Cratchit in Dickens's *A Christmas Carol*), today such services can be provided on the internet by smaller, more entrepreneurial groups and even from a home office. This is part of the global knowledge-based economy.

Skandia is a Stockholm-based insurance and financial service company, founded some 150 years ago. In 1900 Skandia became the first non-British insurance company to enter the US market, but it incurred losses in the San Francisco earthquake of 1906 and in World War I, to the extent that its international business was largely dormant and confined to reinsurance (business accepted for another company to diversify risk). In 2000, the Skandia Group had revenues of 21.7 million krona (US$2.30 million), six times the 1995 figure, and operations in 20 countries. In the mid-2000s it was acquired by Old Mutual and in 2014 the

remaining parts of the firm, after disposals, were renamed Old Mutual Wealth.

In 1986, the Assurance and Financial Services (AFS) Division of Skandia, headed by CEO Jan Carendi, made a big push in the United States. Over the next 12 years it grew by 45 percent per year. By 1998 the AFS Unit had sales of $3.5 billion with fewer than 2,000 employees. It sold a unit-linked variable life insurance product to independent insurance brokers. The product can be sold on the internet. Basically, Skandia purchased mutual funds from other companies but included its own insurance package with them. Skandia was one of the first insurance companies to use such a self-directed unit trust (or mutual fund) that allowed customers to regard life insurance as being like a retirement savings plan.

To derive an ongoing competitive advantage in knowledge management, Jan Carendi transformed the AFS Division of Skandia from a traditional bricks and mortar insurance company into a "clicks and mortar" virtual organization. He was one of the first to appoint a director of intellectual capital, retraining managers to be more flexible, innovative, and responsive to the consumers. While acting as a change agent, Carendi traveled some 200 days a year to pull together a new "federal" model of internal management structure. One aspect of this was a group of independent fund managers; another was a new software package to manage the complex administrative structure.

By the 1980s Skandia consisted of four divisions:

1 an actuarial function, designing insurance products based on risk assessments

2 a sales and marketing group that sold directly to consumers

3 an investment management group that invested premiums

4 an administrative group that managed the customer, accounting, and regulatory paperwork.

Many of the traditional insurance functions were outsourced by Carendi. The fund management and also the sales and distribution functions were outsourced. Both of these required local knowledge of regulations for mutual funds and of personal networks for sales and distribution. Instead, AFS focused on internationally mobile knowledge capabilities, using high tech and the internet.

An overdependence on the US market, from which 60 percent of all Skandia's revenues originate, led to a slower year in 2001. When the high-tech stocks plummeted in 2001 after the dot.com bust, Skandia's customers stopped buying. In July 2001, sales of variable annuities in the United States were halved to $2.5 billion, down from $5.7 billion in the previous year. Diversification into the more stable markets of Germany, Japan, and Spain over the subsequent years may help to recover the company's profitability. Meanwhile, Skandia's actuaries were busy creating new, more cautious products to be ready when US investors are ready to buy again. In 2003, Prudential Financial purchased American Skandia. In 2005 South African/British financial services group Old Mutual Plc launched a $6.5 billion bid to acquire majority control of

Skandia, which was met with resistance from some of Skandia's shareholders and directors. On February 3, 2006, Old Mutual completed its acquisition of Skandia, which was subsequently delisted from the Stockholm and London stock exchanges. In terms of disposals, 2014 was a key year as Old Mutual disposed a number of non-core European business—the Skandia businesses in Austria, Germany, Poland and Liechtenstein. Furthermore, in 2015 Old Mutual Wealth, as the company had been rebranded, went on to dispose of the Skandia businesses in France and Luxembourg. Old Mutual Wealth reported that it had sold these selected Skandia businesses in Europe in order to simplify operations and to focus on a limited number of growing markets. Even though Skandia's largest profitable operation is reported to be in the UK, and in accordance with Old Mutual Global Investors, Old Mutual Wealth has a wide range of operations in Europe and international markets. As of December 2013, the company was reported as overseeing £78.5 billion in customer investments.

The lesson is that reliance on internet-based business on a global scale is just as risky as the centuries-old business cycles. In the past, there were speculative stock market crashes, such as the South Sea Bubble (in 1720). In modern times, we have seen a similar dot.com/high-tech bubble burst in 2001, with profound repercussions, even in the stodgy world of insurance.

Sources: Christopher A. Bartlett, *Skandia AFS*, Harvard Business School, Case No. 9–396–412, 1996; "Skandia: client focus brings spectacular rewards," *Financial Times*, June 23, 2000; Skandia, *Annual Report*, 2000; "Old Mutual gets backing for hostile takeover of Skandia," *Independent*, December 21, 2005; Old Mutual, *Annual Report*, 2014; R. George, "Old Mutual sells Skandia Germany and Austria", *City Wire*, March 27, 2014.

1 Why has insurance changed from local salespeople to an internet-provided "universal" product?

2 Why was Swedish-based Skandia so successful in the US market?

3 Was CEO Jan Carendi "Swedish" or "global" in his management style?

REAL CASE

Ford and Volvo

Before it bought into Mazda and took over the four European auto manufacturers that made up its Premier Brands Group (PAG), Ford had already developed a relatively strong presence in Europe. In contrast to GM's mode of internationalization through M&A, Ford had expanded organically through

the development of local sales, distribution, and manufacturing activities around the world. In Europe, it began with a plant in Manchester, England, in 1911 before moving to the Dagenham site near London in 1932. At its peak, three-quarters of Ford's overseas production was located in

Table 16.8 Ford and its brands, 2014

Primary brands	Ford	Lincoln	Troller
Dealers	10,938	1,042	n/a
Competitors	DaimlerChrysler, Fiat, GM, Honda, Nissan, Toyota, VW, Hyundai/Kia	DaimlerChrysler, GM, Honda, Nissan, Toyota, BMW	Jeep, Toyota, Suzuki
Vehicle retail (approx.)	6,000,000	300,000	n/a
Sales mix	23% N. America 21% Europe 45% Asia–Pacific 6% S. America 5% Rest of world	n/a	n/a

Source: Ford Motor Company, *Annual Report*, 2014.

Europe, with plants in Germany, Spain, the UK, and Belgium. Even then, however, including Brazil, around 50 percent of total production took place in the Americas, primarily in the United States, Mexico, and Canada.

In 2002, Ford's sales mix consisted of 62 percent of sales in North America, 29 percent in Europe, and a weak 5 percent showing in the Asia–Pacific region. This represents the period when Ford maximized its European investments. The Premier Automotive Group (PAG) was created through a series of alliances and takeovers driven partly by the considerable drop in Ford's market share in Europe from 1994 to 1999, from almost 12 percent to just over 9 percent. A broad range of restructurings were initiated by then CEO Jacques Nasser, who stepped in to refocus on the central Ford brand operations and marketing. In 1999, Ford bought Volvo for $6.45 billion, the largest of the PAG companies, adding to Jaguar (bought in 1989), Aston Martin, and Land Rover. Since then it has sold all three. The dismantling of the PAG began in 2006, with Aston Martin sold to a UK group of investors in 2007, Jaguar and Land Rover sold to Tata Motors for $2.3 billion in 2008, and Volvo sold to the Chinese car maker Geely for $1.8 billion in 2010.

At its peak, the overall Ford Group, combining the core brands group and the European-centered PAG, appeared to be one of the more global of the largest auto firms. It was, however, still heavily regional and primarily US oriented. The relative lack of integration among the group companies, particularly Volvo, further underlined its regional structure.

First produced in Gothenburg, Sweden, Volvos were ideally designed to survive the rough roads and winter cold of Sweden. This emphasis on durability was eventually transformed into the concern for passenger safety upon which the company's reputation was built. Before the takeover, Volvo had made 70 percent of its cars in Sweden but 90 percent of its sales abroad. The firm had developed as a high-quality niche manufacturer of safe vehicles, competing against rivals such as Saab, BMW, Audi, and Mercedes. It had its own unique culture and way of developing cars and conducting business. In 2015, Volvo sold over 500,000 vehicles and had a global workforce of over 110,000 people.

Ford bought Volvo in 1999 for $6.45 billion and sold it over ten years later for $1.8 billion. The need to clearly differentiate and segment individual brands was one major factor underlying the structural separation and cultural distinctiveness of the group companies in Ford. While senior management at its Detroit HQ knew this, it is safe to say that they underestimated the challenging complexities of managing a diverse group of brands spread across a different continent.

However, during recent times it seems as though Ford may have learned from mistakes in the past. Understanding the complexity of managing a diverse group of brand across the world, Ford now primarily manages only three brands: Ford, Lincoln, and Troller. Furthermore, Ford seems to be relying less on the US market in comparison to the past. For instance, as of 2014, Ford's automotive sales mix consisted of 23 percent in North America, 21 percent in Europe, 45 percent in Asia–Pacific, 6 percent in South America, and 5 percent in the rest of the world. As of 2014, with accumulated revenues of $135.8 billion, 187,000 employees, and 62 manufacturing plants worldwide, Ford has not only grown but has remained as a global leader within the automotive industry. Table 16.8 shows the range of brands that were under the Ford group in 2014.

Websites: www.volvo.com; www.ford.com

Sources: Economist, "Ford sells Volvo to Geely: devolving Volvo," *The Economist*, March 28, 2010; John Reed and Joe Leahy, "Ford and Tata finalize $2.3bn deal," *Financial Times*, March 26, 2008; Alan M. Rugman and Simon C. Collinson, "The regional nature of the world's automotive industry," *European Management Journal*, vol. 22, no. 5 (2004), pp. 471–82; Ford Motor Company, *Annual Reports*, 2003, 2007, 2014; Alex Taylor III, "Volvo and Saab," *Fortune*, July 21, 1997; Christine Tierney, "Will Volvo become just another Ford?," *BW Online*, December 10, 2001; Christopher Brown-Humes, "Volvo exceeds earnings forecasts," *Financial Times*, February 11, 2002; Volvo Car AB, *Interim Report*, 2015.

1 Discuss why Ford failed to make a success out of the purchase of Volvo.

2 How have Ford learnt from lessons in the past?

NOTES

1 For more on tax havens, see "Gimme Shelter," *The Economist*, January 7, 2000; Nicholas Shaxson and John Christensen, "Time to black-list the tax haven whitewash," *Financial Times*, April 4, 2011; Alice Ross, "Treasure islands," *Financial Times*, January 17, 2011.

2 Also, see Neil Weinberg, "Rent Shokku," *Forbes*, June 7, 1993, p. 108.

3 For more on Honda, see Alex Taylor III, "How Toyota copes with hard times," *Fortune*, January 25, 1993, pp. 78–81.

4 The option contract can also be used to hedge this transaction. American Express could buy 160 call options as listed in the example, for a total premium of US$125,000. For this price, American Express would receive the right to buy pounds at the strike price of US$1.5800 per pound, a worse price than the forward and futures contracts. (Actually, options for lower strike prices are available at much higher premiums.) The option does not look attractive unless American Express wants to speculate that the pound will go down in value even below the forward contract price. If this happens, by not exercising the options, American Express could simply buy pounds in the spot market in 180 days and benefit from the lower price. The option is generally useful if the firm wants to speculate or if the original commercial contract may not be fulfilled, so that the pounds may not be needed after all.

5 A full set of the measures used in capital budgeting appears in basic finance texts, such as Richard A. Brealey and Stewart C. Myers, *Principles of Corporate Finance*, 9th ed. (Boston, MA: McGraw-Hill, 2010).

6 However, if the local-currency price goes up due to the currency revaluation and demand is price inelastic, the total revenue received may go up even if the quantity sold declines.

7 ADRs (American Depositary Receipts) are a derivative instrument based on shares of stock in a company. The issuing company typically sells a large quantity of shares in a block to an investment bank, which in turn holds those shares in its own treasury. The investment bank then issues ADRs whose value is based completely on the original shares, converted into US dollars, in the US market. See, for example, http://daytrading.about.com/cs/educationtraining/a/adrs.htm

8 See Brian Coleman and Thomas R. King, "Euro Disney rescue package wins approval," *Wall Street Journal*, March 15, 1994, p. A3; "Disneyland Paris cuts losses despite fewer visitors," *BBC News*, November 10, 2010; and Scheherazade Daneshkhu, "Euro Disney signs expansion deal," *Financial Times*, September 14, 2010.

9 "Ford to pay $6.47 billion in Volvo deal," *Wall Street Journal*, January 29, 1999, section A, pp. 3, 6; Jorn Madslien, "Changed landscape for global carmakers," *BBC News*, May 10, 2011.

10 Also, see John Templeman and James B. Treece, "BMW's comeback," *Business Week*, February 14, 1994, pp. 42–4; "BMW to invest £500m in UK factories," *BBC News*, June 9, 2011.

11 Keith Bradsher, "Industry's giants are carving up the world market," *New York Times*, May 8, 1998, pp. C1, 4; and Robyn Meredith, "A joining of opposites could help customers," *New York Times*, May 8, 1998, p. C4; www.daimler.com; "DaimlerChrysler board approves Chrysler sales," *Dow Jones*, May 16, 2007.

BIBLIOGRAPHY

Agmon, Tamir, and Lessard, Donald R. "Investor recognition of corporate international diversification," *Journal of Finance*, vol. 22, no. 4 (1977).

Bates, Thomas W., Kahle, Katheleen M., and Stulz, Rene M. "Why do US firms hold so much more cash than they used to?" *Journal of Finance*, vol. 64, no. 5 (October 2009).

Bartram, Soehnke M., Brown, Gregory W., and Minton, Bernadette A. "Resolving the exposure puzzle: the many facets of exchange rate exposure," *Journal of Financial Economics*, vol. 95, no. 2 (2010).

Chang, Shao-Chi, and Wang, Chi-Feng. "The effect of product diversification strategies on the relationship between international diversification and firm performance," *Journal of World Business*, vol. 42, no.1 (2007).

Clark, Terry, Kotabe, Masaaki, and Rajaratnam, Dan. "Exchange rate pass-through and international pricing strategy: a conceptual framework and research propositions," *Journal of International Business Studies*, vol. 30, no. 2 (summer 1999).

Denis, David J., Denis, Diane K., and Yost, Keven. "Global diversification, industrial diversification, and firm value," *Journal of Finance*, vol. 57, no. 5 (2002).

Di Gregorio, Dante. "Re-thinking country risk: insights from entrepreneurship theory," *International Business Review*, vol. 14 (2005).

Dos Santos, Marcelo B., Errunza, Vihang R., and Miller, Darius P. "Does corporate international diversification destroy value? Evidence from cross-border mergers and acquisitions," *Journal of Banking and Finance*, vol. 32, no. 12 (2008).

Eckert, Stefan, and Trautnitz, Georg. "A commentary on risk reduction by geographic diversification," *Multinational Business Review*, vol. 18, no. 1 (2010).

Eden, Lorraine. "Taxes, transfer pricing, and the multinational enterprise." In Alan M. Rugman (ed.), *The Oxford Handbook of International Business* (Oxford: Oxford University Press, 2009).

Eden, Lorraine, Juarez Valdez, Luis F., and Li, Dan. "Talk softly but carry a big stick: transfer pricing penalties and the market valuation of Japanese multinationals in the United States," *Journal of International Business Studies*, vol. 36, no. 4 (July 2005).

Egehoff, William G., Gorman, Liam, and McCormick, Stephen. "How FDI characteristics influence subsidiary trade patterns: the case of Ireland," *Management International Review*, vol. 40, no. 3 (fall 2000).

Errunza, Vihang. "Emerging markets in global finance." In B. Toyne and D. Nigh (eds.), *International Business: An Emerging Vision* (Columbia, SC: University of South Carolina Press, 1997).

Errunza, Vihang, and Senbet, Lemma W. "The effects of international operations on the market value of the firm: theory and evidence," *Journal of Finance*, vol. 36, no. 2 (1981).

Errunza, Vihang, and Senbet, Lemma W. "International corporate diversification, market valuation, and size adjusted evidence," *Journal of Finance*, vol. 39, no. 3 (1984).

European Commission. *Company Taxation in the Internal Market* (Brussels, October 2001).

Gande, Amar, Schenzler, Christoph, and Senbet, Lemma W. "Valuation effects of global diversification," *Journal of International Business Studies*, vol. 40 (2009).

Gao, Ting. "Exchange rate movements and the profitability of US multinationals," *Journal of International Money and Finance*, vol. 19 (2000).

Geringer, J. Michael, Beamish, Paul W., and daCosta, Richard C. "Diversification strategy and internationalization: implications for MNE performance," *Strategic Management Journal*, vol. 10, no. 2 (1989).

Grosse, Robert, *The Future of Global Financial Services* (Oxford: Blackwell, 2004).

Grosse, Robert, with Shannon Mudd and John Mathis. "Dealing with financial crises in emerging markets," *Thunderbird International Business Review*, vol. 44, no. 3 (2002).

Gubbi, Sathyajit R., Aulakh, Preet S., Sougata, R., Sarkar, M. B., and Chittoor, Raveendra. "Do international acquisitions by emerging-economy firms create shareholder value? The case of Indian firms," *Journal of International Business Studies*, vol. 41 (2010).

Hermes, Niels, Smid, Peter, and Lu, Yao. "Capital budgeting practices: a comparative study of the Netherlands and China," *International Business Review*, vol. 16, no. 5 (October 2007).

Jiang, Xu, and Li, Yuan. "The relationship between organizational learning and firms' financial performance in strategic alliances: a contingency approach," *Journal of World Business*, vol. 43, no. 3 (2008).

Johannesen, Niels, and Zucman, Gabriel. "The end of bank secrecy? An evaluation of the G20 tax haven crackdown," *American Economic Journal: Economic Policy*, vol. 6, no. 1 (2014).

Jones, Chris, and Temouri, Yama. "The determinants of tax haven FDI," *Journal of World Business*, vol. 51, no. 2 (2016).

Lee, Seung-Hyun, and Makhija, Mona. "The effect of domestic uncertainty on the real options value of international investments," *Journal of International Business Studies*, vol. 40, no. 3 (2009).

Liebowitz, Seth Jay, Gerde, Virginia W., and Davies, Antony. "Employee-oriented management practices and the firm's financial performance: what causes what?," *Academy of Management Proceedings* (January 2015).

Markides, Constantinos C., and Ittner, Christopher D. "Shareholder benefits from corporate international diversification: evidence from US international acquisitions," *Journal of International Business Studies*, vol. 25, no. 2 (1994).

Markides, Constantinos C., and Oyon, Daniel. "International acquisitions: do they create value for shareholders?," *European Management Journal*, vol. 16, no. 2 (April 1998).

Oxelheim, Lars, Stonehill, Arthur, Randøy, Trond, Vikkula, Kaisa, Dullum, Kare, and Modén, Karl-Markus. *Corporate Strategies to Internationalize the Cost of Capital* (Copenhagen: Copenhagen Business School Press, 1998).

Qi, Yaxuan, Roth, Lukas, and Wald, John K. "How legal environments affect the use of bond covenants," *Journal of International Business Studies*, vol. 42 (2011).

Qian, Gongming, Li, Lee, and Rugman, Alan M. "Liability of country foreignness and liability of regional foreignness: their effects on geographic diversification and firm performance," *Journal of International Business Studies*, vol. 44, no. 6 (2013).

Randøy, Trond, Oxelheim, Lars, and Stonehill, Arthur. "Corporate financial strategies for global competitiveness," *European Management Journal*, vol. 19, no. 6 (December 2001).

Reuer, Jeffrey J., Shenkar, Oded, and Ragozzino, Roberto. "Mitigating risk in international mergers and acquisitions: the role of contingent payouts," *Journal of International Business Studies*, vol. 35, no. 1 (January 2004).

Rugman, Alan M. *International Diversification and the Multinational Enterprise* (Lexington, MA: D.C. Heath, 1979).

Rugman, Alan M. "Implications of the theory of internalization for corporate international finance," *California Management Review*, vol. 23, no. 2 (winter 1980).

Rugman, Alan M. "Twenty-five years of 'international diversification and the multinational enterprise'." In Alain Verbeke (ed.), *Internalization, International Diversification and the Multinational Enterprise—Essays in Honor of Alan M. Rugman* (London: Elsevier, 2005).

Rugman, Alan M., and Eden, Lorraine. *Multinationals and Transfer Pricing* (London: Croom Helm and New York: St. Martin's Press, 1985).

Rugman, Alan M., and Jing, Li. "Real options and the theory of foreign direct investment," *International Business Review*, vol. 16, no. 6 (December 2007).

Rugman, Alan M., and Oh, Chang Hoon. "Regional multinational enterprises and the international financial crisis." In J. Berrill, E. Houston, and R. Sinkovics (eds.), *Firm-level Internationalization, Regionalism and Globalization* (Basingstoke: Palgrave, 2011).

Rugman, Alan M., and Verbeke, Alain. "Strategic capital budgeting decisions and the theory of internalization," *Managerial Finance*, vol. 16, no. 2 (1990).

Song, Sangcheol, Lee, Seung-Hyun, and Makhija, Mona. "Operational hedging in foreign direct investments under volatile and divergent exchange rates across countries," *Journal of World Business*, vol. 50, no. 3 (2015).

Sundaram, Anant. "Management of exchange rate exposure by the multinational corporation." In D. Logue and J. Seward (eds.), *Handbook of Modern Finance* (New York: Warren Gorham Lamont, 2004).

Tschoegl, Adrian E. "FDI and internationalization: evidence from US subsidiaries of foreign banks," *Journal of International Business Studies*, vol. 33, no. 4 (2002).

Wallace, Wanda. "The value relevance of accounting: the rest of the story," *European Management Journal*, vol. 18, no. 6 (December 2000).

Part Five

REGIONAL STRATEGIES

Chapter 17

EUROPEAN UNION

Contents

Objectives of the chapter

The European Union (EU) is one of the world's triad markets. It is the home of one-third of the world's largest 500 firms. Also, many foreign MNEs from Asia and North America are now doing business in the EU or are targeting the area in their expansion plans. This chapter examines the EU environment and reviews some of the major strategy considerations that must be addressed by companies doing business in this economic bloc.

The specific objectives of this chapter are to:

1 *Describe* the Single European Market and the competitive status of the EU in relation to other triad members.

2 *Discuss* how firms carry out an overall strategic analysis of the EU market in terms of competitive intelligence and evaluation of location.

3 *Relate* some of the major strategy issues that must be considered when doing business in the EU, including exporting, strategic alliances and acquisitions, manufacturing considerations, marketing approaches, and management considerations.

The future is Orange

Orange, formerly known as France Telecom until 2013, is a good example of an organization that has grown stronger in its own home-region, rather than aggressively expanding globally. The organization has built up a major presence in the EU primarily through strategic alliances and through the acquisition of competitors. It can now use its strong EU home base as a staging ground to enter the North American and Asian markets, as was discussed in the earlier case on Vodafone (in Chapter 8).

Orange is a leading telecommunication operator in Europe. It offers services covering fixed and mobile communications, data transmission, the internet and multimedia, and other value-added services for individuals, businesses, and other telecommunications operators. It operates in three segments: the Personal Communication Services (PCS), the Home Communication Services (HCS), and the Enterprise Communication Services (ECS). The PCS segment consists of the mobile telecommunication services in central and eastern Europe, Africa, the Middle East, the Caribbean, and Asia; the HCS segment includes fixed-line telecommunication activities (fixed-line telephony, internet services, and operator services), as well as the distribution and support functions provided to the other segments of the group; and the ECS segment provides communication solutions to large and small businesses worldwide. The company operates a number of subsidiaries, and as of 2014 serves over 244 million customers (185 million mobile customers alone), in five continents. With over $40 billion in revenues in 2014 and 156,000 employees (half outside France), the firm is one of Europe's largest telecommunication companies.

Up to 1988, France Telecom (Orange) was a department in the French Ministry of Posts and Telecommunications. It began a process of privatization in 1998, under Lionel Jospin's government, but the French government still owns part of the firm. This causes periodic clashes with EU competition commissioners, including an allegation that the firm was paid the equivalent of over $1 billion in unlawful subsidies in 2004.

The rise of Orange in the European market and its expansion into wireless and internet are the result of a combination of R&D expenditures, alliances, and strategies. Orange has one of the largest research centers in Europe, employing over 5,000 people and holding over 10,000 patents worldwide. R&D efforts strive to facilitate human interaction through telecommunications. Orange has also teamed up with other companies to complement its research efforts. It is working with Ericsson to provide integrated operator

Source: Ulrich Baumgarten via Getty Images

services for the home. An agreement with Motorola will seek to develop "seamless mobility" services for businesses. Meanwhile, it is collaborating with Nokia to provide mobile access to home multimedia content. These types of partnerships are also used to improve the process through which services are provided.

R&D has helped Orange secure a place in the European market. However, the fractured nature of the European market made strategic alliances a necessary element in Orange's international strategy. The EU's 28 members lack not only a common language but also a common regulatory system. Each country awards its own mobile licenses, forcing new entrants to make alliances with license holders. In addition, the previous fixed-line companies continue to own much of the local telecom infrastructure, increasing the benefits of partnering up.

In 1995, Orange (France Telecom) joined Telekom and Sprint to form the Global One alliance, which was expected to serve as a springboard into the US market while protecting Orange's (France Telecom's) home market from competition by Telekom. In 1999, Sprint was purchased by MCI World, effectively voiding the alliance. In the same year, Deutsche Telekom also rescinded its obligations when it sought a merger with Telecom Italia. As a result, Orange (France Telecom) redesigned its international strategy and began to compete directly with Deutsche Telekom in the German market by purchasing 17 percent of E-plus, the country's third-largest cell phone operator. This marked a turning point for Orange's (France Telecom's) international strategy. The company now favors acquisitions over alliances.

In January 2000, France Telecom purchased the Global One alliance from its partners, an event that marked the beginning of a purchasing spree. Later that year, it bought

Orange (UK) from Vodafone. Orange had a presence in 20 countries around the world, including 13 in Europe. France Telecom combined its own mobile business with that of Orange to create Europe's second-largest cell phone company. This acquisition was also a strategic move into the UK market. The firm's biggest competitor, Deutsche Telekom, had already purchased One2One in the UK. With 12.2 million active customers, Orange was the largest mobile operator in the UK, catapulting France Telecom into the big leagues.

Orange (France Telecom) also purchased Equant NV and Freeserve in 2000. Equant NV was combined with Global One under the name Equant. Like other telecommunications firms, Orange experienced a sharp decrease in share value in the early 2000s as a knock-on effect of the dot.com bust; the cost of buying 3G mobile licenses in the UK, Germany, France, and Italy, among others; accumulated debt from the firm's acquisitions; and the lack of a strong market that would allow it to raise funds through the sale of equity. Despite this, and heavy competition from new entrants, France Telecom has been able to turn things around. Its share value has improved considerably and it remains a major European competitor. More recently its expansion has increased with purchases of One GmbH, the third-largest mobile operator in Austria, and 51 percent of Telkom Kenya in 2007. It also won the rights to be the exclusive distributor of the Apple iPhone in France. It is now strategically pre-pared to take advantage of future profits from 4G mobiles, the deregulation of telecommunications and increased competition in local markets, economies of scale on internet service provision, and the growing integration of the EU market.

Orange has come a long way from the days of the government-owned national carrier, France Telecom. In 1995, 75 percent of its revenues were from fixed-line operations, and foreign sales accounted for only 2 percent of revenues. Today, France accounts for 49 percent of revenues and most of this comes from mobile and internet services. Revenue from Spain and Poland accounts for 17 percent, the rest of the world 17 percent, international carriers and shared services 2 percent and enterprise 15 percent. It is becoming more of a multinational, but remains highly dependent on the European market.

Websites: www.orange.com/en_EN/group/; www.francetelecom.com; www.sprint.com; www.equant.com; www.mci.com; www.one2one.co.uk; www.orange.co.uk; www.freeserve.com; www.wanadoo.fr; www.bt.com

Sources: Adam Thomson, "Network spending weighs on Orange as sales and revenues dip in Paris," *Financial Times*, April 28, 2015; "T-Mobile and Orange in UK merger," *BBC News*, September 8, 2009; "France Telecom: battling debt," *BBC News*, April 19, 2001; "French giant targets alliance," *BBC News*, October 12, 1999; "France Telecom clinches Orange deal," *BBC News*, May 30, 2000; "France Telecom takes over Equant," *BBC News*, November 20, 2000; Richard Tomlinson, "5 moves to win the Telecom game," *Fortune*, January 7, 2002; France Telecom, *Annual Report*, 2010; Associated Press, "France Telecom shares decline as government moves to cut its stake," *International Herald Tribune*, June 25, 2007; *Thomson Reuters*, *OneSource*, 2011.

1 Describe the stages by which Orange (France Telecom) has built up a successful strategic base in the EU. What barriers to integration had to be overcome in the EU before France Telecom could buy up rival companies?

2 To what extent has the triad strategy of Orange/France Telecom been the same as that of Vodafone (in Chapter 8)? Are there any differences?

3 In what ways will integration and localization be important issues for conducting mergers in the EU?

4 In what ways are both pricing and positioning important for companies like Orange doing business in the EU?

THE EU ENVIRONMENT

The EU currently consists of 28 countries (see Figure 17.1). These comprise the pre-2004 EU15, ten other European countries that joined in 2004, Bulgaria and Romania which joined in 2007, and Croatia that joined in 2013. The EU15 are closely linked both economically and politically, and this group is more loosely linked to the 13 new members. In terms of monetary policy, 12 of the pre-2004 EU15 share a common currency, the euro, and constitute the Eurozone. Today, the EU28 has a population of almost 508 million and generates an estimated 25 percent share of the world's nominal GDP (US$19.035 trillion). Doing business in this bloc offers huge opportunities, and many MNEs are interested in tapping this giant potential (see Table 17.1).

Table 17.1 Economic profile of the big three (in US$), 2015

	US	JAPAN	EU28
The economy			
GDP	17.97 trillion	4.658 trillion	19.18 trillion
Real GDP growth rate	2.6%	0.6%	1.8%
Inflation	0.2%	0.7%	0.1% (2013 est.)
Workforce			
Population	321 million	127 million	514 million
Population below poverty line	15.1% (2010 est.)	16.1% (2013 est.)	n/a
Labor cost per hour in manufacturing (2012)	27.15	28.94	31.43 (EU15)
Unemployment rate	5.2%	3.3%	9.5%
Merchandise trade			
Trade balance	(749 billion)	(1.4 billion)	(139 billion)
Exports	1.598 trillion	624 billion	2.173 trillion (2012, EU27 est.)
Imports	2.347 trillion	625.4 billion	2.312 trillion (2012, EU27 est.)
Public sector			
Government consumption as % of GDP	17.6%	20.4	21.6% (2012 est.)
Government debt as % of GDP	73.6%	227.9%	n.a

Sources: https://www.cia.gov/index.html; http://www.bls.gov/ilc/#laborforce

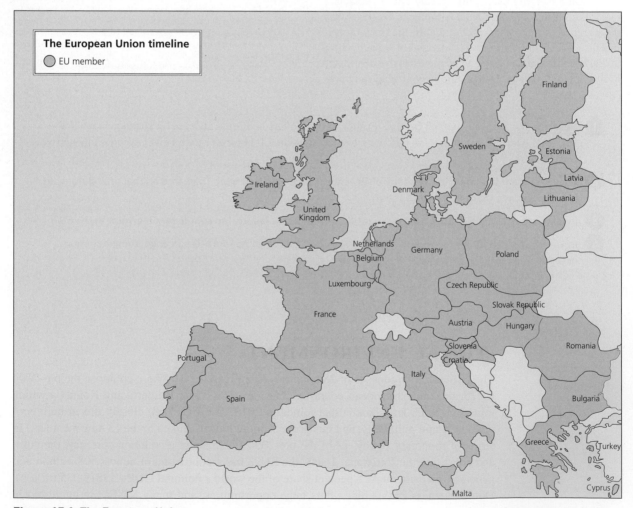

Figure 17.1 The European Union

In 2015–16 a variety of new threats challenged the political and economic cohesion of the EU. The growing flow of migrants from Africa and the Middle East threatened those countries located at the borders of the EU, particularly Turkey and Greece, which had already gone through a series of economic and political upheavals (see the case **International Business Strategy in Action: Greece** in Chapter 4). This triggered heated debates and revealed both a lack of political unification and a lack of a coordinated operational response to the crisis. At the same time the UK, pushing for a range of reforms to further distance itself from the economic, social, and political union, held a referendum to decide whether it should exit the EU altogether.

Emergence of a Single European Market

The origins of the EU go back to the formation of the European Economic Community (EEC) in the late 1950s, at which time there were six founding members: France, West Germany, Italy, Belgium, the Netherlands, and Luxembourg. By the late 1990s, the EU had grown to include Austria, Finland, the UK, Ireland, Denmark, Greece, Spain, Sweden, and Portugal. In 2004, an additional ten countries were added: Poland, the Czech Republic, Hungary, Slovenia, Estonia, Latvia, Lithuania, Cyprus, Malta, and the Slovak Republic. In 2007 Bulgaria and Romania joined, and in 2013 Croatia also joined. Over the last 40 years rapid economic growth has led to a high degree of political and social integration.

The objectives of the EU are:

1 Elimination of customs duties among member states.

2 Elimination of obstacles to the free flow of import and/or export of goods and services among member states.

3 Establishment of common customs duties and unified industrial/commercial policies regarding countries outside the community.

4 Free movement of people and capital within the bloc.

5 Acceptance of common agricultural policies, transport policies, technical standards, health and safety regulations, and educational degrees.

6 Common measures for consumer protection.

7 Common laws to maintain competition throughout the community and to fight monopolies or illegal cartels.

8 Regional funds to encourage the economic development of certain countries/regions.

9 Greater monetary and fiscal coordination among member states and certain common monetary/fiscal policies.[1]

In December 1985, EU leaders adopted a White Paper that contained 279 proposals aimed at achieving a single unified European market by December 31, 1992. Less than two years later the Single European Act (SEA) was passed.[2] A key part of the SEA was the EU **Council of Ministers**, one of the four major institutions of the EU. For each field of discussion, the EU Council of Ministers consists of one minister from each of the member states and is responsible for making major policy decisions for the union. The Council could now pass most proposals with a majority vote, in contrast to the unanimous vote needed previously. This opened the door for much faster progress toward both political and economic integration among member countries. Twelve of the EU15 countries have now adopted a single European currency, the euro, and have committed to a social charter, complete harmonization of social and economic policies, a common defense policy, and related measures that increase the power of the EU bureaucracy in Brussels. The Treaty of Lisbon, which came into force in 2009, was the last amendment to the constitutional basis of the

Council of Ministers
The major policy decision-making body of the EU and one of its major institutions, consisting of one minister from each of the member states

EU. It provided for a greater role for the European Parliament and more ways for national governments and individual citizens to be involved in EU policy making.

Will the EU eventually bring about a **Single European Market (SEM)** in which the above stated goals are achieved? This will depend on the extent of progress in the area of free movement of goods and the practice of government procurement. It will also depend on whether the new member countries, and any others that join in the future, can be harmoniously integrated.

Single European Market (SEM)
A market consisting of all members of the EU, bound together by a single currency, a special charter, complete harmonization of social and economic policies, and a common defense policy

Free movement of goods

There have been no customs duties between most EU members since March 1, 1986. Most technical, safety, and other standards and regulations for trade have now been standardized throughout the EU. However, free movement of goods has been hampered by fragmented local markets. This fragmentation has been created by exploiting language differences between countries and by setting artificially high prices for goods. With the growth of discount stores, mail-order houses, cross-border buying deals, and e-commerce, these differences are gradually being eliminated.

The EU has also created a single currency, the euro,[3] which some believe is beginning to challenge the US dollar's dominance of international trade and finance. In January 2002, the euro officially replaced individual countries' currencies in 12 member states. This had extended to 19 countries in the "Eurozone" by 2014, by which time it had the highest combined value of cash in circulation in the world, surpassing the US dollar. Some key countries, notably the UK, have not joined the single currency community and full financial integration across Europe has proved complex.[4] But the process of financial integration has helped generate new opportunities for both EU businesses and foreign MNEs doing business there.

Practice of government procurement

EU government procurements account for 17 percent of the union's GDP. In the past it has been common to find governments awarding contracts to national firms. However, with the emergence of the SEM and the Government Procurement Agreement (GPA), this is diminishing. The result will be greater efficiency, lower cost, and an economically stronger common market. On the other hand, it is important to realize that, in implementing this strategy, many companies are likely to find themselves losing business to competitors in other EU countries that can provide higher quality and service and lower cost. This development will also probably be somewhat slow in coming because of the possible negative impact of the economic growth of individual countries and the desire to favor national firms when awarding government contracts. In 2004, a British government-commissioned study denounced the difficulties faced by British firms when competing for procurement contracts in other EU nations. Only 10 percent of all government contracts in the EU are awarded to foreign firms, compared to 20 percent in the private sector. It is not that the rules of government procurement are faulty but that governments evade them to favor domestic firms. For example, all contracts above a certain value must be publicly advertised, but at least one government has circumvented this rule by splitting the job into two smaller contracts.

Meanwhile, the EU continues to try to improve cross-border access to government procurement contracts. It has sought to standardize the procurement process to overcome language barriers. For example, the European Commission has proposed a common vocabulary to be used in all public procurement notices that would standardize the procurement process and increase competition.

Enlargement of the EU

The accession of additional members into the EU since 2004 has changed the panorama of the union and raised questions about the feasibility of a truly integrated region, economically and politically. With the exception of the war on Iraq, the EU15 had been able to maintain a relatively common front in regard to foreign policy. The EU's largest members disagreed on whether or not to support a US invasion of Iraq. France and Germany opposed the war while the UK strongly supported it.[5] Despite this, the union has been able to present a unified stance on a number of other international matters, including aid to poorer nations and other wars. The inclusion of new, mostly central European nations, into the union has added a new factor that further complicates reaching a consensus. Most of the new members are pro-American politically and aspire to its economic system, including low corporate taxation. This contrasts with the policies of Germany and France, two founding members, which rely heavily on government involvement and often disagree with US foreign policy. The UK is more aligned with their views, but it stands as a less involved member in the EU when contrasted with France and Germany. Another topic of disagreement is Russia. Both Germany and France have good relations with Russia, whereas the new members view it with distrust. A common foreign policy is now less likely to emerge.[6]

In addition, these new countries have not been fully integrated into the union. The prospect of a flood of cheap labor into the EU15 nations created a negative reaction from EU15 citizens. These new members, therefore, remain outside the Schengen zone of passport-free travel for at least a couple of years and cannot work in most EU15 countries for at least another six years. Indeed, only the UK, Ireland, and Sweden have opened their borders to workers from new member nations. The newer members have also been excluded from receiving the full amount of farm subsidies available to EU15 members. This is partly due to the expense of subsidizing farmers, but also because the lower cost of producing in the new member countries would destabilize the EU15 member's agricultural industry. In addition, the EU, the United States, and Japan are under increasing pressure from less developed countries to eliminate farm subsidies altogether. Offering full subsidies to the 12 new members would only exacerbate the situation if the EU decided to phase out agricultural subsidies. Nonetheless, new members are finding the EU15 a welcoming market for their agricultural products, which are still competitive because of the lower costs of producing in their countries. Future enlargement is likely to follow the same or even more restrictive rights for new members.

Further enlargement also threatens to increase the differences among member countries, stymieing political and economic integration. In particular, the possibility that Turkey might join the union has created a lot of tension within the EU. Turkey's mainly Islamic population is relatively large, and the country has a relatively younger population that could have an impact on the political future of the aging EU. Many nationalist groups within the EU are against Turkey joining the union and, indeed, see any further enlargement as a dilution of their power within the union.[7] It is difficult to predict whether the EU28 has the potential to be as integrated politically and economically as the EU15 did. For the time being, however, there is internal disagreement about further integration.

✔ Active learning check

Review your answer to Active Learning Case question 1 and make any changes you like. Then compare your answer to the one below.

 Describe the stages by which Orange (France Telecom) has built up a successful strategic base in the EU. What barriers to integration had to be overcome in the EU before France Telecom could buy up rival companies?

As a state-owned monopoly, France Telecom originally had a strong presence in its own market but relied heavily on fixed-line operations and had no significant international presence. Faced with deregulation, France Telecom sought to compete regionally but understood that to do so it had to have competitive products and access to international markets. ▶

Investment in R&D allowed the company to expand its product line while strategic alliances were sought to protect its market and expand into others. The Global One alliance with Telekom provided a period of competitive shelter from one of its major EU competitors. By the time this alliance was dissolved in 1999, France Telecom had the capacity to compete alone against major EU telecommunication companies and had begun to acquire companies to solidify its product line and enter new EU markets.

For France Telecom to be able to purchase rival firms, deregulation of the telecommunications markets of individual countries in the EU had to occur. In addition, France Telecom's acquisitions had to overcome antitrust legislation in the EU. The development of the EU Single Market and the strengthening of the competition policy to dismantle protectionist borders within the EU helped France Telecom evolve into Orange.

The competitive status of the EU

The eventual emergence of an integrated EU will help greater Europe compete more effectively with the other triad members. However, several EU countries are currently at a competitive disadvantage in some areas.

Productivity

High wages, salaries, and fringe benefits put some EU firms at a disadvantage in competing with their US and Japanese counterparts. Labor laws in all EU countries make it extremely difficult to fire employees once they have been employed for a year. US companies have much greater freedom and flexibility in hiring and firing their workers on short notice. This means that US employees must remain productive to retain their jobs and that companies can adjust more readily to changes in demand for their product or service. Japanese firms tend to treat their workers as a fixed cost and so find the practice of firing to be unnecessary; employees are grateful to their employers and are willing to work hard to upgrade their skills and increase the company's economic performance.

With some success, EU firms are working to raise their productivity and match that of their major triad competitors. As shown in Figure 17.2, hourly compensation costs for production workers in manufacturing were higher in the main EU economies of France, Germany, and the Netherlands than in the United States. But costs were much lower in the newer EU countries and slightly lower in Japan. Over the last few years, cooperation between EU workers and companies to protect jobs has decreased hourly salaries.

Investment spending

Investment spending in EU countries has traditionally lagged behind. Part of this can be explained by rapid increases in wages and benefits during the 1980s that were not offset by increases in productivity. As a result, EU firms found themselves without the capital to invest and had to resort to borrowing. Demands for loans resulted in higher interest rates, which also put a strain on investors. More recently, EU economies have been doing much better, stabilizing government spending. Despite this, most European countries continue to perform below the US level in terms of overall productivity (see Figure 17.3).

Education

Another area in which EU countries have failed to maintain a competitive edge is education. While all three triad groups spend approximately 5 percent of GDP on education, the approaches are different. In Europe, most vocational training is provided at the high school level, whereas in the United States and Japan it comes later. Moreover, in the United States

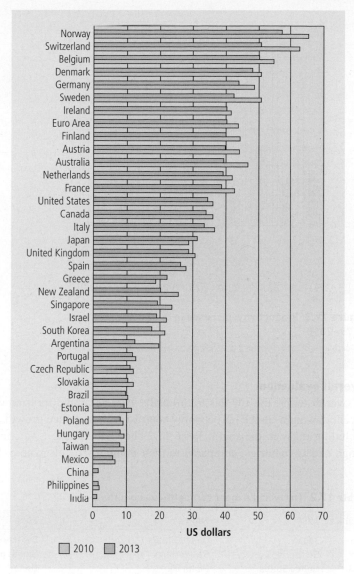

Figure 17.2 Hourly compensation costs in manufacturing, 2010 and 2013

Note: Compensation costs include direct pay, social insurance expenditures, and labor-related taxes. Data for China and India are not strictly comparable with each other or with data for other countries.

Source: The Conference Board, International Labor Comparisons program.

a higher percentage of the population attends college than in Europe or Japan. The European university curriculum is more theoretical than in either the United States or Japan. European educational institutions are also more rigid and less able to adapt to the changing needs of business, and there is less interaction between European educational institutions and industry. Some believe that as a result, many European students receive training that is inappropriate for the employment needs of European business and industry. This in part explains the high unemployment rates in the age group under 25 in many regions of Europe. The major challenge for European countries will be to modify their education systems and make them more flexible, more practical, and better able to adapt to the changing demands of industry.

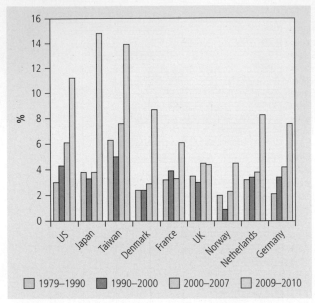

Figure 17.3 Productivity: increase in output per hour, 1979–2010

Source: Bureau of Labor Statistics, http://www.bls.gov/news.release/prod4.t01.htm

Overall evaluation

In overall terms, the EU has traditionally lagged behind its triad competitors, although recent downturns in the US economy contrast with sustained growth in some EU countries, including many in the south. Table 17.2 shows the changes in competitiveness across a range of EU countries, compared to their counterparts elsewhere. In 1989 all the EU15

Table 17.2 The world's most competitive economies

Rank	1989	2008	2014
1	Japan	United States	Switzerland
2	Switzerland	Switzerland	Singapore
3	United States	Denmark	United States
4	Canada	Sweden	Finland
5	Germany	Germany	Germany
6	Finland	Finland	Japan
7	Netherlands	Singapore	Hong Kong SAR (P.R. China)
8	Sweden	Japan	Netherlands
9	Norway	United Kingdom	United Kingdom
10	Australia	Netherlands	Sweden
11	United Kingdom	Korea	Norway
12	Denmark	Hong Kong SAR (P.R. China)	United Arab Emirates
13	France	Canada	Denmark
14	Belgium/Luxembourg	Taiwan (Taiwan Province of China)	Taiwan (Taiwan Province of China)
15	Austria	Austria	Canada
16	Ireland	Norway	Qatar
17	New Zealand	Israel	New Zealand
18	Spain	France	Belgium
19	Italy	Australia	Luxembourg
20	Turkey	Belgium	Malaysia
21	Portugal	Malaysia	Austria
22	Greece	Ireland	Australia

Source: Adapted from IMD and World Economic Forum, *The World Competitiveness Report*, 1989, 2008, and 2014.

countries ranked in the top 22 most competitive economies in the world. By 2008 there were 10 in this category and by 2014 just 9 as newly emerging economies from Asia and elsewhere joined the top ranks. The world is becoming a more competitive place, and some EU countries are finding it hard to keep up.

What changes are likely to occur in the future? One is an increase in acquisitions and mergers among EU firms and between them and companies from outside the bloc. A second change is the emergence of new technologies that will be developed in EU laboratories. A third is additional free trade agreements and other economic arrangements among European countries that are designed to make the EU a stronger, more competitive market.

✔ Active learning check

Review your answer to Active Learning Case question 2 and make any changes you like. Then compare your answer with the one below.

 To what extent has the triad strategy of Orange/France Telecom been the same as that of Vodafone (in Chapter 8)? Are there any differences?

Both Vodafone and Orange/France Telecom have a stronger presence in the European market than in any other triad market. Acquisitions have been a major part of both their strategies to gain technology and market share in their own triad region and in other triad markets. One difference is Vodafone's continued reliance on alliances, such as its joint venture with Bell Atlantic, whereas France Telecom no longer seeks alliances but equity in competitors (i.e., M&A). Another difference is that the extent of Vodafone's international expansion is much larger than Orange/France Telecom's.

CONDUCTING A STRATEGIC ANALYSIS

As we have seen, the EU is likely to be a very competitive market in the future. In preparing to do business in the EU, foreign MNEs must first conduct an overall strategic analysis, focusing on the competitive nature of the industry being targeted. Assuming that the enterprise intends to set up operations by FDI or alternative investments rather than merely export to the market, the analysis must also evaluate location. This section examines both of these activities.

Using competitive intelligence

Competition in the EU has grown over the last few years. Some of the specific strategies employed have included careful market segmentation, increased R&D, and the use of mergers, acquisitions, and alliances to help build market share and improve competitive strength. For example, GM centralized the management of its European operations to save costs and better control regional operations some time ago.[8] Apple monitors prices in Europe and as a result charged about $100 more for a basic iPad in London, England, than in the United States, when it launched the product in Europe in 2010.[9] Competitor intelligence has been an essential part of these developments. This approach employs two complementary paths: external information gathering and internal infrastructural analysis.

External information gathering

The information that is critical for competitor analysis is typically located in a variety of sources. For example, in the UK, Denmark, and Ireland, centralized government-controlled company registration offices provide financial information on registered firms. Other useful sources of competitive information include the Department of Trade and Industry (DTI), trade associations, business information services, and regional and local publications. In France, a great deal of registration information is commonly found in local courthouses. This is also the case in Germany and Italy, where companies must register with the local civil courts in the region where they are headquartered. In these countries, chambers of commerce are also excellent sources of information because they work much more closely with business firms than do their counterparts in the United States. Central databases created by the EU Commission can be used to keep abreast of changes in national legislation, thus keeping companies aware of new laws and regulations. An understanding of the legal, technical, and cultural barriers often used to keep foreign competition at bay can be particularly important in an environmental analysis.

INTERNATIONAL BUSINESS STRATEGY IN ACTION

VW diesel dispute

Established in 1937, the Volkswagen (VW AG) Group is a German multinational automotive enterprise with its headquarters in Wolfsburg, Germany, and subsidiary divisions for the design and manufacture of passenger and commercial vehicles, motorcycles, engines, turbomachinery and financial services. In 2014 it recorded revenues of US$245 billion, 54 percent from car sales. The VW AG group is comprised of many automotive manufacturers such as Audi, Bentley, Lamborghini, Porsche, SEAT, and Skoda. As of 2014, VW had grown to become the second largest automaker in the world, just behind Toyota.

In 2015 the VW Group faced a scandal, dubbed the "diesel dispute," which directly contradicted the company's long-standing values and medium-term strategy: "Our pursuit of innovation and perfection and our responsible approach will help to make us the world's leading automaker by 2018 – both economically and ecologically." The Environmental Protection Agency (EPA) found that many vehicles sold in the US, spanning a range of models (Audi A3, Jetta, Beetle, Golf), were fitted with a device within the diesel engine that could detect when they were being tested and which, in turn, adjusted the performance in order to improve the results. With a large marketing campaign emphasizing low diesel emissions, VW had been pushing to sell vast number of vehicles in the US. However, with findings covering 482,000 vehicles in the US, the EPA found that VW had been fitting this so-called "defeat device" within all its diesel vehicles.

Acknowledging these allegations, the VW Group held its hands up and further admitted that approximately 11 million vehicles sold worldwide had also been fitted with this device. The company was accused not only of cheating the emissions test, but of cheating customers who had bought cars they believed were environmentally friendly. Why had this happened and for how long had it been going on within VW?

Leadership
Following the emergence of these allegations, Martin Winterkorn, who was appointed CEO in 2007, resigned from the organization and was replaced with Matthias Mueller, who was the former boss of Porsche. This, however, was the latest move in a long history of politics and power-play at the top of one of Europe's largest MNEs. For some observers the origins of the scandal can be traced back to 2005, where Winterkorn's predecessor, Bernd Pischetsrieder, and head of VW, Wolfgang Bernhard, were in control of the organization. However, both have claimed their innocence and investigations are turning to the employees hired within the last decade in order to resolve the matter.

The diesel scandal is not the only recent scandal to hit VW, as in 2004 Bernhard was caught in the middle of a bribery scandal concerning payments, which resulted in the resignation of VW's personnel director. Following the bribery scandal, Pischetsrieder and Bernhard attempted to reform the organization in two ways. Firstly, the duo reduced costs within manufacturing bases and emphasized an end to certain labor practices, such as the four-day, 29-hour working week. Secondly, they attempted to reform the organization's culture, focusing on the relationship between management and the works council. However, this proved to be more challenging than initially imagined, as the duo constantly faced a power struggle which resulted in VW's chairman, Ferdinand Piëch, teaming up with labor representatives to remove

Pischetsrieder from his post. Winterkorn replaced Pischetsrieder as CEO and Bernhard left the organization only a few months after the appointment of Winterkorn. Multiple executives and directors have stated that Winterkorn seemed to adopt a culture in which success was down to his own doing and any bad news was pinned on the former leadership duo.

Engine development

Multiple board members have repeatedly suggested that the origins of the diesel dispute can be traced back to 2005, when VW identified a gap in the US diesel market and aimed to target the United States as heavily as possible. However, VW's problem lay in the fact that it did not have a diesel engine which met US vehicle standards. Furthermore, VW went on to withdraw existing diesel models in 2006, as they did not comply with the US's new Tier 2 vehicle standards.

With the aim of developing a new engine that could be used to tap into the US market by 2008, Bernhard appointed Audi's engine developer, Rudolf Krebs, to take on the challenge. But the two quickly came to realize that using a fuel injection system called Pumpe Düse, which was the way VW usually made engines, was not going to work. In order to overcome this obstacle, Bernhard switched to using Mercedes' (his former firm) technology, known as AdBlue. This change in engine technology was seen as controversial, as it did not complement VW's in-house expertise. The adoption of the AdBlue system was put aside, however, when VW appointed Winterkorn as CEO in 2007. He put VW firmly on course to develop the lean NOx trap system in order to reduce emissions. Furthermore, Winterkorn promoted Ulrich Hackenberg and Wolfgang Hatz to take charge of engine and transmission, both of whom were suspended when the diesel dispute hit the headlines.

Who is to blame?

Former employees have stated that 2008 is the critical time in which VW management would have been accountable for the scandal, as this was the year in which VW's engine and software were certified. In addition, former employees have also stated that there would have been multiple occasions for executives to notice that the software team was doubling its workload in terms of programming the engine to act differently when being tested and actually driven. So even though it is possible that a small team of managers may have orchestrated the defect device in order to develop an engine suitable for the US market, arguably management within VW should still be blamed as they were ultimately responsible for the actions of these engineers. It is also difficult to believe that a couple of rogue engineers would have taken it upon themselves to write a software program that reduced emissions when being tested, without the senior members of the team finding out. So a number of unresolved mysteries still lie at the heart of the scandal.

Conclusion

No matter who is to be blamed, Volkswagen's scandal had immediate effects on the organization's reputation and sales. It lost ground to multiple competitors, as shown by Volkswagen's fall in market share across the EU from 26.5 percent in August to 23.3 percent in September 2015. VW remains the market leader in some segments with brands such as Porsche, Audi, Skoda and SEAT still showing signs of growth. But the company has lost the trust it enjoyed among customers as well as regulators and environmentalists— some of them long-standing, loyal believers in the integrity of the VW brand. The leadership faces the challenge of devising a strategy that not only fixes the engine issues, but also creates a culture that wins back trust from both employees and consumers.

Sources: Volkswagen, *Annual Report*, 2015; R. Hotten, "Volkswagen: the scandal explained," *BBC News*, December 10, 2015; "VW crisis: 'Fewer than 10' targeted in emissions probe," *BBC News*, October 16, 2015; P. Kedrosky, "An engineering theory of the Volkswagen scandal," *New Yorker*, October 16, 2015; J. Kollewe, "Volkswagen market share declines in September," *Guardian*, October 16, 2015; R. Milne, "Culture clash gives clue to Volkswagen scandal," *Financial Times*, October 6, 2015; J. Rankin, "VW rejects call to compensate European drivers over emissions scandal," *Guardian*, January 21, 2016.

Coordinated infrastructure
An infrastructure used when there is a high degree of similarity among national markets and business units share resources in an effort to help each other raise overall sales

Market coordination infrastructure
An infrastructure used by firms that compete in similar national markets but do little resource sharing among their businesses

Internal infrastructural analysis

The second step MNEs take is to analyze how to manage their infrastructure. Prescott and Gibbons have described four types of infrastructures that can be used to compete effectively: coordinated, market coordination, resource point sharing, and autonomous.[10] The choice of infrastructure is determined by the similarity of national markets among the MNE's businesses and the extent of resource sharing across businesses.

The **coordinated infrastructure** is used when there is a high degree of similarity among national markets, and business units share resources in an effort to help each other raise overall sales. Computer firms often use this approach. Firms that compete in similar national markets but do little resource sharing among their businesses use a **market coordination infrastructure**. This approach is employed by companies that set up each operation as a separate, independent business, and sometimes by small firms that are geographically dispersed. Firms that compete in dissimilar national markets but share resources such as R&D efforts and manufacturing information use a **resource-sharing infrastructure**. Auto manufacturers use this approach. An **autonomous infrastructure** is used by MNEs that compete in dissimilar national markets and do not share resources. Highly diversified MNEs use this approach.

Resource-sharing infrastructure
An infrastructure used by firms that compete in dissimilar national markets but share resources such as R&D efforts and manufacturing information

Autonomous infrastructure
An infrastructure used by multinationals that compete in dissimilar national markets and do not share resources

Evaluating locations

The European Union is the largest market in the world, but despite the overarching institutions of the EU and the principle of the "single market," the ease of market access for foreign firms varies by industry and country location. The most important location factors tend to be: (1) access to customers, (2) quality of labor, (3) expansion prospects, (4) level of wage costs, (5) attractive environment, (6) access to suppliers, (7) non-financial regional assistance, (8) absence of restrictions for expansion, (9) infrastructure, (10) level of rents, and (11) public transportation.

Another factor often mentioned is the ease with which a company that is not doing well can withdraw. This includes laying off workers, selling facilities, and other factors involved in exiting a market.

Gathering location data and understanding negotiating terms can take a considerable amount of time, but the results often justify the investment. A great deal of useful and accessible data for market-entry evaluation is now online. The World Bank's Doing Business website provides an interactive analysis comparing countries around the world in terms of the relative ease and costs of opening, operating, and closing businesses. Table 17.3 shows how a selected set of European and other (USA and Japan) countries compare according to some key evaluation criteria.

Regional incentives

Investment incentives take a number of forms, including grants, low-interest loans, reduced land prices, and training support for personnel. For example, both Poland and Slovakia offered incentives to the South Korean auto maker Kia to lure investment for a new manufacturing plant. The Czech Republic attracted a large amount of automotive FDI in the mid-2000s and began to supplement manufacturing investment with FDI in services and R&D. In 2008 one the country's first biotechnology clusters began to develop near Prague with 20 foreign companies initiating investments.[11] CzechInvest, the country's investment-promotion agency, and other government departments use tax incentives and cheap loans to attract such investments. These extend the existing advantages of cheap land and labor (relative to western Europe) as well as access to the growing markets of eastern and central Europe.

Typically, incentives are higher when (1) the region is economically depressed, (2) many jobs are being created, (3) the company is making a large investment, and/or (4) the investment is likely to attract other investors. Before agreeing to any contract, however, it is important that the deal be "locked in" and that any repayment of subsidies be made clear up front.

STRATEGY ISSUES

We now focus on a number of strategic issues that need to be considered when doing business in the EU, including (1) an overall strategic analysis, (2) the feasibility of exporting, (3) the value of strategic acquisitions and alliances, (4) marketing considerations, (5) manufacturing approaches, and (6) management considerations. This section briefly examines each issue.

Table 17.3 Comparison of location factors

	Ease of Doing Business rank	Starting a business	Dealing with construction permits	Getting electricity	Registering property	Getting credit	Protecting minority investors	Paying taxes	Trading across borders	Enforcing contracts	Resolving insolvency
Denmark	4	25	5	14	8	23	17	12	7	34	9
Norway	6	22	27	25	5	61	12	15	24	8	8
United States	7	46	41	61	29	2	25	47	16	41	4
United Kingdom	8	45	17	70	68	17	4	16	15	36	13
Finland	9	27	33	33	38	36	76	21	14	17	1
Sweden	11	32	18	7	18	61	32	35	4	21	17
Iceland	12	31	56	9	23	52	28	46	39	3	15
Ireland	13	19	128	67	50	23	6	6	5	18	21
Germany	14	114	8	3	89	23	51	68	18	13	3
Estonia	17	26	20	56	13	23	56	28	6	32	37
Switzerland	20	69	45	5	16	52	78	18	22	22	41
Austria	21	101	78	24	35	52	32	72	19	5	16
Latvia	23	36	47	85	32	23	49	24	28	16	40
Lithuania	24	11	15	105	9	23	78	44	21	14	67
Portugal	25	10	58	47	25	89	51	64	29	27	10
Netherlands	27	21	100	90	58	71	94	23	13	19	12
Japan	29	83	83	28	73	71	35	122	20	26	2
France	31	28	86	60	126	71	17	95	10	10	22
Poland	32	85	137	64	39	17	35	87	41	52	32
Spain	33	74	105	74	66	52	30	76	30	69	23
Slovak Republic	37	77	110	100	11	36	100	100	71	55	31
Bulgaria	38	49	101	125	57	23	14	89	57	75	38
Belgium	42	14	82	99	171	89	40	81	26	10	11
Czech Republic	44	110	139	123	31	23	83	119	58	37	20
Armenia	45	4	81	131	7	36	49	41	110	119	69
Romania	48	38	140	171	63	7	40	52	65	51	46

Source: http://www.doingbusiness.org/ranking, 2015

Overall strategic analysis for the EU

In formulating a strategy for doing business in the EU, we should look at both the process of globalization through economic integration and the need for a firm's national responsiveness.[12] This is done on the matrix in Figure 17.4. The horizontal axis represents political sovereignty and the need for a firm to be nationally responsive. We call this the "national responsiveness" axis. As a political axis, it takes into account both consumer tastes and government regulations. The vertical axis, or "integration" axis, represents globalization through economic integration. This includes the need to develop economies of scale, use a value-added strategy, and reap the benefits of greater coordination and control of geographically dispersed activities.

Quadrants 1 and 4 in Figure 17.4 present relatively simple strategy situations. Quadrant 1 requires a strategy in which the MNE does not need to be concerned with national responsiveness. The company is in a market driven by high integration and its strategy must be focused on achieving price competitiveness. Firms operating in this quadrant are often centralized in structure and thus can use mergers and acquisitions to benefit from high economic integration. Companies selling microcomputers frequently operate in quadrant 1.

In quadrant 4, economic integration is less important than national responsiveness, so the MNE must focus on adapting products to satisfy the specific demands of each country. In this case, integration is minimized in favor of a decentralized strategy of national responsiveness designed to appeal to select niches and target groups. Companies selling food products and designer clothes use this approach.

In quadrant 2, there is low integration and low national responsiveness. The possibilities for obtaining economies of scale and benefits of national or regional responsiveness are small. MNEs operating in this quadrant are vulnerable to triad competitors. There is no advantage in centralized quality control or economies of scale and no ability to adapt activities to individual countries. MNEs selling inexpensive toys that are undifferentiated fall into this quadrant.

MNEs in quadrant 3 use a strategy of high integration and high national responsiveness characterized by strong price competitiveness and select target positioning. This is the

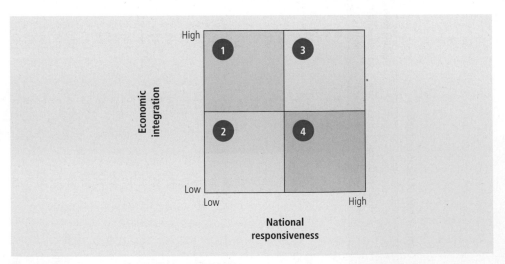

Figure 17.4 Business strategies for the EU

most challenging quadrant to implement; the firm's organization structure is complex, but it is the one in which many successful triad-based adaptive multinationals operate. Auto companies fall into this quadrant.

A close look at events in the EU reveals that Brussels' administrators designed a strategy to help European firms move into quadrant 1. The plan is designed to create a natural entry barrier to outside firms and help ensure the success of local competitors. A survey of the top management of Europe's 300 largest corporations has confirmed this tendency toward integration. The survey found that European managers anticipate greater integration due to such developments as strategic partnerships, mergers, and takeovers as well as increasing economies of scale.[13] As a result, the managers expect the development of more efficient modern industries. The survey also found that European managers were confident that economic integration was a viable strategy for them but would be detrimental to non-European MNEs. Only 9 percent of the managers believed US firms would gain ground in Europe, whereas 42 percent said US firms would lose competitive strength.

Exporting firms operate in quadrant 4. As outsiders in the EU, US firms will find it increasingly difficult to export to Europe and compete on economies of scale in the face of integration by rival EU firms. Not only will costs be higher for exporters, but locally based competitors will have more access to competitive information. As a result, today many exporting firms will be switching from exporting to FDI in order to meet the new nature of competition in Europe.

 Active learning check

Review your answer to Active Learning Case question 3 and make any changes you like. Then compare your answer to the one below.

3 **In what ways will integration and localization be important issues for conducting mergers in the EU?**

Companies successfully operating in different EU countries will seek mergers to achieve some economies of scale in R&D, design, sourcing, and distribution, among others. Nevertheless, the benefits of economies of scale have to be weighed against the need to tailor-make products for customers in different markets. Integration will therefore occur only in some sectors of the merged company.

Exporting

Those firms that continue to export to the EU will have to address a number of legal/financial matters. The following sections examine some of the most important issues (see Table 17.4).

Customs duties and taxes

Goods manufactured outside the EU are subject to customs duties at the point of entry. These duties are determined by an EU-wide tariff system that establishes common rates regardless of entry point. Most duties are based on the value of the good ad valorem, which in turn depends on the stage of assembly or completion of the end product.

Product standards

Products exported to the EU must meet standards and technical regulations. Many of these are common throughout the bloc, but when they are not the product must meet the standards

Table 17.4 Direction of EU trade

	Exports to					Imports from			
	1999		2008		2013/14	1999		2008		2013
Country/region	US$bn	% of total	US$bn	% of total	US$bn	US$bn	% of total	US$bn	% of total	US$bn
EU15	1,371.80	62.65	3,978.24	67.89	5,015.53	1,268.80	59.50	3,851.81	63.00	5,109.25
Austria	48.07	2.19	144.41	2.46	172.60	34.67	1.62	122.42	2.00	166.55
Belgium	110.80	5.06	308.87	5.27	451.92	107.88	5.05	339.99	5.56	467.83
Denmark	29.68	1.35	77.60	1.32	98.37	26.08	1.22	74.09	1.21	111.35
Finland	21.39	0.97	57.30	0.97	77.58	22.33	1.04	57.63	0.94	74.43
France	213.09	9.73	507.00	8.65	671.36	181.15	8.49	385.53	6.30	568.02
Germany	282.76	12.91	771.22	13.16	1,192.75	295.81	13.87	896.25	14.65	1,451.63
Greece	19.24	0.87	53.17	0.90	62.08	5.47	0.25	16.39	0.26	36.27
Ireland	26.78	1.22	64.37	1.09	66.00	40.78	1.91	85.21	1.39	115.33
Italy	129.82	5.92	322.23	5.49	477.29	119.26	5.59	301.23	4.92	517.63
Luxembourg	8.03	0.36	24.53	0.41	23.91	5.09	0.23	25.55	0.41	14.09
Netherlands	117.61	5.37	289.67	4.94	507.48	141.18	6.62	462.12	7.55	567.67
Portugal	32.01	1.46	64.71	1.10	75.07	19.08	0.89	37.79	0.61	62.84
Spain	104.74	4.78	258.30	4.40	333.93	74.92	3.51	190.65	3.11	311.00
Sweden	46.23	2.11	119.15	2.03	159.67	47.86	2.24	116.58	1.90	167.62
United Kingdom	181.93	8.30	375.96	6.41	645.52	147.21	6.90	274.93	4.49	476.99
Other Western Europe	92.45	4.22	213.83	3.64	286.49	89.60	4.20	264.52	4.32	375.26
Iceland	1.44	0.06	3.35	0.05	4.787	1.44	0.06	3.98	0.06	4.99
Norway	24.99	1.14	64.50	1.10	89.99	31.13	1.46	141.06	2.30	153.19
Switzerland	66.00	3.01	145.98	2.49	191.71	57.02	2.67	119.48	1.95	217.08
Developing Europe	159.40	7.27	801.80	13.68	663.07	140.10	6.57	814.10	13.31	667.49
Total Europe	1,623.65	74.15	4,993.87	85.22	5965.09	1,498.51	70.28	4,930.43	80.64	6152.00
Non-European	565.95	25.84	865.43	14.77		633.58	29.71	1,183.27	19.35	
United States	193.49	8.83	367.75	6.27	298.53	174.73	8.19	275.04	4.49	422.44
Japan	37.58	1.71	62.42	1.06	75.69	79.36	3.72	110.82	1.81	79.46
Total	2189.60	100	5859.30	100	6,224.91	2132.10	100	6113.70	100	6,292.28

Notes: EU data for 1999 is EU15, data for 2008 and 2013/14 is EU27. Exports and imports from and to the EU are intra-EU trade.

Source: Adapted from IMF, *Direction of Trade Statistics Yearbook*, 2000 and 2009; Memorandum tables, EU, page 70 (2000) and page 41 (2009); United Nations, *International Trade Statistics Yearbook*, 2014.

of the country to which it is exported. In many cases, products made in outside countries must be modified in order to gain EU entry.[14]

Conducting export operations

In recent years, many US exporters of both goods and services have consolidated their operations with those of European companies, helping them to surmount EU barriers. For example, US accounting firms typically operate through local partnerships. Other examples are management consulting firms with international operations that help address the needs of local clients and law firms with overseas offices.

Those MNEs that do choose to export to the EU must carefully select their agents and distributors. Five steps are critical to this process:

1 Examine the legal and business considerations involved in appointing foreign intermediaries and establish criteria that reflect the particular geographic market.

2 Assemble a list of potential candidates by using the various directories and consulting with other sources of information.

3 Qualify such candidates by applying certain criteria and conducting a preliminary interview.

4 Visit the proposed intermediary to obtain additional information about its resources and facilities, to get a proper feeling for the intermediary's compatibility with the organization, and to check the objectives of the agent or distributor.

5 After selecting an agent or distributor, (a) negotiate an agreement that is fair and mutually beneficial, (b) comply in good faith with the terms of the agreement, (c) continue communication between the parties, and (d) make occasional adjustments in the relationship in response to changing circumstances.

Many small and intermediate MNEs will continue to export to the EU because it is too expensive for them to use any other route. Large MNEs, on the other hand, are turning more and more to strategic acquisitions and alliances.

Strategic acquisitions and alliances

Two of the most popular ways of gaining a foothold in the EU are strategic acquisitions and alliances. (See the case **International Business Strategy in Action: Deutsche Bahn**.) A *Harvard Business Review* study analyzed 49 strategic alliances and concluded that the chances of success are improved if the parties keep five guidelines in mind: (1) acquisitions work better than alliances when developing core businesses; (2) alliances are effective when firms want to gain entry into new geographic markets or businesses that are tangential to the core business; (3) alliances between strong and weak companies typically do not work well; (4) alliances that last are characterized by an ability to move beyond the initially established expectations and objectives; and (5) alliances are more likely to be successful when both sides hold an equal amount of financial ownership. In addition, more than three-quarters of the alliances studied ended with one of the parties acquiring full control.[15]

Making strategic alliances work

It is more common to find MNEs using strategic alliances than using acquisitions. One definition suggests that these are a cooperative arrangement between two or more companies in which:

■ a common strategy is developed in unison and a win-win attitude is adopted by all parties;

■ the relationship is reciprocal, with each partner prepared to share specific strengths with the other, thus lending power to the enterprise;

■ a pooling of resources, investment and risks occurs for mutual gain.

Several important steps are involved in making these arrangements work. One is that each partner must complement the other.[16] If one company is strong in R&D and the other's strengths are in manufacturing and marketing, the alliance may be ideal. On the other hand, if both are strong in R&D and weak in manufacturing and marketing, there is no synergy and the two may end up trying to steal secrets from each other and competing rather than cooperating. Second, the goals of the two groups must be carefully spelled out. Once the partners have agreed on the primary criteria such as new product development, increased market share, and return on investment, they can then decide how to commit their resources. These goals provide a basis for overall direction.

Building working relationships across the two firms is essential for resolving problems and issues that come up. Communication, networking, and interpersonal relationships are extremely useful in ensuring that the spirit of the alliance is kept alive. Mutual understanding, trust, and compromise are important to sustaining alliances over long periods of time,

This needs to be underpinned by a reciprocal respect and understanding of the cultural differences between firms from different parts of the EU and elsewhere. (See Chapter 5 on "International Culture," including the **Active Learning Case: Cultures clash as big pharma gets bigger**.)

Marketing considerations

As the EU develops toward a true economic union, internal barriers to entry and mobility barriers within the bloc should disappear. This will create both challenges and opportunities. In particular, competition is likely to increase as it becomes easier for competitors to invade each other's territories. There is also a complex trade-off between integration and expansion, particularly as the latter encompasses a wider range of economies, institutions, and cultures, which works against some forms of standardization and harmonization.[17] As a result, marketing strategies in the future will have to reflect concern for both pricing and positioning.[18]

INTERNATIONAL BUSINESS STRATEGY IN ACTION

Deutsche Bahn: more than a railroad

Deutsche Bahn is one of the world's largest passenger, freight, and logistics companies. It has a huge passenger railroad station in the center of Berlin and has its executive training center in a Potsdam train museum. Deutsche Bahn Aktiengesellschaft (DB) was founded in 1994, and by 2001 its sales were US$14 billion. During the 2014 financial year DB Group's revenues reached approximately US$44 billion, the Group posted an EBIT of US$ 2.6 billion after adjustments for special items. It was ranked 197 on *Fortune*'s "Global 500" list.

With its head office in Berlin, DB is well known to its 12 million daily passengers who use its extensive Europe-wide train and bus network, served by over 300,000 employees, of which about 196,000 are located in Germany. DB also operates the subway (metro) system in Berlin and Hamburg, as well as many urban bus routes. Indeed, DB manages the densest and most complex rail network in the world and it is the European leader in rail freight and land transportation, beating SNCF, Trenitalia, RCA, and DHL. The rail side of its operation accounts for over 50 percent of total turnover.

Despite attempts to harmonize the rail industry across the EU, there remain many obstacles to European expansion, including the differences in fuels and safety regulations and also language barriers. As a result, rather than expanding across its borders, though there have been some exceptional success stories on that front, such as

Source: Peter Probst/Alamy Stock Photo

the Paris–Frankfurt line, DB's CEO Hartmut Mehdorn has sought to expand within the home country by attracting the potential consumer who does not yet take advantage of the train system. The strategy has been to think outside the box and look at how the train experience can become easier for passengers, businesses, and governments. For example, DB offers a car share program, a rent a car program, and even a bike rental program to its passengers. A state government, on the other hand, might turn to DB to organize its entire transportation system, including rail, subway, rapid transit, and/or buses.

But DB is much more than a railroad company. Outside of rail, which is a base for all its other operations, DB has expanded into air and sea transportation. It is this diversification, according to Mehdorn, that allowed the company to finally turn a profit in 2004, 11 years after the government changed the ownership and management structure of the company. Overall, DB logistics, with its five business units (Rail Freight, Intermodal, Land Transport, Air/Ocean Freight, and Contract Logistics/SCM), is ranked second in the world behind DHL. Including its freight part of its rail business, logistics accounts for 57 percent of the group's revenues (most of the rest is from its passenger business, which, together with air freight, is organized under the Schenker business name). In global air freight, the DB Schenker division ranks just behind DHL and ahead of UPS. Schenker is number three in global ocean freight behind DHL and Kuehne & Nagel.

DB is a home-region, not a global, company even though it operates in over 130 countries. Most of its employees work in Europe, where it has the great majority of its sales (the geographic sales of the group, by region, are not reported). Virtually all of its passenger business is in Europe, and most of its logistic business, and this was further extended by its acquisition of UK-based transport firm Arriva in 2010. The firm has, however, made some investments in North America because its Schenker division acquired the US logistics firm BAX in 2006 for $1.1 billion. In addition to its business in the United States, DB is also involved in China, where it participates in an international consortium building a new rail and road transport system. It has an 8 percent stake in the consortium, which is led by a Chinese state-owned firm, CRCT. With the expansion of the EU into eastern Europe, DB is well positioned to further develop its markets in Europe.

In summary, since the German government decided to distance itself from the management of Deutsche Bahn in 1994, the company has turned itself from a subsidized railroad system into a self-financing "mobility provider" that has now diversified into logistics, buses, sea freight, cars, and even bicycles. While, as of 2007, all of the company's shares were still owned by the government, a process of privatization has taken place since then. Both management and the government see the benefits of going public at a time when the company is well on the way to being much more than a railroad.

Sources: "Transport operator Arriva falls to Deutsche Bahn," *Guardian*, April 22, 2010; "Germany agrees to partly privatize railroad system," *DW-World.de*, November 9, 2006; "Firms seek finance to bid for Saudi project," *Gulf News*, October 5, 2007; Deutsche Bahn, *Annual Report*, 2006–10; Hoover's Online; www.db.de; Deutsche Bahn, *Facts and Figures 2014*, http://www.deutschebahn.com/en/group/ataglance/facts_figures.html; *Fortune*, "Global 500," 2015.

Pricing

The European Commission has estimated that the price of goods and services throughout the EU will decline. Five specific developments will make this work: (1) decreasing costs of doing business, now that internal barriers and restrictions have been removed; (2) the opening up of public procurement contracts to broader competition; (3) foreign investment that will increase production capacity; (4) more rigorous enforcement of competition policy; and (5) general intensified competition brought about by economic reforms.

Price will become an even more important marketing factor to the extent that EU customers develop similar tastes and are willing to accept globally standardized products. As this happens, MNEs will be able to sell the same product throughout the bloc without having to make modifications for local tastes. Unfortunately, whereas some goods can be marketed with this strategy, many will require careful positioning for select target groups.[19]

Positioning

Some global products such as Coca-Cola, Pepsi, and Marlboro cigarettes have universal appeal, but these are more the exception than the rule. For example, in the UK Renault cars are viewed as good economy cars, but in Spain they are perceived as luxury automobiles. Similarly, in the UK and the Netherlands, toothpaste is viewed as a hygiene product and sells much better than in Spain and Greece, where it is marketed as a cosmetic.

As a result, the marketing motto "Plan globally, act locally" will continue to be a useful dictum. A good example is provided by the EU cellular communications market, which offers tremendous opportunities but is also extremely competitive because there are so many submarkets throughout the community. As a result, the mobile communications market will likely end up being divided among a host of major competitors, each of which will position itself for a particular local or regional target group.

Active learning check

Review your answer to Active Learning Case question 4 and make any changes you like. Then compare your answer to the one below.

4 **In what ways are both pricing and positioning important for companies like Orange doing business in the EU?**

Companies like Orange must be prepared to take full advantage of the economies of scale created by EU integration. Production costs decline as the scale of production increases, which is only possible if sales grow. A successful strategy involves both price and cost reductions, so more customers buying more products at lower prices, allowing large-scale production economies to drive down costs and maintain profit margins. This approach, however, is only possible when customers want the same or similar products. Customization and localization erode economies of scale, but customers are still demanding variety, so firms must strike a balance, managing a product portfolio which matches market needs and optimizes the scale of production. This includes producing a range of relatively standardized products for mass EU markets and a range of products customized for individual EU countries where customers in those countries are willing to pay higher prices for this localization.

Direct marketing

Another strategy likely to receive a great deal of attention is direct marketing. Most EU firms tailor their products to narrow markets and direct mail is only now gaining attention. Unlike the United States, where businesses have been using telemarketing and other non-traditional channels for well over a decade, this is a new approach for European consumers, and MNEs will have to surmount a number of challenges if they hope to direct-market their products, such as: (1) consumers speak different languages, so a universal message or strategy will not work throughout the bloc; (2) inclusion of direct-response telephone numbers in television spots is forbidden by the privacy laws of some member states such as Germany; and (3) information about potential clients is fragmented and not easily obtainable. In addition, a high credit card fraud rate has slowed down the growth potential of e-commerce. Nevertheless, direct marketing is likely to play a major role in MNE efforts to create a pan-European marketing strategy.

One study proposes that the overall convergence associated with European market integration will lead firms to emphasize three advertising strategies: creating a uniform brand image, appealing to cross-market segments, and increasing cost performance in advertising.[20]

Manufacturing considerations

As individual country regulations are eliminated and EU members continue to standardize rules and regulations, it will be possible to produce uniform goods for the entire market. This will not come about immediately because of the time needed to change such things as electric systems so that toasters, television sets, and other home appliances can all be manufactured with the same type of plug. However, MNEs will eventually be able to produce many products with standard parts that work in all EU countries. At the same time, manufacturers will continue producing goods that appeal to local market tastes. For example, appliance makers now manufacture self-cleaning ovens for the French because of their tradition of high-temperature cooking. However, they typically leave out this option for the German market, where food is generally cooked at lower temperatures. Some major manufacturing considerations that warrant attention by those doing business in the EU include reducing costs, building factory networks, and entering into R&D alliances.

Reducing costs

There are now over 500 million consumers in Europe and their expenditure represents over half of the EU's GDP. One manufacturing benefit of producing for this size of market is the ability to reduce cost per unit through the use of standardized components and large production runs. Economies of scale are possible, with the cost of components kept to a minimum and large production runs allowing companies to spread fixed costs over more units. This means the cost per item can be sharply reduced. Moreover, economies of scale can be achieved even when production has to be tailored to local conditions. This is accomplished through the use of **delayed differentiation**, in which all products are manufactured in the same way for all countries or regions as late as possible in the assembly process. In these final stages, differentiation is then used to introduce particular features or special components.

Delayed differentiation
A strategy in which all products are manufactured in the same way for all countries or regions as late as possible in the assembly process, at which time differentiation is used to introduce particular features or special components

MNEs also use outsourcing and just-in-time inventory systems to lower the cost of carrying parts and supplies. By tailoring deliveries and shipments to the production schedule, factories are able to minimize their investment in materials and work-in-process. This system is also used by large retailers such as Marks & Spencer in the UK, which employs its electronic network system to keep track of inventory at each store in England, as well as on the continent, and to replenish its outlets as needed.

Another way in which costs are being controlled is by redesigning production processes, thus scrapping old, inefficient techniques in favor of more streamlined methods. This includes careful study of competitive firms in order to identify and copy their successful approaches to cost control. It also entails the elimination of red tape and the use of well-trained, highly motivated work teams.

Factory networks

MNEs in Europe have developed sophisticated networks of factories that both produce components and finished goods and provide distribution and after-sales services. For example, the Philips television factory in Bruges, Belgium, uses tubes that are supplied from a factory in Germany, transistors from France, plastics produced in Italy, and electronic components that come from another factory in Belgium.

These factory networks are also integrated with computer software packages that can operate in multiple European countries without the need for modification. The software packages allow companies to make supply, production, and distribution decisions while satisfying the requirements of the different legal entities in the countries where they operate. Some specific functions they help companies to perform include forecasting, logistics planning, inventory planning, production planning, and central updating of bills of materials. The software provides each factory manager with the specific information needed and does so in the manager's own language. As a result, MNEs are able to coordinate multiple activities and thereby develop an effective pan-European manufacturing system.

R&D alliances

Another emerging manufacturing strategy is participation in cooperative R&D programs. In the EU this is taking two complementary paths. First, many companies are teaming up to share R&D expenses. Siemens and Philips have used this approach to develop computer chips, and IBM has a number of agreements with European firms for developing advanced computer technology.

Second, many firms are trying to get some of these costs funded by participating in European cooperative R&D programs. The EU provides European industry with funding for research in such areas as information technology, biotechnology, and energy. The objective of the program is to stimulate cross-border cooperation and make Europe more productive and competitive in the world market. One of the best-known programs is the **European Research Cooperation Agency** (Eureka, for short), which was launched in 1985 and emphasizes projects in the fields of energy, medicine, biotechnology, communications, information technology, transport, new materials, robotics, production automation, lasers, and the environment.[21] This program has helped develop a European standard for high-definition television (HDTV) and has funded semiconductor research. A central aim is to meet the European objective of raising investment in R&D. EU funding for large-scale projects and coordination across member states also drives economies of scale in R&D, to allow countries to compete in science and technology development with the USA, Japan, and China. Firms that are interested in participating in these cooperative programs typically do so by carrying out six steps:

European Research Cooperation Agency
A research and development alliance that emphasizes projects in the fields of energy, medicine, biotechnology, communications, information technology, transport, new materials, robotics, production automation, lasers, and the environment

1 Find out if the company is eligible for EU-funded programs.

2 Carefully study the EU rules regarding rights of ownership and dissemination of results.

3 Carefully choose the best location for a European R&D center.

4 Determine those competitors and major customers that are already participating in the program.

5 Gather recommendations from the firm's EU and local management.

6 Put together the company's application for funding.

Management considerations

As more firms enter the EU, there is growing concern over their ability to manage Europeans effectively. Many firms enter the market with preconceived ideas about how to interact with their European partners or employees. Some, for example, believe that management styles that have been effective in their country will also work well in Europe. However, as the Japanese have discovered in the United States, effective management approaches must be tailor-made to meet the needs of the local situation. The primary focus must be on adjusting to cultural differences.

Adjusting to cultural differences

There are a number of differences between US and European workers. For example, Europeans are more accustomed to participating in decision making. They have a long history of worker participation programs and of holding seats on the board of directors.

Another difference is employee motivation. Researchers have found that quality of work life is extremely important in Scandinavian countries, whereas opportunities for individual achievement are of particular importance in the UK. French workers are interested in individual achievement but place strong emphasis on security. German workers place a high value on both advancement and earnings.[22] Clearly, no universal list of motivators can be applied throughout the EU. These facts illustrate the importance of MNEs having a global perspective as well as having managers who are focused on the country-specific needs of the area in which they are working.

Barriers to EU market access

Throughout this book, we have explored the need for access to triad markets. Although the EU has become the world's largest market, some EU-based MNEs and governments have sought to restrict access to this area. The overall trend during the postwar period has been toward an increasingly liberalized trade environment, but international managers nonetheless must know how to deal with, or at least anticipate, the use of administrative barriers in foreign markets.

Countervailing duty (CVD)
Import tariff intended to protect domestic producers from harmful subsidization by foreign governments

Anti-dumping duty (AD)
Import tariff intended to protect domestic producers from foreign products sold at less than their cost of production or at lower prices than in their home market

The two most common trade law entry barriers are **countervailing duty (CVD)** laws and **anti-dumping duty (AD)** laws. (These were discussed earlier in Chapters 6 and 10.) While the United States uses CVD as an entry barrier (it had 90 percent of the world's CVD cases in the 1980s), the EU uses AD. Both CVD and AD are import tariffs intended to protect domestic producers from harmful dumping and subsidization by foreign governments. However, it has been demonstrated in several studies that these laws have been "captured" and used by weak firms seeking shelter from strong competition by rival MNEs in the triad.[23]

Table 17.5 shows both the high number of AD cases that were launched and the tendency toward sectoral concentration in the use of AD by EU firms during the period from 2006 to 2014. Many AD cases were brought in the chemical, electronics, iron and steel, and other "mature" sectors that have weak firm-specific advantages (FSAs).

Figure 17.6 shows the rationale for the use of AD and CVD laws by particular firms. As with all free market economies, the EU economy has, at any given point in time, a significant number of firms in difficulty due to the pressure of global competition. These firms are barely able to compete with their more efficient global rivals and find themselves on the verge of exit from the industry. If the main reason for this is international competition, and domestic administrative instruments are in place that would allow such a firm to continue operating by limiting foreign competition, the company is likely to use these instruments. Such a situation is a rare instance when it is logical for a firm to spend time and money on an activity that is not productive from a competitiveness standpoint. By using AD or CVD laws, the uncompetitive firm is able to remain in operation not by improving its firm-specific advantages, but by artificially raising the price at which foreign competitors must sell in the domestic market.

Table 17.5 EU anti-dumping cases investigated by sector, 2006–14

	2006	2007	2008	2009	2010	2011	2012	2013	2014
Chemical and allied	13	2	0	9	7	11	0	1	2
Textiles and allied	2	0	0	3	0	0	0	3	0
Wood and paper	0	0	0	0	2	0	0	0	0
Electronics	5	0	0	1	2	0	2	0	0
Other mechanical engineering	2	0	1	1	1	1	1	0	0
Iron and steel	0	6	11	4	3	6	11	1	9
Others, metal	9	0	5	1	0	1	0	0	3
Other	5	1	3	2	3	2	5	4	2
All products listed	**36**	**9**	**20**	**21**	**18**	**21**	**19**	**9**	**16**
of which anti-dumping	35	9	18	15	15	17	13	4	14
of which anti-subsidy	1	0	2	6	3	4	6	5	2

Source: http://trade.ec.europa.eu/doclib/docs/2014/december/tradoc_152994.pdf

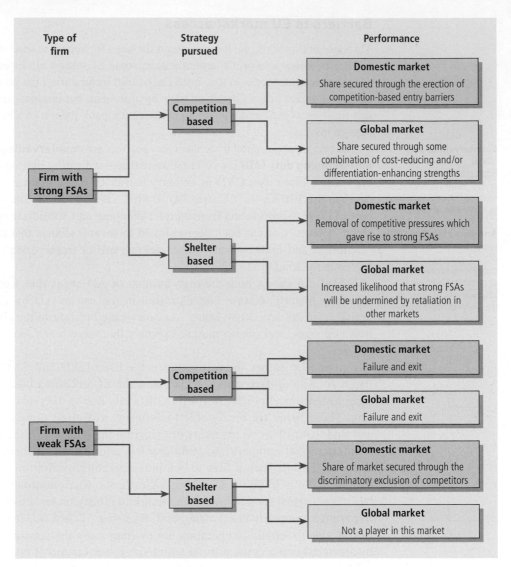

Figure 17.5 Competition and shelter-based strategies

The abusive use of AD and CVD is a particular problem for non-triad members and for MNEs from other parts of the triad because the administration of these trade laws is discretionary and subject to political pressures. Moreover, there is now strong evidence that the administration of these trade laws is biased in favor of domestic plaintiffs and against foreign firms.[24] The technical test of "material injury" due to the subsidies or dumped exports is routinely abused by the responsible administrative agencies in both the EU and the United States. This is an extremely serious problem for global business and serves to reinforce the existence of the triad at the expense of a liberalized world trade and investment system.

KEY POINTS

1 The overall objective of the EU is to create a market in which there are no economic barriers to trade between the member countries. When this is achieved, the EU will be the largest economic bloc in the world. However, there are two areas in particular in which additional progress must be made: free movement of goods and the practice of government procurement. In addition, many new entrants into the EU (and a few of the original members) have yet to be integrated in terms of adopting the euro and are not yet allowed free movement of labor and passport-free travel. They also threaten the possibility of a unified regional foreign policy.

2 The current competitive status of the EU lags that of the United States and Japan in a number of areas, including productivity, investment spending, and education. Greater economic strides will be needed if the region is to compete effectively with its triad counterparts.

3 In preparing to do business in the EU, MNEs should focus on the competitive nature of the targeted industry and the evaluation of location. Competitive intelligence gathering involves external information gathering and internal infrastructural analysis. Location evaluation entails the consideration of such factors as regional incentives, operating costs, and distance from major markets.

4 Many aspects of strategy need to be considered when doing business in the EU, including (a) an overall analysis of the environment, (b) the feasibility of exporting, (c) the value of strategic alliances and acquisitions, (d) marketing considerations, (e) manufacturing approaches, and (f) management considerations. Managers need to weigh the choices of economic integration and/or national responsiveness very carefully.

5 The EU has a large internal market. Firms located in the EU can use non-tariff barriers to entry to keep out rival firms: namely, trade remedy legislation such as countervailing duty (CVD) laws and anti-dumping (AD) laws. Recent research has found that the use of both CVD and AD is a "shelter" strategy designed to protect uncompetitive domestic firms. However, the more successful EU firms concentrate on the development of sustainable firm-specific advantages rather than on the use of CVD and AD laws.

Key terms

- Council of Ministers
- Single European Market (SEM)
- coordinated infrastructure
- market coordination infrastructure
- resource-sharing infrastructure
- autonomous infrastructure
- delayed differentiation
- European Research Cooperation Agency
- countervailing duty (CVD)
- anti-dumping duty (AD)

REVIEW AND DISCUSSION QUESTIONS

1 What are the ultimate objectives of the EU? Identify and describe them.

2 What is the Single European Market and how does it benefit EU firms?

3 What is the competitive status of the main EU economies in terms of labor productivity and investment spending? Based on your answer, what is your overall evaluation of this status?

▶

4 How can firms doing business in the EU use competitive intelligence? Identify and describe two major steps that can be used in this process.

5 What types of regional incentives do countries offer MNEs willing to set up operations in their locales? Identify and describe two of them.

6 In addition to regional incentives, what other evaluation criteria should MNEs employ when deciding where in the EU to establish operations? Identify and describe three of them.

7 In formulating a strategy for doing business in the EU, there are two primary areas of initial consideration: national responsiveness and economic integration. What does this statement mean? Be sure to include a discussion of Figure 17.4 in your answer.

8 What do companies that want to export to the EU need to know about doing business there? Discuss five facts or strategies that would be of value to them.

9 In gaining a foothold in the EU, when is it most effective to opt for an acquisition over an alliance? When is a strategic alliance a better choice? In each case, provide an example.

10 Why will marketing strategies in the EU have to reflect a concern for pricing? A concern for positioning? Give an example of when each would be the most important consideration.

11 What is the likely future of direct marketing in the EU? Defend your answer.

12 What are three major manufacturing considerations for companies doing business in the EU? Identify and describe each.

13 How important is it for EU managers to have a global perspective?

14 How can trade laws be used by EU firms to keep out global competitors?

15 What evidence is there that EU firms use anti-dumping laws?

16 The EU has accepted a number of new members into the union over the course of its development. Are these members fully integrated? What problems might we envisage from new members in the future?

17 How are new entrants into the union likely to affect employment in the EU?

REAL CASE

Accor budget hotels

The largest manager of budget-priced hotels in the world is the French company Accor. In 2014 it owned over 3,717 hotels in 90 countries under the brands Sofitel, Pullman, Novotel, Mercure, Suitehotel, All Seasons, Ibis, Etap Hotel, Formule 1, and Motel 6, and its related activities, Thalassa Sea & Spa and Lenôtre, with a portfolio ranging from luxury to budget class. With a workforce of 180,000 employees, Accor generated revenues of just over US$6 billion in 2014. A total of 42 percent of its hotels were located in France, 24 percent in the rest of Europe, 17 percent in Asia–Pacific and 15 percent

in the rest of world. Accor is a home-region firm with focus on Europe, where almost 70 percent of its total sales are made.

The Accor Group has developed international capabilities, however, as a major service provider to the tourist, business travel, and food business sectors. It is developing an international brand name for the Group's activities in these areas and uses B2B and B2C internet services extensively for the purposes of promotion and managing partnerships. There are 860,000 restaurant managers, supermarket suppliers,

Table 17.6 Accor Hotel portfolio by region, 2014

	Managed		Franchised		HotelInvest (owned and leased)		Total	
	No. of hotels	No. rooms	No. of hotels	No. rooms	No. of hotels	No. rooms	No. of hotels	No. rooms
France	104	12,923	948	70,162	510	57,833	1,562	140,918
Europe	104	14,685	265	29,317	533	80,415	902	124,417
Africa, Middle East, Mediterranean	120	23,921	85	8,964	147	20,097	352	52,982
Asia Pacific	403	89,205	150	18,247	68	10,566	621	118,008
Americas	126	21,437	58	6,967	96	17,567	280	45,971
Total	857	162,171	1,506	133,657	1,354	186,468	3,717	482,296

and other affiliated workers using its B2B services, along with another 300,000 customers/small-business people using B2C.

The company began operations in 1967 and rapidly expanded its Novotel hotels across France. The acquisition of another hotel chain in 1974, Courtepaille, established Accor as a major player in the French market. During the next two years the company moved to develop a market presence in the two- and three-star hotel market segment, opening an Ibis two-star hotel in Bordeaux and acquiring the three-star Mercure hotel chain.

The first significant expansion outside France was the 1973 opening of Novotel in Warsaw, Poland. In 1976, Accor opened its first hotel in Brazil and over the next year it began to rapidly develop in Latin America. In 1979, Accor entered the US market with hotels in Minneapolis and New York; in 1984 a large Novotel was erected in Broadway. To enter the affordable US hotel market, the Motel 6 chain was purchased in 1990. By acquiring Sofitel in 1980 the company entered the African market and strengthened its position in Europe. In 1986, Accor began development in Asia, including China and Thailand. In preparation for the 2008 Olympic Games, Accor entered a joint venture with the Beijing Tourism Group to manage 50 hotels.

Accor is also in the travel business. In France it owns Carlson Wagonlit Travel and Frantour. Acquiring international travel companies has allowed Accor to complement its international hotel expansion plans. The acquisition of Africatours in 1984 allowed Accor to control the stream of tourism in the region. In 1987, Africatours acquired Asia Tours and America Tours. In 2000, Accor purchased a 38.5 percent stake in Go Voyages, an e-travel planner that targets the European traveler. Growing expertise in the hospitality business has also allowed the company to diversify

into other areas, including restaurants and casinos. Table 17.6 shows the global spread of Accor hotels by region and brand.

A report by Datamonitor outlined the Accor Group's main strengths and weakness in 2008. Strengths include: a wide range of product and service offerings, an improving financial position, and a strong focus on customer service. Weaknesses include: underperforming assets, an overdependence on hotels (65 percent of revenues), and a geographic concentration in Europe (75 percent of revenues). The recovering European hotel industry, current expansion in China and India, and the recovering business travel market are all opportunities for the Group. These are offset by the growing range of competitors, particularly in the low-cost travel and leisure segments.

Websites: www.accorhotels.com; www.accor.com; www.fourseasons.com; www.sixcontinents.com

Sources: www.accorhotels.com; Raphael Minder, "Accor may have to rethink casino offer," *Financial Times*, January 3, 2002; Raphael Minder, "Accor to acquire casino group for E258m," *Financial Times*, December 17, 2001; "Casinos on threshold of recomposition," *La Tribune*, January 3, 2002; "Accor agrees Chinese JV to manage around 50 hotels by 2008," *AFX Europe*, December 12, 2001; Anaïs Jouvancy, "European E-travel takes off," *Le Monde Interactif*, November 8, 2000; Accor SA, *Annual Report*, 2010, 2014; Thomson Reuters, *OneSource*, 2011; www.datamonitor.com

1 Why did Accor concentrate on the French and European markets before expanding into other regions?

2 How are acquisitions an important part of Accor's expansion strategy?

3 What are the advantages of increasingly relying on the internet for B2B and B2C?

REAL CASE

Carrefour

French retail giant Carrefour ("crossroads" in French) is the number one retailer in Europe and number two in the world. In 2014, Carrefour made approximately 55 percent of its sales in Europe, but it had 10,860 stores spread throughout 33 countries on four continents, with revenues of US$110 billion and a workforce of 381,227 employees. In 2014, Carrefour SA's total revenue increased by 2.9 percent in comparison to 2013.

Saturated domestic markets, economic growth in Asia and eastern Europe, and improvements in transportation systems are all factors driving large retailers to expand abroad, with mixed success. Tesco has moved into China and the United States, Carrefour has pulled out of some eastern European countries in order to focus on expansion in China, and Wal-Mart is pushing for growth in a range of new markets.

Carrefour SA is a France-based company that is primarily engaged in retail distribution. It operates a network of hypermarkets, supermarkets, hard discount stores, convenience stores, and cash-and-carry outlets, and offers e-commerce services. The company's hypermarkets, Carrefour and Atacadão, offer a range of food and non-food products. Carrefour SA's supermarket chains include, among others, Champion and Norte brands, which primarily offer food, clothing, and household goods. The company's hard discount stores include Dia, Ed, and Minipreço, offering products at discount prices. Its convenience stores, such as Shopi and 8 à Huit, offer a range of convenience products and services. Carrefour SA's cash-and-carry stores, Promocash, Gross, and Docks Market, offer wholesale products for businesses. As of December 31, 2014, the company was 8.11 percent owned by Blue Partners.

Anyone observing Carrefour over the last three decades must concede that international expansion is a key part of its strategic plan. Despite this, in 2008, 47 percent of its sales were in France alone and 81 percent in Europe. The 19 percent of sales outside the region were evenly divided across Asia and Latin America. By 2014, 35 percent of its sales were in France and 55 percent in Europe, 14 percent in Latin America, and 6 percent in Asia. Carrefour is under pressure in its home market of France as rivals keep prices low to gain market share.

In 1996, the French government introduced the "Raffarin law" to restrict the expansion of hypermarkets, with the aim of keeping the French countryside from turning into large warehouse-style retail structures. This in turn would protect the French way of life, in which local food farmers supply small local shops. For Carrefour, this meant that growth of its hypermarket business could come only from acquisitions in its local market or from expanding into foreign markets. Its success at following this strategy has varied considerably because of different competitive environments and cultural differences across regions.

In the United States, Carrefour opened three hypermarkets in Pennsylvania and closed them as a result of local competition. In its home region of Europe, however, Carrefour is the number one retailer in Spain, Portugal, and Greece, and the second largest in Italy.

Carrefour was the first Western hypermarket company to expand into the Asian market in the mid-1990s. By 2001 it was the third largest retailer in China and had operations in Thailand and Japan. The company gambled that Asian customers would be willing to move from their traditional outdoor markets to purchase at air-conditioned and "all under one roof" hypermarkets. These hypermarkets rely on local suppliers that can offer products at the same price level as those supplied to the local competition and cater to the tastes of locals. For their part, local suppliers are all too ready to enter contracts with Carrefour, which promises to put their products on shelves across the Asian region. Moreover, where local contacts are not readily available or insufficient, Carrefour's competitive advantage comes from its economies of scale, centralized purchasing, and power over the supply chain, plus operations and logistics efficiencies.

Because products are offered in a comfortable environment at competitive prices, the local competition is nothing to worry about. In fact, Carrefour is more concerned about competition from other Western retailers such as Wal-Mart

Source: Craig Joiner Photography/Alamy Stock Photo

and Tesco. Tesco and Carrefour raced to open the first hypermarket in the Thai market and basically tied. Both their hypermarkets faced each other in a busy Bangkok street. If they want to survive in the long haul, however, Western companies should always be wary of potential local or regional competitors. In Hong Kong, where Jardine Matheson and Li Ka-shing dominate the market, Carrefour was forced to close operations. The group now sees strong potential for further international growth in the large national markets of China, Brazil, Indonesia, Poland, and Turkey.

But the benefits of international expansion are not completely clear. Carrefour and other large retailers have tended to enjoy higher operating margins in their domestic markets. They have also struggled to leverage scale economies on a global basis because, in order to cater to local tastes, hypermarkets must purchase from local producers. Indeed, in November 2010, Carrefour announced the signing of an agreement with Big C, a subsidiary of Groupe Casino (France), for the divestment of its operations in Thailand for an enterprise value of Ä868 million. Carrefour plans to sell 19 stores in Malaysia and two in Singapore; it shut down its Xi'an outlet in China's Shaanxi Province in July 2010.

On the other hand, Carrefour SA announced the opening of its first Cash & Carry Store in India in December 2010. With a sales area of 5,200 m^2, this store, located east of New Delhi in the Shahdara neighborhood, will offer more than 10,000 stockkeeping units in food and non-food to professional businesses, institutions, restaurants, and local retailers. Carrefour had opened three supermarkets by the end of 2010 and two hypermarkets in 2011 in Romania. The supermarkets were opened in the capital, Bucharest, in the southern town of Târgoviște, and in the northwestern town of Cluj. The hypermarkets slated for a 2011 launch were located in Bucharest and in the northern town of Botoșani.

Since 2011, shares in Carrefour have gradually been falling since Europe's biggest retailer issued a warning that profits in its core French market were set to fall, as it is facing fierce competition from rivals in France.

Sources: www.carrefour.com; "Wal-Mart, Tesco and Carrefour do battle in the East: international retailers find mixed fortunes in their expansion strategies," *Strategic Direction,* vol. 24, no. 2 (2008), pp. 5–7; Peter Child, "Lessons from a global retailer: an interview with the President of Carrefour China," *McKinsey Quarterly,* special edition, 2006, pp. 70–81; Carrefour, *Annual Report,* 2008–14; "French fusion," *The Economist,* September 2, 1999; "A hypermarket," *The Economist,* April 5, 2001; Thomson Reuters, *OneSource,* 2011; "Carrefour shares fall after profit warning," *BBC News,* June 17, 2011.

1 How can Carrefour compete with local retailers in North America?

2 How can Carrefour compete with local retailers in Asia?

3 What strategy does Carrefour need to succeed in Europe?

4 What is Carrefour's basic strategy and structure?

5 Should Carrefour and other large retailers even attempt to expand internationally?

NOTES

1 http://europa.eu/index_en.htm (2016); Spyros G. Makridakis and Michelle Bainbridge, "Evolution of the Single Market," in Spyros G. Makridakis (ed.), *Single Market Europe: Opportunities and Challenges for Business* (San Francisco: Jossey-Bass, 1991), p. 9.

2 Also see Trevor Merriden, "How 'single' is the Single Market?" *Management Review* (March 1998), pp. 27–31.

3 Edmund L. Andrews, "11 countries tie Europe together in one currency," *New York Times,* January 1, 1999, pp. A1, 8.

4 John Grahl and Paul Teague, "Problems of financial integration in the EU," *Journal of European Public Policy,* vol. 12, no. 6 (2005), pp. 1005–21.

5 "EU allies unite against Iraq War," *BBC News,* January 22, 2003.

6 Adriaan J. Schout and Andrew J. Jordan, "From cohesion to territorial policy integration: exploring the governance challenges in the European Union," *European Planning Studies,* vol. 15, no. 6 (2007), pp. 835–51.

7 "Rebels with a cause," *The Economist,* August 3, 2008; "The shape of things to come," *The Economist,* June 23, 2005.

8 "GM creates Europe-wide management," *BBC News,* June 18, 2004.

9 Richard Wray, "Apple reveals UK iPad prices," *Guardian,* May 7, 2010.

10 John E. Prescott and Patrick T. Gibbons, "Europe '92 provides new impetus for competitive intelligence," *Journal of Business Strategy* (November/December 1991), pp. 20–6.

11 "Czech Republic: investment regulations," Economist Intelligence Unit, January 11, 2011, http://www.eiu.com

12 Robert Pearce and Julia Manea, "MNEs' strategies in central and eastern Europe: key elements of subsidiary behaviour," *Management International Review (MIR),* vol. 46, no. 2 (2006), pp. 235–55; Alan M. Rugman and Alain Verbeke, "Europe 1992 and competitive strategies for North American firms," *Business Horizons* (November/December 1991), pp. 76–81.

13 Ibid., p. 78.

14 For more specifics on standards, see www.eurunion.org/eu/

15 Joel Bleeke and David Ernst, "The way to win in cross-border alliances," *Harvard Business Review,* vol. 69, no. 6 (1991), pp. 127–8. See also: *Harvard Business Review on Strategic Alliances* (Cambridge, MA: Harvard Business School Press, 2003).

16 Reshma H. Shah and Vanitha Swaminathan, "Factors influencing partner selection in strategic alliances: the moderating role of alliance context," *Strategic Management Journal*, vol. 29, no. 5 (2008), pp. 471–94; "Strategic alliance: alliances are often said to be like marriages," *The Economist*, November 10, 2009.

17 Stanley Paliwoda, "The marketing challenges within the enlarged Single European Market," *European Journal of Marketing*, vol. 41, nos. 3/4 (2007), pp. 233–44.

18 Urša Golob and Kiement Podnar, "Competitive advantage in the marketing of products within the enlarged European Union," *European Journal of Marketing*, vol. 41, nos. 3/4 (2007), pp. 245–56.

19 Graham Hooley, Brigitte Nicoulaud, and Nigel F. Piercy, *Marketing Strategy and Competitive Positioning*, 5th ed. (Harlow: Financial Times/Prentice Hall, 2011).

20 Shintaro Okazaki, Charles R. Taylor, and Jonathan P. Doh, "Market convergence and advertising standardization in the European Union," *Journal of World Business*, vol. 42, no. 4 (2007), pp. 384–400.

21 See http://www.eurekanetwork.org

22 For more on the cultural differences across Europe, and their consequences, go to Chapter 5.

23 The theory of shelter has been developed in Alan M. Rugman and Alain Verbeke, *Global Competitive Strategy and Trade Policy* (London: Routledge, 1990). A study on the use of EC trade law measures as a shelter strategy is that by Alan M. Rugman and Michael Gestrin, "EC anti-dumping laws as a barrier to trade," *European Management Journal*, vol. 9, no. 4 (1991), pp. 475–82. Related data and analysis of EC trade law cases are reported in Patrick A. Messerlin, "Anti-dumping regulations or procartel law? The EC chemical case," *World Economy*, vol. 13, no. 4 (1990), pp. 465–92.

24 For an overall discussion of triad power and the use of trade laws as barriers to entry, see Francis G. Snyder, *Regional and Global Regulation of International Trade* (London: Hart Publishing, 2002); David Coen, Wyn Grant, and Graham Wilson, *The Oxford Handbook of Business and Government*, Oxford Handbooks in Business and Management (Oxford: Oxford University Press, 2010). Also: Chris Turner and Jacqueline Martin, *Key Facts EU Law*, 3rd ed. (London: Hodder Education, 2011).

BIBLIOGRAPHY

Archibugi, Daniele, and Filippetti, Andrea. *Innovation and Economic Crisis: Lessons and Prospects from the Economic Downturn*, Routledge Studies in Global Competition (London: Routledge, 2011).

Asmussen, Christian Geisler, Pedersen, Torben, and Dhanaraj, Charles. "Host-country environment and subsidiary competence: extending the Diamond Network Model," *Journal of International Business Studies*, vol. 40, no. 1 (2009).

Blevins, Dane P., et al. "Institutional changes within the European Union: how global cities and regional integration affect MNE entry decisions," *Journal of World Business*, vol. 51, no. 2 (2016).

Böhm, Hans, and Scholz, Christian. *Human Resource Management in Europe: Comparative Analysis and Contextual Understanding* (London: Taylor and Francis, 2008).

Brennan, Louis. *The Emergence of Southern Multinationals: Their Impact on Europe* (Basingstoke: Palgrave Macmillan, 2010).

Brenner, Steffen. "Self-disclosure at international cartels," *Journal of International Business Studies*, vol. 42, no. 2, (2011).

Colantone, Italo, and Sleuwaegen, Leo. "International trade, exit and entry: a cross-country and industry analysis," *Journal of International Business Studies*, vol. 41, no. 7 (2010).

Curran, Louise, and Zignago, Soledad. "EU enlargement and the evolution of European production networks," *Research in International Business and Finance*, vol. 26, no. 2 (2012).

Dunning, John H. "The contribution of British scholarship to international business studies," *International Business Review*, vol. 13, no. 2 (April 2004).

Dunning, John H. "Review of *European Union and the Race for Foreign Direct Investment in Europe*," *Journal of International Business Studies*, vol. 37, (2006).

Filatotchev, Igor, and Piesse, Jenifer. "R&D, internationalization and growth of newly listed firms: European evidence," *Journal of International Business Studies*, vol. 40, no. 8 (2009).

Greenaway, David. *The World Economy: Global Trade Policy*, World Economy Special Issues (Oxford: Wiley-Blackwell, 2010).

Guerrieri, Paolo, and Caffarelli, Filippo Vergara. "Trade openness and international fragmentation of production in the European Union: the new divide?," *Review of International Economics*, vol. 20, no. 3 (2012).

Johnson, Debra. *European Business*, 2nd ed. (London: Taylor & Francis, 2009).

Kahancová, Marta. "One company, four factories: coordinating employment flexibility practices with local trade unions," *European Journal of Industrial Relations*, vol. 13, no. 1 (March 2007).

Lawton, Thomas C. "Evaluating European competitiveness: measurements and models for a successful business environment," *European Business Journal*, vol. 11, no. 4 (1999).

Lowson, Robert. "Analyzing the effectiveness of European retail sourcing strategies," *European Management Journal*, vol. 19, no. 5 (October 2001).

Mayrhofer, Ulrike. "Franco-British strategic alliances: a contribution to the study of intra-European partnerships," *European Management Journal*, vol. 20, no. 1 (February 2002).

Nitsch, Detlev, Beamish, Paul, and Makino, Shige. "Entry mode and performance of Japanese FDI in western Europe," *Management International Review*, vol. 36, no. 1 (1996).

Pelkmans, Jacques. "Making EU network markets competitive," *Oxford Review of Economic Policy*, vol. 17, no. 3 (fall 2001).

Radosevic, Slavo, and Kaderabkova, Anna. *Challenges for European Innovation Policy: Cohesion and Excellence from a Schumpeterian Perspective* (Cheltenham: Edward Elgar, 2011).

Reynaud, Emmanuelle, et al. "The differences in values between managers of the European founding countries, the new members and the applicant countries: societal orientation or financial orientation?," *European Management Journal*, vol. 25, no. 2 (April 2007).

Rugman, Alan M., and Collinson, Simon. "Multinational enterprises in the new Europe: are they really global?," *Organizational Dynamics*, vol. 34, no. 3 (2005).

Rugman, Alan M., and Oh, Chang Hoon. "Regional integration and the international strategies of large European firms," *International Business Review*, vol. 20 (2011).

Rugman, Alan M., Theil, Rita, and Verbeke, Alain. "Entry barriers and bank strategies for the Europe 1992 financial directives," *European Management Journal*, vol. 10, no. 3 (September 1992).

Rugman, Alan M., and Verbeke, Alain. "Environmental change and global competitive strategy in Europe." In Alan M. Rugman and Alain Verbeke (eds.), *Research in Global Strategic Management*, Vol. 2: *Global Competition and the European Community* (Greenwich, CT: JAI Press, 1991).

Rugman, Alan M., and Verbeke, Alain (eds.). *Research in Global Strategic Management*, Vol. 2: *Global Competition and the European Community* (Greenwich, CT: JAI Press, 1991).

Rugman, Alan M. and Verbeke, Alain. "Competitive strategies for non-European firms." In B. Burgenmeier and J. L. Mucchielli (eds.), *Multinationals and Europe 1992: Strategies for the Future* (London and New York: Routledge, 1991).

Rugman, Alan M., and Verbeke, Alain. "Europe 1992 and competitive strategies for North American firms," *Business Horizons*, vol. 34, no. 6 (November/December 1991).

Rugman, Alan M., Yip, George, and Jayaratne, Saliya. "A note on the return on foreign assets and foreign presence for UK multinationals," *British Journal of Management*, vol. 19, no. 2 (2008).

Rugman, Alan M., Yip, George, and Kudina, Alina. "The international success of British companies," *Long Range Planning*, vol. 39, vol. 3 (June 2006).

Schmitt, Alexander, and Johannes Van Biesebroeck. "Proximity strategies in outsourcing relations: the role of geographical, cultural and relational proximity in the European automotive industry," *Journal of International Business Studies*, vol. 44, no. 5 (2013).

Ueltschy, Linda C., Laroche, Michel, Rita, Paulo, and Bocaranda, Claudia. "A pan-European approach to customer satisfaction: an optimal strategy?" *Multinational Business Review*, vol. 16, no. 3 (2008), pp. 41–71.

Yip, George, Rugman, Alan M., and Kudina, Alina. "International success of British companies," *Long Range Planning*, vol. 39, no. 3 (2006).

Chapter 18

JAPAN

Contents

Objectives of the chapter

Japan is arguably the odd one out of the three triad regions of the world. Political, social, cultural, and economic differences underpin its unique business infrastructure and the strengths and weaknesses of its firms, relative to competitors from elsewhere. Historically it has undergone a period of unprecedented growth and internationalization and more recently recession, and this process of change helps explain this uniqueness. To understand what is so unusual about the current period for Japan, and why the ongoing corporate restructuring is so fundamental, we need to understand something of this past.

This chapter has a number of aims. By providing an overview of the key economic, political, social, and cultural characteristics of Japan, we can understand more about the Japanese market and the opportunities and constraints it represents for foreign firms. We can also understand more about Japanese corporations: how and why are they different and what are the implications for collaborators and competitors?

Such insights are important for firms defending their own domestic markets against Japanese MNEs, for foreign firms breaking into the Japanese market, and for MNEs acquiring or partnering Japanese firms or recruiting Japanese employees. At a broader level, by making the links between national characteristics and corporate behavior explicit, we can improve our understanding of the sources of differences between countries and help managers operate more effectively at the international level. The approach used here for Japan can be applied to other countries whose markets present opportunities or whose firms present competitive threats.[1]

The specific objectives of this chapter are to:

1 *Examine* the underlying factors—economic, political, social, and cultural—that underlie the distinctiveness of Japan, its business practices, and its corporations.

2 *Understand* why Japan is a difficult but rewarding market for foreign firms to enter.

3 *Identify* key strengths and weaknesses of Japanese firms.

4 *Explore* the ongoing changes in Japan and the implications for Japanese firms, their collaborators, and their competitors.

ACTIVE LEARNING CASE

Doing business in Japan

Japan is the third largest economy in the world after the United States and China. For this and other reasons it is attractive for foreign multinational firms, large and small. It is also very different from other countries—politically, economically, and culturally—and these differences can present major challenges for market entrants.

There are a number of reasons for the imbalance in outward–inward trade and foreign direct investment in Japan. It is a tough, competitive market, characterized until recently by relatively closed interfirm business networks and a unique political, legal, and institutional infrastructure. Surveys and case studies of foreign firms in Japan reveal the difficulties many of them have faced and how they have adapted to succeed. They also reveal how things have changed over the years.

Prior to the "lost decade" of the 1990s, Japan was lucrative but expensive and relatively attractive but restrictive. The major problem for foreign firms was the high basic cost of operating in Japan, including office rents, a high tax burden, staff costs (for local personnel and expatriates), materials, and other inputs. Firms also reported major recruitment problems and difficulties keeping good Japanese staff, partly because the lack of lifetime employment practices and poor social status meant that many Japanese were reluctant to work for foreign firms. Complex employment legislation and very different human resource management practices also added to the effort required to establish an effective local business.

A variety of market restrictions also faced firms, many stemming from the entrenched *keiretsu* networks, both upstream (between buyers and suppliers) and downstream (between producers, distributors, and retailers). Most Japanese firms had long-term relationships with buyers and suppliers characterized by reciprocal trust rather than short-term contractual or price-based arrangements. Breaking these ties by doing business with outsiders could affect these local relationships, so despite the potential for short-term gains, it tended to be avoided. A wide range of government-related obstacles, including binding red tape and uncertain regulations pertaining to foreigners and foreign companies, also created additional constraints for foreign firms in Japan.

In some cases these barriers to foreign entrants were the result of active protectionism, by colluding firms and their trade associations and various other coordinating agencies, or by the Japanese government itself. In the late 1980s and early 1990s political lobbying over alleged restrictive practices, particularly by the US administration, was at its height. In 1989, for example, the Japanese government bowed to US pressure and reformed the Large Retail Store Law to allow

Source: Iain Masterton/Alamy Stock Photo

Toys "Я" Us to open a superstore. This was a high-profile case because of the bilateral negotiations between the United States and Japan that led to the change. Toys "Я" Us went on to open 64 stores. But the Large Retail Store Law still remained to protect small retailers and indirectly supported the tied distribution networks of large *keiretsu*, creating additional barriers for foreign firms. Most recently, aided by further reforms to the legislation, Costco and Wal-Mart from the United States (see the case International Business in Action: Wal-Mart takes Seiyu later in this chapter) and Carrefour of France are aggressively challenging traditional network structures and attempting to eliminate costly local wholesalers.

More often than the direct actions of Japanese government agencies or collusion among corporate groupings, the above constraints for foreign firms in Japan simply stemmed from differences in Japanese business infrastructures, legislative mechanisms, management practices, and consumer preferences. As with any overseas market, foreign firms have to adapt or they will fail to succeed. Foreign managers have also cited competition with Japanese companies and the strictness of orders from Japanese customers in terms of quality, delivery, and after-sales service as key constraints in the past. But these are innate characteristics of doing business in Japan and two key reasons why Japanese firms themselves are so innovative. Successfully developing a business in Japan is an excellent test of a firm's competitive advantages.

The extended downturn in Japan's domestic market in the 1990s and early 2000s made it less attractive but easier to enter Japan. Government deregulation, the loosening of *keiretsu* ties, and changing consumer preferences helped foreign investors. Foreign companies also cited falls in land prices, office rent, and utility costs as specific improvements ▶

in the Japanese business environment. Similarly, reduced distribution costs and improvements in the availability of qualified personnel were also seen as important factors.

The Japanese government has taken steps to improve access for foreign firms, partly to increase consumer choice and stimulate spending and partly to expose local firms to outside competition. Policies aimed at tax reduction and favorable legal and institutional reforms, such as amendments to the Commercial Code of Japan, alongside improvements in labor market flexibility, have helped to increase FDI into Japan.

There are, however, more fundamental changes taking place that are probably more important for foreign entrants. The changing economic climate of the early and mid-2000s, particularly the high costs of manufacturing and depressed consumer demand, has resulted in a growing preference among consumers to buy cheaper, non-Japanese products and a need for Japanese firms to buy from abroad. Long-term *keiretsu* networks have loosened considerably, opening up supplier, distribution, and retailing opportunities to foreign firms. Social and cultural changes also mean that younger Japanese are much more enthusiastic to work for non-Japanese firms, although senior, experienced managers are still relatively difficult to recruit.

More recent entrants to Japan and established foreign firms expanding their presence are a testimony to these changing conditions and the continued promise of the Japanese market. These include the French firm AXA Non-Life Insurance, Miele, the German household appliances company, and Dyson, the British vacuum cleaner manufacturer. Dyson Japan was established in 1998 and has seen a large increase in sales, achieving a 13 percent market share by 2010. In 2013, Dyson's global sales reached approximately US$2 billion (¥230 billion), with Japan as its second largest market, accounting for 20 percent of total sales. Vacuum cleaner sales have been booming in Japan and increased by 6 percent from 2013 to 2014 with approximately 9.31 million units being sold.

The British retailer Tesco increased its commitment to the Japanese market by acquiring the neighborhood supermarket business of Fre'c via its wholly owned subsidiary, C Two-Network Co. in 2004–5. It had already expanded successfully to control 77 stores since its initial entry in 1994, partly by buying C Two -

Network in 2003. Tesco opened its first "Tesco Express" in Japan in 2007, hoping to succeed by promoting its own brand, where many others had already failed. By 2011 it managed 140 stores, selling via both its Tesco brand and a local brand, Tsurukame. However, despite being the world's third largest retailer it was still struggling to develop its presence, and losses in sales inevitably led Tesco to leave the Japanese market in 2012.

Although there has been change in Japan, the key lessons from managers who have experienced this change also emphasize the continued importance of traditional Japanese practices. For newcomers they suggest the following:

- Research the culture, the market, the competition, and the relevant network affiliations.

- Understand that in Japan more than any other market "the customer is king," quality is paramount, and a deep-rooted service philosophy is required.

- Be patient ("wait on the stone") and show long-term commitment; personal and corporate reputation is important and takes time to develop.

- Show sensitivity in all interaction: social gatherings are important and rituals and hierarchy have to be respected.

- Invest to adapt products, services, marketing, and management style.

- Continually innovate, stay ahead of the competition.

- Use Japan to learn, to improve, and to access other Asian markets.

Websites: http://www.jetro.go.jp/; http://www.tesco.co.uk; http://www.bccjapan.com; http://www.meti.go.jp/english/

Sources: Michael Kavanagh, "Australia and Japan sales boost Dyson," *Financial Times*, May 26, 2010; Adam Gale, "Dyson hoovers up Japan," *Management Today*, 16 September, 2014; "UK's Dyson chooses Tokyo for first store," *Nikkei Asian Review*, April 17, 2015; Justin McCurry, "Tesco hopes for Express success in tricky market: Tesco opens first branded store," *Guardian*, September 28, 2007; "Tesco plans to acquire Japanese business," Press Release, Tesco plc, April 27, 2004, at www.tesco.co.uk; "Tesco to leave Japanese market after nine years," *BBC News*, June 18, 2012; S. C. Collinson, *Small and Successful in Japan: A Study of 30 British Firms in the World's Most Competitive Market* (London: Avebury Press, Ashgate Publishing Group, 1996); JETRO, *The 9th Survey on Attitudes of Foreign-Affiliated Companies toward Direct Investment in Japan* (Tokyo: Japan External Trade Organization, 2004), at http://www.jetro.go.jp/en/stats/survey/; JETRO, *Why Japan? Success Stories* (Tokyo: Japan External Trade Organization, 2004), at http://www.jetro.go.jp/en/invest/whyjapan/success_stories/

1 What kinds of challenges are foreign managers likely to meet when trying to set up a subsidiary office in Japan and recruit local employees?

2 How have *keiretsu* networks limited foreign firms entering the Japanese market in the past and how is this now changing?

3 As part of the general growth of foreign direct investment into Japan, why are foreign firms increasingly able and willing to engage in mergers and acquisitions (M&As) with local firms?

4 Despite widespread changes in Japan and the restructuring of Japanese corporations, why is it still important for foreign managers to understand something of the history and the context in which Japanese businesses have evolved?

INTRODUCTION

Between 1950 and 1973 Japanese GDP grew at an unparalleled average annual rate of 8 percent, over three times the growth rates of the UK and the United States in this period and similar to current growth rates in China. The OECD itself noted this by observing: "by the conventional measures of economic performance (income growth, inflation, unemployment) Japan has out-performed all other OECD economies since entry into the organization in 1964."[2] How did this happen?

Since 1973 until recently Japan's average rate of growth has remained at 3 percent per year. Then, in the last half of the 1990s, the Japanese economy grew at half the OECD average (which was 2.8 percent), and by the end of the 1990s it recorded unprecedented negative growth, shrinking by more than 2 percent. More recently it has shown signs of recovery, but it is still undergoing a period of restructuring as it comes to terms with the end of a long era of continued growth and stability.

POLITICAL, SOCIAL, AND CULTURAL CHARACTERISTICS

The 128 million people of Japan are heavily concentrated in the coastal areas and urban regions because of the mountainous nature of the country. Over half of the population lives in and around the three main metropolitan areas of Tokyo, Osaka, and Nagoya, with Greater Tokyo having a population of 37 million.

Up until the end of the 1980s Japan could be characterized politically, socially, and culturally as a highly stable, conservative, and homogeneous country. Economic change since then has been both driven by and a driving force for change across all of these dimensions. To understand the current dynamics affecting the Japanese market, its firms, and its managers we must understand something of its political and social heritage.

A traditionally strong government role in the economy

The branches of the Japanese government are most similar to those in the United States: legislative, executive, and judicial. Legislative power is vested in the Diet, which consists of a popularly elected House of Representatives and House of Councilors. The conservative Liberal-Democratic Party has been in power for most of the postwar period with the support of the powerful business and agriculture lobbies.

Executive power rests with the Cabinet, which is organized and headed by the prime minister, who is elected by the Diet. In addition to the office of the prime minister, there are 17 ministerial divisions in the executive branch. Judicial power is vested in the Supreme Court and there are eight high courts and numerous district courts throughout the country. Overall, Japan is divided into 47 prefectures. Each local political subdivision, including cities, towns, and villages, has its own executive power and operates within the scope of the national law.

Two key ministries were at the heart of Japan's postwar reconstruction, the boom years of rapid growth and, arguably, some elements of its more recent recession. The Ministry of Economy, Trade, and Industry (METI), created in 2001, was previously the Ministry of International Trade and Industry (MITI), which was established in 1951. It was responsible for leading the selective liberalization of the economy and trade particularly in the 1960s and 1970s. It used its strong control to target, promote, and coordinate specific technologies and industry groups to spearhead the national economic development program. The **Ministry of Finance (MOF)** was also highly influential in steering the developing and internationalizing economy via its control over prices and currency exchange in the early days of growth.

Ministry of Finance (MOF)
Works alongside METI and is similarly influential vis-à-vis regulation and restructuring of Japan's capital markets

One of the more unusual systems that helped coordinate decision making and maintain the consensus among METI, MOF, and various key flagship firms was the practice of **amakudari**. This involved the regular movement of senior politicians and civil servants from the public sector into private sector companies, often as highly paid consultants.

Amakudari
(Literally "descent from heaven") The temporary or permanent movement of public sector officials in Japan into private corporations as a mechanism for coordinating national policy and company strategy

These two ministries connected with other ministries and government agencies to influence the evolution of specific forms of business infrastructure, corporate strengths (and weaknesses), and interfirm business practices. The Ministry of Post and Telecommunications (MPT) and METI, for example, jointly guided the development of NTT, the national telecoms carrier; its supplier group, including NEC, Fujitsu, Hitachi, and OKI; and its denationalization and partial break-up during the 1990s.[3]

The early 1990s saw the start of a series of restructurings in Japanese politics, following over a decade when government influence over the economy and, in particular, the strategies of the major firms became increasingly weak. Both the lead political parties and the powerful civil service bureaucracies below them were pushed to justify their roles, responsibilities, and connections with corporate Japan.

However, government in Japan still arguably plays a more important role in the economy and as an influence over corporate strategy than in other OECD countries. Agricultural and foods-related sectors, the construction industry, and financial services, for example, are still very strongly influenced by government via a number of governance mechanisms.

Distinctive cultural characteristics

Although cultural factors are often overemphasized in discussions of Japanese economic strength, there are some distinctive social and cultural elements that underlie the country's success. As described in Chapter 5, the cultural frameworks of Hofstede and Trompenaars indicate a low level of individualism and a high level of uncertainty avoidance compared to Western cultures, reflected in the high priority placed on rituals, routines, and procedures in organizations and society in general. The Japanese are relatively neutral or unemotional in the workplace and prefer more objective rather than subjective forms of decision making. They are also diffuse, in Trompenaars' terminology, with a high correlation between hierarchical relationships in the workplace and social status outside the workplace.

A strong sense of collectivism rather than individualism tends to dominate many aspects of Japanese life. Whether work related or outside work, clubs, groups, and societies exist at all levels and people will tend to belong to several, with a distinct ranking in each according to its focus and their age and experience.

Chu and giri
Chu, meaning loyalty, and giri, meaning duty, obligation, or responsibility, are often used together to denote the traditionally close, trusting relationship between managers and employees; they are also used to describe the ties between older and younger members of a family

Within companies certain characteristics have strong religious roots, including honor, respect, sincerity, loyalty (**chu**), duty, obligation or responsibility (**giri**), ritual, and hierarchy. These are all central pillars of Japanese society in general and are sometimes referred to as the Japanese Code. At various levels, parent–child relationships characterize the hierarchical nature of inter-organizational and interpersonal links, such as government–industry, large firm–small firm, manager–employee, and so on.[4] Respect for elders, ritualistic (and highly complex) language forms and behavior, group activities, and consensus decision making are all important elements. These contrast individualism and meritocratic forms of organization and tend overall to unify the Japanese in their response to **gaijin** or outsiders.

Gaijin
A term used for non-Japanese; while not too offensive it is not particularly polite; gai means outside or foreign, jin means person

Many of these characteristics are nurtured in the strong Japanese school system. This is characterized by a centrally regulated curriculum (dominated by Monbusho, the Ministry of Education, Science, and Culture): conformist attitudes among pupils, teachers, and parents; high standards; and a focus on factual learning and the sciences. As a result of this educational focus, Japan has double the number of scientists and engineers per head of population than the UK.

There is a significant amount of competition to get into good schools but a lack of competition between pupils once in school ("the nail that sticks out will be hammered down" is a local saying frequently used to describe this conformity). There is also a strong correlation between the level and place of education and job opportunities for school or university leavers, particularly at the top end of the business and civil service hierarchies: 50 percent of Japanese school leavers attend university or higher education colleges and 75 percent of the 480 Japanese universities are private.[5]

We get a small insight into the difficulties created for non-Japanese by the complexities of Japanese culture if we consider the *hai* dilemma. *Hai* can mean one of at least four levels of yes: recognition, but not necessarily understanding; understanding, but not necessarily acceptance and agreement; responsibility, meaning understanding, but must consult with others and secure their agreement before acceptance; and agreement, which means understanding, agreement, and acceptance. The non-verbal signals from the speaker have to be understood to determine which yes is being meant.

Hai
"Yes" in Japanese does not necessarily mean "yes I agree," but "yes, I hear what you say"

 Active learning check

Review your answer to Active Learning Case question 1 and make any changes you like. Then compare your answer to the one below.

1 **What kinds of challenges are foreign managers likely to meet when trying to set up a subsidiary office in Japan and recruit local employees?**

One way to answer this question would be to examine the political, economic, and cultural issues in turn. Political challenges include the legislation for registering local companies, licensing, taxation, visas for foreign nationals, and employment regulations. Economic challenges include the costs of premises and business services. But there are other costs, less easy to estimate, that result from the extra time and effort needed to develop customer relationships and adapt to Japanese business practices. All of the above challenges would involve a degree of cultural learning, given that they involve interaction with and an understanding of local people and organizations. Recruiting, managing, and keeping Japanese employees, however, represents one of the biggest challenges for foreign managers. Failure to adapt human resource management practices, incentive schemes, the organizational structure and hierarchy, the definition of roles and responsibilities, and decision-making systems to develop an efficient, motivated local workforce undermines many foreign firms' market-entry strategies in Japan.

ECONOMIC CHARACTERISTICS

Japan is very big and highly competitive. The unusual nature of its rapid growth in the early years stemmed from factors such as the traditional relationship between government and business, its unique capital markets (national finance and investment systems), its traditionally strong **keiretsu** groupings of firms, the role of the corporation in society, and the role of the employee in the firm. These are all linked to its unique social and cultural characteristics, leading many commentators to characterize Japan as having a different form of capitalism.

The size of the Japanese economy, combined with its productivity and the average wealth of its 128 million people, make it the third largest economy in the world after the United States and China. Other general characteristics include its large (though declining) trade imbalance and even larger imbalance in FDI, compared to its triad counterparts (see Tables 18.1, 18.2, 18.3).

Keiretsu
Groupings of Japanese firms with long-term associations and cross-shareholdings; each firm maintains its operational independence but coordinates strategy and often exchanges assets and resources with other firms in its group

Table 18.1 Economic and trade data for Japan, 2009–14

	2009	2010	2011	2012	2013	2014
GDP per head ($ at purchasing power parity)	32,607.87	33,747.64	34,312.11	35,600.73	36,793.194	37,389.79
GDP (% real change p.a.)	−5.0	4.7	−0.5	1.8	1.6	−0.06
Government balance (% of GDP)	−10.4	−10.4	−9.3	−9.8	−8.76	−7.24
Inflation (%)	−1.3	0.72	−0.29	−0.04	0.36	2.80
Public debt (% of GDP)	192.1	215.95	229.84	236.76	242.59	246.20
Hourly direct pay in manufacturing (US$)	n/a	26.01	29.25	28.94	n/a	n/a
Recorded unemployment (%)	5.6	5.1	4.6	4.4	4.00	3.58
GDP by sector	Agriculture: 1.1%, industry: 25.6%, services: 73.2% (2013 est.)					
Exports	$719.2 billion (2013)					
Main exports	Transport, machinery, electrical machinery, motor vehicles, chemicals					
Main export partners	US (18.5%), China (18.1%), Korea (7.9%), Taiwan (5.8%), Hong Kong (5.2%)					
Imports	$838.9 billion (2013)					
Main imports	Mineral fuels, electrical machinery, chemicals, foodstuff, manufactured goods					
Main import partners	China (21.7%), US (8.4%), Australia (6.1%), Saudi Arabia (6.1%), UAE (5.1%)					

Sources: http://www.jetro.go.jp/en/reports/statistics/; http://stats.oecd.org/#; http://www.imf.org/external/pubs/ft/weo/2015/01/weodata/index.aspx

Table 18.2 Japan's FDI imbalance, 2008–14 (millions of US$)

	2008		2009		2010		2011		2012		2013		2014	
	In	Out	In	Out	In	Out	In	Out	In	Out	In	Out	In	Out
Japan	24,426	128,020	11,938	74,699	−1,252	56,263	−1,758	114,363	1,732	122,549	2,304	135,749	2,090	113,629
UK	96,939	111,411	71,140	44,381	50,604	39,502	53,949	107,086	59,375	28,939	47,675	−14,972	72,241	−59,628
US	316,112	311,796	143,604	266,955	197,905	304,399	226,937	396,656	169,680	311,347	230,768	328,343	92,397	336,943

Sources: http://www.unctad.org; http://unctad.org/en/Pages/DIAE/World%20Investment%20Report/Country-Fact-Sheets.aspx; http://unctad.org/sections/dite_dir/docs/wir12_fs_br_en.pdf

This imbalance, coupled with the trade dependence on the US market, resulted in the long-running US–Japan trade conflict during the 1980s. Japan's growth period was marked by increased exports (still reflected in its export profile; see Figure 18.1) and outward FDI, but for some time its domestic market remained relatively closed to competitors for a variety of reasons. More recently, linked to the domestic market recession, imports of cheaper products, particularly from China, have created a more balanced trade profile (see Figure 18.2). Trade and FDI trends in the 2000s show that Japan's economy is becoming more integrated within the Asia region and developing particularly strong economic ties with China. Both output (market-oriented) expansion and input (resource or production-oriented) expansion opportunities are being created for Japanese firms by the growth of the Asian economic region.

Japan is home to around a quarter of the top 100 MNEs. The kinds of sectors represented in this list of top firms, together with Japan's trade profile and sources of outward FDI, all point to a surprisingly narrow range of industry strengths. Its competitive superiority has always been limited to relatively few key sectors, as is the case for most other economies.

Table 18.3 Japan: FDI by country/region, 2010–14 (balance of payments basis, net and flow, US$m)

	Outward					Inward					Net FDI (outward − inward)				
	2010	2011	2012	2013	2014	2010	2011	2012	2013	2014	2010	2011	2012	2013	2014
Asia	22,131	39,492	33,477	40,470	35,390	3,128	1,384	2,895	867	5,402	19,003	38,108	30,582	39,603	29,988
China	7,252	12,649	13,479	9,104	6,741	314	109	72	140	594	6,937	12,540	13,408	8,963	6,147
India	2,864	2,326	2,802	2,155	1,811	4	9	19	18	−1	2,859	2,317	2,783	2,137	1,812
North America	9,016	15,166	35,768	46,505	43,854	3,014	−3,120	−61	1,414	4,361	6,001	18,286	35,830	45,091	39,494
Central and South America	5,346	11,287	10,454	10,197	7,094	−7,724	−1,388	−1,955	−1,363	236	13,070	12,674	12,410	11,561	6,858
Oceania	6,407	8,767	11,075	6,098	5,554	−17	90	125	376	557	6,424	8,677	10,950	5,722	4,997
Europe	15,043	39,841	31,017	32,227	25,873	204	1,203	893	1,061	−2,195	14,840	38,637	30,124	31,166	28,068
Germany	−321	2,165	1,797	2,653	2,815	2,206	18	449	10	626	−2,527	2,147	1,348	2,642	2,189
UK	4,624	14,125	11,882	13,319	8,267	4,817	1,792	1,212	618	91	−193	12,333	10,669	12,701	8,176
France	551	116	2,291	−237	1,486	1,128	3,438	−463	−645	−131	−577	−3,322	2,754	408	1,616
Netherlands	3,288	5,346	8,638	8,636	3,202	−7,733	3	−435	537	−1,469	11,021	5,343	9,073	8,099	4,671
Italy	372	1,007	141	419	77	163	11	−16	88	−91	210	997	157	331	168
Eastern Europe, Russia, etc.	593	628	1,326	322	350	6	0	−15	13	13	588	628	1,341	309	337
Middle East	−348	716	447	91	495	−0	142	−115	9	710	−348	574	562	82	−216
Africa	−372	464	116	−537	1,466	36	−13	−19	−8	6	−408	477	135	−528	1,459
World	57,223	108,808	122,355	135,049	119,727	−1,359	−1,702	1,761	2,358	9,077	58,582	110,509	120,594	132,690	110,650

Notes: "−" (minus sign) indicates net outflow; "0" indicates an amount of less than US$1 million.

"World" includes countries that are not classified into each region. Therefore, "World" is not necessarily equal to the sum of the regional components.

Source: Adapted from Japan External Trade Organization (JETRO), *Reports and Statistics, Japan's Inward and Outward Foreign Direct Investment, 2016.* http://www.jetro.go.jp/en/reports/statistics/

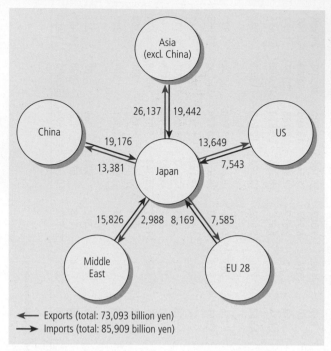

Figure 18.1 Japan's foreign trade by country/region, 2014
Source: Statistical Handbook of Japan (2015).

In the early 1990s just four industries—non-electrical machinery, electrical machinery, transport machinery, and precision machinery—accounted for 75 percent of total Japanese exports. Three product areas—motor vehicles and parts, consumer electronics, and electronic components—were responsible for about one-third of exports. The same industry niches were responsible for the growth of FDI (primarily in production activities) and of foreign sales of Japanese firms.[6] Other data also show how the success of Japanese firms, expressed in terms of the proportion of overseas to total sales, has also been rather limited.[7] Their size, as is the case for many US firms, reflects success in their large domestic and regional markets rather than their global competitiveness.

In his 1990 book *The Competitive Advantage of Nations*, Michael Porter uses Japan to illustrate both the importance of local *rivalry* and *demanding customers* as driving forces behind the evolution of innovative, competitive firms. As shown above, Japan's strong export performance is based on relatively few industries, initially steel and shipbuilding and heavy engineering, then later capital goods production, car manufacturing, electrical engineering, and consumer electronics. In all these sectors very tough competition between many local firms battling for market share (rather than profits) pushed each competitor to develop new products, more rapidly at lower costs. The large number of firms in key industry sectors promoted this rivalry. During its rapid growth phase the country had, for example, nine indigenous car manufacturers (whereas the United States had only three), ten large electronics groups, and over 115 companies producing machine tools, again far more per capita than the United States.

At the same time, tough markets and demanding customers at home pushed Japanese companies to cut costs and emphasize quality, personal service, and buyer-led product customization, all of which came to underlie their global competitiveness during later periods of export-driven growth. Toyota, for example, initially pioneered lean production techniques in the 1950s as a way of lowering costs to undercut local competitors, not to promote international competitiveness.[8]

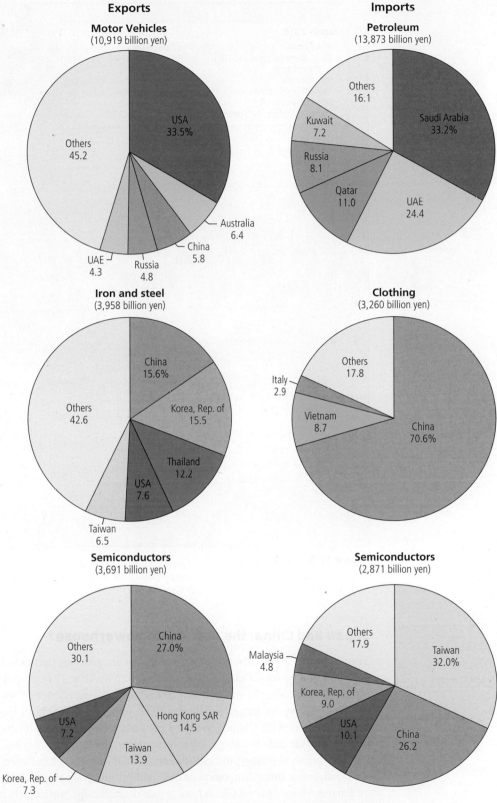

Figure 18.2 Japan's major export and import commodities, 2014

Source: Statistical Handbook of Japan (2015).

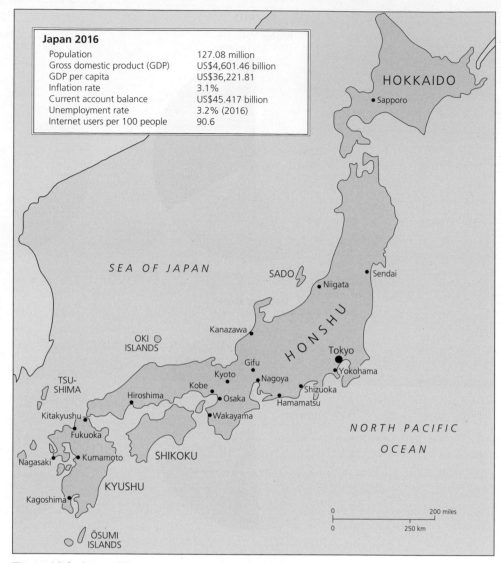

Figure 18.3 Japan, 2014

Sources: World Bank, http://data.worldbank.org/indicator/IT.NET.USER.P2; www.economywatch.com; www.inflationdata.com/articles/historical-inflation-rates-japan-1971-2014/; www.statista.com

Japan and China: the new Asian powerhouse?

Trade and FDI flows between Japan and China are growing particularly quickly, raising the potential of a powerful axis of economic growth in Asia. The combination of Japan's technological leadership in specific industry sectors, its excellence in manufacturing and process innovation, its large, wealthy market, and its footholds in Europe and the United States, together with China's low-cost manufacturing base and its evolving, large but low-income market, sets the stage for a very strong regional partnership. However, the turbulent geo-political history and cultural and social differences between the two nations may well undermine this partnership, or at least limit the pace at which it develops.

Japanese imports from China have grown dramatically, particularly imports of IT products as China surpassed the US to become the major source of IT imports into Japan. Japan is also importing more motorcycles and consumer electronic products made by Chinese manufacturers. Exports from Japan to China have also substantially increased, partly due to buoyant demand for products such as automobiles. At the end of 2007, China overtook the United States to become Japan's major trading partner, accounting for over 17 percent of exports. However, Japan's overall trade deficit with China remained at $18 billion. This had lessened by the end of the decade as significant jumps in bilateral trade took place in 2010–11.

BUSINESS CHARACTERISTICS

Having explored some aspects of the political, social, and economic environment in which Japanese firms have evolved, we now move on to examine some of the factors underlying Japan's economic success. This success in the 1970s and 1980s led to a fear among Western observers that the Japanese had developed an alternative model of market capitalism that would outperform incumbent firms in the United States and Europe. High-profile articles and books on the Japanese threat fed this fear.[9] This also prompted some useful, in-depth research that sought to understand what factors underpinned this success. These include distinctive strengths in manufacturing operations, strong applied research and development (R&D), the *keiretsu* corporate networks, and domestic distribution and retailing systems that connect companies and customers.

Manufacturing strengths

The most detailed comparative studies involving Japanese manufacturers have been carried out in the auto sector, looking, for example, at productivity, manufacturing efficiency, continuous process improvement, design quality, return on R&D, and new product development. The success of Japanese firms in this sector is shown by the fact that on average (up until the end of the 1980s) they produced new models of cars with only 55 percent of the engineering hours required by US and European manufacturers, maintaining development lead times that were over 15 months shorter, and sold the cars at a retail price that was, on average, 30 percent lower than competing models from the United States and Europe.[10]

A variety of attributes underlie Japanese manufacturing competitiveness, and while detailed accounts can be found in numerous other sources, some of the main ones are listed here:

- Attention to quality (built in at every stage of development and production processes), often formalized in quality circles (QCs) and total quality management (TQM), but related much more to each individual employee's concern for flawless output.

- Strong manufacturer–component supplier linkages (coordinated initial development and subsequent innovation), again formalized within just-in-time (JIT) systems but reliant for their success on the close, informal *keiretsu* relationships between buyers and suppliers.

- Ability to cut production costs (using advanced manufacturing technology, JIT, and flexible and lean manufacturing techniques).

- A high level of automation and use of robotics (increasingly used to control costs as the yen appreciated).

- Higher degree of credibility and responsibility given to engineers and technical expertise.

- ***Kaizen***, or continuous improvement, and a focus at all levels on incremental productivity improvement and customer-led product development.

Strong applied R&D

Japan has traditionally spent more than most other countries on R&D, consistently investing over 3 percent of the nation's GDP on R&D. This compares to around 2.5 percent in

Kaizen
Normally taken to mean "continuous improvement" and associated with lean or low-cost, high-productivity manufacturing. A more accurate interpretation is "to dismantle and reassemble a process to make it better." As such *kaizen* was an early form of business process re-engineering

the USA and less than 2 percent on average in the EU28. The recent shift, however, has been the rise of China which overtook Japan in 2010 to become the second-largest R&D investor after the US. In Japan, however, over 75 percent of R&D funding comes from industry, the highest among OECD countries and higher than in China. Contrary to popular myth, the Japanese government has always spent relatively smaller amounts on R&D compared to other advanced countries (this is partly related to the low level of defense spending).

At one time Hitachi, Toyota, Matsushita, NEC, and Fujitsu, the top five R&D spenders in Japan, spent as much (in terms of purchasing power parity) as the total R&D expenditure of the entire private sector in the UK. R&D was predominantly "applied" or near-market R&D. Japan only started to catch up in terms of more basic blue-sky R&D, moving to the scientific frontiers in some technologies, in the last 15 to 20 years.

Keiretsu

The renowned Japanese corporate groupings, or *keiretsu*, characterized by cross-share-holdings and regular meetings between executives, represent more or less closely tied groups of integrated businesses. There are broadly two types of *keiretsu*, the horizontal (**kinyu**) type and the vertical, manufacturing *keiretsu*. Both are undergoing radical change, as described later in this chapter.[11]

Kinyu

Horizontal conglomerates encompassing a wide range of diversified businesses, centered on a dominant bank and/or trading company

Zaibatsu

The pre-war antecedents of some modern-day *keiretsu* in Japan; attempts by the allied forces to break these up after World War II largely failed

Sogo shosha

International trading companies that help other Japanese firms import and export products and services; they were very influential in the rapid growth era in helping local firms break into overseas markets

Many of the former are descended from the pre-war **zaibatsu** conglomerates, which the allied forces attempted to break up in the late 1940s. Three of the top six are direct descendants of the pre-war *zaibatsu*: Mitsui, Mitsubishi, and Sumitomo. The remaining three, Fuyo/Fuji, Sanwa, and Dai-Ichi Kangyo, are more like centralized holding companies. These top six alone directly accounted for about 5 percent of the Japanese labor force and 16 percent of total Japanese corporate sales in the early 1980s. But their cross-shareholding networks and their influence across and down the main corporate hierarchies in Japan were far more prevalent than these figures suggest.

The Fuyo *keiretsu* (*Fuyo-kai*) is shown in Figure 18.4, prior to its restructuring. It typifies the horizontal-type *keiretsu*, with a central bank and **sogo shosha**, or international trading company, and a diversified range of interests. These firms played a major role in bringing Japanese products to the world markets in the growth phase and underpin the global FDI network of many Japanese firms today.

Many of these Japanese banks once dominated the world rankings in asset terms, including Dai-Ichi Kangyo Bank, Sumitomo Bank, Fuji Bank, and Sakura Bank. Commercial banks in Japan have always been oriented more toward corporate clients than individual customers compared to Western banks. Unlike arm's-length shareholders in the West, with short-term repayment horizons, Japanese banks and other shareholders (usually affiliated companies, suppliers, distributors, or associated companies) will have built a long-term commitment to supporting *keiretsu* member companies and their employees. As a result capital markets in Japan have not traditionally emphasized return on investment (ROI) and dividends. Corporations have been much freer from the constraints and demands of shareholders and allowed to manage for long-term growth and continue *keiretsu* connections and loyalty to employees. This form of capitalism has significant benefits in a continually growing economy. But it also has weaknesses and can be an inefficient system for resource allocation as has become much more apparent in Japan's recessionary period. Subsequently, there have been fundamental changes to the structure of capital markets in Japan in recent years, as we will see below.

At one time Mitsubishi was said to be the most tightly woven *keiretsu*, based in Tokyo's business district, Marunouchi, which as a result was called Mitsubishi Village.

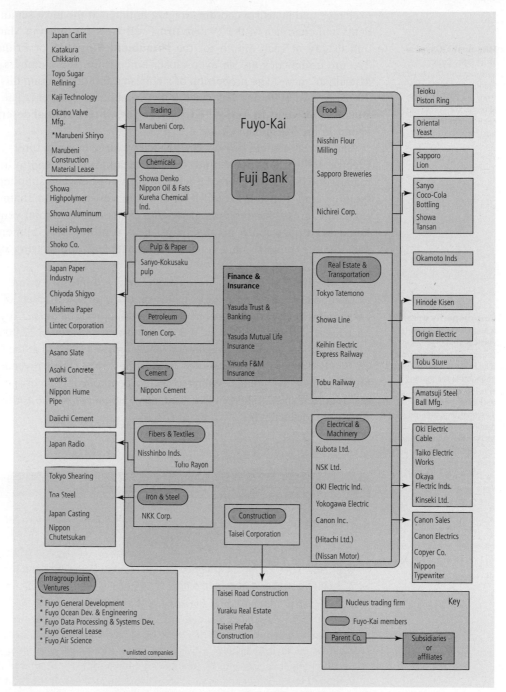

Figure 18.4 The Fuyo *keiretsu* group before restructuring

Source: Sir H. Cortazzi, *Modern Japan: A Concise Survey* (London: Macmillan, 1993), p. 132.

It had over 216,000 employees in businesses ranging throughout the financial, manufacturing, services, and trading sectors from heavy engineering and oil to aerospace and beer. The 29 companies at the heart of the group held an average of 38 percent of each other's shares, a high proportion even for Japanese corporate groups.[12] These companies exchanged directors, cross-financed one another, and engaged in joint investment and cooperative research projects for the benefit of the whole group. Information exchange and interfirm coordination are initiated at the most senior level and the presidents and chairmen of the 29 core firms still meet for lunch in Marunouchi on the second Friday of each month for the **Mitsubishi *Kinyokai***, or Friday Club. Within the 29 core companies are an even closer-knit group, the members of which share the Mitsubishi name. The proportion of stable shareholders among this group stood at over 70 percent in 1996 and has since fallen to about 30 percent. The case **International Business Strategy in Action: Kirin Beer goes international** describes one of the companies in the Mitsubishi Group.

The newer, vertical *keiretsu* are headed by large manufacturers (Hitachi, Matsushita Electric Industrial, Toyota, and NEC, for example) and tend to belong to a particular manufacturing sector. Here the relationships are between suppliers, a flagship manufacturer, and distributors and retailers, in a vertical value chain. Close information exchange, cross-shareholding, personnel exchanges, and joint ventures support excellence in supply-chain management, new product development, standardized IT and logistics, quality and service assurance, and the sharing of management best practices.

At one time Matsushita, for example, had around 500 prime contractors, or first-level suppliers, and over 6,000 smaller suppliers at lower levels of what is known as a **co-prosperity pyramid** or cooperative manufacturing *keiretsu*. Toyota, by comparison, once had 168 first-tier suppliers, 4,000 second-tier, and around 32,000 third-tier, according to one estimate. Small and medium-sized enterprises (SMEs) at the lower levels may rely on two or three top customers for over 50 percent of their revenue, making them both highly cooperative (that is, willing to change component price or specifications to the buyer's requirements at short notice) and very dependent on the fortunes of manufacturers further up the hierarchy.

Mitsubishi *Kinyokai*
The Friday Club in Marunouchi, Tokyo, where the most senior managers from the 29 core firms of the Mitsubishi *keiretsu* gather each month to discuss business

Co-prosperity pyramid
A supply chain linked to a vertical, manufacturing *keiretsu*. It is hierarchical, with firms in the top tiers engaged in technology sharing, personnel exchanges, cross-shareholding, and long-term trading relationships. The further down the hierarchy a firm sits, the more important price becomes and the less such firms are considered *keiretsu* members

---

✔ Active learning check

Review your answer to Active Learning Case question 2 and make any changes you like. Then compare your answer to the one below.

2 **How have *keiretsu* networks limited foreign firms entering the Japanese market in the past and how is this now changing?**

The degree to which *keiretsu* networks will affect foreign firms' success in the Japanese market partly depends on which industry or business they are in. In the past, foreign entrants have found it very difficult to find willing suppliers or distributors because many local firms have been tied into long-term relationships with other *keiretsu* members. Traditionally these long-term relationships have meant that foreign firms will be disadvantaged when competing against local firms, regardless of the relative price or benefits of their product or service. Consumers and corporate purchasing departments have tended to show a strong bias toward local brands and local producers. Since the recession, however, price has become more important as a selection criterion and *keiretsu* structures have loosened, providing more opportunities for foreign firms. Imported products, discount stores (bypassing the complex distribution systems), and direct sales have all become acceptable. Japanese firms of all sizes are actively seeking links with firms outside their traditional networks and outside Japan as part of their changing business strategies.

Kirin Beer goes international

The establishment of the Japan Brewery Company, Ltd. in the late 1880s was a truly international affair. It involved, at various stages and in various roles, a Norwegian, an Englishman, a Scotsman, and a number of Japanese, Americans, and Germans. The symbol of the Kirin, a mythical Eastern cross between a horse and a dragon denoting good fortune, was chosen as its main brand from the start. The firm is the largest beer producer in Japan and one of the four dominant players in the industry alongside Asahi, Sapporo, and Suntory. Its main products are Kirin Lager and Ichiban Shibori, with Kirin Tanrei as Japan's leading *happoshu* (low-malt) beer. Other beverages include canned coffee and tea, fruit juices, and soft drinks. Also active in floriculture and pharmaceuticals, Kirin is part of the Mitsubishi *keiretsu*. In 2014, Kirin revenues were US$18,214 million, of which over 70 percent was generated in Japan.

In recent years the company has been having its share of problems. These all started back in the 1970s when Kirin held 70 percent of the national market. At this time antitrust regulators decided to open the local market to other brewers. As a result, Asahi Beer quickly became the country's second-largest brewer, and since then Asahi has continued to erode Kirin's market share with (1) better product development; (2) a successful marketing strategy with commercials aimed at young, active individuals; and (3) a distribution network that introduced what turned out to be a growing trend among beer consumers—canned beer sold in large supermarkets.

In retrospect, one of Kirin's biggest mistakes was that it was too slow in reacting to competition in a market that it long took for granted. For example, despite Asahi's tactics,

Kirin continued to rely heavily on its traditional sales approach and its long-established network of "mom-and-pop" stores across the country. In truth, the company was confused regarding how to deal with competition and, as a result, made a number of mistakes. When the giant brewer decided to increase its marketing effort and create television ads directed at young people, the strategy was perceived by many viewers as a poor imitation of Asahi's own advertising strategy and the campaign flopped. As a result of such mistakes by Kirin, Asahi continued to gain market share and moved into top position with a 41.7 percent share of the market for beer and *happoshu* in 2004. Since then the two firms have continued to battle for the top spot, with the third-placed supplier, Sapporo, well behind. According to the *Wall Street Journal*, in 2014 Asahi was in the top position of beer market share, holding 35 percent, followed by Kirin with 29.5 percent, Suntory 15.4 percent, Sapporo 11.1 percent, and other firms holding 9 percent.

Partly in an effort to maintain its position in the Japanese market, Kirin has worked to exploit its traditional image. Kirin Lager, Japan's oldest brew, is now being promoted as the classic Japanese premium beer, the type of beer to enjoy with family and friends. And to promote this image with its other brews as well, Kirin has begun increasing its advertising budget. Unfortunately, this new effort faces a number of challenges. The biggest one may well be that most Japanese beer drinkers admit that all beers taste the same to them—so increased advertising may not generate the desired results.

As well as competing actively for domestic market share, Kirin has expanded abroad. Today its products are available in 40 nations including the United States, the European Union, China, Taiwan, and a host of other Asian countries. In most instances Kirin has teamed up with a local brewer. For example, the company entered into a partnership with Anheuser-Busch that allowed Kirin Beer to be brewed in Los Angeles and then shipped to the rest of the country. The company also holds a 46 percent stake in Lion Nathan Limited, a subsidiary in Australia that has important operations in China. Kirin has also invested a 15 percent stake in San Miguel Corporation, the dominant brewer in the Philippines. So the company is off to a good international start. Competitors, however, are also expanding internationally, creating an ongoing need for product differentiation and good brand marketing. So Kirin still has a long way to go. ▶

One of the things that may help the company is that it is part of Mitsubishi, Japan's largest *keiretsu*. As of 2014, the Mitsubishi Group had over 200 operations in 90 countries worldwide. Together with its 626 group companies, Mitsubishi employed a global workforce of over 68,383 people. Although the members of this *keiretsu* operate independently, they can call upon one another for help. For example, when Akai Electric had financial problems, Mitsubishi Bank rescued it. When Mitsubishi Heavy Industries' shipbuilding business ran into trouble, it was able to find work at other group companies for those personnel who were laid off. And the cross-holding structure has also come in handy when warding off takeovers. For example, when Texaco bought Getty Oil, it was prepared to sell Getty's 50 percent share of Mitsubishi Oil to Kuwait Petroleum. However, the members of the Mitsubishi Group got together and outbid the Kuwaitis for Getty's shares. The group has also made important acquisitions and struck major deals in a variety of areas. Mitsubishi companies have participated in the $940 million purchase of the Pebble Beach Golf Course in California, won a $400 million power plant deal in Virginia, and launched a $150 million futures trading joint venture in Chicago. Overall, Mitsubishi has hundreds of interdependent companies, and they are building an empire that stretches from Asia to Europe to the United States. With their help, Kirin may be able to become a major international brewer.

Websites: www.kirin.co.jp; www.mitsubishi.com; www.asahibeer.co.jp; http://www.beverageworld.com/beverageworld/headlines/; http://www.kirin.co.jp/english/annual2003/08source.html; http://www.wsj.com/articles/potential-brewing-giant-could-stir-up-japans-beer-market-1442490813

Sources: Naoko Fujimura, "Asahi tops Kirin in Japan beer sales as demand falls," January 17, 2011, *Bloomberg Businessweek*; "Asahi surpasses Kirin in beer sales," *Japan Times*, July 12, 2007; Emily Thornton, "Japan's struggle to restructure," *Fortune*, June 28, 1993, pp. 84–8; "Japan's beer wars," *The Economist*, February 26, 1998; "A right old brewhaha in Japan," *The Economist*, February 22, 2001; "Japan brewers' shipments rose slightly in 2004," *Kyodo News*, January 18, 2005, Kyodo News International, Tokyo; Kirin Holdings Company Limited, *Annual Report*, 2010, 2014; Thomson Reuters, *OneSource*, 2010; Mintel Global Market Navigator, http://gmn.mintel.com/query/10884473/shares/region; Eric Pfanner and Atsuko Fukase, "A brewing giant may stir up Japan's beer market," *Wall Street Journal*, September 17, 2015.

Distribution, retailing, and customer orientation

Associated with the *keiretsu* industry groupings above are multilayered distribution and retail networks in Japan. At its height it was estimated that there was one retail outlet for every 75 people in Japan (over twice the US ratio) and over 476,000 wholesale stores. These are still organized both by region and by sector and product across Japan and tend to be geared to the large number of small retailers that serve the local markets. This "tied" system of distribution, bound by strong face-to-face ties between sellers and buyers at each level, adds substantial costs to the final product. Again, at its peak, the American Chamber of Commerce in Japan (ACCJ) found that over 48 percent of home electronics products in Japan are sold through exclusively affiliated stores, and about 99 percent of cars are distributed through exclusive dealerships.[13]

Many elements of this complex, high-cost distribution remain in Japan today. Ports in particular are notoriously protected and relatively slower and more expensive than in other OECD countries. The multi-tiered distribution hierarchy has become more simplified, however, driven by the growth in discount stores and cost-reduction measures.[14]

Until recently, the strong patriotic preferences of the average Japanese consumer and, perhaps, the average Japanese middle manager responsible for company purchasing policy provided a firm basis for the country's industrial and distribution infrastructure. Outside the luxury or branded consumer goods markets the Japanese have long had a strong preference for Japanese products.

JAPANESE CORPORATIONS

Japan is home to around 25 percent of the top 100 multinational firms. It is not just a large economy and a large market, but a major source of global competitors. Various stereotypes underlie popular beliefs about Japanese firms that are at best inaccurate and sometimes wholly misleading.

At one extreme, during the 1970s and 1980s, Japanese firms were seen to exemplify the best of all management practices. High-profile articles and books on the Japanese threat fed a general fear about the competitive threat they posed and prompted researchers to identify what was different about Japan and its firms and how such differences might convey sustained competitive advantages.[15] At the other end of the extreme, the economic and corporate failures of the period broadly from 1990 to 2003 have prompted wholesale criticism of the Japanese model.

The truth lies somewhere in between. The Japanese economy, culture, and business system underpin both relative strengths and weaknesses in Japanese companies. The former were very evident during the period of social and political stability and economic growth up to the end of the 1980s. The latter have become more apparent since then.

Very broadly speaking, two kinds of Japanese corporations have existed for some time. On the one hand those firms that have escaped the effects of the extended recession, such as Toyota, Honda, Sony, Canon, Sharp, and Toshiba, have been less dependent on the Japanese market (more internationalized) for some time. They increasingly sold products in markets outside Japan, engaged in FDI abroad, and evolved "less Japanese" styles of management well before the recessionary period. They also represent the industries in which Japan achieved its high levels of export competitiveness in the growth years, which is why we know more about them in the West.[16]

On the other hand, a large number of firms, the majority of Japanese companies in fact, including firms like Nippon Steel, Sumitomo Chemical, Mitsubishi, Kajima, and Dentsu, are less geographically diversified. They have long remained more dependent on the Japanese market, Japanese suppliers, and Japanese ways of doing things.

Confirmation of this division came from the McKinsey Global Institute study which showed that, although labor productivity in Japan's top firms (such as those above) was 20 percent higher on average than in US firms, they only represented 10 percent of the Japanese economy. The other 90 percent of Japanese firms had an average labor productivity that was 60 percent of US levels.

Table 18.4 shows the top 25 Japanese firms in terms of revenues. All but a very few are highly dependent on their domestic market, in that they have less than 20 percent of their sales in each of the triad regions outside their own. Despite the above-mentioned variations in the structures, strategies, and management styles of Japanese firms, there are some common, distinctive characteristics of the stereotypical Japanese firm, relative to its European and American counterparts.

In one of the most extensive studies of the Japanese enterprise system, Fruin highlights high productivity, functional specialization, and manufacturing adaptability as the distinguishing hallmarks of Japanese firms. He identifies these attributes at three connected levels: the factory, the firm, and the interfirm network.[17]

The various social, cultural, and economic characteristics above combine to create certain strengths and weaknesses in Japanese firms. From a wide range of studies[18] we can distill some of the main characteristics of the generic Japanese management style, again traditionally:

Benkyokai
Study associations or work groups for students or colleagues in companies to jointly develop particular areas of knowledge and expertise

- Effective communications internally and with outside firms (decentralized, horizontal information flows) and the use of **benkyokai** or cross-disciplinary, cross-business, and cross-functional workshops.

- Less separation of R&D, design, manufacturing, and marketing functions.

- Lifetime employment, low labor mobility, and substantial investments in training. There is also a strong emphasis on on-the-job training and job rotation within the firm.

- Managers as problem definers, not firefighters, and as educators and mentors, not disciplinarians. This is underpinned by the weak links between performance and pay and the

Table 18.4 The 25 largest Japanese MNEs, 2015 ranking (billions of US$)

Rank	Company	Revenue
1	Toyota Motor	191.1
2	Honda Motor	117.1
3	IX Holdings	111
4	Nissan Motor	106.7
5	Nippon Telegraph & Tel.	104.7
6	Hitachi	91.3
7	Toyota Tsusho	81.5
8	SoftBank	80.6
9	Sony	76.9
10	Marubeni	74.1
11	Panasonic	73.5
12	Mitsubishi Corp.	73.1
13	Tokyo Electric Power	63.9
14	Toshiba	63.2
15	Dai-ichi Life Insurance	60.9
16	Eon	57.6
17	Seven & I Holdings	55.7
18	Nippon Steel & Sumitomo Metal	53.5
19	Itochu	53.1
20	Mitsui & Co.	52.7
21	Mitsubishi UFJ Financial	49.2
22	Idemitsu	46.8
23	Fujitsu	45.1
24	MS&AD	44.3
25	KDDI	42.6
Total		1,870.2

Source: http://www.forbes.com/global2000/list/#header:revenue_sortreverse:true_country:Japan

low wage differentials between workers and managers in the age-related hierarchy. Despite the importance of hierarchy and job titles, average CEO incomes in Japan are rarely more than 10 times the salaries of new recruits. In the United States (and increasingly in the UK) there is a much bigger remuneration gap than this.

■ Strong group/team ethic, loyalty, and motivation combined with competitiveness between teams.

Nemawashi
Literally means "root tying" and is a process of consultation to get agreement on a particular issue before it becomes explicit policy

Ringi
The formalized consensus process of decision making; the *ringisho* is a decision proposal circulated around company departments to be revised or approved before implementation

■ Strict formal hierarchy (based on seniority, rank, and title) combined with strong underlying informal networks and a tendency toward consensus-based (**nemawashi** and **ringi**) decision making (horizontal promotion for high fliers and a lack of outsiders entering the firm at senior levels).

■ General "long-termism" with a focus on growth, employment stability, and market share rather than profits and shareholder dividends.

These are obviously generalizations, but they are factors that tend to exist more or less in a wide range of Japanese firms. Overall, Japanese firms have a strong focus on human resources. A great deal of their strength (and a source of some weaknesses) lies in the employer–employee relationship and the commitment and loyalty shown by each to the other.

This overview of some of the key characteristics of the Japanese has been highly generalized, aiming to select factors that underpin significant differences in Japan relative to other countries. One of the best early books on Japanese firms and business practices, *Kaisha* ("company") by Abegglen and Stalk,[19] sums up some of these distinctive characteristics as the 3Ms:

- *Marketing:* direct links with consumers via retailers and wholesalers and strong customer-led product development.

- *Money:* cross-shareholding and the lack of outside pressure for short-term returns and stock price improvements.

- *Manpower strategy:* worker involvement, loyalty, effective teamworking and devolvement of responsibility combined with hierarchy.

A CHANGING NATION

The past decade has seen a number of major changes in Japan's social, economic, and political structure, and this change continues. The added difficulties brought about in Japan by the current period of chaotic upheaval are partly related to the unusual degree of stability and consensus that the country experienced throughout a long high-growth era that is now over.

Starting in the early 1990s Japan experienced its worst economic recession in the postwar period. Slower growth, reduced investment, declining property prices, and increased unemployment were all secondary effects of earlier declines in profitability, increased domestic costs, and falling domestic demand. These were masked in the late 1980s by rapid growth rates based on strong exports and cheap capital, which ended abruptly when the bubble burst and **endaka** began. The recession was linked to the fast appreciation of the yen, which partly resulted from the 1985 **Plaza Accord** and continued through the mid-1990s, rising 24 percent in value between early 1993 and early 1995.

Between 1990 and 2000, "the lost decade," unemployment grew from 2.1 to 4.7 percent; GDP growth fell from 5.1 to 1.9 percent; motor vehicle production fell by 25 percent; the sales of large department stores slumped by 13 percent; and residential land prices in Tokyo dropped by 55 percent. The knock-on effects continued for some time.

Alongside this economic slump, significant social and cultural developments have resulted in an unprecedented degree of tension between traditional and modern ways of living and working. Some of the broader elements of social change include the aging population, changing diet and changing health problems, a rising crime rate (though from a very low base rate), new attitudes toward work and leisure, and, among some in Japan, a perceived decline in moral values (among others, a new freedom and social openness).

Some of the most obvious changes are seen in the buying patterns of Japanese consumers. Beyond a long-term move to Western foods and clothing styles there has also been a growing preference for "value for money" and an increase in buying from previously frowned-upon foreign firms and discount retail stores. This is partly because of the recessionary pressure on wages but is also an indication that consumers are beginning to realize and object to the fact that Japan's consumer prices were well above the OECD average.

This change in consumer behavior, alongside the increasingly price-oriented, cost-cutting objectives of manufacturers, has challenged the multilayered distribution system that has dominated wholesale and retail networks in Japan. A flatter distribution system has begun to develop, pioneered by discount stores and direct importers.

We will now examine some specific aspects of change in Japan: the restructuring of the capital markets, deregulation, increased inward FDI, and the restructuring of Japanese corporations.

Restructuring capital markets

The changing role of banks and the evolution of Japan's financial services industry created persistent instability in the corporate finance system. During the 1980s and

Endaka

Yen appreciation; the growing value of the yen vis-à-vis other currencies which, among other things, made Japan a relatively expensive place to manufacture

Plaza Accord

An agreement signed by the G5 in 1985 in New York, agreeing to devalue the US dollar against the Japanese yen and the deutsche (German) mark; it triggered the bubble economy and eventual economic recession in Japan in the 1990s

1990s there was a general move toward using capital markets (bonds and equity) for funding investment, particularly among large manufacturing companies in Japan. Partly as a consequence, banking relationships became less stable with far more companies taking loans from more than one bank and changing their main lender. Loose financial discipline in the high-growth, high-investment years resulted in heavy depreciation charges, often on investments that resulted in overcapacity rather than bringing in extra revenue.

The scale of this instability only became clear after the bubble era when the collapse in property prices, which underpinned much of the private sector borrowing, left many companies in financial difficulties. In the late 1990s foreign investors took advantage of the depressed prices to buy property in Japan. This triggered a move toward greater transparency of data relating to property values, occupancy rates, and rents, and made it more difficult to use property to hide personal and corporate finances. Credit recovery, loans, and mortgage services, previously restricted to local firms, were also opened up to foreign participants, with tax laws changed to facilitate this.

That conditions were getting tougher for Japanese firms is evident from the data on debt liabilities and bankruptcies. This prompted widespread changes in corporate governance practices in Japan in the mid-2000s.[20] Average return on equity in 1997 was around 4 percent in Japan compared to 20 percent in the United States, a contrast that preceded the recession but had been accepted as part of the financial system. But while US companies achieve average returns of around 4.5 percent above cost of capital, from 1990 to the mid-2000s Japanese firms (on average) failed to meet the growing costs of capital (that is, they were "value destroyers" rather than "value creators").

As a result of these problems, a process of consolidation, rationalization, and mergers got underway in Japanese capital markets, partly forced on banks by government organizations, as financial deregulation continued (Figure 18.5). Disintermediation has taken place, with companies raising finance from capital markets rather than via traditional *keiretsu* cross-shareholding and bank relationships.[21] Private equity and venture capital also played a growing role, as did foreign investors.

Deregulation, increased M&A, and inward FDI

Although external pressure to deregulate the Japanese from European and US corporations and governments has declined, the pressure from inside Japan has grown. Structural reforms, changes to government policy and the legal codes, plus the changing priorities of Japanese firms and customers have led to a significant increase in inward investment. In particular, foreign M&As, largely unheard of in the past, have grown substantially, as shown in Figure 18.6, but these are still relatively less significant than in other advanced economies. The number of foreign takeover bids each year in Japan exceeded 100 for the first time in 2007 and continued to grow until the end of the decade.[22]

European firms have significantly increased their investments in Japan. French firms were early investors in the late 1990s, making large acquisitions in Japan's automobile, auto parts, and finance/insurance industries. Renault's 36.8 percent stake in Nissan in March 1999 contributed to this (see **Real Case: Renault and Nissan** at the end of this chapter). Three sectors—finance, transport equipment, and telecommunications—accounted for a significant proportion of M&As. But foreign firms have also made attempts to buy into other sectors, including retailing (see the case **International Business Strategy in Action: Wal-Mart takes Seiyu**).

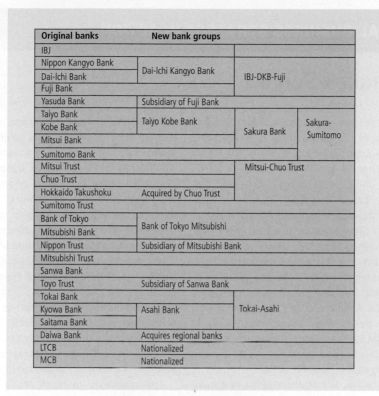

Figure 18.5 Bank group consolidation in Japan

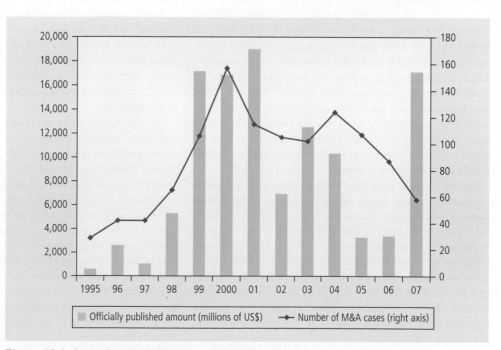

Figure 18.6 Cross-border M&A activity in Japan

Source: JETRO, *White Paper on International Trade and Foreign Direct Investment*, 2007, http://www.jetro.go.jp/en/stats

Wal-Mart takes Seiyu

The Japanese landscape is littered with the remains of foreign firms that misjudged the local market. In March 2002, Wal-Mart purchased a 6 percent stake in Seiyu, the fourth largest supermarket chain in Japan, which has 393 stores selling food, clothing, and general merchandise. The 2001 replacement of Japan's Large-Scale Retail Store Law, which prevented large retail developments, with the more generous Large-Scale Retail Store Location Law has eased Wal-Mart's entry. It retained an option to slowly increase its ownership position in the company to 66.7 percent by 2007. In 2003, after a five-month feasibility study on opportunities in the Japanese market, it took a step in that direction by agreeing to spend $420 million to raise its stake to 34 percent, making Wal-Mart the dominant shareholder. Finally, at the end of 2007 it bought out the remaining shares to become sole owner of Seiyu. (This became the subject of an unusual insider-dealing investigation in Japan in 2010.)

To its Japanese operations, Wal-Mart brought a new management style, strategy, supplier networks, and one of the world's most formidable information and distributions systems. With $244 billion in revenues, Wal-Mart also brought the financial power to update Seiyu's ailing 400 stores. However, since 2003 Seiyu has continued to post annual losses.

Success in Japan's retail market remains anything but assured. The Always Low Prices strategy on which Wal-Mart based its North American success must be adapted significantly to cater to the Japanese market. Japanese consumers insist on standards of quality that Wal-Mart is simply not used to offering in other countries. When, in the early 1990s, the Japanese retail giant Ito-Yokado stocked Wal-Mart biscuits in its stores, they were literally shunned because of their sickly taste and poor quality. Some 40 percent of the biscuits in each packet were said to be broken. Ito-Yokado had to discontinue the product.

Further complicating Wal-Mart's strategy is the resilience of Japan's complex supply system. Carrefour, which entered Japan in 2002, is a good example. The French firm has fallen well short of its original plan to persuade all its Japanese suppliers to adopt the Carrefour direct-purchasing system. This has reflected both a lack of familiarity on the part of Japanese suppliers with such a system as well as the vice-like control over suppliers exerted by large Japanese retailers. Wal-Mart's terrifying reputation for squeezing suppliers' margins until the pips squeak—and then some more—may also make it less attractive as a partner for local firms.

Wal-Mart's success in the United States has also been based on low land prices and labor costs. The price of land in

the outskirts of North American cities and suburbs has allowed the company to build large warehouse-style retail stores with huge parking lots. Japanese land, however, is significantly more expensive. Despite a recession and the stagnation of the Japanese economy, Japanese labor costs are among the highest in the world. That customers demand personal service does not help either. For similar-sized stores, Wal-Mart will have to hire more retail workers in a Japanese store than in the United States.

Lessons learned by Carrefour show that Wal-Mart will also have to differentiate itself from competitors. Carrefour positioned itself in the Japanese market simply as a discount retailer. With little to distinguish its product mix from those of its local rivals, the firm's stores underperformed, forcing a switch in strategy to emphasize its "Frenchness." It now offers a limited range of French products. After its initial stumble, the company expanded in Japan.

The emphasis on fresh produce in Japanese cuisine means that there is high demand for perishable goods and less for the kind of processed foods that are often the staple of Western discount supermarkets. This was also cited as one reason behind the sluggish sales at the US warehouse retailer, Costco, since it entered Japan in 1999.

Another cultural consideration is that the Japanese are hesitant to purchase bulk quantities even if it would save them money. The reason for this is rather simple. While the Japanese remain among the world's wealthiest consumers with a GDP per head of US$32,481, they have on average only 35 m^2 of living space per capita, which is less than half of the Americas.

To date, Wal-Mart has been finding ways to tailor its strategy to the Japanese market. The quality of its products has been raised enough to be acceptable. In renovated Seiyu stores, customers can see their sushi order prepared in front of them, as opposed to the prepackaged variety offered in other countries. To lower land costs, Wal-Mart's stores will have two floors instead of the traditional one floor. Labor costs have been reduced by cutting 25 percent of its workforce through voluntary retirement, saving $46 million on annual wages. It is also relying on its China-based suppliers to stock its Japanese shelves.

But other factors have added to the company's problems, particularly from Japan's continuing economic woes and the tough competitive environment. Uniquely in the developed world, consumer prices in Japan have been falling for some time. Growth has remained sluggish. Yet, that in itself might make this the right moment to enter the market. By the time the country starts to grow again, Wal-Mart will have reno-vated stores, created new relationships with suppliers, linked all Seiyu stores to its computerized logistics system, and learned enough about the Japanese consumer. Its choice of a local partner in the venture should have given it the ben-efit of local knowledge and a large store base. This is an advantage over other foreign retailers like Carrefour and Costco, which have chosen to build up stores from scratch. But other domestic and foreign competitors are readying up and Seiyu continues to lose Wal-Mart money.

Websites: www.walmart.com; www.seiyu.co.jp; and http://www.jetro.go.jp/en/invest/whyjapan/success_stories/

Sources: Lindsay Whipp, "Insider trade probe into Walmart-Seiyu deal," *Financial Times*, November 5, 2010; Hiroko Tabuchi and Kazuhiro Shimamura, "Wal-Mart expects bigger 2007 loss in Japan," *Wall Street Journal*—Eastern Edition, February 13, 2008, p. B14; Tak Kumakura, "Wal-Mart pushes for full ownership of Seiyu," *International Herald Tribune*, October 22, 2007; Wal-Mart, *Annual Report*, 2004; "Can Wal-Mart Woo Japan?," *Business Week*, May 10, 2004; "Wal-Mart moves to control Seiyu," CNN.com, December 12, 2002; and "Wal-Mart's Japanese makeover," *International Herald Tribune*, July 19, 2004.

✔ Active learning check

Review your answer to Active Learning Case question 3 and make any changes you like. Then compare your answer to the one below.

 As part of the general growth of foreign direct investment into Japan, why are foreign firms increasingly able and willing to engage in mergers and acquisitions (M&As) with local firms?

Deregulation by the Japanese government has helped to make it easier in recent years for foreign firms to acquire Japanese firms. Changes in capital markets, some driven by the government, have promoted inflows of foreign capital to reduce the debt burden. Japanese banks are also much more interested in M&A as a means to rescue (or hand over respon-sibility for) failing local companies. More significant factors are, first, the growing opti-mism among foreign firms regarding the future prospects of the Japanese market and their confidence in M&A as a means of access. Second, the rise in M&As can be partly attributed to the changing attitudes of senior Japanese managers who see foreign firms as a means to escape their current economic problems. M&As can help drive some of the strategic changes desired by Japanese managers, such as internationalization and diversification. They can also help push through some of the necessary organizational changes, from de-linking from *keiretsu* relationships to changing internal hierarchies and reward systems.

RESTRUCTURING CORPORATIONS

The initial corporate reaction to the recession was to treat falling profits as part of a cyclical trend that companies could weather using their momentum from the previous decade. Japanese managers had little experience of how to handle the radical restruc-turing and downsizing that became necessary, particularly the problem of labor costs that quickly began to erode domestic manufacturing competitiveness. Labor costs per head in manufacturing were 25 percent higher in 1992 than in 1988, in part because of the rise in white-collar employment, which expanded by a fifth between 1985 and 1992. Managers were particularly slow in reorganizing to overcome their own office and administrative inefficiencies and this, combined with their reticence in cut-ting employees, resulted in the rapid collapse of corporate earnings at the start of the downturn.

The impact of the corporate restructuring was clear from the series of companies announcing job losses at the start of the 2000s, including Toshiba, Fujitsu, Mitsubishi, and Nissan. Most firms cut their university recruitment programs, pushing the unemployment rate for under-24-year-olds to over 10 percent. Some of the largest bankruptcies hit the economy at the start of the decade, including the life insurer Chiyoda Mutual with debts of 2,900 billion yen and the retailer Sogo with debts of 2,000 billion yen.

Despite rationalization, consolidation, and a significant growth of M&As in key sectors, Japanese companies are still having to restructure their operations substantially in the face of longer-term pressures, including:

- more expensive capital;
- growing competition from low-cost Asian producers;
- declining prices of key manufactures, particularly electronics and autos;
- a slowing domestic economy; and
- growing inroads into the domestic economy by foreign competitors.

These developments had a knock-on effect as Japanese firms responded by restructuring internally and changing their interfirm trading relationships. The main changes are summarized below.

The decline of manufacturing and distribution *keiretsu*

Because a large proportion of Japanese SMEs are subcontractors to larger companies, within the multi-tiered hierarchies, recession and reorganization among the giants have had a direct effect on a large number of SMEs. Restructuring effects, coupled with the appreciation of the yen, have passed on down this hierarchy, from primary (direct) subcontractors through second-, third-, and fourth-level indirect suppliers. Automotive firms, including Mazda and Nissan, attempted to cut their first-line subcontractors (from 62 to 16 in Mazda's case), thereby passing on the responsibility for pushing down input prices to companies further down the chain. Both met with greater success in this slimming-down initiative after their respective mergers with Ford and Renault (see **Real Case: Renault and Nissan** at the end of this chapter).

The system of cross-shareholding has become increasingly diluted through reductions in mutual equity stakes. In their drive to cut costs, large manufacturing firms in Japan now avoid giving their usual suppliers a guaranteed volume of business over the long term but are encouraging them to compete with each other with a new emphasis on price as the deciding factor. More inputs are now bought from abroad so a more price-driven domestic market and freer flows of imports have evolved.

There has also been a decline in the use of exclusive agreements with single distributors or sales organizations. In the past these were the norm and in most sectors it was impossible to have multiple agreements or play distributors and retailers against each other to push up sales. Increasingly now, multiple agreements are accepted and the trader–wholesaler–retailer link need not be tied but competitive, with many players competing at each level in a "less imperfect" market.

The growth of outward FDI and offshore manufacturing

Nearly half of all cars and machines made by Japanese-owned companies are made outside Japan. It has been overtaken by China as the largest producer of automobiles and color televisions (Japan is now a net importer). A telling example of the resultant pressures was Nissan's closure of its 30-year-old Zama car plant near Tokyo in March 1995, the first Japanese car plant to be closed since World War II. Ironically, part of the plant, which made 11.2 million vehicles in its lifetime, was turned into a pre-delivery inspection center for Ford vehicles. From 2010 to 2011 Japan became the leading foreign investor in China, with a particular boost after the March 2011 earthquake. Japanese automotive and machinery firms increased their investments into China and exports from China to Japan increased as a result.

The decline of lifetime employment and changing HRM practices

Many of the changes being forced on Japanese managers are culturally taboo but economically inevitable. One of the most significant is the erosion of the lifetime employment system, which is very unlikely ever to return in its traditional form. Unemployment, traditionally very low and carrying a huge social stigma, officially grew to over 5 percent (unofficial estimates put the peak nearer 8 percent).

Early retirements, horizontal movement of employees, rising use of performance-related pay, and significantly reduced wage increases and bonuses at the annual wage negotiations in Japan also signified the new pressures on companies. The largest companies reduced their usual intake of university graduates and introduced merit-based remuneration schemes. These changes also had significant knock-on effects, not least the rise in the already high rate of suicides. In the long term, Japan will have an increasingly flexible labor market, with implications for all aspects of the traditional employee–employer relationship, in-house training, and company loyalty.[23]

Diversification strategies

Diversification strategies have been the cornerstone of many corporate restructuring plans, some successful, others not.[24] NKK, Japan's second-largest steelmaker, is a good example. Its previously loss-making marine engineering division turned in an operating profit of almost 15 percent on sales of almost $100 million (although NKK overall expects to make a loss of five times this amount). The turnaround in this particular division was due to extensive (and risky) investments into areas outside shipbuilding. These include the leisure industry, manufacturing an indoor ski slope and an artificial surfing beach (Wild Blue), using core technologies from NKK's own test divisions. In addition to diversification within manufacturing, the changing cost structure for industrial production has, in particular, accelerated the shift toward services.

 Active learning check

Review your answer to Active Learning Case question 4 and make any changes you like. Then compare your answer to the one below.

4 **Despite widespread changes in Japan and the restructuring of Japanese corporations, why is it still important for foreign managers to understand something of the history and the context in which Japanese businesses have evolved?**

Whether competing with Japanese businesses, collaborating with them, or working for them, their current practices and their distinctive strengths and weaknesses are the result of their historical development in the political, economic, and social context of Japan. Their past is also the clue to their current restructuring, why it is necessary, and why it is not a quick and simple process. Managers in firms looking to enter the Japanese market need to know about the broader context of Japan because this provides insights into the role of government agencies, the business infrastructure, *keiretsu* networks, business etiquette, the culturally influenced preferences of customers, and the many other differences and difficulties that require adaptation. Japanese firms are a product of this unique environment, relatively few have broken away from their dependence on Japan's domestic market, and most retain elements of traditional Japanese management practices. Foreign managers will better understand the strategic options and organizational challenges they face in alliances, joint ventures, and M&As with Japanese companies if they know something of their home environment.

Several studies, including one by Michael Porter and colleagues, have examined the ongoing changes in Japan and analyzed the challenges facing Japanese managers, to suggest the following guidelines for transforming the Japanese company:[25]

- *Create distinctive, long-term strategies.* Rather than imitating close rivals, break out of the consensus and do something different.
- *Expand the focus of operational effectiveness.* That is, improve office-level productivity as well as plant-level efficiency.
- *Learn the role of industry strategy in structure.* Among a number of strategic changes, firms should avoid getting locked into price-based rivalry.
- *Shift the goal from growth to profitability.* Focusing on market share was only possible with "patient capital" (linked to *keiretsu* and traditional capital markets); shareholder pressure will push for performance-related rewards.
- *Reverse unrelated diversification.* Pare down to your core competencies and let other firms do the rest.
- *Update the Japanese organizational model.* Change internal practices away from hierarchy and consensus toward meritocracy and entrepreneurship.
- *Move away from incremental change.* Become more flexible and responsive to suit the new competitive environment.

The few successful international Japanese firms, including Sony and Toyota, are seen as future models by many because they have adapted successfully to the new realities. In fact, it could be argued that their relatively high level of internationalization prior to the domestic market recession gave them the necessary portfolio of overseas markets and sources of inputs, and the global scale and scope advantages needed to weather the local storms. Other firms have failed to adapt, often locked into cultural and institutional routines which were born out of the golden era of economic growth but which are ill-suited to the new realities.[26] Old habits die hard.

CONCLUSIONS

Japan continues in a period of fundamental political, economic, and social transformation. Corporations have been forced by a drawn-out economic recession to alter radically the way they organize and invest. Foreign firms are finding, despite the depressed state of the Japanese market, that there are unprecedented opportunities for alliances and takeovers involving Japanese firms and for introducing new products and services to Japanese customers. There is a new period of internationalization as Japanese firms shift investments out of Japan and attempt to reduce their dependence on local markets, while foreign imports, investment, and M&As are on the increase. Partly because of the significance of the new trading partner and rising power, China, this amounts to processes of regionalization rather than globalization.

Much of this chapter has looked at the traditional way of doing business in Japan, the unique capital markets, *keiretsu*, demanding customers, lifetime employment, and the traditional strengths and weaknesses of Japanese firms. The point of this is that these are enduring facets of Japanese business and they underlie the key distinctiveness that collaborators and competitors need to understand. They also continue to strongly influence the restructuring options open to Japanese firms and the changes in the economy as a whole.

James C. Abegglen, one of the most experienced Western commentators on Japan, sums up this tension between old and new in his book *21st Century Japanese Management: New Systems, Lasting Values.*[27] He describes how success comes from effectively combining the best of old and new. To do this requires some understanding of how adaptability can be promoted in the face of inertia. But it also demonstrates how any in-depth country analysis must take account of the way that distinctive local economic, political, social, and cultural characteristics have evolved in the past and will continue to influence *relative* business practices, markets, and competitiveness in the future.

KEY POINTS

1 The current strengths and weaknesses of Japanese firms result from their evolution in a highly competitive but continually growing domestic economy with unique socio-cultural foundations.

2 The Japanese business environment was traditionally characterized by strong inter-firm rivalry; "patient" long-term finance, partly through cross-shareholding arrangements; *keiretsu* relationships, both vertical and horizontal; complex, multi-tiered distribution systems; demanding customers; and strong government intervention in the early years.

3 Socio-cultural factors that supported the Japanese way of doing business include ideals of obligation, loyalty, hierarchy and ritual, and a strong work ethic, linked to mainstream religion; a strong but conformist education system and "groupism" plus consensus-based decision making in general; and complex language and tacit forms of communication.

4 Japanese firms are traditionally loyal to employees, who tend not to move from company to company; hierarchical and bureaucratic but also consensus oriented; good at integrating between functions and teamwork; good at applied R&D and training; long-termist; and close to suppliers and customers.

5 The Japanese market has traditionally been difficult for foreign investors to break into, partly because of the factors listed above and partly because of the system of governance that tends to favor local firms.

6 Japan is changing. Growing social and political heterogeneity alongside a prolonged economic recession is creating unprecedented tensions and forcing drastic corporate restructuring. *Keiretsu* families are loosening or breaking up; firms are diversifying and divesting; lifetime employment is declining; capital markets are heavily restructuring; and deregulation is the norm.

7 Changes in Japan are creating investment, M&A, and market-entry opportunities for foreign firms.

8 The growing regional Asian economy is centered on the major trading partnership between Japan and China.

Key terms

- Ministry of Finance (MOF)
- *amakudari*
- *chu* and *giri*
- *gaijin*
- *hai*
- *keiretsu*
- *kaizen*
- *kinyu*
- *zaibatsu*
- *sogo shosha*
- Mitsubishi *Kinyokai*
- co-prosperity pyramid
- *benkyokai*
- *nemawashi*
- *ringi*
- *endaka*
- Plaza Accord

REVIEW AND DISCUSSION QUESTIONS

1 List some of the factors underlying the competitive advantages of Japanese firms, developed during the rapid growth era of the 1950s, 1960s, and 1970s.

2 What kinds of social and cultural characteristics of the Japanese underlie their proficiency in manufacturing?

3 How do *keiretsu* structures promote process and product innovation in Japanese firms?

4 Why have inflows of FDI into Japan historically remained lower than FDI outflows?

5 How would a foreign firm wanting to establish a sales and marketing operation in Japan need to adapt to succeed?

6 Why has the economic recession in Japan resulted in outflows of manufacturing investment?

7 What have been the main advantages and disadvantages for many Japanese firms of relying on domestic markets rather than internationalizing?

8 How can we explain Japan's deepening trading relationship with China?

9 What has triggered the restructuring of capital markets in Japan, and what have been the effects on Japanese corporations?

10 How can an economy in recession present new opportunities for foreign investors?

11 What strategic and structural changes are many Japanese firms making in response to the changing economic and competitive environment they face?

12 Why have senior Japanese managers shown a growing admiration for some top foreign CEOs and management gurus?

REAL CASE

Renault and Nissan: no pain, no gain

In March 1999 one of Europe's biggest car makers, Renault, bought a 36.8 percent stake in Nissan, Japan's second largest vehicle manufacturer. It has since increased its stake to 44.4 percent with Nissan taking a reciprocal 15 percent share in Renault. The alliance has deepened following the far-reaching changes put in place by Carlos

Ghosn, installed as President and CEO of Nissan and now revered for having engineered a radical turnaround in the firm's fortunes. Although numerous alliances involving equity participation had taken place before this, notably the Ford–Mazda alliance, the Renault–Nissan case was seen to be a highly unusual foreign "rescue" of a major Japanese firm in dire straits.

Nissan had made losses in six of the seven years prior to 1999, having been hit hardest of all the major car manufacturers in Japan by the decline in domestic sales and the rise in local manufacturing costs. Factory capacity utilization had fallen to 53 percent, and Carlos Ghosn, the new CEO of Nissan (known as "le cost-killer"), set out to cut 21,000 jobs, close five factories, and cut the number of suppliers in half. Close, *keiretsu* relationships with suppliers and distributors were traditionally seen to be a key strength of Japanese manufacturers (Nissan had formerly been part of the Fuyo *keiretsu*), supporting high-quality products, process innovation, just-in-time supply systems, and rapid, customer-led new product development. In a time of recession they represented an overextended supplier and dealer base, undermining profitability.

Internal restructuring also took place, following Ghosn's plan to introduce stock options and bonuses based on achievement and a performance-based promotions scheme, eventually for both employees and managers.

In the case of both external and internal reorganization there are significant clashes with the traditional Japanese way of doing things. First and foremost, job losses represent an enormous problem for managers and employees alike, almost a personal admission of failure on both sides which has social as well as corporate repercussions. The ties of obligation and loyalty associated with lifetime employment are broken. Indirectly, the breakdown of *keiretsu* links with other firms has a parallel effect, also resulting in job losses and the separation of long-term associations, which include personal friendships between managers and employees in both sets of firms.

Internal changes, particularly the introduction of performance-based remuneration and reward, are also radical in the eyes of the Japanese. Lifetime employment is associated with an age-related hierarchy where salaries only grow toward the end of a manager's tenure in the firm, as a reward for long years of service. To lose this reward, either because the firm no longer needs you or because the basis of remuneration is changed, is a drastic shift in the social contract employees entered into. Moreover, losing out to fast-track younger managers who rise up the hierarchy on the basis of their ability is not expected, particularly as talented managers may themselves have had to wait their turn in the past.

The steps taken by Renault change the rules of the game in Japan. Many would say that a sharp shock to push much needed restructuring was the only way. Renault's rescue was called for partly because of Nissan's accumulated losses, which could no longer be supported in a recession, particularly by investors who could no longer afford to ride the storm in a time when capital markets were tightening significantly. But it was also needed because of the inherent problems Japanese managers face in trying to drive such radical restructuring themselves. The senior managers responsible for six years of losses are still in charge alongside Ghosn, having "saved face" because an outsider (a *gaijin*) forced the radical steps needed to turn the company around. Without this outside shock many Japanese firms remain locked into a certain way of doing things because forcing these kinds of changes from the inside on one's work colleagues and friends appears to be too costly. It threatens to destroy the social as well as the business fabric on which the country's impressive historic growth has been founded, and most Japanese do not want to be responsible for this kind of destruction, however creative it might be.

The Renault–Nissan alliance is now heralded as one of the most successful in the business. In the first few years Nissan's $13 billion debt was substantially reduced and it achieved $2.3 billion profits in 2002. The market capitalization of Renault increased threefold and of Nissan more than fourfold. In 2014, the combined companies were the fourth largest global auto maker in terms of unit sales with a market share of 10 percent.

On reflection, it represents the combination of two very different organizations, structurally and culturally. Renault was a strongly home-region-oriented firm, heavily dependent on its home economy, France. Alone it was relatively small, holding just 4.2 percent of the global market, but vying with Volkswagen for European market leadership. Nissan was one of the unusual bi-regional auto firms, with strong sales in the United States and a relatively good market position in countries outside the triad regions. The bar chart in Figure 18.7, together with Figure 18.8, shows the individual and combined sales of both firms. In 2014, the Renault-Nissan alliance sold approximately 8.5 million vehicles. These are similar-sized firms with very different geographic footprints that complement each other well. For the year ended March 31, 2011, Nissan revenue grew 27 percent compared to 2010 and it achieved a record high of US$102,380 million in the past five years. For the year ended March 31, 2015, Nissan's revenue grew by 8.5 percent in comparison to 2014. Furthermore, in 2015, Nissan had a net income of 4.5 percent and a workforce of 149,388 people. Renault ▶

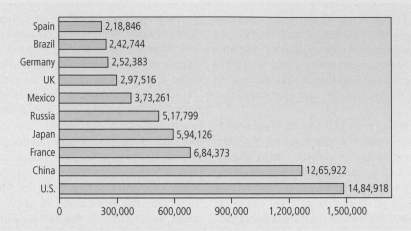

Figure 18.7 Top 10 Renault and Nissan alliance markets, 2015

Source: Groupe Renault, *Annual Report*, 2015.

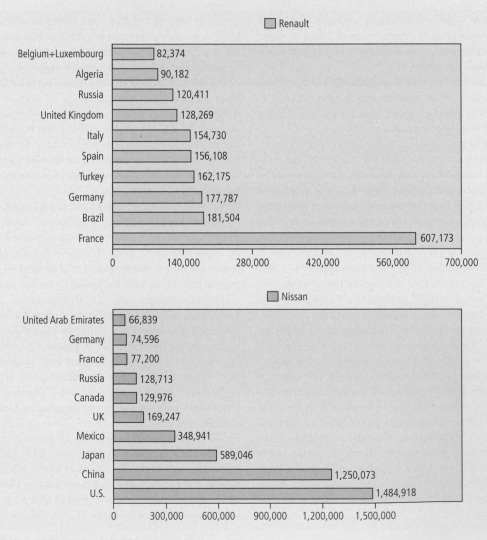

Figure 18.8 Top 10 Renault and Nissan markets

Source: Groupe Renault, *Annual Report*, 2014.

SA's revenue was US$51,611 million for the year ended December 31, 2010. In contrast to Nissan, however, Renault SA's revenues have been flat and even declined. For the year ended December 31, 2014, Renault SA's revenue increased by 0.3 percent and it had an operating profit of 3.9 percent.

A similar pattern of differentiation is true for production. Nissan manufactures just over half of its vehicles in Japan with most of the rest spread fairly evenly among the United States, Mexico, and the UK. It has industrial operations in 20 countries, including manufacturing sites in Taiwan, South Africa, Thailand, the Philippines, and Indonesia. Renault manufactures in 17 countries but makes over 55 percent of its vehicles in France and most of the rest in Europe

Driven by an alliance board, chaired by the CEO of Renault, the two firms have developed shared production facilities in Mexico, Brazil, and Spain; common engineering platforms for entry-level B segment and mid-level C segment vehicles; common powertrain parts and increased sharing of engines and transmissions; and increasingly integrated IT, information, and communications systems.

Renault's competencies in marketing, design, and financing complement Nissan's capabilities in engineering and manufacturing processes. Synergies are enhanced through the exchange of personnel. About 50 employees from Renault originally joined departments such as supplier relations, product strategy, sales and marketing, and finance in Nissan. Similarly, around 50 Nissan employees began work in the areas of quality control, vehicle engineering, manufacturing, and powertrain in Renault.

Beyond this, 250 executives from both firms were assigned to the permanent alliance structures, including cross-company teams and functional task teams, and a further 250 Nissan employees were part of the restructured European sales and marketing divisions of Renault.

Websites: www.nissan.com.jp; www.renault.com

Sources: "Renault-Nissan Alliance facts and figures 2009," www.renault.com/renault_com/en/main; A. M. Rugman, *The Regional Multinationals* (Cambridge: Cambridge University Press, 2005); C. Ghosn and P. Ries, *Shift: Inside Nissan's Historic Revival* (New York: Currency Book/Doubleday, 2005); A. M. Rugman and S. Collinson, "The regional nature of the world's automotive sector," *European Management Journal*, vol. 22, no. 5 (2004), pp. 471–82; R. Kelts, "The cost killer cometh," *Japan Inc.*, October 2003; V. Emerson, "An interview with Carlos Ghosn, President of Nissan Motors, Ltd. and Industry Leader of the Year," *Journal of World Business*, vol. 36 (2001), pp. 3–10; A. Hamey and T. Burt, "'Killer' to make unkindest cut," *Financial Times*, October 18, 1999; Pearson, *Renault Nissan Alliance 2004* booklet; Nissan, *Annual Report*, 2002, 2007–15; Renault SA, *Annual Reports*, 2002, 2007–14; Thomson Reuters, *OneSource*, 2011.

1 What broad economic and specific corporate pressures have resulted in the need for a radical shake-up of Nissan?

2 In the context of traditional Japanese employment and working practices and interfirm relationships, why are the changes being pushed by Renault's Ghosn considered radical?

3 What has accounted for Ghosn's success to date with the Nissan restructuring?

4 In what ways are the two companies better together?

REAL CASE

Sony – diversifying into the automobile industry?

When thinking of Sony one typically thinks of the Walkman and music players, televisions and other home entertainment products including the Playstation, however over recent years the nature of many of these industries has changed. Music players are no longer the lucrative business they once were as they have become part of the package offered in a smartphone, competition in the gaming console sphere has intensified after Microsoft entered the market with its Xbox, and even in the world of TV, Sony is not secure having seen its market share of the LCD market fall from 13.7% in 2005 to 6.5% in 2014.

Smartphones are also an industry which Sony shows signs of divesting from after it stopped developing new smartphones for China and was expecting a 60 billion yen loss from the Xperia in the year to March 2016. It is important to note that while smartphones in general are not Sony's forte, they are one of the sectors key image sensor manufacturers.

Image sensors are the components which convert light into digital information, which in turn then defines the size and density of pixels, the number of megapixels and also the recording frame rate of an output. Sony produces a range of models with some of its higher end products used in handsets such as the Galaxy Note 4. In fact, as its sensor business is doing so well, in June 2015 Sony announced that it was looking to increase its production capacity and would be issuing new shares to fund the strategy. Kenichiro Yoshida, Chief Financial Officer stated that the investment into image sensors would total 210 billion yen (£1.1 million) and in turn was expecting to increase its operating profit fourfold.

Not content with success in the smartphones arena, Sony had set its sights on cars with Shigeo Ohba, the general manager of Sony's image sensor business, predicting that the market for automotive image sensors will greatly increase between 2017 and 2030. It is the concept of self-driving cars which Sony is really planning ahead for, however, with the potential for up to 10 cameras to be installed in each vehicle. Despite the smartphone market exceeding sales of 1 billion units per year across the globe, in comparison just one camera can cost up to five times the price of one smartphone, signalling the potential profitability of the industry for Sony if manages to corner the market. With analysts predicting the demand for automotive cameras to reach 102 million units by 2020, the level of opportunity is clear.

The electrification of vehicles has certainly brought with it exciting prospects for component manufacturers such as Sony, but it seems that that might not be all. In February 2015 it was reported that Sony had purchased a 2& stake in a Japanese start-up company which creates robot cars. In the deal, worth 100 million yen, it is expected that the two parties will work together to create a self-driving car. However it is not just Sony who appears to be considering venturing into the automotive industry, with both Apple said to be pursuing the same strategy with reports of the tech giants snapping up experts to work on 'Project Titan'.

Sources: http://www.statista.com/statistics/267095/global-market-share-of-lcd-tv-manufacturers/; http://www.ft.com/cms/s/0/104c6a56-511e-11e5-8642-453585f2cfcd.html#axzz3lG9tr9j4; http://www.cnbc.com/2015/02/15/sony-follows-tech-peers-apple-google-on-the-car-road.html; http://www.insidercarnews.com/sony-might-be-building-your-next-car/; http://www.bloomberg.com/news/articles/2015-10-07/sony-ceo-hirai-says-electronics-turnaroundpast-midway-point; http://www.forbes.com/sites/ewanspence/2015/02/18/sonys-smartphone-surrender-abandoningthe-xperia/; http://www.forbes.com/sites/marshallphelps/2015/10/17/how-driverless-cars-will-radically-changeevery-aspect-of-our-lives/; http://www.google.co.uk/url?sa=t&rct=j&q=&esrc=s&source=newssearch&cd=8&sqi=2&ved=0CD0QqQIoADAHahUKEwj69KW-1dbIAhWp9HIKHSl6AUE&url=http%3A%2F%2Fwww.informationweek.com%2Fit-life%2Fappleproject-titan-electric-car-may-arrive-by-2019%2Fd%2Fdid%2F1322280&usg=AFQjCNGQ3VmfPtWJPYoc1vWSLgVQyZZlSA&bvm=bv.105814755,d.bGQ.

1   Explain, how Sony has diversified its product range in order to remain competitive?

2   Why has Sony been placing a greater emphasis on the automotive industry in comparison with the smartphone industry?

NOTES

1 This is a recognized approach in management theory. By examining the broader competitive environment within which firms evolve we can identify where specific differences and competitive strengths and weaknesses come from. Evolutionary theories of the firm (Peyton Young), contingency theory (Donaldson), and the theory of nationally bound administrative heritages (Calori et al.) all follow variations of this approach. L. Donaldson, *The Contingency Theory of Organizations* (London: Sage, 2001); R. Calori, M. Lubatkin, P. Very, and J. F. Veiga, "Modeling the Origins of Nationally-Bound Administrative Heritages: A Historical Institutional Analysis of French and British Firms," *Organization Science*, vol. 8, no. 6 (1997), pp. 681–696; and H. Peyton Young, *Individual Strategy* and *Social Structure: An Evolutionary Theory of Institutions* (Princeton, NJ: Princeton University Press, 2001). See also Collinson and Rugman, "The Regional Nature of Japanese Multinational Business," in note 7 below, which applies such theories to explain the limited internationalization of Japanese firms.

2 OECD, *Comparative Economic Performance in OECD Nations* (Paris: OECD, 1989), p. 66, http://www.oecd.org

3 M. Fransman, *Japan's Computer and Communications Industry* (Oxford: Oxford University Press, 1995).

4 C. Nakane, *Japanese Society* (Tokyo: Charles E. Tuttle, 1973).

5 See http://web-japan.org/factsheet/pdf/EDUCATIO.pdf

6 R. D. Pearce and M. Papanastassiou, *The Technological Competitiveness of Japanese Multinationals* (Ann Arbor: University of Michigan Press, 1996); J. H. Dunning and J. A. Cantwell, "Japanese Direct Investment in Europe," in B. Burgenmeier and J. L. Mucchielli (eds.), *Multinationals and Europe 1992* (London: Routledge, 1991).

7 S. Collinson and A. M. Rugman, "The Regional Nature of Japanese Multinational Business," *Journal of International Business Studies*, vol. 39, no. 2 (2008), pp. 215–230; S. Collinson and A. M. Rugman, "The Regional Character of Asian Multinational Enterprises," *Asia Pacific Journal of Management*, vol. 24, no. 4 (2007), pp. 429–446.

8 Sir H. Cortazzi, *Modern Japan: A Concise Survey*, The Japan Times (London: Macmillan, 1993); M. Fruin, *The Japanese Enterprise System* (Oxford: Clarendon Press, 1992); M. Fransman, *The Market and Beyond* (Cambridge: Cambridge University Press, 1990).

9 L. G. Franko, *The Threat of Japanese Multinationals: How the West Can Respond* (Somerset, NY: Wiley, 1983); M. J. Wolf, *The Japanese Conspiracy: Their Plot to Dominate Industry World-wide and How to Deal With It* (New York: Empire Books, 1983); W. G. Ouchi, *Theory Z: How American Business Can Meet the Japanese Challenge* (New York: Horizon Books, 1981); P. F. Drucker, "Behind Japan's Success," *Harvard Business Review,* January/February 1981, pp. 83–90; E. F. Vogel, *Japan as Number One: Lessons for America* (New York: HarperCollins, 1979).

10 M. A. Cusumano and K. Nobeoka, "Structure, Strategy and Performance in Product Development: Observations from the Auto Industry," *Research Policy*, vol. 21 (1992), pp. 265–293; J. P. Womack, D. T. Jones, and D. Roos, *The Machine That Changed the World* (New York: Macmillan, 1990).

11 Sandra Dow and Jean McGuire, "Propping and tunneling: Empirical evidence from Japanese keiretsu," *Journal of Banking & Finance*, vol. 33, no. 10 (2009), pp. 1817–1828; Takchiko Isobe, Shige Makino, and Anthony Goerzen, "Japanese Horizontal Keiretsu and the Performance Implications of Membership," *Asia Pacific Journal of Management*, vol. 23, no. 4 (2006), pp. 453–466.

12 W. Dawkins, "Loosening of the Corporate Web," *Financial Times*, November 30, 1994.

13 Ikuo Takahashi and Helge Fluch, "Retailing in Japan: Overview and Key Trends," *European Retail Research*, vol. 23, no. II (2009); E. Terazono, "Cheap and Cheerful," *Financial Times,* March 15, 1994; "The Emporia Strike Back," *The Economist,* October 29, 1994.

14 JETRO, *Regulations and Domestic Costs Related to the Distribution of Imported Goods* (Tokyo: Japan External Trade Organization, 2005), at http://www.jetro.go.jp/en/stats/survey/

15 See note 10.

16 Collinson and Rugman, "The Regional Nature of Japanese Multinational Business," op. cit.

17 Fruin, op. cit.

18 M. Aoki and R. Dore (eds.), *The Japanese Firm* (Oxford: Oxford University Press, 1994); S. Clegg and T. Kono, *Transformations of Corporate Culture: Experiences of Japanese Enterprises* (New York: Walter de Gruyter, 1998); P. Haghirian, *Understanding Japanese Management Practices* (New York: Business Expert Press, 2010); H. Miyoshi and Y. Nakata, *Have Japanese Firms Changed?: The Lost Decade*, (Basingtoke: Palgrave Macmillan, Palgrave Macmillan Asian Business Series, 2010); M. Sako, *Japanese Labour and Management in Transition: Diversity, Flexibility and Participation* (London: Routledge, 1997); E. Westney, "Japan," in A. M. Rugman and T. Brewer (eds.), *The Oxford Handbook of International Business* (Oxford: Oxford University Press, 2009); R. D. Whitley, "Eastern Asian Enterprise Structures and the Comparative Analysis of Business Organizations," *Organization Studies*, vol. 11, no. 1 (1990), pp. 47–74.

19 J. C. Abegglen and G. Stalk, Jr. *Kaisha: The Japanese Corporation* (Tokyo: Tuttle Publications, 1985).

20 Toru Yoshikawa and Jean McGuire, "Change and Continuity in Japanese Corporate Governance," *Asia Pacific Journal of Management*, vol. 25, no. 1 (2008), pp. 5–24; Toru Yoshikawa, Jean McGuire, and Lai Si Tsui-Auch, "Corporate Governance Reform as Institutional Innovation: The Case of Japan," *Organization Science*, vol. 18, no. 6 (2007), pp. 973–988. The monthly report from the Teikoku

databank for September 2004 lists a total of 1,119 bankruptcies and $3,481 million in liabilities, http://www.teikoku.com/bankruptcy/2004/200409.html; M. Abe and T. Hoshi, "Corporate Finance and Human Resource Management: Evidence from Changing Corporate Governance in Japan," Dokkyo University and RIETI presentation, 2003.

21 Nobuyuki Isagawa, "A Theory of Unwinding of Cross-Shareholding Under Managerial Entrenchment," *Journal of Financial Research*, vol. 30, no. 2 (2007), pp. 163–179.

22 U.S. Department of State, 2011 Japan Investment Climate Statement, Bureau of Economic Energy and Business Affairs; http://www.state.gov/e/eeb/rls/othr/ics/2011/157300.htm

23 David D. C. Chiavacci, "The Social Basis of Developmental Capitalism in Japan: From Post-war Mobilization to Current Stress Symptoms and Future Disintegration," *Journal of Asian Business & Management*, vol. 6, no. 1 (2007), pp. 35–55; Yoshio Yanadori and Takao Kato, "Average Employee Tenure, Voluntary Turnover Ratio, and Labour Productivity: Evidence from Japanese Firms," *International Journal of Human Resource Management*, vol. 18, no. 10 (2007), pp. 1841–1857.

24 Unsurprisingly, the evidence shows, in keeping with theory, that firms pursuing related diversification strategies are doing better than those involved in unrelated diversification. T. Ushijima and Y. Fukui, "Diversification Patterns and Performance of Large Established Japanese Firms," *Working Paper*, Aoyama Gakuin University Graduate School of International Management, Tokyo, 2004; H. Kim, R. E. Hoskisson, and W. P. Wan, "Power Dependence, Diversification Strategy and Performance in *Keiretsu* Affiliated Firms," *Strategic Management Journal*, vol. 25, (2004), pp. 613–636.

25 M. Porter, H. Takeuchi, and M. Sakakibara, *Can Japan Compete?* (Basingstoke: Macmillan, 2000); Panos Mourdoukoutas, *New Emerging Japanese Economy: Opportunity and Strategy for World Business* (Mason, OH: Thomson/South-Western Educational Publishers, August 2005); Arnoud DeMeyer, Peter Williamson, Frank-Jürgen Richter, and Pamela C. M. Mar, *Global Future: The Next Challenge for Asian Business* (Chichester: Wiley, 2005).

26 Collinson and Rugman, "The Regional Nature of Japanese Multinational Business," op. cit.; See also: A. B. Keizer, *Changes in Japanese Employment Practices: Beyond the Japanese Model*, Routledge International Business in Asia Series (London: Routledge, 2011); P. Haghirian and P. Gagnon *Case Studies in Japanese Management* (New York: Business Expert Press, 2011).

27 James C. Abegglen, *21st Century Japanese Management: New Systems, Lasting Values* (Basingstoke: Palgrave Macmillan, 2006).

BIBLIOGRAPHY

Abegglen, James C. *21st Century Japanese Management: New Systems, Lasting Values* (Basingstoke: Palgrave Macmillan, 2006).

Allen, Linda, Chakraborty, Suparna, and Watanabe, Wako. "Foreign direct investment and regulatory remedies for banking crises: lessons from Japan," *Journal of International Business Studies*, vol. 42, no. 7 (2011).

Aoki, Masahiko. "The Japanese firm as a system of attributes." In M. Aoki and R. Dore (eds.), *The Japanese Firm* (Oxford: Oxford University Press, 1994).

Aoki, Masahiko, Jackson, Gregory, and Miyajima, Hideaki (eds.). *Corporate Governance in Japan: Institutional Change and Organizational Diversity* (New York: Oxford University Press, 2007).

Basu, Dipak R., and Miroshnik, Victoria. *Japanese Multinational Companies* (Oxford: Elsevier, 2000).

Chung, C. C., Lee, S-H., Beamish, P. W., and Isobe, T. "Subsidiary expansion/contraction during times of economic crisis," *Journal of International Business Studies*, vol. 41, no. 3 (2010).

Colcera, E. *The Market for Corporate Control in Japan: M&As, Hostile Takeovers and Regulatory Framework* (New York: Springer, 2010).

Collinson, Simon C., and Rugman, Alan M. "The regional nature of Japanese multinational business," *Journal of International Business Studies*, vol. 39, no. 2 (2008).

Delios, Andrew, and Beamish, Paul W. "Joint venture performance revisited: Japanese foreign subsidiaries worldwide," *Management International Review*, vol. 44, no. 1 (2004).

Dent, C. M. *China, Japan and Regional Leadership in East Asia* (Cheltenham: Edward Elgar, 2010).

Dominici, G. *From Business System to Supply Chain and Production in Japan: Lean Production and its Roots in Japanese Business Culture* (Saarbrücken, Germany: VDM Verlag, 2010).

Dyer, J., and Chu, W. "The determinants of trust in supplier–automaker relations in the US, Japan, and Korea: a retrospective," *Journal of International Business Studies*, vol. 42, no. 1 (2011).

Dyer, Jeffrey H., and Hatch, Nile H. "Using supplier networks to learn faster," *MIT Sloan Management Review*, vol. 45, no. 3 (spring 2004).

Furuya, N., Stevens, M. J., Bird, A., Oddou, G., and Mendenhall, M. "Managing the learning and transfer of global management competence: antecedents and outcomes of Japanese repatriation effectiveness," *Journal of International Business Studies*, vol. 40, no. 2 (2009).

Goerzen, Anthony, and Makino, Shige. "Multinational corporation internationalization in the service sector: a study of Japanese trading companies," *Journal of*

International Business Studies, vol. 38, no. 7 (December 2007).

Hasegawa, Y., and Kimm, A. *Rediscovering Japanese Business Leadership: 15 Japanese Managers and the Companies They're Leading to New Growth* (Chichester: John Wiley & Sons, 2010).

Herstatt, C., Stockstrom, C., Tschirky, H., and Nagahira, A. *Management of Technology and Innovation in Japan* (New York: Springer, 2010).

Hong, Jacky F. L., and Snell, Robin Stanley. "Knowledge development through co-opetition: a case study of a Japanese foreign subsidiary and its local suppliers," *Journal of World Business*, vol. 50, no. 4 (2015).

Ito, K., and Rose, E. L. "The implicit return on domestic and international sales: an empirical analysis of US and Japanese firms," *Journal of International Business Studies*, vol. 41, no. 6 (2010).

Jung, J. C., Beamish, P. W., and Goerzen, A. "FDI ownership strategy: a Japanese–US MNE comparison," *Management International Review*, vol. 48, no. 5 (2008).

Kang, Inwon, Han, Shin, and Shin, Geon-Cheol. "A process leading to strategic alliance outcome: the case of IT companies in China, Japan and Korea," *International Business Review*, vol. 23, no. 6 (2014).

Kawai, Norifumi, and Strange, Roger. "Subsidiary autonomy and performance in Japanese multinationals in Europe," *International Business Review*, vol. 23, no. 3 (2014).

Kim, Young-Choon, Lu, Jane W., and Rhee, Mooweon. "Learning from age difference: interorganizational learning and survival in Japanese foreign subsidiaries," *Journal of International Business Studies*, vol. 43, no. 8 (2012).

Kobayashi, Mami. "Ownership structure, shareholder intervention, and success in takeovers," *Japan and the World Economy*, vol. 19, no. 4 (December 2007).

Kotabe, Mike, Martin, Xavier, and Domoto, Hiroshi. "Gaining from vertical partnerships: knowledge transfer, relationship duration and supplier performance improvement in the US and Japanese automotive industries," *Strategic Management Journal*, vol. 24, no. 4 (April 2003).

Kotabe, M., Mol, M. J., and Ketkar, S. "An evolutionary stage model of outsourcing and competence destruction: a triad comparison of the consumer electronics industry," *Management International Review*, vol. 48, no. 1 (2008).

Liker, Jeffrey K., Fruin, W. Mark, and Adler, Paul S. (eds.). *Remade in America: Transplanting and Transforming Japanese Management Systems* (New York: Oxford University Press, 1999).

Lincoln, Edward J. *Arthritic Japan: The Slow Pace of Economic Reform* (New York: Brookings Institution Press, 2001).

McGuire, Jean, and Dow, Sandra. "The persistence and implications of Japanese *keiretsu* organization," *Journal of International Business Studies*, vol. 34, no. 4 (July 2003).

Nobeoka, Kentao, Dyer, Jeffrey H., and Anoop, Madhok. "The influence of customer scope on supplier learning and performance in the Japanese automobile industry,"

Journal of International Business Studies, vol. 33, no. 4 (2002).

Park, Tae-Hoon. "Hierarchical structures and competitive strategies in car development: inter-organizational relationships with Toyota's first-, second- and third-tier suppliers," *Journal of Asian Business and Management*, vol. 6, no. 2 (June 2007).

Pudelko, Markus, and Mendenhall, Mark E. "The Japanese management metamorphosis: what Western executives need to know about current Japanese management practices," *Organizational Dynamics*, vol. 36, no. 3 (2007).

Rose, Elizabeth L., and Ito, Kiyohiko. "Competitive interactions: the international investment patterns of Japanese automobile manufacturers," *Journal of International Business Studies*, vol. 39, no. 5 (2008).

Rosenbluth, F. M., and Thies, M. F. *Japan Transformed: Political Change and Economic Restructuring* (Princeton, NJ: Princeton University Press, 2010).

Rugman, Alan M. "The regional multinationals of Asia." In Y. Kuwana et al. (eds.), *New Frontiers in International Business: Essays in Honor of Kenichi Enatsu*, International Business, vol. 5 (Tokyo, 2008). [Translated and published in Japanese]

Rugman, Alan M. *Rugman Reviews International Business*, Japanese Edition (Basingstoke: Macmillan, 2009). [Translated and published in Japanese]

Slater, Stephanie, and Robson, Matthew J. "Cultural interpretations of destructive acts and trust in Japanese supply channel relationships," *International Business Review*, vol. 21, no. 3 (2012).

Thomas, L. G. III. "Are we all global now? Local vs. foreign sources of corporate competence: the case of the Japanese pharmaceutical industry," *Strategic Management Journal*, vol. 25, nos. 8/9 (September 2004).

Wan, William P., Yiu, Daphne W., Hoskisson, Robert E., and Kim, Heechun. "The performance implications of relationship banking during macroeconomic expansion and contraction: a study of Japanese banks' social relationships and overseas expansion," *Journal of International Business Studies*, vol. 39, no. 3 (2008).

Whitley, Richard, Morgan, Glenn, Kelley, William, and Sharpe, Diana. "The changing japanese multinational: application, adaptation and learning in car manufacturing and financial services," *Journal of Management Studies*, vol. 40, no. 3 (May 2003).

Witt, M. A. *Changing Japanese Capitalism: Societal Coordination and Institutional Adjustment* (Cambridge: Cambridge University Press, 2008).

Witt, M. A., and Redding, G. "Culture, meaning, and institutions: executive rationale in Germany and Japan," *Journal of International Business Studies*, vol. 40, no. 5 (2009).

Zhonghua, W., and Delios, A. "The emergence of portfolio restructuring in Japan," *Management International Review*, vol. 49, no. 3 (2009).

WWW RESOURCES

Japanese Ministry of Economy, Trade, and Industry: http://www.meti.go.jp/english/

Japan External Trade Organization: http://www.jetro.go.jp

Japanese Ministry of Finance: http://www.mof.go.jp/english/

Chapter 19

NORTH AMERICA

Contents

Objectives of the chapter

Within NAFTA, the United States, Canada, and Mexico constitute a thriving economic bloc. More than 34 percent of all US trade is with Canada and Mexico; both those countries conduct well over 75 percent of their international trade with the United States (see Tables 19.1, 19.2, and 19.3 below). Since market access to the United States is fairly open and already well documented, this chapter will focus on the other two members of NAFTA: Canada and Mexico. These countries are very different from the United States and have distinctive business practices. Doing business in these countries requires just as much research and attention to institutional detail as doing business in the EU or Japan.

The specific objectives of this chapter are to:

1 *Examine* the nature of the Canadian and Mexican political and economic systems and their implications for business strategy.

2 *Review* the business environment with primary attention on the industrial, regulatory, banking and finance, and labor relations areas.

3 *Investigate* major economic opportunities that exist in Canada and Mexico and some of the ways of conducting business in these nations.

4 *Consider* specific institutional arrangements, namely, the United States–Canada Free Trade Agreement (FTA) and the North American Free Trade Agreement (NAFTA), which play an important role in shaping opportunities and the business environment in North America.

ACTIVE LEARNING CASE

NAFTA

The North American Free Trade Agreement (NAFTA) came into effect on January 1, 1994. Over the years, it has been the subject of debate and frequent misunderstanding. For example, in the 2008 campaign for the Democratic presidential nomination both Senator Hillary Clinton and Senator Barack Obama pledged to renegotiate NAFTA to add environmental policies and to help labor adjustment. Yet, NAFTA was the first international trade agreement to incorporate both of these issues. NAFTA set up an environmental commission to monitor the impact of environmental regulations on trade and investment. NAFTA also incorporated labor adjustment programs in the form of assistance for retraining and upgrading of individual worker skills.

What then is the actual nature of NAFTA and what has been its impact? While NAFTA is a complex international agreement, it only has two basic principles. First, all tariffs on trade in manufactured goods are abolished. Second, the principle of national treatment is applied to foreign direct investment. Together these two basic principles serve to help open the internal markets of all three countries to greater amounts of trade and investment. In other words, regional economic integration is fostered. Indeed, recent data indicate that Canada and Mexico account for about one-third of all US trade (these countries are the largest trading partners for the United States, ahead of China, Japan, and the EU; see Table 19.1). Both Canada and Mexico have over three-quarters of their trade with the United States (see Tables 19.2 and 19.3).

NAFTA, however, is not a pure free trade agreement, since many sectors are exempted from its provisions. For example, although tariffs have been abolished, the US textile and apparel sector is protected through a system of rules of origin. The latter serve to exclude garments assembled in Mexico from using textile fibers produced in Asia. In a similar manner, automobiles cannot be assembled in Mexico and sold in the United States and Canada unless they have most of their components produced in North America. Similarly, much of the US agriculture sector is still protected from Mexican competition. In the service sector (which now accounts for over 80 percent of all jobs in the United States and Canada), well over half the sectors were exempted from the principle of national treatment. For example, excluded sectors include all

Source: Bettmann/Getty Images

aspects of: healthcare; education; public administration; transportation; and public utilities. This means that each country can enact discriminatory regulations to foster its indigenous firms and exclude foreign nationals from working in these exempted sectors.

In terms of environmental regulations, NAFTA is limited (under multilateral trade rules from the WTO) in its ability to enforce US and Canadian environmental standards upon Mexico. However, NAFTA aims to harmonize environmental standards over time by requiring that Mexico set minimum environmental standards and improve its enforcement to match those of its neighbors within NAFTA. This process is monitored by a trilateral environmental commission headquartered in Montreal, Canada. Research on the environmental aspects of NAFTA by Rugman et al. (1999, 2005) showed that, as US and Canadian automobile suppliers and specialty chemical firms relocated to Mexico under NAFTA, these firms built new plants which incorporated the high environmental standards (ISO 1400) engineered into their production processes. Thus, environmental standards in Mexico are being improved specifically due to NAFTA. Furthermore, each country retains sovereignty over its environmental laws, although compensation can be sought by a foreign investor if a change in such laws results in unfair economic loss, as assessed by the trilateral environmental commission.

As a result of NAFTA there has been a large increase in trade and investment across North America. The region has become even more integrated. Intraregional trade flows have increased significantly over the treaty's first two

Table 19.1 Direction of US trade, 1999–2014

Country/ region	Exports to						Imports from					
	1999		2008		2014		1999		2008		2014	
	US$bn	% of total	US$bn	% of total	US$bn	% of total	US$bn	% of total	US$bn	% of total	US$bn	% of total
Canada	162.95	23.59	260.91	20.07	312.42	19.27	198.82	18.96	339.71	15.68	347.80	14.8
Mexico	86.38	12.50	151.53	11.65	240.25	14.83	109.49	10.44	218.08	10.06	294.47	12.5
Japan	57.73	8.35	66.57	5.12	66.83	4.12	134.00	12.78	143.35	6.61	134.00	5.7
China (incl. Hong Kong)*	25.71	3.72	93.14	7.16	123.66	7.63	98.65	9.40	363.22	16.76	466.75	19.8
EU[†]	151.86	21.98	275.29	21.17	277.30	17.1	199.58	19.03	376.98	17.40	418.34	17.8
All others	206.04	29.83	452.53	34.81	600.01	37	307.86	29.36	724.64	33.45	686.31	29.2
Total	690.68	100.0	1,300.00	100.0	1620.48	100.0	1048.43	100.0	2166.00	100.0	2347.68	100.0

* Data for China in 2014 exclude Hong Kong.
[†] EU data for 1999 are for EU15.
Source: Adapted from IMF, *Direction of Trade Statistics Yearbook*, 2000, 2009 and 2014

Table 19.2 Direction of Canada's trade, 1999–2014

Country/ region	Exports to						Imports from					
	1999		2008		2014		1999		2008		2014	
	US$bn	% of total	US$bn	% of total	US$bn	% of total	US$bn	% of total	US$bn	% of total	US$bn	% of total
United States	208.01	87.64	354.67	77.68	364.48	76.7	143.49	67.00	214.07	52.43	276.16	54.4
EU*	10.43	4.39	34.23	7.50	35.05	7.3	21.52	10.05	50.93	12.47	57.52	11.3
Japan	5.25	2.21	10.42	2.28	9.72	2.0	10.10	4.71	14.43	3.53	13.21	2.6
Triad	223.69	94.25	399.33	87.46	409.25	86.0	175.12	81.77	279.44	68.44	346.89	68.4
Mexico	1.02	0.43	5.49	1.20	4.96	1.0	6.26	2.92	16.73	4.09	28.59	5.6
All others	12.61	5.31	51.71	11.32	60.42	12.7	32.77	15.30	112.07	27.45	131.54	25.9
Total	237.33	100.0	456.54	100.0	474.62	100.0	214.16	100.0	408.25	100.0	507.03	100.0

* EU data for 1999 are for EU15.
Source: Adapted from IMF, *Direction of Trade Statistics Yearbook*, 2000, 2009 and 2014.

Table 19.3 Direction of Mexico's trade, 1999–2014

Country/region	Exports to						Imports from					
	1999		2008		2014		1999		2008		2014	
	US$bn	% of total	US$bn	% of total	US$bn	% of total	US$bn	% of total	US$bn	% of total	US$bn	% of total
United States	120.39	88.27	233.52	80.15	318.36	80.1	105.26	74.14	151.33	49.03	214.81	48.8
Canada	2.39	1.75	7.10	2.43	10.71	2.6	2.94	2.07	9.44	3.05	11.05	2.5
North America*	122.78	90.02	240.62	82.59	329.08	82.8	108.21	76.22	160.77	52.09	225.86	51.3
EU[†]	5.19	3.81	17.00	5.83	19.99	5.0	14.00	9.86	38.33	12.42	47.05	10.6
Japan	0.77	0.56	2.04	0.70	2.61	0.6	5.08	3.58	16.28	5.27	19.30	4.3
All others	2.43	1.78	9.80	3.36	45.45	11.4	10.87	7.65	77.38	25.07	147.77	33.5
Total	136.39	100.0	291.34	100.0	397.13	100	141.97	100.0	308.60	100.0	439.97	100.0

* Excluding Mexico.
[†] EU data for 1999 are for EU15.
Source: Adapted from IMF, *Direction of Trade Statistics Yearbook*, 2000, 2009, and 2014.

▶

decades, from around $290 billion in 1993 to more than $1.1 trillion in 2012. Cross-border investment and travel have also increased significantly. The United States now trades more in goods and services with Mexico and Canada than it does with Japan, South Korea, Brazil, Russia, India, and China combined. Why has NAFTA been so successful?

From the viewpoint of the United States it gains more secure access to the natural resources of Canada and Mexico. In particular, Canada has agreed to continue supplies of oil and gas exports to the United States even in times of economic disruption (in legal terms, existing contractual arrangements will be guaranteed). While Mexico did not incorporate such energy provisions into its NAFTA agreement, it is clear that the United States now has more secure energy supplies from Mexico and internally than it does from the Persian Gulf.

The big gain for Canada and Mexico from NAFTA is better and more secure long-run access to the US market. What are the implications of this for Canadian and Mexican business? In Canada, a new set of Canadian businesses has emerged. These are successful competitors in the US market. These firms include: Bombardier, BCE, Magna (a major automobile supplier), RIM, Onex, and a set of large financial institutions including the Canadian banks. In Mexico, companies such as Cemex and Carso Global Telecom have become major players in the United States. Perhaps more important is that clusters of world-class businesses have developed in Toronto, Montreal, Calgary, and Vancouver in Canada and in Monterrey in Mexico. In short, the business sectors in both Canada and Mexico are being upgraded and modernized, such that these countries are creating new jobs for skilled and educated workers across the integrated geographic space of North America.

Sources: Mohammed Aly Sergie, "NAFTA's economic impact," US Council on Foreign Relations (February 14, 2014), http://www.cfr.org/trade/naftas-economic-impact/p15790; Alan M. Rugman (ed.), *Foreign Investment and NAFTA* (Columbia, SC: University of South Carolina Press, 1994); Alan M. Rugman, John Kirton, and Julie Soloway, *Environmental Regulations and Corporate Strategy: A NAFTA Perspective* (Oxford: Oxford University Press, 1999); Alan M. Rugman, "North American intra-regional trade and foreign direct investment," in Alan Rugman (ed.), *Research in Global Strategic Management*, Vol. 10 of North American Economic and Financial Integration (Oxford: Elsevier, 2004); Alan M. Rugman, *The End of Globalization* (New York: Amacom, 2000, 2001); Alan M. Rugman, "Continental integration and foreign ownership of Canadian industry: a retrospective analysis," in Lorraine Eden and Wendy Dobson (eds.), *Governance, Multinationals and Growth* (Cheltenham: Edward Elgar, 2005); Alan M. Rugman, "Regional multinationals and regional trade policy: the end of multilateralism," in Michele Fratianni, Paolo Savona, and John Kirton (eds.), *Corporate, Public and Global Governance* (Aldershot: Ashgate, 2007).

1 How has NAFTA affected Canada?

2 Has NAFTA increased trade between the United States and Canada? Why is this?

3 How has NAFTA affected Mexico?

4 How has NAFTA affected the United States?

5 Does NAFTA include environmental laws?

INTRODUCTION

In Chapter 10 we saw that governments and the various institutions through which they wield their powers are important external factors in the international business environment. This chapter focuses on institutional factors in the North American market that must be considered when looking at the Canadian and Mexican markets. NAFTA has not abolished all trade barriers between the United States, Canada, and Mexico. There are still major impediments to trade and investment. Furthermore, each of the partners retains its own trade laws. A legal mechanism to appeal trade decisions exists, but this is a compromise position. In contrast, EU member states cannot use trade laws against their partners. So although NAFTA is a step toward trade liberalization, business decisions should not assume that "free trade" makes Canada and Mexico identical to the United States.

CANADA

With a land area of almost 3.85 million square miles (9.98 million km^2), Canada is second in size only to Russia. Divided into ten provinces and three territories (see Figure 19.1), Canada is so large that it encompasses six time zones. The French and British fought over

Canada
Population	35.54 million
GDP (PPP 2014)	US$1,565,812 million
GDP per capita (PPP, constant 2011, international $)	$42,778
Inflation rate	1.9%
Current account balance	−US$37,474 million
Unemployment	6.9%

United States
Population	318.86 million
GDP (PPP 2014)	US$17,419,000 million
GDP per capita (PPP, constant 2011, international $)	$16,284
Inflation rate	1.6%
Current account balance	−US$389,525 million
Unemployment	6.2%

Mexico
Population	125.38 million
GDP (PPP 2014)	US$2,145,089 million
GDP per capita (PPP, constant 2011, international $)	$52,118
Inflation rate	4.0%
Current account balance	−US$26,452 million
Unemployment	4.9%

Figure 19.1 North America, 2014

Note: PPP = purchasing power parity.
Source: http://data.worldbank.org/indicator/SP.POP.TOTL

the country, with control passing into British hands in 1763. Canada became a separate nation in 1867, although it did not fully repatriate its Constitution until 1982. Today it remains a leading member of the British Commonwealth.

Canada's economy

Canada's 35 million people enjoy one of the highest standards of living in the world. Consumer tastes and disposable wealth are very similar to those in the United States. Gross domestic product (GDP) in 2015 was about $1.592 trillion (2016 est.) and at current exchange rates. Over the last 5 years, the rate of economic growth has been in the 0 to 2 percent range. Canada has typically had a positive balance of payments, thanks to its food, energy, and motor vehicle exports. Its primary trading partner is the United States, which provided over 54 percent of Canada's imports and accounted for 76 percent of the country's exports in 2014 (see Table 19.2).

Canada's economic growth historically has been based on the export of agricultural staples, especially grains, and on the production and export of natural resource products such as minerals, oil, gas, and forest products. However, major secondary industries have also emerged; Canada now ranks as one of the top ten manufacturing nations in the world.

The service industry is also expanding rapidly, especially financial services in Toronto. However, the country still faces a major productivity challenge. For each hour Canadians work, they produce 5.8 percent less than their US neighbors.[1]

Almost 80 percent of manufacturing activity is located in Ontario and Quebec—including the entire motor vehicle industry, which is Canada's largest segment—while Calgary has become a major high-tech center. Almost one-quarter of all Canada's exports (and imports) are in autos and auto-related products. The Canada–United States Automotive Products Trade Agreement (Autopact) has encouraged this two-way trade over the last 35 years, allowing free trade in autos assembled in either country, provided there was 50 percent value added in Canada. (Under NAFTA, the content provision rose to 62.5 percent.) Financial institutions and other business service industries are also concentrated in central Canada. The eastern and western areas of the country are more dependent on primary industries: fishing, forestry, and mining in the east; agriculture, ore, and mineral fuels in the west. The country's growth was helped by large inflows of FDI; today, 40 percent of the primary and secondary industries are foreign owned. Yet Canada is wealthy enough now, and its economy is sufficiently mature, to have substantial outward FDI, particularly in the United States.

The United States has more FDI in Canada than in any other country, including the UK. Since 1988 this investment has doubled, and in 2012 it stood at about $326.5 billion. At the same time Canada has invested $250 billion in the United States, more than in any other country.[2] We can see these relationships within individual industries. For example, many US airlines, including American, Delta, and Northwest, fly to Canada, and Air Canada and Canadian Airlines, which merged in 2001, among others, have US routes. So part of the US international airline strategy involves competing with Canadian carriers that are vying for the US market (see the case **International Business Strategy in Action: Bombardier**). There are many other examples of Canadian investment in the United States. Canadian Pacific has purchased the Delaware & Hudson Railway, and Bombardier Inc. bought the Learjet Corporation of Wichita, Kansas. Many other acquisitions are even larger.

✔ Active learning check

Review your answer to Active Learning Case question 1 and make any changes you like. Then compare your answer to the one below.

1 How has NAFTA affected Canada?

NAFTA eliminates tariffs and makes it easier for efficient Canadian firms to operate competitively in the United States. At the same time, it allows efficient US firms to ship their goods into Canada without paying any tariffs and, in the process, helps drive down prices. So NAFTA helps the Canadian economy by encouraging efficiency, lowering prices, and opening up new markets in the United States.

Differences in the business environment

Despite many similarities between the business environments of the United States and Canada, there are also some important differences.

Canada's industrial climate

The Canadian economy is characterized by private enterprise. However, some industries, such as broadcasting and public utilities, are government owned or subject to substantial government regulation.[3] Over the past decade, the trend has been toward privatization and deregulation. In fact, a federal government minister oversees privatization and has been responsible for selling companies that the government feels are no longer essential to meet public policy goals. Firms that have been privatized include Canadair, the de Havilland Aircraft Company, Canadian National Railway's trucking division, Fishery Products International, and Air Canada.

INTERNATIONAL BUSINESS STRATEGY IN ACTION

Bombardier

In 1942 the dreams of a budding young Quebec entrepreneur came true with the incorporation of L'Auto-Neige Bombardier, the world's first snowmobile manufacturer. Although mechanic-turned-industrialist Joseph-Armand Bombardier had great plans for his innovative transportation inventions, he could never have foreseen the course his company would take in the next 50 years.

Today, Bombardier is one of the world's top manufacturers of transportation products, with yearly revenues of $20.1 billion and 74,000 employees for the year ending December 31, 2014. Having begun with snowmobile production, Bombardier is now among the world leaders in commuter and general transportation trains, as well as transport vehicles for industrial and military use, sailboats, motorcycles, and, more recently, smaller aircraft. This extension into numerous other industries has transformed Bombardier from a once small-town Quebec company into a global market competitor and leader with over 90 percent of its total business now conducted outside Canada.

The company operates in two segments: aerospace (through Bombardier Aircraft) and rail transportation (through Bombardier Transportation). BA is engaged in the design and manufacture of aviation products and a provider of related services. BT is engaged in the design and manufacture of rail equipment and systems and a provider of related services. It also provides bogies, electric propulsion, control equipment and maintenance services, as well as complete rail transportation systems and rail control solutions. BA's aircraft portfolio includes a line of business aircraft, commercial aircraft, including regional jets, turboprops, and single-aisle mainline jets, and amphibious aircraft.

Bombardier's success is due mostly to the industrious and business instincts of its former company CEO and current chairman of the board Laurent Beaudoin, who in the past 30 years has followed a strategy of market entry and

Source: Agencja Fotograficzna Caro/Alamy Stock Photo

product improvement through acquisition, instead of relying strictly on R&D. As a result, the company has managed to produce the most technically advanced, innovative, and reliable products on the market and gained substantial market share in many industries, especially with its rubber-wheeled subway car, sold to New York City in the 1980s.

This strategy has been exemplified by Bombardier's entry into the aerospace industry with the acquisition of Canadair in 1986, 12 years after diversifying into the transportation equipment business. The Canadair purchase brought the company a large pool of human resources and technical expertise, which has been applied to develop such "in-house" products as the twin-engine Challenger Business Jet. As a result, Bombardier suddenly held lead positions in numerous niche markets, which ensured ongoing relations with such manufacturing giants as Boeing and McDonnell Douglas. This acquisition quickly resulted in numerous contracts for CF-18 fighters from the Canadian government and contracts for Airbus components from both British Aerospace and France's Aérospatiale.

▶

Further acquisition was a logical step for the company. By acquiring Northern Ireland's Short Brothers, Bombardier extended itself firmly into the European market as a supplier and manufacturer of aerospace technology. At the outset of the 1990s, purchases of both Learjet out of Wichita, Kansas, and Boeing's de Havilland propelled diversification into regional jets and turboprop aircraft. Finally, production of the first-of-its-kind 50-passenger Canadair Regional Jet signified Bombardier's full-fledged entry into the airline industry. With the bulk of its profit already coming from this industry and the shared know-how, technology, resources, and markets of all of these companies pooled under one roof, Bombardier is ripe to become a major player in the aerospace industry.

Over the past ten years, US and Canadian airlines have begun to try to improve their competitive positions through a series of alliances. For example, Air Canada has become part of Star Alliance, a collection of currently 27 international airlines—including United Airlines from the United States—that account for 21 percent of the global market. Similarly, prior to merging with Air Canada in 2000, Canadian Airlines had joined American Airlines and its code-sharing partners around the world in the Oneworld alliance. This is a result of a trend that is grouping the international airline business into several large alliances to compete against each other.

For the North American Airline market, this means an increase in efficiency. In 1993 US carriers were authorized to serve only 44 routes in Canada, and Canadian carriers had a mere 28 routes in the United States. A study at the time revealed that, if the skies between the two countries were allowed to open up, air traffic would double within the next few years. The study also estimated that the resulting increase in tourism and trade would generate $10.3 billion in additional economic activity. These statistics indicate why a new Open Skies agreement between the countries was enacted in 1995 that liberalized the regulatory environment for airlines in both countries. After the establishment of Open Skies, trans-border traffic increased from 13 million passengers in 1994 to 20 million in 2000 and is close to 50 million today. Nonetheless, the 1995 treaty falls short of a full Open Skies agreement because of restrictions on cargo and third-country rights.

Since NAFTA came into effect on January 1, 1994, there has been a further incentive to liberalize trade in services such as airline travel. However, under NAFTA's restricted transportation provisions, national treatment does not apply. This means that a US airline can do business across the Canadian borders only on a point-to-point basis, from, say, New York's LaGuardia to Toronto. It cannot pick up any passengers within Canada. Similarly, Air Canada can fly from Montreal to New York to Miami, but it cannot compete with US airlines on the internal New York to Miami route.

Despite the lack of national treatment, Air Canada has doubled its flights to the United States and more than tripled its number of routes since the Open Skies agreement. Today, Air Canada handles over 40 percent of the Canada–US traffic and attributes close to 3,000 new jobs to the agreement. Air travel was further eased in 1998 by a bilateral agreement to facilitate pre-clearance of customs and immigration services. This will reduce double inspections by customs and immigration officers in both countries. The considerable success of these agreements has led both governments to negotiate similar agreements with other countries around the globe.

Website: www.bombardier.com

Sources: Adapted from Alan M. Rugman, *Foreign Investment and NAFTA* (Columbia, SC: University of South Carolina Press, 1994); www.aircanada.ca; Air Canada, "Air Canada President and CEO urges US airline CEOs towards further liberalization of US–Canada market," press release, December 13, 2001; Canada, Ministry of Transportation, *Canada Transportation Act Review*, July 18, 2001; Bombardier, *Annual Report*, 2010.

Small business is a major part of the economy and accounts for almost 80 percent of all new employment in manufacturing. The service and retail trade industries are characterized by a large number of companies that vary in size; 70 percent of Canadians work in service industries.

Canada's regulatory environment

Commerce and industry in Canada are regulated at every level of government: federal, provincial, and municipal. Many of these regulations are similar to those in the United States.

Competition

Regulation of competition is under the jurisdiction of the federal Parliament. Legislation in this area was revised in the late 1980s to eliminate restrictive trade policies, stimulate production, and promote the international competitiveness of Canadian business. Although there are no price controls in Canada, there is regulation to review monopolies, acquisitions, and mergers. The regulation of anti-competitive practices is handled under the

Competition Act
A Canadian federal law that regulates anti-competitive practices and prohibits actions that will substantially lessen or prevent competition; it is similar to US antitrust laws

Competition Act, which prohibits individuals and companies from practices that will substantially lessen or prevent competition in the marketplace. The Act outlaws bid rigging, price discrimination, or conspiring to unduly lessen competition, and provides for regulation of acquisitions and mergers. If the purchase price is $400 million or more, the parties must refrain from completing the transaction for a time period ranging from 7 to 21 days. During this time the government reviews the situation and decides whether the purchase will prevent or lessen competition (using international comparisons) and thus be uncompetitive in nature. A ruling is then made.

✔ Active learning check

Review your answer to Active Learning Case question 2 and make any changes you like. Then compare your answer to the one below.

② Has NAFTA increased trade between the United States and Canada? Why is this?

The data show that US–Canada trade has increased as a result of NAFTA. Three reasons can be cited. First, the elimination of all tariffs under NAFTA encouraged exports. Second, both countries are more likely to produce those goods and services for which they have a competitive advantage and to buy the others from their neighbor. Third, as the economies of the two countries grow, so will the amount of trade as each begins to adapt operations to the desires of the other and starts to tap this market further.

Exports and imports

Export permits are required for the shipment of goods having strategic value, such as uranium. They are also required to implement the provisions of various international agreements into which Canada has entered. Import documentation is also required, as well as payment of a goods and sales tax (GST) or the federal part of the harmonized sales tax (HST), except for items specified as non-taxable importations. The GST, which went into effect on January 1, 1991, is a value-added tax. On imports, it is collected by Canadian Customs. GST (5 percent) is payable on most goods at the time of importation. Effective July 1, 2010, the HST applies in the participating provinces at the following rates: 13 percent in Ontario, New Brunswick, and Newfoundland and Labrador, 15 percent in Nova Scotia, and 12 percent in British Columbia. The GST applies in the rest of Canada at the rate of 5 percent.[4]

Francization in Quebec

The Canadian federal government has a bilingual policy.[5] But in the province of Quebec, French is the official language for business and education. All firms employing 50 or more people in Quebec must use French at all levels of the organization. Other regulations related to the use of French in Quebec are that: (1) all product labels must be in French, and translations cannot be given greater prominence than the French portion; (2) company names and signs must be in French, but a version of the firm's name in another language may accompany the French version for use outside Quebec; and (3) all signs on the outside of stores must be in French only.[6] Moreover, all education, health services, and other services under provincial jurisdiction are delivered in French. Some exceptions to the French language and sign law policies accommodate the one-fifth of the Quebec population that speaks English. For example, McGill University and Concordia University can operate in English, and English signs can be displayed inside stores, provided they are smaller than French signs.

Banking and finance

Banks in Canada offer a full range of financial services. There are six large Canadian chartered banks with extensive national branch networks that account for 90 percent of the nation's banking industry assets. There are also many smaller (often foreign-owned) banks.[7] All these banks respond to the actions of the central bank, the Bank of Canada, a federal government institution directly responsible for the nation's monetary policy, including (1) regulating credit and currency, (2) controlling and protecting the external value of the Canadian dollar, and (3) regulating the general level of production, trade, prices, and employment, within the scope of monetary policy.

In carrying out its functions, the Bank of Canada buys and sells foreign exchange and sets the interest rate charged to commercial banks. These functions are similar to those carried out by the Federal Reserve in the United States, which helps monitor the US monetary system. The Bank of Canada is also responsible for issuing the country's notes and coins and for managing the federal debt. Canadian interest rates and its exchange rate closely follow those set in the United States, especially in relation to non-North American interest and exchange rates.

Banks operate within the confines of the Bank Act. There are two types: Schedule A and Schedule B. Schedule A banks are Canadian owned and no shareholder has more than 10 percent of the voting stock. Schedule B banks are closely held Canadian-owned or foreign banks. These are allowed to carry on normal banking activities. However, foreign-owned banks cannot, as a group, own more than 16 percent of the total domestic assets of the Canadian banking system. Subsidiaries of US banks are not subject to this restriction because of the US–Canada Free Trade Agreement. In addition, Canadian banks are allowed to operate across the country.

There is also a host of specialized financial institutions that provide limited services throughout the provinces. Examples include savings banks, cooperative credit unions, loan companies, mortgage companies, and insurance companies. Investment bankers provide short-term funds to companies for acquisition or reorganization purposes.

Canada has four major stock exchanges: Toronto, Montreal, Vancouver, and Calgary. Toronto is the major exchange, accounting for approximately 95 percent of dollar trading volume. It is also the financial center of the country.[8]

Labor relations

Canada Labor Code
A federal law that covers areas such as wages, employment practices, work safety, and conciliation of labor disputes

Labor relations are governed by both federal and provincial labor legislation. The **Canada Labor Code** is the federal law that covers such matters as wages, employment practices, work safety, and conciliation in the event of a labor dispute. Provincial governments have similar laws to cover employer–employee relations at the local level.

Unions

With the exception of farmers, domestic help, and white-collar workers, the workforce is heavily unionized. Approximately 30 percent of the total labor force is in unions, compared to approximately 13.5 percent in the United States. Average paid employment (employees) during the first half of 2010 was 14.3 million. However, since union membership rose slightly more rapidly than employment, the unionization rate edged up from 29.5 percent in 2009 to 29.6 percent in 2010. As women experienced disproportionately more gains in unionized jobs, their unionization rate rose to 30.9 percent. The unionization rate for men remained constant at 28.2 percent. As a result, the gap in the rates between men and women widened further in 2010.[9] In some instances the workers are free to choose or reject union membership; in other cases they must become members in order to keep their jobs. The labor–management contract determines these conditions.

As in the United States, once a union has been certified to represent the workers, management must bargain in good faith. The result of such bargaining is a labor–management agreement that determines wage rates, fringe benefits, working conditions, and management rights. Economic nationalism is a strong component of Canadian unionization, and the unions have been major opponents of the FTA, NAFTA, and other economic and political relationships with the United States.

Working conditions

All provinces have legislated minimum wage rates that are periodically adjusted. However, in most sectors wages and salaries are similar to US levels.

A national compulsory contributory pension plan provides retirement benefits to contributors, generally at the age of 65. This age limit varies, however, and there is growing pressure to relax mandatory retirement rules. In addition, many private pension plans are in effect. Other benefits include group life insurance, medical insurance, and subsidized food and housing. Most provincial legislation limits daily or weekly working hours, with mandatory overtime pay for hours worked in excess of these limits. The government also mandates minimum annual paid vacations in almost all industries, which is typically two weeks after a year of employment and up to three or four weeks after longer employment. There are also legislated holidays, which, depending on the city and the province, usually vary between 8 and 12 days.

All provinces prohibit employment discrimination on the basis of race, religion, national origin, color, sex, age, or marital status. There are also provisions for equal pay for equal work, which vary across provinces. They are designed to prevent gender bias in pay levels. For example, Ontario has specific "pay equity" legislation that requires employers to remove gender bias in pay levels; salary adjustments were phased in, starting in 1990. Similar legislation has been enacted in a number of other provinces, including Quebec and Saskatchewan.

Investments

Investment Canada Act (ICA)
A law enacted to significantly reduce restrictions for foreign investors in Canada to create a more open economy

The **Investment Canada Act (ICA)** came into effect on June 30, 1985, and is designed to create a welcome climate for foreign investment by significantly loosening previous restrictions. At the same time, however, some regulations still remain in effect. As noted earlier, investments in certain industries are restricted. For example, a license to operate a broadcasting station can be granted only to a Canadian citizen or corporation whose stock is 80 percent owned by Canadian citizens or Canadian-controlled corporations. Generally, non-residents cannot hold more than 25 percent of the issued and outstanding shares of a chartered bank, a life insurance company, a sales finance firm, a loan company, or a trust company. Nor can a single non-resident together with his or her associates hold more than 10 percent of the issued and outstanding shares of these types of companies. Limits are much less stringent in the securities industry, but the government must be kept apprised of such ownership.

Under the ICA, a non-Canadian wishing to acquire a Canadian firm must apply to the ICA for review and approval, if the assets are valued at more than $5 million or the business relates to Canada's cultural heritage or national identity. In the case of US firms buying Canadian operations, under the provisions of the Free Trade Agreement the ICA review takes place at the $150 million level. So the investment climate is much more conducive to US investors than to any others. When the ICA does conduct a review, a number of factors are considered in determining whether the investment will benefit Canada, including employment, technological benefits, and product innovation.

In addition, numerous provincial statutes place restrictions on foreigners seeking to invest in particular industries or activities. For example, in most provinces individuals have to be Canadian residents for at least a year in order to be registered securities dealers. Similarly, foreigners who are registering ownership of land must disclose their citizenship. In Alberta, British Columbia, Manitoba, Ontario, and Saskatchewan, a majority of the board of directors of corporations must be resident Canadians. However, an indirect takeover of a foreign-owned publisher will require that the firm be sold to a Canadian owner, according to the "Baie Comeau Policy."

Canada's multinationals

It is useful to identify Canada's major companies against the background of global competition and triad power. Some larger Canadian firms like Magna International and Bombardier are well known in the United States.

Table 19.4 ranks the 25 largest Canadian-owned companies in decreasing order of size measured by their sales in 2013. The largest firm is Suncor Energy which had revenues of CAD\$40 billion and is widely recognized as being one of Canada's most successful multinationals. With revenues of \$28.6 billion, Onex Corporation is a global investment conglomerate that operates in multiple industries, including sugar refining, investment, telecommunications, and automotive parts. Other well-known Canadian industrial multinationals at the top of the list are BCE (Bell Canada Enterprise), Bombardier and Magna International.

Table 19.5 lists the largest foreign-owned firms in Canada. These firms also contribute to the performance of the country, creating jobs and wealth for Canadians. However, all

Table 19.4 The largest 25 Canadian-based firms, 2014 ranking (based on 2013 revenue)

Rank	Company	Revenue (millions of CAD\$)	F/T* (%)	Intra-regional sales (%)
1	Suncor Energy Inc.	39,784,000	20.00	94.20
2	Royal Bank of Canada	38,766,000	20.00	90.50
3	Magna International Inc.	35,880,048	79.43	47.00
4	Alimentation Couche-Tard Inc.	35,650,032	86.90	66.70
5	The Toronto-Dominion Bank	33,800,000	54.40	81.10
6	George Weston Ltd.	33,582,000	99.00	100.00
7	Enbridge Inc.	32,918,000	60.20	100.00
8	Power Corp. of Canada	29,642,000	52.10	66.60
9	The Bank of Nova Scotia	28,799,000	41.20	94.40
10	Onex Corp.	28,643,270	n/a	n/a
11	Caisse de dépôt et placement du Québec	23,323,000	n/a	n/a
12	Brookfield Asset Management Inc.	22,919,560	81.50	48.00
13	Bank of Montreal	20,851,000	34.70	95.40
14	BCE Inc., Verdun	20,400,000	n/a	n/a
15	Bombardier Inc.	18,695,530	95.00	32.00
16	Manulife Financial Corp.	18,672,000	75.60	76.70
17	Empire Co. Ltd.	17,612,700	n/a	n/a
18	Canadian Imperial Bank of Commerce	17,139,000	16.30	89.30
19	Canadian Natural Resources Ltd.	16,145,000	8.00	92.20
20	Sun Life Financial Inc.	13,874,000	49.30	50.72
21	Rio Tinto Alcan Inc.	12,836,890	n/a	n/a
22	Rogers Communications Inc.	12,706,000	n/a	n/a
23	Barrick Gold Corp.	12,555,700	97.20	33.00
24	Air Canada, St-Laurent	12,382,000	n/a	n/a
25	Hydro-Québec	12,228,000	n/a	n/a

* F/T refers to foreign sales divided by total sales.

Source: http://www.financialpost.com/news/fp500/2014/index.html

Table 19.5 The largest 15 foreign-owned companies in Canada, 2014 ranking

Rank	Company	Revenue (CAD$)
1	Imperial Oil Ltd., Calgary	32,722,000
2	Husky Energy Inc., Calgary	23,317,000
3	Walmart Canada Corp., Mississauga, Ont.	23,200,000
4	Cenovus Energy Inc.	18,657,000
5	Costco Wholesale Canada Ltd.	16,492,709
6	Agrium Inc.	16,198,810
7	Catamaran Corp.	15,223,497
8	Thomson Reuters Corp.	12,242,973
9	Valero Energy Inc.	12,228,000
10	Honda Canada Inc., Markham, Ont.	11,600,000
11	McKesson Canada Corp., St-Laurent, Que.	10,280,430
12	Direct Energy Marketing Ltd., Toronto	10,020,600
13	Novelis Inc., Atlanta, Ga.	9,821,812
14	Ford Motor Co. of Canada, Ltd., Oakville, Ont.	9,084,600
15	TransCanada Corp., Calgary	8,797,000

foreign-owned firms must be examined in terms of their relationship to their parent companies. A high degree of autonomy, or development of world-class products in Canada, is necessary for a foreign-owned firm to provide sustained benefits to the country. The big auto companies have not done this. However, some energy firms, such as Imperial Oil (owned by Exxon Mobil), have a history of Canadian development. Others, such as Asea Brown Boveri (ABB), have a decentralized organizational structure with a large degree of local autonomy. These smaller but more autonomous Canadian firms (ABB is not on the list) have learned to survive within the global networks of their parent organizations, and their managers can help provide leadership to Canadians.

Another indicator of the nature of international expertise among these firms comes from the degree of their exports. Table 19.4 also reports data on the foreign sales of the largest 25 Canadian-owned firms. Exports from Canadian sales of subsidiaries in the United States and others offshore (excluding the United States) are shown. According to the table, these large companies sell approximately 50 percent of their output abroad. But there is a great deal of variability in terms of their level of multinationality – or dependence on the domestic market vs. international markets. The foreign-owned firms in Canada (Table 19.5) also sell abroad, but information on foreign sales is not readily available. Nevertheless, the four companies that do report this information export about 65 percent of their output.

This demonstrates the tremendous attraction of foreign markets for larger companies in a relatively small market like Canada's, providing further evidence that access to a triad market (in this case, the United States) is critical for success in a global market.

Multilateral agreement on investment (MAI)

Canada will benefit from any type of multilateral agreement on investment. An attempt to negotiate an MAI was made in Paris at the Organization for Economic Cooperation and Development (OECD) over the 1995 to 1998 period. The draft MAI was based on the lines of NAFTA. United Nations, UNCTAD Ministers may take up the need for an MAI.

An MAI includes the principle of national treatment: equal access for foreign investors to the host country's market (but according to host-country rules). A number of sectors are exempted from the national treatment principle. In the same spirit of the FTA and NAFTA, Canada insists on exemptions on healthcare, education, social services, cultural industries, and transportation. All regulations on investment are identified, as are all exemptions to the principle of national treatment. Additionally, dispute-settlement mechanisms are put in place to allow individual investors (and companies) to appeal against government regulations and bureaucratic controls. The MAI helps countries harmonize their regulations, although in the areas of competition policy and tax policy not much progress can be expected (no progress was achieved in NAFTA).

The need for an MAI arises because foreign investment has become an important part of the global economy. Today, the majority of international business is not done by traded goods but through services and investments. More than 75 percent of North Americans work in the service sector, with less than 25 percent in manufacturing. So the new agenda for international agreements is to negotiate rules for trade in services and investment.

Canada's outward stock of FDI is nearly 75 percent in the United States, with which it already has national treatment through the FTA and NAFTA. Thus, its exporting businesses would prefer an MAI with transparent rules.

Business opportunities in Canada

Although the Canadian economy began to slow down during the early 1990s, the country still offers excellent investment and trade opportunities for foreign investors. This is particularly true for US firms, thanks to the US–Canada FTA of 1989 and its extension, the North American Free Trade Agreement (NAFTA), which includes Mexico.

United States–Canada Free Trade Agreement (FTA)
A trade agreement that eliminates most trade restrictions (such as tariffs) between these two countries and extends national treatment to foreign investment

The **United States–Canada Free Trade Agreement (FTA)** was designed to eliminate tariffs and most other trade barriers between the two countries.[10] Some of its specific provisions are:

1 All tariffs on US and Canadian goods were to be eliminated by 1998.

2 Most import and export quotas were to be eliminated by 1998.

3 Use of product standards as a trade barrier is prohibited and national treatment of testing labs and certification bodies is established.

4 Many restrictions on agricultural products, wine and distilled spirits, auto parts, and energy goods have been sharply reduced, if not totally eliminated.

5 The size of the government procurement markets that will be open to suppliers from the other country is slightly increased.

6 Travel by business visitors, investors, traders, professionals, and executives transferred within a firm is facilitated.

7 The opportunity to invest in each other's country is facilitated and encouraged through the adoption of national treatment.

8 A binational commission to resolve disagreements that may arise from the enforcement of the FTA has been established; it dealt with some 20 cases in the first three years of the agreement.[11]

Marketing in Canada

Companies doing business in Canada need to know the distribution practices and advertising and promotion channels. In many cases, these are similar to those in other countries, but there are some important differences.

Distribution practices

Despite the country's vast size, sales to Canadian industries are characterized by short marketing channels with direct producer-to-user distribution. Many industries are dominated by a few large-scale enterprises that are highly concentrated geographically. It is not unusual for 90 percent of prospective customers of an industrial product to be located in or near two or three cities.

The consumer goods market is more diffused than the industrial market, and the use of marketing intermediaries is often necessary. In many cases, complete coverage of the consumer market requires representation in a number of commercial centers across the country. Firms having only one representative or distribution point typically choose Toronto. If the country is divided into two major markets, the other is often Calgary or Vancouver. If the market is divided into three areas, distributors are frequently put in Montreal, Ontario, and Vancouver.

Direct selling is another growing area. This includes the sale of goods from manufacturing premises by mail, home delivery, personal selling, and other non-retail channels. Direct selling now accounts for over $2.18 billion annually in Canada, with 11.2 percent growth in the past five years.[12]

Wholesale and retail trade are also important forms of distribution. Because of the wide dispersion of customers, wholesale trade is critical. However, retail trade is even more important and accounted for more than $393 billion in sales in 2010.[13] Independent stores earn about 88 percent of this, and general merchandisers, including department stores, make up the other 12 percent.[14] Quebec and Ontario account for about 61 percent of all retail sales, and in western Canada, British Columbia and Alberta make up approximately 24 percent of the total.[15] Department stores and supermarkets constitute a large percentage of retail sales. However, as in the United States, they are facing increased competition from discount food stores, showroom retailing, and other forms of self-service retailing. There are also specialized markets for recreation and leisure equipment and associated services, as well as a growing demand for consumer durables. These trends are likely to continue well into the future.

Advertising and promotion

Media used for advertising in Canada include television, radio, newspapers, and magazines. Television and radio advertising are particularly popular because 97 percent of all Canadian households have at least one television, and 99 percent have at least one radio. Hundreds of private firms operate cable television and major broadcasting stations in metropolitan areas, and the country has more than 1,300 television stations and 550 cable television systems, with over 50 percent of the population hooked into a cable system. In addition, the Canadian Broadcasting Corporation (CBC) operates two national television networks, one in English and one in French. There are 1,400 licensed AM and FM radio stations.

More than 100 daily newspapers are published in Canada and are widely used by advertisers, as are trade magazines directed at specific industries such as computers, real estate, banking, and retailing. General interest Canadian magazines such as *Reader's Digest*, *L'actualité*, and *Quest* have raised their share of net advertising expenditures in Canadian periodicals to about 30 percent, approaching the advertising of national newspapers. Two business newspapers, the *National Post* (*Financial Post* section) and *The Globe and Mail* (*Report on Business* section), also are widely read in the business and financial community. More than 450 advertising agencies in Canada can be of assistance in developing advertising and promotion campaigns.

Exporting

One of the most popular ways of doing business in Canada is through exports. As noted earlier, Canada is the United States' largest foreign market. Every year Canadians buy as many US goods as do all the member nations of the EU combined. In fact, over 20 percent of all US exports go to Canada. In recent years the Canadian government has simplified the process for shipping goods into the country. This is particularly true for products coming from the United States, since duties have been eliminated, thanks to the FTA and NAFTA.

Franchising

Canada is the dominant foreign market for US franchisers. Currently more than 300 US franchise firms operate approximately 10,000 franchise units in Canada. A recent report by *Entrepreneur* magazine rated more than 1,100 US franchises, and of those in the top 10, 8 indicated they were seeking to establish franchises in Canada. Thus, there is a great deal of opportunity for those who want to do business in Canada via the franchise route.

Additionally, in recent years Canadian banks have become more responsive to the needs of franchised operations. Chartered banks now offer various loans and repayment plans for franchises. In some cases they also offer payroll and cash management services. So there is considerable opportunity in international franchise operations in Canada.

MEXICO

With a land area of approximately 76,000 square miles (1.9 million km^2), Mexico is equal in size to almost 25 percent of the contiguous United States. It is the second largest nation in Latin America and has a population of over 122 million. The country is a federal democratic republic divided into 31 states and the Federal District (Mexico City). Although it endured political turmoil early in the twentieth century and a recent drug war in the twenty-first century, the government has been stable since World War II. Mexico is a nation where affluence, poverty, natural splendor, and urban blight rub shoulders.[16]

Mexico's economy

Mexico's economy is currently in a state of flux, brought on by new economic relations with the United States. Today Mexico has the strongest economy in Latin America. One of the primary reasons has been the economic policies of Carlos Salinas, who, after becoming president in 1988, introduced liberalization rules regarding foreign investment and privatization. These changes have dramatically improved the economy. GDP growth in 1996 was 5.1 percent, but inflation continued to remain in the range of 25 percent. The GDP growth rate was 1.4 percent and 2.1 percent respectively for 2013 and 2014, but inflation had also been reduced to 4.1 percent.[17] The country has also vigorously promoted exports, especially to the United States, which now counts on Mexico for 25 percent of all imported fruit and vegetables. The *maquiladora* industry (see Chapter 10) is another growing source of economic strength for the country.[18] At the same time, Mexico has become a major region for international investment. In 2014 Mexico attracted 366 greenfield investment projects totaling $33billion of inward FDI (compared to $18 billion in Brazil).[19]

MNE investment

The climate for foreign investment in Mexico has grown increasingly favorable in recent years. Although there were strict controls on foreign investment in the past, deregulation and a series of privatizations have opened up the economy, particularly to US firms. As a result, an increasing number of MNEs are investing in Mexico. Nissan invested $1 billion in a new assembly plant to produce cars for export to both the United States and Japan; Volkswagen invested $950 million to expand its plant; Sears, Roebuck put $150 million into new stores and malls throughout the country, in addition to renovating older units; Wal-Mart purchased Cifra, a successful Mexican retailer; and PepsiCo expanded its snack business by purchasing a majority stake in Gamesa, Mexico's largest cookie maker.

Another reason for increased FDI has been the changes in investment laws that now permit foreigners to hold major equity positions. In the past, foreign ownership in auto parts companies had been limited to 40 percent of equity, but a new decree now sharply reduces the number of firms subject to this law by creating exemptions based on percentages of export sales and sales to individuals. Today, most of the economy is open to full foreign ownership.

Labor

Labor is relatively plentiful and inexpensive. However, MNEs report a serious shortage of skilled labor and managerial personnel, particularly at the middle and upper levels of the organization, and despite numerous engineers. Worker absenteeism in recent years has declined, but turnover remains a serious problem, even in the *maquiladora* sector.

Approximately 30 percent of the total workforce is unionized. In industrial operations with more than 25 workers, about 70 percent of the workforce is in unions. Union control over the members has weakened in recent years, and this trend is likely to continue. However, strikes are not uncommon.

There is a three-tier minimum wage structure in Mexico, but increases have not kept up with the cost of living. The minimum wage in Mexican pesos in Mexico City and surrounding towns in 2011 was 59.82 per day (Zone A, including Baja California, Federal District, State of Mexico, and some large cities), compared to 58.13 pesos (Zone B, including Sonora, Nuevo León, Tamaulipas, Veracruz, Jalisco, and other large cities) and 56.70 pesos (Zone C, the rest of the country).[20]

Government regulations require that at least 90 percent of a firm's skilled and unskilled workers be Mexican nationals, and employers must favor Mexicans over foreigners and union personnel over non-union personnel. On the other hand, these regulations are unlikely to limit investment by MNEs since the government permits hiring exceptions.

Mexico and NAFTA

In conjunction with their privatization policies, Mexico sought to motivate business through increased exposure to international competitive forces and access to the dynamic US market.[21] To this end, the government opened negotiations with the US and Canadian governments in Toronto on June 12, 1991, to create NAFTA. This marked the first time that a less developed country had entered into an agreement with two wealthy countries to create a free trade area. NAFTA went into effect on January 1, 1994, and has had a major impact on Mexico's trade and investment.

Trade in several sectors has experienced considerable growth. In the textile and apparel sectors, quotas on Mexican products were phased out and customs duties on all textile and apparel products were eliminated. For automotive products, Mexico immediately reduced its tariffs on cars and light trucks by 50 percent and pledged to eliminate the remaining duties over ten years. In agriculture, tariff restrictions were lifted on a broad range of goods when NAFTA went into effect.

Mexico's investment climate has also been affected by NAFTA. In the automotive sector, all investment restrictions were eliminated. In transportation, Mexico allowed 49 percent ownership of cars and trucking companies three years after NAFTA went into effect, 51 percent after 10 years, and 100 percent after 10 years. The Mexican finance and insurance sectors have also been liberalized. All these changes have opened up Mexico even more to FDI and, in turn, led to the growth of the Mexican economy and two-way flows of trade and investment with the United States.

As with the US–Canada FTA, binational panels play an important role in resolving trade disputes. Under NAFTA, panels continue to contribute toward trade disputes resolution and now also investment matters. Where investments are concerned, complainants may also take their cases to binding investor–state arbitration.

Regional trade agreements

Other developments involving Mexico as a leader in the movement toward free trade and privatization have included the efforts to create and sustain regional trade agreements based on NAFTA. One of the major regional integration efforts has been the creation of the **Latin American Integration Association (LAIA)**, a free trade group formed in 1980 to reduce intra-regional trade barriers and promote regional economic cooperation. Argentina, Bolivia, Brazil, Chile, Colombia, Ecuador, Mexico, Paraguay, Peru, Uruguay, and Venezuela are all members. The primary objective of LAIA is to create a Latin American common market. In recent years, its slow process toward economic integration has led some members to create sub-regional groups. For example, in the southern cone, Argentina, Brazil, Paraguay, and Uruguay have established a common market called **Mercosur**, which was operational by 1996. In the north, Mexico, Colombia, and Venezuela have a similar agreement, and via NAFTA Mexico is likely to be a key bridge between Latin American countries and the United States. NAFTA has a clause permitting accession of other countries. A second major integration effort is the **Andean common market (Ancom)**, a sub-regional free trade compact designed to promote economic and social integration and cooperation.[22] Bolivia, Colombia, Ecuador, Peru, and Venezuela are all members.

In 1990, US President George Bush launched his **Enterprise for the Americas**, which is aimed at creating an all-American free trade area from Alaska to Argentine Antarctica. The **Free Trade Area of the Americas (FTAA)** that is presently being negotiated by 34 countries would achieve the main objectives of continental integration.[23] If such an idea comes to fruition, it will eliminate the need for LAIA, Ancom, and similar Latin American trade agreements. The United States is aware of the need for reducing, and then eliminating, trade barriers in the Americas if it hopes to establish a viable world market that can compete against the European Union and the Asia–Pacific countries. The idea is also appealing to Latin American countries that see the opportunities associated with linking into the North American diamond and profiting from the economic growth it creates. This development will bring about a Western hemisphere trading bloc and may well become a reality in the early twenty-first century.

Doing business in Mexico

A number of strategic approaches are being used to conduct business in Mexico. (See the case **International Business Strategy in Action: Mexico and NAFTA**.) Two primary reasons for the success of these approaches are the high quality of the workforce and the dramatic improvement in the economy over the last two decades. MNEs operating in Mexico report that the quality of the workforce is excellent. For example, senior-level executives at firms such as Caterpillar, Ford, General Electric, IBM, and Procter & Gamble all report that their Mexican workforces produce high-quality output. Moreover, a Massachusetts Institute of Technology study has named Ford's Mercury Tracer plant in Hermosillo the highest-quality assembly plant in the world. The head of IBM Mexico has stated that "for every dollar you pay a Mexican engineer, you get more from him or her than you'd get in other societies around the world."

At the same time, the market for goods and services is growing rapidly. Many MNEs admit that they are not in Mexico because of the low wage rates but because of rapidly growing demand. Despite a high inflation rate and loss of purchasing power, people want to buy consumer goods and live more like their neighbors to the north. Mexicans are also expressing an interest in high-quality merchandise, with the result that companies are now reducing their reliance on agents and dealers and are instead opening sales subsidiaries and warehouses to provide direct technical assistance. A good example is Toyota, which started

---

Latin American Integration Association (LAIA)
A free trade group formed to reduce intra-regional trade barriers and to promote regional economic cooperation; Argentina, Bolivia, Brazil, Chile, Colombia, Ecuador, Mexico, Paraguay, Peru, Uruguay, and Venezuela are all members

Mercosur
A sub-regional free trade group formed to promote economic cooperation; the group consists of Argentina, Brazil, Paraguay, and Uruguay

Andean common market (Ancom)
A sub-regional free trade compact designed to promote economic and social integration and cooperation; Bolivia, Colombia, Ecuador, and Peru are all members

Enterprise for the Americas
An idea launched by President George Bush to create a free trade area from Alaska to Argentine Antarctica

Free Trade Area of the Americas (FTAA)
A regional trade agreement that is expected to succeed NAFTA and includes 34 countries across North, Central, and South America

a plant in 2005 to produce vans for the US market, but later in the year responded to Mexico's growing demand for vans by producing for the domestic market. With a burgeoning population of 106 million and an economy that is growing even faster, Mexico promises to be a major target area for MNEs in the future. At the same time, these developments help Mexico link itself to the triad via the United States.

INTERNATIONAL BUSINESS STRATEGY IN ACTION

Mexico and NAFTA

Many opponents of NAFTA argued that the agreement would lead to the export of US jobs to Mexico, with a resulting decline in gross national product (GNP). Economists, however, reported that the agreement would help save US jobs and that GNP would rise by $30 billion annually once the treaty was fully implemented. Research has found that the first five years of NAFTA had improved growth and efficiency in all three of its members. Certainly, MNEs in the motor vehicle and parts industry and the telecommunications industry agreed with the economists and have already formulated strategies to address these impending changes.

The US motor vehicle and parts industry expects to see some jobs go to Mexico. Moreover, the export of vehicles from foreign-owned factories in Mexico doubled in the three years after NAFTA. However, prior to NAFTA, Mexican government regulations forced US auto makers to buy Mexican parts, which in many cases did not meet global standards. This led Mexican subsidiaries of the auto makers to run plants at less than maximum efficiency levels. The government also forced the Big Three car companies to export more than they imported into Mexico. NAFTA has allowed companies to act regionally instead of on a country-by-country basis and to reorganize production more efficiently across North America. In an unexpected surge of events, some of the manufacturing previously assigned to Mexico is being brought back into the United States. For example, Ford relocated its production of Thunderbirds and Mercury Cougars from Cuautitlán to its assembly plant in Lorain, Ohio. At the same time, US auto suppliers are doing better because NAFTA requires 62.5 percent of a vehicle's content to originate in North America. This means that foreign suppliers in Asia and Europe are losing out to regional, high-quality firms such as TRW and Dana. Thus, NAFTA is proving to be a boon to the US motor and auto parts industry.

The development of cross-border supply chains associated with automotive, appliances and electronics firms have been driven by the NAFTA agreement. Firms have benefitted from spreading production lines across each country to reduce costs and become more globally competitive, enabled by the tariff reductions of NAFTA. Economists suggest that 40 percent of the content of US imports from Mexico and 25 percent of the content of US imports from Canada are of US origin.

In terms of the direct impact on Mexico, NAFTA was expected to narrow the gap in per capita income with the United States. This did rise in Mexico, but at an annual average rate of 1.2 percent from 1994 to 2013, from $6,932 to $8,397, far slower than other Latin American countries such as Peru, Brazil, and Chile. The agreement was also expected to reduce flows of migrants into the United States from Mexico but this does not appear to have happened.

Doing business in Mexico can take a number of different forms. Four strategies have proven particularly profitable. One is to establish a wholly owned subsidiary. This can be an expensive strategy, but it gives the company total control and allows management to make decisions quickly and efficiently. Quite often a local manager runs the subsidiary, and almost always the majority of the management team are locals. However, headquarters exercises key control.

A second approach is to become part of the *maquiladora* program. This strategy works best for firms aiming to export most of their output back to the United States. The *maquiladora* arrangement allows manufacturing, assembly, and processing plants to import materials, components, and equipment duty free, complete the work with Mexican labor and then ship the finished products back north. Under recent changes in the arrangement, if the company wants, it can sell up to one-third of the output in Mexico and still participate in the program.

A third approach is the so-called shelter program, under which local contractors assume responsibility for all aspects of the manufacturing operation, from site selection to recruitment of personnel to running the factory. After a predetermined time, however, the US company can buy out the shelter operator at a preset price and take over the business.

A fourth approach is a joint venture with a local partner. This combines a foreign company with financial and manufacturing know-how and a local partner that knows how to market the output. A number of US firms have opted for this approach, including Ford, DuPont, and General Electric. In the last case, GE formed a joint venture with Mabe, one of Mexico's largest appliance manufacturers.

▶

In most cases US MNEs will decide in advance which of these four strategies to implement. However, some firms have discovered that the need for such a decision is unanticipated. Take the example of Pace Foods, which went to Mexico City to film commercials for its Pace Picante Sauce. The crew did not want to carry back the jars of Pace's hot sauce that they used in the filming, so they told a local store manager to keep the jars and try to sell them. A few weeks later the company got a call from the manager. He had sold all 350 jars and wanted to know what he should do now. Today Pace has a thriving business selling products in Mexico.

Websites: www.ge.com; www.ford.com; www.pacefoods.com; www.dupont.com

Sources: Mohammed Aly Sergie, "NAFTA's economic impact," US Council on Foreign Relations (February 14, 2014), http://www.cfr.org/trade/naftas-economic-impact/p15790; Alan M. Rugman and John Kirton, "Multinational enterprise strategy and the NAFTA trade and environment regime," *Journal of World Business*, vol. 33, no. 4 (December 1998), pp. 438–54; Alan M. Rugman, John Kirton, and Julie Soloway, *Environmental Regulations and Corporate Strategy* (Oxford: Oxford University Press, 1999); www.ford.com; Joel Millman, "High-tech jobs transfer to Mexico with surprising speed," *Wall Street Journal*, April 9, 1998, p. A18; Laurie P. Cohen, "With help from INS, US meatpacker taps Mexican work force," *Wall Street Journal*, October 15, 1998, pp. A1, 8.

✔ Active learning check

Review your answer to Active Learning Case question 3 and make any changes you like. Then compare your answer to the one below.

③ How has NAFTA affected Mexico?

Mexico's progress under NAFTA will create a market for US goods in that, as the middle and upper classes in the country increase their purchasing power, they will turn more and more to the purchase of US-made goods. From cars to television sets to home appliances, Mexican consumers will be buying products sold by US MNEs. The sale of these goods will create greater interest in Mexico by US multinationals, which will mean even greater opportunities for US firms—and Mexican consumers. The elimination of tariffs under NAFTA ties Mexico into the North American regional triad.

Mexico and the double diamond

To maintain its economic growth, Mexico must continue developing international competitive strength. This is currently being done by linking to the US market. In particular, MNEs must view this market not just as a source for export but also as part of the home market (see Figure 10.6). Specifically, this requires:

1 Developing innovative new products and services that simultaneously meet the needs of US and Mexican customers, with the recognition that close relationships with demanding US customers should set the pace and style of product development.

2 Drawing on the support industries and infrastructure of both the US and Mexican diamonds, realizing that the US diamond is more likely to possess deeper and more efficient markets for such industries.

3 Making free and full use of the physical and human resources in both countries.[24]

To do this, Mexico is relying heavily on a series of strategic clusters. The six major ones, in order of importance, are petroleum/chemicals, automotive, housing and household, materials and metals, food and beverage, and semiconductors and computers. The two that are most internationally competitive and provide the best insights into how the Mexican double diamond is used are the petroleum and automotive clusters.

Petroleum cluster

Mexico's petroleum industry accounted for about 14 percent of all exports in 2014. The country has the third largest proven oil reserves after Venezuela and the United States and is the world's fifth largest producer. The largest firm is state-owned Petróleos Mexicanos (Pemex), which is the world's largest crude oil producer (excluding refining) and one of the world's largest companies. In 2013, Pemex had total assets of over $416 billion, including pipelines, refineries, tankers, aircraft, and rail cars. This huge asset base helps explain why Mexico is a net exporter of energy, principally oil, natural gas, hydraulic power, nuclear and geothermal power, and coal.

The country also has strong petroleum-related industries and infrastructure. At present, 175 companies are operating about 500 basic and secondary petrochemical plants throughout the country and employing approximately 130,000 people.

Domestic demand for oil-related products in Mexico has been rising sharply, forcing Pemex to become considerably more productive. The export market for this oil is expected to remain at current levels for the foreseeable future. The United States will remain Mexico's largest customer. Moreover, although energy was excluded from NAFTA, ongoing discussions have centered on US access to Mexican oil through imports and increased opportunities for US technologies in the energy sector. For major US companies such as ARCO, Chevron, and ConocoPhillips that are selling off some of their domestic properties and looking for exploration opportunities outside the country, Mexico is likely to prove a very attractive location. Turnkey exploration contracts are being used to integrate US expertise and improve Mexican drilling efficiency, thus reducing the cost of oil. This trend will make Mexico one of the lowest-cost producers in the world.

The commodity nature of the energy business provides little opportunity for Mexico to insulate itself from the cyclical changes of both pricing and demand in this cluster. The real opportunities lie in trying to improve efficiencies through various methods: (1) liberalizing exploration programs by allowing more efficient foreign drilling contractors to carry out turnkey operations; (2) reducing the cost base by working with the unions to rationalize jobs that are not required; (3) using foreign technologies in areas where Mexican expertise is lacking; (4) allowing greater participation of foreign firms in producing petrochemicals to expand capacity and competitiveness of commodity products to meet domestic and export demand; (5) using foreign MNEs to bring in technology to produce advanced petrochemicals for use in the US market; and (6) developing alternative, cleaner-burning fuels, such as natural gas and unleaded fuels, to reduce reliance on US imports and comply with international environmental standards.

The potential of this cluster looks promising, even though Mexican proven reserves have recently fallen slightly and the international benchmark price for crude oil has varied from $20 to $150 per barrel. Mexico's vast unexplored areas provide long-term opportunities to continue a strong hydrocarbon-based cluster. Moreover, the proximity of the United States, with its declining proven reserves and growing dependence on imports, will provide Mexico with an export base for improving economies of scale and generating funds for reinvestment in drilling and exploration activities. Thus, Mexico's economic progress will be closely linked to the US diamond.

Automotive cluster

The global auto industry is currently undergoing worldwide restructuring. In the process, Mexico is emerging as a major car and truck producer. Since 1986 the industry has grown rapidly: total unit production in 2002 was 2 million units; however, in 2009, the total unit production was 1,561,052, a drop of 28 percent compared to 2008 due to the world financial crisis leading to fall in exports. The automobile industry accounts for 15 percent of all exports; 85 percent of all Mexican-built cars are exported to the United States.[25] The Big Three US auto makers have been expanding their capacities in Mexico while closing plants in the United States and Canada. Today, Daimler, Ford, and GM account for about 60 percent of all light-vehicle production. At the same time, European and Japanese firms are investing in Mexico in an effort to tap such benefits as low-cost labor, low capital cost, proximity to the world's largest auto market, growth of domestic demand, and accessibility to related support industries.

Mexico has a strong, rich resource base supporting its automotive cluster as well as an abundance of young, skilled, adaptable labor. Foreign auto firms are finding that these workers are particularly effective after they have been trained in total quality management, just-in-time inventory, and related concepts. In addition, unions in Mexico are much more cooperative with management than their counterparts to the north. As a result, this resource base is now producing some of the highest-quality cars and trucks in North America, and the Hermosillo plant is widely regarded as the number one auto factory on the continent.

There are also strong supporting industries and a well-developed infrastructure in the automotive cluster. The auto parts industry has revenues of $2.93 billion and is growing at an annual rate of 10 percent; it employs over 500,000 Mexican workers, a fivefold increase since 1990.[26] Parts companies produce for both the domestic and export markets, and many are a result of FDI by US-based auto part firms. For example, GM has component plants in the country as well as financial participation with Mexican auto part companies. Ford has similar arrangements, as do Volkswagen, Nissan, and a host of other foreign firms.

While the boom of foreign investment in auto parts initially displaced inefficient local parts producers, a handful of efficiently run local companies have emerged to become multinational producers. For instance, with an initial $30 million investment, Mexico's Nemak has opened a plant in the Czech Republic that employs 200 people.

The primary customers for auto output in Mexico are in the local market. However, the percentage of this output that goes for export is rising every year. In particular, with the signing of NAFTA, Mexico's accessibility to the largest auto market in the world is increasing sharply. This accessibility is especially critical to the country since US protectionism is now threatening to raise import barriers. At the same time, Mexican acceptance of US cars manufactured in Mexico is at an all-time high. The same is true in the United States, where the quality reputation of Mexican assembly plants is being felt at the dealer showroom.

✔ Active learning check

Review your answer to Active Learning Case question 4 and make any changes you like. Then compare your answer to the one below.

4 **How has NAFTA affected the United States?**

NAFTA will lead to an increase in trade in the region for three reasons. First, the elimination of all tariffs will encourage exports. Second, all three countries are more likely to specialize in producing those goods and services for which they have a competitive advantage and, in turn, buy the others from their neighbors. Third, as the economies of the member countries grow, so will the amount of trade as each begins to adapt operations to the desires of the other and starts to tap this market. Furthermore, the United States has more secure access to energy and other vital natural resources from Canada and Mexico.

The market potential of the automotive cluster is extremely high. Some problems, however, will have to be dealt with if the country is to continue increasing its competitiveness. Foremost among these is the need for greater technology. One major reason why Mexican autos are cost efficient is the lack of high automation and robotics. It is unlikely that this trend can continue. In addition, the shifting of more and more US and Canadian auto business to Mexico will put major pressure on NAFTA to ensure that these two countries benefit handsomely from this strategy and that other foreign producers, such as the Japanese and Europeans, do not.

Overall, Mexico's economic future is closely linked to that of the United States and Canada. When analyzed in terms of Porter's diamond, some of the country's strategic clusters have already developed worldwide competitive strength. During the 1990s the petroleum and automotive clusters proved to be highly competitive.

Mexico is likely to begin making major inroads into other areas such as semiconductors and computers. Motorola already has a semiconductor plant in Mexico, and HP, IBM, Toshiba, Samsung, NEC, Philips, and others produce computer hardware components in Mexican facilities. As in its automotive success, this is the result of favorable factor conditions, related and supporting industries, demand conditions, and the structure and rivalry of the firms. As a result, Mexico will find that it can link its diamond framework with that of the United States and become a worldwide competitor in still other areas in the process. Porter's diamond framework will prove to be a useful paradigm.[27]

 Active learning check

Review your answer to Active Learning Case question 5 and make any changes you like. Then compare your answer with the one below.

5 **Does NAFTA include environmental laws?**

There are environmental laws in NAFTA, but these are still up for debate. There are issues of sovereignty. Should an international agreement set the standard for environmental laws or should the individual governments make their own laws to be responsive to their national needs? Although an environmental chapter was included in NAFTA, there is a growing concern among NGOs that environmental laws could be used as a non-tariff barrier to trade, keeping out some goods from the rich US market. Both the United States and Canada advocate the use of clean technology in NAFTA and pressing for higher environmental standards and processes in Mexico.

KEY POINTS

1 Canada is the single largest trading partner of the United States. There has been a move toward privatization in the past few years as well as toward deregulation. As in the United States, the government attempts to promote competition, and the North American Free Trade Agreement (NAFTA) with Mexico has recognized the high degree of trade between the two countries.

2 Financial institutions are similar to those in the United States, as are labor relations practices. However, a much larger percentage of Canadian employees are unionized, and the unions have been major opponents of the FTA and the subsequent NAFTA.

3 NAFTA will eventually eliminate most trade barriers between the United States and Canada, which should help open up Canada to more economic development. At the same time, the government welcomes foreign investment, and a wide variety of incentive programs are designed to encourage such investments.

4 The approaches to doing business in Canada are similar to those in the United States, with some important regulatory differences. The chapter identified and discussed both.

5 Mexico has the strongest economy in Latin America, and its close business ties to the United States, as reflected by imports, exports, and US FDI, bode well for its future. The potential of the free trade agreement between the two countries and the growth of the *maquiladora* industry are helping Mexico link its economy to that of the United States. Mexico's petrochemical and automotive clusters are key industries in this linkage and are likely to become world-class competitors in their respective areas.

Key terms

- Competition Act
- Canada Labor Code
- Investment Canada Act (ICA)
- United States–Canada Free Trade Agreement (FTA)
- Latin American Integration Association (LAIA)
- Mercosur
- Andean common market (Ancom)
- Enterprise for the Americas
- Free Trade Area of the Americas (FTAA)

REVIEW AND DISCUSSION QUESTIONS

1 How high is the Canadian standard of living? Of what value is this information to a company interested in doing business in Canada?

2 Is the Competition Act of any concern to US firms, given that the FTA has eliminated most trade restrictions? Explain.

3 What do companies seeking to set up businesses in Canada need to know about labor relations in that country? Identify and discuss three areas of importance.

4 What are the most important provisions of the Free Trade Agreement and how do they affect US firms doing business in Canada?

5 Are there any restrictions on foreign investments in Canada? Identify and describe two of them.

6 What should a firm seeking to enter the Canadian market know about marketing practices there? Identify and describe three practices.

7 How good are franchise opportunities in Canada? Explain.

8 Why is Mexico doing so well economically? Identify two developments that have been particularly helpful in bringing this about.

9 What is the purpose of the LAIA? Of what value is the organization to its members?

10 How might the creation of an "Enterprise for the Americas" affect the LAIA and Ancom? Give an example.

11 How is Mexico using its petroleum cluster to link itself to the North American triad?

12 How is Mexico using its automotive cluster to link itself to the North American triad?

13 Why are these linkages to the North American triad likely to be economically advantageous to Mexico? Cite two reasons.

REAL CASE

Jumex of Mexico

Founded in 1961, Group Jumex is the largest producer of juices and fruit nectars in Mexico. The country has a population of over 120 million people and a hot climate that provides a favorable environment in which Jumex can grow. And grow it has.

Mexico offered other nurturing characteristics to the emerging company in the form of natural resources and market pressures. For one, Jumex has access to an incredible variety of tropical fruits from which it can develop new products. Indeed, the firm offers tamarind, guanábana, and guava nectars as well as the more commonly known mango, peach, pear, and apple.

Tropical fruits are readily available everywhere at a relatively low price, making the blending of juices in customers' homes extremely easy. Juice stands, in which the juice is made on site, are abundant throughout the country. Quality is paramount. Jumex cannot sell products with very little fruit content to Mexicans.

Jumex competes with other domestic producers at home for the juice and nectar market. It also competes with soft drink makers, including Coca-Cola and PepsiCo, for the beverage market. However, Mexican consumers have recently improved the lot of the juice makers, as carbonated drinks are increasingly considered unhealthy.

Competition has made Jumex into an aggressive marketer. The firm uses all types of distribution systems to maximize market share. It works with national wholesalers, regional wholesalers, supermarkets, and small convenience stores to establish a price system that allows them to benefit from selling its products.

Mobile communication was provided to the sales team so that orders could be processed immediately, no matter how far away the distribution center was. This is very important because of the remoteness of many Mexican communities. Prior to this, a salesperson could take two weeks before returning with paperwork to put in an order. Supermarket computerized distribution systems are now integrated with that of Jumex so that their shelves can be stocked as needed.

While most firms have shifted to aluminum, Jumex has maintained the traditional tin can and created a distinct shape that stands out against the competition. A tin can is alleged to be more biodegradable than an aluminum can. To serve different markets, Jumex also packages in plastic, glass, and juice boxes.

Presently, Jumex exports only about 20 percent of its production but it is highly successful. It has operations in Latin America and the Caribbean, North America, Europe, Asia, and Oceania. Distribution and marketing have been adapted to fit each country. In most of Latin America, because of geographic, market, and cultural similarities, the distribution system that was implemented was very similar to that found in Mexico.

Jumex has been surprisingly successful in the US market, where it is now a leading brand of fruit nectars. Part of this success can be attributed to Mexico's lower production costs and the availability of inexpensive natural resources. Another reason is the predominance of Mexican immigrants across the United States, particularly in large urban areas. Whether these are new immigrants or the children of immigrants who travel frequently to Mexico, they know the product and are familiar with the tropical fruits, creating an initial market for the product. Other Latin Americans or immigrants from tropical areas familiar with the brand or the fruits also push demand.

In 2013, understanding the fact that children comprise approximately one third of Mexico's entire population, the Swiss company Capri-Sun decided to enter and become a key player within the Mexican beverage market. Capri-Sun entered the market after securing a licensing agreement with Jumex. It acknowledged the fact that Jumex was already a popular Mexican juice producer, which had acquired an expertise in marketing, and Capri-Sun knew it would stand a greater chance of competing with an already established organization at its side.

In 2014, Mexico introduced a new tax on sugary drinks which resulted in the sales of beverages declining for many firms such as Coca-Cola and PepsiCo. In order to compensate for higher levels of tax, it was reported that bottle production lines had laid off over 1,600 employees in 2014 and raised prices by 16 percent. Furthermore, Coca-Cola FEMSA's juice sales, operating under the Jugos del Valle brand, also experienced a large hit from the introduction of the new tax. However, Jumex decided that it would be too dangerous to pass the tax costs on to consumers, opting to keep its prices the same.

An important factor that has helped Jumex in developed countries is that its products are considered healthier than carbonated drinks and tend to offer more fruit content than many of the company's domestic competitors. However, competition in developed countries is likely to heat up in the future as Ceres, a South African juice producer, Jugos del Valle of Mexico, and new entrants from Asia compete on price, quality, and variety of fruit juices. In the health market sector, organic fruit

▶

juices from developing and developed countries will also offer competition.

Website: www.jumex.com.mx.

Sources: "Soft drinks in Mexico," *Euromonitor*, June 2004; Samuel Bernal, "Jumex le saca jugo al cómputo movil," *Revista Red*, Febrero 2001; www.jumex.com.mx; B. Bouckley, "$2bn brand Capri-Sun: Mexico offers 'enormous growth potential'," April 29, 2013, accessed from www.beveragedaily.com; A. Guthrie, "Mexican soda tax effect waning, Coca-Cola Femsa says," *Wall Street Journal*, October 22, 2014.

1 How has Mexico provided the environment to make Jumex into a competitive fruit and nectar producer in foreign markets?

2 What factors mentioned in this case study have contributed to Jumex's success in the US market?

3 Can you think of any other factors that may have contributed to Jumex's success in the US market?

REAL CASE

GlaxoSmithKline in the United States

Among industrialized countries, the US market for pharmaceuticals is the least regulated and thus the largest in the world. Not surprisingly, European companies like AstraZeneca, Aventis, and GlaxoSmithKline (GSK) depend more heavily on the North American market for their revenues than on Europe as a whole. Europe is a more fragmented market, with individual distribution systems and more layers of regulation, and governments are in the habit of imposing price controls. As a result, Europeans spend 60 percent less per capita on pharmaceuticals than their American counterparts.

With $34.66 billion in revenues and 97,921 employees in 2014, GSK is one of the largest pharmaceutical companies in the world. Although incorporated in the United Kingdom, it is not surprising that GSK manages its operations in the United States. Some 32 percent of its sales originate in this host nation, a fact that is consistent with world trends—the United States accounts for 40 percent of the world market for pharmaceuticals, while the European market accounts for 25 percent. GSK derives 28 percent of its sales from its home-market region. Only 7 percent of its sales come from Japan, 27 percent from emerging markets, and the remainder is derived from ViiV Healthcare (HIV business), other trading, and unallocated activities.

Approximately 30 years ago, British Glaxo was a small company in the dried milk, antibiotics, respiratory drugs, and nutritional businesses. The discovery of Zantac, a drug to treat stomach ulcers, catapulted the company into the mainstream pharmaceutical market and financed its expansion into the US market. As the patent for Zantac was about to expire, Glaxo found itself in a sticky situation. Up to that point the company had relied on internal R&D, but this had failed to develop the R&D capabilities for sustainable long-term growth. In 1995, the company merged with Wellcome, a company known for its strength in R&D and its lack of marketing capabilities. The merger was successful in that the new company now had a stream of new drugs that could be marketed using Glaxo's expertise.

By 2000, Glaxo Wellcome was disappointing investors once again. Drug prospects, at least in the short term, were below the industry average and expected revenues from some of its products never materialized. Yet the merger with SmithKline Beecham was not driven by the same urgency as the previous merger. Both companies had a reasonably stable pipeline and a balanced portfolio of drugs. According to Sir Richard Sykes, then Chairman of Glaxo Wellcome, the deciphering of the human genome would transform the industry and only large companies that could afford to invest in working with this new information would succeed. Together, these two companies are immune to the near-death experience of losing a major blockbuster drug. No one drug accounts for more than 12 percent of the company's revenues.

GSK operates in two product-based industry segments: (1) pharmaceuticals, which include prescription drugs and vaccines; and (2) consumer healthcare, which includes over-the-counter (OTC) medicines, oral care, and nutritional healthcare. Prescription drugs are sold mainly to wholesalers, which dispense them to the public through pharmacies. Consumer healthcare products are sold through pharmacies, wholesalers, or directly to retail outlets. In 2009, GSK acquired a series of R&D-intensive firms, including Stiefel Laboratories, Pfizer's HIV business, the Algerian pharmaceutical, manufacturing and distribution group, and NovaMin Technology. The periodic acquisition and integration of new R&D pipelines and expertise helps the firm refresh its new product development process.

The first step in the development of a drug is R&D. GSK spends $3.1 billion on R&D and has over 13,000 researchers in 17 R&D sites around the world. Once GSK has developed a new drug, it must obtain government approval in every individual nation where the company markets the product, a process that can differ significantly in each jurisdiction. Production and marketing are the next steps for a new drug. GSK's supply chain is divided into a primary chain and a secondary chain. The primary chain manufactures active ingredients for its products and ships them to the secondary chain, which manufactures the end product. There are 13 primary supply-chain sites based in Australia, India, Ireland, Singapore, the United States, and the UK. In Europe, there are 17 secondary supply-chain sites, while North America houses an additional 6 sites. The rest of the world has 32 secondary sites in 19 countries (5 in the Middle East and Africa, 22 in Asia–Pacific, and 5 in Latin America).

Different price regulations at a national level have created some market abnormalities in each region. For instance, Canadian web-based pharmacies have sprung up to service US consumers seeking cheaper alternatives. GSK sent a heavily worded letter to Canadian wholesalers that were selling to these pharmacies and threatened to stop supplies.

In Spain, GSK developed a two-price system: one lower price for products to be sold in Spain and a higher price for those to be exported to other EU member countries. The EU found this practice illegal.

Websites: www.gsk.com; www.aventis.com; www.astrazeneca.com

Sources: Alan M. Rugman, *The Regional Multinationals* (Cambridge: Cambridge University Press, 2005); "The trouble with cheap drugs," *The Economist*, January 29, 2004; GSK, *Annual Report*, 2009, 2014; Thomson Reuters, *OneSource*, 2011; Statista, *Distribution of the Total Global Pharmaceutical Market Value from 2006 to 2014, by Submarket*, 2015.

1 How is GSK's production organized?

2 Is GSK's secondary supply-chain structure global, regional, or local? Why?

3 What is GSK's basic strategy?

4 Why does GSK spread R&D around the world?

5 What factors have made North America the primary market for GSK? Would the situation be different if we measured units sold? Why?

NOTES

1 John R. Baldwin, Jean-Pierre Maynard, and Fanny Wong, "The output gap between Canada and the United States: the role of productivity (1994–2002)," *Statistics Canada Analytical Papers*, January 2005.

2 OECD, Foreign Direct Investment Statistics, FDI Positions by Partner Country. OECD.StatExtracts Online, http://stats.oecd.org, 2010.

3 Also, see Rosanna Tamburri, "Canada considers new stand against American culture," *Wall Street Journal*, February 4, 1998, p. A18; Roger Ricklefs, "Canada fights to fend off American tastes and tunes," *Wall Street Journal*, September 24, 1998, pp. B1, 8.

4 For more information on the GST/HST, see Canada Revenue Agency, http://www.cra-arc.gc.ca/tx/bsnss/tpcs/gst-tps/gnrl/txbl/mprtsxprts/mprtdgds-eng.html, 2010

5 See Rosanna Tamburri, "Canadians clash over cost of diversity," *Wall Street Journal*, April 1, 1998, p. A15.

6 For additional insights into the role of Quebec in US–Canadian economic ties, see Thane Peterson and William J. Holstein, "How a freer Quebec could reshape the continent," *Business Week*, July 9, 1990, pp. 40–3.

7 Government of Canada, Department of Finance, *Canada's Banks*, August 2002, http://www.fin.gc.ca/toc/2002/bank_-eng.asp

8 See www.tse.com

9 Statistics Canada, *Unionization 2010*, http://www.statcan.gc.ca/pub/75-001-x/2010110/article/11358-eng.htm#a2; US Bureau of Labor Statistics, *Union Members Summary*, January 17, 2010.

10 *Summary of the US–Canada Free Trade Agreement* (Washington, DC: US Department of Commerce, International Trade Administration, 1988), p. 12.

11 Ibid., pp. 10–11.

12 See http://www.dsa.ca/home.htm

13 Statistics Canada, *Cansim Database*, Matrix: D657192.

14 Ibid. and Matrix: D657205.

15 Ibid.

16 Also, see Stephen Baker, "Mexico: can Zedillo stem the tide of crisis?" *Business Week*, April 18, 1994, p. 60; "Mexico arrests top leader of Zetas' drug gang," *BBC News*, July 4, 2011; and Mexico country profile, *BBC News*, http://news.bbc.co.uk/1/hi/world/americas/country_profiles/1205074.stm, 2010.

17 CIA, *World Fact Book*, 2010.

18 Also, see Bob Ortega, "Some Mexicans charge north in NAFTA's wake," *Wall Street Journal*, February 22, 1994, pp. B1, 5; Mexico country profile (see note 16).

19 "Mexico foreign direct investment races ahead as Brazil sputters," *Financial Times*, 25 August 2015.

20 See "Labor: minimum daily wages for 2011," http://www.sat.gob.mx/sitio_Internet/asistencia_contribuyente/informacion_frecuente/salarios_minimos/

21 Len J. Trevino, "Strategic responses of Mexican managers to economic reform," *Business Horizons* (May/June 1998), pp. 73–80.

22 Some of the material in this section can be found in "Latin American introduction," *ILT Latin America*, July 1991, pp. 1–13.

23 For more on the FTAA, see www.ftaa-alca.org

24 J. R. D'Cruz and Alan M. Rugman, *New Concepts for Canadian Competitiveness* (Toronto: Kodak Canada, 1992).

25 Susan Carney, "Mexico's low labor costs tempt Detroit carmakers," *Detroit News*, January 7, 2002; International Organization of Motor Vehicle Manufacturers (OICA), http://oica.net/category/production-statistics/, 2009.

26 Geri Smith and Elisabeth Malkin, "Mexico's makeover," *Business Week*, December 21, 1998; Elisabeth Malkin and

Jonathan Wheatley, "Parts shops are tailgating carmakers to Latin America," *Business Week*, October 23, 2000; US Commerce Service, *Buy USA*, http://www.buyusa.gov/mexico/en/automotive_manufacturing.html

27 Alan M. Rugman and Michael Gestrin, "The strategic response of multinational enterprises to NAFTA," *Columbia Journal of World Business*, vol. 28, no. 4 (1993), pp. 18–29.

BIBLIOGRAPHY

Anderson, John, and Sutherland, Dylan. "Developed economy investment promotion agencies and emerging market foreign direct investment: the case of Chinese FDI in Canada," *Journal of World Business*, vol. 50, no. 4 (2015).

Birkinshaw, Julian, and Hood, Neil. "An empirical study of development process in foreign owned subsidiaries in Canada and Scotland," *Management International Review*, vol. 37, no. 4 (1997).

Caliendo, Lorenzo, and Parro, Fernando. "Estimates of the trade and welfare effects of NAFTA," *Review of Economic Studies* (November 2014).

De Hoyos, Rafael E., and Iacovone, Leonardo. "Economic performance under NAFTA: a firm-level analysis of the trade–productivity linkages," *World Development*, vol. 44 (2013).

Eden, Lorraine (ed.). *Multinationals in North America* (Calgary: University of Calgary Press, 1994).

Feils, Dorothee J., and Rahman, Manzur. "Regional economic integration and foreign direct investment: the case of NAFTA," *Management International Review*, vol. 48, no. 2 (2008).

Feinberg, Susan E. "Do world product mandates really matter?," *Journal of International Business Studies*, vol. 31, no. 1 (spring 2000).

Feinberg, Susan E., and Keane, Michael P. "US–Canada trade liberalization and MNC production location," *Review of Economics and Statistics*, vol. 83, no. 1 (2001).

Globerman, Steven, and Shapiro, Daniel M. "The impact of government policies on foreign direct investment: the Canadian experience," *Journal of International Business Studies*, vol. 30, no. 3 (fall 1999).

Globerman, Steven, and Shapiro, Daniel M. "Governance infrastructure and US foreign direct investment," *Journal of International Business Studies*, vol. 34 (2003).

Globerman, Steven, and Walker, Michael (eds.). *Assessing NAFTA: A Trinational Analysis* (Vancouver: Fraser Institute, 1993).

Gomez, Carolina. "The influence of environmental, organizational, and HRM factors on employee behaviors in subsidiaries: a Mexican case study of organizational learning," *Journal of World Business*, vol. 39, no. 1 (February 2004).

Hejazi, Walid, and Safarian, A. E. "NAFTA effects and the level of development," *Journal of Business Research*, vol. 58, no. 12 (December 2005).

Hufbauer, Gary C., Esty, Daniel C., Orejas, Diana, Rubio, Luis, and Schott, Jeffrey J. *NAFTA and the Environment: Seven Years Later* (Washington, DC: Institute for International Economics, 2000).

Hufbauer, Gary C., and Schott, Jeffrey J. *NAFTA Revisited: Achievements and Challenges* (Washington, DC: Institute for International Economics, 2005).

Javalgi, Rajshekhar Raj G., et al. "Foreign market entry mode behavior as a gateway to further entries: the NAFTA experience," *International Business Review*, vol. 19 (2010).

Keane, Michael P., and Feinberg, Susan. "Advances in logistics and the growth of intra-firm trade: the case of Canadian affiliates of US multinationals," *Journal of Industrial Economics*, vol. 55, no. 4 (December 2007).

Kirton, John, and Maclaren, Virginia (eds.). *Linking Trade, Environment and Social Cohesion* (Aldershot: Ashgate, 2002).

Lahrech, Abdelmounaim, and Sylwester, Kevin. "The impact of NAFTA on North American stock market linkages," *North American Journal of Economics and Finance*, vol. 25 (2013).

Lovett, Steven R., Coyle, Tom, and Adams, Russell. "Job satisfaction and technology in Mexico," *Journal of World Business*, vol. 39, no. 3 (August 2004).

Lovett, Steven R., Pérez-Nordtvedt, Liliana, and Rasheed, Abdul A. "Parental control: a study of US subsidiaries in Mexico," *International Business Review*, vol. 18, no. 5 (October 2009).

Rugman, Alan M. *Multinationals in Canada: Theory, Performance and Economic Impact* (Boston, MA: Martinus Nijhoff, 1980).

Rugman, Alan M. "The role of multinational enterprises in US–Canadian economic relations," *Columbia Journal of World Business*, vol. 21, no. 2 (summer 1986).

Rugman, Alan M. *Outward Bound: Canadian Direct Investment in the United States* (Toronto: Canadian–American Committee, and Prentice Hall of Canada, 1987).

Rugman, Alan M. *Multinationals and Canada–United States Free Trade* (Columbia, SC: University of South Carolina Press, 1990).

Rugman, Alan M. (ed.). *Foreign Investment and NAFTA* (Columbia, SC: University of South Carolina Press, 1994).

Rugman, Alan M. (ed.). *North American Economic and Financial Integration* (Oxford: Elsevier, 2004).

Rugman, Alan M. "Thirty years of international business scholarship in Canada," *Canadian Journal of Administrative Sciences*, vol. 25, no. 4 (2008).

Rugman, Alan M., and D'Cruz, Joseph R. "The 'double diamond' model of international competitiveness: the Canadian experience," *Management International Review*, vol. 33, no. 2 (1993).

Rugman, Alan M., and Gestrin, Michael. "The investment provisions of NAFTA." In Steven Globerman and Michael Walker (eds.), *Assessing NAFTA: A Trinational Analysis* (Vancouver: Fraser Institute, 1993).

Rugman, Alan M., and Gestrin, Michael. "The strategic response of multinational enterprises to NAFTA," *Columbia Journal of World Business*, vol. 28, no. 4 (winter 1993).

Rugman, Alan M., Kirton, John, and Soloway, Julie A. *Environmental Regulations and Corporate Strategy: A NAFTA Perspective* (Oxford: Oxford University Press, 1999).

Rugman, Alan M., and Verbeke, Alain. "Multinational corporate strategy and the Canada–US free trade agreement," *Management International Review*, vol. 30, no. 3 (1990).

Rugman, Alan M., and Verbeke, Alain (eds.). *Research in Global Strategic Management*, Vol. 1, *International Business Research for the Twenty-First Century: Canada's New Research Agenda* (Greenwich, CT: JAI Press, 1990).

Rugman, Alan M., and Verbeke, Alain. "Foreign subsidiaries and multinational strategic management: an extension and correction of Porter's single diamond framework," *Management International Review*, vol. 33, no. 2 (1993).

Sargent, John, and Matthews, Linda. "The drivers of evolution/upgrading in Mexico's maquiladoras: how important is subsidiary initiative?," *Journal of World Business*, vol. 41, no. 3 (September 2006).

Schmitz, Troy G., and Lewis, Karen E. "Impact of NAFTA on US and Mexican sugar markets," *Journal of Agricultural and Resource Economics*, vol. 40 (2015).

Ulgado, Francis M. "Location characteristics of manufacturing investments in the US: a comparison of American and foreign-based firms," *Management International Review*, vol. 36, no. 1 (1996).

Waldkirch, Andreas. "The effects of foreign direct investment in Mexico since NAFTA," *World Economy*, vol. 33, no. 5 (May 2010).

Weinstein, Bernard L., and Seman, Michael. "Has the North American Free Trade Agreement fulfilled its promise? An assessment after 15 years," *Regional Science Policy and Practice*, vol. 1, no. 2 (November 2009).

Weintraub, Sydney. *NAFTA at Three* (Washington, DC: Center for Strategies on International Studies, 1997).

Weintraub, Sydney. *Unequal Partners: The United States and Mexico*, Pitt Latin American Series (Pittsburg, PA: University of Pittsburgh Press, 2010).

Wisner, Priscilla S., and Epstein, Marc J. "'Push' and 'pull' impacts of NAFTA on environmental responsiveness and performance in Mexican industry," *Management International Review*, vol. 45, no. 3 (2005).

Chapter 20

EMERGING ECONOMIES

Contents

Objectives of the chapter

More than 100 nations in the world are not triad members; they lie outside North America, Europe, and Japan. An important subgroup of non-triad countries is the "emerging economies," marked by their rapid economic growth and changing involvement in the global economy. They are increasingly important for MNEs of all sizes: as growing markets whose large populations are starting to have more and more disposable income; as increasingly important sources of inputs, including products, technology, and value-adding capabilities as well as commodities and cheap labor; and as a source of competition, as non-triad firms begin to internationalize into triad markets. These developments represent many new opportunities as well as new risks for MNEs. Increased involvement in emerging market regions for managers means coping with more diversity. This includes the broad cultural, political, and economic diversity resulting from the wide range of countries outside the triad. It also includes diversity of business practices and competitors, which MNEs need to adapt to in order to survive.

The specific objectives of this chapter are to:

1 *Examine* the relative attractions, opportunities, and threats in the triad regions and emerging economies for firms looking to internationalize.

2 *Explain* how many emerging economies are becoming more integrated into the global economy, in terms of trade, FDI, and other forms of interaction and interdependence.

3 *Understand* the nature of the new multinationals from emerging economies, as collaborators and competitors.

4 *Examine* the implications of changes in emerging economies for MNE managers in terms of new strategies and organization structures.

Acer Taiwan goes international

Acer Taiwan ranks as one of the largest PC companies in the world. In 2014 the overall Acer Group of companies was comprised of over 7,000 employees, plus dealers, and distributors in more than 100 countries, earning revenues of US$10.39 billion for the year. Around 43 percent of its sales were generated from EMEA (Europe, Middle East, Africa), 24 percent from North America, and 35 percent from Pan Asia–Pacific, making it a balanced multinational in terms of sales. The company is one of the best-known brands in Asia, and a large player in Latin America. In the United States, where HP and Dell dominate, Acer is one of the largest competitors in the consumer electronics market. According to the marketing firm IDC, Acer ranked number 4 in terms of worldwide shipments for total PCs with 7.8 percent market share and number 4 for portable PCs with 10.4 percent market share. Not bad for a company no one knew just a few decades ago.

In 1976 CEO Stan Shih and some of his friends managed to pull together $25,000 to start Multitech. With seven employees, the company began developing small electronic products such as pocket calculators and games. Slowly the company began to grow by commercializing microprocessor technology and its applications. Its initial entrance into the PC market was as a supplier. Multitech began producing computers to be sold under other brand names. Then in 1986 the company launched its own brand name computer, Acer, and it began to sell in Europe and in Japan. While the firm still supplies under other brand names, Acer has become one of the best-known PC brands in the world.

How did a small company from Taiwan gain market share in an industry dominated by well-established computer manufacturers? Two key strategies underpinned its rapid international growth.

First, it focused on learning: actively developing technological know-how, innovation capabilities, and, later, marketing and branding expertise. It invested in engineering training, initially with the help of the Taiwanese government. In the late 1970s it founded the Microprocessor Training Center where 3,000 engineers were trained for Taiwan's information industry. It also entered into a range of subcontracting relationships and joint ventures with major multinational firms in targeted industries. One of the most prominent was its DRAM semiconductor joint venture with Texas Instruments in 1989. To acquire necessary technologies the company bought a host of firms including Counterpoint Computers, Altos, and Kangaroo Computer. It also entered into cross-licensing agreements with firms like IBM and Intel. Innovation was the constant focus. The rapid development of engineering, design, and R&D capabilities helped Acer improve both its production efficiency and its product development capabilities. In 1986 it came out with a 32-bit PC model before IBM. In 1994 it introduced the world's first dual Intel Pentium PC, in 2001 the first Chinese Palm OS, and in 2004 a 64-bit notebook PC.

Second, Acer followed an incremental, niche strategy in order to expand internationally. Stan Shih explains this decision by noting, "It is better to be a big fish in a small pond than a small fish in a big pond." Small markets, especially in Asia, which had not yet been captured by the likes of IBM and Compaq, were a driving force behind Acer's initial international success.

Acer's distribution system was also a novelty. With the product life of computer components at about three months, exporting overseas becomes a problem, but Acer built manufacturing and assembling plants all over the world. The company distributed parts with long product lives by ship, while highly volatile products like processors, PCBs, and memory were shipped by plane. This allowed for just-in-time production that Shih compared to the distribution system of a fast-food chain with perishable and non-perishable ingredients.

The success of the company also owes much to the management structure created by Shih. Unlike traditional Chinese businesses, where management is highly hierarchical and controlled by the owning family, Shih uses decentralized management. Autonomy is important. Managers are encouraged to think like owners, so as to take advantage of all profit opportunities. Additionally, Acer has gone public and employees have the option of buying shares at extremely low prices.

In 2000, Acer spun off its manufacturing operations to focus on globally marketing its brand name products: desktop and mobile PCs, servers and storage, displays, peripherals, and e-business solutions. This began a shift away from production and into design and branding (since 2004 it has produced a "Ferrari" line of notebook PCs), and service-related businesses, partly following the evolution of the industries mapped out by Stan Shih's Smiling Curve in the early 1990s. He predicted that success in the combined computing, IT, consumer electronics, and telecoms industries would increasingly depend on being customer-centric, with customer-driven rather than technology-driven innovation. The firm would need to be committed to providing outstanding service and developing intellectual property such as software, rather than focusing on hardware and production activities.

The retirement of Stan Shih in 2004 led to a significant organizational change at the firm, but it maintained its core strategy under J. T. Wang, who has been Chairman of the Board and Chief Executive Officer in Acer Incorporated since April 20, 2011. A more devolved decision-making structure has evolved across a more international group of senior management, a process accelerated by a number of large acquisitions as well as disposals. Acer's buyout of US-based Gateway in 2007 compares to Lenovo's (successful) takeover of IBM's PC business in 2004 and BenQ's (unsuccessful) takeover of Siemens' PC division more recently. This helped Acer move ahead of Chinese rival Lenovo by strengthening its position in the US retail market and giving it control of Packard Bell in Europe. But the competitive threat posed by mainland Chinese PC and electronics firms remains a key strategic challenge for Acer. In 2010 the firm established its second mainland China manufacturing base in Chongqing and it is now calling this its "global IT center."

Websites: www.acer.com; www.ti.com

Sources: Kathrin Hille and Kevin Allison, "Acer to leapfrog Lenovo with Gateway deal," *Financial Times*, August 27, 2007; "Acer buys Gateway," *Financial Times*, August 28, 2007; Willie Chien, Stan Shih, and Po-Young Chu, *Business Growth Strategies for Asia Pacific* (New York: Wiley, 2005); Daniel Lyons, "Horse power," *Forbes*, February 16, 2004, p. 56; Paul Taylor, "In the CEO's chair: Ky Lee at BenQ," *Financial Times*, March 17, 2004, p. 2; Kathrin Hille, "A head start of being ethnically Chinese," *Financial Times*, April 7, 2004, p. 10; Stanley Shih, "Talking about innovation," *Far Eastern Economic Review*, October 17, 2002, p. 44; Stan Shih, *Growing Global* (Taiwan: Acer Corporation, 2001); Stan Shih, *Me-Too Is Not My Style* (Taiwan: Acer Corporation, 1996); Acer, *Annual Report*, 2006–14; Thomson Reuters, *OneSource*, 2011; Mintel Global Market Navigator, 2011, http://gmn.mintel.com.dblibweb.rdg.ac.uk:4000/snapshots/USA/56/shares/single

1 What was the internationalization strategy of Acer and why was it successful?

2 How are changes in the Asian regional economy, in terms of both growing markets and growing competitors, affecting Acer and how should the firm cope?

3 Why did Acer form strategic alliances with IBM and Texas Instruments?

INTRODUCTION

In Chapter 15 we examined some of the country-level risks common in emerging market countries. Although these stand out because of their rapid growth rate, they share many of the characteristics of non-triad countries in general. Such countries are:

- growing in importance for international managers for both market-seeking investments and resource-seeking investments;

- strongly government controlled, in that government agencies play a central role in negotiating with foreign investors and deciding the local rules of the game;

- less predictable and riskier than triad markets, which investors often underestimate in their pursuit of the high level of rewards on offer;[1] and

- the source of new competitors, as local firms move up the value chain, becoming more sophisticated and more international.

We are concerned with two broad kinds of international expansion in this chapter: first, internationalization from the triad into non-triad regions, whereby established MNEs, whose home base is large and mature, and includes expensive markets, expand to sell more outputs in, or buy more inputs from, cheaper emerging economies; and second, the internationalization of newer MNEs from outside the triad which are looking both to complement home-market resources with assets or capabilities from inside the triad and to sell into the much larger triad countries. For each kind of MNE these two forms of internationalization represent some major strategic threats and opportunities.

TRIAD FIRMS AND EMERGING ECONOMY FIRMS: WHY THE MUTUAL INTEREST?

Triad-based and non-triad-based firms will have similar objectives when exploring market-seeking investments. They both want to increase sales in each other's territories and to do this they must customize products and services to suit these markets, establish (or buy) distribution and sales networks, and raise the profiles of their brands. In many cases they may also need to set up manufacturing, assembly, service, or support activities in each other's markets to avoid import duties and/or to support the needs of customers.

When exploring input-seeking investments, triad-based and non-triad-based firms may also have similar strategies, but they tend to be looking for different kinds of inputs. This is because their home regions provide each with a different set of factor endowments, as described by the Porter diamond model (see Chapter 10).

Figure 20.1 provides a starting point to understand the attraction for triad firms looking to expand into emerging economies and for firms from emerging economies looking to expand into triad regions. The large markets of North America, Europe, and Japan still dominate the global economy, but they are growing slowly relative to emerging markets both large, like India, China, and Brazil, and small, like Poland and Malaysia. Triad regions also tend to be more expensive, in terms of labor costs, infrastructure, land, materials, and supporting industries, relative to non-triad regions. These represent push factors, accentuating the pull of non-triad locations. Combining these differences means that there are strong incentives for triad-based firms both to sell products, services, and other outputs into these growing markets and to source inputs, such as cheap labor or manufactured components and services, from such places.

For new MNEs evolving in non-triad regions, the main attraction of triad markets is the large, mature markets. But many firms also look to these countries to fill gaps in their assets, resources, and capabilities, from technological know-how or specialist components to brands.

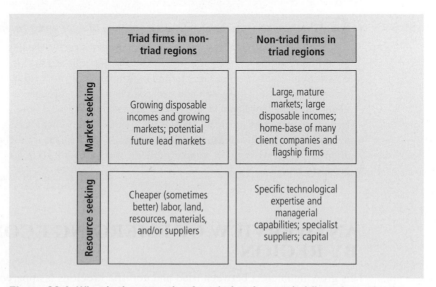

Figure 20.1 What is the attraction for triad and non-triad firms investing in each other's home regions?

Resource-seeking FDI
MNEs invest in production-related activities to benefit from cheaper or better sources of inputs in a particular location; these can include raw materials, components, or labor and expertise

Market-seeking FDI
MNEs invest in distribution, sales, or marketing operations in order to sell products or services (outputs) in particular country markets

FDI into emerging economies for inputs (**resource-seeking FDI**) and outputs (**market-seeking FDI**) takes a variety of forms. Prudential (UK), along with many other triad firms, cut many of its back-office operations in Reading, England, over a decade ago and established a center in Mumbai, India. Although this resulted in around 400 redundancies in the UK, the firm was then able to take advantage of the cheaper (and, in some cases, better) local Indian IT and call-center service workers who have created the local industry reviewed in the **Real Case: The Indian IT, software, and services industry** at the end of this chapter. Contrasting these firms, the **Active Learning Case: Acer Taiwan goes international** shows why and how newer MNEs have broken into triad markets. Yet in many other cases, such as Tesco in the case **International Business Strategy in Action: From Oserian to Tesco**, firms do not see a need to engage in FDI, because they can get access to the advantages of non-triad locations and maintain control over their supply chains by buying and selling through global markets.

More generic international business reasons also exist for expanding into these markets, including risk diversification, the opportunity to extend economies of scale and scope, and the opportunity to leverage existing assets or resources for additional revenues. For example, expanding global production by establishing manufacturing plants in non-triad regions serves to diversify risk by reducing dependence on triad locations where input costs and wages are high—but may also rise further. This allows firms to reap economies-of-scale benefits across the overall production function. Similarly, extending established triad brands into new markets helps build the economies of scale needed to pay for media advertising and other brand-building activities. As sports stars and celebrities, such as Tiger Woods (in the past) and Rory McIlroy (for Nike), develop international reputations, their images can be used to sell products around the world, and companies can earn sufficient revenues to pay for them because they are assets that can be leveraged globally.

✔ Active learning check

Review your answer to Active Learning Case question 1 and make any changes you like. Then compare your answer to the one below.

① What was the internationalization strategy of Acer and why was it successful?

Rather than aiming to break into the triad markets directly, despite the attractions, Acer focused on building a presence in smaller local Asian markets first. In some ways it followed a pattern of gradual, stepwise internationalization. Acer built up from its relatively small home-base diamond in Taiwan and expanded production throughout Southeast Asia. It then undertook a double-diamond strategy for accessing the triad markets of North America and Europe. It formed strategic alliances with the US and European MNEs and used these as a stepping stone to FDI in these key triad markets. It also kept its production-based efficiencies of employee involvement in company growth and ongoing R&D to improve the quality of its products.

AN OVERVIEW OF EMERGING ECONOMIES, BY REGION

This growing interest between triad and non-triad regions is apparent in changing patterns of global FDI. As Table 20.1 shows, just under 50 percent of all FDI now flows into developed countries, mainly the triad. This compares to 85 percent in 1980. Asia, and particularly Southeast Asia, takes the major share of the remaining 37 percent going to developing

Table 20.1 FDI inflows, by host region and economy, 1995–2014 (millions of US$)

Economy/region	1995	2000	2005	2008	2014
World	335,734	1,387,953	916,277	1,697,353	1,467,233
Developed countries	204,426	1,107,987	542,312	962,259	696,854
European Union	114,560	671,417	421,899	503,453	333,084
North America	68,027	380,798	133,265	360,824	301,333
United States	58,772	314,007	99,443	316,112	230,768
Japan	41	8,323	2,775	24,426	2,304
Other developed countries	17,251	29,752	−27,356	83,095	69,987
Developing countries	115,953	252,459	334,285	620,733	670,790
Africa, of which	5,392	8,728	30,672	87,647	53,969
Algeria	0	438	1,081	2,647	2,661
Egypt	595	1,235	5,376	9,495	4,192
Morocco	332	215	2,933	2,388	3,298
Sudan	12	392	2,305	2,601	1,688
Angola	472	879	−24	15,548	−7,120
Chad	33	116	705	834	538
Equatorial Guinea	65	109	1,860	1,290	1,914
Nigeria	1,079	930	3,403	20,279	5,608
South Africa	1,241	888	6,379	9,009	11,018
Latin America and the Caribbean	30,280	97,537	103,663	144,377	186,151
Argentina	5,609	10,418	4,662	8,853	11,301
Brazil	4,405	32,779	15,066	45,058	63,996
Chile	2,956	4,860	6,667	16,787	16,577
Colombia	968	2,395	10,192	10,564	16,199
Ecuador	452	720	1,913	974	731
Peru	2,557	810	2,579	4,808	9,298
Venezuela	985	4,701	2,957	1,716	2,680
Mexico	9,655	16,586	18,055	21,950	44,627
Asia and the Pacific	80,281	146,195	199,951	388,709	427,879
Saudi Arabia	21,877	21,884	1,469	38,223	8,865
Azerbaijan	330	130	1,680	11	2,632
Kazakhstan	964	1,283	1,738	14,543	10,221
China	37,521	40,715	72,406	108,312	123,911
Hong Kong, China	6,213	61,939	35,897	63,003	74,294
India	2,151	2,319	6,598	41,554	28,199
Indonesia	4,346	24,550	5,260	7,919	18,817
Korea, Republic of	1,249	8,572	7,198	7,603	12,767
Malaysia	5,815	3,788	3,967	8,053	12,115
Pakistan	719	305	2,183	5,438	1,333
Singapore	11,591	17,217	20,083	22,725	64,793
Taiwan Province of China	1,559	4,928	1,625	5,432	3,598
Thailand	2,070	3,350	3,687	10,091	14,016
Vietnam	1,780	1,289	2,020	8,050	8,900
Bulgaria	90	1,002	2,223	9,205	1,920
Croatia	114	1,089	1,695	4,383	955
Romania	419	1,037	6,388	13,305	3,602
Russian Federation	2,065	2,714	14,600	70,320	69,219

Source: Adapted from United Nations, *World Investment Report,* 2006, 2009, 2014, key data downloads at http://www.unctad.org (Geneva: United Nations Conference on Trade and Development).

countries, with 22 percent of the world total, compared to a share of just 1 percent in 1980 and 12 percent in 1990. Africa receives approximately 4 percent. Overall, though, FDI is the largest source of external finance for all developing countries and on average now amounts to over one-third of their GDP, compared to just 10 percent in 1980. As described below, patterns of inward FDI are varied, with some countries or regions showing significant growth while others experience no growth and even decline.[2]

Given the market-seeking and resource-seeking aims of MNE investors, we can see that the varying levels of attractiveness of different non-triad investment destinations are the result of differences in market size and growth rates and the opportunities they present for firms looking for sourcing and production advantages. Opportunities for accessing these kinds of advantages can be enhanced by government **liberalization policies**, which can help to reduce the limitations and constraints on foreign firms' investments and business activities. Liberalization, for many governments in emerging economies, signals a move away from a centrally controlled or coordinated economy, toward a more free market economy. This shift is often accompanied by the widespread privatization of state-owned firms. Again this presents opportunities for MNEs—for example, in telecoms, utilities, or energy industries—to buy into newly privatized firms or establish joint ventures and alliances to access resources or the local market. India provides a clear illustration of this with FDI inflows amounting to over $2 billion between 1991 and 1995, after liberalization, compared to well below $1 billion in the two decades leading up to 1990.

Non-triad countries and regions differ, both in their initial economic attractiveness to MNEs and in the ways that governments are liberalizing parts of the economy; together these explain many of the differences we observe in regional patterns of FDI. Table 20.2 shows that, in the same time period, outflows of FDI from developing countries have grown fairly dramatically. Again Southeast Asia is responsible for the dominant share. China's stock of outward FDI has grown from $2.5 billion in 1990 to over $25 billion in 2000, and over $60 billion in 2007. It has since grown at a staggering rate, to over $148 billion in 2008 and over $2,600 billion in 2013. In addition to this, however, a significant proportion of the much larger outward flows from Hong Kong originally come from mainland China.

We will now briefly review the recent experience of each of the main non-triad regions in terms of inward FDI and look at some examples that provide insights into the drivers of FDI flows. In preparation for the discussion below about MNEs from emerging economies, we will also briefly look at some of the largest firms in these countries that are expanding within and beyond their regions.

Liberalization policies
Government policies that move away from planned economies toward more free market systems; they are marked by the privatization of state-owned businesses, a lowering of tariff and non-tariff barriers, and reductions in the constraints placed on foreign firms' investments and business activities

Table 20.2 FDI from developing countries, 2000–13 (billions of US$)

Region/economy	FDI outflows (annual average)		FDI outflow 2013	FDI outward stock			
	2000–4	2005–8	2013	2000	2005	2008	2013
Developing economies	70.2	227.0	454.1	862.3	1,273.6	2,356.6	4,993.3
Africa	0.4	7.5	12.4	44.1	53.9	97.9	162.4
South Africa	16.7	1.5	8.0	32.3	38.5	62.3	110.9
Latin America and the Caribbean	13.9	53.4	114.6	204.3	345.3	561.4	1,312.3
Brazil	2.5	14.5	3.5	51.9	71.5	162.2	293.3
Chile	1.5	3.7	10.9	11.2	21.3	31.7	101.9
Mexico	2.4	5.2	12.9	8.3	28.0	45.3	143.9
Asia and the Pacific	55.8	166.0	326.0	613.8	874.3	1,697.2	3,512.7
South, East, and Southeast Asia	51.8	136.5	292.5	597.2	837.6	1,564.4	3,153.0
China	2.7	27.0	101.0	27.7	46.3	147.9	613.6
Hong Kong, China	27.5	48.3	91.5	388.4	470.4	775.9	1,352.3
India	1.2	12.6	1.7	1.8	9.5	61.7	119.8
Korea, Republic of	3.6	10.2	29.2	26.8	36.4	95.5	219.1
Malaysia	1.5	8.5	13.6	15.8	44.4	67.5	134.0
Memorandum							
World	645.1	1,552.0	1,410.7	6,069.8	10,129.7	16,205.6	26,312.6

Source: UNCTAD, *World Investment Report*, 2006, 2009, and 2014, at www.unctad.org

Asia–Pacific and the Middle East

As shown in Table 20.1, Asia–Pacific and the Middle East received approximately 30 percent of global FDI flows in 2014, the most of any non-triad region. But FDI is highly concentrated, with 10 out of the 55 economies in the region (for which reliable data are available) accounting for over 90 percent of FDI. China and Hong Kong (China) received just under half of the total regional FDI, indicating their growing attractiveness to investors.

We focus on China in the next chapter, but there are examples of events and factors elsewhere in the region that help explain these patterns of investment. Many of the countries in the region continue to liberalize their economies and privatize state-owned assets, both of which are attractive to MNEs. Cross-border M&A has grown steadily, as has the significance of intra-regional M&A, as opposed to investments driven by triad-based firms. But a few large acquisitions and divestments can make a big difference to individual country markets. Following significant growth of FDI into South Korea in the early to mid-2000s, 2006 saw a drop as both Wal-Mart and Carrefour divested from the country to focus on other Asian markets.

FDI into India has decreased between 2008 and 2014, however FDI inflows increased around sixfold between 2005 (US$6,598 million) and 2008 (US$41,554 million). A growing economy, continued liberalization, and the attractiveness of evolving IT, software, and services industries (see **Real Case: the Indian IT, software, and services industry**) all provided momentum. GM and IBM increased their presence as did Wal-Mart, Toyota, and Nissan.

The oil-rich countries of Bahrain, Jordan, Kuwait, Oman, and Saudi Arabia also experienced recent upturns in inward FDI, almost exclusively related to their oil industries. Less political turmoil would clearly have resulted in larger inflows to the Middle East region in recent decades.

Intra-regional investments
Investments in the local region rather than in other triad or non-triad regions, such as when Chinese firms invest in other Southeast Asian economies

Finally, there are two clear trends that indicate the dynamism of the Asia region. First, the growth of **intra-regional investment** is particularly driven by the regional giants India and China joining countries like Malaysia, South Korea, Taiwan, and Singapore as active investors, but also by the growth of Japanese investment in the region. Second, FDI in services is growing rapidly and now represents over 50 percent of FDI stock in the Asia region. Many of the high-growth economies are becoming increasingly service oriented and have developed efficient institutional and infrastructural conditions for attracting finance, telecoms, and commerce-related activities. In accordance with its commitments to the liberalization of services under its WTO accession agreement, China is opening its service industries to FDI. Restrictions on FDI in industries such as banking and finance, telecoms, logistics and distribution, transportation, and retail and wholesale trade are being removed.

MNEs from Asia–Pacific

The Asia–Pacific region has a large proportion of the 50 largest non-financial MNEs from developing countries listed by UNCTAD (see Table 20.3). The largest number from any one country come from Hong Kong (China). Top of the list is Hutchison Whampoa, a diversified conglomerate which focuses on the Asia region. Other major firms from the region include Petronas (oil and petroleum; Malaysia), Singtel (telecoms; Singapore), Samsung Electronics and LG Electronics (South Korea), and Jardine Matheson Holdings (diversified; Hong Kong).

Outward FDI from India has increased significantly in recent years. Indian companies undertake cross-border M&As to gain access to new technologies and expertise, and to build stronger positions in global markets. Steel industry takeovers have been hitting the headlines in recent years, with Mittal Steel's takeover of European firm Arcelor for

Table 20.3 The top 50 non-financial TNCs from developing economies ranked by foreign assets, 2013[a] (millions of US$, number of employees)

Ranking by: Foreign assets	TNI[b]	Corporation	Home economy	Industry[c]	Assets Foreign	Assets Total	Sales Foreign	Sales Total	Employment Foreign[d]	Employment Total	TNI (Percent)
1	19	Hutchison Whampoa Limited	Hong Kong, China	Diversified	85,721	103,715	24,222	31,339	206,986	250,000	80.9
2	93	CITIC Group	China	Diversified	78,602	565,884	9,561	55,487	25,285	125,215[e]	17.1
3	16	Hon Hai Precision Industries	Taiwan Province of China	Electrical & electronic equipment	65,471	70,448	128,650	132,429	810,993	1,290,000	84.3
4	70	Petronas – Petroliam Nasional Bhd	Malaysia	Petroleum expl./ref./distr.	49,072	163,275	71,939	94,543	5,244	46,145	39.2
5	63	Vale SA	Brazil	Mining & quarrying	45,721	131,478	38,326	47,694	15,680	85,305	44.5
6	59	China Ocean Shipping (Group) Company	China	Transport and storage	43,452	56,126	19,139	29,101	4,400	130,000	48.9
7	91	China National Offshore Oil Corp	China	Petroleum expl./ref./distr.	34,276	129,834	21,887	83,537	3,387	102,562	18.6
8	58	América Móvil SAB de CV	Mexico	Telecommunications	32,008	75,697	37,395	58,950	67,525	158,719	49.4
9	67	Lukoil OAO	Russian Federation	Petroleum and natural gas	31,174	98,961	113,801	139,171	18,144	120,300	42.8
10	20	Cemex S.A.B. de C.V.	Mexico	Non-metalic mineral products	30,730	36,808	11,717	14,986	35,387	45,087	80.1
11	92	Petróleos de Venezuela SA	Venezuela, Bolivarian Republic of	Petroleum expl./ref./distr.	27,462	218,424	46,899	123,223	4,877	126,945	18.2
12	80	Samsung Electronics Co. Ltd.	Korea, Republic of	Electrical & electronic equipment	26,077	169,702	19,294	179,060	123,563	227,000	26.9
13	39	Singapore Telecommunications Ltd	Singapore	Telecommunications	25,768	32,242	9,541	14,633	10,496	23,176	63.5
14	83	Hyundai Motor Company	Korea, Republic of	Motor vehicles	25,443	113,906	11,754	75,211	38,318	98,348	25.6
15	44	Jardine Matheson Holdings Ltd	Hong Kong, China	Diversified	24,284	63,460	29,732	39,593	217,556	360,000	57.9
16	54	SABIC – Saudi Basic Industries Corp.	Saudi Arabia	Petroleum expl./ref./distr.	23,540	90,089	33,377	50,422	25,391	40,000	51.9
17	85	Gazprom JSC	Russian Federation	Petroleum and natural gas	23,425	396,454	92,016	153,863	27,400	431,200	24.0
18	24	Wilmar International Limited	Singapore	Food, beverages and tobacco	23,088	41,920	33,622	45,463	90,575	93,000	75.5

19	2	China Resources Power Holdings Company Ltd	Hong Kong, China	Energy	22,938	22,938	8,049	8,049	38,018	38,118	99.9
20	42	Tata Motors Ltd	India	Automobile	21,575	31,281	26,519	34,765	20,379	62,716	59.2
21	17	Ooredoo QSC	Qatar	Telecommunications	20,304	26,104	7,601	9,303	15,289	17,130	82.9
22	88	Formosa Plastics Group	Taiwan Province of China	Chemicals	19,994	101,998	14,405	78,130	24,287	102,763	20.6
23	62	New World Development Ltd	Hong Kong, China	Diversified	19,857	36,918	2,411	4,582	14,751	47,000	45.9
24	100	China National Petroleum Corporation	China	Petroleum expl./ref./distr.	19,284	541,083	11,296	425,720	31,442	1,656,465	2.7
25	29	CapitaLand Ltd	Singapore	Construction and real estate	18,926	30,885	1,706	2,642	10,500	12,000	71.1
26	32	Abu Dhabi National Energy Co PJSC	United Arab Emirates	Utilities (Electricity, gas and water)	18,198	33,377	5,660	7,566	2,547	3,300	68.8
27	6	Noble Group Ltd	Hong Kong, China	Wholesale trade	17,748	19,700	94,045	94,045	14,440	15,000	95.5
28	26	Genting Bhd	Malaysia	Other consumer services	17,719	21,940	3,411	5,599	43,559	58,000	72.3
29	97	Petróleo Brasileiro SA	Brazil	Petroleum expl./ref./distr.	16,927	331,078	14,071	144,275	7,640	85,065	7.9
30	49	Gerdau SA	Brazil	Metal and metal products	15,684	26,072	11,677	19,475	19,211	41,869	55.3
31	31	MTN Group Ltd	South Africa	Telecommunications	15,263	21,409	10,651	16,486	19,690	27,000	69.6
32	69	Bharti Airtel Limited	India	Telecommunications	15,153	30,783	4,442	14,796	10,514	24,725	40.6
33	46	Tata Steel Ltd	India	Metal and metal products	14,994	27,027	17,658	24,803	37,638	80,534	57.8
34	55	CLP Holdings Ltd	Hong Kong, China	Utilities (Electricity, gas and water)	14,855	29,513	9,152	13,519	2,236	6,581	50.7
35	66	Sinochem Group	China	Petroleum expl./ref./distr.	14,704	45,488	55,555	71,891	9,828	48,414	43.3
36	22	Quanta Computer Inc	Taiwan Province of China	Electrical & electronic equipment	14,494	19,479	29,770	34,757	89,567	121,917	77.8
37	89	POSCO	Korea, Republic of	Metal and metal products	13,997	74,289	14,168	56,632	5,505	35,094	19.8
38	14	China Resources Enterprises Ltd	Hong Kong, China	Food and beverages	13,426	16,448	15,148	16,274	200,450	211,000	89.9
39	1	Golden Agri-Resources Ltd	Singapore	Food	13,286	13,286	6,052	6,052	47,000	47,000	100.0
40	3	First Pacific Company Ltd	Hong Kong, China	Electrical & electronic equipment	13,256	13,880	5,991	5,991	80,897	80,941	98.5
41	23	YTL Corporation Bhd	Malaysia	Utilities (Electricity, gas and water)	13,010	16,154	4,920	6,499	6,405	9,000	75.8
42	95	Sun Hung Kai Properties Ltd	Hong Kong, China	Other services	12,615	60,277	403	8,799	6,242	35,000	14.4

Table 20.3 (continued)

Ranking by: Foreign assets	TNI[b]	Corporation	Home economy	Industry[c]	Assets		Sales		Employment		TNI (Percent)
					Foreign	Total	Foreign	Total	Foreign[d]	Total	
43	27	Steinhoff International Holdings Ltd	South Africa	Other consumer goods	12,453	16,090	8,008	10,374	49,632	79,900	72.2
44	56	Lenovo Group Ltd	China	Electrical & electronic equipment	11,962	16,882	19,335	33,873	8,092	35,026	50.3
45	73	Fomento Económico Mexicano SAB	Mexico	Food, beverages and tobacco	11,919	22,752	6,292	18,125	35,560	182,260	35.5
46	11	Shangri-La Asia Ltd	Hong Kong, China	Other consumer services	11,496	11,920	1,781	2,057	27,552	28,700	93.0
47	40	Hindalco Industries Ltd	India	Diversified	11,325	22,186	11,249	14,765	11,618	20,238	61.5
48	13	Li & Fung Ltd	Hong Kong, China	Wholesale trade	11,254	12,015	19,010	20,222	24,104	28,465	90.8
49	25	Gold Fields Ltd	South Africa	Metal and metal products	10,931	11,200	3,078	3,528	18,030	44,230	75.2
50	94	Oil and Natural Gas Corp Ltd	India	Petroleum expl./ref./distr.	10,930	46,630	3,233	29,901	3,908	32,923	15.4

Notes:
[a] All data are based on the companies' annual reports unless otherwise stated and correspond to the financial year from 1 April 2012 to 31 March 2013.
[b] TNI, the Transnationality Index, is calculated as the average of the following three ratios: foreign assets to total assets, foreign sales to total sales, and foreign employment to total employment.
[c] Industry classification for companies follows the United States Standard Industrial Classification as used by the United States Securities and Exchange Commission (SEC).
[d] In a number of cases foreign employment data were calculated by applying the share of foreign employment in total employment of the previous year to total employment of 2012.
[e] In lieu of 2012 figures, 2011 data have been used.

$32 billion ranking as the world's largest cross-border M&A transaction in 2006. In the same year, the Tata conglomerate acquired the Corus Group for $9.5 billion. It went on to buy Jaguar and Aston Martin from Ford in 2008, to add premium brands to its low-cost automotive portfolio. Further discussion about new multinationals from non-triad regions appears below.

Central and eastern Europe

Despite years of political and economic change, including liberalization, in the Central and East European (CEE) region, it still attracts a relatively small percentage of global FDI inflows. Poland, the Czech Republic, and Hungary receive larger shares of FDI than other countries in the region but have experienced declines in recent years, as has the Russian Federation. These, plus five other CEE countries (Estonia, Latvia, Lithuania, Slovenia, and Slovakia), joined the EU in May 2004 and saw FDI inflows shrink, but things have improved since then.

Some countries are attracting auto sector FDI, including the Czech Republic, with an investment from Toyota–PSA, and Slovakia, with investments from PSA, Kia, and Hyundai. Volkswagen Slovakia is already that country's largest company and biggest employer by far. Slovakia has a population of just over 5.4 million people, yet has developed into a leading producer of autos, with an output of over one million cars in 2014, from having no auto industry whatsoever before 1991, when VW took over Skoda's businesses in Bratislava in the Czech Republic. VW has invested around $1.3 billion in Slovakia, and Hyundai's investments are expected to total $1.5 billion eventually. But in all these cases the MNEs were attracted to the region not just because of the combination of cheap labor, good infrastructure, and proximity to Europe's large markets, but also because of the over $1 billion in subsidies and regional development loans they received to sweeten the deal.[3]

In terms of outflows of FDI from the CEE region, the Russian Federation has dominated for some time as the major source. A key question for analysts is whether these capital flows represent genuine strategic investments in other parts of the world or capital flight from a politically tense Russia.

MNEs from central and eastern Europe

The largest MNEs in the CEE region are Russian, most of them nationally owned at one time or another and many of them based on the country's abundant natural resources. The Russian oil and gas giants (Gazprom, Rosneft, and Lukoil) have started to expand abroad, including Gazprom's investments in the German energy sector to get direct access to end-users (also see the **Real Case: Yukos and the Russian oligarchs** in Chapter 15). Telecoms, aluminum, and other industries also feature in the international expansion of CEE firms.

Latin America and the Caribbean

Approximately 12.5 percent of global FDI went to the Latin America region in 2014, the highest proportion since 1980 and still lower than inflows to China and Hong Kong (China) that year. Inward FDI has grown since then, but the percentage of global FDI going to this region has fallen. The three largest economies of Argentina, Brazil, and Mexico have seen large fluctuations in inflows in the recent past. To various degrees these economies have had a difficult decade in terms of economic growth and recession. A spate of privatizations during the late 1990s gave a temporary boost to inward FDI for these and other regional economies and a number of MNEs increased their involvement in Latin America during this period. An example is Endesa, the Spanish-owned electricity utility, which is the leading supplier in six countries and serves approximately 10 million customers (50 percent of its global market) in the region. Through its regional subsidiary Enersis, Endesa bought into or bought out national companies in Argentina, Brazil, Chile, Peru, Colombia, and the Dominican Republic to develop massive economies of scale in energy production, distribution, and services in the region.[4]

Regional-level, as opposed to national-level, competition has evolved in other industries, sometimes pitting home-based MNEs against foreign-owned incomers. In telecoms, for example, Mexico's América Móvil and Spain's Telefónica are battling it out for regional domination, both having boosted their holdings when US telecom firms went through a divestment phase. Although the former dominates the Mexican mobile telephony business, it has a long way to go to catch up with Telefónica. Telefónica Móviles, the Spanish firm's regional mobile telecom subsidiary, has a presence in 13 countries in the region, is the market leader in 7 and second in 5, and serves a total of over 40 million customers.[5]

Brazil and Mexico still receive the highest amounts of FDI and, as we would expect, one-third of all FDI into the region came from the United States. Many Latin American countries now face increased competition for US manufacturing investment from China and the Asia region. This is particularly true of Mexico, whose linkage to the North American triad via NAFTA was discussed in Chapters 10 and 19, where the Mexico–US double diamond was explained. Various periods have seen a decline in the number of *maquiladora* enterprises (which once accounted for almost 50 percent of Mexico's merchandise exports) and associated jobs losses. Combined with the decline in inward FDI, this called into question the attractiveness and competitiveness of the region in comparison to a fast-evolving Asia.

MNEs from Latin America

Of the 50 largest non-financial TNCs from developing countries listed by UNCTAD (Table 20.3), a relatively small number are from the Latin American region. As with the central and eastern European MNEs (and contrasting those from the Asia–Pacific region) many of the largest are natural resources based. These include the largest of all, Cemex (construction materials; Mexico), Petróleos de Venezuela (Venezuela), Petrobras (Brazil), Companhia Vale do Rio Doce (mining; Brazil), Metalúrgica Gerdau (metal products; Brazil), and Perez Companc (oil and petroleum; Argentina).

Africa

As home to most of the world's least developed countries (LDCs), Africa has always recorded low levels of inward FDI because of its relative lack of attractiveness to MNEs. Political instability, weak infrastructure, poor labor skills, and macroeconomic fragility have plagued many parts of the continent for decades. Except for the larger economies of Egypt and South Africa, and the oil producers such as Equatorial Guinea, Angola, Nigeria, and the Sudan, most of the remaining LDCs normally receive less than $200 million FDI per year.

As shown in Table 20.1, only approximately 3.5 percent of total global FDI went to Africa in 2014, and this tends to be concentrated in resource-rich economies. Oil, diamonds, gold, and platinum in particular have been the main attraction for MNEs. Exxon Mobil, for example, has offshore oil projects in Nigeria, and the French firm Total Oil Nigeria has plans to invest $10 billion in the Nigerian oil industry.[6] For most of Sub-Saharan Africa, however, inflows are limited, although South Africa stands out as a major recipient due to its relatively healthy economy. Chinese investment into Africa, particularly targeting sources of raw materials and resources, is very much in the news. FDI worth an estimated $30–40 billion, much of it from state-owned enterprises, has flowed into Sub-Saharan Africa, but accurate data are not yet available.

FDI in telecoms and services recently overtook investment in mining and extraction in South Africa. At the same time it has extended its investments in other parts of the continent, with firms like BHP Billiton (mining) and Eskom (utilities) expanding into other African markets. Two of South Africa's telecom firms are also majority shareholders in the largest mobile telecom firm in Africa, a joint venture between Telecom SA, VenFin, and Vodafone (35 percent stake) with over 10 million subscribers and almost $2.5 billion in revenues. It competes with MTN Group from South Africa, Orascom (Egypt), Orange (France Telecom), and Celtel International (the Netherlands), all of which are gradually taking market share from the fixed-line industry dominated by national telecom firms. In some industry sectors, despite the lack of inward FDI, there are growing business links between Western firms and local African firms. The Kenya cut flower industry is one example (see **International Business Strategy in Action: From Oserian to Tesco**).

INTERNATIONAL BUSINESS STRATEGY IN ACTION

From Oserian to Tesco: the Kenyan cut flower industry

Kenya is one of the leading exporters of flowers in the world, accounting for approximately 35 percent of the market share in Europe. Kenya's roses, carnations, and summer flowers are famed for being long-lasting and extremely popular in other nations such as Russia and the United States. This industry took off in the first half of the 2000s, with export growth accelerating rapidly in the late 1990s and achieving 27 percent between 2001 and 2005. How did this global competitive advantage evolve in one of the world's least developed countries?

Horticultural and cut flower exports provide well over US$1 billion to Kenya's economy. In 2013, Kenya's floriculture industry exported 125,000 tons, worth over US$600 million. The country has approximately 10 percent of the global export market. Ecuador and Colombia are key competitors and the Netherlands still dominates with over 50 percent. The major markets are Germany, the UK, and United States, but the major proportion of exports goes to the Dutch auction houses in Holland. Direct sales via supermarket chains, particularly in the UK, have increased dramatically, however.

The country's flower industry employs about 70,000 people, and it has been reported that the industry supports over 500,000 people in Kenya. The average basic wage in the flower industry is around US$5,000 compared to Kenya's average GDP per capita of US$800. Most of the flower growing is in the areas of Naivasha, Thika, and Kiambu, where over 2,000 hectares are used for flower production. Although over 30 varieties of flowers are grown in Kenya, roses make up two-thirds of Kenya's flower exports, followed by carnations, statice, and alstromeria. The real start of the industry happened in 1994 with the formation of the Kenya Flower Council to support the operations of a number of fast-growing businesses.

Local factor conditions

The successful cultivation of flowers requires the following elements:

- good physical conditions: high light intensity, abundant water, clean soil, good climate;
- appropriate seeds and planting material;
- capital for investment and working capital;
- productive labor;
- expertise in growing techniques;
- good management and organization;
- pesticides and other chemicals;
- energy for heating;
- infrastructure;
- a high level of quality consciousness all along the production and post-harvesting chain.

Perhaps more than any other internationally traded good, time-to-market is critical in the cut flower industry. Strict control of humidity, temperature, and air quality is essential for delivering an attractive product to the market. Growers rely heavily on the post-harvest chain of handlers, storage, and transport, and in the absence of a "cold chain" it is not possible for equatorial producers to sell to the main northern markets.

Air freight adds significantly to the total cost and makes up by far the largest component of overall cost to African producers. Air freight, marketing, handling in Europe, and packaging make up 50 percent of all costs for Kenyan growers. In the Netherlands, however, transport accounts for just 14 percent of the costs, but labor makes up 35 percent of costs. ▶

Although cheap labor and a good growing climate are advantageous for growing flowers, some countries have done well for some time without these local factor endowments. The Netherlands does not have climatic, land, or labor advantages but has been a dominant player in the industry for a long time. This is partly due to the power of the Dutch auction houses, which have long overseen the international flower trade.

In Porter's terminology (in the diamond model discussed in Chapter 10), acquired factor conditions, such as the cold transport infrastructure, plant breeding and greenhouse technologies, and production management capabilities were required before Kenya could leverage its natural endowments and the cheap labor advantage to compete in the open market. It is only in the last 15 to 20 years that these acquired factors have developed.

Another "diamond of advantage" factor, the influence of government, has had a significant effect over the last two decades. A cycle of political instability has arguably limited investment as internal and external funders do not have confidence in the sustainability of the flower-growing industry.

The Oserian Development Company

Oserian ("place of peace" in Maasai), one of the largest privately owned flower farms in the world, was among the first commercial exporters of cut flowers from Kenya. Although it began growing flowers in the early 1980s, the company dates from 1967 and was started and is still operated and partly owned by Hans and Peter Zwager. It has over 200 hectares under cultivation next to Lake Naivasha in the Rift Valley and exports over 300 million stems per year. These are mainly sold by East African Flowers (EAF) BV, through the Tele Flower Auction (TFA) in Holland, to other buyers around the world; or by World Flowers in the UK, direct to Tesco. Crops include roses, spray carnations, gypsophila, chrysanthemums, statice, hypericum, euphorbia, delphinium, and perezi. The farm employs about 5,000 people; 85 percent are permanent employees and over 60 percent live on the farm with their families. The facilities include three kindergartens, two primary schools, a secondary school, shopping centers, social halls, and a medical center.

Industry structure: Tesco and the growing power of the supermarkets

Although the Dutch auction houses have traditionally been the focal point of the world flower industry, large retailers are building direct links with growers around the world, using their purchasing power to gain better control over product price, delivery, and quality. African producers appear to be the main beneficiaries of this change in purchasing habits. Supermarkets are interested in African flowers because they are inexpensive and because growers are willing to accept a set price. To the growers this arrangement is attractive because supermarkets buy large quantities at pre-arranged prices. But in order to live up to their side of the bargain, African growers must invest in optimal production methods. Often this includes investments in greenhouses, forced ventilation and heating, and, in all cases, greater attention to quality.

Over the past decade Kenya's direct imports to the UK have grown, partly due to the establishment of direct links with Marks & Spencer and Tesco. The British spend more than $3 billion a year on fresh cut flowers and indoor plants; 85 percent of all flowers sold in the UK are imported, of which about 20 percent come from countries outside the EU.

Around one-quarter of roses sold in the UK are purchased directly from Kenya, mainly by the major supermarkets. Tesco, one of the top three supermarket chains in the world, is the UK's number one food retailer and the largest retailer of flowers and plants. Tesco has been selling houseplants and flowers for the last two decades and sales keep growing, hence the need for reliable ties with suppliers. Tesco became an associate member of the Kenya Flower Council in early 2000 as its direct links with suppliers like Oserian began to grow. By cutting out the Dutch auction houses, Tesco found that it could work directly with growers to reduce prices and improve quality and also pass on customer needs to more directly influence new developments.

Fairtrade

Tesco and Oserian deepened their buyer–supplier alliance by opening a line of Fairtrade roses. These are grown by Oserian and one other farm in Kenya (Finlay Flowers in Kericho), which have been certified to comply with employment, social, and environmental conditions laid down in the Fairtrade agreement.

The agreement was set up in response to concerns among customers and expressed in the media about the conditions under which flowers are grown. This included the employment conditions of workers and the environmental effects on the land and particularly water availability, around, for example, Lake Naivasha. Although Fairtrade roses are slightly more expensive, they represent a differentiated product designed to appeal to ethically minded customers. Tesco does not take an additional profit as 8 percent of the overall export price goes directly to the farms, allocated by joint management and employee committees, to improve employee conditions. This premium is worth up to US $200,000 per year to the two farms involved. This concern for social ethics has strengthened as Oserian became part of the Mavuno Group in 2010 and expanded its direct sales to more global markets.

As of 2015, the Kenyan farmers started lending their floral expertise to neighboring country Rwanda. As part of a government partnering scheme, the two nations aim to build a

35-hectare flower park which is 60 km away from Rwanda's capital city, Kigali. The aim of this partnership is to produce over 3 million stems per year, which will provide employment and hopefully pump approximately US$200 million into Rwanda's economy by 2017.

Sources: Milena Veselinovic, "Got roses this Valentine's Day? They probably came from Kenya," *CNN Africa View*, March 16, 2015; http://www.oserian.com; A. Odhiambo, "Oserian deal with Dutch firm sparks rivalry," *Business Daily*, April 2011; "Roses are red: Kenya's flower industry," *The Economist*, February 7, 2008; Gathoni Muraya, "Local flower market quietly booming," *Business Day Africa*, March 28, 2007; C. S. Dolan, S. Jafee, and R. Thoen, "Equatorial rose: the Kenyan–European cut flower supply chain," in R. Kopiki (ed.), *Supply Chain Development in Emerging Markets* (Boston, MA: MIT Press, 2004); Mary Hennock, "Kenya's flower farms flourish," *BBC News*, February 14, 2002; Chris Collinson, *The Business Costs of Ethical Supply Chain Management Report No. 2607*, Natural Resources and Ethical Trade Programme (Chatham: National Resources Institute, 2001), at http://www.nri.org/NRET/2607.pdf; further material from the KFC at http://www.africaonline.co.ke/kfc/index.html; industry data from the Horticultural Crop Development Authority (HCDA), Nairobi; http://www.tesco.com/corporateinfo/

MNEs from Africa

Just five of the 50 largest non-financial TNCs from developing countries listed by UNCTAD (Table 20.3) are from Africa, and they are all South African. Sasol (industrial chemicals), Gold Fields (metal products), Naspers (consumer services), Steinhoff (consumer services), and Sappi (paper products) are major players in their respective sectors throughout the region. At least part of the explanation for the lack of large indigenous firms from other African countries lies in their colonial past and the history of domination by Western multinationals as investors in local mineral or agricultural resources.[7]

SHIFTING PATTERNS OF COMPARATIVE AND COMPETITIVE ADVANTAGE

As we have seen from the breakdown of FDI flows above, FDI into non-triad regions tends to be concentrated in a few countries within each region. Moreover, although FDI still tends to be related to primary resources, such as oil, minerals, and agricultural commodities in many of these countries, there is a growing volume of manufacturing and service-related FDI. This is particularly true for a group of emerging markets or **newly industrialized countries (NICs)**, which have broken the cycle of underdevelopment to achieve economic growth and wealth creation, partly through increased integration with other parts of the global economy. This group includes relatively wealthy countries like South Korea, Singapore, Hong Kong (China), and Taiwan (China), which were together called the "four Asian Tigers" in the 1980s when they began to achieve high rates of economic growth. But there are also other growing economies, particularly in the Asia–Pacific region, that appear to be moving along the same growth path. Why are these economies growing? How are they able to compete with triad firms, export, and sell in triad markets? Why are they attractive as locations for triad FDI? These are important questions as the emergence of these economies, particularly the two giant markets of China and India, is giving rise to some of the most important competitive opportunities and threats for MNEs of all types.

To understand current patterns of growth in many emerging markets, we need to briefly review some of the theoretical explanations for the evolving patterns of national-level comparative and competitive advantage (we did this in Chapter 6 and some of the following summarizes our earlier description). In the original landmark study of wealth creation and national competitiveness, the economist Adam Smith stated:

> What is prudence in the conduct of every private family, can scarce be folly in that of a great kingdom. If a foreign country can supply us with a commodity cheaper than we ourselves can make it, better buy it of them with some part of the produce of our own industry, employed in a way in which we have some advantage. The general industry of the country, being always in proportion to the capital which employs it, will not thereby be diminished ... but only left to find out the way in which it can be employed with the greatest advantage.[8]

Newly industrialized countries (NICs)
A subgroup of emerging market economies that have experienced rapid economic growth, normally accompanied by political and social change; the forerunners were the four Asian "Tiger" economies: Singapore, South Korea, Taiwan, and Hong Kong. The rapid growth, increased trade and FDI, and integration of China in the global economy show that it is approaching this status

Adam Smith's theory of absolute advantage suggested that each nation should *specialize* in producing goods it had a *natural* or *acquired* advantage in producing (and therefore could produce more efficiently than other countries). Exports of these goods would pay for the import of goods that other countries produced more efficiently. There were therefore *net gains from trade* for all countries involved. Smith also became famous for his analysis of specialization and competitive advantage at the firm level.

Over time Smith's views were extended, for example, by David Ricardo's theory of comparative advantage. A notable shift toward looking at sources of competitive advantage and regional variations in these to explain global patterns of competitiveness came in the early 1900s. Two Swedes—Eli Heckscher (in 1919) and Bertil Ohlin (in 1933)—are responsible for developing a basic model that was further refined by the American economist Paul Samuelson. The H–O or HOS model (or theory of factor endowments) takes us beyond the simple assumptions made by Ricardo about labor productivity to look at the *relative availability* of different factors of production (primarily land, labor, and capital) and therefore their *relative price* (rent, wages, and interest) in each country. These will determine the products in which a country has a comparative advantage, and in which it will therefore tend to specialize and trade.

The HOS model maps out the initial conditions for regional specialization in capital-intensive or labor-intensive industries according to local factor advantages, but it is also a dynamic model, showing how economic conditions change as countries interact through trade. These theories underpin the Porter diamond model (see Chapter 10). They are also incorporated into the interestingly named **Flying Geese model** by Japanese academic Kaname Akamatsu.[9]

Flying Geese model
A model suggesting that Asian countries are following Japan's historical economic transition, specializing in particular industries (steel to textiles to clothing to autos to electronics) during particular growth stages. At a particular point in time we should expect to see these industries located in different Asian countries, depending on their resource endowments, labor costs, and capabilities

Flying Geese model

The Flying Geese model (Figure 20.2) suggests that Asian economies are following similar development paths, but are at different stages along this path, following the lead "goose," Japan. Over time each country, or group, will gain and then subsequently lose specific comparative advantage in a particular industry. Japan has shifted from iron and steel to textiles to clothing to autos to electronics. The four Tiger economies—Hong Kong, South Korea, Singapore, and Taiwan—followed a similar trajectory, although quicker. Other ASEAN (Association of South-East Asian Nations) members such as Indonesia, Malaysia, the Philippines, and Thailand are a little further behind, but the sequence of specialization is similar. In each country the transition is marked by a shift of

Figure 20.2 Flying Geese model: changing national-level specialization

Figure 20.3 Flying Geese model: the shifting location of industrial production

employment from one sector to another, within the broader move from agriculture to manufacturing and then to services. Overall, rising skills and improved technological capabilities, increased capital investment, and wage inflation (as predicted by the HOS model) drive, and are driven by, the change process.

If we look at a particular industry, the location of production activities and subsequent exports and trade flows change as different economies change their specialization (Figure 20.3). China now dominates as the world's biggest exporter of textiles and clothing, Korea has a thriving automobile sector, and Singapore and Taiwan have very successful electronics industries. These have grown to the point that Japan, now a net importer of televisions, is losing its lead in many product areas (Figure 20.4). The overall pattern of change is also in line with Vernon's international product life cycle theory (described in Chapter 6).[10]

Figure 20.4 Flying Geese model: the pattern of shifting comparative advantage

Figure 20.5 Accelerated structural transformation (are the geese flying faster?)

The timescale over which individual countries develop the economic conditions, resources, and capabilities to specialize in a particular industry sector appears to be shortening. Comparative advantage between nations is also therefore shifting faster than in the past (Figure 20.5). It took Toyota and Sony 30 to 35 years to evolve into leading firms in their industries, whereas Samsung (South Korea) and Acer (Taiwan) took 20 to 25 years. Firms like WIPRO, Infosys, and TCS, which are lead firms in the Indian software industry, achieved superior competitive positions (albeit in niche areas of customized software and IT services) in 15 to 20 years.

The Flying Geese model is far from perfect and has been widely criticized on a number of counts. Many studies note that the sequential transfer of industrial specialization does not follow the same pattern in each country, or that it tends to be more of a parallel process whereby emerging economies seem to develop capabilities and grow exports across several industries at the same time. The example of the Indian IT and services industry (see the **Real Case: The Indian IT, software, and services industry**) also demonstrates that leapfrogging is possible. Here an LDC has evolved competitive advantages in an advanced service sector without going through the stages depicted by the model.

For the most critical observers, the model is associated with a desire by Japan to see itself as the lead "goose" in the region from a political and perhaps military perspective (particularly given that its origins date back to the 1930s), as opposed to a useful representation of patterns of economic transformation.

There are, however, some insights we can gain into the processes affecting the changing global locations of different industries and business activities and into the changing relative competitive advantages between countries. With this in mind we need to think about the future for China—the evolving specializations of Chinese firms and the resulting competitive threats for other firms. China represents a powerful combination of cheap and well-educated labor, good infrastructure, a growing domestic market, and massive inflows of capital and technology from abroad. These are driving the rapid development of comparative and competitive advantage in a range of industries, including clothing, autos, white goods, and electronics. What we may be seeing is parallel development across these sectors, rather than sequential, stage-wise development following the lead goose (as shown in Figure 20.5). This theme is taken up in Chapter 21.

Active learning check

Review your answer to Active Learning Case question 2 and make any changes you like. Then compare your answer to the one below.

2 **How are changes in the Asian regional economy, in terms of both growing markets and growing competitors, affecting Acer and how should the firm cope?**

Among a range of threats and opportunities, China looms large in both respects. Acer has taken a step in the right direction by moving away from manufacturing, where Chinese firms have natural advantages, and into customer-oriented design, development, and services. Acer's advantages also lie in its global distribution and marketing and its brand. These are firm-specific advantages (FSAs), which Lenovo and other Chinese firms will take some time to develop. The evolving political relationship between Taiwan and mainland China or the People's Republic of China is also an important factor, influencing some of the strategic options open to firms like Acer. But other parts of Asia, including Japan, are changing and the firm could do well to develop an international strategy that focused more on the regional than the global.

Emerging economies as sources of innovation

A natural extension to the above theories on comparative and competitive advantage is to examine innovation as a relative (and sustainable) source of advantage at the national, industry, and firm level. Traditional theories about the MNE tended to view the triad as a source of innovation and non-triad regions as recipients in a simple outward diffusion model. But other studies, which go beyond the Flying Geese model, have shown how firms that develop the independent capacity to innovate, continually upgrading their FSAs and reducing their reliance on location-specific endowments (CSAs), such as cheap labor, can achieve more sustainable competitive advantages.[11]

Specific combinations of country-specific advantages (CSAs) and firm-specific advantages (FSAs) explain Japan's competitive advantage in auto exports, Taiwan's semiconductor industry, and Indian IT and software businesses, for example (see also Figure 20.6). Local conditions (the CSAs) also "breed" certain organizational forms, assets, capabilities,

Globalizing...	Assets	Capabilities	Connections	Reputation
Innovation and technology	Patents, licenses, IPR; specialized tools hardware, software, etc.	Low-end (maintenance) to high-end (blue-sky R&D) expertise	Strategic alliances; buyer and supplier links; R&D networks/ global capability inputs	Credibility, trust, track record, recognition
Marketing and brands	Own valued brands, logos, trademarks, awards, etc.	Brand management protection, development expertise	Formal co-branding; supplier or buyer, distribution, and retailing affiliations	Reputation for quality, price, innovation, etc.; market positioning, brand recognition; market presence

Figure 20.6 Firm-specific advantages (FSAs) for the new multinationals

or expertise (FSAs) that turn out to be relative strengths in other markets. Honda's original export success in the United States came from its ability to make smaller, fuel-efficient autos, which it was forced to do to succeed in the domestic Japanese market during the postwar period. Porter cites demanding customers, industry rivalry, and efficient and effective supply chains (the *keiretsu* structures described in Chapter 18) as key local drivers of the innovative capabilities of Japanese auto firms.[12] Both product and process innovation tend to be important. Continuously learning how to produce better (cheaper, more desirable) products and services in better (cheaper, more efficient, faster) ways is the key. But the dual effects of CSAs and FSAs that lead to international competitiveness can arise by chance as well as by design, and usually result from an unanticipated combination of both.

As the **Real Case: The Indian IT, software, and services industry** below and the case **International Business Strategy in Action: From Oseran to Tesco** above both show, firms in developing and emerging economies have an increasing range of opportunities to exploit local endowments and develop new competitive advantages. However, the openness of the global economy means that local players have to compete with MNEs which are also looking to exploit specific CSAs and often have equal access.

The Brazilian biofuels industry, for example, has evolved over decades because petroleum has traditionally been expensive and sugar cane cheap and available. Following the government's PróÁlcool program of incentives, the country gets more than 30 percent of its automobile fuels from sugar cane-based ethanol (mainly from bagasse which is cane waste); 85 percent of new cars in Brazil can run on biofuels. In a world where governments, consumers, and companies aim to move toward more environmentally friendly sources of energy, Brazil has emerged as a leader in agricultural processing and automotive technologies related to ethanol-based fuels. However, in contrast to India's IT sector, or China's white goods industry, the few, small-scale automotive producers in Brazil appear to have lost out to the multinationals, failing to exploit their own country's head-start in ethanol fuel technologies. GM is seizing the opportunity by establishing a number of joint ventures in Brazil to co-develop better automotive technology in this field. It is gaining a lead in duel-fuel systems and all of its cars produced in Brazil are "Flex Fuel" vehicles. Rather than being attracted by low costs, GM's choice of location for its R&D was driven by the need to access the best capabilities available globally.

International studies, including the *World Competitiveness Report*, use science and technology indicators, such as patenting output, to assess and compare the growing innovative capacity of different countries in different industries and technologies. In recent years Singapore, Taiwan, Korea, Malaysia, Chile, and the Czech Republic have all ranked well as up-and-coming innovators.[13] The development of world-class universities and other attributes of advanced national science and technology infrastructures (or "national innovation systems") has made some emerging economies attractive to R&D FDI from MNEs. China ranks third as a preferred location for foreign R&D investment, after the United States and the UK, while India, Singapore, and Brazil are all in the top 20.[14] Microsoft, Siemens, and Philips have invested heavily into the Republic of Korea, for example, because of the available range of expertise in high-technology fields. Microsoft's Mobile Innovation Lab develops wireless technologies and software for mobile devices. Siemens bought into DASAN Networks and develops communications and information systems technology for its global markets. Following acquisitions of parts of the LG Group, Philips has developed an R&D center focused on TV technology. This influx of high-technology investment further adds to the importance of emerging economies as sources, rather than passive recipients, of innovation.

MARKET ACCESS TO THE TRIAD

For non-triad firms the triad regions encompass by far the largest, wealthiest, and most sophisticated markets in the world. Access can be subject to complex arrangements with varying degrees of economic trade liberalization and protectionism that are inherent in the institutional and political structures of these regions. The triad represents both globalization and sovereignty dimensions. The EU is the most politically integrated, in terms of institutional structures, and the Japanese-based bloc is the least. NAFTA is a free trade agreement, not a common market, but NAFTA contains provisions for the accession of Latin American and Caribbean and Central American nations, and it may then evolve into stronger political linkages like the EU model.

To develop global industries, non-triad nations need both trade and investment from the triad nations and also access to the markets of at least one of the triads. This implies that the focus of business strategy for firms in a smaller, non-triad nation should be to secure inward triad investment and market access for exports to a triad bloc. This can be done by direct business contact of a double-diamond type, but it is helped and reinforced by formal linkages arranged by the governments. As demonstrated in the previous chapter, both Canada and Mexico have already gone down this route.

Korean *chaebols*
Traditionally family-dominated, diversified conglomerates. Family ownership has been reduced and many are now focused in particular business sectors, reducing their diversity. There are parallels with Japanese *sogo shosha* in terms of early government support and their relationship with dominant national banks

In general, NAFTA is the basis for a trading bloc of the Americas; the EU is the locus for eastern European and African nations; Japan is the hub for many Asian businesses. Some smaller, non-triad nations may attempt to open the doors to two triad markets. For example, both South Korea and Taiwan have equal trade and investment with the United States and Japan. Firms from these countries need two double diamonds (see **International Business Strategy in Action: Korean *chaebols***). Australia still has a large amount of trade with the UK and the EU, but its trade with Japan and other Asian nations is increasing rapidly. Indeed, the geographical basis of the triad serves to reinforce the dependence of neighboring nations on their dominant regional economic partner.

INTERNATIONAL BUSINESS STRATEGY IN ACTION

Korean *chaebols*: Hyundai and Samsung

Between 1970 and 2000, South Korea's GDP grew by 750 percent. Industrial production increased at an even higher rate and grew to account for over 95 percent of GDP by 2004. GDP per capita grew from $100 in 1963 to $10,000 in 1995 and over $25,000 in 2014. The so-called "Miracle on the Han River" has made the country the 12th largest in the world in terms of GDP, and it continues to grow faster than most advanced economies.

In South Korea's transition to industrialization, a transition that many other poor countries have tried to make with little success, *chaebols* played a major role. South Korea still maintains a healthy rate of growth, although it is not as rapid as in the boom years. Despite their central role in the transition years the influence of the *chaebols* has declined. Their opaque, interdependent structures and cross-shareholdings have been increasingly questioned by South Koreans themselves, as well as by outsiders.

There are 17 South Korean firms in the Global Fortune 500 (2015) including the five largest *chaebols*: Samsung Electronics, Hyundai Motor, SK Holdings, POSCO, and LG Electronics. Across the world, these companies have become household names, producing everything from ships to autos to electronics. During the 1960s, *chaebols* prospered under a government-fostered development plan. When Park Chung-hee became South Korea's president after a military *coup d'état*, he instituted an import-substitution strategy that favored large local producers and provided them with cheap credit, tax breaks, and other benefits. After Park Chung-hee's death, low-interest loans continued to be made available to *chaebols* because of ties with banks. Since banks could not let a borrower the size of *chaebols* ▶

fail, credit was made available regardless of profitability, depriving the non-*chaebol* business sector from much needed credit.

In the 1990s, the *chaebols* took on debt to finance large expansion projects. The Asian financial crisis in 1997–8 reduced their revenues to such an extent that these companies could no longer pay their creditors. For a long time, *chaebols* managed to conceal their troubles by providing member companies with intra-conglomerate loans. In addition, foreign and domestic investors became increasingly aware of murky financial reporting practices. By the end of the crisis, Daewoo had become bankrupt.

In 1997, the IMF was called to bail out the South Korean economy after an unprecedented drop on the Korean won created a debt crisis. As part of the bailout, South Korea was to restructure its *chaebols*. Debt-to-equity ratios had to be reduced. Financial reporting had to become transparent. Most importantly, non-core businesses were to be spun off. To oversee the transformation of the *chaebols* and, in turn, the Korean economy, the Financial Supervisory Commission (FSC) was established in 1998. Although *chaebols* have reduced their debt-to-equity ratios, unreliable financial reporting continues to occur. Most importantly, many *chaebols* continue to resist selling off their non-core businesses.

Hyundai Motor and Samsung Electronics are two of the most successful and international firms from South Korea, but they have taken different development paths to get where they are.

Chaebols had their origins in the vision of individuals. In 1946 Chung Ju-yung, who worked as a delivery boy for a rice mill in the 1930s, purchased an auto repair shop that was the early foundation of the Hyundai group. In 1947 Hyundai Engineering and Construction was established to take advantage of reconstruction contracts at the

end of World War II. By 1976, Hyundai had brought its country into the auto business with the introduction of the Pony.

Hyundai Automotive spun off from its conglomerate parent and merged with Kia to form one vehicle company, now the fifth largest in the world in terms of (8 million) unit sales. In recent years it has experienced significant increases in overseas sales, particularly in the United States and Europe. As an indication of its standing, Hyundai won top place as the most reliable car manufacturer in an influential consumer survey in the United States, joining Japanese car manufacturers in the top spots for the first time. It has also made significant inroads into the Chinese market, particularly in 2008 with its joint-venture partner Beijing Automotive. In 2014, Hyundai Motor's revenues were US$90 billion, representing an impressive growth of 1.35 times from US$67 billion in 2006. In 2014, Hyundai Automotive generated 35.2 percent of its revenue from Asia, 17.9 percent from North America, 14.1 percent from Korea, and19.6 percent from other regions. Hyundai Automotive is a home-region MNE, but within the last five years it has been focusing more on global markets.

In 1938, Lee Byung-chul founded Samsung and began exporting food to China, and not long after that he opened a light manufacturing business. The 1970s saw Samsung enter the chemical and heavy manufacturing industries. In the 1980s, the company entered the aerospace and telecommunications industry. During this decade, Samsung also became a major world supplier of semiconductors.

Samsung Electronics is one of the largest and most profitable South Korean companies, with sales of $106 billion in 2007, $134 billion in 2010, and $190 billion in 2014. Samsung Electronics generates 10 percent of its total sales from Korea, 16 percent from China, 20 percent from Asia and Africa, 33 percent from America, and 21 percent from Europe. Although it ranks with Panasonic and Hewlett-Packard among the top three global firms in electrical appliances and electronics, it is now the largest electronics firm in the world by some accounts.

The 1997 Asian crisis forced Samsung to switch its focus from cheap consumer electronics to the top end of the market. The firm sold over 100 non-core businesses and let go 30 percent of its employees, a significant step in a country with traditionally militant trade unions. The refocusing on R&D, design, and marketing has since paid off. Driven by its four design centers in London, Tokyo, San Francisco, and Seoul, Samsung won more prizes from the

Industrial Design Society of America in 2005 than any other firm. It was world number two in cell phones, and number one in DRAM memory chips, flash memory chips, hard drives, and TFT-LCDs. Key innovative products include LED-backlit LCD TVs, Galaxy S cell phones, and the Galaxy tablet which rivals the iPad.

Contrasting the route taken by Hyundai Automotive, Samsung Electronics is still part of the Samsung *chaebol*, the largest in South Korea, with businesses ranging from ship-building, engineering, and chemicals to financial services, hotels, and a theme park. The conglomerate is nearly four times larger than its nearest rivals LG and SK and accounts for about one-third of the country's stock market capitalization. The group is controlled through a complicated web of shareholdings that bind its 27 subsidiaries, although over 60 percent of Samsung Electronics shares are in the hands of foreign investors.

This opaque structure still worries minority shareholders, who have seen their returns eroded from the widespread *chaebol* practice of using profitable businesses to subsidize weaker affiliates and fund risky expansion. Samsung would arguably be in an even stronger position today had it not been called upon to bail the group out of failed investments in the past, including an attempt to break into the auto sector which lost the group credibility as well as cash.

Websites: www.daewoo.com; www.hyundai.com; www.hyundai-motor.com; www.samsung.com; www.samsungelectronics.com; www.seriworld.org

Sources: Jason Leow and Gordon Fairclough, "Hyundai freshens China effort," *Wall Street Journal*, April 8, 2008; "As good as it gets? Special report on Samsung Electronics," *The Economist*, January 15, 2005; C. Wright, "After the crisis, the fight back," *Financial Times*, March 1, 2005, p. 6; A. Ward, "Hyundai wins 'most reliable' ranking in US," *Financial Times*, September 6, 2004, p. 15; A. Fifield, "Seoul to clamp down on *chaebol*," *Financial Times*, March 1, 2005, p. 15; A. Fifield and J.-A. Song, "SK Corp steps up its cautious courtship," *Financial Times*, December 1, 2004, p. 12; Samsung, *Annual Reports*, 2007–14; Thomson Reuters, *OneSource*, 2011; "The Global Fortune 500," 2011 ranking, *Forbes*, July 25, 2011 issue; Hyundai Motor, *Annual Reports*, 2006–14; http://www.statista.com/statistics/275520/ranking-of-car-manufacturers-based-on-global-sales/

Later in this chapter we take a look at the Indian software and IT services industry. Within this industry there are small but significant examples of how success in one particular niche market can support triad access for firms in unrelated sectors. In March 2000 the UK's Tetley Tea Group was acquired by Tata Tea Limited. Coming more than 50 years after the end of 200 years of British colonial rule that had supported British-owned tea estates in India, this shift of power is an appropriate symbol for the twenty-first century. But the takeover was only made possible because of the financial success of Tata's IT division, Tata Consultancy Services (TCS). Both are part of the Tata Group, one of India's biggest publicly quoted conglomerates. Tata Tea was originally a tea estates company and is now India's second most popular tea brand, with a 21 percent share of the Indian branded teas market, 54 tea estates, and 59,000 employees. Senior management at Tata Tea said:

> We wanted to create a global brand, because the marketplace was global and in a global market-place only global brands survive, local players get marginalized. We did not want to get marginalized, so we had to either build a global brand or acquire one.

TCS is "Asia's largest global software and services company" (according to its own PR), whose revenues have doubled every two years over the past six years. TCS is the "jewel in the crown" of the Tata conglomerate, making net profits of over $489 million in the year of the Tetley acquisition. Over 90 percent of these revenues come from the firm's software exports, which are double those of its nearest domestic rival. TCS has 11,000 professionals in 50 countries and sells customized software systems, consultancy services, and, increasingly, e-business products and services to a wide range of businesses partly through alliances with Western giants like Microsoft, IBM, and Netscape. The revenues and enhanced market capitalization gained from the software side provided the financial leverage to move up the value chain in the tea industry, taking over a major Western brand to enter into the UK market. This could be described as a case of "reverse colonization" and there are many more like it to come.[15]

✔ Active learning check

Review your answer to Active Learning Case question 3 and make any changes you like. Then compare your answer to the one below.

 Why did Acer form strategic alliances with IBM and Texas Instruments?

Acer was not familiar with the North American market and was a new kid on the computer block. So it formed strategic alliances, whenever possible, with the dominant US MNEs. In doing so, Acer learned about the US triad market and how to distribute its products there. It also gained new technological capabilities for both process (manufacturing) innovation and product design and development. Acer was then able to move ahead of these once-dominant US firms once it combined its efficiency in production with its new market knowledge of the rich North American customers.

KEY POINTS

1 Emerging economies are increasingly important for MNEs: as growing markets; as sources of cheaper or better production inputs; and as a source of competitors in the shape of new MNEs as non-triad firms internationalize.

2 Emerging economies tend to be controlled more strongly by their governments and are less predictable and riskier than triad markets.

3 Emerging market countries need investment from, and access to, a triad bloc in order to develop global industries. Inflows and outflows of global FDI show that there is growing integration between countries inside and outside the triad.

4 Current trends such as privatization, liberalization, and legislative changes that are designed to encourage foreign direct investment (FDI) are helping emerging economies to tap their economic potential. Intra- and inter-regional trade agreements can also be helpful in both creating mini common markets and smoothing international trade.

5 FDI into Asia is concentrated in the ten fast-growing economies. There is strong intra-regional trade and FDI growth and a marked increase in the importance of service industries; 36 out of the 50 largest non-financial TNCs from developing countries are from the Asia–Pacific region.

6 Despite years of liberalization, the central and eastern European region attracts relatively small amounts of FDI. Better prospects appear to be ahead for countries that have joined the EU.

7 Latin America and the Caribbean region receive a small percentage of global FDI (less than China). Intra-regional competition is strong but manufacturing exporters are losing out to China.

8 Africa receives less than 4 percent of global FDI and remains relatively unattractive and risky for most investors. South African MNEs are expanding across the region in particular industry sectors.

9 The newly industrialized countries (NICs), a subgroup of non-triad economies, have experienced rapid economic growth and increased trade and FDI, partly by specializing in particular industries and developing comparative and competitive advantages.

10 NICs and other emerging markets in Asia are seen by some to be following the Flying Geese model of economic development. The Indian software industry appears to counter this pattern of sequential industry specialization as well as contradicting the main tenets of Porter's diamond of competitive advantage.

11 Emerging economies are growing in importance as sources of innovation and as locations for R&D investment by MNEs.

Key terms

- resource-seeking FDI
- market-seeking FDI
- liberalization policies
- intra-regional investments
- newly industrialized countries (NICs)
- Flying Geese model
- Korean *chaebols*

REVIEW AND DISCUSSION QUESTIONS

1 Why do MNE managers need to develop an understanding of changing economic conditions in non-triad regions?

2 What characteristics do we tend to associate with emerging economies that are important considerations for foreign investors?

3 How have emerging economies liberalized to encourage FDI?

4 How does inward FDI help emerging economies and their domestic industries?

5 Which non-triad regions and countries have achieved the most rapid economic growth in the last 10 to 20 years and what factors have helped their development?

6 Why does Africa receive relatively little inward FDI?

7 What insights does the Flying Geese model of economic development provide for understanding current and future trade and investment flows? What are its weaknesses as a model?

8 How did Indian IT, software, and services firms evolve beyond their reliance on cheap labor to develop firm-specific advantages and internationalize?

REAL CASE

The Indian IT, software, and services industry

With an average per capita GDP of around $5,700 (2015) in PPP terms, India is a less developed country (LDC). It has low literacy rates and high infant mortality rates. There are just 18 internet users for every 100 people. Yet it also boasts one of the fastest-growing knowledge-based industries in the world.

The Indian IT software and services industry has outstripped all other industries, becoming the largest industry in India in terms of market capitalization. During the late 1990s it grew by an average of 50 percent year on year. It is increasingly important to overall GDP and, more significantly, as a contributor to India's exports. Almost 3 million ▶

software professionals and a further 6 million people directly and indirectly are employed by the Indian software industry. India controls over 20 percent of the global customized software market, specializing in high-quality solutions and IT services for corporate customers in the banking, finance, and insurance sectors. It is not currently a player in the market for off-the-shelf, packaged software, which is dominated by US firms.

As we know, exports provide a clear indicator of global competitive advantage. Indian software industry exports have grown from under $5 million in 1980 to $700 million in 1996, $6 billion in 2000, $12 billion in 2004, over $30 billion in 2007 and over $80 billion in 2014 (see Figures 20.7 and 20.8). The top firm, Tata Consultancy Services (TCS), a division of the Tata conglomerate, has 335,620 employees and a revenue of $15.5 billion for the year ended March 31, 2014. As of 2014, the organization has grown to become the tenth largest IT service provider in the world. The number two firm, Infosys Technologies, managed 187,976 employees and revenue of US$9 billion for the year ended March 31, 2014.

However, the sources of advantage underpinning the growth rate and success of the Indian IT industry are not explained by many of the standard international business frameworks, such as the Porter diamond model. Few, if any, of the factors that led to the genesis of the industry were initially present in India. There was no local demand; related and supporting industries, such as telecoms and computing, were highly underdeveloped; the national communications infrastructure was among the worst in the world; and the main factor of production, the skills and knowledge of software programmers and IT business

managers (an acquired factor endowment), was initially not home-grown.

The industry began with Indians returning from higher education, IT training, and often work experience in the United States and Europe. Many of the industry founders, such as Wipro Chairman Azim Premji, Ramalinga Raju of Satyam, and S. Ramadorai of TCS, were educated at US universities (although others, such as F. C. Kohli of TCS and Infosys Chairman Narayana Murthy, were not). They noticed the rising demand for customized software programmers and IT expertise in the banking, insurance, financial services, and other industries in the West, and saw India as a potential low-cost provider of this expertise. They returned to India and built firms to meet the software needs of the triad, primarily the United States.

Factors that were on their side were the English language skills of the Indians, as this is the main software programming language; the time difference that allowed a 24-hour software development project cycle; new global information and communications network infrastructures; fears over the Y2K or year 2000 problem; and the low cost of labor. "Body shopping," the contracting of Indian programmers and their physical relocation to work with clients abroad, accounted for 90 percent of industry revenues in 1989. The average cost of a software programmer in India in the late 1990s was still about one-twelfth the cost of a US or European programmer. But wage rates were relatively much lower in the early stages of the industry's growth cycle and increased at around 25 percent per year from the mid-1990s. The cost of a programmer in China or Russia is now around 20 percent lower than in India, and the same lack of barriers to entry will help firms based in these countries to mount a new competitive threat.

Figure 20.7 India's IT Industry: rapid growth in the early years

Source: NASSCOM Report, http://www.nasscom.in

Figure 20.8 The growth of the Indian IT market: local and global

Note: E = estimates.
Source: NASSCOM, TechSci Research.

As the industry evolved, government support, particularly the development of software technology parks (the STPI network), the promotion of technical training, and subsidies to ICT infrastructure, became important. Also significant were the activities of US and European multinationals. Initially Western firms subcontracted programming and other tasks to Indian firms to exploit the cheap labor advantage. Many, like Texas Instruments, Microsoft, and Computer Associates, made substantial investments to build local operations to work within the emerging industry clusters in Bangalore and Madras. These global firms promoted innovation both as customers and as suppliers to local firms. They transferred hardware and software technology and assisted in the development of local technological capabilities through technical and management training, investment in R&D, new product and services development, and joint ventures. They also prompted and sometimes assisted in the development of local ICT infrastructure.

Perhaps the most important factor underlying the continued success of the industry is its evolution from an industry based on cheap labor and low costs to one based on value-added expertise, including specialist software and IT systems design and development capabilities. Indian software firms have moved up the value chain, shifting the basis of their competitive advantage from just cost to a combination of cost, quality, and high-end R&D expertise. There have been a range of positive effects on the local economy, not least the growth of direct and indirect employment in the sector, as shown in Figure 20.9.

Indian firms are also now themselves actively subcontracting to lower-cost providers in China and elsewhere as they move away from contract programming as a major source of their revenues and into e-commerce and web-related products and services. They are leveraging their advantages in cost and skills through joint ventures with big, established players in the computing, telecom, and consumer electronics industries. The Infosys–Microsoft joint venture, focusing on MS .NET products, is an example of this, as is the Mahindra–British Telecom venture. An estimated 300 multinational companies have been engaged in R&D rather than contracting work in India. Intel, Microsoft, Cisco Systems, Samsung Electronics, Oracle, SSA Global, and others have set up R&D activities in Hyderabad, Mumbai, and Bangalore.

As a result of these developments, the industry has divided into a variety of subsectors. The IT software and services sector is still the largest and the key export

IT-BPM: Highest impact sector for India

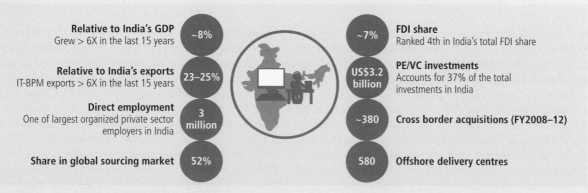

Figure 20.9 How the IT sector impacts India

Note: BPM: business process management; ISP: internet service provider; MNC: multinational company; GIC: global in-house center
Source: NASSCOM.

revenue earner, but growth has slowed. A domestic software and telecom industry, with a thriving venture capital industry, has also emerged in India. This is evidence of a strong and growing industry cluster that has evolved, unusually, *after* the export success of key firms in the industry. IT-enabled services (ITES) and business process outsourcing (BPO) services, including call centers, transcriptions services, and back-office processing such as billing, taxation, and accounting, have been growing rapidly. Hubs of these services are Mumbai, Bangalore, Chennai, Kolkata, Hyderabad, Kochi, Ahmedabad, and Pune. Some of the key players in this market are AMX, Convergys India Services, GE Capital, Standard Chartered, Dell, Healthscribe India, EXL Service, Daksh eServices, Wipro Spectramind, and 24/7 Customer.

The development of the ITES/BPO subsector has brought home some of the threats as well as opportunities of living in a globally connected world for people in Europe and the United States. According to the UK's Communication Workers Union, for example, 33 firms including Barclays, British Airways, Lloyds TSB, Prudential, and Reuters have collectively outsourced 52,000 jobs serving UK customers to India. Norwich Union, the UK's largest insurer, has built up a workforce of 3,700 people in India and plans to double this in the near future. This is a sign of the times, and as global firms discover new ways of accessing cheaper and/or better expertise in other parts of the world, some groups of people will experience new opportunities to join and benefit from the global economy while others will feel increasingly vulnerable to the threat of new competition.

Sources: NASSCOM, *The IT-BPO Sector in India: Strategic Review for 2011*, Executive Summary. NASSCOM, http://www.nasscom.in/upload/Publications/Research/140211/Executive_Summary.pdf; NASSCOM, "Indian IT/ITES industry: impacting economy and society 2007–08," NASSCOM Foundation Report, 2008; "Soaring salaries hit India IT group margins," *Financial Times*, September 12, 2007; "Offshoring pays off for UK companies," *Telegraph*, January 25, 2005; "India makes it to the global R&D map," *Financial Express*, December 6, 2004; D. Gardner, "Bangalore-based software company to use US web platform for e-commerce solutions," *Financial Times*, September 15, 2000; K. Merchant, "Hidden gem seeks share of limelight: information technology," *Financial Times*, August 9, 2000; K. Merchant and D. Gardener, "New Delhi woos Silicon Valley Indians: IT successes encouraged to invest," *Financial Times*, September 15, 2000; http://indiainfoline.com; http://www.nasscom.in/; http://www.indiainvest.com; https://ict4dblog.wordpress.com/2015/04/28/indian-itsoftware-sector-statistics-1980–2015-time-series-data/.

1 How well does the Porter diamond framework explain the beginnings of the Indian IT and software services industry?

2 Why has this kind of industry not developed in other parts of the world, where triad companies also outsource IT activities (such as Barbados)?

3 What are the threats and opportunities for Western software firms arising from this shift in the competitive landscape, and how are they strategically responding to these?

REAL CASE

Bumrungrad International in Thailand

Medical tourism (medical travel, health tourism, or global healthcare) is not as new as we might think. Spa towns and sanatoriums promoted international travel for health reasons across Europe and beyond, from the eighteenth century onwards. But the industry has entered a new phase as a globally competitive business worth an estimated US$35 billion. Levels of quality, safety, and reliability in locations beyond the triad are now good enough to create choice for patient–customers and for price to become a key factor. As Table 20.4 shows, there is a clear economic incentive for private and public healthcare clients to "shop around."

The growing costs of employer healthcare schemes in the United States are one reason for the growing popularity of medical tourism. Canada and Mexico have developed thriving businesses based on their proximity to the US market. A few US employers have also begun to build incentives into their benefit packages to encourage employees to travel abroad for healthcare. This includes paying for travel and subsistence for time away from work in return for cheaper medical bills. The Maine-based retailer Hannaford Brothers, for example, will cover the total costs for employees to travel to Singapore for knee and hip replacements, including travel for a companion accompanying the patient. Cuba attracts 20,000 medical tourists per year, but for obvious reasons these have come from Latin America and Europe rather than the United States.

There are, of course, added risks for many people in venturing beyond their borders in search of low-cost

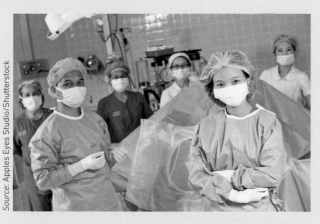

Source: Apples Eyes Studio/Shutterstock

Bumrungrad International

David Boucher, a 49-year-old American, chose to have a colonoscopy at Bumrungrad International Hospital in Bangkok. His company gladly paid the $640 bill, saving over $250 on the costs of the same procedure in the United States. What is significant is that David Boucher was an assistant vice president of healthcare services at Blue Cross & Blue Shield of South Carolina. His firm is part of the largest group provider of healthcare insurance services in the United States, providing coverage for more than 100 million people. His main reason for undergoing the procedure in Thailand was to advertise the increasingly international options open to his firm's 1.5 million customers. He has been involved in signing a range of alliances with overseas hospitals and in discussions with local corporations and employee groups about this strategic response to the growing costs of healthcare in the United States. In 2008 Blue Cross took the initiative in medical "offshoring" by creating a partnership with Bumrungrad Hospital through its Companion Global Healthcare subsidiary.

Bumrungrad ("care for the people") International was founded in 1980 and advertises itself as the largest private hospital in Southeast Asia. In 2010 it had 34 outpatient clinics, which included 250 examination rooms with the capacity to service of over 4,000 patients per day. By 2014 it had grown to have a workforce of over 3,000 employees, achieving a turnover of about $400 million. It had 580 beds and over 30 specialized treatment centers, serving over 1 million patients each year. Over half of its patients are international and come from over 200 different countries. Bumrungrad is a publicly traded company listed on the Thai Stock Exchange. The majority shareholders are Bangkok Bank PCL and the Sophonpanich family.

Several key factors explain Bumrungrad's success. The country has a history of prioritizing healthcare perhaps dating

medical procedures. These can be exacerbated by the legal complexities of extending insurance cover across borders. In an attempt to alleviate some of the risk and uncertainty, international healthcare accreditation, offered by organizations like the US-based Joint Commission International (JCI) and the associated Society for International Healthcare Accreditation (SOFIHA), is increasingly important.

There are also ethical issues beyond the economics of supply and demand, not least the problem that wealthy medical tourists divert scarce medical resources and expertise away from the poorest and neediest in developing countries. Massive investments in initiatives like the "Medicity" project in the Gurgaon region near New Delhi focus on providing top-class healthcare for the rich, in the world's poorest areas. Supporters cite the multiplier effect of medical clusters, which include employment and subsequent investment in local people and infrastructure. Critics simply see a further widening of global income and welfare disparities.

Table 20.4 Comparing the international costs of medical procedures

Medical procedure	Cost in the US* ($)	Cost in alternative locations ($)
Heart-valve replacement	200,000	10,000 (India) including airfare and vacation
Coronary artery bypass surgery	100,000	12,000 (Bumrungrad Hospital, Thailand)
Full facelift	20,000	1,250 (South Africa); can be part of a "medical safari"
Knee replacement	15,000	5,000 (Colombia); including costs of hospital stay
In vitro fertilization	12,000	5,000 (Panama)
Dental bridge	5,500	500 (India)
Lasik eye surgery	3,700	730 (India and elsewhere)
Colonoscopy	900	640 (Bumrungrad Hospital, Thailand)
Root canal	800	300 (Panama)

* For most examples these are listed as the minimum cost in US hospitals.

Sources: Various.

▶

back to Prince Mahidol of Songkla, who gained an MD degree from Harvard Medical School in the early twentieth century. Ongoing support from the Thai government and members of the country's ruling elite has made medicine and healthcare a national priority. The founders of Bumrungrad Hospital have focused on service quality and international credibility partly through their recruitment and incentives practices and by aiming for recognized accreditation. The hospital has more than 200 surgeons who are board-certified in the United States and it was the first hospital in Asia to be accredited by the US-based Joint Commission International (JCI).

To counter any potential criticism over the ethics of diverting medical resources to a top-class, but relatively expensive (for locals) hospital, the Bumrungrad Hospital Foundation was established in 1990. It helps the less privileged in Thailand gain access to free medical treatment and healthcare services. The Foundation has provided free medical help to over 100,000 Thais, including 122 pediatric heart operations.

Sources: Laurie McGinley, "Health matters: the next wave of medical tourists might include you," *Wall Street Journal*, February 16, 2008; Bruce Einhorn, "Outsourcing the patients," *Business Week*, March 13, 2008; Rory Carroll, "First World results on a Third World budget," *Guardian*, September 12, 2007; http://www.bumrungrad.com (accessed 2016); http://www.patientsbeyondborders.com/hospital/bumrungrad-international-hospital (2016); Thomson Reuters, *OneSource*, 2011.

1 How is the growing provision of alternative sources of health services around the world likely to affect the triad-based providers, public and private?

2 Explain the rise of Bumrungrad International and the Thai medical tourism industry in terms of country-specific advantages (CSAs) and firm-specific advantages (FSAs).

3 Should healthcare "offshoring" be viewed or treated any differently from any other globalizing industry, such as software or BPO services?

NOTES

1 D. W. Conklin, "Analyzing and managing country risks," *Ivey Business Journal*, vol. 66, no. 3 (2002), pp. 360–2; S. E. Feinberg and A. K. Gupta, "MNC subsidiaries and country risk: internalization as a safeguard against weak external institutions," *Academy of Management Journal*, vol. 51 (2008).

2 Emerging market and developing country economies overall have grown by an average of over 6.5 percent in recent years, which is much faster than historical trends and much faster than developed economies; "Coming into flower," *The Economist*, October 16, 2004; For the most recent data see: www.unctad.org and http://www.vcc.columbia.edu/content/emerging-market-global-players

3 See http://www.slovakembassy-cd-london.co.uk/gfx/documents/Automotive.pdf (2007); Robert Anderson, "Autos: success from nowhere at all," *Financial Times*, Special Report Slovakia, May 26, 2004, p. 3; Mark Landler, "Slovakia vies to create 'Detroit' of Europe," *International Herald Tribune*, April 14, 2004, p. 11; Chris Wright, "Automakers jump into fast lane of expansion," *Automotive News* (Detroit), May 3, 2004, p. 26 P.

4 See http://www.endesa.com

5 See http://www.telefonica.es/accionistaseinversores/

6 UNCTAD's 2007 *World Investment Report* focuses on multinational firms, extractive industries, and development, and provides an excellent overview of the extent and impacts of FDI in these sectors worldwide (www.unctad.org).

7 For further discussion see S. C. Collinson, "M&A as imperialism?," in D. Angwin (ed.), *Images of M&A* (Oxford: Blackwell, 2006).

8 Adam Smith, *The Wealth of Nations*, Book IV: 2, Modern Library edition, 1776.

9 K. Akamatsu, "Historical patterns of economic growth in developing countries," *The Developing Economies*, vol. 1 (1962), pp. 3–25; Kálmán Kalotay, "The European flying geese: new FDI patterns for the old continent?" *Research in International Business and Finance*, vol. 18, no. 1 (2004), pp. 27–49. For other analyses, at the industry and firm levels, see L. Kim, "Crisis construction and organizational learning: capability building in catching-up at Hyundai Motor," *Organization Science*, vol. 9 (1998), pp. 506–21; F. J. Contractor (ed.), *Economic Transformation in Emerging Countries: The Role of Investment, Trade and Finance* (Oxford: Elsevier, 1998); Michael Hobday, *Innovation in East Asia: The Challenge to Japan* (Aldershot: Edward Elgar, 1995); Sanjaya Lall, *Learning from the Asian Tigers: Studies in Technology and Industrial Policy* (Basingstoke: Macmillan, 1996); Dosi Giovanni et al., *The Economics of Technical Change and International Trade* (Hemel Hempstead: Harvester Wheatsheaf, 1990); Kim Linsu, *Imitation to Innovation: The Dynamics of Korea's Technological Learning* (Boston, MA: Harvard Business School Press, 1997).

10 Raymond Vernon, "International investment and international trade in the product cycle," *Quarterly Journal of Economics* (May 1996), pp. 190–207.

11 See the references in note 9 above, and Linsu Kim and Richard R. Nelson, *Technology, Learning and Innovation: Experiences of Newly Industrialising Economies* (Cambridge: Cambridge University Press, 2000).

12 This was one of Porter's original examples from the study of factors underlying export success in particular industries in particular economies which are summarized in the "diamond of advantage." Michael E. Porter, *The Competitive Advantage*

of Nations (New York: Free Press, 1998). More recent research shows how the overdependence on CSAs by some Japanese firms has led to an inability to adapt and internationalize in response to changing domestic economic conditions; S. Collinson and A. M. Rugman, "The regional nature of Japanese multinational business," *Journal of International Business Studies*, vol. 39, no. 2 (2008), pp. 215–30.

13 See the *World Competitiveness Report* and discussions about the Innovation Capacity indicators at www.weforum.org

14 UNCTAD, *World Investment Report 2005: Transnational Corporations and the Internationalization of R&D* (Geneva: UNCTAD), www.unctad.org

15 See Collinson, "M&A as imperialism?"; K. Merchant, "Hidden gem seeks share of limelight: information technology," *Financial Times*, August 9, 2000; http://www.indiainfoline.com/sect/itso/ch20.html; http://www.tata.com/0_people/interviews/20001227_krishna_kumar1; http://www.tata.com/tcs/index.htm

BIBLIOGRAPHY

Aybar, Bülent, and Ficici, Aysun. "Cross-border acquisitions and firm value: an analysis of emerging-market multinationals," *Journal of International Business Studies*, vol. 40 (October/November 2009).

Backman, Michael, and Butler, Charlotte. *Big in Asia: 25 Strategies for Business Success* (New York: Palgrave Macmillan, 2004).

Bound, Kirsten, Leadbeater, Charles, O'Connor, Simon, Webb, Molly, and Wilsdon, James. *The Atlas of Ideas: Europe and Asia in the New Geography of Science* (London: DEMOS, 2007), http://www.demos.co.uk

Bresnahan, Timothy, and Gambardella, Alfonso (eds.). *Building High-Tech Clusters: Silicon Valley and Beyond* (Cambridge: Cambridge University Press, 2004).

Buck, Trevor. "Modern Russian corporate governance: convergent forces or product of Russia's history?" *Journal of World Business*, vol. 38, no. 4 (November 2003).

Casanova, Lourdes. *Global Latinas: Latin America's Emerging Multinationals* (New York: Palgrave Macmillan, 2009).

Chang, Eunmi. "Individual pay for performance and commitment HR practices in South Korea," *Journal of World Business*, vol. 41, no. 4 (December 2007).

Chang, Sea-Jin. *Financial Crisis and Transformation of Korean Business Groups: The Rise and Fall of Chaebols* (Cambridge: Cambridge University Press, 2003).

Christensen, Clayton M., Hang, Chang-Chieh, Chai, Kah-Hin, and Subramanian, Annapoornima M. "Editorial: managing innovation in emerging economies: an introduction to the special issue," *IEEE Transactions on Engineering Management*, vol. 57, no.1 (February 2010).

Corredoira, Rafael A., and McDermott, Gerald A. "Adaptation, bridging and firm upgrading: how non-market institutions and MNCs facilitate knowledge recombination in emerging markets," *Journal of International Business Studies*, vol. 45, no. 6 (2014).

De Meyer, Arnoud. *Global Future: The Next Challenge for Asian Business* (Singapore: Wiley, 2005).

Doh, Jonathan P., Rodriguez, Peter, Uhlenbruck, Klaus, Collins, Jamie, and Eden, Lorraine. "Coping with corruption in foreign markets," *Academy of Management Executive*, vol. 17, no. 3 (2003).

Doh, Jonathan P., Teegen, Hildy, and Mudambi, Ram. "Balancing private and state ownership in emerging markets' telecommunications infrastructure: country, industry, and firm influences," *Journal of International Business Studies*, vol. 35, no. 3 (May 2004).

Engardio, Peter. *Chindia: How China and India Are Revolutionizing Global Business* (New York: McGraw-Hill, 2006).

Farrell, Diana, Remes, Jaana K., and Schulz, Heiner. "The truth about foreign direct investment in emerging markets," *McKinsey Quarterly*, no. 1 (2004).

Fiegenbaum, Avi, Bavie, Dovev, and Shoham, Aviv. "Competitive positioning of foreign MNEs in domestic markets: theoretical extensions and evidence from the Israeli market," *Management International Review*, vol. 44, no. 3 (2004).

Filatotchev, Igor, Strange, Roger, Piessc, Jenifer, and Lien, Yung-Chih. "FDI by firms from newly industrialised economies in emerging markets: corporate governance, entry mode, and location," *Journal of International Business Studies*, vol. 38, no. 4 (July 2007).

Filatotchev, Igor, Wright, Mike, Uhlenbruck, Klaus, Tihanyi, Laszlo, and Hoskissen, Robert E. "Governance, organizational capabilities, and restructuring in transition economies," *Journal of World Business*, vol. 38, no. 4 (November 2003).

Friedman, Thomas L. *The World Is Flat: A Brief History of the Twenty-first Century* (New York: Farrar, Straus, & Giroux, 2005).

Gaffney, Nolan, Karst, Rusty, and Clampit, Jack. "Emerging market MNE cross-border acquisition equity participation: the role of economic and knowledge distance," *International Business Review*, vol. 25, no. 1 (2016).

Gill, Indermit Singh, and Kharas, Homi J. *An East Asian Renaissance: Ideas for Economic Growth* (Washington, DC: World Bank, 2007).

Giuliani, Elisa, et al. "Emerging versus advanced country MNEs investing in Europe: a typology of subsidiary global–local connections," *International Business Review*, vol. 23, no. 4 (2014).

Goedhart, Marc H., and Haden, Peter. "Emerging markets aren't as risky as you think," *McKinsey Quarterly*, special edition issue 4 (2003).

Goldstein, Andrea. *Multinational Companies from Emerging Economies: Composition, Conceptualization and Direction in the Global Economy* (New York: Palgrave Macmillan, 2nd ed., 2009).

Gray, Kenneth R. "The ins and outs of doing business in Europe: Germany, France, Russia, and the emerging markets of eastern Europe," *Thunderbird International Business Review*, vol. 47, no. 1 (January/February 2005).

Grosse, Robert, and Trevino, Len J. "New institutional economics and FDI location in central and eastern Europe," *Management International Review*, vol. 45, no. 2 (2005).

Hafsi, Taieb, and Farashahi, Mehdi. "Applicability of management theories to developing countries: a synthesis," *Management International Review*, vol. 45, no. 4 (2005).

Hamm, Steve, *Bangalore Tiger* (New York: McGraw-Hill, 2006).

Judge, William Q., Naoumova, Irina, and Koutzevol, Nadejda. "Corporate governance and firm performance in Russia: an empirical study," *Journal of World Business*, vol. 38, no. 4 (November 2003).

Jwa, Sung-Hee, and Lee, Kwon (eds.). *Competition and Corporate Governance in Korea: Reforming and Restructuring the Chaebol* (Cheltenham: Edward Elgar, 2004).

Krivogorsky, Victoria, and Eichenseher, John W. "Effects of top management replacement on firms' behavior: empirical analysis of Russian companies," *Management International Review*, vol. 45, no. 4 (2005).

Kumar, Sameer, Jamieson, Jacky, and Sweetman, Mathew. "Software industry in the fastest emerging market: challenges and opportunities," *International Journal of Technology Management*, vol. 29, no. 3/4 (2005).

Li, Ming Hua, Lin Cui, and Jiangyong Lu. "Varieties in state capitalism: outward FDI strategies of central and local state-owned enterprises from emerging economy countries," *Journal of International Business Studies*, vol. 45, no. 8 (2014).

Li, Peter Ping, "Toward a learning-based view of internationalization: the accelerated trajectories of cross-border learning for latecomers," *Journal of International Management*, vol. 16, no. 1 (March 2010).

Lieberthal, K., and Lieberthal, G. "The great transition," *Harvard Business Review*, vol. 81, no. 10 (October 2003).

London, Ted, and Hart, Stuart L. "Reinventing strategies for emerging markets: beyond the transnational model," *Journal of International Business Studies*, vol. 35, no. 5 (September 2004).

Luo, Yadong. "Market-seeking MNEs in an emerging market: how parent–subsidiary links shape overseas success," *Journal of International Business Studies*, vol. 34, no. 3 (May 2003).

Luo, Yadong. "Building a strong foothold in an emerging market: a link between resource commitment and environment conditions," *Journal of Management Studies*, vol. 41, no. 5 (July 2004).

Luo, Yadong. "Autonomy of foreign R&D units in an emerging market: an information processing perspective," *Management International Review*, vol. 46, no. 3 (2006).

Manea, Julia, and Pearce, Robert. "MNEs' strategies in central and eastern Europe: key elements of subsidiary behaviour," *Management International Review*, vol. 46, no. 2 (2006).

McCarthy, Daniel J., and Puffer, Sheila M. "Corporate governance in Russia: a framework for analysis," *Journal of World Business*, vol. 38, no. 4 (November 2003).

McManus, John, Li, Mingzhi, and Moitra, Deependra. *China and India: Opportunities and Threats for the Global Software Industry* (Oxford: Chandos, 2007).

Meyer, Klaus E. "Perspectives on multinational enterprises in emerging economies," *Journal of International Business Studies*, vol. 35, no. 4 (2004).

Meyer, Klaus E., and Peng, Mike. "Probing theoretically into central and eastern Europe: transactions, resources, and institutions," *Journal of International Business Studies*, vol. 36, no. 6 (November 2005).

Meyer, Klaus E., and Peng, Mike W. "Theoretical foundations of emerging economy business research," *Journal of International Business Studies*, vol. 47 (2015).

Nguyen, Quyen T. K., and Rugman, Alan M. "Internal equity financing and the performance of multinational subsidiaries in emerging economies," *Journal of International Business Studies*, vol.46 (2014).

Oh, Chang Hoon, and Rugman, Alan M. "Regional multinationals and the Korean cosmetics industry," *Asia Pacific Journal of Management*, vol. 24, no. 1 (2007).

Pak, Yong Suhk, and Park, Young-Ryeol. "A framework of knowledge transfer in cross-border joint ventures: an empirical test of the Korean context," *Management International Review*, vol. 44, no. 4 (2004).

Pangarkar, Nitin, and Lim, Hendry. "Performance of foreign direct investment from Singapore," *International Business Review*, vol. 12, no. 5 (October 2003).

Park, Young-Ryeol, and Pak, Yong Suhk. "What they learned from the crash: a comparison of Korean firms, FDI before and after the 1997 financial crisis," *Management International Review*, vol. 46, no. 1 (2006).

Prahalad, C. K. *The Fortune at the Bottom of the Pyramid* (Upper Saddle River, NJ: Wharton School/Pearson, 2005).

Prestowitz, Clyde. *Three Billion New Capitalists: The Great Shift of Wealth and Power to the East* (London: Basic Books, 2006).

Puffer, Sheila M., and McCarthy, Daniel J. "The emergence of corporate governance in Russia," *Journal of World Business*, vol. 38, no. 4 (November 2003).

Puffer, Sheila M., and McCarthy, Daniel J. "Can Russia's state managed, network capitalism be competitive? Institutional pull versus institutional push," *Journal of World Business*, vol. 42, no. 1 (March 2007).

Ramamurti, Ravi. "Developing countries and MNEs: extending and enriching the research agenda," *Journal of International Business Studies*, vol. 35, no. 4 (July 2004).

Ramamurti, Ravi, and Doh, Jonathan P. "Rethinking foreign infrastructure investment in developing countries," *Journal of World Business*, vol. 39, no. 2 (May 2004).

Ramamurti, Ravi, and Singh, Jitendra V. (eds.) *Emerging Multinationals in Emerging Markets* (Cambridge: Cambridge University Press, 2010).

Redding, Gordon. "The thick description and comparison of societal systems of capitalism," *Journal of International Business Studies*, vol. 36, no. 2 (March 2005).

Roth, Kendall, and Kostova, Tatiana. "Organizational coping with institutional upheaval in transition economies," *Journal of World Business*, vol. 38, no. 4 (November 2003).

Rugman, Alan M. "How global are TNCs from emerging markets?" in Karl Sauvant (ed.), *The Rise of Transnational Corporations from Emerging Markets: Threat or Opportunity* (Cheltenham: Edward Elgar, 2008).

Rugman, Alan M. "Globalization, regional multinationals and Asian economic development," *Asian Business and Management*, vol. 9, no. 3 (September 2010).

Rugman, Alan M., and Collinson, Simon. "The regional character of Asian multinational enterprises," *Asia Pacific Journal of Management*, vol. 24, no. 4 (2007).

Rugman, Alan M., and Doh, Jonathan P. *Multinationals and Development* (New Haven, CT: Yale University Press, 2008).

Rugman, Alan M., and Lee, In Hyeock (Ian). "Multinationals and public policy in Korea," *Asian Business and Management*, vol. 8, no. 1 (March 2009).

Rugman, Alan M., and Oh, Chang Hoon. "Regional multinationals and the Korean cosmetics industry," *Asia Pacific Journal of Management*, vol. 24, no. 1 (March 2007).

Rugman, Alan M., and Oh, Chang Hoon. "Korea's multinationals in a regional world," *Journal of World Business*, vol. 43, no. 1 (January 2008).

Rugman, Alan M., and Oh, Chang Hoon. "The international competitiveness of Asian Firms," *Journal of Strategy and Management*, vol. 1, no. 1 (2008).

Sanfilippo, Marco. "FDI from emerging markets and the productivity gap: an analysis on affiliates of BRICS EMNEs in Europe," *International Business Review*, vol. 24, no. 4 (2015).

Sartor, Michael A., and Beamish, Paul W. "Offshoring innovation to emerging markets: organizational control and informal institutional distance," *Journal of International Business Studies*, vol. 45 (2014).

Sauvant, Karl P. *The Rise of Transnational Corporations from Emerging Markets: Threat or Opportunity?* (Cheltenham: Edward Elgar, 2009).

Sukpanich, Nessara, and Rugman, Alan M. "Multinationals and the international competitiveness of ASEAN firms." In Philippe Gugler Julien Chaisse (eds.), *Competitiveness of the ASEAN Countries, Corporate and Regulatory Drivers* (Cheltenham: Edward Elgar, 2010).

Treviño, Len J., and Mixon, Franklin G. "Strategic factors affecting foreign direct investment decisions by multinational enterprises in Latin America," *Journal of World Business*, vol. 39, no. 3 (August 2004).

Tsai, Terence, and Cheng, Bor-Shiuan. *The Silicon Dragon: High-Tech Industry in Taiwan* (London: Edward Elgar, 2006).

Tsang, Eric W. K. "Influences on foreign ownership level and entry mode choice in Vietnam," *International Business Review*, vol. 14, no. 4 (August 2005).

Wyk, Jay Van. "Doing business in South Africa," *Thunderbird International Business Review*, vol. 46, no. 4 (July/August 2004).

Zhao, Meng, Park, Seung Ho, and Zhou, Nan. "MNC strategy and social adaptation in emerging markets," *Journal of International Business Studies*, vol. 45 (2014).

WWW RESOURCES

http://globaledge.msu.edu/ibrd/marketpot.asp
http://www.tdctrade.com
http://asnic.utexas.edu
http://www.lanic.utexas.edu
http://reenic.utexas.edu

http://www.africaguide.com
http://www.africaonline.com
http://www.vcc.columbia.edu/content/emerging-market-global-players

Chapter 21

CHINA

Contents

Objectives of the chapter

In the 1950s China's economy was the size of Sudan's. Now, following 40 years of liberalization, it is the second largest economy in the world. Political change has led to economic and social change, which in turn is driving further political change and increasingly turbulent interdependencies with other parts of the globe. Rapid economic growth has led to an expanding domestic consumer market alongside continued poverty and growing disparities in wealth and income across the population of over 1.4 billion people.

The scale, scope, and speed of these changes are unprecedented and the resulting range of commercial and competitive opportunities and threats should be of interest to every manager and every firm worldwide. In this sense China's rise represents a major test of adaptability for firms looking to break into its growing domestic market and for those defending home markets against Chinese imports and FDI. In order to survive, many firms need to understand the evolving strengths and weaknesses of Chinese businesses, identify the resulting complementarities and competitive conflicts, and reposition themselves accordingly.

The specific objectives of this chapter are to:

1 *Understand* the nature of the Chinese economy, the role of government, and the characteristics of China's domestic market and its corporations.

2 *Examine* the opportunities and constraints facing Western firms investing in China and the ways in which successful firms have adapted to succeed there.

3 *Analyze* the degree to which Chinese firms are internationalizing, how and where they are selling and/or investing abroad, and what kinds of relative competitive advantages they appear to have.

4 *Reflect* on the implications of China's rise, in "real-world" terms and for academic analysis and understanding of firm performance and business processes.

ACTIVE LEARNING CASE

Oxford Instruments in China

The Oxford of ancient spires and ivory towers is well known among the Chinese. The successful, high-tech spin-off Oxford Instruments (OI) is less well known, but the company has worked to change this. Having sold a range of its products in China for over 10 years and experienced a 30 to 40 percent growth in sales year after year, senior managers at OI decided it was time to invest more heavily. The company opened representative offices in Beijing and Shanghai during the last decade and employed 20 people (including two expatriates). Then, between April 2003 and August 2004, OI registered as a **wholly foreign-owned enterprise (WFOE)** and established a manufacturing facility. This was a major investment for a medium-sized firm with a limited turnover. But it was a necessary step given that over 90 percent of OI's sales were from outside the UK, with approximately 10 percent in China. Moreover, its managers learned a number of important lessons along the way.

A key reason for investing directly in the Chinese market, moving to a higher level of both commitment and risk, was to get closer to the growing number of Chinese customers. OI chose to build on the strong platform of representative offices through the establishment of a repair and service center for supporting its microanalysis detector customers in China. It also wanted to provide a platform for the assembly of top-level products. To establish a business entity capable of delivering these kinds of activities, it needed some outside help. One way to reduce the risks of FDI is to hire local specialists who know about the local rules of the game and with the relationships and connections to help smooth the way. Another route is to hire experts who understand the international legal and regulatory conditions relating to an FDI project. In fact, when initiating its investment plans in China, OI did both. An international law firm was hired to ensure that global regulatory standards were followed. A local sponsor was also brought in (at a significantly lower cost) to help with the submission of the investment application to government authorities.

The establishment process itself was relatively straightforward. Step 1 was to register the company name. Step 2 was the submission of a feasibility report and articles of association to show the firm would be profitable and (most important) produce good tax returns. The WFOE, Oxford Instruments (Shanghai) Co., Ltd., was then given government approval and granted a trading license around three months after the start of the process. Post-registration procedures, including securing the "red"

Source: Simon Collinson

company chop (an official company seal or signature stamp), took a little longer.

Further development of an effective and efficient HQ–subsidiary organization structure and good working relationships between head-office management and local managers in China were seen to be key priorities in the early stages of the China venture. The UK side defined a common internal financial reporting structure and shared the group business strategy, which the senior management in China was then allowed to revise and tailor to the local context and culture. The existing OI China chief representative, a Chinese national employed by OI for five years, was named as the general manager of the new organization. The leadership of this existing member of the OI team, with experience of working both in a related industry and in an English-speaking environment, to head up the China operation was important for creating the necessary HQ–subsidiary relationships. As with any international expansion, an overarching question for OI was (and continues to be): what business processes and decision-making responsibilities do we move to China and what do we keep in the UK?

Key constraints and challenges cited by OI include time- and resource-consuming Chinese bureaucracy at various levels, including central, regional, and local governments, and individual firms (one customer required 11 different VAT invoices for a single sale). It was important for OI to link the new Shanghai facility into its global IT infrastructure, but the ▶

instability of the local internet required the company to invest in alternative (and more costly) connection methods. As OI continues to grow in China, the task of developing the necessary range of capable, experienced local managers in the sales and marketing functions as well as in operations will continue to be a focus.

Perhaps more significant than these problems have been OI's concerns about protecting its intellectual property rights (IPR) in China. OI's R&D assets and technological capabilities underpin its primary competitive advantage. It has had to take steps to avoid losing these to local Chinese competitors. Some formal protection and registration steps are available, and these have been taken by OI, but this provides limited protection in China. More effective protection of IP is gained through placing an emphasis on the careful recruitment of staff in China and the retention of the development and some manufacturing of key technologies at home in the UK. OI's customers are mainly top universities and organizations with high-level scientific research requirements. These customers are often co-developers of new technologies, so OI has built a range of cooperative alliances in which mutual trust and reciprocity are essential.

Many people talk about the importance of relationships in China. One interpretation is that in the process of developing relationships the Chinese are effectively performing a "credit check." In the absence of stable or reliable formal contracting rules, regulations, processes, and institutions, more emphasis is placed on interpersonal trust as the reliable basis for doing business. What rules there are in China tend not to be applied consistently. This leaves plenty of scope for influencing processes and decisions, which places even more of a premium on having the right connections.

At an early stage in the project, the following light-hearted "rules" for doing business in China were presented by a speaker at a "Making it in China" session at the University of Cambridge:

Rule 1: China is a highly regulated country, in which one needs to learn, understand, and follow countless regulations.

Rule 2: China presents a chaotic and unpredictable operating environment in which anything is possible; in fact there are no rules.

Rule 3: Rules 1 and 2 are simultaneously valid.

Understanding these local rules of the game has clearly paid off for OI. In 2008 the company won the UK Exporter of the Year Award "for the company demonstrating the utmost energy, novelty, patience and persistence, in the field of exports from UK to China during the year." It has achieved an average annual growth of 50 percent of export sales to China. From its original Beijing office it has expanded to Shanghai (where it also has a customer support center), Guangzhou, and Chengdu. China has become the fastest-growing market for OI across the world. From annual sales of less than $1 million in 1997, annual sales to China in 2014 exceeded over $54 million. The company overall employs over 2,300 people in over 15 countries and earns annual revenues of over $500 million.

Website: http://www.oxford-instruments.com

Sources: Oxford Instruments, Annual Report, 2010–14; Thomson Reuters, OneSource, 2011. This case has been partly compiled by the authors from a presentation by and discussions with Daniel Ayres, the project manager for the establishment of the manufacturing WFOE in Shanghai. Our sincere thanks to him and Oxford Instruments for allowing us to use the case here.

1 Why has OI invested in China? In what ways does its strategy fit with current trends in China?

2 Which "mode of entry" did OI select in China and what kinds of operational and practical challenges did it face?

3 What kinds of threats and opportunities might OI face from new multinational firms from China and what strategic responses should it be considering?

Wholly foreign-owned enterprise (WFOE)

A wholly foreign-owned enterprise is a limited liability company under Chinese company law and the preferred mode of investment for foreign MNEs looking to manufacture in China. WFOEs are also known as WOFEs (wholly owned foreign enterprises)

INTRODUCTION

With over 1.4 billion people, China (see Figure 21.1) has the largest population in the world, more than Latin America and Sub-Saharan Africa combined. Although it is an ancient civilization, the economy was only recently liberalized and opened up to trade and investment following Prime Minister Deng Xiaoping's reforms in 1978. Since then it has been moving from a closed centrally planned communist state toward an open market economy, and is increasingly participating as a major player in the modern world. While the rest of the world increasingly relies on China's economic growth to maintain global

Company chop
An official company seal or signature stamp used to verify company documents, contracts, and often financial transactions

Figure 21.1 South and East Asia

economic momentum, China itself is feeling the political and social strains of this unprecedented era of change. Its burgeoning economy attracts growing amounts of FDI as foreign firms take advantage of opportunities to produce products cheaper and sell into its expanding domestic market. Chinese firms are also evolving to compete not just in their own market but also abroad, as a new group of multinationals flexes home-grown advantages beyond the "middle kingdom."

UNPRECEDENTED SCALE, SCOPE, AND SPEED OF GROWTH

Lists of facts and figures that highlight the China phenomenon abound. It is the second largest economy, vying with the United States for the top spot in terms of trade and FDI, the largest producer of rice, wheat, cotton and tobacco, red meat, coal, and aluminum. It has over $3.5 trillion in foreign reserves (by far the largest in the world), 160 cities with more than 1 million people, the largest number of atheists of any country, and over 1.25 billion subscribers to wireless phone services. It accounts for over 30 percent of the world's luxury goods, and manufactures 88 percent of the world's toys, 66 percent of the world's bicycles, over 50 percent of the world's motorcycles, 70 percent of the world's mobile phones, 60 percent of the world's shoes, and over 30 percent of the world's coal (but reports 80 percent of worldwide deaths related to coal mining).

A particular boost came in 2001 when China joined the World Trade Organization (WTO) and began to attract record levels of FDI. **WTO accession** carried with it the commitment to phase out non-tariff barriers, provide trading rights to foreign companies, and change conditions on foreign investment, and this has been happening.[1]

The results have been impressive. GDP grew at an average of 8 percent per year, reminiscent of Japan's "catching-up" period in the 1960s and 1970s. In recent years up until 2011, China achieved annual growth rates close to 10 percent; however, since 2011 annual growth levels have been steadily declining (see Table 21.1). Exports and imports, as well as FDI, have surged but with a positive imbalance (exports exceeding imports) resulting in growing foreign reserves and contributing in particular to the massive deficit of the United States. China is now ranked as the second largest economy in nominal GDP terms and second largest in PPP terms.

The new era of export-led growth has resulted in economic and social development nationally, with a significant overall reduction in poverty across the whole of China (adjusted for purchasing power, China has grown to be over 70 percent richer than India). But growth has been concentrated in the industrialized east and in urban areas, where per capita disposable income is more than three times higher than that in the rural areas and growing faster, at almost 13 percent compared to less than 10 percent in rural areas. The country is still classed as "lower-middle income" and 130 million Chinese fall below the international poverty line.[2]

Trade and FDI are major indicators of the level to which an economy is integrated in the global economy and interdependent with other economies. The liberalization process in China centered on opening up the country in terms of inward and outward trade and FDI. In 2009, the global economic downturn reduced foreign demand for Chinese exports for the first time in many years down to $1.204 trillion (2009 est.), but China rebounded quickly, outperforming all other major economies in 2010 with GDP growth around 10 percent. China's external trade recently reached $1.506 trillion. This represents almost 40 percent of GDP. Note, though, that over 50 percent of these exports came from foreign-owned or foreign-invested firms (see Table 21.2). The Chinese government's 12th Five-Year Plan, adopted in March 2011, pledged to continue reforming the economy and emphasized the need to increase domestic consumption in order to make the economy less dependent on exports for GDP growth in the future. However, China likely will make only marginal progress toward these rebalancing goals in this decade.

China faces a number of economic problems, including inflation and local government debt, which swelled as a result of stimulus policies, and is largely off-the-books and potentially of low quality. The "middle income trap" is also a significant concern, whereby the economy becomes locked into a dependence on low-cost production and low-cost services,

WTO accession
Admission to the World Trade Organization; in return for the right to access and to engage in fair trade with other national markets, the country must liberalize its own markets

Table 21.1 China: key economic indicators, 2009–14

	2009	2010	2011	2012	2013	2014
GDP per capita ($bn at PPP)	10,813.814	12,085.451	13,482.080	14,789.517	16,173.272	17,617.321*
GDP (% real change pa)	9.214	10.410	9.300	7.763	7.751	7.361*
Government structural balance ($bn)	(636.789)	(515.027)	278.620	121.023	(443.482)	(443.954)
Inflation (%)	(0.700)	3.300	5.400	2.646	2.624	1.988
Official Unemployment (%)	4.300	4.100	4.100	4.100	4.050	4.090
Current account balance (% GDP)	4.764	3.997	1.861	2.568	1.931	2.021a

Note:
* estimated figures.
Source: IMF.

Table 21.2 China: key trade indicators, 2014

Major exports	% of total	Major imports	% of total
Machinery and transport equipment	45.8	Machinery and transport equipment	37.0
Miscellaneous manufactured articles	26.4	Mineral fuels, lubricants	16.2
Goods classified chiefly by material	17.2	Crude materials	14.3
Leading markets	**% of total**	**Leading suppliers**	**% of total**
US	16.9	South Korea	9.5
Hong Kong	16.2	Japan	8.8
Japan	6.8	US	7.8

Sources: Adapted from CIA, *The World Factbook*, 2014 estimates.

which support low-added-value jobs and therefore relatively low incomes. This cycle of low-value demand and supply can evolve into an economic "catch-22."[3]

China differs considerably from Japan, during its rapid economic growth phase, in this respect. So, while exports are normally seen as an indicator of local competitive advantage, this is not so straightforward in the case of China. Location endowments certainly convey some specific advantages, notably the lower costs of manufacturing that result from the availability of cheap labor. It is clear that the liberalization process has allowed foreign multinationals access to this resource and, certainly in some industries, they are better equipped than local "infant" industry firms to leverage this advantage. So, a significant proportion of China's export boom has been driven by foreign firms "migrating" existing manufacturing facilities from elsewhere into China and gaining the benefits of lower-cost exports to existing markets in the triad regions.

The attractiveness of China to MNEs, and the scale of their involvement, are shown by the sheer volume of FDI inflows over the past 20 years (see Table 21.3). In 2014 China recorded US$128 thousand billion of FDI inflows (many times higher than that of Japan, which has always attracted relatively low amounts of direct investment). China's total stock of FDI is more than four times that for Japan, again despite its relatively recent economic liberalization. The section below will discuss inward investment into China, followed by a review of the constraints facing firms trying to get into its growing domestic market.

Other firms are benefiting, without investing significantly in China, by extending their supply chains to take advantage of low-cost suppliers. At one point in the mid-2000s Wal-Mart imported over $25 billion in one year from China, making it the sixth largest importer of any "economy," with a larger volume than that of Russia. Wal-Mart's import volume has since decreased and it is beginning to redress the trade imbalance in a small way by expanding its network of retail stores in China. (See the **Real Case: Job losses and offshoring to China** in Chapter 6.)

Table 21.3 China: direct investment flows, outward and inward (billions of US$), 2011–14

	Outward FDI flows				Inward FDI flows			
	2011	2012	2013	2014	2011	2012	2013	2014
China	74,654	87,804	101,000	116,000	123,985	121,080	123,911	128,500
India	12,456	8,486	1,679	9,848	36,190	24,196	28,199	34,417
United States	396,569	311,347	328,343	336,943	229,862	169,680	230,768	92,397
East Asia	213,680	215,497	225,254	302,520	233,878	212,428	221,450	248,180
Asia and Oceania	314,580	301,017	336,368	431,749	427,562	404,537	430,671	468,070
Developing economies	357,570	357,249	380,784	468,148	639,135	639,022	670,790	681,387
World	1,587,448	1,283,675	1,305,910	1,354,046	1,563,749	1,402,887	1,467,233	1,228,263

Sources: UNCTAD, *World Investment Report*, 2011–14.

Outward FDI from China has grown significantly in recent years (see Table 21.3), partly as a result of the strong government push for international expansion (the "Going Global" strategy pursued by MOFCOM: see below) and the rising use of mergers and acquisitions (M&As) by Chinese firms to access Western markets, technologies, and brands. The final section in this chapter will examine a new breed of Chinese multinational firm.

THE ROLE OF GOVERNMENT

China has evolved from a closed, centrally planned system towards an open, market-oriented economy. Reforms started in the late 1970s with the phasing out of collectivized agriculture, and expanded to include the gradual liberalization of prices, fiscal decentralization, increased autonomy for state enterprises, the foundation of a diversified banking system, the development of stock markets, the rapid growth of the non-state sector, and opening up to foreign trade and investment.

Government reforms and the maintenance of the critical balance between liberalization and continued government control, guiding the development of capitalist enterprises and market incentives, are major factors responsible for the economic success currently experienced by China. They will continue to be critical factors for the sustainability of growth and development, as both the domestic and international contexts become increasingly turbulent. Comparisons between China and Russia are common and can be instructive. One study characterizes the differences as follows:

> China gave priority to administrative reform, aligned bureaucratic incentives at all levels with growth and development objectives, and enhanced enterprise and local autonomy while preserving the capacity of the center to exercise control. This approach transformed government bodies into real owners of the reform process and led to privatization over time that was largely welfare enhancing. Russia, on the contrary, gave priority to economic over state restructuring. Major reforms including mass privatization were implemented in an environment of a weak state, which did not have the capacity to protect its ownership rights and coordinate reforms. As a result, privatization was a wasteful process associated with asset stripping and consequently with lack of legitimacy of newly established property rights.[4]

The Chinese government has emphasized market-led growth by raising personal incomes and consumption while helping newly privatized industries to increase productivity through technology transfer and improved management. These aims, together with a policy of export-led growth, have been supported by the influx of FDI, also driven by the liberalization process. Multinational investors have pushed up exports while creating alliances and joint ventures which have helped local firms develop the necessary assets and skills to become more productive (although some studies argue that the effect has been to limit the competitiveness of local enterprises as they have become subordinate suppliers to Western MNEs).

China's central and provincial governments have worked on a "three-step development strategy," since the 1980s. This has involved regional development initiatives, now focused on controlling growth in the east of the country and subsidizing growth inland. "Key national projects" have supported infrastructure development on a massive scale, and the targeting of strategic industries, assets, and technological capabilities. Over time these kinds of government-directed initiatives have become increasingly international, as part of the "**Going Global**" strategy. Premier Wen Jiabao has strengthened this approach, building on the initial impetus by Premier Zhu Rongji in 2001, as part of the government push for the development of national industry champions and the procurement of natural resources abroad. Both underpin a broader agenda of economic nationalism including energy security, geo-political positioning, and national competitiveness.

Going Global
A key strategy of the Chinese government as part of the 11th Five-Year Plan, to internationalize target industry sectors and companies

Another major policy objective in China is to boost high-technology industry sectors. In 2010 PRC President Hu Jintao stated: "A nation's technological competitiveness determines its place and future in international competition." Efforts are led by the National Development and Reform Commission as part of the country's 12th Five-Year Plan. Key industries, including information technology, biotechnology, aerospace, new materials, high-tech services, new energies, and marine science and technology, are the focus of this initiative. The government is also both facilitating local technology-based start-up firms and encouraging high-tech FDI by upgrading the R&D infrastructure to develop innovative, patentable technologies. There has been a huge expansion in the number of researchers in China since 1999. China now counts more researchers than Japan, and is on its way to potentially overtake the EU in this regard. The country is already second only to the United States in terms of advanced technology exports, and it overtook Japan to become the second-largest investor in R&D (spending $121 billion in 2010). Since 2010 China has continued to be the second largest investor in R&D and it was recorded as spending $284 billion in 2014.

In the coming years China plans to reduce its external imbalances; boost domestic demand, particularly consumer demand, and rebalance investment and consumption; further promote balanced external sector development; speed up financial reform; and further improve the exchange regime "in a gradual and controllable manner." There are, however, a range of ongoing problems, including: large disparities in per capita income between regions; unemployment, particularly affecting previous employees of **state-owned enterprises (SOEs)** and migrants; corruption and other economic crimes; poor health and safety standards (for employees and consumers); environmental damage and social problems related to the economy's rapid transformation; and a rapidly aging population, due to the one-child policy.

The government retains substantial control over some areas of the economy (such as energy and transportation, financial markets, news media, infrastructure, land, and property) and is influential in others (aerospace, telecoms, construction, retailing, and creative media) and less involved in others (automotive and consumer products). This means there are different levels and types of control exerted in different spheres of life. Add to this the variety of levels of government, from central to provincial to city and town, and the fact that these are no longer "harmoniously aligned." Also add the fact that the application or implementation of laws and regulations varies greatly according to the specific location, situation, and people involved, and we begin to get an idea of the reasons why China plays by different rules of the game (see **Active Learning Case: Oxford Instruments in China** above).[5]

State-owned enterprises (SOEs)
Companies that are owned, financed, and controlled by government

MNE INVESTMENT INTO CHINA

The massive growth of FDI into China has created the largest array of international mergers and acquisitions, alliances, joint ventures, and partnerships ever witnessed. These are clearly a major source of complementary assets, resources, and capabilities for the Western multinationals and the local companies involved, which engage in a reciprocal give-and-take as part of the process of market entry.

China holds the double attraction for MNEs of a cost-effective source of production inputs, particularly cheap labor, and a growing consumer market. These strategic drivers equate to two simple forms of investment rationale: input-oriented investments and output-oriented investments. The former are designed to gain access to local resources, endowments, and country-specific advantages (CSAs) that will help the firm develop, produce, or deliver a product or service cheaper or better in some way. The latter are designed to expand sales by tapping into new and/or growing markets. Greater profitability should result from either or both, if they prove successful.

Airbus in China

Source: epa european pressphoto agency b.v./Alamy Stock Photo

Passenger volumes in China's air transportation industry are expected to grow annually by 11 percent over the next 20 years. This will make it the world's second largest aviation market, requiring an additional 1,790 aircraft to cope with the increased volume. Forty-nine new airports and 701 airport expansion projects are also expected under China's Five-Year Plan. The Chinese government maintains a strong degree of control over the civil aviation industry. Respective agencies aim to improve the reliability and efficiency of the transport infrastructure and promote competitiveness among domestic firms. The General Administration of Civil Aviation of China (CAAC) is the government agency responsible for the non-military aviation industry. It has rationalized the country's airlines, completing mergers with the "Big 3"—Air China, China Eastern, and China Southern—and some of the smaller airlines.

CAAC and other agencies are also central to the expressed aim of the Chinese government to develop an indigenous "Made-in-China" aircraft to rival Boeing and Airbus. There is no doubt this can be done and the economic rationale is less relevant at this stage than the political symbolism. The government has begun funding this as a prestige project and will continue to do so until it succeeds. There are question marks, however, over how long it will take and how reliable, safe, and therefore marketable the final product will be.

The government's determination, coupled with the inherent advantages of low-cost production and the rapid rate of technology transfer and local learning, have impressed one experienced Chinese expatriate in the aerospace industry. He proposed:

> Within the next 15 years there will be three major commercial aerospace corporations; Boeing, Airbus and a Chinese firm. Soon after there may well be two; one of which will be the Chinese firm.[6]

One senior British executive in China described the "Stairway to Heaven." The three stages toward local technological maturity in aerospace manufacturing:

- Stage 1 "Made-to-print": local manufacturers follow simple designs for low-end (and later, high-end) manufacturing.
- Stage 2: Local firms take on responsibility for product modules or "build-kits," including some redesign and process innovation.

- Stage 3: Full engineering partnerships with Western firms, with shared design and development, local responsibility for technology, quality, etc., and risk and revenue sharing (suppliers as shareholders in ongoing development processes).

Foreign firms in China, including Airbus and Boeing, Rolls-Royce and General Electric, are part of this plan. In order to gain access to the growing domestic market, estimated to be worth over $300 billion over the next 20 years, they have had to establish partnerships with local Chinese manufacturers. These involve subcontracting, technology transfer, and training with an expressed aim of increasing the local content of aircraft.

AVIC1 (Aviation Industry Corporation of China) and AVIC2 are responsible for all aerospace manufacturing in China. AVIC1 concentrates on large aircraft and is the main organization charged with developing a complete Chinese-made aircraft. However, rather than one unified "China" interest group there are local rivalries and factions competing with each other to become the lead player, not a simple them-and-us situation. As in other industries in China, local competition drives learning. There is "collaborative competition" guided, more or less, by the government, depending on the industry. On October 28, 2008, AVIC1 and AVIC2 officially merged because the previous separation resulted in split resources and led to redundant projects. The major focus of AVIC is to efficiently develop indigenous military technologies and to eventually compete with Boeing and Airbus in the civilian airline industry. During the Airshow China 2008, AVIC appeared in public for the first time. In the Singapore Air Show in February 2010, AVIC introduced the Comac 919 aircraft for the first time outside the mainland. The aircraft, which will be designed and built entirely in China, will compete directly against industry stalwarts A320 and Boeing 737 after completing flight trials.

Airbus subcontracts around $60 million per year to five Chinese firms and this is expected to double over the next five years. Components made in China include A320 wing parts, passenger doors, and landing gear bays. Two major joint ventures are at the center of Airbus operations in China, in the cities of Xi'an (Xi'an Aircraft Corporation with 28,000 employees) and Shenyang (Shenyang Aircraft Corporation with 20,000 employees). Both the local firms are state-owned enterprises (SOEs) operating under the AVIC1 umbrella organization. The head of the Xi'an plant is also the local town mayor.

The company has transferred manufacturing technology and put in place a range of training programs to develop the local capabilities at these plants, and among local component suppliers. While improved productivity is important, the quality and reliability of the components produced here are far more important, given the safety-critical nature of the final product.

Process improvement and innovation at the plant level are monitored or measured by a number of indicators. These include output and productivity measures, such as improvements in scrap yield and customer reject rates. The increased use of quality circles, "lean" management systems, and techniques such as the use of "visibility boards" which map out operations on the plant floor and monitor process changes, all indicate improvements in managerial and process-related capabilities. Other advances, such as a move from the use of 2-D to 3-D design drawings, demonstrate engineering, design, and product development innovations—all of which show how local Chinese managers, engineers, and plant-level personnel are learning through their interaction with Western counterparts.

Sources: S. C. Collinson, B. Sullivan-Taylor, and J. L. Wang, "Adapting to the China challenge: lessons from experienced multinationals," Advanced Institute of Management (AIM) Research Executive Briefing, London (2007), http://www.aim-research.org/publications/adaptingtochina.pdf; Aude Lagorce, "China's next bid for glory: aviation supremacy," *Wall Street Journal*, April 14, 2007 ; AVIC, http://www.avic.com.cn; Juliana Liu, "Chinese planes challenge Boeing and Airbus," *BBC News*, February 7, 2010.

First and foremost, China has a reputation as a cheap manufacturing hub, so cost advantages are still the primary motivator for many companies. The average factory wage (around $200 per month, but varying by region and type of employment) is far less than in more industrialized Pacific Rim countries such as Taiwan and much lower than anywhere in the triad regions. In addition to low labor costs, other positives of sourcing in China include: lower capital costs and low-cost product design and R&D; large manufacturing capacities; and, for some, improvements in quality. The negatives include: communication problems, low product quality, long initial start-up times, intellectual property theft, increased management complexity, and operational and supply-chain challenges.

At the same time, the rapid growth of the economy and the country's growing purchasing power are increasing consumer purchasing power as well as channeling investment into transportation, energy, utilities, communication systems, and other parts of its infrastructure. In response to these attractions, MNEs have made a large number of investments in China and the country now hosts the largest number of MNE affiliates of any economy, employing around 24 million people.

Most investments have been in the form of equity joint ventures or WFOEs. However, because of the evolving legislation governing foreign investment into China, there has been a noticeable shift in the mode of market entry by foreign firms toward M&As and WFOEs. Ten Asian locations (Hong Kong, Macau, Taiwan province, Japan, the Philippines, Thailand, Malaysia, Singapore, Indonesia, and South Korea) account for around 60 percent of FDI inflows. This shows a strong regional effect, with Japan, China, and the larger satellite Asian economies evolving a strong, mutually beneficial growth cycle of trade and FDI. The United States, Japan, and the EU account for roughly similar proportions of FDI in China. Around 70 percent of FDI each year is in manufacturing industries and cumulative FDI in China's high-tech industry is over $120 billion, with more than 700 foreign-affiliated high-tech companies operating R&D facilities in China. But service-related FDI is also growing. Investment in China's burgeoning retail industry, for example, is very healthy. Based on a first-mover strategy, Carrefour (France) has become the fifth largest retailer in China, while Wal-Mart (United States), which ranked the 14th largest, recently expanded its presence in China through the acquisition of Trust-Mart.

But the major distinguishing feature of China's inward FDI is the wide range of firms and industries involved. The top MNEs from all industries have a presence, including Occidental Petroleum (coal mining), Motorola (producing semiconductors and mobile phones), General Motors and VW (joint ventures with a Shanghai automotive company), Dow Chemical (a polyurethane production joint venture), Heinz (a baby-food plant), Procter & Gamble (a joint venture producing laundry and personal care products), Hewlett-Packard (electronics joint ventures), RJR Nabisco (manufacturing Ritz crackers, among other food products), Airbus and Boeing (a series of joint ventures), Rolls-Royce (aero engines), Seagram (whisky and wine), Babcock & Wilcox (a joint venture making boilers), and Mitsubishi (a venture to build elevators). Other firms on this growing list include Bell Telephone, DaimlerChrysler, General Bearing, Gillette, Lockheed, Pabst Brewing, Peugeot, Squibb, VW, and Xerox. P&G even spent $300 million in one year just marketing one product: Oil of Olay!

A regional investment pattern is also increasingly strong. For example, in terms of sales, Taiwanese firm Hongfujin Precision Industry (Shenzhen), a subsidiary of Hon Hai Precision Industry (also known as the Foxconn Group), has surpassed Motorola (China) in size, becoming the largest foreign affiliate in China. Overall, the firm employs close to 1 million Chinese, mainly in the coastal region of Shenzhen. But it has plans to move manufacturing into cheaper regions away from the east coast, including Chengdu and Wuhan. However, Foxconn has been involved in several controversies—most relating to how it manages employees in China, where it is the largest private employer. The decision to increase staff numbers and to move inland followed the suicides of 13 Chinese employees in 2010. On May 20, 2011, an explosion and fire broke out at one of the factories in Chengdu. The incident affected the iPad 2 assembly line and caused three deaths and 15 injured workers. The incidents threatened to tarnish the image of top global brands, such as Apple, Dell and Nokia, for which Foxconn produces laptops and smartphones. However, despite all these unfavorable news headlines, China still attracts electronics manufacturing companies, such as Taiwanese firms Quanta Computer and Inventec which are prominent in the list of top foreign affiliates in China. An increasing number of transnational corporations (TNCs) have established regional headquarters in Chinese cities such as Beijing and Shanghai. IBM relocated its global procurement headquarters to Shenzhen some time ago and is unlikely to move this inland.

Some firms have been successful in China. Although it is not doing so well elsewhere in the world, GM has generated profits for some time from its China operations. It accounts for an estimated 80 percent of the group's Asia–Pacific operations, which make about a fifth of the firm's net profits. Sales in China, driven by the Buick Saloon and Excelle Sedan, gave GM a market share approaching 10 percent to challenge Volkswagen, the long-time market leader (although most analysts predict overcapacity problems, reducing profits for all car firms in China in the coming years).[7]

Other firms investing in China believe, despite losing money, that they have invested in "a foot in the door" to the most important growing region in the world. But there is a third group of firms that have failed either to break into the market or to gain any return on their investments in China. Many following something of a "herd mentality" to get into China have failed to do their homework and been surprised to find how different, difficult, and risky the country is for inward investors (see the next section). Among those firms which failed miserably in China was New Zealand's Fonterra. Fonterra used to own 43 percent in the joint venture with Sanlu Group. Sanlu was a state-owned Chinese dairy products company based in Shijiazhuang, the capital city of Hebei Province. It was one of the oldest and most popular brands of infant formula in China before it went bankrupt. In September 2008, Sanlu was involved in an adulterated milk powder scandal, affecting some 294,000 Chinese infants and killing six. Their baby milk powder had been tainted with melamine, which can cause kidney stones and other complications. It received a bankruptcy order from Shijiazhuang Court on 24 December 2008 and several of its top managers were sentenced to long prison terms. As a direct consequence of the criminal contamination of milk in China, Fonterra recognized an impairment charge of $139 million against the carrying value of its investment in Sanlu. Following this impairment charge, Fonterra's best estimate of the book value of its investment in Sanlu was approximately $62 million, which was 69 per cent below its previous carrying value. In the process, Fonterra learnt a painful lesson in international business.

A spate of acquisitions and investments in the beer industry in the mid-2000s bears a strong resemblance to a period in the mid-1990s when foreign firms rushed to enter the Chinese market and lost out. Between 1993 and 1996 international beer firms invested over $1 billion in the Chinese market and found that capacity far outstripped demand, prices were unsustainably low, and production plants were small scale and inefficient. Although the local breweries were virtually bankrupt, local governments, concerned about rising unemployment, were pumping money into them, making it impossible for foreign firms to compete. Fosters, Carlsberg, Bass, and Asahi all bailed out at a loss, leaving the two largest local players, Tsingtao and Yanjing, to increase their dominance. Carlsberg alone lost $2 million between 1998 and 2000 before selling out.[8]

In 2002 China overtook the United States as the largest beer market in the world and foreign firms rushed to invest once again. In 2004 Anheuser-Busch acquired the Harbin Brewery Group Ltd., Heineken NV bought 21 percent of Guangdong Brewery Holdings Ltd., Scottish & Newcastle plc acquired a minority stake in Chongqing Beer Group, and Interbrew SA acquired a majority stake in Zhejiang Shiliang Brewery Co. Ltd. Then, in 2011 Anheuser-Busch InBev announced a deal to acquire 100 percent of Liaoning Dalian Daxue Brewery Co., Ltd. of China to expand its market share there. Most are doing much better in the Chinese market this time around, but local players are strong and beginning to look at market opportunities abroad.

Foreign R&D investment

MNEs, particularly those in IT hardware, the automotive industry, and pharmaceuticals and biotechnology, invest massively in R&D. Some of the largest investors, such as Ford Motor, Pfizer, DaimlerChrysler, Siemens, Toyota Motor, and GM, spend more on R&D than the vast majority of developing countries. Only China, Taiwan, South Korea, and Brazil come close to these individual firms in terms of total, national-level R&D expenditure. So the recent shift of R&D investment from the triad to emerging market economies and especially to China is significant. The share of foreign affiliates in R&D in the developing world increased from 2 percent to 18 percent between 1996 and 2002, and has continued to grow.[9] China is the most favored destination for MNEs looking to invest in R&D abroad.

There are now over 300 foreign R&D centers in the country. In many cases inward investors are competing for privileged access to the Chinese market and will offer high-technology investments to gain government support for projects. GM's automotive R&D center, for example, was established in the late 1990s when global car companies were fighting to get the best joint ventures with a few, government-supported local firms. Boeing (United States) and Airbus (a European consortium) were also under pressure to transfer technologies and established local training in return for access.

Electronics and ICT (information and communication technology) firms were among the earliest entrants. Motorola established the first China-based R&D center of any MNE in 1990 and now has 15 centers there, employing over 1,500 engineers. Microsoft has five centers with Microsoft Research Asia (MRA), one of the largest R&D centers in the world, responsible for the firm's basic R&D for the Asian region. Nokia also has five centers in China, making its initial investment in 1998. General Electric located one of only three of its global R&D centers in Shanghai in 2003.

Pharmaceutical firms have followed suit, including $100 million research centers for both Novartis and GSK in the late 2000s. The former, based in Shanghai, focuses on the infectious causes of specific types of cancer endemic in China and Asia. It also works to combine Western technology and drug-discovery approaches with the traditional methods of Chinese medicine.[10] For pharmaceutical firms the relatively low costs of field trials in China is one reason to invest.

More generally, the shortage of science, technology, and engineering expertise in the West is a major driver. While the EU is said to have a shortfall of around 700,000 science and engineering personnel, China hosts around 750,000 (second only to the United States), who are also cheaper to employ. Alongside this input-oriented or resource-oriented rationale for FDI in R&D, there are output-oriented or market-oriented reasons for R&D investments. These include the fact that industrial partners have moved to China. So, for example, much of the R&D conducted by Motorola's semiconductor and component divisions requires close collaboration with customers. Existing, Western-based customers have moved manufacturing activities to China and new customers are also emerging in China and the Asian region. These trends combine to create a strong incentive for Motorola to move its R&D "center of gravity" away from the West. China is also becoming a lead market for some technologies. Again, taking the Motorola example, advanced consumer use of mobile phone services in China makes it a lead market for user-led innovation, prompting firms to locate R&D activities there to keep up with adoption trends.

Over the longer term we can expect benefits for research institutes, universities, and local firms as MNE R&D networks supplement and support China's national system of innovation. The Chinese government has identified foreign R&D investments as a critical part of China's technology development strategy, originally outlined in the 10th Five-Year Plan (2001–5), now a core part of subsequent Five-Year Plans. China overall spends more than double the UK on R&D, and this has been growing at around 9 percent per year in recent years, in line with GDP growth. The country has 20 million people in higher education and has established more than 60 industrial parks dedicated to Chinese graduates returning from overseas to set up businesses. Well-educated graduates and a very good science and technology infrastructure, relative to other developing and emerging countries, are important national assets for China. These are now underpinning the growth of high-tech firms, such as Beijing Yuande Bio-Medical, from Beijing Medical University; Datang Microelectronics, from Beijing's Telecoms Research Institute; and Innova Superconductor and Tsinghua Solar, both from Tsinghua University.[11]

 Active learning check

Review your answer to Active Learning Case question 1 and make any changes you like. Then compare your answer to the one below.

1 **Why has OI invested in China? In what ways does its strategy fit with current trends in China?**

OI's investment in China was mainly "market seeking," in that the firm had experienced growing sales through exports to China in the past and expected to further increase sales by establishing a presence in the market, alongside its customers. This investment has paid off well, with both exports and locally manufactured product sales growing well. FDI to establish local customer services and representative sales offices has supported this success. OI is benefiting from cheaper local assembly costs for some products and has recently developed some R&D partnerships. These count as "resource-seeking" investments. Its strategy has continued to fit well with current trends in China. The growth in local demand for its products comes from both Chinese firms and foreign MNEs, including OI's customers in the United States and Europe that have moved operations to China. China may also evolve into an important source of inputs for its worldwide product development and R&D efforts in the future.

GETTING INTO CHINA

According to folklore in China, "the mightiest dragon cannot crush the local snake"[12]—in other words, local advantage can help a great deal in fending off larger and wealthier "predators." In response to the very different market conditions and complex local rules of the game in China, it is more common for multinationals to use intermediaries in the process of establishing a local presence here than elsewhere in the Pacific Rim. Government agencies such as those connected to the Ministry of Foreign Trade and Economic Cooperation offer such assistance, as do banks, law firms, and a vast range of consultancies.

As discussed above, the Chinese economy is centrally planned to some degree and the rights of all firms and individuals are strongly influenced by central, regional, and local government agencies. The government has a priority list of desired investments: ventures involving advanced technology, exports, or the generation of foreign exchange are given the highest priority. Understanding the policy agenda and the people responsible for formulating, revising, and implementing it is critical for market-entry strategies and continued survival in China. Local policy is also connected to high-level political forces that are important to understand. For example, at the international level, China has been running a large trade surplus with the United States in recent years, and there is every reason to believe that, unless this situation is corrected, the US government will limit Chinese imports. The European Union has also been talking about limiting clothing imports from China because of the threat to local manufacturers (effectively because they are "too competitive"). These political reactions could result in a backlash against triad MNEs in China. These and other sources of country risk that can affect the success of an overseas investment should also be taken into account when considering the mode of entry adopted by MNEs.

In terms of mode of entry, firms can invest via a range of FDI mechanisms, including Sino-foreign joint ventures, joint exploitation, and exclusively foreign-owned enterprises (or WFOEs), foreign-funded shareholding companies, and joint development companies:

1 Sino-foreign joint ventures, also known as joint shareholding corporations, generally require the capital from the foreign party to be at least equal to a 25 percent share in the enterprise, according to Chinese regulations.

2 Cooperative businesses, also called contractual cooperation businesses, have the rights and obligations of different parties embedded in the contract. The foreign partner generally supplies all or most of the capital while the Chinese party supplies land, factory buildings, and other facilities.

3 Exclusively foreign-owned enterprises take the form of limited liability companies, and regulations formally call for these to "adopt international advanced technology and facilities" or "all or most of the products must be export-oriented."

4 Joint exploitation, development, and production enterprises relate to maritime and overland oil exploitation.

5 Foreign-funded shareholding companies involve Chinese and foreign shareholders holding the shares of the company and accepting liability according to proportional ownership. The shares held by foreign investors must account for more than 25 percent of the total registered capital.

Lessons from foreign firms that established operations in China some time ago and have developed some experience adapting to the local business environment illustrate some of the key difficulties. A survey by the US Embassy in Beijing and Gallup received 286 responses from American investors in China.[13] About half said they were profitable and a further half of the remaining firms were investing more in anticipation of future profits. They reported a number of difficulties that created additional risks or costs, or required adaptation. The biggest problems were said to be, in order of importance:

- transparency of laws and regulations;
- cost of doing business;
- customs procedures/export procedures; and
- foreign exchange regulations/exchange rate risk.

Drawing on a number of surveys, some key issues for foreign entrants are as follows:

- Market-access rights from equity holdings to taxation levels vary by industry and are changing rapidly. At least three, often more, levels of government, including local, regional, and central government agencies, have a direct and strong influence over the local rules of the game and give preferential treatment to local firms and to particular kinds of foreign investors.

- Chinese tax laws and other regulations governing business practices are complex. Despite the expense, it is necessary to use attorneys, accountants, and consultants familiar with Chinese requirements.

Guanxi
Denotes personalized or informal networks of relationships in China. They can be important preconditions for smoothing the way or gaining favors or advantages, particularly when both society and the economy are dominated by central government. There are parallels with the concept of social capital

- Contracting tends to be based around relationships and connections (**guanxi**) rather than formal, legal documents. These are the basis of mutual trust, with due diligence on potential business partners performed by checking their network connections, as opposed to formal market mechanisms. Relationships with the right connections are critical. Developing *guanxi* connections with the wrong partners creates obligations that may act as a trap. Contracts are just a starting point for doing business, not the end goal.

- Intellectual property rights (IPR) are not well protected, legally or via any local business ethics. Investors need to carefully consider the implications of this, including the possibility of local firms getting and using key assets such as brands, patents, and business systems. One example of technology theft is in the high-speed bullet train project. Foreign companies were apparently lured in and encouraged to hand over their technology with promises of a share of China's domestic market. One of the bullet trains was subsequently involved in a serious accident, leaving 40 dead and more than 200 people injured in Zhejiang, eastern China, on July 23, 2011. The train having been built by a joint venture between Chinese firm CSR Corp. and Canadian firm Bombardier, the accident led to a revealing series of accusations. These included allegations of mass corruption that went all the way to the top of the railway ministry, then later technical problems. The Japanese firm Kawasaki and Germany's Siemens were involved and they had warned the Chinese companies for years about the dangers of scaling up this kind of technology at this rapid pace. The underlying aim of Chinese companies is to combine foreign technology with native low-cost labor and capital to undercut foreign firms in international markets. In this case, the domestic market was used as a testing ground and the Chinese firms became involved in high-speed projects in Venezuela and Turkey. Exports were meant to provide the payback. The accident, however, is a blow to China's marketing efforts. Foreign train manufacturers were already challenging the legality of Chinese exports, which included their technology. Now potential purchasers in the United States, Thailand, and Russia may be even harder to convince.

- Keeping face and being respectful are important. Group orientation and steeper hierarchies characterize Chinese organizations.[14]

- Learning the language may be important in order to provide insights into the local business culture. But too much of a willingness to do things the local way can be seen as a sign of compromise and ultimately weakness. Respect and credibility often come from asserting one's own practices and rules of the game.

- The role of the Chinese partner in the success or failure of a joint venture or alliance cannot be overemphasized. Good partners will have the connections to overcome obstructive red tape and enable success; bad partners may have no power or knowledge to deal with obstructive bureaucrats, may violate confidentialities, and/or may establish competing businesses.

- Although there is a large, cheap general labor pool, skilled managers, particularly those with marketing expertise, are difficult to find and keep. Engineers and technicians are similarly difficult to hold onto.[15]

In some business sectors, joint ventures are required, or were required until recently, by the Chinese government. In a joint venture the local partner is typically responsible for providing the land and buildings and for carrying out local marketing. The MNE is expected to contribute the equipment, technology, and capital and to be responsible for export marketing. In those cases where the multinational is manufacturing for sales in China, high-quality products, excellent service, and good promotional efforts are critical to success. Researchers have found that outstanding service and effective promotion can often make up for some lack of quality. However, price reductions and special sales terms are unlikely to offset poor quality. Similarly, while customer relations are important, they are often not enough to make up for poor quality or poor service. The Chinese want to buy the best quality available.

In light of these challenges, joint ventures have a number of both benefits and problems. Majority-owned joint ventures give foreign firms an element of control combined with the benefits of gaining immediate access to experienced managers and their local relationship networks. Experienced managers report on the benefits of being able to access local business knowledge, including customer and supplier connections and getting assistance with local officials and regulations. Local firms and/or experienced local experts are normally important for helping customize and adapt existing products and services for local markets, and for developing new ones targeted at the Chinese market. Table 21.4 outlines some of these synergies between foreign and local firms.

Table 21.4 Common examples of synergies between foreign multinationals and local Chinese firms

Type of partnership	Foreign multinational firm provides . . .	Local Chinese firm provides . . .
Manufacturing joint venture or subsidiary–local supplier alliance	• Finance • Technology, production systems, management systems (control, coordination best practices, performance measurement, IT, etc.) • Management expertise, engineering, and plant-level training	• Land, labor, facilities, finance • Links to/knowledge of suppliers, buyers, contractors, distributors • Access to local resources, materials • HRM expertise, recruitment capabilities • Local government connections, knowledge of local regulations
Product development joint venture	• Finance • Technology and product development tools, processes, best practices, and expertise • Links to other sources of expertise inside and outside the firm	• Facilities • Finance • Some engineering, technical expertise • Knowledge of regulations, IPR protection strategies, and relevant connections • Links to/knowledge of customer preferences and distribution channels

✔ Active learning check

Review your answer to Active Learning Case question 2 and make any changes you like. Then compare your answer to the one below.

❷ Which "mode of entry" did OI select in China and what kinds of operational and practical challenges did it face?

OI registered as a wholly foreign-owned enterprise (WFOE) and established a manufacturing facility through this route rather than via a joint venture. Its major challenges, like many foreign firms in China, included the need to: understand and comply with local regulatory and legal conditions and deal with Chinese central and local authority bureaucracies; develop relationships with local customers and adapt to their contracting behaviors; recruit and train (and retain) local experts; develop an effective working relationship between the local offices and the UK-based divisions; and protect its intellectual property rights.

Studies show that recruiting, managing, and motivating personnel rank very high among key difficulties faced by foreign managers, even when working with local partners. Skill shortages and weaknesses in Chinese management, and the resulting low levels of labor productivity, also presented significant problems. But this can also reflect a failure on the part of foreign managers to (1) differentiate between labor costs and productivity in preparation for investing in China,[16] and (2) sufficiently adapt management and working practices to get the best out of a Chinese workforce.

According to experienced expatriates, one of the most remarkable aspects of China is the sheer drive and motivation of its people. In general they are very hard working and ambitious. Local cultural values and China's past history have a strong influence on workplace behavior, underlying a reluctance to take the initiative and the need for detailed instructions, for example. But a massive appetite for learning, advancement, and the rewards of capitalism among the people are central to China's growth drive. Cheap labor is one of China's major attractions, but experienced labor is increasingly scarce and there is a talent war for particular kinds of employees. As a result labor rates are increasing and firms are putting in place a range of strategies to retain good employees. Rises in wage costs may well outpace improvements in the productivity of the country's workforce, which could result in lower export competitiveness.[17]

OUTWARD INVESTMENT AND THE NEW MULTINATIONALS FROM CHINA

As mentioned above (see Table 21.3), outflows of FDI from China have grown rapidly over the last decade, albeit from small beginnings. For some observers, growing outward FDI is a sign of the impending competition from emerging Chinese MNEs set to dominate particular global industries in the near future. For others, this "infant stage" of international expansion is set to continue for some time with Chinese firms still ill-equipped to significantly expand overseas operations.

Private Chinese companies are stepping up their outward investment, but large SOEs account for the bulk of FDI outflows from China. The government is pushing for internationalization under its current "Going Global" campaign, which is central to the current Five-Year Plan set by the CPC Central Committee. As a result, much outward FDI (over 70 percent in most years) comes from large Chinese companies under the state-owned Assets Supervision and Administration Commission of the State Council. Total amounts are still, however, a small proportion of global FDI and dwarfed by the stock of inward FDI in China.[18] One study suggests that China's outward FDI tends to come from "state-controlled enterprises with government sanctioned monopoly status" and is biased toward tax havens and neighboring economies.[19] The existing capital markets and corporate ownership structures tend to promote international expansion among larger firms championed by the government, particularly in the areas of energy and raw materials (which China is short of), rather than firms that may have particular strategic advantages.

Chinese firms are certainly appearing increasingly prominently in lists of corporate rankings. Table 21.5 shows the top 25 Chinese firms in the *Forbes* ranking of the global top 2,000 corporations.

But the "Forbes 2000" list and many other rankings which show a growing presence of Chinese firms simply measure size and/or profitability, not the degree of internationalization. Larger Chinese firms are arguably the result of the growing domestic market, not international expansion. When we examine the distribution of assets and sales of these large Chinese firms, we see that they do remain highly dependent on their domestic and regional markets.[20]

Studies that examine the degree to which Chinese firms have internationalized suggest that they are still heavily reliant on country-specific advantages (CSAs) and have yet to develop the requisite firm-specific advantages (FSAs) to break into overseas markets to any great extent. More significantly, the rationale for focusing on domestic and regional (Asian) market opportunities appears to be a significant influence shaping outward FDI.[21]

When they do venture abroad, Chinese firms follow the same logic as other MNEs. They are driven by the two main targets: input-oriented investment (for resources) and output-oriented investment (for market access). As regards the former, a notable increase

Table 21.5 Top 25 Chinese (mainland) firms in the "Forbes 2000" list, 2015 ranking

Rank	Company	Revenue (US$bn)
1	Sinopec	427.6
2	PetroChina	333.4
3	ICBC	166.8
4	China Construction Bank	130.5
5	Agricultural Bank of China	129.2
6	China State Construction Engineering	120.3
7	Bank of China	120.3
8	China Mobile	104.1
9	SAIC Motor	99.5
10	China Railway Group	96.8
11	China Railway Construction	94.1
12	Ping An Insurance Group	73.5
13	China Life Insurance	71.4
14	China Communications Construction	58.5
15	People's Insurance Company of China	55.7
16	Bank of Communications	53.6
17	China Telecom	52.7
18	China Unicorn	46.2
19	China Merchants Bank	45.5
20	CNOOC	44.6
21	Lenovo Group	44.3
22	China Minsheng Banking	40.0
23	China Shenua Energy	39.6
24	Industrial Bank China	39.4
25	China CITIC Bank	38.3
Total		2,525.9

Note: Data are for 2015, based on revenue, accessed from http://fortune.com.

in Chinese investments in Africa has been driven by the growing demand for energy resources and raw materials in China. In recent years up to 40 percent of the global growth in oil demand has come from China, hence large-scale investments in Nigeria and other African countries with oil reserves. In 2008 a reciprocal deal worth a massive $9 billion was designed to give the Democratic Republic of Congo badly needed infrastructure in return for access to its raw materials. It involved the building of around 2,400 miles (4,000 km) of road, 2,000 miles (3,000 km) of railroad, plus 32 hospitals, 145 health centers, and two universities. China will get access to an estimated 10 million tons of copper and 400,000 tons of cobalt in return.[22]

When we examine output-oriented or market-facing investment, it is interesting to note the changes in the kinds of exports and FDI coming out of China, as indicators of its changing competitive advantage. In 1985 just 2.6 percent of Chinese exports were categorized as high technology, whereas almost 50 percent of exports were based on primary products or manufactured products based on natural resources. Today, well over 30 percent of exports are high technology and less than 10 percent are from the latter category above. The initial boost in higher-value exports came from MNEs using China as an export base for their products. But high-technology, high-value products are increasingly exported by local Chinese firms that are moving up the learning curve.

Local Chinese firms and other firms based outside the triad are able to learn via subcontracting relationships and joint ventures with larger multinational firms. In this sense MNEs are, to a certain extent, "breeding" their future competitors through the technology and capability transfer that takes place within these interfirm relationships. This may be an unintended consequence of an alliance, or it may be made explicit, through: the transfer of equipment, know-how, and training; the licensing of patents or brands; and other activities that are part of the negotiated contract. Western MNEs often trade their own knowledge, technology, assets, resources, and networks in order to get access to local knowledge, technology, assets, resources, and networks as part of a market-entry or expansion strategy.[23]

From 2011 onwards, Chinese businesses invested a growing volume of FDI in acquisitions, trade deals, and loan agreements abroad. They had the dual aims of accessing large (though mature) consumer markets and buying assets, technology and expertise to complement their home-based cheap labor and other CSA endowments.

Overall, this means that China is evolving beyond its dominance as a global exporter of textiles, clothing, and toys, and into areas such as autos (see the **Real Case: Nanjing Auto makes the MG** below), white goods (see the case **International Business Strategy in Action: Haier goes global** below), consumer electronics, and mobile phones. In telecoms, for example, Chinese firms Huawei Technologies, Zhongxing Telecom, and Datang Telecom are but three government-backed, high-tech competitors which are quickly gaining ground against foreign equipment manufacturers, including Ericsson, Lucent, Nortel, and Cisco Systems. Huawei commands the greatest market share in China for optical systems equipment, outselling all foreign competitors.[24] Although Motorola and Nokia still dominate China's mobile handset manufactures, domestic enterprises such as Bird, TCL, and Konka are chipping away the leaders' market share. In the semiconductor sector, US government analysts judge China now to be only two years or less behind US manufacturing technology and only one generation behind the commercial state of the art. Huge Dragon and China's largest manufacturer of high-definition televisions Konka are other examples of up-and-coming local firms. Similarly in computer software, local firms Founder, Red Flag, UFSoft, Neusoft, Kingdee, and Top Group are both partnering and competing with Microsoft, Oracle, IBM, and Sun Microsystems in niche areas.[25]

Lenovo, a high-profile Chinese firm, made the news in the early days of foreign M&As when it bought IBM's PC business for $1.75 billion. This was a landmark deal for China, not least because of IBM's status as the archetypal US computer firm. Lenovo, originally called Legend when it was spun off from the Chinese Academy of Sciences in the mid-1980s, makes about 30 percent of PCs in China and is number two in laser printers. The sale gave IBM $650 million in cash, along with an 18.9 percent stake in Lenovo worth $600 million. The merged firm had sales of about $12 billion a year, as well as a five-year license for IBM's PC brands. Lenovo's PC operations were then moved to be headquartered in upstate New York, rather than Beijing, and the company opened an R&D center in California's Silicon Valley, as a "listening post."[26] Lenovo is now listed among China's leading "power brands," many of which are in the white goods and consumer electronics sectors, such as Galanz, Changhong, SVA, TCL, and Haier.[27]

As Chinese firms aim to move higher up the value chain, design and R&D activities will become increasingly important, as well as access to advanced market economies abroad. For some fledgling MNEs this means investing overseas to acquire technologies, build or buy distribution networks and brands, and develop a wider portfolio of expertise, in keeping with the framework described in Chapter 20 (see Figure 20.6).

For some observers the growth of a new breed of multinationals from emerging economies warrants a new theoretical approach or set of explanatory frameworks. This is necessary, say some, because the current frameworks have developed out of the experience of Western-based MNEs and their international operations in other mature economies of the triad, and expansion into emerging and developing economies. Although the two main types of FDI, input-oriented (resource-seeking) and output-oriented (market-seeking) FDI, are still relevant, the motivations of MNEs from emerging economies are significantly different. Studies indicate that they are internationalizing to compensate for current competitive disadvantages, such as technological capabilities and brands, rather than exploiting existing advantages to expand abroad. (The case of Nanjing Auto's takeover of MG supports this view: see the **Real Case: Nanjing Auto makes the MG** below.)[28]

INTERNATIONAL BUSINESS STRATEGY IN ACTION

Haier goes global

Haier is arguably one of the fastest-growing consumer products multinationals ever. It began life in 1984 as a government-owned refrigerator manufacturer and grew 68 percent per year on average between 1984 and 2005 to become one of the world's largest white goods manufacturers alongside Whirlpool, AB Electrolux (Sweden), BSH Bosch und Siemens Hausgeräte GmbH (Germany), GE Consumer (US), and GD Midea Holding Co., Ltd. (China).

With a workforce of over 70,000 employees, it has established 15 manufacturing complexes and 30 overseas plants, 8 design centers, and a network of over 60,000 sales agents worldwide, and has a warehouse capacity of 2,000,000 square meters. It has also become one of the

Source: Lou-Foto/Alamy Stock Photo

most successful brands China has so far produced and controls more than 30 percent of China's refrigerator, washing machine, and freezer markets. In 2014, Haier sales were US$32.8 billion. Although the majority of sales were generated in China, it has explicitly followed an aggressive internationalization strategy.

Haier began exporting products to overseas markets in 1990. Six years later it started to internationalize through FDI in Southeast Asia before moving further abroad to the larger triad markets (see the milestones in Table 21.6). It deliberately followed a step-by-step international expansion strategy aimed at "building volume and gaining international experience" in Asia, starting with a joint venture in Indonesia in 1996.

A major first-step was taken in 1999, with a greenfield investment in South Carolina, making Haier the largest Chinese-invested company in the United States, a decision made at a time when the US home appliance industry was in a downturn and most appliance manufacturers there were moving their manufacturing bases to other low-cost countries, including China. More recently Haier has established manufacturing operations in India. This allowed it to save up to 30 percent of the cost of locally sold refrigerators by avoiding import duties, as well as service its growing Indian customer base more efficiently.

As of 2015, Haier had established 4 R&D bases, 7 industrial parks, 24 manufacturing plants, and 24 trading companies outside China. Furthermore, Haier has entered the top ten chain channels in Europe and USA with its markets across over 100 countries and regions. Its product range extends from refrigerators and freezers to commercial air-conditioners, microwave ovens, washing machines, dishwashers, televisions, mobile phones, and computers. As well as manufacturing in the United States, Italy, Pakistan, Jordan, India, and Nigeria, it has localized aspects of product design, distribution, and sales processes to suit its international markets. The company also set itself a target of doubling foreign sales in subsequent years.

An audacious strategy to outbid rivals, including Samsung, to acquire General Electric's appliance unit for $5.4 billion in 2016 showed not only how bold the firm had become, but also how it had matured in terms of its strategic approach to international expansion.

Table 21.6 Haier goes global

Date	Haier's internationalization milestones
1990	Exports first batch of refrigerators to Europe, focusing on Germany
1993	Haier refrigerators and other products enter the Middle East market
1995	Begins exports to the US, first in OEM form, later under the Haier brand. Also establishes a local assembly plant in Southeast Asia
1996	Enters the Indonesian market through a joint venture (its first outside China)
1997	Enters Malaysia and the Philippines with greenfield investments
1999	Greenfield investment worth $30 million in Camden, South Carolina, signals the start of Haier America Refrigerator Corp. Ltd. and Haier's first overseas factory
2000	The first "Made in America" refrigerators come off the production lines in the US
2001	A second overseas factory is established in Pakistan
	Acquires a refrigerator plant in Italy and sets up a joint venture in Nigeria
2002	Haier products enter the Australian and New Zealand markets
	Establishes trading companies in Malaysia and Thailand
	A joint venture between Haier and Japan's Sanyo is established in Japan
2003	Manufacturing operations in Jordan produce washing machines for the Middle East markets
	Haier enters the home computer market
2004	Haier home computers are sold into the French market
	An electronics manufacturing operation is established in Dubai
2005	Wholly owned subsidiary set up in Australia
2007	Buys an Indian refrigerator factory and begins manufacturing in India
2008	Haier (Thailand) buys Sanyo's refrigerator factory in Thailand
2009	25-year anniversary celebrated in Qingdao, China, and European HQ in Varese, Italy
2010	Distribution, sales, and service centers established in the UK and other triad countries
2011	Haier announces the acquisition of Sanyo's white goods business in Japan and Southeast Asia
2016	Acquisition of General Electric's appliance unit for $5.4 billion

Learning to internationalize

Haier has successfully managed to overcome some of the key challenges for Chinese firms looking to "go global." Key to this has been the strong emphasis on quality, technological innovation, and brand building. Foreign alliances and partnerships have also been an important factor, supporting access to, or the internal development of, the relevant assets and capabilities underlying these strengths.

The strong emphasis on quality dates back to a famous incident involving the CEO of the Haier Group, Zhang Ruimin, in the mid-1980s. At what was the Qingdao Refrigerator Factory, he used a hammer to smash up a number of defective refrigerators in front of managers and workers to drive home the importance of zero-defect manufacturing. Technological innovation, both process related and product related, has also been a cornerstone of senior managements' philosophy and the firm reinvests a growing proportion of sales revenue into R&D. The company has worked with over 200 foreign manufacturing firms in the home appliance design sector. It has also led over 60 national R&D and technology development projects as part of the Chinese government's push for local capability development in target industries.

In addition to a highly active brand-building strategy for the domestic China market, Haier has actively promoted its corporate and product brands overseas. In the US market, for example, it gained recognition through a high-profile sponsorship deal with the National Basketball Association (NBA) and for a period was the sole sponsor for the televised NBA competition.

One senior manager describes Haier's internationalization strategy as a three-stage process:

First, we should set up a large overseas production and sales network. Second, all Haier's products that meet the local market demand should move into the major sales channels. And last, the company should produce mainstream products in local markets.

Haier is clearly advancing down the route to becoming more global in terms of sales and FDI. However, it is difficult to assess whether profits have flowed from this expansion process. We need to ask how much the firm still depends on the two key country-specific advantages (CSAs) that all Chinese firms need to break away from: (1) the cheap-labor advantage, and (2) the home-market advantage, which provides profits from consumers, retailers, and distribution networks which the firm knows well.

Website: http://www.haier.com

Sources: Reuters, *Haier's GE unit buy highlights growing China M&A maturity*, January 26, 2016; Giulia Segreti, "Purchase opens doors and minds," *Financial Times*, April 25, 2011; Jeannie Jinsheng Yi and Shawn Xian Ye, *The Haier Way: The Making of a Chinese Business Leader and a Global Brand* (Paramus, NJ: Homa & Sekey, 2003); H. Liu and K. Li, "Strategic implications of emerging Chinese multinationals: the Haier case study," *European Management Journal*, vol. 20, no. 6 (2002) pp. 699–706; Florence Chong, "Why China must have world-class brands? It is not a question for debate. It is a must!?" *Asia Today International*, April 4, 2006; Ying Fan, "The globalisation of Chinese brands," *Marketing Intelligence and Planning*, vol. 24, no. 4 (2006), pp. 365–79; Haier, *Annual Report*, 2010–14; Thomson Reuters, *OneSource*, 2011; Euromonitor International, 2011, http://www.portal.euromonitor.com/Portal/Pages/Magazine/IndustryPage.aspx; Mintel Global Market Navigator, 2011, http://gmn.mintel.com/query/10928149/shares/region

This view is opposed by others who see existing frameworks as sufficient, perhaps with minor adaptations, to explain and predict the behavior of Chinese firms. Despite differences in underlying culture, capital markets, economic history, and the context from which these firms have emerged, the existing explanations for internationalization are still perfectly adequate.[29]

✔ Active learning check

Review your answer to Active Learning Case question 3 and make any changes you like. Then compare your answer to the one below.

3 **What kinds of threats and opportunities might OI face from new multinational firms from China and what strategic responses should it be considering?**

OI is arguably already in a good competitive position in that its profitability stems mainly from its technological capabilities and investments in R&D, rather than low costs. Most large Chinese firms are building from an initial low-cost advantage, so while OI might experience some competition in its low-end businesses, it seems secure for now in the more technologically sophisticated business lines. IPR theft is a continuing threat and may help newcomers catch up rapidly in some key niche areas. But while any high-technology start-ups or established instrumentation firms in China might eventually be able to compete on the basis of new technology developments, they are weak in terms of customer relationships and brand recognition, and therefore have limited access to markets outside China. There may be opportunities for OI to partner with smaller start-ups to develop new products, or build relationships with larger customers to provide products, technical services, and support as they internationalize.

KEY POINTS

1 One of the most important trends of our time is the economic development of China and its growing importance in terms of trade and FDI, as a cheap manufacturing base, as a growing market, and as a source of competitive opportunities and threats for all MNEs. Its economic growth and rising influence in the global economy may, however, be slowed or halted by social and political forces, domestic or international.

2 In terms of the scale, scope, and speed of economic growth, China is unprecedented. It is larger and growing faster, across a broader range of industries, than Japan during its rapid development phase.

3 The Chinese government at various levels has a strong influence over the economy, business practices, and the opportunities open to MNEs. The "Going Global" policy and initiatives to develop target industries and indigenous innovation capabilities are central to the plans of central government.

4 Inward and outward FDI have grown. MNEs are attracted to the growing domestic market and opportunities for cheaper manufacturing. MNEs are also establishing R&D activities in China.

5 MNEs looking to get into the Chinese market need to be aware of its particular differences and difficulties, including changing regulations governing foreign investors; customs, tax, and foreign exchange procedures; specific cultural traits and the importance of *guanxi*; the problems with intellectual property rights; and the need to secure good partnerships and local expertise.

6 The current concern is that China and other emerging economies are increasingly competitive in manufacturing, taking investment and jobs from the triad regions. The key concern in the near future will be with their competitiveness in high-technology and knowledge-based businesses.

7 Some Chinese firms are expanding abroad. The extent and impacts of this internationalization of a "new breed" of MNEs are hotly debated.

Key terms
- wholly foreign-owned enterprise (WFOE)
- company chop
- WTO accession
- Going Global
- state-owned enterprises (SOEs)
- *guanxi*

REVIEW AND DISCUSSION QUESTIONS

1 What indicators point to the increasing importance of China and Chinese firms in the global economy? Describe two factors that have helped China's recent economic growth.

2 What makes China an attractive location for inward FDI by MNEs?

3 Give some examples of the national development policies pursued by the Chinese government. Explain how these affect the options open to foreign firms investing in China.

4 What makes China an attractive location for foreign R&D activities?

5 What modes of market entry are open to foreign firms investing in China?

6 What guidelines must MNEs follow when doing business in China? Identify and briefly describe three specific difficulties for foreign firms breaking into the Chinese market.

7 What are the main pros and cons of establishing a joint venture with a local firm for an MNE looking to sell products to the growing consumer market in China?

8 Do you think China will remain a manufacturing hub? How might Chinese firms develop competitive advantages in high-technology and service industries, and what are the implications for triad-based MNEs?

9 What kinds of Chinese firms account for most outward FDI from China?

10 Explain why Chinese firms are investing in Africa.

11 Do you think Chinese MNEs warrant a new theoretical approach to understanding multinational firms and their reasons for internationalizing?

REAL CASE

Citigroup in China

The banking industry faces many barriers to globalization. Overcoming cultural differences and dealing with varying regulations and financial systems make it very difficult to establish a truly global bank. Citigroup (or Citi), formed in 1998 by the merger of Citicorp and Travelers Group, is a leader in international banking and one of the largest companies in the world, in terms of assets. In 2014 it had $76.9 billion in revenues and 241,000 staff around the world (compared to 375,000 at its peak in 2008) and served over 200 million customer accounts in more than 100 countries. Furthermore, as of 2014, Citigroup had reduced its business scope by shedding over 60 non-core businesses. Some 45 percent of its income originates in the United States, 15 percent from Europe and Middle East, 19 percent from Latin America, and 21 percent from Asia.

Citigroup enters a developing country via mergers and acquisitions where possible, and implements its own marketing strategy. In the first stage of development, it caters to the global customer (usually a large corporation) by providing short-term loans, cash management, and foreign exchange services. During a country's second stage of development, as demand grows in the face of a burgeoning middle class, Citigroup begins to offer personal financial products.

In China, the political climate has limited Citigroup expansion plans in the Asia region. Citigroup opened its first office in China in 1902 but was thrown out by the new communist government of Chairman Mao in 1949. Even after it was allowed back into the country, its business was restricted mainly to foreign currency. China's market potential, however, always attracted the bank, and when the country began ▶

to show interest in opening its borders and joining the World Trade Organization, Citigroup stepped in as a key broker in negotiations with the US government. The bank's efforts are paying off. In the 1990s, the Chinese began to open their economy and make commitments for further reforms. By 2001, import tariffs had been lowered to an average of 15 percent from 44 percent in 1992, and they continued to decrease, averaging 9 percent by 2006 and less in subsequent years.

Deregulation is allowing Citigroup to implement its emerging-market strategy in China. In the initial phase, the bank marketed only to large foreign corporate clients. By 2004, it had expanded its customer base to include travelers, business people, wealthy Chinese with foreign exchange needs, and local businesses. Citigroup's international network has also made it attractive to Chinese MNEs operating in other markets. Among these is Lenovo, a Chinese PC manufacturer that today controls over 25 percent of the domestic market and has begun to expand abroad. Other examples include Konka (electronics), Haier (consumer appliances), and China Telecom. Local banks do not have the same level of international service.

Deregulation not only allows Citigroup to open fully functional branches to cater to the wealthy and, increasingly, to the middle class, but also attracts more foreign clients. UPS and FedEx, for instance, are both looking to open 100 percent-owned delivery systems in China. Home to the largest number of mobile phone subscribers in the world and nowhere near saturation, China also expects to attract telecom service providers and product manufacturers. In short, opportunities for foreign investment in China are creating a large number of MNE subsidiaries from which Citigroup can draw its client pool.

Citigroup's second marketing stage for emerging markets is expanding into personal banking. To some degree, Citigroup now offers consumer banking, corporate and investment banking, and insurance in the Chinese market. The bank does not yet provide a full range of consumer services to the entire population. Indeed, its banking fees are kept high for all but very large deposits to attract only the wealthier segments of the population. In 2010 it launched its "Citigold Private Client" services into China, Singapore, and Hong Kong, targeted at high-net-worth individuals. It also developed its online banking services.

In 2002, the firm was first allowed to offer foreign exchange services to Chinese nationals but it is not yet allowed to offer consumer banking in yuan. In 2004, it partnered the Shanghai Pudong Development Bank to offer a dual-currency credit card that could be used in yuan and US dollar transactions, the first of its kind in China. The credit card business is tricky in China because there is no reliable credit rating agency, but by moving forward with this service, Citigroup's goal is to create brand awareness that will allow it to dominate the market once it matures. The bank is likely to move consumers into mortgages, personal loans, pension funds, and other financial products in the final stage of its market-entry strategy.

Although Citigroup has a definite first-mover advantage in the Chinese market, it still faces competition from domestic banks. These include the Industrial and Commercial Bank of China and other large foreign competitors such as HSBC, which also has extensive experience in the region. The Pudong deal was relatively small compared to rivals' acquisitions and it has continued to look for bigger opportunities. Mainland China recently generated only 2 percent of Citigroup's Asian revenues, as against higher percentages from smaller economies, including Hong Kong (12 percent), South Korea (14 percent), and India (10 percent). It clearly has much work to do to build a position in China commensurate with its global standing.

Websites: www.citigroup.com; www.fedex.com; www.ups.com; www.legend.com.cn; www.konka.com; www.haier.com; www.chinatelecom.com.cn; www.icbc.com.cn; www.hsbc.com

Sources: Citigroup, *Annual Report*, 2010–15; "ICBC tops Citigroup as world's biggest," *China Daily*, July 23, 2007; "Year of the Citi in China?" *Business Week*, January 23, 2006; Anthony Spaeth, "China's Legend in the Making," Time.com, May 8, 2000; "Citigroup allowed to build mansion in Shanghai," *People's Daily*, December 4, 2000; Michael Shari, Brian Bremner, Heather Timmons, and Becky Gaylord, "Citibank conquers Asia," *Business Week* (online edition), February 26, 2001, p. 44, "Foreign bank integration accelerates in China," *The Banker*, May 3, 2004; "Citibank business in Beijing," *China Daily*, March 26, 2004; "Another first: Citibank wins foreign exchange approval," *China Daily*, March 20, 2002; Thomson Reuters, *OneSource*, 2011.

1 How can a foreign organization such as Citigroup make an initial assessment of a host-country market (such as China) in deciding how to do business there? What is involved in this process?

2 What kinds of opportunities and constraints does Citigroup face in China? Despite its early-mover advantages, why does it appear to have limited presence there?

3 Why is the Chinese government an important influence in banking and the financial services industry? How has it tended to intervene in the market to assert its influence?

REAL CASE

Nanjing Auto makes the MG

China became a net exporter of cars for the first time in 2005, due in part to the large-scale inward investment from non-Chinese car manufacturers, channeled into joint ventures with local firms in this industry. But exports account for a small proportion of total sales. By 2015 annual production in China had reached 21 million and demand from the domestic automotive market had grown fast enough to make China the largest automotive market in the world.

VW entered China well ahead of the competition through a joint venture with the government-owned Shanghai Automotive Industry Corporation (SAIC) in 1984. A second joint venture with the First Automotive Works (FAW) in 1991 helped it reach a dominant position (56 percent market share) in the growing Chinese car market before other foreign competitors were even allowed to enter. GM was a later entrant and had been involved in a range of technology transfer initiatives before being allowed to establish manufacturing operations in 1997 through a $1.6 billion joint venture with SAIC. GM reached a 10 percent market share to challenge VW. But both GM and VW faced growing competition from new foreign entrants after the 2001 WTO deregulation rulings began to take effect. Ford, Honda, Toyota, Hyundai, and Suzuki all entered the market in the early to mid-2000s. More significantly, local car makers also started to come into their own around this time.

SAIC, which merged with Nanjing Automotive Corporation (NAC) in 2008, Chery Automobile, and FAW are the largest local producers. SAIC has a string of joint ventures, including with VW and GM, while FAW has partnerships with Mazda and Toyota, in addition to its main ally, VW. In contrast, Chery is one of the more independent local players, as is Geely Automotive Holdings. Initially established as a fridge maker, Geely has steadily accelerated sales and expanded its manufacturing operations to reach a 5 percent share of the mainland market.

Low cost is the one key advantage at this stage for indigenous car firms, gained through cheap labor, available land, and capital (in China much of it initially from the government). This only temporarily makes up for weaknesses in most other areas, from manufacturing technology, process innovation, and product design, to sales and branding. But the industry has moved up the value chain in its short history. Low-cost advantages are increasingly complemented by capabilities in design, engineering, manufacturing, marketing, and management which are driving process and product innovation. Most firms have partly developed and partly

bought into these assets and capabilities through joint ventures with Western car-makers. More unusually, NAC accessed them directly by acquiring one of the oldest and best-known car firms in the UK, MG.

Based in Longbridge in the heart of the West Midlands manufacturing region, MG was part of MG-Rover, a corporation that combined two famous British car brands that dated back to the early 1900s. A turbulent history of takeovers and management failures had brought the firm to collapse in the early 2000s, despite the strength of its design, engineering, and technology divisions and the loyalty of its customers. In May 2005 NAC bought the MG brand name, physical assets including the powertrain technology, and the manufacturing rights to the MG range of cars in a deal worth over $80 million. In parallel, NAC's then competitor SAIC announced it would build the Rover 75 (relaunched as the Roewe) in China using the rights it had bought from MG-Rover in 2004.

NAC shipped the MG assets to China and, in the space of a year, by March 2007 the firm had set up production in the Pukou High-Tech Development Zone in Nanjing and locally made cars were rolling off the plant line. The aim was to develop the plant to eventually produce 200,000 autos, 250,000 engines, and 100,000 gear boxes, with an explicit strategy to keep costs low by expanding and improving the local Chinese supply chain. To do this it has embarked on a wide range of recruitment and training programs, which involve ex-MG-Rover plant managers, engineers, designers, and other employees from the UK operation and from suppliers. These are providing the Chinese with the capabilities not just to operate the plant, but to improve the product design, manufacturing quality, and cost and to conduct R&D and engineering development to create future automotive products.

The acquisition provides an interesting illustration of how far the kinds of advanced assets and capabilities required to produce and sell complex products can be bought and transferred across continents. It begs the question: how far can changes in ownership drive geographic shifts in competitive advantage? What it shows is that knowledge, expertise, and skills have to be transferred alongside hardware and technology for the full set of manufacturing process and product competencies to be developed by the recipient firm. This takes a long time, during which the recipient remains dependent on knowledge and expertise from the firm and/or regional "cluster" of firms in which the original capabilities evolved.

▶

Source: Matthew Lewis/Getty Images

Source: David Lyons/Alamy Stock Photo

Sources: This case was partly developed on the basis of interviews conducted as part of a larger study of MNEs in China. See S. C. Collinson, B. Sullivan-Taylor, and J. L. Wang, "Adapting to the China challenge: lessons from experienced multinationals," Advanced Institute of Management (AIM) Research, Executive Briefing, London, 2007, http://www.aimresearch.org/publications/ adaptingtochina.pdf; http://www.mg-uk.co.uk; Jason Subler and Shen Yan, "Chinese carmakers merge to take on multinationals," *Guardian,* December 27, 2007; "The world's big carmakers have unwittingly created a new Chinese rival," *The Economist,* February 22, 2007; Yu Qiao, "Global, local firms jostle for position," *China Daily,* April 21, 2007. OICA 2015 Production Statistics, http://www.oica.net/ .category/production-statistics/.

Some of these capabilities will be transferred via training programs and by recruiting some of the MG-Rover managers, designers, and engineers directly to work in China. Others will be accessed by redeveloping some functions at the original Longbridge plant in the UK, linked to the main manufacturing plant in China. Subsequent plans by NAC for Longbridge have included an R&D, engineering, and test center for MG models; HR recruitment and purchasing and logistics centers to serve China and Longbridge; a sales and marketing base for the UK and Europe; and eventually a local assembly plant for European markets. NAC is effectively developing a new multinational network to leverage the location-specific complementarities between the Midlands and Nanjing. It hopes to produce cars for both markets, taking on competitors in both regions. With one acquisition a new MNE is born.

1 How have foreign car firms historically established themselves in the Chinese market (what form of FDI?), and why is this mode of market entry normally used?

2 List some examples of firm-specific advantages (FSAs) that are held by foreign car manufacturers and some examples of country-specific advantages (CSAs) in China relevant to this industry.

3 What are the relative costs and benefits of acquiring particular kinds of FSAs, in the way that NAC has done, compared to establishing a joint venture?

NOTES

1 The WTO Agreement on Trade-Related Investment Measures (TRIMs) is still being implemented. It should eventually lead to the end of Chinese requirements on trade and foreign exchange balance, local content, and export performance for foreign investors. The Chinese government is also committed to relaxing foreign investment restrictions in many important service industries, including distribution services, telecommunications, financial services, and professional services; http://www.wto.org

2 "The Great Divide," *The Economist*, March 5, 2005.

3 Arie Y. Lewin, Martin Kenney, and Johann Peter Murmann (eds.), *China's Innovation Challenge: Overcoming the Middle Income Trap* (Cambridge: Cambridge University Press, 2016).

4 Jeffrey B. Miller and Stoyan Tenev, "On the role of government in transition: the experiences of China and Russia compared," *Comparative Economic Studies*, vol. 49 (2007), pp. 543–71.

5 A range of texts listed in the Bibliography can provide background on the evolving role of government in China. There are many online sources of information as well, including the official central government website: http://english.gov.cn and other semi-official or at least non-controversial sites, including http://www.chinatoday.com/gov/a.htm and http://www.china.org.cn. There are many other sites that are more critical of the regime in China.

6 This was a respondent in an extensive survey of multinational firms in China across a variety of industries; S. C. Collinson, B. Sullivan-Taylor, and J. L. Wang, "Adapting to the China challenge: lessons from experienced multinationals," Advanced Institute of Management (AIM) Research, Executive Briefing, London, 2007, http://www.aimresearch.org/publications/adaptingtochina.pdf

7 Jason Dean and Peter Stein, "Inland China beckons as Hon Hai seeks fresh, cheaper labor force," *Wall Street Journal*, September 4, 2010; "China surprise," *The Economist*, April 2, 2005; also see Kim Woodard and Anita Qingli Wang, "Acquisitions in China: a view of the field," 2004, at http://www.chinabusinessreview.com/public/0411/woodward.html

8 Tim Clissold gives an extensive and amusing account of the local rules of the game in his book *Mr. China* (London: Constable & Robinson, 2004). It is based around his experience as a British investor who teamed up with a Wall Street banker in China in the early 1990s. Together they invested over $400 million in a range of industries (including auto components and beer) in China and lost most of it because of the lack of legal and institutional infrastructure, fraud, and their own naivety regarding Chinese business practices; Fonterra, www.fonterra.com; "Fonterra takes 69pc Sanlu writedown," *Business Day*, 24 September, 2008; http://www.stuff.co.nz/business/industries/642763

9 UNCTAD, *World Investment Report Transnational Corporations and the Internationalization of R&D*, 2005; UNCTAD, *Globalization of R&D and Developing Countries*, *Proceedings of the Expert Meeting Geneva*, January 24–6, 2005.

10 Kerry Capell, "Novartis in China: East meets West in R&D," *Business Week*, November 6, 2006.

11 Ming Zeng and Peter J. Williamson, "The hidden dragons," *Harvard Business Review*, October 2003, pp. 92–9.

12 This is a quote from Tim Clissold's book, *Mr. China*, taken from "The Battle of Ningshan" in *Journey to the West*, an unattributed sixteenth-century Ming dynasty novel.

13 The US Commercial Service based in China, part of the US Department of Commerce, provides a Country Commercial Guide. This is continually revised and updated, informed by ongoing studies and surveys. See http://www.usembassy-china.org.cn/fcs/ccg_2008_secured.pdf

14 Among numerous how-to texts on coping with Chinese culture to "make it big" in the Chinese market, see, for example, John L. Graham and Mark N. Lam, "The Chinese negotiation," *Harvard Business Review* (October 2003), pp. 82–91; Tom Orlik, "China's runaway investment train," *Wall Street Journal*, July 26, 2011; Saira Syed, "The price of high-speed ambitions," *BBC News*, July 28, 2011.

15 This list partly comes from interviews and discussions, including several with Alice Huang, Managing Director of Enter Consulting, a firm based in Shanghai that supports inward investors. See Collinson et al., "Adapting to the China challenge."

16 This is a common theme in studies, stemming from the tendency for firms to focus due-diligence efforts on cost cutting and "sell" investment propositions internally and externally on the basis of simple financial metrics. Comparative data on labor costs per hour are relatively easy to gather. Productivity is context specific and influenced by multiple factors and much more difficult to anticipate.

17 See Lewin et al., *China's Innovation Challenge*; see also "How rising wages are changing the game in China," *Business Week*, March 27, 2006. This pattern, of rising costs of particular kinds of labor, was predicted by Eli Heckscher (in 1919) and Bertil Ohlin (in 1933) in an economic model that was further refined by the American economist Paul Samuelson. The H-O or HOS model (or theory of factor endowments) took trade theory beyond the simple assumptions made by Ricardo about labor productivity to look at the relative availability of different factors of production (primarily land, labor, and capital) and therefore their relative price (rent, wages, and interest) in each country. These will determine the products in which a country has a comparative advantage, and in which it will therefore tend to specialize and trade. See, for example, J. R. Markusen, *Multinational Firms and the Theory of International Trade* (Boston, MA: MIT Press, 2004).

18 Chen Hua, "China's FDI meets challenges," *China Business Weekly*, April 21, 2005, http://www.chinadaily.com.cn/english/doc/2005-04/21/content_436121.htm; "Chinese Exporters Seek New Openings," *BBC News*, March 1, 2001.

19 Randall Morck, Bernard Yeung, and Minyuan Zhao, "Perspectives on China's outward foreign direct investment," *Journal of International Business Studies*, vol. 39 (2008), pp. 337–50.

20 These data come from Alan M. Rugman, "Do we need a new theory to explain emerging market multinationals?" Paper prepared for the Columbia University "Five Diamond International Conference: Thinking Outward: Global Players from Emerging Markets," April 2008, pp. 28–9, New York.

21 Ibid.

22 For a lively overview of this unusual partnership, see BBC's *Newsnight* reports on China in Africa at http://news.bbc.co.uk/2/hi/programmes/newsnight/7343060.stm. The debate regarding the net effects of China's investment continues and parallels long-running discussions regarding the developmental costs and benefits of previous periods of colonialism.

23 S. C. Collinson, "Who benefits when MNEs partner with local enterprises in China?," in Lewin et al., *China's Innovation Challenge*.

24 Peter Marsh, "Chinese investment in Europe: focus on deals high up value chain," *Financial Times*, April 26, 2011; Hong Liu and Kequan Li, "Strategic implications of emerging Chinese multinationals: the Haier case study," *European Management Journal*, vol. 24, no. 6 (2002), p. 699; Yubing Wu, "China's refrigerator magnate," *McKinsey Quarterly*, no. 3 (2003), http://www.mckinseyquarterly.com

25 In fact China's software industry is comparable in size to India's but is not export oriented. All the major firms are

focused on serving local customers and foreign firms based in China.

26 Jerry Biediger et al., "Strategic action at Lenovo," *Organizational Dynamics*, vol. 34, no. 1 (2005), pp. 89–102.

27 Ying Fan, "The globalization of Chinese brands," *Marketing Intelligence and Planning*, vol. 24, no. 4 (2006), pp. 365–79.

28 See Collinson, "Who benefits when MNEs partner with local enterprises in China?," and other chapters in Lewin et al., *China's Innovation Challenge*. Another study that supports this view is John Child and Suzana B. Rodrigues, "The internationalization of Chinese firms: a case for theoretical

extension?," *Management and Organization Review*, vol. 1, no. 3 (2005), pp. 381–410. Another that takes a slightly different perspective, but still sees emerging economy MNEs as "special cases," is John A. Mathews, "Dragon multinationals: new players in 21st century globalization," *Asia Pacific Journal of Management*, vol. 23 (March 2006), pp. 5–27.

29 See Rugman, "Do we need a new theory to explain emerging market multinationals?" and Rajneesh Narula, "Globalization, new ecologies, new zoologies, and the purported death of the eclectic paradigm," *Asia Pacific Journal of Management*, vol. 23 (June 2006), pp. 143–51.

BIBLIOGRAPHY

Anderson, Jonathan, and Hu, Fred. *The Five Myths about China and the World* (Hong Kong: Goldman Sachs, 2003).

Buckley, Peter, Clegg, Jeremy L., Cross, Adam R., Liu, Xin, Voss, Hinrich, and Zheng, Ping. "The determinants of Chinese outward foreign direct investment," *Journal of International Business Studies*, vol. 38, no. 4 (2007).

Breslin, Shaun. *China and the Global Political Economy* (Basingstoke: Palgrave-Macmillan, 2007).

Breslin, Shaun. "The political economy of development in China: political agendas and economic realities," *Development*, vol. 50, no. 3 (2007).

Chen, Kun, and Kenney, Martin. "Universities/research institutes and regional innovation systems: the cases of Beijing and Shenzhen," *World Development,* vol. 35, no. 6 (2007), pp. 1056–74.

Chen, Roger. "Corporate reputation: pricing and competing in Chinese markets: strategies for multinationals," *Journal of Business Strategy*, vol. 25, no. 6 (2004).

Cheong, Young R., and Xiao, Geng. "Global capital flows and the position of China: structural and institutional factors and their implications." In J. J. Teunissen (ed.), *China's Role in Asia and the World Economy: Fostering Stability and Growth* (The Hague: Forum on Debt and Development (FONDAD), 2003).

Child, John. "China and international business." In Alan M. Rugman and Thomas L. Brewer (eds.), *The Oxford Handbook of International Business* (Oxford: Oxford University Press, 2009).

Child, John, and Tse, David K. "China's transition and its implications for international business," *Journal of International Business Studies*, vol. 32, no. 1 (spring 2001).

Chung, Goo Hyeok, Du, Jing, and Choi, Jin Nam. "How do employees adapt to organizational change driven by cross-border M&As? A case in China," *Journal of World Business*, vol. 49 (2014).

Clissold, Tim. *Mr. China: A memoir* (London: Collins, 2006).

Coase, Ronald, and Wang, Ning. *How China Became Capitalist* (Basingstoke: Palgrave Macmillan, 2011).

Collinson, Simon C., "Cross-border M&A by the new multinationals: different reasons to 'go global'." In P. J. Williamson, R. Ramamurti, A. C. C. Fleury, and M. T. L. Fleury (eds.), *The Competitive Advantage of Emerging Market Multinationals* (Cambridge University Press, Cambridge, 2013).

Collinson, Simon C. "Who benefits when MNEs partner with local enterprises in China?" In Arie Y. Lewin, Martin Kenney, and Johann Peter Murmann (eds.), *China's Innovation Challenge: Overcoming the Middle Income Trap* (Cambridge: Cambridge University Press, 2016).

Collinson, Simon C., and Narula, Rajneesh, "Asset recombination in international partnerships as a source of improved innovation capabilities in China", *Multinational Business Review*, vol. 22, no. 4 (2014).

Deng, Ping, "Why do Chinese firms tend to acquire strategic assets in international expansion?," *Journal of World Business*, vol. 44, no. 1, (2009).

Doh, Jonathan P., Rodriguez, Peter, Uhlenbruck, Klaus, Collins, Jamie, and Eden, Lorraine. "Coping with corruption in foreign markets," *Academy of Management Executive*, vol. 17, no. 3 (2003).

Doh, Jonathan P., Teegen, Hildy, and Mudambi, Ram. "Balancing private and state ownership in emerging markets' telecommunications infrastructure: country, industry, and firm influences," *Journal of International Business Studies*, vol. 35, no. 3 (May 2004).

Dunning, John. "Comment on dragon multinationals: new players in 21st century globalization," *Asia Pacific Journal of Management*, vol. 23 (June 2006).

Eberhardt, Markus, McLaren, Julie, Millington, Andrew, and Wilkinson, Barry. "Multiple forces in component localization in China," *European Management Journal*, vol. 22, no. 3 (June 2004).

Engardio, Peter. *Chindia: How China and India Are Revolutionizing Global Business* (New York: McGraw-Hill 2006).

Enright, Michael J., Scott, Edith E., and Chang, Ka-mun. *Regional Powerhouse: The Greater Pearl River Delta and the Rise of China* (Singapore: Wiley, 2005).

Farrell, Diana, Remes, Jaana K., and Schulz, Heiner. "The truth about foreign direct investment in emerging markets," *McKinsey Quarterly*, no. 1 (2004).

Fernandez, Juan Antonio, and Underwood, Laurie, *China CEO: Voices of Experience from 20 International Business Leaders* (Singapore: Wiley, 2006).

Fishman, Ted C. *China Inc.: How the Rise of the Next Superpower Challenges America and the World* (New York: Scribner, 2006).

Goedhart, Marc H., and Haden, Peter. "Emerging markets aren't as risky as you think," *McKinsey Quarterly*, special edition issue 4 (2003).

Gray, Kenneth R. "The ins and outs of doing business in Europe: Germany, France, Russia, and the emerging markets of eastern Europe," *Thunderbird International Business Review*, vol. 47, no. 1 (January/February 2005).

Hamilton, Stewart, and Zhang, Jinxuan. *Doing Business with China: Avoiding the Pitfalls* (Basingstoke: Palgrave Macmillan, 2011).

Hu, Helen Wei, and Cui, Lin. "Outward foreign direct investment of publicly listed firms from China: a corporate governance perspective," *International Business Review*, vol. 23, no. 4 (2014).

Hu, Mei-Chih, and Matthew, John A. "National innovation capacity in East Asia," *Research Policy*, vol. 34 (2005).

Humphery-Jenner, Mark, and Suchard, Jo-Ann. "Foreign venture capitalists and the internationalization of entrepreneurial companies: evidence from China," *Journal of International Business Studies*, vol. 44, no. 6 (2013).

Jefferson, Gary, Bai, Huamao, Guan, Xiaojing, and Yu, Xiaoyun. "R&D performance in Chinese industry," *Economics of Innovation and New Technology*, vol. 15, nos. 4/5 (2006).

Kafouros, Mario, and Wang, Elizabeth Yi. "Technology transfer within China and the role of location choices," *International Business Review*, vol. 24, no. 3 (2015).

Keeley, James, and Wilsdon, James. *China: The Next Science Superpower?* Demos Reports (2007), http://www.demos.co.uk/files/China_Final.pdf

Kumar, Sameer, Jamieson, Jacky, and Sweetman, Mathew. "Software industry in the fastest emerging market: challenges and opportunities," *International Journal of Technology Management*, vol. 29, nos. 3/4 (2005).

Kynge, James. *China Shakes the World: A Titan's Rise and Troubled Future—and the Challenge for America* (New York: Houghton Mifflin, 2006).

Li, Jing, and Li, Yong. "Flexibility versus commitment: MNEs' ownership strategy in China," *Journal of International Business Studies*, vol. 41, no. 9 (2010).

Li, Kai, Griffin, Dale, Yue, Heng, and Zhao, Longkai. "National culture and capital structure decisions: evidence from foreign joint ventures in China," *Journal of International Business Studies*, vol. 42, no. 4 (2011).

Lin, Hao-Chieh, and Hou, Sheng-Tsung. "Managerial lessons from the East: an interview with Acer's Stan Shih," *Academy of Management Perspectives*, vol. 24, no. 4 (2010).

Ling, Zhijun, and Avery, Martha. *The Lenovo Affair: The Growth of China's Computer Giant and Its Takeover of IBM-PC* (Singapore: Wiley, 2006).

Liu, Xiaohui, Lu, Jiangyong, Filatotchev, Igor, Buck, Trevor, and Wright, Mike. "Returnee entrepreneurs, knowledge spillovers and innovation in high-tech firms in emerging economies," *Journal of International Business Studies*, vol. 41, no. 7 (2010).

London, Ted, and Hart, Stuart L. "Reinventing strategies for emerging markets: beyond the transnational model," *Journal of International Business Studies*, vol. 35, no. 5 (September 2004).

Luo, Yadong. "Building a strong foothold in an emerging market: a link between resource commitment and environment conditions," *Journal of Management Studies*, vol. 41, no. 5 (July 2004).

Luo, Yadong, and Tung, Rosalie. "International expansion of emerging market enterprises: a springboard perspective," *Journal of International Business Studies*, vol. 38, no. 4 (2007).

Ma, Xufei, Delios, Andrew, and Lau, Chung-Ming. "Beijing or Shanghai? The strategic location choice of large MNEs' host-country headquarters in China," *Journal of International Business Studies*, vol. 44, no. 9 (2013).

Ma, Xufei, Tong, Tony W., and Fitza, Markus. "How much does subnational region matter to foreign subsidiary performance? Evidence from Fortune Global 500 Corporations' investment in China," *Journal of International Business Studies*, vol. 44, no. 1 (2013).

Mathews, John A. *Dragon Multinational: A New Model for Global Growth* (New York: Oxford University Press, 2002).

McManus, John, Li, Mingzhi, and Moitra, Deependra. *China and India: Opportunities and threats for the Global Software Industry* (Oxford: Chandos, 2007).

Meyer, Klaus E. "Perspectives on multinational enterprises in emerging economies," *Journal of International Business Studies*, vol. 35, no. 4 (2004).

Meyer, Klaus E. "International research in transitional economies." In Alan M. Rugman and Thomas L. Brewer (eds.), *The Oxford Handbook of International Business* (Oxford: Oxford University Press, 2009).

Navarro, Peter, and Autry, Greg. *Death by China: Confronting the Dragon and a Global Call to Action* (Upper Saddle River, NJ: Prentice Hall, 2011).

Nolan, Peter. *Transforming China: Globalization, Transition and Development* (London: Anthem, 2004).

OECD. *OECD Reviews of Innovation Policy: China Synthesis Report* (Paris: OECD, 2007).

Ping Li, Peter. *Disruptive Innovation in Chinese and Indian Businesses: The Strategic Implications for Local Entrepreneurs and Global Incumbents* (London: Routledge, 2012).

Pollitte, Wesley A., Miller, Joseph C., and Yaprak, Attila. "Returns to US firms from strategic alliances in China: a knowledge-based view," *Journal of World Business*, vol. 50, no. 1 (2015).

Prestowitz, Clyde. *Three Billion New Capitalists* (New York: Basic Books, 2006).

Pun, Ngai. *Made in China: Women Factory Workers in a Global Workplace* (Durham, NC: Duke University Press, 2005).

Quer, Diego, Claver, Enrique, and Rienda, Laura. "Business and management in China: a review of empirical research in leading international journals," *Asia Pacific Journal of Management*, vol. 24 (2007).

Redding, Gordon. "The smaller economies of Asia and their business systems," in Alan M. Rugman (ed.), *The Oxford Handbook of International Business* (Oxford: Oxford University Press, 2009).

Rugman, Alan M., and Doh, Jonathan. *Multinationals and Development* (New Haven, CT: Yale University Press, 2008).

Rugman, Alan M., and Li, Jing. "Will China's multinationals succeed globally or regionally?" *European Management Journal*, vol. 25, no. 5 (2007).

Shi, Weilei Stone, Sunny Li Sun, Brian C. Pinkham, and Mike W. Peng. "Domestic alliance network to attract foreign partners: Evidence from international joint ventures in China," *Journal of International Business Studies*, vol. 45, no. 3 (2014).

Story, Jonathan. *China uncovered: what you need to know to do business in China* (London: Financial Times, Pearson, 2010).

Sull, Donald N. *Made In China: What Western Managers Can Learn from Trailblazing Chinese Entrepreneurs* (Boston, MA: Harvard Business School Press, 2005).

Sun, Pei, Mellahi, Kamel, and Thun, Eric. "The dynamic value of MNE political embeddedness: the case of the Chinese automobile industry," *Journal of International Business Studies*, vol. 41, no. 7 (2010).

Taylor, Robert (ed.). *International Business in China: Understanding the Global Economic Crisis* (London: Routledge, 2011).

Tian, Xiaowen, and Slocum, John W. "What determines MNC subsidiary performance? Evidence from China." *Journal of World Business*, vol. 49 (2014).

Tsui-Auch, Lai Si, and Möllering, Guido. "Wary managers: unfavorable environments, perceived vulnerability, and the development of trust in foreign enterprises in China," *Journal of International Business Studies*, vol. 41, no. 6 (2010).

Williamson, Peter J., and Zeng, Ming. "Strategies for competing in a changed China," *MIT Sloan Management Review*, vol. 45, no. 4 (summer 2004).

Wu, Aiqi, and Hinrich Voss. "When does absorptive capacity matter for international performance of firms? Evidence from China." *International Business Review*, vol. 24, no. 2 (2015).

Wyk, Jay Van. "Doing business in South Africa," *Thunderbird International Business Review*, vol. 46, no. 4 (July/August 2004).

Yong Gao, Gerald, and Pan, Yigang. "The pace of MNEs' sequential entries: cumulative entry experience and the dynamic process," *Journal of International Business Studies*, vol. 41, no. 9 (2010).

Zeng, Ming, and Williamson, Peter J. *Dragons at Your Door: How Chinese Cost Innovation Is Disrupting Global Competition* (Boston, MA: Harvard Business School Press, 2007).

Zheng Zhao, Anand, Jaideep, and Mitchell, Will. "A dual networks perspective on interorganizational transfer of R&D capabilities: international joint ventures in the Chinese automotive industry," *Journal of Management Studies*, vol. 42, no. 1 (2005).

Zhibin Gu, George. *China's Global Reach: Markets, Multinationals, and Globalization* (Palo Alto, CA: Fultus Corporation, 2006).

Zhou, Kevin Zheng, and Xu, Dean. "How foreign firms curtail local supplier opportunism in China: detailed contracts, centralized control, and relational governance," *Journal of International Business Studies*, vol. 43, no. 7 (2012).

WWW RESOURCES

http://globaledge.msu.edu/ibrd/marketpot.asp
http://www.stats.gov.cn/english/index.html
http://english.gov.cn
http://www.chinatoday.com
http://www.china.org.cn

http://www.usembassy-china.org.cn
http://www.tdctrade.com/main/china.htm
http://asnic.utexas.edu/
http://www.aimresearch.org/publications/adaptingtochina.pdf
http://news.bbc.co.uk

GLOSSARY

Acceptance zone. An area within which a party is willing to negotiate.

Achievement oriented. Where status is earned rather than a right; recruitment and promotion opportunities tend to be more dependent on performance, as in a meritocracy.

Adjusted present value (APV). An NPV that takes into account sources of country risk that might impact a project's expected future cash flows.

Ad valorem duty. A tax which is based on a percentage of the value of imported goods.

Advertising. A non-personal form of promotion in which a firm attempts to persuade consumers to a particular point of view.

Amakudari. (Literally "descent from heaven.") The temporary or permanent movement of public sector officials in Japan into private corporations as a mechanism for coordinating national policy and company strategy.

Ambidexterity. The ability of a firm to be aligned and efficient in its management of today's business demands while simultaneously being adaptive to changes in the environment.

Andean common market (Ancom). A sub-regional free trade compact designed to promote economic and social integration and cooperation; Bolivia, Colombia, Ecuador, and Peru are all members.

Andean Community. An economic union consisting of Bolivia, Colombia, Ecuador, and Peru.

Anti-dumping duty (AD). Import tariff intended to protect domestic producers from foreign products sold at less than their cost of production or at lower prices than in their home market.

Arbitrageur. A person or firm that deals in foreign exchange, buying or selling foreign currency with simultaneous contracting to exchange back to the original currency; arbitrageurs thus do not undertake exchange risk.

Arm's-length price. The price that exists or would exist on a sale of a given product or service between two unrelated companies—as contrasted with an intracompany transfer price.

Ascription oriented. Where status is more of a right than earned; recruitment and promotion opportunities tend to be more dependent on seniority, ethnicity, gender, religion, or birth.

Association of South-East Asian Nations (ASEAN). An economic union founded in 1967 that includes Brunei Darussalam, Cambodia, Indonesia, Lao PDR, Malaysia, Myanmar, the Philippines, Singapore, Thailand, and Vietnam; this economic bloc focuses not on reducing trade barriers among members but, rather, on promoting exports to other nations.

Autonomous infrastructure. An infrastructure used by multinationals that compete in dissimilar national markets and do not share resources.

Backward integration. The ownership of equity assets used earlier in the production cycle, such as an auto firm that acquires a steel company.

Balance of payments (BOP). The value of all transactions between a country's residents and the rest of the world; the three broad BOP categories are the current account, capital account, and official reserves.

Balance sheet hedging. The use of financial instruments denominated in foreign currency to eliminate exchange rate (translation) risk from the balance sheet of a company.

Benkyokai. Study associations or work groups for students or colleagues in companies to jointly develop particular areas of knowledge and expertise.

Business managers. Managers responsible for coordinating the efforts of people in a corporate organization: for example, in a matrix structure.

Canada Labor Code. A federal law that covers areas such as wages, employment practices, work safety, and conciliation of labor disputes.

Capital account. A category of the BOP that consists of transactions that involve financial claims.

Caribbean Basin Initiative. A trade agreement that eliminates tariffs on many imports to the United States from the Caribbean and Central American regions.

Cartel. A group of firms that collectively agree to fix prices or quantities sold in an effort to control price.

Center-for-global, local-for-local, local-for-global, and global-for-global. Structural archetypes for the location of three innovation-related activities: sensing, responding, and implementing. These result from the need for some innovation activities to be centralized and/or standardized and others to be de-centralized and/or customized (or "localized").

Centrally determined economy. An economy in which goods and services are allocated based on a plan formulated by a committee that decides what is to be offered.

Chu and giri. Chu, meaning loyalty, and giri, meaning duty, obligation, or responsibility, are often used together to denote the traditionally close, trusting relationship between managers and employees; they are also used to describe the ties between older and younger members of a family.

Civil society. A group of individuals, organizations, and institutions that act outside the government and the market to advance a diverse set of interests.

Clearing account. A centralized cash management bank account in which one MNE affiliate reviews payment needs among various MNE affiliates and arranges to make payments of net funds due from each affiliate to others through the clearing account.

Cluster analysis. A marketing approach to forecasting customer demand that involves grouping data based on market area, customer, or similar variables.

Codetermination. A legal system that requires workers and their managers to discuss major strategic decisions before companies implement the decisions.

Collectivism. The tendency of people to belong to groups who look after each other in exchange for loyalty.

Common market. A form of economic integration characterized by the elimination of trade barriers among member nations, a common external trade policy, and mobility of factors of production among member countries.

Communication. The process of transferring meanings from sender to receiver.

Communism. A political system in which the government owns all property and makes all decisions regarding production and distribution of goods and services.

Company chop. An official company seal or signature stamp used to verify company documents, contracts, and often financial transactions.

Comparative advertising. The comparing of similar products for the purpose of persuading customers to buy a particular one.

Competition Act. A Canadian federal law that regulates anti-competitive practices and prohibits actions that will substantially lessen or prevent competition; it is similar to US antitrust laws.

Competitive intelligence. The gathering of external information on competitors and the competitive environment as part of the decision-making process.

Competitive scope. The breadth of a firm's target market within an industry.

Compound duty. A tariff consisting of both a specific and an ad valorem duty.

Concurrent engineering. The process of having design, engineering, and manufacturing people working together to create a product, in contrast to working in a sequential manner.

Consolidation. The translation of foreign affiliate accounts and addition to home-country accounts for the purpose of reporting the complete (global) condition of a company; consolidation of foreign affiliate accounts that are denominated in other currencies necessarily produces translation risk.

Container ships. Vessels used to carry standardized containers that can be simply loaded onto a carrier and then unloaded at their destination without any repackaging of the contents of the containers.

Contract management. A process by which an organization (such as the government) transfers operating responsibility of an industry without transferring the legal title and ownership.

Control. The fundamental function of management that involves developing profit plans for the firm and its divisions and then deciding what to do when actual operating results differ from those planned.

Controlling. The process of determining that everything goes according to plan.

Coordinated infrastructure. An infrastructure used when there is a high degree of similarity among national markets and business units share resources in an effort to help each other raise overall sales.

Co-prosperity pyramid. A supply chain linked to a vertical, manufacturing *keiretsu*. It is hierarchical, with firms in the top tiers engaged in technology sharing, personnel exchanges, cross-shareholding, and long-term trading relationships. The further down the hierarchy a firm sits, the more important price becomes and the less such firms are considered *keiretsu* members.

Corporate culture. The shared values, traditions, customs, philosophy, and policies of a corporation; also, the professional atmosphere that grows from this and affects behavior and performance.

Corruption. The misuse of public power for private benefit.

Cost-of-living allowance. A payment to compensate for differences in expenditures between the home country and the foreign location.

Cost strategy. A strategy that relies on low price and is achieved through approaches such as vigorous pursuit of cost reductions and overhead control, avoidance of marginal customer accounts, and cost minimization in areas such as sales and advertising.

Council of Ministers. The major policy decision-making body of the EU and one of its major institutions, consisting of one minister from each of the member states.

Council of the European Union. The major policy decision-making body of the EU; it consists of one minister from each of the 28 member states and is one of four major institutions of the EU.

Countertrade. Barter trade in which the exporting firm receives payment in products from the importing country.

Countervailing duty (CVD). Import tariff intended to protect domestic producers from harmful subsidization by foreign governments.

Country risk analysis. Examines the chances of non-market events (political, social, and economic) causing financial, strategic, or personnel losses to a firm following FDI in a specific country market.

Court of Auditors A court that has one judge appointed from each EU member country; this court monitors the financial aspects of the union.

Court of Justice. A court that has one judge appointed from each EU member country; this court serves as the official interpreter of EU law.

Cultural assimilator. A programmed learning technique designed to expose members of one culture to some of the basic concepts, attitudes, role perceptions, customs, and values of another culture.

Cultural convergence. The growing similarity between national cultures, including the beliefs, values, aspirations, and the preferences of consumers, partly driven by global brands, media, and common global icons.

Culture. The sum total of the beliefs, rules, techniques, institutions, and artifacts that characterize human populations or the collective programming of the mind.

Culture clash. When two cultural groups (national or corporate) meet, interact, or work together and differences in their values, beliefs, rules of behavior, or styles of communication create misunderstandings, antagonism, or other problems.

Currency diversification. An exchange risk management technique through which the firm places activities or assets and liabilities into multiple currencies, thus reducing the impact of exchange rate change for any one of them.

Currency inconvertibility. The inability of a firm to transfer profit from a subsidiary in a host country to other areas of the organization or to shareholders because of host-government restrictions on profit remittances.

Currency option. A derivative financial instrument where the owner has the right but not the obligation to exchange money denominated in one currency into another currency at a pre-agreed exchange rate on a specified date. The right to buy is the call option and the right to sell is the put option. It allows the company to take advantage of favorable movements in exchange rates. Options are the only form of hedging that does this.

Current account. A BOP category that consists of merchandise trade, services, and gifts (unilateral transfers).

Customs union. A form of economic integration in which all tariffs between member countries are eliminated and a common trade policy toward non-member countries is established.

Debt–equity ratio. The value of a firm's total debt divided by the value of its total equity; a higher ratio implies greater leverage, and potentially greater risk.

Decision making. The process of choosing from among alternatives.

Delayed differentiation. A strategy in which all products are manufactured in the same way for all countries or regions as late as possible in the assembly process, at which time differentiation is used to introduce particular features or special components.

Demand-Flow™ Technology (DFT). A production process that is flexible to demand changes.

Democracy. A system of government in which the people, either directly or through their elected officials, decide what is to be done.

Differentiation strategy. A strategy directed toward creating something that is perceived as being unique.

Diffuse. A tendency for workplace relationships and obligations, including relative status and hierarchical position, to extend into social situations and activities outside of work.

Distribution. The course that goods take between production and the final consumer.

Divestiture. (Also see *Privatization*.) A process by which a government or business sells assets.

Dumping. The selling of imported goods at a price below cost or below that in the home country.

Dynamic capability. The firm's ability to integrate, build, and reconfigure internal and external competences to address rapidly changing environments.

Economic globalization. The growing interdependence of locations and economic actors across countries and regions.

Economic integration. The establishment of transnational rules and regulations that enhance economic trade and cooperation among countries.

Economic risk. The risk of financial loss or gain to an MNE due to the effects of unanticipated exchange rate changes on future cash flows that are denominated in foreign currencies.

Economic union. A form of economic integration characterized by free movement of goods, services, and factors of production among member countries and full integration of economic policies.

Embargo. A quota set at zero, thus preventing the importation of those products that are involved.

Emotional. An acceptance of emotion and subjectivity as the bases for some decision making and a preference for explicit displays of emotions and feelings in the workplace.

Empowerment. The process of giving employees increased control over their work.

Endaka. Yen appreciation; the growing value of the yen vis-à-vis other currencies which, among other things, made Japan a relatively expensive place to manufacture.

Enterprise for the Americas. An idea launched by President George Bush to create a free trade area from Alaska to Argentine Antarctica.

Esprit de corps. The spirit of a group that makes the members want the group to succeed.

Estimation by analogy. A method of forecasting market demand or market growth based on information generated in other countries, such as determining the number of refrigerators sold in the United States as a percentage of new housing starts and using this statistic in planning for the manufacture of these products in other world markets.

Ethnocentric predisposition. The tendency of a manager or multinational company to rely on the values and interests of the parent company in formulating and implementing the strategic plan.

Ethnocentric solution. A centralized decision-making framework in which financial decisions and control for foreign affiliates are largely integrated into home-office management.

Ethnocentrism. A belief in the superiority of one's own ethnic group; the dominance of the home-country culture in decision making, human resource management, and overall corporate culture in a multinational firm.

Eurobond. A bond denominated in foreign currency issued in any country's financial market; most eurobonds are issued in London or in Luxembourg (for tax reasons).

Eurocurrency. A bank deposit in any country that is denominated in a foreign currency. A yen-denominated bank deposit in Germany is a euro–yen deposit, a form of eurocurrency.

Eurodollar. A dollar-denominated bank deposit outside the United States.

European Coal and Steel Community (ECSC). A community formed in 1952 by Belgium, France, Italy, Luxembourg, the Netherlands, and West Germany for the purpose of creating a common market that would revitalize the efficiency and competitiveness of the coal and steel industries in those countries.

European Commission. A 28-member group chosen by agreement of member governments of the EU; the Commission is the executive branch of the EU.

European Council. Composed of the heads of state of each EU member country as well as the president of the European Commission. Meetings of the Council take place at least twice a year and their purpose is to resolve major policy issues and to set policy direction.

European Free Trade Association (EFTA). A free trade area currently consisting of Iceland, Liechtenstein, Norway, and Switzerland; past members included the UK (before it joined the EU).

European Monetary Union (EMU). The agreement among, initially, 11 of the European Union countries to eliminate their currencies and create the euro; European Union countries do not necessarily have to join the EMU.

European Parliament. A group of 750 representatives elected directly by voters in each member country of the EU plus the EU President; the Parliament serves as a watchdog on EU expenditures.

European Research Cooperation Agency. A research and development alliance that emphasizes projects in the fields of energy, medicine, biotechnology, communications, information technology, transport, new materials, robotics, production automation, lasers, and the environment.

European Union (EU). A treaty-based institutional framework that manages economic and political cooperation among its 28 member states: Austria, Belgium, Bulgaria, Croatia, Cyprus, the Czech Republic, Denmark, Estonia, France, Finland, Germany, Greece, Hungary, Ireland, Italy, Latvia, Lithuania, Luxembourg, Malta, the Netherlands, Poland, Portugal, Romania, Slovakia, Slovenia, Spain, Sweden, and the UK.

Exchange controls. Controls that restrict the flow of currency.

Exchange rate. The value of one currency in terms of another; for example, US $1.2378/€1.

Exchange risk. The risk of financial loss or gain due to an unexpected change in a currency's value.

Exchange risk adaptation. An exchange risk management technique through which a company adjusts its business activities to try to balance foreign currency assets and liabilities, and inflows and outflows.

Exchange risk avoidance. An exchange risk management technique through which the firm tries to avoid operating in more than one currency.

Exchange risk transfer. An exchange risk management technique through which the firm contracts with a third party to pass exchange risk on to that party, via such instruments as forward contracts, futures, and options.

Expatriates. Individuals who reside abroad but are citizens of the multinational's parent country; they are citizens of the home, not the host, country.

Export tariff. A tax levied on goods sent out of a country.

Exports. Goods and services produced by a firm in one country and then sent to another country.

Expropriation. The governmental seizure of private businesses coupled with little, if any, compensation to their owners.

External economies of scale. Efficiencies brought about by access to cheaper capital, highly skilled labor, and superior technology.

Factor endowment theory. A trade theory which holds that nations will produce and export products that use large amounts of production factors that they have in abundance and will import products requiring a large amount of production factors that they lack.

Five partners. A business network consisting of five partner organizations: the flagship firm (a multinational enterprise), key suppliers, key customers, key competitors, and the non-business infrastructure.

Flagship firms. Multinational firms characterized by global competitiveness and international benchmarks.

Flying Geese model. A model suggesting that Asian countries are following Japan's historical economic transition, specializing in particular industries (steel to textiles to clothing to autos to electronics) during particular growth stages. At a particular point in time we should expect to see these industries located in different Asian countries, depending on their resource endowments, labor costs, and capabilities.

Focus strategy. A strategy that concentrates on a particular buyer group and segments that niche based on product line or geographic market.

Foreign bond. A bond issued by a foreign company in another country's financial market.

Foreign direct investment (FDI). Equity funds invested in other nations. It is different from portfolio (financial) investment in that FDI is undertaken by MNEs which exercise control of their foreign affiliates.

Foreign exchange. Foreign currency-denominated financial instruments, ranging from cash to bank deposits to other financial contracts payable or receivable in foreign currency.

Foreign exchange brokers. A company that provides specialized services to commercial banks in the interbank foreign exchange market, essentially functioning to unite interested buyers and sellers of foreign currency-denominated bank deposits; brokers intermediate about half of all wholesale foreign exchange transactions in New York and London.

Foreign exchange traders. Bankers who deal in foreign exchange, buying and selling foreign currencies on behalf of clients and/or for the bank itself; typically they deal in foreign currency-denominated bank deposits.

Foreign investment controls. Limits on foreign direct investment or the transfer or remittance of funds.

Foreign investment review agency. A government agency that reviews applications for foreign direct investment projects and approves or disapproves the projects, according to standards established by the government.

Foreign Sales Corporation Act. Legislation designed to allow US exporters to establish overseas affiliates and not pay taxes on the affiliates' income until the earnings are remitted to the parent company.

Foreign trade zones. Areas where foreign goods may be held and processed and then re-exported without incurring customs duties (same as a free trade zone).

Formal institutions. Rules that may be in the form of legal code, laws, and promulgations, government decrees that are legally laid out and codified.

Forward integration. The purchase of assets or facilities that move the company closer to the customer, such as a computer manufacturer that acquires a retail chain that specializes in computer products.

Forward rate. An exchange rate contracted today for some future date of actual currency exchange; banks offer forward rates to clients to buy or sell foreign currency in the future, guaranteeing the rate at the time of the agreement.

Free trade area. An economic integration arrangement in which barriers to trade (such as tariffs) among member countries are removed.

Free Trade Area of the Americas (FTAA). A regional trade agreement that is expected to succeed NAFTA and includes 34 countries across North, Central, and South America.

Free trade zone. A designated area where importers can defer payment of customs duty while further processing of products takes place (same as a foreign trade zone).

Fronting loan. A third-party loan in which an MNE home office deposits funds with a financial institution, which then lends to the MNE's affiliate in a country where the MNE faces political risk or currency transfer restrictions.

Funds positioning techniques. Mechanisms such as transfer pricing, intercompany loans, and timing of payments that are used to move funds from one affiliate to another in a multinational firm.

Gaijin. A term used for non-Japanese; while not too offensive it is not particularly polite; *gai* means outside or foreign, *jin* means person.

General Agreement on Tariffs and Trade (GATT). A major trade agreement that was established to negotiate trade concessions among member countries, and since superseded by the WTO agreements.

Geocentric predisposition. The tendency of a multinational to construct its strategic plan with a global view of operations.

Geocentric solution. A decision-making framework in which financial decisions and evaluation related to foreign affiliates are integrated for the firm on a global basis.

Geocentrism. Neither home- nor host-country culture dominates decision making, human resource management, and overall corporate culture in a multinational firm.

Gestion. The skill or practice of controlling, directing, or planning something, especially a commercial enterprise or activity.

Global area structure. An organizational arrangement in which primary operational responsibility is delegated to area managers, each of whom is responsible for a specific geographic region.

Global functional structure. An organizational arrangement in which all areas of activity are built around the basic tasks of the enterprise.

Global product structure. An organizational arrangement in which domestic divisions are given worldwide responsibility for product groups.

Global sourcing. The use of suppliers anywhere in the world, chosen on the basis of their efficiency.

Globalization. The production and distribution of products and services of a homogeneous type and quality on a worldwide basis.

Going Global. A key strategy of the Chinese government as part of the 11th Five-Year Plan, to internationalize target industry sectors and companies.

Grande école. One of the "grand" or great schools considered to be the pinnacle of French higher education, highly selective and prestigious and the main source of the country's business and political leaders.

Guanxi. Denotes personalized or informal networks of relationships in China. They can be important preconditions for smoothing the way or gaining favors or advantages, particularly when both society and the economy are dominated by central government. There are parallels with the concept of social capital.

Hai. "Yes" in Japanese does not necessarily mean "yes I agree," but "yes, I hear what you say".

Hardship allowance. A special payment made to individuals posted to geographic areas regarded as less desirable.

Heckscher–Ohlin theory. A trade theory that extends the concept of comparative advantage by bringing into consideration the endowment and cost of factors of production and helps to explain why nations with relatively large labor forces will concentrate on producing labor-intensive goods, whereas countries with relatively more capital than labor will specialize in capital-intensive goods.

Hedge. A strategy to protect the firm against risk, in this case against exchange rate risk.

Home-country nationals. Citizens of the country where the multinational resides.

Horizontal integration. The purchase of firms in the same line of business, such as a computer chip firm that acquires a competitor.

Host-country nationals. Local people hired by a multinational.

Humane orientation. Cultures that emphasize helping others, charity, and people's wider social obligations.

Ideology. A set of integrated beliefs, theories, and doctrines that helps to direct the actions of a society.

Import tariff. A tax levied on goods shipped into a country.

Imports. Goods and services produced in one country and bought in by another country.

Indigenization laws. Laws which require that nationals hold a majority interest in all enterprises.

Individualism. The tendency of people to look after themselves and their immediate family only.

Industrial democracy. The legally mandated right of employees to participate in significant management decisions.

Informal institutions. Rules that are not always laid out in the form of written instruction, but come out of usage and tradition, and are often unwritten and tacit.

Initial screening. The process of determining the basic need and potential of the multinational's goods and services in foreign markets.

Innovation. The renewal and enlargement of the range of products and services and the associated markets; the establishment of new methods of production, supply, and distribution; the introduction of changes in management, work organization, and the working conditions and skills of the workforce.

Institutions. The sets of common habits, routines, established practices, rules, or laws that regulate the interaction between individuals and groups.

Integrative techniques. Strategies designed to help a multinational become a part of the host country's infrastructure.

Interdependence. Mutual reliance between groups of actors; individuals, firms, countries, or regions.

Intermodal containers. Large metal boxes that fit on trucks, railroad trains, and aircraft and help reduce handling costs and theft losses by placing the merchandise in a tightly sealed, easy-to-move unit.

Internal economies of scale. Efficiencies brought about by lower production costs and other savings within a firm.

International business. The study of transactions taking place across national borders for the purpose of satisfying the needs of individuals and organizations.

International division structure. An organizational arrangement in which all international operations are centralized in one division.

International Fisher effect. The theory of exchange rate determination that states that differences in nominal interest rates on similar-risk deposits will be eliminated by exchange rate changes.

International human resource management (IHRM). The process of selecting, training, developing, and compensating personnel in overseas positions.

International joint venture (IJV). An agreement between two or more partners to own and control an overseas business.

International logistics. The designing and managing of a system to control the flow of materials and products throughout the organization.

International market assessment. An evaluation of the goods and services that the multinational can sell in the global marketplace.

International marketing. The process of identifying the goods and services that customers outside the home country want and then providing them at the right price and place.

International Monetary Fund (IMF). The international organization founded at Bretton Woods, New Hampshire, in 1944 that includes most countries of the world and offers balance of payments support to countries in crisis along with financial advice to central banks.

International monetary system. The arrangement between national governments/central banks that oversees the operation of official foreign exchange dealings between countries.

International product life cycle (IPLC) theory. A theory of the stages of production of a product with new "know-how": it is first produced by the parent firm, then by its foreign subsidiaries, and finally anywhere in the world where costs are the lowest; it helps explain why a product that begins as a nation's export often ends up as an import.

International screening criteria. Factors used to identify individuals regarded as most suitable for overseas assignments.

International trade. The exchange of goods and services across international borders.

Intra-regional investments. Investments in the local region rather than in other triad or non-triad regions, such as when Chinese firms invest in other Southeast Asian economies.

Investment Canada Act (ICA). A law enacted to significantly reduce restrictions for foreign investors in Canada to create a more open economy.

Just-in-time inventory (JIT). The delivery of parts and supplies just as they are needed.

Kaizen. Normally taken to mean "continuous improvement" and associated with lean or low-cost, high-productivity manufacturing. A more accurate interpretation is "to dismantle and reassemble a process to make it better." As such *kaizen* was an early form of business process re-engineering.

Keiretsu. Groupings of Japanese firms with long-term associations and cross-shareholdings; each firm maintains its operational independence but coordinates strategy and often exchanges assets and resources with other firms in its group.

Kinesics. A form of non-verbal communication that deals with conveying information through the use of body movement and facial expression.

Kinyu. Horizontal conglomerates encompassing a wide range of diversified businesses, centered on a dominant bank and/or trading company.

Korean *chaebols*. Traditionally family-dominated, diversified conglomerates. Family ownership has been reduced and many are now focused in particular business sectors, reducing their diversity. There are parallels with Japanese *sogo shosha* in terms of early government support and their relationship with dominant national banks.

Latin American Integration Association (LAIA). A free trade group formed to reduce intra-regional trade barriers and to promote regional economic cooperation; Argentina, Bolivia, Brazil, Chile, Colombia, Ecuador, Mexico, Paraguay, Peru, Uruguay, and Venezuela are all members.

Leontief paradox. A finding by Wassily Leontief, a Nobel Prize-winning economist, which shows that the United States, surprisingly, exports relatively more labor-intensive goods and imports capital-intensive goods.

Liberalization policies. Government policies that move away from planned economies toward more free market systems; they are marked by the privatization of state-owned businesses, a lowering of tariff and non-tariff barriers, and reductions in the constraints placed on foreign firms' investments and business activities.

Lighter aboard ship (LASH) vessels. Barges stored on a ship and lowered at the point of destination.

Localization of production. The manufacturing of goods in the host market.

Localization of profits. The reinvestment of earnings in the local market.

London interbank offered rate (LIBOR). The interest rate on large-scale foreign currency-denominated deposits offered from one bank to another in London.

Macro political risk. A risk that affects all foreign enterprises in the same way.

Managerial development. The process by which managers obtain the necessary skills, experiences, and attitudes that they need to become or remain successful leaders.

***Maquiladora* industry.** Named after the practice of millers charging a *maquila*, or "miller's portion," for processing other people's grain, this is a free trade zone that has sprung up along the US–Mexican border for the purpose of producing goods and then shipping them between the two countries.

Market coordination infrastructure. An infrastructure used by firms that compete in similar national markets but do little resource sharing among their businesses.

Market-driven economy. An economy in which goods and services are allocated on the basis of consumer demand.

Market growth. The annual increase in sales in a particular market.

Market indicators. Indicators used for measuring the relative market strengths of various geographic areas.

Market intensity. The richness of a market or the degree of purchasing power in one country as compared to others.

Market-seeking FDI. MNEs invest in distribution, sales, or marketing operations in order to sell products or services (outputs) in particular country markets.

Market size. An economic screening consideration used in international marketing; it is the relative size of each market as a percentage of the total world market.

Masculinity. The degree to which the dominant values of a society are success, money, and material things.

Material handling. The careful planning of when, where, and how much inventory will be available to ensure maximum production efficiency.

Matrix structure. An organizational arrangement that blends two organizational responsibilities such as functional and product structures or regional and product structures.

Mental maps. Cognitive representations of the nature and attributes of the spatial environment, showing how "psychic distance" operates in practice for SME managers.

Mercantilism. A trade theory which holds that a government can improve the economic well-being of the country by encouraging exports and stifling imports to accumulate wealth in the form of precious metals.

Mercosur. A sub-regional free trade group formed to promote economic cooperation; the group consists of Argentina, Brazil, Paraguay, and Uruguay.

Micro political risk. A risk that affects selected sectors of the economy or specific foreign businesses.

Ministry of Economy, Trade and Industry (METI). A Japanese ministry charged with providing information about foreign markets and with encouraging investment in select industries and, in the process, helping to direct the economy. From the post-war period to 2001 it was known as the Ministry of International Trade and Industry (MITI).

Ministry of Finance (MOF). Works alongside METI and is similarly influential vis-à-vis regulation and restructuring of Japan's capital markets.

Mitsubishi *Kinyokai*. The Friday Club in Marunouchi, Tokyo, where the most senior managers from the 29 core firms of the Mitsubishi *keiretsu* gather each month to discuss business.

***Mittelstand*.** About 3.4 million small and medium-sized firms defined as having less than €50 million turnover that make up the heart of the German economy.

Mixed economies. Economic systems characterized by a combination of market- and centrally driven planning.

Mixed structure. A hybrid organization design that combines structural arrangements in a way that best meets the needs of the enterprise.

Modular integrated robotized system (MIRB). A software-based production process that relies entirely on robots.

Modular manufacturing. A manufacturing process that consists of modules that can be easily adapted to fit changing demand.

Monetary exchange rate. The price of one currency stated in terms of another currency.

Multilateral netting. Payment of net amounts due only between affiliates of an MNE that have multiple transactions among the group, which can be partially netted out among them, so then only the net funds need to be transferred.

Multinational enterprise (MNE). A multi-plant firm that controls and coordinates operations in at least two countries; or a firm that engages in value-added international business activities, that has affiliates in more than one country, and whose operations and activities in different locations are actively coordinated by one or more headquarters organizations.

National responsiveness. The ability of MNEs to understand different consumer tastes in segmented regional markets and to respond to different national standards and regulations imposed by autonomous governments and agencies.

Nationalization. A process by which the government takes control of business assets, sometimes with remuneration of the owners and other times without such remuneration.

***Nemawashi*.** Literally means "root tying" and is a process of consultation to get agreement on a particular issue before it becomes explicit policy.

Neo-mercantilism. A trade theory which holds that a government can improve the economic well-being of the country by encouraging exports and stifling imports.

Neutral. A preference for unemotional, objective analysis of a situation or a decision and for limited displays of emotions and feelings in the workplace.

Newly industrialized countries (NICs). A subgroup of emerging market economies that have experienced rapid economic growth, normally accompanied by political and social change; the forerunners were the four Asian "Tiger" economies: Singapore, South Korea, Taiwan, and Hong Kong. The rapid growth, increased trade and FDI, and integration of China in the global economy show that it is approaching this status.

Nominal interest rate. The actual rate of interest offered by a bank, typically given as an annual percentage rate.

Non-governmental organizations (NGOs). Private sector groups that act to advance diverse social interests (see also *Civil society*).

Non-tariff barriers. Rules, regulations, and bureaucratic red tape that delay or preclude the purchase of foreign goods.

North American Free Trade Agreement (NAFTA). A regional free trade agreement among Canada, the United States, and Mexico.

Official reserves. Funds owned by national monetary authorities that are used for bringing BOP accounts into balance.

Open innovation. Interactive, collaborative networks of product or service providers and customers or users which help firms innovate more efficiently.

Particularism. Judging a situation and adjusting rules and procedures according to the specific situation or individuals involved.

Personal selling. A direct form of promotion used to persuade customers to a particular point of view.

PEST framework. Examines the political, economic, socio-cultural, and technological conditions in particular country markets.

Plaza Accord. An agreement signed by the G5 in 1985 in New York, agreeing to devalue the US dollar against the Japanese yen and the deutsche (German) mark; it triggered the bubble economy and eventual economic recession in Japan in the 1990s.

Political risk. The probability that political forces will negatively affect a multinational's profit or impede the attainment of other critical business objectives.

Political union. An economic union in which there is full economic integration, unification of economic policies, and a single government.

Polycentric predisposition. The tendency of a multinational to tailor its strategic plan to meet the needs of the local culture.

Polycentric solution. A decentralized decision-making framework in which financial decisions are largely allocated to foreign affiliates and financial evaluation of affiliates is done in comparison to other firms in that context.

Polycentrism. Each subsidiary, division, or function reflects the culture of its host country; local managers' cultural predispositions and decision making dominate over those of home-country managers in a multinational firm.

Power distance. A cultural dimension that measures the degree to which less powerful members of organizations and institutions accept the fact that power is not distributed equally.

Privatization. The process of selling government assets to private buyers.

Process mapping. A flowchart of every step that goes into producing a product.

Product managers. Managers responsible for coordinating the efforts of their people in such a way as to ensure the profitability of a particular business or product line.

Production system. A group of related activities designed to create value.

Promotion. The process of stimulating demand for a company's goods and services.

Protective and defensive techniques. Strategies designed to discourage a host country from interfering in multinational operations.

Proxemics. A form of non-verbal communication that deals with how people use physical space to convey messages.

Psychic distance. A measure of the similarity or difference between two cultures; also commonly defined as the measurable distance between the home market and a foreign market resulting from the perception of cultural and business differences.

Purchasing power parity. The theory of exchange rate determination that states that differences in prices of the same goods between countries will be eliminated by exchange rate changes.

Quota. A quantity limit on imported goods.

Real interest rate. The nominal interest rate adjusted for price changes. Domestically, this means adjusting for inflation; internationally, this means adjusting for exchange rate (currency price) changes.

Regiocentric predisposition. The tendency of a multinational to use a strategy that addresses both local and regional needs.

Regional managers. In a geocentric matrix, managers charged with selling products in their geographic locale.

Regression analysis. A mathematical approach to forecasting that attempts to test the explanatory power of a set of independent variables.

Repatriation. The process of returning home at the end of an overseas assignment.

Repatriation agreement. An agreement that spells out how long a person will be posted overseas and sets forth the type of job that will be given to the person upon returning.

Resource managers. In a matrix structure, managers charged with providing people for operations.

Resource-seeking FDI. MNEs invest in production-related activities to benefit from cheaper or better sources of inputs in a particular location; these can include raw materials, components, or labor and expertise.

Resource-sharing infrastructure. An infrastructure used by firms that compete in dissimilar national markets but share resources such as R&D efforts and manufacturing information.

Return on investment (ROI). A percentage determined by dividing net income before taxes by total assets.

Ringi. The formalized consensus process of decision making; the *ringisho* is a decision proposal circulated around company departments to be revised or approved before implementation.

Roll-on-roll-off (RORO) vessels. Ocean-going ferries that can carry wheeled cargo such as automobiles, trailers, and trucks that drive onto built-in ramps and roll off at the point of debarkation.

Secular totalitarianism. A system of government in which the military controls everything and makes decisions that it deems to be in the best interests of the country.

Sequential. Cultures that view time in a sequential or linear fashion; order comes from separating activities and commitments.

Single European Act (SEA). An Act passed by the EU that contains many measures to further integrate the member states, along economic and political dimensions, and that allows the Council of Ministers to pass most proposals by a majority vote, in contrast to the unanimous vote that was needed previously.

Single European Market (SEM). A market consisting of all members of the EU, bound together by a single currency, a special charter, complete harmonization of social and economic policies, and a common defense policy.

Small and medium-sized enterprises (SMEs). Defined by governments using different criteria for policy purposes. SMEs are firms with fewer than 250 employees in Europe, but fewer than 500 in the United States. Indian manufacturing firms qualify as SMEs if they invest less than US$2 million in plant and equipment.

Socialization. The process of enculturation, or the adoption of the behavior patterns of the surrounding culture.

Sogo shosha. International trading companies that help other Japanese firms import and export products and services; they were very influential in the rapid growth era in helping local firms break into overseas markets.

Special drawing right (SDR). The currency of the IMF; accounts at the IMF are denominated in SDRs, and the IMF has issued about $204 billion of SDRs as currency since its inception in 1969.

Specific. A tendency to limit workplace relationships and obligations, including relative status and hierarchical position, to the workplace.

Specific duty. A tariff based on the number of items being shipped into a country.

Speculator. A person or firm that takes a position in foreign exchange with no hedging or protection mechanism to try to gain from expected exchange rate changes.

Spot rate. The exchange rate offered on the same day as the request to buy or sell foreign currency; actual settlement (payment) may occur one or two days later.

Standardized training programs. Generic programs that can be used with managers anywhere in the world.

State-owned enterprises (SOEs). Companies that are owned, financed, and controlled by government.

Strategic alliance. A business relationship in which two or more companies work together to achieve a collective advantage.

Strategic business units (SBUs). Operating units with their own strategic space; they produce and sell goods and services to a market segment and have a well-defined set of competitors.

Strategic cluster. A network of businesses and supporting activities located in a specific region, where flagship firms compete globally and supporting activities are home based.

Strategic fit. A strategic management concept which holds that an organization must align its resources in such a way as to mesh effectively with the environment.

Strategic planning. The process of evaluating the enterprise's environment and its internal strengths and then identifying long- and short-range activities.

Strategy formulation. The process of evaluating the enterprise's environment and its internal strengths.

Strategy implementation. The process of attaining goals by using the organizational structure to execute the formulated strategy properly.

Synchronic. Cultures that view events in parallel over time; order comes from coordinating multiple activities and commitments.

Systems of innovation (SI). These stress the "importance of 'systemic' interactions between the various components of inventions, research, technical change, learning and innovation. The national systems of innovation (NSI) bring to the forefront the central role of the state as a coordinating agent" (Soete et al., *Systems of Innovation*, 2010).

Tailor-made training programs. Programs designed to meet the specific needs of the participants, typically including a large amount of culturally based input.

Tariff. A tax on goods shipped internationally.

Tax havens. Jurisdictions that offer the MNE a lower tax rate (or no tax) than in other places, so that MNEs can locate some of their business activities there and thus reduce overall tax payments.

Theocratic totalitarianism. A system of government in which a religious group exercises total power and represses or persecutes non-orthodox factions.

Theory of absolute advantage. A trade theory which holds that nations can increase their economic well-being by specializing in goods that they can produce more efficiently than anyone else.

Theory of comparative advantage. A trade theory which holds that nations should produce those goods for which they have the greatest relative advantage.

Third-country nationals. Citizens of countries other than the one in which the multinational is headquartered or the one in which they are assigned to work by the multinational.

Time-to-market accelerators. Factors that help reduce bottlenecks and errors and ensure product quality and performance.

Totalitarianism. A system of government in which one individual or party maintains complete control and either refuses to recognize other parties or suppresses them.

Trade adjustment assistance. Assistance offered by the US government to US businesses and individuals harmed by competition from imports.

Trade creation. A process in which members of an economic integration group begin to focus their efforts on those goods and services for which they have a comparative advantage and start trading more extensively with each other.

Trade diversion. Occurs when members of an economic integration group decrease their trade with non-member countries in favor of trade with each other.

Training. The process of altering employee behavior and attitudes in a way that increases the probability of goal attainment.

Transaction risk. The risk of financial loss or gain to an MNE due to unanticipated exchange rate changes affecting future cash flows from transactions that are denominated in foreign exchange.

Transfer price. The price used for an intracompany payment for shipment of products or services from one affiliate to another in an MNE; these prices can be used to reduce taxes, move funds to desired locations, and so on.

Transit tariff. A tax levied on goods passing through a country.

Transition strategies. Strategies designed to help smooth the move from foreign to domestic assignments.

Translation risk. The risk of losses or gains on the MNE's balance sheet, due to unhedged exchange rate changes during an accounting period.

Transnational network structure. An organization design that helps MNEs take advantage of global economies of scale while also being responsive to local customer demands.

Transparency. The *clarity* and *consistency* of policies and legislation applied in the governance of businesses.

Trend analysis. The estimation of future demand by either extrapolating the growth over the last three to five years and assuming that this trend will continue or by using some form of average growth rate over the recent past.

Uncertainty avoidance. The extent to which people feel threatened by ambiguous situations and have created institutions and beliefs for minimizing or avoiding those uncertainties.

Unconventional cargo vessels. Vessels used for shipping oversized and unusual cargoes.

United States–Canada Free Trade Agreement (FTA). A trade agreement that eliminates most trade restrictions (such as tariffs) between these two countries and extends national treatment to foreign investment.

Universalism. The uniform application of rules and procedures, regardless of situation, context, or individuals involved.

Upstream and downstream. Common terms in production process industries, such as oil and gas, metals, and bio-pharmaceuticals. They represent the beginning and end stages of the production process. Upstream production is the process of exploring and extracting raw materials, whereas the downstream stage involves processing the materials into a finished product and selling it.

Value chain. The way in which primary and support activities are combined in providing goods and services and increasing profit margins.

Vertical integration. The ownership of assets involved in producing a good or service and delivering it to the final customer.

Virtual integration. A networking strategy based on cooperation within and across company boundaries.

Weighted-average cost of capital (WACC). The firm's cost of obtaining funds from the various sources available. Each source of funds is weighted (multiplied) by the percentage of total capital it provides. Thus, the WACC is W_1 (cost of using retained earnings) + W_2 (cost of bank borrowing) + W_3 (cost of other source of funds), where each cost is stated as an annual percentage rate and each W is the percentage of total capital from that source.

Weighted Country Risk Assessment Model. Combines an investment project appraisal with country risk analysis.

Wholly foreign-owned enterprise (WFOE). A wholly foreign-owned enterprise is a limited liability company under Chinese company law and the preferred mode of investment for foreign MNEs looking to manufacture in China. WFOEs are also known as WOFEs (wholly owned foreign enterprises).

Work councils. Groups that consist of both worker and manager representatives and are charged with dealing with matters such as improving company performance, working conditions, and job security.

Working capital. Short-term financial instruments such as bank deposits and marketable securities that can be optimized by the MNE on a global basis.

World Bank. The world's largest development bank, formed along with the IMF at Bretton Woods in 1944. Its original name was the International Bank for Reconstruction and Development (IBRD). The World Bank assists developing countries with loans and economic advising for economic development.

World Trade Organization (WTO). An international organization that deals with the rules of trade among member countries; one of its most important functions is to act as a dispute-settlement mechanism.

WTO accession. Admission to the World Trade Organization; in return for the right to access and to engage in fair trade with other national markets, the country must liberalize its own markets.

Zaibatsu. The pre-war antecedents of some modern-day *keiretsu* in Japan; attempts by the allied forces to break these up after World War II largely failed.

INDEX

Items in **bold** are also in the Glossary

3M company 98, 354
24/7 Customer 676
AB Electrolux 143, 701
AB LM Ericsson 130
ABB (Asea Brown Boverie) 319, 324,
    332, 341, 353, 631
Abbey 472
Abegglen, JC 600–1, 608–9
Abramovich, Roman 505
absolute advantage, theory of 186–8,
    664, **721**
ABX 375
Accenture 143
Accor hotels 576–7
accountancy Big Four practices 261–2
accounting for country risk 489–90
accounting standards 514
Acer 371, 383, 649–50, 652, 667, 672
Acer Taiwan 649–50, 652
acquisitions *see* mergers and
    acquisitions (M&As)
Acro Aircraft Seating 5
adaptability 450–1
Adidas 180, 417–19, 430, 433, 438–9
adjusted present value (APV) 489, **713**
adjustment strategies 453–4
advertising 428, 430, **713**
Aer Lingus 143
Aeroméxico 130
Aerospatiale 625
Africa *see also* individual countries
    China 660, 700
    colonialism 25, 663
    European Union 669
    foreign direct investment (FDI)
        653–4, 660–3
    least developed countries (LDCs)
        660
    liberalization 26
    natural resources 660–1, 663
    oil industry 660
    political instability 660
    ports and port services in sub-
        Saharan Africa 506–8
    services industry 661
    state-owned enterprises 660
    telecommunications
        industry 266, 661

African Development Bank (ADB) 478
Africatours 577
Agfa 23
agriculture 15, 29, 33–4, 200–2, 359,
    663–5
AIG 180
Air Asia 180
Air Berlin 143
Air Canada 624, 625, 626
Air China 690
Air France 197
Air Liquide 362
air transport
    costs 400
    economic environment 360–1
    freight 399
    global financial crisis of 2008 149
    integrative techniques 501
    international trade 197–8
    predictability 399–400
    state subsidies 148–9
    time 399
    WTO sanctions 148–9
Airbus 197–8, 360–1, 482, 625,
    690–1, 693
Airtel 258
Airtouch Communications 256
Akai Electric 598
Akamatsu, Kaname 664
Alcan 323
Alcatel 411–12
Alcatel Lucent 328
Aldi 78–9, 173
Ali, Muhammad 417
Alibaba 69
Alkon 313–14
All Seasons 576
AllAlloy Pte Ltd 72
Allergan 154
alliances *see* strategic alliances
Allied Irish Banks 219
allowances 458, 459, 468–9
Alrosa 493
Altos 649
Aluminium Company of America 453
Amazon 69, 350–1
Ambev 18
America Movil 660

America Tours 577
American Airlines (AA) 197, 624, 626
American Chamber of Commerce in
    Japan (ACCJ) 598
American Depositary Receipt (ADR)
    241, 537
American Express (AMEX) 350,
    529–31
American Skandia 543
AmerisourceBergen 82
Amnesty International 136
amusement parks 336
AMX 676
Andean Community/Common Market
    (Ancom) 133, 141, 636, **713**
Anderson, Andrew 209, 338
Andorra as a tax haven 522
Anglo American Corporation 241, 493
AngloGold Ashanti 241–2
Anheuser-Busch 180, 343, 360, 496–7,
    597, 693
Anheuser-Busch InBev 18, 360, 496–7,
    693
anti-dumping duty (AD) laws 193,
    201–2, 230, 573–5, **713**
anti-globalization movement 137–8,
    158, 353–4, 493
AP Moller-Maersk (APM) 372
apartheid 493
APM Terminals 373
Apple 82, 328, 360, 411
    admired company, as one of world's
        350–1, 353–4
    Apple Computer 371, 559
    China 692
    iPad 354, 383, 559, 671
    iPhone 328, 354, 551
    Japan 337
    marketing 92
    strategic alliances 143
arbitrage 226–7, **713**
Arc Tyrex 279
ArcelorMittal 655, 659
Arco 639
Argentina 129, 359, 659
Armani 390
Arriva 569
Asahi Breweries Ltd 343, 597, 693